CRITICAL ACCLAIM FOR THE BERKELEY GUIDES

"[The Berkeley Guides are] brimming with useful information for the low-budget traveler — material delivered in a fresh, funny, and often irreverent way." **—The Philadelphia Inquirer**

"...hip, blunt and lively....these Cal students boogie down and tell you where to sleep in a cowboy bunkhouse, get a tattoo and eat cheap meals cooked by aspiring chefs." **—Atlanta Journal Constitution**

"...Harvard hasn't yet met `On the Loose's' pledge to plant two trees in Costa Rica for every one felled to print its books—a promise that, given the true grit of these guides, might well mean a big new forest in Central America." **—Newsweek**

"[The Berkeley Guides] offer straight dirt on everything from hostels to look for and beaches to avoid to museums least likely to attract your parents...they're fresher than Harvard's Let's Go series." **—Seventeen**

"The books are full of often-amusing tips written in a youth-tinged conversational style." **—The Orlando Sentinel**

"So well-organized and well-written that I'm almost willing to forgive the recycled paper and soy-based ink." **—P.J. O'Rourke**

"These guys go to great lengths to point out safe attractions and routes for women traveling alone, minorities and gays. If only this kind of caution weren't necessary. But I'm glad someone finally thought of it."

—Sassy

"The very-hip Berkeley Guides look like a sure-fire hit for students and adventurous travelers of all ages. This is real budget travel stuff, with the emphasis on meeting new places head on, up close and personal....this series is going to go places." **—The Hartford Courant**

"The guides make for fun and/or enlightening reading."

—The Los Angeles Times

"The new On the Loose guides are more comprehensive, informative and witty than Let's Go ." **—Glamour**

OTHER BERKELEY GUIDE TITLES

the BERKELEY guides

THE BUDGET TRAVELER'S HANDBOOK

PACIFIC NORTHWEST & ALASKA

ON THE LOOSE

SECOND EDITION

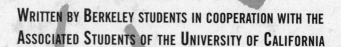

WRITTEN BY BERKELEY STUDENTS IN COOPERATION WITH THE
ASSOCIATED STUDENTS OF THE UNIVERSITY OF CALIFORNIA

PACIFIC NORTHWEST & ALASKA
ON THE LOOSE

Editors: Lauren M. Black, Emily W. Miller
Editorial Coordinators: Laura Comay Bloch, Sharron S. Wood
Executive Editor: Scott McNeely
Production Editor: Tracy Patruno
Map Editor: Bob Blake
Creative Director: Fabrizio La Rocca
Cartographer: David Lindroth Inc.; Eureka Cartography
Text Design: Tigist Getachew
Cover Design and Illustration: Rico Lins

SPECIAL SALES

Contents

What the Berkeley Guides Are All About

Three years ago, a motley bunch of U.C. Berkeley students spent the summer traveling on shoestring budgets to launch a new series of guidebooks—*The Berkeley Guides.* We wrote the books because, like thousands of travelers, we had grown tired of the outdated attitudes and information served up year after year in other guides. Most important, we thought a travel guide should be written by people who know what cheap travel is all about.

You see, it's one of life's weird truisms that the more cheaply you travel, the more you inevitably experience. You're bound to experience a lot with *The Berkeley Guides,* because we believe in living like bums and spending as little money as possible. You won't find much in our guides about how a restaurant prepares its duck à l'Orange or how a hotel blends mauve curtains with green carpet. Instead, we tell you if a place is cheap, clean (no bugs), and worth the cash.

Coming from a community as diverse as Berkeley, we also wanted our books to be useful to everyone, so we tell you if a place is wheelchair-accessible, if it provides resources for gay and lesbian travelers, and if it's safe for women traveling solo. Many of us are Californians, which means we like trees and mountain trails. It also means we emphasize the outdoors in every *Berkeley Guide*, including lots of info about hiking and tips on protecting the environment. (As the saying goes: "Take only pictures and leave only footprints.") To further minimize our impact on the environment, we print our books on recycled paper using soy-based inks.

Most important, these guides are for travelers who want to see more than just the main sights. We find out what Seattlites and Alaskans do for fun, where they go to eat, drink, play Frisbee, or just hang out. Most guidebooks lead you down the tourist trail, ignoring important local issues, events, and culture. In *The Berkeley Guides* we give you the info you need to understand what's going on around you, whether it's the latest on the indie-grunge thing or the region's obsession with the Portland Trailblazers.

The Berkeley Guides began by covering Eastern Europe, Mexico, California, and the Pacific Northwest and Alaska. In the course of research our writers slept in whorehouses in Mexican border towns and landed bush planes above the Arctic Circle. The second year was no different: Our student writers weathered guerrilla attacks in the Guatemalan Highlands, motorcycle wrecks in Ireland, and a strange culinary concoction in Belize known as "greasy-greasy." The result was five new guidebooks, covering Central America, France, Germany, San Francisco, and Great Britain and Ireland. This year, things were even more crazy. One writer got an ulcer, one lost her skirt on a moped, two crashed their motorbikes, while another spent hours digging through a dumpster to reclaim a batch of "misplaced" manuscript. Bloodied but unbowed, *The Berkeley Guides* brings you four new guidebooks, covering Europe, Italy, Paris, and London, not to mention completely revised and updated editions of our first- and second-year guides.

We've done our best to make sure the information in *The Berkeley Guides* is accurate, but time doesn't stand still: prices change, places go out of business. Call ahead when it's really important, assuming, of course, that the place has a phone.

Thanks to You

The Pacific Northwest and Alaska are huge, and it takes an enormous amount of effort to cover the whole region. We couldn't have done it without the help of hundreds of folks in hundreds of towns and cities; some are listed below but many others—whom our writers met briefly on ferries, buses, and in strange, unprintable places—also helped out. We would like you to help us update this book and give us feedback from the road. Drop us a line—a postcard, a scrawled note on some toilet paper, whatever—and we'll be happy to acknowledge your contribution below. Our address is 515 Eshleman Hall, University of California, Berkeley, CA 94720.

JoAnne Aimes (Queen Charlotte Islands); Alaskan Hotel (Juneau); Elizabeth and Breezy-Feneezy Annis (all over the road); Len and Miriam Atkins (Seaview); Lanning Blanks (Portland); Jennifer Bloch (Seattle); Tamara Britt (Valdez); Mrs. Bruno (Bridgeport); Chilkat Guides Limited (Haines); Steve Cohen, Metro Washington Park Zoo (Portland); Monica Cole, Oregon Museum of Science and Industry (Portland); Jane Cottrell (Cape Perpetua Visitor Center); Steve Cutts (Queen Charlotte Islands); Days of '98 Theatre (Skagway); Richard Denner (Ellensberg); Patricia and Peter Dwillies (Pier House, Campbell River); Matt Elliott (Longview); ERA Helicopters (Juneau); Fishermen Vince and Patrick (Cordova); Diantha Frankord (Queen Charlotte Islands); Sabine Friends (Fairbanks); Glacier Bay Airways (Juneau); Glacier Bay Tours and Cruises (Juneau); Karla Hart and Shari Paul, Alaska Rainforest Tours (Juneau); Jack Heald (Cave Junction); Polly, James, Seth, Eli, Kate and Meg Just-Gottesmans (North Plains); Pete Kent, World Forestry Center (Portland); Les Kreuger (Truckee); Kyriakos, Paula, Michelle, Debra; Denman Island Guest House; LaVonne's Fish Camp (Kotzebue); Evan Lemmerman, (Anchorage); Ricky Little Raging Waters (the road); Mona Luna (Anchorage); Sheelagh Mullins (Cordova); Dave and Donna Nanney, Chilkat Eagle Bed and Breakfast (Haines); Dean Noles (Homer); Eliah D. Novin (Honey Hill); Mark Omlid (Kodiak); Perserverance Theatre (Juneau); The Rain Forest Youth Hostel (Forks); Rose the Eskimo Granny (Kotzebue); Marco Rósen (Beaver Creek); Don Routley (Nanaimo Travel Infocentre); Helen Sheehan (Queen Charlotte Islands); Mike and Maureen Shipton, Greystone Manor (Courtenay); Rich Smythe (Barrow); Ron Spector (Eugene); Dean Still and the crew (Aprovecho); Dale Swire (Ashland); Chris Tait (Queen Charlotte Islands); Temsco Helicopters (Skagway); The U.S. Forest Service (Mt. St. Helens); Rick Vanderlaan (Spokane); Deborah Wakefield (Portland Oregon Visitors' Association); Cheryl Walters (Oregon Dunes National Recreation Area Information Center); Katrina Winn (Anchorage); and all the U.S. Forest Service offices and chambers of commerce throughout the Pacific Northwest.

Special thanks to Ezra Glenn, who helped put this book in motion.

Finally, we'd like to thank the Random House folks who helped us with cartography, page design, and production: Steven Amsterdam, Bob Blake, Denise DeGennaro, Tigist Getachew, Tracy Patruno, Fabrizio La Rocca, and Linda Schmidt.

Berkeley Bios

Behind every restaurant blurb, write-up, lodging review, and introduction in this book lurks a student writer. You might recognize the type—perpetually short on time, money, and clean underwear. Six Berkeley students spent the summer in Washington, Oregon, British Columbia, and Alaska researching and writing *The Berkeley Guide to the Pacific Northwest & Alaska*. Every two weeks they sent manuscript back to their ever-patient editors in Berkeley, who squashed it into shape.

The Writers

Gary Blond lived in Italy and Japan and worked with orangutans on the island of Borneo before giving his life over to the Berkeley Guides. Gary had thought he had seen the proverbial all until one night in Portland when, in his tireless search for worthy places to recommend, he found himself at the U.F.O. museum lying on a vibrating psychiatric couch, staring at a wall of ticking clocks and a mannequin's head covered in plastic flies. During his exploration of Portland and the Oregon Coast, Gary also had the occasion to watch his life flash before his eyes when he lost his brakes for a few moments while driving down a steep winding hill on the Oregon Coast—a moment he'd rather forget.

Veteran Berkeley Guides writer **Marisa Gierlich** proved an intrepid traveler once again. But nothing in France or Sweden could have prepared her for the potholes and precipitation of the Alaska Highway and the Yukon. She and her Jeep may never be the same. Marisa recently graduated from Berkeley and was last seen tromping across Montana.

In the upper latitudes of Alaska, **Alison Huml** tried to go native: She pitched her razor and change of clothes, scarfed down towering piles of sourdough pancakes, and slept on fishing boats. Nonetheless, she couldn't hide her Lower 48 roots. Alison nearly lost it on her hosts' dining-room table when she sampled *muskeg* (whale skin à la blubber)—reminiscent of a rubber tire spread with Crisco. Like a true Californian, she also pulled out her sneakers for a jog in the frigid Arctic air of Barrow (sled dogs strained at their chains and snapped as she passed, and a passel of Eskimo kids chased her, yelling, "you stupid white lady!"). Alison's more positive remembrances include her stay at a Kotzebue fish camp, where an Eskimo granny taught her about tundra vegetation, and her close encounter with a grizzly while hiking in Denali National Park. Alison hopes to return to Alaska to wear down the soles of her boots before heading to law school.

Denny's poster girl **Kate Isaacson** once spent $16 in a single day at the drive-in espresso stands of Western Washington. From the driver's seat of her white Cabriolet convertible (license plate KTSGRVN), this polymorphous-perverse native of California covered nearly every inch of Washington State (except Seattle) without ever losing her caffeine buzz. In the course of her journey, Kate found plenty of fellow neurotics to kvetch with, as she collected enough material for her next three novels (all currently in progress). Her spotted owl-feather shawl was the talk of every town, alternately inciting bar-room brawls and inspiring free rounds of drinks on the house. Among her sordid escapades were a night on the town with Spokane's homeless, temporary membership in a hippie colony on Orcas Isle, and countless lost nights of reveling with local loggers in their natural habitat. An aspiring writer, Kate is currently looking for employment that will utilize her miraculous ability to sleep on command and ingest large doses of caffeine with minimal side effects. Either that or the Harlequin Romance shtick.

After two seasons of charting Czech culture for *The Berkeley Guide to Eastern Europe*, **Helen Lenda** was excited to explore the wilderness in southeast Alaska and British Columbia. Given her childhood in rainy Seattle, she was prepared for the assorted rain showers, downpours, and drizzles of the Alaskan Panhandle—although the morning she awoke to a lake of rainwater in her tent was a bit much. With over 100 hours spent aboard ferries, Helen became intimately familiar with every vessel in the Alaska Marine Highway fleet, and deeply impressed by the ferry system timing: The 4 AM stopover in Tenakee Springs allowed just enough time for a quick soak in the village's hot springs.

Having spent his youth in London, **Josh Lichtner** assumed that he would be dispatched to some urban wasteland, but true to the perverse nature of the Berkeley Guides' editorial staff, he was instead set loose on the wilds of Oregon. From white-water rafting on the Rogue River to mountain biking in the Cascades to horse trekking in the high desert to camping and hiking in the Oregon "Alps," he savored a variety of the state's outdoor recreational activities. The highlight of his trip was an ill-fated attempt to hike down into Hell's Canyon to the Snake River with his girlfriend and her dog. The three intrepid explorers lost the trail, experienced sun-stroke and dehydration, and spent nine hours hiking cross-country to get back out again. This near-death experience has not dampened Josh's lust for adventure: At the tender age of 33, he still hikes through the Berkeley campus in an all-out effort to complete his history B.A.—proving that there is life after 30.

The Editors

After being sucked back into *The Berkeley Guides* fold from a writing stint in England, **Emily W. Miller** found herself once again toiling behind a Mac Classic (oh, the technology). Her dejá vu was not a fantasy—she spent last summer in the same office crunching out witticisms about Italy. She and coeditor Lauren developed a highly dysfunctional, symbiotic relationship, bordering on the pathological. They now both answer to the name Joe-Bob. Emily graduated with honors from U.C. Berkeley, and what good has it done her?

Lauren M. Black used and abused *The Berkeley Guides* as a mere stopover on her way from U.C. Berkeley undergrad studies to law school. Lauren's relationship with the Pacific Northwest & Alaska book started out rocky (don't ask), but she grew to love her job (kinda like a junkie loves her junk). Lauren lived vicariously through her writers; she particularly enjoyed Josh's rafting trip down the Rogue, and has yet to get her breath back after bungee jumping on Vancouver Island. Back in Berkeley, Lauren shared many memorable Diet Cokes, smiles, and tears with her coeditor, Emily, despite a freakish disparity in height.

The Pacific Northwest

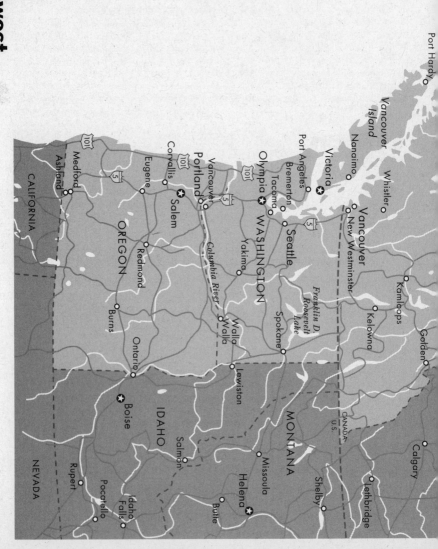

100 miles
150 km

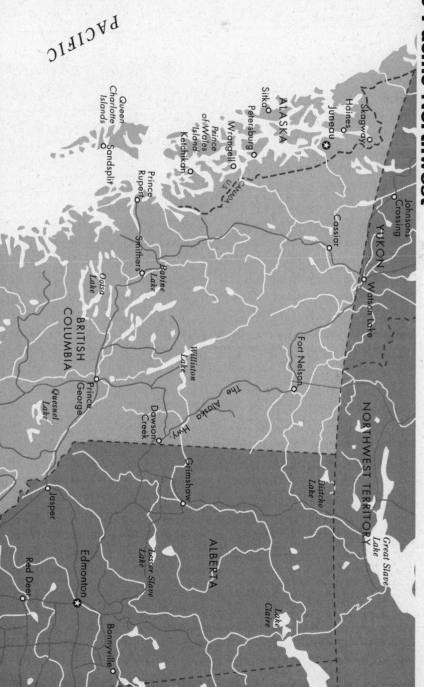

The Pacific Northwest

PACIFIC

Queen
Charlotte
Islands

Sandspit

Sitka

ALASKA

Haines

Juneau

Skagway

Johnsons
Crossing

YUKON

Petersburg

Wrangell

Prince
of Wales
Island

Ketchikan

CANADA
US

Prince
Rupert

Cassiar

Watson Lake

Smithers

Ootsa
Lake

Babine
Lake

BRITISH
COLUMBIA

Fort Nelson

Williston
Lake

The Alaska Hwy

NORTHWEST TERRITORY

Prince
George

Quesnel
Lake

Dawson
Creek

Grimshaw

Bistcho
Lake

Great Slave
Lake

Jasper

Edmonton

Lesser Slave
Lake

ALBERTA

Lake
Claire

Red Deer

Bonnyville

Alaska

ARCTIC OCEAN

Barrow

Chukchi Sea

Colville R.

G

E

S

BROOKS

Anaktuvuk
Pass

Noatak
National
Preserve

Cape Krusenstern
National
Monument

Gates of the Arctic
National Park
and Wildlife
Preserve

RUSSIA

Kobuk Valley
National
Park

Kotzebue

Bettles

Dalton

ARCTIC   CIRCLE

Bering
Land Bridge
National
Preserve

Teller

Bering

Kanuti Flats
National
Wildlife
Refuge

Koyukuk
National
Wildlife
Refuge

I

N

Strait

Council

Livengo

Nome

Yukon   River

Baker

Saint
Lawrence
Island

Norton Sound

Nowitna National
Wildlife Refuge

Innoko
National
Wildlife
Refuge

KUSKOKWIM   MOUNTAINS

Denali
National Park

Bering
Sea

Kuskokwim
R.

Denali
(Mt. McKinley)

Cantwe

R

ALASKA

R

Willow

Pal

Anchorage

Yukon Delta
National
Wildlife
Refuge

Bethel

TAYLOR
MOUNTAINS

Lake Clark
National Park
and Preserve

Tyonek

Whittier

Nunivak
Island

ALASKA

Kenai

Lake
Illiamna

F

R

Seward

Togiak
National
Wildlife
Refuge

Cook

Inlet

Kuskokwim Bay

Dillingham

Homer

Kenai National
Wildlife Refuge

Kenai
Fjords
Nation
Park

Katmai
National Park
and Preserve

Bristol Bay

Port Lions

Chugach
National
Forest

ALASKA PENINSULA

Anaichak
National Monument
and Preserve

Kodiak
National
Wildlife
Refuge

Kodiak

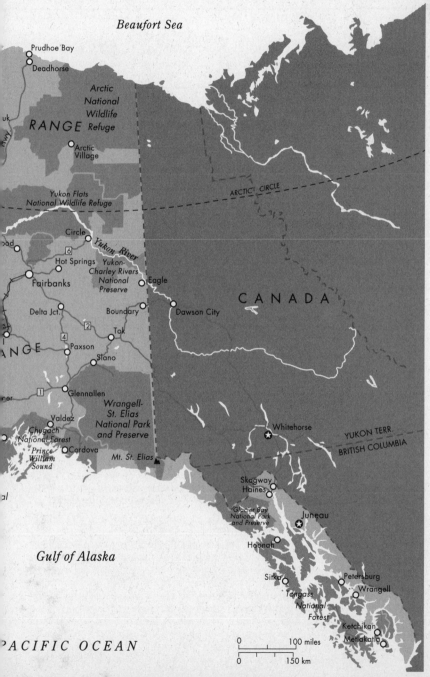

Alaska

Beaufort Sea

Prudhoe Bay
Deadhorse

Arctic
National
Wildlife Refuge

RANGE

Arctic
Village

Yukon Flats
National Wildlife Refuge

ARCTIC CIRCLE

Circle

Yukon River

Hot Springs

Yukon-
Charley Rivers
National
Preserve

Eagle

CANADA

Fairbanks

Delta Jct.

Boundary

Dawson City

Tok

Paxson

Slano

Glennallen

Wrangell-
St. Elias
National Park
and Preserve

YUKON TERR.

Valdez

Whitehorse

Chugach
National Forest

BRITISH COLUMBIA

Cordova

Prince
William
Sound

Mt. St. Elias

Skagway
Haines

Glacier Bay
National Park
and Preserve

Juneau

Gulf of Alaska

Hoonah

Sitka

Petersburg

Wrangell

Tongass
National
Forest

Ketchikan
Metlakatla

PACIFIC OCEAN

0   100 miles

0   150 km

Introduction

The first thing you notice about cities like Seattle, Portland, and Vancouver is nature. It's everywhere—you can't get away from it even if you want to. Mountains rise up in the distance, water swirls in bays and inlets, and pristine forests wend through the city centers. Nowhere else in the Lower 48 or Canada does nature smack you so hard in your pale, urban face. Even if you're a three-pack-a-day basket case, it's tough to find excuses why you shouldn't hike up the nearest mountain or bike through a forest. Why? Because it's inevitably right there, so close you can't miss it. Bicycle trails run through northwest cities like cobwebs; you've never seen so many cyclists in Day-Glo in your life; and joggers are so numerous they now have their own street signs. If you thought California was into this stuff, you should see the Pacific Northwest. Hiking, biking, skiing, boating, and fishing are practically mandatory up here.

Forty-five percent of all garbage is recycled in Seattle, the first city in the United States to put such a massive program into effect. People here feel guilty if they throw away anything that's glass, paper, plastic, aluminum, or tin.

But whatever you do, don't say you're planning to move here because you're likely to be strung up by your ankles and beaten with birches. Call them selfish, but the residents of the Pacific Northwest are getting mighty pissed off with newcomers (largely Californians) moving in and hogging valuable space. If you've got an out-of-state car, don't be surprised if people scrawl nasty things about where you can shove it or suggest that Poland is awfully nice this time of year. If you're just visiting, fine, but don't get too comfortable, especially if you're a Californian.

The Pacific Northwest is suffering from flavor-of-the-month syndrome. Twenty years ago everyone in America moved to California; 10 years ago they got bored and moved to the Sunbelt; now it's the Pacific Northwest's turn. Hollywood jumped on the bandwagon and started spewing out TV shows like *Northern Exposure*, *Frasier*, and *Twin Peaks* that portrayed everyone in the region as beautiful half-wits or at least passionate about logs. As a result, you've got a bunch of yahoos from the rest of the country roaring up here to live in harmony with the wilderness, only to realize that the cement foundation of their new tract home is sitting on it.

Seattle now has the seventh-worst traffic congestion in the country, yet it only ranks 20th in population. Forests are being bulldozed for development, and farms in the Cascade Mountains are rapidly making way for condos. Yet the whole brouhaha about city growth is comparatively new. In contrast, environmentalists and loggers have been pulling one another's beards for decades, wrangling over how the huge forests of the Pacific Northwest should best be used: To be left leafy and alone, or chewed up and made into toothpicks and little paper cups. Things have really heated up since the spotted owl threatened to die, starting a huge legal battle pitting the biggest employers in the region against a coalition of environmentalists, outdoors enthusiasts, and even some small businesses. As a result, the Feds declared large swaths of the old-growth forest off-limits to loggers, which is like telling Attila the Hun to stay out of Rome. Not surprisingly, passions run high: Loggers have zero tolerance for people who care more about owls than jobs, and will happily tell you so over a beer. Some environmentalists have responded by whacking spikes into trees, which do ugly things to chain saws and the people wielding them.

Alaska is another story altogether. Up here it's not so much a question of living in harmony with nature as surviving it. Nature has very much got the upper hand, and the romance of the untamed American frontier is alive and well. Roads are few—only one road runs into the Arctic Circle—and many small settlements are accessible only by boat, bush plane, or dog sled. When the weather moves in, communities can be cut off for weeks, and winters are dark and viciously cold. Vast areas of Alaska comprise pristine wildernesses where you're far more likely to run across caribou, bears, and moose than other humans. Heading into the bush for a camping trip requires a lot more than a sleeping bag, a box of matches, and a bag of marshmallows. But the land is as beautiful as it is harsh, and you won't soon forget the immense glaciers that inch out of the mountains down to the sea, the ice-covered peaks of the Alaska Range, the hundreds of miles of flat tundra, or the untouched forests of spruce and birch.

Alaskans wear furs because they're functional, not fashionable, and you're likely to get a shotgun up your nose if you run around throwing fake blood on everyone and shouting "murderer."

Not surprisingly, Alaskans aren't your average suburban hand-wringers who fret about the condition of their nails. People who stockpile moose in their freezer are funny that way. Hunting and fishing are still a means of feeding yourself here, not just sport. The standard hazing process for gaining the right to call yourself Alaskan is living through a winter here. And there are three possible outcomes of such an event: You will run screaming to Hawaii and become a surfer; you will drink yourself into oblivion; or you will be a convert. Actually the last two options are not mutually exclusive, since a lot of Alaskans, both Native Americans and newcomers, have a big problem with the bottle.

One-fifth the size of the contiguous United States, Alaska has the smallest population of any state—a little over 550,000, almost half of whom live in the Anchorage area (nicknamed "Los Anchorage" after that mecca of urban sprawl, Los Angeles). Only a handful of other towns have populations over 5,000, so the allure for travelers is the miles of wide-open spaces and glacier-capped mountains rather than cultural events and monuments. Except for the towns in Southeast Alaska and the Kenai Peninsula, most of the settlements are nothing more than a collection of trailers, rusting garbage, and satellite dishes. Nome ain't Rome when it comes to baroque architecture.

Life in Alaska revolves around the land, the sea, and the state's natural resources: wildlife, fishing, timber, and oil. State politics are contentious, because so many interest groups are competing for the use of these resources. Hunting and fishing rights are currently a hot issue as subsistence hunters and fishermen (most of whom are Native Americans) clash with commercial and sports interests over rights to harvest fish and game. Another burning issue is oil exploration and drilling. In the 1970s the trans-Alaskan pipeline and the oil from Prudhoe Bay created a large number of high-paying jobs and led to a real improvement in state services. Now that much of the oil has been pumped out of Prudhoe Bay, oil companies are looking at potential fields in the Arctic National Wildlife Refuge, and Alaskans find themselves torn between the need for jobs and the desire to preserve the environment and lifestyles of the region's native people.

Predominantly anarchists, Alaskans want to be free to pursue whatever lifestyle they choose and resent anyone infringing upon that right. If you don't step on their toes, the typical Alaskan is friendlier and more down-to-earth than people elsewhere in the country. People will lend you their truck without taking your firstborn as collateral; and they won't look at you like a panhandler if you approach them in the street. Hitchhiking, which is considered dangerous in most of the Lower 48 states, is still a fairly common way of getting around in Alaska, and many people are willing to offer rides to backpackers. Just think twice about getting into a car with anyone named Hannibal who has a predilection for Chianti and fava beans, because there are also some real hard cases in Alaska—"end-of-the-roaders" who've come up from the Lower 48. Some are on the lam, others are avoiding alimony payments, and still others are just antisocial.

BASICS

If you've ever traveled with anyone before, you know the two types of people in the world: the planners and the nonplanners. You also know that travel brings out the very worst in both groups: Left to their own devices, the planners will have you goose-stepping from attraction to attraction on a cultural blitzkrieg, while the nonplanners will invariably miss the flight, the bus, and the point. This Basics chapter offers you a middle ground, providing enough information to help plan your trip without saddling you with an itinerary or invasion plan. Keep in mind that companies go out of business, prices inevitably go up, and, hey, we're only too human; as one Nixon official so eloquently said, "mistakes have been made."

Planning Your Trip

WHEN TO GO

Everything is more crowded and expensive in July and August. Of course, these are the only months when the Pacific Northwest is warm and sunny, so join the crowds or wait till early autumn, when the warmth lingers and the people leave. It goes without saying that the best time to hit the ski areas is December–March; in Alaska, it's possible to ski downhill and cross-country as late as May. Most ski areas, though, are uncomfortably crowded during Christmas and Easter breaks.

CLIMATE Alaska doesn't close down and freeze into an enormous ice cube in winter. In fact, as any local will tell you, being in Alaska in winter is the only way to find out what the state is *really* like. After the tourists have turned tail, birch, aspens, and willows give a spectacular autumn show. Perhaps most importantly, during the off-season you don't have to worry about Alaska's nefarious mosquitoes.

In the lower states, the severity of weather depends on where you are in relation to the Cascade Mountains, and how far north you go. The Pacific Northwest's image of being perpetually soggy is more or less accurate along the coast, to the west of the Cascades; but inland, to the east of the mountains, it's unusual to get more than six inches of rain per year. As for the region's reputation for freezing weather, the coastal areas stay mild, with summer highs in the 70s and winter temperatures about 40°F. Snow is uncommon in the lowlands and, if it falls, it's usually in December and January. To the east of the mountains the temperatures are more extreme; into the 80s on summer days, and hovering around 0° in winter. Obvious fact: Expect the weather to get progressively colder as you move north from Oregon to Washington to Canada.

Not-so-obvious fact: The farther north you go, the longer the hours of daylight in summer. In Barrow, at the northern tip of Alaska, the sun doesn't set for 82 days between late May and early August. In summer, daytime temperatures in Alaska can climb to the 90s inland, but the weather can change quite quickly, and the odd cold day accompanied by sleet should be expected. In the winter months you're left with only a few hours of daylight; temperatures average –10°, but may dip as low as –60° or –70°.

Average daily high and low temperatures stack up as follows:

City	January: High/Low	July: High/Low
Anchorage:	22°F/7°F	66°F/50°F
Portland:	44°F/33°F	79°F/55°F
Seattle:	45°F/35°F	76°F/56°F
Vancouver:	41°F/32°F	72°F/55°F

FESTIVALS AND SEASONAL EVENTS

➢ **OREGON** • A tip for Oregon-bound summer travelers: If itineraries are not your thing, but you do have the overwhelming urge to make it to a few festivals, stick to the coast—there are festivals everywhere.

MID-FEB.–LATE OCT.: **Oregon Shakespeare Festival** in Ashland, held every year since 1935, features contemporary and classic plays on indoor and outdoor stages. *Box 158, Ashland, OR 97520, tel. 503/482–4331 or 800/547–8052.*

EARLY JUNE: **Portland Rose Festival** is a 24-day extravaganza featuring the nation's second-largest rose parade and the largest children's parade. Since 1907 the city has celebrated the rose as "symbolic of Portland's fresh outlook and unwavering individuality." *Tel. 503/227–2681.*

EARLY JULY: **World Championship Timber Carnival,** in Albany during the Fourth of July weekend, throws a traditional slant on an increasingly controversial way to make a living. Call 800/526–2256 for more info. The **Old Oregon Country Faire** (tel. 503/343–4298) is a rollicking three-day hippie fest in Elmira that throws you right back to the '60s. The crowd grows every year as people camp out in tents, set up craft booths, and mellow out to music.

JULY: **Oregon Brewers Festival** began just a few years ago in Portland and is billed as America's largest beer party, with microbreweries from all over the country pouring their house beers. *Tel. 503/281–2437.*

EARLY AUG.: **Mt. Hood Festival of Jazz**, in Gresham, features outdoor performances, with new acts every hour. *Tel. 503/666–3810.*

LATE AUG.–EARLY SEPT.: **The Oregon State Fair**, held in Salem over the 11 days before Labor Day, has all the trappings of a state fair, including concerts, flea markets, and sporting events. *Tel. 503/378–3247.*

➢ **WASHINGTON** • MID-APR.–EARLY MAY: **Wenatchee Apple Blossom Festival**, held in the "Apple Capital of the World," features parades, races, and carnivals all over town. *Box 850 Wenatchee, WA 98807, tel. 509/662–3616.*

MAY: **Viking Fest** (tel. 206/779–4848) is a Norwegian celebration in Poulsbo. **Northwest Folklife Festival in Seattle** (tel. 206/684–7300) is one of the largest folk fests in the United States, bringing together musicians and artists from all over.

MID-JULY: **Bite of Seattle** is an outdoor food fest at the Seattle Center with the city's finest restaurants selling scrumptious samples (about $4 a serving). *Tel. 206/232–2982.*

MID-JULY–EARLY AUG.: **Seafair**, or Mardi Gras Seattle-style, includes a torchlight parade through downtown and many water-related events, such as hydroplane races on Lake Washington. *Tel. 206/728–0123.*

SEPT.: **Western Washington Fair** has been going on for years in the town of Puyallup, drawing crowds with its offerings of food, song, exhibits, and prize animals. *Tel. 206/845–1771.*

➤ **ALASKA** • EARLY MARCH: **Iditarod Sled Dog Race** (tel. 907/376–5155), though under scrutiny for alleged animal abuse, is legendary. Mushers and teams of dogs start in Anchorage and finish—nearly 1,200 miles and two mountain ranges later—in Nome, where celebrations ensue. Wassila, 35 miles from the start, may be the best spot to experience the race; they hold **Iditarod Days** (tel. 907/376–1299), festivities that center around the "restart."

September–April is the best time to see the Aurora Borealis light up the sky.

APRIL: **Alaska Folk Festival** is a free, week-long, nighttime folk-music celebration where regular folks take turns performing their brand of music for 15 minutes, sometimes longer. *Tel. 907/789–0292 or 907/586–1670.*

LATE MAY: **Little Norway Festival** celebrates the hearty Scandinavian forebears of the people of Petersburg. *Tel. 907/772–3646.*

LATE AUG.–EARLY SEPT.: **Alaska State Fair**, held in Palmer, is typical of state fairs with its homemade baked goods and entertainment; the Anik Glacier makes a nice backdrop for the fair. *Tel. 907/745–4827.*

➤ **BRITISH COLUMBIA** • MARCH–APRIL: **Pacific Rim Whale Festival** takes place during gray whale migratory months. *Tel. 604/725–3414.*

MID-JULY: **Harrison Festival of the Arts** is a week-long shebang celebrating African roots with music, art, and workshops. *Box 399, Harrison Hot Springs, BC V0M 1K0, Canada, tel. 604/796–3664.*

LATE JULY: **Vancouver Sea Festival** (tel. 604/684–3378) has, you guessed it, a parade, fireworks, and a carnival, in addition to many water-related activities and boat shows, including the **International Bathtub Race** (tel. 604/753–7223 or 604/754–8474), a highly acclaimed but weird competition where fiber-form vessels are raced from Nanaimo to Vancouver.

MID-AUG.–EARLY SEPT.: **Pacific National Exhibition** (tel. 604/253–2311), the big-deal fair in Western Canada, features big-name entertainment and the like.

➤ **YUKON** • LATE AUG.: **Discovery Days,** held the weekend closest to August 16, is a four-day celebration commemorating the discovery of gold and the ensuing gold rush in Dawson City. *Discovery Day Committee, Box 308, Dawson City, Yukon Territory Y0B 1G0, Canada, tel. 403/993–5434 or 403/667–5340.*

TOURIST OFFICES

Aside from offering the usual glossy tourist brochures, state and local tourist offices can answer general questions about travel and refer you to other organizations for even more info. When writing, ask for brochures on specialized activities, such as boating, horseback riding, or biking—they may not be included in a generic information package.

NORTH AMERICA

➤ **ALASKA** • **Alaska Division of Tourism** distributes a free "Alaska State Guide." *Box 11080, Juneau, AK 99811, tel. 907/465–2010.*

➤ **OREGON** • **Oregon Tourism Division** distributes free travel guides and maps. The "Oregon Parks Guide" indicates which campgrounds have wheelchair access. *Oregon Economic Development Dept., 775 Summer St. NE, Salem, OR 97310, tel. 800/547–7842 or 800/543–8838 in OR.*

➤ **WASHINGTON** • **Washington State Tourism Office** sends out an excellent free booklet called "Destination Washington." *101 General Administration Bldg. AX-13, Olympia, WA 98504, tel. 206/586–2088 for general info or 800/544–1800 for free booklet.*

➢ **CANADA** • **Travel British Columbia** has free accommodation, travel, and outdoor-adventure guides, a road map that highlights national parks, and a guidebook for disabled travelers. *1117 Wharf St., Victoria, BC V8W 2Z2, tel. 604/387–1642 or 800/663–6000.*

Tourism Yukon distributes a free vacation guide and road map. *Box 2703, Whitehorse, Yukon Y1A 2C6, tel. 403/667–5340 or 800/661–0494 in Canada.*

OFFICES ABROAD Foreign visitors who want some "official" tourist information about the United States can check with the **U.S. Travel and Tourism Administration (USTTA)** (Dept. of Commerce, 14th and Constitution Aves. NW, Washington, DC 20230, tel. 202/482–2000). Information about Canada is available from the **Tourism Industry of Canada** (10 Rideau St., Ottawa, Ontario K1A OH5, tel. 613/238–3883 or 613/787–4000).

➢ **CANADA** • USTTA. *Suite 602, 480 University Ave., Toronto, Ontario M5G 1V2, tel. 416/595–5082. Other location: 241095 W. Pender St., Vancouver, BC, tel. 416/595–0335.*

➢ **UNITED KINGDOM** • USTTA. *Box 1EN, London W1A 1EN, tel. 0171/495–4466.* **Canada House, Tourism Division.** *Trafalgar Sq., London SW1Y 5BJ, tel. 0171/930–6857.* **Tourism British Columbia.** *1 Regent St., London SW1Y 4NS, tel. 0171/930–6857.*

➢ **AUSTRALIA** • USTTA. *APO GPO Box 478, Sydney 2001, tel. 02/233–4055.* **Canadian Consulate, Tourism Desk.** *6th floor, 111 Harrington St., Sydney 2000, tel. 02/364–3000.*

BUDGET TRAVEL ORGANIZATIONS

Student Travel Australia (STA) has 120 offices worldwide and offers low-price airfares to destinations around the globe, as well as rail passes, car rentals, you name it. STA issues the ISIC (International Student Identity Card) and their own STA Travel Card (about $6) for recent graduates, which proves eligibility for some travel discounts (*see* Student I.D. Cards, *below*). Write or call one of their offices for a slew of free pamphlets on services and rates.

Council on International Educational Exchange (CIEE) is a nonprofit organization dedicated to the pursuit of work, study, and travel abroad. Through its two subsidiaries, **Council Travel** and **Council Charter,** CIEE offers discounted airfares, rail passes, accommodations, and guidebooks. They also issue the ISIC, IYC, ITC, and youth hostel cards (*see* Student I.D. Cards, *below*). University travel centers may also carry CIEE's *Student Travels* magazine, a gold mine of travel tips (including work and study-abroad opportunities). **Council Charter** (tel. 212/661–0311 or 800/223–7402) buys blocks of seats on commercial flights and sells them

STA Offices

• **NORTH AMERICA. ARIZONA:** *Scottsdale (tel. 602/596–5151 or 800/777–0112).* **CALIFORNIA:** *Berkeley (tel. 510/642–3000); Los Angeles (tel. 213/934–8722); San Francisco (tel. 415/391–8407); Santa Monica (tel. 310/394–5126); Westwood (tel. 310/824–1574).* **MASSACHUSETTS:** *Boston (tel. 617/266–6014); Cambridge (tel. 617/576–4623).* **NEW YORK:** *East Village (tel. 212/477–7166); Columbia University (tel. 212/854–2224).* **PENNSYLVANIA:** *Philadelphia (tel. 215/382–2928).* **WASHINGTON DC** *(tel. 202/887–0912).*

• **INTERNATIONAL. AUSTRALIA:** *Adelaide (tel. 08/223–2426); Brisbane (tel. 07/221–9388); Cairns (tel. 070/314199); Darwin (tel. 089/412955); Melbourne (tel. 03/349–2411); Perth (tel. 09/227–7569); Sydney (tel. 02/212–1255).* **NEW ZEALAND:** *Auckland (tel. 09/309–9995); Christchurch (tel. 03/379–9098); Wellington (tel. 04/385–0561).* **UNITED KINGDOM:** *London (tel. 0171/938–4711).*

at a discount. Call for prices and availability. *205 E. 42nd St., New York, NY 10017, tel. 212/661–1414.*

Educational Travel Center (ETC) books low-cost flights (most departing from Chicago) to destinations within the continental United States and around the world. ETC also issues American Youth Hostel cards. For more details request their free brochure, *Taking Off. 438 N. Frances St., Madison, WI 53703, tel. 608/256–5551.*

Travel CUTS is a full-service travel agency that sells discounted airline tickets to Canadian students and issues the ISIC, IYC, and HI cards. Their 25 offices are on or near college campuses. *187 College St., Toronto, Ont. M5T 1P7, tel. 416/979–2406.*

Y's Way International. This network of YMCA overnight centers offers low-cost accommodations (average overnight rate of $26) in the Pacific Northwest to travelers of all ages. Their booklet, "The Y's Way," details locations, reservation policies, and package tours. *356 W. 34th St., New York, NY 10001, tel. 212/760–1707.*

Hostelling International (HI) is the grandmammy of hostel associations, offering single-sex dorm-style beds ("couples" rooms and family accommodations are available at certain HI hostels) and kitchen facilities (about $4–$22 per night) at nearly 5,000 locations in 70 countries around the world. A one-year membership is available to travelers of all ages and runs about $25 for adults (renewal $20) and $10 for those under 18. A one-night guest membership is about $3. Family memberships are available for $35, and a lifetime membership will set you back $250. For more info, *see* Hostels, in Staying in the Pacific Northwest and Alaska, *below. 733 15th St. NW, Suite 840, Washington, DC 20005, tel. 202/783–6161.*

Other associations aiding and abetting hostel-goers include **American Youth Hostels (AYH)** (733 15th St., Suite 840, Washington, DC 20005, tel. 202/783–6161); **Hostelling International Canada (HIC)** (205 Catherine St., Suite 400, Ottowa, Ont. K2P 1C3, tel. 613/237–7884); **Youth Hostel Association of England and Wales (YHA)** (Trevelyan House, 8 St.

Council Travel Offices

ARIZONA: Tempe (tel. 602/966–3544). **CALIFORNIA:** Berkeley (tel. 510/848–8604), Davis (tel. 916/752–2285), La Jolla (tel. 619/452–0630), Long Beach (tel. 310/598–3338 or 714/527–7950), Los Angeles (tel. 310/208–3551), Palo Alto (tel. 415/325–3888), San Diego (tel. 619/270–6401), San Francisco (tel. 415/421–3473 or 415/566–6222), Santa Barbara (tel. 805/562–8080). **COLORADO:** Boulder (tel. 303/447–8101). **CONNECTICUT:** New Haven (tel. 203/562–5335). **FLORIDA:** Miami (tel. 305/670–9261). **GEORGIA:** Atlanta (tel. 404/377–9997). **ILLINOIS:** Chicago (tel. 312/951–0585), Evanston (tel. 708/475–5070). **INDIANA:** Bloomington (tel. 812/330–1600). **LOUISIANA:** New Orleans (tel. 504/866–1767). **MASSACHUSETTS:** Amherst (tel. 413/256–1261), Boston (tel. 617/266–1926 or 617/424–6665), Cambridge (tel. 617/497–1497 or 617/225–2555). **MICHIGAN:** Ann Arbor (tel. 313/998–0200). **MINNESOTA:** Minneapolis (tel. 612/379–2323). **NEW YORK:** New York (tel. 212/661–1450, 212/666–4177, or 212/254–2525). **NORTH CAROLINA:** Chapel Hill (tel. 919/942–2334). **OHIO:** Columbus (tel. 614/294–8696). **OREGON:** Portland (tel. 503/228–1900). **PENNSYLVANIA:** Philadelphia (tel. 215/382–0343), Pittsburgh (tel. 412/683–1881). **RHODE ISLAND:** Providence (tel. 401/331–5810). **TEXAS:** Austin (tel. 512/472–4931), Dallas (tel. 214/363–9941). **UTAH:** Salt Lake City (tel. 801/582–5840). **WASHINGTON:** Seattle (tel. 206/632–2448 or 206/329–4567). **WASHINGTON D.C.** (tel. 202/337–6464).

Stephen's Hill, St. Albans, Herts. AL1 2DY, England, tel. 01727/855215); **Australian Youth Hostels Association (YHA)** (Box 61, Strawberry Hills, Sydney 2012, New South Wales, tel. 02/212–1266); and **Youth Hostels Association of New Zealand (YHA)** (Box 436, Christchurch 1, tel. 03/799–970).

STUDENT I.D. CARDS

Students traveling around the United States and Canada should not expect big discounts— except possibly on air travel if they purchase tickets through special student-travel agencies such as Council Travel or STA (*see* Budget Travel Organizations, *above*). Still, bring your student I.D. card with you for those occasional discounts on bus travel, admission to some museums, movie theaters, and club cover charges.

The **International Student Identity Card (ISIC)** entitles students to special fares on local transportation and discounts at museums, theaters, sports events, and many other attractions. If purchased in the United States, the $17 cost for the popular ISIC card also buys you $3,000 in emergency medical coverage; limited hospital coverage; and access to a 24-hour international, toll-free hotline for assistance in medical, legal, and financial emergencies. In the United States, apply to CIEE or STA; in Canada, the ISIC is available for C$15 from Travel CUTS (*see* Budget Travel Organizations, *above*). In the United Kingdom, students with valid university I.D.s can purchase the ISIC at any student union or student-travel company. Applicants must submit a photo as well as proof of current full-time student status, age, and nationality.

The **STA Travel Card** is available to travelers age 35 and under for $6. With it, you'll gain access to discounted student fares and *Discount Counter*, a coupon book that offers dollars-off coupons for a limited number of subscribing businesses' services. Purchase the STA card *before* departing.

The **Youth International Educational Exchange Card (YIEE)** is issued to travelers (students and nonstudents) under age 26 by the Federation of International Youth Travel Organizations (FIYTO). It provides services and benefits similar to those given by the ISIC card. The card is available for $16 from CIEE or FIYTO. *81 Islands Brugge, DK-2300 Copenhagen S, Denmark.*

MONEY

CURRENCY The United States and Canada both use dollars ($) and cents (¢), but the value of each differs on the world market, as do the illustrations printed on the bills—the U.S. dollar has presidents, the Canadian has the queen and prime ministers. Commonly used paper currency comes in $1, $5, $10, and $20 bills in both the United States and Canada. Canada recently introduced the C$2 bill and began phasing out the C$1 bill in favor of a C$1 coin nicknamed the "loonie" because of the loon stamped on one side. Coins in both countries come in denominations of 1¢ (penny), 5¢ (nickel), 10¢ (dime), and 25¢ (quarter). Throughout this book we will refer to Canadian currency with a preceding "C" (e.g., C$10, C$50).

In Canada do not use a personal check from a U.S. bank—there's a heavy surcharge.

At press time, the exchange rates for U.S. dollars were as follows:

Canada (C$)	Britain (£)	Australia (AUS$)	New Zealand (NZ$)
$1 = C$1.35	$1 = 62p	$1 = AUS$1.36	$1 = NZ$1.64
C$1 = 74¢	£1 = $1.61	AUS$1 = 74¢	NZ$1 = 61¢

Many Canadian restaurants, businesses, and hotels accept U.S. currency (though U.S. businesses do NOT accept Canadian dollars) and usually respect the current exchange rate. You can get cash from ATMs (Automated Teller Machines) in both countries, but many small towns don't have them. In such cases, a Visa or MasterCard comes in handy for getting cash advances—as long as you don't mind paying a hefty service charge and/or interest fee (*see* Credit Cards, *below*).

TRAVELING WITH MONEY Cash never goes out of style, but traveler's checks and a major U.S. credit card are usually the safest and most convenient way to pay for goods and services on the road. Depending on the length of your trip, strike a balance among these three forms of currency, and protect yourself by carrying cash in a money belt or "necklace" pouch (available at luggage and camping stores) or front pocket; keeping accurate records of traveler's checks' serial numbers; and recording credit-card numbers and an emergency number for reporting the cards' loss or theft. Carrying at least some cash (hard currency) is wise; most budget establishments will accept cash only, and, outside of urban areas, changing traveler's checks may prove difficult. Bring about $100 (in as many single bills as possible) in cash; changing dollars will be easier than cashing traveler's checks.

TRAVELER'S CHECKS Traveler's checks can be used for purchases in the same way as a personal check (always ask first), or they can be exchanged for cash at banks, some hotels, tourist offices, American Express offices, or currency-exchange offices. American Express checks are the most widely accepted; other brands are sometimes refused. Some banks and credit unions will issue checks free to established customers, but most charge a 1%–2% commission fee. Members of the **American Automobile Association (AAA)** can purchase American Express traveler's checks from the AAA commission-free. Buy the bulk of your traveler's checks in small denominations (a pack of five $20 checks is the smallest); many establishments won't accept large bills, and, even when they do, breaking a large check for small purchases leaves you carrying too much cash. Call any of the toll-free or collect telephone numbers listed below for more information about where to purchase traveler's checks and how widely they are accepted in your destination.

Many fleabag hotels and hole-in-the-wall restaurants don't accept traveler's checks, and will look at you funny if you hand them plastic.

American Express card members can order traveler's checks in U.S. dollars and six foreign currencies by phone, free of charge (with a gold card) or for a 1% commission (with your basic green card). In three to five business days you'll receive your checks: up to $1,000 can be ordered in a seven-day period. AmEx also issues **Traveler's Cheques for Two**, checks that can be signed and used by either you or your traveling companion. If you lose your checks or are ripped off, true to Karl Malden's repeated pledges, AmEx has the resources to provide you with a speedy refund—often within 24 hours. Ask for the *American Express Traveler's Companion,* a handy little directory of their offices, to find out more about particular services at different locations. *Tel. 800/221-7282 in U.S. and Canada.*

Citicorp traveler's checks are available from Citibank and other banks worldwide in U.S. dollars and some foreign currencies. For 45 days from the date of check purchase, travelers have access to the 24-hour International S.O.S. Assistance Hotline, which can provide English-speaking doctor, lawyer, and interpreter referrals; assistance with loss or theft of travel documents; traveler's check refund assistance; and an emergency message center. *Tel. 800/645-6556 in U.S. or 813/623-1709 collect outside U.S.*

MasterCard International traveler's checks, issued in U.S. dollars only, are offered through banks, credit unions, and foreign-exchange booths. Call for information about acceptance of their checks at your travel destination and for the local number to call in case of loss or theft. *Tel. 800/223-7373 in the U.S., 609/987-7300 collect from outside the U.S.*

Thomas Cook brand of MasterCard traveler's check is available in U.S. dollars and foreign currencies. If purchased through a Thomas Cook Foreign Exchange office (formerly Deak International), there is no commission. For more info, contact MasterCard (*see above*).

Visa, as a sponsor of the 1992 Olympics, boosted its name recognition and acceptance worldwide. When two giants in the traveler's check universe (BankAmerica Corporation and Barclays) embarked on a joint venture, their baby was born as **Interpayment Visa Travelers Cheques,** which are actually imprinted with the name of the financial institution that sells the checks. Don't be fooled: You're getting Visa traveler's checks, widely known and available in at least 10 currencies. *Tel. 800/227-6811 in U.S. and Canada or 813/623-1709 collect from outside U.S.*

➤ **LOST AND STOLEN CHECKS** • Unlike cash, once lost or stolen, traveler's checks can be replaced or refunded *if* you can produce the purchase agreement and a record of the checks' serial numbers (especially of those you've already cashed). Sign all the checks when you buy them; you'll endorse them a second time to exchange them for cash or make purchases. Common sense dictates that you keep the purchase agreement separate from your checks. Caution-happy travelers will even give a copy of the purchase agreement and checks' serial numbers to someone back home. Most issuers of traveler's checks promise to refund or replace lost or stolen checks in 24 hours, but you can practically see them crossing their fingers behind their backs.

CREDIT CARDS Major credit-card companies have tightened requirements and aren't passing out $1,000 credit lines to students and low-income applicants the way they did in the material-world '80s. If you want plastic (not a bad idea on the road), check at university bookstores or student unions for special student offers from American Express and other companies. If a more economically able family member or friend is willing, he or she may apply for a second card for you that is linked to their account. Plastic money is not free: Annual fees for basic credit cards range from nothing to upwards of $55, and the interest rate on unpaid monthly balances runs 10%–20%. For a survey that details annual fees and interest rates, send a self-addressed, stamped, business-size envelope to the nonprofit outfit **Consumer Action** (116 New Montgomery St., Suite 233, San Francisco, CA 94105, tel. 415/777–9635).

Visa and MasterCard (but not always American Express) are both accepted at many banks, though each bank sets its own limits on the amount of money you can withdraw and which cards are accepted; policies may even vary from branch to branch. Typically, the daily withdrawal limit is about $300. A small commission fee—no more than if you were exchanging traveler's checks—is charged. Expensive restaurants and hotels will accept credit cards, as will car-rental agencies and ATM machines—look for the card logo on windows.

GETTING MONEY ON THE ROAD

Provided there is money at home to be had, there are at least five ingenious ways to get it:

• Have it sent through a large **commercial bank** that has a branch in the town where you're staying. Unless you have an account with that large bank, though, you'll have to initiate the transfer at your own bank, and the process will be slower and more expensive.

• If you're an **American Express** cardholder, cash a personal check at an American Express office for up to $1,000 ($2,500 for gold cardholders) every 21 days; you'll be paid in U.S. traveler's checks or, in some instances, in cash. **Express Cash** further allows American Express cardholders to withdraw up to $1,000 every 21 days from their personal checking accounts via ATMs (*see* Cash Machines, *below*).

• An **American Express** *MoneyGram*^SM can be a dream come true if you can convince someone back home to go to an American Express MoneyGram^SM agent and fill out the necessary forms.

Making the Most of Your Parents' Credit Card

Even if you have no job, no credit, no cards, and no respect, you can still tap into fabulous services offered by the Visa Assistance Center if one of your parents has a Visa Gold or Business card and you are a dependent of 22 years or less and at least 100 miles from home. Write down the card number in a safe, memorable place and call the center for emergency cash service, emergency ticket replacement and lost-luggage assistance, medical and legal assistance, and an emergency message service. Helpful, multilingual personnel await your call 24 hours a day, seven days a week. In the U.S. call 800/759–6262; from Canada and abroad call 919/370–3203 collect.

You don't have to be an AmEx cardholder to send or receive a MoneyGram℠: simply pay up to $1,000 with a credit card or cash (and anything over that in cash) and, as quick as 10 minutes later, it's ready to be picked up. Fees vary according to the amount of money sent but average about 3%–10%. You have to get the transaction reference number from your sender back home and show ID when picking up the money. For locations of American Express Money-Gram℠ agents call 800/926–9400 or contact the nearest AmEx agent.

- **MasterCard** and **Visa** cardholders can get cash advances from many banks, even in small towns. The commission for this handy-dandy service is about 6½%. If you get a PIN number for your card before you leave home, you might even be able to make the transaction with an ATM machine.

- Have funds sent through **Western Union** (tel. 800/325–6000), with fees ranging from 4% to 9%, depending on the amount sent. If you have a MasterCard or Visa, you can have money sent up to your card's credit limit. If not, have someone take cash, a certified cashier's check, or a healthy MasterCard or Visa to a Western Union office. The money will reach the requested destination in minutes but may not be available for several more hours or days, depending on the whim of the local authorities.

CASH MACHINES Virtually all U.S. banks belong to a network of **ATMs** (Automated Teller Machines), which gobble up bank cards and spit out cash 24 hours a day in cities throughout the world. Some are affiliated with the Cirrus system, some with PLUS and Exchange, a very few with STAR. These bank substitutes are better in theory than practice; ATMs may not always function or even exist outside of big cities. If the transaction cannot be completed, chances are that the computer lines are busy (try to avoid Friday afternoons), and you'll just have to try again later. If you know your PIN number as a word, learn the numerical equivalent before you leave, since some ATM keypads show no letters, only numbers. On the plus side, *To find out if there are any cash machines in a given city, call Cirrus (tel. 800/424–7787) or PLUS (tel. 800/843–7587) and dial your way through a push-button phone maze.*
ATMs spew U.S. and Canadian instantly at a generally excellent rate of exchange. That said, some banks do charge a 1%–3% fee per ATM transaction, so consider withdrawing larger chunks of cash rather than small bundles on a daily basis.

A **Visa** or **MasterCard** can also be used to access cash through certain ATMs (provided you have a PIN for it), but the fees for this service are usually higher than bank-card fees. Also, a daily interest charge usually begins to accrue immediately on these credit-card "loans," even if monthly bills are paid up.

Express Cash allows American Express cardholders to withdraw up to $1,000 in a seven-day period (21 days in parts of Canada) from their personal checking accounts via a worldwide network of ATMs. Gold cardholders can receive up to $2,500 in a seven-day period (again, 21 days in parts of Canada). Each transaction carries a 2% fee, with a minimum charge of $2 and a maximum of $6. Apply for a PIN and set up the linking of your accounts at least two to three weeks before departure. Call 800/CASH–NOW for an application.

WHAT TO PACK

As little as possible. Besides the usual suspects—clothes, toiletries, camera, a Walkman, and a good book—bring along a day pack or some type of smaller receptacle for stuff; it'll come in handy not only for day excursions but also for those places where you plan to stay for only one or two days. You can check heavy, cumbersome bags at the train or bus station (or leave it at your motel/hostel) and just carry the essentials with you while you go looking for lodging.

WHERE TO PUT IT ALL By distributing the weight of your luggage across shoulders and hips, backpacks ease the burden of traveling. You can actually choose among three types of packs: external-frame packs (for longer travels or use on groomed trails), internal-frame packs (for longer travels across rougher terrain), and travel packs (hybrid packs that fit under an airline seat and travel well in cities or the back country). Although external frames achieve the best weight-distribution and allow airspace between you and your goodies, they're more awkward and less flexible than packs with an internal frame. Since an external-frame backpack will run you about $100–$225 (internal frames are about $50 more), be sure to have it fitted correctly when you buy it. Check to see that it is waterproof, or bring an extra waterproof poncho to throw over it in downpours. An inside pocket is great for dirty laundry or food storage, and straps for a sleeping mat are good for those who will be roughing it. Straps, zippers, and seams are the most vulnerable points on a bag; check that straps are wide, adjustable, and offer some padding; check the stitching on zippers and seams; and look for a wide zipper. A zipper that can be locked never hurts.

THE SLEEP SHEET:

Take a big sheet. Fold it down the middle the long way. Sew one short side and the long, open side. Turn inside out. Get inside. Sleep.

BEDDING Hostels require that you use a sleep sheet, and, though some rent them, some don't. If you have a backpack, consider a sleeping mat that can be rolled tightly and strapped onto the bottom of your pack; these make train- and bus-station floors a tad more comfy.

LAUNDRY For the average person, hotel rooms are the best place (certainly the cheapest) to do laundry. A bring-your-own laundry service includes: a plastic bottle of liquid detergent or soap (powder doesn't break down as well), about six feet of clothesline (enough to tie to two stable objects), and some plastic clips (bobby pins or paper clips can substitute). Porch railings, shower curtain rods, bathtubs, and faucets can all serve as wet-laundry hangers if you forget the clothesline. Be sure to bring an extra plastic bag or two for still-damp laundry and dirty clothes.

Dr. Bronner's Magic Soap is safe for both clothes and your bod, and the label is cool reading material on long train rides.

TOILETRIES Use a separate, waterproof bag for containers that seal tightly; the pressure on airplanes can cause lids to pop off and create instant moisturizer slicks inside your luggage. Bring all the paraphernalia you need to conduct chemical warfare on your contact lenses, if you wear them. Bring some toilet paper with you and have some in your pockets at all times. Bring tampons, deodorant, soap, shampoo, toothpaste, and any prescription drugs you might need. Condoms and birth control are also important. Finally, bring insect repellent, sunscreen, and lip balm from home. **Avon "Skin So Soft"** body moisturizer is the best bug repellent in the world, even if it's not marketed as such. Repeat: This stuff *really* works. Check the phone book under AVON and make an appointment with your friendly Avon person. Another option is **Green Ban's** environmentally-sound insect repellent: stinky, but moderately effective.

Alaskan Fashion Tips

Unless you're traveling by car, you'll need to pack lightly but still meet the demands of the extreme northern climate. One thing is in your favor: Dress is extremely casual in Alaska. Blue jeans and a T-shirt are appropriate attire even in the priciest restaurants around Fairbanks. Moreover, you'll fit in better with the locals if you leave makeup, hairspray, hair gel, and razors at home. If you're coming to the interior in summer, you need to be prepared for temperatures between 40° and 70°F, give or take 10°F. Bring clothing that you can layer, and by all means bring wool socks, one or two wool shirts, a wool hat, and even a pair of wool pants if you plan to adventure into the far north. Summer days are generally warm and dry, but freezing rain is not unheard of. You'll also probably encounter some genuinely hot days, so bring along a comfortable pair of hiking shorts. Throw in sunscreen—the sun will be out for 20 hours or more a day and, yes, it is possible to get a midnight sunburn.

CAMERAS AND FILM While traveling, keep film as cool as possible, away from direct sunlight or blazing campfires. On a plane, unprocessed film is safest in your carry-on luggage—ask security to inspect it by hand. (It helps to keep your film in a plastic bag, ready for quick inspection.) Inspectors at American airports are required by law to honor requests for hand inspection, so don't be afraid to demand your rights (if you've got no contraband hiding in your luggage, that is). All airport scanning machines used in U.S. airports are safe for any number of scans from five to 500, depending on the speed of your film. The higher the film speed, the more susceptible it is to damage.

FIRST-AID KITS For about 97% of your trip, a first aid kit may mean nothing to you but extra bulk. However, in an emergency you'll be glad to have even the most basic medical supplies. Prepackaged kits are available, but you can pack your own from the following list: bandages, waterproof surgical tape and gauze pads, antiseptic, cortisone cream, tweezers, a thermometer in a sturdy case, an antacid such as Alka-Seltzer, something for diarrhea (Pepto Bismol or Immodium), and, of course, aspirin. If you're prone to motion sickness or are planning to use particularly rough modes of transportation during your travels, take along some Dramamine. No matter what your coloring, if you'll be exposed to sunlight for any length of time, pack sunscreen to protect against cancer-causing rays. Women: If prone to vaginal infections, you can now buy over-the-counter medication (Monistat or Gynelotrimin) that will save you prolonged grief on the road. However, self-medicating should only be relied on for short-term illnesses; seek professional help if any medical symptoms persist or worsen.

MISCELLANEOUS Stuff you might not think to take but will be damn glad to have: (1) extra day-pack for valuables or short jaunts; (2) a flashlight, good for electricity failures, reading in the dark, and exploring caves; (3) Walkman, entertainment for bus and train rides; (4) a pocket knife for cutting fruit, spreading cheese, removing splinters, and opening bottles; (5) water bottle; (6) sunglasses; (7) several large zip-type plastic bags, useful for wet swim suits, towels, leaky bottles, and rancid socks; (8) travel alarm clock; (9) needle and small spool of thread; (10) batteries; (11) some interesting books.

RESOURCES FOR WOMEN

Unfortunately, not everyone is as open-minded about independent women as we know they should be—solo women travelers often have to put on a tough, surly exterior to avoid unwelcome advances. You can play it safe—avoid seedy bars and hitchhiking—or carry mace (which is technically illegal in Canada). Hitchhiking alone is a bad idea, and women who stop to pick up roadside hitchers should also exercise caution. Your best bet is to hook up with fellow travelers whom you feel you can trust, and stick together in questionable areas. In larger cities, hotlines, support groups, and women-oriented bookstores are your best resources.

PUBLICATIONS For a complete listing of women's periodicals, presses, and cafés, try the *Directory of Women's Media* ($30), published by the National Council for Research on Women. *530 Broadway, 10th floor, New York, NY 10012, tel. 212/274–0730.*

Excluding the lesbian-oriented *Women's Traveller* (*see* Resources for Gays and Lesbians, *below*) and *Are You Two...Together?*, the only major travelogue for women is *Women Travel: Adventures, Advice, and Experience* ($12.95), published by Prentice Hall and available at bookstores. Over 70 countries receive some sort of coverage, with journal entries and short articles. As far as practical travel information goes, it offers few details on prices, phone numbers, and addresses. Thalia Zepatos' *A Journey of One's Own* ($13), subtitled "Uncommon Advice for the Independent Woman Traveler" and available at most bookstores, is fun to read but has little information on specific regions. Still, for women it's a good resource for general travel information.

ORGANIZATIONS National Organization for Women is a feminist organization committed to equality for women. NOW is also a good resource and referral center for just about any women's issue. *4649 Sunnyside Ave. N, Seattle, WA 98103, tel. 206/632–8547. Also: 8700 SW 26th St., Portland, OR 97219, tel. 503/452–0272.*

Women's Resource Center at the University of British Columbia. *1144 Robson St., Vancouver V6E 1B2, Canada, tel. 604/685–3934.*

WAVE. Women Against Violence offers counseling, support, and referral for women who have been raped or abused. *Box 88584 Chinatown Postal Outlet, Vancouver V6A 4A7, Canada, tel. 604/255–6344.*

Women Welcome Women (WWW) is a non-profit organization aimed at bringing together women of all nationalities. WWW can get you in touch with women around the globe who are interested in every variety of women's issues. *Contact F. Alexander, 8/A Chestnut Ave., High Wycombe, Buckinghamshire HP11 1DJ, England.*

The **Young Women's Christian Association (YWCA)** offers social-service programs and accommodation referrals to women. *620 Sutter St., San Francisco, CA 94102, tel. 415/775–6502; in Los Angeles, tel. 213/365–2991.*

RESOURCES FOR GAYS AND LESBIANS

Gay men and women enjoy a certain amount of freedom in the larger cities. Despite these supportive environments, gay-bashing continues to occur, so always try to be aware of your surroundings if you're with your same-sex lover. Outside big cities, attitudes are decidedly more conservative and biased. Publications focusing on gay issues can be found in gay community bookstores and cafés.

PUBLICATIONS *The Advocate* ($3) is an excellent, national, bimonthly gay magazine. The focus is less on travel and more on contemporary gay issues. *Liberation Publications, 6922 Hollywood Blvd., Los Angeles, CA 90028.*

Another excellent resource is the **Damron Address Book** ($13.95 plus shipping), which focuses on gay male travel in the United States and Canada. *Box 422458, San Francisco, CA 94142, tel. 415/255–0404 or 800/462–6654.*

INN Places ($14.95 plus $3.50 shipping) thoroughly covers the U.S. and is the guide to get for up-to-date listings of gay agencies, hotels, and clubs. *Ferrari Publications, Box 37887, Phoenix, AZ 85069, tel. 602/863–2408.*

Spartacus bills itself as *the* guide for the gay traveler, with practical tips and reviews of hotels and agencies in over 160 countries. It's a bit expensive at $29.95, though you do get snappy color photos and listings in four languages. *Tel. 800/462–6654.*

One of the best gay and lesbian travel newsletters is **Out and About**, with listings of gay-friendly hotels and travel agencies, plus health cautions for travelers with HIV. A 10-issue subscription costs $49; single issues cost about $7. *For subscriptions tel. 800/929–2268.*

The most comprehensive lesbian publication is **Women's Traveller** ($10), a dense guide to bars, hotels, and agencies throughout the United States and Canada. *Box 422458, San Francisco, CA 94142, tel. 800/462–6654.*

ORGANIZATIONS The best way to locate organizations is to browse through one of the publications listed above. For info and referrals try **Phoenix Rising** (tel. 503/223–8299) in Portland or the **Lesbian and Gay Community Line** (tel. 506/489–2266) in Spokane. Other cities have community centers that serve as meeting places for locals; check individual chapters and local phone books.

International Gay Travel Association (IGTA) is a nonprofit organization with worldwide listings of travel agencies, gay-friendly hotels, gay bars, and travel services aimed at gay travelers. *Box 4974, Key West, FL 33041, tel. 800/448–8550.*

RESOURCES FOR THE DISABLED

Accessibility may soon have an international symbol if an initiative begun by the Society for the Advancement of Travel for the Handicapped (SATH) catches on. A bold, underlined, capital **H** is the symbol that SATH is publicizing for hotels, restaurants, and tourist attractions to indicate that the property has some accessible facilities. While awareness of the needs of travelers with disabilities increases every year, budget opportunities are harder to find. Always ask if discounts are available, either for you or for a companion. In addition, plan your trip and make reservations far in advance, since companies that provide services for people with disabilities go in and out of business regularly.

The national park system offers the **Golden Access Passport,** a free, lifetime entry pass that exempts travelers with disabilities and their families or friends from all entry fees and 50% of use fees for camping and parking in federal parks and wildlife refuges. You aren't allowed to register by mail or phone, but you can apply in person with medical proof of disability at all National Park Service and Forest Service offices, Forest Service ranger station offices, national parks that charge fees, Bureau of Land Management Offices, and Fish and Wildlife Service offices. For info, contact the **Outdoor Recreation Information Center** (915 2nd Ave., Suite 442, Seattle, WA 98174, tel. 206/220-7450).

ACCOMMODATIONS Most large hotel chains, such as **Best Western, Embassy Suites, Radisson,** and the cheaper **Motel 6** can accommodate wheelchair users but rarely offer them discounts. **Red Roof Inns** (in U.S. and Canada, tel. 800/843-7663) have wheelchair-accessible rooms and special alarm systems for their deaf and blind guests. Whenever possible, reviews in this book will indicate if rooms are wheelchair accessible.

GETTING AROUND The **American Public Transit Association** (tel. 202/898-4000) in Washington, D.C., has information on transportation options in all U.S. cities for travelers with disabilities.

➢ **BY PLANE** • Most major airlines are happy to help travelers with disabilities make flight arrangements, provided they are notified up to 48 hours in advance. Some airlines, such as **Air Canada** (tel. 800/776-3000 or 800/361-8071 in Canada), **Delta** (tel. 800/221-1212, TDD 800/831-4488), and **USAir** (tel. 800/428-4322, TDD 800/245-2966), offer a discounted "companion fare" if a passenger with disabilities needs attendant help or medical attention. Ask about discounts and check-in protocol when making reservations.

➢ **BY TRAIN** • **Amtrak** (tel. 800/872-7245, TDD 800/523-6590) offers a 25% discount on one-way coach fares for travelers with disabilities. However, you must show written verification of your disability. If notified when reservations are made, Amtrak will provide assistance for travelers at stations. Both **B.C. Rail** (tel. 604/631-3500) and **VIA Rail** in Canada (tel. 604/669-3050, 800/561-3949, or 800/561-8630 from Vancouver) allow disabled passengers with a doctor's note to bring along a companion for free. **Alaska Railroad** (tel. 800/544-0552) can accommodate travelers in wheelchairs on their Anchorage–Denali and Denali–Fairbanks routes, but they give no discounts.

➢ **BY BUS** • **Greyhound-Trailways** (tel. 800/752-4841, TDD 800/345-3109) allows a disabled traveler and a companion to ride for the price of a single fare. No advance notice is required, although you will need to show proof of disability (such as a doctor's letter) to receive the special fare. **Greyhound Lines of Canada** (tel. 604/662-3222 or 403/265-9111) offers free passage for the companions of blind passengers. City transit systems (like Seattle) sometimes have permit deals that allow discounts on different transportation options.

➢ **BY FERRY** • The following ferry companies offer special discount cards to disabled travelers. Write for full details. Also call **Washington State Ferries** (tel. 206/464-6400 or 800/843-3779 in WA, TDD 800/833-6388) for an application for a free half-fare permit.

Alaska Marine Highway. *Attn: Pass Desk, Box 25535, Juneau, AK 99802-5535, tel. 800/642-0066.*

B.C. Ferries. *1112 Fort St., Victoria V8V 4V2, Canada, tel. 604/669-1211.*

➢ **BY CAR** • If you plan to rent a car in the U.S., you'll find that some major car-rental companies are able to supply hand-controlled vehicles with a minimum of 24 hours' advance notice. Given a day's notice, **Avis** (tel. 800/331-1212) will install hand-controlled mechanisms at no extra charge. **Hertz** (tel. 800/654-3131, TDD 800/654-2280) asks for 48 hours advance notice and a $25 cash or credit-card deposit to do the same. **National** (tel. 800/328–4567, TDD 800/328–6323) and **Thrifty** (tel. 800/367–2277) have hand-controlled cars at certain locations and ask for at least two days' notice to serve mobility-impaired renters.

PUBLICATIONS *Access to the World: A Travel Guide for the Handicapped*, by Louise Weiss, is highly recommended for its worldwide coverage of travel boons and busts for the disabled. It's available from Henry Holt & Co. (tel. 800/488–5233) for $12.95; the order number is 0805001417.

Twin Peaks Press specializes in books for the disabled, such as *Travel for the Disabled*, which offers helpful hints as well as a comprehensive list of guidebooks and facilities geared to the disabled. Their *Directory of Travel Agencies for the Disabled* lists more than 350 agencies throughout the world. Each is $19.95 plus $2 ($3 for both) shipping and handling. *Box 129, Vancouver, WA 98666, tel. 206/694–2462 or 800/637–2256 for orders only.*

ORGANIZATIONS **Disabled Outdoors Foundation** is a nonprofit organization that works to increase recreational opportunities for outdoor enthusiasts with handicaps. Its executive director also serves as editor and publisher of a quarterly magazine, *Disabled Outdoors Magazine* (for subscriptions dial 708/358–4160), teeming with information on fishing, camping, boating, and what have you. U.S. subscription rates are $10 for one year, $18 for two years. *320 Lake St., Oak Park, IL 60302.*

Mobility International USA (MIUSA) is a nonprofit organization that coordinates exchange programs for disabled people around the world. MIUSA also offers information on accommodations and organized study programs for members ($20 annually). Nonmembers may subscribe to the newsletter for $10. *Box 10767, Eugene, OR 97440, tel. and TDD 503/343–1284.*

Outdoors Forever is a new nonprofit organization that works to make the outdoors more accessible to people with physical limitations. Call or write for more information about their magazine, *Outdoors Forever,* or their publications on equipment, techniques, and organizations that plan outings. *Box 4832, East Lansing, MI 48823, tel. 517/337–0018.*

WORKING IN THE PACIFIC NORTHWEST AND ALASKA

The Pacific Northwest (Alaska in particular) is a heavyweight in the fishing industry, drawing many a college student and hearty traveler into its employ each summer. Most fishing jobs require experience, unless the company is desperate to hire replacements. The best fishing jobs are available in July; try Kodiak, Cordova, Bristol Bay, Dillingham, Pelican, and the Homer-Ketchikan run. Later in the summer, try the Southeast. Most canning jobs don't require experience, and, although the majority are arranged before the season, you can always try to get a last-minute, on-the-spot job. Contacting one of the many fishing organizations in the Pacific Northwest may also put you in touch with job opportunities. The **Women's Fishing Network**, a volunteer educational organization that publishes an informative newsletter, can match both women and men with job possibilities. Offices are located in Seattle (tel. 206/742–2810) and Alaska (Box 103920, Anchorage, AK 99510).

LEGAL REQUIREMENTS In order to work legally in the United States, you must have a social-security number, which is the birthright of U.S. citizens. Obtaining a green card, which entitles foreigners to work and reside in the United States, is a long shot for most visitors. Another option is to participate in an **Exchange Visitor Program (EVP)** (*see* Work Programs, *below*). Canada is equally tough on foreign workers; unless foreigners are involved in a government- or school-sponsored exchange program, potential workers must have a prospective Canadian employer arrange for a work permit. With a little persistence (and chutzpah), illegal work (i.e., with no papers in hand) can be found. But be warned that if you're caught working illegally you *will be* deported and perhaps permanently denied entrance into the United States and/or Canada.

WORK PROGRAMS Exchange-visitor programs are authorized by the U.S. government to provide foreign students with legal jobs. Most jobs are not big money-makers and come with restrictions, usually on the amount you can earn and the length of time you can stay. CIEE (*see* Budget Travel Organizations, *above*) publishes two excellent resource books with complete details on work/travel opportunities. An excellent resource is CIEE's **Work, Study, Travel Abroad: The Whole World Handbook** ($13.95), which gives the lowdown on scholarships, grants, fellowships, study abroad programs, and work exchanges. The U.K.-based Vacation Work Press publishes two other first-rate guides: **Directory of Overseas Summer Jobs** (£9) and Susan Griffith's **Work Your Way Around the World** (£12). The first lists over 45,000 jobs worldwide; the latter has fewer listings but makes a more interesting read. Look for them at bookstores, or contact the publisher directly at *9 Park East End, Oxford OX1 1HJ, England, tel. 01865/241978.*

The U.S. Forest Service has jobs in the great outdoors. Contact the **U.S. Forest Service Pacific Northwest Region** (Box 3623, Portland, OR 97208, tel. 503/326–3816) or the **Alaska U.S.D.A. Forest Service** (Box 1628, Juneau, AK 99802, tel. 907/586–8857).

For British travelers, **British Universities North America Club (BUNAC)** operates in conjunction with CIEE to provide temporary work permits. *16 Bowling Green Lane, London EC1R OBD, England, tel. 0171/251–3472.*

The "Au-Pair in America" program offered by the **American Institute for Foreign Study (AIFS)** places foreign nannies in American households. *102 Greenwich Ave., Greenwich, CT 06830, tel. 203/869–9090 or 800/727–2437, ext. 6123.*

Camp America places visitors in camps throughout the United States, including some in California. Positions range from camp counselors to administrative assistants. *Dept. WW 37A, Queens Gate, London SW7 5HR, England, tel. 0171/581–7373.*

Australians and New Zealanders should look into the **SWAP Program**, which arranges temporary work visas valid for up to six months in the U.S. *Box 399, Carlton South, Melbourne, VIC 3053, Australia.*

Canadians should contact **Travel CUTS**, which offers a version of the CIEE program to Canadian students who want to work abroad for up to six months. *SWAP, 243 College St., 5th floor, Toronto, Ontario M5T 2Y1, tel. 416/977–3703.*

VOLUNTEER WORK If you can afford to work for nothing, more power to you. And the first call you should make is to the **CIEE Voluntary Service Department**, which can get you a job as a teacher, house builder, archaeological dig helper, whatever, throughout the U.S. An excellent

Exciting Careers in Fish Canning

Lots of ads appear in student publications for summer jobs in Alaska, though the cannery business is down from the good old days (early 1980s) when anyone who made it up to Alaska could find a fairly lucrative, if grueling, job in a cannery or on a fishing boat. Don't blame us if there aren't any jobs, though it's worth the cost of a phone call to find out. Many cannery employment agencies charge around $15 for listings or "instruction manuals," but this service has the ring of a serious scam. One unnamed agency specializes in fishing, cannery, logging, construction, and oil company jobs (tel. 206/736–7000, ext. 400B).

M & L Research (Box 84008-PX, Seattle, WA 98124) offers a 68-page, cannery-and-fishing employment booklet ($10.95)—complete with a 60-day unconditional, 100% money-back guarantee. Sounds good, but one has to wonder, why wouldn't you simply read it, then ask for your money back?

resource is CIEE's **Volunteer!** ($8.95), a comprehensive guide to volunteer opportunities world-wide. *205 E. 42nd St., New York, NY 10017, tel. 212/661–1414, ext. 1139.*

Service Civil International (SCI) and **International Voluntary Service (IVS)** work for peace and international understanding through two- to three-week work camps in the United States. Applicants must be 16 or older and pay a $35 processing fee. Send for a free brochure. *Innisfree Village, Rte. 2, Box 506, Crozet, VA 22932, tel. 804/823–1826.*

Volunteers for Peace (VFP) sponsors two- to three-week international work camps in the United States for around $150. Send for their *International Workcamp Directory* ($10); it lists over 800 volunteer opportunities. *43 Tiffany Rd., Belmont, VT 05730, tel. 802/259–2759.*

If you're itching to work in the great outdoors, contact the **U.S. Forest Service, Pacific Northwest Region, Volunteer Coordinator**, which has programs throughout Washington and Oregon. *Box 3623, Portland, OR 97208, tel. 503/326–3651.*

Sierra Club Service Trips are subsidized work outings in the Pacific Northwest, including some to Mt. Hood and Mt. Rainier. *730 Polk St., San Francisco, CA 94109, tel. 415/923–5630.*

Info for Foreign Visitors

PASSPORTS AND VISAS

CANADIAN CITIZENS Canadian citizens must show proof of citizenship and identity to enter the United States (a passport, birth certificate with raised seal, or voter registration card are preferred). Passport applications, available at any post office or passport office, cost C$35 and take one to two weeks to process. For additional information while in the United States, contact the **Canadian Embassy** (501 Pennsylvania Ave. NW, Washington, DC 20001, tel. 202/682–1740). Consulates are located in Atlanta, Boston, Chicago, Cleveland, Dallas, Detroit, Los Angeles, Minneapolis, New York City, San Francisco, and Seattle.

U.K. CITIZENS You need a valid 10-year, £15 passport to enter the United States. Application forms, which take about four weeks to process, are available from the **Passport Office** (Clive House, 70 Petty France, London SW1H 9BR, tel. 0171/279–4000 or 0171/279–3434 for recorded info), or from most travel agents, main post offices, and regional passport offices. A British Visitor Passport is not acceptable.

Visas are required for visits of more than 90 days. Apply four weeks in advance to a travel agent or the **U.S. Embassy Visa and Immigration Department** (5 Upper Grosvenor St., London W1A 2JB) or, for residents of Northern Ireland, to the **U.S. Consulate General** (Queen's House, Queen St., Belfast BT1 6EO). Visas can be given only to holders of 10-year passports—although visas in expired passports remain valid. Submit a completed Nonimmigrant Visa Application (Form 156), a copy of your passport, a photograph, and evidence of your intended departure from the United States after a temporary visit.

AUSTRALIAN CITIZENS Australian citizens need a valid passport and visa to enter the United States. Passports cost AUS$76, less for children; applications are available at any post office or passport offices. While in the United States, Australians may obtain additional information from the **Embassy of Australia** (1601 Massachusetts Ave. NW, Washington, DC 20036, tel. 202/797–3000). Consulates are located in Chicago, Honolulu, Los Angeles, and New York City.

NEW ZEALAND CITIZENS New Zealand citizens need a valid passport to enter the United States. Ten-year passports, which cost NZ$35 and take about 3 weeks to process, are available from the **New Zealand Passport Office** (Documents of National Identity Division, Department of Internal Affairs, Box 10526, Wellington), as well as regional passport offices and post offices. To stay more than 90 days, you'll need a visa as well; contact the American Embassy or Consulate nearest you. In the United States, you can get more information from the **New Zealand Embassy** (36 Observatory Circle NW, Washington, DC 20008, tel. 202/328–4800). The embassy has a second office in Los Angeles.

INTERNATIONAL FLIGHTS

FROM CANADA The following airlines have direct and connecting flights from Toronto, Calgary, Montreal, and Vancouver to Seattle and Portland: **Air Canada** (tel. 800/776–3000), **United** (tel. 800/538–2929), **Canadian Airlines International** (tel. 800/426–7000), **Northwest** (tel. 800/447–4747), and **American** (tel. 800/433–7300).

FROM THE U.K. Airlines serving the U.S. from Great Britain and/or Ireland with direct, non-stop flights to Portland, Seattle, and/or Vancouver include **British Airways** (tel. 800/247–9297 in U.S. or 0181/897–4000 in U.K.), **United Airlines** (tel. 800/538–2929 in U.S. or 0181/990–9900 in U.K.), and **Air Canada** (tel. 800/776–3000 in U.S. or 0181/759–2636 in U.K.).

FROM DOWN UNDER Qantas (tel. 800/227–4500 in U.S., 02/957–0111 in Sydney, or 09/357–8900 in Auckland) and **United** (tel. 800/538–2929 in U.S., 02/237–8888 in Sydney, or 09/379–3800 in Auckland) fly from Sydney to L.A. and San Francisco and from Auckland to L.A; you'll have to catch a connecting flight to the Pacific Northwest. **Air New Zealand** (tel. 800/262–1234 in U.S. or 09/357–3000 in New Zealand) flies nonstop from Auckland to L.A. and Vancouver. **Japan Airlines** (tel. 800/525–3663) flies from Sydney (tel. 02/283–1111) and Auckland (tel. 09/379–9906) to Seattle via Tokyo.

CUSTOMS AND DUTIES

Visitors 21 and older can bring into the United States (1) 200 cigarettes or 50 non-Cuban cigars (sorry, Fidel) or 2 kilograms of smoking tobacco, (2) one U.S. quart of alcohol, and (3) duty-free gifts to a value of $100. Forbidden are meat and meat products, seeds, plants, and fruits. Avoid illegal drugs like the plague.

CANADIAN CUSTOMS Exemptions for returning Canadians range from C$20 to C$300, depending on how long you've been out of the country: For two days out you're allowed to return with C$100 of goods; for one week out you're allowed C$300 worth. You'll be taxed 20% for items exceeding these limits (more for items you ship home). In any given year you're allowed one C$300 exemption. Duty-free limits are: up to 50 cigars, 200 cigarettes, 2 pounds of tobacco, and 40 ounces of liquor—all must be declared in writing upon arrival at customs and must be with you or in your checked baggage. To mail gifts back home, label the package "Unsolicited Gift—Value under C$40." Of course, if the value of the package is more than C$40 and you're caught, you'll pay hefty fines to retrieve your package from customs. For more scintillating details, request a copy of the Canadian Customs brochure "I Declare/Je Déclare" from the **Revenue Canada Customs, Excise and Taxation Department** (2265 St. Laurent Blvd. S., Ottawa, Ont. K1G 4K3, tel. 613/957–0275).

U.K. CUSTOMS Travelers age 17 and over returning to the United Kingdom may bring in the following duty-free goods: (1) 200 cigarettes or 100 cigarillos or 50 cigars or 250 grams of tobacco, (2) 1 liter of alcohol over 22% volume or 2 liters of alcohol under 22% volume, plus 2 liters of still table wine, (3) 60 ml of perfume and 250 ml of toilet water, (4) other goods worth up to £36. For further information or a copy of "A Guide for Travellers," which details standard customs procedures as well as what you may bring into the United Kingdom from abroad, contact **HM Customs and Excise** (Dorset House, Stamford St., London SE1 9PY, tel. 0171/928–3440).

AUSTRALIAN CUSTOMS Australian travelers 18 and over may bring back, duty free: (1) 1 liter of alcohol, (2) 250 grams of tobacco products (equivalent to 250 cigarettes or cigars), (3) other articles worth up to AUS$400. If you're under 18 your duty-free allowance is AUS$200. To avoid paying duty on goods you mail back to Australia, mark the package "Australian Goods Returned." For more rules and regulations, request the pamphlet "Customs Information for Travellers" from a local **Collector of Customs** (Box 8, Sydney NSW 2001, tel. 02/226–5997).

NEW ZEALAND CUSTOMS Although you may be greeted with a "Haere Mai" ("Welcome to New Zealand"), travelers over the age of 17 are faced with the following duty-free restrictions: (1) 200 cigarettes or 250 grams of tobacco or 50 cigars or a combo of all three up to 250 grams, (2) 4½ liters of wine or beer and one 1.1-liter bottle of spirits, (3) goods with a combined value of up to NZ$700. For more details ask for the pamphlet "Customs Guide for Travellers" from a New Zealand consulate.

PHONES AND MAIL

INTERNATIONAL CALLS Calls between the United States and Canada are not considered international calls and can be dialed as regular long-distance numbers. To call any other country, dial 011, the country code, the city code (dropping the initial zero if there is one), then the actual number. If you get stuck, dial 00 for a long-distance operator, who can help you. The country code for **Great Britain** is 44, **New Zealand** 64, and **Australia** 61.

When calling, remember to account for time differences from PST (Pacific Standard Time): England is eight hours ahead; New Zealand 19 hours ahead; and Australia, with three time zones, 16–18 hours ahead. The cheapest times (PST) to call England are 6 PM–7 AM, New Zealand 11 PM–10 AM, and Australia 3 AM–2 PM. A three-minute call from anywhere in the United States during those bargain times will cost about $2.18 (England), $4.07 (New Zealand), or $3.30 (Australia). For the exact rate, call the **AT&T** long-distance operator (tel. 00), **U.S. Sprint** (tel. 800/877–4646), or **MCI** (tel. 800/444–3333).

SENDING MAIL HOME International rates for sending letters to destinations beyond the North American continent begin at 50¢ for the first half-ounce and 95¢ for the first full ounce. Add 39¢ per ounce for letters heavier than 1 ounce. Rates are slightly cheaper for mail to Canada (40¢ for the first ounce) and Mexico (45¢ for the first ounce). You can also stop by any post office and buy ready-to-mail aerogrammes. For 45¢ you get paper, envelope, and postage all in one; the charge for the second ounce is 45¢, and each ounce thereafter is 39¢. Post cards cost 40¢. Allow one to two weeks delivery time for international mail.

Coming and Going

When your travel plans are still in the fantasy stage, start studying the travel sections of major Sunday newspapers: Courier companies, charter flights, fare brokers, and driveaway companies often list incredibly cheap deals. Travel agents are another obvious resource, as they have access to computer networks that show the lowest fares before they're even advertised. However, budget travelers are the bane of travel agents, whose commission is based on the ticket prices. That said, agencies on or near college campuses—try STA or Council Travel (see Budget Travel Organizations, *above*)—actually cater to this pariah class and can help you find cheap deals.

Flexibility is the key to getting a serious bargain on airfare. If you can play around with your departure date, destination, amount of luggage carried, and return date, you will probably save money. Options include charter flights, flying standby, student discounts, courier flights, and APEX (Advanced Purchase Excursion) and Super APEX fares; read on to help get through this maze. Another useful resource is George Albert Brown's *Airline Traveler's Guerrilla Handbook*

Bikes in Flight

Although you may get a bit wet, the Pacific Northwest's enticing greenery lures the serious bike rider to hit the road. Most airlines accommodate this urge by shipping bikes, provided they are dismantled and put into a box, as luggage. Call to see if your airline sells bike boxes (around $10). International travelers can substitute a bike for the second piece of checked luggage at no extra charge; otherwise, it will cost $100 extra. Domestic flights are less gracious and charge bike-toting travelers a $45 fee (not including the $10 for the box).

(Blake Publishing Group, 320 Metropolitan Sq., 15th St. NW, Washington, DC 20005, tel. 800/752–9765; $14.95), an in-depth account of how to find cheap tickets, change cheap tickets, and generally beat the system.

Hot tips when making reservations: If the reservation clerk tells you that the least expensive seats are no longer available on a certain flight, ask to be put on a waiting list. If the airline doesn't keep waiting lists for the lowest fares, call them on subsequent mornings and ask about cancellations and last-minute openings—airlines trying to fill all their seats sometimes add additional cut-rate tickets at the last moment. When setting travel dates, remember that off-season fares can be as much as 50% lower. Ask which days of the week are the cheapest to fly on—weekends are often the most expensive.

CONSOLIDATORS AND BUCKET SHOPS

Consolidator companies, also known as bucket shops, buy blocks of tickets at wholesale prices from airlines trying to fill flights. Check out any consolidator's reputation with the Better Business Bureau before starting; most are perfectly reliable, but better safe than sorry. Then register with the consolidator and, usually in conjunction with their staff, work up a list of possible destinations and departure dates. The week before you leave, the consolidators will contact you and give you a list of the flights they think they can get you on. You're obligated to accept one of these flights, even if it wasn't your first choice. If you don't, the consolidators probably won't put too much effort into getting you on another flight. If everything works as planned, you'll save 10%–40% on the published APEX fare.

It goes without saying that you can't be too choosy about which city you fly into. Other drawbacks: Consolidator tickets are often not refundable, and the flights to choose from often feature indirect routes, long layovers in connecting cities, and undesirable seating assignments. If your flight is delayed or canceled, you'll also have a tough time switching airlines. One last suggestion: Confirm your reservation with the airline both before and after you buy a consolidated ticket.

Airfare Busters. *5100 Westheimer Ave., Suite 550, Houston, TX 77056, tel. 713/961–5109 or 800/232–8783.*

Airhitch. *2790 Broadway, Suite 100, New York, NY 10025, tel. 212/864–2000; 1341 Ocean Ave., Suite 62, Santa Monica, CA 90401, tel. 310/458–1006.*

Discount Travel International (DTI). *169 W. 81st St., New York, NY 10024, tel. 212/362–3636. 801 Alton Rd., Suite 1, Miami Beach, FL 33139, tel. 503/538–1616.*

Globe Travel. *507 5th Ave., Suite 606, New York, NY 10017, tel. 800/969–4562.*

UniTravel. *1177 N. Warson Rd., Box 12485, St. Louis, MO 63132, tel. 314/569–2501 or 800/325–2222.*

Up & Away Travel. *347 Fifth Ave., Suite 202, New York, NY 10016, tel. 212/889–2345.*

CHARTER FLIGHTS

Charter flights have vastly different characteristics, depending on the company you're dealing with. Generally speaking, a charter company buys a block of tickets on a regularly scheduled commercial flight and sells them at a discount. Despite a few potential drawbacks—among them infrequent flights, restrictive return-date requirements, lickety-split payment demands, frequent bankruptcies—charter companies inevitably offer the cheapest tickets around, especially during high season when APEX fares are most expensive. Make sure you find out a company's policy on refunds should a flight be canceled by either yourself or the airline. Summer charter flights fill up fast and should be booked a couple months in advance.

Council Charter (tel. 212/661–0311 or 800/800–8222) has the scoop on hundreds of different charter and reduced-fare flights. **DER Tours** (Box 1606, Des Plains, IL 60017, tel. 800/782–2424) is a full-service travel store, with rail passes, discounted airfares, and listings of charter flights. **MartinAir** (tel. 800/627–8462) is an airline that operates like a charter. Restrictions apply, and availability is limited during summer. Definitely call a few weeks in advance. **Tower Air** (tel. 800/34–TOWER) specializes in domestic and international charters. On the plus side, you get to deal with the airline directly. On the downside, Tower is notorious for overbooking. **Travel Charter** (tel. 810/641–9677 or 800/521–5267) caters to students bound for Europe, though some of their charters are loaded with restrictions. **Travel CUTS** (*see* Budget Travel Organizations, *above*) is part of the CIEE umbrella, which means it's a reputable place for Canadian students to book their charter.

Staying in the Pacific Northwest and Alaska

GETTING AROUND

As you likely have observed, the Pacific Northwest is huge, but getting around is not that difficult. Most roads are good; trains, ferries, and buses crisscross; the cities have relatively good mass-transit systems; and the people are friendly. Depending upon what you want to see, you can combine a few forms of travel: flying to Seattle, say, taking a bus to Vancouver, catching a ferry to Alaska, and so on.

BY CAR Traveling by car is the most popular and convenient way to travel throughout British Columbia, Washington, and Oregon; generally the roads are well maintained and not overly crowded. Because natural beauty is the primary attraction, a car is also a traveler's best friend, allowing the flexibility to stop and enjoy the scenery or to explore parks and recreation areas at leisure. However, if you're mostly interested in seeing the cities, a car may be more of a hassle (traffic, parking, expenses) than a convenience, and you may be better off taking advantage of the excellent public transportation that the cities offer.

The U.S. interstate highway network provides quick and easy access to the Pacific Northwest in spite of imposing mountain barriers. From the south, I–5 runs from the U.S.–Mexico border through California, into Oregon and Washington, and ends at the U.S.–Canada border. From the east, I–90 stretches from Boston to Seattle. I–84 runs through the midwest states to Portland. If you're planning to drive to Alaska, you better have lots of time and a whole collection of dumb car games to play. From Seattle, it takes about seven days to travel the 2,500 miles to Anchorage.

Collaboration, Invasion, and the Alaska Highway

When Japanese bombers attacked the U.S. naval base at Dutch Harbor, Alaska, in June 1942, the threat of a serious Japanese invasion loomed large in the minds of many U.S. and Canadian residents. To counter the Japanese threat, the U.S. military began a large build-up of forces in Alaska, facilitated by the construction of the Alaska Highway. This engineering feat ultimately involved the labor of some 10,600 American troops (among them, some 3,700 blacks), and about 7,500 (mostly Canadian) civilian construction workers. Temperatures hovered at −40° while the intrepid work force completed the 1,500-mile highway in just 8 months, 12 days. But with the opening up of British Columbia and Alaska, epidemics of diseases unknown to the indigenous peoples soon wreaked havoc with native populations. Traditional subsistence economies were also shattered when northern Indians and Eskimos rushed to take highway jobs.

Cars enter Canada on I–5 at Blaine, Washington, 30 miles south of Vancouver. Two major highways enter British Columbia from the east, the **Trans-Canada Highway** (the longest in the world—more than 5,000 miles from St. John's, Newfoundland, to Victoria, British Columbia) and the **Yellowhead Highway**, which runs from the Rocky Mountains to Prince Rupert through northern British Columbia. Border-crossing procedures are usually quick and simple although, according to a few young, cash-strapped types (seen as potential drug smugglers by customs officials worldwide), Canadian customs has been known to take a car or two apart.

Within Alaska, the **Alaska Highway**—alternatively known as the Alaska–Canada Highway, or the Al-Can for short—covers 1,500 miles from Fairbanks down to Dawson Creek, Yukon, crossing some 100 rivers and five mountain ranges. Although the highways in Alaska have a notorious reputation for wrecking cars with their gravel, frost coating, and various other pitfalls, this reputation is exaggerated. That's not to say that the Alaska Highway is any kind of Autobahn; the drive is still *very* trying on the driver and the vehicle. The other highways in the interior—the **Dalton Highway** to Prudhoe Bay, **George Parks Highway** between Anchorage and Fairbanks (including Denali National Park), **Steese Highway** to Circle, and **Richardson Highway** to Valdez—are not as well maintained as the Alaska Highway, but are still manageable. Nevertheless, make sure your car is in good shape before committing to Alaska; pack spare tires and fan belts; bring along chains if it's anytime near winter; and remember that gas is more expensive up here than it is in the lower 48 States, and that most of Alaska simply cannot be reached by road. In the Southeast and around Prince William Sound, you'll find yourself relying on ferries. Only one road, the Dalton Highway, ventures above the Arctic Circle, and the entire west coast (including Nome) can only be reached by air.

➤ **AUTOMOTIVE ASSOCIATIONS** • If you're going to be traveling in the United States and Canada by car, becoming a member of the Automobile Association of America (AAA) or one of its affiliates is the best investment you can make. Membership costs $55 for the first year and $38 annually thereafter. Members receive free maps and tour books, personalized itinerary plans, free emergency road service, and discounts at hotels, motels, "attractions," and some restaurants. If you belong to any type of auto club abroad, AAA may honor your membership; otherwise consider joining while you're here. Be sure to request the free *Tour Book to Oregon and Washington*.

American Automobile Association (AAA). *1000 AAA Dr., Heathrow, FL 32746, tel. 407/444–7000 or 800/222–4357.*

British Columbia Automobile Association (BCAA) has 24-hour emergency road service for members of AAA or BCAA, and free maps. *Tel. 604/293–2222 or 604/268–5000.*

➤ **CAR RENTALS** • National car-rental agencies include **Alamo** (tel. 800/327–9633), **Budget** (tel. 800/527–0700), **Dollar** (tel. 800/800–4000), and **Thrifty** (tel. 800/367–2277). Most charge about $25–$45 a day (often with unlimited mileage) to renters over 25 with a major credit card. In the off-season, a week's rental with unlimited mileage can be as low as $120. Expect to pay more ($10–$15 a day) for the privilege of being under 25 years old; very few companies (except Budget) rent to anyone under 21. Reserving a car a few days in advance and renting it for a week or more may get you a better guaranteed rate. Some companies charge nothing to return the car to another location, others charge $100–$150 extra. Optional insurance ($9–$12 a day) is a good idea. Some credit cards, such as American Express, provide

Music to Drive By

"Route 66" (Manhattan Transfer, DePeche Mode), "Keep on Truckin'" (Eddie Kendricks), "Truckin" (the Grateful Dead), "Convoy" (C. W. McCall), "Little Red Corvette" (Prince), "Wreck on the Highway" (Bruce Springsteen), "Baby, You Can Drive My Car" (the Beatles), "Driving My Life Away" (Eddie Rabbitt), "On the Road Again" (Willy Nelson), "Pink Cadillac" (Aretha Franklin), "Too Much Magic Bus" (The Who), and anything by Tom Waits.

automatic auto-insurance coverage if you charge your rental, but be sure to read the small print. Companies like **Rent-A-Wreck** (tel. 800/535–1391), which specializes in cheaper, older, and uglier cars, sometimes undercut the national companies on rates—but make sure the lower rental cost is not eclipsed by added mileage charges or mileage limits.

➤ **BUYING A CAR** • Some people try to beat car-rental costs by buying a car and selling it when they leave. Although buying does provide an alternative to sinking money into a rental, hassles to consider include registration, insurance, and repairs. Registration means enduring long lines at the **Department of Motor Vehicles (DMV),** where you must present the car title, bill of sale, and state-required smog certificate. Registration fees are a percentage of the cost of the car—usually anywhere from 7% to 12%. Some states also require proof of insurance policy liability; policy costs vary depending upon the county. Unless you're an amateur mechanic, do not invest in a car needing repair work. Because mechanic labor fees run $50–$80 an hour, even simple repairs will probably top $100.

BY BUS **Green Tortoise Adventure Travel** is not just a bus ride; it's often the most memorable part of your vacation. It's also *the* cheap alternative to humdrum public transportation. Green Tortoise's buses crawl their way to cities up and down the West Coast and are equipped with sleeping pads, kitchens, and stereos. They also offer a summer trek to Alaska, winter tours to Mexico and Baja, and other package trips across the continental United States. Reservations are recommended, especially for the weekly trips between San Francisco and Seattle (a one-way ticket costs $50). The buses often stop for a gourmet cookout, sauna, or swim. You'll need to reserve a seat five to seven days in advance and pay the driver in cash. *Tel. 800/867–8647 or 415/956–7500.*

Green Tortoise is the smelliest, cheapest, wackiest, most laid-back way to travel up and down the West Coast.

Greyhound-Trailways (tel. 800/752–4841) in the United States and **Greyhound Lines of Canada** (tel. 604/662–3222 or 403/265–9111) are two separate companies and overlap only from Seattle to Vancouver. Bus service is available to Washington and Oregon from various points in the United States. Similarly, service to British Columbia is available from the rest of Canada. Bus service in North America—though fairly economical—is somewhat grungy and depressing. Discount passes are available; contact the Greyhound-Trailways International Travel office nearest you. Cheapest fares are offered during the "low season" (January–June).

Alaska Denali Transit (tel. 907/766–3145) runs buses out of Anchorage to Homer and Kenai. In the Yukon, **Norline Coaches** (tel. 403/668–3355) offers service between Whitehorse and Dawson City. Around Alaska there are also a variety of smaller shuttle-bus companies that ser-

AlaskaPass

Long distances between destinations in Alaska can make travel hugely expensive. Enter the AlaskaPass. This new company (tel. 907/766–3145 or 800/248–7598) offers a comprehensive bus/ferry/train pass geared to independent travelers. If you plan well, the various passes can even save you money getting here from Seattle or Vancouver. AlaskaPass offers different pass options; for example, an 8-day pass runs $499, while a pass allowing 21 days of travel over a 45-day period is about $929. The company provides you with schedule information for all the carriers honoring their card and helps you set an itinerary to suit your needs. They also have fixed itineraries that whisk you around Alaska so you can see as much of the state as possible in a short period of time. The pass can be a valuable money-saver, but to make sure that it really is a bargain, you'll need to plan carefully and leave enough room in your itinerary to take alternative routes and spend extra time in the areas you find most worthwhile.

vice Denali and a number of small communities around the state. Check the Coming and Going section of specific towns and cities for more detailed information.

Gray Line of Alaska (tel. 907/277–5581 or 800/544–2206) carries passengers between Haines, Skagway, and Whitehorse, and makes several stops in between. Buses between Anchorage and Fairbanks ($109 one-way) and Anchorage and Denali ($67 one-way) operate May–September. Generally, buses run about three days a week. The AlaskaPass is accepted with a $5 fee.

➤ **BUS PASSES** • Greyhound's **Ameripass,** valid on all U.S. routes, can be purchased in advance in cities throughout the U.S.; spontaneous types can also buy it up to 45 minutes before the bus leaves from the terminal. The pass allows purchasers unlimited travel within a limited time period: seven days ($250), 15 days ($450), or 30 days ($550). Foreign visitors can get slightly lower rates. You can extend the pass for $15 per day but must do so when you purchase the ticket. Greyhound Lines of Canada offers the **Canpass**, valid for unlimited travel within Canada, in the following increments: seven days (C$280) and 15 days (C$490).

BY TRAIN **Amtrak** (tel. 800/USA–RAIL), the only passenger rail service in the U.S., offers daily service to Oregon and Washington from California and the East. The *Empire Builder* takes a northern route from Chicago to Seattle. The *Pioneer* travels from Chicago to Portland via Denver and Salt Lake City. The *Coast Starlight* begins in Los Angeles, stopping in Western Oregon and Washington before pulling into Seattle. You can't catch a train across the border from Seattle. **VIA Rail Canada** (tel. 800/561–3949 or 800/561–8630 from Vancouver) runs the cross-country *Canadian* three times a week from Toronto to Vancouver. Trains also run from Vancouver to Prince Rupert via Jasper, Alberta. Via Rail offers 10% youth (under 29) discounts.

Willing to do anything for a free ride, some folks jump freight trains—going so far as to call the train companies, pretending they want to send a package, and asking the time, track, and number of departing trains. A very bad idea.

➤ **RAIL PASSES** • Amtrak's **All-Aboard Pass** is good for people who plan their itinerary in advance. The pass, which is actually a booklet of tickets, allows Amtrak riders special fares for three stops made in 45 days of travel within a region. For travel in or through Oregon and Washington, request the All-Aboard Pass for the Western United States region ($199, $179 off-season), and choose your own route. Ticket agents need to know your dates of travel and intended destinations for ticketing, so call Amtrak in advance. Amtrak also provides free but limited shuttle services for pass-holders whose routes don't connect.

Amtrak's **USARail Pass** works to the advantage of the foreign budget traveler (it's not available to U.S. or Canadian citizens) because it requires no formal itinerary, works on any of Amtrak's U.S. routes, and allows for spontaneous planning (within a specified time period). A 15-day pass costs $318 ($218 off-season), a 30-day pass $399 ($319 off-season). Buy them at an international travel agency before entering the United States, or from an Amtrak office (passport and visa required for purchase).

BY FERRY Ferries are convenient, relaxing, and sometimes the only viable way to travel between Seattle, Vancouver, and parts of Alaska. Most ferries will transport cars (with drivers), accommodate disabled passengers, and allow pets (with some restrictions). In addition to the companies mentioned below, there are many smaller, passenger-only ferries. Usually only cash and traveler's checks are accepted. The base rate for foot passengers is fairly cheap—usually $20–$30 for a three-to-five-hour ferry ride between towns. But the costs add up once you factor in surcharges for transporting bikes or kayaks (an extra $10–$15 between stops on the Marine Highway). Vehicles cost anywhere from $15 to $700 to get from point to point, depending upon the length of the vehicle and the distance you're traveling.

Washington State Ferries is the largest ferry system in the United States, with 25 vessels and 10 routes to a few of the region's most scenic destinations: Puget Sound, the Olympic Peninsula, and the San Juan Islands. One-way fares average $3.50 per person, $5.90 per car and driver. *Colman Dock, Pier 52, Seattle, WA 98104, tel. 206/464–6400; or from within WA, tel. 800/843–3779.*

BC Ferry, otherwise known as the "Friendship Fleet," does the ferry thing for British Columbia's mainland and the islands along the coast. Fares average about C$6.25 per person, C$23.25 per car. *Tel. 604/669–1211.*

The **Alaska Marine Highway** is the yellow brick road of Alaska, providing basic transportation not only for visitors but also for local residents in many of the small island communities along Alaska's coast. The company runs ferries from Bellingham, Washington, to Southeast Alaska through the Inside Passage, a corridor that winds its way through the many coastal islands. Ferries provide year-round service for pedestrians and vehicles from Ketchikan to Skagway and to many ports in between. The other links of the ferry system are in Prince William Sound (including Cordova), Kodiak, Homer, Seward, and down the chain of Aleutian Islands to Dutch Harbor. Summer traffic on the ferry system is heavy, and reservations for transporting cars from port to port must be made well in advance. From the fall through the spring the system cuts back its service. *Tel. 800/642–0066.*

BY PLANE If you're short on time and long on desire to see the major cities, air travel is the quickest and cheapest option. Many people opt to fly from Portland to Seattle or Vancouver, or from Seattle to Anchorage. Check **Alaska Air** (tel. 800/426–0333) for good deals. In Alaska, small aircraft remain an essential and integral part of transportation. Small companies throughout the state service the bush and outlying island communities. Planes are used to fly sport fishermen, forest-service employees, petroleum engineers, hikers, and local residents to otherwise unreachable spots. Schedules are ruled by the weather, however, and in some areas—especially Southeast Alaska—the fog and cloud cover can ground aircraft for days. A trip out on a small plane can be an adventure in itself, offering you a chance to view the countryside from a different vantage point. **Alaska River Charters** (tel. 907/455–6827) has bush planes that may give you the most thrilling ride of your life and the only opportunity to see truly unspoiled wilderness. **Mark Air** (tel. 907/266–6802) services over 300 communities.

➢ **AIR PASSES** • **Council Travel** (*see* Budget Travel Organizations, *above*) offers two reasonably cheap ways of flying within the U.S. The **USAir Pass** is for students only, and allows you to fly between three U.S. cities for $395. The **Visit America** pass is available to foreign residents only; it entitles the holder to three stops, one-direction only, in a 60-day period for $200–$300. However, you must purchase it *before* arriving in the U.S.

Delta (tel. 800/221–1212) offers two separate passes for foreign visitors. The **Discover America Pass** allows three ($389), four ($489), five ($589), or six ($619) stops over a 60-day period in U.S. cities served by Delta—including Seattle, Portland, and Vancouver. You must purchase this pass before arriving in the U.S.; contact a travel agent or your favorite student travel office. Delta's **Standby Pass** allows unlimited standby travel within a 30-day ($549) or 60-day ($899) period. You fly coach class and must arrive at the airport early enough to get your name on the standby waiting list. This pass must also be purchased before arriving in the U.S.

BY BIKE Bicycling your way through the Pacific Northwest is perhaps the cheapest, most environmentally sound, and, depending upon your physical condition, most enjoyable way to see the area. Campgrounds cost less for cyclers, and hostels will make room for you even if they're full. In the summer, many adventurous and fit cyclists tour British Columbia, where biking is allowed on virtually every highway (even freeways), but the hills can be vicious. In southeast Alaska, exploring cities like Juneau and Ketchikan on bike allows you to reach some of the outlying attractions that are otherwise accessible only by car or on a tour. Remember, you'll probably get stuck riding in wet weather some (or most) of the time, so plan your gear accordingly.

Bicyclists should be experienced or go with someone who is—perhaps a touring group. Wear a helmet and bring along repair tools and a spare tube or patch kit. If you go on your own and plan on biking only part of the way, some train lines (like Amtrak) will transport your bike, in addition to yourself, for a small charge. One of the best books on the subject is *Bicycling the Pacific Coast* (by Tom Kirkendall and Vicky Spring, $12.95). For touring info, contact one of the following:

Backroads Bicycling Touring. *1516 5th St., Berkeley, CA 94710, tel. 800/245–3874.*

Bicycling Association of British Columbia. *1200 Hornby St., Vancouver, BC V6Z 2E2, tel. 604/737–3034.*

Portland Wheelman Touring Club. *Box 40753, Portland, OR 97240, tel. 503/257–7982.*

Rocky Mountain Cycle Tours. *Box 1978, Canmore, AB TOL OMO, tel. 403/678–6770.*

HITCHHIKING Although it's illegal in some places and always a little risky, hitching is the cheapest way to get around, and it's a common mode of travel in the Pacific Northwest. The best places to hitch are well-traveled highways, though some freeways forbid hitching on the entrance/exit ramps and on the freeway itself.

Hitching requires a flexible itinerary: Tales abound of hitchers getting stuck for days in such places as Tok, Alaska (you're right: you've never heard of it), waiting for a ride. If you do decide to thumb it, travel with a friend, especially if you are female. Catching a ride in campgrounds, diners, or youth hostels is one technique. Holding up a sign lends an air of legitimacy to your request. If thumbing at roadside, make sure the spot allows room for cars to pull over easily and, needless to say, you should look as unthreatening as possible. Offer gas money and be somewhat destination-flexible but never accept a ride if you are unsure about the driver. Always be aware of location and have a backup plan for emergency situations (fake car-sickness, etc.). Remember that you can always refuse a potential ride, and if your instincts tell you something is not right, say no thanks (or tell the driver you're going farther than he or she is). Start hitching early in the day; most people who start their days at 6 AM are living honest lives. If you're from a foreign country (of course, clever people can pretend), sew a patch of your country's flag to your pack. You'd be surprised how many Alaskans have traveled overseas and are more enthusiastic about picking up a foreign traveler.

On Vancouver Island, hitching is widely practiced and accepted, although it may not be any safer than anywhere else. In Alaska, hitching is still fairly popular and acceptable, but it's easiest as a method of getting around within a region; longer, cross-country rides can be difficult to score. Reaching remote areas is the chanciest proposition, but check individual chapters for more detailed information on local hitching conditions.

PHONES

For local directory assistance, dial 411. For long-distance help, dial the area code plus 555–1212. Local directory-assistance calls are free from any pay phone. If you don't know the area code or need help with local calls, dial the operator (0); for long-distance or international calls, dial 00. To find out if a particular business has an 800 number, call 800/555–1212. For info on international phone services, *see* Phones and Mail, in Info For Foreign Visitors, *above*.

Charges for collect calls are higher than for normal long-distance calls, so if you want to keep your friends, give them your number so they can call you back. Not all pay phones accept incoming calls, so read the fine print on the phone before trying this. Station-to-station is the standard collect call; anyone answering at the number you dial can accept the charges. Less common, and even more expensive, is a person-to-person call, which authorizes only the person whose name you give to the operator to accept the charges. On the up side, you won't be charged if the person you want to reach is out.

AREA CODES:

- *Alaska: 907*
- *British Columbia: 604*
- *Oregon: 503*
- *Eastern Washington: 509*
- *Western Washington: 360*
- *Yukon: 403*

To avoid collect calls or pockets bulging with change, you may want to use a calling card. They're issued by national long-distance companies (AT&T, U.S. Sprint, MCI, and Metromedia) to U.S. and Canadian citizens with current telephone service and allow you to make calls from any phone and be billed at a later date. Though there is usually no initial fee, each time you use a calling card you pay an additional service charge ranging from about 40¢–80¢, depending on how far you're calling.

MAIL

SENDING MAIL In the United States international rates for sending letters are 50¢ for the first half-ounce and 45¢ for the second half-ounce (i.e., one ounce equals 95¢) and 39¢ for each ounce thereafter. Post cards cost 40¢. Allow one to two weeks' delivery time. From Canada, letters and postcards to the United States cost C46¢ for up to 30 grams, and C67¢ for 30–35 grams. International mail and postcards from Canada cost C80¢ for up to 20 grams, C$1.20 for 20–50 grams. Sending packages domestically and internationally through **United Parcel Service** (UPS) (tel. 800/222–8333) often proves to be cheaper than sending them through the post office.

RECEIVING MAIL Being in transit does not mean you have to go without that little love note from your squeeze back home. In the United States and Canada use the following format for addressing mail: Name of addressee c/o General Delivery, Main Post Office, City and State/Province, U.S./Canada, Zip Code (U.S.)/Postal Code (Canada). Contact the nearest post office for more details. Most post offices are open weekdays 9–5, half-day on Saturday, and will hold your mail for up to 30 days before returning it to the sender. **American Express** offices also hold mail (but no packages) for 30 days for those cardholders or traveler's-check holders who present their cards/checks when claiming mail. Call American Express (tel. 800/528–4800) to obtain locations.

WHERE TO SLEEP

Saving money on lodging means more money for the important things in life: microbrewery beer, hot tubs, bush plane excursions, and all-you-can-eat salmon feasts. Hostels and campgrounds are the cheapest way to go and often the most interesting in terms of scenery and meeting interesting fellow travelers. Learn the pros and cons of various campgrounds, hostels, or motels from other travelers and be willing to break your itinerary to follow a promising word-of-mouth rave.

Throughout the book, the lodging price categories refer to the cost of a double room plus tax. Likewise, in the Food sections, the price categories refer to the cost of a main course with a drink. If you're a soda addict or insist on a king-size bed, all bets are off.

MOTELS AND MOTEL CHAINS Best Western (tel. 800/528–1234), **Days Inn** (tel. 800/325–2525), **Quality Inns** (tel. 800/228–5151), **Super 8 Motels** (tel. 800/843–1991), and **Travelodge** (tel. 800/255–3050) are splattered all over the Pacific Northwest. **Motel 6** (tel. 505/891–6161) has locations in Oregon and Washington, as does **Nendel's** (tel. 800/547–0106), which is also in British Columbia.

BED-AND-BREAKFASTS Bed-and-breakfasts are usually out of the budget range, but if you want to splurge on something that smacks of dear old home, spend your money here. B&Bs are privately owned homes or restored architectural beauties, and the room price varies accordingly. As the name implies, all B&Bs provide breakfast, which can range from a pastry and coffee to a five-course feast. The rooms themselves are usually without telephones and televisions, and you're usually required to share bathrooms with other guests.

Bed-and-breakfasts are a booming business in British Columbia. Several agencies list homes all over the province. For a big list, try the **British Columbia Bed and Breakfast Association** (Box 593, 810 W. Broadway, V57-4E2, tel. 604/276–8616) or the **Best Canadian Bed and Breakfast Network** (tel. 604/738–7207). Many of the B&Bs are located a ways from bus stations in B.C., so you may need a car, although some B&B owners will come and pick you up. Rooms typically cost $50 and up.

Canada has farm hostels that allow you to stay and work a few hours a day in return for free (or very cheap) food and lodging in a wonderful spot. Check with the tourist board for referrals.

Reservation agencies for all of Alaska include **Accommodations in Alaska: The Friendly Choice** (Box 110624, Anchorage 99511–0624, tel. 907/345–4761), **Alaska Private Lodgings** (Box 200047, Anchorage 99520–0047, tel. 907/248–2292), and **Alaska Sourdough Bed and Breakfast** (889 Cardigan Circle, Anchorage 99503–7027, tel. 907/563–6244).

In Washington both **Accommodations Northwest** (Box 982, Anacortes, WA 98221) and the **Washington Bed and Breakfast Guild** (2442 N. W. Market St., Seattle, WA 98107) publish brochures with short descriptions, addresses, and phone numbers of B&Bs statewide. Neither, however, includes prices. In Oregon, check with the **Bed and Breakfast Directory** (tel. 503/476-2932). **Northwest Bed and Breakfast** (610 S.W. Broadway, Suite 606, Portland, OR 97205, tel. 503/243-7616) handles B&Bs throughout the Pacific Northwest.

HOSTELS Hostels are a wonderful form of cheap lodging. The **American Youth Hostel Association** (Dept. 801, Box 37613, Washington, DC 20013-7613, tel. 202/783-6161), part of the Hostelling International umbrella, accepts travelers of all ages and has listings of hostels in Washington, Oregon, and Alaska. Most tend to be near cities or along the coast. Lodgings are almost always clean and comfortable and often in beautiful settings and buildings. One concession is AYH's strict rules (which sometimes vary from hostel to hostel): Alcohol, drugs, and smoking are forbidden; curfews, sometimes as early as 10 PM, are enforced; and a simple chore is required of each visitor. The maximum stay is three days unless an extension is granted. In the summer season it's a good idea to book ahead. Some hostels will allow you to use your sleeping bag, although officially they require a sleep sack that can be rented for about $1 a night. All hostels have a kitchen, common room, and often useful listings that detail budget things to do in the area. One major drawback is the lock-out most have from 9 to 5, during which all guests must leave the premises. It is usually not necessary to be a member ($25 for one year) to secure a bed, but nonmembers pay $11 while members pay $8. AYH publishes a U.S. handbook (free for members, otherwise $5) that details the location and individual amenities of each hostel. **Hostelling International Canada (HIC)** (205 Catherine St., Suite 400, Ottawa, Ont. K2P 1C3, tel. 613/237-7884) is the Canadian version of the AYH.

The **YMCA** and **YWCA** also operate hostels with facilities that range from dorm-style rooms to high-school gyms outfitted with beds in summer. Age limits and prices vary, so call ahead. *733 15th St. NW, Washington, DC 20005, tel. 202/783-6161. Also: 2160 Yonge St., Toronto, Ont. M4S 2A1, tel. 800/922-9622.*

UNIVERSITY/STUDENT HOUSING During the summer, universities often rent out dorm rooms by the night or the week; however, it's usually under the pretense that you're staying on some sort of school-related business. If they ask, say you're thinking of attending school there. Generally, universities are not a real bargain. Dorm rooms are dreary and costs are high—$30 to $40 for a single or double. If you're interested in a school not listed in this guide, contact the university's housing office.

LODGING ALTERNATIVES

➤ **ROUGHING IT** • Crashing for free is definitely possible in certain areas of this region if you're willing to take a few risks. Sleeping on someone's private property is always a bad idea unless you get their permission. Public places such as bus stations and train stations are rarely open 24 hours and are rarely safe after hours. Your safest and most comfortable option is sleeping in the great outdoors—and there's plenty of outdoors in the Northwest! Often the main danger here is not humans but bears; even close to town, it's important to take proper precautions, such as hanging all food from trees. In some Alaskan fishing towns you should ask about

Canadian Tax Tips

Room taxes in Canada are so confusing that even hotel owners may not fully understand the rules. First there's the provincial hotel tax (PHT), which varies from province to province: British Columbia tacks on an 8% room tax and, sometimes, an additional 2% municipal tax. Next, there's your basic goods and services tax (GST) (i.e., sales tax), which is 7% across the country. Nonresidents are entitled to a GST rebate on rooms. If you're keeping close tabs on the cash flow (and we know you are), ask if the GST and/or the PHT are included or added to your room rate—we wouldn't want you to get a rude shock when you check out.

camping in one of the small tent cities used by seasonal workers—it's a great way to meet people and learn about local issues firsthand (*see* Chapter 11 for more info).

➤ **APARTMENT STAYS** • If you have a group of friends and want to stay in one place for a few weeks, consider renting or subletting an apartment. Contact the area's chambers of commerce for agencies that specialize in vacation apartment stays.

➤ **OTHER OPTIONS** • **Crash Network**. It costs nothing to join the Crash Network, and once you do, your name and essential info gets published in the Crash Directory ($5). With this in hand, you call or write in advance to potential crashees and ask if you may stay for a few days—for free. All crashers must follow the Crash Code: (1) Treat each other with respect, (2) No stealing, (3) Don't eat crashee's food unless offered, and (4) Don't bring friends over without prior consent of crashee. As it says in the brochure, "if you understand the Crash Code and use a little bit of patience, you and your fellow human should be able to work everything out between yourselves." *519 Castro St., Suite 7, San Francisco, CA 94114.*

Servas. Formed in the aftermath of World War II, Servas is a membership organization that enables you to arrange a stay with host families. Servas is dedicated to promoting peace and understanding around the globe. Becoming a member makes you eligible for their host list directory for any country you desire. Servas is not for tourists or weekend travelers; peace-minded individuals who want more than a free bed can write or call for an application and an interview. You can arrange a stay with a Servas host or host family in advance or just try your luck when you reach the country. Membership is $55 per year, and a one-time deposit of $25 is required. *In the United States: 11 John St., Suite 407, New York, NY 10038, tel. 212/267–0252. In Canada: 229 Hilcrest Ave., Willowdale, Ont. M2N 3P3, tel. 416/221–6434. In the U.K.: 83 Gore Rd., London E97 HW. In Australia: 16 Cavill Ct., Vermont South, 3133 Victoria, tel. 803–5004. In New Zealand: 15 Harley Rd., Takapuna, Oakland, tel. 594442.*

Intervac U.S. This company can hook you up with people willing to exchange time in their home for time in yours. It's really intended for professors and professionals temporarily living in the U.S. or abroad, but it's worth ordering the free information newsletter. *Box 590504, San Francisco, CA 94159, tel. 415/435–3497 or 800/756–4663.*

World For Free (WFF). Like the Crash Network, WFF helps like-minded people find contacts in foreign cities. The $25 membership fee gets you listed in the WFF Address Book, which means people may start calling or writing you tomorrow to crash at your pad. You are never obligated to house a WFF member, though the whole point is to be nice and to help travelers in need. After joining you also get a copy of the latest WFF Address Book, which you can use to contact other members and arrange accommodations by phone or mail. *Box 137, Prince Street Station, New York, NY 10012, fax 212/979–8167.*

CAMPING

Camping is an essential part of any trip to the Pacific Northwest. Particularly in Alaska—where food, accommodations, and transportation are expensive—camping is the cheapest and easiest way to save money. Even in winter, when the region is covered with snow, ski-touring is an unfor-

McMotel

Like the golden arches, the big "6" looming on every main drag acts as a beacon to budget travelers. While connoisseurs of fine mattresses and fragrant body lotions will say that Motel 6 is the McDonald's of the motel industry, there's something to be said for a 200-hotel chain whose $20–$40 rates are always posted on a big sign. Even if you don't stay there, you can use Motel 6 as a gauge of the general lodging rates in various cities; the pricier the Motel 6, the trendier (and more expensive) the town.

gettable experience, giving you the opportunity to feel, taste, and smell the wilderness at its most pristine. In summer and spring, the Northwest fills with wildflowers, and a host of outdoor activities opens up. The wildlife is generally harmless, although potentially harmful bears do roam in the wild. Never sleep with food in your tent or backpack, and remember that any boulder you climb to strategically secure your food, a bear can climb, too. If you're camping in the backcountry, put food in sealed containers or plastic bags inside a sleeping bag sack and hang it from a tree branch at least 20 feet above ground. Make sure the branch is thin enough that it will not support a black bear (grizzlies cannot climb trees) and that the tree is far from where you're sleeping. Many designated campsites have food lockers designed to be bear-proof.

A good book (which covers Washington and Oregon only) to peruse is *Pacific Northwest Camping* (Foghorn Press, 555 De Haro, Suite 220, San Francisco, CA 94107, tel. 415/241–9550; $16.95). Also check with the **Sierra Club** (730 Polk St., San Francisco, CA 94109, tel. 415/776–2211) for a good selection of guides.

CAMPING GEAR Equipment, from clothes to tents, is much cheaper in the lower 48 states than in Alaska or Canada, so you should stock up on gear (and even food if possible) at large outdoor stores like **REI** (1700 45th St. E, Sumner, WA 98352, tel. 800/426–4840), which has stores up and down the west coast. **The North Face** (tel. 206/622–4111) has factory outlets in large northwestern cities, where supplies and gear are much cheaper than at their regular stores. Call for outlet locations. **Patagonia, Inc.** (259 W. Santa Clara Ave., Ventura, CA 93001, tel. 805/643–8616 or 800/336–9090) has both a store and a catalog featuring outdoor gear. The **Mountain Equipment Co-op** (428 W. 8th St., Vancouver, B.C. V59 1N9, tel. 604/872–7858) is the best place to buy gear in Canada (other locations are in Calgary and Toronto)—membership costs $5 and is worth it. The **Three Vet Store** (2200 Yukon St., Vancouver, B.C. V5Y 3P2, tel. 604/872–5475) requires no membership and has good equipment.

If you're coming to Alaska or British Columbia in the winter, you'll need the warmest clothing you can find. The necessities include a fully lined parka, fully lined boots and gloves, long underwear, wool socks, and wool or synthetic blends that are breathable and wick (repel) moisture away from your skin. No matter where you're headed, if you're planning on camping or backpacking, consider most of the following items as essentials:

• Sleeping bags are a first concern. Both down and synthetic bags will keep you warm in cold, dry weather, but down becomes useless when wet, whereas Polarguard HV and Qualofil stuffing provide warmth (uncomfortable though they may be) even when sopping wet, thus protecting you against hypothermia. If you do have a down bag, take the precaution of wrapping it in a plastic bag.

• Tent or tarp to keep out those friendly mosquitoes and black flies.

• A silver-bottom ground cloth for placing under your tent or under your sleeping bag on those clear nights when you want to sleep under the stars. It also doubles as an emergency poncho in a rainstorm or as insulation in a snowstorm.

• A propane stove, a Coleman, a Whisperlite, or a small backpacking stove will save you large sums of money. Extra canisters of fuel are relatively easy to find in hardware and grocery stores (but not in the Alaskan bush).

• Some rope or webbing, especially if you're camping (bears . . . food . . . bears eat your food . . . you no food).

• A candle lantern ($12–$18)—and don't forget matches in a waterproof pouch. Gas lanterns are too heavy and use too much fuel.

• Duct tape, indispensable for fixing all sorts of broken, torn, or leaky things—tents, clothes, water bottles, even fingers.

• Snow-sealed hiking boots; though heavy, they're the only pair of shoes you need to go anywhere and get through anything. If you have the space, pack a pair of thongs or sandals—they're good for the muddy floors of campground showers.

- Some polypropylene or chinchilla gear, or wool sweaters. Bring mittens and a couple of hats: a wool one for night and a baseball cap or something with a brim for excessive rain or sun. Your mother was right: 90% of your body heat is lost right off the top of your head.

- Rain gear, dummy. You're in the Pacific Northwest.

- Mild liquid soap (like Dr. Bronner's) that can be used for hair, face, teeth, dishes, and clothes alike.

- Toilet paper—you never know when (or where) you gotta go.

- Water-purification tablets or iodine crystals ($8). If you can afford $30–$60, a water purifying hand-pump makes life easy; try the ones made by PUR, which are lightweight and can purify a gallon of water in about 10 minutes.

- Also useful are a can opener, a bottle opener, a multiblade knife (like a Swiss army knife), a first-aid kit, a mug (all-purpose eating and drinking container), and a water bottle (pack a few of these if possible). It's hard to get fresh water in some places (like on the north shore of the Charlotte Islands or in remote parts of Alaska), so you might want to stock up when you can.

STAYING HEALTHY It's always a good idea to bring a first-aid kit (*see* What to Pack, in Planning Your Trip, *above*). If you plan on hiking, bring Moleskin (thicker than a Band-aid) and tape to cover blisters. Combating mosquitoes is best accomplished by donning heavy clothes that cover as much of your skin surface as possible, and covering yourself with insect repellent. Poison oak, with its evil oily three-leaf stem that causes severe itching and rash, blankets much of the Pacific Coast. To avoid the bushy plant, watch for its leaves, which are shiny green in the spring and rich orange and red in the fall. If you happen to fall into a bush, wash your skin with cold water (don't use soap) and do not scratch. Although drinking water fresh from a stream won't kill you, you may think longingly of death if you contract giardia (a.k.a. Beaver Fever), a microscopic protozoan that causes excruciatingly painful stomach cramps and diarrhea. Always use a water filter (cheap plastic ones cost around $35) or boil the water for at least five minutes. Water-purification pills do not always kill giardia. Bring some water with you and drink a lot to avoid dehydration. For snowy hikes beware of frostbite—when you have it your skin turns white, waxy, and cold (ewww!). Never, ever rub frostbite (you will damage the skin); instead, warm it gently with body contact or dry cloth, and get to a doctor for treatment.

PROTECTING THE ENVIRONMENT So many people use (and abuse) the great outdoors that it's necessary to offer some simple guidelines. In the Pacific Northwest (and Alaska especially), where grizzlies still roam, keeping a clean camp is a matter of survival and not just

How to Avoid Hypothermia

Hypothermia, when your body temperature falls below normal, kills many campers each year because it goes unrecognized. It's likely to occur if you've been exposed to cold water (rain, river, lake) and cold air temperature. The first symptom is an apathetic, sleepy feeling followed by confusion, collapse, and, finally, death. Precautions to take:

- *Maintain your energy supply by eating high-calorie foods and avoid becoming overly fatigued.*

- *Wear layered clothing. Wool and synthetics are best. Cotton next to the skin draws heat from the body when it's wet, and down is completely ineffective when wet.*

- *Seek shelter from the wind and rain and stay dry! Put on any extra dry clothing you've had the foresight to pack protected in a plastic bag.*

some feel-good environmental ideal. Remember the basics: Always travel on trails and, if possible, camp on previously used sites to avoid trampling vegetation and causing soil erosion. Always pack out the garbage you create and bury human waste 8 inches deep, at least 200 feet from water, your camp, and trails. To wash anything, use only biodegradable soap and a container. Never wash directly in a stream or lake, but at least 50 feet away in your container. Very few parks allow you to build fires in the wilderness; if you must, make sure to put it out completely before leaving the site. If you bring a stove, get a free fire permit at the nearest ranger station. *How to Shit in the Woods* (Ten Speed Press, Box 7123, Berkeley, CA 94707; $5.95), by Kathleen Meyer, is a good book on a not especially pleasant but important skill.

NATIONAL AND STATE PARKS

If green is your favorite color, you will be awed, no, overwhelmed by its abundance in the national and state parks in the Pacific Northwest, at least in the summer. In Washington, one-third of the land is public, and in Alaska animals have 54 million acres on which to roam. National parks, like Alaska's Denali and Katmai, Washington's Olympic, and Oregon's Crater Lake, are unequivocally beautiful. Although they allow recreation, they were established for the purpose of preservation. Amazingly, Alaska, with two-thirds of all U.S. national park lands within its borders, is allocated only 3% of the U.S. Park Service budget.

National park campgrounds are fairly well kept but often crowded. National forests, which are less protected "multiple-use land" areas, have less spectacular but also less crowded campgrounds. State parks (usually historically or geologically significant and smaller than national parks) lie somewhere in between in terms of the quality of the scenery and campground maintenance. Many campgrounds do not accept reservations, but those in the most popular spots will take bookings eight weeks in advance. For reservations, call **MISTIX** (tel. 800/365–2267 for national parks, 800/280–2267 for national forests, 800/444–7275 for state parks).

VISITOR INFORMATION The Sierra Club recently published the first-rate *Easy Access Guide to National Parks* ($16). **The National Park Foundation** (Box 57473, Washington, DC 20037), a Congressional group, publishes a guide to 375 national parks that includes basic accessibility information; send $13.95 for shipping and handling. A map and guide listing types of facilities and activities available at each park (including accessibility info) is also available from the **U.S. Department of the Interior** (National Park Service, Box 37127, Washington, DC 20013).

The **USDA Forest Service Outdoor Recreational Center** in Seattle offers the best selection of brochures on state parks, national parks, and the U.S. Forest Service. *915 2nd Ave., Suite 442, Seattle 98174, tel. 206/220–7450. Open weekdays 8:30–5.*

Alaska's State Bird and How to Avoid It

There is good news and bad news concerning mosquitoes. First the good news: They're around only three months of the year. As for the bad news: Those three months are June, July, and August, when most of you will be visiting. If you're here in the summer, the sooner you face the fact that you'll be bitten, the better off you'll be. To reduce the number of bites, you can always try garlic, but don't leave home without some sort of repellent, too. You should absolutely buy Avon Skin so Soft—the only effective repellent around. If you're too lazy to look up "Avon" in the phone book and call for details on where to buy it, we wash our hands of you. For the latest in fashions, pack a mosquito hat with netting that covers your head and face, particularly if you're heading into the backcountry. An after-bite product with ammonium hydroxide will help stop the itching.

Oregon State Parks and Recreation Division. *1115 Commercial St. NE, Salem, OR 97310, tel. 503/378–6305.*

Washington State Parks and Recreation Commission. *7150 Clearwater La., KY–11, Olympia, WA 98504, tel. 206/753–5755.*

Alaska Public Lands Information Center is the place to go the minute you set foot in Tok, Anchorage, or Fairbanks to make reservations in a state or national park (except Denali). Remember, you'll be making these reservations 7–21 days in advance, but you'll stand a good chance of getting the campgrounds of your choice. *605 W. 4th Ave., Suite 105, Anchorage, AK 99501, tel. 907/271–2737; 250 Cushman, Suite 1A, Fairbanks, AK 99701, tel. 907/451–7352; Box 359, Tok, AK 99780, tel. 907/883–5667.*

WHAT IT WILL COST Both national and state parks charge entrance fees per car that vary depending upon the facilities the park has to maintain. Entrance fees cost about $5–$6 a car in both park systems. National forests tend to be more lax; often there is no ranger to collect fees, just a self-pay metal bin operating on the honor system. The $25 **Golden Eagle Pass** grants entrance to any national park during the calendar year and is available through the mail from the National Park Service and the Forest Service. The **Golden Access Passport** is a free, lifetime-entry pass that exempts travelers with disabilities and their families or friends from all entry fees and 50% of use fees for camping and parking. With medical proof of disability, you can pick one up in person at most federally run parks and refuges.

FURTHER READING

If you can, get your hands on assorted Tom Robbins novels; Ken Kesey's **Sometimes a Great Notion**, about logging and psychosis in the Pacific Northwest; Ursula Le Guin's books, particularly **The Lathe of Heaven**, which is set in Portland; **The Journals of Lewis and Clark**; Harold Davis's **Honey in the Horn; Coyote Was Going There**, a collection of Oregon Native American coyote and trickster legends; Oregon poet Robert Davies's **Tracks in Oregon**; Robert Pirsig's classic **Zen and the Art of Motorcycle Maintenance**, philosophical travels through the Pacific Northwest and a disillusioned perspective of Crater Lake; Jack London's super-groovy (in a sixth-grade kinda way) **Call of the Wild**, set in Alaska; Ivan Doig's **The Sea Runners,** an adventure set in 1853, when Alaska belonged to Russia; John McPhee's **Coming into the Country**, which describes three different areas of Alaska; John Keeble's **Yellowfish** and **Dialogues with Northwest Writers;** Alaskan Natalie Kusz's award-winning memoir **Road Song**, about a family's move from Los Angeles to Alaska in 1969.

PORTLAND

2

By Gary Blond

In a debate about whose city is better, it would be difficult to defeat a resident of Portland. Sure, you'd score points by bagging on Portland's perennial rains, or by asserting that any city without a major league baseball team is clearly un-American. Before you could say much, though, the Portland resident would assail you with factlets about the city's beautiful scenery, clean air, fine parks, excellent public transportation, ambitious public arts program, and world-class zoo. In the face of such an unstoppable barrage, you'd undoubtedly be reduced to muttering sentences beginning lamely with "Yeah, well . . . " and trailing off into awkward silence. No city is a Shangri-La—and Portland certainly isn't immune to the ills that plague other American towns—but in terms of sheer livability, Portland more than holds its own against its urban siblings.

Probably the only city in the nation with more trees than asphalt, Portland's the place where a nature fix rarely requires a drive of more than five or ten minutes. Parks and gardens dominate the scenery, from the world's smallest, Mills, which occupies a downtown traffic island, to the nation's largest forested urban park, a 4,800-acre affair just northwest of the city proper. On clear days, Oregon's tallest peak is visible to the east in the guise of snow-capped Mt. Hood, while the lopsided shape of famed Mt. St. Helens can be seen to the north. Dividing the city in half is the wide and mighty Willamette River, spanned by ten bridges.

Portlanders love to tell the story of their city's naming. No profound orations, epic struggles, or prophetic visions marked this moment—just a couple of early settlers, Asa Lovejoy (a native of Boston) and Francis Pettygrove (a native of Portland, Maine), flipping a coin. Pettygrove won. And though its establishment may have been haphazard, little since has been left to chance. Creative city planning has made this an extremely user-friendly environment, with one of the best and most extensive systems of mass transit in the nation, and an easy-to-learn grid of streets and numbered avenues. Downtown, public drinking fountains run continuously so you won't be bothered with the taxing task of turning a handle or pushing a button.

Every spring, Blazermania envelopes Portland, and residents converse about nothing else. Learn a few key phrases and players' names or you'll be very, very lonely.

Another point of pride for Portlanders is the city's public arts program. More than 40 statues, sculptures, and murals decorate downtown, the result of an aggressive policy that funnels a portion of construction moneys from every state building into the commission and preservation of artwork. In terms of museums, Portland's stand up to the finest in the Pacific Northwest. The Portland Art Museum has an outstanding collection of Asian and Native American art, as well as many Western masters like Picasso and Monet.

33

Despite its considerable size, Portland often seems like a cozily eccentric small town. For almost a decade, the city was run by a bearded veteran tavern owner named Bud, a guy whose first appearance in the public sphere was to pose as a flasher for the infamous 1978 poster "Expose Yourself to Art." Six years later he was elected mayor of Portland (and faithfully continued to pedal to work on his bike). In the late '60s, Portland's forward-thinking planners imposed height restrictions on buildings—at a time when most urban centers were stacking 'em as high as the reinforced steel would allow. Today, the low skyline makes for a friendlier and less alienating city, and in Portland's case, it also preserves the outstanding views.

Though there are no mammoth skyscrapers, Portland has plenty of urban pockets with their own distinctive styles. Visit the Hawthorne District, for example, and you'll leave the city thinking a good number of its residents do nothing with their time but look for new places to pierce themselves. Portland's diversity is most evident at night: On almost any evening, you can catch live jazz, blues, country and western, or alternative rock—or just belly up to a neighborhood bar with a pint of locally brewed beer. Especially novel are Portland's theater-pubs, where for a mere $1 you can see a second-run movie on a full-size screen, and, for a few dollars more, buy pizza and beer to go with it.

Unlike some anxious and self-conscious cities, which steer visitors from one cheery, sanitized sight to another, Portland wears its seedier industrial sectors on its sleeve. You'll run across bustling microbreweries in a stretch of deserted warehouses, junkies roaming the fringes of a historic district, and trendy neighborhoods—particularly those east of the Willamette River—surrounded by rundown blocks. Portland's problems may pale in comparison to those of many other urban centers, but what better proof of a city that has much to offer than a city that has nothing to hide.

Basics

AMERICAN EXPRESS This downtown office holds mail for American Express card members and check holders. They'll also cash out-of-town checks. *1100 S.W. 6th Ave., tel. 503/226–2961. Open weekdays 8:30–5:30.*

LUGGAGE STORAGE At the **Portland International Airport,** coin-operated lockers (75¢ for 24 hrs) are located on the main floor concourse. Storage for a day or more can be had at **D.J.'s Delivery Service** (tel. 503/281–9464), which can accommodate any kind of baggage—even frozen stuff. Charges are $2–$5 per bag per day, depending on the size (and temperature). D.J.'s is located near baggage claim carousel one. **Amtrak** (800 N.W. 6th Ave., tel. 800/872–7245) holds stuff for ticketed customers only. The first 48 hours are free; after that they charge $1.50 per bag per day. At the **Greyhound Station** (550 N.W. 6th Ave., tel. 503/243–2350), ticketed customers can store their bags for $4 the first day and $5 for each additional day.

VISITOR INFORMATION The **Portland Oregon Visitors Association** distributes two helpful publications free of charge: the *Portland Book,* which gives a decent overview of citywide attractions, and the Powell's Bookstore *Walking Map of Downtown Portland,* which offers a self-guided tour of downtown's major sights. Tickets to major shows and sporting events can be purchased at the **Ticketmaster** outlet. And be sure to look around downtown for the wandering teams dressed in kelly green. No, they're not Girl Scouts, but **Portland guides,** who will happily answer questions and provide directions. *25 S.W. Salmon St., tel. 503/222–2223. Near Tom McCall Waterfront Park. Open weekdays 8–6:30, Sat. 8:30–5, Sun. 10–4.*

COMING AND GOING

BY CAR Portland is 180 miles south of Seattle and 672 miles north of San Francisco via I–5. Boise, Idaho lies 434 miles east via I–84. U.S. 30 and U.S. 26 are the main routes west to the coast; U.S. 26 continues southeast past Mt. Hood to central Oregon. The Portland Oregon Visitors Association (*see above*) provides free highway maps of the state.

Portland has scores of rental car companies offering a wide range of rates and options. The best deal on short drives can be found at **Rent-A-Wreck** (9785 Shady Lane, Tigard, tel.

503/624–1804), though you must be 21 or older and have a credit card. Prices are $20 a day in winter, $23 a day in summer; weekly rates start at $120. The first 100 miles are free, and each additional mile is 15¢. **Thrifty Car Rental** (632 S.W. Pine St., tel. 503/227–6587) also requires a credit card and that renters be at least 21. Cars cost about $25 a day with unlimited mileage.

BY BUS Greyhound (550 N.W. 6th Ave., tel. 503/243–2311 or 800/231–2222) runs 11 buses a day to Seattle (4 hrs, $19); eight a day through the Willamette Valley to Eugene (2½ hrs, $13) and to San Francisco (17 hrs, $72); six to Los Angeles (23 hrs, $102); three east through the Columbia Gorge to Boise, Idaho; and four a day to various points along the Oregon coast. Exact prices and trip lengths vary according to season and day of travel. The Greyhound station is accessible from downtown by Tri-Met Buses 31–33, 54, and 56–59 (see Getting Around, below).

Adventurous souls should forgo Greyhound for an unforgettable voyage aboard the **Green Tortoise** (no office in Portland, tel. 800/867–8647), which tools leisurely up and down the coast with stops for passengers to hike or swim. Coaches contain sleeping mattresses, but no toilets or showers. It's the closest you could ever hope to come to recreating Ken Kesey's cross-country, Electric-Kool-Aid bus trip. Green Tortoise usually picks up at the intersection of S.W. College Street and 6th Avenue (near Portland State). The bus to Seattle ($15) runs every Tuesday and Saturday; the bus to Eugene ($10) and San Francisco ($42) operates every Sunday and Thursday. Call ahead for updated information and to make reservations.

BY TRAIN Amtrak stops at **Union Station** (800 N.W. 6th Ave., tel. 800/872–7245), one block north of the Greyhound depot and 13 blocks north of Pioneer Courthouse Square. Three trains make the daily trip to Seattle (4 hrs, $23). Trains depart once daily for Eugene (3 hrs, $24), San Francisco (19 hrs, $131), Los Angeles (29 hrs, $160), and other cities up and down the West Coast, as well as Chicago (2 days, $217). Precise fares and travel times vary, so call ahead. To reach downtown from the station, you can catch Tri-Met Buses 31–33, 54, or 56–59. Other points in Portland and its suburbs are serviced by the MAX Light Rail (see Getting Around, below).

BY PLANE The efficient **Portland International Airport** (tel. 503/335–1234) is 13 miles northeast of downtown, a drive of about 20 minutes in average traffic. For many airlines, this rarely crowded airport is a hub for flights to Asia. **ATMs** and a **currency exchange office** (tel. 503/281–3045) are on the airport's main level. The exchange office is open daily 5:30 AM–7 PM. On the main and baggage-claim levels, two **visitors centers** (open daily 6 AM–11:30 PM) dispense information on accommodations and attractions. For information on luggage storage, see above.

➤ **AIRPORT TRANSIT** • To reach downtown Portland by public transportation, take **Tri-Met Bus 12** (see Getting Around, below). Weekdays, buses depart every 15 minutes (5:30 AM–8:50 PM) or half hour (8:50 PM–11:50 PM). Weekend service is every half hour from 5 AM to midnight. The trip ($1) takes approximately 40 minutes. **Raz Transportation** (tel. 503/246–3301) offers service (about $7) to downtown, the Lloyd Center area, and the train and bus depots. Buses leave every half hour 5 AM–midnight. **Taxi** fare to downtown runs $21–$25.

HITCHHIKING Hitching from Portland can be difficult. Check the ride boards posted at the student unions of **Portland State** (724 S.W. Harrison St., tel. 503/725–3000), **Lewis and Clark College** (615 S.W. Palatine Hill Rd., tel. 503/768–7000), or **Reed College** (see Worth Seeing, below).

GETTING AROUND

Portland is bordered and bisected by rivers: The **Columbia River,** on the town's northern outskirts, separates Portland from Vancouver, Washington, while the **Willamette River,** spanned by ten bridges, splits the city into eastern and western halves. Passing through the city's historic district and crossing the Willamette, **Burnside Street** acts as dividing line between Portland's northern and southern sections. Avenues run north to

Burnside Street and the Willamette River divide the city into four quarters. If you see a street labeled "N.W. Glisan," you know it's north of Burnside and west of the Willamette.

south; streets run east to west. **Front Avenue** borders the Willamette's western bank; **Water Avenue** runs the length of its eastern shore. Numbered avenues run parallel to Water Avenue; their numbers increase as you head east. More numbered avenues run roughly parallel to Front Avenue and increase consecutively as you head west.

Downtown Portland lies in the southwest quadrant (i.e., west of the Willamette and just south of Burnside Street). Most of the city's sights are clustered within this easily walked 20-block area. Try strolling, for example, south from the Saturday Market at Old Town to the excellent Oregon Art Institute. In the **northwest quadrant,** a 15-block walk will take you through the brewery area to Nob Hill, a hip and gentrified neighborhood with a heavy concentration of trendy shops, restaurants, and bars. (Northwest streets are laid out in alphabetical order.) But that's about all the exploring you'll want to do on foot.

East of the Willamette, the **southeast quadrant** contains scores of middle-class neighborhoods, as well as a funky enclave of cafés, ethnic eateries, and specialty shops along Hawthorne Boulevard. The mostly residential **northeast quadrant** contains Memorial Coliseum, the Oregon Convention Center, and the tiny but fascinating American Advertising Museum.

The city is blessed with a simple and efficient public transportation system, **Tri-Met** (tel. 503/238–RIDE), which operates daily from approximately 5 AM to midnight. You have two options: **Buses** run anywhere and everywhere. Nearly all of them cut conveniently through downtown's **Transit Mall,** on S.W. 5th and 6th avenues between S.W. Salmon and Alder streets. The **MAX** (Metropolitan Area Express) light rail, a sort of modernized trolley, follows a single route from downtown Portland east to the suburb of Gresham, passing through key tourist stops like Pioneer Courthouse Square and Old Town. Show a transfer slip or validated ticket stub (good for one hour) and you can switch midtrip from bus to MAX, or vice versa. All Tri-Met rides in Portland's downtown—inside the loop made by the Willamette River and I–405, but excluding the area north of Union Station—fall within the **Fareless Square,** where, as the name suggests, you won't pay a dime. Otherwise, travel costs $1, or $1.30 if your destination is one of the more remote suburbs. Pick up a **transit map** ($2.50), specific route brochures (free), or special ticket packages (*see* By Bus, *below*) at Tri-Met's Customer Service Office in Pioneer Courthouse Square (S.W. 6th Ave., btw Morrison and Yamhill Sts.), open weekdays 9–5. All MAX light rail and Tri-Met buses are wheelchair accessible.

BY BUS Nearly all of the 74 Tri-Met bus lines pass through downtown Portland's Transit Mall (*see above*), which makes finding the right one fairly easy. Southbound buses stop on 5th Avenue, and those going north stop along 6th Avenue. Fare is usually $1; you may also purchase 24-hour passes ($3.25) or 10-ticket packages for one zone ($8), two zones ($9), or all zones ($12) at the Tri-Met office (*see above*). Most of Portland's sights lie within a single zone, but you may want to spend the extra dollar if you're planning a thorough exploration of the city's east side. Be sure to keep your transfer or receipt; it's also valid on MAX (*see below*) and can save you from the wrath of patrolling Tri-Met inspectors.

From downtown, Bus 15 travels west on S.W. Washington Street to N.W. 23rd Avenue, then continues north through Nob Hill to the tip of Forest Park. Bus 20 follows Burnside Street, passing the north side of Washington Park (though the park's zoo is served by Bus 63). Routes connecting downtown Portland with points east of the Willamette River include Bus 14 (south to the Hawthorne District), Bus 9 (north to Broadway and south to Powell Avenue), and Bus 12 (north to Sandy Boulevard). For bus connections with Greyhound and Amtrak stations, *see* Coming and Going, *above;* for more information on fares, free rides, and other Tri-Met regulations, *see above.*

BY MAX LIGHT RAIL MAX was designed for eastside commuters bored by lengthy bus rides. (Westside residents will get the same treatment when a new MAX line opens in 1998.) It's also a good way to see the city—if your destination lies along the single existing MAX route, which passes through Pioneer Courthouse Square and Old Town before finally arriving at the northeastern suburb of Gresham. Trains originate at a downtown station on S.W. 11th Avenue at Yamhill Street. Conductors don't collect fares or check tickets, so you'll need to purchase a ticket or validate a prepaid one at the station's ticket machine before boarding. (Save the stub, since periodic sweeps by merciless Tri-Met inspectors result in fines for the empty-handed.)

Validated MAX tickets also allow you to board Tri-Met buses. For more information on fares, schedules, free rides, and other Tri-Met regulations, *see above*.

BY CAR Portland is a car-friendly city. With a set of wheels and a fair sense of direction, touring the urban sprawl east of the Willamette won't be a problem; however, stick to the commercial thoroughfares, since side roads tend to end and then start up again a few blocks away. Downtown, expect to pay for daytime parking, either at a coin-op meter or at one of the many outdoor parking lots (usually $10 or less per day). Watch for weekend bargains. The *Portland Book* (*see* Visitor Information, *above*) includes a fairly detailed city map. Though helpful, it omits several outlying areas—and forces you to learn about one-way streets the hard way. Detailed road maps (about $2.50) are available at most bookstores and gas stations.

BY TAXI If you need a taxi, spend the 20¢ on a phone call or proceed immediately to one of the designated stands downtown (usually located in front of posh hotels). With **Portland Taxi** (tel. 503/256–5400) and **Broadway Deluxe Cab** (tel. 503/227–1234 or 800/248–8294), rates are $1.50 per mile, with a flat $2 initial charge. Between downtown and Union Station, a cab ride costs about $3; it's about $6 between downtown and Nob Hill.

Portland is a no-hail town; cabs normally don't stop on the street, even if you hurl yourself at the windshield.

Where to Sleep

Don't feel obligated to stay in the section of Portland you're planning to visit. Most of the city's attractions are downtown, where lodging tends to be seedy. Since public transportation is swift, frequent, and thorough, opt for a few extra minutes on the bus instead. Typically, budget travelers congregate at the city's lone youth hostel in the southeast section (*see* Hostels, *below*) or at motels on one of the outlying commercial strips: East of the Willamette, try **N.E. Sandy Boulevard** (east of 33rd Avenue), or **N.E. 82nd Avenue.** West of the river, **S.W. Barbur Boulevard** tends to have accommodations that are slightly cleaner, brighter, and cheaper than eastside digs—though they're just as generic. For something a bit more homey, try a bed-and-breakfast. They tend to be more expensive, but a few in the northeast quadrant have rooms for $50–$65.

DOWNTOWN

Staying downtown puts you within walking distance of many of Portland's attractions, but in the thick of the city's drug trade. Consider walking with a friend at night. Even if overexposure to Oliver Stone has made you think vice is romantic, you may do well to avoid the area just north of W. Burnside Street, near Old Town. Downtown's best lodging deals are just outside the trendy shopping district, west and north of Pioneer Courthouse Square. As seedy as it is cheap, **S.W. 3rd Avenue** harbors some bottom-of-the-barrel choices. If you'd rather not worry about the tougher urban elements, try one of the lower-priced B&Bs in the northeast district or an inexpensive motel along Barbur Boulevard in the southwest.

➤ **UNDER $25** • **YWCA.** If you have two X chromosomes, you might want to stay in one of the Y's spartan rooms, just around the corner from the Renoirs and Monets at the Portland Art Museum. Prices are $18 for a shared double, $24 for a single. Or, if you're really desperate, you and your sleeping bag can take a spot in the communal room for just $10. Expect a mix of travelers and long-term residents. *1111 S.W. 10th Ave., at Main St., tel. 503/223–6281. Walk 3 blocks south and 3 blocks west of Pioneer Courthouse Square. Women only. Luggage storage.*

➤ **UNDER $50** • **Ben Stark Hotel and International Hostel.** If you're short on cash, consider one of the bland rooms at the Ben Stark, which does a better job of keeping bad elements away than most of the other budget hotels downtown. You're eligible for a space in the hostel only if you carry an international passport or can fake a convincing foreign accent. Those who pass the test pay $15 to stay in the hostel section. Hotel-style rooms run $29–$46; the more expensive ones have private baths. *1022 S.W. Stark St., tel. 503/274–1223. 3 blocks north*

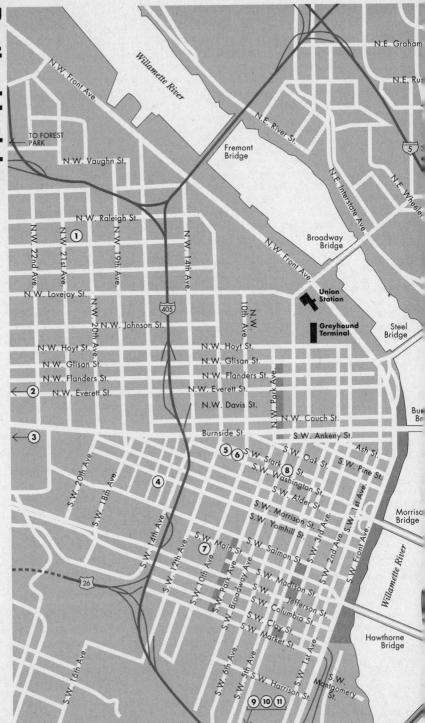

Portland Lodging

Willamette River

N.W. Front Ave.

TO FOREST PARK

N.W. Vaughn St.

Fremont Bridge

N.E. River St.

N.E. Graham

N.E. Rus

N.E. Wheele

I-5

N.W. Raleigh St.

N.W. 22nd Ave.

N.W. 21st Ave.

①

N.W. 19th Ave.

N.W. 14th Ave.

N.E. Interstate Ave.

Broadway Bridge

N.W. Front Ave.

N.W. Lovejoy St.

N.W. 20th Ave.

N.W. Johnson St.

Union Station

Greyhound Terminal

Steel Bridge

405

N.W. 10th Ave.

N.W. Hoyt St.

N.W. Glisan St.

N.W. Flanders St.

②

N.W. Everett St.

N.W. Hoyt St.

N.W. Glisan St.

N.W. Flanders St.

N.W. Everett St.

N.W. Davis St.

N.W. Park Ave.

N.W. Couch St.

Bu Br

③

Burnside St.

S.W. Ankeny St.

S.W. 20th Ave.

S.W. 18th Ave.

④

S.W. 14th Ave.

⑤ ⑥

S.W. Oak St.

S.W. Stark St.

⑧

S.W. Washington St.

S.W. Alder St.

S.W. Morrison St.

S.W. Yamhill St.

S.W. 3rd Ave.

S.W. 2nd Ave.

S.W. 1st Ave.

S.W. Front Ave.

Ash St.

S.W. Pine St.

Morriso Bridge

Willamette River

26

S.W. 16th Ave.

S.W. 12th Ave.

S.W. 10th Ave.

⑦

S.W. Main St.

S.W. Park Ave.

S.W. Broadway Ave.

S.W. Salmon St.

S.W. Madison St.

Jefferson St.

S.W. Columbia St.

S.W. Clay St.

S.W. Market St.

S.W. 6th Ave.

S.W. 5th Ave.

S.W. 3rd Ave.

S.W. Harrison St.

S.W. 1st Ave.

S.W. Montgomery St.

Hawthorne Bridge

⑨ ⑩ ⑪

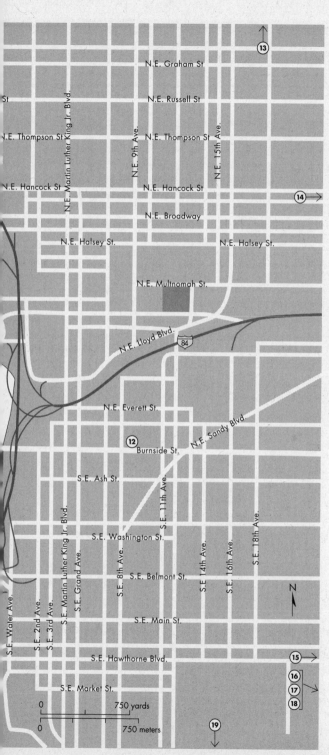

Aladdin Motor Inn, **11**

Ben Stark Hotel and International Hostel, **6**

Capitol Hill Motel, **10**

Carriage Inn Apartel, **1**

The Clinkerbrick House Bed-and-Breakfast, **14**

Econo Lodge, **17**

Georgian House Bed-and-Breakfast, **13**

Imperial Hotel, **8**

MacMaster House, **3**

Mallory Motor Hotel, **4**

Mark Spencer Hotel, **5**

Motel 6, **16**

Oxbow Park Campground, **18**

Pittock Acres Bed-and-Breakfast, **2**

Portland International Hostel (HI), **15**

Rose Manor Inn, **19**

Scandia Lodge, **9**

Thriftlodge, **12**

YWCA, **7**

and 3 blocks west of Pioneer Courthouse Square. 83 hotel rooms, some with bath; 3 dorm rooms. Luggage storage, safe deposit boxes, laundry.

➤ **UNDER $65** • **Mark Spencer Hotel.** The questionable characters in front of the Spencer belie the spacious, well-furnished, and very comfortable rooms within. All rooms have full kitchens, and suites have walk-in closets and furniture like desks and sofas. If you don't mind a bit of urban theater below your window, this is definitely one of the best deals in downtown Portland. Mention this book and you'll receive a discount rate of $45–$65. *409 S.W. 11th Ave., at Stark St., tel. 503/224–3293 or 800/548–3934. 3 blocks north and 4 blocks west of Pioneer Courthouse Square. 101 rooms. Luggage storage, laundry, cable TV.*

➤ **UNDER $85** • **Imperial Hotel.** This is the least expensive luxury hotel in the heart of downtown Portland. Though it's not as opulent as its next-door neighbors, it still comes complete with a uniformed doorman. The newly remodeled rooms are clean and comfortable, with singles ranging from $60 to $75, doubles from $70 to $85. *400 S.W. Broadway, at Stark St., tel. 503/228–7221. 3 blocks north of Pioneer Courthouse Square. 170 rooms. Luggage storage, restaurant/lounge, free valet parking.*

MacMaster House. This sprawling, turn-of-the-century, colonial-style home sits atop King's Hill, just minutes from both downtown and Washington Park. Oriental rugs and antique furniture attest to the eclectic tastes of innkeeper, Cecilia Murphy, and her sidekick Domino, the friendly dalmatian. Most rooms ($70–$80) have fireplaces, and all guests enjoy a full breakfast. *1041 S.W. Vista St., near W. Burnside St., tel. 503/223–7362. 7 rooms, 5 with shared baths.*

Mallory Motor Hotel. If the area has you a bit freaked, make your way to the elegant and charming Mallory, in a relatively safe, quiet area west of Pioneer Square. A personable staff distinguishes this from similar luxury hotels with a more affected, upper-crust attitude. Though not lavish, rooms are large and comfortable, ranging from $45 to $75. Reservations are recommended year-round. *729 S.W. 15th Ave., at Yamhill St., tel. 503/223–6311 or 800/228–8657. 8 blocks west of Pioneer Courthouse Square. 144 rooms. Cable TV, restaurant/lounge, free parking. Wheelchair access.*

SOUTHWEST

Though southwest Portland is mainly residential, some motels are clustered along **Barbur Boulevard,** a few miles south of downtown but quickly reached by I–5. The digs here aren't quite as decrepit as the motels on Portland's other strips. They're also farther from the city, so criminal types are unlikely to be lurking. Just don't expect interesting nightlife; the best you'll get here is a decent restaurant or two, a movie theater, and a slew of fast-food joints.

➤ **UNDER $50** • **Aladdin Motor Inn.** You couldn't wish for a more attentive motel staff than that at the Aladdin, and rooms are clean and comfortable. If you flash the good book (this Berkeley Guide, of course), a double costs $34–$39 in winter and $39–$49 in summer. Kitchenettes are a few bucks more. The trip to city center is quick and painless if you catch Bus 12, which stops nearby. *8905 S.W. 30th Ave., at Barbur Blvd., tel. 503/246–8241 or 800/292–4466. 52 rooms. Coin-op laundry. Wheelchair access.*

Capitol Hill Motel. If the Aladdin's booked, head for the canopied, hut-like things across the street. Rooms are clean and not too shabby, though those offended by the lingering odor of cigarette smoke should seek sleep elsewhere. During summer, doubles cost $35–$45 weekdays and $40–$48 weekends. *9110 S.W. Barbur Blvd., tel. 503/244–1400. 15 rooms. From downtown, take Bus 12. Luggage storage.*

➤ **UNDER $65** • **Scandia Lodge.** The wooden exterior and token pine trees make this a credible copy of an alpine lodge—a serious accomplishment considering its location right next to Barbur Boulevard. Prices range from about $48 for a single to $65 for a large suite, all with kitchens or kitchenettes. *10450 S.W. Barbur Blvd., tel. 503/244–0151. From downtown, take Bus 12. 42 rooms. Heated pool.*

NORTHWEST

Portland's quiet northwest quadrant is an ideal place to stay. Besides being easily accessible from downtown, the northwest is home to scenic Forest Park and the hip neighborhood of Nob Hill (for more on both, *see* Worth Seeing, *below*). Your lodging choices here are scattered over a large area, so choose your destination before you head out here, and consider making reservations.

➤ **UNDER $65** • **Carriage Inn Apartel.** Featuring what may be the longest hallway in Portland (it's almost a block long) and clean, spacious rooms with kitchens and couches, this Nob Hill inn is a pretty good deal despite a drab exterior and gloomy brown-and-maroon room decor. Doubles run $49–$56; stay for a week and you'll get the seventh day free. *2025 N.W. Northrup St., btw 20th and 21st Aves., tel. 503/224–0543. From downtown, take Bus 17. 68 rooms. Laundry, free parking, cable TV. Wheelchair access.*

Even if your name were Dorothy and you clicked your heels together three times, you couldn't find a place more like home than the Pittock Acres Bed-and-Breakfast.

➤ **UNDER $85** • **Pittock Acres Bed-and-Breakfast.** In the forested hills west of downtown, this modern B&B was formerly part of the Pittock estate (*see* Museums and Galleries, in Worth Seeing, *below*). The traditional Victorian and country decor, attractively landscaped yard, and hospitable owners make a stay here extremely pleasant. The giant, hearty breakfasts can be tailored to your health specifications. Room are $60–$80. *103 N.W. Pittock Dr., tel. 503/226–1163. From downtown, take Bus 20. 4 rooms, 2 with bath. No smoking.*

SOUTHEAST

The vast southeastern quadrant spans several middle-class residential neighborhoods as well as the tenaciously alternative Hawthorne District and the Reed College campus (*see* Worth Seeing, *below*). Most motels line the commercial strip of **S.E. 82nd Avenue;** a few may be found on **S.E. Powell Boulevard.** The city's lone youth hostel is in the area on Hawthorne Boulevard. When hotel hunting, keep in mind this district's size: It's about 40 blocks from S.E. 82nd Avenue to the heart of the Hawthorne District.

Most of the motels on S.E. 82nd Avenue are seedier than a watermelon.

➤ **UNDER $50** • **Motel 6.** Convenient to downtown and Hawthorne Boulevard, this chain motel has clean but ultimately forgettable rooms. In summer, their spartan singles and doubles are $37 and $43, respectively. *3104 S.E. Powell Blvd., tel. 503/238–0600. From downtown, take Bus 9 south. 69 rooms. Heated pool.*

Rose Manor Inn. The Rose's recently remodeled rooms are large, clean, and bright. Cost is $49–$54 (with kitchen) or $43–$47 (without). The Museum of Science and Industry (*see* Worth Seeing, *below*) is just a few minutes away by car. *4546 S.E. McLoughlin Blvd., tel. 503/236–4175 or 800/252–8333. From downtown, take Bus 17 to S.E. Holgate Blvd. and 17th Ave., then walk 1½ blocks west. 76 rooms. Swimming pool.*

➤ **UNDER $65** • **Econo Lodge.** Most of the motels on 82nd Avenue could benefit from creative bulldozing, but this one's quite nice and clean—if you don't mind the cemetery across the street. Doubles are $40–$50 in winter and $45–$55 in summer. *4512 S.E. 82nd Ave., at Holgate St., tel. 503/774–8876. From downtown, take Bus 17 south. 38 rooms. Wheelchair access.*

NORTHEAST

Ten blocks east of the Willamette River lies Lloyd Center, America's first mall; sadly, there's not much else to northeast Portland. If you're planning to sleep here, treat yourself to a B&B. Most are located in the peaceful residential neighborhoods north of N.E. Broadway. If you're on a budget, you'll have to settle for one of the generic motels lining **N.E. Sandy Boulevard.**

➤ **UNDER $50** • **Thriftlodge.** This motel's probably the blandest-looking in town, but you probably weren't planning to snap a picture of it anyway, were you? Rooms are fairly clean and comfortable, and the motel is within walking distance of downtown. In summer, doubles are $43–$47. *949 E. Burnside St., tel. 503/234–8411 or 800/525–9055. From downtown, take Bus 19. 79 rooms. Swimming pool.*

➤ **UNDER $65** • **The Clinkerbrick House Bed-and-Breakfast.** Since you asked, the odd name describes the melted and deformed fire brick that gives the exterior of this Dutch colonial home the appearance of an old lava flow. Inside you'll find three tidy rooms and two friendly innkeepers, Bob and Peggie Irvine. Rooms are $50–$65, including full breakfast and use of the upstairs kitchen. *2311 N.E. Schuyler St., tel. 503/281–2533. From downtown, take Bus 9 to N.E. 24th Ave. and Broadway, then walk ½ block north. 3 rooms, 1 with bath.*

➤ **UNDER $85** • **Georgian House Bed-and-Breakfast.** The English garden at this attractive Georgian-style colonial recently made the cover of *Better Homes and Gardens*, but don't let that intimidate you. Charming guest quarters and delicious full breakfasts are presided over by a jovial innkeeper, Willie Ackley. Rooms are $65, $85 with private bath. *1828 N.E. Siskiyou St., tel. 503/281–2250. From downtown, take Bus 8 to N.E. 15th Ave. and Siskiyou St., then walk 4 blocks east. 4 rooms, 1 with bath.*

HOSTELS

Portland International Hostel. In the center of the bohemian Hawthorne District, Portland's only hostel boasts kitchen facilities, a travel center, a picnic-perfect backyard, and off-street parking. Special activities include barbecues ($2, summertime only) on the wide front porch and all-you-can-eat pancake breakfasts ($1). Beds are $12 for HI members and $15 for non-members. You can't (as in they won't let you) outstay your five-day welcome. *3031 S.E. Hawthorne Blvd., at 30th Ave., tel. 503/236–3380. From downtown, take Bus 14 south. 36 beds. No curfew, lockout 10 AM–5 PM. Luggage lockers, reservations recommended in summer.*

Though it's technically illegal, it is possible to slumber under the towering Douglas firs of Forest Park—but you'll get nailed for sure if you start blowing up the air mattresses and charring weenies over the Coleman. From downtown Portland, you can reach America's largest urban forest by taking N.W. Lovejoy Street west to Cornell Road. Or, take Bus 15 from S.W. Washington Street to the park's southern edge. And leave the weenies at home.

CAMPGROUNDS

Portland may be surrounded by plenty of trees, fields, and streams, but you won't find many campgrounds nearby. Consider one of the hundreds of sites in the Columbia River Gorge and around Mt. Hood (*see* Chapter 4, Western Oregon and The Cascades) if you're hell-bent on camping: For example, beautiful **Champoeg State Park** (tel. 503/678–1251) is just 22 miles south of the city. Closer to Portland, you can choose from 2 RV parks: **Reeder Beach** (26048 N.W. Reeder Rd., Sauvie Island, tel. 503/621–3970), a few miles north of town off U.S. 30, welcomes tent-carriers at $15 a night; and **Rolling Hills** (20145 N.E. Sandy Blvd., tel. 503/666–7282) has tent sites for $13. Both have rest rooms, showers, and drinking water.

Oxbow Park. A heavily forested nature preserve on the banks of the Sandy River, this campground 17 miles from downtown Portland provides the perfect escape for those who like to hike, fish, or swim. Tent sites are $9. *3010 S.E. Oxbow Pkwy., Gresham, tel. 503/663–4708. From Rte. 84 east, take 238th St. exit and drive 5 mi south, then go east 7 mi on Division St. 45 sites. Drinking water, toilets.*

Food

You can eat well in Portland without spending serious bucks. It's a casual kind of city where even the residents prefer high-quality diner food to mediocre nouvelle cuisine: sandwich shops, ethnic restaurants, and pubs serving burgers and freshly brewed beer dominate the scene.

Unfortunately for those traveling on foot, many of the most interesting and inexpensive dining options lie outside Portland's pedestrian-friendly downtown, east of the Willamette River on Hawthorne Boulevard and west of the river on N.W. 21st and 23rd avenues in Nob Hill. Downtown, choose between the fast-food stands of Old Town, a smattering of places in Chinatown, and several unique restaurants around 2nd Avenue.

DOWNTOWN

You'll find cheap and hefty meals at Old Town's **Saturday Market** (*see* Worth Seeing, *below*). Open Saturdays *and* Sundays, the outdoor booths hawk hot burritos, souvlaki sandwiches, pierogi, seafood salads, spring rolls, and spicy Thai noodles, all at less than $4 a pop. From Pioneer Courthouse Square (S.W. Morrison St. at Broadway), walk about 4 blocks east and 6 blocks north, then follow your nose. Next door to the Saturday Market, the pint-sized **New Market Village** is open daily; fast-food Mexican and Chinese meals are served in an old brick building. Those craving Greek food have a choice of two excellent restaurants in Old Town: **Berbati** (19 S.W. 2nd Ave., tel. 503/226–2122), which has a quiet and simple elegance, or **Alexis** (215 W. Burnside St., tel. 503/224–8577), where a belly dancer performs weekends. You'll shell out $8–$14 for an entrée at either place. To quell hunger pangs quickly and cheaply, you might try the **Galleria Mall** (S.W. 9th Ave., at Morrison St.), the **Pioneer Place** food court (S.W. 5th Ave. at Morrison St.), or the food stands at **Pioneer Courthouse Square** (*see* Getting Around, *above*).

➤ **UNDER $5** • **Macheezmo Mouse.** "Fresh, Fit, Fast" is the motto of the eight Portland Macheezmo restaurants, all riding the new wave of fast food by offering inexpensive, healthy Mexican fare. Their low-calorie, low-fat, high-carb "speedo chicken burrito" makes a great lunch at $3.25. Tips on reducing dietary fat, sodium, and cholesterol abound on recycled-paper brochures; thankfully, thrill seekers are still permitted to order extra sour cream. *Downtown: 723 S.W. Salmon St., tel. 503/228–3491; Pioneer Place: S.W. 5th Ave. and Yamhill St., tel. 503/248–0917. For other locations, tel. 800/275–2213.*

➤ **UNDER $10** • **Abou Karim.** Excellent Lebanese fare at affordable prices is the pride of this Old Town eatery, decorated with posters, photographs, and paintings from the tiny Middle Eastern country. At lunch time, $2.50 will buy you a falafel sandwich or an order of babaganoush (baked eggplant topped with tahini, lemon juice, and garlic). Prices go up slightly for dinner; kebab plates of all sorts (chicken, beef, and lamb) cost about $6.25. Reservations are advised on weekends. *221 S.W. Pine St., at 2nd Ave., tel. 503/223–5058. 4 blocks east and 5 blocks north of Pioneer Courthouse Square. Wheelchair access. Open Mon.–Thurs. 11–9, Fri. 11–10, Sat. noon–10.*

Dan and Louis Oyster Bar. The long wooden tables, wide-open rooms, and seafaring instruments and artifacts will make you think you're eating in a Navy mess hall from years past (1907 to be exact; that's when the place opened). It gets a tad rowdy at night, so you'll sit at your communal table, mingle, and enjoy it. Not surprisingly, the menu features seafood ($6–$12), but landlubbers can order hamburgers or chicken. Or you can make a meal of one of their substantial seafood soups ($3–$8), like the delicious Garibaldi crab stew. *208 S.W. Ankeny St., tel. 503/227–5906. 5 blocks east and 7 blocks north of Pioneer Courthouse Square. Open Sun.–Thurs. 11–10, Fri. and Sat. 11–11.*

Fong Chong Restaurant. At lunchtime, Portlanders flock here for dim sum—that's Chinese finger food to you. Each order of dim sum costs $1.70, and the menu's list of 200-plus items means you can indulge in more than just pork buns. Avoid the Americanized stuff like chow mein and chop suey and dive head first into their tasty Szechwan and Cantonese dishes. The service is manic, with waiters sliding food onto the tables with amazing precision and speed. Solo travelers should be extra careful when visiting this area at night. *301 N.W. 4th Ave., at*

Everett St., Chinatown, tel. 503/220–0235. 7 blocks north and 3 blocks east of Pioneer Courthouse Square. Open daily 11–10.

Hamburger Mary's. This eclectic three-room restaurant has everything but the kitchen sink suspended from its walls and ceilings. And someday, they may hang that, too. Burgers are the specialty here; try the excellent Hamburger Blue ($5.75), topped with bleu cheese and ham. Vegetarians can choose from a few non-cow options. 840 S.W. Park Ave., tel. 503/223–0900. 1 block west of Pioneer Courthouse Square. Open daily 7 AM–2 AM.

➤ **UNDER $15** • **Jake's Famous Crawfish.** You know the food is fresh if they print a new menu each day, and they do at Jake's. The classic brass and wood decor makes it clear that business has been thriving for generations. You'll save bucks if you avoid the expensive dinner menu and stick to lunch, like the hearty salmon triple decker club sandwich ($7.50). There's also a well-stocked bar where you can order clam linguine and other favorites from a special $2 menu (plus a $2 drink minimum). The bar menu is available weekdays 3 PM–6 PM, and nightly 9:30 PM–11 PM. 401 S.W. 12th Ave., tel. 503/226–1419. 5 blocks west and 3 blocks north of Pioneer Courthouse Square. Open Mon.–Thurs. 11:30 AM–11 PM, Fri.–Sat. 11:30 AM–midnight, Sun. 4:30 PM–10 PM. Reservations recommended.

NORTHWEST

The hip neighborhood of Nob Hill is extremely popular with restaurant-goers; count on a fight for parking any night of the week. Choose from loads of tasty and reasonable options along rollicking **N.W. 23rd Avenue**, or from along quieter **N.W. 21st Avenue**, where you'll find slightly lower prices.

➤ **UNDER $5** • **Escape From New York Pizza.** This popular little restaurant (one long counter and a few tiny tables) cooks perfect pizza and nothing else. Expect big droopy slices ($1.50) with plenty of grease. And when you're done eating, give yourself the finger to make your New York experience complete. 622 N.W. 23rd Ave., tel. 503/227–5423. From downtown, take Bus 15 west. Open daily 11:30 AM–11 PM.

Garbanzo's. After you figure out just what that wire's doing on the wall (here's a hint: it's called "art"), take a seat and enjoy the tasty Middle Eastern sandwiches, such as the chicken falafel, all for under $4. An extra $3 gets you a tasty side salad of tabbouleh, mixed vegetables, or potatoes. Garbanzo's is one of Portland's rare late-night eateries, open until 1:30 AM on weekdays and 3 AM on weekends. For other options, see box, below. 2074 N.W. Lovejoy St., at 21st Ave., tel. 503/227–4196. From downtown, take Bus 17 north. Opens daily at 11:30 AM.

➤ **UNDER $10** • **Kornblatt's Delicatessen.** For the best deli food in town, schlepp over to Kornblatt's, where delicious smells of warm bagels and smoked fish waft out the front door. Omelets are $6, a bagel with lox is $7, and deli sandwiches average $6. The gratis bowl of kosher pickles should keep you busy until your food arrives. The neighborhood crowds tend to linger over their tables on weekends, so come early or prepare to wait. 628 N.W. 23rd Ave., tel. 503/242–0055. From downtown, take Bus 15 west. Open summer, weekdays 7 AM–10 PM, weekends 7 AM–11 PM; winter, weekdays 7 AM–9 PM, weekends 7 AM–10 PM.

SOUTHEAST

The southeast district is filled with small restaurants that may not look promising from the outside but really come through when the food is served. **Hawthorne Boulevard** has many of the best cafés and ethnic eateries, but don't neglect some of the more out-of-the-way establishments.

➤ **UNDER $5** • **Dots Café.** Remember the Brady Bunch episode in which Greg moved into his father's study and remade it as a "groovy" bedroom? Throw in a pool table and a couple of bohemian thrift-shop items and you've got the decor of Dots, a little café packed with Reed students and hippie folk enjoying the inexpensive food and extraterrestrial atmosphere. Nothing on the menu (hamburgers, sandwiches, and Mexican dishes) costs over $5.50. *2521 S.E. Clinton St., at 26th Ave., tel. 503/235–0203. From downtown, take Bus 4 to Division St. and 26th Ave., then walk 2 blocks south. Open daily 9 AM–2 AM.*

➤ **UNDER $10** • **Bangkok Kitchen.** Authentic Thai food—and only Thai food—is served at Bangkok Kitchen; try asking for soy sauce or chow mein if you want to get yelled at. Sauces are uncommonly hot, so unless you're a masochist, choose mild. Their excellent noodle dishes cost about $5. *2534 S.E. Belmont St., at 26th Ave., tel. 503/236–7349. From downtown, take Bus 15 east. Open lunch and dinner Tues.–Fri., dinner Sat.*

Bread & Ink Café. Long ago, chefs at the Hawthorne District's Bread & Ink threw out the can opener and microwave in favor of preparing food from scratch. Staples like bread, ketchup, mayonnaise, and even mustard are all homemade. Fresh pasta and fish entrées are always top-notch, as are deli staples like cheese blintzes ($6) and Nova Scotia lox ($6). The eclectic dinner menu changes about every six weeks and draws from Italian, Mexican, and Greek cuisine. *3610 S.E. Hawthorne Blvd., tel. 503/239–4756. From downtown, take Bus 14 south. Open daily 7 AM–3 PM and 5:30 PM–9:30 PM; Fri. and Sat. until 10 PM.*

Esparza's Tex-Mex Cafe. Occupying a lonely corner south of E. Burnside Street, this neighborhood favorite evokes the feeling of Texas in the '50s, with vinyl booths and a jukebox blaring golden oldies. Chef and owner Joe Esparza concocts some of the tastiest and most creative Tex-Mex in all of Portland: Joining the standard lineup of enchiladas and burritos are surprises like smoked buffalo with two-pepper sauce ($10) and tacos with calf brains ($10). Most dishes fall into the $7–$10 range. *2725 S.E. Ankeny St., at 28th Ave., tel. 503/234–7909. From downtown, take Bus 19 north or Bus 20 east. Open Tues.–Thurs. 11:30 AM–10 PM; Fri. and Sat. until 10:30 PM.*

Jarra's Ethiopian Restaurant. Students from Reed College flock to this southeast district institution with a reputation for seriously spicy offerings in a no-frills setting. Dishes topped with *wat* sauce often lead to heavy sweating; swallow your pride and order the milder *alicha*. Entrées ($7.50–$10.50) come with plenty of spongy injera bread to sop up your food. *1435 S.E. Hawthorne Blvd., tel. 503/230–8990. From downtown, take Bus 14 south. Open Tues.–Fri. 11:30 AM–2:30 PM, Tues.–Sat. 5 PM–10 PM.*

Best Places for Late-Night Grub

- **Brasserie Montmarte (656 S.W. Park Ave., tel. 503/224–5552)** serves pastas ($6–$9) and hosts live jazz (no cover charge). Open until 3 AM on weekends.

- **Dot's Café (2521 S.E. Clinton St., at 26th Ave., tel. 503/235–0203)** offers inexpensive hamburgers and sandwiches in an off-beat setting. Open until 2 AM daily.

- **Garbanzo's Falafel (Westside: 2074 N.W. Lovejoy St., at 21st Ave., tel. 503/227–4196; Eastside: 3433 S.E. Hawthorne Blvd., at 34th Ave., tel. 503/239–6087)** is the best place in town for falafel (under $4) and Mediterranean-style salads. Open until 1:30 AM Sunday–Thursday, until 3 AM Friday and Saturday.

- **La Casa de Rios (4343 S.E. Hawthorne Blvd., tel. 503/234–2038)** serves tamales and enchiladas in a cozy setting with a pink-brick interior. It's popular with the artsy Hawthorne crowd. Open until 11 PM daily.

- **Le Bistro Montage (301 S.E. Morrison St., at 3rd Ave., tel. 503/234–1324)** satisfies late-night cravings for Cajun cuisine ($9–$11). Open until 4 AM daily.

Le Bistro Montage. Whether it's for the Cajun cuisine or the late-late-late night hours, this New Orleans-style bistro is a hit. Choose from a potpourri of jambalayas ($9–$11) or one of the more unusual dishes like catfish linguini with Cajun gravy ($9). If you're destitute, chow down a bowl of spicy macaroni (a mere $2). *301 S.E. Morrison St., at 3rd Ave., tel. 503/234–1324. Open daily 6 PM–4 AM.*

NORTHEAST

The northeast lacks a cohesive restaurant area like the southeast's Hawthorne Boulevard (*see above*), but the food here tends to be equally good. **Broadway** has several appealing cafés and pubs, including **McMenamins on Broadway** (1504 N.E. Broadway, tel. 503/288–9498), purveyor of burgers, sandwiches, and pastas (all under $6) served at long wooden tables. **Sandy Boulevard** has a few fast-food options and several swanky higher-priced restaurants as well.

➤ **UNDER $10 • American Dream Pizza.** Don't let the sneakers suspended from the ceiling distract you from the main event at this lively two-room joint: pizza, sold by slice or by pie. Choices include giant calzones ($5.50), plain cheese pizza ($3.50–$8), and the formidable "Bill Walton," a pizza topped with every vegetable imaginable ($15 for a medium pie). Wash it all down with a pitcher of microbrewed beer. *4620 N.E. Glisan St., at 47th Ave., tel. 503/230–0699. From downtown, take Bus 19 north. Open Mon.–Tues. 4–10, Wed.–Sat. 11:30–10, Sun. 3–10.*

Merchant of Venice. Tentatively Italian (the music is mainly reggae and rock), this intimate café and deli serves gourmet pizza by the slice or pie and traditional pasta dishes (à la carte, $4.50; full dinner, $5.50–$6). Feel free to scribble on the paper tablecloths with the crayons provided—unless you've brought your own. *1432 N.E. Broadway, at 15th Ave., tel. 503/284–4558. From downtown, take Bus 9 north to N.E. Wiedler St. and walk 1 block north. Open Mon.–Thurs. 11–9, Fri.–Sat. 11–10.*

DESSERT/COFFEEHOUSES

Portland's coffee infatuation is second only to that of its northern neighbor, Seattle. Those in search of their daily (or hourly) caffeine fix will find an overwhelming abundance of coffee shops; there are even a few drive-throughs. For a quick and tasty brew, visit one of the **Starbucks** outlets all over town; Portland's own **Coffee People** (Nob Hill: 533 N.W. 23rd Ave., at Hoyt St., tel. 503/221–0235; Eastside: 3500 S.E. Hawthorne St., at 35th Ave., tel. 503/235–1383; 5 other locations citywide) offers an even larger selection of coffees and has a pleasant ambience. In Old Town, ultra-hip **La Patisserie** (208 N.W. Couch St., at 2nd Ave., tel. 503/248–9898), open daily until midnight, serves cheap, unique sandwiches in a whimsical forest-like setting of wood logs and large, leafy plants. Also downtown, the **Heathman Bakery and Pub** (901 S.W. Salmon St., at 9th Ave., tel. 503/227–5700) caters to a more refined clientele with tasty pizzas ($7.25–$9.25) from their wood-burning oven.

Papa Haydn. Entrées, though excellent, cost about $15 here; budget travelers will want to skip immediately to Papa Haydn's decadent desserts. Perennial favorites include Boccone Dolce ($4.50), a concoction of baked Swiss meringue, semi-sweet chocolate, whipped cream, and fruit. Or try any of the chocolate-raspberry offerings—a taste of heaven for only $5. Expect a long wait. *Westside: 701 N.W. 23rd Ave., at Irving St., tel. 503/228–7317; Eastside: 5829 S.E. Milwaukee Ave., at Yukon St., tel. 503/232–9440. Open Tues.–Thurs. 11:30–11, Fri. and Sat. 11:30–midnight, Sun. 10–3. Wheelchair access.*

If you complain about the service or selections at the Rimsky-Korsakoffee House, the feisty staff will give you a map to Denny's and throw you out.

Rimsky-Korsakoffee House. No signs mark the entry to this aggressively hip coffee house, discouraging casual and uninformed passersby from accidentally straggling in. Those who succeed can nibble on scrumptious desserts ($3.25) at tables that slowly rotate or gently bob up and down. Live piano and violin music entertains nibblers most nights; other surprises you'll have to discover for yourself. *707 S.E. 12th Ave., at Alder St., tel. 503/232–2640. Open daily 7 PM–midnight, Fri. and Sat. until 1 AM.*

Exploring Portland

Portland's major attractions are concentrated downtown, west of the Willamette River. If you don't pause to eat, go to the bathroom, or browse for tacky postcards, you can probably complete your whirlwind tour in a single day, visiting the Portland Art Museum, Oregon History Center, Niketown, Old Town, several funky neighborhoods, a brewery or two, and the behemoth Powell's Bookstore. But to appreciate the city without feeling rushed, allow at least a couple of days. Downtown Portland can and should be toured on foot, starting perhaps by the Portland Art Museum and working your way north and east toward Old Town and the Willamette River. At Powell's, pick up the invaluable *Walking Map of Downtown Portland* (free); it's also available at Powell's Travel Bookstore (701 S.W. 6th Ave., tel. 503/228–1108) in Pioneer Courthouse Square, and at the Portland Oregon Visitors Association (*see* Visitor Information, *above*). If you're feeling beat, head for the Transit Mall (*see* Getting Around, *above*); city buses are free of charge throughout downtown.

Make a point of seeing the city's outlying parks and neighborhoods if you have a few days; many consider these Portland's greatest assets. West of downtown lies **Washington Park,** with its zoo and colorful gardens; **Forest Park,** with acres of pristine wilderness; and the neighborhood of **Nob Hill,** the West Coast version of New York City's artsy, eclectic Greenwich Village. East of the Willamette, worthwhile stops include the **Oregon Museum of Science and Industry** and the bohemian **Hawthorne District.** Conveniently, Bus 63 travels east–west across the city's two halves, from Washington Park to the Museum of Science and Industry.

WORTH SEEING

BLITZ-WEINHARD AND THE MICROBREWERIES Blitz-Weinhard's massive brewing complex produces the much-acclaimed Henry Weinhard's Private Reserve, Oregon's favorite low-cost brew. Offered Thursday and Friday afternoons, the free 45-minute tour takes you through the beer-making process from hops to lager and ends with (grab your steins, folks) free samples. Don't bother with a reservation; it's first come, first served. *1133 W. Burnside St., tel. 503/222–4351. From Pioneer Courthouse Square, walk 4 blocks west and 4 blocks north.*

Microbreweries are as ubiquitous as coffee houses in many Portland neighborhoods. They will cheerfully try to spark your addiction to a product that makes Coors taste like warm spit by offering tours and tastings, often gratis. **Bridgeport Ales** (1313 N.W. Marshall St., tel. 503/241–7179) offers free tours and tastings on many Saturdays and Sundays; call ahead to be sure. In the northwest industrial district, the **Portland Brewing Company** (2730 N.W. 31st St., at Industrial St., tel. 503/226–7623) offers free Saturday afternoon tours of its small Bavarian-style building and has a stylin' brew house tap room where you can sample their product (a pint costs $2.75) while admiring the large copper brewing kettles. From downtown, you can reach the PBC on Bus 17. If you want to tour the whole town with a tankard of ale, pick up a list of beer makers at the Portland Oregon Visitor's Association (*see* Visitor Information, *above*).

FOREST PARK Forest Park is the 4,800-acre crown jewel in Portland's incredible park system, as well as the largest forested urban park in the nation. Twenty-seven-mile **Wildwood Trail** runs through its heart, past towering stands of Douglas firs. Wildwood is restricted to explorers on foot; a network of other trails is also open to mountain bikers and equestrians. And despite the park's size, numerous side trails make short loop trips possible for those needing a half-day's blissful break from the city. The downtown office of the **Portland Parks and Recreation Department** (1120 S.W. 5th Ave., Room 1302, tel. 503/823–2223) can give specific information on hikes and trails through the park. *From downtown, take Bus 15 from S.W. Washington St.; by car, take N.W. 23rd Ave. to Thurman St. and go west. Admission free. Open daily dawn–dusk.*

THE GROTTO If even a whiff of religion makes you balk, then strike the Grotto from your sightseeing list. Staffed by the Order of the Servants of Mary, the 64-acre "place of solitude, peace, and prayer" has trails winding through a forest of towering firs, past sculptures of biblical figures, including a candle-surrounded replica of Michelangelo's *Pietà*. On a clifftop accessible by elevator ($1.50), you'll find a paved trail that passes ponds, gardens, more biblical statuary, and tiny chapels. Services are held daily. *8840 N.E. Skidmore St., at cnr Sandy*

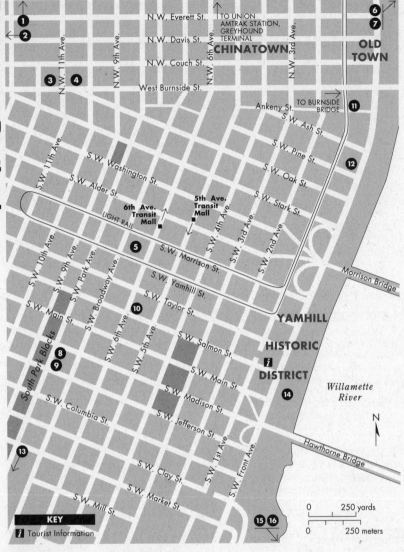

Downtown Portland

N.W. Everett St.

N.W. Davis St.

N.W. Couch St.

West Burnside St.

TO UNION AMTRAK STATION, GREYHOUND TERMINAL

CHINATOWN

OLD TOWN

N.W. 11th Ave.

N.W. 9th Ave.

N.W. 6th Ave.

N.W. 3rd Ave.

Ankeny St.

TO BURNSIDE BRIDGE

S.W. Ash St.

S.W. Pine St.

S.W. Washington St.

S.W. Alder St.

S.W. 11th Ave.

S.W. Oak St.

S.W. Stark St.

6th Ave. Transit Mall

5th Ave. Transit Mall

LIGHT RAIL

S.W. 4th Ave.

S.W. 3rd Ave.

S.W. 2nd Ave.

S.W. Morrison St.

Morrison Bridge

S.W. 10th Ave.

S.W. 9th Ave.

S.W. Park Ave.

S.W. Broadway Ave.

S.W. 6th Ave.

S.W. 5th Ave.

S.W. Yamhill St.

S.W. Taylor St.

S.W. Main St.

S.W. Salmon St.

YAMHILL

HISTORIC

DISTRICT

South Park Blocks

S.W. Columbia St.

S.W. Madison St.

S.W. Main St.

S.W. Jefferson St.

Willamette River

N

S.W. Clay St.

S.W. 1st Ave.

S.W. Front Ave.

Hawthorne Bridge

S.W. Market St.

S.W. Mill St.

0   250 yards

0   250 meters

KEY

i Tourist Information

Blitz-Weinhard Brewery, **3**

Cowboys Then and Now Museum, **7**

Forest Park, **1**

Grotto, **6**

Niketown, **10**

Oregon History Center, **9**

Oregon Maritime Center and Museum, **12**

Oregon Museum of Science and Industry, **15**

Pioneer Courthouse Square, **5**

Pittock Mansion, **2**

Portland Art Museum, **8**

Powell's City of Books, **4**

Reed College, **16**

Skidmore Fountain, **11**

Tom McCall Waterfront Park, **14**

Washington Park, **13**

Blvd. and N.E. 85th Ave., tel. 503/254–7371. From downtown, take Bus 12 north. Park admission free. Open daily 9–8 in summer, 9–5:30 in winter.

HAWTHORNE DISTRICT In recent years, trendy new boutiques and restaurants have been infiltrating the bohemian preserve of Hawthorne Boulevard, but the street still hasn't sold its soul to the Gap. Neighborhood dives still fill with barflies, and cafés and used-book shops and record stores still attract a crowd that probably knew Abbie Hoffman on a first-name basis. Here you'll see yuppies hanging out side by side with the nose-ring crowd. It all makes for an interesting afternoon of coffee-sipping, people-watching, and window-shopping. Most of the Hawthorne action takes place between S.E. 32nd and S.E. 40th avenues. At night, check out a second-run movie ($1) at the **Baghdad Theater & Pub** (*see* After Dark, *below*). *From downtown, take Bus 5 south.*

METRO WASHINGTON PARK ZOO The zoo is Oregon's most popular tourist attraction, and deservedly so: Its brilliant Africa Rain Forest exhibit houses exotics like fruit bats and pythons; in the Bamba du Jon Swamp building, realistic thundershowers pound the backs of smug-looking crocodiles every hour. Other residents include primates, bears, giraffes, tigers, penguins, insects—and the world's largest captive herd of breeding Asian elephants. Summer concerts include jazz (Wednesdays) and bluegrass (Thursdays) from 7 to 9 PM. They're free with zoo admission and always attract huge picnic-toting crowds. The Zoo Train ($2.50) is a pleasant way to reach the adjacent Rose and Japanese gardens (*see* Washington Park, *below*). *4001 S.W. Canyon Rd., Washington Park, tel. 503/226–1561. From downtown, take Bus 63 west; by car, follow signs from U.S. 26. Admission: $5.50. Open daily 9:30–7.*

NIKETOWN This bizarre attraction tries to combine art and retail in one slick package. High-tech video displays compete with pneumatic tubes and tanks of fluorescent fish for your attention. Besides gawking at Michael Jordan's shoes and a statue of Andre Agassi, you can choose from an assaulting array of Nike-emblazoned shoes and clothing. (Given the inflated prices, you may wish to browse, not buy.) The odd store hours represent the height, shoe size, or jersey numbers of various sports superheroes; Niketown employees will happily decipher them for you. *930 S.W. 6th Ave., at Salmon St., tel. 503/221–6453. Walk 2 blocks south from Pioneer Courthouse Square. Admission free. Open Mon.–Thurs. 10–7:01, Fri. 10–8, Sat. 10–6:52, Sun. 11:25–6:23.*

If visiting Niketown has convinced you that wearing their shoes will make you a sports superstar, the Nike Factory Store (3044 N.E. Martin Luther King Jr. Blvd., tel. 503/281–5901) carries its illustrious goods at less prohibitive prices.

NOB HILL This lively northwest neighborhood was given its name in the 1880s by a native of San Francisco who thought it resembled his old stomping grounds. Portland's upper class moved in soon after and began building fine Georgian and Victorian homes. These days, many well-to-dos still live here, but the feeling isn't stuffy—it's more like a bustling and fashionable small town. Two commercial streets, N.W. 21st and N.W. 23rd avenues, make up the area's core and offer a range of conventional and off-beat enterprises, from fashionable clothing boutiques to hip restaurants and coffee shops. On weekend evenings, the streets fill with university students taking advantage of the high concentration of trendy bars. *From downtown, take Bus 17 north to N.W. 21st Ave., or Bus 15 west to N.W. 23rd Ave.*

OREGON HISTORY CENTER Unlike some other dull and dreary history museums, the Oregon History Center makes state history interesting. Its whimsical collection of artifacts from Oregon's past ranges from stagecoaches and dugout canoes to political campaign buttons and a Wheaties box with Portland Trail Blazer Clyde Drexler on the cover. A visit to the center's outstanding research library is included in the admission price. *1230 S.W. Park Ave., tel. 503/222–1741. Across from the Portland Art Museum (see below). Take Bus 57 or 59. Admission: $4.50, $1.50 students. Open Tues.–Sat. 10–5, Sun. noon–5.*

OREGON MUSEUM OF SCIENCE AND INDUSTRY (OMSI) Perched on the Willamette's east bank, OMSI features six halls filled with hundreds of interactive exhibits. If you can't find something to pique your interest here, then you truly hate science. Don't miss the earthquake simulator that puts you right in the middle of a 5.5-magnitude quake (perfect for homesick Californians); the fascinating display of human prenatal development with 41 real embryos and fetuses ranging in development from 28 days to 32 weeks; and a guided tour of the USS *Blueback,* a naval submarine featured briefly in the movie *The Hunt for Red October.* The submarine tour ($3.50, 40 min) is a must for anyone wishing to be stripped of the romantic notion that life aboard an underwater vessel is as fun as the Beatles' song. The museum's unusual domed movie screen, Omnimax ($7), takes you into orbit with the space shuttle or on a flight through the Grand Canyon. *1945 S.E. Water Ave., tel. 503/797–4000. From downtown, take Bus 63. Museum admission: $7; additional attractions half price with general museum admission. Open summer, daily 9:30–7, until 9 PM on Thurs. and Fri.; winter, daily 9–5:30, until 9 PM on Thurs. and Fri.*

PIONEER COURTHOUSE SQUARE This public square is the heart and soul of downtown Portland. On sunny afternoons, the steps fill with lunching office workers, addled tourists, and happy slackers simply cooling themselves in the mist of the square's purple-tiled fountain. It's a great place to enjoy live music (free) during summer: "Peanut Butter and Jam" sessions (Tuesdays and Thursdays noon–1) feature a wide range of musical performers, while "Starbucks by Starlight" concerts (Mondays 5–7 PM) provide a great opportunity to sample live jazz in the gathering dusk. *701 S.W. 6th Ave., cnr S.W. Broadway and Morrison St., tel. 503/223–1613.*

PORTLAND ART MUSEUM As befitting this gateway to the Pacific Rim, Portland's museum has an excellent collection of Asian artifacts and paintings. Additionally, look for interesting collections of graphic art and Native American works. Fans of the classics will appreciate French and Italian masterpieces, including Rodin, Renoir, Monet, and Degas, while mavens of modern art will enjoy deconstructing the aesthetically pleasing but occasionally vexing works by modern artists. *1219 S.W. Park Ave., tel. 503/226–2811. Take Bus 57 or 59. Admission: $4.50 adults, $2.50 students. Open Tues.–Sat. 11–5, Sun. 1–5; 1st Thurs. of the month, 11–9.*

POWELL'S CITY OF BOOKS Give yourself several hours to explore the shelves of new and used books at Powell's; with over 750,000 volumes, it's the largest bookstore in the country. The friendly staff and free store map make a visit enjoyable rather than overwhelming. And though you won't find any fancy oak furnishings and tweedy pseudoacademics, you may finally locate that long-sought, out-of-print discourse on Ché Guevara. The in-store **Anne Hughes Coffee Room** is the perfect place to contemplate your selections over espresso and pastries. *1005 W. Burnside St., tel. 503/228–4651 or 800/878–READ. From Pioneer Courthouse Square, walk 3 blocks west and 4 blocks north. Open Mon.–Sat. 9 AM–11 PM, Sun. 9–9.*

REED COLLEGE Though fairly small, Reed is regarded as one of the best private liberal arts schools on the West Coast, if not the country. Reed's student body is just about as progressive and P.C. as a student body can be: No fraternities or sororities here, no rah-rah football games, and in place of traditional collegiate sports, students often gather to play Ultimate Frisbee on the big green field near the main entrance. If you're looking for nightlife, campus kiosks are the place to find out about local bands and bars. *3203 S.E. Woodstock Blvd., at 28th Ave., tel. 503/771–1112. From downtown, take Bus 19 south.*

Attractive and wooded, and with a small lake at its center, the peaceful Reed College campus invites you to just exist—and discuss the fact that perhaps you don't.

SKIDMORE OLD TOWN HISTORIC DISTRICT The oldest buildings in Portland fill a 20-block area bordered by Oak Street on the south, Davis Street on the north, Front Avenue on the east, and Third Avenue on the west. Most of these historic structures date from the area's heyday in the second half of the 19th century; when businesses began moving south and west in the 1890s, Old Town eventually fell into disrepair. A recent renovation project has rehabilitated the buildings and plazas, restoring Victorian cast-iron facades and Romanesque archways. At the historic district's core is **Skidmore Fountain** (1st Avenue and Ankeny Street), built in 1888 to slake the thirst of both men and horses. You can pick up a map at the Portland Oregon Visitors Association (*see* Visitor Information, *above*) if you'd like to take a self-guided walking tour. Be careful here at night; as streets empty out, the junkies get busy, especially around Burnside Street just west of the Burnside Bridge.

The best time to visit Old Town is either Saturday or Sunday, when craft and food vendors set up their stalls for **Saturday Market** (btw S.W. 1st and Front Aves., and Burnside and Ankeny Sts.), open Saturday 10–5:30 and Sunday 11–4:30. Like the Pike Place Market in Seattle (*see* Chapter 6), this bustling outdoor bazaar is full of bizarre trinkets, like puppets, boomerangs, beaded jewelry, and walking sticks; there's also heaps of cheap food. The weird and wonderful **24-Hour Church of Elvis** (219 S.W. Ankeny St., tel. 503/226–3671) occupies a small storefront near the market. It's got Versateller-like talking machines (25¢) that usually coughs out some sort of "prize" (like a miniature dollar bill redrawn with the faces of Merv Griffin, Gary Hart, and Donna Rice). The church also performs legal weddings ($25) and dispenses souvenir T-shirts; the standard shirt is $10, the deluxe glow-in-the-dark version $15. Knock on the door if you're interested. On the north side of W. Burnside Street around N.W. 4th Avenue you'll find **Chinatown:** Besides an elaborately carved gate and a few decent restaurants, there's not much to see. Take a quick walk through and stop for dim sum at the **Fong Chong Restaurant** (*see* Food, *above*), but don't linger.

WASHINGTON PARK This beautiful forested park covers 332 acres of hills west of Portland. On its grounds you'll find **Metro Washington Park Zoo** (*see above*), the **World Forestry Center** (*see below*), and the **Hoyt Arboretum** (tel. 503/823–3655). Ten miles of trails meander around the arboretum's grounds, through a collection of more than 800 species of trees and shrubs; free guided tours take place April though October, weekends at 2 PM. Near the arboretum's south end begins the 27-mile **Wildwood Trail,** continuing north to **Forest Park** (*see above*). The adjacent **Oregon Vietnam Veterans Living Memorial** lists Oregonians who died in the war in its Garden of Solace. The city's favorite flower is showcased in the **International Rose Test Garden;** during summer, 600-plus varieties perfume the air. June's the best time to view the blooms. Farther along, you'll find the ornate **Japanese Gardens** (tel. 503/223–4070), which offer traditional manicured landscapes with streams, waterfalls, tiny bridges, and koi-filled ponds, as well as a stark Zen garden of sand and stone designed to encourage meditation. The Japanese Gardens charge admission ($5, $2.50 students) and are open daily 9–8 in summer, daily 10–4 in winter. *From downtown, take Bus 63 west; by car, follow signs from U.S. 26. Open daily dawn-dusk.*

WORLD FORESTRY CENTER The Forestry Center embarks daily on a Mission Impossible: To educate visitors about forest protection and management without environmentalists accusing it of being too friendly to loggers and loggers claiming that it's too friendly to environmentalists. Despite the inane 70-foot talking tree you see as you enter the center, you'll find interesting exhibits here on old growth and rain forests, logging and forest management, and a well-done show called the "Forests of the World." A clever interactive game developed by the Smithsonian Institute allows you to play at making the difficult decisions of a forest manager—usually with unpopular consequences. *4033 S.W. Canyon Rd., Washington Park, tel. 503/228–1367. From downtown, take Bus 63; by car, follow signs from U.S. 26. Admission: $3. Open summer, daily 9–5; winter, daily 10–5.*

MUSEUMS AND GALLERIES

Portland houses several unique collections covering highly specialized topics like cowboy history and American advertising, in addition to the larger museums: the **Oregon History Center, Oregon Museum of Science and Industry,** and **Portland Art Museum,** all reviewed above. Art galleries, of which Portland has many, are clustered around the Old Town and Yamhill historic districts (between S.W. Front and 3rd avenues), and in the Pearl district (north of W. Burnside Street between N.W. 8th and 14th avenues). On the first Thursday of every month, about 25 museums and galleries hold evening hours; some serve free refreshments. Weigh the possibility of a complimentary canapé and chardonnay dinner against the frustration of fighting the crowds—the free food and drink go fast.

AMERICAN ADVERTISING MUSEUM The only museum in the country dedicated exclusively to advertising traces the charmed life of print ads from the late 17th century to the waning years of the 20th. Understandably, you might want to skip all that for the exhibits on TV and radio's greatest commercial campaigns. This irony-free museum takes its subject very seriously; those who choose to sing cereal jingles aloud do so at their own risk. *600 N.E. Grand Ave., tel. 503/230–1090. 1 block from the Oregon Convention Center. Admission: $3. Open Wed.–Fri. 11–5, weekends noon–5.*

COWBOYS THEN AND NOW MUSEUM This tiny museum is filled with enough cowboy kitsch to make Silver heigh-ho in the opposite direction. Curators have wrangled up a timeline of cowboy history, numerous cowboy artifacts, and several short cowboy films (which play continuously). Double your fun with a visit to the 100-year-old chuck wagon tended by Zack, a mannequin that speaks on cowboy life with the aid of an actor's face projected onto its own. Though Zack says nothing worth hearing, it's fascinating to watch him do it. *729 N.E. Oregon St., tel. 503/731–3333. Admission free. Open Wed.–Fri. 11–5, weekends noon–5.*

OREGON MARITIME CENTER AND MUSEUM Maritime history types (you know who you are) will enjoy the center's displays of model ships and vintage photos, and exhibits of navigation instruments and ship hardware. Museum admission price also includes a tour of the 1947 steamer *Portland*, moored just outside. If you're determined to see only one maritime museum in your lifetime, however, visit the one in Astoria (*see* Chapter 3) instead, which has a more extensive, better-preserved collection. *113 S.W. Front St., tel. 503/224–7724. Admission: $4, $2 students. From Pioneer Courthouse Square, walk 6 blocks east and 6 blocks north. Open summer, Wed.–Sun. 11–4; winter, Fri.–Sun. 11–4.*

PITTOCK MANSION The lavish 16,000-square-foot Pittock Mansion, perched on a hilltop high above Portland, is all that you'd expect of a grand, old house designed for a real-life Citizen Kane (in this case, the founder of the newspaper *The Oregonian*). Built in 1914, the French Renaissance-style residence is loaded with opulent turn-of-the-century furnishings. If you're strapped for cash and can't foresee a career as an interior decorator, just enjoy the grounds and panoramic views of Portland for free. *3229 N.W. Pittock Dr., near W. Burnside St., tel. 503/248–4469. From downtown, take Bus 20 west. Admission: $4. Open daily noon–4.*

PARKS AND GARDENS

Portland has one of the best park systems in the nation, with plenty of extremes: **Forest Park** and **Washington Park** are the city's two largest preserves (*see* Worth Seeing, *above*), with over 5,000 acres combined. On the other end of the spectrum, **Mill Ends Park** occupies a single S.W. Front Street traffic island—qualifying it as the world's smallest city park.

CRYSTAL SPRINGS RHODODENDRON GARDEN Though it's particularly spectacular when the brightly hued rhododendrons are blooming (April–early June), the garden's lake, fountain, little waterfall, and friendly flock of ducks make it a nice place to visit any time of year. *S.E. 28th Ave., at Woodstock St., tel. 503/823–3640. Across the street from Reed College. From downtown, take Bus 19 south. Admission: $2, daily 10 AM–6 PM, except Tues. and Wed.; otherwise, free. Open daily, 6 AM–9 PM.*

LEACH BOTANICAL GARDEN This 9-acre shaded garden has 1½ miles of trails following pleasant Johnson Creek, looping past 1,500—count 'em, 1,500—species of plants. *6704 S.E. 122nd Ave., tel. 503/761–9503. From downtown, take Bus 5 south, then transfer to Bus 71. By car, exit I-205 on Foster Rd., go east to S.E. 122nd Ave, then turn south. Admission free. Open Tues.–Sat. 9–4, Sun 1–4.*

MT. TABOR PARK An island of forest surrounded by a sea of southeast Portland suburbs, Mt. Tabor Park covers a now-extinct volcano. You can get a nice look at Mt. Hood from here, but most views of the city are blocked by towering Douglas firs—certainly a worthwhile trade-off. *S.E. Salmon St. and 60th Ave., tel. 503/823–3648. From downtown, take Bus 15.*

OXBOW PARK Set on the Sandy River's banks, Oxbow Park has large grassy picnic areas perfect for a game of catch or Frisbee, as well as places to hike, fish, and swim. Camping is permitted, too (*see* Where to Sleep, *above*). *3010 S.E. Oxbow Pkwy., Gresham, tel. 503/663–4708. From Rte. 84 east, take 238th St. exit and drive 5 mi south, then go east 7 mi on Division St. Admission: $3 per car.*

TOM MCCALL WATERFRONT PARK The Waterfront Park (named after the most progressive governor in Oregon's history) runs the length of the Willamette's west bank between S.W. Madison and Ankeny streets. It's one of the best places in the city to romp on a warm, sunny day. Most people congregate on one end at the Salmon Street Plaza, joggers and bikers race back and forth, and kids and odd-looking adults splash in the Salmon Street fountain. Festivals fill the park in summer; during one, the **Rubber Ducky Derby** (June), hundreds of little yellow toy ducks are dropped into the river for a mega-slow quarter-mile race.

TRYON CREEK STATE PARK Tryon Park, covering 645 acres just south of downtown, is second only to Forest Park (see Worth Seeing, above) in terms of pristine beauty. Twenty miles of hiking and equestrian trails and paved bike paths weave through Douglas firs, western red cedars, and bushy stands of hemlock; most trails begin at the park's nature center, near the main entrance. If you're alert and very, very lucky, you may spot owls, beaver, or black-tailed deer. *11321 S.W. Terwilliger Blvd., tel. 503/653-3166. From downtown, take Bus 38 south; by car, exit I-5 at Terwilliger Blvd. and go south. Open daily dawn–dusk.*

BEACHES

Though it lies 70 miles east of the Pacific, Portland has several first-rate beaches—thanks to its many rivers. There's a sandy stretch for everyone, from families to nudists to nudist families.

NORTHEAST MARINE DRIVE Though it may seem an unlikely spot for sunbathing, the airport's northern boundary makes a surprisingly decent beach, with a view of planes descending to the airport and windsurfing maniacs maneuvering on the Columbia River. From either I-5 or I-205, exit onto Marine Drive; the beach (which isn't visible from the road) is just southeast of the parking lot for the M. James Gleason Boat Ramp.

ROOSTER ROCK At the western edge of Columbia Gorge lies Rooster Rock, about 20 miles east of Portland in the town of Corbett. Sunbathers lay out like lizards, *au naturel*, anywhere east of the parking area. West of the parking lot, everyone wears swimsuits. Most people, though, just head to Sand Island, about a 15-minute walk from the parking lot. *Tel. 503/695-2261. From I-84, follow signs to Columbia Gorge State Park. Admission: $3 per car May–Sept., free Oct.–Apr.*

SAUVIE ISLAND Sauvie Island in the Columbia River could be called a beach-goer's Eden, with various stretches for nude and clothed sunbathers and tremendous views of Mts. Hood and Saint Helens. This is also a terrific place to stop and pick your own strawberries, blueberries, and blackberries. To reach the beaches, take U.S. 30 west to the Sauvie Island exit. Purchase a $3 parking permit at the island's **Cracker Barrel Grocery Store** (15005 N.W. Sauvie Island Rd., tel. 503/621-3960) if you plan to park on public roads.

STATUES AND SCULPTURES

City funds and some private donations have brought statues or sculptures to almost every downtown street corner (for every state building erected, 1.33% of construction costs go to Portland's public art program). Most local bookstores sell a "Public Art Walking Tour" booklet ($2) that guides visitors to the most interesting works.

And the runner-up in the contest for Largest Hammered-Copper Sculpture in the World: Portlandia, second only to Lady Liberty in New York City.

Fittingly, a tour of public art should begin at the **Portland Building** (1120 S.W. 6th Ave.), which houses the **Metropolitan Center for Public Art**. Over the entrance to this controversial postmodern structure is *Portlandia*, a massive copper sculpture of a trident-wielding goddess. At **Pioneer Courthouse Square** (see Worth Seeing, above), you'll view the most playful public art in the city: the *Weather Machine*, a 25-foot tower that indicates weather conditions and temperatures using mythological figures and colored lights; and Seward Johnson's *Allow Me* sculpture, a life-sized bronze businessman with umbrella and outstretched hand. Many works of art line the **Transit Mall** (along S.W. 5th and 6th Aves.); the most notorious is Norman Taylor's nude *Kvinneakt* (S.W. 5th Ave., btw Stark and Washington Sts.), which former mayor Bud Clark made famous in his "Expose Yourself to Art" poster. Don't ask—just go to the nearest poster shop and check it out. Other highlights include the regal bronze statues of Abraham Lincoln and Theodore Roosevelt, occupying spots on tree-lined S.W. Park Avenue at Madison Street.

FESTIVALS

February–March. The **Portland International Film Festival** (Portland Art Museum, 1219 S.W. Park Ave., tel. 503/221–1156) features hot new films from around the world, shown subtitled and in the original language. Admission is $6 per film.

May. The **Cinco de Mayo Festival** (S.W. Front Ave., tel. 503/823–4000), celebrated on or near the May 5, is in remembrance of Mexico's victory against French invaders in 1862. Live music and delicious food are part of the outdoor festivities.

June. Residents have been celebrating the annual **Portland Rose Festival** (tel. 503/227–2681) since 1907; it's grown to a 24-day citywide marathon honoring Portland's favorite flower. Three weeks of concerts, flower shows, and car or boat races culminate with the nationally renowned Grand Floral Parade on the second Saturday in June.

July. No need to BYOB to the **Oregon Brewers Festival** (Tom McCall Waterfront Park, tel. 503/778–5917), which gathers beer makers from across North America, then mixes in live music and plenty of barbecue. Admission is free—the ale isn't.

August. Portland's chefs show off at **Bite . . . A Taste of Portland** (Tom McCall Waterfront Park, tel. 503/248–0600), where the city's best restaurants peddle their creations. A $2 donation benefiting the Oregon Special Olympics will gain you admittance; food averages $3.50 a plate.

August–September. **Artquake** (tel. 503/227–2787) provides an accessible weekend of classical and pop music, visual art, theater, dance, and culinary arts staged around Pioneer Courthouse Square. With a $2 donation, all artquake activities are free.

October. The two-day **Salmon Festival** (Oxbow Park, Gresham, tel. 503/797–1850) celebrates the fall Chinook salmon run with a wildlife-theme art show and a salmon bake.

November. Downtown's **Meier & Frank Holiday Parade** (tel. 503/241–5328), held the day after Thanksgiving, includes floats, marching bands, horse-drawn carriages, Santa Claus, and about 23,000 excited spectators lining the mile-long route.

December. The **Portland Parade of Christmas Ships** sails in formation around the Willamette and Columbia rivers every night for several weeks prior to Christmas. Contact the Portland Oregon Visitors Center (tel. 503/222–2223) for tips on where to best view the spectacle.

After Dark

The nighttime emptiness of Portland's streets can be misleading; all sorts of activity takes place after dark. Finding a happening neighborhood tavern or a lounge with plenty of atmosphere should be a virtual no-brainer, since beer—particularly the microbrewed stuff—is a serious matter with Portlanders. Fans of live music have their pick of jazz, blues, reggae, and alternative sounds, with most cover charges under $5. And square dancing is on the rise, so drop that attitude (and don another). The city also has several second-run movie houses charging at most $1.50 for admission and often serving pizza, beer, and other pub fare. You'll find the greatest number of bars downtown and in Nob Hill, around N.W. 21st and 23rd avenues. Portland's east side is less lively. If you go out there, choose your destination before starting, and don't plan on much bar hopping.

Get into the groove before you walk into the clubs: Locals Only (61 S.W. 2nd Ave., tel. 503/227–5000) sells the work of Northwest, and primarily Portland, musicians.

The mainstream city newspaper, *The Oregonian*, lists weekly events in the "Arts and Entertainment Guide" of its Friday calendar section. The *Portland Downtowner* also covers local events, trends, and culture; the biweekly *Rocket* covers the Northwest music scene. The latter two are available free at many stores and clubs around town.

For half-price concert and theater tickets on the day of the show, visit **PDX TIX** in the Galleria mall. They accept cash only. *921 S.W. Morrison St., tel. 503/241–4902. Open Oct.–June, Thurs.–Sat. noon–6, Sun. noon–5.*

BARS With nine microbreweries and one megabrewery in town (*see* Worth Seeing, *above*), it's difficult to visit Portland without drinking beer. Pubs and taverns are everywhere; almost all pour the local stuff. If you're perplexed by the array of ambers, bitters, stouts, and ales, start with the medium-bodied **Portland Ale** (Portland Brewing Company) or **Blue Heron Bitter** (Bridgeport).

In the industrial area north of W. Burnside Street, the **Bridgeport Pub & Brewery** (1313 N.W. Marshall St., tel. 503/241–7179) serves its cask-conditioned and draught ales in two spacious rooms. Take advantage of special drink prices (Mondays and Tuesdays) and live music (Saturdays). Farther west, **Kingston Saloon** (2020 W. Burnside St., btw N.W. 20th Ave. and 20th Pl., tel. 503/224–2115) is perfect for sports freaks, with countless TVs and cheap pitchers of domestic beer ($6). In the heart of Nob Hill, the **Blue Moon Tavern** (432 N.W. 21st Ave., tel. 503/223–3184) is furnished with a large wood-burning stove and long tables reminiscent of a German beer hall. It's owned by the McMenamin brothers, a pair who run about 30 pubs in the Portland area. Expect lots of twenty-somethings on weekends. A few blocks to the north, **The Gypsy** (625 N.W. 21st Ave., at Irving St., tel. 503/796–1859) attracts a Generation X crowd who enjoy the bar/restaurant/pool hall's groovy '60s-style decor and '90s music. Downtown, **Paddy's Bar & Grill** (65 S.W. Yamhill St., tel. 503/224–5626) has an upscale appearance (oak bar, brass fittings, and a huge display of liquor bottles) but reasonably priced food and booze. Also downtown, **Bush Garden Japanese Restaurant** (900 S.W. Morrison St., tel. 503/226–7181) is probably the most authentic Japanese restaurant in the city. Karaoke begins nightly at 9.

East of the Willamette, hip hordes crowd **The Space Room** (4800 S.E. Hawthorne Blvd., tel. 503/235–8303) on weekend evenings. Despite the name, the decor could hardly be less 2001—it's strictly smoky, old-time cocktail lounge (though their incredibly stiff cocktails do induce the floaty feeling of being in orbit). Hit the **East Avenue Tavern** (727 E. Burnside St., tel. 503/236–6900) if you're looking for a taste of Old Ireland; the Dublin-born owner, Mike Beglin, serves Guinness and Bass ales with a wee bit o' live Irish music on some weekends (cover $3–$6). It's an intimate atmosphere ideal for striking up conversation with one of the locals.

DANCING Portland may not have many places to dance, but it does have variety. At most clubs, you'll find both live and recorded music, with covers from $2 to $6. Some joints with DJs are free; check the calendar sections of the local papers for the latest.

The Drum. This place rounds 'em up for live country-and-western music and line or square dancing, pardner. They've got dance lessons ($1) from 7:30 to 9:30, Sunday–Thursday. Don't write this place off as a geriatric jam; it's a mixed-age crowd with the majority of patrons in their late twenties. *14601 S.E. Division St., tel. 503/760–1400. From downtown, take Bus 4 from S.W. 5th Ave. Cover: $2 Fri. and Sat. after 8:30.*

Lotus Card Room and Cafe. In front, it's a restaurant serving standard American fare; in back, there's a crowded disco. The music here is always loud, usually recorded, and follows a different theme each night: alternative Wednesdays, hip hop Fridays, and disco Sundays, to name a few. *932 S.W. 3rd Ave., at Salmon St., tel. 503/227–6185. No dancing Mon. and Tues. Cover: $3 after 10 PM Fri.–Sat., $1 after 10 PM Wed., Thurs., and Sun.*

Panorama. This popular joint caters to a mixed straight and gay crowd, with recorded music ranging from house to techno to disco. If the Panorama seems too eclectic to you, boogie over to **The Brig:** It's a hoppin' gay club connected to the Panorama and owned by the same people. The cover charge gets you into both clubs. *341 S.W. 10th Ave., tel. 503/221–7262. Open Thurs. and Sun. until 2:30 AM; Fri. and Sat. until 4 AM. Cover: $2 Thurs., $3 Fri.–Sat.*

Red Sea. A restaurant/club combination, Red Sea serves Ethiopian food in the front room and plays reggae and calypso for a swaying mixed-age crowd in the back. There's live music every

Thursday, when cover is $4. Friday and Saturday cover is $2. *318 S.W. 3rd Ave., tel. 503/241–5450. Restaurant open Tues.–Sat.; nightclub open Thurs.–Sat.*

LIVE MUSIC Portland clubs *appear* unpromising: Jazz and blues establishments look more like grungy lounges, and rock acts often play in cramped neighborhood pubs with no real stage. In terms of performance quality, however, there are no weaknesses in Portland's music scene. The jazz and blues selection sizzles, but if it's the alternative scene you seek, you won't be disappointed, either. Many clubs include a few traditional rock acts each week; fans should consult a newspaper (*see* After Dark, *above*) for information.

On the alternative rock circuit, Northwest bands to look for include **Sweaty Nipples** and the **Spinanes. Curtis Salgado** plays a fierce blues harmonica, while **Glen Moore, Thera Memory,** and **David Friesen** are talented local jazz musicians. The **Cathedral Park Jazz Festival** (under St. Johns Bridge, tel. 503/284–5446), held in July, is Oregon's largest free jazz festival, while the **Mt. Hood Festival of Jazz** (Mt. Hood Community College, Gresham, tel. 503/666–3810), held in August, is Oregon's largest jazz festival, period. Blues enthusiasts should check out the **Waterfront Blues Festival** (Tom McCall Waterfront Park, tel. 503/282–0555), held every July 4th weekend: For a donation of $3 and two cans of food, you'll spend four mellow days listening to acts from around the country jam. Proceeds benefit the Food Bank. During fall and winter, the **Portland Art Museum** (1219 S.W. Park Ave., tel. 503/225–2811) hosts live blues and jazz in its sculpture court on Wednesday evenings; tickets cost $4.50.

➤ **ROCK** • Pool sharks and party-minded types will appreciate **Belmont's Inn** (3357 S.E. Belmont St., tel. 503/232–1998), which has an excellent dance floor and pool hall. The $2–$5 cover gets you live music ranging from traditional rock to R&B and blues.

La Luna. If you can survive the insane line, you'll have a blast at La Luna; some of the hottest acts in town play here. The downstairs is open to an all-ages crowd four or five nights a week (finally, the under-21 crowd can chuck their fake IDs). Upstairs, look for drink specials like $1 beers on Tuesdays. Monday is "Queer Night"; the rest of the week you'll groove with a primarily straight crowd. *215 S.E. 9th Ave., at Pine St., tel. 503/241–5862. Bar open Mon.–Sat. 7–2 AM. Downstairs schedule varies. Cover: $4 and up.*

Satyricon. Satyricon is *the* place for alternative rock, though you'll need to brave a fairly raunchy neighborhood to get here. Once safely inside, you can rock the night away for $3–$7. Mondays, when new bands take the stage, are free; on Sundays ($1 cover), check out the unusual medley of performance artists, soloists, and acoustic musicians. *125 N.W. 6th Ave., at Davis St., tel. 503/243–2380. Open daily 10 PM–2 AM. Cover varies.*

➤ **JAZZ AND BLUES** • **Brasserie Montmartre.** Though this lounge is elegant, it has a casual and altogether comfortable feel. Free nightly jazz includes shows by some first-rate locals, typically duos on weekdays and larger groups on the weekends. *626 S.W. Park Ave., btw Morrison and Alder Sts., tel. 503/224–5552. Open weekdays 11:30 AM–2 AM, Fri. until 3 AM, Sat. 10 AM–3 AM, Sun. 10 AM–2 AM.*

Candlelight Cafe and Bar. The hottest blues room in town packs in a primarily local crowd. It's a mellow bar where patrons shoot pool while top blues musicians perform only 20 feet away. The younger set (under 21) is welcome until 9:30 PM; everyone will appreciate the lack of cover charge or drink minimum. *2032 S.W. 5th Ave., at Lincoln St., tel. 503/222–3378. Open daily 10 PM–2:30 AM. Wheelchair access.*

Dandelion Pub. Top-notch blues acts—like Curtis Salgado and Duffy Bishop—and an unpretentious atmosphere packs 'em in here Wednesday through Saturday. There are no bands on Tuesdays. *1033 N.W. 16th Ave., at Marshall St., tel. 503/223–0099. Open Tues.–Sat. 3 PM–2:30 AM. Cover: $4 Fri. and Sat.*

Jazz de Opus. Take a sip, lean back, and relax to the smooth sounds of some local jazz greats: Leroy Vinnegar, Dan Fanhle, and Thera Memory have all been known to weave their magic here. The club draws prime visiting acts, too. Live jazz can be heard from 9 PM to 1 AM every night but Monday. *33 N.W. 2nd Ave., at Couch St., tel. 503/222–6077. $3 drink minimum.*

➤ **CLASSICAL** • The **Oregon Symphony** (711 S.W. Alder St., tel. 503/228–1353) performs more than 100 concerts a year at downtown's Arlene Schnitzer Concert Hall. Seats run $10–$50, but students may purchase half-price tickets one hour before evening concerts. The **Portland Opera** (1516 S.W. Alder St., tel. 503/241–1802) offers five productions a year at the Portland Civic Auditorium. Prices are $20–$90; discount student tickets are sold a half hour before the show. The **Oregon Ballet Theatre** (Portland Civic Auditorium, tel. 503/227–6867) is a small company that performs classical and contemporary works. **Chamber Music Northwest** (522 S.W. 5th Ave., Suite 725, tel. 503/223–3202) produces a superb festival (late June–late July) that features world-class performers. Tickets cost $10–$23.

CINEMAS Portland is king of cheap, second-run movie houses. And, as befits a town that brews gallons of beer, several sell pints with the popcorn. You can't miss the pleasantly gaudy facade of the **Hollywood Theater** (4122 N.E. Sandy Blvd., tel. 503/248–6977), where $1.50 still buys a double feature. The city's two hybrid pub-theaters both charge $1 admission to see fairly current flicks, though you must be over 21 to enter: **Baghdad Theater** (3702 S.E. Hawthorne Blvd., tel. 503/230–0895) serves pizza ($2–$3 per slice) and beer; **Mission Theater and Pub** (1624 N.W. Glisan St., at 17th Ave., tel. 503/223–4031) serves beer, burgers, and sandwiches. If you prefer classic films on a small screen, try the bar at Nob Hill's **L'Auberge Restaurant** (2601 N.W. Vaughn St., tel. 503/223–3302), on Sunday night only; admission is free.

Outdoor Activities

HIKING There are plenty of fine hiking opportunities around Portland, even inside the city proper. The ambitious may want to try the 27-mile Wildwood Trail at Forest Park (*see* Worth Seeing, *above*). Less taxing is a jaunt through conifer forests at **Hoyt Arboretum** in Washington Park (*see* Worth Seeing, *above*), which has 10 miles of trails. **Tryon Creek State Park** (*see* Parks and Gardens, *above*) has 20 miles of trails, include several easy ½-mile nature walks and a 1-mile trail down to the creek. For more information on scenic hikes, try the city's Bureau of Parks and Recreation (tel. 503/823–2223).

BIKING A moderate climate, beautiful scenery, and fairly level terrain make Portland a great city to see with your ass firmly planted on the seat of a bicycle. The mountain biking group **PUMP** (tel. 503/223–3954), or Portland United Mountain Pedalers, can suggest interesting bike routes in the city and throughout Oregon. Otherwise, roll over to **Forest Park** (*see* Worth Seeing, *above*), where a bevy of seldom-traveled roads wind through stunning conifer forests. If you've filled your quota of tree-viewing, cruising along **Tom McCall Waterfront Park,** the Portland approximation of a California beach boardwalk, provides an excellent opportunity to people-watch. **Cascadden's Mountain Sports** (1533 N.W. 24th Ave., tel. 503/224–4746) rents mountain bikes by the hour ($9 for 2 hours), day ($25), and week ($75).

Sure, Nike's "Just Do It" catch phrase probably originated with a flatulent New York ad executive begging someone, anyone, to pull his finger, but it's more pleasant to imagine that Portland's wonderful hiking and biking opportunities were the true inspiration for the Oregon-based company's slogan.

FISHING Its position at the confluence of the relatively unpolluted **Willamette** and **Columbia rivers** makes Portland a superb place to fish. On the Columbia, look for salmon, trout, and big, ugly sturgeon. In addition to salmon, the Willamette is known for steelhead, and cutthroat and rainbow trout. However, Portland residents aren't so generous with their fish: You won't find equipment rentals anywhere in the city. If fishing is a life-or-death issue for you, **Fisherman's Marine Supply** (901 N. Columbia Blvd., tel. 503/283–0044) sells equipment and can arrange fishing trips. All it takes is a whole lotta cash.

SPECTATOR SPORTS Perennial NBA championship contenders, the **Portland Trail Blazers** (700 N.E. Multnomah St., tel. 503/234–9291) are definitely the hottest ticket in town. The season begins in October and usually runs through May.

Blazer games sell out within hours (and sometimes, minutes) of going on sale, but you can occasionally score a pair of tickets through the classifieds or from one of the random dudes hanging about the stadium entrance—either way, you'll pay dearly.

The **Portland Winter Hawks** (Memorial Coliseum, 1401 N.E. Weidler St., at Broadway, tel. 503/235–8771) compete September–March in the World Hockey League. Though it's not exactly the NHL, it's enough to entertain.

Fans of the racetrack have several options: The **Portland International Raceway** (West Delta Park, 1940 N. Victory Blvd., tel. 503/285–6635) has sportscar (year-round) and Indy (once yearly) events. At **Portland Meadows** (1001 N. Schmeer Rd., tel. 503/285–9144) thoroughbred and quarter horses race regularly, October–April. The **Multnomah Greyhound Park** (N.E. 223rd Ave., at Glisan St., tel. 503/667–7700) offers greyhound racing Tuesday–Sunday from May to August.

Near Portland

Portland makes an ideal base camp from which to explore the stellar attractions of northwest Oregon and southwest Washington. East of the city are the forests, waterfalls, and farmlands of the Columbia River Gorge, and the Mt. Hood National Forest, famed for its rivers, alpine forests, and superb ski resorts. For more info on both areas, *see* Chapter 4. Cross the Washington border just north of Portland and you'll find the historic city of Vancouver, with its fort and 19th-century houses.

VANCOUVER, WASHINGTON

Despite its location just across the Columbia River from bustling Portland, the city of Vancouver has a historic, small-town feel. Proudly restored old buildings, infused with the pioneer flavor that is a legacy of early explorers Lewis and Clark, serve as the city's major attractions. And, as if you could possibly not realize that you're in the American west, city businesses, in perpetual fear of being confused with the *other* Vancouver (in British Columbia, Canada), emblazon every brochure and pamphlet with three essential letters: USA.

The two-story **Clark County Historical Museum** displays re-creations of turn-of-the-century buildings, including a country store, post office, and doctor's office. Downstairs, there's a one-room exhibit of railroad paraphernalia and model trains. Retired railroaders are on hand to answer questions. *1511 Main St., tel. 206/695–4681. Admission free. Open Tues.–Sun. 1–5.*

Fort Vancouver, overlooking the Columbia River, was established in 1825 by the rebellious Dr. John McLaughlin, who bucked his bosses at the fur-trading Hudson Bay Company to give settlers lodging and medical attention on credit—which should qualify him as the patron saint of budget travelers. The original fort, a one-time center of the Pacific Coast fur trade, was abandoned in 1860 and burned to the ground in 1866. (According to rumor, the U.S. Army had engaged in a bit of arson to clear grazing land for soldiers' horses.) One hundred years later, the stockade and five major buildings were reconstructed with painstaking attention to detail, rangers were gussied up in period costumes, and the fort reopened to tourists. Ignore the folks with video cameras and you'll swear you've suddenly been transported to the 19th century. *From I-5, take Mill Plain Blvd. exit and follow signs ½-mi east. Admission: $2. Open summer, daily 9–5; winter, daily 9–4.*

Fort Vancouver is the place to be on the Fourth of July, with plenty of free, live music throughout the day and the largest fireworks display west of the Mississippi at night. Sure, the parking situation is worse than at the original Woodstock, but other than that, it's a great time.

The **Fort Vancouver Visitors Center** (1501 E. Evergreen Blvd., tel. 206/696–7655) has a small collection of fort artifacts and will show you a 15-minute video of the fort's history on request. Entry to the visitors center museum is free.

Just north of Fort Vancouver, **Officer's Row** (E. Evergreen Blvd., tel. 206/693–3103) can be seen just fine from a car window. Built between 1850 and 1906, these 21 Victorian houses, now restored, served as residences for officers assigned to the Vancouver Barracks. If you do have time, stop for a tour of the **Marshall House** (1301 Officer's Row, tel. 206/693–3103); from 1936 to 1938 this was the home of General George Marshall, author of the eponymous plan to rebuild Europe and the Pacific after World War II. The tours (free) are offered weekdays 9–5 and select weekends 11–6. At the **Grant House,** a new **Folk Art Center** (1101 Officer's Row, tel. 206/694–5252) has a pleasant café and rotating displays of artwork by locals past and present.

Within easy walking distance of Fort Vancouver and Officer's Row, the **Pearson Air Museum** adjoins the oldest continuously operating airfield in the United States. The first airplane landed here in 1905; in 1937, Pearson made aeronautical history when the first nonstop transpolar flight touched down on its runway. The museum displays vintage aircraft, including a 1917 Curtiss "Jenny" and a Vietnam-era army attack helicopter. *1105 E. 5th St., tel. 206/694–7026. Admission: $2. Open Wed.–Sun. noon–5.*

VISITOR INFORMATION The **Vancouver/Clark County Visitors and Convention Bureau** provides extensive information on Vancouver, and some on Clark County as well. *404 E. 15th St., Suite 11, 98663, tel. 206/693–1313. Off I–5, btw D and E Sts. Open Mon. 9–5, Tues.–Fri. 8–5.*

GETTING AROUND Vancouver's attractions are spread out and not easily accessible by foot. The public bus system, **C-Tran** (108 E. 7th St., btw C and Washington Sts., tel. 206/695–0123), runs Monday–Saturday 5:45 AM–9:45 PM, Sunday 8:15 AM–5:45 PM. The fare is 60¢. Taxi services in town include **Cab One** (tel. 206/260–1212) and **Vancouver Cab Company** (tel. 206/693–1234). Don't bother trying to hail one on the street—they won't stop.

WHERE TO SLEEP While most cheap lodgings are scattered around Vancouver, you'll find several budget motels just north of the city on **N.E. Highway 99,** parallel to I–5.

Value Motel. The cheapest (and smallest) rooms in town run a mere $20; though bathrooms are shared, you'll have privacy in fall and winter, when the motel is rarely full. Standard doubles with bath, larger and farther away from highway noise, cost about $38. *708 N.E. 78th St., tel. 206/574–2345. From I–5, take 78th St. exit. 122 rooms, 82 with bath.*

Vancouver Lodge. Considering its prime location downtown—within walking distance of Fort Vancouver and Officer's Row—the lodge's clean and harmless doubles ($42–$55) are a very good deal. Each room has a refrigerator and coffee maker. *601 Broadway, at 6th Ave, tel. 206/693–3668. 48 rooms.*

➤ **CAMPING** • **Battle Ground Lake State Park** (18002 N.E. 249th St., tel. 206/687–4621 or 800/562–0990), about 20 miles northeast of Vancouver, has a pleasant beach and nearby equestrian trails (*see* Elsewhere Near Portland, *below*). There are 50 sites; choose between developed ($11) or primitive ($5). On the east fork of the Lewis River, **Paradise Point State Park** (tel. 206/263–2350 or 800/562–0990) has a 2-mile hiking trail and decent beach about a half-mile away. It's easy to reach (take I–5 north to exit 16), though the noise from the highway could hardly be considered soothing. The 79 spots run $10 for a standard site and $5 for primitive.

FOOD **Pacific Grill and Chowder House.** Stifle the urge to belt out a few lusty lyrics from "Pirate's Life for Me" while being shown to a table here; this is not Disneyland, just a Red Lion Inn restaurant with dim lighting and a few flashy seafaring props—not to mention an incredible view of the Columbia River. You can order most entrées for less than $10, so long as you leave the fish in the sea at dinnertime. The curly pasta with spring vegetables ($8.75) makes an unbeatable meal. *100 E. Columbia Way., tel. 206/694–8341. Open daily 6 AM–2 PM and 5 PM–10 PM, Fri. and Sat. until 11 PM. Wheelchair access.*

Who Song and Larry's Cantina. This downtown restaurant whips up tasty Mexican dishes in festive surroundings; just remember to grit your teeth and speak kindly to the serenading waiters in goofy hats. Alternately, enjoy margaritas and great views of the Columbia River from one of the outdoor decks. Most dinners cost $7–$10. *111 E. Columbia Way, tel. 206/695–1198 or, from Oregon, 503/285–7395. Open Mon.–Thurs. 11–10, Fri. and Sat. 11–11, Sun. 10–10. Reservations recommended.*

The Wiener Wagon. You'll find the cheapest lunch in Vancouver at this green and white cart, a downtown fixture since 1975. Vegetarians will want to bypass the tasty wieners ($1–$2.50) for the Veggie Delight: almost anything you can stuff into a pita for under $2. *Cnr. 12th and Main Sts. Lunch only.*

ELSEWHERE NEAR PORTLAND

BATTLE GROUND AND BATTLE GROUND LAKE STATE PARK Twenty-one miles northeast of Vancouver (take Highway 503) is the town of Battle Ground. Ironically, not a single skirmish, battle, war, or even a tussle has been fought here. Three miles to its east lies **Battle Ground Lake State Park;** still no historic trenches and cannons to photograph, but there is a pleasant lake for swimming and sunning. It's stocked each spring with rainbow trout, all but assuring an easy catch for those with fishing equipment. The park maintains 10 miles of forested trails for hikers and horseback riders and 50 tent sites for campers (*see* Camping, in Vancouver, *above*). A 2½-hour scenic tour ($10) on the **Lewis and Clark Railway** (1000 E. Main St., tel. 206/687–2626 or 503/227–2626) winds along some of the Pacific Northwest's oldest train tracks. Trains depart from Battle Ground (the town) and make a short stop at **Moulton Falls County Park** (*see below*). The train departs Tuesday–Sunday at 10 AM and 1:30 PM in summer; weekends at 10 AM and 1:30 PM in fall and spring. The winter schedule varies.

At the 333-acre **Moulton Falls County Park** (tel. 206/699–2467), several developed trails lead over swinging bridges, past waterfalls and a few calm, inviting pools perfect for a cooling dip. In summer look for steelhead trout jumping the falls on their annual migration upriver to spawn. *From Battle Ground, take Rte. 503 5 mi north to Rock Creek Rd., turn right, and follow signs to park.*

If for no other reason, visit Battle Ground for a meal at **Fatty Patty's.** Some servings are so huge that exhausted finishers win a free T-shirt. In particular, look for pancakes ($2.25) bigger than the giant plates they ride in on, and Jimmy's Swine Burger ($9.95), a triple-patty, seven-inch-wide monster served with a platter of french fries and a salad. *813 W. Main St., tel. 206/687–3904. Open Mon. 5 AM–3 PM, Tues.–Fri. 5 AM–9 PM, Sat. 6 AM–9 PM, Sun. 7 AM–3 PM.*

RIDGEFIELD North of Vancouver, the **Ridgefield National Wildlife Refuge** encompasses 3,000 extremely diverse acres of marshland, bog, forest, and pasture. During winter months, as many as 275,000 migrating waterfowl make this their temporary home. You'll also see black-tailed deer, beaver, coyote, foxes, and nonmigratory birds such as red-tailed hawks and great blue herons. An easy 1.9-mile loop trail begins at the refuge entrance, leading hikers through a forest of oak and Douglas fir and skirting around the edges of the wetlands. If you stop for a moment, you'll hear nothing but the mutter of birds and the gentle sound of tall grasses swaying in the breeze. *Tel. 206/887–4106. From I–5, take Exit 14 and follow signs. From Ridgefield, follow N. Main Ave. 1 mi north.*

OREGON COAST   3

By Gary Blond

When describing the Oregon Coast, those inclined toward emphatic terms like "spectacular" and "gorgeous" run little risk of overstatement; the scenery is simply *that* mesmerizing. From California all the way to the Washington border, the coast's main thoroughfare, U.S. 101, takes you past 363 miles of unspoiled beaches, jagged offshore rock formations, scenic state parks, historic lighthouses, and coastal sand dunes. The highway doesn't always hug the coast, but short detours onto turnoff roads take you to prime coastal viewpoints.

This coastal paradise does not come without a price, though. On the Oregon Coast, payment is extracted most frequently in the form of rain—so much rain that you could fill an entire swimming pool with a year's worth of it. And the scenery itself isn't without imperfections; your view is sometimes marred by ugly clear-cut forests, with the stumps of fallen trees sticking up like tombstones in a massive cemetery. Of course, loggers frustrated by recent restrictions might not be so sentimental—think twice before whining about the clear-cutting to an Oregonian with an I LOVE SPOTTED OWLS . . . FRIED bumper sticker on the back of his truck.

The coast is dotted with towns, some small and some even smaller. Local economies are dominated by logging, fishing, and tourism—most commonly a combination of all three. In addition to the economic similarities, a few other notable constants run through them: Nightlife is a rare commodity, retirees aren't, and local teenagers are totally bored. But none of these things should drag you down too much; the coast's true appeal resides in the great outdoors. Popular activities include dune buggying, storm watching, beachcombing, hiking, clam digging, crabbing, and whale watching. If you can, explore the coast in early fall, when summer weather lingers but crowds have thinned out. Winters can be fun for storm watchers and are temperate if you stick to the southern end, but otherwise they're wet and dreary. If you do make a winter trip, pack an umbrella and pray your motel has cable. The route mapped out below follows U.S. 101 from south to north, but the coast is equally spectacular whichever way you go.

Basics   VISITOR INFORMATION Most towns covered in this chapter have well-stocked chambers of commerce with at least some information on the rest of the coast; see individual sections below for more information.

If you begin your trip in the south, visit the **State Welcome Center,** about 2 miles north of Brookings, for literature and recommendations on the entire coast and the rest of Oregon as well. *1650 U.S. 101, at Harris Beach State Park, tel. 503/469–4117. Open May–Oct., daily 9–5.*

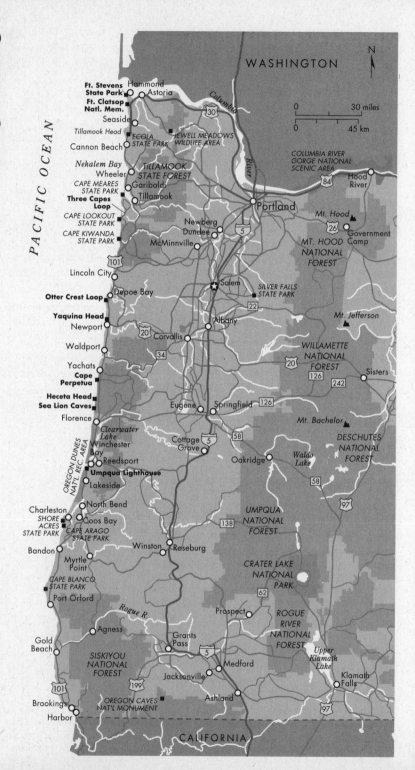

Oregon Coast

PACIFIC OCEAN

N

WASHINGTON

Ft. Stevens State Park
Ft. Clatsop Natl. Mem.
Hammond
Astoria
Seaside
Tillamook Head
Cannon Beach
ECOLA STATE PARK
JEWELL MEADOWS WILDLIFE AREA
Columbia River
30

0   30 miles
0   45 km

COLUMBIA RIVER GORGE NATIONAL SCENIC AREA

Hood River
84

Nehalem Bay
Wheeler
CAPE MEARES STATE PARK
Three Capes Loop
Garibaldi
Tillamook
TILLAMOOK STATE FOREST

Portland
5

Mt. Hood
26
Government Camp

CAPE LOOKOUT STATE PARK
CAPE KIWANDA STATE PARK

Newberg
Dundee
McMinnville

MT. HOOD NATIONAL FOREST

101

Lincoln City
Depoe Bay
Otter Crest Loop
Yaquina Head
Newport

Salem
SILVER FALLS STATE PARK
22

Mt. Jefferson

20
Corvallis
Albany

Waldport

WILLAMETTE NATIONAL FOREST

34

Yachats
Cape Perpetua

20
126
242
Sisters

Heceta Head
Sea Lion Caves
Florence

Eugene
Springfield
126

Mt. Bachelor

Clearwater Lake
Winchester Bay
Reedsport
Umpqua Lighthouse
Lakeside
OREGON DUNES NATL. REC. AREA

Cottage Grove
5
58

Oakridge
Waldo Lake

DESCHUTES NATIONAL FOREST

58

97

Charleston
SHORE ACRES STATE PARK
CAPE ARAGO STATE PARK
North Bend
Coos Bay

Bandon
Winston
Roseburg

138

UMPQUA NATIONAL FOREST

Myrtle Point
CAPE BLANCO STATE PARK
Port Orford

CRATER LAKE NATIONAL PARK

62

Agness
Rogue R.
Prospect

ROGUE RIVER NATIONAL FOREST

Gold Beach

SISKIYOU NATIONAL FOREST

Grants Pass
5

Upper Klamath Lake

101

199
Jacksonville
Medford
Klamath Falls
97

Brookings
Harbor
OREGON CAVES NAT'L MONUMENT
Ashland

CALIFORNIA

On the northern end, the **Seaside Chamber of Commerce and Visitors Bureau** serves as a state welcome center, with an extensive selection of pamphlets and a friendly staff. *7 N. Roosevelt St., on U.S. 101, tel. 503/738–6391 or 800/444–6740. Open May–Oct., Mon.–Sat. 8–6, Sun. 9–5; Nov.–Apr., weekdays 9–5, weekends 10–4.*

GETTING AROUND

The two best ways to see the coast are by car and by bike. Buses are a far less attractive option; they skip all the coastal detours off U.S. 101 and roar past beaches and scenic viewpoints without stopping. There are small airports with limited service in Astoria, Newport, and Florence, and a larger one in North Bend/Coos Bay (tel. 503/756–2170) with regular flights to Portland. Ambitious hikers with lots of time on their hands might try the 360-mile Oregon Coast Trail (*see below*), which follows U.S. 101 much of the way but also includes a lot of beach walking.

BY CAR Most travelers drive along the coast, following **U.S. 101** north to Astoria or south to Brookings. Although traffic jams are rare, U.S. 101 is a winding two-lane road for much of the way, so don't expect to break any speed records. If you want to stop and enjoy coastal offerings, you should allow at least three days for the 363-mile trip. You can do the drive in a day and still see some spectacular scenery framed through your car window, but frequent stops and detours off the main road will be out of the question. Pay attention to your gas tank; you'll only find gas stations within the towns, not between them. Also remember that U.S. 101 takes on additional names when passing through towns: In Brookings it's Chetco Avenue; in Gold Beach it's Ellensburg Street; and in Port Orford it's Oregon Street.

Renting a car on the coast can be expensive, especially in summer, and rental outfits are few; try to find wheels in Eugene or Portland instead.

About 50 miles inland is the north–south **I–5,** which parallels U.S. 101. Below Bandon, two major roads link the highways: **Route 42** runs from Roseburg (on I–5) to Coquille, where it splits, meeting up with U.S. 101 in Bandon and just south of Coos Bay; and **U.S. 199** goes southwest from Grants Pass to Crescent City (on the northern California coast). From Portland, you can take **U.S. 30** along the Columbia River to Astoria, **U.S. 26** to just north of Cannon Beach, **Route 6** to Tillamook, and **Route 18** to just north of Lincoln City. To reach the coast from Eugene, take **Route 126** to Florence. If you're heading south, U.S. 101 continues into California, passing Crescent City en route to San Francisco. If you're heading north, U.S. 101 travels up the Washington coast and circles the Olympic Peninsula. Stop at one of the state welcome centers (*see* Visitor Information, *above*) to pick up a free *Oregon Coast Magazine's Guide to U.S. 101,* which leads travelers on a mile-by-mile tour of the coast.

BY BUS Greyhound (tel. 800/231–2222) runs two buses a day between Portland and San Francisco. The route follows U.S. 101 through Lincoln City, Newport, Florence, Coos Bay, Brookings Harbor, and other towns. The trip from Portland to Lincoln City takes almost 3 hours and costs about $13; to go from Lincoln City to Brookings Harbor takes more than six hours and costs about $30. This Greyhound route covers the southern and central coast; to get from Lincoln City to the northernmost towns by bus, however, you need to travel east to Portland and then west again—a waste of time and money.

RAZ Transportation (tel. 800/666–3301) makes a northwest Oregon loop every morning from Portland to Seaside, up the coast to Astoria, and back east to Portland; every afternoon it makes this same loop in the opposite direction. The Astoria–Portland trip costs $15; from Seaside to Portland you'll pay $19; and the Seaside–Astoria leg is $4.

BY BIKE You won't find a more scenic ride than the well-marked **Oregon Coast Bike Route,** which runs right alongside U.S.101, with occasional detours onto county roads and city streets. The route covers 368 miles and requires, on the average, six to eight days of biking; because of the hilly terrain and spectacular views, most people don't bike more than 60 miles a day. For more information, consult the "Oregon Coast Bike Route Map and Guide," put out by the Department of Transportation (Bicycle/Pedestrian Program Manager, Room 210, Transportation Building, Salem 97310, tel. 503/378–3432) and available at most chambers of commerce.

Despite the south-to-north route outlined in this book, you should begin in the north and cycle southward if you plan on traveling between May and October, when winds blow from the northwest; the north-to-south route also puts you on the ocean side of the road, so you don't have to cross U.S. 101 to access viewpoints. During summer, mild temperatures—usually between 60°F and 80°F—and reduced rainfall make for good conditions, but the road is more crowded; on the other hand, winter storms can be hazardous. The best time to go is early fall.

HIKING The **Oregon Coast Trail** begins at the California border and runs 360 miles, alternating from beach to highway to county road, all the way to Ft. Stevens State Park, just west of Astoria. There are breathtaking hikes along the entire route, but highlights include the beach trails of the southern coast and, in the north, the 2-mile uphill hike through Ecola State Park to an ocean viewpoint. Make sure you have plenty of water on the long stretches of beach, and bring along rain gear and warm clothing, even in summer. Most chambers of commerce carry the "Oregon Coast Trail Guide," which indicates hiker/biker campgrounds and gives details on each segment of the trail. For a free copy, write to Trails Coordinator, Oregon State Parks, 525 Trade St. S.E., Salem 97310, or call 503/378–5012.

HITCHHIKING Hitching is legal in Oregon, but it's not always easy. Hitchhikers have better luck on U.S. 101 than on I–5, but the going is slow and, like anywhere in the United States, risky. Almost any time of year you can expect rainy weather, though you're likely to keep much drier in summer. The best places to catch a ride on U.S. 101 are on the outskirts of towns, where speed limits are lower.

WHERE TO SLEEP

The coast has some reasonably priced bed-and-breakfasts and some great camping; otherwise, you're stuck with generic motels ($30–$50) along U.S. 101. Youth hostels are practically nonexistent on the coast. During summer, campgrounds and motels are often filled, especially on weekends. Make reservations well in advance. Motel rates are often discounted about $10 during winter—ask if they don't offer.

You might as well start practicing now: "I'd like some clam chowder," or "I think I'll have the fish and chips." With the exception of sandwiches and hamburgers, these are about your only budget dining options on the coast.

For campers, making reservations can be complicated. Only nine state-park campgrounds on the coast accept reservations, and then only from Memorial Day to Labor Day. Contact any coastal chamber of commerce for a reservation form, and include a $20 reservation fee with the application, $6 of which is nonrefundable. In all other cases, campsites are available on a first-come, first-served basis. For more information, contact the **State Park Campsite Information Center** (tel. 800/452–5687 in OR, or 503/731–3411 out of state and in Portland). **MISTIX** (tel. 800/444–7275) also offers reservations at selected sights—watch for a service charge. If you haven't reserved, try to arrive no later than noon, and favor inland campgrounds, which tend to be less crowded. Plenty of private campgrounds and RV parks will accept reservations, but these are rarely as attractive as the state and federal parks and don't save you much (if any) money.

OUTDOOR ACTIVITIES

As you might expect, the sporting life centers around the ocean. Besides the activities listed below, popular pastimes include dune buggying in the Oregon Dunes National Recreation Area (*see* Oregon Dunes, *below*) and fishing in Oregon's ocean, lakes, and rivers.

CLAMMING AND CRABBING Clamming seems basic at first glance: you spot your prey, dig it out with a narrow shovel, and flip it in the bucket. There's plenty more where it came from, up and down the coast. But if you've never gone clamming before, ask for some information at a chamber of commerce. The Oregon Department of Fish and Wildlife puts out a pamphlet that covers digging technique, identification of clams, when to go, and what to wear. The best time to clam is low tide, when conditions are less hazardous, clams are feeding, and you can see what you're digging. Sports stores along the coast rent shovels for about $5 a day. And don't wear your brand-new Reeboks for this; prepare for some mud-smearing fun.

The most coveted clam—and the most difficult to dig—is the razor. High concentrations of razors can be found around Seaside and Cannon Beach on the north coast, and there are small populations around Newport, Coos Bay, and Gold Beach. Other clams, such as gapers, cockles, littlenecks, and soft-shells, inhabit the coastal bays; Charleston, near Coos Bay, is a particularly good spot.

Crabs are found in coastal bays and at river mouths. You can catch them using crab rings or pots, which are baited, sunk, and then pulled up after about 20 minutes. In most areas, you need to rent a small boat and drift out into the water, but several spots have crabbing docks. Renting a boat with crab rings and bait costs about $35. A relatively new way to catch crabs uses a crab snare, which you attach to a fishing pole, allowing you to crab much in the way that you would fish. You can buy snares for about $10. There's a daily catch limit of 12 male crabs, each at least 5¾ inches. Female crabs, which have a roundish flap on their bellies as opposed to a narrow one, must be returned to the water immediately.

WHALE WATCHING This popular pastime takes one of two forms: You either stand at certain elevated spots along the shore with your fingers crossed, or you pay about $10 to get on a charter for an hour. The small town of Depoe Bay, between Newport and Lincoln City, has several operators and a year-round population of whales, though other spots along the coast also offer trips. If you'd rather not pay, try the lookout at Ecola State Park near Cannon Beach, the Depoe Bay Sea Wall, Yaquina Head in Newport, the Devil's Punch Bowl north of Florence, or Shore Acres State Park near Coos Bay. Go in the early morning and watch for the spray of water; if you're lucky, you'll see a whale breech (hurl itself out of the water, exposing nearly its whole body).

South Coast

Before the dust can settle on the California side of the border, travelers have begun the 122-mile journey along Oregon's rugged and spectacular south coast. It's easy to drive the route in a day, but don't even think of letting the scenery succumb to a windshield whiz-by; Oregon's south coast is no place to make good time. You might miss the bizarre and inspiring ("Was that Bob Hope?") rock formations fashioned over the centuries by the moody Pacific, or the pleasure of taking a stroll through the Shrader Old-Growth Forest in Gold Beach. And don't assume that because you can't see it from the road, it must not be there; U.S. 101 has a nasty way of hiding the coast's most striking scenery. Get onto the many little detour roads—they'll lead you to stunning, unobstructed viewpoints. For more information on coming and going, *see above.*

Eye on the Storm

Winter and spring on the coast can be downright nasty, but for some this is a definite plus. Raging storms make for dramatic coastal scenery—surf crashing onto rocks sending geysers high above the ocean, and finally the sun parting storm clouds and filling the sky with color. Given the right weather and high tide, you can storm-watch almost anywhere along the coast, but the best results are at elevated spots with lots of rocks down below. Try the seawall at Depoe Bay, or Shore Acres State Park near Charleston. It's also fun to see what goodies the storm brings in—like the glass fishing floats that sometimes fall off Japanese fishnets and wash ashore. Just be careful if you storm-watch from the beach; stay away from the logs washed ashore because waves can suddenly come in and move them.

If you're worried about money, you can do the south coast without breaking the bank. The only hostel around here is in Bandon, but abundant campgrounds often put you right next to the most scenic spots. Many of the south coast's pleasures—hiking, exploring tide pools, beachcombing, and storm and whale watching—won't cost you a thing. Food in restaurants can be expensive, especially if you order fish, but breakfasts are generally filling and cheap, and local markets come to the rescue for lunch and dinner. In the end, it may very well turn out that your biggest expense on the coast is developing all the photographs you've taken.

Brookings

With only a narrow stretch of the Chetco River to separate them, the towns of Brookings and Harbor are so close they're often grouped under the single heading Brookings. These Siamese cities don't provide a double dose of pleasure, though; in themselves, they don't even merit a visit. Harbor, on the south side of the river, has a busy but uninteresting port; and Brookings, on the north bank, is little more than a residential community surrounding a motel-filled strip of U.S. 101. Why, then, would you even consider a stop in Brookings-Harbor? The operative word is proximity: Just outside town you can kick up your hiking boots in some of Oregon's most rugged and spectacular coastal scenery, or drop a line in the well-stocked Chetco River. And Brookings-Harbor lies in what locals like to call the "Banana Belt," because of the 70° temperatures it can experience during any month of the year. The gentle breezes have brought retired people to the area in droves. While the local party scene may better suit your grandmother, Brookings is one hell of a place to spend some time outdoors.

VISITOR INFORMATION **Brookings-Harbor Chamber of Commerce.** *16330 Lower Harbor Rd., at the Harbor port, tel. 503/469–3181. Open summer, weekdays 9–5, Sat. 9–1.*

Chetco Ranger Station. They've got maps and information on the Siskiyou National Forest, which is just inland from the south Oregon coast. *555 5th St., Brookings, tel. 503/469–2196. Open weekdays 7:30–4:30.*

WHERE TO SLEEP Hands down, camping is the cheapest and most attractive budget option. Most of the town's rather dull (and expensive) motels lie along noisy U.S. 101. On the highway at the south end of town, the **Beaver State Motel** (437 Chetco Ave., tel. 503/469–5361) is the least expensive on the strip, with clean doubles for $28–$39 in winter and $42–$55 in summer. But if you don't mind paying for a heated indoor pool and sauna, the **Bonn Motel** (1216 Chetco Ave., on U.S. 101, tel. 503/469–2161) is your best bet. The rooms are big and clean and have free HBO, though you shouldn't be surprised if the specially designated nonsmoking rooms smell faintly of smoke. Winter rates of $34–$38 soar to $65–$85 during summer.

Chetco Inn. At this old-fashioned inn, where Clark Gable once stayed, you'll feel like you're sleeping in an antique country home, complete with fluffy heart-and-flower decorations in each creaky room. Though the effect may seem a bit hokey, this is the cheapest place in town, with doubles ranging from $27 in winter to $30–$50 in summer. *417 Fern St., tel. 503/469–5347. 1 block east of U.S. 101. 41 rooms, most with bath. Laundry. Wheelchair access.*

➤ **CAMPING** • **Harris Beach State Park.** For those who enjoy full camping amenities and the crowds of RVs that come with them, this lovely park provides easy access to sheer cliffs and unspoiled beaches. Some tent sites offer shady solitude. Fees are $15–$17, and reservations are advised. *2 mi north of Brookings on U.S. 101, tel. 503/469–2021. 156 sites, some hiker/biker sites. Showers. Wheelchair access.*

Loeb State Park. A stone's throw from the Chetco River, this wooded campground offers an opportunity to trek along some quality trails and feed the friendly fish (*see* Outdoor Activities, *below*). Southern sites offer spectacular views of the river and surrounding hills. All sites are $14. If Loeb is full, head about 7 miles east on Chetco River Road to the more primitive and cheaper **Little Redwood** campground ($5 per night), operated by the Chetco Ranger District. *Loeb State Park: Chetco River Rd., tel. 503/469–2021. From U.S. 101 just south of Brookings, 8 mi east on Chetco River Rd. 53 sites. Showers $2 for noncampers. Wheelchair access.*

FOOD **Marty's Pelican Bay Seafoods.** On the Harbor side of the river, this local favorite offers the winning combination of a lively atmosphere and colossal portions. Seafood (mainly shellfish) runs $5–$8, and the big and popular pelican burger (ham, beef, and two kinds of cheese) is $7.75. *16403 Lower Harbor Rd., tel. 503/469–7971. Open Mon.–Sat. 4 AM–9 PM, Sun. 5 AM–3 PM.*

Pickle Barrel Sandwich and Seafood Company. This restaurant serves both lunch and dinner, but most locals reserve their highest praise for the hearty sandwiches at lunch. Try the garbage grinder (small $4.25, large $5.45), a toasted sandwich with salami, ham, pepperoni, provolone, mozzarella, and several other less meaty goodies. *702 Chetco Ave., on U.S. 101 in Brookings, tel. 503/469–6401. Open Mon.–Sat. 11–3 and 5–9.*

Rubio's Mexican Restaurant. If you crave zesty Mexican food and a margarita to wash it down, this is the place for you. Full dinners run $7.25–$11, but if you eat à la carte you can knock about $3 off those prices. And if you don't mind traveling with a burdensome object (no offense to any traveling partners), you can even buy one of the piñatas you see hanging on the walls. *1136 Chetco Ave., on U.S. 101 in Brookings, tel. 503/469–4919. Open Mon.–Sat. 11–8.*

WORTH SEEING You might begin your tour of the Brookings area with a quick look at the **Chetco Valley Museum** (15461 Museum Rd., 2½ mi south of Chetco River, tel. 503/469–6651), on a hill overlooking U.S. 101 and a mere hundred feet from the largest cypress tree in the United States. (The tree may prove the highlight of your visit.) The exhibits, housed in a onetime inn built in 1857, focus on the pioneer history of the area; admission is $1. At the north end of the Chetco River bridge, you'll find the 26-acre **Azalea State Park** (off North Bank Rd. 3 blocks east of U.S. 101, tel. 503/238–7488, or 800/452–5687 in summer). If you come here between April and June, wild azaleas will be in bloom. From here take North Bank Road, which becomes Chetco River Road, to reach **Loeb State Park** (tel. 503/238–7488, or 800/452–5687 in summer), a good spot for hiking (*see* Outdoor Activities, *below*), picnicking, and swimming in the Chetco River.

If you love flowers, Azalea State Park is for you. If not, you'll exclaim an obligatory "How pretty!" and then quickly forget you ever went here.

About 2 miles north of Brookings on U.S. 101, **Harris Beach State Park** (tel. 503/469–2021) offers the northbound traveler a first extensive view of Oregon's south coast and proof that it wasn't overrated after all. From Harris Butte, a short walk from the parking lot, you can see 25 miles of rock-strewn shoreline. You can also walk down to the beach, explore tide pools, climb (at your own risk) the funky-looking rocks, and watch (with binoculars) as cormorants and pelicans fly around Oregon's largest coastal island—called, appropriately enough, Bird Island. This federally protected preserve is clearly visible from the parking lot, but there's no access to it.

Samuel H. Boardman State Park (tel. 503/238–7488, or 800/452–5687 in summer) begins about 4 miles north of Brookings and stretches 8 miles along the coast, with more than ten viewpoints off U.S. 101. The turnoff at **Indian Sands** (Mile 348.5) provides an especially clickworthy outlook. From here you can catch a trail to the sand dunes below (*see* Outdoor Activities, *below*). Ten miles past the last viewpoint in Boardman State Park, **Cape Sebastian** (tel. 503/238–7488, or 800/452–5687 in summer) sits 700 feet above the sea. A narrow road winds through dense pines to the north parking area, where you'll catch sweeping coastal views to the north and the south. A trail from this parking lot takes you down to the beach—about a 3-mile round-trip.

OUTDOOR ACTIVITIES Nearly all the state parks on the south coast have hiking trails, not to mention those along the beaches and in the Siskiyou National Forest. In Loeb State Park (*see* Worth Seeing, *above*), the easy ¾-mile **Riverview Nature Trail** follows the Chetco River, crossing the North Bank–Chetco River Road and connecting with the steeper but more beautiful **Redwood Nature Trail**, a wet and mossy 1-mile loop past towering redwoods. Brochures at the Riverview and Redwood trailheads provide a self-guided tour.

The short but mildly strenuous **Indian Sands Trail** begins at the south side of the Indian Sands parking lot in Samuel H. Boardman State Park (*see* Worth Seeing, *above*). Follow this trail to the sand dunes, at which point you can take a right and follow the wooden COAST TRAIL posts until you come to the edge of a cliff. Here you'll be rewarded with an impressive coastal view, complete with the sound of waves crashing against the rocks below—an excellent place to sit and wax philosophic.

Gold Beach

This small town about 30 miles north of Brookings has little charm or appeal. Nearly everything, from the pioneer cemetery to the high-school sports stadium, lies on U.S. 101, the main commercial strip. Do not pass go—head straight for the **Rogue River,** the main attraction in the vicinity. The Rogue's sands were once mined for gold, giving the town its name; the river has since become a gold mine for the companies that operate very popular jet-boat excursions through its scenic waters. If boating isn't your thing, you can hike or ride a horse along the river. The Gold Coast Ranger District Office (*see* Visitor Information, *below*) has information on scenic driving tours through the Siskiyou Forest and along the Rogue River.

VISITOR INFORMATION Gold Beach Visitor Center/Gold Coast Ranger District Office. *1225 S. Ellensburg Ave. Visitor Center: tel. 503/247–7526 or 800/525–2334. Ranger Office: tel. 503/247–6651. On U.S. 101 in the south end of town. Open weekdays 8–5.*

WHERE TO SLEEP There's nothing woodsy, or even grassy, about commercial Gold Beach, but at **Ireland's Rustic Lodges** (1120 S. Ellensburg Ave., tel. 503/247–7718) you'll find a property full of manicured lawns and pine lodges. You can choose spacious and comfortable rooms facing U.S. 101 ($35–$40), cottages ($45–$50), or oceanfront rooms with fireplaces ($55–$60). If all of Ireland's 40 rooms are booked, try **The Landing** (94749 Jerry's Flat Rd., on U.S. 101, tel. 503/247–6105), upstairs from the restaurant of the same name. The rooms are so close to the river that you can almost feel the spray of passing speedboats. Adequate but unspectacular singles with traditional country-style furniture and wood-beam ceilings run $25; similarly decorated doubles go for $30.

➤ **CAMPING** • **Quosatana.** Near the Rogue River, which you can hear behind the trees, this clean Siskiyou National Forest campground offers widely spaced sites ($7) and easy access to good fishing. *Tel. 503/247–6651. About 14 mi NE of Gold Beach on Jerry's Flat Rd. 43 sites. Flush toilets, drinking water. Open Apr.–Oct.*

FOOD The Golden Egg. Overlooking the Gold Beach High School football field (Go Panthers!), this casual little restaurant is your best bet for breakfast and lunch. Omelets ($5–$8) are made to order with anything from crab and shrimp to green chiles and avocado. Burgers and sandwiches go for around $5. *710 S. Ellensburg Ave., on U.S. 101, tel. 503/247–7528. Open daily 6 AM–3 PM.*

Port Hole Café. Decorated with the portholes promised in its name, this café serves huge salads ($7) with names like the Barge, the Galleon, and the Mayflower, as well as sandwiches and hamburgers ($3.50–$6). If the food isn't enough to lure you in, come for the view of the port. *Port of Gold Beach, tel. 503/247–7411. Open daily 11–8.*

OUTDOOR ACTIVITIES If you have the money, you might consider the obligatory boat or raft excursion along the Rogue River. A six-hour, 64-mile trip on a jet boat costs about $30 with either **Jerry's Rogue Jets** (tel. 503/247–4571 or 800/451–3645) or **Rogue River Mail Boat Hydro-Jets** (94294 Rogue River Rd., tel. 503/247–7033 or 800/458–3511). If you choose the latter, you'll actually get to join the crew as they deliver the mail to the little river community of Agness.

➤ **HIKING** • For one of the most scenic hikes in the area, take the **Shrader Old-Growth Trail.** This fairly easy 1-mile loop winds past tremendous moss-covered Douglas firs, Port Orford cedars, and gentle streams. To reach the trail from Gold Beach, take Jerry's Flat Road 9½ miles to the well-marked turnoff road, which begins just past the entrance to the Siskiyou National Forest. The trail starts exactly 2 miles up this winding gravel road.

➢ **HORSEBACK RIDING** • **Indian Creek Trail Rides** (Jerry's Flat Rd., ½ mi from U.S. 101 along Rogue River, tel. 503/247–7704) leads guided tours over coastal mountains. One-hour trips cost $18, two-hour trips $30.

➢ **CLAMMING AND CRABBING** • **Rogue Outdoors** (560 N. Ellensburg Ave., on U.S. 101, tel. 503/247–7142) rents clam shovels for $1–$3 and crab rings for $3. If you're a novice, the owner would be more than happy to offer some friendly advice.

Port Orford

Port Orford is small—so small, in fact, that it doesn't have a signal light, so small that you can almost drive through it without even knowing you were there. Were it not for an arresting view of the coast and Battle Rock (see Worth Seeing, below) from U.S. 101, you probably wouldn't even think to stop your car. But Port Orford has more than a roadside view. For its size, it offers a surprisingly large number of crafts galleries; as fishing and logging jobs continue to disappear you can expect to see more of these galleries popping up. If art isn't your thing, head over to the harbor and watch boats being hoisted by crane out of the water (wind conditions don't allow them to be safely moored at sea).

As the most westerly city in the contiguous United States, Port Orford gets a tremendous amount of rain each winter and a great deal of wind each summer. It is definitely the bad-hair capital of the Oregon coast.

VISITOR INFORMATION **Port Orford Information Center.** *520 Jefferson St., by Battle Rock Park, tel. 503/332–8055. Open daily 9–5.*

WHERE TO SLEEP Budget travelers will like Port Orford's accommodations—well, the prices, at least. The **Port Orford Motel** (1034 Oregon St., on U.S. 101, tel. 503/332–1685), an ugly blue motel on the north end of town, has small but adequate doubles, some with kitchens, for $29. Just hope the person before you didn't smoke cigars. The L-shaped **Shoreline Motel** (206 6th St., across from Battle Rock Park, tel. 503/332–2903) could easily have had a great view of the ocean but doesn't because it was built with the L facing the wrong way. Small but clean doubles run $28 during the off-season and $38 in summer. Across the street from the Shoreline Motel, the **Battle Rock Motel** (136 S. 6th St., on U.S. 101S, tel. 503/332–7331) actually does have an ocean view and, as its name suggests, a view of Battle Rock as well. Doubles similar to the Shoreline's in quality will run you $25–$35, depending on the season and the room.

➢ **CAMPING** • **Humbug Mountain State Park.** When Captain William Tichenor got lost here in the good old days, he probably used a couple of stronger expletives to describe his plight than the park's name suggests. Fortunately, Tichenor's bad experience doesn't reflect on the quality of this clean, well-located campground. Sites ($15–$17) may not be as secluded or woodsy as those at inland campgrounds, but they're right next to the challenging Humbug Mountain Trail (see Worth Seeing, below). *U.S. 101, about 5 mi south of Port Orford at Mile 307, tel. 503/332–6774. 108 sites. Open mid-Apr.–Oct.*

Cape Blanco State Park. This clean, well-maintained campground offers $15–$17 sites sectioned off by trees and shrubs, with lots of room for RVs. A short road from the camp leads down to the wide and lonely beach below. *Tel. 503/332–6774. From U.S. 101 4½ mi north of Port Orford, take Cape Blanco State Park Rd. for 4 mi. 58 sites. Showers.*

FOOD Port Orford has very few restaurants, budget or otherwise. If you're going to stay here for any extended period of time, consider buying groceries at **Buck's Sentry Market** (1555 Oregon St., tel. 503/332–1185).

Whale Cove. In addition to serving the best food in Port Orford, this establishment continually demonstrates the relevance of its name; it's not unusual to see binocular-equipped patrons looking out the windows in the hopes of spotting a gray. If you've come unprepared, the owner may lend you a pair of binoculars. Chicken and seafood dinners run $7–$10; a burger at lunch is less than $5. *U.S. 101 across from Battle Rock Park, tel. 503/332–7575. Open winter, daily 8–8; summer, daily 7 AM–9 PM.*

Wheelhouse Restaurant. Big portions and reasonable prices distinguish this friendly, if decoratively uninspired, restaurant across the street from the Whale Cove. You can get an omelet with a Frisbee-size hotcake for less than $5. *521 Jefferson St., at Battle Rock Park, tel. 503/332–1605. Open Mon.–Sat. 6 AM–8 PM, Sun. 7–7.*

WORTH SEEING The first thing you see when you enter the city from the south is **Battle Rock,** the site of a battle between white settlers and the local Tututni Indians in 1851. Make your way to the top of the rock for an impressive view of the south coast. For another good coastal lookout head to the Coast Guard station in **Heads Wayside State Park** (tel. 503/238–7488 or 800/452–5687); go two blocks west on 9th Street and follow the signs. A quarter-mile paved trail leads through a wooded area to the edge of a bluff that juts out over a churning lagoon.

North of Port Orford, a well-marked road leads 5 miles west from U.S. 101 to **Cape Blanco State Park** (tel. 503/332–6774), the westernmost point in Oregon. Here forests of Sitka spruce border the sea, driftwood clutters the beach, and sea otters and gray whales patrol the rocky coastline. Oregon's oldest working lighthouse, a 59-foot white tower built in 1870, perches above the ocean. To explore the teeming tide pools below, look for the ½-mile **Coast Trail** (marked by a post) on the right side of the road as you approach the lighthouse, about ⅛ mile past the campground turnoff. Pay attention; this trail is easy to miss.

One of the most popular—and challenging—hikes in the area follows the 3-mile **Humbug Mountain Trail** (trailhead at Mile 306.5) past tall rhododendrons up to a coastal lookout. The view from the top is nice, but for most it doesn't justify the toil of the journey.

Bandon

Unlike its neighbors to the south, Bandon is more than a glorified strip of U.S. 101. To get to where it's at in this town 31 miles north of Port Orford, you have to leave the highway and explore **Beach Loop Drive,** at the traffic light on U.S. 101. The road takes you past **Face Rock,** which looks strikingly like a face, and **Cat and Kittens rocks,** which look almost nothing like a cat and kittens. Bandon's other center of action is the **Old Town,** sandwiched between 1st and 2nd streets along the Coquille River. The site of the original business district, Old Town was destroyed by fire in 1936 and reconstructed in the 1980s. All the shops have the requisite wooden exteriors, but the effect is not nearly as cheesy as you'd expect. Make a point of visiting **Cranberry Sweets** (cnr of 1st and Chicago Sts., tel. 800/527–5748) for inventive cranberry candies and chocolate in unusual flavors—at $6.50 a pound, the cinnamon chocolate may just be worth the splurge.

You have to give Bandon credit for resisting the temptation to spell the "Old" in Old Town with an "e" at the end.

Across the Coquille River from the Old Town, **Bullards Beach State Park** has a long beach and an octagonal lighthouse built in 1896. Don't bother wandering inside; there's not much to see. Instead, watch the waves crash against the jetty right outside the lighthouse. Don't be surprised if you see a seal or two sticking its head out of the water to figure out exactly what kind of creature you are. On the return trip to Bandon (south on U.S. 101), stop at the **Bandon Cheddar Cheese Factory** (680 E. 2nd St., just north of Old Town, tel. 800/548–8961). Although watching cheese being made through a gift-shop window is not all that exciting, hungry visitors can take advantage of free samples. Less mature travelers (especially kids) may love a visit with the lions, tigers, bears, chimps, and other creatures of the wild at the **West Coast Game Park Safari** (Rte. 1, tel. 503/347–3106), 10 miles south of Bandon on U.S. 101. Its petting zoo offers hands-on fun, especially when the bear and leopard cubs are around. Admission is $6.

VISITOR INFORMATION **Bandon Chamber of Commerce.** The helpful staff can give you loads of brochures and information on the whole coast. *300 S.E. 2nd St., at Chicago Ave., tel. 503/347–9616. Open May–Oct., daily 10–4:30; Nov.–Apr., daily 10–5.*

Coquille Chamber of Commerce. Get details here on the annual melodrama festival that runs from Memorial Day through Labor Day. *119 N. Birch St., tel. 503/396–3414. Take Rte. 42S inland from Bandon for 17 mi. Open weekdays 1–4.*

WHERE TO SLEEP You'll find the usual roadside motels along U.S. 101, especially around the junction with Route 42S. Travelers with more to spend can stay at the motels on Beach Loop Drive, most of which overlook the ocean. Your best bet, though, is the **HI Sea Star** (375 2nd St., in Old Town, tel. 503/347–9632). This hostel is stocked with skylights, a wood-burning stove, and just enough knotty pine to make you feel like a member of the Swiss Family Robinson. At about $12 per night for HI members and $15 for nonmembers, this is the best deal on Oregon's south coast. Rooms for couples are available for about $2 extra per person; all guests share a well-equipped kitchen, a clean bathroom, and a woodsy common lounge. Reservations are advised in summer.

If you don't mind splurging a bit for the best view in town, consider the **Sunset Motel** (1755 Beach Loop Dr., tel. 503/347–2453, or 800/842–2407 for reservations). From here, you look out on magnificent crags at the ocean's edge and at the eerily human Face Rock. Rooms with a view start at around $58, but for $38 you can get an economy room without a view that's still only steps away from the scenery. Other amenities include laundry facilities and an indoor Jacuzzi.

➤ **CAMPING** • **Bullards Beach State Park.** This sprawling campground at the mouth of the Coquille River puts you right near Bandon and offers a plethora of fishing, crabbing, beachcombing, and hiking opportunities. Though you'll find lots of RVs here, the $16–$17 sites offer some measure of privacy. If you don't want to pay for RV amenities you'll never use, try the **Horse Camp** a little farther down the road, which has eight primitive sites for $9. *Bullards Beach: Tel. 503/347–2209. 1 mi north of Bandon on U.S. 101. 192 sites. Showers.*

FOOD Finding a cheap and decent restaurant in Bandon is no easy task, especially around dinnertime. If take-out food works for you, try the **Fish Market** (249 1st St., tel. 503/347–4282) by the boat basin in Old Town. Healthy portions of fish-and-chips go for less than $5, and nothing on the menu is over $7. The market closes on Wednesday, but it's open 11–6 every other day.

Lord Bennett's Restaurant and Lounge. This upscale restaurant is no place for budget travelers to go for dinner, but at lunch there are few places better. Not only do you get a knockout view of the ocean and Face Rock, you also get something almost unheard of for the budget traveler: a cloth napkin! Scallops cost $6 and the crab sandwich is $7. *1695 Beach Loop Dr., tel. 503/347–3663. Wheelchair access. Open 11–3 and 5–10.*

Minute Café. This Old Town café serves tasty greasy-spoon fare that attracts a local following. A huge slice of fresh strawberry pie (in season) will set you back $2. As long as you skip the grilled oysters ($8.50 a plate), you can do dinner for about $7. *145 N. 2nd St., in Old Town, tel. 503/347–2707. Open 5:30 AM–7 PM.*

OUTDOOR ACTIVITIES Those seeking salmon in the Coquille need not closet their rods at the end of summer; runs continue through October 15th. Other fish in these fecund waters range from striped bass and rainbow trout to shad and perch. For $4, you can rent a rod and reel at **Port O'Call** (*see below*). The staff can also give you seasonal information on the best fishing spots.

➤ **HORSEBACK RIDING** • **Bandon Riding Stables** (Beach Loop Drive, just north of Face Rock, tel. 503/347–3423) offers trips along the beach; you'll pay about $20 for one hour, $25 for 1½ hours.

➤ **CLAMMING AND CRABBING** • Mud clams dominate the scene at Bullards Beach; if you're after crabs, check out the Coquille River near town. For clam shovels and crab rings at $4 per day, and a little friendly advice, try **Port O'Call** (155 1st St., at Baltimore St., tel. 503/347–2875).

NEAR BANDON

SEVEN DEVILS ROAD If you want to escape U.S. 101 for a while, take this detour to the little fishing town of Charleston, just west of Coos Bay and North Bend (*see below*). On the way, you'll pass forests, clear-cut valleys, farmland, and the South Slough National Estuarine

Research Reserve (*see* Worth Seeing, in Charleston, *below*). You can get directly onto Seven Devils Road from U.S. 101 a few miles north of Bandon, but this isn't advised unless you have a fondness for narrow gravel roads. Instead, drive a few miles farther on U.S. 101 until you see a sign (just north of Mile 253) pointing to Charleston. After about 6 miles, this turnoff becomes Seven Devils Road—but without the gravel.

Charleston

Take one whiff of Charleston and you'll know the extent of this little town's fishing industry. Unfortunately, as the fishing trade declines in this part of the country, the town's future becomes more and more uncertain. One thing that's still true is that Charleston is a peaceful place to stay for those trying to avoid the maddening (relatively speaking) crowds of Coos Bay and North Bend. And staying in Charleston will put you near the fascinating South Slough National Estuarine Research Reserve and the beautiful Shore Acres State Park (*see* Worth Seeing, *below*). Even for a person who doesn't like fish, that's not a bad silver lining.

VISITOR INFORMATION Charleston Visitor Center. *Boat Basin Dr. and Cape Arago Hwy., east of the South Slough Bridge, tel. 503/888–2311. Open daily 10–5.*

WHERE TO SLEEP Captain John's Motel. This sprawling motel a short walk from the marina is popular with fishermen docking in Charleston. Hospitable owners George and Danuta Drodzdowicz offer exceptionally clean and spacious rooms and a complimentary breakfast of banana bread and coffee. They'll also tell you all you need to know about Charleston and Coos Bay. Doubles rent for $41–$48, depending on the season and the size of your bed. *8061 Kingfisher Dr., at Boat Basin Dr., tel. 503/888–4041. From Cape Arago Hwy., turn north onto Boat Basin Dr. and go about ⅛ mi. 47 rooms. Fish-cleaning facilities.*

➤ **CAMPING** • At **Bastendorf Beach Park** (Cape Arago Hwy., about 2 mi from Charleston, tel. 503/888–5353), hoopsters will enjoy the basketball court and kids will dig the playground. Everyone else can picnic overlooking the ocean and sleep in secluded sites ($11–$13). Even so, **Sunset Bay State Park** (Cape Arago Hwy., tel. 503/888–4902), a mile west, has more trees and is just plain more attractive. It's 3 miles west of Charleston and 1 mile east of Shore Acres State Park; nearby lies a sheltered cove. Sites run $15–$17.

FOOD The food selection in Charleston is not unlike the town itself: very small. Either stick with markets or try the **Sea Basket** (Charleston Boat Basin, tel. 503/888–5711), a two-room fast-food joint on the water that's all about fish. It's cluttered with nets and fishing photos, the signs of a serious fisherman's hangout; you may be tempted to clank hooks with those who surround you. As might be expected, you can get hearty fish-and-chips for under $6; a clam chowder and salad bar goes for about $5.

WORTH SEEING The **South Slough National Estuarine Research Reserve** is one of the few undeveloped parts of the Coos Estuary (where the river meets the sea). The mix of fresh and salt water supports an ecosystem of plants (sedges and pickleweed among them) and animals (beavers, bobcat, blue heron, and elk). Several hiking trails, including the interesting **Estuary Study Trail** (*see* Outdoor Activities, *below*), lead around nearly 5,000 acres of land; and an interpretive center high above the estuary offers films, slide shows, guided walks, and several exhibits on estuarine ecology. *Tel. 503/888–5558. 4 mi south of Charleston on Seven Devils Road. Admission free. Interpretive center open Sept.–May, weekdays 8:30–4:30; June–Aug., daily 8:30–4:30.*

Four miles north of South Slough, Seven Devils Road meets the **Cape Arago Highway.** A right turn here takes you into Charleston, at the mouth of the estuary, while a left leads out toward the rugged coast. You might stop first for a picnic at **Sunset Bay State Park** (tel. 503/888–4902), situated in a serene cove protected by sandstone cliffs. The water here is unusually warm for the coast; you can actually swim in it for a minute or two before your legs go numb. About a mile north of Sunset Beach is **Shore Acres State Park** (tel. 503/888–3732), the former estate of lumber baron Louis J. Simpson, where for a $3 admission fee you can check out an observation shelter overlooking the raging Pacific, terraced sandstone cliffs that descend to tide pools, surf thundering against natural reefs, and an impeccable botanical garden. A trail from the garden leads down to a secluded cove with a white-sand beach. The park is open daily dawn to dusk. Less than 2 miles farther on the Cape Arago Highway is **Cape Arago State Park** (tel. 503/888–4902), which has more spectacular coastal views and lots of sea lions barking and basking on the rocks below. Here the highway ends and loops back on itself, taking you past Charleston to the towns of Coos Bay and North Bend.

Picnic tables overlooking the water at Cape Arago State Park make for an ideal lunch spot, but keeping your napkin from flying off the table in the ever-present wind may become the bane of your existence.

OUTDOOR ACTIVITIES If you don't mind paying $55 for six hours of deep-sea fishing, contact **Betty Kay Charters** (7960 Kingfisher Dr., at the Charleston boat basin, tel. 503/888–9021 or 800/752–6303). They also lead whale-watching trips. You can rent crab rings ($3 each) at **Bob's Sport Fishing,** which is sharing space with Betty Kay until they relocate elsewhere. Call to verify the location (tel. 503/888–4241).

➤ **HIKING** • For unusual topography, try the South Slough National Estuarine Reserve (*see* Worth Seeing, *above*). The dinky 10-minute trail from the Interpretive Center won't do much for you, but the **Wasson Creek** and **Winchester Creek trails,** both just under a mile round-trip, pass marshlands, Sitka spruce, beaver dams, and—if you're lucky—an elk herd. The best hike, though, is the 3-mile (round-trip) **Estuary Study Trail,** which takes you past all the estuary habitats: uplands, salt marsh, tide flats, and open channel. The walk itself should take less than an hour and a half, but don't forget to account for the hangout factor—you'll definitely want to spend some time at the bottom by the mud flats watching for birds and other critters.

Coos Bay and North Bend

You don't have to be an environmentalist to recognize the significance of the wood-chip "mountains" along U.S. 101 in Coos Bay or the huge stockpile of logs along the water near the McCullough Bridge. It's unmistakably clear to all who visit this wooden wonderland that the logging industry plays a major role in the economies of Coos Bay and North Bend. It's also clear, however, that as logging opportunities diminish, these adjacent towns will have to rely on tourism for a financial boost. As of yet, they haven't quite figured out how to bring the tourists in—other than to tout their proximity to the Oregon Dunes, which begin just north of town. Fortunately for Coos Bay and North Bend, that's a powerful lure.

VISITOR INFORMATION **Coos Bay Chamber of Commerce.** *50 Central St., tel. 503/269–0215 or 800/824–8486. On U.S. 101 downtown. Open weekdays 9–5, Sat. 10–4.*

North Bend Visitor Information Center. *1380 Sherman Ave., on U.S. 101, tel. 503/756–4613. Open daily 9–4 .*

WHERE TO SLEEP Virtually all the cheap lodging is along the highway, so you have to contend with franchises and the sights and smells of heavy industry. You're better off finding a campground, or heading to Captain John's in Charleston (*see above*). If you're stuck, try the **Motel 6** in Coos Bay (1445 N. Bayshore Dr., on U.S. 101, tel. 503/267–7171). The rooms here are larger than those of a standard Motel 6, and you'll find a Jacuzzi, sauna, and weight room. Singles run $30–$36 and doubles $36–$42.

If you want to avoid the noise of U.S. 101, head straight for the **Lombard Bed and Breakfast** in North Bend (2310 Lombard St., west of Broadway btw Newmark St. and Virginia Ave., tel. 503/756–3857). It's not an old Victorian house, but the comfortable, unpretentious home has a pretty garden, and you get full breakfast, as well as interesting conversation with the down-to-earth hostess, Charlotte Skinner, an ex–Peace Corps volunteer. Best of all, the rates are phenomenally low for a B&B: $30 for the single room and $35 for the double.

FOOD **Blue Heron Bistro.** With a sloping wood-paneled ceiling, foreign beer paraphernalia on the walls, and classical music in the background, this place has some heavy-duty character. And if you think the decor sounds good, wait until you try the homemade breads, pastries, and pastas. Prices, however, tend to be a bit steep; dinners run $7–$12. For lunch, try the blackened snapper on a homemade onion roll ($6.50). *100 Commercial St., on U.S. 101 in Coos Bay, tel. 503/267–3933. Open Sat.–Thurs. 8:30 AM–9 PM, Fri. 8:30 AM–10 PM.*

Gussie's Place. This 24-hour restaurant and lounge is *the* nightspot for the Coos Bay/North Bend rock-and-roll crowd. The restaurant in front has filling chicken, steak, and seafood dinners ($7–$10), and the popular lounge in back features local rock bands (no cover), a dance floor, and a bar. A room off the lounge has video poker and blackjack tables. *1088 Newmark St., west of Ocean Blvd. in Coos Bay, tel. 503/888–2022.*

Virginia Street Diner. Neon abounds at this spacious '50s-style diner about ¼ mile from U.S. 101. The theme is overdone, but the food is good and cheap. Take a seat at a booth and enjoy chicken-fried steak ($5.50) with a milkshake or a Green River (7-Up with ice cream). Most dinners cost $5–$6. *1430 Virginia St., North Bend, tel. 503/756–3475. From U.S. 101, west on Virginia St. Open daily 6 AM–10 PM.*

WORTH SEEING Coos Bay and North Bend (which, along with Charleston, are often referred to as the "Bay Area") make up the largest population center on the Oregon Coast. But despite the size, there aren't a whole lot of things to do within city limits. If you want to see work by regional artists, pay a visit to the unexciting **Coos Art Museum** (235 Anderson Ave., Coos Bay, tel. 503/267–3901). The **Coos County Historical Society Museum** (1220 Sherman Ave., on U.S. 101 in North Bend, tel. 503/756–6320) offers history buffs a standard mix of Native American and pioneer exhibits, as well as an old locomotive once used by the Coos Bay Lumber Company. If you've spent nights dreaming of a set of myrtlewood golf clubs, now is the time to check out the **House of Myrtlewood** (1125 S. 1st St., off U.S. 101 at the south end of Coos Bay, tel. 503/267–7804); they offer a free tour of the factory behind their store. But don't waste much time in this industrial area—head instead for the dunes (*see below*). **Spinreel Dune Buggy Rentals** (9122 Wildwood Dr., 11 mi north of North Bend, tel. 503/759–3313) rents Odysseys, a type of one-person buggy, for one hour at $30; the second hour is $25.

Oregon Dunes

Like the Christmas present you find only as you take down the tree, Oregon's dunes, which begin just north of North Bend, hit right when you begin to feel like you've seen it all. Thousands of years ago, glacial activity flattened this landscape, leaving the area susceptible to large accumulations of sand. Local rivers deposited their sediment, winds spread the deposits eastward, and in the end dune buggies were formed. Actually, great sand dunes were the result, but the dune buggies may seem a natural part of the scenery if you're traveling near North Bend or Florence, where off-road vehicles (ORVs) are permitted. The Oregon Dunes National Recreation Area stretches for 41 miles between these two cities, though, and once you get out a bit, the dunes cease to make that annoying revving sound. From Spinreel to Tugman State Park and from the Umpqua River to the Siltcoos Recreation Area, ORV's are forbidden, allowing regular folks the chance to peacefully follow designated hiking trails through the dunes. These windswept sand hills can extend several miles eastward, encompassing lakes, shallow creeks, wind-sculpted trees, and changing vegetation.

Of course, you'd hardly know any of this existed if you stayed on the highway, which hides the dunes just to the west and makes the area seem primarily forested. Fortunately, several campground turn-offs and the **Oregon Dunes Overlook** (Mile 200.7) provide nice views and quick access to the sand. On the east side of U.S. 101, you'll find scenic lakes with camping facilities and hiking trails. These are sources for trout, bass, and perch—and good swimming holes as well.

Most of the action centers around the Winchester Bay/Reedsport area, where fishing occupies much of the work force. If you want to stay the night, camping is your best budget option, though you should avoid the campgrounds in areas that allow ORVs unless you don't mind the raucous crowds that come with them. As for food, the Oregon Dunes area offers little. In Florence (*see below*), the pickings are much less slim, so consider eating there. For transportation information, *see* Basics, *above.*

VISITOR INFORMATION Oregon Dunes National Recreation Area Information Center. This center, run by the U.S. Forest Service, provides exhaustive information about the dunes and lots of brochures and trail maps. Ask to see the 20-minute video on local wildlife and the natural history of the dunes. *855 U.S. 101, tel. 503/271–3611, South of Umpqua River in Reedsport, next to Lower Umpqua Chamber of Commerce. Open Memorial Day–Labor Day, weekdays 8–6, weekends 9–6; Labor Day–Memorial Day, weekdays 8–4:30.*

Umpqua Lighthouse Coastal Visitor Center. *Umpqua Lighthouse Rd., ½ mi west of U.S. 101, tel. 503/271–4631.*

Lakeside

About 11 miles north of the Oregon Dunes National Recreation Area (the *other* NRA) is the turnoff for the tiny town of Lakeside; follow 8th Street east for a mile into town. Lakeside has only one attraction in its immediate vicinity, but it's an appealing one: **Tenmile Lakes.** This pristine, bass-filled body of water spreads its tentacles in many directions—it's got an amazing 178 miles of shoreline. Most of the lake is accessible only by boat (*see* Outdoor Activities, *below*).

VISITOR INFORMATION Lakeside Chamber of Commerce. *200 N. 8th St., tel. 503/759–3011. Open weekdays 8–5.*

WHERE TO SLEEP Budget travelers should immediately head to North Eel Creek Campground (*see below*), one of the best between North Bend and Florence. If you have an aversion to camping, your only alternative is the **Lakeshore Lodge** (290 S. 8th St., by the Lakeside Marina, tel. 503/759–3161). With a restuarant and lounge, this large establishment caters to the regulars who come to Tenmile Lakes to fish and sail. All the rooms have lake views; singles start at $41, doubles at $47.

➤ **CAMPING** • **North Eel Creek Campground.** Because this section of the dunes prohibits off-road vehicles, this campground is much more peaceful and sedate than other Oregon Dunes NRA campgrounds. It also puts you right at the Umpqua Dunes trailhead. Many of the sites ($10) offer total seclusion, and one backs right up against a big sand hill. *½ mi north of Lakeside on U.S. 101, tel. 503/759–3692. 52 sites. Flush toilets, drinking water. Open all year.*

FOOD There are very few restaurants in town and none is anything to write home about. Check out Lakeside's only market, **McKay's** (200 S. 8th St., at Park St., tel. 503/759–3411), instead.

OUTDOOR ACTIVITIES Don't miss the 2½-mile **Umpqua Dunes Trail,** accessible from North Eel Creek Campground (*see above*), the best of all trails for those in search of a Saharalike experience. Here you'll find the tallest dunes in the area—some as high as 400 feet. The first ¼ mile takes you past a wooded area that opens up into a sea of sand. The trail isn't marked on the open sand, so you have to walk up the highest dune to get your bearings. Route markers will only become visible once you reach the north end of a tree island to the west.

➤ **BOATING** • At Tenmile Lakes, the **Lakeside Marina** (end of 8th St., 1 mi east of U.S. 101, tel. 503/759–3312) has canoes at $5 for the first hour and $2 per hour thereafter. You can also rent a motorboat for $6 an hour (two-hour minimum) or $30 a day.

Winchester Bay

Winchester Bay is reeling, but not in the fishing way. To the contrary, recent state legislation, in an attempt to preserve the dwindling salmon population, has declared a statewide ban on all salmon fishing beginning each year in June. Unfortunately for those who work here, that's right when the salmon arrive. The effect of the ban on a town that relies heavily on salmon fishing is obvious and devastating. Most of the charter-boat companies that used to flourish here have closed up shop, and many people are wondering how long they'll have their jobs. That said, there are still plenty of reasons to visit Winchester Bay. For one, the town is a mile or so from some of

OREGON COAST

Oregon's best dune-buggy terrain. Also, you can visit the **Umpqua Lighthouse,** part of a state park of the same name. The red-capped lighthouse is closed to the public, but from its vantage point high on a hill overlooking Winchester Bay you get long-range views of the ocean, the mouth of the Umpqua, and sometimes even whales. As for would-be anglers, you may not catch salmon, but as they say, there are other fish in the sea.

Why the heck do signs referring to Winchester Bay and Salmon Harbor always seem to lead to the same place? Well, technically Salmon Harbor is the part right along the water, and Winchester Bay refers to the residential area beyond. A vote to merge the two sections under one name went nowhere; both names have loyal supporters.

VISITOR INFORMATION Winchester Bay doesn't have its own chamber of commerce, but you can get information on this and the surrounding area at the **Reedsport Chamber of Commerce** just 4 miles away (*see* Reedsport, *below*).

WHERE TO SLEEP Your options are limited. You can always find a clean room at the **Harbor View Motel** (540 Beach Blvd., tel. 503/271–3352), across from the harbor at 4th Street. If you don't mind falling asleep to a foghorn's lullaby, join the regular fishing clientele, who are attracted by the lowest rates in town—$26 for a single, $29–$34 for a double.

FOOD Winchester Bay is yet another small coastal town with little in the way of budget dining. Before you turn to nibbling your nails for nourishment, check out **Pizza Ray's and Suzy's,** on the harbor two blocks from U.S. 101 (705 Beach Blvd., tel. 503/271–2431). This inexpensive pizza parlor is part of a coastal chain; there's another branch in Reedsport. The tasty mini pizza (good for one person) costs only $3.75–$4.50, depending on the number of toppings.

OUTDOOR ACTIVITIES If you haven't hit the sand yet, all is not lost. **Dunes Odyssey Rentals** (75303 U.S. 101, at Salmon Harbor Blvd., tel. 503/271–4011) rents Odysseys and Quads for $30 for the first hour and $5 less for each subsequent hour ($15 from the fourth hour on).

➤ **CRABBING** • The crabbing dock is on Salmon Harbor Drive (Route 251), between Winchester Bay and the Umpqua Lighthouse. You can rent rings for $2 a day at **Stockade Tackle Shop** (cnr of 4th St. and Beach Blvd., tel. 503/271–3800).

➤ **FISHING** • The lakes provide some of the best fishing in the area. Bass, perch, and trout populate these waters, but you won't find a place that rents rods. If you don't have your own and feel like spending some money, try an ocean-bound charter from **Gee Gee, Inc.** (465 Beach Blvd., tel. 503/271–3152), which has five-hour trips for $50.

Reedsport

Reedsport, a logging town just north of Winchester Bay, could easily be dismissed as just another characterless coastal strip town. Look a little closer, though, and you'll see that it's making a valiant attempt to distinguish itself. For several years Reedsport has been home to the *Hero,* the first large Antarctic research vessel ever built, which was in service from 1968 to 1985. In 1993 Reedsport capitalized on the boat's presence by building the **Umpqua Discovery Center** (409 Riverfront Way, take U.S. 38 to 3rd St., tel. 503/271–4816) to display exhibits on the Antarctic. Along with the Discovery Center came a couple of restaurants, and presto, Reedsport has an attractive, albeit tiny, boardwalk on the river. The tours of the *Hero,* which cost $3 and are the only way to get on board, are particularly interesting because the last crew left almost everything behind.

About 3 miles east of town on Route 38, the **Dean Creek Elk Viewing Area** is home to about 120 Roosevelt elk, who roam the meadows across the road from the Umpqua River. Weighing in at up to 1,200 pounds, these elk, the largest land animals in Oregon, are hard to miss. Viewing stations and turnoffs have been set up to facilitate gazing. The drive to and beyond the viewing area along Route 38 is quite beautiful, with the Umpqua River coming right up to the road in some places.

VISITOR INFORMATION Reedsport/Lower Umpqua Chamber of Commerce. *Cnr of U.S. 101 and Rte. 38, tel. 503/271–3495, or 800/247–2155 in OR. Open weekdays 9–5, Sat. 10–5; also Sun. 10–5 in summer.*

WHERE TO SLEEP Salbasgeon Inn. All rooms at this out-of-the-way inn have knockout views of the Umpqua. You can play horseshoes or badminton in the enormous backyard along the river; fish for salmon, steelhead, and perch; or enjoy the forests of Franklin Ridge opposite the river. Spotless doubles begin around $50 in winter and go up to $65–$70 in summer. The only drawback is the sound of an occasional logging truck barreling down Route 38. *45209 Rte. 38, tel. 503/271–2025. 7 mi east of Reedsport. 12 rooms, 4 kitchen suites. Wheelchair access.*

Salty Seagull Motel. From the outside, the rooms at this roadside motel seem deceptively small. Most guests are pleasantly surprised to find each room equipped with a bedroom, a living room, two TVs, and a full kitchen. Units run $35 in winter and $50 in summer. *1806 U.S. 101, tel. 503/271–3729. Just over the Scholfield Creek Bridge from downtown. 6 rooms. Coin laundry.*

Tropicana Motel. Despite the name, there are no palm trees here and you don't get free orange juice in the morning. What you get is a clean, comfortable room for $32 in winter, $40 in summer. The motel also has a swimming pool, though it's so small its looks more like a cold Jacuzzi. *1593 U.S. 101, tel. 503/271–3671. Just east of Winchester Ave. 41 rooms. Luggage storage, pool, whirlpool.*

➤ **CAMPING** • **Tahkenitch Campground.** This shady, popular campground just across U.S. 101 from Tahkenitch Lake is also the trailhead for the Tahkenitch Dunes and Threemile Lake trails (*see* Outdoor Activities, *below*). The sites ($10) are refreshingly free of dune-buggy people. *Tel. 503/271–3611. 7 mi north of Reedsport on U.S. 101. 35 sites.*

FOOD Don's Diner and Ice Cream Parlor. This popular restaurant serves hamburgers and the occasional sandwich. Nothing on the menu is expensive: The sandwich, salad, and pie combo costs only $5. If you have room for more, take a few steps to the ice cream parlor and do some real cholesterol damage. *2115 Winchester Ave., tel. 503/271–2032. Open daily 10–10.*

Windjammer Restaurant. This shipshape restaurant—note the fleet of meticulously crafted boat models and the shipwreck-theme placemats—serves reliable seafood at moderate prices. Chow down on spicy catfish fillet ($7.50) or top-sirloin steak ($9). *1281 Hilway Ave., off U.S. 101, tel. 503/271–5415. Open daily 6 AM–9 PM.*

OUTDOOR ACTIVITIES The **Tahkenitch Fishing Village** (10 mi north of Reedsport on U.S. 101, tel. 503/271–5222) rents canoes for four hours ($10) and for the day ($15); motorboats cost $25 for four hours and $35 for the day.

➤ **HIKING** • The **Threemile Lake Trail** and the **Tahkenitch Dunes Trail** both begin at the south end of Tahkenitch Campground (*see above*), about 8 miles north of Reedsport, and then separate after ¼ mile. Despite the spectacular scenery along the way, these trails are surprisingly unfrequented. On the Threemile Lake Trail you climb through a conifer forest and slowly advance toward the beach and narrow Threemile Lake. The 2-mile Tahkenitch Dunes Trail takes you across dunes to the shore of Tahkenitch Creek by the ocean. A 1½-mile walk along the beach connects the two trails, so enthusiastic hikers can make a 6½-mile loop.

North Central Coast

During this 78-mile stretch of U.S. 101, the highway winds high above the ocean on roads so scenic you'll think you're in a luxury car commercial (except for the luxury car, of course). With the pounding surf of the Pacific on your west and the towering old growth of the Siuslaw National Forest on your east, you'll pass 800-foot-high Cape Perpetua, which on a clear day has views of more than half the Oregon coastline. To the south lie the first-rate sand dunes of Florence, and farther north you'll find the something-for-everyone town of Newport, with its thriving waterfront, excellent aquarium, and wide sandy beaches. From Newport you can reach the whale-watching town of Depoe Bay by driving north on U.S. 101 or by taking the Otter Crest Loop, which rises 500 feet to Cape Foulweather for tremendous coastal views. From Depoe Bay, a short 15-minute drive takes you into Lincoln City and the end of this leg of the coast. Along the way you'll become intimately acquainted with sea lions and harbor seals, and you may even spot a whale (or two or three). The hostel in Newport provides a great break from camping. Don't expect much in the way of budget dining from Yachats, Waldport, or Depoe Bay; if you can hold out until Newport or Lincoln City, though, you should be all set. For information on Coming and Going, *see* Basics, *above*.

Florence

Recently, Florence was welcomed into the warm embrace of the McDonald's franchise community—yes, this town has arrived. Florence's tourist trade is on the rise, too, though the jet set here is a bit gray around the temples. The increased popularity is no surprise: In the town's immediate vicinity are freshwater lakes, beautiful beaches, the Siuslaw River, and dunes so close you can see them from downtown. Florence even has an Old Town to attract the there-must-be-something-to-see-down-there crowd. If you're coming from Eugene, Florence is little more than an hour's drive down Route 126. All told, it's surprising that McDonald's didn't come sooner.

VISITOR INFORMATION **Florence Chamber of Commerce.** *270 U.S. 101, tel. 503/997–3128. Open daily 9–5.*

WHERE TO SLEEP **Money Saver Motel.** This clean but characterless motel puts you just one block from Old Town and the scenic Siuslaw River Bridge. It lives up to its name; a double costs $48–$52 in summer and goes down $16 in winter. *170 U.S. 101, tel. 503/997–7131. 40 rooms. Wheelchair access.*

Park Motel. Time to break out the "Fleischman Forever" T-shirt—this place is straight off the Northern Exposure set. Despite the generous use of rustic knotty pine, you need not hang your food off the high branch here—the rooms are exceptionally comfortable and clean. In summer, a single is $43 and a double $57, but the price goes down to $30 and $36 during winter. *85034 U.S. 101S, 1½ mi south of Florence Bridge, tel. 503/997–2634. 14 rooms. Luggage storage. Wheelchair access.*

Villa West Motel. This well-maintained motel provides a base from which to explore the dunes. The $58 price tag for a summertime double goes down to $38 in winter. This is a good place for people who want clean rooms and don't mind freeway noise. *901 U.S. 101, at Rte. 126, tel. 503/997–3457. 3 blocks from Greyhound Station, 8 blocks from Old Town. 22 rooms.*

➤ **CAMPING** • **Carl G. Washburne State Park.** The 1,089-acre park straddles the highway, with campsites surrounded by forest on the inland side. A trail goes under the highway and down to the beach. Sites run $15–$17 and don't bother with reservations—they don't accept them. *Tel. 503/547–3416 or 503/997–3851. 3 mi north of Sea Lion Caves. 66 sites. Showers.*

Honeyman Memorial State Park. Campers have access to three different lakes, the beach, and the adjacent dunes. On nearby Cleowax Lake, the dunes fall right down to the water, allowing people to cruise, roll, or slide into it. Sites at this extremely popular campground run $15–$17. *3 mi south of Florence on Cleowax Lake, tel. 503/997–3641. 381 sites. Hot showers ($2 for non-campers). Reservations recommended Memorial Day–Labor Day.*

Siltcoos Recreation Area. The access road to the beach leads past four separate campgrounds: Lodgepole, Lagoon, Waxmyrtle, and Driftwood. Despite the myriad camping options, those not enthralled by the dune-buggy scene may be happier elsewhere. Of the campgrounds, Lodgepole and Lagoon are farthest from the beach, but you'll have more forest and more privacy. Disabled travelers should try the fully wheelchair-accessible Driftwood. Only Waxmyrtle accepts reservations, and then only in summer. All sites run $8–$10. *Tel. 800/280–2267. Siltcoos Beach and Dune Access Rd., 7 mi south of Florence on U.S. 101. 177 sites. Driftwood open year-round, others June–Sept.*

Tyee. The only Oregon Dunes National Recreation Area campground on the east side of U.S. 101, Tyee offers fishing, swimming, and waterskiing on nearby Siltcoos Lake. Sites are right along the Siltcoos River—a peaceful setting, although the traffic on U.S. 101 still makes itself heard. All 14 sites ($10) include water and you'll do your business on vault toilets—be sure to go before you leave home. No reservations accepted. *No phone. 6 mi south of Florence on U.S. 101. 14 sites.*

FOOD Because of its sizable retired community, Florence goes to sleep pretty early. If you want late-night grub, your only option is the 24-hour **Fisherman's Wharf Restaurant and Lounge** (1341 Bay St., tel. 503/997–2613). This place provides what little nightlife Florence has; you can hear live rock and country music from 9 PM to 2 AM on Friday and Saturday nights. If you're looking for a quick and tasty bite, try the fresh fish and excellent clam chowder at **Mo's** (1436 Bay St., in Old Town, tel. 503/997–2185), which overlooks the Siuslaw River. No dinner is more than $8, and all include the famous chowder. Stop by daily 11–9.

Alpha-Bit Café. If you're headed to Eugene and I-5, take a side trip to the '60s at this café/bookstore in Mapleton (about 10 miles inland from Florence). Started by members of Alpha Farm, an alternative community in nearby Deadwood, Alpha-Bit has a mostly grains 'n' greens menu (no red meat), and good coffee for a mere 25¢ per cup. Sink your teeth (well, sorta) into a grainburger for $3.50. *10780 Rte. 126, at Rte. 36, tel. 503/268–4311. Open Mon.–Thurs. 10–6, Fri. 10–9, Sat. 10–6.*

Blue Hen Café. Owned by Orie and Gordon Jenks, a self-proclaimed "bit past middle age" couple, this home-turned-restaurant is best known for its chicken and chowder, but it also serves hamburgers, sandwiches, and salads. Everything is excellent, and most dishes are in the $4–$6 range. *1675 U.S. 101N, tel. 503/997–3907. Wheelchair access. Open Mon.–Sat. 7 AM–8 PM, Sun. 7–7.*

WORTH SEEING Most of Florence lies on the north side of the Siuslaw River Bridge, but before you cross over the double arch you may want to take a quick peek into the **Siuslaw Pioneer Museum.** Housed in an old Lutheran church, the museum features items that were donated by local folks with pioneer pasts, some of whom work here as volunteers. *85294 U.S. 101, Mile 192, tel. 503/997–7884. Donation: $1. Open Tues.–Sun. 10–4.*

At the Pioneer Museum, be sure to check out the antique Girl Scout uniforms, which are displayed on sexy, decidedly un-Girl Scout-like mannequins.

Florence's **Old Town** lies on the north bank of the river, a few blocks east of U.S. 101. **Bay Street,** its short main drag, parallels the Siuslaw and passes beneath the bridge. On the eastern end of Bay Street, about three blocks from the bridge, is a busy marina, and in between are restaurants, galleries, and antiques stores. There's nothing earth-shattering to see, but the stores make for good browsing. One surprisingly interesting stop is the **Western Fly Fishing Museum** (280 Nopal St., tel. 503/997–6349), about two blocks up Nopal Street from Bay Street. William Cushner, the museum's founder, was a picture framer with almost no fishing experience, but he loved framing flies in a way that made them appear suspended—just as a fish would see them. Cushner passed away in 1992; his son-in-law, Jack Smrekar, now runs the museum. You can check out the creations for $2.50.

OUTDOOR ACTIVITIES Visiting the dunes without making a buggy trip is like going to an ice cream parlor and ordering water. If you're going to blow some sand, Florence is a good place to do it.

➤ **DUNE-BUGGYING** • **Sand Dune Frontier** (83960 U.S. 101S, tel. 503/997–3544), about 4 miles south of Florence, gives half-hour dune buggy tours for $6 in ORVs that seat about 10 people. They also have Odysseys for about $30 an hour. While you're waiting for the tour or for your buggy, you can play a round or two at their miniature golf course. **Sandland Adventures Inc.** (cnr of 10th St. and U.S. 101, 1 mi south of Florence, tel. 503/997–8087) offers Odysseys for about $30 an hour and dune-buggy tours led by professional drivers that start at around $15.

➤ **HIKING** • Seven miles south of Florence, on the east side of U.S. 101, the 2-mile **Siltcoos Lake Trail** winds through dense forest to some good trout fishing and six free primitive campsites. On the other side of the highway, about a mile down the Siltcoos Dune and Beach Access Road, lies the **Waxmyrtle Trail,** which begins at the entrance to the Waxmyrtle Campground (*see* Where to Sleep, *above*). This trail follows the Siltcoos River 1½ miles to the ocean. If you're quiet and pay attention, you might spot an osprey or blue heron feeding in the salt marshes.

➤ **HORSEBACK RIDING** • If you're traveling with a stud, you can keep him at **C&M Stables,** 8 miles north of Florence. If your stud isn't a horse, the two of you might prefer a guided sunset beach ride—the stable provides the horses ($30 for 2 hrs). C&M also offers a variety of nature rides, including a breathtaking winter tour. Call for information and reservations. *90241 U.S. 101N; tel. 503/997–7540.*

➤ **BOATING** • The **Honeyman Park Lodge** (tel. 503/997–9143) on Cleowax Lake in Honeyman State Park, about 3 miles south of Florence on U.S. 101, offers pedal boats ($7 per hour), canoes ($7 per hour), and rowboats ($7 per hour).

➤ **CRABBING** • In Florence, crabbers should head to the dock at the end of the South Jetty Road or the dock at Old Town Park. **Siuslaw Charters** (020 Nopal St., tel. 503/997–8961) rents rings for $5 a day.

NEAR FLORENCE

You can get a final look at the dunes just before they taper off at the **Sutton Recreation Area** (tel. 503/268–4473), about 3 miles from Old Town. Sutton Beach Road leads west 2 miles to the **Holman Vista,** which offers views of the ocean, the dunes, and Sutton Creek—it makes for an interesting photo opportunity. Stop off a short distance farther on U.S. 101 to check out the carnivorous specimens at the **Darlingtonia Wayside** (just south of Mile 185, no phone), a sanctuary for insect-eating Darlingtonia plants, otherwise known as cobra lilies, which trap bugs and then slowly digest them. Six miles north of these fly-feasting flora you'll find **Sea Lion Caves** (91560 U.S. 101, tel. 503/547–3111). This 125-foot-high cave and its outside ledges are the only year-round home on the American mainland for the endangered Steller sea lions. The admission fee ($5.50) is steep, but you won't feel robbed.

> *At Darlingtonia you can have fun screaming, "For the love of God, don't!" at all the insects that wander into the maws of these carnivorous plants.*

HECETA HEAD One-fifth of a mile north of the Sea Lion Caves you'll come to a turnout with a distant view of the **Heceta Lighthouse.** Join the thousands who have hastily reached for their cameras to photograph this stunning 1894 lighthouse on its forested promontory overlooking the sea. For a closer look, continue to **Devil's Elbow State Park** (tel. 503/731–3411, or

Buckle up for Safety

The hair-raising, tonsil-straining excitement of dune cruising in an off-road vehicle (ORV) or all-terrain vehicle (ATV) should be regarded with a measure of caution. In the interest of fun 'n' safety, the rental companies usually offer customers a crash course. But just in case, make sure to get a copy of the Off-Road Vehicle Guide to Sand Areas of the Siuslaw National Forest from the Oregon Dunes National Recreation Area office (see visitor information in the Oregon Dunes, above). A few basic pointers: The terrain is full of dips and other surprises, so think twice before declaring yourself GI Joe and ripping across the dunes in search of enemy territory. And whatever you do, obey the signs indicating areas closed to off-road vehicles. Out here, flora and fauna are a whole lot more than a couple of Disney characters.

800/452–5687 in summer) less than a mile north. You can relax on the small beach here, have a picnic, and, at low tide, climb and explore the rocks. But the real attraction is the ½-mile trail that winds up a hill to the old Heceta Lighthouse. Views from the trail take in forested coastline, foaming sea, and islands inhabited by hundreds of nesting seabirds. On the way, you'll pass the Queen Anne-style **Heceta House,** which lodged the families of the two assistant lighthouse keepers until 1963, when the lighthouse became automated. Legend has it that the house is haunted by a former caretaker's wife named Rue searching for her baby girl, who died on the premises. The lighthouse, a white structure with a red top, gives off the strongest light of any beacon on the coast. It's open to the public Thursday–Monday, noon–5.

Yachats

Despite having the best name on the coast (say it YAH-hots; no Yiddish gutteral sound required), this laid-back town of some 600 residents doesn't offer a whole lot to do. If you don't want to visit nearby **Cape Perpetua** (*see* Near Yachats, *below*) and aren't into peaceful strolls along the beach, then make sure you've got a good book handy. In the early morning or late afternoon, head east out of town on **Yachats River Road** and you might see elk grazing along the river. Yachats is one of the only places in the world where sea-bound smelt, which resemble sardines, come toward shore to spawn. Between April and October, the smelt hit the shoreline, and fishermen with special triangular nets go out to meet them. The **Smelt Fry** attracts many visitors on the first weekend after July 4, as does the **Kite Festival,** held at the mouth of the Yachats River in October.

VISITOR INFORMATION Yachats Visitor Center. *441 U.S. 101, tel. 503/547–3530. Open daily 10–4.*

Cape Perpetua Visitor Center. *2400 U.S. 101S, tel. 503/547–3289. Open winter, weekends 10–4; summer, daily 9–5.*

WHERE TO SLEEP In the Yachats-Waldport area, cottages are the lodging of choice. These can be expensive, but the determined traveler should find a reasonable deal. The **Yachats Rock Park Cottages** (431 W. 2nd St., tel. 503/547–3214) put you in walking distance of the beach and come with full kitchens, puzzles, games, old books, and cable television. Rates run $42–$56. At the **Wayside Lodge** (5773 U.S. 101N, 2½ mi north of Yachats, tel. 503/547–3450) you get nicer rooms and a much better view than at Rock Park, but you pay more; most cottages run $60–$65 in summer (one studio cottage goes for $45).

See Vue. On a cliff with an unobstructed view of the sea, the See Vue virtually drips with character; each room has its own name with a corresponding decorative scheme. For a nostalgic look into someone else's genealogical past, try Granny's antique-laden room. Most rooms are $46–$52 in summer and $36–$42 in winter. *95590 U.S. 101, tel. 503/547–3227. 6 mi south of Yachats. 10 rooms.*

➤ **CAMPING** • **Cape Perpetua.** This pleasant national forest campground along Cape Creek, in the shadow of the highest point on the Oregon Coast, makes an ideal base camp for many hikes. Quiet, well-spaced sites run $10. *3 mi south of Yachats off U.S. 101, tel. 503/547–3289. 37 sites. Closed Oct.–Apr.*

FOOD Food is a big problem for the budget traveler in Yachats. Most restaurants are overpriced, and the town has only one market. If you don't have the energy to drive 8 miles to Waldport for less expensive but unexceptional food, then do the dining thing at **Leroy's Blue Whale** (580 U.S. 101 at 6th St., tel. 503/547–3399). Almost all the steak, seafood, and chicken dinners cost less than $8, and for $5 you get a big and very filling plate of fish-and-chips.

NEAR YACHATS

CAPE PERPETUA Three miles south of Yachats, suspended high over the Pacific, 800-foot **Cape Perpetua** offers breathtaking coastal views—on a clear day you can see Coos Bay and all the way to Lincoln City on the north. At the base, the **Cape Perpetua Visitor Center** (*see* Visitor

Information, *above*) has exhibits on forests and oceans and a friendly staff. From here you can hike the solitary 4-mile **Cummins Creek Trail,** which leads through an old-growth Sitka spruce forest and just begins to explore the 9,300-acre Cummins Creek Wilderness. Also departing from the visitor's center, the moderately strenuous 1½-mile hike to the top of Cape Perpetua ascends through a dense forest, with signs along the way explaining ecological cycles and historic events in the area. If an easy half-mile jaunt sounds a bit more your speed, make your way from the visitor's center along the trail to the **Spouting Horn.** As the surf crashes onto the rocks beneath the cliffs, water is forced through a spout, or horn, at the top of a cave, spraying a fine sea mist skyward.

For a spectacular view without all the legwork, drive up the 2-mile road that starts about 300 yards past the visitor center on U.S. 101. A mile into the drive the road forks; unless you want a 22-mile tour of the surrounding forest and a whole heap of confusion ("It can't possibly be this far?!"), go left here to the top of the cliff. If you still have the energy to visit one more attraction, check out the **Devil's Churn,** less than a mile north of the visitor center, where a crevice in volcanic rock foams with pounding surf at high tide. A short trail leads from the parking lot to the center of the action.

WALDPORT If you're feeling clammy and crabby, and maybe a little bit fishy, you'll feel right at home in Waldport. To reach the bay shore, head east on Route 34 just before U.S. 101 crosses the bay, and turn left on Mill Street directly across from the high school. For $40 you can rent a boat and fishing supplies for three hours at the **Dock of the Bay Marina** (1245 Mill St., tel. 503/563–2003). Other than bay activities, there isn't a lot to do in quiet Waldport. You may want to head inland along the Alsea River on scenic Route 34. The turnoff for the **Drift Creek Wilderness** (tel. 503/563–3211) is about 7 miles out on the highway; you continue north for a mile on forest roads, then park your car and hike through old-growth forest, tall ridges, and meadows. For more information on hikes, contact the **Waldport Ranger Station** (1049 S.W. Pacific Coast Hwy., on U.S. 101, ½ mi south of town, tel. 503/563–3211).

From Waldport, U.S. 101 leads over the Alsea Bay Bridge and north to **Seal Rock State Park** (Mile 150.7), where you can enjoy the sounds and sights of pounding surf, explore tide pools, and (if you're lucky) watch seals on offshore rocks. Just to the north, in the residential town of **Seal Rock,** you'll find **Sea Gulch** (U.S. 101, tel. 503/563–2727), an incredibly tacky but genuinely amusing theme park landscaped with about 400 life-size wooden figures right out of the Wild West. Ray Kowalski and his three sons sculpt the gunslingers and loggers by chainsaw and arrange them along a quarter-mile trail, with props and—hopefully intentional—misspelled signs ("Dangur Kwiksand") along the way. If you don't want to pay the rather exorbitant $4.50 for all this, you can check out the carvings in front for free.

➢ **WHERE TO SLEEP AND EAT** • The **Waldport Motel** (170 S.W. Arrow St., on U.S. 101, tel. 503/ 563–3035) has the cheapest (doubles $40 in summer) and sometimes noisiest rooms in town. Half the rooms have full kitchens. If you don't mind spending a little extra, the **Alsea Manor Hotel** (190 S.W. Arrow St., tel. 503/563–3249) offers cleaner and altogether nicer rooms, equipped with sturdy, traditional furniture, for $51–$58 in summer. Campers should check out the quiet campground at **Tillicum Beach** (4½ mi south of Waldport on U.S. 101, tel. 503/563–3211), which has $10 sites, many with ocean views. Otherwise, try the **Blackberry Campground** (15 mi east of Waldport on Rte. 34, tel. 503/563–3211) on the Alsea River, with sites from $7 to $9. As for food, good budget restaurants are hard to find, but you can get a large helping of spaghetti and mozzarella cheese, plus garlic bread and a trip to the salad bar, for only $5 at **At'sa Pizza** (427 U.S. 101, in Seastrand Mall, tel. 503/563–3232).

Newport

Newport grew up around the turn of the century as a thriving resort for Portlanders. It still retains the atmosphere of a busy seaside vacation town, with shops and restaurants on the bay, sandy beaches, oceanfront hotels, and an active nightlife, although these days plenty of year-round residents hang their hats within the town's boundaries, and fishing dominates the economy slightly more than tourism. The highway above the bayfront cuts through the middle of town, about 10 blocks from the ocean, and has the regular array of motels and franchises. The **Bayfront,** resting beneath the highway, follows Bay Boulevard along the north shore of Yaquina Bay, past an odd mix of open-air fish markets, canneries, merchants hawking fish cocktails, charter boats unloading their catch, and some too-kitschy-to-be-true tourist traps. Avoid **Ripley's Believe It or Not,** the **Waxworks,** and the **Underseas Gardens,** all of which offer up pure cheese at a steep admission price. If you're looking for nightlife, visit **Pip Tide** (836 S.W. Bay Blvd., tel. 503/265–7797), which has live Top 40 music, inexpensive drinks, and an appropriately rowdy clientele. Or sample home-brewed beer next door at the **Bayfront Brewery** (748 S.W. Bay Blvd., tel. 503/265–3188).

VISITOR INFORMATION **Greater Newport Chamber of Commerce.** *555 S.W. Coast Hwy., on U.S. 101, tel. 503/265–8801 or 800/262–7844. Open summer, weekdays 8:30–5, weekends 10–4; winter, weekdays 8:30–5.*

WHERE TO SLEEP It's the rarest of creatures on the Oregon Coast, but Newport's got one: a hostel! You'd think that your lodging decision would already be made, but wait—Newport also has the most inventive B&B on the Oregon Coast, a worthwhile splurge if ever there was one. If neither of these options entices you, your best bet is to look for a cheap but clean room on U.S. 101, just north of the Yaquina Bay Bridge. In summer, make reservations; you won't have much luck scraping up a room on a Saturday night in August. Three of the better values for the money are **Willer's Motel** (754 S.W. Coast Hwy., tel. 800/945–5377), which has eager-to-please owners and doubles starting at $36 in summer; **Newport Motor Inn** (1311 N. Coast Hwy., tel. 503/265–8516), with $38 doubles in summer; and the **City Center Motel** (538 S.W. Coast Hwy., tel. 503/265–7381), where doubles start at $40 in summer.

Brown Squirrel Hostel. This little-known hostel, located in a one-time church, provides clean surroundings and a large communal kitchen and living room. You sleep within quick walking distance of the beach. Beds are $10 for members and nonmembers. *44 S.W. Brook St., tel. 503/265–3729. From cnr of Olive St. and U.S. 101, go 4 blocks west. 20 beds. Laundry.*

Sylvia Beach Hotel. If you can afford it, do yourself a favor and stay in this "novel" bed-and-breakfast overlooking the Pacific. Each room is named after a famous author, with inventive decorative schemes to match. An overhanging pendulum will be the last thing you see before drifting off to sleep in the eerie Poe Room. Rooms, all with private bath, range from $60 to $130, but the real steals are the bunks at $20 a person. In the morning, look for a hearty breakfast buffet. *267 N.W. Cliff St., tel. 503/265–5428. 20 rooms, 2 bunk rooms. No smoking. Reservations necessary.*

➤ **CAMPING** • **Beverley Beach State Park.** An underground pedestrian tunnel connects this well-groomed campground to the beach across the highway. Sites are $16 to $18. *7 mi north of Newport, tel. 503/265–9278. 279 sites, some hiker/biker sites. Showers.*

South Beach State Park. This huge family-oriented campground is only a quarter-mile from the beach. Roll up your sleeves and join your fellow campers for some clam digging, sunbathing, and fishing. And get used to that group feeling—sites ($17) are neither very shaded nor particularly private. *5580 South Coast Hwy., 2 mi south of Newport on U.S. 101, tel. 503/867–4715. 254 sites, some hiker/biker sites. Showers. Open all year.*

FOOD **The Chowder Bowl.** Most tourists flock to Mo's (*see* Florence, *above*), the area's most publicized chowderhouse, but if you want to avoid the crowds and still enjoy some tasty chowder ($2 a cup) and fish-and-chips ($6), check out this laid-back place instead. *728 N.W. Beach Dr., in Nye Beach, tel. 503/265–7477. Open summer, daily 11–9; winter, daily 11–8.*

J&R Ranch BBQ. For tangy western-style barbecue at reasonable prices, this little roadside restaurant is mmm . . . mmm good. Chicken, pork, beef, or rib dinners will only set you back $5–$8. *3607 S. Coast Hwy., on U.S. 101, tel. 503/867–3410. ¼ mi south of Yaquina Bay Bridge. Open daily 11–8.*

Whale's Tale. Shunning the bayfront tradition of deep-frying everything, the chefs here broil and poach their heart-happy dishes, using seafood so fresh it will almost flop right off your plate. Poppyseed pancakes ($2.25) and eggs Newport (with hollandaise, shrimp, and ham) at

$7 are favorites for breakfast, while the vegetarian garden burger and shrimp sandwich are worthy lunchtime selections. Lunch entrées hover around $7, but dinner prices soar. *452 S.W. Bay Blvd., tel. 503/265–8660. Center of the bayfront.*

WORTH SEEING Most of Newport rests on the north side of Yaquina Bay Bridge, but two sights on the south side deserve visits. Oregon State University's coastal research takes place at the **Hatfield Marine Science Center,** where you can stick your hand in a couple tanks and touch sea urchins, starfish, and even a Pacific octopus. Knowledgeable orange-jacketed volunteers explain the marine activity on hand, and some informative displays give you the lowdown on topics such as fishing, marine mammal beaching, and estuary life. *2030 Marine Science Dr., tel. 503/867–0100. Admission free. Open summer, daily 10–6; winter, daily 10–4.*

The newer attraction on the south side of the bridge is the **Oregon Coast Aquarium.** Each gallery focuses on a different coastal habitat—from rocky shores to coastal waters and wetlands. The facility stresses interaction and education; you can touch pools of crabs, starfish, mussels, and sea anemones (though you can do the same for free at the Hatfield Marine Science Center). The reasons to shell out the big bucks here are the playful, cuddly-looking sea lions, harbor seals, and sea otters, and the positively un-cuddly moon jellyfish. *2820 S.E. Ferry Slip Rd., tel. 503/867–3474. Near the south shore of Yaquina Bay Bridge off U.S. 101. Admission: $7.75. Open summer, daily 9–6; winter, daily 10–4:30.*

Just over the bridge on the north side of the bay, the **Yaquina Bay Lighthouse,** with a keeper's dwelling inside, hovers over the vessels pulling in and out of Newport. It turned out its light in 1874, after only three years of service, and is now open to the public. Some people believe the tower is haunted by a girl named Muriel; in truth, however, Muriel was only a fictional character in a century-old short story set at the lighthouse (you can watch a poorly produced short video that reenacts the tale). The park surrounding the lighthouse offers a wide beach and good views of ships passing under the Yaquina Bay Bridge. *Tel. 503/265–5679. Admission free. Open summer, daily 11–5; winter, weekends noon–4.*

If the lighthouse hasn't satiated your appetite for turn-of-the-century architecture, visit the **Historic Nye Beach Area,** where wealthy Portlanders have old Victorian vacation homes overlooking the sandy beach. Here you'll find the **Newport Visual Arts Center,** which offers changing exhibits of paintings, sketches, and crafts by local artists. *839 N.W. Beach Dr., tel. 503/265–5133. Admission free. Open summer, daily noon–4; winter, daily 11–3.*

OUTDOOR ACTIVITIES If you dig crabs, **Newport Tradewinds** (653 S.W. Bay Blvd., on the bay downtown, tel. 503/265–2101) rents rings and bait for $5 a day. They also run Pacific-bound fishing charters at $50 per five hours. If you have your own rod, try the Alsea River for salmon and steelhead trout, and the Yachats River for cutthroat trout.

NEAR NEWPORT

YAQUINA HEAD LIGHTHOUSE In 1874, the old Yaquina Bay Lighthouse in Newport (*see above*) was retired as the area's beacon, and the torch was passed to this lighthouse, which is still functioning from its perch 162 feet above the sea, about 3 miles north of Newport on U.S. 101. While Yaquina Head may not feature a ghost, its natural surroundings more than compensate. The basaltic headland on which the lighthouse stands was once an ancient lava flow, and it has withstood the coast's battering waves and harsh weather conditions ever since. Views extend as far south as Cape Perpetua, and the offshore rocks and islands give you surprisingly close-up views of seals, murres, and puffins. Whale watching is quite rewarding from here, too, even in summer. A stairway leads down from the headland to the black cobble beach, where tide pools teem with hermit crabs, purple urchins, and starfish. The lighthouse is open 9–4, and free tours are given on the half-hour in summer from 9 to noon.

Depoe Bay

As a tourist town, Depoe Bay has two claims to fame: It has the smallest navigable harbor in the world—interesting if you're into maritime trivia, but not a reason to visit—and it's the self-proclaimed whale-watching capital of the world, which creates a bit more of a splash. If you've never seen a gray whale and have the urge, this is the best place to get on a charter. Also, because of U.S. 101's proximity to the sea, there are no buildings to mar your ocean view in Depoe Bay. Even the seawall partitioning the highway and the rocky shore does little to deter the pummeling waves, as you'll see at the **Spouting Horn,** where water deflecting off sea caverns spurts high into the air, making sidewalk onlookers much wetter than they'd like.

VISITOR INFORMATION **Depoe Bay Visitors Center.** *620 U.S. 101, south of the bridge, tel. 503/765–2889. Open daily 10–3.*

WHERE TO SLEEP Unfortunately for budget travelers, inexpensive lodging is not nearly as common as whale sightings in Depoe Bay. You may be better off staying in Lincoln City and making a day trip here. If you must stay in town, the **Four Winds Motel** (356 U.S. 101NE, tel. 503/765–2793) is about the least expensive place you're going to find: Small but clean rooms go for $32–$35 on summer weekdays and $41–$53 on summer weekends.

FOOD Depoe Bay is a budget diner's nightmare. Not only are the restaurants expensive, but you don't even have a decent market to fall back on. The only reasonable establishment in town is **Oceans Apart Restaurant** (177 U.S. 101NW, tel. 503/765–2513), which features plenty of mahi-mahi dishes in the $8 to $10 range and some odd Hawaiian-style creations like a tropical omelet with pineapple, cream cheese, and macadamia nuts ($5.75).

OUTDOOR ACTIVITIES Hour-long expeditions cruise the coast in search of grays and almost always find one. Trips cost about $9 and usually include interesting tales and educational tidbits, compliments of your ship's captain. Two of the biggest companies offering tours are **Dockside Charters** (270 S.E. Coast Guard Pl., tel. 503/765–2545) and **Tradewinds Sportfishing** (On U.S. 101, north end of the bridge, tel. 503/765–2345 or 800/445–8730).

NEAR DEPOE BAY

OTTER CREST LOOP The scenic 4-mile **Otter Crest Loop** leaves U.S. 101 about 8 miles north of Newport and heads west to the coast. The first stop along the short route is **Devil's Punchbowl,** a large, circular sandstone formation with a hole at the top that you can gaze through without leaving the parking lot. Ocean water enters through narrow holes in the rock; when the waves get choppy, the water swirls around, giving the impression of a cauldron. After you've watched for a minute or so and taken the requisite photo, step inside **Mo's West** (925 1st St., tel. 503/765–2442) at the other end of the parking area for some peanut butter and chocolate Punchbowl pie ($2). Have them show you where Bruce Springsteen sat when

Captain James Cook, the English navigator who explored the Pacific Northwest, gave Cape Foulweather its unfortunate name when he landed there on a blustery day in 1778. One can only imagine how much worse the name would be if Cook had also been seasick.

he ate there. If you want to go down to the beach, take the stairway east of the parking lot. A little over a mile farther on the Otter Crest Loop, **Cape Foulweather** perches 500 feet above the ocean. From here you can take in tremendous southern views of sandstone cliffs, lush inland forests, and curving coastline. Winds sometimes reach 100 miles per hour.

Lincoln City

Lincoln City, a collection of five villages that expanded and finally merged in 1964, has been panned as a tasteless 7-mile strip of motels and fast food joints. While it's true that you'd be hard-pressed to call Lincoln City a charmer, it's not without attractions. For one, if you're too lazy to clean the underwear and socks you've been wearing for the past few days, then you can head over to the **Factory Stores at Lincoln City** (1510 E. Devil's Lake Rd., cnr of U.S. 101, tel. 503/996–5000), where a Hanes Factory Outlet sells "slightly imperfect" underwear at reduced prices. You'll also find some 40 more outlets, including Eddie Bauer, London Fog, and Levi's.

When you're done stocking up, head east of the town center on U.S. 101 to 6th street to **Devil's Lake** (tel. 503/994–2002), in the state park of the same name. A local Siletz Indian legend tells of an evil spirit inhabiting the waters and sucking native warriors beneath the surface. If you're not a native warrior, though, you might want to swim, fish, camp, rent boats, and explore the forested lake. From Devil's Lake to the ocean flows the D River, supposedly D shortest river in D world. Aside from lake activities, Lincoln City also offers miles of kite-flying beaches with steady winds (thanks to the town's position at the 45th parallel, midway between the pole and the equator). Residents take advantage of the prime conditions by holding a kite-flying festival every spring and fall. If you just want a peaceful beach to walk on, head to the tiny town of **Neskowin,** about 15 miles north of Lincoln City.

VISITOR INFORMATION Lincoln City Visitor and Convention Bureau. *801 U.S. 101, tel. 503/994–8378 or 800/452–2151. Open weekdays 8–5, Sat. 8:30–5, Sun. 10–4.*

WHERE TO SLEEP Call it a blessing or a curse, but Lincoln City has over 50 motels, most located along U.S. 101, with some clusters on Northwest Harbor and Northwest Inlet avenues. Two places to try if the listings below don't pan out are **Captain Cook's Motel** (2626 U.S. 101, tel. 503/994–2522), with clean rooms for $36–$40 in summer, and the **Budget Inn** (1713 N.W. 21st St., left turn at KFC, tel. 503/994–5281), with large doubles that are less noisy than most for $35–$50 in summer.

Billows Motel. Perched on a cliff 90 feet above the ocean, this old motel offers large rooms with truly magnificent ocean views and kitchen facilities to sweeten the deal. The rooms ($50) are clean, although the motel's antiquated exterior might lead you to believe otherwise. *1721 N.W. Harbor Ave., tel. 503/994–2937. Take N.W. 21st St. from U.S. 101 to N.W. Harbor Ave. 6 rooms.*

Sea Echo. It's your standard blah motel, but the rooms are extremely clean and the owners particularly friendly. Doubles, some with ocean views, run $32–$41 in summer. *3510 U.S. 101, tel. 503/994–2575. 12 rooms.*

➤ **CAMPING** • **Devil's Lake State Park.** Winding paths lead to secluded, woodsy sites a short hike from the lake. Nearby, you can go fishing or rent boats. Sites run $16–$18. *N.E. 6th*

Getting to the Bottom of Oregon's Anti-Gay Initiatives

For the last decade Oregonians have been embroiled in an increasingly contentious and nasty debate, spearheaded by the Oregon Citizens Alliance (OCA) and bathed in the rhetoric of Christian fundamentalism. The state has been besieged by referendums and local ballot measures about what place homosexuals have in this traditionally progressive state. Though it has not had success with statewide measures, the OCA has successfully pushed through "anti–special rights" initiatives in 25 predominantly rural communities. The group claims to not be anti-gay, but rather to object to what it perceives as special treatment of gays—such "special rights" as equal access to housing and the right for openly gay people to teach. (There seems to be a fundamental misapprehension on the part of the OCA as to what constitutes a special right and what is, in fact, a civil right.) The state has declared the OCA initiatives unconstitutional and the group, in turn, is suing the state—and preparing another statewide ballot measure. The OCA's measures have drawn a spirited response from Oregon's progressive community. Those concerned for civil rights in Oregon will be happy to hear that there are, ironically, more openly gay, lesbian, and bisexual candidates running for public office here than in any other state of the union.

St., tel. 503/994–2002. About 100 yards east of U.S. 101 in Lincoln City. 100 sites. Hot showers. Hiker-biker sites. Open all year.

FOOD Lincoln City has no shortage of restaurants and fast-food joints, though finding a cheap place that's also palatable isn't always so easy. If you'd rather handle your cooking on your own, **Trillium Natural Foods Grocery** (1026 S.E. Jetty Ave., tel. 503/994–5665) sells organic produce and organic foods in bulk.

Dory Cove. Locals rave about this seaside restaurant just north of town. Specialties include thick clam chowder ($2 a cup) and beer-battered cod with fries ($7.50). Be ready to wait up to an hour during peak periods. *5819 Logan Rd., tel. 503/994–5180. North end of town, follow Logan Rd. until you reach the beach.*

Otis Café. This small-town café was a local secret until a host of reviewers, including the *New York Times,* discovered its eminently affordable waffles, burgers, and fresh-baked breads. Success has not spoiled the Otis Café, but plan on kicking back for a while before eating, especially on weekend mornings. Nearly everything on the menu is less than $6; the cinnamon roll ($1.25) is a meal in itself. *Tel. 503/994–2813. On Rte. 18, 1 mi east of U.S. 101, 3 mi north of Lincoln City.*

OUTDOOR ACTIVITIES The **Blue Heron Landing Marina** (4006 W. Devil's Lake Rd., tel. 503/994–4708), on Devil's Lake, rents 12-foot motor boats for $20 per two hours, paddle boats for $6 per half hour, and canoes for $8 per hour.

North Coast

The northernmost portion of the coast, encompassing Tillamook and Clatsop counties, is 120 miles of land rich in the kind of historic lore that elementary-school teachers like to talk about. For instance, the Lewis and Clark expedition, commissioned by President Thomas Jefferson to find a "Northwest Passage" to the Pacific, settled in Clatsop during the winter of 1805. Astoria, at the mouth of the Columbia River, was the first permanent U.S. settlement west of the Rockies. But even if you can't get excited by all this Americana, you'll appreciate the area's natural appeal. From tree to shining sea, the north coast offers some incredibly diverse attractions, including the spectacular Three Capes Loop drive and the pastoral town of Tillamook, seat of a thriving dairy industry. As Tillamook County's snappy motto puts it, you get "Trees, Cheese, and Ocean Breeze" in one stretch of coast. Before finally bidding adieu to the water in gritty Astoria, you ascend 700 feet up Neahkahnie Mountain in Oswald West State Park and pass the countless fishing villages that surround Tillamook Bay and Nehalem Bay.

Money on this part of the coast does not have to be a dirty word. Seaside has the highest concentration of inexpensive motels on the north coast, but there's a youth hostel just over the Astoria Bridge in Washington that's worth keeping in mind. If you don't want to camp and overpriced motels cramp your style, avoid Cannon Beach like the plague (a day trip is okay). For information on coming and going, *see* Basics, *above.*

Three Capes Loop

About 20 miles north of Lincoln City and 7 miles north of the residential beach town of Neskowin, U.S. 101 meets up with the 35-mile Three Capes Loop, named for Cape Kiwanda, Cape Lookout, and Cape Meares, which lie on the route. The coastal scenery on this detour is blessed with a wild beauty relatively unscathed by the commercial muck that plagues much of the coast. In order to make the most of this farmland-and-forest route, force yourself out of your car and explore the capes on foot.

CAPE KIWANDA Just north of **Pacific City,** you'll find Cape Kiwanda, a massive sand hill that tapers off into a sandstone cliff as it moves out over the sea. While other sandstone cliffs in the area have been washed away by the battering surf, Kiwanda has endured, in part because the 327-foot rock about a half-mile offshore—called Haystack II, in deference to the monolith of the same name in Cannon Beach—has absorbed many tidal blows headed toward the cape. You wouldn't know this from the photographs taken here during storms, though, when the ocean's attack on the hardy sandstone cliff seems vicious. In nice weather you can join the hang gliders who use Kiwanda's north face as a launch pad, or hike up the cape from the beach. To get here, you have to park in the lot a few hundred yards to the south and then walk down the beach.

On this same beach at sunrise, you can watch Pacific City's renowned fleet of flat-bottomed fishing boats, called dories; this is one of the few places in the world where fishermen launch their boats directly into the ocean from the beach. Pacific City, on the Nestucca River, also has some good fishing; you can rent equipment for angling, clamming, and crabbing at **Pacific City Sporting Goods** (35030 Brooten Rd., tel. 503/965–6466).

CAPE LOOKOUT From Cape Kiwanda, the Three Capes Loop winds through farmland, dunes, and forested valleys before reaching the poorly marked trailhead for the 2½-mile Cape Lookout hike. (The main entrance to the state park is about 3 miles north.) The only indication of this trail from U.S. 101 is a sign pointing to a WILDLIFE VIEWING AREA, which directs you to a parking lot by the trailhead. The narrow, 400-foot-high Cape Lookout juts several miles into the ocean and can only be reached by foot. Near the beginning of the trail, you pass a plaque dedicated to the crew of a World War II bomber that crashed against the cape in 1943. The rest of the hike includes forests of western hemlock, western red cedar, red alder, and Sitka spruce. The real thrill comes after 10 minutes or so, when you're treated to dramatic views of rugged coastline as far south as Cascade Head. Though the views from the tip of the cape disappoint, it's still an easy and pleasant trail to hike.

Back on the Three Capes Loop, you pass a couple of interesting viewpoints before reaching the main entrance to **Cape Lookout State Park** (tel. 503/842–4981). Here you'll find a campground with 197 beachside tent sites for $15 per night. Past the park, the road curves inland around Netarts Bay and then runs through the residential town of Netarts on the way to **Oceanside**, about 8 miles past Cape Lookout State Park. Most of the houses in this quiet but ritzy town are built into a hillside, with the most expensive-looking ones on top of a cliff. The only restaurant in town, **Roseanna's Café** (1490 Pacific St., tel. 503/842–7351), gives you wonderful ocean views and great seafood, but also a hefty bill for dinner; at lunch prices are much more reasonable, with gourmet sandwiches running $5–$8. The **Oceanside Inn** (1440 Pacific St., tel. 503/842–2961 or 800/347–2972) has exceptionally clean rooms with kitchens, ocean views, and beach access. Room prices run $45–$85, and reservations are highly recommended. The rooms at **Oceanfront Cabins** (1610 Pacific St., tel. 503/842–6081) aren't quite as nice as those at the Oceanside Inn, but they, too, come with kitchens, and they cost just $50–$65. With binoculars you can spot sea lions on nearby rock islands from either hotel.

CAPE MEARES The northernmost cape on the Three Capes Loop is only about 2½ miles from Oceanside. Here you won't have to work as hard for views; from the parking area, you take in cliffs with trees growing from ledges, odd offshore rock formations, driftwood scattered on beaches, and deep coves carved by the sea. Seals, sea lions, and a variety of coastal birds frequent the rocks below, and in the distance the rocky shore stretches for miles to the south. A short walk west on a paved path leads to the **Cape Meares Lighthouse,** built in 1890, which is open daily 11–4 in summer. Another short hike leaves from the parking area and heads through old-growth forest to the **Octopus Tree,** a mammoth Sitka spruce with no central trunk, just several gargantuan limbs that sprout from its base—it's often compared to a candelabra. One native legend claims that it occupies a sacred burial ground and that the twisted branches were once used to hold the canoes of the deceased. From Cape Meares, the Three Capes Loop runs southeast along the shore of murky Tillamook Bay. Views of the bay take in fishermen in small boats and, in the distance, the small towns of Bay City and Garibaldi.

Tillamook

For those who underestimate the power of cheese, a visit to Tillamook should set the record straight. If not for cheese, why else would more than 800,000 tourists each year be drawn to this town of 4,000, with none of the ocean scenery that its coastal neighbors offer? True, Tillamook's pastoral setting is appealing, but visitors aren't here to look at the grass—they're here to check out the **Tillamook County Creamery Association** (4175 U.S. 101N, north end of town, tel. 503/842–4481), where you watch from an upstairs viewing area as blocks of nationally acclaimed Tillamook cheese move through a maze of conveyor belts and past a busy assembly line of uniformed, hair-netted workers. After witnessing this process, you can stick toothpicks into free samples of the factory's cheeses, and (if you're like most people) buy some, too. If what you really want is to taste free cheese samples without crowds and noise, head instead to the **Blue Heron French Cheese Company** (2001 Blue Heron Dr., off U.S. 101 on the north side of town, tel. 503/842–8281). The company no longer produces its Blue Heron Brie in this facility, but you can still sample it here, and you'll taste some wonderful jams, jellies, and mustards.

Less known but perhaps more interesting than Tillamook's cheesy attractions is the **Tillamook Naval Air Station Museum** (4000 Blimp Blvd., tel. 503/842–1130). At the museum, housed in a massive World War II blimp hangar, the largest clear-span wood building in the world (large and open with beamed ceilings), is a collection of World War II naval planes. To get here, take U.S. 101 2 miles south of Route 6 and follow the signs. Admission is $5, but if you don't want to pay you can peer into the hangar from behind a fence outside.

VISITOR INFORMATION **Tillamook Chamber of Commerce.** *3705 U.S. 101N, tel. 503/ 842–7525. Next to Tillamook Creamery just north of town. Open summer, daily 9–5; winter, weekdays 9–5, Sat. noon–4:30, Sun. 10–2.*

WHERE TO SLEEP Inexpensive, adequate accommodations are tough to find in Tillamook. You'll get the best price in town at the **Tillamook Inn** (1810 U.S. 101N, tel. 503/842–4413), which has small but clean rooms at $37 per single and $46–$50 per double in summer. If you want to move up a couple notches in quality but only one notch in price, the **Mar-Clair Inn** (11 Main Ave., on U.S. 101, tel. 503/842–7571 or 800/331–6857) has very clean and comfortable rooms that run $52 for a single and $58–$60 for a double in summer. Guests have the use of a pool, hot tub, sauna, and game room. If you're more of a bed-and-breakfast kind of person, Tillamook has a nice one: the **Blue Haven Inn** (3025 Gienger Rd., tel. 503/842–2265), set right in the middle of cow country. This attractive old house, built in 1916, has three guest rooms, all with comfortable antique furnishings and unique names and themes. Two rooms go for $60, and one with private bath is $75. The price includes a full gourmet breakfast of your choice. To reach the inn from town, head south down U.S. 101 for 2 miles and go west on Gienger Road.

FOOD **Blue Heron Deli.** If the free samples have you crying out for more, try the deli counter in the Blue Heron French Cheese Company. Here you can nibble on fromage favorites like the Blue Heron classic (creamy brie cheese and smoked turkey on a fresh-baked roll; $5.50) or the generous cheese and fresh-fruit plate ($4). Try to sit outside—right next to the tiny petting zoo. *2001 Blue Heron Dr., tel. 503/842–8281. Off U.S. 101 north of downtown. Open summer, daily 8–8; winter, daily 9–5.*

La Casa Medello. If mouse bait doesn't interest you, venture here for tasty and reasonable Mexican fare; full dinners run $6–$8. The restaurant does a fairly commendable job of looking Mexican, and with its dim lighting you won't even notice that the flowers are fake. *1160 U.S. 101N, tel. 503/842–5768. Open daily 11–8:30.*

Moran's Diner. Anyone who enjoys a casual local diner with hearty, predictable food and locals perched on swivel chairs at the counter will like Moran's. Egg dishes go for less than $5, turkey sandwiches for $4. It takes about 20 minutes to eat, pay, and leave, although you can lounge around sipping free coffee refills if you want. *1850 U.S. 101N, tel. 503/842–8280. About 1 mi north of Tillamook. Open 6 AM–2 PM.*

OUTDOOR ACTIVITIES Two relatively short trails lead to **Munson Creek Falls,** the highest waterfall in the Coast Range. The ¼-mile lower trail takes you to the base of the falls, while the much tougher ⅜-mile upper trail climbs to a point near the middle of the falls for prime views of mossy cliffs and raging white water. The upper trail is badly overgrown and in poor condition, with a couple of little bridges towards the end seemingly days away from total collapse. Caution, as you might have guessed, is advised. The access road leaves U.S. 101 7 miles south of Tillamook and continues 1½ miles to the marked trailhead.

NEAR TILLAMOOK

GARIBALDI About nine miles north of Tillamook on the north side of Tillamook Bay lies the little town of Garibaldi. Until the 1933 Tillamook Burn (a fire that destroyed 270,000 acres of area forest) Garibaldi had a thriving logging industry. Today, the large smokestack you see as you enter town is almost all that remains of it; Garibaldi now functions primarily as a fishing town, with the busiest harbor between Depoe Bay and Astoria. **Siggi-G Ocean Charters** (611 Commercial St., at the boat basin, tel. 503/322–3285) offers eight-hour bottom-fishing trips for $65 and eight-hour halibut trips for $95. If you'd rather take advantage of Tillamook Bay's excellent crabbing and clamming, **Garibaldi Marina** (302 Mooring Basin Rd., at the boat basin, tel. 503/322–3312) rents crab rings for $3 per day and clam shovels for $2 per day. Four miles north of Garibaldi **Jetty Fishery** (27550 U.S. 101N, tel. 503/368–5746) rents crab rings for $5 a day and has a wonderful crabbing dock.

Your best and just about only bet for spending the night is the **Harbor View Inn** (302 7th St., across from boat basin, tel. 503/322–3251), with doubles from $45–$50. If you have equipment, you can save a lot of money by camping at **Barview Jetty County Park** (tel. 503/322–3522), about 2 miles north of Garibaldi on U.S. 101. Forested tent sites at this large campground near the beach cost $12 per car. The **Bayfront Bakery and Deli** (302 Garibaldi Ave., on U.S. 101, tel. 503/322–3787) is a good place to get tasty, inexpensive baked goods. Deli sandwiches go for $3.55, homemade bagels with cream cheese for 85¢. Its summer hours are 2:30 AM–5:30 PM Wednesday–Saturday and Sundays 2:30 AM–4 PM. They're closed Sundays and Mondays in winter.

NEHALEM BAY North of Garibaldi, U.S. 101 passes through a couple of lackluster burbs: **Rockaway Beach,** a quiet seaside town of 1,000 with little to offer but the beach itself; and the three-block village of **Wheeler,** the southernmost community on Nehalem Bay, which has a couple restaurants and shops that might warrant a quick potty-stop, but nothing more. U.S. 101 meets up with Route 53 about a mile past Wheeler, and you can take this road a mile northeast to the **Nehalem Bay Winery** (34965 Rte. 53, tel. 503/368–9463), in the historic old Mohler Creamery. Here you step up to the driftwood counter and sample a variety of wines, from blackberry to pinot noir to the wonderful white Riesling. Because of its location and unusual wines, this winery attracts more visitors than any other on the Oregon Coast. Tasting is free daily 10–6.

About 2½ miles north of Wheeler, U.S. 101 cuts through the heart of tiny **Nehalem,** a community of about 250 on the north fork of the Nehalem River. This old-fashioned town has several antiques shops and art galleries, but the most intriguing store is the **Mystery Treasure House** (35870 U.S. 101, next to Nehalem Food Mart, tel. 503/368–6219), which sells odd gifts and features a big bookcase lined with used mystery novels. The books are kept company by thousands of fantasy figurines, including scores of gnomes and the intrepid Sherlock Holmes. If you're hungry, **Chadwicks** (across from Mystery Treasure House, tel. 503/368–5557) serves up tasty lunch sandwiches for less than $5 on an outdoor deck overlooking the tranquil Nehalem River. (For dinner, however, the pasta and seafood dishes break the $10 barrier.) The rustic **Bunk House** (36315 U.S. 101N, tel. 503/368–6183), adjoining an espresso shop about a mile north of Nehalem, offers old but clean doubles, some with kitchens, for an incredibly low $20–$35 in summer. Reserve at least a month in advance during peak season.

Just north of the Bunk House on U.S. 101, an access road leads 1½ miles west to **Nehalem Bay State Park** (tel. 503/368–5943, or 800/452–5687 in summer). The park occupies a 4-mile sand spit at the mouth of the bay; if you didn't get your fill of sand dunes on the central coast, here's another chance. Clamming and crabbing are popular activities, and beachcombing has been known to turn up some interesting objects, including beeswax from a 16th-century Spanish ship. The **Nehalem Bay State Park Campground** (tel. 503/368–5943) has 291 sites for $16. The sites are fairly close together and not very private, but they put you near the beach. If you want to save money, you can stay at the park's primitive Horse Camp for $9, but you must have a horse to reserve a site; otherwise, it's first come, first served.

North of Nehalem, U.S. 101 swings back toward the coast, passing **Manzanita,** an expensive beach town. Less than a mile north of Manzanita is **Neahkahnie Beach,** popular with strollers and sunbathers and an obsession for treasure hunters (legend tells of a Spanish shipwreck off the shore here more than two centuries ago).

OSWALD WEST STATE PARK About a mile north of Neahkahnie Beach, the road begins to climb **Neahkahnie Mountain,** located within Oswald West State Park (tel. 503/368–5943, or 800/452–5687 in summer). Along a short stretch of road—reaching as high as 700 feet above the ocean—are several viewpoints overlooking the coast. If you feel like climbing to the top of Neahkahnie Mountain from here, you'll find the easy-to-miss trailhead post for the **Neahkahnie Summit Trail** across the highway from an unmarked gravel turnoff ⅔ mile north of the viewpoint honoring Oswald West. The 1½-mile hike up the mountain cuts through dense vegetation and misty old-growth forests. At the 1,631-foot summit, the trail leaves the lush, eerie forest for jaw-dropping views of the coast—as far as Cape Meares to the south and Tillamook Head to the north. The trail is steep and often muddy, so don't get caught wearing your flip-flops.

According to accounts by local Indians, the crew of a wrecked Spanish ship buried their valuable cargo in boxes at the foot of Neahkahnie Mountain. Hopefuls have been digging here for years, but the only artifacts unearthed so far have been a goblet and a few other trinkets.

Past the trailhead, U.S. 101 descends the mountain and brings you to the main entrance of **Oswald West State Park.** The first parking lot you'll see belongs to the **Oswald West State Park Campground** (tel. 503/368–5943), where 36 primitive sites ($9) nestled among huge Sitka spruce and cedar can be reached by ⅓-mile trail. Wheelbarrows are provided to help you cart your gear through the park. The campground has drinking water and toilets and is very popular with the twenty- to thirty-something crowd. From the sites, you can walk to secluded **Short Sand Beach,** which borders a calm inlet called Smuggler's Cove in the shadow of Neahkahnie Mountain. Also starting at the campground is a fantastic 2-mile hike through old-growth Sitka spruce forest to the edge of **Cape Falcon,** 300 feet above the water. During a 1982 storm with winds in excess of 150 mph, many of the giant trees were flattened—which you may not even notice, thanks to replanting efforts.

About 5 miles north of Oswald West on U.S. 101, **Hug Point State Park** (tel. 503/238–7488, or 800/452–5687 in summer) is a secluded cove partially enclosed by forested cliffs. The park has several mini-caves to crawl into, as well as a tiny 10-foot waterfall.

Cannon Beach

This one-time artists' community 4 miles north of Hug Point State Park is picking up speed in its race to become a full-blown tourist magnet. The main drag, Hemlock Street, remains a browser's paradise full of shops and galleries; and Cannon Beach is still the place to catch up on all that live theater you've missed while on the coast. But as the town becomes more popular and the cost of living increases, artists who were previously able to make ends meet have been forced to flee for more affordable climes.

Cannon Beach is a good-looking town; buildings are required by law to be aesthetically pleasing, and the word "neon" isn't even spoken aloud.

The beach itself is the town's major lure, though it's far enough from the highway that you may forget it's even there. **Haystack Rock,** a protected marine garden and the reigning monarch of the midtown beach, is a damned impressive sight at 235 feet tall. You can check out the teeming tide pools on the rock during low tide. Overhead, rare birds such as the tufted puffin make their nests. Many would-be explorers have been stranded at high tide, so be sure to consult the tide tables at the chamber of commerce. Cannon Beach usually holds its wildly popular **Sand Castle Day** on the first Saturday in June (or on the Saturday after that if the tides are better). During the festival, your odds of finding a place to stay without a reservation are slightly worse than nil.

VISITOR INFORMATION **Cannon Beach Chamber of Commerce.** *Cnr of 2nd and Spruce Sts., tel. 503/436–2623. Open summer, daily 9–5; winter, daily 11–5.*

WHERE TO SLEEP There's no shortage of motels in Cannon Beach; most of them lie along South Hemlock Street, one block from the beach. Keep in mind, however, that during summer the town's popularity keeps the price of rooms sky-high. Unless you're traveling during the off-season, save money by camping or staying in Seaside, north of Cannon Beach.

Blue Gull Inn. These clean, remodeled rooms, within easy walking distance of the downtown shops and galleries, range from $50 to $65 in summer. Some pleasant perks include a sauna, free laundry, and candy on your bed when you arrive. Some rooms have a kitchen. *487 S. Hemlock St., tel. 503/436–2714. 1 block from the beach. 21 rooms.*

Hidden Villa Motel. Scottish-born owner Patrick Kealey provides comfortable beds and fully furnished kitchens in all units. The motel is about a block east of South Hemlock Street, so the rooms remain quiet. Expect to pay $35 in winter and $75 in summer. *188 E. Van Buren St., tel. 503/436–2237. 6 rooms.*

➢ **CAMPING • Saddle Mountain State Park.** In the shadow of northwestern Oregon's tallest mountain, this secluded campground surrounded by dense forests offers a very challenging hiking trail to the summit. Tent sites are $10 per person. *Tel. 503/861–1671. 10 mi east of Cannon Beach on U.S. 26, then 7 mi north on access road. 10 sites. Flush toilets, drinking water. Closed Nov.–Feb.*

FOOD Nearly all of Cannon Beach's budget options are on North Hemlock Street. The **Cannon Beach Bakery** (144 N. Hemlock St., tel. 503/436–2592) bakes breads in a gas-fired brick oven and offers a variety of wonderful pastries. Get 'em while they're hot Wednesday–Monday in summer and Thursday–Monday in winter. For some fishes to go with your loaves, try **Osburn's Grocery Store and Delicatessan** (north end of Hemlock St., tel. 503/436–2234), which has a bevy of sandwich options, including a popular vegetarian sandwich for $4.50. For cheap burgers, sandwiches, and beers, stop by **Bill's Tavern** (188 N. Hemlock St., at 2nd St., tel. 503/436–2202), where a large pitcher of Henry Weinhard's costs $5. If you want breakfast, try the hearty omelets (about $6) at **Lazy Susan Café** (126 N. Hemlock St., tel. 503/236–2816), open every day but Tuesday for breakfast and lunch.

WORTH SEEING A mile north of town, a winding access road leads through forested **Ecola State Park** (tel. 503/436–2844, or 800/452–5687 in summer) and out to **Ecola Point** for good views of Cannon Beach and Haystack Rock. Do yourself a favor and have a picnic here; despite the $3 day-use fee, the grass and the view are both divine. From here, you can drive to **Indian Beach,** in a secluded cove surrounded by offshore volcanic rocks. From here a 2-mile hike to Tillamook Head offers good views of "Terrible Tilly," the retired Tillamook Rock Lighthouse, located on an offshore basalt island (*see* Outdoor Activities, *below*). Built in 1879, Terrible Tilly withstood a number of storms that sent waves crashing over her top. She was retired in 1957.

Unlike many coastal lighthouses, Terrible Tilly has no ghost story surrounding her; as if to compensate, the lighthouse is now being used as a columbarium—a place to store the ashes of the deceased.

OUTDOOR ACTIVITIES If you have loads of energy and endurance and not much else to do, try the 7-mile hike across **Tillamook Head** that begins at Indian Beach in Ecola State Park (*see above*) and runs all the way to the southern edge of Seaside. Initially, you'll pass through lush rain forests of spruce, salal, and hemlock. About 2 miles out is a backpackers-only campsite; from here a barely visible trail leads west past an old World War II bunker to the edge of Tillamook Head, giving you good views of Terrible Tilly about a mile offshore.

A 2½-mile path up **Saddle Mountain,** the highest peak in northwestern Oregon, takes you past grassy meadows of wildflowers and rare flora to the 3,283-foot summit. On a clear day you'll see Mount Hood and the Three Sisters to the east, and Nehalem Bay and the Pacific to the west. The last half mile of the trail is a real bitch; don't even try it unless you have experience and/or regard Carl Lewis as a peer. To get to the trailhead, go 10 miles east of Cannon Beach on U.S. 26, and continue north on the access road for seven miles to the campground.

NEAR CANNON BEACH

JEWELL MEADOWS WILDLIFE AREA If you want to see some Roosevelt elk, follow U.S. 26 (which branches off U.S. 101 3 miles north of Cannon Beach) east for 21 miles to the Jewell Junction, and then take the unmarked state road north 9 miles to Jewell. From this small town, it's only a mile west (toward Astoria) on Route 202 to the first viewpoint for the 1,200-acre Jewell Meadows Wildlife Area (tel. 503/755–2264) on Fishhawk Creek. Elk, coyote, black-tailed deer, and red-tailed hawks live in the meadows and forests. Because Jewell is a wildlife refuge, it's closed to hikers and campers. If you don't mind skipping Seaside (*see below*) and a few sights along the way, Route 202 goes northwest to Astoria.

Seaside

Once a seedy variation on Coney Island, Seaside has recently cleaned up its act and shed some of its garishness for a more family-oriented atmosphere. The droves of tourists, however, have remained a part of the package. Less than 4 miles north of the U.S. 26 junction lies the town's main attraction—its long, flat beach, with a boardwalk called the **Prom** running alongside. The Prom is ideal for jogging, cycling, walking, or watching others sweat. Turn-of-the-century houses, built when Seaside was a vacation spot for the Portland elite, line the east side of the Prom. The town's main thoroughfare, **Broadway,** runs east–west and meets the Prom at the **Turnaround,** a traffic circle with a statue of Lewis and Clark at its center. The statue marks the endpoint of the pair's expedition, which extended no farther south along the coast.

From the Prom, a stroll east on Broadway takes you through Seaside's so-called "Million Dollar Walk"—four blocks of arcades, miniature golf, bumper cars, shops, crowded restaurants, and all the taffy you can eat. Sure, it's touristy, but you can enjoy it in small doses. You might want to check out the **Seaside Aquarium** (200 N. Prom, tel. 503/738–6211), just north of the Turnaround. Built in 1937, this two-room aquarium definitely looks its age, but it's worth paying the $4.50 admission if you're into this sort of thing. In the outer room, you can feed harbor seals and get splashed as they dive for the food. In the inner room you'll see four Pacific octopuses swimming around and doing their best to look freakishly unreal. The aquarium is open weekdays 9–6 and weekends 9–8 in summer, and Wednesday to Sunday 9–5 in winter.

BASICS **Seaside Chamber of Commerce and Visitors Bureau.** This state welcome center has brochures and maps covering all of Oregon. *Tel. 503/738–6391 or 800/444–6740. Northeast cnr of Broadway and U.S. 101. Open summer, Mon.–Sat. 8–6, Sun. 9–5; winter, weekdays 9–5, weekends 10–4.*

WHERE TO SLEEP The most expensive rooms line the beachside Prom. In summer, make reservations or arrive by 1 PM. If the hotels below are filled, make your way to the **Coast River Inn** (800 S. Holladay Rd., tel. 503/738–8474), with clean doubles for $45–$60 in summer; or the *very* purple **Driftwood Motel** (825 N. Holladay Rd., tel. 503/738–5597), where old but functional rooms with kitchens run $35–$60 in summer.

Riverside Inn Bed and Breakfast. This wonderful inn combines the private baths and color TVs of a motel with the personalized rooms and homey feel of a bed-and-breakfast. All rooms come with books, and some have kitchens. Guests may eat breakfast on the deck overlooking the Necanicum River. Rates are $50–$85 in summer and $45–$80 in winter. *430 S. Holladay Rd., tel. 503/738–8254 or 800/826–6151. 11 rooms. From Broadway, south on S. Holladay Rd.*

Royale Motel. The large, clean rooms in this motel on the Necanicum's west bank run $36–$43 in winter and $45–$56 in summer. All the rooms have big windows and plenty of light. *531 Avenue A, tel. 503/738–9541. 1 block south of Broadway. 26 rooms.*

Sundowner Motor Inn. The clean rooms and the location (a block from the beach and bustling Broadway) lift the Sundowner out of standard motel limbo. All the rooms have refrigerators, and guests can use the small indoor pool and whirlpool. Doubles run $50–$60 in winter and $60–$70 in summer. *125 Ocean Way, tel. 503/738–8301. 1 block north of Broadway. 22 rooms.*

➤ **CAMPING • Ft. Stevens State Park.** This massive campground offers forested sites near beaches and lakes. If your Tevas have been twitching for some action, try the 8 miles of biking and hiking paths that crisscross the park. Tent sites are $16; during summer, reservations are advised. *Ridge Rd., Hammond, tel. 503/861–1761. 9 mi north on U.S. 101, then take well-marked road to state park. 262 tent sites. Hot showers.*

FOOD If you can't decide what kind of food you want, head to **Broadway,** where everything from seafood and burgers to pancakes and ice cream comes at a reasonable price. For nightlife, try the **Shilo Inn Lounge** (Prom and Broadway, tel. 503/738–8481), where a DJ cranks out tunes (cover $1) every night starting at 9. You can hit the tiny dance floor or just enjoy a sterling view of the ocean. The crowd gets younger as the night progresses. Beer on tap starts at $1.25, and mixed drinks begin at $3.

Dooger's Seafood and Grill. This popular and often crowded restaurant offers its best deals during lunch, when a halibut sandwich costs $4.50 (or $5.50 with a cup of chowder). At dinner, expect prices to climb into the $10–$12 range. You can wait as long as an hour on weekend nights. *505 Broadway, tel. 503/738–3773.*

The Pig 'n' Pancake. Despite the name, this restaurant is more than a breakfast place; you can get steak, seafood, chicken, and pasta dishes, most of which fall into the $6–$9 range. Don't count breakfast out, however; for $3.25 you get 16 silver dollar–size pancakes. *323 W. Broadway, tel. 503/738–7243. Open summer, daily 6 AM–11 PM; winter, daily 6 AM–10 PM.*

OUTDOOR ACTIVITIES At the **Prom Bike Shop** (80 Ave. A, tel. 503/738–8251) you can rent mountain bikes and super-cool three-wheel funcycles for about $5 an hour; two-seat "trikes" go for $8 an hour.

NEAR SEASIDE

FORT STEVENS STATE PARK Travel 9 miles north of Seaside on U.S. 101 and then 5 miles northwest on the marked turnoff road to reach the worthwhile **Ft. Stevens State Park** (tel. 503/861–1671). This one-time military installation now features the requisite museum plus an enormous day-use area with scenic lakes, campgrounds, and a long stretch of beach. Ft. Stevens was built at the mouth of the Columbia River during the Civil War. During World War II a Japanese submarine fired shots nearby, without knowing the fort was there, but fortunately did no damage to the place. After the war, Ft. Stevens was deactivated as a military base, but its old gun emplacements are still outside the museum. The museum includes military artifacts, exhibits on the fort's history, and an interesting seven-minute home movie made in 1941 by a Ft. Stevens soldier showing off his big gun. In summer you can take guided tours of the underground Battery Mishler and 45-minute narrated tours of the grounds in a 1952 army cargo truck. *Ridge Rd., Hammond, tel. 503/861–2000. Day use $3, battery tour $2, truck tour $2.50. Call ahead for tour times. Open summer, daily 10–6; winter, Wed.–Sun. 10–4.*

Just south of the historic area, **Coffenbury Lake** is a good place to drop a line or take a dip. Near the beach parking lot, which is about a mile from the camping area (*see* Where to Sleep, in Seaside, *above*), lies the skeleton of the *Peter Iredale,* an English sailing ship that was beached during a storm in 1906. You might also follow the **South Jetty Road,** which branches off Ridge Road, to a raised viewing platform at Parking Area C. Here, at the northwestern tip of Oregon, you can see the Columbia River and Mt. St. Helens on a clear day. When the weather doesn't cooperate, give storm watching a try—watch the waves pound the jetty, sending spray high into the air.

FT. CLATSOP NATIONAL MEMORIAL The memorial, several miles north of Ft. Stevens off U.S. 101, marks the site where Lewis and Clark spent a miserably rainy winter in 1805–6.

The original fort disappeared long ago, but it was reconstructed in 1955 from details in the explorers' journals. You may get to see buckskin-clad rangers build canoes, demonstrate candle making or muzzle loading, and give fun (really!) interactive talks. The new visitor center offers movies and displays about Lewis and Clark and the Native Americans of the lower Columbia River. *Tel. 503/861–2471. From U.S. 101N, follow signs for 3 mi on Alternate U.S. 101. Admission: $2. Open mid-June–Labor Day, daily 8–6; off-season, daily 8–5.*

Astoria

Established in 1811, this historic town at the mouth of the Columbia River goes unnoticed by most visitors, despite its world-class museum, miles of beaches, and Victorian homes on a hillside overlooking the water. Add to these the distinction of being the first permanent U.S. settlement west of the Rockies, and most towns would have sold their soul to tourism long ago. But Astoria maintains its identity as a gritty fishing and logging town, whose past adds character without rendering Astoria a lifeless model from the 19th century. On busy **Commercial Street** downtown, you won't find many boutiques or upscale restaurants—just sandwich joints, hole-in-the-wall cafés, movie theaters, and functional shops.

VISITOR INFORMATION **Astoria-Warrenton Chamber of Commerce.** Pick up the informative "Explorer's Guide to the History of Astoria." *111 W. Marine Dr., on U.S. 30, tel. 503/325–6311. Open summer, Mon.–Sat. 8–6, Sun. 9–5; winter, weekdays 8–5, weekends 10–4.*

WHERE TO SLEEP Astoria has almost as many B&Bs as it does motels, and their prices are a bit more reasonable than on the rest of the coast. The chamber of commerce has a complete listing. Travelers on a tight budget, however, should head immediately to the hostel (*see below*). If you've exhausted these options, check out the motels on Marine Drive just west of downtown.

Ft. Columbia State Park Hostel. On the Washington side of the Columbia River, this hostel was once a military infirmary at the army fort, and guests still sleep on hospital beds. Five miles of hiking trails adjoin this hopping hostel, and the beach is only five minutes away. Rates are $9 for members and $12 for nonmembers; those traveling by bike pay $2 less. *Ft. Columbia State Park, tel. 206/777–8755. Cross Astoria Bridge and follow U.S. 101 west 2½ mi. 24 beds in 3 rooms. Curfew 10 PM (loosely enforced). Open March–October.*

Lamplighter Motel. Sandwiched between the Pig 'n' Pancake restaurant and the chamber of commerce (how's that for location?), this motel has clean rooms with cable TV—just like living with your parents. You'll pay $38–$42 for a double in winter and $48–$58 in summer. *131 W. Marine Dr., at Hume St., tel. 503/325–4051. 29 rooms.*

Windover House B&B. For great views of Young's Bay and the Columbia River, look no further than this attractive house (circa 1917) with antique furnishings and Danish decorations. Warm hospitality and a full breakfast add to the appeal of this place, though the three cats could make life a nightmare for allergic types. Rooms run $60–$70. *550 W. Lexington Ave., tel. 503/325–8093. From Marine Dr. take 8th St., right on Lexington Ave. 3 rooms.*

FOOD Astoria has no shortage of fast-food restaurants, but if franchises don't flip your burger you can do fine at the cafés and sandwich shops on the downtown segment of Marine Drive.

Andrew and Steve's Café. To stay in business for nearly 80 years, a restaurant must be doing something right. At this rather ordinary-looking café, tasty food does the trick: A steak sandwich runs about $6.50 and sautéed vegetables over fettucini alfredo are about $7. For dessert, try the homemade pie at $2 a slice. *1196 Marine Dr., tel. 503/325–5762. Open daily 6 AM–9 PM.*

Columbian Café. This tiny one-room café is among the best finds on the coast. Everything on the menu costs less than $6, and thankfully, the food is significantly fresher than the pleasantly jaded waiters and waitresses. Try fish and vegetarian dishes such as a spinach frittata ($4) or mushroom-and-cheese crepe ($4.50). On cold, wet days, wash your meal down with hot apple cider. *1114 W. Marine Dr., at 11th St., tel. 503/325–2233. No dinner Mon. or Tues.; closed Sun. No credit cards.*

Ship Inn. At this restaurant on the south bank of the Columbia River, you can eat while watching ships and seabirds. Sandwiches run $4.50–$6, but the specialty is the British standby fish-and-chips in unusual varieties. Try a filling half-order—maybe squid-and-chips?—for a little over $5. *1 2nd St., at W. Marine Dr., tel. 503/325–0033. Open daily 11:30–9:30.*

WORTH SEEING Intentionally or not, most visitors will check out the massive **Astoria Bridge,** which stretches 4.1 miles to Washington state. **Marine Drive,** which runs alongside the river, passes beneath the bridge, and **Coxcomb Hill** looms over the river, with most of the town on its flanks. Many of the old Victorian houses are on the northern slope of the hill, between Duane and Grand avenues and 8th and 17th streets. At the top of the hill is one of Astoria's main attractions: the 125-foot **Astoria Column.** If you have the energy to walk up 164 winding steps to its top, you'll be treated to a panoramic view of the area. The lazy can enjoy the town's second-best view from the base of the column. A weathered frieze on the outside of the column depicts the period when European Americans "discovered" Oregon and the accompanying massive migrations. The column is open from dawn to dusk and admission is free. To get there, head up 16th street from Marine Drive and follow the signs.

Down the hill by the river is the **Columbia River Maritime Museum,** Astoria's star attraction. Inside this large, wave-shaped museum you can see the the entire bridge of the World War II destroyer USS *Knapp* (which helped take Okinawa), and the conning tower and working periscopes of the submarine USS *Rasher.* Get a bird's-eye view from the periscope, where you can watch the ships on the river outside the museum. Your museum admission also allows you to wander around the lightship *Columbia,* rendered obsolete in the '70s and now floating alongside the museum. *1792 Marine Dr. at 17th St., tel. 503/325–2323. Admission: $5. Open daily 9:30–5.*

WESTERN OREGON AND THE CASCADES

4

By Josh Lichtner

To most out-of-staters, traveling in western Oregon means touring the Oregon coast. According to this myth, the farther inland you go, the more ordinary the surroundings. But if you look at any decent map, you'll immediately notice the grand swath of green that stretches the entire length of the state some 100–150 miles inland from the ocean. This splash of color would be the wondrous Cascade Mountains, made up of dormant volcanoes several million years old. The range runs as far north as British Columbia and south into California. Among its peaks you'll find literally hundreds of campgrounds; rivers and lakes for swimming, fishing, and rafting; and a worthy hiking trail around every bend. Just east of Portland you can visit the Cascades' tallest peak, Mt. Hood (11,235 feet). For an even more striking sight, run—don't walk—to Crater Lake, in the southern part of the state. The lake earned its name when mighty Mt. Mazama blew its top and rainwater and snow runoff combined to fill the gaping hole. The sight of its deep blue water, circled by ridges 8,000 feet high, can be dizzying.

Providing a diversion from the sometimes harsh natural beauty are towns like Ashland, with its ongoing Shakespeare festival, and collegiate Eugene. I–5 runs north–south through the state, connecting Medford, Grants Pass, Roseburg, Eugene, Salem, and Portland. On the southern end of this corridor, the Rogue River Valley offers some of the best hiking, fishing, swimming, and white-water rafting in the state. Farther north you'll encounter the fertile Willamette Valley, home to several first-rate wineries. The climate on the west side of the Cascades tends to be wet and cool from fall to spring, with sunny skies and 80° days in June. The damp westerly winds never make it over the mountains, however, so the east side is dry and hot in summer, and dry and cold in winter. Between late fall and early spring, areas near the mountains receive a lot of snow. Expect some crowds in summer, but nothing near what you'll encounter on the coast.

Sculptured peaks, empty craters, and caves formed from hardened lava offer evidence of the region's volatile past.

As for outdoor activities, well, it just don't get much better than Western Oregon. Cyclists should stick to U.S. 97, which runs from Klamath Falls to the Columbia River (east of The Dalles). Avoid Routes 66 and 138 to the south; they are narrow and dangerous. Before you hit the pavement, contact the **Oregon Department of Transportation** (210 Transportation Building, Salem 97310, tel. 503/378–3432) for their free *Oregon Bicycling Guide.* If you want to fish, try to bring your own equipment; rentals are scarce and damned expensive. Licenses cost $6.75 a day, $30 a week, and $40 for the season. For the lowdown on hiking in the area, try *Exploring Oregon's Wild Areas,* available in bookstores throughout Oregon.

Western Oregon

0   60 miles
0   90 km

WASHINGTON

Columbia R.

Astoria
Seaside
Cannon Beach

30

26

Columbia River Gorge National Scenic Area

N

Tillamook National Forest

Portland
Beaverton

Milwaukee

84

Hood River

The Dalles

Mt. Hood

35

197

97

Tillamook

6

McMinnville

5

213

Maupin

26

PACIFIC OCEAN

101

18

22

Salem

Lincoln City

99W

22

Newport

20

Corvallis

Albany

34

Madras

97

Sweet Home

20

Willamette National Forest

Sisters

Prineville

Redmond

Suislaw National Forest

126

McKenzie R.

Bend

Florence

Eugene

Springfield

58

Deschutes R.

Newberry Crater

Oregon Dunes National Recreation Area

Reedsport

38

Willamette Pass

La Pine

97

31

North Bend
Coos Bay
Coquille

Oakland
Sutherlin

138

Umpqua National Forest

Crater Lake National Park

Silver Lake

Myrtle Point

101

42

Roseburg

5

Crater Lake

Crater Lake

Summer Lake

62

Fremont National Forest

Rogue R.

Siskiyou National Forest

Grants Pass

199

Upper Klamath Lake

Beatty

140

Gold Beach

Oregon Caves National Monument

Jacksonville

Medford

Ashland

Illinois Valley
Brookings

Takilma

Rogue River National Forest

Klamath Falls

CALIFORNIA

CASCADE RANGE

GETTING AROUND

BY CAR Many attractions lie on side roads and scenic loops, so driving is the only option if you want to take in a lot in a short time. However, drivers need to take certain precautions: You can travel 100 miles on some of these roads without seeing a gas station, so keep an eye on the tank and fill up when you pass through a town. Between late fall and early spring, you're advised—and often required—to have snow tires and to carry chains when crossing the Cascades; some passes may close. Contact local chambers of commerce for up-to-date information on conditions. U.S. 97 runs the length of the state on the east side of the Cascades, and I–5 runs along the west side. Many east–west routes connect U.S. 97 with I–5.

If you're hitching, your best bet is to stay off of I–5 and use the smaller highways. Heading north or south, try U.S. 99, which parallels I–5. On east–west journeys almost every route will get you a ride sooner or later.

BY BUS AND TRAIN Buses and trains are best if you're headed for a specific destination and don't really want to see anything. **Greyhound** (tel. 800/231–2222) connects most major cities in the region. The bus from Eugene to Grants Pass (3½ hrs) costs $20 one-way· from Eugene to The Dalles (6½ hrs) you'll pay $27.25. **Amtrak** (tel. 800/872–7245) has once-a-day service in Oregon between Portland and Klamath Falls, stopping along the way in Salem, Albany, Eugene, and Chemult. The trip from Portland to Klamath Falls (7½ hrs) costs $64 one-way.

BY PLANE Many major cities in the region have tiny airports servicing only California and the Pacific Northwest. The **Eugene Airport** (28855 Lockheed Dr., tel. 503/687–5430) is the exception; you can fly from here to almost anywhere in the United States, and to several places in Europe and Asia as well.

WHERE TO SLEEP

You'll find plenty of national forest campgrounds in the areas around the Cascades. Mostly on quiet county and forest service roads, these sites offer privacy in a wilderness setting. The state parks are also secluded, though they cost more and aren't as numerous as on the coast. The only state parks in this region that accept reservations are **Detroit Lake** (tel. 503/854–3346 in summer, 503/854–3406 off-season), east of Salem, and **Cove Palisades** (tel. 503/546–3412), north of Bend—and the latter only takes reservations in summer. Of course, you'll find motels just about anywhere you go; prices start at around $28, but expect to pay more in many areas. If you have the cash, check out the many bed-and-breakfasts in the Cascades region. Although rates start at around $45, lots of these places will charm the bejeezers off you, and the price includes an often enormous breakfast. For a fairly comprehensive list of B&Bs, pick up a copy of the *Oregon Bed-and-Breakfast Directory* at any chamber of commerce or visitor center, or call 800/841–5448 and ask them to send you copy before your trip. There aren't many hostels in the Cascades region, but the few that exist are listed here.

Rogue River Valley

Back in the days of the Wild West, gold seekers came to this part of southwest Oregon to find their fortune. Nowadays, they've been replaced by wilderness seekers intent on white-water thrills and rugged beauty. The Rogue—one of only eight U.S. rivers to be designated "wild and scenic" by Congress—originates in the Cascades, flows south and then west through Grants Pass, and ultimately empties into the Pacific at Gold Beach (*see* Chapter 3). Along the way, calm waters alternate with roaring rapids, and sun-scorched green cliffs rise up from the river, forming canyons inhabited by deer, black bears, otters, wild turkeys, and bald eagles. Guided boat trips are easy to find, but you can also see much of the river by car and nearly all of it on foot.

With the notable exception of Ashland and its thriving theater scene, the emphasis here should be on the great outdoors. Cheap hotels and restaurants are concentrated in Grants Pass and Medford, but neither town offers much besides convenience. Near Medford, you can check out historic Jacksonville, a boomtown during the 19th-century gold rush. Southwest of Grants Pass are redwood forests and the Oregon Caves National Monument, with 3 miles of underground passages. The Rogue River Valley gets far less rain than most areas west of the Cascades—there's almost none in summer, when temperatures hover around 90°. Budget travelers should follow the sun to one of the area's many campgrounds—without a doubt the best way to experience the region. The **Rogue River National Forest Supervisor's Office** (333 W. 8th St., Medford, tel. 503/858–2200), open weekdays 7:45–4:30, provides maps, brochures, and advice.

COMING AND GOING

Cars and bikes are the vehicles of choice in the Rogue River Valley. If you're coming from the coast, take U.S. 199 northeast for 86 miles from Crescent City, California, to Grants Pass. About 30 miles of I–5 separate Grants Pass and Medford, and I–5 links the two cities with Seattle, Portland, Salem, and Eugene to the north, and San Francisco to the south. Route 140 connects Medford with Klamath Falls, 76 miles east.

BY BUS Greyhound (460 N.E. Agness Ave., Grants Pass, tel. 503/476–4513 or 800/231–2222) runs seven buses a day between Grants Pass and Medford (40 min, $5), and five between Eugene and Grants Pass (3½ hrs, $19). **Western Transport Lines** (tel. 503/772–3818 or 800/861–1025), based in Medford, has once-a-day service between Medford and Klamath Falls (1½ hrs, $17) and between Grants Pass and Crescent City (2½ hrs, $17).

BY TRAIN The closest **Amtrak** (tel. 800/872–7245) stop is in Klamath Falls.

BY PLANE The **Medford/Jackson County Airport** (tel. 503/776–7222), the major hub in southwest Oregon, has flights to California and northwestern cities on Horizon and United airlines.

OUTDOOR ACTIVITIES

HIKING This fantastic terrain offers everything from casual strolls in the woods to tough multi-day wilderness treks. The National Forest Supervisor's Office in Medford (*see above*) offers good maps and equally fine advice. The **Rogue River Trail** begins about 16 miles from the mouth of the Rogue and follows the river for 127 miles through the Siskiyou and Rogue River national forests all the way to Crater Lake National Park. The 40-mile stretch between Foster Creek (near Agness) and Grave Creek (northwest of Grants Pass) overlooks the river at its wildest points. You can access this portion of the trail by taking the Merlin–Galice Road to Galice, 15 miles northwest of Grants Pass, and continuing north for about 4 miles to Grave Creek.

The **Upper Rogue River Trail,** northeast of Medford along Routes 62 and 230, covers 75 miles and offers more scenic hiking past funky lava formations and thick old-growth forests. You might begin by taking the moderate 4.6-mile hike from the River Bridge Campground to the Woodruff Bridge Picnic Area. On the northern half of this trail, the river shoots through the narrow channel of Takelma Gorge, bordered by dark lava cliffs. To reach the trailhead from Medford, travel 39 miles northeast on Route 62 and then 1 mile northwest on Forest Service Road 6210. At its southern end, the Upper Rogue Trail passes **Lost Creek Lake,** which is also near several good hikes. The 2½-mile uphill hike to **Viewpoint Mike** climbs through stands of oak and Douglas fir and past some basalt columns from the eruption of Mt. Mazama several thousand years ago. At the end of the hike, you can see Crater Lake in the distance. The trailhead is about 30 miles northeast of Medford just off Route 62.

At 9,495 feet, the summit of Mt. McLoughlin often has you floating above the clouds.

Even during summer, ambitious hikers should try the 5-mile trail up the highest peak in southern Oregon, **Mt. McLoughlin.** The trail ascends through a forest of Shasta fir and mountain hemlock, passing an occasional elk or deer. It's cold and sometimes snowy and rainy up here, so bring warm clothing and plenty of water. To reach the trailhead from Medford, travel east for about 35 miles on Route 140 and take Forest Service Road 3650 north for about 3 miles.

RIVER TRIPS The wildest section of the Rogue River is the 40-mile stretch northwest of Grants Pass, between Grave Creek and Agness. Accessible only by boat or on foot, this section earns a Class IV rating (Class VI being the most difficult and dangerous). Those who have lived to tell advise the inexperienced to make this run with a guide. One-day excursions encounter fairly tough rapids, but you need to make a three-day commitment if you want to venture onto the wildest part of the river. Most white-water outfitters give you the option of inflatable one-person kayaks; paddle rafts, in which members of the group do the rowing; and oar-powered rafts, propelled by the guide. Call or write for reservations. **Orange Torpedo Trips/Whitewater Cowboys** (Box 1111, Grants Pass 97526, tel. 503/479–5061 or 800/635–2925) offers half-day runs for $35 and full-day trips for $50. Try to ride with Gene, the Old Man of the Rogue River; he's been rafting since 1946. **Rogue Wilderness, Inc.** (Box 1647, Grants Pass 97526; tel. 503/479–9554) has half-day trips for $40; full days run $50 and include a picnic lunch. These companies will do multi-day trips if you have the people and/or the bucks.

A slightly cheaper but less exciting way to experience the Rogue is by jet boat. These powerful vessels seat more than 20 and cruise at a clip of about 30 miles per hour, but (and this is a biggie) they're restricted from the wildest section of the river. **Hellgate Excursions** (953 S.E. 7th St., Grants Pass, tel. 503/479–7204) has two- and five-hour trips for $20 and $38, respectively; each passes the sheer cliffs of Hellgate Canyon, and the longer trip tackles some white-water rapids as well. **Jet Boat River Excursions** (8896B Rogue River Hwy., tel. 503/582–0800) offers a $10, hour-long introductory trip.

The cheapest way to get onto the water is in an inner tube, but check the nature of the river *before* you get in. Any waterway with a rating of Class III or above means that if you want to see your next birthday, you need experience or a guide. You're legally required to wear a life jacket at all times.

FISHING Anglers have quite a few options in the Rogue River Valley. The river itself teems with salmon during spring and fall runs and with steelhead trout in summer, fall, and winter. One of the best spots to fish is **Valley of the Rogue State Park,** just east of Grants Pass on I–5. If you'd prefer more solitude, try **Applegate Lake,** southwest of Medford in the Rogue River National Forest, or **Lost Creek Lake,** north of Medford on Route 62. The Rogue's many tributaries are also good sources for salmon and trout. Permits run $6–$7.50 a day and $40 for the whole season; they can be purchased at WalMart, Payless, and other, uhh . . . fine stores. Some resorts rent equipment, but in general, rentals are expensive and hard to find; your best bet is to bring or buy your own gear.

SKIING Winter visitors can hit the slopes of **Mt. Ashland** (1745 Rte. 66, tel. 503/482–2897), about 18 miles south of the town of Ashland. Here you'll find 23 downhill runs and 40 acres of night skiing areas. Lift tickets cost $16 on weekdays and $24 on weekends. To reach the resort from Ashland, take I–5 south to the Mt. Ashland exit and follow the paved road about 8 miles. Ski season usually runs from Thanksgiving to mid-April.

Ashland

At the head of the Rogue River Valley, lodged between the spectacular Siskiyou and Cascades mountain ranges, Ashland makes up for its remote location with great scenery, proximity to numerous recreation areas, and a thriving drama scene. The **Oregon Shakespeare Festival** (*see box, below*), held from mid-February to October, has turned the town into an arena for theater of all kinds, from experimental to traditional. Ashland is also home to **Southern Oregon State College** (Siskiyou Blvd., 1 mi southeast of downtown, tel. 503/552–7672), which some locals cite as Oregon's party school. Call or check the notice boards on campus for upcoming events. During winter, Ashland offers challenging and cheap downhill skiing at **Mt. Ashland** (*see* Outdoor Activities, *above*) and cross-country skiing just about anywhere there's snow.

There are several ways besides the festival to entertain yourself in town, many free and all centering around **Lithia Park,** which spreads south from the central plaza into the hills. During festival season, look for a slew of performances under the umbrella term **Festival Noons.** These include lectures by actors, directors, and scholars; music by past and contemporary composers; and dance performances. Tickets ($3) must be purchased at the Festival Box Office (*see box, below*); performances begin (surprise) at noon. For free you can attend **Talks in the**

Park, each an informal hour of questions and answers with directors, costume designers, stage managers, actors, composers, and other theater folk. Sessions begin at noon in Bankside Park, just outside Gate 1 of the Elizabethan Theater. You can also take backstage tours ($8); buy tickets at the Festival Box Office.

VISITOR INFORMATION **Ashland Chamber of Commerce.** *110 E. Main St., next to Black Swan Theater, tel. 503/482-3486. Open summer, weekdays 9–5.*

Ashland Ranger District, Rogue River National Forest. This is a good source for maps and trail information. *645 Washington St., tel. 503/482-3333. 1 block from intersection of Rte. 66 and I-5. Open weekdays 8–4:30.*

WHERE TO SLEEP If you're in the position to choose, pick Ashland over Medford or Grants Pass. Between the hostel, the motels, and the camping, visitors can always find a cheap place to stay here. But watch out—hotel rates climb $10–$20 during summer and holidays. For a hearty dose of character, try the lovely old **Columbia Hotel** (262½ E. Main St., downtown, tel. 503/482-3726). Simple doubles with a country-floral motif go for $28 in winter and $46 in summer if you're willing to share a bath (rooms with private bath are $52–$72). The 24 rooms can book up two to three months ahead for summer weekends, so try to reserve early.

For the cheapest lodging, head to the **HI Ashland Youth Hostel** (150 N. Main St., Ashland 97520, tel. 503/482-9217), a big old house with a well-kept garden. A dorm bed costs $13 ($11 for HI members) and a private double room runs $29. The 39 beds fill up, so send a check three to seven days ahead of your stay to reserve a space. You can get a shower for $2 if you're just passing through. The office is open 8–10 AM and 5–11 PM; keep in mind the midnight curfew.

B&Bs tend to be quite pricey, but they offer an interesting alternative to the generic motels. One of the cheaper B&Bs (and certainly one of the more eccentric) is **Dale Swire's Victory House** (271 Beach St., tel. 503/488-4428). Dale's dedication to the 1940s embraces almost every facet of his home: Each room is named after a wartime leader, pictures of gunboats and bombers line the hallways, the hearty meatless breakfasts honor wartime rationing, and you can take a dip in the FDR hot tub. Prices start at $54 in winter and are higher in summer depending on which "presidential suite" you choose. To get here from downtown take East Main Street to Siskiyou Boulevard and go about ½ mile to Beach Street.

➤ **CAMPING** • By far the nicest campground is the **KOA** (tel. 503/482-4138), 3½ miles east of Ashland on Route 66, with 30 tent sites ($16–$21) available March–October. Sites are fairly secluded, and you get hot showers and a game room. A general store/deli is next door,

Another Great Way to See Men in Tights

It was almost 60 years ago that Ashland local Angus Bowmer suggested the idea of an outdoor Shakespeare performance. Skeptics organized a boxing match to cover the losses, but the play turned out to be a hit. The original makeshift stage has since grown into three stunning theaters, with 11 plays drawing over 350,000 visitors every year. Ashland's Oregon Shakespeare Festival runs from mid-February to late October and features a variety of contemporary and traditional plays, in addition to the requisite dramas by Will the Quill. During summer, the best place to see a performance is at the outdoor Elizabethan Stage, which opens in June. Tickets, which run $17.50–$26.50, can be purchased at the Festival Box Office (15 S. Pioneer St., 1 block south of Main St., tel. 503/482-4331). If you're short on funds, standing-room-only tickets for the outdoor venue are just $9 a pop, or you can hope for a bargain from one of the many people who stand near the box office selling extra tickets on the day of the performance.

and Emigrant Lake is just a short walk away. You absolutely need a reservation during summer. If the KOA is full, try **Emigrant Lake County Park** (tel. 503/482–5935), a little farther east on Route 66. Sites are $12, but be warned—this is a very spartan campground; during summer, when the 42 first-come, first-served sites fill up, privacy is impossible. At least there are hot showers and the lake is only a couple hundred yards away. Look for two 280-foot water slides near the campground (10 rides for $4, $15 for the whole day).

FOOD Despite the predominance of high-priced tourist eateries, Ashland has a surprising array of reasonably priced restaurants and coffeehouses, especially in the downtown area around Main Street. The **Ashland Bakery-Cafe** (38 E. Main St., tel. 503/482–2117) and **Brother's Restaurant and Deli** (95 N. Main St., tel. 503/482–9671) serve the usual breakfast favorites (locals swear by Brother's), and **Geppetto's** (345 E. Main St., tel. 503/482–1138) features tremendous portions of American and Italian fare. Try the cheese wontons ($3) or build your own baked potato (around $3).

You'll find the hands-down best cuppa joe in town at **Garo's Java House** (376 E. Main St., tel. 503/482–2261), open weekdays 8 AM–11 PM and weekends 9 AM–midnight. This hip joint, the brainchild of two San Francisco transplants, features not only coffee drinks but also focaccia sandwiches ($4.75), live jazz on Sunday nights, and good people-watching. Farther from the downtown area, near the college, is the **Mihamu Teriyaki Grill** (1253 Siskiyou Blvd., tel. 503/488–3530). You'll forget what it looks like before you've made it out the door, but this Japanese restaurant serves delicious teriyaki dinners for under $5. If you don't fancy eating out, pick up groceries at the **Ashland Community Food Store Co-Op** (37 3rd St., just off of E. Main St., tel. 503/482–2237), open daily 9–8.

Medford

Like Grants Pass (*see below*), Medford is little more than a good hub for visiting sights in the area; even the visitor center directs tourists to attractions that lay conspicuously outside town. Long, smoggy commercial strips lead into the bustling core of the city, which has a slightly gentrified feel. If you like places with a few hip restaurants and tree-lined boulevards, Medford gets the edge over Grants Pass. Hospitals, lumber mills, and fruit-packing factories are major employers here. The **Bear Creek Corporation** (2836 S. Pacific Hwy., 1 mi south of Medford, tel. 503/776–2362) gives free tours of its fruit-packing and rose-growing operation.

VISITOR INFORMATION *Medford Visitors and Convention Bureau. 101 E. 8th St., tel. 503/779–4847. Open weekdays 9–5.*

GETTING AROUND Downtown Medford is bordered by Jackson Street to the north, 12th Street to the south, Oakdale Avenue to the west, and Riverside Avenue to the east. The **Rogue Valley Transit District** (3200 Crater Lake Ave., tel. 503/779–2877) provides bus service in town as well as to and from Jacksonville and Ashland. The base fare is 75¢; ask the driver if your trip includes any zone changes (which cost more). Hitchhikers headed to Jacksonville should wait on Main Street at the western end of town; for Grants Pass, Crater Lake, and Klamath Falls, try the northern part of Riverside Avenue; for Ashland, the southern part of Riverside. **Greyhound** and **Western Transportation Lines** share a bus station (212 N. Bartlett Ave., tel. 503/779–2103 or 800/231–2222).

If you've come to the Rogue River Valley poorly prepared, you can thank your lucky stars as you make your way to McKenzie Outfitters (130 E. 8th St., tel. 503/773–5145), the largest camping and recreation store between California and Eugene.

WHERE TO SLEEP Motels cluster on Riverside Avenue, on the east side of the downtown area. Between Jackson and Maple streets on Riverside, you'll find a cluster of dull, functional, and cheap places. The **Cedar Lodge** (518 N. Riverside Ave., tel. 503/773–7361), with a pool, a patio, and clean rooms, wins the award for most accommodating; doubles cost $40–$45 during peak season. The **Tiki Lodge** (509 N. Riverside Ave., tel. 503/773–4579) is slightly cheaper, with doubles for around $38 in summer. Central Avenue, just west of Riverside, has equally unspectacular choices. The **City Center Motel** (324 S. Central Ave., tel.

503/773–6248) charges only $32 for a double; for a few dollars more, you get a much cleaner room at the **Sierra Inn** (345 S. Central Ave., tel. 503/773–7727). Those who wish to bypass roadside motels and splurge on a B&B should head to nearby Jacksonville or Ashland; the latter also has a hostel.

➤ **CAMPING** • Camping is somewhat scarce in the immediate vicinity. You can take Route 238 about 14 miles southwest of town past Jacksonville to **Cantrall-Buckley Park** (at Ruch, take upper Applegate turnoff to Hamilton Rd., tel. 503/776–7001). The 30 sites ($10) are unexceptional, but nearby Applegate River makes up for the campground itself. Route 62 passes several generic private campgrounds on its way north to Crater Lake, but save yourself for the 20-plus sites at **Rogue Elk Park** (Rte. 62, tel. 503/776–7001), about 27 miles from Medford. Forested spots ($8) with plenty of space border the Rogue. Going east on Route 140 toward Klamath Falls, you can stop off at Fish Lake in the Rogue River National Forest. Two national forest campgrounds and one private campground provide a total of about 50 sites right on the water, with nearby hiking trails leading into the forest. Of the three, **Doe Point Campground** (Rte. 140, 33 mi east of Medford, tel. 503/482–3333) offers the best bet for a little privacy, with 25 sites ($9) on the quiet north shore of the lake.

FOOD **C.K. Tiffin.** The hippest spot in town comes complete with an old redbrick wall covered with art posters and painted old-time advertisements. The menu offers unmistakably healthy fare, including a grain burger with Caesar salad ($4.95) and rice pilaf with seasoned beans ($2.95). Breakfasts are a deal at $3.50 or less. *226 E. Main St., downtown, tel. 503/779–0480. Open weekdays 7–3.*

Grub Street Grill. The booths, carpet, and patio chairs are all green, and the imitation garden decor is a little hokey; but this place serves excellent sandwiches with names that someone probably takes very seriously. Try the Killer Diller French Dip ($5.50), the My Thai Chicken Sandwich ($5.50), or the Veggie Delight with guacamole ($4.85). For the evening crowd, there's a sports pub in back and lots of microbrews on tap. *35 N. Central St., tel. 503/779–2635. Open Mon.–Thurs. 10–9, Fri. 10–10, Sat. noon–10.*

Samovar Restaurant adds a few Russian touches (read: wooden dolls) to Medford's usual Denny's aesthetic, and a creeping plastic vine clinging to a white trellis nicely divides the restaurant into two garish pink spheres instead of one.

Samovar Restaurant and Bakery. Even if the only Russian word you know is "vodka," chances are you'll find something great among the Russian and Middle Eastern dishes here. For breakfast, try the cheese blintzes ($4.50); for lunch, the Siberian pelmene (poached pasties stuffed with meat and topped with sour cream; $4.25) makes a filling and tasty meal. *101 E. Main St., at Front St., tel. 503/779–4967. Open Mon. 7:30–3, Tues.–Sat. 7:30–3 and 5–9.*

NEAR MEDFORD

JACKSONVILLE About 5 miles west of Medford on Route 238, this well-preserved example of an 1850s gold-rush town offers all the charm of a breezy Sunday afternoon. About 80 late-19th-century buildings remain, including the Methodist-Episcopal Church, the County Jail (now the Children's Museum), and the Rogue River Valley Railway Depot. Poke around the shops lining the wooden boardwalk or visit the **Jackson County Museum** (206 N. 5th St., tel. 503/773–6536), the one-time county seat (until it moved to Medford), which displays the usual pioneer artifacts for a $2 admission fee. The best time to visit Jacksonville is between June and early September, during the annual **Peter Britt Festival** (tel. 503/773–6077 or 800/88–BRITT), a medley of folk, pop, country, jazz, and classical music. In years past visitors have rubbed elbows with such greats as Wynton and Branford Marsalis, Emmylou Harris, and Fats Domino. Tickets ($14–$27) go on sale by mail in early March. After June 1 try **Jacksonville Books** (California St.). For more information contact the **Jacksonville Chamber of Commerce** (185 N. Oregon St., tel. 503/899–8118).

Grants Pass

The best thing to be said for Grants Pass is that it makes you appreciate the incredible surrounding countryside all the more. If it weren't for its location on the Rogue River and its proximity to the Oregon Caves National Monument, Grants Pass would barely be noticed. But with almost 40 hotels and more than 100 places to eat, this city takes good care of budget travelers. After you've met basic needs, head out of town; in addition to U.S. 199 (see Near Grants Pass, *below*), there are several roads worth checking out. The Merlin–Galice Road meets up with the Rogue and passes the bizarre rocks and steep cliffs of **Hellgate Canyon,** about 10 miles from Grants Pass. There's nothing scenic about I-5, but it does lead 12 miles east to **Valley of the Rogue State Park,** where you can picnic alongside the river and—if you're brave—take a dip. Keep going another few miles on I-5 to reach Route 234, which leads to the **Oregon Vortex/House of Mystery** (4303 Sardine Creek Rd., Gold Hill, tel. 503/855-1543). For a steep $6 you can witness a change in the earth's magnetic field (well, that's what they say) that makes balls roll uphill.

If you're in Grants Pass on a Saturday between March and November, or a Tuesday beginning in June, head to the **Growers' Market** (4th and F St., behind post office), the largest open-air agricultural market in Oregon, open 9 AM–1 PM. Check out the crafts as well as the fresh, wholesome grains and greens.

VISITOR INFORMATION **Grants Pass/Josephine County Visitors and Convention Bureau.** *1501 N.E. 6th St., tel. 503/476-5510 or 800/547-5927. Open summer, daily 8–5; winter, weekdays 8–5.*

GETTING AROUND The two central one-way thoroughfares in Grants Pass are 6th Street, which runs southwest, and 7th Street, which heads northeast. Unless you're at the northernmost end of town, you can cover the whole city on foot. Hitchhikers heading toward the Oregon Caves and Crescent City should try the southern end of 6th Street; those heading east to Medford should wait on U.S. 199 at the eastern end of town. **Greyhound** and **Western Transportation Lines** share a bus station (460 N.E. Agness Ave., tel. 503/476-4513).

WHERE TO SLEEP Plenty of inexpensive motels lie along 6th and 7th streets in the heart of Grants Pass. The **Crest Motel** (1203 N.E. 6th St., northern end of town, tel. 503/479-0720) offers simple rooms with cable TV at dirt-cheap prices (doubles $26). If motel hell doesn't appeal, you can camp (see below) at a forested spot along the Rogue River.

Knight's Inn. Reasonable prices and large, clean rooms give this place a slight advantage over other cheapo motels in the area. Room rates ($30–$40) include cable TV, HBO, and coffee. Some rooms have kitchenettes. *104 S.E. 7th St., at G St. on south end of town, tel. 503/479-5595. 32 rooms. Wheelchair access.*

Riverside Inn. If escaping the drab, commercial confines of Grants Pass is a priority, make your way to this place on the Rogue River at the southern end of town. Most of the well-kept rooms have river views and some have balconies. You'll appreciate the charming song of ducks and geese on the riverbanks below—unless it's six in the morning. Rooms without a view range from $55 in the winter to $65 in the summer; with a view, you pay $65–$125. *971 S.E. 6th St., tel. 800/334-4567. 173 rooms. Wheelchair access, pool, whirlpool.*

➤ **CAMPING** • Although several campgrounds offer excellent alternatives to the dull motels in Grants Pass, your time and money might be better spent traveling farther afield (see Oregon Caves *and* Crater Lake, *below*). **Valley of the Rogue State Park** (12 mi east of Grants Pass on I-5, tel. 503/582-1118) is just a hop, skip, and a jump from a 3-mile stretch of the Rogue where you can join the fish for a swim, or drop a line and reinforce the hierarchy of the food chain. Unfortunately, I-5 is also nearby and auto noise can be a problem. The 173 sites ($15) fill quickly in summer, so arrive early. **Indian Mary Park** (12 mi west of Grants Pass on Merlin–Galice Rd., tel. 503/474–5285), a more secluded campground on the Rogue, has 89 sites ($7) with beach access. Campers can toss a ball at the park's baseball diamond or romp on hiking trails. Midway between Grants Pass and the Oregon Caves, the **Last Resort** (off U.S. 199, 2 mi east on Lake Selmac Rd., tel. 503/597–4989) is a small campground with 43 sites at $12 a night. Right on the shores of Lake Selmac, this place drips with water-sports opportunities. The woodsy sites are a healthy distance from U.S. 199, so noise isn't a problem.

FOOD On 6th and 7th streets, plenty of fast-food joints offer the full spectrum of greasy fare. For hearty sandwiches on homemade bread (less than $5), head to **Dottie's Diner** (314 S.E. H St., tel. 503/474–2561). Even better is the **Sunshine Natural Food Cafe and Market** (128 S.W. H St., 1 block west of 6th St., tel. 503/474–5044), open weekdays 9–6 and Saturday 10–5, which features tasty organic fare and the best espresso drinks this side of Seattle. The Awesome Salad ($3.95) lives up to its name with a combination of beans, tabouli, pasta, olives, and lettuce. Also look for turkey tacos ($4.75), vegetarian sandwiches ($4), and peanut-butter-and-jelly sandwiches ($1.75). If you think "organic" is something for your lawn, then perhaps you'd be better off at the **Powderhorn Cafe** (321 N.E. 6th St., downtown, tel. 503/479–9403), home of such delights as the Caveman Special Burger (with bacon, ham, cheese, and a fried egg; $5.25). Stop by Monday–Saturday 6 AM–3 PM.

NEAR GRANTS PASS

U.S. 199 Also called the Redwood Highway, this scenic road runs southwest from Grants Pass through the Illinois River Valley. It's bordered by the Siskiyou National Forest to the west and the Rogue River National Forest to the east. Needless to say, you'll see plenty of towering trees, especially near the California border, where the redwoods appear. Heading southwest, mosey on down to the **Kerbyville Ghost Town,** a replica of the 19th-century gold-rush town of the same name. It's one of the few places where miners still profitably pan for gold, and for about $4 Sourdough Ken will teach you how. You'll find Ken and a cast of grizzled but friendly cowfolk in the town bar (22300 Redwood Hwy., tel. 503/592–4939). If you're there on a Sunday or a Wednesday night you can likely check out a jam session for free. Also ask about trail rides ($15 an hour) and the Friday night ride and cookout ($20).

A few miles farther south, about 25 miles from Grants Pass, the town of Kerby is the proud home of the **Kerbyville Museum** (24195 Redwood Hwy., tel. 503/592–2076 or 503/592–4478 in winter). They're technically open only from May–September, but they'll make an exception for anyone motivated enough to call. Stop by for a hefty dose of memorabilia from the frontier days, along with a random collection of bottle openers, ancient pianos, and arrowheads. Best of all, it's free.

OREGON CAVES NATIONAL MONUMENT From Cave Junction, a few miles south of Kerby on U.S. 199, Route 46 leads 20 miles east to the Oregon Caves National Monument. Situated in Siskiyou National Forest only 48 miles from Grants Pass, the monument is one of Oregon's best-kept secrets. The caves were discovered by a hunter whose dog had chased a bear through a hillside opening. Following the harried hound, the man happened upon 3 miles of passages and rooms—all shaped out of marble. The caves formed from seashells turned to limestone about 220 million years ago, when the ocean still covered this area. Millions of years later, under the heat and pressure from nearby volcanic eruptions, the limestone was transformed into marble. These days visitors have access to about a mile of cave trails, leading past stalagmites and stalactites that sometimes meet in the middle to form columns. If your guide doesn't offer, ask him to hit the dimmer switch so you can check out the caves in their natural state—the darkness is so intense that many people lose their balance. Bring a heavy sweater, since temperatures can hover around 41°, and prepare for an uphill hike through the caves. *Tel. 503/592–3400. Admission $5.75. Open summer, daily 8–7; winter, daily 8:30–4; Sept. and May–June 8, daily 8:30–5.*

If you're tired and have a few bucks to spare, make your way to the **Oregon Caves Chateau** (20000 Caves Hwy., tel. 503/592–3400), conveniently located just below the cave's entrance. This magnificent 1930s lodge offers peace and quiet, two fireplaces, nearby waterfalls, and plenty of trees right in the middle of the Siskiyou National Forest. At $79 per double and $88 for a four-person suite ($10 less in winter), it's well worth the splurge. For reasonably priced breakfasts (all under $5) try the restored 1930s diner downstairs. Pass by the elegant and pricey dining room upstairs just to steal a glance at the stream that runs through it.

For those on a tight budget, Jack Heald's **Fordson Home Hostel** (250 Robinson Rd., Cave Junction, tel. 503/592–3203), on 20 acres of densely wooded land right near the caves, is a great choice. Jack is understandably proud of his working saw mill, organic garden, and solar shower, not to mention a vortex that does strange things to trees and people. You'll make his day if you ask about his collection of toy tractors or the 28 actual antique Fordson tractors scattered around the property. Beds are $10 for AYH members, $12 for nonmembers. Campsites cost $3. To get here from Route 46 east, go right at the second Holland Loop turnoff and left on Robinson Road.

Otherwise, several campgrounds offer wooded sites alongside creeks between May and September. **Cave Creek** (Forest Service Rd. 4032, 4 mi from caves, tel. 503/592–2166) costs $5 a site, and **Grayback** (on Rte. 46, 10 mi from caves, tel. 503/592–2166) is $7. If you stay at the former, be sure to explore the trail from the campgrounds through the forest to the caves.

ROGUE RIVER NATIONAL FOREST This 630,000-acre stretch of creeks, lakes, oak woodlands, and conifer forests consists of two separate pieces of land—one northeast of Grants Pass, bordering Crater Lake National Park, and the other along the Oregon-California border, southwest of Ashland. Both sections offer good camping and hiking, but one of Oregon's nicest campgrounds, Huckleberry Mountain, is in the northern section (*see* Crater Lake, *below*). You can access this portion of the forest on Route 62, which leads to Crater Lake, or Route 140, which goes to Klamath Falls. Be sure to catch **Mt. McLoughlin** (*see* Outdoor Activities, *above*) and **Fish Lake,** both on Route 140. The **Rogue River** runs alongside Route 62. You can reach the southern section of the forest on Forest Service roads that branch off from I–5 south of Ashland and from Route 238 southwest of Jacksonville. Look for **Applegate River, Applegate Lake** and **Mt. Ashland** (*see* Outdoor Activities, *above*).

Crater Lake National Park

With its freakish lava formations, alpine meadows, and deep canyons, Crater Lake National Park is a prime destination for both casual hikers and serious backpackers. Because of its high elevation in the southeastern Cascades, the park is covered in snow much of the year—the snowmelt usually occurs in mid-June. On a clear day, though, regardless of the time of year, even the mildest hike will amaze you. In addition to the superlative color of the lake itself—a deep blue reminiscent of some sickly-sweet crème de menthe drink—you can explore the towering Pinnacles, in a craggy canyon 8 miles from Rim Drive. In the western part of the lake, **Wizard Island**—actually a cinder cone—sticks its head 760 feet out of the water, and in the southeast you can check out the small, weatherworn island of basalt called the **Phantom Ship.**

Thanks to the lobbying efforts of William Gladstone Steel, Crater Lake and the surrounding 183,224 acres became a national park in 1902. But compared to Yellowstone and Yosemite, it hasn't quite hit the big leagues, with only a single lodge (now being renovated) and less than a half-million visitors per year. That means you can explore to your heart's content without having to worry about crowds—although your visit may still take a while, because roads are steep and windy, and many points can be accessed only on foot. Don't break any speed laws heading north of the lake; all you'll find is a mouthful of volcanic dust and wide, barren flatlands. To the west lies better cheesy-postcard material: meadows with glacier lilies and western pasqueflowers; forests of Douglas fir, sugar pine, and mountain hemlock; and streams running

About 7,000 years ago, Mt. Mazama literally blew its head off, sending ash as far as Canada and leaving a huge caldera. When the massive hole sealed over, water began to collect, and eventually Crater Lake was formed. At 1,932 feet, it's the deepest lake in the United States.

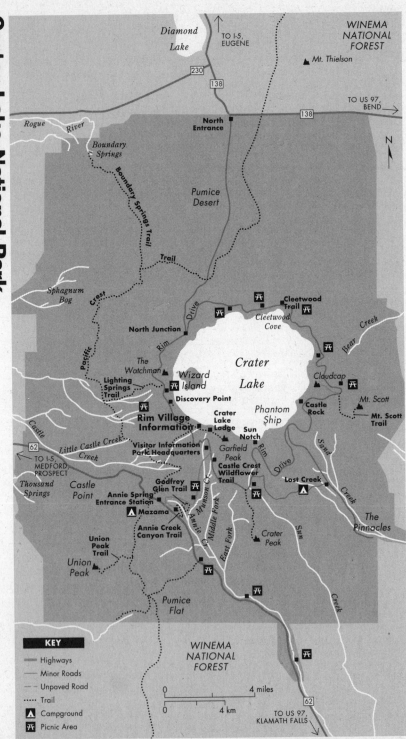

Diamond Lake

TO I-5, EUGENE

WINEMA NATIONAL FOREST

230

138

▲ *Mt. Thielson*

TO US 97, BEND →

Rogue River

North Entrance

138

Boundary Springs

N

Pumice Desert

Boundary Springs Trail

Trail

Sphagnum Bog

Crest

Pacific

North Junction

Rim Drive

Cleetwood Trail

Cleetwood Cove

Bear Creek

The Watchman

Wizard Island

Crater Lake

Cloudcap

Lighting Springs Trail

Discovery Point

▲ *Mt. Scott*

Rim Village Information

Crater Lake Lodge

Phantom Ship

Castle Rock

Mt. Scott Trail

Sun Notch

Castle Creek

62

Visitor Information Park Headquarters

Garfield Peak

Rim Drive

Sand Creek

Little Castle Creek

TO I-5, MEDFORD, PROSPECT

Castle Crest Wildflower Trail

Lost Creek

Thousand Springs

Castle Point

Godfrey Glen Trail

Annie Spring Entrance Station

Annie Creek

Middle Fork

Sun Creek

The Pinnacles

▲ **Mazama**

Annie Creek Canyon Trail

East Fork

Crater Peak

Union Peak Trail

▲ *Union Peak*

Pumice Flat

WINEMA NATIONAL FOREST

62

TO US 97, KLAMATH FALLS

KEY

— Highways
— Minor Roads
-- Unpaved Road
···· Trail
▲ Campground
🏕 Picnic Area

0 _____ 4 miles
0 _____ 4 km

through pumice canyons. **Union Peak** and **Crater Peak,** both more than 7,000 feet high, rise up over the southern end of the park, and in the southeast corner stand the cool pillars of hardened volcanic ash called the Pinnacles. East of the lake, pine forests and meadows surround **Mt. Scott,** the tallest peak (8,926 feet) in the park.

The park is well designed for those with disabilities, with scores of scenic vistas along Rim Drive, the road that circles the lake. Between June and September you pay $5 to enter by car and $3 on foot, bike, or motorcycle. If you stay on Route 62, which passes through the southwestern portion of the park, you won't get stuck with the fee, but you won't get to see the lake either.

BASICS

VISITOR INFORMATION Visitor Information Center and Park Headquarters. The center provides loads of educational and logistical information on the park, as well as free backcountry permits. Sharing duties with park rangers are the friendly and informative staff from the **Crater Lake Natural History Association.** They'll send you a mail-order catalogue of maps and books about the park. *Tel. 503/594–2211. 4 mi off Rte. 62, 3 mi south of Rim Village. Open daily 9–5.*

WHEN TO GO Crowds are rarely a problem. If you want to avoid tourists altogether, early fall is a good time to visit; during winter and spring, some park roads are closed because of snow. Winter temperatures often fall below zero. July and August produce the nicest weather, with temperatures in the high altitudes ranging from 75° to 80°, though the valleys surrounding the park may see 110° days. At any time of year, you could encounter sub-freezing nights.

GENERAL STORES **Mazama Village Camper's Service Store** (tel. 503/594–2511), at Mazama Village and Campground near the south entrance, is the only store inside the park. Come here for food and limited camping supplies; there's also a small laundromat. Weather permitting, it's open daily 8–8 from June to September, daily 8 AM–10 PM in May and October. About 25 miles west of the park on Route 138, **Diamond Lake Resort** (tel. 503/793–3333) carries the big Fs—food and fishing tackle—daily 7 AM–10 PM in summer and daily 8–6 in winter. **Union Creek Resort** (tel. 503/560–3565), about 25 miles southwest of the park on Route 62, has a similar stock. Union Creek is open daily 8–8 in summer, but winter hours vary; take your chances or call ahead.

COMING AND GOING

BY CAR You can enter the park from the north or the south. From Roseburg on I-5, Route 138 runs east to the northern entrance, where a park road takes you up to the rim of the lake. This is the best route if you're coming from Portland (6 hrs, 250 mi). In the south, the 80-mile, two-hour trip from Medford follows Route 62 northeast along the Rogue River to the southern entrance. From Klamath Falls, take U.S. 97 north for 25 miles and then Route 62 northwest for 25 miles. The two-hour drive from Bend goes south on U.S. 97, then west on Route 138.

BY BUS OR TRAIN Greyhound (tel. 800/231–2222) stops in Roseburg, Chemult, Bend, Klamath Falls, Medford, and Grants Pass. No buses go to the park from any of these points, though, so you have to hitchhike or rent a car. **Amtrak** (tel. 800/USA–RAIL) stops in Chemult, about 40 minutes' drive from the park, but this small town doesn't even have a car-rental outlet. If you're traveling by train, get off at Klamath Falls and rent a car.

WHERE TO SLEEP

Rooms are scarce in and around the park. If you plan to stay the night, your best bet is a park campground or one of the national forest campgrounds just outside. Otherwise, Klamath Falls, only 50 miles away, has plenty of cheap lodging. For protection from the elements inside park boundaries, **Mazama Village** (Rte. 62, tel. 503/594–2511) is your only choice. A quarter mile inside the south entrance near park headquarters, you'll find spacious rooms, each with two queen-size beds, at $70 for two people, $79 for three, $84 for four, and $89 for five.

Outside the park are two resorts, each about 25 miles from Crater Lake. On a mountain lake north of the park, the **Diamond Lake Resort** (off Rte. 138 and Rte. 230, tel. 503/793–3333) offers rustic accommodations and boat rentals. Motel rooms are $54; cabins start at $85, but you can squeeze six people into them at no extra charge. You're probably better off in the **Union Creek Resort** (Rte. 62, tel. 503/560–3565), just southwest of the park in the Rogue River National Forest. The nine rooms in this lodge, all made of solid wood, run $35–$45. For a quieter setting away from the road, try the smaller cabins, which start around $40. Larger cabins ($45–$65) have decks overlooking Union Creek. On the Wood River just outside the park, the **Fort Klamath Lodge Motel** (52851 Rte. 62, 6 mi south of park entrance, tel. 503/381–2234) is a good option if you're here between May and October. Comfortable doubles with real pine paneling cost $35; for $45 you can get a two-bedroom apartment that sleeps four and has a kitchenette.

CAMPING In addition to the two park campgrounds (*see below*), you'll find several decent spots a bit farther out. If altitude sickness isn't a problem, check out **Huckleberry Mountain** (Forest Service Rd. 60, tel. 503/560–3623), in the Rogue River National Forest at an elevation of more than 5,000 feet. It's only 4 miles south of Route 62 and 15 miles from the park entrance; best of all, the 25 sites are free. Bring water, since the pumps don't always work. North of the park, the Umpqua National Forest offers two massive campgrounds with water, toilets, and showers on Diamond Lake, just off Routes 138 and 230 within 6 miles of the park entrance. **Broken Arrow** (Forest Service Rd. 4795, south end of lake, tel. 503/498–2531) has 148 sites ($6), and **Diamond Lake** (Forest Service Rd. 4795, east end of lake, tel. 503/498–2531) has 240 sites ($7). **Union Creek Campground** (tel. 503/560–3623), opposite Union Creek Resort (*see above*), is another attractive site with camping alongside Union Creek and the Upper Rogue River. The 99 sites ($7) have water and toilets but no showers.

Lost Creek Campground. Lost Creek has tent sites only (no RVs!) and is much more secluded than its neighbor Mazama (*see below*). Sites with water and pit toilets, but no showers, are $5 per night. It's about halfway down the road from Rim Drive to the Pinnacles, in the southeast section of the park. *Tel. 503/594–2211. 16 sites. Open July–Sept. No reservations.*

Mazama Campground. At the Annie Spring entrance, this is the larger of the park's two campgrounds. With hot showers, a store, and even a mini-laundromat, it's no wonder RV owners like the location; expect some heavy traffic in summer. The most private tent spots ($11) are on the outer loops above Annie Creek Canyon. *Off Rte. 62, tel. 503/594–2511. 198 sites. Open June–mid-Oct. No reservations.*

FOOD

The lack of development around Crater Lake may preserve its natural splendor, but the dining scene here sucks. Your best bet is to buy groceries at a market or general store (*see* Basics, *above*) and picnic at a site on Rim Drive; the Vidae Falls area offers a great Alpine setting overlooking Sun Creek. Otherwise, head to the restaurants in Medford or Klamath Falls.

INSIDE THE PARK Rim Village Cafeteria. This is the best place in the park for a sit-down meal, but only by default (there are no other options). The deli/lounge, right in the main parking lot, offers mediocre pub fare ($5–$7), including burgers, mini-pizzas, and fried seafood. Beer, wine, and cocktails satisfy that nagging thirst. *Tel. 503/594–2511. Open summer, 8 AM–7 PM; no dinner Oct.–June.*

NEAR THE PARK Beckie's Cafe. This tiny roadside joint next to the Union Creek Resort (*see* Where to Sleep, *above*) has served up cheap home cookin' for more than 60 years. The pies are the best things on the menu; if huckleberry's out of season, try Very Berry à la mode ($3). *25 mi southwest of Crater Lake on Rte. 62, Prospect, tel. 503/560–3565. Open summer, Sun.–Thurs. 8 AM–8 PM, Fri.–Sat. 8 AM–9 PM; winter hours vary, call ahead.*

Diamond Lake Resort. The café on the ground floor offers a predictable, informal, sit-down meal for just a little more than you'd want to pay; the all-you-can-eat soup and salad bar ($4.95) is the best choice here. If you have an extra $30 you're just dying to spend, hit the upstairs Dinner House, where excellent prime rib goes for $17.95. You'd probably be better off at the standard **South Shore Pizza Parlor** (tel. 503/793–3330) across the lake. *25 mi from Crater Lake, off Rtes. 138 and 230, tel. 503/793-3333. Café open weekdays 5 AM–9 PM, weekends until 10 PM.*

EXPLORING CRATER LAKE

You can get a taste of the park even if you stay in your car—the 33-mile Rim Drive circles Crater Lake, and an 8-mile trip leads out to the Pinnacles. But to reach the more remote regions of the park, you need to hike. For a thorough exploration of the park and the lake— including the guided boat tour given by the park service—figure on spending at least a day. Biking around Rim Drive allows for easier access to the viewpoints, but the road is more than 7,000 feet high, with steep, narrow stretches and no shoulder; this trek is a challenge, to say the least. Bicycles are forbidden on park trails, and there are no rentals in the park.

ORIENTATION PROGRAMS At the Sinnott Memorial Overlook in Rim Village, park rangers give 15-minute presentations on the geology and volcanic history of the lake. Talks are offered only four times a day, so check with rangers for times. A 20-minute introductory video at park headquarters, shown every hour, previews the major attractions. On a clear day, skip the video and see the sights firsthand.

GUIDED TOURS The park service offers a two-hour narrated boat ride around the lake. Private boats are forbidden, so the tour is your only chance to see the lake up close. If you have the time and money ($10) and the day is clear, the tour is definitely worthwhile. You pass the **Phantom Ship,** a craggy basalt island on the southern shore, and stop off for five minutes at **Wizard Island,** a cinder cone that rises 760 feet above the water. You can choose to stay on the island and return on a later boat; popular activities here include hiking, picnicking, fishing, and swimming (though 45° water can be disheartening). From early July to early September, a 40-passenger boat leaves hourly 10–4 from Cleetwood Cove, on the north side of the lake. To reach the boat landing from Rim Drive, you have to hike down the mile-long Cleetwood Trail (*see below*).

SHORTER HIKES Most trails begin on Rim Drive and are clearly marked. To reach the lake, take the mile-long **Cleetwood Trail.** At the bottom of the steep descent, you can catch the boat tour (*see above*), fish, or just stick your toes in the icy blue water. It's about a 20-minute trip down to the lake, but allow as much as an hour for the uphill climb back to Rim Drive. The short, steep **Watchman Trail** leaves Rim Drive on the western side of the lake and climbs a little less than a mile to the Watchman, an 8,035-foot precipice. From here, you look down about 2,000 feet over Wizard Island and its lagoon. Signs in the parking area at the Wizard Island Overlook point you to the trailhead.

Just off the winding road that leads up to Rim Drive from the Annie Spring entrance on Route 62 is the easy **Castle Crest Wildflower Trail,** which follows Munson Creek for just under a mile. During summer, this trail passes some of the park's most colorful meadows. A sign pointing toward the trailhead is across the street from the Steel Center at park headquarters.

LONGER HIKES On the eastern side of the park, the 2½-mile (one-way) **Mt. Scott Trail** begins at about 7,800 feet and climbs more than 1,000 feet to the highest point in the park. Views to the west take in the lake and the dappled cliffs that surround it; to the east you'll see the broad Klamath Valley. The moderately difficult trail has several steep sections, and the high elevation can quite literally take your breath away. The trailhead is on the east side of Rim Drive, midway between the Cleetwood Trail and Rim Village.

The **Pacific Crest Trail** stretches from Canada to Mexico, and more than 30 challenging miles of it run through the park's canyons and forests. You can pick up the trail just east of the park's north entrance, passing through the Pumice Desert and around the western side of the lake, and finally leaving the park southeast of Union Peak. Pacific Crest hikers who want to see the lake should take the 4-mile (one-way) **Lightening Springs Trail,** which leaves the Pacific Crest Trail in the western half of the park, climbs about 1,500 feet, and meets up with Rim Drive a mile south of the Watchman. Some hikers begin at Rim Drive and head down to the Pacific Crest Trail, continuing on to the south end of the park.

In the northwest section of the park, the 8-mile (one-way) **Boundary Springs Trail** cuts a path between the Pumice Desert to the east and a forest of Douglas fir and mountain hemlock to the west, ending finally at Boundary Springs, the source of the Rogue River. You can access the trail by parking on the road that leads from the north entrance to Rim Drive, and then following the Pacific Crest Trail about 3 miles west to the Boundary Springs Trailhead. Signs on the road are easy to miss, so watch closely.

PARK ACTIVITIES

FISHING Rainbow trout, brown trout, and kokanee salmon were introduced to Crater Lake in the 19th century. Those who covet these creatures usually cast their line from the boat landing or, if they take the boat tour (*see* Guided Tours, *above*), from Wizard Island. Your park permit doubles as a fishing license, but don't expect a fruitful day; it's difficult to find the fish in Crater Lake. If the equipment you have on you won't suffice, the closest place to rent is **Diamond Lake Resort** (*see* Basics, *above*).

Crater Lake's deep blue water consists mostly of snow runoff, and the water stays at about 45°F year-round, which makes swimming a numbing experience. The intrepid usually take their dips on warm summer days in the lagoon on Wizard Island.

CROSS-COUNTRY SKIING There are no maintained trails in the park, but from November to June cross-country skiers cruise Rim Drive. Rent equipment at **Rim Village** (tel. 503/594–2511); skis cost $11 for the day, $8 for a half day, and $3.50 for an hour. Most people tackle only a section of Rim Drive, since the entire circle takes about two or three days and roads often close after heavy storms. Ski season starts in late October and runs through April, snow permitting.

SNOWSHOEING Most people stick to Rim Drive, since snowdrifts and steep inclines can make treks elsewhere in the park very difficult. You can rent shoes at **Rim Village** (tel. 503/594–2511); prices are similar to those for skis (*see above*).

Near Crater Lake

KLAMATH FALLS This town on U.S. 97, at the south end of Upper Klamath Lake, is an interesting place to wile away an afternoon or two before visiting Crater Lake. At the **Klamath County Museum** (1451 Main St., tel. 503/883–4208), open Monday–Saturday 9–5:30, and Sundays until 5 in summer and Monday–Saturday 8–4:30 in winter, you can explore the region's natural history and check out artifacts of the settlers and Native Americans for free (donations welcome). Especially impressive is the collection of Native American grinding tools. Inside the museum, a **visitor information center** has info on the entire state of Oregon. If you're into western kitsch, the **Favell Museum** (125 West Main St., tel. 503/882–9996), open Monday–Saturday 9:30–5:30, should be worth the $4 admission fee. About three blocks away, the **Baldwin Hotel** (31 Main St., tel. 503/883–4208), converted from a hardware store in 1911 and now restored to its early splendor, is an interesting stop. It's open Tuesday–Saturday 10–4 from June to September, and admission is $4 ($3 for students). During summer, a free 45-minute trolley ride takes you from the Baldwin past the historic buildings of the downtown area to the Klamath County Museum.

The town's current transition from logging town to tourist mecca has not been smooth, but it's no doubt a whole lot easier than the one the Modoc and Klamath tribes underwent when white trappers and settlers arrived in the region in the mid-1800s.

If you prefer scenic drives to relics, take the 110-mile **Lower Klamath Loop Tour,** which follows U.S. 97 south past the California border and returns to Klamath Falls via Route 139 and Route 39. Or try the 52-mile **Upper Klamath Lake Tour,** which heads north along Route 140, takes you through the town of Fort Klamath, and comes back along Route 62 and U.S. 97. Both loops pass farms, forests, and marshlands, and offer excellent opportunities to see waterfowl and bald eagles.

➤ **WHERE TO SLEEP** • Klamath Falls has a slew of affordable motels on U.S. 97, South 6th Street, and Main Street. The absolute cheapest is the **Brae Crest Motel** (3006 Green Springs Dr., near junction of Rte. 140 and U.S. 97, 1 mi south of town, tel. 503/884–9812). Threadbare but functional rooms with a fridge and a TV go for just $26—what more could you ask? If you want to stay in the heart of town, head for the **Maverick Motel** (1220 Main St., tel. 503/882–6688), which has clean doubles for about $35. If you feel like living it up a little before you hit the parks, the **Klamath Manor B&B** (219 Pine St., tel. 503/883–5459 or 800/956–5459), one block from Main Street in the downtown area, is the place to do it. The $55 doubles at this plush restored house are quiet and comfy, and the breakfasts are insanely good. The warm and eager hosts can help you find your way around Klamath Falls.

➤ **FOOD** • The **Klamath Grill** (715 Main St., tel. 503/882–1427), in all its faux wood-paneled glory, is the hands-down local favorite for breakfast. Pancake or French toast specials with eggs and meat sell for less than $3.75. At lunch, the grilled sandwiches run under $5. Chow down weekdays 6 AM–2:30 PM and weekends 7–2. The sandwiches at **Inge's Cheese Haus** (4023 S. 6th St., tel. 503/884–1810), open weekdays 11–7 and Saturday 11–3, would make a New York deli proud. For less than $5 you get a big sandwich, all the homemade soup you can eat, and a dollop of potato salad. Your best bet for dinner is **Sergio's Mexican Restaurant** (327 Main St., tel. 503/883–8454), which serves damn tasty fare at slightly inflated prices Monday–Saturday 11–10 and Sunday 11–9. The enchiladas suizas (chicken enchiladas topped with melted cheese and sour cream; $6) are delicious, and the restaurant defies Klamath Falls tradition with its tasteful decor and subdued lighting. If you're heading on to Crater Lake, then Klamath Falls is the place to stock up on food. Several supermarkets line South 6th Street, and there's a **Safeway** (N. 8th St., at Pine St., tel. 503/882–2660) downtown.

ROUTE 138 AND UMPQUA NATIONAL FOREST The 100-mile trip between the north entrance of Crater Lake and the town of Roseburg follows scenic Route 138 along the North Umpqua River, through the heart of the Umpqua National Forest (tel. 503/672–6601). It's about a 2½-hour journey if you drive straight, but you'll probably want to check out the forest's incredible offerings—waterfalls, mountain lakes, unique volcanic formations, hot springs, and groves of Douglas fir and cedar. **Diamond Lake,** about 5 miles from the north entrance, has snow-capped mountains as a backdrop and some of the best recreation in the Cascades region, including hiking, fishing, swimming, boat rentals, horseback riding, snowmobiling, and skiing. About 25 miles west of Diamond Lake you'll reach Toketee Lake. You can turn north here and follow Forest Service Road 3401 to the **Umpqua Hot Springs** (tel. 503/498–2531), a free four-person concrete tub carved into a 60-foot cliff, with 106° waters. As Route 138 winds toward Roseburg, you pass **Toketee Falls,** where the North Umpqua River plummets 120 feet through basalt columns; and **Colliding Rivers,** site of the dramatic confluence of the North Umpqua and Little rivers.

Bend and the Eastern Cascades

To most people driving north on U.S. 97 from Klamath Falls and Crater Lake National Park, Bend comes as a rude shock. But leave behind the gas fumes, fast-food franchises, and malls of "the Strip" (as U.S. 97 is known in town), and you'll get a shock of a happier nature. Downtown Bend is lovely, with good restaurants, pubs, and cafés, and the peaceful, tree-shaded **Drake Park** on the eastern bank of the Deschutes River. Bend offers all the outdoor recreation opportunities of more popular Oregon towns in a much less crowded environment. Fast becoming one of the mountain-biking capitals of the world, the area has over a million acres of land open to bikers; the Deschutes National Forest is actually adding mountain-bike trails, whereas most parks are banning two-wheeled trekkers.

Bend lies between the snow-capped Eastern Cascades and the bleak, beautiful desert farther east. The Pacific Northwest is known for its wet weather, but on the east side of the Cascade

Range all that wetness goes away. Damp clouds, blocked by the Cascade peaks, dump all their water on the western side, leaving Bend dry. Summer is much hotter here than in the rest of the region, though temperatures do drop at night; in winter, snow accumulates only at high elevations.

BASICS

VISITOR INFORMATION Bend Chamber of Commerce and Central Oregon Welcome Center. Here you'll find ultrasleek display units loaded with information on the entire state. The on-site forest ranger can answer your questions about the Deschutes National Forest. *63085 U.S. 97, tel. 503/382–3221. Open Mon.–Sat. 9–5, Sun. 11–3.*

Deschutes National Forest Office. Come for information on hiking and camping in the national forest, including an excellent free guide to mountain-biking trails and a $3 forest map. *1645 U.S. 20, tel. 503/388–2715. Open weekdays 7:45–4:30.*

COMING AND GOING

U.S. 97, with most of the franchises and motels, runs north–south through Bend. The downtown area lies about eight blocks west of the highway, along Bond and Wall streets; you can easily handle this area on foot. Most roads, even if they don't have shoulders, leave plenty of room for bikers. For train travelers, the nearest **Amtrak** station is in Chemult, about 60 miles south of Bend.

BY CAR U.S. 97 travels north from Bend to Madras, connecting with U.S. 197 and leading into The Dalles (131 mi). Going south, U.S. 97 passes Sunriver, La Pine, and Chemult, and finally reaches Klamath Falls (137 mi). At a fairly low elevation, U.S. 97 gets minimal snow. Traveling west over the mountains on U.S. 20, Route 126, and Route 242 can be treacherous in winter, spring, and fall (242 is always closed in winter). Check conditions with the chamber of commerce (*see above*) before setting out. The route from Bend to Eugene (128 mi) follows U.S. 20 to Route 126, or, weather permitting, U.S. 20 to slow and scenic Route 242 and on to Route 126. To get to Portland from Bend (160 mi), take U.S. 97 to U.S. 26.

BY BUS Greyhound (2045 U.S. 20, tel. 503/382–2151 or 800/231–2222) connects Bend and Klamath Falls (3 hrs, $18), stopping in several towns along the way. You can also ride to Eugene (3 hrs, $20) and Portland (4½ hrs, $20).

WHERE TO SLEEP

You'll find most of Bend's cheap sleeps on U.S. 97 at the south end of town. Prices escalate as you move north. Campers will find secluded spots in the La Pine area (about 30 mi south on U.S. 97) and on the Cascade Lakes Highway (about 25 mi west).

➢ **UNDER $35 • Edelweiss Motor Inn.** They're a little threadbare, but the clean doubles at the Edelweiss are a great deal ($28–$35) within easy walking distance of downtown. This place has been around forever, and the owners haven't gotten around to installing phones. *2346 N.E. Division St., tel. 503/382–6222. From U.S. 97, west on Revere St. and right on Division St. 28 rooms, some with kitchens.*

Sonoma Lodge. Spacious rooms, hospitable owners, and a complimentary banana-bread breakfast give this roadside motel a definite edge over its neighbors. Doubles cost $30–$50, depending on the season and the number of beds you need. Some rooms come with kitchens. *450 S.E. 3rd St., on U.S. 97, tel. 503/382–4891. 18 rooms.*

➢ **UNDER $50 • Bend Riverside Motel.** Once you locate your room in this massive, five-building facility, you'll probably find it cozy, comfortable, and quiet. The motel sits right on the Deschutes River, several blocks from U.S. 97. Some rooms overlook the river, while others have views of a city park. Doubles cost a slightly high $49–$69, but the peaceful location makes this place a good value. *1565 N.W. Hill St., tel. 503/389–2363 or 800/284–2363. From U.S.*

97, west on Revere St. to Deschutes Pl., which leads to the motel. 200 units. Laundry, heated pool, sauna, whirlpool, tennis court. Wheelchair access.

Mill Inn Bed & Breakfast. A pleasant budget option if ever there was one, this B&B has a four-bunk room for $15 a person (you can get the whole shebang for $50 if you've got a party of four). There are also private rooms with twin beds ($39), queen rooms ($44), and king rooms ($60). Everyone shares a large common area, a hot tub, and some very friendly hosts. *642 N.W. Colorado Ave., tel. 503/389–9198. From U.S. 97, take Franklin St. west, and then Bond St. south, to Colorado Ave. 9 rooms, 4 with shared bath. Wheelchair access.*

HOSTELS **Bend Alpine Hostel (HI).** On the west side of town, far from the incessant roar of U.S. 97, this brand-spankin'-new hostel offers 40 beds, including a family room and a couples room (no extra charge). You get easy access to the free Mt. Bachelor shuttle one block away, and a slew of ski and bike rental outlets are nearby. Members pay $12, nonmembers $15; there's $1 discount for those who arrive by bicycle. *19 S.W. Century Dr., tel. 800/299–3813. From U.S. 97 take Greenwood St. (which changes names several times) west to 14th St.; it turns into Century Dr. Reception open 7:30–9:30 AM and 4:30–11 PM. Kitchen, laundry. Wheelchair access.*

CAMPING Three small, free campgrounds open July–October lie close together in the Deschutes National Forest, on or near alpine lakes. **Todd Lake** (tel. 503/388–5664), with 11 sites, is 6,200 feet above sea level and features panoramic views of the Cascades. To get here, go 25 miles west on the Cascade Lakes Highway and a mile north on the forest service entrance road, and take the short hike to the sites. **Soda Creek** (tel. 503/388–5664), with 10 sites, is between two meadows about 25 miles west on the Cascade Lakes Highway and 100 yards south on Forest Service Road 400. With nine sites, **Devil's Lake** (tel. 503/388–5664), 27 miles west on the Cascade Lakes Highway, benefits from good hiking trails and one of the prettiest lakes in the region.

If you have the bucks (nine of them), grab one of the 55 sites at **Cultus Lake** (tel. 503/388–5664), about 50 miles west on the Cascades Lakes Highway. You'll camp next to a crystal-clear lake surrounded by trees; just don't look for the showers (there aren't any). You can enjoy several excellent trails near the grounds (the lovely Cultus Lake Loop Mountain Bike Trail starts here), and the lake has canoe, rowboat, and kayak rentals.

Another area with plenty of campsites is south of Bend around Paulina Lake and East Lake, though you'll do better along the Cascade Lakes Highway (*see above*). **Little Crater** (22 mi south on U.S. 97 and then 15 mi east on Rte. 21, tel. 503/388–5666), on the east shore of Paulina Lake, is one of the most popular spots. The 50 sites ($12) are available May–October. Closer to Bend, attractive **Tumalo State Park** (5 mi northwest on U.S. 20, tel. 503/388–6055) has 68 sites ($17) on the banks of the Deschutes River, surrounded by lawns and dense woods.

FOOD

Stick to U.S. 97 for diners and fast food; otherwise, head west on Franklin Avenue to Bond and Wall streets, where you'll find the better restaurants. You can grab an espresso at the hip **Cafe Paradiso** (945 N.W. Bond St., tel. 503/385–5931), which has light meals for around $3.50 and live music on Friday and Saturday nights.

➤ **UNDER $5** • **Deschutes Brewery and Public House.** Bend's contribution to the Northwest's microbrewery scene comes alive at night, with sports on the tube and live blues and country bands on weekends. Windows showcase the vats, and you can tour the brewery on Saturday by calling in advance. The low-priced menu is what you'd expect of a pub—sandwiches (under $5) and burgers ($3–$5). A pint of ale goes for $2. *1044 Bond St., at Greenwood Ave., tel. 503/382–9242. Open Mon.–Thurs. 11 AM–11:30 PM; Fri.–Sat. 11 AM–12:30 AM, Sun. 11–10.*

Jake's Diner. You'll know you've found it when you see the monster trucks in the parking lot. Diner aficionados will appreciate the large counter, the revolving showcase of pies, and the menu's claim that "the largest portions in Central Oregon" are served here. Try the chicken fillet on a hoagie with a hefty side of fries ($5). *61260 U.S. 97S, tel. 503/382–0118. South end of town. Open 24 hrs.*

Vive La Crêpe. You wouldn't exactly expect Bend to have a crepery, but here it is—direct from France (well, sorta). You can get both savory and sweet versions of these flat French pancakes. The Nutella crepe ($2.50), with a mind-blowing chocolate and hazelnut spread, makes a great snack. *824 N.W. Wall St., downtown, tel. 503/388–0159. Open daily 10–6.*

If you feel like some easy skanking, Pasha's (61 N.W. Oregon Ave., tel. 503/382–5859) features live reggae music most nights. Leave your spliffs outside, though—there's a police station about a block away.

Westside Bakery and Café. With a large bakery counter in front and three dining rooms in back, this casual café is *the* local breakfast spot. Take the several minutes' wait for a table as a good sign. Breakfasts include a wide variety of omelets and griddle cakes, as well as specials like Belgian waffles with blackberries ($4.75). For lunch try a huge sandwich ($4.75 whole, $3.25 half). If you're still hungry (yeah, right), pick up a fresh loaf of bread or some bagels for a picnic in the mountains. *1005 N.W. Galveston St., tel. 503/382–3426. From U.S. 97, take Franklin Ave. west; it turns into Galveston. Open Mon.–Sat. 7–3, Sun. 7–2.*

OUTDOOR ACTIVITIES

HIKING If you're coming from the south, you might start by taking the mile-long **Benham Falls Trail,** near the Lava Lands Visitor Center (*see* box, *below*). The trail is actually misnamed, considering that it doesn't pass a waterfall. It does, however, follow the Deschutes River at one of its wildest points. To reach the trail, go south for 11 miles on U.S. 97, then go 4 miles west to the picnic area and walk across the footbridge. For a longer hike through Alpine meadows, with majestic Mt. Jefferson in the distance, try a section of **Metolious River Trail,** which follows a tributary of the Deschutes. You reach the trail by traveling about 30 miles northwest of Bend past Sisters on U.S. 20, turning north at the Camp Sherman exit, and following signs. Strong hikers can tackle the 3-mile (one-way) hike to the top of **Black Crater,** an old volcanic peak west of Sisters on Route 242. The trail leads to a pristine lake and ultimately to spectacular views of Mt. Washington and the Three Sisters Mountains. To reach the trailhead, go north for 20 miles to Sisters and turn west on Route 242; the trail begins between Miles 80 and 81. Contact the Deschutes National Forest Office (*see* Visitor Information, *above*) for maps and information.

Those equipped with rod and reel can choose between the Deschutes River, the Metolious River, and many Alpine lakes. You may catch trophy-size rainbow, steelhead, or eastern brook trout.

BIKING With one million plus acres of cyclable terrain, Bend is rapidly becoming a mountain-biker's mecca. There are plenty of places to rent bikes, and most shops will sell you a trail map (about $3.50), but the Deschutes National Forest Office (*see* Visitor Information, *above*) gives away an extensive booklet covering the best trails for free. **Skjersaa's Ski Shop** (130 S.W. Century Dr., near Bend Alpine Hostel, tel. 503/382–2154) has the best bikes at competitive rates ($12 for 6 hrs, $15 for 24 hrs); high performance bikes cost more ($20 for 24 hrs). They supply the helmets, but you must bring your own water bottle and gloves.

This is mostly virgin territory, and you can still ride all day without seeing anyone. The **Deschutes River Trail** begins in town: The first 7.5 miles follow Route 46 west; then take a left on Forest Service Road 41 and follow signs to Lava Falls, turn left onto Forest Service Road 4120, and after the overflow parking lot (¾ mi) turn left onto the single track. The ride parallels the river for 6 miles, alternating between single and double track. The views are spectacular, and the ride's not too tough.

HORSEBACK RIDING Several companies offer guided trail rides. **Sunriver Stables** (Center Dr., Sunriver, tel. 503/593–1221, ext. 4420) has half-hour tours for $15, hour-long rides for $22, and two-hour trips that cross the Deschutes River for $38. **Eagle Crest Equestrian Center** (Eagle Crest Resort, Redmond, tel. 503/923–2072) leads a one-hour trip through junipers and sagebrush ($17) and a 1½-hour sunset ride ($25).

RAFTING The Deschutes and McKenzie rivers aren't as famous for their rapids as the Rogue (*see* Rogue River Valley, *above*), but they can be just as exciting. **Sun Country Tours, Inc.** (Sun River Resort, tel. 503/382–6277) and **Hunter Expeditions** (61535 U.S. 97S, Suite 16; tel. 503/389–8370) offer half-day trips on the Deschutes for about $30. Sun Country's all-day trips are $75, and Hunter's are $60.

SKIING **Mt. Bachelor** (tel. 800/829–2442) is one of the premier skiing peaks in the Northwest, with 56 downhill runs, 10 cross-country trails, a snowboard park, and an average annual snow base of about 175 inches. Lift tickets cost about $33 a day; if you plan to stay a while,

And You Thought the Lamps Were Cool

To understand the landscape of central Oregon, you need to know something about its volcanic history. The Cascades were formed thousands of years ago from the sheer force of a volcanic explosion (or, in the case of the larger mountains, from lava flow and ash buildup). In turn, they coughed up more lava, changing the course of rivers, creating lakes and caves, and leaving gaping craters. The Lava Lands Visitor Center (58201 U.S. 97S, tel. 503/593–2421), 11 miles south of Bend on U.S. 97, lays it all out for you, explaining the molten origins of the odd formations nearby. Stop by daily 9–5 between April and October. From the center, you can head up the paved road to the 500-foot summit of Lava Butte. If the weather doesn't suck, the platform on top of this old cinder cone commands incredible views of the Cascades. A short trail passes over hardened lava flow as it circles the crater. If just thinking about the 1½-mile hike up the butte leaves you out of breath, there's also a shuttle ($1.50) that departs from the center every half hour.

After an eruption, the surface of a lava flow sometimes hardens while the molten mass continues to flow underground. Once the liquid leaves the tube, a cave is formed. Oregon's longest uncollapsed tube is the Lava River Cave (tel. 503/593–2421), about 12 miles south of Bend on U.S. 97. From mid-May to mid-September, you can explore it for $2. A 2½-mile round-trip trail leads through the cramped passages and cavernous halls. It's cool in here even during summer, when temperatures outside hover in the 90s. If you're still curious about lava caves, head southeast on China Hat Road, which leaves U.S. 97 at the southern end of Bend. About 8 miles out, you'll see signs for Arnold Ice Cave, Boyd Cave, and Wind Cave. Bring a flashlight if you want to explore them, and wear warm clothes—temperatures hover around 40°. You can rent lanterns for about $1.50 at the Lava River Cave.

Two miles south of the Lava River Cave lies the Lava Cast Forest, where hardened lava shows the outlines of trees that were run over by molten flows. About 13 miles past the forest, Route 21 leads to the Newberry Crater, a 5-mile-wide caldera formed by powerful eruptions several thousand years ago. The crater now contains a lava flow of obsidian (black glass), a waterfall that tumbles from the rim of the crater, and two trout-filled lakes (East and Paulina). During summer, a paved road leads up to Paulina Peak, the highest point in the volcano (almost 8,000 feet), for spectacular views of the lakes and the Cascades in the distance.

inquire about multi-day packages. To get here from Bend, head west for about 22 miles on the Cascade Lakes Highway. The **Mt. Bachelor Shuttle** (tel. 503/382–2442) will transport you to the mountain for free from their offices about 5 miles west of Bend on the Cascade Lakes Highway.

Near Bend

SISTERS On a clear day, the 20-mile drive from Bend to the village of Sisters offers some of the best mountain views in the region. Three Fingered Jack, Mt. Washington, and the Three Sisters are a few of the snowy peaks that rise up in the distance. The road passes farmland and horse ranches before arriving in the high-plains tourist town of Sisters, which sits about 3,100 feet above sea level. The town tries to capture the feel of the Old West, with columned storefronts and quaint signs lining Cascade Street, the main thoroughfare. The theme reflects the ranching lifestyle of the town's inhabitants (of course, it also attracts the tourist dollar). You can browse in the crafts shops and antiques stores, or pick up a Stetson at **Leavitt's Western Wear** (145 W. Cascade St., tel. 503/549–6451). Sisters is also well known for its llama farms. Check out the animals (raised for wool and to carry packs) less than a mile west of town on Route 242. Bend's visitor center (*see above*) can give you info on llama farms that offer free tours.

Cascade Street has several decent places to eat. The cheapest is **Ali's** (Town Square Mall, 100 W. Cascade St., tel. 503/549–2547), where you can get innovative soups and bagels for under $3. Excellent pita-bread sandwiches with fillings like curried chicken salad or turkey-apple salad run about $5. If you're looking for a place to stay, call the **Conklin Guest House** (69013 Camp Polk Rd., tel. 503/549–0123), a B&B with a dorm room that sleeps eight ($25 per person).

HIGH DESERT MUSEUM Part zoo and part cultural museum, this interesting 150-acre complex pays tribute to the nature and history of the area between the Cascades and the Rocky Mountains. One of the many highlights of the eclectic collection is the **Earle A. Chiles Center,** a walk-through exhibit that traces the region's history from about 8,000 years ago to the time of the gold rush. Along the way, you pass life-size dioramas depicting ancient natural landscapes, Native American life, and wild frontier towns of the 19th century. Outside, 20 acres of hiking trails lead past river otters, porcupines, and live birds of prey—all displayed in their natural habitats (well, almost). There are no restaurants here, so bring your lunch. *59800 U.S. 97S, tel. 503/382–4754. 6 mi south of Bend. Admission: $5.50. Open daily 9–5.*

SMITH ROCK STATE PARK This 623-acre park (tel. 503/548–7501) sits right on the canyon of the **Crooked River,** which winds its way through sedimentary rock and finally empties into Lake Billy Chinook. Several hikes in the park offer spectacular views of the river, the rugged and colorful rocks, and the Cascades in the distance. The best trail follows the Crooked River around the base of **Smith Rock,** ending at Monkey Face, a rock formation that resembles (you guessed it) a monkey's head. As you explore, check out the climbers who scale the cliffs—Smith Rock's sheer crags and arduous ascents put it in the world-renowned category. To reach the park from Bend, take U.S. 97 north for 22 miles to Terrebone, then turn right at the sign and go 2½ miles. After soaking up the scenery, you can drive north on U.S. 97 to Culver and then west for 5 miles to **Cove Palisades State Park** (tel. 503/546–3412), in a canyon on Lake Billy Chinook. It's a favorite spot for hiking, swimming, boating, and waterskiing.

Willamette Valley

In the fertile **Willamette Valley** (say Wil-AM-it, damn it!), which stretches from Portland over 100 miles south to Eugene, dozens of wineries cultivate the cold-weather pinot noir, Riesling, and chardonnay grapes, creating wines that win gold medals in international competitions. Over two-thirds of all Oregonians hang their hats in the valley, many of them around Salem, the state capital, and Eugene, home of the University of Oregon and altogether the hippest city in the region. The McKenzie River flows west from the Cascades, emptying into the Willamette River near Eugene. Rafters ride the rapids here, and hikers explore the banks and surrounding forests. Rolling farmland, rivers, lakes, and forests make the valley a great place to tour by car or bike. Although I-5 will get you where you're going in a hurry, back roads and river highways like Route 99W provide a much better way to see it all. If you come during spring or summer, camping is the cheapest and best way to experience the area's beauty. From late June through early October, days are sunny and warm; but at other times, especially in winter, rain is a given.

COMING AND GOING

BY CAR I–5 and Route 99 (which splits into 99W and 99E) run north–south through the valley, while U.S. 20, Route 22, and Route 126 run west to the coast and east to the Cascades. To reach the Crater Lake area, take Route 58 southeast from Eugene to U.S. 97. The most scenic road is Route 99W, which runs parallel to I–5, hitting most major towns but bypassing Salem.

BY BUS Greyhound (tel. 800/231–2222) has several routes through the Willamette Valley. One heads southwest from Portland to Lincoln City on the coast, with stops in Newberg, McMinnville (1½ hrs, $7), and elsewhere. Greyhound's major route in the Willamette Valley goes south from Portland on I–5 through Salem, Albany, Corvallis, Eugene, and Roseburg, and then continues on to Grants Pass and into California. From Portland to Eugene (3 hrs) you'll pay $13; from Salem to Eugene (2 hrs) it's $10.

BY TRAIN Amtrak (tel. 800/872–7245) runs one train a day north and south through the valley, stopping in Portland, Salem, Albany, and Eugene. The Portland–Eugene trip (3 hrs) costs $24.

BY PLANE The **Eugene Airport** (28855 Lockheed Dr., tel. 503/687–5430) has flights to cities throughout the United States, as well as Europe and Asia.

Eugene

At first it makes you paranoid (perhaps your fly is down, or you have a booger hanging from your nose), but soon you understand it—the people in Eugene smile. They smile when they know you, they smile when they don't, they probably smile alone in the dark. And it's not some creepy Stepford thing; this town, where college students, yuppies, loggers, and latter-day flower children coexist peacefully, is Oregon's friendliest, cleanest city and one of the most laid-back spots you'll ever visit.

With an enrollment of about 20,000 students and the largest payroll in the city, the **University of Oregon** is at the root of the town's unique flavor. You'll probably want to spend some time touring its museums and ivy-covered buildings, and hanging out in the small restaurants and coffee shops near campus. The historic neighborhood around **Skinner Butte Park,** on the banks of the Willamette River, also merits a look. Eugene lies at the confluence of the McKenzie and Willamette rivers, between the Cascade Mountains to the east and the Coast Range to the west. Hiking trails meander through the hills around the city, and white-water rafting operators run frequent trips on the McKenzie (*see* Near Eugene, *below*).

VISITOR INFORMATION **Lane County Convention and Visitors Association.** *305 W. 7th Ave., tel. 503/484–5307, 800/452–3670 in OR, or 800/547–5445 outside OR. Open June 4–Labor Day, weekdays 8:30–5, weekends 10–4.*

Willamette National Forest Service. Here you can get advice about trails and camping. *211 E 7th Ave., downtown, tel. 503/465–6522. Open weekdays 7:45–4:30.*

GETTING AROUND Most worthwhile sights lie just south of the Willamette River in a compact area. It's only a six-block walk from the downtown mall, which is bordered by 8th and 10th avenues and Charnelton and Oak streets, to Skinner Butte Park on the southern bank of the Willamette. It's about 12 blocks from the mall to the University of Oregon, just east of downtown. Public transportation and bike routes are among the best in the country, so you don't need a car to get around. For information on Greyhound and Amtrak, *see* Coming and Going, *above.*

➤ **BY BUS** • City buses leave from **Eugene Station** (10th Ave. and Willamette St.) on the south edge of the mall. Bus 1 makes a continuous loop around the downtown area. The fare for most trips is 75¢; you need exact change. Day passes ($1.90) and five-token packs ($3.25) are available at 7-Elevens and other markets. Call the **Lane Transit District** (tel. 503/687–5555) for more information.

WHERE TO SLEEP Most of Eugene's affordable motels are on Franklin Boulevard and its extension, Broadway Avenue. This strip runs east–west through the heart of the city. If the places below are full, try the **Franklin Inn** (1857 Franklin Blvd., tel. 503/342–4804) or the **Campus Inn** (390 E. Broadway Ave., tel. 503/343–3376); both have rooms for $40–$45. Otherwise, head out to Gateway Avenue in nearby Springfield for cheap motels. The **Pacific 9 Motor Inn** (3550 Gateway St., take Exit 195 from I-5, tel. 800/722–9462) has clean doubles ($32) and singles ($27).

66 Motel. This clean, relatively quiet place a block north of the university is one of the best deals in town. Rooms ($28–$37) have firm beds, TVs with remote control, and private showers. *755 E. Broadway Ave., tel. 503/342–5041. Take Bus 11 from downtown; or walk 7 blocks east on E. Broadway Ave. from the mall. 66 rooms.*

Manor Motel. If 66 Motel is full, try this clean, adequately furnished spot three blocks northwest of the university. Doubles ($33) come with refrigerators and full baths. Singles cost about $25. *599 E. Broadway Ave., tel. 503/345–2331. Take Bus 11 from downtown; or walk 5 blocks east on E. Broadway Ave. from the mall. 25 rooms. Heated pool, basketball hoop. Wheelchair access.*

➤ **HOSTELS • Lost Valley Hostel (HI).** Although there is no hostel within Eugene, you'll find a very mellow one in the nearby town of Dexter, about 30 minutes outside of Eugene. The hostel is on the 85-acre grounds of the Lost Valley "intentional community," which specializes in organic gardening and sustainable forestry, and runs various educational projects and conferences. There are plenty of hiking trails on and around the property. On weeknights, guests can join the community in organic vegetarian dinners (around $6.50). The clean, awfully close rooms run $12 a night for normal people, $9 for AYH members. *81868 Lost Valley Ln., Dexter, tel. 503/937–3351. I-5 south to Route 58, right on Rattle Snake Creek Rd., right on Lost Valley Ln. 10 beds. Reservations required.*

➤ **CAMPING •** The campgrounds closest to Eugene are practical and not very scenic, but less than an hour southeast of town you'll find incredible spots (with toilets and water) in the Fall Creek Corridor, which runs along Fall Creek in the Willamette National Forest. The best of the bunch is the $8-a-night **Bed Rock** (tel. 503/937–2129), 15 miles east of Lowell on Road 18. The creek here has several large swimming holes and plenty of awesome diving rocks—don't drink and jump. From Eugene take I-5 south to Route 58, follow signs through Lowell, and take Big Fall Creek Road/Road 18.

KOA, a chain of campgrounds offering all the necessities and nothing too memorable, operates two campgrounds nearer to Eugene, but they pale in comparison to the Fall Creek Corridor. Sights at **KOA Eugene** (8 mi north of Eugene in Coburg, tel. 503/343–4832), near the Willamette River, run a fairly expensive $15 a night. **KOA Sherwood Forest** (12 mi south of Eugene in Creswell, tel. 503/849–4110) has sites for about $10.

FOOD Eugene has a lion's share of health-food stores and vegetarian restaurants. Downtown, **Govinda's** (270 W. 8th Ave., tel. 503/686–3531) offers an all-you-can-eat vegetarian buffet on weekdays; lunches run $5.50 and dinners $6.50. There's also a salad bar ($3.50). Heartier budget munchies such as burgers and pizza can be found on 13th Avenue or Franklin Boulevard. For ethnic eats, head to the **Fifth Street Public Market** (5th Ave., btw High St. and Pearl St.), where nine inexpensive restaurants crank out food on the second floor.

➤ **UNDER $5 • Glenwood Restaurants.** Both of their very popular locations are packed at breakfast (and lunch and dinner). Try the Nova Scotia scramble ($3.95), a satisfying mix of lox, cream cheese, and eggs. Lunchers will find hearty sandwiches, stir fry, and pasta for under $6. *1340 Alder St., at 13th St. 1 block from the university, tel. 503/687–0355. Open 24 hours. Other location: 2588 Willamette St., at 26th St., tel. 503/687–8201. Open weekdays 6:30 AM–9 PM, weekends 7 AM–9 PM.*

Keystone Café. This hippie greasy spoon is another essential breakfast and lunch spot. You won't choose it for the decor; it's the large portions that keep 'em coming. At breakfast, the Powerhouse ($3.90), a mixture of home fries, tofu, cheese, sour cream, and mushrooms, is a good bet. For lunch you can try the tempeh burger (some soy thing; $4.70). *395 W. 5th Ave., at Lawrence St., tel. 503/342–2075. Open daily 7–3.*

➢ **UNDER $15 • Café Navarro.** Voted Eugene's best new restaurant in '93 and the best ethnic restaurant in '94, Navarro serves Caribbean and Latin food in a tasteful split-level room with parrot-print curtains and a swirl of reggae and Latin song. Lunches run $3.95–$5.95 and dinners cost $7.50–$13.95. If you can, come for dinner and try the pescado borracho (red snapper marinated in ginger-orange sauce and basted with Cajun spice; $11.95). *456 Willamette St., tel. 503/344–0943. North of 8th Ave., down the street from Amtrak station. Open Tues.–Sat. 11–3 and 5–9:30, Sun. 9–3.*

Cafe Zenon. Yet another stylish downtown joint at which to see and be seen while sipping your espresso, this place is popular with the up-market, used-to-be hippie crowd and college students. In addition to delicious desserts and coffee, the café serves top-notch Euro-Latin-Afro meals (whatever that means) at reasonable prices. The Cajun chicken and pasta salad ($7) is a good bet. Lunch will run you $7 or so, dinner $10–$15; fabulous desserts are about $3.25. *899 Pearl St., at E. Broadway Ave., tel. 503/343–3005. Open Mon.–Sat. 8 AM–midnight, Sun. 10 AM–midnight.*

WORTH SEEING Skinner Butte Park, along the southern and western banks of the Willamette River, is a good place to start your tour of Eugene. A 15-minute walk or a short drive leads up to some killer views of Eugene—that's Spencer Butte rising over the city. After descending, take a quick look at the Victorian houses on the lower slopes of the hill. The Willamette was a major shipping and transportation route in the late 19th century, and Eugene grew out of this neighborhood near the river's southern bank. About three blocks south of here is the **Fifth Street Public Market** (5th Ave., btw High and Pearl Sts.), where galleries, craft shops, boutiques, and restaurants share space in a converted mill. On weekends between April and December, follow the hip (and live) grooves a few blocks south to the outdoor **Saturday Market** (8th Ave., at Oak St.), with tie-dyed everything, cheap prepared food, jewelry, and organic edibles.

Spread out on a green campus just east of downtown, the **University of Oregon** is the state's premier public institution of higher learning. On a stroll around campus, you'll pass open quads and old redbrick buildings covered in ivy, some dating back to the 19th century. It's such an idyllic scene that Hollywood chose this as the site of the famed Faber College in the

A Magical Affair

Fusing eclectic live music, unique arts and crafts, New Age workshops, and outrageous vaudeville entertainment, the Oregon County Fair (tel. 503/343–6554) has been bringing together the best aspects of the '60s for over 25 years. For just $7–$10, depending on the day of your visit, you can roam freely through a 26-acre playground of sunny meadows and shady oaks 13 miles west of Eugene. Join the throngs of long-haired youth and elders—some costumed, some barely clothed—in spontaneous revelry, but also stop occasionally to check out the belly dancers, jugglers, clowns, political satirists, and musicians who serve as the official entertainment. This is the place to witness an Acrosage demonstration, an acrobatic form of massage that must be seen to be believed. If you're anywhere in the state of Oregon during the second week of July, try to attend for at least a day. Even seasoned travelers, well versed in fairs, festivals, carnivals, and other gala events, say they've never seen anything quite like it.

'70s classic *Animal House*. Tours leave at 10:30 AM and 2:30 PM from **Oregon Hall** (tel. 503/346–3014 or 503/346–3009). The free **Museum of Art** (tel. 503/346–3027), on the west side of campus, has an impressive permanent collection of Asian art, including an entire room devoted to Japanese dolls. Housed in a cedar replica of a Native American longhouse, the free **Museum of Natural History** (E. 15th St., near Agate St., tel. 503/346–3024) specializes in regional artifacts. Both museums are open Wednesday–Sunday noon–5. On the other side of Franklin Boulevard, check out **Millrace Stream**. You can rent canoes at the **Canoe House** (tel. 503/346–4386).

For those with culture on their agendas, Eugene hosts a top-notch Bach Festival for two weeks around the end of June. Contact Hult Center's Bach Office (1 Eugene Center, tel. 503/687–5000) for tickets and information.

The Autzen Footbridge leads over the Willamette River just north of the university. Follow signs from here to the **Willamette Science and Technology Center (WISTEC)**, which uses cool interactive displays to teach science (Hey, Mom! It's fun *and* I'm learning!) and includes the largest planetarium between San Francisco and Vancouver, featuring laser and star shows. *2300 Leo Harris Pkwy., tel. 503/687–3619. Admission: $3. Open Wed.–Sun. noon–6.*

AFTER DARK Eugene has a spirited nightlife every night of the week. To find out the haps, put down your latte long enough to read the *Eugene Weekly,* available free at most cafés, restaurants, and stores. Locals favor **W.O.W. Hall** (291 W. 8th St., downtown, tel. 503/687–2766), with an eclectic blend of dance, performance, and music (industrial to folk); tickets run $5–$10. The **Good Times Café and Bar** (375 E. 7th St., 1 block from Fifth Street Market, tel. 503/484–7181) specializes in blues and rock. Covers run $1–$8, sometimes more if a big act blows through town. For the college crowd and the parasites that prey on them, **Guido's** (801 E. 13th St., 1 block from campus, tel. 503/343–0681) features all request DJ dancing every night, as well as pool tables, video games, and lots of noise. There's no cover, and the full bar has plenty of specials priced to get you ripped and ready for that wet T-shirt competition.

OUTDOOR ACTIVITIES Eugene has several good hikes within a few miles of city limits. A great way to get a bird's-eye view of the city is to climb 2,065-foot **Spencer Butte,** which dominates the southern sky. You can reach the butte by taking Bus 23 or 24 from the downtown mall to Fox Hollow Road and Donald Street. Follow Fox Hollow until it intersects with **Ridgeline Trail,** then head right on the trail and stay to the left when it splits. For another worthwhile—and flatter—hike, stay on Ridgeline Trail and check out stands of old-growth Douglas fir, rare Calypso orchids, and deer. For an expansive view of the Willamette Valley and the distant Cascades, try the mile-long hike to the summit of **Mt. Pisgah** in Howard Buford Park, about 5 miles southeast of Eugene. The trail alternates between conifer forest and grasslands. Bus 26 will get you within 2 miles of the park; get off at Seavey Loop Road and follow it east.

The Eugene area is also a good bet for bike touring. The 195-mile **Willamette Valley Bicycle Loop** runs through many of the most scenic areas in the region. For more information, contact the visitor center (*see above*). You can rent bikes at **Pedalpower** (535 High St., btw 7th and 5th Sts., tel. 503/687–1775) for $3 an hour or $15 a day. Or try **Blue Heron Bikes** (877 E. 13th Ave., near the university, tel. 503/343–2488), which charges $2.50 an hour, $12 a day, and $15 overnight (mountain bikes cost more). Both stores have information on local mountain-biking trails.

Just east of Eugene is Springfield, a town that has dubbed itself the "Gateway to the McKenzie River." You should probably take the sobriquet seriously and pass right through.

NEAR EUGENE

MCKENZIE RIVER For some spectacular visuals, explore the river and its surrounding areas. Take a motor tour east from Eugene on Route 126; not only do you get the awesome river, but for the same price we'll throw in two—that's TWO—impressive mountain ranges: the Cascades and the Sisters. If you'd prefer to shoot the rapids, several operators run trips. **Take Me Rafting** (1085 Laurel Ave., Springfield, tel. 503/741–0658) has half-day excursions on the McKenzie for about $28, full days for $50, and two-hour scenic floats on the Willamette River for only $12. You can also try **McKenzie River Raft Co.** (tel. 503/747–6078) and **Oregon Whitewater Adventures** (tel. 503/747–5422).

OAKLAND History buffs can make the trip to Oakland, about 55 miles south of Eugene off I–5. This small rural town became prominent in the 1850s as a stopover point for the stagecoach line connecting Portland and Sacramento. Later, it was a trading and transportation center for regional commerce—prunes around the turn of the century and turkeys between the wars. The **Chamber of Commerce** (117 3rd St.) has self-guided tour maps of the town's buildings, which date from the late 19th century. The original buildings were destroyed in a fire. The **Oakland Museum** (136 Locust St.) focuses on town history, and several antiques stores and small shops focus on your wallet.

Salem

Unless you're here to lobby against a bill, there's no reason to stop—let alone spend a night—in Salem. Eugene and Portland (an hour south and north of the capital, respectively) will both treat you much better. If you do end up in Salem, don't expect much more than decent food and a couple of ways to kill an

Salem, the state capital, is Oregon's Brasília: a center of government but not much else.

Appropriate Technology for an Inappropriate World

Cutting right against the grain of prevailing American mores, the folks at the Aprovecho Institute not only develop ultra-efficient, ultra-cheap technology, but they turn around and give it away free. This extraordinary community of scientists, builders, organic farmers, and foresters receive no profits and perceive thievery of their concepts as the highest of praise.

On 40 acres of forest, meadows, and organic gardens just 30 miles south of Eugene, Aprovecho develops earth-affable technology, including high-yield organic farming, sustainable forestry, and what the group calls Appropriate Technology. Appropriate Technology sets out to maximize the renewable resources of (primarily) third-world nations while employing local skills, material, and financial resources—all this without upsetting native culture and practices and always maintaining compatibility with local wishes and needs (whew!). The group rakes in praise for their rocket stove, a highly efficient twig-burning stove constructed out of 5-gallon tin cans. They always have new projects going, including the forthcoming Icy Ball—a $30 heat refrigeration unit aimed at third-world medical clinics.

If you want to know more about what goes on at Aprovecho, the institute holds open house 2:30–7 PM the first Sunday of each month. The staff will give you a tour of the entire spread, including demonstrations and explanations of Appropriate Technology. For lengthier visits, Aprovecho offers five-day work weeks, where for $10 a day you can work alongside interns on all of Aprovecho's projects. For more information and directions, contact Dean Still at the institute (80574 Hazelton Rd., Cottage Grove 97424, tel. 503/942–8198).

afternoon. For 12 days around Labor Day you can soak up the atmosphere at the traditional and staid **Oregon State Fair** (tel. 503/378–3247), which pales in comparison to Eugene's County Fair (*see* Eugene, *above*). Undoubtedly the area's top attraction, **Silver Falls State Park** (*see* Near Salem, *below*), lies 25 miles east of town. If you need to fill up a free afternoon, visit the **Oregon State Capitol** (900 Court St. N.E., tel. 503/378–4423), with its 23-foot Oregon Pioneer statue. Free tours are offered weekdays 8–5, Saturday 9–4, and Sunday noon–4 in summer. Nearby **Willamette University** (900 State St., tel. 503/370–6300), a private liberal-arts school with 2,000 students, has frequent concerts, speakers, and sports events. Only history buffs will be turned on by **Mission Mill Village** (1313 Mill St. S.E., tel. 503/585–7012), where $5 gets you a tour of a mid-19th-century house, church, and wool mill; but the **Salem Convention and Visitors Association** (tel. 503/581–4325), open weekdays 8:30–5 and Saturday 10–1, is on the grounds.

Despite its gridded layout, downtown Salem can be confusing; many streets are one-way or end abruptly. Commercial Street runs south along the Willamette River on the western border of downtown; it's the best orientation point if you're lost. The intersection of Court Street and Liberty Street (1 block southeast of Commercial St.) is the downtown hub; within a few blocks of here lie shops, cafés, restaurants, and a dynamite bagel and fruit-juice bar (*see below*).

WHERE TO SLEEP Relative to other cities its size, Salem has poor pickins. If you do decide to spend the night, look on Market Street, at the north end of downtown. **Holiday Lodge** (off I-5 at Market St. exit, tel. 503/ 585–2323 or 800/543–5071) has clean, comfy rooms with cable TV and phones—but it's right next to the highway. At $40 for two this is about as cheap as you'll find in Salem.

State House B&B. A great alternative to motels, the State House gives you a lovely room ($45–$65), a huge breakfast, and a peaceful setting on Mill Creek. For all you Brits, the owners have a pro dart shop next door. If you're traveling in a pack, ask about the bungalows across the creek, which go for $60–$70 and comfortably sleep four or more. *2146 State St., 1 mi southeast of downtown, tel. 503/588–1340 or 800/800–6712. 4 rooms, 2 bungalows.*

Tiki Lodge. This motel has nice modern rooms ($55), a pool, and cable TV, but you could be in just about any city in the United States. *3705 Market St. N.E., at I-5 exit downtown, tel. 503/581–4441. 50 rooms.*

YWCA. Women can take advantage of clean, spartan rooms that go for only $18. Unfortunately the house manager prefers long-term guests, so consider yourself lucky if there's a one-night vacancy. *768 State St., downtown, tel. 503/581–9922. 36 rooms.*

➤ **CAMPING • Champoeg State Park.** If you can't get a site at Silver Falls (*see below*), try this campground on the south bank of the Willamette River, southeast of Newberg and about 25 miles north of Salem. Hiking and biking trails wind through the meadows and oak groves, and you can fish, boat, and swim on the river (*see* Near Salem, *below*). There are only six tent sites ($9); otherwise, you have to pay $16 for an RV site. *From I-5, take Exit 278 and drive 8 mi west, tel. 503/633–8170. 48 sites. Hot showers.*

Silver Falls State Park. In one of the most beautiful areas of Oregon, Silver Falls offers tent sites ($15) that fill quickly in summer. Procrastinators and people who live by the seat of their pants will appreciate the fact that reservations are not accepted. Campers can explore the nearby waterfalls (*see* Near Salem, *below*). *25 mi east of Salem via Route 22 and Route 214, tel. 503/873–8681. 51 sites. Showers. Open Apr.–Oct.*

FOOD The wine industry has attracted some sophisticated restaurants, but the food isn't up to Portland or Eugene standards.

➤ **UNDER $5 • Arbor Café.** A hot spot with the 9 to 5 crowd, this downtown cafe does a very brisk lunch trade. Enjoy a vegetarian or meat sandwich (under $5) in the airport-inspired lounge. The tomato, pesto and provolone sandwich ($3.50) will send you flying. Caffeine junkies will appreciate the extensive espresso menu ($1–$2). *380 High St. N.E., tel. 503/*

588–2353. Downtown across from Salem Center. Open Mon.–Thurs. 7:30 AM–9 PM, Fri. 7:30 AM–11 PM, Sat. 9 AM–11 PM.

Ritz Diner. Popular for breakfast and lunch, this simple diner serves unpretentious eats for less than $5. At breakfast try biscuits and gravy ($2.75, $3.45 with eggs); for lunch you can do the usual burgers and sandwiches thing. *135 Lancaster Dr. S.E., at State St., tel. 503/370–7810. 1½ mi from downtown. Open Mon.–Sat. 6 AM–8 PM, Sun. 8–1.*

Rolling Bagels and Fountain of Juice. Just when you thought you could justifiably consider a milkshake a balanced meal, up pops this organic bagelry and juice bar. In a large, modern-meets-hippie downtown location, you get excellent bagels with exotic spreads ($3.75) and healthy juice concoctions—finally a place to get your wheat grass fix. *220 Liberty St. N.E., near Court St., tel. 503/371–0176. Open weekdays 7–6, Sat. 8–5.*

➤ **UNDER $10** • **Kwan's Cantonese Cuisine Restaurant.** You're greeted by a towering, 14½-foot wooden Buddha who keeps watch over the ornate gift shop. Dinner will set you back $7–$10, but lunch specials like chicken with black mushrooms are a great deal at around $5. Rub Buddha's tummy and make a wish. *835 Commercial St., tel. 503/362–2711. Open daily 11–10.*

Days of Wine and Roses

With over 50 producers to choose from, the Willamette Valley has become a popular spot for wine tasting. Many wineries are located in beautiful country and almost all of them provide picnic facilities. So pack a lunch and take off for a day of wine, sun, and scenery; but remember, the wineries offer you only tastes (about 1 oz.); they're here to sell you wine, not give it away. If your glass is still half-empty after visiting the places below, get the "Discover Oregon Wineries" brochure at local chambers of commerce.

In the southern Willamette Valley, stick to Route 99. If your idea of wine is a gallon of Gallo between friends, your first stop should be the Honeywood Winery (1350 Hines St., Salem, tel. 503/362–4111). One of eight wineries in the Salem area, this place specializes in unusual fruit wines such as spiced apple, rhubarb, and strawberry—sweeeet. Two miles west of Albany off U.S. 20, Springhill Cellars Winery (2920 N.W. Scenic Dr., tel. 503/928–1009) rakes in the honors for its pinot noir, chardonnay, and Riesling. Stop by weekends 1–5 from April to September. To continue your wine ride, follow Scenic Drive north to Springhill Road, which heads west (changing names several times along the way) to the town of Airlie. At Airlie Wineries (15305 Dunn Forest Rd., tel. 503/838–6013), open weekends noon–5 from March to December, you'll find picnic tables and a view over the valley that would make your mother cry.

In the northern valley, too, many of the best wineries are off Route 99W. Set off on Worden Hill Road, which leaves 99W at the town of Dundee, just south of Newberg. Make the obligatory stop at ritzy Knudsen Earth (Worden Hill Rd., tel. 503/538–3318), one of Oregon's biggest wineries, open daily 10:30–5:30 in summer and daily 11–5 in winter. Farther south on 99W, in the town of Lafayette, take Mineral Springs Road north to Chateau Benoit (Mineral Springs Rd., tel. 503/864–2991 or 503/864–3666), open daily 10–5, which makes award-winning sauvignon blancs.

NEAR SALEM

ROUTE 22 AND SILVER FALLS STATE PARK Salem makes an ideal base for scenic drives west to the coast and east to the Cascades. The two-hour (round-trip) drive east on Route 22 passes through farmland and woods before reaching the Willamette National Forest, about 40 miles from Salem. As the old-growth forests of Douglas fir, maple, and alderwood take over, you'll get some incredible views of Oregon's second highest peak, Mt. Jefferson. The picture gets even more spectacular as the road nears its junction with U.S. 20 and Route 126. To experience the wonders of the changing seasons, make this trip during fall.

Don't go home without at least passing through **Silver Falls State Park** (20024 Silver Falls Hwy., tel. 503/873–8681). To get here, turn off Route 22 onto Route 214 about 10 miles east of Salem, and go 15 miles. You'll find 10 serious waterfalls surrounded by verdant rain forest. By car you can only access two of the falls, but you can hike past all of them on an easy 10-mile loop trail. Or take the 2-mile loop trail that leads behind the 93-foot Lower South Falls and past the 177-foot South Falls. Both trails begin at the main parking lot. North Falls, the most spectacular of the bunch, drops past a giant cavern and crashes on the rocks below. The cavern offers the best viewing; take the 10-minute trail down from the overlook. The park is open daily 8–4:30.

If you return to Route 22 and continue east, you'll pass **Detroit Lake State Park** (tel. 503/854–3346 in summer or 503/854–3406 off-season), a good spot for swimming, fishing, and waterskiing. You can rent boats at **Kane's Hideaway Marina** (530 Clester Rd., Detroit, tel. 503/854–3362). From Detroit, Forest Service Road 46 (across from marina entrance) heads north to the **Cleator Bend Campground** (tel. 503/854–3366), with $8 tent sites. You can cross the bridge here and follow signs to **Breitenbush Hot Springs Retreat** (tel. 503/854–3314). A dip in their therapeutic pools, surrounded by forests and meadows, costs $8; to stay the night in a cabin, you'll pay $45–$75 per person.

Breitenbush may not be for everyone, but the countryside is fantastic, and a little New Age touchy-feely won't kill you.

CHAMPOEG STATE PARK Historic **Champoeg State Park** (tel. 503/633–8170) lies 4 miles outside Newberg, a small town about 24 miles south of Portland on Route 99W. In case you've been wondering, this is the site where, in 1843, American and French-Canadian settlers cast off the rule of the Brits and the Hudson's Bay Company and established a provisional government in Oregon. Take Route 219 south from Newberg to the park turnoff; admission on summer weekends and holidays is $3.

MCMINNVILLE Within stumbling distance of much of the surrounding wine country, McMinnville makes an easy base from which to drink, drink, and be merry. Its attractive **Downtown Historic District** has buildings dating from the 19th century to the Great Depression. Self-guided tour maps are available at the **Chamber of Commerce** (417 N. Adams St., tel. 503/472–6196), open weekdays 9–5. For tasty sandwiches under $5, head to **Jake's Deli** (1208 S. Baker St., at Rte. 99W, tel. 503/472–8812). To get to McMinnville, take Route 99W south from Portland through Newberg and Dundee.

If you head north on 99W to the nearby town of Newberg, you'll find the **Spring Creek Llama Ranch** (14700 N.E. Spring Creek Lane, tel. 503/538–5717) tucked away on 24 acres of meadows and forest. Join a crew of 15 (llamas, of course) for a relaxing stay in this modern ranch house. The very comfortable rooms ($55–$75) come with a hearty breakfast. Call ahead for directions to this secret spot; reservations aren't always necessary.

Mt. Hood National Forest

Oregon's tallest mountain rises 11,235 feet from the valley floor and provides a smashing addition to Portland's skyline on clear days. Mt. Hood is only 55 miles east of Portland, but it's surrounded by a huge national forest. The area is Portland's playground: During winter, skiers take to the slopes or venture onto the mountain's cross-country trails; in summer, vacationers flock to the lakes and rivers. Scenic trails wind through the forest, and on clear days the views of Mt. Hood leave even the crustiest of hikers with a silly smile on their face. The two centers of activity on the mountain are Timberline Lodge and Government Camp. Heading west on U.S. 26 from Government Camp, you'll pass little towns like Welches and Sandy that offer the best deals on lodging and food.

BASICS

VISITOR INFORMATION The **Mt. Hood Information and Visitor Center,** just west of the mountain in Welches, doubles as a U.S. Forest Service Station, providing information on hiking trails, accommodations, and outdoor recreation. They'll send you free info if you ask. Those who plan to head out into one of the forest's six wilderness areas can also come here for the requisite free wilderness permit (also available at certain trailheads). For hiking suggestions and difficulty ratings ask for the free pamphlet "Day Hikes Around Mt. Hood." *65000 U.S. 26E, Welches 97067, tel. 503/622–4822 or 503/622–3191, ext. 611. About 15 mi from summit heading towards Portland. Open daily 8–4:30.*

The time estimates in "Day Hikes Around Mt. Hood" are really conservative; if you're in decent shape, divide by two.

WHEN TO GO As you can imagine, Mt. Hood's character changes dramatically from season to season. Cold, cloudy days in winter give way to warm, clear weather in summer, when temperatures often reach the comfortable 80s. Snow does occasionally fall in summer, so never get too set in your plans and come prepared. Hiking is best in late summer and fall because many paths are snowed in until July. If you can, come on a weekday to avoid the crowds.

➤ **FESTIVALS** • The two-day **Mt. Hood Festival of Jazz** (tel. 503/666–3810) takes place each August in Gresham. At the **Sandy Mountain Festival** (tel. 503/668–5900), which happens during the second weekend in July, you'll find craft booths, food, and country music in a wilderness setting.

GENERAL STORES The **Village Store** (88821 E. Government Camp Loop, tel. 503/272–3355), open 8 AM–10 PM in summer and 8–7 in winter, offers a very limited selection of basic groceries and pharmacy items. For a much better selection at about half the price, head west on U.S. 26 to the Hoodland Plaza in the town of Welches. At the **Thriftway** supermarket (68280 U.S. 26E, tel. 503/622–3244), open Monday–Saturday 7 AM–10 PM, Sunday until 9 PM, you can find just about anything you need and then some. In the same shopping center you'll find **Erb Ally** (68266 U.S. 26E, tel. 503/622–4106), which meets your organic needs with fresh baked breads, grains, nuts, fresh juices, and of course, tofu.

COMING AND GOING

BY CAR In winter you often need chains for the 55-mile drive on U.S. 26 from Portland. Some gas stations and stores let you buy them and then sell them back if you don't use them. For weather conditions call the Zigzag Ranger Station (tel. 503/622–3191).

BY BUS Greyhound (tel. 503/243–2317 or 800/231–2222) runs from Portland to Government Camp ($8.50) once a day, stopping in Gresham, Sandy, Brightwood, Wemmes, Zigzag, and Rhododendron. The Huckleberry Inn in Government Camp (tel. 503/272–3325; *see* Where to Sleep, *below*) acts as the agent for the area.

WHERE TO SLEEP

As a general rule, the closer you get to the mountain, the more expensive the accommodations. For the best deal, head to towns on the fringe of the forest like Brightwood and Sandy, both of which have several reasonable motels. The national forest contains about 80 campgrounds, some of them perennial RV hangouts and others primitive and pristine. They've set up a reservation service (tel. 800/280–CAMP) for the more modern campgrounds. Only call if you know which campground you want; this is not an info line.

➤ **UNDER $55 • Huckleberry Inn.** If you don't mind gobs of kids from ski camp during summer, try the clean and fairly modern rooms here, some of which can hold up to six people. The best deal is the coed dorm room, with bunks at $16 a night. The base price for regular rooms is $50 for two; add $12 for each additional person. If proximity to the snow is not a priority, you can do much better a little way down the mountain. *U.S. 26 Business Loop, Government Camp, tel. 503/272–3325. 15 rooms.*

Oregon Ark Motel. If pine paneling, wood stoves, and 30 acres of meadows, ponds, and woods appeal to you, then not only are you normal, but you've come to the right place. The rooms ($30–$50) are big and clean, the TVs have cable, and the owners go out of their way to make you comfortable. Not only that, you're only 20 minutes from Mt. Hood's summit. Look for the ark with the two giraffes. *61700 U.S. 26E, Brightwood, tel. 503/622–3121. 15 rooms.*

Shamrock Inn. You have several options at this newly remodeled, comfortable motel in Sandy, just west of the national forest. Small budget rooms with a queen-size bed cost $35; rooms with a kitchen run $48; and suites with a living room, kitchen, and one or two bedrooms are $60–$80. *59550 U.S. 26E, Sandy, tel. 503/622–4911. 20 units. Laundry. Wheelchair access.*

➤ **UNDER $65 • Timberline Lodge.** Even if you don't plan on staying here, make the 6,000-foot ascent to experience the epic proportions of the lodge's beams and ceilings—they just don't grow trees like they used to. Built in 1937 by the WPA (part of FDR's New Deal), the Timberline sits about halfway up the mountain, commanding views of over 100 miles. The second-floor lobby offers some serious hangout space; you won't be the only non-guest kicking it by one of the stone fireplaces. The Forest Service runs free tours at 11 AM, 1 PM, and 3 PM daily. The least expensive rooms (around $60) have shared baths, and all guests have access to the pool, sauna, and Jacuzzi. Reservations are suggested. *Timberline Rd., tel. 503/272–3311, 503/231–7979, or 800/547–1406 for reservations. 59 units.*

Stanley Kubrick liked the remote setting of the Timberline Lodge enough to film outside scenes from "The Shining" here (red rum, red rum).

CAMPING With almost 80 campgrounds, Mt. Hood is a camper's dream, though most of the sites are closed in winter. The northern portion of the national forest has beautiful views but tends to be crowded. For solitude, choose one of the less accessible campgrounds farther south. The visitor center (*see above*) has maps and can advise you on sites and availability; there's a reservation line (tel. 800/280–CAMP) for some grounds.

➤ **NORTH • Devil's Half-Acre.** On the old Barlow Road, this was the final overlook of the Old Oregon Trail. Of the campgrounds off Barlow, Devil's Half-Acre offers the best opportunity to stop and smell the wildflowers. Note that this is a "dispersed camping" site—it's free, but your only amenities are the trees and bushes that surround you. *Tel. 503/328–6211. From U.S. 26, head 3 mi north on Rte. 35 to Barlow Pass, follow to Pioneer Woman's Grave, and immediately turn onto Forest Rd. 3530. 5 sites. Open May–Oct.*

Green Canyon Campground. At this campground on the banks of the Salmon River, you fall asleep to the sounds of nearby waterfalls. As the name suggests, the Salmon has great fishing, and you can swim (if you're a member of the Polar Bear Club). Tent sites are free but there's no water, and you'll do your business on vault toilets. *Tel. 503/622–3191, ext. 311. From Zigzag, head 5 mi south on Salmon River Rd./ Rd. 2618. 15 sites. Open May–Sept.*

Trillium Lake Campground. Hold onto your bathing cap—the lake here is actually warm enough for swimming. You can also fish, and there's a special ramp for disabled anglers. Tent sites with a view of Mt. Hood run $10 ($12 for lakeside sites). This place is popular, so call the 800 number listed above for a reservation. *Tel. 503/666–0704. Go 2 mi east of Government Camp on U.S. 26, turn on Forest Rd. 2656, and go 1 mi. 55 sites. Open May–Sept.*

➤ **SOUTH** • **Hideaway Lakes Campground.** For a quick trip off the beaten track, try this serene campground at the edge of a crystal-clear lake. This is a favorite site for serious anglers; bring your rod along and throw another trout on the barbie. Hikers can wander the nearby trails. Tent sites run $8. *Tel. 503/630–4256. From Estacada, go 27 mi southeast on Rte. 224, 8 mi east on Forest Rd. 57, 3 mi northeast on Forest Rd. 58, and northwest on Forest Rd. 5830. 9 sites. Open June–Sept.*

FOOD

Many of the nicer lodges have restaurants, but most are expensive and the food's terrible—you should consider taking out life insurance before you consume. Stick to the towns on the west side of the mountain along U.S. 26 for decent, cheap fare; or pick up food at a market (*see* Basics, *above*).

➤ **UNDER $5** • **Honey Bear Express.** This little deli, espresso bar, and ice cream parlor has great sandwiches for less than $4 (but then, everything tastes great after a day on the mountain). Try a Wy'east ($3.95)—that's a veggie feast of cream cheese, walnuts, black olives, and cucumbers on dark rye with secret sauce. *68272 U.S. 26E, in Hoodland Park Plaza, tel. 503/622–5726. Open daily 9–5.*

➤ **UNDER $10** • **Barbeque Shack.** It's time to toss aside that salad fork and dust off the steak knife. This place features an all-you-can-eat chicken barbecue ($5.95) on Monday nights, all-you-can-eat spaghetti with red sauce ($1.95) on Wednesday nights, and great pork ribs ($5.25) every night. The portions are huge, and the atmosphere's all country. On Friday and Saturday nights you can ya-hoo! with a thigh-slapping band. Breakfasts are under $5 and feature (you guessed it) plenty of meat. *63750 U.S. 26E, in Wemme just east of Welches, tel. 503/622–3876. Open Sun.–Thurs. 7 AM–11 PM, Fri.–Sat. 7 AM–1 AM.*

Calamity Jane's. You can get filling steak and fish entrées, but burgers ($3–$5) are the specialty here. Huge, artery-clogging milkshakes ($2.75) may be enough for two. *42015 U.S. 26, 1 mi east of Sandy, tel. 503/668–7817. Open Sun.–Fri. 11–10, Sat. 11 AM–midnight.*

Mogul Mountain Pizza. Next door to the Honey Bear (*see above*), this place makes excellent pizzas. There's only one small table, so plan on getting it to go. A large Mt. Shasta (with mushrooms, olives, sliced tomatoes, green peppers, and onions; $15.50) will easily feed three hungry people. *68278 U.S. 26E, in Hoodland Park Plaza, tel. 503/622–4323. Open Wed.–Mon. 4–9 PM.*

➤ **UNDER $15** • **Mt. Hood Brew Pub.** Toss back a few of the home brews or other featured microbrews at this cozy pub and restaurant right below the summit in Government Camp. The pricey food is quite tasty and more than a little weird. You may—or may not—want to top your pizza ($9.50 and big enough to feed one very hungry person) with combos like the Brewmaster, which includes smoked salmon, capers, chives, and cream cheese. Sandwiches cost around $5.50. *87304 E. Government Camp Loop, at U.S. 26E, tel. 503/272–3724. Open daily noon–10.*

EXPLORING MT. HOOD

Most visitors use cars to get around this vast national forest. The two main roads are Route 35, which runs north–south from the town of Hood River (actually on the Columbia River) to just east of tiny Government Camp; and U.S. 26, which runs east–west from Sandy to Government Camp before heading southeast and exiting the forest.

HIKING The Mt. Hood area has a vast system of trails; hikers should stop at the visitor center (*see* Basics, *above*) to pick up guides. Many of the high-country trails are closed until early June, so be sure to check with the Forest Service before heading out. If you have time and energy, attempt one of the more difficult trails—they have significantly less traffic than the easy ones. The **Pacific Crest Trail,** which stretches from Mexico to Canada, goes through the forest. The Mt. Hood portion, called **Trail 600** (no points for originality there) begins at the Timberline Lodge (*see* Where to Sleep, *above*) and winds for 41 miles around the base of the mountain; plan on a three-day journey. In general, the trails in the Mt. Hood Wilderness get the heaviest use. For more solitude, head to the **Badger Creek Wilderness Area** (tel. 503/467–2291), southeast of Mt. Hood. Disabled hikers might want to try the **Lost Creek Nature Trail,** a ½-mile paved trail designed for wheelchairs but open to everyone. To reach the trailhead, head 4 miles north of Zigzag on Lolo Pass Road, turn east on Forest Road 1825, and go 2 miles to the end of the road.

Avoid Bagby Hot Springs, in the southern part of the forest. According to the July '94 issue of Outside magazine, it's a close runner-up for being one of the 16 most dangerous parks in the United States. Skinheads and their pals often use the springs and the surrounding area for target practice.

Burnt Lake Trail. If your back hurts just contemplating a moderate hike, then hobble away from this challenge; it receives the "most difficult" rating from the Forest Service. On the 7.3-mile round-trip, you'll climb approximately 1,500 feet, following Lost Creek to Burnt Lake—it's a pretty amazing journey. To reach the trailhead from Zigzag, head 4 miles north on Lolo Pass Road, turn east on Forest Road 1825, and follow it to the end.

Cooper Spur Loop. This steep but ultimately rewarding 8-mile loop climbs 2,500 feet to Cooper Spur, putting you nearly face to face with Mt. Hood. Mt. Adams lies to the north and Mt. Jefferson to the south. Use Trails 600 and 600A to reach the spur, but return only by Trail 600A. To get to the trailhead from the Cooper Spur Inn (27 mi south of Hood River on Rte. 35), go 10 miles west on Forest Road 3512.

Ramona Falls Loop. On this 4.4-mile loop you'll wander through dry forests, old-growth stands, and extensive rhododendron patches on a gradual climb to Ramona Falls. Take a well-deserved breather at the incredible waterfall at the midpoint. The trail is one of the most traveled in the state, so try to hike it during the week. To reach the trailhead from Zigzag, head 4 miles north on Lolo Pass Road, turn east on Forest Road 1825, and then take Forest Road 100 for 1.6 miles. The last section is extremely rutted; you may want to park and walk the last mile.

Umbrella Falls–Sahalie Falls Loop. This 5-mile loop through meadows and Alpine forest has incredible views of Mt. Hood. The trail begins at the Hood River Meadows parking lot on Route 35, 8 miles north of the intersection with U.S. 26. Take Trail 645 for half a mile, turn left on Trail 667, and continue 2 miles to Umbrella Falls. Return on Trail 667C.

SCENIC DRIVES AND VIEWS The **Mt. Hood–Columbia River Gorge Loop** (locally called "the Loop") packs loads of memorable scenery into one trip. The challenge is to try not to see all of it framed through a car window. The drive begins in Portland and follows U.S. 26 east for 55 miles. As the road crosses the south slope of Mt. Hood, you can take a detour to Timberline Lodge (*see* Where to Sleep, *above*). Turning north onto Route 35, you pass through 42 miles of Alpine forests and the Hood River Valley before reaching the town of Hood River. From here, I–84 takes you west 62 miles back to Portland. On the final leg of the trip, you can check out Bonneville Dam and the spectacular waterfalls of the Columbia Gorge (*see* Exploring the Columbia River Gorge, *below*).

FOREST ACTIVITIES

MOUNTAIN BIKING You can spin your wheels on any trail that does not expressly prohibit bikes (they're forbidden in all designated wilderness areas and the trails leading to them). **Mt. Hood Skibowl** (87000 U.S. 26E, tel. 503/262–3206, ext. 244) has trail maps, rents bikes ($26 half day, $38 full day), and for $2–$3 will chairlift you and your bike up into the mountains for the descent of your life. While you're up there, you can also try many rim trails. For advice on biking roads, contact the visitor center (*see* Basics, *above*).

ROCK CLIMBING Mt. Hood is the second most climbed peak in the world (after Japan's Mt. Fuji), but it's not for any old fool—the deep crevasses, rock falls, and capricious weather could make your life a mini-hell. Unless you're an accomplished climber with an axe, a rope, crampons, a helmet, and knowledge of the mountain, relent and go with a guide. From May to September, **Timberline Mountain Guides** (Timberline Lodge, tel. 503/636–7704) offers two-day classes starting at $180 a person that include a climb up the South Side to the summit. You can get basic instruction for about $80 a day. Call in advance for reservations. Even if you decide to go sans guide, make sure you register at Timberline Lodge.

SKIING Mt. Hood is very popular with the snow crowd year round. The slopes close for only two months—September and October—and even then there's snow above Timberline Lodge. Of late, snowboarding has really taken off here, so in addition to the ski bums, you're likely to run into lots of super-stylin' kids sporting funkier fashions than just about anywhere else in the state. The downhill skiing and snowboarding season runs from November through August. Nordic skiing takes place through the winter and early spring, depending on snow conditions. The best place to rent equipment is **Valian's Ski Shop** (Government Camp Business Loop, tel. 503/272–3525). Downhill gear goes for $12 a day and nordic for $9; snowboards with boots rent for $25. If you plan on snowboarding during summer, bring your own; shops won't risk you trashing their boards in low-snow conditions.

➤ **DOWNHILL** • **Mt. Hood Meadows** (off Rte. 35, Mt. Hood, tel. 503/337–2222) is the largest ski area on Mt. Hood, with over 60 trails and a vertical drop of 2,777 feet. Lift-ticket prices of $28–$31 also make it the most expensive. Beginners will appreciate the area around Buttercup Lift; more accomplished skiers should try Heather Canyon. The U.S. Ski Team does its summer training at **Timberline** (off U.S. 26, tel. 503/231–7979) on Palmer Glacier. This area closes only during September and October. Timberline claims a 3,000-foot-plus vertical drop, but the upper lift never runs in winter and the lower lifts stop in summer. The expert runs won't challenge strong skiers, but beginners and intermediates should do fine here. Lift tickets run about $26 in winter. **Mt. Hood Skibowl** (off U.S. 26, tel. 503/272–3206) offers a 1,500-foot vertical drop and lots of night skiing. Skibowl lacks good intermediate slopes, but high intermediates should do fine on the many expert runs. Lift tickets run about $20 for a full day; night skiing is less expensive.

➤ **CROSS-COUNTRY** • You need a Sno-Park permit ($2 a day, $9.50 a season) to park at the trailheads; most sporting-goods stores carry them. If you're near Timberline Lodge (*see* Where to Sleep, *above*), try the trail from there to Zigzag Canyon or down to Government Camp. **White River Sno-Park** on Route 35 offers access to trails down White River Canyon. From the **Mt. Hood Meadows** parking lot off Route 35, it's a 2.4-mile trip to Elk Meadows, and you get a great view of Mt. Hood on clear days.

Columbia River Gorge

Just east of Portland, the West's largest river carves a 1,000-foot-deep, 70-mile canyon out of the rugged Cascade Mountains. On the western end of the Columbia River Gorge you'll encounter temperate rain forests, cascading waterfalls—and windsurfers galore. If you close your eyes and concentrate, you can probably hear them grabbing their sailboards and stampeding here. The gorge's two dams have tamed the **Celilo Falls**, leaving behind a canal-like stretch of river that has grown into a windsurfing mecca. You can also swim from alternately sandy and marshy shores, and fish for sturgeon, salmon, bass, and trout. Hikers can explore some truly choice trails, where losing oneself in the incredible scenery is a matter of course. On the eastern end of the gorge, in the town of The Dalles, there aren't many windsurfers, but then there isn't much of anything in this barren desert. The towns of Hood River and The Dalles offer lots of restaurants and a moderate selection of adequate motels.

BASICS

VISITOR INFORMATION At the **Columbia Gorge National Scenic Area Ranger District** (902 Wasco St., Suite 200, Hood River, tel. 503/386–2333) and the **U.S. Forest Service Information Center** (Multnomah Falls, off I–84, tel. 503/695–2372), you can get hiking, biking and camping information. Ask for *Columbia Gorge Magazine,* which highlights the area's main attractions. The "Oregon Routes of Exploration" pamphlet includes a brief history of the gorge and a good map. Hikers and backpackers might want to buy the U.S. Forest Service map of the Columbia Wilderness for $2.

The **Hood River Chamber of Commerce** (Port Marina Park, Hood River, tel. 503/386–2000 or 800/366–3530), open weekdays 9–5 year-round and weekends 10–4 from April to October, has loads of information about hiking and mountain-biking trails. It's off I–84 at Exit 64. **The Dalles Convention and Visitors Bureau** (901 E. 2nd St., The Dalles, tel. 503/296–6616 or 800/255–3385) is open weekdays 9–5 year-round, and Saturday 10–5 and Sunday 10–3 in summer.

COMING AND GOING

The gorge begins near the town of Troutdale, 17 miles east of Portland off I–84, and stretches 70 miles east to the town of The Dalles. The historic **Columbia Gorge Scenic Highway** was built around 1910 and heralded as an engineering marvel. It parallels I–84 in the western part of the gorge and provides a scenic alternative to the interstate, passing several amazing waterfalls. In winter, however, the road becomes treacherous and icy.

You haven't been windwhipped until you've been caught in a Columbia Gorge downpour with winds of 100 mph. Bring a wind- and water-resistant jacket, and if you plan to hike, expect mud thick enough to coat your tennies any time of year.

BY BUS Greyhound (tel. 800/231–2222) has stations in The Dalles (201 Federal St., at 1st St., tel. 503/296–2421) and Hood River (1203 B St., tel. 503/386–1212). A trip between the two stations costs $4. Every day, a bus heads east through both stations toward Idaho, and another goes west to Portland (about $7 from Hood River). From The Dalles, a bus goes south once a day to Bend ($19).

BY TRAIN Amtrak (tel. 800/872–7245) runs alongside I–84 and stops in Hood River (110 Railroad Ave.) and The Dalles (201 E. Federal St.). The 23-mile trip from Hood River to The Dalles costs $4, and the 62-mile trip from Hood River to Portland is $14.

WHERE TO SLEEP

The chambers of commerce in Hood River and The Dalles have lists of B&Bs, which typically charge $50–$75. Campgrounds tend to be packed in summer, especially on weekends, so reserve your site or get a move on it. If you're having trouble finding a site, make your way toward Mt. Hood along Route 35, or into Washington, using the bridge at Hood River or the one near Cascade Locks. Check with the visitor centers (*see* Basics, *above)* for more hints on campsite availability. If you decide to stay in a motel, be warned: Prices are $10–$20 higher in summer. The Dalles is ugly and the pickings are slim; head to Cascade Locks or Hood River first.

➣ **THE DALLES • Huntley Inn.** Decent rooms ($42–$56) with Continental breakfast thrown in have made this inn successful. The hot tub and heated pool don't hurt either. *2500 W. 6th St., tel. 503/296–1191 or 800/448–5544. 71 units. No-smoking rooms.*

Williams House Inn. This ornately furnished turn-of-the-century B&B smacks of the Victorian era. Despite the Williams' down-home conversation, the house is so formal that a stroll across the plush carpet seems somehow inappropriate. But the two cozy bedrooms, particularly the suite, will put you at ease. Rooms cost $55–$75. *608 W 6th St., tel. 503/296–2889. 3 rooms, none with bath.*

➣ **HOOD RIVER • Prater's Motel.** At the beginning of Hood River's main drag, this motel has roomy, clean units looking out on the Columbia River. At $45 for a double, it's about as cheap as Hood River gets. Decided to pitch a tent yet? *1306 Oak St., tel. 503/386–3566. From I–84, take Exit 62 to Oak St. 7 rooms.*

Vagabond Lodge. The modern, clean, elegantly furnished rooms facing the back (around $70) look across a grove of Douglas fir to marvelous views of the Columbia River. The older units in front—which are perfectly fine—run $42 and up. Call months ahead for summer-weekend reservations. *4070 Westcliff Dr., Hood River, tel. 503/388–2992. 40 units.*

➤ **CASCADE LOCKS** • **Bridge of the Gods Motel.** Hardly as epic as the name suggests, this place offers clean accommodations without any of the hustle and bustle of Hood River. Doubles run $36–$40. *630 U.S. 30, tel. 503/374–8628. 7 rooms.*

Scenic Winds Motel. The best deal on the Oregon side of the gorge, the Scenic Winds gives you a $38 cabin set back off the road in the peaceful town of Cascade Locks. On top of that, you get a TV—what more could you ask? *10 Wa-Na-Pa St., tel. 503/374–8390. 10 rooms. No credit cards.*

HOSTELS **Bingen School Inn.** Just when you thought you'd left your school days behind you, up pops this elementary school–cum–hostel, complete with chalkboards and those annoying blond-haired surfer dudes. Good rates, plus a kitchen, a TV lounge, and a gym, attract the windsurfing crowd and anyone else looking for the best deal around. You can rent windsurfing equipment (everything but the wet suit) for $35 and mountain bikes for $15 a day. Beds go for $11, private rooms for $29. *Cnr Humbolt and Cedar Sts., Bingen, WA, tel. 509/493–3363. Cross the Hood River toll bridge (50¢) to Washington State and head 2 mi east on Rte. 14 to Cedar St. 45 beds, 6 private rooms, all with shared bath.*

CAMPING **Columbia River Gorge Resort.** You couldn't call it secluded, but this well-located place lets you escape the freeway noise that plagues some state campgrounds. Tent sites are $14. *Along I–84 east of Mosir, tel. 503/478–3750. Over 500 sites. Showers, toilets.*

Eagle Creek Campground. Within swooping distance of the scenic Eagle Creek Trail (*see* Hiking, *below*), this campground offers relatively remote and unspoiled sites ($5). *Tel. 503/386–2333. Eagle Creek exit off I–84 east, 2 mi west of Cascade Locks. 19 sites. Open May–Sept.*

Wyeth Campground. Set in the woods, with several excellent trailheads nearby, this is a great place to hang for a day or two. The grounds are exposed, but the sites ($8) aren't on top of each other. *Tel. 503/386–2333. 7 mi east of Cascade Locks off I–84. 14 sites. Fire rings, picnic tables, vault toilets. Open May–Sept.*

FOOD

Head to Hood River for the best deals—local restaurants cater to starving, broke windsurfers who like to claim that their $1,000 boards are their last possessions. Picnickers can hit the 24-hour supermarkets in Hood River and The Dalles, located on the respective main drags as you enter town.

UNDER $5 **Carolyn's Restaurant.** Locals cite this as the place to have breakfast in Hood River, and if you're looking for standard fare at moderate prices, maybe you should take the suggestion. For something a little different, try the chocolate-chip pancakes ($4.55). Sandwiches run under $5. *1313 Oak St., west end of town, tel. 503/386–1127. Open 6 AM–3 PM.*

The Dalles can be a depressing culinary experience unless you're into fast food—or worse, fast food masquerading as quality dining.

Salmon Row Pub. With several microbrews on tap, tasty $10 pizzas, and a throng of locals, the Salmon Row is the place to come when you want to loosen up. On Friday and Saturday nights the locals may be a bit legless . . . er, drunk, but you can always sit behind one of the cedar-shingled partitions. See no evil, hear no evil. *500 Wa-Na-Pa St., first exit in Cascade Locks from I–84, tel. 503/374–9310. Open daily 11–11.*

Sugar Bowl. This tavern looks seedy from the outside and only slightly less so inside, but the all-you-can-eat soup and salad bar is only $5. For something a little less healthy, try the ¼ pound hamburger with tasty onion rings ($5.25). *504 W. 9th St., The Dalles, tel. 503/296–2956. Open weekdays 11–10, Sat. 4 PM–10 PM.*

`UNDER $10` **Yaya's International Cafe.** Run by a friendly family—from the South Bronx no less—this restaurant features an excellent multicultural menu that draws heavily on Greek cuisine and features a wide array of vegetarian dishes. Try the Mad Greek sandwich ($4.25), with Genoa salami, ham, turkey, provolone cheese, swiss cheese, and various green things. *207 Oak St., Hood River, tel. 503/386-1996. Open daily 11-10.*

EXPLORING THE COLUMBIA RIVER GORGE

`HIKING` The best way to see the gorge and surrounding forests is on foot. Most hikes begin at trailheads along the Columbia River Scenic Highway. The paths, which usually head south toward Mt. Hood, are steep at first but eventually level out to upward-sloping plateaus. You may want to buy a map at the Columbia Gorge Ranger District or the Forest Service Information Center (*see* Basics, *above*) and create your own itinerary. The Forest Service has recently begun classifying hiking trails by degrees of difficulty. When they say difficult, they mean it; here you'll find some steep climbs. Many trails are now open to bikers as well; contact the Forest Service for the latest update. Wheelchair users can head to **Starvation Creek,** just 4 miles past Exit 51 off I-84. It's only half a mile from the parking area to a waterfall and a fully equipped rest area.

If you plan to spend some time here, get a copy of 35 Hiking Trails: Columbia River Gorge, by R. and D. Lowe (Touchstone Press, Box 81, Beaverton, OR 97075). At $7.95, it's an excellent resource for the serious hiker.

➤ **SHORTER HIKES** • Horsetail-Oneonta Loop. This 2.7-mile loop leads behind upper Horsetail Falls, offering views of the Oneonta Gorge. The easy grade and the great scenery attract quite the family crowd, so try to come on a weekday. The trail begins at Horsetail Falls on the Scenic Highway; from I-84, use Exits 28 or 35 to reach the highway.

Wahclella Trail. Those who don't feel up to anything strenuous should consider this gentle 2-mile (round-trip) hike past Punchbowl Falls. To get here take the Exit 40 toward Bonneville Dam.

➤ **LONGER HIKES** • Angels Rest Trail. Fields of wildflowers and forests of alder, maple, and conifer line this 2½-mile (one-way) hike along old logging roads. Sounds pretty idyllic—but the operative words here are "vertical gain." If you're not scared off, the actual hike isn't that tough. At Angel's Rest Summit, you can often see across the gorge to Mt. St. Helens. The trail begins at Bridal Veil Falls on the Scenic Highway; from I-84, use Exits 28 or 35 to reach the highway.

Eagle Creek Trail. This kick-your-ass trail follows Eagle Creek for 13 miles between steep cliffs, through dense rain forests, and past several falls before emerging at Wahtum Lake. At Tunnel Falls, 6 miles in, the trail passes through a tunnel behind the roaring cascade. Allow 8–10 hours each way—and remember it can get very cold up here. Take Exit 41 on eastbound I-84 (no exit accesses the trail from the west side of the highway).

Wyeth Trail. This 5.6-mile (one-way) hike climbs through old-growth forests and meadows dotted with wildflowers to incredible North Lake. Make sure to check out the stellar views of the gorge. The steep trail gains almost 4,000 feet and the trip is better made by those who use the word "Nautilus" in everyday conversation. The hike will take you a whole day, so pack plenty of food and water. Take Exit 51 from I-84 eastbound or westbound; the trail leaves from the campground of the same name.

`SCENIC DRIVES` Interstate 84 runs east–west through the gorge on the southern bank of the Columbia River, which divides Oregon and Washington. The Washington State Highway (Rte. 14) hugs the river on the north bank. For a great drive, follow the old **Columbia River Scenic Highway,** which parallels I-84 along the western section of the gorge. The highway splits off from I-84 at Exit 16 in Troutdale, 17 miles east of Portland. (If you're heading west on I-84 and want to follow this tour in reverse, take Exit 35.) The road climbs up to the Vista House at **Crown Point,** a great place for panoramic views of the gorge. Five miles down the road, you can park and take the short hike to **Bridal Veil Falls.** Three miles farther east, the brooding **Wahkeena Falls** cascade 242 feet to a small pool below. **Multnomah Falls,** a mile farther, plunges 620 feet, making it the second highest year-round falls in the United States. A paved path crosses the lower part of the falls and winds up to the top, making the entire experience wheelchair accessible. Another 2 miles takes you to **Oneonta Falls** and **Oneonta Gorge.** In order to see these falls, you have to stone-hop or wade down the narrow gorge. A half-mile farther, **Horsetail Falls** drops 221 feet in a single flow. After rejoining I-84, continue east about 5 miles to the **Bonneville Dam** (tel. 503/374–8820), a hydroelectric project completed in 1939. You can watch ships navigating a 500-foot lock and salmon hurling themselves up fish ladders. Take a self-guided tour daily 9–5, in summer until 8.

WORTH SEEING Many visitors finish their tour of the gorge on the Washington side of the river, at the extraordinary **Maryhill Museum** (35 Maryhill Museum Dr., Goldendale, WA, tel. 509/773–3733), open daily 9–5 from March to November. This early-20th-century manor house, turned into a museum in 1926, has an entire room of sculptures and drawings by Auguste Rodin, displays of Native American artifacts from across the continent, and a strange and wonderful collection of chess sets dating back to the 17th century. The museum is west of Goldendale, across the river and 15 miles east of The Dalles on Route 14. Admission is $4.

➤ **HOOD RIVER** • Centrally located between The Dalles and Troutdale, Hood River has grown from a sleepy town to a windsurfing hot spot. Californians and other out-of-staters flock here, often snatching up what to them is unbelievably cheap real estate. As a result, the town has become more expensive and sophisticated, with merchants catering to big-city folks. The old-timers are caught between anger at the intrusion and satisfaction with the growing economy. For travelers, this is about as non-nature-oriented as the action gets in the gorge.

Hood River Vineyards (4693 Westwood Dr., tel. 503/386–3772) produces pinot noir and Riesling and offers summer tours daily 11–5. If you prefer grains to grapes, try the home-brewed ale at the **Whitecap Brewpub** (506 Columbia St., tel. 503/386–2281). **Horsefeathers** (115 State St., tel. 503/386–4411) has a thriving bar scene where you can get drunk with total strangers. The **Mt. Hood Railroad** (110 Railroad Ave., tel. 503/386–3556) will cruise you through the apple and pear orchards of the Hood River Valley to the base of Mt. Hood and back. At $20, it's expensive, but as the Hood River Chamber of Commerce puts it, the scenery is gorge-ous.

➤ **THE DALLES** • At the eastern end of the Gorge, The Dalles has seen little of the boom that windsurfing brought to Hood River. In many ways this is not surprising—hot and dry in summer, and dreary all year round, this town is UGLY. On top of that, there are few activities here that merit a stop. If you happen to be in the area, divert absolute boredom with a trip to the **Fort Dalles Museum** (500 W. 15th St. at Garrison St., tel. 503/296–4547), open weekdays 10:30–5 and weekends 10–5 from March to October. For $2 (students free) you'll see an interesting collection of turn-of-the-century vehicles, horse-drawn hearses and pioneer memorabilia. Mid-July brings the **Fort Dalles Days Rodeo,** along with a country-western dance and parade. For great views of the gorge, head to **Sirosis Park,** on a bluff above the town. **The Dalles Dam** (tel. 503/296–1181), off Exit 87, has a tour train for viewing the fish ladders and hydropower facilities. Both are open daily 9–5.

OUTDOOR ACTIVITIES

In the past decade, the Columbia River Gorge has become one of the top windsurfing spots in the world. On a blustery day, stylin' dudes decked out in neon wet suits cover the entire river from Cascade Locks to The Dalles. Rest assured, there's also plenty of fishing and hiking (*see* Exploring the Columbia River Gorge, *above*) along the river. White-water raft operators run river trips on the Deschutes and White Salmon rivers, both tributaries of the Columbia.

MOUNTAIN BIKING Of late, mountain biking has really taken off in the gorge, thanks to the opening of many trails by the Forest Service. This is great biking country, with plenty of challenging trails and lots of dirt. The Forest Service Information Center (*see* Basics, *above*) has a list of legal trails. You can rent bikes at the Bingen School Inn (*see* Where to Sleep, *above*).

WINDSURFING High winds in deep river channels will challenge the expert, while sheltered coves cater to beginners. Consider yourself forewarned: This is not exactly a budget activity. Several shops in Hood River offer lessons, rent equipment, and can advise you about the best spots on any given day. Try **Front Street Sailboards** (207 Front St., tel. 503/386–4044), where a board will cost you $40 a day; for $59, you can have a three-hour lesson with all equipment included. The **Sailboard Warehouse** (13 Oak St., tel. 503/386–9434) rents boards at similar rates.

FISHING The Columbia River teems with salmon, bass, walleye, and 6-foot sturgeon; two of its tributaries, the John Day and the Deschutes, offer heavy steelhead runs as well. **River's Bend Outfitters** (604 E. 11th St., The Dalles, tel. 503/296–5949) and **Johnson's Oregon Guide Service** (2028 Lambert St., The Dalles, tel. 503/296–2744) are among several licensed companies that offer transportation, fishing gear, boats, and expert advice—but you'd better call as far ahead as possible. As they say around here, this is a "spendy" way to go; it'll cost you $125 a day. And remember your state permit, available at local tackle shops.

RAFTING The Deschutes River has popular Class III and IV runs near the Columbia River Gorge. Approach them with respect—and some healthy fear. Unless you're experienced, take a guide. Many outfitters are based in the town of Maupin, 40 miles south of The Dalles on U.S. 197. For around $60 a day you can experience the ride of a lifetime. **C.J. Lodge and White Water Rafting** (304 Bakeoven Rd., Maupin, tel. 503/395–2404) offers a wide variety of trips with good equipment and experienced guides. The White Salmon River, which runs into the Columbia on its Washington side, has waters that approach Class V; you don't want to be here without someone who knows what she's doing.

EASTERN OREGON AND THE HIGH DESERT

5

By Josh Lichtner

Get ready to experience the Great Outdoors. Eastern Oregon isn't known for its mini-malls and symphony halls—it's known for vast deserts, deep gorges, mountains that take you into different weather zones, and towns with a mighty population of six. These lands have been mined by early Chinese settlers, trampled by dusty cowboys on horseback, and trekked over by pioneers on the Oregon Trail. The land is just about the only reason to come here. There are few places on the West Coast where you can lose yourself so entirely in the wilderness, with human contact ranging from barely any to none at all.

Eastern Oregon is called the High Desert because much of the region sits on a plateau more than 3,000 feet above sea level, and the highest mountains reach nearly 10,000 feet. But desert is a misleading term. Compared with the sodden coastal strip, it *is* arid: The central mountains around the John Day Fossil Beds are barren, full of sharp ridges, burnt colors, and bare rock. But hundreds of rivers, creeks, and streams flow through the region, too, giving way to grasslands and forests of ponderosa pine and Douglas fir. The Wallowa mountains in northeastern Oregon are sometimes called America's Alps because of their sheer height. Yet, just 30 miles east of the Wallowas is Hells Canyon, a desolate gorge that plunges 8,000 feet to the Snake River.

Much of Oregon's early history was played out in these mountains and valleys. The Oregon Trail, the 2,000-mile route that early pioneers followed west from Missouri, crosses the northeastern part of the state. You can still see the ruts made by the wagon wheels of settlers battling their way over the Blue Mountains. In the 1860s, gold was found here—a discovery that forever changed the face of eastern Oregon. The Native Americans were the big losers in this bonanza of exploration and exploitation. Driven from their land by settlers and prospectors, tribes such as the Nez Percé took up arms—and were defeated. Much of the land now belongs to the government, which manages millions of acres of national forest and wilderness for you to hike around in or set up camp.

If your idea of aerobic exercise is inhaling a Camel, stick to the coffee houses of Portland. Come to eastern Oregon for the camping, hiking, fishing, biking, and skiing. The national forests and the wilderness areas boast thousands of miles of trails and unpaved roads that are almost always deserted. The summer season lasts June–October; after that, campgrounds close and the trails become heavy with mud or snow. In fall, hunters descend on the area in pursuit of elk, deer, bear, and other helpless woodland critters. Although there are a couple of downhill ski places in northeastern Oregon, the area is better suited to cross-country skiing. In winter, skiers can take advantage of the trails and forest roads that pass through huge pine forests.

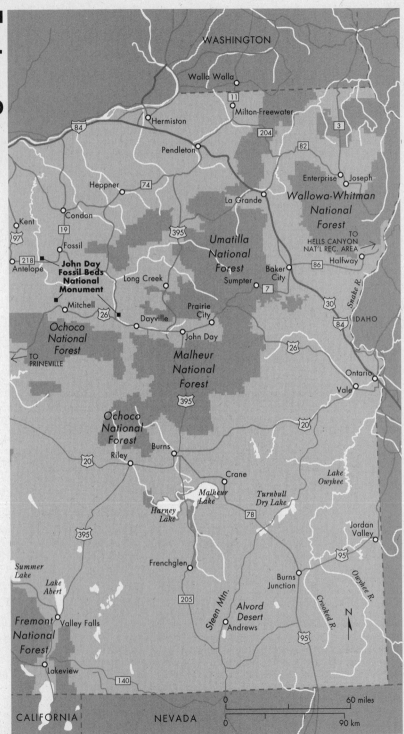

Eastern Oregon

WASHINGTON

Walla Walla
11
Milton-Freewater
Hermiston
204
84
3
Pendleton
82
Enterprise Joseph
Heppner 74
La Grande
Wallowa-Whitman
National
Forest
Kent
97
Condon
19
TO
HELLS CANYON
NAT'L REC. AREA
Umatilla
National
Forest
Fossil
218
Antelope
John Day
Fossil Beds
National
Monument
Long Creek
395
Sumpter
Baker
City
86 Halfway
30
Snake R.
Mitchell
26
Dayville
Prairie
City
7
IDAHO
Ochoco
National
Forest
John Day
84
TO
PRINEVILLE
Malheur
National
Forest
26
Ontario
Vale
Ochoco
National
Forest
395
20
Burns
Riley
20
Crane
Lake
Owyhee
Malheur
Lake
Turnbull
Dry Lake
Harney
Lake
78
Jordan
Valley
395
Frenchglen
95
Summer
Lake
205
Burns
Junction
Owyhee R.
Lake
Abert
Steen Mtn.
Alvord
Desert
N
Crooked R.
Fremont
National
Forest
Valley Falls
Andrews
95
Lakeview
140
0   60 miles
CALIFORNIA   NEVADA   0   90 km

GETTING AROUND

It may make you feel like an environmental scab, but a car makes life much easier in the wilds of Oregon. The public transport system isn't very extensive, and the distances are too long for most bikers and hikers. If you have a choice, go with a four-wheel-drive beast. Sure, you can get around driving on paved streets, but if you want to get out into the boonies, you need to travel unpaved forest roads, some of which sport their own mountain ranges and mud baths. From Portland, you've got three good options for traveling through eastern Oregon: I-84 runs straight east along the Columbia River and dips down to La Grande, Baker City, and into Idaho; U.S. 26 goes southeast to Prineville and then directly east through the Ochoco and Malheur National Forests; and U.S. 26 to U.S. 97 leads to Bend in central Oregon; from there U.S. 20 heads southeast to Burns. **Greyhound** (tel. 800/231–2222) provides regular service along I-84 between Portland and Boise, Idaho, stopping at many of the little towns along the way. **Amtrak** (tel. 800/872–7245) follows I-84 from Portland to Boise.

During the winter, rural roads often get snowed in, and in the summer, you'll undoubtedly experience a delay caused by the ever-present road work throughout the region. Mileage charts offer little help when planning trips in the east: Roads are steep, curvy and often in some state of disrepair.

Ochoco National Forest

Together with the adjoining Crooked River National Grassland, the Ochoco National Forest accounts for nearly a million acres of land, smack in the middle of Oregon. Except for the annual influx of hunters during the fall, this forest of ponderosa pines remains relatively deserted, making it a great spot for hikers seeking a little solitude. The forest includes three wilderness areas, and there are no maintained trails or developed campsites. This arid landscape, receiving only 20–40 inches of rain a year, is marked by steep-sided canyons, towering volcanic plugs, and sharp ridges. The great herds of elk that used to roam the Ochocos and were hunted almost to extinction are slowly returning, and you can also see wild horses, eagles, and possibly even a wildcat or cougar. Although you'll sweat through some scorching days in summer, the nights can get bitterly cold; the best months to experience the forest are June–October; otherwise, expect snow and terrible road conditions. If you plan to do any serious hiking or backpacking here, you should invest in a Forest Service map ($3) or enlarged fire map of the area ($3.50) from the Prineville Ranger District Station (*see below*).

VISITOR INFORMATION

The Prineville Ranger District Station provides information about hiking, camping, rockhounding, mountain biking, and fishing. *3160 N.E. 3rd St., Prineville, tel. 503/447–9641.*

Prineville/Crook County Chamber of Commerce. *390 N. Fairview St., at 3rd St., Prineville, tel. 503/447–6304. Open summer, weekdays 9–5, weekends 11–4; winter, weekdays 9–5.*

COMING AND GOING

The Ochoco National Forest lies about 15 miles east of Prineville, the main town in the area and a good place to base yourself. You don't need reservations or permits to camp and hike in Ochoco, and you can park for free in the designated areas near the trailheads. Prineville itself is just three hours from Portland by car down U.S. 26, and 45 minutes northeast of Bend.

BY BUS **Greyhound** (Town Pump, 1005 Madras Hwy., Prineville, tel. 503/447–3646) runs once a day from Prineville west to Madras and Redmond, where passengers connect with the

Fill up on gas in Prineville or in Mitchell—gas stations around here are few and far between.

main north–south line serving Portland and Bend. **People Mover** (229 N.E. Dayton, John Day, tel. 503/575–2370) stops in Prineville on its U.S. 26 service from Bend to John Day, two hours to the east. The bus makes the round-trip journey once every Monday, Wednesday, and Friday; the fare is $17 one-way.

GETTING AROUND

Because this mountain range is so isolated, public transport is extremely limited. The **People Mover** (*see above*) goes through the national forest on its way to John Day, and the drivers will drop you off if you ask. Driving and biking remain the most feasible options, though. Bikers usually stick to U.S. 26 because of its wide lanes and sparse traffic. Route 380, the small road that runs about 50 miles from Prineville to Paulina (a remote site with camping facilities and a ranger station) is also paved.

Most roads in the forest are gravel or dirt—some of which are suitable for mountain bikes, and some of which will give even your car a real workout. Don't get on these roads if it looks like rain, unless you want to be driving a mudmobile.

WHERE TO SLEEP

Unless you camp, your options are pretty much limited to Prineville or Mitchell (on the other side of the forest, 50 miles east on U.S. 26). Be sure to reserve rooms early in summer, when most accommodations fill up. Although Prineville is the bigger town and has several supermarkets and restaurants (*see* Food, *below*), Mitchell has more character—it's a funky old desert town with a great motel. Besides, everything in Mitchell is within walking distance (as in no more than two blocks away).

PRINEVILLE Carolina Motel. The rooms at this ordinary hotel are spacious and almost soundproofed with vinyl padding, though you may get the vague impression of being lodged in a coffin. Despite this aesthetic oddity, the rooms are clean, and at $40 a night for a double room, this is as good as it gets in Prineville. *1050 E. 3rd St., tel. 503/447–4152. 26 rooms.*

Ochoco Inn. This generic, small-town motel comes fully equipped with a grumpy owner. Any takers? Since it costs $42 a night, you might as well save yourself two bucks and go enjoy the mortuary decor of the Carolina (*see above*). *123 E. 3rd St. at Main St., tel. 503/447–6231. 34 rooms.*

MITCHELL The Sky Hook Motel. At this carefully tended inn perched above the small town of Mitchell, you can hang out in the vegetable and flower gardens after a day's hike. The owners are friendly, the rooms well furnished, and—oh boy—you can even get single-channel TVs and kitchenettes. This place stands head and shoulders above most motels. Doubles go for $35. *101 U.S. 26, tel. 503/462–3569. 6 rooms.*

CAMPING Just pitch your tent wherever your fancy takes you; wilderness permits aren't required, and absolute solitude is easy to find. Just pay attention to your route: Getting lost is a distinct, frightening possibility. The developed campsites offer a slightly more civilized atmosphere; you get pit toilets but little relief from noisy neighbors on holidays and weekends. Most of the campgrounds are open June–September, but be prepared for frost or rain even in summer. For information on additional campgrounds, contact the **Ochoco Forest Supervisor** (3160 N.E. 3rd St., Prineville, tel. 503/447–6247). Skip **Ochoco Lake State Park** and head for nicer ones down the road. Ochoco Lake's dam broke, and now there's no lake, making the nearby campsites unappealing. Snowfall permitting, the lake should be full again by 1996. Tent sites are $10.

Ochoco Campground. Near the Ochoco Ranger Station and the trailhead for the Lookout Mountain Trail (*see* Hiking, *below*), this campground is a wonderful place to see elk, wild horses, and mule deer. Tent sites cost $6. *Tel. 503/447–9645. From Prineville, 12 mi east on U.S. 26, right on Forest Road 22 for 7 mi. 6 sites. Closed Sept.–Apr.*

Walton Lake Campground. Catch your z's in the woods at this developed site on Walton Lake. The swimming is great, and you can catch the trailhead for the Round Mountain Trail here. This site fills up on weekends and holidays, so come during the week or get here early. Sites cost $4. *Tel. 503/447–9645. From Prineville, 12 mi east on U.S. 26, then 15 mi south on Forest Rd. 42. Toilets, drinking water.*

White Rock. At the edge of the Mill Creek Wilderness, this free, undeveloped campground requires that you carry your water in and your trash out. Catch the Wildcat Trail (*see* Hiking, *below*) here. *9 mi east of Prineville on U.S. 26, left on Mill Creek Rd. for 7 mi, right on Rd. 3350 for 3 mi, and left on Rd. 300. Closed Nov.–Mar.*

Wildcat Campground. On the edge of the spectacular Mill Creek Wilderness (*see* Exploring Ochoco National Forest, *below*), Wildcat is the trailhead for the Twin Pillars Trail (*see* Hiking, *below*). With Mill Creek running nearby and ponderosa pines towering above, this is a great place to stay. Tent sites cost $6. *From Prineville, 9 mi east on U.S. 26, north on Mill Creek Rd. for 11 mi to Road 33. 17 sites. Toilets. Closed Nov.–Mar.*

Wolf Creek Campground. In the remote southern part of the Ochoco Range, this campground lies about 6 miles from the old-growth forest, gorges, and crags of Black Canyon Wilderness. At Black Canyon Creek, anglers can catch steelhead trout, and others can swim with them. Sites are $4. *68 mi SE of Prineville on U.S. 26. Take left fork 3 mi east of Paulina to Rd. 42. 11 sites. Toilets. Closed Nov.–Mar.*

FOOD

Nothing beats catching your own trout and grilling it over an open fire—especially not most of the restaurants around the national forest. The supermarkets and restaurants listed below are in Prineville, this region's locus of civilization. To stock up before heading into the woods, stop at **Eriksons Entry Supermarket** (315 W. 3rd St./U.S. 26, tel. 503/447–6291) or **Thriftway Supermarket** in Ochoco Plaza (E. 3rd St./U.S. 26, east end of town, tel. 503/447–6423).

Dad's Place. A typical American diner on Main Street, Dad's offers no-nonsense food at no-nonsense prices. For an eye-opener, try the No. 7 biscuit sandwich ($3.50), with ham, bacon, cheese, and egg on a toasted biscuit—you'll be scarfing oat bran for the rest of your life to get rid of this one. For lunch they have burgers galore, and such haûte cuisine as the French dip for $4.50. *229 N. Main St., tel. 503/447–7059. Open weekdays 5 AM–2 PM, Sat. 7 AM–1 PM.*

The Sandwich Factory. A Ph.D in linguistics would help in deciphering the long, confounding menu at this roadside shack. Selections are numbered/alphabetized from 1 through WD-5. Try an un-vegetarian special sandwich ($4 whole, $2.75 half), which is the same as the vegetarian special but with meat, and thus is a 1SB instead of a plain old 1S. The factory also serves espresso, something called Yo-cream, and breakfast sandwiches that are the same as ordinary sandwiches only served earlier (??). *277 North Court, at E. 3rd St., tel. 503/447–4429. Open weekdays 7:30 AM–8 PM, Sat. 9–7.*

EXPLORING OCHOCO NATIONAL FOREST

➤ **MILL CREEK WILDERNESS** • The main attractions of this rugged 17,500-acre wilderness are the volcanic plugs that rise up out of the surrounding pine forest; hot volcanic gases hollowed the plugs, and subsequent erosion of surrounding soil left hardened caves. The most spectacular of them all is **Steins Pillar,** a 350-foot stone toothpick that towers above the Mill Creek Valley. One of the main hikes through Mill Creek leads to the **Twin Pillars,** two adjacent columns of stone. East Fork Mill Creek, which runs through the middle of the wilderness, is a good place to catch rainbow trout. If you're quiet, you might see elk, deer, and wild turkeys. You'll find the trailhead leading into this wilderness at Wildcat Campground (*see* Camping, *above*).

➤ **BRIDGE CREEK WILDERNESS** • Despite its diminutive size, this 5,400-acre wilderness is a great place to get away from it all. The terrain here is less steep than in the Mill Creek Wilderness, and there are no maintained trails, which means you'll run into fewer people. Take in spectacular views of the forest, with only woodpeckers, prairie falcons, and goshawks for company. This is also a favorite wintering area for the park's growing population of elk. The terrain changes constantly from wooded slopes to grassy plateaus and meadows, watered by a maze of small streams. South of Bridge Creek is **Big Summit Prairie,** which blooms from late May through June with wildflowers bearing such fancy names as Mules Ear, Wyethia, Biscuit Root, and Yellow Bells. Bridge Creek Wilderness is a few miles east of Mill Creek; you can get to it from U.S. 26 near Mitchell.

➤ **BLACK CANYON WILDERNESS** • East of Bridge Creek, Black Canyon Wilderness is probably the most remote of the three wilderness areas—you'll rarely see anyone tromping across the rugged 13,400-acre landscape here, although the area is popular with hunters in fall. Black Canyon Creek drops more than 3,000 feet through a terrain of jagged ridges, steep gorges, and old-growth forest. In May and June, wildflowers flourish. From Dayville, east of Mitchell, head south for 11 miles on Forest Road 74.

HIKING For additional information on hikes, contact the Ochoco Forest Supervisor in Prineville (*see* Camping, *above*).

Black Canyon Trail. Less demanding than the three hikes described below, this trail follows Black Canyon Creek through the cliffs of steep Black Canyon. This hike is easy but long—about 12 miles each way. So be prepared, bring plenty of water, and turn back if you've had almost enough. The first part of the trail crosses the creek several times, so bring shoes that don't mind getting wet. You have to cross the south fork of the John Day River to get to the trailhead, but it's only a foot deep in the summer. *From Dayville on U.S. 26, take Forest Rd. 47 about 7 mi south to trailhead.*

Lookout Mountain. Open meadows at the top of this peak allow you to see for hundreds of miles, including an amazing view of the Cascades to the west, the Ochocos to the north, and the Maury Mountains to the south. The trail begins at 3,900 feet and gradually climbs another 3,000 feet over its 7 miles. *From Prineville, go 12 mi east on U.S. 26, then south 9 mi on Forest Rd. 42 to trailhead, next to Ochoco Ranger Station.*

Round Mountain. This National Recreation Trail is a gradual climb from Walton Lake up the eroded remnants of an extinct volcano. The hike is 9 miles one-way and climbs over 2,000 feet. The most scenic portion of the trail is the 5-mile climb from Walton Lake to the top of Round Mountain. The spectacular view from the top more than compensates for the sweat you work up on the way. *From Prineville, go 12 mi east on U.S. 26, then 15 mi south on Forest Rd. 42 to Walton Lake Campgrounds.*

Twin Pillars Trail. Two rocky columns (*see* Mill Creek Wilderness, *above*) lie at the end of this 17-mile round-trip hike. The trail begins at Wildcat Campground and climbs about 1,700 feet through lodgepole pine and ponderosa pine. This hike is long, but not too difficult. *From Prineville, go 7 mi east on U.S. 26, north on Mill Creek Rd., and continue 12 mi to Wildcat Campground.*

DRIVES AND VIEWS If you don't have the time or inclination to go traipsing through the wilderness, drive around the **Big Summit Prairie Loop.** This 43-mile drive starts at the ranger station at the junction of Forest Roads 42 and 22 and takes you in a loop past Lookout Mountain, Round Mountain, Walton Lake, and Big Summit Prairie. From the ranger station, take Forest Road 42 until you reach Road 3010; it will connect you to Road 22, which loops you back to the ranger station. You can also do the same loop backwards, starting out on Road 22. For another great drive, take Road 22 all the way through the forest to Mitchell; the 45-mile drive, mostly on well-maintained dirt roads, passes through the forest and ends in rolling farmland. You'll find excellent camping along the way—just venture onto one of the many dirt roads that intersect Road 22, and remember which way you came from.

FOREST ACTIVITIES

FISHING This area is a prime place to fish for steelhead and rainbow trout. Steelhead fishing is best in March and April in Trout, Bear, Rock, Cottonwood, and Black Canyon creeks. Rainbow trout can be found in Walton and Delintment lakes and Antelope Reservoir. Fishing permits cost $6.75 a day, $30 a week, or $40 a season, and are available at local sporting-goods stores and big supermarkets.

MOUNTAIN BIKING While mountain biking is not nearly as popular here as in the Deschutes National Forest, the Ochoco forest offers trails aplenty, as well as miles of Forest Service roads that are fun and challenging to ride. Pick up the pamphlet "Mountain Biking in Central Oregon," a guide to trails in Ochoco National Forest, from the Prineville Ranger District Station (see Visitor Information, above). This guide lists ten trails, six of which are single-track.

ROCKHOUNDING Rockhounding, searching for semi-precious or unusual stones, is very popular in the Ochocos. The annual "Prineville Rockhound Pow-Wow," held in June, brings rockhounds and dealers from all over to trade, buy, and sell stones. If you plan to go out rock-hounding, pick up the free brochure from the Prineville Ranger District Station (see Visitor Information, above), which maps out the best locations for "prospecting." You can expect to find "thunder eggs," beautiful egg-shaped rocks with swirling patterns, as well as agate, obsidion, fire-obsidian, petrified wood, and red and green jasper.

WINTER SPORTS Two loops have recently been developed in the forest for cross-country skiers, both of which start at Bandit Springs State rest area, 29 miles east of Prineville on U.S. 26. One loop is designed for beginners and the other for intermediate to advanced skiers. Ask at the Prineville Ranger District Station (see Visitor Information, above) for the handout on trails, which includes handy advice as to what to do if you're lost.

Near Ochoco National Forest

JOHN DAY FOSSIL BEDS

Whether or not you're interested in fossils, the John Day Fossil Beds National Monument will provide you with at least a day's worth of free, sweaty, and often awe-inspiring entertainment. Although hot and frequented by rattlesnakes, the John Day trails are well worth hiking. The monument's three "units" or sections—**Clarno, Painted Hills,** and **Sheep Rock**—are notable as much for their rugged beauty as their paleontological significance. The beds were formed as a result of volcanic activity during the Cenozoic Era, a period stretching back five to 50 million years, and provide a remarkable record of the era's animal and plant life. The missionary Thomas Condon discovered the beds around 1870. Coming a decade after Darwin published his theory of evolution, Condon's discovery brought a veritable stampede of scientists to the area. Today, scientists continue to find fossils of everything from saber-toothed tigers to pollen and nuts.

During the summer temperatures here soar, and nothing sounds better than a dip in the John Day River. Between Clarno and Sheep Rock, pull onto the dirt shoulder on Route 19, just east of the junction with Route 207, and walk down the bank to a sandy beach bordering a deep section of the river.

Scientists have unearthed the oldest fossils at **Clarno,** whose fossil beds date back about 40 million years. Back then, this part of the world was a subtropical oasis, filled with palms, ferns, and thick vegetation. You can see the fossilized evidence of this ancient forest along two short trails that run from the **Palisades,** an area of ancient eroded mud slides.

Painted Hills offers some of the most dramatic landscape of the fossil beds: The eroded hills reveal dramatic striations of red, gold, bronze, and green created by minerals in the clay. The colors are best at dawn or dusk, or just after rain. The ¾-mile **Carroll Rim Trail** gives you a bird's-eye view of the hills. The fossils at Painted Hills date back about 30 million years and reveal a climate that had become noticeably drier than that of Clarno's era. Although none of the trails at Painted Hills are wheelchair accessible, the parking lot at the trailhead offers a fantastic view of these sand hills. If you have time to visit only one of the units, you should probably head to **Sheep Rock,** which has a large information center (open daily 8:30–6), interesting exhibits, and great scenery. The most impressive attraction is the **Blue Basin,** a canyon whose sinuous spires look like the turrets of drip sandcastles. The half-mile, wheelchair-accessible **Island in Time Trail**

winds through the Blue Basin, and trailside exhibits shed light on the basin's fossils, which date back about 25 million years. The 2-mile **Blue Basin Overlook Trail,** which loops around the rim of the canyon, offers some fantastic views.

COMING AND GOING Painted Hills lies just 6 miles north of U.S. 26 along a small paved road; the turnoff is 3 miles west of Mitchell. Sheep Rock is east of Mitchell on U.S. 26, and only about 5 miles west of Dayville. Set in a remote region north of U.S. 26, Clarno is much more difficult to reach. From Sheep Rock, take Route 19 north to the village of Fossil, and then go west for 20 miles on Route 218.

Although the Oregon Tourism board claims you can do the John Day Fossil Beds "loop" in eight hours, this doesn't leave much time to enjoy the scenery or take a hike through the various beds. Distances here are immense and the roads are steep, winding, and often under construction during the summer. There is no actual loop here, and whichever way you choose to see the area, you'll be covering at least 200 miles of country roads, about 60 miles of which

Rolls Royces and Orange Robes

In a surreal episode of Oregonian history, Bagwhan Sri Rajneesh, the Indian guru best known for his fleet of Rolls Royces, moved his ashram in the early 1980s from Poona, India, to a patch of land between the small town of Madras (excuse the cosmic irony) and the even smaller town of Antelope, 23 miles west of Clarno on Route 218. At first the Rajneeshee, mostly white, upper-middle-class professionals looking for New Age solace, tried to be friendly with their neighbors and just do their own thing. They set up an intricate town for themselves called Rajneeshpuram, with thousands of residents and visitors, an intricate water and sewage system, a school, and a newpaper. Some of the down-to-earth Antelopians (there were only 45 of them) were undoubtedly nervous about these "weird hippies" or "religious freaks," who always wore bright "sunset colors" of orange, red, and purple, but most locals allowed them to live their lives unmolested—at least until things started getting really strange.

What started as an ashram with a charismatic leader and a dogma adapted to appeal to (wealthy) westerners soon began to seem more like a greedy conglomerate. The Rajneeshee, outnumbering the residents of Antelope, soon took over their town, changing its name to Rajneesh, gaining control of the school system, and defying any government regulations limiting construction at Rajneeshpuram. Before long, the Rajneeshee started amassing weapons and threatening any local or official who opposed their plans of never-ending expansion. Before the whole situation had a chance to explode, though, Rajneesh's histrionic, greedy, and paranoid primary aide was found guilty of trying to poison local commissioners, wire-tapping phones, and a list of other crimes. Bhagwan, aware that he was about to be deported by immigration officials because he had lied on his entrance visa (he had claimed he was in poor health, but failed to see a doctor once here), caught a plane back to India, where he eventually died. Now the Antelope General Store and Café hands out maps to the spiritual ghost town 12 miles from town. The property is in the hands of a mortgage company and is strictly private, so unless you are into a little trespassing, don't bother schlepping out here.

will be backtracking. A good strategy would be to see Clarno and the Palisades and then head to the Painted Hills and spend the night at the excellent Sky Hook Motel in Mitchell; the next day you could hit Sheep Rock and the information center (or you could do this in reverse, depending on which direction you're coming from).

Malheur National Forest

The rugged and beautiful Malheur forest has not always been such a benign destination. The name Mal heur (bad hour) was coined by French trappers who suffered constant misfortune in the area at the hands of the Native Americans and Mother Nature. In 1862 gold was discovered in the Blue Mountains that now make up much of the Malheur (pronounced "MAL-here") National Forest. Miners swarmed into the area, displacing the resident Paiute people who stood between them and the region's rich claims. Bustling towns quickly sprang up in the **John Day Valley,** a long valley ringed on three sides by mountains, but when the gold gave out, the miners drifted out of the mountains and left only deserted settlements and abandoned mine shafts. Today, the tiny towns that line U.S. 26 in the John Day Valley—**John Day, Prairie City, Canyon City,** and **Mount Vernon**—try to cater to prospectors after different riches: hiking, skiing, fishing, and hunting. None of these towns are worthy of more than a brief stopover, though—the forest is the main draw. The campgrounds (all free) are lovely, and the hiking is superb.

The Malheur National Forest is vast: It covers 1,460,000 acres, and the nearest town with over 10,000 residents is over 100 miles away. In winter, bald eagles soar over snow-covered mountains; in spring, the hills are alive with flowers of every color; and in summer, streams and creeks provide relief for weary hikers. More than 240 miles of trails crisscross the forest, passing through rolling grasslands and thickly wooded stands of pine, fir, and cedar, which serve as home to black bears, bighorn sheep, elk, mule deer, and wolverines.

VISITOR INFORMATION

The Grant County Chamber of Commerce in John Day has information on the towns in the John Day Valley and the mountains beyond it. *281 W. Main St./U.S. 26, behind old wooden church, tel. 503/575–0547. Open weekdays 9–12 and 1–5.*

Bear Valley and Long Creek Ranger Districts. Get detailed information on camping, hiking, trail conditions, and recreation in the forest. They also sell a mountain biking trail guide listing 22 trails ($4.95). Since they have no free handouts on trails, talk to one of the rangers here and pick up a forest service map ($3). *528 E. Main St./U.S. 26, just east of John Day, tel. 503/575–2110. Open weekdays 7:15–5.*

Prairie City Ranger District. This office has the beautiful Strawberry Mountain Campground and adjoining trails within its jurisdiction. Stop off here and get detailed information about camping and trail conditions; they also sell the forest service map of the whole forest, as well as a large scale map of the Strawberry Mountain and Monument Rock Wilderness ($4). *U.S. 26, Prairie City, tel. 503/820–3311. Open weekdays 7:15–4:45.*

Malheur National Forest Supervisor. This office in John Day can give you a general overview of the forest and some trail and campground information. *139 N.E. Dayton St., tel. 503/575–1731. Open weekdays 7:15–5.*

COMING AND GOING

This extremely isolated area has limited public transport. In summer, a reliable car, preferably air-conditioned, is a virtual necessity, although many people bring in bikes to ride around the scenic countryside. If you're coming from Portland, you have two ways to reach the Malheur National Forest: You can follow U.S. 26 all the way through the Cascades and the Ochoco

National Forest into the John Day Valley, which is flanked by the Malheur Forest; or you can take I–84 east along the Columbia River to Pendleton, and then U.S. 395 south into the forest. The town of John Day, which is the primary hub for exploring the forest, is 127 miles south of Pendleton, in the center of the John Day Valley. Many of the forest trailheads lie at the end of dusty gravel roads running off U.S. 26 and U.S. 395—be careful, these roads are rough on cars, and you should be certain to carry water in summer and tire chains in winter. If you're heading for the southern end of the forest, consider taking U.S. 20 east from Bend to the town of Burns (*see* Southeastern Oregon, *below*), which lies about 15 miles south of the forest.

BY BUS **People Mover** (229 N.E. Dayton, John Day, tel. 503/575–2370) runs along U.S. 26 from Bend to John Day and back on Monday, Wednesday, and Friday. The drivers will drop you anywhere along the 145-mile route for $17 one way.

WHERE TO SLEEP

Only resolute homebodies would refuse to take advantage of the terrific, free campgrounds in the national forest, but you can find a few adequate motels in the John Day Valley, mostly in the towns of John Day and Mount Vernon, which lie 8 miles apart on U.S. 26; or in Canyon City, about 5 miles south of John Day on U.S. 395. Motel prices in Mount Vernon are at least $12–$15 cheaper than in John Day. If you're approaching this area from the John Day Fossil Beds, there is an excellent, cheap B&B in the one-horse town of Dayville, 35 miles west of John Day on U.S. 26 (*see below*). If you're exploring the southern portion of the Malheur National Forest, consider staying in **Burns,** at the junction of U.S. 20, U.S. 395, and Route 78. Motels fill up quickly in the summer, so try to reserve ahead.

MT. VERNON **Blue Mountain Lodge.** Right on U.S. 26, this motel doesn't look like much from the outside, but the rooms are spacious, and they come with cable TV and comfortable beds. Best of all, this is the cheapest place around—double rooms go for $27, and singles are $22. *150 Main St., tel 503/932–4451. 14 rooms.*

What's In a Name?

You've been in the area for a while—you've visited the John Day fossil beds, swam in the John Day River, driven through the John Day Valley, passed through the towns of Dayville and John Day—you must be wondering who the hell John Day was. No, he didn't discover the fossil beds (that was Minister John Condon), he didn't discover the John Day Valley or the John Day River, and he didn't even found any of the towns bearing his name. No, John Day was just the man who was unfortunate enough to join John Jacob Astor on an ill-fated 1810 expedition to open a fur-trading post on the Columbia River. By the time these men reached the Snake River, late in 1811, winter was beginning. Conditions became so dire that the expedition was split up into four smaller groups in order to maximize chances of survival. After an awful winter, only John Day and Ramsey Crooks were left alive. On reaching the Mah-hah River, Native Americans attacked the travelers, taking everything, including their clothes. But the two intrepid and very naked men managed to make it back to the Columbia River, where they were rescued by bemused fur trappers some two years after the original expedition had started. Whether because of the humor inherent in poor Mr. Day's epic trek, or because of his perserverence and bravery (or a little of both), the Mah-hah River was renamed the John Day, as was just about everything else around here. One can only wonder what was so wrong with Ramsey Crooks that not even a creek was named after him.

Mount Vernon Motel. If the Blue Mountain Lodge is full, head around the corner to this little ramshackle motel. The adequate rooms will set you back $32 a night for a double. *195 N. Mountain Blvd., off U.S. 26, tel 503/932–4712. 6 rooms. No credit cards.*

JOHN DAY **Budget 8 Motel.** The rooms in this generic motel are big, clean, and entirely forgettable. A room for two runs about $40 in the summer and $36 in the winter. *711 W. Main St./U.S. 26 E., tel. 503/575–2155. 14 rooms.*

DAYVILLE **Fish House Inn B&B.** In the little town of Dayville, this wonderful B&B is well worth a detour. The two cottages behind the main house are gorgeous: You get big rooms, shaded porch window seats, and private bathrooms in an idyllic country setting. The friendly hosts provide fresh-roasted coffee, barbecues, and a huge country breakfast. The cottages rent for $50 and $45; if these are full, stay in the main house, where smaller rooms rent for $35 and $40. *U.S. 26, tel 503/987–2124. 35 mi west of John Day, 5 mi east of John Day Fossil Beds Info Center. 5 rooms, 3 with bath. No credit cards.*

CAMPING The Malheur National Forest offers campers a choice of 20 free developed campgrounds, as well as a host of undeveloped ones. The best developed site is Strawberry Campground (*see below*). The majority of the campgrounds lie in the section of the forest south of John Day and U.S. 26, in or around the Strawberry Mountain Wilderness. You can access many of these sites from **Prairie City,** a small settlement 13 miles east of John Day on U.S. 26. Only the water from developed sites is safe to drink; boil all other water first. For a full listing of campgrounds, pick up the campground information pamphlet from any Ranger District or Supervisors Office (*see* Visitor Information, *above*). Most of the campgrounds are open between May 30 and October 15 or early November.

Magone Lake Campground. Set on the banks of a shimmering lake north of the John Day Valley, this campground is sometimes populated by the RV set, but if you like boating, swimming, or fishing, this is a good choice. *Tel 503/575–2110. 9 mi north of Mt. Vernon on U.S. 395, east on Forest Rd. 36 for 8 mi, and north on Forest Rd. 3618 for 2 mi. 22 sites.*

Middle Fork Campground. The middle fork of the John Day River runs by this primitive campground. You must bring in your own water. *Tel. 503/820–3311. 15 mi east of Prairie City on U.S. 26, 1 mi north on Rte. 7, and 5 mi NW on U.S. 20 to Susanville. 11 sites.*

Strawberry Campground. Set in the splendid Strawberry Mountains, this free campground is worth the drive out here. Try to get one of the sites by the creek, although you can't go wrong here. Nearby trailheads lead to stunning views and lakes. Trout fishing is good nearby, too. *11 mi south of Prairie City on Forest Rd. 6001. 11 sites.*

FOOD

Thriftway (U.S. 26, tel. 503/575–1899), at John Day Plaza in Chester, on the western end of town, is the largest supermarket in the area, and you should avail yourself of its services if you're camping. Otherwise, the food around here could be characterized as ordinary to bad, with the exception of Victoria Station (*see below*).

There are two restaurants in Mt. Vernon, and they're across the street from one another. Flip a coin: Heads, you're at **The Wounded Buffalo** (100 E. Main St., tel. 503/934–4277), where you can get such delicacies as cheese on toast ($3.25) or a BLT ($4); tails, you're munching at **L/O's Silver Spur Restaurant** (Main St., tel. 503/934–4545). Their French toast ($2.75) or flapjacks ($3) will fill you up but good. The pies, at $1.50 a slice, are another good bet.

The Cave Inn. This place turns out some tasty pizzas. A medium No. 4 combo, a feast of meat, will feed three and costs $12.50; the veggie combo costs $11. *830 Canyon Blvd., John Day, tel. 503/575–1083. Open daily 3 PM–10 PM.*

Sweet Buns Bakery. This is one of the most bizarre restaurants you're likely to encounter anywhere. The restaurant is located in a furniture showroom, and it's not exactly clear where the dining stops and the sales begin. Make an offer on your table and chair while you drink the 5¢ coffee and eat a burrito ($3.75). You can get tacos, burgers, homemade soup, and a lovely little bedroom set ($199). *201 W. Main St., in John Day Minimall, tel. 503/575–1054. Open Mon.–Thurs. 8–6, Fri. and Sat. 8 AM–9 PM, Sun. 10–9.*

Victoria Station Coffee, Espresso Bar, and Bakery. For your stimulants, head to this tasteful country café, where you can pick up a drive-through latte ($1.75) or opt to sit down and have a slice of excellent pie ($2.25) or a fresh-baked pastry. They also do a lunch special—salad and pie with coffee for $5.25, or delicious quiche with fresh bread and frozen cranberries ($5). *103 S.W. 1st St., behind Dairy Queen, John Day, tel. 503/575–0838. Open daily 7–4 PM.*

EXPLORING MALHEUR NATIONAL FOREST

➢ **STRAWBERRY MOUNTAIN WILDERNESS** • Southeast of John Day is the 68,300-acre Strawberry Mountain Wilderness. It's the more frequented of the park's two wilderness areas, but it's not exactly rush hour around here—you won't see many people on the 150 miles of trails, except perhaps during hunting season. If you have limited time in the area, make this your first destination. The Pine, Indian, Strawberry Canyon, Bear, Lake, Wall, Roberts, and Big creeks have their headwaters in the Strawberry Mountains, which range from 4,800 feet to the 9,038-foot **Strawberry Mountain,** the region's crown jewel. The alpine lakes in the mountains are stunning, too. Keep your eyes peeled for Rocky Mountain elk.

➢ **MONUMENT ROCK WILDERNESS** • Some 30 miles east of John Day, the Monument Rock Wilderness is extremely remote and offers some of the region's best scenery. **Table Rock,** a 7,815-foot mountain that lies just outside the boundary of the wilderness, offers the best views of the ponderosa pine forests, which dominate the lower regions, and the subalpine forests, which thrive atop the mountain peaks. Look for Douglas fir, white fir, lodgepole pine, and quaking aspen. The wilderness is also home to the rare wolverine. To reach the Monument Rock Wilderness, take County Road 62 south from Prairie City, turn left on Forest Road 13, and left again on Forest Road 1370; otherwise, take Forest Road 16 south from Unity, a small settlement that lies 36 miles east of Prairie City on U.S. 26.

➢ **ALDRICH MOUNTAINS** • West of Strawberry Mountain, the barren peaks of the Aldrich Mountains are home to mountain lions and deer. Sagebrush grows on the southern slopes, and Douglas firs tower over the northern slopes. There are no maintained trails or trail markers up here, but you can still hike in this beautiful country—ask at the ranger's station in Prairie City (*see* Visitor Information, *above*) for suggested hikes. You can reach 6,988-foot Aldrich Mountain via Forest Road 21, which branches off U.S. 26 about 18 miles west of John Day. Take Forest Road 21 south for about 10 miles before turning right onto Road 2150 for another 10 miles. This last stretch is a bit rough; unless you have a pickup truck or four-wheel drive, you might want to hike the last mile up to the lookout point.

If your hiking muscles are sore, a dip in the **Blue Mountain Hot Springs** (tel 503/820–3744) may be just the ticket. The spring is 11 miles east of Prairie City on County Road 62; it's unmarked, so watch your odometer. The springs are open daily 10–6, and admission is $2. If you're already hot, go west of John Day on U.S. 26 to the WR2 Forest Products parking lot for access to the **swimming hole** in the otherwise shallow John Day River.

Bring along insect repellent in the early summer; the mosquitoes are fearsome up here, especially at Little Strawberry Lake.

HIKING Two extremely rewarding hikes leave from Strawberry Campground (*see* Where to Sleep, *above*). The first is a 6-mile round-trip hike that winds past placid Strawberry Lake and beautiful, turbulent Strawberry Falls to **Little Strawberry Lake.** The second is an 8-mile round-trip hike that crosses Slide Creek and takes you through forest and steep alpine meadows before looping around **Slide Lake,** which is perfect for swimming. Along the way you get great views of the John Day Valley, as well as the surrounding craggy mountain peaks. As you approach Slide Lake look for the waterfall on your left—you'll actually hear it before you see it. The first four miles, all uphill, are arduous, and you should allow at least three or four hours for the whole trip. For a great view of the John Day Valley and the Blue Mountain range, hike 6 miles to the summit of **Strawberry Mountain.** The trailhead is on Forest Road 60, 2 miles before Strawberry Campground. The country here is very rugged, and all of these hikes require a lot of uphill walking; bring plenty of water and wear decent boots.

If you're one of those people who likes nature in small doses, the 1-mile **Cedar Grove Trail** is probably for you. This easy trail passes rocky crags and hills covered in dense forest. The cedar trees here are the only ones for hundreds of miles. To get to the trailhead, take U.S. 26 west from John Day for 18 miles to its junction with Forest Road 21; take Forest Road 21 south 9 miles, turn right on Forest Road 2150, and drive another 5 miles.

HISTORIC BUILDINGS AND SITES **Kam Wah Chung & Co. Museum.** This restored building was a trading post on the Dalles Military Road in 1866–67 and then served as a general store, a Chinese labor exchange for the mines, a Chinese doctor's shop, and an opium den. The museum is quite extraordinary, with a completely stocked Chinese pharmacy, items that would have been sold at the general store, and re-created living quarters. Nothing in the house postdates the 1940s, and some artifacts are from the late 1800s. This museum is a testament to the often-forgotten early Chinese community in Oregon, and it's well worth a visit. *Canton St., John Day, no phone. Admission: $2. Open May–Oct., Mon.–Thurs. 9–noon and 1–5, weekends 1–5.*

FOREST ACTIVITIES

The main reason to come here is to camp and hike, but in summer, you'll find good **fishing** for rainbow and brook trout in the forest's many streams and lakes. The season begins in April, but the fishing gets even better in May, June, and July. Die-hard anglers can even go ice-fishing here. You'll need to pick up a license from a sporting goods store, True Value Hardware (161 E. Main St., tel. 503/575–8632) in John Day, or a supermarket (*see* Food, *above*) for $6.75 a day, $30 a week, or $40 a season. Malheur National Forest is an excellent—and largely unused—area for **winter sports,** particularly cross-country skiing and snowmobiling. Many of the slopes are gentle, and skiers have hundreds of miles of forest roads to explore. In fall, the forest becomes a shooting gallery for **hunters,** some of whom are out to get Bambi and his furry friends with semiautomatic weapons.

If you bear any resemblance to a woodland animal, you'd better stay in bed—hunters are gunning for everything from black bears to bighorn sheep.

Northeastern Oregon

If you have only limited time to spend in eastern Oregon, head for the northeast. Nowhere else in the state is there such a diversity of landscapes or, for that matter, such dramatic terrain. Only 30 miles separate **Hells Canyon,** the deepest canyon in North America, from the soaring heights of the **Wallowa Mountains.** The former is arid and desolate, watered only by the Snake River slithering along the canyon floor; the latter has all the verdant beauty of the Alps, complete with green meadows and snow-capped peaks. Cars aren't going to be much help to you in these remote areas—for the most part, you have to hike or ride a horse in, or take a boat down the Snake, in the case of Hells Canyon. Don't expect much in the way of civilization: Most of the land up here is national forest, and huge tracts of it are wilderness. Unless you're allergic to dirt, you'll want to camp here, and much of the camping is free.

The **Oregon Trail** passed through this corner of the state, snaking its way up the Grande Ronde Valley between the peaks of the Wallowa Mountains on one side and the Blue Mountains on the other, before finally crossing the Blue Mountains north of La Grande. The discovery of gold in these same mountains in the 1860s sparked a second invasion of settlers. The largest towns in the region today—Baker City, La Grande, and Pendleton—were all beneficiaries of the boom that followed. However, the little mining settlements that fueled the boom were abandoned as soon as the gold ran out. If you travel into the mountains, you can still see these crumbling ghost towns and even some of the old mining gear. People who live in these towns are down-to-earth, friendly, and fiercely proud of their pioneer heritage. Because of the distances and terrain, this is not country you can just breeze through—plan at least a week in this region to sample some of the beautiful country it has to offer.

BASICS

VISITOR INFORMATION The **Forest Supervisor of Wallowa-Whitman National Forest** provides general information about camping and outdoor activities in the national forest, which covers much of the Blue Mountains, including the Elkhorn Range, as well as the Wallowa Mountains and Hells Canyon. For specific info, go to the ranger districts listed throughout this chapter. *Box 907, Baker City, tel. 503/523–6391. Open weekdays 8–5.*

The **Forest Supervisor of Umatilla National Forest** (2517 S.W. Hailey Ave., Pendleton, tel. 503/278–3716) can tell you all about huntin', shootin', fishin', campin', and hikin' in the Blue Mountains, including the North Fork John Day Wilderness and the Wenaha-Tucannon Wilderness.

The **Hells Canyon National Recreation Area Headquarters** at the Wallowa Mountains Visitors Center provides campground and hiking information about Hells Canyon. It also has a list of companies that run boat trips down the Snake River. *88401 I–82, Enterprise, tel. 503/426–4978. Open weekdays 7:30–5.*

COMING AND GOING The major highway in the area is I–84, connecting the towns of Pendleton, La Grande, and Baker with Portland to the west and Boise, Idaho, to the southeast. If you're coming along U.S. 26 from Bend in central Oregon, you can either turn off onto U.S. 395 at Mount Vernon to reach Pendleton, or follow Route 7 east to Baker. Once you're on the interstate, you have several options for reaching the Wallowa Mountains and Hells Canyon, but I–82 from La Grande is probably the easiest. Be sure to bring tire chains in winter.

➤ **BY BUS** • Greyhound (tel. 503/523–5011) travels between Portland and Boise along I–84 twice daily, stopping in Pendleton, La Grande, and Baker City. The fare from these towns to Portland or Boise is $30–$35. **Wallowa Valley Stage Line** (La Grande Station, 2108 Cove Ave., tel. 503/963–5165) operates daily service (except Sunday) between La Grande and Joseph, a small settlement on the edge of the Eagle Cap Wilderness in the Wallowa Mountains, for $11 one way.

➤ **BY TRAIN** • Amtrak (tel. 800/872–7245) has Monday, Wednesday, and Saturday service to and from Portland on a route that runs parallel to I–84, stopping at Pendleton, La Grande, and Baker City. The trip from Baker City to Portland costs about $62, from Baker City to Boise $32.

➤ **BY BIKE** • County and state roads provide easy access to most regions, making this an excellent area for biking. The roadside scenery is spectacular, but remember that this area is mountainous and arid, so always carry water and be prepared to huff and puff. A great trip for cyclists is the 70-mile route along I–82 from La Grande to Joseph in the Wallowa Mountains. Only extremely fit riders should attempt the arduous ride on Route 39 that begins 8 miles east of Joseph and heads south over several peaks to a junction with Route 86, 7 miles east of Oxbow. Pick up the "Oregon Bicycling Guide Map" that highlights these and other routes throughout the state. Most visitor information centers and ranger district offices give these out free.

OUTDOOR ACTIVITIES

➤ **HIKING** • The Wallowa Mountains, Hells Canyon, and the Blue Mountains offer more than a thousand miles of hiking trails, some reaching over 9,000 feet. Hells Canyon is mostly inaccessible by car and instead explored by rafters and intrepid hikers.

➤ **BOATING** • Jet boat or white-water raft trips running down the Snake River are the best way to see Hells Canyon, the deepest gorge in North America. Jet boats usually leave from Clarkston, Washington, or Lewiston, Idaho, about 90 miles north of Enterprise, Oregon. Float trips are also available on the Minam, John Day, and Grande Ronde Rivers in the spring and summer; they start at around $90 a day. For information on other trips, contact the Hells Canyon Chamber of Commerce (*see* Hells Canyon National Recreation Area, *below*).

➤ **SKIING** • **Anthony Lakes** (61995 Quail Rd., Island City, tel. 503/963–4599) offers downhill skiing from late November through the first week in April, with 22 runs and an 800-foot vertical drop. Lift tickets for adults are approximately $20. You can rent alpine ($14 a day) and cross-country ($10) skis and snowboards ($16) at the rental store at Anthony Lakes Resort. Six miles of groomed cross-country trails, along with several snowmobiling paths, are maintained in the area. Anthony Lakes is 20 miles west of North Powder, off I–84. Free cross-country trails also line the **Wallowa** and **Blue Mountain Ranges**. Contact one of the chambers of commerce for more information.

Baker City

Back in 1890, Baker City was bigger than either Spokane or Boise, profiting handsomely from the money that poured in from the nearby mining towns of Sumpter, Granite, Cornucopia, and Copperfield. Brothels, saloons, and hell-raising were the mainstays of a rough-and-tumble lifestyle that lasted as long as the boom. Today, Baker is a logging and ranching town with a reassuring, small-town atmosphere.

Although it may not be the best place from which to explore the Wallowa Mountains and Hells Canyon, consider stopping here to work out your plan of attack. Baker's visitor center offers the most comprehensive information on the parks in northeastern Oregon. Furthermore, the town is a great base for exploring the Elkhorn Ridge and the other mountains in the western section of the Wallowa-Whitman National Forest, including the Anthony Lakes area. The town has its share of cheap motels, a superb B&B, and good camping nearby, not to mention the slick and informative Oregon Trail Interpretive Center. Ghost towns and abandoned gold mines abound, and several hikes and drives—and even an old steam engine—give you a good feel for the country (*see* Near Baker City, *below*).

The **National Historic Oregon Trail Interpretive Center,** which opened up in 1992 about 5 miles out of town, does a fine job re-creating pioneer life of the mid-1800s. A tour of the center begins at a simulated section of the Oregon Trail, complete with wagon-wheel ruts and teams of oxen. You not only survey the hard life on the trail, you experience it yourself with a bossy wagon-master who helps you choose your gear for the journey. Then you're led through the trail as the pioneers experienced it—though maybe a little more safely this time—while examining such issues as camp life, marital strife, and the settler's impact on Native Americans. An indoor theater presents movies and plays that further explain the way settlers lived. *Tel. 503/523–1843. From I–84, take Rte. 86, get off Exit 302, and follow signs. Admission free. Open daily 9–4.*

The **Oregon Trail Regional Museum** in town complements the Interpretive Center by focusing on artifacts associated with the early pioneers. The enormous back room is filled with covered wagons, an old fire-fighting wagon, and pioneer tools. The museum also boasts one of the most impressive rock collections in the west, including 650-pound hunks of quartz, thunder eggs, agates, and jaspers, as well as phosphorescent rocks that glow neon under black light. The museum also displays an impressive selection of Native American artifacts, butterflies, nails (as in hammer and), and quilts. *2490 Grove St., at Campbell St., tel. 503/523–9308. Admission: $1.50. Open daily 9–4.*

VISITOR INFORMATION The **Baker County Visitor and Convention Bureau** is the welcome center for the entire region. It also has a small pioneer museum and a very helpful staff. *490 Campbell St., just off I–84, tel. 503/523–3356 or 800/523–1235. Open weekdays 8–6, weekends 9–1.*

Baker Ranger District provides specific camping, hiking, and recreation information. Pick up their free "Recreation Report" and their "Travel Opportunity Guide Map" ($3). *3165 10th St., U.S. 30, tel. 503/523–6391. Open weekdays 7:45–4:30.*

COMING AND GOING Baker City lies on I–84 (a.k.a. U.S. 30), 42 miles south of La Grande and 130 miles west of Boise. Route 7 runs southwest to U.S. 26 and John Day, while Route 86 runs northeast to Hells Canyon. Both **Amtrak** (2803 Broadway, tel. 800/872–7245) and

Greyhound (515 Campbell St., tel. 503/523–5011) serve the town. If you're hitchhiking, the best place to snag a ride is at the rest stop 10 miles north of town or at the freeway on-ramp in Baker.

WHERE TO SLEEP Most of the lodging in Baker City is grouped along Campbell Street, just off I–84, and along 10th Street (U.S. 30 N.), where motels are about $10 cheaper. The **Western Motel** (3055 10th St., tel. 503/523–3700 or 800/481–3701) is your best bet in town. Cozy rooms with vibrating beds (25¢), cable TV, and air-conditioning go for $29 a double and $25 a single. For about $32 a night, **Green Gables Motel** (2355 10th St., tel. 503/523–5588) gives you large, slightly musty, and very green rooms for $30–$35. Bigger, more plush rooms at **Royal Motor Inn** (2205 Broadway, tel. 503/523–6324 or 800/547–5827), with cable TV and use of the small heated pool and the nearby athletic club, go for $35–$38.

Bruno Ranch Bed & Breakfast. This has to be one of the best deals in Oregon, situated on 540 acres adjoining the Wallowa National Forest. Mrs. Bruno lavishes her guests with huge country breakfasts, tours of her place, and some of the warmest company you're likely to encounter in the entire state. The rooms are rustic and comfortable, and guests are welcome to use the large den with a fireplace and a pool table. This is a place to come and get away from it all: The nearest town of any size is Baker, 25 miles north. A room with breakfast costs $27 for two, $20 for one. Primitive tent sites are $5. *Box 51A, Bridgeport, tel. 503/446–3468. From Baker City, take Hwy. 7 west and Hwy. 245 south to Bridgeport turnoff; take first right to ranch.*

Unless your idea of luxury is a Motel 6 and remote control, Mrs. Bruno's B&B is paradise.

Powder River Bed and Breakfast. The two clean and unpretentious rooms make you feel instantly at home. Cozy double rooms with private bath go for $60, full breakfast included (let them know if you have any dietary oddities). You can combine your stay with some fishing, since the owners also run the Powder River Tackle Company. *Rte. 7, Box 500, tel. 503/523–7143. 1 mi south of railroad overpass heading toward Sumpter and Unity.*

Go West: The Oregon Trail

If you went to an American high school, chances are you didn't escape before having the Oregon Trail stuffed down your gullet. Now that you're actually in Oregon, all those statistics and dates start to take on meaning. Maybe you've sampled the rugged, hot landscape yourself, camping in the steep Blue Mountains, and hiking up Mt. Hood or along the mighty Columbia River, all of which were obstacles en route to the fertile Willamette Valley. Strangely enough, the pioneers passed several other fertile valleys on the trail, such as the Grand Route (site of La Grande), but they were so programmed to head to the Willamette Valley that these other areas weren't settled until the subsequent gold rush.

For those of you who slept through history class, here's a refresher: From 1841 to 1861, about 300,000 people made the 2,000-mile journey from western Missouri to the Columbia River and the Oregon coast, looking for rich agricultural land in the west. Almost 20,000 of them died, victims of disease, drowning, cold, hunger, or attacks by Native Americans. It cost about $400 to buy the oxen and wagon necessary for the trip, and another $225 to buy supplies sufficient for three people. Among the recommended supplies were three rifles at $20 each, three pistols at $15 a pop, 600 pounds of bacon ($30), 1,080 pounds of flour ($20), and 100 pounds of coffee ($8).

➤ **CAMPING** • The premier camping spots near Baker are undoubtedly the three grounds at **Anthony Lake** (tel. 503/523–4476). The alpine scenery here is fantastic, and the hiking's great. Anthony Lake Campground is the biggest of the three, with 37 units at $5 a night. Mud Lake, a few hundred yards from Anthony Lake, has seven sites at $3 a night. The nicest spot on the mountain is at Grande Ronde Lake, where sites are $3 if the water is turned on, and free if no water is available (you can get water 1 mile down the road at Anthony Lake). All sites have fire rings and toilets. To reach Anthony Lake from Baker, head 17 miles north on I–84, get off at the North Powder exit, and head 21 miles west to the lake.

The nearest campgrounds in the area are at Phillips Reservoir, a large lake about 15 miles southwest of Baker, but none of these come close to the ones at Anthony Lake. **Miller Lane** (seven sites) and **Southwest Shore** (18 sites) are free but have no piped water or any other amenities. **Union Creek** (58 sites), charging $8 a night, has full hook-ups and boat docks nearby. To reach the first two campgrounds, drive 24 miles southwest on Route 7 from Baker, turn south on Forest Road 2226, and continue about 3 miles. The last campground is on Route 7, 17 miles from Baker City. All the campgrounds are open from May to November.

FOOD If you like your food fried, you won't go hungry in Baker, which harbors the usual fast-food suspects. You can buy food to take camping at the **Albertsons** on Resort Street, one block west of Main Street.

Baker City Cafe—Pizza à Fetta. This gourmet pizza place, featuring freshly thrown dough and Italian sodas, seems out of place in Baker City, but once you try the pesto or the three-tomato pizza ($19 for a large), you'll be thankful it's here. Pizza is sold by the slice or the pie. Pasta dishes, including lasagna ($6.25) and excellent salads with rosemary vinaigrette dressing ($5.25), are also available. *1915 Washington St., 1 block from Main St., tel. 503/523–3641. Open weekdays 11–8, weekends 11–9.*

Front Street Café. This place offers a cool and relaxing escape, great salads and sandwiches, and hot and iced espresso drinks. Try the flaming salad with your choice of grilled meat ($4.95 small, $5.95 huge) or a charbroiled mesquite bacon burger ($5). *1840 Main St., tel. 503/523–7536. Open Mon.–Sat. 7 AM–8 PM, Sun. 7–4.*

The Gold Skillet. For absolutely unsophisticated, honest American breakfasts and lunches, this is the place. A full stack of pancakes with sausage costs $3.90, and lunch specials featuring some sort of meat and potatoes cost $4.50. *781 Campbell St., across from the visitor center, tel. 503/523–4657. Open Tues.–Sun. 5 AM–2 PM.*

OUTDOOR ACTIVITIES Baker's location between the Wallowa Mountains and the Elkhorn Range of the Blue Mountains makes it a good base from which to explore the surrounding region. (For more information about activities in the Eagle Cap Wilderness and the Wallowa Mountains, *see* The Wallowa Mountains, *below*.) The Baker County Visitor and Convention Bureau (*see* Visitor Information, *above*) can give you the low-down on all kinds of activities and hikes in the area.

➤ **HIKING** • Hiking trails crisscross the Elkhorn Ridge to the west of Baker City. You'll find the trailheads for many of the area's best trails at **Anthony Lake**. The Baker Ranger District gives out the *Anthony Lakes Recreation Guide,* which lists several hikes. The most rewarding is a 7-mile loop trail from Anthony Lake via **Gunsight Mountain and Angell Peak,** climbing through granite mountains, alpine meadows, and snowy fields as late as July, with views of five lakes, the surrounding valleys, and the Cascades. Bring food, plenty of water, and, in summer, insect repellant. The trailhead is just east of the Anthony Lake Campground. Take Trail 1661 to Trail 1612 and then Road 185 back down to the lake. The 1-mile hike up to the lake lookout is very steep, but worth it for the views of eight alpine lakes as well as the surrounding Elkhorn peaks. Take Road 210 from Route 73, 5 miles east of Anthony Campground, and turn onto 187 until you see the trailhead sign. To reach Anthony Lake from Baker City, head 17 miles north on I–84, get off at the North Powder exit, and head 21 miles west to the lake.

The **Granite Creek Trail** is a more difficult 3½-mile trail that serves as one of the main routes into the rugged 107,000-acre North Fork John Day Wilderness. You'll find chinook salmon and steelhead in the North Fork, and you might cross paths with cougar, black bear, bald eagles, and mule deer. The trailhead is 10 miles north of the town of Granite on Forest Road 1035 (*see also* Hiking, in La Grande, *below*).

➤ **DRIVES AND VIEWS** • Elkhorn Drive is a 106-mile route that makes a loop from Baker City through the Elkhorn Range of the Blue Mountains. Along the way, you pass numerous old gold-mining towns, the Sumpter Valley Railroad, and the Anthony Lakes Ski Area. The real highlight of the trip, though, is the Elkhorn Range itself, whose sharp ridges and peaks top 8,000 feet. At that altitude, only white-bark pine can survive, but on the lower slopes spruce, larch, Douglas fir, and ponderosa pine all proliferate. The route, which is signposted all the way, starts on Route 7 out of Baker City. Instead of returning to Baker, you can carry on to La Grande by taking Route 73 all the way to I–84. Pick up a map at the Baker City Chamber of Commerce.

Instead of traveling with the big rigs up I–84, consider taking the scenic 130-mile byway from Baker City to the Columbia River. The route, which leaves the Elkhorn Drive at the ghost town of Granite, heads northwest through the North Fork John Day Wilderness and the Umatilla National Forest before rejoining I–84 about 9 miles east of Arlington (and just west of a bombing range). The area along the route supports the largest herd of Rocky Mountain elk in the country. Much of the signposted drive runs along Route 74.

NEAR BAKER CITY

SUMPTER Thirty miles west of Baker along Route 7 is the town of Sumpter, which played a key part in the development of the region. Gold was discovered in the Powder River Valley in 1862 by five ex-Confederate soldiers, who named their claim site after Fort Sumter in South Carolina. In the early days, most of the prospectors working in "placer" mines (mines in which they panned for gold) in Sumpter were Chinese. When the railroad reached the town in 1896, the population exploded as miners poured in to work the "hard rock" mines (mines from which the gold ore must be dug out). By 1903, Sumpter had 3,500 residents who patronized 16 saloons, several newspapers, and even an opera house. In August 1917, a devastating fire destroyed the town. Today, you can still see the old dredge that was used to dig the gold-bearing gravel out of the river. Every Memorial Day weekend, Labor Day weekend, and 4th of July, Sumpter hosts a huge **flea market**, which attracts thousands of people who come to rummage through the junk and crafts, looking for modern-day hidden ore. If you decide to attend, remember that these country roads were not built to handle such a shopping frenzy—be prepared for traffic jams and parking problems. For more information about the flea markets or Sumpter in general, call 503/894–2362.

OXBOW (COPPERFIELD) Seventy-five miles northeast of Baker, up Route 86, is a town once called Copperfield (now Oxbow), the baddest town in the area at the turn of the century. The town, with its collection of brothels, bars, opium dens, and gambling halls, was the site of an ongoing war between workers building the Oxbow Dam and employees of the railroad. The situation became particularly ugly when the residents told the governor, who had threatened to impose martial law, that he'd be killed if he showed his sorry hide in Copperfield. Equal opportunity employer that he was, the governor sent his female secretary, Ms. Hobbs, instead. She declared martial law, hinting that her seven burly escorts might perform rudimentary plastic surgery on town officials if they didn't resign. The town burned to the ground several months later under suspicious circumstances and was never reconstructed.

SUMPTER VALLEY RAILROAD A restored steam engine carries tourists on a 6-mile stretch of the original narrow-gauge Sumpter Valley Railway, which ran through the Blue Mountains from Baker City to Prairie City, 80 miles to the southwest. The railroad, which was started in 1891 and closed in 1947, carried timber, passengers, and gold ore down the steep grades via a series of switchbacks and narrow bridges. Today, you can board the wood-burning train at the Sumpter Valley Railroad Restoration Depot near McEwen, about 25 miles southwest of Baker on Route 7, for a ride to the old mining town of Sumpter (*see above*). The trip is short, and the price a little high, but train aficionados will want to take this trip. Trains run four times daily on weekends and holidays, from Memorial Day to the end of September. *Tel. 503/ 894–2268. Fare: $5 one-way, $8 round-trip.*

La Grande

With a population of 12,000, the town of La Grande isn't exactly a bustling metropolis, but you'll find more here than gas and eats. If you roll into town during the summer, you'll probably be greeted by fluttering rainbow-colored flags lining Adams Avenue, the town's main drag. But don't get the wrong idea: The cowboys here are the real deal, not the Village People, and the townspeople have no idea they are proudly displaying a well-known symbol of gays and lesbians. (The Chamber of Commerce responded to questions: "Oh no, we're not *that* progressive here.") The flags herald La Grande's "Crazy Days," the town's big summer sidewalk sale. Now that that's cleared up, La Grande is definitely a tad more progressive than its neighbors. Eastern Oregon State College, the only four-year college in eastern Oregon, is located here and brings a certain sophistication that other towns in the area lack. But culture isn't the big draw here: People flock to La Grande because it's the best base for seeing the Blue Mountains, the Wallowas, Hells Canyon, and the Grande Ronde Valley. The Umatilla and Wenaha-Tucannon Wilderness to the north and the North Fork John Day Wilderness to the south offer compelling views, hiking trails, and fishing.

VISITOR INFORMATION The La Grande Chamber of Commerce offers information on La Grande and the surrounding area. *2111 Adams Ave., Suite B, tel. 503/963–8588 or 800/848–9969. Open weekdays 8–noon and 1–5.*

For information about specific areas around La Grande, contact the **Walla Walla Ranger District** (1415 W. Rose, Walla Walla, tel. 509/522–6290), the **North Fork John Day Ranger District** (Box 158, Ukiah 97880, tel. 503/427–3231), or the **La Grande Ranger District** (3502 U.S. 30, 1 mi south of town, tel. 503/963–7186).

COMING AND GOING La Grande lies at the intersection of I–84 and Route 82, 50 miles southeast of Pendleton and 42 miles north of Baker City. From I–84, I–82 runs west to Adams Avenue, the town's main thoroughfare. I–82 is probably the best way to reach the Eagle Cap Wilderness in the Wallowa Mountains and Hells Canyon. Joseph, the small town at the foot of the Wallowa Mountains, is 71 miles east along I–82. Both **Amtrak** (Depot and Jefferson Sts., tel. 800/872–7245) and **Greyhound** (2108 Cove Ave., tel. 503/963–5165) stop at La Grande on their Portland–Boise routes. **Wallowa Valley Stage Line** (same address as Greyhound) offers daily service (except Sunday) along I–82 to Joseph for about $11.

WHERE TO SLEEP Most of the motels are grouped near I–84 or on Adams Avenue in town, and camping along the Grande Ronde River is free and easy.

Moon Motel. This is the best of the budget lot, and free use of the athletic club across the street is included in the price (doubles $29, singles $25). Rooms are small and funky (in the negative sense), but you do get color TV and air-conditioning. *2116 Adams Ave., tel. 503/963–2724. 9 rooms.*

Stang Manor Bed and Breakfast. Housed in a 10,000-square-foot mansion built by a timber baron, Stang Manor manages to be big and comfortable at the same time. Check out the large common area, including the blue Victorian dining room. The wide lawn out front is a great place to relax in the sun. Four rooms with bath go for $70–$90. *1612 Walnut St., tel. 503/963–2400.*

Wendell's Corner. This no-frills motel offers big doubles for a bargain basement $28; singles are $24, and you can get a two-room, three-bed unit for $45 a night and pack in as many people as you like (within reason). *2309 E. Adams Ave., tel. 503/963–4424. 10 rooms.*

➤ **CAMPING** • You'll find great camping along the Grande Ronde River about half an hour west of La Grande. Four free campsites have pit toilets, water, and fire rings. The two best are **River** (Forest Rd. 51, tel. 503/963–7186) and **Woodley** (no phone). To get to River, take I–84 north to Route 244 and head west until you hit Forest Road 51. To get to Woodley, continue on Forest Road 51 and take Forest Road 5125 to the campground; the last 5 miles are gravel. The other two campgrounds are on Forest Road 51 before you get to River Campground. The campgrounds are open May–November.

Hilgard Junction State Park. Basically a crowded overnight stop for RVs, this campground is notable for its accessibility, not its scenery or serenity. Sites are $9. *Head west on I–84 for 8 mi to Hilgard Junction. 18 sites. Open year-round.*

FOOD In addition to the usual fast-food fare, La Grande actually offers fairly decent food at budget prices.

Mamacita's. This restaurant serves the best food for the best prices in the nicest setting in town (beat that). Daily lunch specials go for $2.95 and include enchiladas, salads, and tacos; for $4.95, the dinner combos are also a great deal. The range of dishes is pretty standard, but the people at Mamacita's cook it well and serve it cheerfully. *110 Depot St., tel. 503/ 963–6223. Open Mon.–Thurs. 11–2 and 5:30–9, Fri. 11–2 and 5:30–10, Sat. 5:30–10, Sun. 5:30–9.*

Smokehouse Restaurant. The slow, indifferent service is pretty bad, but the locals swear by this place. The food *is* pretty good: Flapjacks are $3, and all the usual egg dishes go for around $5. *2208 E. Adams Ave., tel. 503/963–9692. Open daily 6 AM–9 PM.*

Ten Depot Street. Though many of the dishes here exceed $10, you can save money by ordering "blue-plate specials" ($4.50) featuring meat, potatoes, vegetables, and soup of the day. You can also pick from a selection of salads, including Greek ($4.95), Oriental chicken ($4.95), and the delicious Oregon Caesar ($5.95). They always offer a $1 featured dessert; try the scrumptious sour cream apple pie. *10 Depot St., tel. 503/963–8766. Open weekdays 11:30–2:30 and 5:30–10, Sat 5:30–10.*

OUTDOOR ACTIVITIES For a wealth of information on fishing, outfitters for trips to Hells Canyon and Eagle Cap Wilderness, and free shuttles to Hells Canyon, stop by **Grande Ronde Angler** (1306 Adams Ave., tel. 503/963–7878). John Ecklund, the owner and consummate outdoorsman, also owns **Little Creek Outfitters,** which offers one- to seven-day trips that combine fishing and rafting on the Grande Ronde River. Trips start at $75 a day, including food, fishing gear, and John's company.

➤ **HIKING** • For the pioneers on the Oregon Trail who drove their wagons through La Grande, the Blue Mountains were a deadly obstacle on their journey west. Today, the mountains overlooking La Grande, laced with hiking and riding trails, are the area's biggest attraction. The 177,000-acre **Wenaha-Tucannon Wilderness,** part of the Blue Mountains straddling the Oregon–Washington border, has 203 miles of trails from which you can see elk and even the occasional mountain lion or bald eagle. Trails wind through deep canyons and past rocky outcroppings. The hike down **Elk Flat Trail** to the Wenaha River plunges over 2,000 feet through the Wenaha River Canyon in just a few miles. To get to the trailhead, head 20 miles north of La Grande on I–82 to Elgin. From Elgin continue north on Forest Road 62 just over 30 miles to the Elk Flats Campground.

Several trails pass through vast timber stands and grasslands in the **North Fork Umatilla Wilderness,** north of La Grande. The **Lick Creek Trail** tends to be less crowded than the others. The trail climbs more than 2,000 feet in 3 miles, passing open grassland and large stands of trees. To get to the trailhead, go about 20 miles west on I–84 to the Kamela exit, and then head east on Forest Road 31 for about 25 miles until you intersect Forest Road 32; turn left and continue several miles to the trailhead at Umatilla Campground (*see* Camping, in Pendleton, *below*).

Other good hikes follow trails to the **North Fork John Day River,** which flows through the North Fork John Day Wilderness, southwest of La Grande. To get to the trail that follows Big Creek to the John Day River, take I–84 about 9 miles west, and then drive 13 miles southwest on Route 244; turn south on Forest Road 51 for another 30 miles until you reach Forest Road 52; the trailhead and Big Creek Campground are a few miles down this road.

➤ **HOT SPRINGS** • **Lehman Hot Springs,** about 45 miles southwest of La Grande on Route 244, features a giant swimming pool fed by natural hot springs, set right in the forest. Water temperatures get progressively hotter as you approach the source. You can also camp here for $5 a site. *Tel. 503/427–3015. In Ukiah; from La Grande, take I–84 north to Route 244 west heading toward Ukiah. Admission: $5.*

The Wallowa Mountains

When you first see the Wallowas towering over the small town of Joseph, they seem unreal. Without foothills or any other forewarning, the Wallowas rise abruptly skyward, prompting some to call them "Heaven's Gate" or "The American Alps." Almost the entire range is protected within the Eagle Cap Wilderness Area, leaving the forests and lakesides untrammeled by roads. Wallowa Lake, near the small town of Joseph on Route 82, is a center for summer activities and consequently crowded and touristy. Your best bet is to head for the mountains and lose yourself (figuratively) in the wilderness.

From La Grande, I–82 passes through the towns of Elgin, Wallowa, Lostine, Enterprise, and Joseph en route to Wallowa Lake where it dead-ends. The road is packed during the summer with RVs and cars, and the small towns along the way support diners and motels to handle the crowds, as well as plenty of antiques shops. If you plan to spend some time browsing, save yourself for the small town of **Joseph**. Its Main Street is lined with antiques and handicraft shops, as well as ten art galleries displaying bronze and silver castings from the four metal foundries in town. **Valley Bronze of Oregon** (18 Main St., tel. 503/432–7445) has a very slick showroom displaying western and nature-themed sculptures; they also offer twice-daily tours of their foundry, where you can see the process of bronze casting from conception through molding to the finished product. The biggest annual event in Joseph is the three-day **Chief Joseph Days Rodeo and Commemorative Dance and Encampment** (last weekend in July), which features rodeo, music, and other Native American events. This event pays homage to the town's namesake—young Chief Joseph, leader of the Nez Percé Indians, who made a last ditch run for freedom in 1877 and were finally stopped by U.S. soldiers 30 miles short of the Canadian border. Chief Joseph Days tickets cost $10 and should be ordered in advance (Box 13, Joseph, OR, tel. 503/632–1015). Along the same lines, the free **Wallowa County Museum** (Main St., no phone), open daily 10–5 in spring and summer only, has a small but poignant collection of artifacts and photographs chronicling the Nez Percé Wars, as well as early pioneering artifacts.

VISITOR INFORMATION For specific information about Eagle Cap Wilderness and Hells Canyon, the **Wallowa Mountains Visitors Information Center** houses three agencies (Eagle Cap Rangers District, Hells Canyon Recreation Area, and Wallowa-Whitman National Forest) under one roof in a very modern building just outside of Enterprise. This is the future of visitor centers, with videos of the area, a film library open to the public upon request, lots of pamphlets, an excellent topographical map of the entire area. The center sells 12 maps at $3 each—for a general overview of the area, get the Wallowa-Whitman National Forest North-Half map, but if you plan to do any serious hiking—especially in the hazardous Hells Canyon area—get the appropriate detailed map. *88401 I–82, 1 mi north of Enterprise, tel. 503/426–5546 or 503/426–5591 (24-hr info line). Open summer, Mon.–Sat. 7:30–5, Sun. 10–5; winter, weekdays 7:30–5.*

The **Wallowa County Chamber of Commerce** in the small town of Enterprise offers information on sights and activities in the "American Alps." *I–82, tel. 503/426–4622. Open Mon.–Sat. 10–3.*

Joseph Chamber of Commerce offers everything the Wallowa office does and more. They have a wealth of information about attractions in Joseph, including foundries, art galleries, the Chief Joseph Days Rodeo, lodging, and outdoor recreation. *204 N. Main St., I–82, tel. 503/432–1015. Open weekdays 11–4.*

COMING AND GOING Forest roads give hikers plenty of options for reaching Eagle Cap Wilderness from either La Grande or Baker City—pick up a map from the Wallowa Mountains Visitor Center for detailed information. The most popular route to the Wallowas is to go east on I–82 from La Grande to Joseph, the nearest town to Eagle Cap Wilderness, or to continue on I–82 another 6 miles to Wallowa Lake, a resort near the Eagle Cap Wilderness boundary where many trails begin. Forest Road 8210 from Lostine and Forest Road 8250 from Wallowa—two small towns on I–82—also lead to campgrounds and trailheads. If you're coming from Baker City, you can either go east on Route 86 and then north on Route 39 to gain access to the Wilderness, or take Route 203 east to Medical Springs and then Forest Road 67.

➤ **BY BUS** • **Wallowa Valley Stage Line** (2108 Cove Ave., La Grande, tel. 503/963–5165) runs one bus daily from La Grande to Joseph for about $11; during the summer you can ride all the way to Wallowa Lake for $12.50 one way.

WHERE TO SLEEP Camping is the best way to see the Wallowas and Eagle Cap Wilderness—campgrounds are cheap, plentiful, and located in spectacular settings. But if you're aching for a real bed, there are plenty of motels and hotels around, too. During the summer, the entire county is often booked solid, so call ahead. Plenty of comfortable lodges line the south shore of Wallowa Lake, but they tend to be expensive, as do many of the places in Joseph and Enterprise. If you have a car, it's easy enough to stay in less crowded Minam or Wallowa, on I–82 north of Joseph, within 40 miles of Eagle Cap Wilderness.

➤ **WALLOWA LAKE** • **Eagle Cap Chalets.** If you've decided to go the civilization route, this motel keeps you close to the miniature golf and go-cart racing around Wallowa Lake for as low as $51. You can also rent a condo that sleeps four for $80, or a cabin (some with fireplaces, all with kitchens) for $57 and up—$15 a head if you bring along six very close buddies. *59879 Wallowa Lake Hwy./I–82, tel. 503/432–4704. 37 rooms.*

Wallowa Lake Lodge. Set right in the middle of the tourist village, this fancy hotel also has cabins with kitchens, and some with fireplaces, for $65 and up. *60060 Wallowa Lake Hwy/I–82, tel. 503/432–9821. 33 cabins.*

➤ **JOSEPH** • **Chandlers' Bed, Bread & Trail Inn.** The wood pile out back and a cedar exterior make this place feel more like a ski lodge than a bed-and-breakfast. That's the way owners Jim and Ethel like it: informal and comfortable. Rates start at $60, and smoking is not permitted. *700 S. Main St. tel. 503/432–9765. 4 rooms.*

Indian Lodge Motel. This is the oldest motel in the county, but it has been totally remodeled. Rooms are comfortable, albeit generic, with TVs, coffee machines, and air-conditioning. Doubles start at $43, singles at $33. *Box B, I–82, tel. 503/432–2651. 16 rooms.*

Mountain View Motel and R.V. Park. This motel is a couple of notches below the rest, but in summer you can't be choosy around here. The rooms are small and paneled with fake wood. Doubles start at $35, singles at $28, and four people can share a unit with kitchen for $50. *83450 I–82, 2 mi north of Joseph, tel. 503/432–2982. 9 rooms.*

➤ **ENTERPRISE** • **Melody Ranch Motel.** Western-themed rooms in this motel are nice and clean and have good beds and small bathrooms. Doubles start at $40, singles at $30. Cabins with kitchens are available at a higher rate. *402 W. North St., tel. 503/426–4986. 14 rooms.*

➤ **WALLOWA** • **Mingo Motel and Hot Tub.** This is the best deal around: Doubles cost $36, singles cost $29, and you get large rooms, cable TV and use of the hot tub—which, after a couple of days hiking and camping, is just what the doctor ordered. *2nd and Alder Sts., tel. 503/886–2021. 11 rooms.*

➤ **MINAM** • **Minam Motel.** Rates begin around $38 at this basic motel, but you pay extra for fully furnished kitchens. *I–82, tel. 503/437–4475. 8 rooms.*

➤ **CAMPING** • Campers can choose from more than a dozen developed campgrounds on the periphery of the Eagle Cap Wilderness. Contact the Forest Supervisor or any of the individual Ranger Districts (*see* Visitor Information, in La Grande, *above*) for a complete listing of campgrounds.

Coyote. This remote campground set in a ponderosa pine forest is the favorite of many of the rangers around here. You'll have to drive on dirt roads to get here, but in summer your car should make it fine. Bring your own water. *40 mi NE of Enterprise; take Hwy. 3 to Forest Rd. 46; last 26 mi are dirt roads.*

Hurricane Creek Campground. This is a free campground with no piped water. Though Hurricane Creek runs right by it, you shouldn't drink the water. A trailhead nearby leads to the popular Lakes Basin in the Eagle Cap Wilderness. *4 mi west of Joseph on Forest Rd. 8205. Closed Nov.–May.*

Indian Crossing. Right on the Inmaha River, this excellent site offers good fishing, hiking, and solitude—for free. *51 mi east of Enterprise; take I–82 to Hwy. 350 heading to Imnaha, then Forest Rd. 39 to 3960; last 10 mi are gravel.*

FOOD Wallowa County certainly isn't Oregon's culinary capital, but if you're looking for basic American food, you won't be disappointed. If you're camping, the best place to stock up on marshmallows and weiners is the **Safeway** at the north end of Enterprise—you can't miss it as you enter town.

➤ **ENTERPRISE • The Common Good Marketplace.** This combination health food store, juice bar, and café serves homemade soups ($2.95), excellent chicken curry and Greek salads ($4.95), and a selection of meat and veggie sandwiches in a relaxed atmosphere. *100 Main St./I–82, tel. 503/426–4125. Open Mon.–Sat. 9–4.*

➤ **JOSEPH • The Wagonwheel Restaurant.** This nicely decorated restaurant with a patio and a friendly staff serves up good food, such as Belgian waffles with whipped cream ($3.25), daily lunch specials ($5.95), and an all-you-can-eat salad bar ($4.95 lunch, $5.95 dinner), as well as steaks and delicious homemade soups. *500 Main St., tel. 503/432–9300. Open weekdays 6 AM–11 PM, weekends 7 AM–11 PM.*

➤ **WALLOWA LAKE • Vali's Alpine Deli and Restaurant.** The owners of this place are a Hungarian couple who have been serving authentic Eastern European food for 19 years—their persistence has paid off, and now you're advised to make a reservation for dinner. A different dish, such as chicken paprika with dumplings and salad ($7.85) or Hungarian kettle goulash with fried bread ($7), is served each night. *Wallowa Lake Hwy./I–82, tel. 503/432–5691. Open summer, daily 10–noon and 5:30–9; winter, weekends 10–noon and 5:30–9.*

EXPLORING THE WALLOWA MOUNTAINS The 358,460-acre **Eagle Cap Wilderness Area** is the largest wilderness in Oregon, encompassing most of the Wallowa Range. Because of its size, many of the more remote areas are accessible only to hard-core backpackers or horseback riders. It's rugged country, too: The granite peaks, interspersed with glaciated valleys and alpine meadows and lakes, range between 5,000 and 10,000 feet. Thick forests blanket the low valleys, but higher up the vegetation becomes more sparse, with only hardy alpine trees able to survive. Within the wilderness are bighorn sheep, elk, deer, and mountain goats. Printed trail maps are hard to come by here, and the ones that do exist leave a lot to be desired. Visit the Wallowa Visitors Center (*see* Visitor Information, *above*) and grill the rangers on where to hike before you go. Several trailheads are located at the turnaround at the end of I–82, known as Power House Road. From here you can hike the steep 8-mile round-trip route to Aneroid Lake, where you'll catch a great view of Wallowa Lake and the surrounding mountains. Another good, easier hike is the 6-mile trail to the upper falls on beautiful B.C. Creek. Along the way you pass rock slides and the lower falls. This area abounds with beautiful apline lakes; ask at the visitor information office for a list detailing the lakes' camping, hiking, and fishing opportunities.

Most hikes in the Wallowas are fairly steep and long, running through river valleys that wind between some of the tallest peaks in Oregon. For a marvelous view of the Wallowa Valley, trudge 7 miles from the south end of Wallowa Lake to the shoulder of **Chief Joseph Mountain.** The 3,000-foot climb is taxing, but the view is worth it.

➤ **PACK TRIPS •** Guided pack trips are a popular option for those who aren't prepared to go it alone. The crews take care of food and shelter, leaving you with nothing to do but enjoy the scenery. **Hurricane Creek Llama Treks** (Rte. 1, Box 123, Enterprise, tel. 503/432–4455) helps you explore the Wallowas or Hells Canyon accompanied by a pack-laden llama. Trips cost over $100 a day and begin in the late spring. **Eagle Cap Wilderness Pack Station** (59761 Wallowa Lake Hwy., Joseph, tel. 503/432–4145), on the south end of Wallowa Lake, offers a more conventional way to see the peaks, using horses or mules. Trips range from one hour (about $15) to several days (about $115 a day).

➤ **VIEWS AND DRIVES •** If you're not willing to sweat for a view, take the **Wallowa Lake Tramway** (Rte. 1, tel. 503/432–5331) to the top of 8,200-foot **Mt. Howard.** Views of Wallowa

Lake and Valley are great on the way up in the steepest gondola in North America. The fare to the top is also steep at $10. If you're not satisfied with the view from Mt. Howard, you can hike to the 9,447-foot **East Peak,** only about 2 miles away. Another relatively easy way to see some of the natural splendor of the area is to take the **Wallowa Mountain Loop.** The trip from Joseph to Baker takes about 3½ hours and takes you through the national forest, the Eagle Cap Wilderness, and part of Hells Canyon Recreation Area, passing over mountains, heavily wooded areas, a section of forest devastated by fire, and several creeks and rivers. From Joseph take Highway 350 to Imnaha for 8 miles, turn right onto Forest Road 39, and continue until you meet Highway 86, which leads to Halfway and on to Baker City.

Hells Canyon National Recreation Area

Gazing down the deepest gorge in North America, you'll find it hard to believe that these desolate, impassable cliffs occupy the same state as the snow-capped Wallowas, only 30 miles west. Straddling the Oregon–Idaho border, Hells Canyon offers conifer forests and alpine lakes at its rim, and grim desert-like conditions 8,000-feet below at the Snake River. This was the home of Chief Joseph and the Nez Percé Native Americans, who fished for abundant salmon on the Snake River. The Nez Percé and the salmon are gone, run off by the bullets and dams of the settlers. Bighorn sheep, mountain lions, and elk still dwell in the canyon, sharing it with pine martens, golden eagles, and lots of rattlesnakes. Nearly a thousand miles of trails cross the area, offering several backpacking loops. But as you stand at the top gazing down into the gorge, don't be lulled by the forest and cool breezes, for once you get down,

One otherwise savvy Berkeley Guides writer found out the hard way that any hike into this treacherously beautiful country can be hell. If the extreme heat and lack of potable water don't get you, the snakes very likely will.

out from under the cover of the trees, you quickly realize that the canyon was not only named for its incredible depth, but also for its extreme harshness. So think like a camel and bring a lot of water with you, make sure you have a good map, and know what you're getting into.

VISITOR INFORMATION The **Hells Canyon Chamber of Commerce** (Box 841, tel. 503/785-3393) in Halfway has information on float trips and accommodations in the area. For information about other outdoor activities and camping in the region, contact the Wallowa Visitors Center, which houses the **Hells Canyon National Recreation Area Headquarters** (*see* Visitor Information, in The Wallowa Mountains *above*).

COMING AND GOING Hells Canyon is barely accessible by car. Gravel roads provide the only route to the most interesting sights in the area. I–82, a paved road running from Joseph to Imnaha on the border of the park, is the main access route. From the south, Forest Road 39 off Route 86 is a viable alternative. No public transport extends to this area. If you don't have a car already, your best bet is renting one in a town like La Grande and driving here. Try to enter this area with a full tank, because gas is expensive and hard to find here.

WHERE TO SLEEP The recreation area itself has no hotels, though the accommodations in Enterprise, Joseph (*see* Where to Sleep, in The Wallowa Mountains, *above*), and Halfway are all within an hour's drive of Hells Canyon. Campgrounds are the preferred option here; they are cheap and readily available.

Halfway Motel. The rooms at this place are adequate; some have cable TV, and some have kitchens. Try to stay in one of the new rooms, which cost $42 for a double; the older rooms go for $32. Reservations are recommended year-round. *171 S. Main St., across from U.S. bank, Halfway, tel. 503/742-5722. 31 rooms.*

➤ **CAMPING** • You'll find two incredible campgrounds on the gravel road that leads from the small town of Imnaha to Hat Point. The first 8 miles of this road are very rough, but once you've passed this hurdle, you'll be glad you made the trek.

Hat Point Campground. At the end of the trail, and seemingly the end of the world, this free campsite has no water, but it does have an awe-inspiring view of Hells Canyon, as well as of the Imnaha River valley. Climb the six-story fire lookout tower for a 360° panoramic view of this fabulous country. Be sure to bring plenty of water, especially if you plan to hike down into Hells Canyon. *Tel. 503/426–4978. From Joseph, take Rte. 350 to Imnaha, drive through town to Forest Rd. 4240, and continue for 23 mi to Hat Point.*

Indian Crossing Campground. Set on the banks of the Imnaha River, this serene campground is also a trailhead for paths heading into the Eagle Cap Wilderness. Tent sites are $4. *From Joseph, head 8 mi east on Rte. 305, south on Forest Rd. 39 for 29 mi, then west on Forest Rd. 3960 for 9 mi. 15 sites. Closed Dec.–May.*

Saddle Creek Campground. This campground offers spectacular views of Hells Canyon and the Seven Devils Mountains of Idaho. Still, Hat Point (*see above*) is a better destination. *Tel. 503/426–4978. Drive 19 mi on Forest Rd. 4240 and stop 5 miles before Hat Point. 6 sites. No water. Closed Dec.–June.*

EXPLORING HELLS CANYON Hells Canyon has more than 1,000 miles of trails. Most are long and steep and lack water sources, so be sure to pack enough to drink—sunstroke and dehydration are distinct possiblities down here. Check with rangers before you attempt a hike down here; buy the $3 Hells Canyon map; and consider bringing a snake-bite kit.

Hat Point offers two very steep and dangerous hikes down to the Snake River. Unless trails are improved, we advise you not to do these hikes—or to do them only as far as the meadows; after that it's all downhill—and very hot. Other major trailheads are at Dug Bar and Hells Canyon Reservoir on the Oregon side, and Pittsburgh Landing on the Idaho side. The roads to these trailheads are rocky, steep, and narrow. A 4½-mile hike to the **Snake River** through the rugged **Imnaha Valley** begins 20 miles north of Imnaha at Imnaha Bridge on Forest Road 4260. A few miles north of this trailhead is the 3.7-mile **Nee-Me-Poo Trail** to Dug Bar on the Snake River, which follows in the steps of Chief Joseph and the Nez Percé's flight toward Canada. Most of the other good hikes require overnight stays. Both of the packing outfits listed previously (*see* Pack Trips, in The Wallowa Mountains, *above*) also run trips into Hells Canyon.

➤ **BOATING** • Given Hells Canyon's lack of good roads, the best way to see it may be by raft or jet boat. Jet-boat trips typically depart from Clarkston, Washington or Lewiston, Idaho to the north. White-water raft trips typically leave from Hells Canyon Dam. **Hells Canyon Jet Boat Tours White Water Rafting** (Oxbow, tel. 503/785–3352) offers one-day jet-boat trips from Hells Canyon Launch, just outside Hells Canyon Dam, for $70. White-water trips start at $90 a day. Otherwise, try **Beamer's Landing** (Lewiston, ID, tel. 800/522–6966), which offers one-day and overnight excursions. A complete list of other boat-trip operators is available from the Hells Canyon information offices (*see* Visitor Information, *above*).

➤ **DRIVES AND VIEWS** • **Hat Point Lookout** boasts the best view, but the hour-long 24-mile drive on rutted gravel roads up steep canyons is its hefty price. Forest Road 4240 to Hat Point begins at the town of Imnaha, 30 miles east of Joseph on Route 350. **McGraw Lookout** is more accessible and offers a view almost as good as Hat Point's. McGraw Lookout is east of Forest Road 39 on Forest Road 3965. Little-seen **Buckhorn Lookout** offers sweeping views of the Imnaha River Valley. Head 42 miles northeast of Joseph on Zumwalt Road (Route 697) to get here.

Pendleton

Except for during the huge Round-up Rodeo in September, Pendleton (population 15,000) doesn't feel like the biggest town in eastern Oregon, and that's just the way locals like it. Once a stop along the Oregon trail, and later a busy horse-rustling town, Pendleton now seems more like a ghost town during long summer evenings when the streets are deserted. Pendleton is relatively isolated, set amid miles of fields, quite a distance from the Umitilla and Wallowa-Whitman National Forests. But this Old West town makes a good stop-over, with plenty of cheap lodging and several sights to see, including the Round-Up Hall of Fame, the famous Pendleton Woolen Mill, and the sprawling Pendleton Underground, which celebrates the rough and tumble days of the frontier, when many of Pendleton's illicit businesses took refuge underground along with a sizable portion of the town's persecuted Chinese population.

VISITOR INFORMATION The **Pendleton Chamber of Commerce** gives out plenty of useful brochures, but is loath to admit any preferences among restaurants or motels. *25 S.E. Dorion St., tel. 503/276–7411. Open weekdays 9–5.*

For more information about hiking and outdoor activities around Pendleton, contact the very helpful **Umatilla National Forest Supervisor's Office** (2517 S.W. Hailey Ave., 1 block south of Exit 209, Pendleton, tel. 503/278–3716); they will point you to the best camping sites and give you information about the 600 miles of mountain biking trails. Two other offices, both located in Washington State, deal with the Umatilla forest: **Pomeroy Ranger District** (Rte. 1, Box 53F, Pomeroy, tel. 509/843–1891) and the **Walla Walla Ranger District** (1415 W. Rose St., Walla Walla, tel. 509/522–6290).

COMING AND GOING I–84 runs through Pendleton, connecting with Portland 207 miles to the west, and La Grande 52 miles to the east. U.S. 395 runs south to John Day, 129 miles away. To the north, Route 11 leads 42 miles to Walla Walla, Washington. **Greyhound** (320 S.W. Court, tel. 503/276–1551) runs twice a day west to Portland for $27 and east to Boise for $40. Two daily buses head north to Walla Walla, Washington ($12.25). **Amtrak** (17 S.W. Frazer Ave., tel. 800/872–7245) runs parallel to I–84, heading east on Monday, Wednesday and Saturday and west on Sunday, Tuesday, and Thursday (once daily). The fare is about $36 to Portland, $56 to Boise.

➤ **HITCHHIKING** • If you're heading west, you may have more luck hitching on Route 37 north to Route 730 west than on I–84 itself. U.S. 395 and 11 are good routes for catching rides going south.

GETTING AROUND The town is very simply laid out with streets running north to south and avenues east to west. The intersection of Court Avenue and Main Street is the center of town.

WHERE TO SLEEP Pendleton offers plenty of rooms for a town of its size, but all of them are booked a year ahead of time for the Round-Up in September. Otherwise, rooms here are fairly easy to find. You'll find the mass of motels on Court Avenue downtown, but these are a little more expensive than the ones on S.E. Court Avenue, slightly out of town.

➤ **UNDER $30** • **Pillars Motel.** The dilapidated facade and scrawled sign out front rid you of any false hopes—but at $20 a single and $26.60 a double, you get what you pay for. The rooms are old and small but clean, and the motel is within walking distance of the Woolen Mills, if not the center of town. *1816 S.E. Court Ave., east end of town, tel. 503/276–6241. 14 rooms. No credit cards.*

➤ **UNDER $40** • **Longhorn Motel.** This motel is extremely convenient, right in quiet downtown Pendleton. These big, clean, comfortable rooms are nicer on the inside then the exterior might suggest. Singles are $30, doubles $36. *411 S.W. Dorion St., tel. 503/276–7531. 36 rooms.*

Motel 6. Generic, clean, and rather small rooms with cable TV start at $30. *325 S.E. Nye St., off I–84 Exit 210, tel. 503/276–6120. 122 rooms. Heated pool.*

Pioneer Motel. Right across the street from the Pillars (*see above*), this motel is a little classier and a little more expensive. Fairly large rooms with cable TV and only a touch of funk go for $27 (single) and $32 (double). *1807 S.E. Court Ave., tel. 503/276–4521. 30 rooms.*

➤ **UNDER $50** • **Chaparral Motel.** The Chaparral has immaculate rooms, good beds, and an excellent, friendly staff. Kitchenettes and refrigerators are available, as are non-smoking rooms. Doubles cost $46; singles are $36. *620 S.W. Tutuilla St., tel. 503/276–8654. Take exit 209 from I–84. 50 rooms.*

➤ **CAMPING** • The nearest campground is 25 miles from Pendleton.

Bull Prairie Lake Campground. This terrific campground, two hours from Pendleton, is secluded and so far undiscovered by most people. It's at the southeast end of the Umatilla Forest and offers easy access to the John Day Fossil Beds. Come here to hike, fish, and swim. Tent sites are $4 a night. *Forest Rd. 2039, tel. 503/676–9187. From Pendleton take U.S. 395 south, then Rte. 4 west to Heppner; from here take Rte. 207 south past Hardman into forest. Pit toilets, drinking water, fire rings.*

Emigrant Springs State Park. Set on a historical site along the Oregon Trail, this full-service campground has hot showers and a lot of trailers and RVs. Tent sites are $9. *Tel. 503/983–2277. From Pendleton, 25 mi east on I–84. 51 sites. Closed Nov.–Mar.*

Jubilee Lake. This is the most popular campground in the Umatilla forest, and it gets crowded on weekends and holidays. Come during the week for great camping next to the lake at $9 a site. Surrounded by the forest, this campground is also close to good fishing, swimming, and hiking. *Tel. 509/522–6290. From Pendleton, take Rte. 11 northeast to Weston, then Rte. 204 past Tollgate to Forest Rd. 64; 70-min drive from Pendleton. Wheelchair access.*

Umatilla Forks Campground. Surrounded by forest on the banks of the Umatilla River, this free campground offers swimming, fishing, and hiking trails nearby. *32 mi east on County Rd. N32, which goes through Mission and Cayuse. 29 sites. Closed Nov.–May.*

FOOD You'll find mostly meat-and-potatoes fare here, with a couple of mediocre Mexican restaurants thrown in for good measure. A few good breakfast and lunch places line Main Street.

Cimmiyotti's. Eat here just to enjoy the turn-of-the-century Old West decor, complete with chandeliers and fuzzy wallpaper. Cimmiyotti's specializes in well-prepared steaks and Italian food, although the portions are small. The best deals are the 6-ounce sirloin served with baked potato, salad and bread ($7.75) and lasagna with soup or salad and garlic bread ($7.75). *137 S. Main, tel. 503/276–4314. Open Mon.–Sat. 4 PM–midnight.*

Cookie Tree Bakery and Café. You can get cheap breakfasts ($1 daily specials) on cheap plates with cheap flatware. The lunches aren't expensive either. Come eat either meal in a very informal atmosphere. *30 S.W. Emigrant Ave., downtown, tel. 503/278–0343. Open weekdays 6 AM–4 PM.*

Rainbow Cafe. Even if you don't eat, drink, or pass out here, you owe it to yourself to step through the swinging door and into the past. This combination bar, pool hall, and diner is a glimpse of how the west was fun. Take a seat at a booth, or sit at the counter surrounded by crusty locals eating such delicacies as a fried egg sandwich ($1.65), a tall stack of hot cakes ($2.50), and fried chicken ($4.50). Nothing here is over $5. *209 S. Main St., tel. 503/276–4120. Open daily 6 AM–2:30 AM.*

WORTH SEEING

➤ **ROUND-UP** • This is the main reason to come to Pendleton. The September Round-Up (tel. 503/276–2553 or 800/457–6336) is one of the "Big 4" rodeos (Walla Walla, Lewiston, and Ellensburg are the other three), attracting top rodeo performers and fans from all over. The Round-Up runs for four days and features rodeos, wild horse races, barbecues, parades, and milking contests. The **Happy Canyon Pageant and Dance,** held each night during the Round-Up, begins with a re-creation of the settlement of the area and is followed by a dance, featuring live country and western music and some gambling. Tickets for the various events cost $6–$11. If you plan to attend, order your tickets and reserve lodging months in advance—over 50,000 people descend on Pendleton for this event. The Round-Up grounds and ticket office are located on Court Avenue on the eastern side of town.

Round-Up Hall of Fame Museum. If you're here while the Round-Up is not, stop by the grounds for a quick look at the Hall of Fame Museum. This small but excellent collection of rodeo memorabilia features photos spanning the rodeo's 84-year history, including pictures of the Rodeo

Queens (all white) and the Princesses (all Native American), as well as saddles, guns, and rodeo costumes. *Court Ave., at Round-Up grounds, tel. 503/276–2553. Admission free. Open daily 10–5.*

➤ **WOOLEN MILLS** • Aside from the rodeo, Pendleton is probably best known for its woolen mills, producing superb Indian blankets and Pendleton shirts and sportswear. Once the clothing of choice for cowboys, Pendleton clothing has gained popularity among regular folk. If you're interested in how this intricate material is made, pay a visit to the mill. The free tour lasts about 20 minutes and details the weaving process from start to finish. If you have some extra cash, you can buy a factory-second blanket from the mill's store for under $50. Tours are given four times a day. *1307 S.E. Court Place, tel. 503/276–6911. Go north on Hwy. 11 until you hit S.E. Court Place; turn right. Open weekdays 8 AM–4:45 PM, Sat. 8 AM–1 PM.*

➤ **THE UNDERGROUND** • A 90-minute tour gives visitors an idea of what Pendleton was like a century ago, when the town boasted 32 saloons and 18 brothels. The first part of the tour heads into the town's subterranean labyrinth, which once hid illegal businesses and housed Chinese laborers in 16 square blocks of underground rooms. The guides do a tremendous job of bringing Pendleton's history to life. The "Cozy Rooms Bordello Tour" focuses on the life of Madame Stella Darby, the town's best-known madam. If you're claustrophobic, don't take this tour; otherwise, it's worth your time and money. Tours leave at various times during the day, and reservations are recommended. *S.W. Emigrant St., tel. 503/276–0730. Admission: $11, $6 for half-tour. Open summer, daily 9–4; winter, Mon.–Sat. 9:30–3.*

➤ **HISTORIC HOMES** • Many of the large homes built around the turn of the century are still standing, ranging from simple farmhouses to stately Queen Anne homes. Some of the more recent homes are built in Colonial Revival style. The Chamber of Commerce (*see* Visitor Information, *above*) has a good self-guided walking and driving tour of the homes; pick up a pamphlet at their office.

Southeastern Oregon

Many travelers who've never been to the Pacific Northwest before assume that all of Oregon is as damp and densely forested as its western coast. But most of the vast southeastern stretches of Oregon more closely resemble the deserts of Nevada. As you pass east of the Cascades, the trees dwindle in number, the landscape turns from green and brown to burnt orange, and the sun seems to inflate to twice its previous size. Southeastern Oregon receives less than 10 inches of rain per year, and you could probably fry an egg on your car hood most summer afternoons. Even in summer, however, temperatures often drop dramatically at night, and winters can bring severe storms, often closing roads and mountain passes. Apart from gas money, you're not likely to spend much over here: Lodging is cheap, and you can camp for free. The major attractions lie in a 100-mile corridor running south from Burns, including the **Malheur Wildlife Refuge, Steen's Mountain,** and the **Alvord Desert.** This is rough, rugged, beautiful country, and even if the cowboys and ranchers strike you as somewhat closed, if you travel with an open mind, you'll find the people here hospitable and warm—just a little wary of outsiders. Bend (*see* Chapter 4) is the last major town you'll pass en route to southeastern Oregon from the west. **Burns** is about 100 miles east of Bend and serves as the hub for most of the region. It's a small provincial town—the kind with one bookstore selling nothing but Bibles—but it serves as a useful base for exploring the Ochoco National Forest to the north (*see* Ochoco National Forest, *above*) and the Malheur National Wildlife Refuge to the south.

The night sky in southeastern Oregon is disorientingly clear. From the desert, far from any source of man-made light, you can view the dense white strip of the Milky Way as you've never seen it before.

VISITOR INFORMATION

Malheur Field Station (tel. 503/493–2629; *see* Where to Sleep and Exploring, *below*) is open mid-March through September and can provide you with information on all sorts of outdoor activities in the region—hiking, swimming, and lava-tube exploration, to name a few—and give you detailed directions to the more remote desert destinations that would otherwise be impossible to find.

Burns Ranger District and Snow Mountain District (HC 74, Box 12870, Hines, tel. 503/573–7292), open weekdays 8–4:30, and the **Burns District Bureau of Land Management** (HC 74–12533, U.S. 20 West, Hines, tel. 503/573–5241), open weekdays 7:45 AM–4:30 PM, have information about outdoor activities and camping. Both are on U.S. 20, just west of Burns in the town of Hines.

The Burns Chamber of Commerce offers basic tourist information about the area. *18 W. D St./U.S. 395, next to county museum, tel. 503/573–2636. Open weekdays 9–5.*

COMING AND GOING

U.S. 20 is the only major road into eastern Oregon, taking you from Bend through Burns to Ontario on the Idaho border. You won't find many pit stops between these towns, so make sure your car is in good condition and full of gas, and bring along extra water. Another way to reach Burns is via U.S. 26 to John Day and then south on U.S. 395. Take Route 205 south from Burns to reach Malheur Field Station. Many of the small gravel roads in southeastern Oregon, including the road to Steens Mountain, are open only from mid-July through October.

WHERE TO SLEEP

Camping is the way to go here; you'll find several good campgrounds surrounding the Malheur Wildlife Refuge and on Steens Mountain. If you want a roof over your head and a hot meal, your best bet is Burns and the neighboring town of Hines, both of which have motels and family-style restaurants. You can get double rooms for $30–$40 in Burns at **Motel 6** (997 Oregon Ave., tel. 503/573–3013), the **Orbit Motel** (U.S. 20 and U.S. 395 N, tel.503/573–2034), or the **Silver Spur Motel** (789 N. Broadway, tel. 503/573–2077). In Hines, check out the **Knotty Pine Motel** (U.S. 20 W, tel. 503/573–7440) for $32 doubles. If you're exploring the southwest area in Lake County, consider heading for **Lakeview,** which also has its share of motels and diners.

Frenchglen Hotel. Sixty miles south of Burns and about 35 miles south of the Malheur Field Station along Route 205, the Frenchglen Hotel is one of the best stopovers in southeastern Oregon. Much of the sturdy furniture in the hotel's small but comfortable rooms was handmade by the owners. For a real treat, make reservations for dinner: Wonderful family-style dinners cost $12–$15 and begin promptly at 6:30. Doubles go for about $42. *Rte. 205, in Frenchglen, tel. 503/493–2825. Take Rte. 205 south from Burns. 8 rooms, none with bath. Closed Nov. 16–Feb. 28.*

Malheur Field Station. Set in the middle of the wildlife refuge and surrounded by some of the most barren country you could hope to see, the Field Station is a must for anyone who missed out on either World War II or boarding school. Built originally as Job Corps housing, this spartan facility is legendary. From the airplane-hanger dimensions of the gym to the huge dining hall and barrack-style dorms (with the original 1940s beds—bring a sleeping bag), you can't help but expect a siren blast at any moment. Despite the spartan aura, this is a great place from which to explore the wildlife refuge and Steens Mountain. Dorm beds are $12, and you can get a trailer for two or more at the same rate. The meals are all-you-can-eat (breakfast $5.75, buffet-style pack lunch $5.50, dinner $7). You can also work for room and board with advance approval: A 4½-hour workshift equals one night's room and board. *See* Exploring, *below,* for details of the Field Station classes and workshops. *Malheur Bird Refuge, tel. 503/493–2629. Take Rte. 205 south from Burns about 26 mi to the marked turn-off on other side of Malheur Lake. Laundry, gym. Closed Nov.–Feb.*

CAMPING The Bureau of Land Management (BLM) owns lots of land in southeastern Oregon; you can stay cheaply at one of their designated campgrounds, or pay nothing to sleep on a random patch of their land. Just pull off the road and set up camp. The BLM hands out a free map of Oregon and their land at the Burns office (*see* Visitor Information, *above*).

Blitzen River Crossing. This is the by far the best spot on the mountain, and it's absolutely free. Set in a grassy, wooded gulch next to the river, this idyllic spot has been a local favorite for years. The river is partly dammed here, and you'll find deep swimming holes. Rock fire rings are already in place. *Steens Loop Rd., at Blitzen Creek.*

Fishlake. In the Steens Mountain Area, situated by the well-stocked Fish Lake, this is the nicest developed campground on the mountain, charging $4 a site. *Steens Loop Rd., tel. 503/573–5241. Fire rings, free wood, toilets, fishing, swimming. Closed Nov.–Feb.*

FOOD

While in Burns you might want to check out **Steens Mountain Café** (195 N. Alder St., at Jefferson Ave., 1 block east of U.S. 395, tel. 503/573–7226), which serves family-style Basque lunches ($7.50) and dinners ($10.50), as well as sandwiches ($3.50). The meals are enormous, and you can get a doggy bag for the next day's lunch. **The Frenchglen Hotel** (*see* Where To Sleep, *above*) has great breakfasts and lunches for around $5. If you're headed out to the Malheur Wildlife Refuge and/or Steens Mountain, you might want to stock up on groceries at the **Safeway** in Burns (U.S. 395 S., tel. 503/573–6767), open daily 5 AM–11 PM.

EXPLORING SOUTHEAST OREGON

MALHEUR WILDLIFE REFUGE About 32 miles south of Burns, the Malheur Wildlife Refuge is home to over 280 species of birds, luring almost as many bird-watchers as migrating fowl. Though its shoreline has shrunk considerably in the last few years, Malheur Lake is still one of the nation's largest inland marshes. Head to the refuge's **information center/headquarters,** 6 miles east of Route 205, where you can pick up leaflets and talk to the friendly staff on where you're likely to see the hundreds of birds that live in the refuge. While at the center, their small museum's collection of stuffed birds, eggs, and desert rodents is worth a gander. The information center will also supply you with a free map of the refuge. The 30-mile Central Patrol Road, which cuts right through the heart of the refuge, is your best bet for viewing birds. Every year over the first weekend of April, the refuge hosts the Annual John Schartt Migratory Bird Festival and Art Show, which attracts thousands of ornithologists, birdwatchers, and just plain old bird fanciers. There are speakers, workshops, and guided tours of the refuge—this is a big deal in the world of ornithology and offers an excellent opportunity for the novice to learn about migratory birds. Write in advance for registration and event information (H.C. 72 Box 245, Princeton, OR 97721, tel. 503/493–2612).

MALHEUR FIELD STATION In addition to providing room and board to travelers (*see* Where To Sleep, *above*), the Field Station holds a series of weekend courses and workshops, as well as one three-week course, each year between June and August. Recent courses have focused on field botany, field microbiology, bird-watching, ecology of deserts, and Native American fiber arts.

Hiking trails and nature walks abound in this area; you can get a trail guide at the Field Station for the **South Coyote Butte Trail,** which offers good overviews of the sparse desert vegetation and takes about an hour. The desert is swelteringly hot most of the day, so plan on moderate hikes and bring a hat, some sunscreen, and plenty of water. You can also get directions from the field station to numerous local petroglyphs and volcanic crater swimming lakes, as well as the self-guided tour of the **Diamond Craters,** a series of collapsed volcanic domes. Be wary of rattlesnakes while out in this country. If you see one, be calm and give it the right of way. Also check with the Field Station for directions to the **lava tubes,** a series of dark, cool, underground caves. Be sure to let someone know you're exploring these potentially treacherous tubes.

STEENS MOUNTAIN At 9,700 feet, Steens Mountain is tough to miss, especially on the eastern side, where the sheer mountain rises from the flat basin of the Alvord Desert. On the western side—the side from which most people are likely to see it—Steens Mountain slopes gently upward over a space of about 20 miles. From this side, its immense size is what makes it so impressive. Steens Mountain is actually a huge fault block, created when the ancient lava that covered this area fractured. From Frenchglen, you can drive to the top of Steens Mountain on a very rough gravel road known as the **Steens Loop Road,** open mid-July through October. Looking out over Kiger Gorge on the southeastern rim of the mountain, you can see the dramatic evidence of the carving power of glaciers. A few miles further along the loop road you'll come to the equally stunning East Rim viewpoint. It's more than 5,000 feet down to the valley floor, and you can see the desolate Alvord Desert clear into Idaho and Nevada. On the drive up, you can often spot prairie falcons, golden eagles, kestrels, bighorn sheep, coyote, and deer. This is fantastic country, worthy of more than just a scenic drive—trailheads along the road are stocked with pamphlets describing the nature and length of the hike. The more daring can take a dramatic hike down into the Kiger Gorge. Be warned that although it may be 90°F or more in the desert valleys below, up on the mountain it often snows in June and even July—bring a warm jacket.

ALVORD DESERT In old Westerns, parched cowboys always seem to be crossing numbingly flat deserts with a wall of mountains in the far distance. Well, the Alvord Desert covers the numbingly flat bit, and the wall of mountains is the eastern face of Steens Mountain. Today, the Alvord is popular with wind sailors, who scoot across the hard-packed sand, and glider pilots, who use the flat basin as a runway. In winter, snowmelt from Steens Mountain can turn the basin into a shallow lake. In the 1800s, Chinese workers used sagebrush to fire the enormous vats of a Borax processing plant here. To get to the desert, take Route 205 south from Frenchglen for about 50 miles; the road ends at a T-junction; go left to Alvord Desert and the tiny settlement of Andrews. Bring plenty of water—once the wind sailors and glider pilots go home, this desert is deserted, and you're on your own.

OUTDOOR ACTIVITIES

In addition to sightseeing, camping, and hiking, the southeast also offers good fishing and big-game hunting. Many of the lakes and rivers hereabouts are stocked—especially in the Steens Mountain area. For excellent fishing try the appropriately named **Fish Lake** off Steens Loop Road. One of the best and most memorable ways to see the area is on horseback. **Glacier Mountain Outfitters** (Burns, tel. 503/573–3814) offers one-hour ($20), four-hour ($60), and two- to three-day trail rides ($125 a day, all food included).

SEATTLE

6

By Marissa Levin with Kate Isaacson

No matter how hard Seattleites have labored in recent years to keep their city off national lists of the best cities in America, the crowds keep coming, and the stretchmarks of urban expansion keep appearing. In contrast to life 100 years ago, when early settlers of this one-time remote logging outpost had to beg for new arrivals (especially women), the Seattle of the 20th century struggles to shoehorn in a tide of new residents toting their suitcases full of sky-high expectations. The gimme generation has taken to wheeling into town and asking for it all: fame and fortune as rock stars, clean air in a cosmopolitan setting, big paychecks, low rents, and plenty of good coffee served in styrofoam-free establishments. From the Klondike Gold Rush of the 1890s to a Pacific Rim position as super-city of the 1990s, Seattle sure has come a long way.

But despite its burgeoning population, the city's distinctive districts remain admirably individualistic. **Capitol Hill,** northeast of Downtown, is the center of Seattle's gay life and offers funky restaurants, cafés, bars, and nightclubs; the **University District** is home to some 50,000 University of Washington students and faculty—and another excellent collection of taverns and restaurants; other city sectors like **Fremont, Ballard,** or **Belltown** seem more like small-town neighborhoods than slices of urban pie, with their locals-only dive bars, clubby clubs, and strings of cluttered secondhand shops. The center of many Seattleites' lives is the **Pike Place Market,** where tourists and locals commingle (one buys souvenir T-shirts, the other picks up freshly caught fish). While the market scene is never anything but chaos, the attending mix is symbolic of a citywide

This is the kind of city that takes an old power station and turns it into a majestic park overlooking Lake Union: Gas Works Park.

harmony. It's the kind of camaraderie becoming increasingly frayed as 7-Eleven society sweeps Seattle of mom-and-pop stores. But who's eating whom? Starbucks Coffee was just a bunch of local folks until it was sucked into the big-time corporate dollar chase. Bands like Pearl Jam, Soundgarden, and Alice in Chains once struck lonely chords of the "Seattle Sound"—but that sound has been swallowed whole by the national music scene. Grunge, in a chewed-up and regurgitated form, is now for (and by) everyone. Striking is the memory of the skinny, shaggy, raging blond, in his old Converse tennies and worn jeans, who warbled about generational angst. He isn't here any more, and he isn't coming back.

But don't cry for Seattle. The so-called Emerald City still exists. Under the perennial clouds and amidst endless drizzle, Seattle may be short on A-list sights like museums or missions or historic battlegrounds, but it compensates with acres of delightful and accessible parks and lakes, many within the city limits. Further afield, you need only to hop a short ferry ride from

Downtown Seattle

Mercer St.

Seattle Center

Stadium

Coliseum

Monorail Terminal

Thomas St.

Space Needle

Denny Park

Denny Way

1st Ave. N.
Warren Ave. N.
2nd Ave. N.
Broad St.
Taylor Ave. N.
6th Ave. N.
Aurora Ave. N.
Dexter Ave. N.
8th Ave. N.
9th Ave. N.
Westlake Ave. N.
Terry Ave. N.
Boren Ave. N.

Mercer St
Thomas St
John St.
Denny W

Clay St.
Cedar St.
Vine St.
Wall St.
Bailey St.

99

MONORAIL

6th Ave.
5th Ave.
4th Ave.
3rd Ave.
Blanchard St.
Bell St.

②

③

BELLTOWN

2nd Ave.
1st Ave.
Western Ave.
Lenora St.
Virginia St.

④
⑤
⑥
⑦
⑧

9th A
8th Ave.
7th Ave.
Stewart St.

i

AE

Olive W

Monorail Terminal

Pine St.

6th

4th Ave.
3rd Ave.
5th Ave.

Pike St.

Alaskan Way

Waterfront

KEY

AE American Express Office

i Tourist Information

Ferry Lines

Elliott Bay

Pike Pl.

Pike Place Market

⑨
⑩
⑪
⑫

⑬

⑭
⑮ ⑯

Union St.

Post Office

University

Western Ave.
1st Ave.
2nd Av

99

State Ferry Terminal

TO WINSLOW/ BAINBRIDGE ISLAND

TO BREMERTON

170

Sights ●

Bill Speidel's Underground Tour, **20**

Center on Contemporary Art, **15**

Frye Art Museum, **21**

Omnidome Film Experience, **10**

Piers 54–56, **13**

Pier 59, **11**

Seattle Art Museum/ Downtown, **16**

Seattle Aquarium, **9**

Victor Steinbrueck Park, **8**

Waterfront Park/ Pier 57, **12**

Lodging ○

Commodore Motor Hotel, **5**

Green Tortoise Backpackers Hostel, **1**

Kings Inn, **2**

Marvin Gardens Inn/ Apartments, **3**

The Moore, **4**

The Pacific Plaza Hotel, **18**

Pensione Nichols, **7**

Seattle International AYH Hostel, **14**

St. Regis Hotel, **6**

YMCA, **19**

YWCA, **17**

Greater Seattle

Sights ●

Ballard Locks, 3
Burke Memorial Washington Museum, 7
Henry Art Gallery, 8
Museum of Flight, 19
Museum of History and Industry, 10
Seattle Art Museum, 12
University of Washington, 9
Washington Park Arboretum, 11
Wing Luke Museum, 18
Woodland Park Zoo, 2

Lodging ○

College Inn Guest House, 6
Corner House, 15
Gaslight Inn, 17
Prince of Wales Inn, 16
Salisbury House, 13
University Inn, 1
University Motel, 4
University Plaza Motel, 5
Vincent's Guest House, 14

N. 80th St.
522
N.E. 75th St.
20th Ave. N.
N.E. 65th St.
Green Lake
99
N.E. 55th St.
3rd Ave.
Phinney Ave.
Woodland Park
Eastern Ave.
5
N.E. 50th St.
UNIVERSITY DISTRICT
Fremont Ave.
Meridian Ave.
Stone Way
N.E. 45th St.
Lake Washington Ship Canal
Gas Works Park
Portage Bay
Union Bay
Queen Ann Ave.
Lake Union
520
Boyer Ave.
10th Ave.
Volunteer Park
11
W. Mercer St.
99
E. Valley St.
CAPITOL HILL
12th Ave.
E. Thomas St.
Denny Way
DOWNTOWN
Western Ave.
Virginia St.
Olive Way
Madison St.
Rainier Av. S.
17th Ave.
23rd Ave.
E. Union St.
E. Cherry St.
Empire Way
KEY
Rail Lines
Pioneer Square
E. Yesler Way
Jackson St.
Elliott Bay
0   500 yards
0   500 meters
Amtrak/ King St. Station
INTERNATIONAL DISTRICT
S. Dearborn St.
S. Lake Way
90
S. Holgate St.
17th Ave. S.
900
Harbor Island
E. Marginal Way S.
1st Ave. S.
4th Ave.
S. McClellan St.
Beacon Ave. S.
167
Delridge Way
99
Duwamish Waterway
5
15th Ave. S.
S. Columbian Way
Empire Way S.
900

Downtown to reach a peaceful, hikable island in the Puget Sound. Or, drive an hour or two to reach the Olympic or North Cascade Mountains. When "the mountain is out" (Seattle lingo for nice weather), the city comes alive with kayakers, in-line skaters, hikers, and picknicking idlers. If you're wondering whether Seattle is still a cool place to visit: Of course it is. If you think it can stay that way with zillions of new residents each year: Get real. Right now, Seattle's still got the perfect balance of intellectual stimulation (the University of Washington), natural wonders (plentiful city parks), political interest (the pan-Washington debate over the tree and the owl), arts (those soggy days mean 100% attendance at basement rehearsals), and caffeine (a jillion caffeholic fill-up stations) to still be beautiful. Who knows what keeps this city so down-to-earth despite a thousand sycophants scratching at its doors? Whatever it is, let's hope it lasts another year.

Basics

AMERICAN EXPRESS This Downtown office holds mail for American Express cardmembers and check holders. They'll also cash out-of-town checks and help with travel arrangements, even outside Washington. *600 Stewart St., at 6th Ave., Downtown, tel. 206/441–8622. Open weekdays 9–5.*

LUGGAGE STORAGE Seattle attracts a lot of transient types, so finding an empty locker can be tough. The **King Street Station** (*see* Coming and Going by Train, *below*) will store bags for Amtrak ticket holders ($1.50 per bag per 24 hrs) for up to 60 days. **Sea-Tac Airport** (tel. 206/433–5333) charges a daily rate based on the size of your luggage (generally $2.50–$5). Empty lockers are scarce at the **Greyhound Station** (*see* Coming and Going, *below*), where storage is available to all around the clock. If you do get lucky, lockers cost $1 for the first 24 hours and $3 per day after that.

MEDICAL AID Northwest Hospital's 24-hour hot line **MED-INFO** (tel. 206/633–4636) provides free referrals. For inexpensive or free care, try **Providence Medical Center** (500 17th Ave., at E. Jefferson St., First Hill, tel. 206/320–2000) or the **Women's Health Care Center** (1833 Harvard Ave. E, at Denny St., Capitol Hill, tel. 206/328–1700).

VISITOR INFORMATION The Visitor Information Bureau has an overwhelming supply of brochures, including bus and ferry information; for the short-term visitor, this is overkill. (Don't expect the grouches working behind the desk to be particularly helpful, either.) Do pick up "The Seattle Guide," which includes a city map and comprehensive weekly listings. The free magazine is also available at most hotels and art galleries Downtown. *800 Convention Pl., Downtown, tel. 206/461–5840. Enter east of 7th Ave. on Union St. Open weekdays 8:30–5; also open weekends 10–4 in summer.*

The **Greater University Chamber of Commerce** can provide information about the University District. *4714 University Way NE, tel. 206/527–2567. Open weekdays 9–5.*

COMING AND GOING

BY CAR Two major freeways link Seattle with the rest of the country: I–5 goes north to Vancouver (2½ hrs); and south to Portland (3 hrs), Eugene (5 hrs), San Francisco (14 hrs), and Los Angeles (22 hrs). I–90 passes Lake Washington and the city's eastern suburbs, continuing east to Spokane (5½ hrs) and, eventually, all the way to Boston. U.S. 2 connects Seattle with the northern Sierras.

BY BUS On the northern fringe of Downtown, **Greyhound** (811 Stewart St., at 8th Ave., tel. 206/628–5526 or 800/231–2222) provides frequent service to Portland (3½ hrs, $19), San Francisco (20 hrs, $69), Los Angeles (26 hrs, $119), and other points along the coast. The route east hits Spokane (6 hrs, $26) and Chicago (2 days, $169). Exact prices and trip lengths vary according to season and day of travel. Connect with local buses at the Convention Place Bus Tunnel Station (9th Ave. and Olive Way), two blocks south and east of the Greyhound terminal: Bus 10 will take you to Pike Place and Pioneer Square, at the heart of Downtown; Bus 7 runs to Capitol Hill and the University District. For other local routes, *see* Getting Around, *below. Greyhound ticket window open daily 12:30 AM–1:30 AM, 5:30 AM–2:30 PM, and 3:45 PM–7:30 PM.*

A more unusual option is the **Green Tortoise** (tel. 800/TORTOISE or 800/227–4766), which tools leisurely up and down the coast with stops for passengers to hike or swim. Coaches contain sleeping mattresses, but no toilets or showers. Buses depart twice weekly (Sunday and Thursday, 8 AM) for Portland (5 hrs, $15 one-way), Eugene (8 hrs, $25), San Francisco (1 day, $49), and Los Angeles (2 days, $69) from 9th Avenue and Stewart Street, near the Greyhound Station. Reservations are required for overnight trips.

BY FERRY Many Washington residents commute to Seattle from one of the nearby islands or the peninsulas across the sound, so ferry service is frequent and reliable. From Downtown's **Colman Dock/Pier 52** (801 Alaskan Way), several **Washington State Ferries** (tel. 206/464–6400 or 800/843–3779 in Washington) cruise daily to Bainbridge Island (35 min) and, on the Olympic Peninsula, Bremerton (1 hr). One-way rates for car and driver are $7.10 during peak season (mid-May–Oct.), or $5.90 off-season. Walk-on passengers ($3.50) pay only for the outward-bound leg of the trip. Passenger-only ferries depart daily for Vashon Island (25 min) during weekday rush hours and on Saturdays; fare is $3.50 per person. Ticket lines are often long during weekday rush hours and in summer, and reservations are not accepted, so allow plenty of time before your departure. Bikers take note: The Seattle–Vashon ferry only permits five bicycles on each boat, so arrive extra early or kiss your bike goodbye. Buses 11, 302, and 305 connect the ferry terminal with other points around Downtown.

The **Fauntleroy Ferry Terminal** in West Seattle is an alternative for visitors to Vashon Island who can't live without cars. Round-trip fares for the 15-minute trip are $9.55 per car and driver during peak season (mid-May–Oct.) or $7.95 off-season. Walk-on passengers pay $2.30. There's also service to Southworth (at the southern end of the Kitsap Peninsula); rates are the same as Seattle–Bremerton (*see above*). To reach the Fauntleroy Terminal, take Highway 99 south to the West Seattle Freeway and follow the signs. For information on ferries to Vancouver Island, *see* Chapter 10.

BY TRAIN Amtrak stops at **King Street Station** (3035 S. Jackson St., at 3rd Ave., tel. 206/382–4120 or 800/872–7245) on the southern edge of Downtown. Three trains make the daily trip to Portland (4 hrs, $23). Trains depart once daily for San Francisco (23 hrs, $153), Los Angeles (1 ½ days, $157), and other sights along the coast, as well as Chicago (2 days, $217). Precise fares and travel times vary, and trains often sell out well in advance, so call ahead.

Connect with local buses at the International District Bus Tunnel Station (S. Jackson St. and 5th Ave.), two blocks west of King Street Station. Bus 7 continues to Capitol Hill. Bus 71, 72, or 73 will take you to the University District; at night these buses begin their routes at 3rd Avenue and Washington Street (two blocks north of the train station). To reach any of the lodging Downtown around 1st Avenue, walk two blocks to 1st Avenue and Jackson Street and take Bus 15, 18, 22, or 23 north. For info on other local bus routes, *see* Getting Around, *below*.

BY PLANE The **Seattle-Tacoma International (Sea-Tac) Airport** (tel. 206/433–5217) is 30 minutes south of Downtown on I-5. **Alaska Airlines** (tel. 800/426–0333 or 206/433–3100) flies the West Coast from Mexico to Alaska. Both **Horizon** (tel. 800/547–9308) and **Southwest Airlines** (tel. 800/466–7747) serve the Pacific Northwest and western Canada. Other major airlines that fly here include **United** (tel. 800/241–6522), **American** (tel. 800/433–7300), **Delta** (tel. 800/221–1212), **Northwest** (tel. 800/225–2525), and **Continental** (tel. 800/525–0280).

The airport's useful **Visitor Information Center** (tel. 206/433–5218), open daily 9:30 AM–7:30 PM, is located on the baggage claim level. The **Thomas Cook currency exchange** office (tel. 206/248–0401), open daily 6 AM–10 PM, is on the airport's main level, near the entrance to Concourse B.

➤ **AIRPORT TRANSPORT** • **Metro Transit's** buses offers the best deal ($1.10) on travel between Sea-Tac and Downtown. Pickups are outside the baggage claim areas. Express Bus 194 makes the trip in 30–40 minutes and operates continuously Monday–Saturday from early morning until 7:20 PM. Bus 179 makes the same trip in 40 minutes, from morning to just after midnight, stopping frequently along 2nd Avenue on the way to the airport and along 4th Avenue on the return. Bus 184 is the late-night bus, making two trips nightly between midnight and 5 AM. **Gray Line Airport Express** (tel. 206/626–6088) offers service ($7) to major hotels Downtown, such as the Sheraton, Hilton, and Stouffer Madison, daily 5 AM–midnight. Pickups are outside the United Airlines and the international baggage claim areas. Reservations are not necessary. **Shuttle Express** (tel. 206/622–1424 or 800/487–RIDE) offers 24-hour door-to-door service for $14.

Before you hit the road with your thumb in the air, remember: Seattle is the runaway capital of the nation. If some psycho is looking for company, this could be his first stop.

HITCHHIKING Although hitchhikers are treated kindly by most Seattleites, ride boards are generally a better way to find a car going your way. Check the boards at the Downtown **AYH Hostel** or at the **University of Washington Student Union** (*see* Hostels, in Where to Sleep, and the University District, in Worth Seeing, *below*). Don't try to catch a ride on the freeways (I–5 and I–90), where hitchhiking is strictly prohibited. Instead, stand near an on-ramp. And before you take any ride, assess the situation carefully—Seattle has its share of loonies.

GETTING AROUND

The Downtown area is sandwiched between Puget Sound and I–5 and revolves around **Pike Place Market** (bordered by Western and 1st avenues and Virginia and Pike streets). North of the market you'll hit **Seattle Center** (bounded by 1st and 5th avenues N, Mercer Street, and Denny Way), home of the Space Needle; and to the market's south is **Pioneer Square** (1st Avenue, between Cherry and S. Jackson streets), a historic quarter with shops and a hopping bar scene. Streets run east–west, while avenues go north–south. Outside the immediate Downtown area, streets are preceded with directional abbreviations (e.g., E. James Street), while avenues are followed by suffixes (e.g., 16th Avenue NE). There are plenty of confusing exceptions that make a good map essential.

Wherever you go in Seattle, you'll see a perplexing maze of waterways and hills. Knowing the various bodies of water will help orient you: **Puget Sound** borders the city to the west (and eventually meets the Pacific Ocean far north of here), while giant **Lake Washington** borders it on the east. Just north of Downtown is **Lake Union,** which has two man-made arteries, together known as the **Lake Washington Ship Canal.** These connect the Sound with Lake Washington and divide the city into northern and southern halves. In the southern section you'll find the neighborhoods of **Queen Anne** and funky **Capitol Hill,** as well as **Downtown.** To the north are the neighborhoods of **Ballard,** residential **Fremont, Wallingford,** and the student-filled **University District.** Farther north is **Green Lake,** the city's most bustling park.

BY BUS Between 4 AM and 9 PM, all public transportation is free within the Downtown **Ride Free Area,** bounded by Battery Street on the north, I–5 on the east, S. Jackson Street on the south, and the Waterfront on the west. At all other times and in all other places, bus fare is regularly 85¢, or $1.10 during weekday rush hours (check specific bus schedules for times). If you're confused, don't worry: The onboard fare collection boxes post prices, and bus drivers are usually helpful. Trips to areas outside the Seattle city limits are $1.10, $1.60 during peak hours. On weekends and holidays you can purchase a **Day Pass** from the driver for $1.70.

Downtown, buses circulate frequently: approximately every 10 minutes on weekdays and every 15 minutes on weekends. Catch most buses near Pioneer Square, on 1st, 2nd, 3rd, and 4th avenues between Pine and University streets. Seattle also has a brand-new electric bus that travels underground, north–south along 3rd Avenue between Pine and S. Jackson streets. You can ride this bus (it's included in the city's Ride Free Area) or catch a regular bus from one of the five tunnel stations: Convention Place (9th Ave. and Olive Way); Westlake Center (3rd Ave. and Pine St.); University Street (3rd Ave. and University St.); Pioneer Square (3rd Ave. and James St.); and the International District (5th Ave. and S. Jackson St.).

Between Downtown and the University District, the quickest daytime route is on Express Bus 71, 72, or 73. At night, Bus 74 or 83 makes the same run with more stops. Downtown, Bus 7 climbs Pike and Pine streets, continuing north to Broadway (Capitol Hill's main artery) and the University District before looping back to Downtown. Buses 10 and 43 also connect Downtown with Capitol Hill. For information on getting to and from specific destinations, call the 24-hour **Metro Rider Information Hotline** (tel. 206/553–3000 or 800/542–7876 in Washington). Comprehensive **Metro maps** and **timetables** are available at 7-11 stores, Bartell Drugstores, and any of the major shopping centers around town.

BY MONORAIL The monorail, operated by **Metro Transit** (tel. 206/553–3000 or 800/542–7876 in Washington), was built for the 1962 World's Fair. It runs between Westlake Center (5th Ave. and Pine St.) and Seattle Center (*see* Worth Seeing, *below*) on Downtown's northern boundary. Service is at 15 minute intervals, Sunday–Thursday 9–9, Friday and Saturday 9 AM–midnight. Fare is 85¢ each way.

BY STREETCAR The **Waterfront Streetcar** is a convenient, inexpensive, and fun way to travel (of course the 10 million other tourists packed into the trolley with you probably read the same thing). The vintage 1927 Australian trolley runs along Alaskan Way between Pier 70 (at Broad Street) and the International District (at S. Jackson Street). Downtown attractions such as the Waterfront, Pike Place Hillclimb, Pioneer Square, Seattle Center, and the Downtown shopping area are all either on its route or only a short walk from one of the stations. The trolley runs daily at 20-minute intervals and is operated by **Metro Transit** (tel. 206/553–3000). Fare is 85¢. Stations and streetcars are wheelchair accessible.

BY BIKE Many Seattleites get around town by bicycle. Before you follow suit, some advice: Don't underestimate the hills (if you're out of shape you'll be happier planting your butt on a bus seat), and always wear a helmet. Urban biking is no pushover peddle in the park, and Seattle is a wet, hilly, and hectic place to do it. Try to obey all traffic rules because Seattle cops (some on mountain bikes themselves) treat bikers no differently than drivers. Now that we've nagged and annoyed you, know that touring Seattle by bike is a great idea. You can visit remote neighborhoods and get a good workout at the same time.

Several Seattle bike trails deserve mention. The 2-mile **Elliott Bay Bikeway** runs along the Waterfront from Pier 86 to Pier 70 and offers great views of the Sound; the **Alki Beach 12-mile trail** has great views of the Olympics; and the 12-mile **Burke-Gilman Trail** cuts through the University District to follow the northwest shore of Lake Washington. Additionally, on the third Sunday and first Saturday of the month May–September, **Lake Washington Boulevard** is closed to cars from the University of Washington Arboretum to Seward Park.

➤ **BIKE RENTALS** • The least expensive rental shops are **Montlake Bicycle Shop** (2223 24th Ave. E, Capitol Hill, tel. 206/329–7333) and **R and E Cycles** (5627 University Way NE, University District, tel. 206/527–4822). Near Alki Beach, **Alki Bicycle Company** (2611 California Ave. SW, West Seattle, tel. 206/938–2322) offers mountain bikes ($9 per hr), touring bikes ($7 per hr), tandems ($8 per hr), and in-line skates ($4 per hr). **Gregg's Green Lake Cycle** (7007 Woodlawn Ave. NE, Green Lake, tel. 206/523–1822) has mountain bikes and touring bikes from $4 per hour to $25 per day.

BY TAXI If you've been stranded at night by the bus (they generally don't run after 2 AM), call **Broadway Cabs** (tel. 206/622–4800) or **Graytop Cab** (tel. 206/282–8222). Cost is an initial $1.20 plus $1.40 for every mile. A trip from Downtown to the University District will cost about $10, and to Broadway on Capitol Hill, about $5.

Don't flag down private cabs (recognizable because they don't paint a company name on the door)—these unregulated taxis overcharge more than most U.S. defense contractors.

BY CAR In sprawling Seattle, a car can be a big advantage, especially if you don't have a lot of time. Unfortunately, many of the visitor information maps focus exclusively on Downtown or simply lack detail. If you're a member of **AAA**, request a free *Tour Book to Oregon and Washington* from your local chapter; otherwise, invest $2 in a detailed map, available at any bookstore.

➤ **CAR RENTALS** • Most of the major rental companies have locations at the airport and in Downtown Seattle. Rates may differ from one office to the other, so call ahead. Credit cards are almost always required of renters. Some companies, such as **Hertz** (tel. 800/654–3131) and **Avis** (tel. 800/331–1212), will not rent to people under 25; others will make you pay a surcharge.

The cheapest company is **Best Rent-A-Car** (1305 Stewart St., tel. 206/343–2378), which has rates beginning at $19.95 per day (and no surcharge for the under-25 crowd). The first 150 miles per day are free, and each mile thereafter costs 10¢. **Dollar Rent A Car** (701 Stewart St., tel. 206/682–1316) has subcompacts with unlimited mileage for $23.95–$32.95 a day, depending on availability. They do not rent to drivers under age 25. A cheaper option is **Thrifty** (801 Virginia St., tel. 206/625–1133), which rents compact cars for $19.99–$35.99. Drivers ages 21–24 must pay an extra $10 per day.

Where to Sleep

Ever since the sound and style of grunge swept the country, curious people have been flocking to Seattle from every corner of the earth. Reservations are crucial during the summer and a bright idea in other seasons. Although super-cheap options are rare, several reasonably priced lodgings exist in the **University District** and **Capitol Hill.** Most of the major hotels are Downtown near the commercial bustle of Pike Place Market and the constant beer-fest of Pioneer Square. If you're yearning to throw out your sleep sheet and take a break from wearing flip-flops in the shower, try one of the pricier Downtown hotels or head for a bed-and-breakfast in the cool neighborhood of Capitol Hill.

DOWNTOWN

This is the place to be, whether you're a 9-to-5 suit or a latter-day hippie. Hotels in this densely populated neighborhood of office buildings, restaurants, and shops are usually inexpensive and sometimes come with views of Elliott Bay. Downtown can be sleazy at night (especially around 1st and 2nd avenues in the Pike Place Market; near King Street Station; and in the less inhabited parts of Pioneer Square), but you will have easy access to the Seattle social scene. Fill daytime hours lounging at one of numerous cafés and evenings checking out the scene at a neighborhood bar. The usual precautions against mugging and theft certainly apply, but there's no need for paranoia. While Seattle may have its tough side, it doesn't compare with the streets of New York or Los Angeles.

UNDER $40 **Commodore Motor Hotel.** The choice here is between taking a bed in the dormitory, or getting a private room with the same amount of space at a higher price. (As an added bonus, the private rooms have unappealing bathrooms and showers.) Private single rooms are $42. Rooms with shared baths are $33 (single) or $37 (double). Dorm beds ($12) are available only to HI members. *2013 2nd Ave., at Virginia St., tel. 206/448–8868. 5 blocks from Greyhound Station. 102 rooms; 8 dorm beds. Laundry, luggage storage. Wheelchair access.*

Marvin Gardens Inn/Apartments. These "efficiency suites" (which are merely normal-sized motel rooms crammed with as much stuff as possible) are ideally located in the center of town. They're one of the best deals in the city if you plan to stay for a week or more, particularly if you split the weekly ($210) or monthly ($545) rates between two or more people. The sterile rooms come with full-sized bed, private bath, TV, telephone, and weekly maid service. *2301 3rd Ave., at Bell St., tel. 206/443–1030 or 800/443–3031. 67 units. Laundry. Wheelchair access.*

St. Regis Hotel. This hotel doubles as low-income housing for recovering alcoholics. Expect chipped paint, stained walls, and a smoke-filled lobby with sundry sprawling regulars. At least you'll get a surprisingly quiet single ($30) or double ($40). Most rooms share baths. *116 Stewart St., at 2nd Ave., tel. 206/448–6366. 4 blocks from Greyhound Station and 1 block from Pike Place Market. 185 rooms, most with shared bath. Laundry. Wheelchair access.*

YMCA. It may be a bit older-looking than the YWCA (*see below*), but it's also quieter. Secure, convenient, and big, the YMCA can sleep over 300 people of both sexes. Beds in the dorms ($18.50) are reserved for HI members. Anybody may stay in one of the singles ($34, or $46 with bath) or a shared-bath double ($40), though room rates are about $8 lower for HI members. Those staying in the dorms must bring their own linens or a sleeping bag. *909 4th Ave., btw Marion and Madison Sts., tel. 206/382–5027. 3 blocks south and 1 block east of University St. Tunnel Station. From Greyhound Station, take the tunnel bus; or take Bus 25 or 70–74 to Madison St. Laundry, luggage storage ($1 per bag, per day). Wheelchair access.*

YWCA. Cleaner and safer than any of the area's cheap motels, the Y doubles as temporary residence for single mothers and battered women. Bare formica rooms open to women only are spacious and come with their own linen and towels; singles are $31 ($186 per week), and doubles are $42 ($252 per week). Free local calls, use of the exercise room, and 24-hour front-door security (administered by a depressingly clueless staff) are all included. Reservations are recommended. *1118 5th Ave., at Seneca St., tel. 206/461–4888. 3 blocks east of University St. Tunnel Station. From Greyhound Station, take the tunnel bus; or take Bus 25 or 70–74. 27 rooms, all with shared bath. Laundry. Wheelchair access.*

UNDER $50 **The Moore.** Not much has changed at this Seattle relic since it was built in 1907. Rooms are relatively clean and commodious, and some have partial views of Puget Sound. Resign yourself to chipped paint on the ceilings and peeling walls unless you request one of eight newly renovated rooms. Doubles are $39 (shared bath) or $45 (private bath). Rooms with kitchenettes are $34 (single) and $44 (double). Don't expect much hospitality from the folks at the front desk, and definitely skip the restaurant. *1926 2nd Ave., at Virginia St., tel. 206/448–4851. 5 blocks south and 1 block west from Greyhound Station. 137 rooms, most with bath.*

UNDER $60 **Kings Inn.** Clean and affordable, Kings Inn is your basic generic motel. Simply expect nothing from the cocky people who run this place and you won't be disappointed. Rooms are $50 (single) or $60 (double). Suites ($80) sleep four and include kitchenettes. *2106 5th Ave., at Lenora St., tel. 206/441–8833. 2 blocks north of Greyhound Station. 69 rooms. Wheelchair access.*

UNDER $85 **The Pacific Plaza.** Across the street from the main library, the Pacific Plaza is worth a few extra dollars. Rooms may feel kind of corporate, with dark wood furniture and nicely tiled bathrooms, but who would scorn the Danish pastries and Starbucks coffee served every morning? Typically, doubles are $75–$94. Call ahead to inquire about frequent weekend discounts. *400 Spring St., btw 4th and 5th Aves., tel. 206/623–3900. From Greyhound Station, take Bus 25 or 70–74. 160 rooms. Luggage storage.*

Pensione Nichols. Just up the hill from Pike Place Market, this B&B is a beautifully decorated, well-run establishment perfect for those who have seen enough gray motel carpeting for a lifetime. Energetic hostess Lindsay Nichols uses antiques from her mother's shop downstairs to decorate the bedrooms and the spacious living room, where a superb continental breakfast is served. Singles are about $60, doubles $85; suites are $120–$160. Reserve well in advance in summer. *1923 1st Ave., btw Stewart and Virginia Sts., tel. 206/441–7125. 6 blocks from Greyhound Station. 11 rooms, most with shared bath. Luggage storage.*

CAPITOL HILL

This is the fashionable neighborhood for those who have rejected the whole 2½ kids/picket fence/station wagon ideal but who won't move to a commune out in the middle of nowhere. It's a center for the gay community and home to some of the most interesting accommodations in the city. Not everyone can afford to live in Capitol Hill, though, and the same goes for travelers—a double room in one of its turn-of-the-century bed-and-breakfasts usually costs $75–$100. In addition to the B&Bs listed below, try the **Gaslight Inn** (1725 15th Ave. E, at Howell St., tel. 206/325–3654) or **Salisbury House** (750 16th Ave. E, at Aloha St., tel. 206/328–8682), or contact the **Seattle Bed and Breakfast Inn Association** (tel. 206/547–1020), which offers listings but does not make reservations.

UNDER $30 **Vincent's Guest House.** This backpacker's hostel/B&B is the cheapest place to stay in the area, hands down. It's also the most fun, with a constant tide of young travelers enjoying the low weekly rates ($70–$140), frequent barbecues, and free bagel breakfasts.

Beds in the tidy dorms cost $12 per night. Singles are $25, $30 with private bath, and doubles are $5 more. *527 Malden Ave. E, btw Thomas and Roy Sts., tel. 206/323-7849. From Downtown, take Bus 10 to E. John St. and 15th Ave., then walk 1 block north and ½ block west. 8 rooms. Laundry, luggage storage (75¢ per day). Wheelchair access. No credit cards.*

UNDER $60 **The Corner House.** This elegant pink B&B on Capitol Hill's east side deserves a special mention. Hosts Oliver Osborne and Julianne Nason provide bountiful breakfasts and cozy rooms with antique furnishings. They charge $55 for one of the two doubles, or $20 for a bed in their large room, which sleeps three or four. The small number of rooms makes reservations crucial, especially in summer. Amble, the cat, may cause problems for anyone with allergies. *102 18th Ave. E, at Denny Way, tel. 206/328-2865. From Downtown, take Bus 43 to 19th Ave. E and John St., then walk 1 block west and 1 block south.*

UNDER $100 **Prince of Wales.** In this casual, incredibly friendly Victorian B&B, rooms (some are suites with two big beds) have names: The King, The Queen, The Prince, and The Princess go for $85–$110. Single occupants pay slightly less. Owner Carol Norton cooks a healthy, low-fat breakfast and will let you play with her dog and two cats. *133 13th Ave. E, at John St., tel. 206/325-9692 or 800/327-9692. From Downtown, take Bus 43. 4 rooms.*

THE UNIVERSITY DISTRICT

Accommodations around the U-district (as it's referred to by locals) would always be full if Parents' Weekend was more than just an annual thing at the University of Washington. Certainly students can't afford most of the motels and hotels here. Budget choices are limited to crashing on a friend's couch or staying at one of the **fraternity** (tel. 206/543-1800) or **sorority** (tel. 206/543-1810) **houses,** which rent out cheap rooms in the summer. It's not the most convenient or interesting area unless you're a prospective student or visiting parent, and though you'll find cheap places to eat and shop, nightlife is basically nonexistent. Fortunately, buses run frequently to Downtown and Capitol Hill.

UNDER $60 **College Inn Guest House.** The College Inn caters to a youngish crowd. The downstairs pub is a popular hangout, and the upstairs rooms are favored by University of Washington students with significant others in town for a romantic weekend. Tastefully furnished singles ($35–$49), doubles ($60–$70), and bed space in one of two dorm-style triple rooms ($27 per person) all include continental breakfast. *4000 University Way NE, tel. 206/633-4441. From Downtown, take Bus 7 or 71–74 to N.E. Campus Pkwy. and Brooklyn Ave., then walk 1 block east and 1 block south. 25 rooms. Luggage storage. Reservations required.*

University Motel. Suites, incredibly worn but clean, sleep up to 10 people here; some include fully furnished kitchenettes. (You can pick up groceries at the nearby Safeway, or flirt with gourmet cooking using fresh food from the Pike Place Market Downtown.) The manager accepts only guests over age 21 and does practice his right to refuse service to those he dislikes—which seems to include almost everyone. Rooms are $50 for one guest, plus $6 for each additional person. *4731 12th Ave. NE, tel. 206/522-4724. From Downtown, take Bus 71–74 to University Way NE and 47th St., then walk 2 blocks west; or take Bus 7 via Capitol Hill. 21 rooms.*

UNDER $80 **University Inn.** This inn close to campus offers two starkly different wings: The north has dark, antiseptic-smelling hallways and rooms (single $65, double $75) that capture traffic noise from Roosevelt Way. Rooms in the newer south wing are an additional $10—but the fresher, almost pleasant, atmosphere is worth the extra cash. *4140 Roosevelt Way NE, tel. 206/632-5055. From Downtown, take Bus 7, 43, or 71–74 to N.E. Campus Pkwy., then walk 2 blocks north. 102 rooms. Luggage storage, outdoor pool, kitchenettes ($10 extra). Wheelchair access.*

University Plaza Hotel. You'll see visiting professors and business types relaxing in the University Plaza's lounge. The Hiltonesque rooms are quiet, comfortable, and clean. Singles start at $70 and doubles at $75; suites are $165. *400 N.E. 45th St., at 4th Ave., tel. 206/634-0100. 135 rooms. Luggage storage, outdoor pool. Wheelchair access.*

HOSTELS

Some bed-and-breakfasts and motels double as hostels, devoting one or two large rooms to cheap beds in dorm rooms (see Commodore Motor Hotel, YMCA, Vincent's Guest House, and College Inn Guest House, above).

Green Tortoise Backpacker's Guest House. Two blocks from Seattle Center (see Worth Seeing, below), this small, quiet, and clean hostel is a world removed from the frenzy of Downtown. It's located in Seattle's Queen Anne sector: nothing chic, but a real neighborhood. Dorm beds cost $11–$12, depending on proximity to a bathroom. Private rooms are $30, $35 with private bath. 715 2nd Ave. N, at Roy St., Queen Anne, tel. 206/322-1222. From Downtown, take Bus 1,2, or 13 to 1st Ave. N and Mercer St., then walk 2 blocks east and 1 block north. 75 beds. Laundry, luggage storage, kitchen, garden. No credit cards.

Seattle International AYH Hostel. Steps from Pike Place Market and the Waterfront, this Club Med of budget lodging is cheap, clean, friendly, and filled with extra amenities. In addition to providing tight security, the helpful staff leads a daily orientation (7:30 PM) for newly arrived visitors. Only HI members may stay June–September ($14); nonmembers are welcome during the rest of the year ($17). Year round, it's an excellent place to socialize with foreign travelers. Reservations require a one night deposit. 84 Union St., at Western Ave., Downtown, tel. 206/622-5443. 11 blocks south and west from Greyhound Station. 137 beds. Lockout 11 AM–2 PM. Reception open daily 7 AM–midnight. Laundry, luggage storage, kitchen, lockers, sleep sheets ($2), TV room.

ROUGHING IT

Seattle is not as laid back and relaxed as it used to be, and big-city problems have slowly encroached over the last several years. Tons of panhandlers—most of them restless young kids who came in search of Kurt Cobain and never returned home—roam the streets, begging for money and hurling insults at passersby. In retaliation, the city recently passed an ordinance that outlaws sidewalk-sitting in commercial areas 7 AM–9 PM daily.

City parks close at night. Technically, you can be arrested if you decide to sleep in one. However, the police usually won't bother with illegal campers unless there's a complaint—and even then they almost always issue a warning first. Consider the risks carefully before setting up camp: Unless you like danger, avoid Capitol Hill's Volunteer Park, site of several recent assaults, and the small parks Downtown. If you don't mind the hard floor, smoke-clouded air, and wandering drunks, you can call the Greyhound Station (see Coming and Going, above) home 24 hours a day.

Food

It's not difficult to eat cheaply in Seattle. During the day and early evening, you can't go wrong at **Pike Place Market**, where vendors sell everything from burritos and souvlaki to pasta salad, pizza, and pastries. Buy produce and fresh fish here and cook your own dinner if you're staying at one of the many motels with kitchenettes. At the **Waterfront,** touristy restaurants and fast-food joints serve seafood to diners enjoying views of Elliott Bay and the Olympic Mountains. Around the university campus, a seven-block stretch of **University Avenue** is packed with inexpensive restaurants and fast-food joints, while on **Capitol Hill** streets to explore include E. Broadway (specializing in Thai and fast food) and 15th Avenue E, which has a good collection of breakfast places and more intimate establishments. In general, Seattle is loaded with Mexican and vegetarian restaurants, both of which tend to be cheap.

Throw cholesterol cares to the wind when you eat at **Dick's** (Capitol Hill: 115 Broadway, at E. Denny Way, tel. 206/323-1300; University: 111 N.E. 45th St., at 1st Ave., tel. 206/632-5125), a Seattle institution. Food is served through a take-out window, and diners enjoy views of a parking lot, a

Spicy-food junkies will revel in the large number of affordable Thai restaurants in town, especially around Capitol Hill. The International District offers the best values on Asian cuisines like Cantonese, Szechuan, Japanese, Vietnamese, and Cambodian.

string of stores, and a never-ending flow of cars and drunks. It's not bad when you consider that a burger, shake, and fries cost only $3. If Dick's greasy fare doesn't grab you, consider the seafood at **Ivar's Salmon House** (Queen Anne: 333 Elliott Ave. W, tel. 206/284–7040; University: 4755 12th Ave. NE, tel. 206/527–7961, and 401 N.E. North Lake Way, at 4th Ave., tel. 206/632–0767). An order of fish and chips costs just over $4.

Those who have a kitchen at their disposal but have no interest in pushing through the crowds at Pike Place Market should head to one of the supermarkets around the city. Gourmet **QFC**, which has freshly made basics and some truly bizarre produce (in addition to the usual brand-name stuff) isn't much pricier than the grocery shopper's standby, **Safeway**. The two can usually be found in pairs about a block apart. Closest to Downtown are the ones in the Queen Anne district: From 1st Avenue take Bus 15 or 18 and get off at 1st Avenue N and Republican Street. In Capitol Hill, you'll find them on Broadway E, accessible from Downtown on Bus 7 or 10.

PIKE PLACE MARKET

At Downtown's Pike Place Market, bordered by Western and 1st avenues and Virginia and Pike streets, wall-to-wall restaurants, food stalls, and fresh produce stands feature an awesome array of ethnic foods, baked goods, locally caught seafood, and seasonal fruits and vegetables. To eat inexpensively Downtown, skip the restaurants and buy the makings for a mega-sandwich here. Take-out stands are cheapest ($3 and up), but almost all meals cost less than $10. Tables and public benches are found throughout the market. Or, on one of those rare Seattle days when the sky is clear, take your purchases to **Steinbrueck Park** (near the market's north end) and picnic on the lawn overlooking Elliott Bay—you may find some unsavory characters here, but it's generally safe during the day. Other cheap Downtown options include **Burrito Express** (Pike St. and 1st Ave., no phone), in front of the Economy Market Atrium, which serves gigantic veggie, chicken, or beef burritos ($3.35) and soft tacos ($3.25). **Cucina Fresca** (1904 Pike Pl., tel. 206/448–4758) is a good place to pick up the makings for a low-cost gourmet Italian picnic. The hot garlic bread ($1.20) is unforgettable if you *really* like garlic. Pasta salads ($4) and fresh focaccia bread ($1.75) are also excellent.

UNDER $5 **Café Counter Intelligence.** Overlooking the Pike Place Market, this tiny, artsy third-floor café whips up extra-special breakfasts, gourmet vegetarian meals, and unique milk-shakes and espresso drinks—like their devastating Dutch chocolate shake ($3.25). The rice cream ($4.50) is similar to rice pudding but made tastier by a topping of cinnamon and honey. Waffles ($4) arrive decked with fresh fruit, and the cinnamon toast ($2.75) is perfect for small appetites. Because the café is hard to find, it's one place where you won't have to worry about crowds. *94 Pike St., Suite 32, tel. 206/622–6979. On 3rd level of the Corner Market Building. Open Wed.–Sat. 9–5, Sun. 10–3.*

El Puerco Lloran. One of the most authentic Mexican restaurant in Seattle, El Puerco offers bay views, indoor and outdoor seating, and festive decor. Listening to traditional music as you sit at a tiny folding table beneath brightly painted walls, you'll swear you're in Tijuana. A modest menu of homemade foods is served at south-of-the-border prices; three taquitos with beans and rice is $4.50. Salsa is free, but tortilla chips will cost you. *1501 Western Ave., tel. 206/624–0541. At the Pike Place Market Hillclimb. Open Mon.–Sat. 11:30–9, Sun. noon–7.*

Pier 54 is home to the original Ivar's Acres of Clams (tel. 206/624–6852), a chain of fish bars serving fried cod, salmon, clams, and shrimp at very reasonable prices. A bowl of clam chowder is $2.69; oysters and chips are $4.80.

Emmett Watson's Oyster Bar. Inexpensive chowders and a selection of over 50 beers make this courtyard restaurant a thrill for seafood lovers. Oysters and chips ($4.75) and their infamous Puget Sound salmon soup with aioli ($5.95) definitely make this place worth a visit. *1916 Pike Pl., tel. 206/ 448–7721. Open daily 11:30 AM–9 PM.*

Kosher Delight. This is the best (and only) place in Seattle to satisfy an itch for authentic deli food. They sell sandwiches ($5), falafel ($3.95), and Dr. Brown's, too! *1509 1st Ave., at Pike St., tel. 206/682–8140. Open Sun.–Fri. 7–6; shorter hrs on Fri. in winter.*

UNDER $10 **Abruzzi Pizza House.** Though not much to look at from the outside, Abruzzi employs two guys from Italy who cook some of the best Italian food in town. Spread out in one of the big open booths and enjoy enormous portions of pasta ($7) and pizza ($8 and up). Expect a line for takeout on weekdays. *604 Pike St., at 6th Ave., tel. 206/624–8122. Across from the Sheraton Hotel. Open Mon.–Sat. 11–9.*

Café Septieme. This totally trendy café really can't get over itself, but the food is delicious, so bear with the attitude. The brioche raisin French toast with fruit and sausage ($5.75) is a breakfast best. At lunch and dinner, look for the Caesar salad ($5.50) and vegetarian lasagna ($7.50). *2331 2nd Ave., tel. 206/448–1506. Open weekdays 7 AM–midnight, weekends 9 AM–midnight.*

Crocodile Café. This café has slipped from its former position as the town's hippest spot, but it still has funky decor, good food, and the occasional evening jam session by a local band. Sandwiches hot ($6.25) and cold ($5.45) come with a fat side of fries, and the ratatouille omelet ($6.25) is enough food for an entire day. The "homefries from heck" with onions and salsa ($4) are rumored to be a great hangover cure. *2200 2nd Ave., at Blanchard St., tel. 206/448–2114. Open Tues.–Fri. 7 AM–10 PM, Sat. 8 AM–midnight, Sun. 9–3.*

Gravity Bar. Whoever designed the Gravity Bar couldn't decide between using *The Jetsons* and *Land of the Lost* as a decorating motif, but there's no confusion about the purpose of this restaurant. The juice bar offers wheat grass specials like the Mama Hopper (apple, banana, ginger, and wheat grass), and the Crispi sandwich ($6) is an amazing mix of pesto, goat cheese, and tomatoes. *113 Virginia St., btw 1st and 2nd Aves., tel. 206/448–8826. Open Mon.–Thurs. 11–9, Fri. 11–10, Sat. 10–10, Sun. 10–8.*

The Gravity Bar, where vegetarianism and hip decor coincide, is a candidate for the coolest eatery in Seattle.

Mama's Mexican Kitchen. On the northern fringe of Downtown, this Mexican joint—complete with mariachis and piñatas—has become a meeting spot for the "in" crowd who hang in the Belltown neighborhood. If it's nice out, sit on the sidewalk and slurp Mama's strawberry margaritas ($3) and super nachos ($5). Big eaters should choose the enchilada and taco combo or a tamale plate with rice, beans, and salad ($7.50). *2234 2nd Ave., at Bell St., Belltown, tel. 206/728–6262. Open Mon.–Sat. 11 AM–midnight, Sun. 5 PM–11 PM.*

UNDER $15 **Kells.** Kells is an Irish pub/restaurant serving hearty traditional dishes that wash down well with a pint of ale—a meat pie is $9, and Dublin coddle, a concoction of sausage, potato, cabbage, onion, and pepper, is $5.95. Wednesday through Saturday nights, live Irish folk music turns this Emerald City haunt into a rowdy outpost of the Emerald Isle. Entrées range from $8 to $20. *1916 Post Alley, btw Virginia and Stewart Sts., tel. 206/728–1916. Food served daily 11:30 AM–2:30 PM and 5–9 PM.*

PIONEER SQUARE

Sadly, the restoration of historic Pioneer Square (1st Avenue between Cherry and S. Jackson streets) did not include the restoration of bygone prices. Though bars abound, most restaurants in this neighborhood are out of a budget traveler's range. At a few isolated places, however, you'll find good food without having to empty your wallet. **Bagel Express** (205 1st Ave. S, near Yesler Way, tel. 206/682–7207) is your basic bagel stop with a terrific tuna melt ($3.05) and bagel "eggspress" ($2.30). In the Howard Building, **Pioneer Square Pizza** (614 1st Ave., tel. 206/343–9103) sells pizzas by the slice ($1.75) and by the pie ($7.50 and up).

UNDER $5 **Walter's Waffles.** This place makes a daytime excursion to Pioneer Square worthwhile. A plain waffle ($1.50) with cinnamon and sugar is fine, but the chocolate-dipped ones will make your day—particularly with a rich cup of latte ($2). Grilled Italian sandwiches, like the turkey and cheese with mozzarella and oregano ($4.75), are excellent. *106 James St., at 1st Ave., tel. 206/382–2692. Open weekdays 7–5, Sat. 10–4.*

UNDER $10 **New Orleans Creole Restaurant.** This joint does it up with romantic lighting and rich velvet curtains covering the walls. Enjoy nightly blues and jazz (*see* After Dark, *below*) while sipping a Richard Beal mint julep ($3.50) and dining on pan-fried oysters ($5.50), crawfish bisque ($2), or the Lousiana shrimp and oyster jambalaya ($9.25), which is big enough for two. *114 1st Ave. S, tel. 206/622–2563. Open daily 4 PM–11 PM.*

CAPITOL HILL

You have a couple of different options when you want to find a place to eat in the neighborhood of Capitol Hill (generally bounded by E. Denny Way on the south, I–5 on the west, and various bodies of water on the north and east). You can cruise **Broadway E** between Denny Way and Mercer Street to find funky budget joints where dudes and dudettes clad in leather and Doc Martens tend to socialize. Six blocks to the east, the quieter and less crowded **15th Avenue E** also yields a wealth of eclectic, low-priced offerings. Either can be reached from Downtown on Bus 10. If you can get over the name, **Macheezmo Mouse Healthy Mexican Food** (211 Broadway E, at John St., tel. 206/325–0072) is great for a cheap, filling meal. Burritos ($4) and enchiladas ($4) are made with fresh ingredients. It's a fairly sterile environment, so take it to go and eat outside.

UNDER $5 **Bagel Spot.** Indecisive people will hate the Bagel Spot, where freshly made bagels (45¢) come in billions of flavors, and spreads include varieties like strawberry and jalapeño. Most sandwiches are around $3.50. *408 Broadway E, tel. 206/325–9407. Open weekdays 7–6, weekends 8–6.*

Pagliacci. Hungry or not, you can't walk past Pagliacci without suddenly being stricken by the desire to eat. Fresh, fragrant, and cheap offerings like the sundried tomato pizza ($2.25 per slice) or pesto pasta salad ($2.25) may have something to do with it. *426 Broadway E, tel. 206/324–0730. Open Sun.–Thurs. 11–11, Fri.–Sat. 11 AM–1 AM.*

UNDER $10 **Broadway Grill.** This place is popular for its late-night hours and sidewalk patio. More than just a char-a-slab-of-beef establishment, they serve terrific appetizers like wood-broiled veggie skewers ($8.95) and grilled chicken sesame salad ($7.95), as well as dishes like the grilled brie and chicken sandwich ($6.95). *314 Broadway E, tel. 206/328–7000. Open weekdays 10 AM–2 AM, weekends 9 AM–2 AM.*

Coastal Kitchen. The Coastal Kitchen takes an around-the-world-in-ninety-days approach: Every three months a different coastal cuisine—like the Italian Riviera or Mexico's Pacific coast—is highlighted. For lunch and dinner, the creative sandwiches ($5–$6.75) and various pastas make tasty choices, but the real meal here is breakfast, served daily until 3 PM. Blueberry pancakes ($4.25) are most popular; Charleston breakfast shrimp ($7.35) with sausage, cornbread, and eggs may be pricier, but it's amazing. *429 15th Ave. E, at Republican St., tel. 206/322–1145. Open Mon.–Thurs. 8:30 AM–10 PM, Fri. 8:30 AM–11 PM, Sat. 8:30–3 and 5–11, Sun. 8:30–3 and 5–10.*

Deluxe Bar and Grill. On a sunny day, sit on the outdoor patio and enjoy one or two or more of the great beers of Seattle with this restaurant's extremely good pub food, like the barbecue burger ($5.95) or a huge portion of onion rings ($5.25). Don't expect to get in and out too quickly; the constant crowds mean that service can be slow. Happy hour happens twice every weekday, 3 PM–7 PM and 11 PM–1 AM. *625 Broadway E, tel. 206/324–9697. Open daily 11 AM–2 AM.*

Hamburger Mary's. Hamburger Mary's serves amazing breakfasts day and night. Sure, you can get boring eggs benedict ($6.50), but why bother when the same price brings you veggie benedict (grilled tomatoes, onions, peppers, and mushrooms instead of that same ol' slab o' ham). Their "world's greatest hamburger" is pretty damn close to perfection; order it with any of your favorite toppings for $5. Those who spurn charred cow flesh can opt for the grilled veggie delight ($4.95). This place has a fun atmosphere and a major gay clientele. *1525 E. Olive Way, at Denny Way, tel. 206/325–6565. Open daily 7 AM–2 AM.*

Jack's Bistro. This lively indoor/outdoor bistro serves light meals for under $4 and full dinners for under $10. Worth trying are the curry chicken salad ($5.50) and fettuccine gorgonzola ($8.95). Breakfast is their most popular meal. *405 15th Ave. E, tel. 206/324–9625. Open Tues.–Sat. 8 AM–10 PM, Sun.–Mon. 8 AM–3 PM.*

Siam on Broadway. On weekend nights prepare to wait up to an hour for a table at this tiny restaurant, the local favorite for Thai food. Entrées vary in spiciness from mild to four-alarm. The vegetables in peanut sauce ($5.75) get high honors. *616 Broadway E, btw Mercer and Roy Sts., tel. 206/324–0892. Open Mon.–Thurs. 11:30–10, Fri. 11:30–11, Sat. 5–11, Sun. 5–10.*

Wildrose. For some inscrutable reason, the chefs at Wildrose whip up an interpretation of Thanksgiving dinner every day. Take the turkey and cranberry on a sandwich ($4.50), with freshly baked bread or with a side of fried polenta ($5.25). Though the kitchen closes at 10 PM, once the bar starts to fill (around 8), it's hardly a relaxing spot to dine. Wildrose is a favorite of the gay community. *1021 E. Pike St., tel. 206/324–9210. Open Sun.–Thurs. 11 AM–midnight, Fri. and Sat. 11 AM–2 AM.*

INTERNATIONAL DISTRICT

The current title of this neighborhood, formerly called Chinatown, more accurately reflects the diversity of cultures crowded into the 10–15 blocks around Kingdome Stadium at Downtown's southeastern corner. You'll find a variety of inexpensive restaurants on the stretch between S. Weller and Washington streets and 2nd and 12th avenues.

UNDER $10 **Chau's Chinese Restaurant.** The Cantonese-style seafood dishes at Chau's make the rest of the district's restaurants seem about as exciting as three-week-old fish. Go for the food, not the atmosphere—you're here to eat the steamed oysters with garlic sauce ($6.50) and the Dungeness crab ($7 per pound), not enjoy the tacky decor. *310 4th Ave. S, at Jackson St., tel. 206/621–0006. Open weekdays 11 AM–midnight, Sat. 4 PM–12:30 AM, Sun. 4 PM–11 PM.*

House of Hong. Choose from an extensive menu offering over 75 dishes at this elegant Cantonese establishment, where lunch specials are $5–$6. On weekends, crowds come for the excellent dim sum. *409 8th Ave. S, at Jackson St., tel. 206/622–7997. Open Sun.–Thurs. 11–10, Fri. and Sat. 11 AM–midnight.*

A Little Bit of Saigon and **Pho 88.** The mom-and-pop atmosphere of the area's smaller establishments may be lacking at this giant Vietnamese eatery and the adjacent take-out shop, but the soups (about $3) and beef dishes ($3–$6) are a favorite of transplanted natives; rarely will you hear a word of English spoken here. There's not much here for vegetarians. *1036A S. Jackson St., tel. 206/325–3663 (Saigon) and 206/325–0180 (Pho 88). In the Asian Plaza. Both open daily 9 AM–10 PM.*

THE UNIVERSITY DISTRICT

Dominating the scene along **University Way NE** between 40th and 52nd streets is a diverse group of ethnic restaurants frequented by a mixture of students and faculty (and the occasional person completely unaffiliated with the University of Washington). You can reach "The Ave," as it's referred to by locals, on Buses 70–74 from Downtown. Since restaurants cater to slim student budgets, it's an excellent trip to take if you're short on cash. Prices are generally under $5 for a full meal. Neighborhoods bordering the U-District, such as **Fremont** and **Wallingford,** tend to be inhabited by young families and upwardly mobile singles—making them equally fertile grounds for restaurants.

Just dogs (and tons of 'em) cross the counter at **Shultzy's Sausages** (4142 University Way NE, tel. 206/548–9461), a gourmet hot dog stand where franks ($2.50–$3.50) dress in unexpected condiments like marinara and parmesan. **Bruegger's Bagel Bakery** (4517 University Way NE, tel. 206/545–0828) will slap sandwich stuff—tuna, turkey, or ham—on a bagel ($3.50), sell it naked (49¢), or cover it with one of several flavored cream cheeses.

UNDER $5 **The Black Cat Cafe.** A collectively run vegetarian restaurant, this is the place to enjoy latte ($1.10) and pastries while reading the massive assortment of local and national political publications, or catch a free movie (10:30 PM most Saturdays) and dig into some homemade ice cream. Food—always fresh and usually organic—can be prepared either vegetarian or vegan. House favorites include veggie biscuits and gravy ($2) and *chilagurres*—eggs scrambled with tortillas, salsa, and potatoes ($4.50). It's a great place to meet people if you're traveling alone. *4110 Roosevelt Way NE, tel. 206/547–3887. 4 blocks west of University Way. Open Tues.–Sun. 10–9.*

Cedar's Restaurant. Come here for authentic Middle Eastern and Mediterranean food like gyros and falafel ($3). Just to keep things exciting, there are occasional specials like gyros with feta cheese ($4). Business is primarily take-out, so there's only a small eating area. *1319 N.E. 43rd St., at University Way, tel. 206/632–7708. Open daily 11:30–8:30.*

Flowers. The best bargain in town may be the vegetarian hot buffet (11 AM–4 PM) at Flowers, where an all-you-can-eat lunch ($5.50) includes noodles, curries, rice dishes, and sautéed vegetables. Dinner includes sandwiches ($5) such as turkey and roasted eggplant, and serious dishes like chicken kabobs with fresh vegetables ($6). After dark there's a cool bar scene with occasional live entertainment, $1 tequila shots (Wednesdays), and $1 beers (Thursdays). *4247 University Way NE, tel. 206/633–1903. Open daily 11 AM–2 AM.*

Poco Loco. Seating may be scarce (actually, it's nonexistent), but Poco Loco does boast big and very tasty burritos ($3.50); choose from vegetarian, chicken, or beef. Crispy tacos are a steal at $1.75 each. *4518 University Way NE, tel. 206/548–9877. Open daily 11–6:30.*

Proud Bird. The Bird serves inexpensive, savory Cantonese and Mandarin Chinese cuisine. Try the chow mein ($4) or Mongolian beef ($4). All dishes come with egg roll, potsticker, steamed rice, fortune cookie, and plenty of green tea. With all that, who cares if the decor lacks style? *4234 University Way NE, tel. 206/632–7248. Open Sun.–Thurs. 10–10, Fri.–Sat. 11 AM–midnight.*

UNDER $10 **Sunlight Café.** The down-to-earth patrons at this extremely popular vegetarian café describe themselves as the "counter culture," since they're always to be found downing chow at Sunlight's counter. On weekends, customers line up at the door for the eggless sesame crunch waffle ($3); the favored daily lunch is the combo soup, salad, and bread ($5). All dinner entrées (around $8) are served with salad and soup, and portions are huge. *6403 Roosevelt Way NE, at 64th St., tel. 206/522–9060. 4 blocks west of University Way. Open daily 7 AM–10 PM.*

Best Late-Night Noshing Spots

- *Steve's Broiler (1937 4th Ave., Downtown, tel. 206/441–5377) tends to attract more drinkers than eaters, though the popular lounge/diner serves fine steaks, fish, and omelets. Open 24 hours.*

- *The Sea Garden (509 7th Ave. S, International District, tel. 206/623–2100) serves excellent Cantonese seafood. Expect to wait for a table, even late at night. Open weekdays until 2 AM, weekends until 3.*

- *Trattoria Mitchelli's (84 E. Yesler Way, Pioneer Square, tel. 206/623–3883) is a favorite of pub crawlers seeking midnight supper, so expect a wait. Most of the creative pizza and pasta dishes are under $8. Open daily until 4 AM.*

- *Tai Tung (659 S. King St., International District, tel. 206/622–7372) can't be topped for a quick and filling bowl of Chinese noodles ($4). Open Mon.–Sat. until 3 AM, Sun. until 1 AM.*

- *Triangle Tavern (3507 Fremont Pl. N, Fremont, tel. 206/632–0880), though primarily a bar, serves up generous sandwiches and other grub ($4–$6) with sides of Caesar salad. Open Mon.–Sat. until 2 AM, Sun. until midnight.*

DESSERT/COFFEEHOUSES

The yuppies of the '80s may have had health clubs, junk bonds, and cocaine, but in the '90s we've got stellar coffeehouses, poetry readings, and wicked triple lattes—largely thanks to Seattle. Seattle's addiction to good coffee made from freshly roasted beans is an addiction that has recently spread to grip the entire country. And while the number of coffee concoctions can be seemingly infinite, every Seattle resident will passionately tout his or her favorite (lattes seem to have the biggest following). But the whole coffee craze is not just about consuming caffeine—it's also about the café. Cafés have taken over as the city's social centers, where everyone mixes, regardless of age, sexual preference, or background. To find out what's going on at cafés around town, pick up *The Bean* (free), a monthly compilation of great café reads—ranging from book reviews to short fiction. It's available at most newsstands and coffeehouses.

Seattle's coffee craze began in 1970 with three entrepreneurs selling gourmet beans and home-brewing machinery from a shop called **Starbucks.** Other players soon entered the scene, but Starbucks has continued to sells its brews from what seems like every block in Seattle (and now other parts of the country as well). At most outlets you'll find a steel coffee bar where you can stand or sit, a few sleek tables, and shelves of bagged beans and coffee paraphernalia for sale. It's not the kind of coffeehouse where you'd pass an entire day, so don't expect to settle down with a book. *Pike Place Market: 1912 Pike Pl., tel. 206/448–8762; Downtown: 1100 4th Ave., at Spring St., tel. 206/467–7773; Capitol Hill: 434 Broadway E, tel. 206/323–7888; University: 4555 University Way NE, tel. 206/634–1390; many other Starbucks locations throughout Seattle and the rest of the known world.*

PIKE PLACE MARKET **SBC Coffee.** Originally called Steward Brothers' Coffee and later renamed Seattle's Best, this is one of the city's major suppliers of gourmet beans. Most of the five SBC outlets in the Seattle area are modern-looking, but the one at Pike Place Market has a rustic feel—and plenty of outdoor tables excellent for people-watching. SBC serves hot cider as well as coffee. *Pike Place Market: 1530 Post Alley, at Pine St., tel. 206/467–7700; Downtown: 506 Union St., btw 5th and 6th Aves., tel. 206/622–7286; Westlake Center: 400 Pine St., at 4th Ave., tel. 206/682–7182.*

CAPITOL HILL **B&O Espresso.** Designed to resemble a late-18th-century drawing room, this classy café is filled with wide tables and wingback chairs covered in rich floral fabrics. Neighborhood residents pop in at least once, if not twice, a day: First to fuel up before work, and then again for a late-night latte ($1.50) and a piece of insanely good pie ($3.50) or a brownie ($2.20). Breakfast also brings in the regulars, especially for the sour cream waffles with fruit and cream ($3.95). The two other locations (Capitol Hill: 401 Broadway E, tel. 206/328–3290; West Seattle: 2352 California Ave. SW, tel. 206/935–1540) have the same great desserts, but not the same great ambiance. *204 Belmont Ave. E, at Olive Way, tel. 206/322–5028. Open Mon.–Thurs. 7:30 AM–midnight, Fri. 7:30 AM–1 AM, Sat. 9 AM–1 AM, Sun. 9 AM–midnight.*

Bauhaus. This combination bookstore/coffeehouse is trying hard (maybe too hard) to achieve an intellectual, alternative atmosphere. The book selection is very interesting, and the lattes ($1.35) are great—just don't be surprised if you overhear overdressed patrons yammering about Djerassi. *301 E. Pine St., at Melrose Ave., tel. 206/625–1600. Just east of I–5. Open weekdays 6 AM–1 AM, weekends 8 AM–1 AM.*

Dilettante Chocolates. Mouth-watering chocolates and desserts are the specialty at Dilettante. Stay away unless you're serious about sweets; the real goodies, like the Grand Marnier truffle torte, cost about $5. If you can, settle for a glazed brownie (under $2) and a latte ($1.50). A recent expansion means there's plenty of room to stretch out and watch the crowds. *416 Broadway E, tel. 206/329–6463. Open Mon.–Thurs. 7 AM–midnight, Fri. 7 AM–1AM, Sat. 8 AM–1 AM, Sun. 8 AM–midnight. Also at Pike Place Market (retail store only): 1603 1st Ave., at Post Alley, tel. 206/728–9144. Open daily 11–5.*

Harvard Espresso Gallery. Here's a true pro-neighborhood institution: The same local artist is always featured on its walls. Sip a hazelnut liqueur ($2) and indulge in a chocolate brownie ($1.50) while mulling over a game of chess, either on the balcony or at a table outdoors. *810 E. Roy St., at Broadway, tel. 206/323–7598. Across from the Harvard Exit Theater. Open Sun.–Thurs. 8:30 AM–11 PM, Fri. and Sat. 8:30–midnight.*

Pacific Dessert Company. This dessert lover's paradise could also be Oprah Winfrey's biggest nightmare, since everything here is sinfully tasty and fattening. The chocolate cake ($3.50) and tarts ($2.50 each) may even change your life (or at least enhance your weight). Start your day with a latte ($2), and skip pouring that pink packet into the coffee—at this point, it won't help. *420 E. Denny Way, tel. 206/328–1950. Open weekdays 7–7, Sat. 8 AM–9 PM, Sun 8–6.*

Café Paradiso. This increasingly popular late-night coffeehouse at times feels more like a nightclub than a café. There's always a show of local art, too. When it's not packed, Paradiso's a great place to catch up on some reading or shmooze with the regulars. Beyond coffee drinks ($1.50) and pastries, they serve excellent snacks like bagels ($2) and calzones ($2.50–$4.50). *1005 E. Pike St., tel. 206/322–6960. Open Mon.–Thurs. 6 AM–1 AM, Fri. 6 AM–4 AM, Sat. 8 AM–4 AM, Sun. 8 AM–1 AM.*

PIONEER SQUARE Torrefazione. Many locals insist that Torrefazione has raised the art of coffee-brewing to new heights. While it's more yuppie than hip, a seat by the coffee roaster or along the cobblestone street does give the full effect of being in an urbane Italian café. Latte costs $1.35. *320 Occidental Ave. S, at Jackson St., tel. 206/624–5773. Also in Capitol Hill: 622 Olive St., tel. 206/624–1429. Open weekdays 7–6, Sat. 9–6.*

THE UNIVERSITY DISTRICT Café Allegro. The strongest coffee in the U-District is poured at hard-to-find-Allegro, where boisterous political discussions abound. The front room (smoking permitted) is noisier and offers better vantage points than the less-crowded back room (smoking prohibited). Leave notes for lost friends on the bulletin board at the register. Lattes are $1.60. *4214 University Way NE, btw 42nd and 43rd Sts., tel. 206/633–3030. From N.E. 45th St. go south on University Way; Allegro will be in the alley on the left. Open weekdays 7 AM–11 PM, Sat. 7:30 AM–11 PM, Sun. 8:30 AM–11 PM.*

Espresso Roma. Students have a love/hate relationship with the cheap coffee found at this spacious, funky café. Though the coffee is sub-par and the room is messy, it's still fun to come here with a boisterous group (or even by yourself for a highly rated evening of eavesdropping). Provocative local art covers the gray cement walls, and large windows provide a panorama of The Ave. Huge lattes and enormous brownies are about $1.50 each. *4201 University Way NE, at 42nd St., tel. 206/632–6001. Also in Capitol Hill: 202 Broadway E, tel. 206/324–1866. Open weekdays 7 AM–11 PM, weekends 8:30 AM–11 PM.*

Grand Illusion Espresso and Pastry. Filled with students chatting or taking a snooze, this smoke-free vegetarian café lures locals with its fresh, homemade food. The soup-and-bread special ($2) changes daily, but the Russian cabbage borscht is a perennial favorite. Food can be taken out to the wooden terrace or into the attached theater (*see* After Dark, *below*). Most espresso drinks are around $1.60. *1405 N.E. 50th St., tel. 206/525–9573. Open weekdays 8:30 AM–11 PM, weekends 8:30 AM–11:30 PM.*

The Last Exit on Brooklyn. One of Seattle's oldest coffeehouses is filled with leftovers from the Beat Generation, who sip lattes ($1) and feast on one of more than 20 kinds of sandwiches, including the ever-popular peanut butter and jelly (under $2). Entertainment includes customers strumming their guitars or playing the café's piano; heated games of chess and solitaire; and an open mike on Monday nights. Tables in the backyard are available for enjoyment on those rare sunny days. *5201 University Way NE, tel. 206/526–9155. Open Mon.–Thurs. 7 AM–11 PM, Fri. 7 AM–1 AM, Sat. 8 AM–1 AM, Sun. 9 AM–midnight.*

Exploring Seattle

Before setting out, devise a sightseeing strategy. If your time is limited, focus on the major sights and attractions Downtown along Elliott Bay: **The Seattle Center, Pike Place Market, the Waterfront, Pioneer Square,** and the **International District.** All of the above sights lie along the Waterfront Streetcar route and (except for the Seattle Center) within the city bus Ride Free Area (*see* Getting Around, *above*). Of course, if you have more time you'd be crazy to limit yourself to Downtown. **Discovery Park,** one of the city's most beautiful attractions, overlooks Puget Sound well north of the urban snarl. To the

Bracketed between Puget Sound and Lake Washington, and punctuated by several more large lakes, Seattle isn't just about grunge and good coffee: It's about water. All you need is a sunny afternoon to join in the fun with a hike around Discovery Park or a canoeing session out on Lake Union (see Parks and Gardens, below).

northeast, **Capitol Hill,** with its funky restaurants and bars, outrageous parade of fashions, and prominent gay and lesbian communities, is an excellent neighborhood for a day's stroll. Add another day or two and you can also explore the area north of **Lake Union,** hitting the zoo, Green Lake Park, and all the shops along University Way.

WORTH SEEING

ART MUSEUM—DOWNTOWN This new $62 million structure was designed by acclaimed postmodernist architect Robert Venturi, who recently completed a wing for the National Gallery in London. The new building, which uses motifs of Pacific Northwestern Native Americans, tripled the museum's previous exhibition space. Inside, the imposing marble staircase leads past funerary sculpture to a mezzanine-level café, while special exhibits occupy the second floor. Japanese, Chinese, Korean, and pre-Islamic art—including a full-scale replica of a Japanese tea room—fill half of the third floor; the other half focuses on Native American art from the Pacific Northwest. Fourth floor exhibits concentrate on works from ancient Egypt to modern Europe. There's also an outstanding collection of contemporary Northwestern art. Outside, look for the amusing three-story-tall *Hammering Man* sculpture by Jonathan Borofsky, at the corner of University Street and 1st Avenue. *100 University St., btw 1st and 2nd Aves., tel. 206/654–3137 or 206/654–3100. 2 blocks south of Pike Place Market. Admission: $6, $4 students. Open Tues.–Sat. 10–5, Thurs. 10–9, Sun. noon–5. Wheelchair access.*

BALLARD LOCKS Built between 1911 and 1917 to facilitate ship travel between Puget Sound and Washington and Union Lakes, the locks (known formally as the Hiram M. Chittenden Locks) are like water elevators, lowering or raising boats to appropriate levels as they pass between fresh and salt water. A fish ladder performs a similar function for salmon traveling between the ocean and the freshwater hatcheries where they spawn. You'll spy salmon swimming the various ladder rungs through special underground viewing windows; most of the fish swim by between mid-June and October. When you've had enough, check out the 7-acre **Ornamental Gardens** (free) on the north side of the grounds. And just east of the locks is the Scandinavian neighborhood of **Ballard,** a mecca for fans of both blues music (*see* After Dark, *below*) and old neighborhood taverns. The locks are a 20-minute drive from Downtown. *3015 N.W. 54th St., west of Ballard Bridge, tel. 206/783–7001 or 206/783–7059. From Downtown, take Bus 17. Admission free. Grounds open daily 7 AM–9 PM; visitor center open summer, daily 10–7, winter, Thurs.–Mon. 11–5.*

BILL SPIEDEL'S UNDERGROUND TOUR After the Great Seattle Fire of 1889, jittery municipal leaders decided to make life easier for firefighters by flattening the city. Laborers cut peaks and raised valleys, filled in entire city blocks, and transformed first floors into basements almost overnight. The 1½-hour Underground Tour explores the "dirt, corruption, sewers, and scandal" of the old first-floor sidewalks and storefronts that are now a half-dozen feet below historic Pioneer Square. Given by young comedians (who are actually very funny), the tours begin at Doc Maynard's Public House, a carefully restored 1892 saloon, and include a 20-minute comic overview of Seattle's history. From there, into the sewers you go. Rodent-haters should skip the underground portions; rats cruise those passages like they own the place. Tours run three to seven times daily. *610 1st Ave., Pioneer Square, tel. 206/682–1511 or 206/682–4646. From Downtown, take Bus 15, 18, 22, or 23 to Yesler Way. Admission: $5.95, $4.30 students.*

BOEING FIELD AND THE MUSEUM OF FLIGHT Despite what you might believe, Boeing, not Starbucks, is Seattle's major economic base. The company—the world's leading aircraft manufacturer—has a monstrously big assembly factory on the 62-acre Boeing Paine Field; tours give you an incredibly interesting peek at the nuts and bolts of flight. Since space on the free 90-minute tour fills up quickly, arrive early. *Tel. 206/342–4801. From I–5, take Rte. 526 (Exit 189) and go west 3½ mi to tour center exit. Call for tour times.*

After the tour, wing it over to the adjacent **Museum of Flight,** which describes the history of planes with lots of written information. The Great Gallery houses 20 airplanes, some dating to the turn of the century. The Red Barn exhibit, about the birth of Boeing, explains the company's role in the development of flight. *9404 E. Marginal Way S, tel. 206/764–5720. From Downtown, take Bus 174 or 950. Admission: $6. Open daily 10–5, Thurs. until 9.*

DISCOVERY PARK Most Seattleites consider the 15-minute drive from Downtown a small price to pay for a day at Discovery Park, bordering Puget Sound north of Elliott Bay. A few officers' homes and an old cemetery are the only reminders of the 520-acre park's former role as a military base. Now, nature reigns. Wide grassy hills and an open meadow are perfect for picnicking and kite-flying. In the surrounding thick forest, miles of trails and coastal paths wind, occasionally emerging on scenic overlooks. (On sunny days, look for brilliant Mt. Rainier from vantage points along the park's southern coast.) A walking tour of the **2.8-mile loop trail** favored by joggers will introduce you to the park's varied terrain. The southern stretch of the park's 2-mile beachfront is sandy, while the rocky northern section is home to marine life like crabs and periwinkles. For a map and detailed trail information, stop by the **visitor center** just inside the East Gate. *3801 W. Government Way, tel. 206/386–4236. From Downtown, take Bus 19 or 33. Open daily dawn–dusk.*

GREEN LAKE On sunny days, all of Seattle pours into this park about 5 miles north of Downtown. Its primary function (which should sorely disappoint solitude-seekers and nature

Near the main entrance to Green Lake Park, at Woodlawn Avenue N and Ravenna Street, is Spud Fish & Chips (6860 E. Green Lake Way N, tel. 206/524–0565), where crispy sea-critter combos cost less than $4. Cross the street to eat on the grassy slope of the park.

Best Ways to Spend a Warm Day

- *Join the rest of Seattle on the water (in a dinghy, on an inner tube, or atop anything else that floats). The best spot is behind the U.W. Stadium, where Lake Washington runs into Puget Sound.*

- *Picnic on the green at Discovery Park. And bring a camera—if it's clear and sunny, the view of Mt. Rainier is gorgeous.*

- *Fly a kite in Gas Works Park.*

- *Stroll the old tree-lined streets around Volunteer Park.*

- *Bike the Burke-Gillman Trail along the western shore of Lake Washington.*

- *Sunbathe and swim at Madison Park Beach on Lake Washington. (It's not the cleanest water around, but that doesn't stop Seattleites from taking the plunge.)*

lovers) is as a forum for body scoping and lots of self-conscious sporting activity. Circle Green Lake on the 3-mile path and you'll pass basketball and volleyball courts, a softball field, swimming and fishing areas, a pitch-and-putt golf course, tennis courts, and lots of sunbathers. On the east shore is the **Green Lake Activities Center** (tel. 206/527–0171), which rents **paddleboats** ($5 per hour), weather permitting. Bikers and in-line skaters share the path with pedestrians, so watch out if you're on foot. *Community Center: tel. 206/684–0780. From Downtown, take Bus 16 to Woodlawn Ave. N and Ravenna St. Open daily dawn–dusk.*

THE INTERNATIONAL DISTRICT Immigrants from Japan, China, the Philippines, Vietnam, and Laos have all settled in this 10- to 15-block neighborhood at Downtown's southeastern end, filled with authentic restaurants, family-run stores, herbalists' shops, and the offices of practicing acupuncturists. The district is bordered by **S. Washington Street** on the north, **S. Welter Street** on the south, **2nd Avenue S** on the west, and **12th Avenue S** on the east. Chinese workers were the first to move here, after completion of the Transcontinental Railroad in the 1860s, and the district was then known as Chinatown. The name changed six or seven years ago to reflect the area's true composition. Having withstood anti-Chinese riots in the 1880s and the internment of Japanese-Americans during World War II, this neighborhood now flourishes as the Pacific Northwest's pan-Asian cultural center.

The best way to explore the lively streets of the International District is on foot—slowly—taking in the diverse cultures and lifestyles represented. Strips of unusual shops are often tucked behind main avenues on tiny alleys, so explore inquisitively. And if you're lucky, you'll catch the occasional street performance. On **S. Jackson** and **King streets**, grocery stores offer fresh vegetables and fruits and some specialty items at incredibly low prices. Reach the district from other parts of Downtown by taking the Waterfront Streetcar from one of the piers. Or catch a Metro bus: Bus 1 (which becomes Bus 36) passes Pike Place Market and then continues east along S. Jackson Street.

PIERS 54–56 The area between Piers 54 and 56, a few blocks south of the Aquarium and Omnidome (*see below*), is crowded with seafood restaurants and Pacific Rim import shops selling tourist trinkets, pricey basketry and dishware, and the usual cheesy T-shirts. Avoid all except the macabre gift shop/museum **Ye Olde Curiosity Shop** (tel. 206/682–5844) on Pier 54. In addition to the usual overpriced Washington mementos (like those ubiquitous mugs and silver spoons), you'll find a collection of oddities, including Sylvester, Sylvia, and Gloria, the perfectly preserved mummies; shrunken heads; a whale's jawbone; and a stuffed calf with two heads. On Pier 55, **Argosy Cruises** (tel. 206/623–1445) offers a narrated one-hour cruise ($12.50) of Elliott Bay and a 2½-hour excursion ($21.50) through Seattle's Ballard Locks (*see above*). But don't throw down your money for a harbor tour too quickly: Remember, Washington State Ferries (*see* Getting Around, *above*) charges $3.50 for the same ride to Bainbridge Island (minus the soundtrack, of course). From the piers, you can catch the Waterfront Streetcar (*see* Getting Around, *above*) north to Myrtle Edwards Park (*see* Parks and Gardens, *below*) or south to Pioneer Square and the International District.

PIKE PLACE MARKET The Pike Place Market is the heart of Seattle. Not only is it the biggest tourist draw in the city, it's also the daily stomping grounds of real, live Seattleites—who aren't gonna let a bunch of Hawaiian shirts and Eddie Vedder wannabes stand between them and their Alaskan king salmon, fresh spices, flowers, produce, and cheeses. At the southern edge of the Pike Place Market (at the intersection of Pike Place and Pike Street), you'll find a conglomeration of fresh food stands. Walking north through the market you'll pass artisans selling everything from batik clothes to handmade knives and cutting boards; there are so many, they sometimes outnumber the tourists. Staircases with neon signs reading MORE SHOPS lead from the market's enjoyable outdoor section to a maze of cheesy shops, most of which you can skip. But look for the main set of stairs at the market's southwestern corner: They lead down to the Waterfront, where musicians play their instruments and wait for stardom.

The market has been around since 1907, when Washington farmers began boycotting the city's profiteering middlemen in favor of selling their products directly to the public. Despite numerous ups and downs and a foiled attempt at renovation in the '60s, the market has grown ever since. Pick up a "Visitor's Guide to the Public Market" at the **visitor information booth** near the neon-lit PIKE PLACE MARKET sign for more information on the market's history and the independent businesses that thrive here.

To list all the worthwhile joints in the area would take chapters, but one deserves special mention: On the west side of Pike Place, at its intersection with Pike Street, the **Pike Place Fish Company** (86 Pike Pl., tel. 206/682–7181) displays freshly caught salmon, catfish, monkfish, and other delicacies spread over ice. It seems like every other stand in the market—until someone buys a fish. A merchant then sends the creature flying over customers' heads and into the hands of the cashier. The show is free and fun, even if you don't buy. The Pike Place Market is open Monday through Saturday 9–6, and Sunday 11–5. It's accessible from other points Downtown on Bus 15, 18, 22, or 23.

PIONEER SQUARE At night, historic Pioneer Square is the place to go for noisy restaurants, boisterous beer-swilling, and even some good music. During the day, however, it's much more refined: Upscale boutiques, bookstores, and restaurants line the area's four central blocks along **1st Avenue S** between Cherry and S. Jackson streets. Polished brick buildings, some with Romanesque features and terra-cotta trim, suggest that Pioneer Square hasn't changed much since the turn of the century. Actually, when the city's business district relocated during the early decades of the 20th century, the square slowly filled with cheap hotels and whorehouses. A massive restoration project in the early 1970s brought back its historic feel without making it seem antiseptic.

Just south of Pioneer Square is the park where the Seattle Mariners play baseball. Never a popular stadium, the ugly Kingdome reached its nadir in 1994 when huge ceiling tiles fell onto the fortunately empty playing field. Since then, the remaining tiles have been quietly removed and the dome put back in use. Play ball.

Pioneer Square is as old as Seattle itself. In 1853 the clever Henry Yesler installed a steam-powered lumber mill at the base of what is now Yesler Way. Loggers would cut wood at the top of a nearby hill and send it skidding down to the mill along the waterfront. Soon the lawless area around the mill came to be known as the "skid road" area; "road" then became "row," and the rest is etymological history. In 1889, Seattle's Great Fire tore through the neighborhood and reduced the original mill-town buildings to ashes. The oldest structures standing today date from the 1890s and early 1900s and include the iron pergola over **Pioneer Square Park** (1st Ave. at Yesler Way); the Romanesque Revival **Interurban Building** (102–108 Occidental Ave. S); the **Pioneer Building** (1st Ave. at Yesler Way), with its elegant facades and detailed iron grillwork; and **Smith Tower** (506 2nd Ave.), whose 42 floors made it the tallest building west of the Mississippi when it was completed in 1914.

Pioneer Square is about 10 blocks south of Downtown's sights like the Waterfront or Pike Place Market. If you don't want to walk, you can catch Bus 15, 18, 22, or 23 at any stop between Yesler Way and S. Jackson Street.

THE SEATTLE AQUARIUM/OMNIDOME FILM EXPERIENCE The main attraction at Waterfront Park (*see* Parks and Gardens, *below*) is the aquarium, a well-designed maze of exhibits that includes a special glass-paneled underwater dome where you'll observe octopuses, dogfish, eels, and rays cruising serenely by. At the exhibit on sea wildlife, visitors occasionally get to hold some of the animals. And the exhibit dedicated to protecting the environment is also enlightening, though you'll walk away feeling a bit guilty for flushing the toilet. The best time to visit the aquarium is when its inhabitants are being fed (at 11 AM, 11:30, 1:30 PM, 2, and 5). Outside the main entrance (which means it's free), the "Window on Elliott Bay" exhibit features local sea creatures. *Pier 59, at the Pike St. Hillclimb, tel. 206/ 386–4320. Admission: $6.75. Open late May–Sept., daily 10–7; Oct.–late May, daily 10–5.*

The Omnidome Film Experience, adjacent to the aquarium, employs a 100-foot curved dome screen and six 200-watt speakers to surround you with the sights and sounds of the powerful 1980 Mt. Saint Helens eruption. There's also a changing program of nature films about the ocean and its inhabitants. Films are 30 minutes in length. *Pier 59, tel. 206/622–1868. Admission: $6 for 1 film; $8 for 2; $11 for film plus entrance to aquarium. Showings every 40 min weekdays 10 AM–9:20 PM, Fri. and Sat. 10 AM–10:25 PM. Schedule may vary in winter; call ahead.*

SEATTLE CENTER AND QUEEN ANNE HILL The city built the 74-acre Seattle Center for the 1962 World's Fair. About 15 blocks north of the Pike Place Market, the complex is bounded by 1st and 5th avenues N, Mercer Street, and Denny Way. It's still quite heavily used by Seattleites, who see plays at **Intiman Theater;** cheer their basketball team, the Sonics, at the **Coliseum;** take their kids to the **Children's Museum** (*see* Museums and Galleries, *below*); or attend one of the three summer festivals held on its grounds (*see* Festivals, *below*). Most people, however, regard the concrete structure as an ugly reminder that their beautiful Seattle has finally gone Big City. *Tel. 206/684–7200. From Westlake Center, take the monorail; or take Bus 15, 18, 22, or 23 along 1st Ave.*

If you haven't yet noticed the Seattle Center's famous **Space Needle** you should get your nose out of your navel. The 607-foot-tall steel structure that has come to symbolize the city looks more like a giant 1950s-style floor lamp than the graceful "architecture of the future" that it was suppose to represent when completed in 1962. You can ride the elevator to the observation deck on top and take in great views of the city—and even spy Mt. Rainier, Mt. Baker, and the northern Cascades on a clear day. Two restaurants (one with very high prices and the other with very bad food) have tables on the Needle's rim. Trying hanging out at the Emerald Suite's bar for a while; the altitude and the restaurant's gentle rotation (one full rotation every 58 minutes!) may produce an extra buzz. *Tel. 206/443–2100. Elevator: $6.50. Observation deck open daily 8 AM–midnight.*

The Seattle Center's other major attraction is the **Pacific Science Center,** at the southern end of the complex. Exhibits include a replica of a Native American ceremonial house from a Pacific Northwestern tribe; a laser light show; and nature films on the 3½-story-tall screen in the **IMAX Theater**. It's all really fun if you're in the "I'm a tourist and proud!" state of mind. IMAX and laser show matinees are $2 plus museum admission; evening shows are $5.50 (IMAX) and $6 (laser show). Show times vary, so call for a schedule. *200 2nd Ave. N, tel. 206/443–2880; IMAX schedule: tel. 206/443–4629; Laser show: tel. 206/443–2850. Science Center admission: $6. Open summer, daily 10–6; winter, weekdays 10–5, weekends 10–6.*

One block west of the Center's 1st Avenue exit is Queen Anne Avenue, which climbs to the top of **Queen Anne Hill,** one of the highest peaks in Seattle. It's part of a ritzy residential neighborhood with plenty of big houses built in the Queen Anne style of architecture—hence the area's name. If you have a car, head up Highland Drive for views of the city, the Sound, and the Cascades. The best spot to park and gawk is **Kerry Viewpoint,** at 2nd Avenue W and Highland Drive.

THE UNIVERSITY DISTRICT In typical collegiate fashion, the University of Washington (called "U-dub," as in UW) and its 50,000-plus students and staff have commandeered a massive section of the city. The concentration of student housing, bookshops, cafés, campus buildings, ethnic restaurants, and vintage clothing stores clustered on the streets and avenues north of campus are referred to by locals as the "U-District"; they're an excellent escape from the tourristed areas Downtown. Because businesses in the U-District are geared toward students on tight budgets, it's generally cheaper than Downtown, too. The main drag, **University Way NE,** runs north–south, one block west of campus. From Downtown, Buses 71–74 travel directly to University Way. Buses 7 and 43 arrive in the U-District via Capitol Hill.

People watching from a café window on "The Ave," as University Way is known, can be fun: You'll see leather-clad rockers, frat-types in "Go Huskies" T-shirts, wild-haired bohemians, and tweedy-looking professors all pass by.

The **University of Washington,** founded in 1860, lies at the center of the U-District. Mammoth **Husky Stadium**—where UW plays pretty decent football—is on the southeastern end of campus and makes a good landmark if you get lost. Pick up a campus map at the **University of Washington Visitor Information Center** (4014 University Way NE, at Campus Pkwy., tel. 206/543–9198), open weekdays 8–5. Though the occasional student demonstration stirs up campus, on the whole it's a fairly mellow place. Tree-lined boulevards, grassy quads, and impressive classical buildings give the campus a very traditional look.

On campus, **Red Square** is the nerve center for student activity and politics. (The "red" refers to its brick paving, not students' political inclinations.) Officially, it's called Central Quadrangle—and some maps refer to it as "Central Plaza Garage." Never mind. On sunny days the steps are filled with students sunbathing, studying, or just hanging out. Come here to scope out the scene—or to carry on a heated exchange with one of several staunch '60s-protest types who never quite came off that last trip. Walk east and you'll eventually reach the **Student Union Building,** or **HUB** (the "H" stands for Husky, the school's mascot). On the ground floor you'll find some nondescript places to eat, a bowling alley, and a ride board.

At the center of Red Square, what looks like a minimalist's giant interpretation of a pencil is actually the Broken Obelisk, a steel sculpture by Barnett Newman.

That building masquerading as a cathedral just east of Red Square is the neo-Gothic **Suzzalo Library.** Veer right and pass the Drumheller Fountain to get to the lawns of **Rainier Vista,** which afford spectacular views of Mt. Rainier (weather permitting). Then head west on Stevens Way to visit the **Medicinal Herb Garden,** the largest of its kind in the western hemisphere. Herbs and other interesting plants native to the Pacific Northwest, as well as from around the world, sprout and blossom here—including the real wallflower (*cheiranthus cheire*) and California and Oriental poppies. And no, the University does *not* farm hemp.

At the western end of the campus lies the **Henry Art Gallery.** Founded in 1927, it was the first public art museum in Washington. The permanent collection includes 19th- and 20th-century American and European paintings, as well as many Japanese ceramics and textiles. Temporary exhibits tend to be controversial and innovative and are often accompanied by special lectures, workshops, and films. *15th Ave. NE, at 41st St., tel. 206/543–2280. Admission: $3.50, $2 students. Open Tues.–Wed. and Fri.–Sun. 11-5, Thurs. 11–9. Admission on Thurs. by donation.*

Built in 1885, **The Burke Memorial Washington State Museum** is the oldest university museum in the West. The outstanding Native American collection includes intricate masks and ceremonial blankets. Other exhibits highlight geological and zoological features of the Pacific. Downstairs, the **Boiserie Café** is a favorite hangout of professors and students. *N.E. 45th St., at 17th Ave., tel. 206/543–5590. Suggested admission: $3, $2 students. Open Fri.–Wed. 10–5, Thurs. 10–8.*

After dark take a walk south from N.E. 45th Street along Memorial Way to the university's **Observatory** (tel. 206/543–0126). Built in 1895, its glass dome rotates on two cannonballs recycled from the Civil War. On Mondays and Thursdays the public is invited to look through the observatory's 6-inch telescope (or, when the weather isn't cooperating, see an astronomy slide show). The free viewings are fall and spring 8–10, winter 7–9, and summer 9–11.

VOLUNTEER PARK High above the mansions of north Capitol Hill sits 45-acre Volunteer Park. On warm days, neighborhood residents gather on its pleasant lawns to picnic, sunbathe, read, or play volleyball. Climb the park's water tower (near the 14th Avenue entrance) for some good views of the surrounding mountain ranges. Facing the eastern shore of the park's small reservoir is the original Seattle Art Museum (*see* Museums and Galleries, *below*), and on the park's northern border is Lake View Cemetery, where actor Bruce Lee is buried. Ask the officer at the front gate how to find the grave if you're a fan. At the north end of the park, the **Conservatory** (tel. 206/684–4743), open daily 10–7, houses exotic plants and flowers, all expertly maintained and displayed. The secondhand shops and small restaurants just past the park's exit on **15th Avenue E** are also worth poking through. Volunteer Park is now closed from dusk to dawn, due to too much frisky business in the bushes. *Park entrance: E. Prospect St. and 15th Ave. From Downtown, take Bus 10.*

WOODLAND PARK ZOO This natural-habitat zoo ranks as one of the best in the country. The new African Savannah exhibit has monkeys, hippos, zebras, giraffes, and springbok (African gazelles), but the area's large enough so that many of the animals hide from view. (Can you blame them?) There are bats in the Nocturnal House and brilliantly colored poisonous snakes and frogs at the Tropical House. In all cases, zoo curators have taken pains to provide space and surroundings similar to the animals' natural habitats. The Woodland Park Zoo is west of the U-District and just south of Green Lake. *5500 Phinney Ave. N, tel. 206/684–4800. From Downtown, take Bus 5 north. Admission: $6. Open summer, daily 9:30–6; winter, daily 9:30–4.*

The zoo's south gate opens onto Fremont Avenue N. Follow this 15 blocks south to the funky neighborhood of **Fremont,** with its drawbridge over the busy Lake Washington Ship Canal. Around the bridge are several blocks of interesting secondhand stores, skate shops, restaurants, and bars—good for an evening's exploration. Be sure to look for the sculpture *Waiting for the Interurban* by Richard Beyer, a short distance from the bridge on North Lake Way. Seattle's favorite piece of public art is designed to look like five people waiting at a bus stop.

MUSEUMS AND GALLERIES

Seattle is not a haven for traditional Western art, and it doesn't strive to be one. Its strength lies instead in various fine collections of Asian, Native American, and African works, as well as the contemporary art of the Pacific Northwest. Most art galleries can be found around Pike Place Market, Pioneer Square, or the neighborhood of Belltown (near Seattle Center). On the first Thursday of every month is the **Pioneer Square Art Walk,** when galleries throw open their doors to the unwashed masses from 5:30 to 9. Some offer wine and cheese or live music—it's quite a scene, and it's all free. Most participating galleries show new works by talented local artists. On occasion, artists appear to speak about their work.

Look over your shoulder or down at your feet for public art on Downtown sidewalks and plazas. Seattle has sunk a sizable chunk of money into its public arts program of late, and the results are impressive. One million bucks were poured into providing cool art for the bus tunnels (*see* Getting Around, *above*) alone: In the **Pioneer Square Station** (3rd Avenue and James Street) is a mural of Seattle's history, while the **International District Station** (5th Avenue and S. Jackson Street) features Chinese calendar symbols. While Downtown, stop to admire Henry Moore's massive sculpture, *Vertebrae* (4th Avenue at Madison Street). *Seattle Arts,* a monthly magazine put out by the Seattle Arts Commission, publishes information on upcoming events, interviews with artists, and announcements of upcoming public-art contests. Pick one up at the Visitor Information Bureau (*see* Visitor Information, *above*), or at a museum or gallery. Besides those listed below, the city's museums include the Burke Museum, Pacific Science Center, Seattle Museum–Downtown, and the University of Washington's Henry Art Gallery, all mentioned in Worth Seeing, *above*.

The number of galleries Downtown is mind-boggling—and most have contemporary art far more interesting than the museums. To top it all off, they're free. Pick up a list of galleries at the Visitor Information Bureau (*see* Visitor Information, *above*) or at one of the galleries. A few of the best are: **AG 47 Gallery** (163 S. Jackson St., tel. 206/623–3812), **Art Mavens** (416 Occidental Ave. S, tel. 206/682–7686), and **In Sights** (416 Occidental Ave. S, tel. 206/624–6411).

CENTER ON CONTEMPORARY ART (COCA) This cutting-edge gallery, two blocks from the Pike Place Market, has mostly multimedia exhibitions, with an emphasis on experimental visual art and music. Most of the artists work with techno cyberspace. *1309 1st Ave., btw Union and University Sts., tel. 206/682–4568. Admission: $2. Open Tues.–Sat. 11–6. Open some evenings for special exhibits.*

FRYE ART MUSEUM The museum's permanent collection once belonged to Charles Frye, one of Seattle's great early industrialists, and his wife Emma. It includes 290 works by early-18th- and late-19th-century masters, such as Edouard Manet, Childe Hassan, and Adolphe William Bouguereau (whose cheesy, proto-modernist paintings are ironically now back in fashion). You can also see the painting that started it all, "Little Girl with Pigs," which the Fryes purchased at the 1893 Chicago World's Fair. The Frye Museum stands among Seattle's hospitals on First Hill (also called "Pill Hill"), just east of Downtown and south of Capitol Hill. It's not a particularly striking structure, but the art is worthwhile. *704 Terry Ave., at Cherry St., First Hill, tel. 206/622–9250. From Downtown, take Bus 12 to Madison St. and Terry Ave. and walk 3 blocks south. Admission free. Open Mon.–Sat. 10–5, Sun. noon–5.*

MUSEUM OF HISTORY AND INDUSTRY Just across the Montlake Bridge from the University of Washington, this popular museum collects artifacts from Seattle's colorful history: pieces from Henry Yesler's lumber mill, early photos and documents, and an exhibit on the Great Fire of 1889. The "Passages Northwest" exhibit explores the history of the whole region.

The best part of the museum is the hands-on exhibit with games and historic clothes to try on—actually, they're for kids, but it's still fun. *2700 24th Ave. E, Montlake, tel. 206/324–1125. From Downtown or Capitol Hill, take Bus 43. Admission: $3. Open daily 10–5. Admission on Tues. by donation.*

SEATTLE ART MUSEUM—VOLUNTEER PARK Although much of the museum's collection has been moved to a new building Downtown, this recently renovated art deco structure in pretty Volunteer Park still houses most of the city's Asian art, including Chinese jade, Japanese textiles, and ancient ceramics and paintings. For more on the Downtown Seattle Art Museum and on Volunteer Park, *see* Worth Seeing, *above. 14th Ave. E, at Prospect St., Capitol Hill, tel. 206/654–3100. From Downtown, take Bus 10. Admission: $2. Open Tues.–Wed. and Fri.–Sat. 10–5, Thurs. 10–9, Sun. noon–5.*

SEATTLE CHILDREN'S MUSEUM Although everything here is arranged for people under 4 feet tall, this is a truly fun break from touring the Seattle Center (*see* Worth Seeing, *above*). The child-sized city neighborhood is incredibly detailed, down to the fire engine with detachable ladder. The Imagination Station is the thing to see here for reasons we can't explain. *Seattle Center, tel. 206/298–2521. In the lower level of the Center House. Admission: $3.50. Open Tues.–Sun. 10–5.*

WING LUKE ASIAN MUSEUM Named for the first Asian-American to be elected to public office in Washington state (the Seattle city council in 1962), the Wing Luke Museum provides insight into the history and culture of Seattle's large and growing Asian-American community. Photographs, seasonal exhibits, and work by modern artists heighten the experience. *407 7th Ave. S, at Jackson St., International District, tel. 206/623–5124. From Downtown, take Bus 1 (which becomes Bus 36). Admission: $2.50, free Thurs. Open Tues.–Fri. 11–4:30, weekends noon–4.*

PARKS AND GARDENS

Few other American cities have parks as nice as Seattle's. Park lands range from untamed forests and windswept beaches to manicured swaths of grass perfect for sports and socializing. City parks are open from dawn to dusk and are absolutely free. The major ones—Discovery, Green Lake, and Volunteer—are discussed in Worth Seeing, *above.* The city's **Recreation Information Line** (tel. 206/684–4075) can answer questions about the Seattle parks.

ALKI BEACH PARK This West Seattle park has one of the city's most popular beaches for sunning and (if you're impervious to cold) swimming. There's also a 12-mile bike trail with great views of the Olympics, and a bike rental shop is conveniently located nearby (*see* Getting Around by Bike, *above*). *Beach entrance: Alki Ave. SW, at 63rd Ave. From Downtown, take Bus 37 or 56; or follow West Seattle Fwy. to Admiral Way SW and turn right on 63rd Ave.*

GAS WORKS PARK The Gas Works Plant was transformed from power station to city park in the early '60s. Pipes, wheels, and other remnants of the old gas plant are now used by children to climb and play on, giving the Fremont park an industrial/artsy feel. People also visit the park to fly their kites (it's on the windy north shore of Lake Union), picnic, or watch sailboats from the grassy slopes bordering the lake. On Tuesday evenings folks gather to watch boats compete in Duck Dodge, a friendly race that's more of an excuse to party than anything else. *Park entrance: N. North Lake Way, at Wallingford Ave., Fremont. From Downtown, take Bus 26 to N. 35th St. and Wallingford Ave., then walk 2 blocks south.*

GOLDEN GARDENS PARK After a visit to the Ballard Locks (*see* Worth Seeing, *above*), stop by Golden Gardens, a local favorite for watching Seattle's spectacular sunsets. Several trails wind through the forested eastern section, but the sunset watch takes place on the sandy beach bordering Shilshole Bay and overlooking the Olympic Mountains. It's a great place to dig for clams, picnic, or take a swim (if you can bear the arctic conditions). *Park entrance: N.W. 85th St. and 32nd Ave., Sunset Hill. From Downtown, take Bus 17.*

MYRTLE EDWARDS AND ELLIOTT BAY PARKS This pair of waterfront parks stretching north from Alaskan Way at Bay Street (just beyond Downtown's Pier 70) has pleasant benches and lawns, as well as paved biking and jogging trails. Both offer a welcome respite from the crowded city streets and a chance to enjoy the water. *From Pike Place Market, walk 11 blocks north, or take Waterfront Streetcar.*

RAVENNA When exploring University Way, many visitors quit at around 50th Street, where university-oriented stores and cafés give way to less exciting stuff. Students know better. About 14 blocks north of campus is Ravenna Park, packed with Douglas fir, western red cedar, and hemlock, all surrounding a narrow, steep-walled creek. Many hiking and biking trails lead through the 54-acre park. *Park entrance: N.E. 58th St. and 16th Ave. From Downtown, take Bus 71–73.*

SCHMITZ PARK This West Seattle park, just inland from Alki Beach (*see above*), offers one of the finest forest walks in Seattle. The park trail leads into a ravine and through stands of old-growth hemlock, cedar, and Douglas fir. There's also some decent mushroom-picking, but be absolutely sure you know what you're doing—a bad fungus can be deadly. *Park entrance: Admiral Way SW, at Stevens St. From Downtown, take Bus 56, or follow West Seattle Fwy. to Admiral Way SW.*

SEWARD PARK Seward Park borders vast Lake Washington on the city's southeastern edge. Most of the action here—biking, jogging, and picnicking—takes place to the park's south, while a secluded 2-mile trail traverses the thickly wooded areas to the north. It's as popular with South Seattle residents as Discovery Park (*see* Worth Seeing, *above*) is with Seattleites who live farther north. *Park entrance: S. Orcas St., at Seward Park Ave. From Downtown, take Bus 39 south.*

WARREN MAGNUSON PARK Jutting into Lake Washington from the city's northeast, "Sand Point" (as it's called by locals) offers the best beach in Seattle for quiet sunbathing. Relax, soak up the sun, and look south to Evergreen Point Floating Bridge (the longest floating bridge in the world), which connects Seattle with Bellevue and eastern Washington. Bring a bus schedule: You don't want to get stuck here at night, no matter how pretty it is. *Park entrance: Sand Point Way NE, at 70th St. From Downtown, take Bus 74 north (weekdays only).*

WASHINGTON PARK/ARBORETUM Most of Washington Park is given over to the University of Washington Arboretum, a botanical research facility (open to the public) with over 5,000 varieties of plants, trees, shrubs, and vines. At the park's southern end is the **Japanese Garden** (tel. 206/625–2635), with tranquil grounds including a waterfall, carp-filled lake, charming bridges, and an authentic tea house. Washington Park is also a popular spot for cyclists, but don't cruise around here alone after dusk—the park's late-night visitors tend to be pretty creepy. *2300 Arboretum Dr. E, Capitol Hill, tel. 206/325–4510. From Downtown, take Bus 43. Japanese Garden admission: $1.50. Arboretum open daily 7 AM–sunset; Japanese garden open daily 10–sunset; park visitor center open daily 10–4.*

WATERFRONT PARK Between Piers 57 and 59 (just south of the aquarium), this maritime park remains relatively serene despite the nearby boardwalk's throngs of tourists; come here to regain composure after an afternoon of sightseeing. The large wooden observation deck offers excellent views of Puget Sound and the surrounding mountains. *Just west of Pike Place Market, btw Stewart and University Sts.*

Seattleites who want to get out on the city's waterways tend to create some pretty wacky floating devices—tying the neighbors' lawn furniture together, or roping up some spare tires from Dad's garage.

CHEAP THRILLS

When the sun shines, do as the locals do: Head to a park or hit the water. Neither is ever too hard to find—but the second option is often a lot pricier. To find a floating vessel that won't cost you an arm and a leg, visit the **UW Waterfront Activity Center** (tel. 206/543–9433), on Montlake Boulevard NE near Husky Stadium. They'll rent you a rowboat or canoe ($3.50 per hour) as long as you can produce a valid driver's license.

Back to reality. The sun may shine between July and September, but the rest of the year it's dismal and gray in Seattle. When it's too chilly to play *Poseidon Adventure* on Lake Washington, Seattleites head to some of the numerous **microbreweries** that have set up shop in the Pacific Northwest over the last decade. In order to qualify for the "micro" prefix, a brewer must produce less than 20,000 kegs of beer a year—quality, not quantity, is key. The Fremont neighborhood's **Redhook Brewery** (3400 Phinney Ave. N, at 34th St., tel. 206/548–8000) is one of the best microbreweries around. Tour (free) the facility and then hit the company's **Trolleyman Pub,** which serves up the freshly brewed Wheat Hook, Black Hook, and Extra Special Bitter. Take your pint ($2.75) to a couch near the fireplace and forget about the weather outside. **Rainier Brewery** (3100 Airport Way S, tel. 206/622–2600), off I–5 well south of Downtown, also has free tours and tastings weekdays 1–6.

The **Out To Lunch** series of free daily concerts (noon–1:30 PM) features jazz and R&B from late June through September. Most venues are outdoors: Westlake Center Plaza (4th Ave. and Pine St.), Union Square (6th Ave. and Union St.), Post Alley (near the Waterfront, btw Madison and Spring Sts.), and the Rainier Square Neighborhood Roof Garden Plaza (5th Ave., btw Union and University Sts.). For a schedule and locations, call 206/623–0340.

Aspiring rock artists (or the morbidly minded) will want to make the trek to the town of Renton's **Greenwood Memorial Park** (380 Monroe Ave. NE), the final resting place of Jimi Hendrix, Seattle native and greatest guitarist of all time. From Downtown, take Bus 147 south and ask the driver to drop you close to the entrance.

Pioneer Square bookstore **Tabula Rasa** (621 Western Ave., tel. 206/682–5185) offers a tour of its vast collection of rare books, from miniatures to old diaries. The owners, John and Gizella, are also bookbinders and willing to share their knowledge of this vanishing art.

Most Seattle neighborhoods hold open markets during the summer months. Visit one to meet Seattle locals, chow on some cheap eats, and even score a few bargain offbeat souvenirs:

Capitol Hill Street Market. *10th Ave. E and Pike St., tel. 206/860–8618. Open weekends 10–5.*

International District Weekend Market. *401 S. Jackson St., at the Metro Station Plaza, tel. 206/624–3426. Open Sat. 10–4.*

University District Farmers Market. *N.E. 50th St. and University Way, tel. 206/527–2567. Open Sat. 9–2.*

FESTIVALS

➤ **FEBRUARY** • During Seattle's week-long celebration of **Mardi Gras,** Cajun, jazz, and R&B music is performed at Pioneer Square and in neighboring bars. The free attractions also include food and crafts booths, a parade, and all kinds of music in the streets.

➤ **MAY** • The **Seattle International Film Festival** (tel. 206/324–9996) features mainstream and experimental films and attracts hip hordes from all over. It's based at Capitol Hill's **Egyptian Theater** (801 E. Pine St., tel. 206/323–4978 or 206/324–9996).

The **Northwest Folklife Festival** (Seattle Center, tel. 206/684–7300) is a massive hippie-fest held over Memorial Day weekend: It's a fun scene with sporadic hacky-sack games, booths vending Guatemalan clothing or Oregon-grown herbs, and all kinds of music for hours on end.

➤ **JULY** • **Fourth of July.** Seattle goes nuts for the 4th. Most of the fireworks are at dusk on Lake Union; the best place to watch is Gas Works Park (*see* Parks and Gardens, *above*). Arrive early.

Bite of Seattle (Seattle Center, tel. 206/232–2982), held the third week of July, brings together booths representing over 50 of Seattle's top restaurants for public munching and nibbling. Admission is $3, and you pay for noshing along the way. For $6.50, you get to taste the creations of ten selected restaurants.

Seafair culminates with the hydroplane race finals, but what you should really watch for are the floating spectators that fill Green Lake. Many literally tie themselves to each other so they won't float away in a drunken stupor. Even if you don't have a boat to socialize on, a walk out onto the dock will usually get you an invitation for a drink and a smoke.

Beginning in mid-July, the three-week extravaganza that is **Seafair** (tel. 206/728–0123) includes milk-carton races on Green Lake, hydroplane expeditions, triathlons, ethnic food festivals, and a Torch Light Parade. Though it's a celebration of community, many residents head for the hills to avoid all the noise and commotion.

➢ **AUGUST** • Seattle's best-known festival is **Bumbershoot,** boasting an eclectic gathering of musicians, craftspeople, writers, poets, comedians, and actors. Past performers have included B.B. King, the Neville Brothers, and Allen Ginsberg. It all happens on Labor Day. *Seattle Center, tel. 206/622–5123. Admission: $9 in advance, $10 at the door.*

Seattle's Original Hempfest. It doesn't take much imagination to figure out what goes on here (Hint: It's not braiding rope.) The musical guests are always the latest hot bands, the fest is free, and no alcohol is allowed. It's usually held at Gas Works Park, but for detailed information, check the magazine *The Rocket (see* After Dark, *below).*

Shopping

Seattle has become a big-time shopping city, with stores selling everything from secondhand collectibles to fine jewelry. Downtown is strictly for serious gold-card shoppers; upscale chain stores abound in the **Pacific First City Center** (1420 5th Ave., at Pike St.). As you head west, shops become funkier and more affordable.

Finding gifts at Pike Place is no problem. Pick from the usual: T-shirts, posters, low-priced jewelry, scarves—and boxed smoked salmon.

At **Pike Place Market,** you can find some reasonable deals on sweaters, jewelry, and crafts. Vendors must be put on a waiting list and be approved by a committee before selling their hig-quality, handmade wares here. Lately, **Pioneer Square** has made the transition from shopping to drinking mecca, but among the many remaining rug stores are some great music outlets and bookstores.

Beyond the city's Downtown shopping district, **Capitol Hill,** the **University District,** and the neighborhood of **Fremont** have many of the best bargains. The first two represent a wide range of stores, while Fremont's commercial district spans a scant few blocks and specializes in used goods, some stranger than others.

DOWNTOWN Don't you feel a little geeky walking into Seattle's coolest clubs in your jeans, hiking boots, and favorite college T-shirt? Even if you're not a Morrissey fan, tolerate the choice of music at **Fast Forward** (1918 1st Ave., tel. 206/728–8050) to check out their great selection of men and women's club wear. They have unique, funky jewelry, hats, and almost any other accessory you could think of. **Local Brilliance** (1535 1st Ave., tel. 206/343–5864) sells trendy but unusual clothing made locally. The handmade jewelry isn't half as pricey as it looks. **Marshal's** (1000 1st Ave., at Madison St., tel. 206/624–7000) is an athlete's dream: Athletic clothing and footwear, fishing and camping equipment, hunting supplies, and alpine gear are all sold at very low prices. The world music that fills **Zamboanga Gallery Store** (1906 Pike Pl., at the Stewart House Bldg., Stall 7, tel. 206/448–9345), across from the Pike Place Market, will put you in the mood for browsing their selection of African instruments, Guatemalan textiles, Israeli jewelry, and Indian dolls. The stuff is pricey but fun to look at.

From Downtown, head northwest on 2nd Avenue about six blocks and you'll come to the neighborhood of **Belltown**—the center of teen and twenty-something grunge life. These cool types buy their beloved tunes at **Wall of Sound** (2237 2nd Ave., at Bell St., tel. 206/441–9880), where patrons can listen before they buy. The cool chicks collect their clothes at **Pin Down Girl** (2224 2nd Ave., at Bell St., tel. 206/441–1248), where patient digging through bins and racks will yield anything from last year's Nikes to a vintage Penzoil jacket.

PIONEER SQUARE Hole-in-the-wall **Bedazzled Discs** (101 Cherry St., tel. 206/382–6072) specializes in alternative music. There's a huge funk section and a number of hard-to-find CDs as well. Come here for the scoop on raves, clubs, and indie shows. Around since the dawn of time, **Bud's Jazz Records** (102 S. Jackson St., at 1st Ave., tel. 206/628–0445) sells jazz and only jazz, from collectors' items to latest releases. The incredibly knowledgeable staff is happy to share their expertise. Really missing the *Starsky and Hutch* lunch box you lost in the third grade? Find another at **Ruby Montana's Pinto Pony, Ltd.** (603 2nd Ave., tel. 206/621–PONY).

Their warehouse space is filled with collectibles, especially salt and pepper shakers, cookie jars, and anything made during the '70s.

CAPITOL HILL Capitol Hill has the best shops in town for vintage clothing and alternative tunes. As a bonus, there are numerous establishments where you can suck down a microbrew between buying frenzies. And take note of the bronzed shoeprints imbedded in the cement at most corners of **Broadway E**, one of the neighborhood's main shopping strips. They're instructions for specific dances (like the waltz) and are part of Seattle's ambitious public art program.

Fifteenth Avenue (between Union and Roy streets) has some truly unique stores. **The Cauldron** (526 15th Ave. E, tel. 206/325–7368) sells "Lucifer protection" potions, oddly shaped daggers, and do-it-yourself voodoo equipment. It also holds open circles and readings. Across the street but at the other extreme, **Metropolis Vintages** (423 15th Ave. E, tel. 206/322–2297) sells reasonably priced used clothing from the Victorian era.

Stores on and around Broadway tend to be more expensive, but several warrant a look. One block south of Broadway, the **Chicken Soup Brigade Thrift Store** (207 Harvard Ave. E, at John St., tel. 206/329–4563) donates to AIDS patients all proceeds from its sale of secondhand clothes. West of Broadway, **Dig This** (1720 E. Olive Way, tel. 206/324–7841) has a terrific selection of vintage jewelry, scarves, and hats. **Orpheum** (618 Broadway E, tel. 206/322–6370) sells new and used compact discs (rock, jazz, blues, reggae, pop, soul, and rap). Get the scoop here on clubs and local jams.

Two blocks east of Broadway, **REI (Recreational Equipment, Inc.) Co-op** (525 11th Ave. E, btw Pike and Pine Sts., tel. 206/323–8333) is *the* store to purchase anything under the sun (or clouds) for sporting in summer and winter. They also offer good rental rates for boots, packs, and other equipment; organize bike and ski trips; and maintain a popular trade-and-sell bulletin board. Around the corner (just look for the idle pack of skaters) is **Crescent Downworks** (1100 E. Pike St., tel. 206/329–9248), one of the best skate- and snowboard shops in the city, a source for sport and fashion accessories. **Capitol Hill Surplus** (910 E. Pike St., tel. 206/325–3566) has camping supplies at similar prices to REI, so compare before buying.

Seattle's Best Bookstores

- *Elliott Bay Book Company. Possibly the most comprehensive bookstore in existence, Elliott Bay carries every genre of writing imaginable—many available at discount prices in the store's Bargain Loft. Ask for a schedule of in-store readings. 101 S. Main St., at 1st Ave., Pioneer Square, tel. 206/624–6600.*

- *Magus. The oldest and best used bookstore on "The Ave" is staffed by dedicated bibliophiles. You'll usually get store credit for selling used books; late in the week, they'll sometimes pay cash. 1408 N.E. 42nd St., at University Way, University District, tel. 206/633–1800.*

- *McCoy Books. Enjoy a really good espresso while checking out the best in new American fiction. McCoy's doesn't carry used books, but they compensate with a giant newsstand. They also list readings that are scheduled around town. 117 Pine St., btw 1st and 2nd Aves., Downtown, tel. 206/623–5354.*

- *Pioneer Square Books. This is the best place in town to purge your backpack of heavy books. They buy at good prices and trade at even better ones. You'll also find a number of out-of-print books here. 213 1st Ave., Pioneer Square, tel. 206/343–BOOK.*

THE UNIVERSITY DISTRICT One of the busiest shopping areas in town is **The Ave** (University Way NE, from 41st to 50th streets), crammed with book, record, and vintage-clothing stores. Businesses cater to student tastes and budgets (though quite a few other Seattleites find it appealing, too). Unfortunately, The Ave swarms with young runaways, whose aggressive panhanding can sometimes make a trip depressing and frustrating.

Bulldog News (4208 University Way NE, tel. 206/632–6397; also in Capitol Hill: 401 Broadway E, tel. 206/328–2881) stocks almost 3,000 different periodicals, including a wide selection of foreign publications. **Beauty and the Books** (4213 University Way NE, tel. 206/632–8510) may not look big until you stumble on the back room and basement. Haphazard boxes of books, layers of dust, and a littering of half-empty coffee cups are all part of its dilapidated charm. **Cellophane Square Records** (1315 N.E. 42nd St., at University Way, tel. 206/634–2280) is a treasure trove of new and used records, tapes, and compact discs. In addition to the ubiquitous alternative rock titles, it stocks a surprising selection of jazz and blues. In addition to being one of the best used clothing stores in Seattle, the **Clotheshorse Trading Co.** (4241 University Way NE, tel. 206/632–7884) will patch any clothes you bring in (take them off first, please) at prices $5 and up.

The only headshop in town, **Off the Wall** (4514 University Way NE, tel. 206/548–8903) is understandably busy. They sell what headshops all over the world sell: metal and wood pipes, bongs (in portable or four-foot models), sex toys, T-shirts, and strange posters.

After Dark

Seattle tends to be relatively low-key at night—especially given its position as progenitor of '90s music and lifestyle. Bars close at 2 AM, and even on weekends most of the streets are empty well before then. But what Seattle lacks in stamina, it more than makes up for in quality and variety. Its theaters have received heaps of national praise over the past few years, and its alternative music scene is the envy of every other American city, inspiring dozens of record execs to search anxiously for the "next Seattle sound." To keep up with the music scene, pick up *The Rocket,* a free monthly, or the recently-introduced *Hype.* The *Seattle Weekly* (75¢), published every Tuesday, is excellent for listings on galleries, theaters, and classical music performances. Both of the big city newspapers, *The Seattle Times* and *The Post-Intelligencer*, publish pull-out calendar sections on Sundays. Many theater and concert tickets can be purchased by phone in advance through **Ticketmaster** (tel. 206/628–0888), though they'll impose a stiff "convenience charge."

Half-price theater and concert tickets are available at **Ticket/Ticket.** Purchases must be made on the day of the show, in-person, and with cash only. *Downtown: At the Pike Place Market Information Booth, 1st Ave. and Pike St., tel. 206/324–2744. Open Tues.–Sun. noon–6. Capitol Hill: At Broadway Market, 401 Broadway E, 2nd floor, tel. 206/324–2744. Open Tues.–Sun. 10–7.*

BARS Microbrews are all the rage across the Pacific Northwest. Visiting Bud drinkers will be in for a big shock: Brews that look and smell like malty soy sauce are the beer of choice in Seattle. Drink prices are pretty much the same all over the city: Most pints are around $3, and mixed drinks are $4.

➤ **PIONEER SQUARE** • **Pioneer Square** is the site of Seattle's amazing **pub crawl.** Every Thursday–Saturday, a single cover charge ($7) is good for several participating bars, all within easy staggering distance of each other. Among the participants are **Fenix Café** (111 Yesler Way, tel. 206/447–1514) and the **Central Tavern** (207 1st Ave. S, tel. 206/622–0209). For other participants, *see* Music, *below.*

J&M Café. This Pioneer Square hangout is easy to spot—it's the one with the crowds, day and night. The clientele consists largely of drunken fraternity dudes, rowdy sports fans, binging off-duty military boys, and pole-toting fishermen just back from Alaska. Not surprisingly, things sometimes get out of hand. *201 1st Ave. S, tel. 206/624–1670. Open daily 11:30 AM–2 AM.*

The Pacific Northwest Brewing Company, Ltd. A cross between an upscale bar and grill and an English-style pub, this inviting microbrewery serves six draft ales ($3 a pint) and an assortment of appetizers and full meals ($7 and up). The crowd here is pretty mainstream. On sunny days, take a table outdoors along Occidental Mall. *322 Occidental Ave. S, tel. 206/621–7002. Open summer, Sun. and Mon. 11:30–9, Tues.–Thurs. 11:30–10, Fri. and Sat. 11:30–2; winter, Sun. and Mon. 4–9, Tues.–Thurs. 4–10, Fri. and Sat. 4–2.*

Pioneer Square Saloon. Students from UW escape to this alley bar, as yet undiscovered by tourists. It's surprisingly mellow and non-hormonal for a place frequented by a bunch of college students. There's an acoustic show on Wednesday nights to make your pint (around $3) that much more enjoyable. *73 Yesler Way, tel. 206/628–6444. Open daily noon–2 AM.*

➢ **CAPITOL HILL** • Nightlife in the neighborhood of Capitol Hill is expanding at an exponential rate, and crowds from all over town head here at night to hang out in its bars, clubs, and cafés. It's also the center of the gay community, who not only party, but also work, live, and play in these parts. At the Capitol Hill cafés along E. Pine and Pike streets (around Martin Luther King Jr. Way) hangs a predominently lesbian crowd; there's always a buzz about what's going on around town that night.

Comet Tavern. Two pool tables, graffiti-covered walls, and wooden tables carved with names and plenty of curses set the scene for the young crowd of Comet regulars, most of whom consider mainstream society a contagious disease. *922 E. Pike St., at Broadway, tel. 206/323–9853. From Downtown, take Bus 7, 10, or 14. Open daily noon–2 AM.*

The Deluxe Bar and Grill. This place is perfect—who needs more than microbrews on tap, a lively crowd, and awesome burgers? For a night of serious drinking in a happening (but not quite rowdy) environment, this is your best bet. *625 Broadway E, at Roy St., tel. 206/324–9697. From Downtown, take Bus 7 or 10 . Open daily 11 AM–2 AM. Happy hour 3 PM–7 PM and 11 PM–1 AM.*

Linda's Tavern. New to the neighborhood, Linda's has been welcomed with cheers all around. Attracting a fairly flamboyant bunch, this place may look like trouble—but it's not. Linda's blasts off on weekends, when there's a line for pool and standing room only at the bar. *707 E. Pike St., tel. 206/325–1220. Open daily 4 PM–2 AM.*

➢ **PIKE PLACE MARKET** • If you've passed the entire day around Pike Place Market, passing the evening here, too, might constitute overkill. There are plenty of restaurants that will tempt you, but very few bars. **Kells** (*see* Food, *above*) is always popular, very Irish, and offers live music on the weekends. The **Virginia Inn** (1937 1st Ave., at Virginia St., tel. 206/728–1937) is a comfortable place with a gallery of local art and seven microbrews on tap ($3.25 a pint). Kell's attracts the older whisky- and scotch-drinking crowd; the Virginia has cornered the market on traveling yuppies.

Pike Place Brewery. The three secrets of Pike Place's success: an awesome location (around the corner from the AYH hostel and just under the Market); really good ales (try the Pike Place Pale Ale *and* the East India Pale Ale); and a cheerful, athletic-looking staff. The tasting room is only open during the day, but whoever said drinking had to be a nighttime activity? *1432 Western Ave., tel. 206/622–3373. Open Mon.–Sat. 10 AM–4 PM.*

➢ **BELLTOWN** • This revitalized area just north of Downtown has become a popular haunt of authentic and would-be artists. It's also one of the best neighborhoods in the city for finding divey bars. Include in your wanderings the congenial **Two Bells Tavern** (2373 4th Ave., tel. 206/441–3050); **Ditto Tavern** (2303 5th Ave., tel. 206/441–3303), which holds open-mike poetry readings on Sunday nights; and the **Crocodile Café** (2200 2nd Ave., at Blanchard St., tel. 206/448–2114), which has a diner in one room, a bar in another, and live alternative music in a third. For more on the Crocodile, *see* Rock, *below*.

➢ **THE UNIVERSITY DISTRICT** • In general, student nightlife takes place outside the U-District. However, the few bars, movie houses, and theaters near the university are always packed with students on weekends.

Big Time Brewery and Alehouse. Decorated with vintage beer memorabilia, this microbrewery attracts a graduate school crowd during the afternoon and a younger set on Friday nights. The Atlas Amber Ale is a favorite; pints are $2.25, and most of their sandwiches and chili are around $4. *4133 University Way NE, tel. 206/545–4509. Open daily 11:30 AM–12:30 AM. Wheelchair access.*

Lox Stock and Bagel. Popular with fraternity boys, the Lox reels in a young and thirsty mob with its evening happy hour (4–7 PM), where plenty of pints (75¢) and nachos (free) can be enjoyed to live music. They also have pool tables, darts, and two big-screen TVs. On Tuesday and Saturday nights, a DJ makes it look more like a modern *American Bandstand* than a mainstream bar. *4552 University Way NE, tel. 206/634–3144. Open Mon.–Sat. 11 AM–2 AM.*

➤ **FREMONT** • Fremont's bars enjoy popularity with UW students who've given up on the lackluster scene in the University District. Everyone comes to the **Red Door Ale House** (3401 Fremont Ave. N, tel. 206/547–7521) for at least one round before making their way to other neighborhood haunts. **Triangle Tavern** (3507 Fremont Pl. N, tel. 206/632–0880) offers patio seating for enjoyment of its wide selection of beers. **Trolleyman Pub** (*see* Cheap Thrills, *above*) is the Redhook Brewery's popular tavern—nothing but the company brew here. Quite a few blocks from the rest is **La Boheme** (6119 Phinney Ave. N, tel. 206/782–3002). The diverse, funky clientele take advantage of the fact that this is the local bar with the most microbrews on tap.

MUSIC Seattle's music scene is coming down from a tidal wave of national adoration that started up about four years ago. Sure, there's still plenty of raw talent, but the ghosts of bands past weigh heavily on these new musicians. Nonetheless, you'll find few gaps in the Seattle scene. With a minimum of effort, you can find a good performance almost any night. Several jazz and blues clubs attract nationally known performers, while most rock clubs feature strong local acts. The neighborhood of Belltown specializes in grunge and alternative rock, while Pioneer Square and the northwestern neighborhood of Ballard harbor the majority of clubs for blues, R&B, and jazz. In Pioneer Square, a $5–$7 cover paid at one place is also good for admission to several other clubs, so you're free to make the rounds; for more information, *see* Bars, *above*. For any type of music, the biggest names perform at **Paramount Theater** (907 E. Pine St., Capitol Hill, tel. 206/682–1414), **Moore Theater** (1932 2nd Ave., Downtown, tel. 206/443–1744), or the **Coliseum** (tel. 206/684–7202) in Seattle Center (*see* Worth Seeing, *above*).

➤ **ROCK** • **Colour Box.** The best local bands (primarily alternative rock) headline here. There is no cover charge on Sunday (acoustic) and Tuesday (new music) nights. Otherwise, Colour Box is part of Pioneer Square's joint cover system (*see* Bars, *above*). *113 1st Ave. S, Pioneer Square, tel. 206/340–4101.*

They Ain't Playin' Snooker

Although it's one Seattle activity that hasn't gotten a lot of talk or press, pool is practically the official city sport. Everyone in these parts plays pool like a shark and is well prepared to hustle you out of all your money. Though every corner dive has a table, a few places in particular are famous for packing in pool lovers:

- *211 Club (2304 2nd Ave., Belltown, tel. 206/443–1211), on the second level of a warehouse, has plenty of character and ample pool tables for both regulars and rookies.*

- *Jillian's Billiard Club and Café (731 Westlake Ave. N, Queen Anne, tel. 206/223–0300) is an upscale place with two floors of tables, a menu heavy on gourmet food, and plenty of microbrews.*

- *R Place (619 E. Pine St., Capitol Hill, tel. 206/322–8828) is a bar with a big gay scene and an authentic pool-hall atmosphere. The people here are more serious about socializing and less serious about playing pool.*

Crocodile Café. When it opened in 1991, this club quickly developed a reputation as the hippest spot in too-cool Belltown—and it's still the place to catch some of the hottest bands in town. The crowd depends on what type of music is playing that night; it's a mix of alternative rock, reggae, and some experimental folk and jazz. *2200 2nd Ave., at Blanchard St., Belltown, tel. 206/448–2114. Cover: $5. For recorded schedule, call 206/441-5611.*

Moe Mo' Roc 'n Cafe. This is one of the most happening spots in Capitol Hill, with progressive and rather off-the-wall performers dominating the stage. The crowd is built to match. Live music is performed Wednesday–Saturday. *925 E. Pike St., Capitol Hill, tel. 206/324–2406.*

Off Ramp Music Cafe. Although the Off Ramp books top alternative artists, a few always slip in who will probably never make a record deal. It's a popular spot for locals who want their music without a scene, and it's frighteningly loud. Live music happens nightly. *109 Eastlake Ave., btw Denny Way and Republican St., tel. 206/628–0232. Just north of Downtown and west of I–5. From Downtown, take Bus 70–73 or 7. Cover: $4 and up.*

OK Café and Hotel. Cutting-edge punk and grunge shows, mostly by local bands, make this a very cool place. Cover is $5–$7 and will get you admission to several other Pioneer Square joints (*see* Bars, *above*). *212 Alaskan Way S, Pioneer Square, tel. 206/623–9800.*

RCKCNDY. This is probably the hottest place in Seattle to see and be seen. A lot of the patrons genuinely like alternative music, while others are trendy pretenders hoping to meet a Vedder look-alike. RCKCNDY usually books the best of local bands. *1812 Yale Ave., tel. 206/623–0470. Just north of Downtown.*

Under the Rail. This place usually attracts recognizable names for good shows in an intimate space. Though more theater than bar, the Rail does serve beer and wine. *2335 5th Ave., Downtown, tel. 206/448–1900.*

➢ **JAZZ** • **Dimitriou's Jazz Alley.** The center of Seattle's jazz scene and one of the top clubs in the country, this sleek spot gets virtually every big name that passes through town. The crowd is incredibly diverse. *2037 6th Ave., Downtown, tel. 206/441–9729. Cover: $8 and up.*

Latona Tavern. Just a few blocks southeast of Green Lake, Latona's is a cheap, intimate neighborhood bar playing local jazz and occasional blues Thursday–Sunday. *6423 Latona Ave. NE, University District, tel. 206/525–2238. Cover: $1.*

New Orleans Creole Restaurant. Though not as prominent as Jazz Alley, this place does get its share of big names. Serious listeners should come early and get a table near the stage. They also serve some mean New Orleans seafood (*see* Food, *above*). The $5 to $7 cover is also good at other Pioneer Square clubs (*see* Bars, *above*). *114 1st Ave. S, Pioneer Square, tel. 206/622–2563.*

➢ **BLUES** • In Pioneer Square, **Doc Maynard's** (610 1st Ave. S, tel. 206/682–4649) and **Larry's** (209 1st Ave. S, tel. 206/624–7665) are both part of a $5–$7 cover deal that includes entrance to five other Pioneer Square bars and clubs. (For other participants, *see* Bars, *above*.) Bands typically rock the jam-packed crowds with blues and R&B standards.

The Ballard Firehouse. This haunt populated with locals is the preferred place to see blues; the crowd is generally respectful rather than rowdy. You'll find a younger crowd when alternative bands perform, but plan to dance your ass off no matter who's playing. *5429 Russell Ave. NW, Ballard, tel. 206/784–3516. From Downtown, take Bus 17 or 18. Cover: around $5.*

The Owl Café. Much smaller and narrower than the Firehouse (*see above*), this joint feels awfully crowded when it fills on weekends. Standard twelve-bar blues acts are featured: Though nothing surprising, they get the house jumping anyway. *5140 Ballard Ave. NW, Ballard, tel. 206/784–3640. From Downtown, take Bus 17 or 18. Cover: $5.*

DANCING **Casa U-Betcha.** By day this is a popular restaurant, but on Friday and Saturday nights it busts out with world beat tunes spun by a local DJ. It's a great place to learn some really cool and unusual dances. *2212 1st Ave., Belltown, tel. 206/441–1989.*

Down Under. The outrageous design and constant light show at this old-school club make for a good time, even if you have no intention of grooving on the packed, sweaty dance floor.

They're only open Friday and Saturday nights, when DJs spin techno-pop dance tunes, and Tuesday night, when salsa is the music of choice. *2407 1st Ave., Belltown, tel. 206/728–4053. Cover: $5–$6 weekends, $1–$4 Tues.*

Neighbors. This primarily gay dance club plays lots of techno and disco. You can boogie non-stop until at least 4 AM on weekends. *1509 Broadway E, Capitol Hill, tel. 206/324–5358. Cover: $1–$3.*

The Re-bar. Pro-gay Re-bar is by far the most interesting dance club in Seattle. The music changes nightly (usually funk, soul, or hip hop), but regardless of the tunes, writhing, sweaty bodies pack the dance floor by 10 PM. Live music happens every Tuesday. *1114 Howell St., at Boren Ave., Downtown, tel. 206/233–9873. Just west of I–5. Cover: $3.*

Romper Room. Romper Room has an artsy, avant-garde appearance, and so do many of its patrons. It's full of alternative rockers and stoners who are ready to hit the dance floor. *106 1st Ave. N, Queen Anne, tel. 206/284–5003. Near Seattle Center. Cover: $3–$5.*

Vogue. Although not as hip as it once was, Vogue's still hot. You've got your gothic, your reggae, or your basic live bands every night of the week. It's dark and loud, perfect for those who can't spend another night in a coffeehouse. *2018 1st Ave., Downtown, tel. 206/443–0673. Near Pike Place Market. Cover: $4–$5.*

The Weathered Wall. People rock out to all kinds of sounds in one part of the Wall's massive entertainment center. In another, performance art and live music happen. If nothing else, there's excellent people-watching; the crowd is a mishmash of types. *1921 5th Ave., Downtown, tel. 206/448–5688. Cover: $3–$6.*

CLASSICAL MUSIC The **Seattle Symphony Orchestra** performs at the city's Opera House under the direction of acclaimed conductor Gerard Schwartz. Tickets cost $10–$42; discount tickets are available to students an hour before the show. *Seattle Center, tel. 206/443–4711.*

The **Seattle Opera,** considered one of the best in the country, offers less-expensive, "silver-cast" performances with lesser-known performers in the leads. Tickets are $16–$45. "Gold-cast" performances cost $38–$78. *Seattle Center, tel. 206/443–4711.*

COMEDY CLUBS The **Comedy Underground.** Though not as famous as the Improv (*see below*), the Underground is also good for a few hearty laughs. They host open-mike nights every Monday and Tuesday. Advance-purchase tickets are available through Ticketmaster. *222 S. Main St., Downtown, tel. 206/622–4550. Near Pioneer Square. Cover: $10. Shows Sun.–Thurs. at 9; additional show Fri. and Sat. at 11 PM.*

The Improv. This club hosts the city's top stand-up acts, many of whom appear on cable TV's *Evening at the Improv.* Tickets are available at the Improv box office or through Ticketmaster. *1426 1st Ave., Downtown, tel. 206/628–5000. Near Pike Place Market. Cover: $6–$15 plus 2-drink minimum. Showtimes: daily at 8:30 PM; additional show Fri. and Sat. at 10:45.*

THEATER Seattle is considered by some to be stronger in theater than in any other performing art. Twelve professional companies make their home here, some playing in elegant Broadway-style houses, others in more intimate, college-type venues. Consult the *Seattle Weekly* for current listings; half-price tickets are available at Ticket/Ticket (*see above*).

The Seattle Repertory Theatre (Bagley Wright Theater, 155 Mercer St., Seattle Center, tel. 206/443–2222) has won a Tony Award as the best regional theater and continues to stage first-rate productions of everything from classical drama to modern comedy. If you're low on funds, catch a show preview ($8–$13.50). Weekday and matinee performances are also cheap.

People working the stands in Pike Place Market always have an opinion on the city's smaller theater companies, since most of them are aspiring actors. If you're seeking advice on which show to see, consult a likely looking flower vendor or one of the employees at Ticket/Ticket (*see After Dark, above*). Seattle Center's **Intiman Theater** (2nd Ave., at Mercer St., tel. 206/626–0782) specializes in international works, while **A Contemporary Theater** (100 W. Roy St., at 1st Ave., Queen Anne, tel. 206/626–0782) and **Empty Space Theater** (3509 Fremont Ave. N, at 35th St., Fremont, tel. 206/547–7633) both showcase regional playwrights.

For something more experimental, visit the **New City Theater** (1634 11th Ave., near Pine St., Capitol Hill, tel. 206/323–6800), which also has a monthly showing of short films. Performance tickets are often under $10. **On the Boards** (153 14th Ave., at Fir St., Capitol Hill, tel. 206/325–7901) hosts a popular event every month called "12 Minutes Max," in which amateurs are each given 12 minutes to perform.

FILM Seattle loves movies, and the Seattle **Film Festival** (*see* Festivals, *above*) has become one of the most prestigious in North America, with top-name directors and critics on hand. But movie mania here has a certain sophistication to it—many people won't see a film just anywhere—and several small theaters maintain their distinctive personalities despite the proliferation of multiplex cinemas.

In Capitol Hill, the **Egyptian Theater** (801 E. Pine St., at Broadway, tel. 206/323–4978), a transformed Masonic auditorium, screens a mix of foreign-language, mainstream, and artsy films. The **Harvard Exit** (807 E. Roy St., at Broadway, tel. 206/323–8986), about 10 blocks north of the Egyptian, offers similar fare on its two screens. The creaky antique furniture in the sitting room will make you believe legends of a resident ghost.

The best movie deal is at Downtown's UA Cinema 150 (2131 6th Ave., at Blanchard St., tel. 206/443–9591), which shows both recent second-runs and older arty movies for $2 three times daily. Needless to say, the theater is rarely empty.

In the University District, **Neptune Theater** (1303 N.E. 45th St., tel. 206/633–5545) usually shows double features, mostly classics. The **Grand Illusion Cinema** (1403 N.E. 50th St., tel. 206/523–3935) is a tiny, unorthodox film house seating about 90 people. It specializes in foreign animation and independent films, and lets you enter with espresso or quiche from the café next door. Films are shown daily at 5 and 9, and weekends at 1 PM. Admission is $5.

Near Seattle
Within easy striking distance of Seattle is some of the most spectacular coastal and mountain scenery in the country. In this section, we stick fairly close to the water, concentrating on **Puget Sound, Whidbey Island,** and the **San Juan Islands,** with a few other attractions thrown in for good measure. Chapter 7, Western Washington, covers the Olympic Peninsula, with its mountains, beaches, and rain forest. Chapter 8, The Cascades and Eastern Washington, takes you to the North Cascades, a short drive east from Seattle and an excellent getaway for skiing, hiking, and camping.

Puget Sound

Life is good on the shores of Puget Sound, the body of water that stretches up from Seattle, filled with little islands and skinny peninsulas. For the residents of the villages, farms, and towns that dot the Sound's islands, Seattle may be just an hour's commute from here but seem light years away. Life moves at a more leisurely pace, slowed by ferry schedules, changing seasons, and the overwhelming desire to sit back and take it all in. In few other places do people appear to live so comfortably with nature. For the budget traveler, Puget Sound offers the prospect of magnificent scenery, cheap food, and spectacular camping. Don't visit Seattle without hopping a ferry to see the Sound.

BAINBRIDGE ISLAND

The slow pace of Bainbridge Island discourages obsessive touring, but beautiful mansions, a winery, peaceful gardens, two state parks, and the small-town atmosphere of **Winslow** on the island's east coast all make the half-hour ferry trip from Seattle worthwhile. Most residents of Bainbridge Island are wealthy but laid-back. You'll encounter inflated B&B and restaurant prices here, but camping in the wilderness is always a deal. Many Seattleites cruise over for weekend brunch and return the same afternoon. You, too, can visit the island as a day trip, or you can continue to the nearby Kitsap (*see below*) and Olympic peninsulas.

Strait
of Georgia

USA
CANADA

Saturna
Island

Patos
Island

Sucia
Island

Waldron
Island

Eastsound
Village

Moran
State
Park

Lummi

Lummi
Island

Bellingham
Bay

Ferndale

Laurel

542

Marietta

Lake
Whatcom

Bellingham

11

Stuart
Island

Deer
Harbor

Orcas
Island

East Sound

Doe Bay

Roche
Harbor

Orcas

Samish
Bay

5

English Camp
Nat'l Park

San Juan
Island

Shaw
Island

Odlin
County
Park

Blakely
Island

Cypress
Island

Guemes
Island

Burlington

Friday Harbor

San Juan
Islands

Spencer Spit
State Park

Mt
Vernon

Lime Kiln Point
State Park

Decatur
Island

Anacortes

20

American
Camp
Nat'l Park

Lopez
Island

Fidalgo
Island

La Conner

5

CANADA
USA

Deception Pass

Deception Pass
State Park

534

Strait of Juan de Fuca

Whidbey
Island

Skagit
Bay

Oak Harbor

Stanwood

TO
VICTORIA,
B.C.

San de Fuca

20

532

Camano
Island

Coupeville

Ebey's Landing National
Historic Reserve

Ft. Casey
State Park

Keystone

Saratoga Passage

Port
Susan

Dungeness

Ft. Worden State Park

Port Townsend

Admiralty
Bay

Greenbank

Mabana

TO
PORT
ANGELES

Sequim

Ft. Flagler
State Park

Langley

101

Sequim Bay
State Park

Gardiner

Hadlock

Freeland

525

Discovery
Bay

20

Mutiny
Bay

Clinton

Everett

Useless
Bay

Mulkiteo

N

OLYMPIC
NATIONAL
PARK

Leland

104

Port
Ludlow

Puget
Sound

Lynnwood

Shine

Kitsap
Peninsula

0   30 miles

0   45 km

TO BAINBRIDGE ISLAND,
VASHON ISLAND

Edmonds

TO
SEATTLE

Just up the hill from the ferry terminal is **Winslow,** a small town with charming cafés, antiques shops, clothing stores, and restaurants. After browsing, travel less than a third of a mile up Route 305 to the **Bainbridge Island Winery** (682 Rte. 305, tel. 206/842–9463) and have a picnic in the garden overlooking the vineyard. On the northeast end of the island is the **Bloedel Reserve** (7571 N.E. Dolphin Dr., tel. 206/842–7631), where $4 gets you into 150 acres of lakes, meadows, and carefully groomed gardens. Make arrangements at least a week in advance. Not far from here, about 3 miles off Route 305, is **Fay-Bainbridge State Park** (tel. 206/842–3931), encompassing 17 acres of the island's northeast end. The park is a good spot for fishing, beachcombing, and swimming, provided that numbingly cold water doesn't bother you. On the southern end of Bainbridge, about 6 miles southwest of Route 305 on Pleasant Beach Road, **Ft. Ward State Park** (tel. 206/842–4041) offers a mile of beach, a boat launch, scuba diving, clam digging, hiking on forested trails, and views of the water and the Olympic Mountains.

VISITOR INFORMATION The **Bainbridge Island Chamber of Commerce** (166 Winslow Way, Winslow, tel. 206/842–3700) has free maps and can steer you toward the best shops, beaches, and bike routes.

COMING AND GOING **Washington State Ferries** (tel. 206/464–6400 or 800/542–0810 in Washington) make the 35-minute trip at least once an hour from the Colman Dock at Pier 52 in Seattle to the island's Winslow terminal. Walk-on passengers ($3.50) pay for the westward trip and return at no cost. One-way rates per car and driver are $7.10 during peak season (mid-May–Oct.) or $5.90 off-season. Ticket lines are often long during weekday rush hour and in summer, and reservations are not accepted, so allow plenty of time before your departure. Route 305 heads north from the Winslow ferry terminal to the bridge crossing **Agate Pass** (less than 10 miles away), which connects Bainbridge to the Kitsap Peninsula.

GETTING AROUND Bainbridge Island is 12 miles long and 4 miles wide. Cycling around Bainbridge is fun, fast, and highly recommended. On foot, you'll be limited to Winslow and the winery. **Kitsap Transit's** (tel. 206/373–2877) Bus 90 travels north from the ferry terminal on Route 305, making stops along the way to Poulsbo on the Kitsap Peninsula (*see below*). Fare is 50¢.

WHERE TO SLEEP AND EAT The only accommodations on the island are bed-and-breakfasts. **Bombay House** (8990 Beck Rd. NE, tel. 206/842–3926) is on the southern part of the island, about 4 miles from Winslow. This beautifully restored Victorian home sits on a hill overlooking the water and is fairly close to Ft. Ward State Park. Doubles go for $55–$85. If they're full, try the **Cedar Meadows Bed and Breakfast** (10411 N.E. Old Creosote Hill Rd., tel. 206/842–5291), where each of the four doubles goes for $60–$80. The house is surrounded by six wooded acres and offers bikes, a croquet lawn, and common room with a TV and VCR. If you call ahead, the owners will pick you up from the ferry.

You don't have to stray far from the ferry terminal to eat well on Bainbridge. Winslow has a slew of restaurants, ranging from pizza joints to seafood places. By far the best is the **Streamliner Diner** (397 Winslow Way, tel. 206/842–8595), which serves hearty breakfasts, as well as soups, salads, and the like for lunch. Expect hefty portions, a fun atmosphere, and long lines on weekends. Entrées are about $5.

KITSAP PENINSULA

The Kitsap Peninsula is popular with Seattleites because it's a short ferry ride from home, full of state parks and long, unpopulated stretches of coastline—though most visitors treat it as a mere thoroughfare between Seattle and the Olympic Peninsula. You may, however, wish to give it a closer look. The eastern side of the Kitsap Peninsula, bordered by Puget Sound, is dotted with tiny port towns and their bustling marinas. As you travel along the coast, views of the Olympic National Forest to the west provide a stunning backdrop. Off Route 305 you'll find **Poulsbo,** a tiny, touristy Norwegian-theme sea town. Though kitschy, it's also the most interesting and flavorful town on the peninsula. **Bremerton** and **Port Orchard,** south of Poulsbo on Route 3, are major navy port towns with interesting collections of military people and museums, but not too much more. In Bremerton, you can take a self-guided tour ($5) aboard the destroyer *Turner Joy*, which was instrumental in the escalation of the Vietnam War. From mid-May through September, **Kitsap Harbor Tours** (tel. 206/377–8924) offers a 45-minute guided "Mothball Fleet" boat tour ($6) of the Bremerton shipyard every hour on the half hour from 10:30 AM to 4:30 PM daily. The **Bremerton Naval Museum** (130 Washington Ave., tel. 206/479–7447), next to the Bremerton tourist office (*see below*), contains memorabilia from the Naval Yard, including a Japanese torpedo. On the east coast between Poulsbo and Bremerton, **Silverdale** is the largest city on the peninsula, offering a mall, a beach, and a variety of inexpensive restaurants and entertainment.

Suquamish, a Native American reservation off Route 305, is where Seattle's namesake, Chief Sealth, lies buried. In August the town hosts Chief Seattle Days, a festival drawing people from all over the Northwest for canoe races, dance competitions, and a salmon bake.

VISITOR INFORMATION The **Bremerton/Kitsap County Visitor and Convention Bureau** (120 Washington Ave., Suite 101, Bremerton, tel. 206/479–3588), one block uphill from the ferry terminal, provides brochures about Bremerton and the Olympic and Kitsap peninsulas. **The Greater Poulsbo Chamber of Commerce** (19131 8th Ave. NE, Poulsbo, tel. 206/779–4848) offers the usual gamut of tourist information. Both offices are open weekdays 9–5. **Poulsbohemian Coffeehouse** (19003 Front St., Poulsbo, tel. 206/779–9199) acts as a satellite office for the chamber of commerce, with information on both the Kitsap and Olympic Peninsulas. Of course, they also serve coffee (*see Food, below*).

COMING AND GOING **Washington State Ferries** (tel. 206/464–6400 or 800/542–0810 in Washington) sail every day from Seattle's Colman Dock/Pier 52 to Bainbridge Island (*see above*) and then continue on to Bremerton. The trip takes an hour. Walk-on passengers ($3.50) pay only for the outward-bound leg of the trip. One-way rates per car and driver are $7.10 during peak season (mid-May–Oct.) or $5.90 off-season. Ticket lines are often long during weekday rush hour and in summer, so allow plenty of time before your departure. To sail from the Seattle area to the northern end of the peninsula, take the **Edmonds–Kingston** route, which costs the same and runs about as frequently. You can drive or bike directly from Kitsap's northwest to the tip of the Olympic Peninsula via the **Hood Canal Floating Bridge.** To reach the bridge, take Route 104 west from Kingston.

GETTING AROUND East of the peninsula is Puget Sound; east of that, Seattle. Route 305 begins on Bainbridge Island, crosses a bridge to Poulsbo on the peninsula, and then meets Route 3 to the northeast. Route 3 runs north–south, up to the Hood Canal Bridge (*see* Coming and Going, *above*), and down through Silverdale, Bremerton, and Port Orchard. South of Port Orchard, Route 3 eventually joins U.S. 101 on the Olympic Peninsula (half-way between Olympic National Park and Olympia). From Bremerton, Route 16 leads south through Gig Harbor to Tacoma and I–5. The **Seattle–Olympic Peninsula bike trail** connects much of the Kitsap Peninsula. To explore a good chunk of it, ask about the **Hood Canal Loop** at the Bremerton tourist office (*see* Visitor Information, *above*).

Kitsap Transit (tel. 206/373–2877) has a crosstown express, Bus 11, which will take you from Bremerton to Poulsbo (50¢). Bus 11 leaves the Bremerton Ferry Terminal daily 6 AM–8 PM at a quarter past the hour. The **Jefferson County Bus Line** (tel. 206/385–4777) connects Poulsbo to Port Townsend and serves other northern destinations. Call for schedules and rates.

WHERE TO SLEEP Lodging in Bremerton is limited. Some of the cheapest rooms are at the **Chieftain Motel** (600 National Ave., tel. 206/479–3111), where they charge by the bed, not by the person. Pack your fleet sardine-style into a big bed for $32, or two beds for $38. This is the motel where Bremerton's teens come to party, so prepare for noise. Most of the lodging in Poulsbo is extremely expensive, but the **Continental Inn** (1783 Rte. 308, tel. 206/779–5575), just south of town, has fully equipped rooms for $39 (singles) and $43 (doubles). From Bremerton take Route 3 north to Route 308 east. Six miles north of Poulsbo, off Route 3, the **Kitsap Memorial State Park** (tel. 206/779–3205) has 43 developed sites ($10) and five primitive walk-in sites ($7.50). The park offers some woodsy trails, but the sites have little privacy and are usually dominated by RVs.

FOOD Poulsbo's Front Street, lined with great international restaurants, is the best place to dine on the peninsula. Stop at the **Poulsbohemian Coffeehouse** (19003 Front St., tel. 206/779–9199) for pastries, cappuccino, great seats that overlook the water, and a small tourist information center. Continuing south, stop in for locally famous Scandinavian breads and baked goods at **Sluy's Bakery** (18924 Front St., tel. 206/697–BAKE). **Thomas Kemper Brewery and Taproom** (22381 Foss Rd. NE, tel. 206/697–7899) is an excellent place to tour the brewery and have lunch or dinner—they serve a range of beers and pub foods like brewer's burgers ($4.50) or beer-boiled bratwurst ($5.50). Non-carnivores can try the scrumptious veggie burger ($5.50). Hidden at the end of a brick alley, **Jose's Café** (18830 Front St., tel. 206/779–7676) serves huge, excellent burritos (about $5) and inexpensive combo plates loaded with beans, rice, and chips.

OUTDOOR ACTIVITIES The **Olympic Outdoor Center** (26469 Front St., tel. 206/697–6095) in Poulsbo offers a variety of whitewater- and sea-kayaking trips, ranging from a few hours to a few days, for all levels of experience. Day trips run $40–$65; multiday trips are $110–$250.

VASHON ISLAND

This rural Puget Sound island, southwest of Seattle, offers a pleasant escape from the city's chaos. Vashon's charm lies in its winding roads, quiet beaches, small towns, and bustling AYH hostel. Most of the island is undeveloped, so be adventurous and take a few detours off the main road. It's the perfect place to go biking or hole up for a few days if you're looking for peace, quiet, and green, green scenery.

Vashon is close enough to Seattle that you can tour the island all day and still make it back to the city for dinner.

The ferry lets you off on the northern tip of the island. From here, it's about 3 ½ miles south to **Vashon,** a four-block village of antiques stores and the occasional coffee shop. Berries are a specialty here: In mid-July, the two-day **Strawberry Festival** draws a big crowd with its parade and handicraft displays. **Tok's U-Pick Fields,** right off the main highway in downtown Vashon, lets you forage for your own strawberries and raspberries throughout the summer. About 2 miles south of downtown Vashon is the **Blue Heron Arts Center** (19704 Vashon Hwy. SW, tel. 206/463–5131), the center of the island's cultural scene and a prime spot to shop for locally made pottery, wooden boxes, jewelry, and hand-painted scarves. Less than a mile further south the highway meets S.W. Ellisport Road, which leads into Dockton Road SW. This road continues south to **Dockton Park,** one of the island's best beaches. (Though it's connected to Vashon by a natural sandbar, this area is called **Maury Island.**) If you're looking for a great walk, stay on the highway a few extra miles to reach the **Burton Peninsula.** Trails here wind through thick forest, and a little-traveled road makes the 3-mile loop along its outer rim.

VISITOR INFORMATION There is no visitor center, but you can pick up the *Island Grapevine* at major stores and markets around the island. The free paper has all the information you'll need on community events and organizations.

COMING AND GOING **Washington State Ferries** (tel. 206/464–6400 or 800/542–0810 in Washington) makes regular trips (walk-on passengers only) from Colman Dock/Pier 52 in Seattle to **Heights Dock** at the northern tip of Vashon Island (25 min) during weekday commuter rush hours and on Saturdays; there is no service between Pier 52 and Vashon Island on Sundays. Fare is $3.50 per person. An alternative for visitors to Vashon Island who can't live without cars is to take the ferry from the Fauntleroy Terminal in West Seattle (*see* Coming and Going by Ferry, in Seattle, *above*), a trip of 15 minutes. Round-trip fares are $9.55 per car and driver during peak season (mid-May–Oct.), or $7.95 off-season; walk-on passengers are $2.30. Ticket lines are often long during weekday rush hour and in summer, so allow plenty of time before your departure. The Seattle–Vashon ferry only permits five bicycles on each boat, so arrive extra early if you're bringing your two-wheeled friend. To reach Tacoma, take the ferry from the **Tahlequah Dock** at the island's southern tip. The 15-minute trip costs as much as the Fauntleroy–Heights Dock route.

GETTING AROUND Vashon's beauty and small size (it's about 12 miles from end to end) make biking a fine mode of transportation. As in many Puget Sound areas, the hills can be a challenge. Traveling by foot, you'll probably miss out on the southern half of the island unless you plan to stick around for more than a day. Beginning at the Heights Dock, on the northernmost end of Vashon, a single highway (with several changing names) runs south down its center, eventually turning into Tahlequah Road. This leads to the Tahlequah Ferry Terminal on the south end of the island. **Metro Bus Service** (tel. 800/542–7876) Buses 118 and 119 run along the island north–south, from ferry terminal to ferry terminal. Some buses go only as far as Burton Peninsula, however, so ask before boarding.

WHERE TO SLEEP Motels are not plentiful on Vashon Island. Luckily, there's a good AYH hostel for frugal travelers to fall back on, because most lodging comes in the form of fairly expensive B&Bs. If you have the money, though, many of these are well worth it. **The Old Tjomsland House Bed and Breakfast** (17011 Vashon Hwy. SW, at 171st St., tel. 206/463–5275) is a late-19th-century farmhouse set back from the main highway, just north of downtown Vashon. Jan and Bill Morosoff offer hearty breakfasts, good conversation, and plenty of privacy. Two rooms go for $55 each, and there's a cottage for $75.

Vashon Island Ranch/AYH Hostel. Some people like Vashon so much that they'll stay here while visiting Seattle and commute into the city. Just west of downtown Vashon, the hostel sleeps up to 40 people in its log lodge and five Sioux-style tepees. It also provides discounts on ferry tickets, free bikes, free firewood, and free all-you-can-eat pancake breakfasts. Tepees are equipped with beds and fire pits and are usually reserved for couples, while the two-bunk rooms in the lodge are each strictly single-sex. At $9 for HI members and $12 for nonmembers, this hostel is one of the best deals around. *12119 S.W. Cove Rd., off Rte. 5, tel. 206/463–2592. Kitchen facilities. Closed Oct.–May.*

FOOD Vashon Island isn't exactly teeming with restaurants, but a few centrally located places offer filling meals at affordable prices. In downtown Vashon, the **Malt Shop and Charburger** (17635 100th Ave. SW, tel. 206/463–3740) serves 14 kinds of burgers, all for less than $5, plus thick shakes and malts. About a block north of the Blue Heron Arts Center (*see above*) is **M.O.M.S.** (19120 Vashon Hwy. SW, tel. 206/463–5990), or Market on Main Street, which has sandwiches for under $4. For pasta, stir-fry, Mexican fare, and weekend brunches, try the **Sound Food Restaurant** (20246 Vashon Hwy. SW, tel. 206/463–3565), about two blocks south of M.O.M.S.

OLYMPIA

Olympia is both the capital of Washington and the home of Olympia Beer—what more could you ask for in a town? Sitting demurely on the southernmost shore of Puget Sound, this small city houses an impressive collection of legislative buildings, as well as some fine old mansions around the downtown area. It's also home to liberal Evergreen State College, where you'll see a mixture of young, Birkenstock-wearing folks and buttoned-down future candidates for state legislature.

Depending on whether or not the state legislature is in session when you arrive, Olympia will feel either like a sleepy town, or like a sleepy town bustling with rhetoricians in three-piece suits.

The **Capitol Hill** area holds some interesting sights for the government-minded, most prominent of which is the **Legislative Building** (Capitol Way, btw 10th and 14th Aves.). Free tours start at the main foyer on the hour, 10 AM–3 PM daily. The building has a 287-foot dome that closely resembles the Capitol Building in that other Washington, across the continent. Its grounds feature rose gardens and Japanese cherry trees, especially beautiful when in bloom (around the end of April). Next door, the **Governor's Mansion,** erected in 1908, is the oldest building on Capitol Hill. The red-brick, Georgian-style mansion is still called home by Washington's current governor. Portions of the interior are furnished with a collection of Federal-period antiques; free tours are given on most Wednesday afternoons. Reservations (tel. 206/586–TOUR) are required. While you're in the neighborhood, check out the **State Library** (just behind the Legislative Building) which houses all sorts of state documents, as well as some good local artwork.

Farther along Capitol Way is the **State Capitol Museum** (211 W. 21st Ave., tel. 206/753–2580), a branch of the Washington State Historical Society. The 70-year-old building is closed for renovation until May 1995; when it reopens, it will house seasonal exhibits of local art, history, and natural history and a permanent display of rare Native American baskets. A **Japanese Garden** (cnr Union and Plum Sts., tel. 206/357–3370), created with assistance from Yashiro, Japan—Olympia's sister city—features a waterfall, bamboo grove, koi-filled pond, and lawns decorated with stone lanterns. It's an excellent diversion if you've had one too many Corinthian columns. The garden is open daily 10–10.

VISITOR INFORMATION The **State Capitol Visitor Center** is the best source for tourist information on Olympia, the Olympic Peninsula, and western Washington. *Cnr 14th Ave. and Capitol Way, tel. 206/586–3460. Open summer, weekdays 8–5, weekends 10–4; winter, weekdays 8–5.*

The **Greater Olympia Visitors Convention Bureau** (316 Schmidt Pl., tel. 206/357–3370) supplies words of wisdom on how to visit Olympia's sights on a budget. The **Washington State Parks and Recreation Commission** (7150 Clearwater Ln., tel. 206/753–5755) can give you the lowdown on parks around the Olympic Peninsula, in the San Juan Islands, and elsewhere.

COMING AND GOING Olympia lies at the southern tip of Puget Sound, at the intersection of I–5 with U.S. 101. Driving north on I–5 you'll skirt Olympia's downtown and continue northeast to Seattle. Drive south and you'll reach Portland. To reach the Olympic Peninsula, follow U.S. 101 northwest. To get to the center of Olympia, take the **State Capitol/Downtown Exit 105** from I–5.

➤ **BY BUS** • **Greyhound** (707 E. 7th Ave., at Capital Way, tel. 206/357–5541 or 800/231–2222) buses stop in Olympia several times daily on the way north to Seattle (2 hrs, $10) or south to Portland (3 hrs, $19); buses also travel east to Spokane (8½ hrs, $49). Precise fares and travel times vary. Lockers in the terminal are available to ticketholders ($1 per day). If you're not in a hurry, Olympia's **Intercity Transit** (*see* Getting Around, *below*) will take you to Tacoma (1 hr, $1.50), where you can transfer to a bus into Seattle.

➤ **BY TRAIN** • **Amtrak** (6600 Yelm Hwy. SE, tel. 800/USA–RAIL) trains pass through Olympia twice daily, on a coastal route that continues north to Seattle (2 hrs, $13), and south to Portland (2½ hrs, $19) and eventually to Los Angeles (1½ days, $108). Exact prices and trip lengths vary according to season and day of travel. The station is an inconvenient 8 miles south of town, but **Intercity Transit** (*see* Getting Around, *below*) runs an on-call bus line between the station and town.

GETTING AROUND Intercity Transit (tel. 206/786–1881) provides bus service around Olympia Monday–Saturday 6 AM–7 PM. For service from 7 PM to 11 PM and on Sundays and holidays, call their **Custom Bus** (tel. 206/943–7777). Fare on any bus is 50¢, or $1.00 for an all-day pass.

WHERE TO SLEEP Campgrounds and a few chain motels are the cheapest sleeping options in the area. Ever-reliable **Motel 6** (400 W. Lee St., tel. 206/754–7320) has a branch in the town of Tumwater, just south of Olympia. Singles run about $28, doubles about $34. From I–5 south, take Exit 102, turn left on Trosper Road, right on Capitol Way, and then right onto W. Lee Street. At the center of Olympia is the **Golden Gavel Motor Hotel** (909 Capitol Way, tel. 206/352–8533), which has clean singles for $34–$41 and doubles for $40–$48, depending on the season. From I–5, it's at Exit 105. The **Cinnamon Rabbit Bed and Breakfast** (1304 7th Ave. SW, tel. 206/357–5520), a quiet house near the waterfront, offers the comforts of home (and then some): pleasant rooms, full breakfasts, and a hot tub. Singles are $52, doubles $57.

➤ **CAMPING** • The closest and prettiest campsites are in **Millersylvania State Park,** about 10 miles south of the city on I–5 (take Exit 95). The 164 tent sites ($10 per night), some of which are wheelchair-accessible, have access to tables, stoves, pay showers, and toilets, as well as a stretch of old-growth forest. **Capitol Forest,** west of Olympia on U.S.101 (exit at Blacklake Boulevard), has three primitive campgrounds: Yew Tree, Middle Waddle, and Margaret McKenny. Most have toilets, but none has drinking water. Areas near the entrance roads get crowded in the summer, so pick up your tent and head into the heart of the forest on one of the rarely used trails. The indispensable "Capitol Forest Fire Trail and Campground Map" ($1) is available at the **State Department of Natural Resources** (1111 Washington St. SE, Olympia, tel. 206/902–1234).

FOOD You'll find a range of affordable food in the city center at the intersection of 4th and 5th avenues with Capitol Way. Here you can feast on quality Chinese, Thai, Vietnamese, Greek, Italian, and health food. The **Sweet Oasis Mediterranean Bakery and Café** (507 Capitol Way, tel. 206/956–0470) offers excellent Greek salads ($3.50), Mediterranean soup and salad specials ($3.75–$4.75), and falafel, hummus and tabbouleh plates ($4.25), served with hot pita bread. For dessert, try a jolt of Arabic coffee ($1.75) with a sweet slice of baklava. At **Saigon Rendez-Vous Restaurant** (117 W. 5th Ave., at Capitol Way, tel. 206/352–1989) expect terrific Vietnamese and Chinese cuisine, including an entire menu of meatless dishes. Lunch specials are $5.25–$6.25, dinners $5–$8. The Saigon's greatest hits include greaseless egg rolls and to-die-for chicken with lemon grass. For organic produce, try the well-stocked **Olympia Food Co-op** (West Olympia: 921 N. Rogers St., tel. 206/754–7666; East Olympia: 3111 Pacific Ave., tel. 206/956–3870), open 9–8 daily.

AFTER DARK Downtown Olympia bustles with students from Evergreen State College. Walk up and down 4th and 5th avenues near Capitol Way and you'll find taverns, cafés, ancient diners, and a wide selection of live music. **Columbia Street Public House** (200 W. 4th Ave., at Columbia St., tel. 206/943–5575) is a popular local hangout with a scattering of wooden tables and chairs, dim lighting, and a hip young crowd. The daily happy hour (4–6 PM) features $2 microbrews and cheap food. An eclectic music lineup includes bluegrass (Mondays), Irish folk (Wednesdays), jazz (Thursdays), and jazz and R&B (Saturdays). There's a $2 cover charge on Saturdays.

To get wired and bond with local characters, try Batdorf and Bronsori (513 Capitol Way S, tel. 206/786–6717), the perfect café for java snobs— they roast their own beans in the back room.

Olympia has a growing gay community, now a big part of the bar and music scene. **Thelka** (116 E. 5th Ave., tel. 206/352–1855) draws an unpretentious twenty-something crowd of gays and straights with a DJ, darts, and pool. Cover charge is $1 (Thursdays) or $2 (Fridays and Saturdays). Enter through the back alley. The **Fish Bowl Pub** (515 Jefferson St. SE, tel. 206/943–6480) serves the Fish Brewing Company's unique Fish Tale Ales and "fish food" like smoked salmon and cream cheese ($4.25) to a mellow, generally young clientele. Wednesdays is Grateful Dead night; patrons bring their Dead tunes and crank up the good karma.

On the tail of the Seattle Grunge Sound came the "Olympia Sound," spearheaded by local, independent label K Records and various home-grown bands. Coming soon to a radio station near you.

The **Capitol Theater** (206 E. 5th Ave., tel. 206/754–5378) screens two to three second-run domestic and foreign films daily. Admission is $5. **State Tri-Cinemas** (204 E. 4th Ave. tel. 206/357–4010) shows movies on six screens twice daily. Most of the films are fairly recent, but all seats in this slightly run-down place are only $1.

WHIDBEY ISLAND

Skinny Whidbey Island floats just east of the Olympic Peninsula at the mouth of Puget Sound. Residents claim to have the best of both worlds: Quiet island life with easy bridge access to the mainland. But as the largest island in the continental United States, Whidbey has almost as many miles of tract houses as it does of gorgeous scenic coastline, and its size creates a less-than-intimate, sprawling suburban feel. Sure, folks here can get to Seattle without the fuss of a ferry, but the road goes both ways: Seattleites find the escape to Whidbey just as easy. Consequently, Whidbey Island doesn't come close to providing the kind of idyllic respite one finds in the San Juan Islands (*see below*), just a ferry ride to the north. Instead, it's the perfect getaway for civilization-dependent types who aren't quite ready to give up the conveniences of chain hotels, 24-hour grocery stores, and freeway on-ramps. **Oak Harbor,** Whidbey's northernmost city, is dominated by a naval base and is rather bland and uninspiring. Further south, the seaside towns of **Coupeville, Langley,** and **Freeland** are much more compelling, with historic

Victorian homes, restored downtown districts, friendly neighborhoods, and long stretches of coastline to explore by kayak or on foot. With the exception of good-looking, plentiful camp-grounds, budget lodging is limited.

VISITOR INFORMATION The **Central Whidbey Chamber of Commerce** actually holds court in the offices of **Center Isle Real Estate** (5 S. Main St., Coupeville, tel. 206/678–5434), open daily. It can supply information about the town of Coupeville and its surroundings. The **North Whidbey Chamber of Commerce** (5506 Rte. 20, just north of Oak Harbor, tel. 206/675–3535) has information about the island, as well as the town of Oak Harbor. The **Langeley Chamber of Commerce** (124½ 2nd St., tel. 206/221–6765) gives out information on the town's sights and accommodations.

COMING AND GOING You can reach Whidbey Island either by car or by ferry. The island, 20 miles north of Seattle, is connected to the mainland at its northern tip by **Deception Pass Bridge.** From the Canadian border, take I–5 south to Route 20 west and follow the signs. Head-ing north, take I–5 to Route 536 west, which joins Route 20.

➤ **BY FERRY** • **Washington State Ferries** (tel. 206/464–6400 or 800/542–7052 in Wash-ington) run between **Clinton** (on the southern tip of the island) and **Mukilteo** (just north of Seat-tle), a trip of 20 minutes. Walk-on passengers ($2.30) pay only for the westward leg of the trip. One-way rates for car and driver are $4.80 during peak season (mid-May–Oct.), $4 off-season. To reach Mukilteo from Seattle, take I–5 north to Exit 182. Ferries also run from **Port Townsend** (at the tip of the Olympic Peninsula) to **Keystone** (at Whidbey's midpoint). The ride is 30 min-utes one way.

Walk-on passengers ($1.75) pay for both outbound and return voyages. One-way rates for car and driver are $7.10 during peak season (mid-May–Oct.) or $5.90 off-season. Lines for the ferry are common on weekends and Friday afternoons, especially in summer; arrive early. Fer-ries generally depart for Whidbey every half hour from 5 AM to 1 AM in summer, and somewhat more erratically in winter.

GETTING AROUND Sprawling Whidbey Island has fairly comprehensive (and free) bus ser-vice, so travel here doesn't necessitate a car—though bringing one wouldn't hurt. One highway runs south down the length of this narrow island, changing names from **Route 20** to **Route 525** at its midpoint. If you're planning to bicycle, allow several days to cover all the territory. Maps are essential regardless of your chosen form of transport, since many roads are poorly marked. Pick up free maps at island tourist offices or on the ferries. In Coupeville, **All Island Bicycles** (302 Main St., off Rte. 20, tel. 206/678–3351) rents 18-speed mountain bikes by the hour ($8) or day ($19.95). In Oak Harbor, **All Star Rent-a-Car** (5769 Rte. 20, at Cemetery Rd., tel. 800/722-5216 or 206/675-7498) has daily ($19.95) and weekly ($129.95) rates. Drivers ages 21–24 pay an extra $3 per day.

Welcome to Whidbey. Now Go Home.

In the 1970s, Whidbey Island was a mecca for hippies, artists, and other crunchy or burnt-out types who fled the drudgery of Seattle life in search of a simpler existence. You can see the remnants of idealism in the many art galleries and multicolored mail-boxes painted with peace signs—and in the locals who gripe about "Californians" buy-ing up all of the oceanfront property. Whidbey residents apply the term "Californian" liberally, to anyone who's made money in another part of the world (usually by selling a speck of overvalued land) and who then arrives on the island to build a big house and live the good life. Ironically, many so-called Californians are actually wealthy Seattleites buying vacation homes. Don't mention the "C" word, though, and you'll do fine.

➤ **BY BUS** • **Island Transit** (tel. 206/678–7771 or 206/321–0625) provides free bus service to various points around the island: east and west Oak Harbor, Coupeville, Greenbank, Freeland, Langley, Clinton, and the Keystone and Clinton ferry terminals. Buses run Monday–Saturday hourly from about 7:30 AM until 8 PM. Pick up schedules and maps at most large business establishments.

WHERE TO SLEEP Whidbey's four excellent state campgrounds offer the best lodging options on the island. Otherwise, Oak Harbor has a few nondescript roadside motels with rooms for around $40–$50, and a few bed-and-breakfasts with exorbitant prices. The rest of the island (Coupeville, Langley, and Freeland) is strictly stocked with expensive Victorian B&Bs, with doubles hovering around $100 per night. The **Whidbey Island B&B Association** (tel. 206/679–2276) can make recommendations if you so desire.

➤ **COUPEVILLE** • **Colonel Crockett Farm Bed and Breakfast.** Although a stay in this 135-year-old Victorian farm house costs a bit more than a motel (doubles $65–$75, suites $85–$95), the building is beautiful and ideally located near Penn Cove harbor and downtown Coupeville. A hot breakfast is included. *807 N. Main St., Coupeville, tel. 206/678–3711. 5 rooms.*

The Coupeville Inn. With panoramic views of Coupeville and Penn Cove, the rooms here are well decorated, with private balconies, TVs, and phones. Doubles start at $50 (higher in summer); you'll pay extra for what you can see out the windows, too. Continental breakfast is included. *200 Coveland St., Coupeville, tel. 206/678–6668. 24 rooms.*

Tyee Motel and Cafe. This fairly isolated motel has clean but tacky rooms that are the cheapest in southern Whidbey Island. Each room varies drastically, so if you get one with brick walls and plastic chairs, ask to see another. The friendly management runs the restaurant next door, and there's a grocery store across the street. Singles are $34, doubles $38. *405 S. Main St., Coupeville, tel. 206/678–6616. 9 rooms. Wheelchair access.*

➤ **LANGLEY** • **Drake's Landing.** Langley's most affordable lodging also has some of the best views. At the edge of town and across the street from the harbor, the five rooms here (all with full bathrooms) are well decorated with quilts and woodwork. Small doubles go for $45–$55. *203 Wharf St., Langley, tel. 206/221–3999. From Downtown, follow 1st St. to the waterfront.*

➤ **FREELAND** • **Mutiny Bay Resort Motel.** Each of Mutiny's five cabins with kitchens ($50–$65) sleep up to five people. Or spring for one of four gorgeous, glass-walled chalets ($100), which sleep seven; these have fireplaces, TVs, fully equipped kitchens, and excellent views of the sound. The motel has a private fishing dock and pole rentals, too. *5856 Freeland Ave., Freeland, tel. 206/331–4500. Reservations recommended.*

➤ **OAK HARBOR** • **Queen Ann Hotel.** Located in Oak Harbor's historic shopping district, the Queen Ann offers quiet, well-maintained rooms equipped with cable TV and coffee makers. The city beach is within easy walking distance. Doubles range from $47 to $53. *1204 W. Pioneer Way, Oak Harbor, tel. 206/675–2209. 22 rooms, 4 with kitchens. Indoor pool and hot tub.*

➤ **CAMPING** • The four state park campgrounds on Whidbey fill quickly in summer. They're open year-round and usually charge a per-campsite fee plus $5 per extra vehicle. However, a fifth campground is free: **Rhododendron Park,** run by the Department of Natural Resources, offers eight semi-private campsites, drinkable water, pit toilets, and several hiking trails. It's just 2 miles south of Coupeville on Route 20. For general camping information, call the **Washington State Parks Department** (tel. 800/562–0990).

Deception Pass State Park. Washington state's most popular park packs in about three million visitors per year. With more than 17 miles of saltwater shoreline, three freshwater lakes, and over 20 miles of forest trails, Deception Pass is a must-visit even for those who don't plan to stay overnight. The park's secluded inlet and long but crowded sandy beach are perfect for picnicking, while campsites ($11) are canopied by dense forest. Special hiker/biker spots are $5. The park is at the northernmost point of the island, just over Deception Pass Bridge. *Tel. 206/675–2417. From Oak Harbor, take Rte. 20 7 mi north. 230 sites. Saltwater fishing, showers, rest rooms, fire rings. Wheelchair access.*

Ft. Casey State Park. Built during the late 1890s, this former U.S. Army post was one of three artillery installations that once guarded the Strait of Juan de Fuca and the entrance to the Puget Sound. You can explore the guns and bunkers, visit an interpretive center, stroll mile-long Keystone Spit, or admire the lighthouse at Admiralty Head. Sites ($11) are near the beach and hiking trails. *1280 S. Ft. Casey Rd., Coupeville, tel. 206/678–4519. 35 sites. Tables, showers, rest rooms, fire rings, fishing.*

Ft. Ebey State Park. Ft. Ebey is less crowded with both people and trees than is Deception Pass to the north. Trails lead to the nearby beach, the old fort batteries, and several forested "kettles," depressions left behind by the huge, slowly melting glaciers of 10,000–12,500 years ago. Most noticeable of these ice age remnants is Lake Pondilla, a large kettle with fishing, birdwatching, swimming, scuba diving, and picnicking areas. Sites ($11) are cramped but relatively well shrouded with shrubs and bushes. The most private are the tents-only walk-in sites ($5). *Tel. 206/678–4636. From Coupeville, take Rte. 20 2 mi east to Libby Rd. 50 sites. Showers, tables, rest rooms, fire rings. Wheelchair access.*

South Whidbey State Park. This campground on the southwestern coast has waterfront sites ($11) close to hiking trails, fishing, and swimming. *4128 S. Smuggler's Cove Rd., tel. 206/321–1559. Between the towns of Greenbank and Freeland on Rte. 525. 54 sites. Showers, tables, fire rings, and rest rooms.*

FOOD Seafood dominates most restaurants' menus. In Coupeville, virtually all eating establishments serve some version of clam chowder. Elsewhere, expect plenty of smoked salmon. You'll find the best selection of restaurants in Coupeville and Langley; Oak Harbor has fast-food and chain restaurants, as well as a decent supermarket.

➤ **COUPEVILLE • Christopher's.** Coupeville's resident chef extraordinaire is only 21, but his cooking is praised up and down the island and beyond. The Pacific Northwestern cuisine includes medallions of beef tenderloin with blueberry sauce ($16.95), fresh Canadian halibut filets with lemon and fresh dill ($15), and chicken loganberry ($13.95). The tiny restaurant is set up like someone's home, with two small, individually decorated rooms. It's definitely worth the splurge. *23 Front St., Coupeville, tel. 206/678—5480. Open Wed.–Fri. 5 PM–9 PM; also open Fri. 11:30 AM–2:30 PM.*

Coupeville Café and Harbor Store. This café in a historic wharf building (circa 1900) offers cheap food and drinks and the best seats in town—picnic tables right at the pier's end. Create your own sandwich ($3.95) with bread from the in-store bakery, or try a house specialty, like fried prawns or ginger chicken ($6.95). The café's peeling, Pepto-pink paint actually adds to the casual ambiance. *26 Front St., Coupeville, tel. 206/678–3625. Open daily 9–5.*

Toby's Tavern. A small, dark, no-frills joint, Toby's offers a pool table, bar stools (monopolized by seafaring locals), and several red vinyl booths that overlook the water. For a real feel of Whidbey culture, come at night, when the bar is packed with characters. The menu is strictly pub fare, such as sandwiches ($5), fish and chips ($7.95), and the town's ubiquitous chowder ($2.50). Nonsmokers may find this place irritating. *8 Front St., Coupeville, tel. 206/678–4222. Meals served daily 11–9; drinks served 11–midnight.*

➤ **OAK HARBOR • Café Galerie.** Galerie is a gem in the mud of boring downtown Oak Harbor. The airy café offers indoor seating at wrought-iron park benches among local works of art. Enjoy big deli sandwiches ($4.45), soups ($1.45), refreshing fruit shakes ($1.95), and homemade pie (95¢ a slice) along with views of the boat-filled marina. It's a popular destination for the after-theater crowd. *1083 W. Pioneer Way, Oak Harbor, tel. 206/675–5921. Open daily 7–7.*

➤ **LANGLEY • The Doghouse Backdoor Restaurant and Tavern.** A Whidbey institution, the Doghouse is part waterfront bar, part family-oriented restaurant. Both sections serve what's locally considered the best hamburger on the island ($5). Vegetarians can try a no-meat burger ($5.25) or tasty ghivetch ($4.25), veggies sautéed in broth and topped with melted cheese. The view of Saratoga Passage from the back is a spectacular distraction from the pool tables and locals socializing in the tavern up front. *230 1st St., Langley, tel. 206/321–9996. Open Mon.–Thurs. 11–8:30, Fri. and Sat. 11–9:30, Sun. 11:30–8:30.*

WORTH SEEING Whidbey's four **state parks** offer great opportunities for hiking, fishing, cycling, and camping. **Ft. Casey** and its gun batteries are reminders of the island's long relationship with the military, an effect of its strategic position at the mouth of Puget Sound. Less

Langley, situated on a bluff overlooking the Saratoga Passage, is the island's postcard-perfect seaside village, with numerous antiques shops, clothing boutiques, art galleries, cafés, and restaurants, and a friendly, Birkenstock-clad citizenry.

bellicose are the collection of well-preserved homes and businesses in the towns of **Coupeville** and **Langley,** all beautifully restored Victorian gables and gingerbread. As a rule, towns become more quirky and interesting the further south you travel.

➤ **COUPEVILLE** • Coupeville, a salty and untouristy seaside village on southern Whidbey Island, could claim the title of Most Rustic Island Town. One of Washington's oldest settlements, it really hasn't changed much in appearance since the 1800s. The main drag (and practically the only drag) overlooks Penn Cove and includes several Victorian homes, an old wharf, and a handful of log cabins built during the 1850s. You'll also find several shops and restaurants, as well as the **Island County Historical Museum** (908 N.W. Alexander St., tel. 206/678–3310), with exhibits on local history. Both the town and nearby Ft. Ebey State Park (*see* Where to Sleep, *above*) are part of the **Ebey's Landing National Historic Reserve** (tel. 206/678–4636), a protected 22-acre expanse of farmland, parks, trails, and over 90 registered historical structures. There's very little left of Ft. Ebey—just one old gun emplacement—but the park's scenery makes it worth a visit. Walk along the dry, almost desert-like bluffs overlooking the water or explore the damp forests inland.

➤ **DECEPTION PASS STATE PARK** • If you arrive from the north by car, don't whip by this place with your head in the clouds. Likewise, if you come from the south, try to make it all the way to the northern tip of the island to see this spectacular pass. When Captain George Vancouver first explored the area, he believed Whidbey and Fidalgo islands were a peninsula, so he named this small body of water dividing the two Deception Pass. Walk out along the bridge for a spectacular view, especially around sunset. The trails and shelters in the park were built by the Civilian Conservation Corps. You can also visit the **interpretive center** (tel. 206/675–2417) for more information on park activities.

➤ **GREENBANK** • Just south of town, the **Meerkerk Rhododendron Gardens** (3135 S. Meerkerk Ln., tel. 206/678–1912) offer 53 acres of walking trails among 1,500 native and hybrid species of rhododendrons. The best time to see flowers is in April or May. Admission is free, and the gardens are open daily 9–4. About three-quarters of a mile north of Greenbank, **Loganberry Farms** (657 Wonn Rd., tel. 206/678–7700) cultivates loganberries, from which they make fine liqueurs and port. Visit the rustic farm where the berries are grown, take a self-guided tour of the harvesting and fermentation process, and then enjoy free samples of the finished products. The **Loganberry Festival** (usually the last weekend of July) brings together craftspeople, entertainers, and musicians.

➤ **FT. CASEY STATE PARK** • One of three artillery posts established in the 1890s to guard Puget Sound, Ft. Casey served as a training center during World Wars I and II before

Even if—by some major defect in your personality—you aren't interested in Ft. Casey's batteries of mounted guns, it still has a fine waterfront setting for throwing around a Frisbee or flying a kite.

ultimately retiring as a park in 1950. Parts of *An Officer and a Gentleman* were filmed here, amid the old gun batteries, endless lawns, and winding beach trails. The park also has 35 campsites (*see* Where to Sleep, *above*), picnic areas, and a boat launch. The **Keystone Underwater State Park,** adjacent to the harbor, is a popular area for scuba diving; you can rent equipment at the **Whidbey Island Dive Center** (9050 900th Ave. W, Oak Harbor, tel. 206/675–1112), where a day's gear will run from $50 to $80. The **Ft. Casey Interpretive Center,** open Wednesday–Sunday 10–6, is located in Admiralty Lighthouse. Tours of the fort are given on summer weekends at 2 PM. *Interpretive Center: 1280 S. Ft. Casey Rd., Coupeville, tel. 206/678–4519. Park open daily 8 AM–dusk.*

➤ **OAK HARBOR** • Oak Harbor—named for the once-plentiful trees now replaced by fast-food stands—lacks the aesthetic qualities of Langley or Coupeville, but what did you expect of a navy town? (If you answered "muscled men with crew cuts roaming the island in a horny dementia," you're obviously familiar with the scenario.) The island's commercial and military center, it was originally settled by Dutch and Irish immigrants in the 1800s. Several windmills and the annual tulip festival, **Holland Happenings** (late April), serve as reminders of Oak Harbor's heritage. The town hosts several other festivals each year, the biggest of which is **Race Week** (mid-July), one of the top 20 regattas in the world. Sailboats from all over fill its marina and the streets come alive. Just south of Oak Harbor is **Whidbey Island Naval Air Station,** source of all the short-haired men and the whooshing planes overhead. Every summer, a **Navy Air Show** (tel. 206/257–2286) dominates life in northern Whidbey for a short stretch of days.

San Juan Islands

Welcome to island paradise, Pacific Northwestern style. Once you've seen the blue waters, rugged landscape, undeveloped coastline, and quirky island communities, you, too, may contemplate never leaving. The San Juan Islands greet visitors with wildlife that's still wild and citizens who are still friendly. Of the 172 islands with names, less than a third are inhabited, and only four are accessible by ferry. The rest of the pocket-sized islands are accessible only by private boat, kayak, or plane. Of course, tourists are quickly discovering the San Juans, clogging the roads and filling the ferries in July and August, and wealthy property owners from Seattle and California are staking more permanent claims. To the seasoned urbanite, peak tourist season will seem amazingly serene on the San Juans, but for a less tumultous trip, try to visit either in spring or early fall.

All kinds of people have come to the San Juans to escape their respective rat races—lawyers-turned-fishermen, ex-hippies, and struggling artists—making the islands simultaneously provincial and progressive.

If you can slow down and rid yourself of the desire for four-star accommodations, you certainly won't deplete your cash reserves here. The islands offer one **AYH hostel,** on Orcas Island, and many wildly beautiful (and cheap) camping spots. Pack a picnic and you'll barely have to spend any money on food. And most of the "tourist attractions"—bald eagles, wildflowers, sunsets, and orca whales—are free. Ultimately, it's the landscape that wins over most visitors. Drier and sunnier than the mainland, the San Juans offer for exploration grassy meadows and sunny beaches, damp coniferous forests, wineries, a few towering mountains, and several pastoral stretches dotted with tiny, self-sufficient farms. People come from all over for the cycling, boating, and kayaking, or just to roam the parks and forests.

COMING AND GOING **Washington State Ferries** (tel. 206/464–6400 or 800/843–3779 in Washington) run between Anacortes (90 minutes north of Seattle) and Sidney, British Columbia, stopping at four of the San Juans along the way: Lopez, Shaw, Orcas, and San Juan Islands. Fares are collected on westbound ferries only; eastbound return is included in the ticket price. The fare from Anacortes to Sidney is $6.90 per passenger. Per car and driver, the fare is $35.65 during peak season (May–mid-September) and $29.70 during off-peak. The fare to individual islands is $4.95 per passenger. Per car and driver it is $14.75–$20.30 (peak) or $12.30–$16.80 (off-peak), with Lopez being the cheapest and San Juan the most expensive. To save a few bucks, plan on going to San Juan Island (or Sidney) first, and then loop back to Orcas, Shaw, and Lopez islands free of charge on your return. To reach Anacortes from Seattle, take I–5 north to Route 20 west and follow the signs.

During weekends, holidays, Friday afternoons, and most July and August days, you can easily spend up to three hours waiting with your car at the Anacortes Ferry Terminal. Unfortunately, you can't make reservations for passage to any of the islands; reservations are only accepted for direct trips between Anacortes and Sidney, May–September. Not all ferries stop at each island, and sailing times (and frequencies) vary by season, so call ahead, or pick up a schedule, available at tourist offices and ferry terminals. Generally, if you're not traveling during commuter traffic times (i.e., early morning or late afternoon on weekdays), or going westbound on Friday and eastbound on Sunday, you should be able to arrive about 30–40 minutes prior to your departure and have no problems. Otherwise, allow at least 60–90 minutes at Anancortes (or one of the islands) and two hours at Sidney.

From June to September, **San Juan Island Shuttle Express** (355 Harris St., Suite 105, Bellingham, tel. 206/671–1137) provides passenger service once daily (9:15 AM) from the Cruise Terminal in Bellingham (*see* Elsewhere Near Seattle, *below*), about 25 miles south of the Canadian border, to Orcas Island and to Friday Harbor on San Juan Island. The trip is 2¼ hours; the round-trip cost is $33, or $27 for students.

➤ **BY PLANE** • The following companies fly very costly charters to the San Juans: **Harbor Airlines** (tel. 800/359–3220), **West Isle Air** (tel. 800/874–4434), and **Kenmore Air Harbor** (tel. 800/543–9595).

GETTING AROUND Although it's expensive to take your car to the islands, it's worth doing unless you're an extremely fit cyclist. On San Juan Island the ferry lets you off in town, but on Orcas and Lopez Islands, the major sights are at least a 10- to 20-minute drive from the ferry terminal. Options for carless folk are: hitchhiking (relatively safe and common on all the islands), renting a bike or scooter (most islands offer rentals at the ferry terminals), or calling a cab.

SAN JUAN ISLAND

The residents of San Juan Island have a love/hate relationship with the rest of the world. Although the economy is largely tourist driven, you wouldn't know it from dealing with the aloof locals. Still, they wouldn't offer great outdoor activities, like kayaking, cycling, boating, and a whale-watching park; and they wouldn't put on the fabulous **San Juan Island Dixieland Jazz Festival** every year (in late July) if they didn't want at least a few humble visitors.

Free Willy was filmed on San Juan, though locals are notoriously hush-hush about this fact. If you see the film, notice that the island's name has been obscured on the Chamber of Commerce building so as to avoid a sudden influx of frenzied, child-toting mobs.

Because of its proximity to Victoria, B.C., San Juan Island receives more visitors than any of the other three San Juan islands accessible by ferry. **Friday Harbor,** the largest town in the San Juans, revolves around the yuppie-driven summer resort economy. **Spring Street,** stretching up from the ferry terminal, is loaded with cute but pricey restaurants, clothing boutiques, art galleries, cafés and a few pubs. Shops and restaurants cater to tourists (the island population doubles during the summer), but you'll find plenty of locals here, too.

VISITOR INFORMATION The friendly and informative staff at the **Chamber of Commerce** (125 Spring St., Friday Harbor, tel. 206/378–5240) prefer to answer questions rather than throw brochures at you.

GETTING AROUND San Juan Island is large in comparison with the other San Juan Islands. While it is possible to see the island by bike, you'll want to take two or three days to do so. For the most part, it's pleasant cycling territory (many roads run along the ocean) with mild hills. To avoid the steepest ones, travel west on Beaverton Valley Road from the ferry terminal and south on Westside Road (along Mitchell Bay). **Primo Taxi and Tours** (tel. 206/378–887) runs a shuttle ($4) between Roche Harbor and Friday Harbor, 7:20 AM–5:55 PM in summer (shorter hours in winter). They also have a taxi service (tel. 206/378–3550) that operates daily from 6 AM to 3 AM.

Island Bicycles (380 Argyle St., Friday Harbor, tel. 206/378–4941) rents everything from one-speeds to mountain bikes by the hour ($2–$5) or by the day ($8–$20). Bicycle maps are $3. Those who aren't up to biking can rent mopeds at **Susie's Moped Rentals** (Churchill Sq., Friday Harbor, tel. 206/378–5244 or 800/532–0087), near the ferry landing, per hour ($10) or per day ($40).

WHERE TO SLEEP Unless you want to pay $100 for a room, your lodging options on San Juan Island are nil, nada, zero, zilch. The Roche Harbor Resort has abundant charm but is isolated and (as you'd expect from a resort) fairly expensive. B&Bs are plentiful but pricey: Rates start at about $65 per night, but most rooms cost around $75–$100. For the prices and phone numbers of hotels and B&Bs on San Juan, call **San Juan Central Reservations** (tel. 206/378–6678) or pick up a list of B&Bs at the Chamber of Commerce (*see* Visitor Information, *above*). If you're camping and feel particularly grungy, the **public rest rooms** at the port in Friday Harbor have showers.

Roche Harbor Resort. A popular boating resort, Roche Harbor has changed little since its construction in the 1880s. A standard room with a shared bath in the Hotel de Haro is $48 in the low season (October–March) and $70 in the high season (April–September). Rates for suites and rooms with a harbor view are $70–$110. Cottages ($100–$110), which sleep four–six people, are available for rent during the high season. A four-night minimum is imposed on the cottages in July and August. *4950 Tarte Memorial Dr., tel. 206/378–2155. At the island's north end, 10 mi NW of Friday Harbor. Grocery store, restaurant, swimming pool. Closed Thanksgiving–Easter.*

➤ **CAMPING • Lakedale Campground.** By far the largest of the island's campgrounds, Lakedale also offers the most amenities. Swim, fish, and hike, or explore Nava and Dream Lakes in one of the rentable kayaks, canoes, or paddleboats ($3.50–$5.50 per hour). Most of the sites are noisy, especially when families infest the place in July and August. Regular sites are $18, and walk-in spots are $5.50. There are also two "tent cabins" ($30–$40 each). *2627 Roche Harbor Rd., tel. 206/378–2350. 4 mi north of Friday Harbor. 120 tent sites, 6 walk-in sites. Drinking water, coin-op showers. Closed Oct. 15–Apr. 1.*

San Juan County Park. Whales swim by this waterfront campground daily. It's more secluded than Lakedale and also less riddled with RVs—probably because it's miles and miles from both Friday and Roche harbors. Sites cost $14, $4.50 for walk-in spots. Reservations are recommended in summer. *380 Westside Rd., tel. 206/378–2992. 20 sites. Drinking water available, but limited.*

Town & Country Park. A mile north of the Friday Harbor ferry landing, this RV park maintains a secluded area for cyclists and other tent carriers. The hillside tent sites ($10) are under a stand of tall trees at the edge of a meadow. *595 Tucker Ave., Friday Harbor, tel. 206/378–4717. 11 tent sites; 27 RV sites. Drinking water, coin-op showers, laundry, fire rings.*

FOOD The island has plenty of perfect picnic spots. To pick up the fixings, stop by **King's Market** (160 Spring St., Friday Harbor, tel. 206/378–4505), the island's largest grocery store. For a hot meal, the best (and actually, the only) choices are also in Friday Harbor. Take the stairs down from the sidewalk to **Way of Life Whole Foods Market/Vegetarian Juice Bar** (35 1st St. S, Friday Harbor, tel. 206/378–5433) for a glass of wheatgrass juice ($1.50 per ounce), vegetarian and vegan lunch food (around $5), or breakfast offerings such as granola or muesli with fruit ($3.75).

Front Street Ale House. This big, friendly pub 'n grub tavern is packed with rambunctious locals and cheery tourists feasting on slamming chili ($4.95), shepherd's pie ($6.95), and monster nachos ($6.95). The microbrewed wheat beer Eichenberger Itefe-Weizen (just ask for an "Ike"), served in a traditional Bavarian glass, is one of the best around. Entrées ($4–$8) include salads, sandwiches, and seafood. There's a special late-night menu, too. *1 Front St., tel. 206/378–2337. Open weekdays 8 AM–midnight, weekends 8 AM–1 AM. Kitchen open until 10 PM; snacks served until midnight.*

Front Street Café. This café/ice-cream parlor, gussied up with fussy wallpaper and Tiffany lamps, is just steps away from the ferry terminal. They serve sandwiches ($4.95) and salads ($2.25–$3.25) for lunch, and breakfast items like granola and banana ($3.50) or a bagel with lox ($5.50). It's the perfect place to grab breakfast and an espresso, though lines here can be as long as those for the ferry. *101 Front St., Friday Harbor, tel. 206/378–2245. Open daily 7 AM–9:30 PM.*

Katrina's. In back of the Funk 'n' Junk antiques store, this place serves homemade meals at a few backyard tables. The eclectic, sometimes-vegetarian or vegan menu changes daily, depending on the chef's whims. Dishes such as Eggplant Mezzaluna with sundried-tomato pesto ($4.75) include soup or salad and freshly baked bread. *65 Nichols St., Friday Harbor, tel. 206/378–7290. Open weekdays noon–5.*

WORTH SEEING Unless you arrive on a private boat, you'll probably begin your visit in Friday Harbor, the islands' commercial center. In summer, the town swarms with tourists—many of whom just ferry out for the day and then leave at dusk. Once you've satisfied the browsing urge in Friday Harbor, explore the island's farmlands and rolling hills. Heading north from town and circling the island you'll easily catch all the main attractions: Roche Harbor, English Camp, Limekiln Lighthouse, Whalewatch Park, False Bay, and American Camp, in that order. Several are discussed here; for the rest, *see* Outdoor Activities, *below*.

➤ **ROCHE HARBOR** • Built in the 1880s as a limestone-mining village, Roche Harbor retains much of its old flavor in its present incarnation as a resort. In its heyday as a watering hole for the jet set, Teddy Roosevelt and many other notables came to visit. The historic Hotel de Haro (*see* Roche Harbor Resort, in Where to Sleep, *above*) displays period photographs and artifacts in its lobby. If you're interested, ask the staff for a map that points out remnants of the mining industry and the eerie memorial to McMillian, **The Mausoleum.** Designed by the man himself as a sort of neo-Greek temple, the monument embodies the family's religious beliefs and McMillian's own devotion to the Masonic Order. Sons and daughters are each symbolized by a chair, doubling as the crypt for his or her ashes. The number of steps and their layout are also symbolic, as is the surreal broken column, supposedly illustrating the unfinished state of man's work when life is cut short. *10 mi northwest of Friday Harbor.*

➤ **WHALE MUSEUM** • A pod of about 98 orcas swim the waters around San Juan Island. Because these do not migrate and are always within a 200-mile radius of their home, you have a pretty good shot at seeing them any time of year. At the museum, photos and a family tree identify each of the resident whales, excepting the two or three most recent newborns; whalewatching trips and tours are also possible. For an extra $25–$40, you can adopt one of these magnificent sea mammals, though you're not allowed to take it home with you. *62 1st St. N,*

The Pig War

Early in San Juan Island's history, ownership of the island was claimed by both the English and the Americans. Tensions escalated into a full-scale but arcane confrontation, known as The Pig War, when an American farmer shot and killed an Englishman's pig. The two governments sent in the troops to establish camps, where dozens of bored soldiers passed 13 years between 1859 and 1872. No one was ever killed or injured, and in the end the two sides even took to planning social events together. A visit to either the camps or The Pig War Museum (at Tucker and Guard streets in Friday Harbor) fills in the political details and gives an idea of what life was like for the soldiers. Live reenactments of troop action (or rather, inaction) are presented during summer by the National Park Service; check at the Chamber of Commerce in Friday Harbor for a schedule of the performances.

Of the two military encampments, English Camp at the island's north end is the better preserved, with buildings and even a restored English garden. An on-site slide presentation tells the Pig War story. At the more desolate American Camp, situated at the end of the island's beautiful southern peninsula, the few historical remains make a good excuse for a walk through grassy meadows or along the seashore. These twin San Juan Island National Historic Parks (tel. 206/378–2240) are open all year.

Friday Harbor, tel. 206/378–4710. Admission: $3, $2.50 students. Open late-May–Sept., daily 10–5; Oct.–May, daily 11–4.

AFTER DARK Because of the seasonal tourist flow, Friday Harbor attracts numerous bands and performers throughout July and August. On the last weekend in July is the island's **Dixieland Jazz Festival** (tel. 206/378–4224 or 206/378–5509); with some of the world's best Dixieland jazz bands, it's the apex of the summer season. **Herb's Tavern** (cnr Spring and 1st Sts., Friday Harbor, tel. 206/378–9106) is a favorite local hangout with billiards and big tables good for socializing.

OUTDOOR ACTIVITIES Kayakers and scuba divers can frolic in the San Juan waters along with whales and sea otters. Many visitors come to the island to explore its marine parks, accessible only by boat. **Emerald Seas Aquatics** (180 1st St., Friday Harbor, tel. 206/378–2772) runs half-day boat dives ($50) for certified scuba divers only. (If you're here for a week, you can take a certification class for $275.) They also organize kayaking expeditions in the tranquil waters of nearby Griffin Bay, which include an introductory lesson and use of a kayak for either two ($15) or four ($25) hours. **Crystal Seas Kayaking** (tel. 206/378–7899) offers morning, afternoon, and sunset tours for up to six participants. The $39 tours (4–5 hours) pass marine life like whales, porpoises, seals, eagles, and smaller shoreline creatures. At the Cannery building in Roche Harbor Resort (see Where to Sleep and Worth Seeing, above), **San Juan Central Reservations** (tel. 206/378–2155, ext. 258) offers guided kayak trips ($42), which include free admission to the Whale Museum (see Worth Seeing, above).

If you spend any amount of time on the island, you have a good chance of spotting orcas, or killer whales. Many of the charters that operate out of Friday Harbor are irresponsible about keeping a respectful distance from these sensitive marine mammals, but you can see them from the shore safely and easily at **Limekiln State Park,** an official whale-watching park on the island's western shore. **False Bay,** just south of Limekiln, is a favorite hangout for bald eagles. There are several cleared inland trails, but you'll probably want to stick close to shore and keep your eye out for whales and other sealife.

ORCAS ISLAND

The largest of the San Juan Islands, Orcas Island boasts the longest shoreline, as well as many acres of forested, hilly terrain. Most Orcas Island residents are products of urban flight; they've renounced big-city life in favor of this close-knit island community situated among stretches of stark, largely undeveloped wilderness, rocky coastline, and sand beaches. As with other islands, residents include a high percentage of artists, musicians, and otherwise creative people, but Orcas is distinct in its large population of younger bohemian adventurers, who thrill to explore the San Juans' most geographically diverse island on foot or by kayak. It's little wonder the area is so popular: There's a welcoming AYH hostel at the edge of **Doe Bay;** campsites are affordable and plentiful all over the island; and cafés and markets in **Eastsound** provide inexpensive, healthy food. Looming 2,400 feet above sea level, **Mt. Constitution** in Moran State Park offers what are possibly the best ocean views in the continental United States. Stop by the unstaffed **Travel Infocenter** (Main St., tel. 206/376–2273), next to the Orcas Island Museum in Eastsound, to pick up free maps and brochures.

GETTING AROUND Orcas is shaped like a horseshoe, with the **Orcas Island Ferry Landing** (tel. 206/376–4389) at its southwestern tip. The AYH hostel and a mineral springs resort are on the southeastern end, and the village of **Eastsound** (the heart of island commerce) is at its center. If you're planning to get around on a bike, be warned: Orcas's hills are steep. The drive from tip to tip can also be lengthy because of Orcas's unique shape.

Arrive early in the day if you hope to rent a mountain bike at **Wildlife Cycles** (A St. and North Beach Rd., Eastsound, tel. 206/376–4708), since the demand is usually greater than the supply. Rentals are by hour ($5) or day ($20); topographical maps are available for a charge, but biking maps are free. If you've got more cash than energy, rent a moped at **Key Moped Rentals** (tel. 206/376–2474) for $10 per hour or $40 per eight-hour day. Key's rental offices are located at Orcas Landing, Rosario Resort, and in Eastsound on Langell Street north of Island

Market. **Adventure Limo/Taxi Service** (tel. 206/376–4994) provides shuttle service from the ferry landing to Doe Bay ($37) and to Eastsound ($20).

WHERE TO SLEEP Reservations are essential on Orcas Island. Although you may have luck at the last minute at the hostel or one of the overflow camping areas in Doe Bay, to stay at **Moran State Park Campground** in the spring or summer, you'll need to make reservations in January. The cheapest lodging is in Eastsound.

Outlook Inn. This Victorian inn on the edge of Eastsound features a variety of rooms decorated in the styles of the 19th century. The east wing, refurbished in 1980, offers TVs and private bathrooms. Rooms in the other wing may be more weathered, but they're still comfortable— and some of the best deals in town. Doubles (with shared baths) are $70 ($35 in winter). The new rooms are $120 ($50 in winter). *Main St., Eastsound, tel. 206/376–2200. 28 rooms, 17 with shared bath.*

West Beach Resort. Big groups (or those who just want to save some money by cooking instead of dining out) will appreciate the resort's 13 beachfront cabins, which come with kitchens, fireplaces, and full bathrooms. The price ($95 summer, $72 winter) includes round-trip shuttle service from the ferry or airport. This is the place to stay if you want to explore the shoreline, rent a kayak, or just relax on the sand. *Box 510, Rte. 1, tel. 206/376–2240. 3 mi west of Eastsound on Enchanted Forest Rd.*

➤ **HOSTELS** • **Doe Bay Village.** A haven for young hippies and outdoorsy people of all ages, this resort on at the eastern tip of Orcas Island is true bliss for the piss-poor adventurer. The resort is a patchwork of various accommodations tucked between two forested hills, with a small beach perfect for kayak launches. Secluded campsites ($10.50) sit on the edge of the water and offer unparalleled scenery. The anything-but-private AYH hostel consists of a two-story room (ground floor and loft) with a lot of beds ($14.50 per person, $12.50 HI members) and bodies. Most guests stay in one of the waterfront cottages, which range from your basic cabin with bed ($40.50) to more deluxe models equipped with kitchens ($50–$92), some of which sleep up to eight people. Guests may also use the resort's mineral baths and saunas ($3). *Tel. 206/376–2291 or 206/376–4755. From Ferry Landing, take Horseshoe Hwy. northeast through towns of Eastsound and Olga (about 28 mi) to Doe Bay Rd. 6 dorm beds, 1 private room, 22 cabins. Reservations recommended for cabins and hostel. Kayak trips, hot tub, café, mineral baths, and spa services.*

Doe Bay Village is the bohemian center of the San Juan Islands, a combination of never-say-meat crunchy types and backpacking college students.

➤ **CAMPING** • **Moran State Park.** Moran State Park, much quieter than Doe Bay, has possibly the best camping you'll find on the islands. The 151 sites ($11 each) fill up fast, especially on weekends and in summer, so make reservations (by mail) well in advance. The campground wraps around a lake and sites are close to several hiking trails. Even if you don't have reservations, consider stopping by for a look at the park's sights and to ask about vacancies or cancellations. *Star Rte., Box 22, Eastsound, Orcas Island, 98245, tel. 206/376–2326. From Ferry Landing, take Horseshoe Rd. north through Eastsound and follow signs. Closed Labor Day–Memorial Day (some sites are open year-round).*

Obstruction Pass. Nine free, primitive campsites are tucked away in this remote but popular 80-acre park, administered by the Department of Natural Resources. Leave your car in the parking lot and hike the narrow, bumpy half-mile trail to the sites, which are perched on a wooded cliff overlooking the water. The beauty of the campground makes up for the lack of running water. *Obstruction Pass Rd., off Horseshoe Hwy., tel. 800/527–3305. Pit toilets, beach, tidepool access.*

FOOD The widest selection of food is in Eastsound (around the ferry landing) or in Olga. Small markets can be found at Obstruction Pass, Doe Bay, and Deer Harbor. The best way to eat on Orcas is over an open fire, but if your camping repertoire is limited to canned beans and marshmallows, Eastsound has several self-service cafés and markets with standard sandwiches, burgers, and variations on the granola theme. A **Farmer's Market** is held every Saturday morning in front of the Eastsound museum. **Island Market** (Langell St., Eastsound, tel. 206/376–6000) is the best-stocked grocery store on the island. **Orcas Homegrown Market** (N. Beach Rd., Eastsound, tel. 206/376–2009) sells organic produce, fresh seafood, and freshly made salads and sandwiches from the in-store deli.

Café Olga. Located in the Orcas Island Artworks (*see* Worth Seeing, *below*), this café has become extremely popular with tourists. The result is cramped tables, long waits, and inflated prices, although the healthy food remains creative and tasty. Indoor seating is surrounded by artwork, while the outdoor patio is surrounded by forest. Come for moderately priced breakfasts like eggs rancheros ($5.95). Lunch options include homemade soup ($4.95), crescent rolls with lox, cream cheese and a salad ($7.75), or roasted cashew and chicken salad ($7.50). *Horseshoe Hwy., at village intersection, Olga, tel. 206/376–5098. Open Mar.–Dec., daily 10–6.*

Doe Bay Café and Restaurant. Overlooking the water at Doe Bay Village (*see* Where to Sleep, *above*), this funky health food café is staffed by a friendly team of music-blaring hippies who live on the grounds and work for room and board. As a result, you'll find the atmosphere extremely casual. Tables are covered with butcher paper and jars of crayons (to facilitate your island regression); you'll also find omelets ($7), hot cereal ($3), and strong coffee ($1.15), and a daily dinner menu with vegetarian and vegan treats like Thai veggies in peanut sauce ($6.95) and pasta with garlic, basil, vegetables, and herbs ($6.95). Local acoustic musicians often show up to play during dinner. *Tel. 206/376–4755. From Ferry Landing, follow Horseshoe Hwy. northeast through Eastsound and Olga (about 28 mi) to Doe Bay Rd. Open summer, daily 8–11 and 6–9; winter, Mon.–Thurs. 8–9:30 and 6–8 (buffet only), Fri.–Sun. 8–11 and 6–9.*

Doty's A-1 Café and Bakery. Place your order over the long glass pastry case and then take a seat inside or out on the patio. The hamburgers ($2.75), chicken breast and herb sandwich ($3.50), and fries are all pretty reliable. You can also get a standard homemade breakfast, like french toast ($2.75), coffee (25¢), and great baked goods. *7 North Beach Rd., Eastsound, tel. 206/376–2593. Open Mon.–Sat. 6:30 AM–8 PM, Sun. 7–5.*

WORTH SEEING In the center of Eastsound is the **Orcas Island Historical Museum** (Main St., tel. 206/376–4849), a compound with six early settlers' cabins and a water tower. Each cabin was disassembled in 1956 and moved piece by piece to its present location. The museum's exhibits include a hodgepodge of early homesteaders' artifacts, from recipes to primitive medical and dental tools. The adjacent lawn has picnic tables perfect for lunch and postcard writing. Admission is $1. Nearby is the simple and elegant **Emmanuel Church,** built in 1886 to resemble an English countryside chapel.

In the town of Olga, the **Orcas Island Artworks** (Horseshoe Hwy., btw Eastsound and Doe Bay, tel. 206/736–5098), is a strawberry-packing plant turned exhibition hall. Locals sell jewelry, wood carvings, paintings, and homespun yarns (among other things). The building also houses Café Olga (*see* Food, *above*).

Doe Bay Steam Sauna and Mineral Baths offers three cement baths filled with water from a natural thermal spring. Clothes are optional, though most guests whip it all off, even in broad daylight. More vexing may be the water's natural residue, which looks gross. Don't worry: It's harmless, and anyway, there's a new shower house just up a short trail. Most weekend evenings the tubs approximate a human can of sardines, with a jovial if cramped group of bathers. The adjacent aromatic cedar sauna is great for sore biking muscles. The baths and sauna are located in Doe Bay Village (*see* Where to Sleep, *above*). *Tel. 206/376–2291. Admission: $5, $3 for village guests. Open daily 8 AM–11 PM.*

OUTDOOR ACTIVITIES Orcas Island has a unique hilly and forested terrain, great for hiking and cycling; fishing and kayaking are popular, too. Topping your list of places to explore should be a drive, hike, or cycle to **Mt. Constitution.** Drive the island from tip to tip on **Horseshoe Highway,** then take a kayak trip for a change of perspective, or collapse and read a book.

Moran State Park's 14 hiking trails loop around a peaceful lake and range from short to strenuous. Pick up a free map and trail pamphlets at the park's registration booth, near the entrance. The 2½-mile walk around **Cascade Lake** is fairly level and leisurely; ambitious hikers

Don't leave Orcas Island without getting to the top of Mt. Constitution. Besides having marvelous views, it's the world's best place to hear tourists from Kansas emit high-pitched screams of delight.

can take the steep 4.3-mile trail up 2,027-foot **Mt. Constitution** (which can also be scaled by car). From the watchtower look for the Cascade and Olympic mountain ranges, Mt. Baker and Mt. Rainier, and the Canadian Gulf Islands, including Vancouver Island. You may also spot orca whales at sea. The park opens for day use at 6:30 AM in summer and at 8 AM in winter, and closes at dusk. For information on camping at Moran, *see* Where to Sleep, *above. From Eastsound, take Horseshoe Hwy. southeast and follow signs.*

➤ **SEA KAYAKING** • **Island Kayak Guides** (Doe Bay Village, tel. 206/376–2291) organizes half-day ($30) and full-day ($60) trips to surrounding islands for beginning kayakers. **Shearwater Adventures** (Eastsound, tel. 206/376–4699) offers three-hour kayak trips to offshore Eastsound, the Wasp Islands, and Orcas Island's north shore. Full-day trips ($65) go to Sucia Island or the marine state parks of Jones and Clark Islands. Overnight tours and beginning and intermediate classes are also available. For a different type of sea excursion, **Osprey Tours** (514 Enchanted Forest Rd., Eastsound, tel. 206/376–3677) offers guided tours in traditional Native American Aleutian-style sea kayaks. The best part is the big, birdlike Aleut hat you get to wear while you paddle around for a half day ($35), full day ($75), or overnight ($165) trip.

NEAR ORCAS ISLAND If Orcas is too heavily colonized for your wild tastes, make a day trip to one of the uninhabited smaller islands nearby. With a boat or kayak you can enjoy several marine parks. **Sucia Island** is actually a cluster of 11 islands 2½ miles north of Orcas. The trails, bays, and bluffs can be treacherous, so be sure to pick up a navigational map and watch the weather warnings.

LOPEZ ISLAND

If you want to pretend you're a local, cover your out-of-state license plates and wave. Believe it or not, Lopezians wave at everyone and everything. Some people barely raise a finger, while others muster up a vigorous arm swing—but all of them do it.

Lopez may get a lot of nutty types on adventure bike tours, but is otherwise the least visited of the major San Juan Islands. If you want typical tourist amenities, head to San Juan or Orcas instead.

It's a friendly and idyllic little island, and except for a few stores and restaurants in **Lopez Village,** it's almost entirely undeveloped. You won't find any chain hotels or restaurants, plastic paraphernalia embossed with whales, or even a tourist office. You will find gorgeous, undisturbed wilderness and a laid-back community of artists, writers, wine makers, and other urban escapees. Restaurants and B&Bs tend to be pricey, but the campgrounds are fine, and the rest of the island can be enjoyed on even the most severely curtailed budget. Pack your hiking, biking, or kayaking gear, plan to cook your own food, and if you want the friendly locals to remain friendly, *don't* tell your friends what a great time you had on Lopez Island.

VISITOR INFORMATION Lopez doesn't have a tourist office, but the **Lopez Historical Museum** (Lopez Village, tel. 206/468–2049) gives out maps and brochures. Pick up an invaluable Lopez Island guide/map at any real estate office, the **Spencer Spit State Park** (*see below*) ranger station, or the reservation office at the **Islander Lopez** (Fisherman Bay Rd., tel. 800/736–3434), 15 minutes south of the ferry terminal. Either by accident or intention, road signs on Lopez aren't always reliable, so you'll definitely need a map.

GETTING AROUND The **Lopez Ferry Terminal** is on the northern tip of the island. Lopez is the first ferry stop from the mainland town of Anacortes (a trip of about 40 minutes). Though there's no public transportation on the island, the uncrowded and relatively flat roads make biking a breeze. The **Bike Shop on Lopez** (Lopez Village, tel. 206/468–3497) rents 10-speeds ($16 per day) and mountain bikes ($20). Reserve a bike in advance and the shop will deliver it to you at the ferry terminal. **Angie's Cab Courier** (tel. 206/468–2227) can take you from the ferry to Lopez Village for $6.50.

WHERE TO SLEEP Lopez has a number of chichi B&Bs with prices to match. Budget accommodation is basically limited to camping. Two excellent parks compensate for the absence of inns, but be warned: None of the island's campgrounds has hot water. Six miles southeast of Lopez Village, **Marcan's Blue Fjord Cabins** (Elliott Rd., at Jasper Cove, tel. 206/468–2749) are an escapist's dream—fully equipped and completely removed from civilization. Two people pay $68 in winter, $78 in summer, and there is a two- to three-day minimum stay.

The Sunset Guest House. This simple cabin (two bedrooms and a loft) in Lopez Village is situated on a small bluff overlooking the water. You must reserve months in advance for summer, and at least three weeks in advance in any other season. For two people the rate is $65 per night; add $5 for each additional person. *Lopez Village, behind the post office, tel. 206/ 468–2688. No credit cards.*

➤ **CAMPING • Spencer Spit State Park.** Several hiking trails meander through this lovely state park on the island's east side, but most campers stick close to the shore. There's the "spit" (a long, narrow finger of sand that stretches away from the beach), worth the 10-minute hike from the road, and several sections of beach ideal for clamming. Secluded sites ($11) are surrounded by trees and roaming deer; two open-air huts ($15 each) are a great deal if you're traveling with a group or without a tent. Reservations are only accepted for one of the huts, so plan to arrive early on summer weekends. The park is open 6:30 AM–dusk, and guests must self-register. *Tel. 206/468– 2251. From Ferry Landing, turn left onto Port Stanley Rd. and follow signs. 25 sites. Pit toilets, showers.*

If you're planning to camp in Lopez during the summer, shop on the mainland for that life-saving 10-pound can of bug repellent and any other supplies. There aren't any camping stores on the island, and Lopez Village rolls up the sidewalks promptly at 7 PM.

Odlin County Park. This campground is better equipped than Spencer Spit, although you still face cold showers and pit toilets. Camp on the beach or next to a baseball diamond. The sites are given out on a first-come, first-served basis and cost $10. *Tel. 206/468–2496. 1 mi from Ferry Landing on main road. 30 sites.*

FOOD Lopez has only a handful of eating establishments and they're all surprisingly good. The **Lopez Village Market** (tel. 206/468–2266), the only grocery store in town, is open daily and has a large selection of staples. **Blossom** (tel. 206/468–2204), also in Lopez Village, is a tiny natural-foods market with a variety of organic fruits and vegetables. Most of the island's restaurants are near the market at the center of town.

With a funky, laid-back staff, **Holly B's Bakery** (Lopez Village, tel. 206/468–2133) is your only option for cup of coffee or an inexpensive bite to eat. Holly B whips up scrumptious cinnamon buns ($1.80) and excellent homemade breads. The **Lopez Island Pharmacy and Soda Fountain** (tel. 206/468–2616) serves good, cheap sandwiches ($2–$4), malts ($3), and homemade ice cream ($1.20). Eat at the counter in the pharmacy or outside on the deck under an umbrella. To reach the pharmacy, take Fisherman's Bay Road south from the ferry landing and turn right at the hardware store.

The Bay Cafe. Lopez's favorite eatery is a real splurge, but the excellent food combined with views of the San Juan Channel is definitely worth it. Entrées include sesame chicken breast ($13) and scampi with basil frittata and a warm sun-dried tomato vinaigrette ($15). The atmosphere is romantic, the food fresh and delicious. Make a reservation several days in advance to be sure of getting a table. *Lopez Village, tel. 206/468–3700. Across from the post office. Open summer, Wed.–Mon. 5:30 PM–8:30 PM; winter, Wed.–Sun. 5:30 PM–8 PM.*

Gail's. Gail's offers vegetarian dishes from a changing multi-ethnic menu, prepared with vegetables grown in the owner/chef's garden. The restaurant has a warm atmosphere enriched by the soft sounds of jazz and the smell of freshly baked challah bread. Eat from a special early-dinner menu (until 7 PM) and walk away with a full stomach for under $8, or show up later and pay $10–$20 per dinner entrée. (Serious budget travelers take note: Soups are $3 per bowl, and great salads are $5.) For lunch, create your own deli sandwich ($4.95) or try a daily special (around $7). *Lopez Village, tel. 206/468–2150. From Ferry Landing, take Fisherman Bay Rd. to the Community Pavilion and turn right. Open summer, weekdays 11–4 and 5:30–9, weekends 8–4 and 5:30–9; winter, weekdays 8 AM–2 PM, weekends 8 AM–2 PM and 5:30–8:30 PM.*

WORTH SEEING You could spend one day on Lopez Island and see the essentials, or one week hanging about and meeting locals. There isn't much in the way of typical tourist attractions, so kick back and enjoy what's here. If you're an itinerary freak, it's easy to make a loop tour of the island.

The hodgepodge collection at the **Lopez Historical Museum** (Lopez Village, tel. 206/468–2049) includes a few items of interest and some impressive model ships. There's a fun "Please Touch" table with hands-on items for children (and adults). The museum gives out brochures, including a map and self-guided tour of historical landmarks, which point out some of the island's oldest homes, churches, and school buildings. The nearby **Chimera Lopez Artists Cooperative Gallery** (tel. 206/468–3265) displays art by talented locals.

OUTDOOR ACTIVITIES The residents of Lopez take wilderness preservation very seriously. Long hours of community debate often ensue on issues as small as whether or not to maintain a trail to Shark Reef. As a result, you'll find the coastal areas of Lopez marvelously underdeveloped and rich in sealife. Several parks and picnic areas line the island's coasts and are easily accessed by flat, open roads. Exploration by bike is ideal, though conditions for kayaking aren't so bad, either. The folks at **Lopez Bicycle Works and Kayaks** (Fisherman Bay Rd., tel. 206/468–2847) will cheerfully rent you a kayak by the hour ($15) or day ($50), or escort you on a guided sunrise, sunset, moonlight, or half-day tour ($30–$40). Their bikes are $5 an hour, $23 for 24 hours.

Shark Reef, an isolated, craggy strip of coast, is excellent for spotting marine life like seals, heron, and sea lions, and several rocky tide pools hide smaller creatures. Park in the small lot south of the village on Shark Reef Road, and follow the unmarked trail that begins next to the outhouse about 15 minutes through a thick forest to reach the water's edge. There's no camping, but the trail winds along the coast and provides views so gorgeous that what begins as a quick peek usually evolves into an all-day affair. Bring lunch.

Another prime spot for wildlife-viewing is **Spencer Spit State Park,** a 130-acre marine park on the northeast shore of the island. Come here for beautiful beaches and numerous trails and picnic areas. Follow the 10-minute trail downhill from the parking lot to Spencer Spit, where you can cook lunch at one of the fire pits or walk out onto the long sand spit to investigate the resident birds and small sea animals. You can swim here, though the water is brisk; it's more fun just to watch the boats go by. Other picnic areas are at **Agate Beach** and **McArdle Bay.** For information on camping at Spencer Spit, *see* Where to Sleep, *above.*

NEAR LOPEZ ISLAND

➤ **SHAW ISLAND** • The fourth of the San Juan Islands accessible by ferry, Shaw Island, is the least visited for a reason: The locals are mostly Franciscan nuns who don't warm to visitors. They keep to themselves and ignore guests.

Even if you don't visit the island, check out the landing when your ferry pulls in for a stop. Both the ferry landing and general store are run by some business-minded nuns; on a windy day, you'll see their habits flying in the breeze as they help dock the ferry. You may want to come for a bike trip by day, but forget about overnight hospitality.

Elsewhere Near Seattle

SNOQUALMIE VALLEY

The Snoqualmie Valley, just 25 miles southeast of Seattle, was settled by farmers in the 1850s for its advantageous transportation route through a break in the Cascades. The area today has a plethora of historical sites and museums, hiking trails, and beautiful, lush surroundings, including **Snoqualmie Falls,** a waterfall that boasts a drop 100 feet greater than Niagara's. So, history buffs come by the truckload, right? Outdoor enthusiasts rush here to hike old railroad tracks and to climb the great **Mt. Si**, right? Well, sometimes, but the truth is, most Snoqualmie Valley tourists belong to the cult of David Lynch fans who come to see the real life set of the one-time movie/TV series/national phenomenon *Twin Peaks*.

If you haven't seen the series, things may seem strange here. Fellow travelers and local waitresses will direct you, without provocation, to "The corner where the guy with the mask always stood," (North Bend Boulevard and Route 202), "The R.R. Diner" (The Mar T Café in North Bend), "The Great Northern Hotel" (Salish Lodge at the top of Snoqualmie Falls), and "The Road House" (The Colonial Inn in Fall City). Without even asking, you'll be informed that there is no Twin Peaks, but rather Mt. Si, and that Mt. Si only has one peak, known locally as "the haystack." After you've heard enough Laura Palmer references, head to the hills of the surrounding national forests, where camping and a well-established trail system await.

One weekend every year, usually near the end of summer, Snoqualmie hosts the **Twin Peaks Fan Festival,** an obsessive fest for fixated "Peak Freaks" or "Peakeans" (they will answer to either) who are finding it hard to come to grips with the series' cancellation two years ago. The weekend features Roadhouse parties, cherry pie feasts, a log lady relay race, look-alike contests (where you have the option of impersonating either an object or a character—hmmm), and the opportunity to meet such screen legends as "Boy Behind Mask" (Jonathan Leppell) and The Log Lady (Catherine Coulson). You can participate in individual events and pay separately for each, or pay a whopping $108 to participate for the whole Peak experience (food and sightseeing included). For information contact: Peaks of Romeo, 8900 N. Dutchess Ln., Romeo, MI 48065, tel. 810/752–5142. They'll reply by mail if you send a SASE.

VISITOR INFORMATION The **Gift Shop** at the **Salish Express Café** (tel. 206/831–6525) next to Snoqualmie Falls sells a handy $10 *Twin Peaks* map. Otherwise, the best place to stop is the tiny **North Bend Information Center** (318 North Bend Blvd., tel. 206/888–3411), open summers, daily 9–1 and 2–6—look for the hut on the north side of the road, 1 mile up Route 202 from I–90. The **Snoqualmie Pass Visitor Information Center** (I–90 Exit 52, Snoqualmie Pass, tel. 206/434–6111); the **North Bend District Ranger Station** (4204 S.E. North Bend Way, North Bend, tel. 206/888–1421); and the **Mt. Baker-Snoqualmie National Forest Supervisor's Office** (21905 64th Ave. W, Mountlake Terrace, tel. 206/775–9702) can provide information on snow recreation, hiking, fishing, and camping in the Snoqualmie Valley.

COMING AND GOING From I–90, take Route 202 (Exit 31) and travel northwest about 1 mile to reach the town of Snoqualmie. You'll pass through downtown North Bend, with the largest collection of food and lodging options in Snoqualmie Valley. Or take Route 203 (Exit 27) directly north to Fall City.

You can also reach the Snoqualmie Valley from Seattle on a public bus. Buses 210–213 depart from downtown Seattle (2nd Avenue at Pike Street or 4th Avenue at Lenora Street) for Snoqualmie Valley hourly, 6 AM–9:30 PM daily. The Seattle–Fall City–Snoqualmie Falls–North Bend route takes 1 hour and 10 minutes and costs $1.60 during peak hours (weekdays 6–9 AM and 3–6 PM), $1.10 during off-peak hours.

WHERE TO SLEEP The cheapest lodging is in North Bend. Try the **North Bend Motel** (322 E. North Bend Way, tel. 206/888–1121), for a no-frills, plywood-and-acrylic room. Singles go for $34–$36, doubles are $36–$38. Also in downtown North Bend, the **Sunset Hotel** (227 W. North Bend Way, tel. 206/888–0381) has similarly uninspiring rooms, though they are farther from the main highway. Doubles here are also $36–$38. Some rooms have kitchenettes.

➢ **CAMPING** • The closest place to camp near town is **Snoqualmie River Campground** (tel. 206/222–5545); it's the first left after the Fall City Bridge on Route 202 south. The flat, open sites ($14 per night) offer no privacy, but the campground is so big you can usually find a secluded spot on the river. Showers, drinking water, and river swimming are the perks here.

FOOD Driving to the falls on Route 202, you'll pass by **Isadora's Antiques and Adornments** (132 Railroad Ave., at Rte. 202, tel. 206/888–1345), a café, espresso bar, and antiques shop that serves great, healthy lunches. Try the hummus plate ($3.95), the gourmet pizza of the day

($3.75), or the homemade soup with bread ($3.95). For soups, sandwiches, and freshly baked breads, hit **George's Bakery & Delicatessen** (127 W. North Bend Way, tel. 206/888–0632), which makes a mean turkey and havarti cheese sandwich on a rosemary sourdough roll; with soup or salad, it's a mere $3.

WORTH SEEING Visit the **Snoqualmie Valley Historical Museum** (320 North Bend Blvd. S, North Bend, tel. 206/888–3200), half a mile from I–90 off Exit 31, to check out interesting antiques and historical displays. The musem is open Thursday–Saturday 1–5; suggested donation is $1. If you plan to stay in the area for a few days, purchase the museum's *28 Historic Places in the Upper Snoqualmie Valley* ($4.50), which will enable you to embark on self-guided side trips. Or leave your car in the 20th century and climb aboard the **Puget Sound & Snoqualmie Valley Railroad** (tel. 206/746–4025), built in 1890. Following a loop between the depots in Snoqualmie and North Bend, you'll travel the same valley route as the pioneers did. Trains creep along the canyon wall, with one side a swarm of ferns and shrubs, the other a precipice with chilling views. This is not a trip for acrophobiacs. Tickets are $6.30 round-trip, and the train runs April–October.

You can't leave the area without at least a cursory drive past the magnificent, 268-foot-high **Snoqualmie Falls.** Follow Route 202 5 miles north from I–90 (or until you hear the equivalent of several hundred fire hoses at full blast). Every Boy Scout in the state has climbed **Mt. Si,** the mountainous watchtower of the Snoqualmie Valley. A relatively steep trail climbs 3,500 feet in 4 miles, past the Snoqualmie Valley Viewpoint and **Snag Flat** (a single stand of old-growth forest, survivor of a past forest fire), and ends at the summit, offering great views of Mt. Ranier and the Olympics. The trail traverses cooling forests, so despite several tortuous switchbacks, it's not too strenuous. Traveling northwest on Route 202, take a right onto North Bend Way, left onto Mt. Si Road (after the ranger's station), cross the bridge, and park. The trailhead is a quarter-mile downriver, just past the fifth house on the right.

If the idea of a punishing hike up a hill doesn't thrill you, visit **The Herb Farm** (32804 Issaquah–Fall City Rd., Fall City, tel. 206/784–2222). You can walk the grounds where 639 herbs and edible plants are grown; sample edible flowers; or take part in one of several classes offered weekly, such as tea preparation ($22), herbal cooking ($24, includes lunch), Northwest native herbal medicine ($22), and herbal papermaking ($29). The farm also offers a basic introduction on how to identify, grow, and use 16 major herbs ($15, includes $5 worth of plants). Free tours of the grounds are offered weekends at 1 PM, April to mid-September. The grounds are open from dawn to dusk year round.

OUTDOOR ACTIVITIES The statewide **Volkssport Association** sponsors several local walking and biking competitions, which cost about $5 each to enter. Pre-registration is not required. A booklet listing course ratings, wheelchair accessibility, start times, and route directions is usually available at area businesses. For more information, contact Jennifer Little (tel. 206/222-5715).

The **Ski Acres Mountain Bike and Hiking Center** (tel. 206/236–1600) sells lift tickets ($8 per full day), rents mountain bikes ($24 per day), and gives mountain-bike instruction ($40 per day) in the Snoqualmie Pass. *From I–90, take Exit 54 and follow signs.*

➤ **HIKING** • The national "Rails to Trails" movement, now in its second decade, transforms unused train tracks into "highways" for non-motorized traffic, like cyclists, hikers, and joggers. In the Snoqualmie Valley, the 6½-mile **Preston–Snoqualmie Trail** follows an old Northern Pacific Railroad route from the town of Preston to a viewpoint near Snoqualmie Falls. Find the trailhead at the I–90 Preston exit or on Lake Alice Road, one-half mile past the Fall City Cemetery. The trail is maintained by the **King County Parks Department** (tel. 206/296–4232), which will publish a comprehensive state trail map (about $3) in early 1995. Hiking maps and guides for the area are also available at REI (*see* Shopping, in Seattle, *above*).

➤ **SKIING** • About 15 miles east of North Bend on I–90, the Alpental, Snoqualmie, Ski Acres, and Hyak ski areas of **Snoqualmie Pass** (locally known as "The Pass") have collective plans to drastically develop their ski trails and tourist facilities within the next five years. (Hyak, for example, recently unveiled a new snowboard park featuring a 100-yard-long halfpipe.) Ski season is generally mid-November–mid-April; lift passes are $12–$16 (weekdays) or $26 (weekends). Of the 65 major runs at The Pass, most are at the intermediate level, with elevation ranges from 3,675 to 5,400 feet. Shuttle service and overnight lodging are available. *Tel. 206/232–8182 for information, or tel. 206/232–1600 for snow conditions.*

BELLINGHAM

Bellingham is a surprisingly lively little town with a funky bohemian edge, on Puget Sound 90 miles north of Seattle. You'll find many of the 9,000 students of Western Washington University tromping around the historical district of **Fairhaven.** This cool sector on the south side of town is filled with used-book stores, cafés, vendors of batik clothing, and a mix of outdoorsy students and unpretentious families in a sort of peaceful suburban cocktail. Driving north, consider exiting the highway before Bellingham to take the 23-mile **Chuckanut Drive** (Route 11) along the coast. You'll pass the nude beach of **Teddy Bear Cove** and wind up at the southern end of Bellingham, in Fairhaven.

VISITOR INFORMATION The **Bellingham Chamber of Commerce** offers the usual tourist brochures. *904 Potter St., at Lincoln Rd., tel. 206/671–3990. Open summer, daily 9–6; winter, daily 8:30–5:30.*

COMING AND GOING Bellingham is about 45 miles south of Vancouver, B.C., and 90 miles north of Seattle on I-5. **Greyhound** (tel. 206/733–5251 or 800/231–2222) has four buses daily from Seattle to Bellingham; a round-trip ticket costs $18.

WHERE TO SLEEP AND EAT Motels are plentiful in Bellingham, especially along North Samish Way (Exit 252 off I-5). Decent doubles at the centrally located **Shangri-La** (611 E. Holly St., tel. 206/733–7050) start at $30 and include TV, phone, and fridge. From there, it's a short walk to both the university and downtown shopping and dining.

Cobblestone Café. For an innovative all-organic meal, beat a path to this tiny café, where creative dishes are served in the quiet, intimate dining room or outside on a small terrace. At lunch you'll find perfect midday meals, like the salad niçoise ($5.50) or the grains salad ($7.50), with wild rice, fruit, nuts, sautéed vegetables, and quinoa. Sandwiches come with delicious sautéed basil potatoes: Try the cobble ghanouj ($6.50), a pita stuffed with roasted eggplant, tomato, peppers, and greens, or a bowl of oyster stew ($7.50). *1308 11th St., tel. 206/650–0545. Open Tues.–Thurs. 11–3 and 5–9, Fri.–Sat. 11–3 and 5–9:30, Sun. 10–3.*

The major café scene in town is undoubtedly at Tony's (1101 Harris Ave., at 11th St., tel. 206/733–6319), a grungy, comfortable place packed with shaved heads of both genders, PDPs (publicly displayed piercings), and a cool alternative crowd.

OUTDOOR ACTIVITIES Bellingham is a great base for all sorts of outdoor activities. During the winter, ski at **Mt. Baker** (Business office: 1017 Iowa St., Bellingham, tel. 206/734–6771) in the North Cascades. Lift tickets are $15 (half day) or $20 (full day); on the mountain, rentals are $11.50 (downhill skis and poles) or $20 (snowboards). For information on **ski lessons** call George Savage (tel. 206/592–5550). The area opens for skiing in early November and usually closes in mid-May. From Bellingham, take Route 542 north past Kendall and follow the signs. The **American Alpine Institute** (1212 24th St., Bellingham, tel. 206/671–1505) runs backpacking and climbing trips into the North Cascades.

WESTERN WASHINGTON   7

By Kate Isaacson

Western Washington has a landscape for every mood. The pensive may want to watch a winter storm at Long Beach or wander through a dripping rain forest on the Olympic Peninsula; the environmentalist can get his or her dander up in the lumber towns of Kelso and Longview; and the philosophical can gaze at the endless flow of the Columbia River and consider the fact that we are each of us merely a drop. But no matter what your mood when you visit this part of the state, you should devote your time to the outdoors. The area draws urbanites and granolas alike to its topographically rich bosom; and while you may feel drawn that Snowplow museum in that town you missed when you blinked, don't forego your hikes or kite-flying expeditions for it.

Even in a state overflowing with postcard-perfect mountains, lakes, rivers, and forests, the Olympic Peninsula stands out. Surrounded by water on three sides—the Pacific Ocean to the west, the Strait of Juan de Fuca to the north, and the Hood Canal to the east—this rich and rare environment encompasses several types of terrain in a relatively small area. In **Olympic National Park,** the heart of the peninsula, outdoor enthusiasts can hike the snow-capped peaks of the Olympic Mountain Range, challenge the rapids of the Dosewallips or Elwha rivers, discover the true meaning of "wet" while hiking through the Hoh Rain Forest, or explore the pristine Pacific beaches at **Ozette, La Push,** and **Kalaloch.** The peninsula's attractions don't stop with the park. Rare natural sights include the Dungeness Spit (the world's longest) and Cape Flattery, the extreme northwest corner of both the peninsula and the continental United States. The Victorian town of **Port Townsend** and the seaport town of **Port Angeles** are among the few urban centers here, featuring major grocery stores, restaurants, motels, and transit systems. The rest of the Long Beach Peninsula is a string of beach towns, crowded with happy, kite-flying, bird-watching fools.

Even if you're allergic to grass, trees, and sunshine, and consider renting a movie an acceptable sunny-day activity, you'd better get your butt outdoors when you visit this part of the state. It doesn't matter how much of a city slicker you were before your trip: After a couple of weeks camping and communing with Washingtonians, you too will find yourself allowing trivial matters such as personal hygiene to take a back seat to the really important things in life, like cracking spotted owl jokes and drinking Olympia beer right out of the can. You should also know that the phone company will soon change the region's area code to 360 (yes, that's 360). Of course, they will not say when. Optimists by nature, we've changed the appropriate phone codes throughout this chapter. The upshot: If you can't get through, try the old code (206).

Washington

Vancouver Island

Strait of Georgia

CANADA
U.S.A.

Bellingham

Mt. Baker Nat'l. Forest

North Cascades National Park

Newhalem
Concrete
Diablo Lake

Marblemount

Victoria

San Juan Islands

Burlington

Mt. Vernon

Glacier Peak Wilderness Area

Cape Flattery
Neah Bay
Clallam Bay

Strait of Juan de Fuca

Whidbey Island

Makah Indian Res.

112

Dungeness
Coupeville
Port Townsend

Fort Flagler State Park

Snoqualmie National Forest

Lake Ozette

Lake Crescent

Port Angeles
Sequim
Gardiner

Everett

Forks

Olympic National Park

101

101

Gold Bar
Index

2

Stevens Pass

La Push

Skykomish R.
Skykomish

Hoh Indian Reservation

Seattle

405

Bremerton
Port Orchard
Bellevue

Queets

Quinault Indian Reservation

16

Renton

90

R

E

Shelton

Tacoma

Buckley

8

410

410

Aberdeen
Montesano

Olympia

7

Mt. Rainier National Park

5

Longmire

Paradise

Leadbetter Point
Osterville
Nahcotta
Ocean Park
Long Beach

South Bend

Chehalis

Elbe
Ashford

706

12

101

6

Morton

Packwood

Seaview
Ilwaco

Naselle

12

Mt. St. Helens National Volcanic Monument

Gifford Pinchot National Forest

Yakima Indian Reservation

PACIFIC OCEAN

Altoona
Skamokawa
Cathlamet

4

Astoria

Longview

Kelso

Mt. St. Helens

Cougar

White Salmon

Golden

Mary

Vancouver

14

84

Portland

Washington

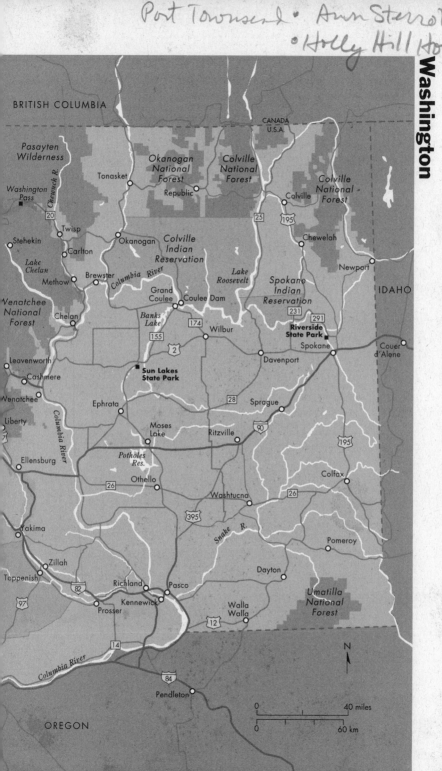

BRITISH COLUMBIA

Pasayten
Wilderness

Okanogan
National
Forest

Colville
National
Forest

CANADA
U.S.A.

Colville
National
Forest

Chewuch R.

Tonasket

Washington
Pass

Republic

Colville

20

25   195

Twisp

Chewelah

Stehekin

Okanogan

Carlton

Colville
Indian
Reservation

Newport

IDAHO

*Lake
Chelan*

Brewster

Methow

Columbia River

*Lake
Roosevelt*

Spokane
Indian
Reservation

Wenatchee
National
Forest

Chelan

Grand
Coulee

Coulee Dam

231   291

**Riverside
State Park** ■

Coeur
d'Alene

Banks
Lake

174

Wilbur

Spokane

155

Leavenworth

2

Davenport

Cashmere

■ **Sun Lakes
State Park**

Wenatchee

Columbia River

Ephrata

28

Sprague

90

Liberty

Moses
Lake

Ritzville

195

Ellensburg

Potholes
Res.

26

Othello

Colfax

Washtucna

26

Yakima

395

Snake R.

Pomeroy

Zillah

Toppenish

82

Richland

Pasco

Dayton

97

Kennewick

*Umatilla
National
Forest*

Prosser

Walla
Walla

12

14

Columbia River

N

84

Pendleton

0   40 miles

0   60 km

OREGON

233

Olympic Peninsula Coast

Olympic National Park seems to send out subliminal messages to anyone who's ever donned a pair of hiking boots: Come to me, hike me, climb me. You'll see these nature disciples driving U.S. 101, wilderness-bound and determined, passing port towns, Indian reservations, beaches, rivers, inlets, and forests without wavering for an instant. Those who actually want to see some of the coast first should follow the highway west from **Port Townsend,** the hip town at the northeastern tip of the peninsula, along the northern coastline and the Strait of Juan de Fuca to **Neah Bay.** South of here, U.S. 101 twists southward along 57 miles of Pacific Coast—the longest stretch of undeveloped coastline in the continental United States—before reaching Aberdeen and curving eastward to Olympia.

Despite diverging interests, both the indigenous populations of the peninsula and the Anglo settlers who came later have approached this landscape with fearful respect. You would be wise to do the same, making sure you know what you're doing (and where you're going) before you set out on any ambitious cross-country treks. With a little planning and a good map, however, you can spend a day or a lifetime exploring the wet wilderness, iconoclastic towns (such as artsy Port Townsend and shit-kickin' Forks), and rugged coasts of this remote region.

Peninsula dwellers ought to have just as many terms for rain as Eskimos have for snow. Rainfall ranges from an annual 142 inches in the Hoh Rain Forest to about 15 inches in Sequim.

VISITOR INFORMATION Port Ludlow's **Olympic Peninsula Gateway Visitor Center** (9000 Beaver Valley Rd., tel. 360/437–0120) dispenses brochures, trail information, and maps between 9 AM and 4 PM every day. In Port Angeles, the **Clallam County Parks Department** (in courthouse, tel. 360/452–7831) provides information on camping and picnic areas north of the Olympic National Park and west of Sequim.

COMING AND GOING From Seattle, there are two ways to reach the peninsula by car: Take the car ferry to Bainbridge Island and drive Route 305 across the Hood Canal Bridge; or take Interstate 5 south toward Tacoma, switch to Route 16 up to Bremerton, pick up Route 3, and follow it across the Hood Canal Bridge. Either route takes about an hour and 45 minutes, but the ferry means less driving. You can reach the northern towns of Port Townsend and Port Angeles via **Greyhound** or ferry. Without a car, though, your access to the smaller towns on the west coast is limited by the fact that public transit extends only as far south as La Push.

Washington State Ferries (tel. 800/843–3779) charge $1.65 for foot passengers and $7.10 for a vehicle and driver. The following ferries serve the Olympic and Kitsap peninsulas: Seattle–Bainbridge, Seattle–Bremerton, Edmonds–Kingston, Mukilteo–Clinton, and Keystone–Port Townsend. The Keystone–Port Townsend route may close or suffer delays in severe weather; call 206/464–6400 to find out.

GETTING AROUND **Clallam Transit** (2417 W. 19th St., Port Angeles, tel. 800/858–3747) serves all of Clallam County, from Sequim in the east, to La Push on the west coast, to Neah Bay in the northwest. The peninsula's other transit system, **Jefferson County Transit** (1615 Sims Way, Port Townsend, tel. 360/385–4777 or 800/773–7788) runs along the eastern coast as far south as Brinnon, then as far west as Sequim (where it connects with Clallam Transit) and to Poulsbo, where it connects with **Kitsap Transit** (tel. 360/373–2877). All buses in the state are, by law, wheelchair accessible. In the Port Townsend area, disabled people who need to be picked up should call Jefferson County's **Paratransit Service** (tel. 800/436–RIDE), which operates weekdays 10–6, for 60¢ local rides.

➤ **BY CAR** • Due to limited bus routes, driving is the easiest way to get around. U.S. 101 rings the peninsula in an upside-down U; where it diverges from the coast you can use smaller county roads. **Budget Rent A Car** has branches in Port Townsend (3049 Sims Way, tel. 360/385–7766) and Port Angeles (111 E. Front St., tel. 360/452–4774 or 800/345–8038). Both charge $48 per day for up to 100 miles—after that you pay 30¢ per mile.

Port Townsend

Jutting out on the northeast corner of the rugged Olympic Peninsula, Port Townsend is something of an anomaly, filled with working painters and potters, and scores of Victorian houses. This little seaport town, bordered by the Strait of Juan de Fuca to the north and Puget Sound to the east, was once slated to be Washington's primary port of entry. But the Union Pacific Railroad decided not to serve the town, and it was cut out of the economic loop. The population plummeted, and big urban infrastructure projects were abandoned, some already half-completed. (You can still see 14 miles of unused streetcar tracks running around town.)

Port Townsend has the largest population of artists, Birkenstock wearers, and Birkenstock-wearing artists on the Olympic Peninsula.

In the 1960s, residents decided to refurbish their Victorian homes, a task that has paid off economically: The town's prosperity derives mainly from tourism. Some things may have gotten a little too cutesy, but behind the prettily restored facades you'll find a thriving artist community. Travelers can sip espresso with the locals, explore the art galleries, meander through historical neighborhoods, catch a jazz concert, or relax in one of the old-fashioned pubs and just watch the world pass by.

In summer the town erupts with festivals, or rather becomes one continuous celebration. The **Centrum Foundation** (tel. 360/385–3102) stages an annual summer-long arts festival at Fort Worden State Park, staging workshops for artists and big-name musical performances (the Seattle Symphony Orchestra and the Duke Ellington Orchestra have participated in past years). Port Townsend's most popular event is the **Jazz Port Townsend Festival** (tel. 800/733–3608), held in late July. Buy tickets ($10 and up) from **Quimper Sound** (901 Water St., tel. 360/385–

2454) in person or by phone. The tourist office (*see* Visitor Information, *below*) can fill you in on the innumerable other festivals that happen every summer.

VISITOR INFORMATION The **Port Townsend Chamber of Commerce** gives out free maps, brochures, and advice on what to see. Pick up the free brochure *72 Points of Interest in Historic Port Townsend;* it has a good map and a detailed self-guided tour that includes all the major sights in town. *2437 E. Sims Way, tel. 360/385–2722. About 15 blocks west of downtown. Open weekdays 9–5, Sat. 10–4, Sun. 11–4.*

COMING AND GOING To drive from Port Townsend to Port Angeles and the Olympic National Park, take Highway 20 to U.S. 101. **Greyhound** (tel. 206/624–3456) runs buses from Seattle as far as Port Ludlow (1 per day, $6.50), where you can transfer to **Jefferson County Transit** (tel. 360/385–4777) Bus 7, which will take you into Port Townsend for 75¢.

Washington State Ferries (tel. 800/843–3779) has daily ferries from Port Townsend to the islands in Puget Sound; **Clipper Navigation, Inc.** (tel. 206/448–5000) offers daily high-speed ferry service between Port Townsend, Seattle, and Victoria, B.C. One-way Seattle–Port Townsend fare is $21; Port Townsend–Victoria is $38.

GETTING AROUND Downtown Port Townsend is laid out on a grid, with the two main streets, Water Street and Washington Street, running parallel to the harbor. **Jefferson County Transit** (tel. 360/385–4777) operates in town between 8 AM and 6 PM. Bus 3 makes a continual loop within Port Townsend (2 per hour). Bus 5 travels from downtown to Fort Worden once an hour. Bus fare is 50¢, and you can buy a day pass, good in all zones, for $1.50.

WHERE TO SLEEP If it's Victorian B&Bs you want, head for the hills above Water and Washington streets. If you're traveling in the off season, almost every innkeeper in town will be willing to cut you a deal. A cheaper option is to stay in one of the two hostels or camp in Fort Flagler or Fort Warden state parks (*see below*).

Palace Hotel. Smack in historic downtown, this one-time house of ill repute has 17 large, well-restored rooms with vaulted ceilings and Victorian antiques. You'll fork over $50–$87 in winter, $55–$95 in summer; the expensive rooms have private bath and views of the water. Continental breakfast is included, and some rooms have kitchenettes. *1002 Water St., at Tyler St., tel. 360/385–0773. 17 rooms, 12 with bath.*

Point Hudson Lodge. Built in 1934, Point Hudson Lodge was once a quarantine hospital that, during World War II, served as an onshore navy patrol base. Today it's one of the cheapest hotels in town and has the added advantage of being close to an isolated strip of beach. The small rooms ($35–$49 in winter, $46–$59 in summer) are sparsely decorated but clean. Big bonus: Every guest gets a free pass to a nearby health spa. *Point Hudson Resort., across from marina, tel. 360/385–2828. From downtown, drive east down Water St. to end. 24 rooms, 18 with bath. Laundry, wheelchair access.*

➤ **HOSTELS** • **Fort Flagler State Park (HI).** If you're looking for peace and solitude, stock up on supplies and head out to the tip of the peninsula. The managers are mellow and friendly, and you're more likely to find a space here than at the crowded hostel at Port Townsend (*see below*). Like Port Townsend, Fort Flagler offers beach access and views, and charges $9 to HI members, $12 to nonmembers. Cyclists pay $2 less at both hostels. *7850 Ft. Flagler Rd. No. 17, Nordland, tel. 360/385–1288. Take Hwy. 20 to Hwy. 195, then take Hwy 116E to park. Kitchen, laundry, luggage storage. Reservations advised.*

Port Townsend Hostel (HI). Set on a hillside overlooking the Strait of Juan de Fuca, this hostel is in Fort Worden State Park, only 2 miles northwest of downtown Port Townsend. The place gets crowded and rowdy in summer. Beds cost $9 for HI members, $12 for nonmembers. *272 Battery Way, tel. 360/385–0655. Follow signs from Hwy 20. 30 beds. Kitchen. Reservations advised.*

➤ **CAMPGROUNDS** • Reserve ahead for a site at **Fort Worden State Park** (tel. 360/385–4730). The campground, on the shores of Puget Sound just north of Port Townsend, sits amidst 440 acres of woods. Showers, picnic and swimming areas, and a lighthouse are within walking distance. Two campers in one tent pay $14.50 per night. At **Old Fort Townsend State**

Park (off Rte. 20, btw Port Townsend and Port Hadlock, tel. 360/385–3595), you can dig for clams ($5 license required) or putter around the beach. Sites go for $10; trails, picnic tables, bathrooms, and showers are all nearby. Southeast of Port Townsend on the tip of Marrowstone Island, **Fort Flagler State Park** (10341 Flagler Rd., Norland, tel. 360/385–1259) has well-maintained sites ($11 per night, plus $5 reservation fee) that are close to trails, restrooms, showers, and a beach. To get here from Port Townsend, take Route 20 to Route 19 South, then Route 116 West, which leads to the park entrance.

FOOD For quick and filling grub, try some fish and chips (about $4) from the nameless shack on the Quincey Street Dock. **The Food Co-op** (1033 Lawrence St., tel. 360/385–2883) sells everything from flavored tofu and organic paprika to quart-size containers of yogurt and freshly ground peanut butter. There's a ride board outside that also has flyers advertising bands, readings, and theater events around town. **Aldrich's** (940 Lawrence St., at Tyler St., tel. 360/385–0500) is an old-fashioned grocery store with a salad bar, fresh produce, and a deli serving homemade vegetarian soup ($2.75) and tasty sandwiches ($2.75). **Waterfront Naturals and Juice Bar** (810 Water St., tel. 360/385–3290) serves just about any kind of juice you could imagine, as well as a few you couldn't: The Sunrise Smoothie (orange and lemon juice, garlic, ginger, and olive oil) goes for $3.50.

If you prefer to sit while you eat, grab one of the few table at **Dogs-A-Foot** (Water St., at Madison St., no phone), a weeniemobile that peddles tofu dogs ($1.50), Italian sausages with sautéed peppers and onion ($3.25), and a number of other variations on the time-honored classic. Those looking for a little more ambiance should amble over to **Lanza's** (1020 Lawrence St., tel. 360/385–6221), where the tables are hewn from rock, and live jazz plays Wednesday–Saturday nights. You can create your own gourmet pizza here, or order a house specialty like smoked chicken pizza with spinach, sun-dried tomatoes, roasted garlic, mozzarella, and pesto ($8.30). Lanza's is open Monday–Thursday 5 PM–8:30 PM, Friday and Saturday 5 PM–9 PM. Another good bet is **Salal Café** (634 Water St., at Quincey St., tel. 360/385–6532). This employee-owned restaurant, open Wednesday–Monday 7 AM–2 PM, is usually packed with artsy types. Omelets and pastas take up about half the menu, but everyone orders the potatoes sautéed with vegetables, cheddar cheese, and garlic.

WORTH SEEING Just walk around town for an eyeful of what remains of Port Townsend's glory days. The "Genuine Bull Durham Smoking Tobacco" ad on the **Lewis Building** (Madison St., at Water St.) is one of many charming relics. **Guided Historical Tours** (820 Tyler St., tel. 360/385–1967) introduces groups to the city's Victorian houses, saloons, or waterfront. The **bell tower** on Jefferson Street, at the top of the Tyler Street stairs, is the last of its kind in the

A Hip Cuppa Joe

For a small town, Port Townsend is truly bursting with cafés. Of the many places where you can sit and observe your comrades in Slackdom, the following are two of the best. The Uptown Oasis Co. serves the best cappuccino ($1.40) in town and is a gathering place for all sorts of odd and interesting characters. Build your own smoothie ($2.70) or try some of the fresh-baked pastries. 720 Tyler St., at Lawrence St., tel. 360/385–2130. Open Mon.–Sat. 7:30–6, Sun. 9 AM–1 PM.

The Boiler Room is hidden down an alley, past dumpsters, and behind a tiny, hobbit-like door. It offers mismatched furniture, local art, jolting espresso ($1), and snacks such as veggie pizza ($3). Wear your dark glasses and you'll fit right in with the groovy locals. Tyler St., north of Water St., tel. 360/379–8247. Turn right behind Victorian Sq. Mall, walk through parking lot past Back Alley Tavern, and turn right. Open Tues.–Thurs. 11–11, Fri. and Sat. 11 AM–midnight, Sun. 5 PM–11 PM.

country. Built in 1890, it used to call volunteer firemen to duty; now it houses artifacts from the city museum, including a creepy 19th-century horse-drawn hearse. **Chetzemoka Park** (Jackson St., at Blaine St.), also on the bluffs, provides grassy napping spots with great views of Admiralty Inlet.

Fort Worden State Park (tel. 360/385–4730 or 206/385–5582), built on Point Wilson in 1855 to defend Puget Sound, was converted into a state juvenile center in 1953 and became a state park in 1972. The neatly manicured 440-acre grounds include a row of restored Victorian officers' houses, the Marine Science Center, a World War II balloon hangar, and a sandy beach that leads to the **Point Wilson Lighthouse**.

The **Jefferson County Historical Museum** is in the original city jail; Jack London crashed here for a night on his way to the Klondike gold rush in 1897. The museum houses Native American artifacts, more than 5,000 historic photos of the Olympic Peninsula, and exhibits on Port Townsend's maritime history. Come to get a quick glimpse of the history of the town, its founders, and early settlers. *210 Madison St., at Water St., tel. 360/385–1003. $2 donation requested. Open Mon.– Sat. 11–4, Sun. 1–4.*

CHEAP THRILLS When you're sick of sightseeing, disappear into **William James Bookseller** (829 Water St., tel. 360/385–7313), where almost every nook has a comfortable chair and you can take in classical music while you read up on the Northwest. In front of the store, several boxes of books are free for the taking. On summer Saturdays, you can get into the organic spirit at the **Port Townsend Farmers' Market;** it happens next to the police station on Water Street. Local farmers sell veggies, fruits, herbs, and flowers, while others hawk artwork and fresh-baked bread.

Stop by the Port Townsend Tattoo Studio at 938 Water Street and ask Mike Wingate how he got a grant from the state of Alaska to learn tattooing. His gallery includes photos of clients like Mr. X, a corporate accountant who has all of his body tattooed except areas visible when wearing a suit. If you decide to go under the needle, prices start at $32.

AFTER DARK Weekend nights at the **Back Alley Tavern** (923 Washington St., behind Terry Bldg., tel. 360/385–2914) you can hear live rock and R&B for a $3–$5 cover. Come on a weeknight and gulp down one of 15 beers on tap or play pool with locals upstairs. The **Town Tavern** (639 Water St., tel. 360/385–4706) is a friendly bar with a pool table. They've also got plenty of beer and live R&B Friday and Saturday night (cover: $4–$5).

OUTDOOR ACTIVITIES The goofy staff at **P.T. Cyclery** (215 Taylor St., south of Water St., tel. 360/385–6470) rents mountain bikes for $6 per hour or $20 per day; AYH members get a 10% discount. The **Outdoor Connection,** inside the **Sport Townsend** sporting-goods store (1044 Water St., tel. 360/379–9711), organizes free hiking and biking tours. Guided kayak tours are $35 for about three hours or $70 for a full day with lunch.

NEAR PORT TOWNSEND

FORT FLAGLER STATE PARK A 15- to 20-minute drive south of town takes you to the northern tip of Marrowstone Island and **Fort Flagler State Park** (tel. 360/385–1259). The turn-of-the-century gun placements and bunkers are interesting, but the main attractions are the beaches and wooded hiking trails. The water is freezing here, but the camping is good (*see* Where To Sleep, *above*).

GARDINER Once upon a time, an eccentric man bought an expanse of beachfront property in Gardiner and built his fantasy castle. Larger-than-life trolls support the foundations, and smaller mythical creatures keep the fence posts in place. To get here from Port Townsend, drive west on U.S. 101 (toward Port Angeles), then north on Gardiner Beach Road. When you reach the beach, turn left. This is a private residence, so you'll have to gawk from the curb.

SEQUIM/DUNGENESS Sequim, which sits in the shadow of the Olympic Mountains, is known for having the mildest climate and least rainfall of any town in these soggy parts. Settled in 1851, this farm area is now one of the fastest-growing communities on the North

Olympic Peninsula—many of the new arrivals are retirees attracted by the warm weather. Stop here long enough to watch the birds and seals, hike along the nearby saltwater canal or in the mountains, and see the Dungeness Spit (*see below*). For tourist info, contact the **Sequim Visitor Information Center and Chamber of Commerce** (1192 E. Washington St., btw U.S. 101 and Rhodofer Rd., tel. 360/683–6197), half a mile east of town.

Most of Sequim's attractions lie to the north, including the **Dungeness Recreation Area** (tel. 360/452–7831), where you can camp; the **Dungeness Spit Wildlife Refuge** (tel. 360/457–8451), home to at least 30,000 migrating waterfowl; and the **Dungeness Spit,** a 6-mile-long natural finger of sand that points into the ocean. It still grows up to 30 feet every year as a result of erosion. The spit protects the bay, which is filled with Dungeness crab, from crashing surf. The **Dungeness Lighthouse** (open daily 9–4) was built at the end of the spit, but the spit grew, and now the lighthouse is only *near* the end. To get here from Sequim, go west on U.S. 101 and turn north on Kitchen-Dick Lane, which turns into Lotzgesell Road and brings you to the entrance. Carless souls can ride **Jefferson County Transit** Bus 8, which runs five times a day on weekdays and twice on Saturday from Port Townsend to Sequim (75¢). To get from Sequim to Port Angeles, take **Clallam Transit** Bus 30. The best time to visit is during the spring and fall bird migrations. The recreation area is open until sunset, and the entrance fee is $2 per car.

A few wineries in the area offer free tours and tastings. Drop by Neuharth Winery (148 Still Rd, tel. 360/683–9652) for a tour, or call and make a reservation to see, smell, and taste the goods at Lost Mountain Winery (730 Lost Mountain Rd., tel. 360/683–5529).

West of the Dungeness River, you can drive through the **Olympic Game Farm** (383 Ward Rd., Sequim, tel. 360/683–4295). The most famous resident is a 30-year-old female brown bear named Bozo, better known as Ben from the television series *Grizzly Adams.* To get here from the Dungeness Recreation Area, take Lotzgesell Road to Ward Road, about 5 miles north of Sequim. Admission is $4, but you can peek through the fence for free.

Port Angeles

Think of Port Angeles as a sort of traveler's purgatory: You've got plenty of cheap food and places to stay, but heaven is always just a short drive away. Bordered on the north by the Strait of Juan de Fuca and on the south by the Olympic National Park, Port Angeles does offer a few points of interest. **Ediz Hook,** about 4 miles west of town off U.S. 101, is one of three natural sand spits (fingers of land formed when a repetitive tidal pattern pushed sand in a particular direction over a long period of time) on the Olympic Peninsula. It's a fine place to take a walk by the water and check out the numerous marine critters. From Port Angeles, head west on U.S. 101 and follow signs to the U.S. Coast Guard Observation Point, which is on the end of the spit. You'll think you took a wrong turn when you hit the lumber mill, but press on. Still, a spit is a spit, and most likely you'll soon want to be on your merry way to more pleasant points on the peninsula. From Port Angeles you have easy access to Neah Bay, Victoria (1–1½ hours by ferry), and, most importantly, the Hurricane Ridge Olympic National Park entrance, about 6 miles due south.

VISITOR INFORMATION **Port Angeles Chamber of Commerce.** *121 E. Railroad Ave., tel. 360/452–2363. Open Oct.–May, weekdays 10–4; June–Sept., daily 8 AM–9 PM.*

COMING AND GOING Port Angeles lies right on U.S. 101, an hour's drive west of Port Townsend.

➤ **BY BUS** • **Trailways** (215 N. Laurel, tel. 360/452–8311 or 800/366–3830) runs two buses daily between Seattle and Port Angeles (3¼ hrs, $15.30 one-way). From Port Angeles you can catch **Clallam Transit** buses (639 Monroe Rd., tel. 360/452–4511 or 800/858–3747) to various points on the northern peninsula, including Neah Bay, La Push, and Forks. Bus fare is 50¢–75¢ depending on the length of the journey. Clallam Transit also runs guided tours in summer and has winter service to the Hurricane Ridge ski area ($6).

➤ **BY FERRY** • The ferry terminal is right on the waterfront, at the foot of Laurel Street. **Black Ball Transport** (tel. 360/457–4491) ferries go between Port Angeles and Victoria, B.C. (1½ hrs, $25 per vehicle, $6.25 per passenger one-way). Four leave daily April–August; half that operate September–March. **Victoria Rapid Transit** (tel. 360/452–8088) also runs between Port Angeles and Victoria (2–4 daily, $20 per vehicle one-way). Reserve ahead on weekends.

WHERE TO SLEEP Port Angeles boasts a good collection of chain hotels, as well as some independent hotels that range from sleazy to charming. As you approach town from the west, U.S. 101 becomes Front Street, where you'll find most lodgings; the rest are one street south on First Street. Prices are invariably lower in the off-season.

Aggie's Port Angeles Motor Inn. The no-frills rooms in this huge complex are within walking distance of downtown and City Pier. Selling points include a restaurant downstairs and recently lowered rates: Singles go for $38; doubles run $48–$54. *602 E. Front St., tel. 360/457-0471. 114 rooms, all with bath. Wheelchair access.*

Flagstone Motel. Many of the rooms here have views of the harbor or Mt. Olympus, not to mention cable TV. Even better, the hotel features a heated pool and sauna, and fresh coffee and sweet rolls are served in the morning. If that's not enough, drop a quarter into the metal box by the bed and let the "magic fingers" do their thing. Singles are $34–$42; doubles, $40–$51. *415 E. 1st St., across from post office, tel. 360/457-9494. 45 rooms.*

➤ **HOSTELS** • **The Spa.** Staying at this central, independent hostel is guaranteed to work out all the kinks in your karma: Everyone sleeps on mats or futons ($12.50 each) on the floor of a large, peach-colored room. Wake to a breakfast of oatmeal and organic orange juice served in the garden tea room. Call between 10 AM and 9 PM to reserve a mat (and a session with the masseuse, if your budget allows). *511 E. 1st St., tel. 360/452-3257. Take Bus 22. Around 6 mats. Lockout 11–5 PM.*

At The Spa, you're encouraged to go granola and make use of the library of health books, the Finnish steam baths, and the on-site masseuse.

➤ **CAMPING** • Call the **Port Angeles Parks and Recreation Department** (tel. 360/457–0411) for the scoop on sleeping outdoors. Public shower areas are available at **William Shore Memorial Pool** (225 E. Fifth St., tel. 360/457-0241) during pool hours.

City-owned **Lincoln Park** is the closest campground to town. Tree-lined sites ($7) are semi-clean, semi-private, and close to short hiking trails. The park has showers and toilets. Pay at the entrance, or else the caretaker will wake you up in the middle of the night. To reach the campgrounds take Bus 24 from Oak Street toward Cherry Hill. If you're driving, head west on U.S. 101, go south on the truck route and turn right on Lauridson Boulevard (Highway 112). The **Salt Creek Recreation Area** (tel. 360/928–3441), 12 miles west of Port Angeles and 3 miles north of Highway 112 on Camp Hayden Road, has big sites on a bluff overlooking the Strait of Juan de Fuca. The nearby beach is good for swimming, diving, fishing, and tide-pool exploration. Pay the $10 fee and you'll get free showers and use of a kitchen.

FOOD The Lincoln Street waterfront has a motley assortment of overpriced, touristy restaurants in addition to the usual greasy fish joints. First Street is your best bet for eateries with more evenly matched price/quality ratios. For a tasty snack, try **Steve's Bakery** (110 E. 1st St., tel. 360/457-4003), where Steve himself bakes everything from scratch. You can sit with the locals (including Steve's family) and enjoy a cinnamon roll (65¢) with a 50¢ cup of coffee. Across the street, **Country Aire Grocery** (117 E. First St., tel. 360/452-7175) stocks a healthy supply of natural and organic foods. If all else fails, there's always the 24-hour **Safeway** (115 E. 4th St.) in the residential district.

Coffee House. With purple arches, a 17-foot warehouse ceiling, and chili-pepper-shaped lights around the windows, the Coffee House is just the place to enjoy an eclectic vegetarian/gourmet meal. The homemade soups are terrific; try to come on Friday for the fresh seafood bisque ($2.95). Sandwiches (from $6), salads, and standard burgers and fries are also available. *118 E. 1st St., btw Lincoln St. and Laurel St., tel. 360/452-1459. Open Mon.–Sat. 7 AM–8 PM., Sun. 8–5.*

First Street Haven Restaurant. This narrow little restaurant feels like a crowded living room—everyone knows everyone. Fill up on Haven Veggie Browns (hashbrowns with sautéed green peppers, onions, zucchini, mushrooms, and a topping of melted cheddar and Swiss, avocado, and sour cream) for less than $6. *107 E. 1st St., at Laurel St., tel. 360/457–0352. Open weekdays 7 AM–4 PM, Sat. 8 AM–4 PM, Sun. 8 AM–2 PM.*

Pete's Pancake House. Pete bears a striking resemblance to Grizzly Adams and doesn't really care if you eat here or not. His food is good, cheap, and filling, his menus are dirty, his staff has an attitude, and he serves a mammoth peanut butter-and-jelly omelet ($5.25). *110 E. Railroad Ave., tel. 360/452–1948. Across from Victoria Ferry Terminal. Open 24 hours a day.*

AFTER DARK With a few exceptions, Port Angeles is calm after the sun sets. If you've had enough of the harbor views, head to a bar, catch a movie at **Lincoln Theater** (132 First Street, tel. 360/457–7997), or go late-night browsing at **Port Books & News** (104 E. First Street, tel. 360/452–6367), which offers free coffee year-round and frequent readings in summer.

Smitty's (536 Marine Dr., west of downtown, tel. 360/452–2432) is mainly a sports bar for locals, but in summer the place gets packed. Entertainment ranges from comedy to karaoke to live bands from Seattle; the cover fluctuates accordingly. Thursday and Friday afternoons between 4:30 and 6:30 is happy hour, which features lots of free food. **Zak's** (125 W. Front St., tel. 360/452–7575) is a fun bar popular with a young, laid-back crowd. With nine beers on tap (including five microbrews), two pool tables (free Tues. and Thurs. after 6 PM), and three dart boards, you should be able to keep yourself entertained.

OUTDOOR ACTIVITIES **Olympic Raft and Guide Service** (239521 U.S. 101, 8 mi west of town, tel. 360/452–1443) runs trips down the Elwha River and Queets Corridor as well as through the Hoh Rain Forest. All excursions last around 2½ hours, cost $35 per person, and are ideal for novices. **Pedal 'n Paddle** (120 E. Front St., tel. 360/457–1240) rents mountain bikes for $8 an hour, $22 a day. They also guide kayakers on trips around the harbor for $35 per person.

NEAR PORT ANGELES

LAKE CRESCENT Local Indian legend says that the Storm King vented his anger at two warring tribes by throwing a piece of himself (a rock) at them. The rock dammed a stream and created the beautiful Lake Crescent. You'll get a completely different story from the men in suits, who claim the lake was carved by slow-moving ice. Either way, Lake Crescent, just 16 miles west of Port Angeles on U.S. 101, is great for trout fishing and tranquil contemplation. From here, you can hike the **North Shore Trail** along an old railroad bed or do the mile-long jaunt to Barnes Creek and the beautiful **Marymere Falls.**

NEAH BAY AND CAPE FLATTERY For a perfect day trip from Port Angeles, drive 71 miles west on U.S. 101, link up with Highway 112, and head toward Neah Bay. The drive itself takes you over the Elwha and Hoko rivers, past heavy forests and rocky coastline, before you reach **Neah Bay.** The tiny village, on the shores of the Strait of Juan de Fuca, is an ancient fishing and whaling center, home to Makah Indians since at least 1,000 BC. Today the Makah have the largest reservation (44 square miles) on the peninsula, and the only one developed for tourism. Stop at the **Makah Cultural Resource Center** (tel. 360/645–2711), which will be on your left as you enter the town from the east on Highway 112. For a $4 admission fee you can check out exhibits of traditional clothing, various weapons and tools, toys, canoes, and a full-scale log house complete with real (smelly) meat hanging to dry. Mark your calendars for the last weekend in August, when the annual **Makah Days,** the largest Native American festival on the Olympic Peninsula, takes place. The festival features traditional dancing and singing, salmon bakes, and canoe races. If you don't want to drive all the way back to Port Angeles or Forks, you can stay on the reservation at the Makah-owned **Cape Flattery Resort** (tel. 360/645–2251). For $12.50 you'll sleep on a new, clean bunk bed in a comfortable house close to a bowling alley, a gym, a bingo parlor, and free Makah cultural programs. The tip of Cape Flattery is just a 9-mile hike away.

Cape Flattery is land's end—the extreme northwest point of the continental United States, where the Strait of Juan de Fuca meets the Pacific Ocean. Dense stands of fir and cedar cover the cape, and cliffs more than 300 feet high provide mind-blowing views across the water. To get to the cape, drive west on Highway 112 to the end of Neah Bay, turn right after the building with the totem pole, and follow the signs. You'll come to a narrow dirt road covered with potholes. By the time you reach the trailhead, you'll have discovered the exact width of your car. Bring along a pair of shoes with good traction to navigate the soggy trail, and plenty of warm clothes.

LAKE OZETTE Lake Ozette, 50 miles west of Port Angeles, is the third-largest natural freshwater lake in Washington. The best reason to come here is the 2-mile **Indian Village Trail** loop to **Ozette**, a 2,000-year-old site that was once a year-round Makah fishing and whaling village. In 1970, tidal erosion exposed a group of 500-year-old homes that had been preserved in a mudslide, and the area was swamped with archaeologists. Today the artifacts are on display at the **Makah Cultural Resource Center** (*see above*).

To reach Lake Ozette from Port Angeles, drive west on Highway 112, turn left on Hoko Ozette Road (past Sequim), and continue 22 miles to the **Ozette Ranger Station** (tel. 360/963-2725), where the loop hike to Ozette begins. Be sure to check out the large granite rocks in the area, many of which bear old petroglyphs (rock carvings). You can camp free at the trailhead, but it's often crowded and noisy; call the ranger station for information on backcountry camping and permits.

FORKS You have now entered the vortex of the spotted owl debate. For the pro-logging perspective, head to the **Forks Timber Museum** (U.S. 101, tel. 360/374-9663), built in 1989 by a local high school shop class and supported by local volunteers. The **Forks Information Center** (1411 Forks Ave. S., tel. 360/374-2531), open daily 9-5 in summer, with shorter hours in winter, is at the southern edge of town on U.S. 101, across from the Forks Airport. To get to Forks, drive 56 miles southeast of Port Angeles on U.S. 101.

If you want to feel at home in Forks, start leaving the G off the ends of your present participles (e.g. "I am eatin' a spotted owl").

Absolutely nothing is happening in Forks, but being the only real outpost of hotels, motels, and Taco Bells between Port Angeles and Aberdeen, it's a cheap and convenient stop on the way to Olympic National Park or Olympic National Forest. At the **Rain Drop Café** (U.S. 101, at E. A St., tel. 360/374-6612), you can feast on huge tacos ($1.95) and creamy peanut butter-and-chocolate milkshakes ($1.25) daily 5 AM-9 PM. The **Far West Motel** (251 N. Forks Ave., on U.S. 101, tel. 360/374-5506), where rooms start at $30, is the cheapest acceptable indoor sleep around.

HOH INDIAN RESERVATION The reservation was established in 1893 for the Hoh Indians—a Quileute band that has been recognized as a separate tribe; currently 75 permanent residents live here. To learn more about tribal life, head to the **Hoh Tribal Center,** 3 miles off U.S. 101. The staff provides literature about Hoh history and will let you crash on a comfortable chair in their spacious, fire-warmed lodge. They can also direct you to the homes of artisans if you want to buy baskets, paintings, or beadwork.

Olympic National Park

The Olympic National Park and the surrounding Olympic National Forest encompass over 1.5 million acres of mountains, trees, meadows, glaciers, rivers, coastline, and lakes. You name it, it's in there. The high point (literally) of the park is Mt. Olympus, which rises 7,965 feet above the forest floor. To the west, the Olympic Coastal Strip includes 57 miles of isolated beaches loaded with diverse marine life. Keep in mind that dangerous headlands and tides can make hiking along certain stretches of coastline dangerous or impossible. Contact the nearest park- or forest-ranger station for up-to-date information on the area you plan to hike. And boy do you have choices: More than 600 miles of hiking trails take you through the park's different vegetation zones, including one of the only virgin temperate rain forests in the northern hemisphere and the largest intact stand of coniferous forest in the continental United States. If your legs refuse to go a step farther, have a seat in a kayak or raft and take off down one of the area rivers. In wintertime take advantage of the area's cross-country and downhill skiing.

The Olympic National Forest is open for limited logging, hunting, fishing, and off-road camping. The National Park is more strictly regulated: There's no hunting or logging, and camping is allowed in designated areas only. Although 15 roads enter from different directions, all of them dead-end after a few miles, meaning horses and hiking boots are the only means of transportation in most of the park's interior.

The jagged Olympic Mountains, which loom over the park, trap passing storm fronts, causing the forests and highlands to soak up as much as 150 inches of rain and snow a year—sometimes as much as 11 inches in a single day.

BASICS

GENERAL STORES The main shopping area for the northern areas of the park is Port Angeles. **Brown's** (112 W. Front St., tel. 360/457–4150) in Port Angeles is the place to stock up on camping food and supplies. For groceries, visit the 24-hour **Safeway** in Port Angeles (*see above*). You can also find most necessities at stores in the town of Forks, including **Ron's Food Mart** (171 Forks Ave., tel. 360/374–6451). Otherwise stores are few and far between. In the park, you can pick up food, gas, camping supplies, and fishing tackle, or rent boats at the **Fairholm General Store** (221121 U.S. 101 W., tel. 360/928–3020), at the west end of Lake Crescent.

At the Hoh Rain Forest entrance, on Upper Hoh Road, you'll pass **Peakle** (tel. 360/374–5254), a small camping store, and **Westward Hoh Resort** (tel. 360/374–6657), an even smaller grocery store. Small general stores at Sol Duc Hot Springs Resort and Kalaloch Lodge (*see* Where To Sleep, *below*) sell gas, food, fishing tackle, and camping supplies. At the south shore of Quinault Lake, stop at **Quinault Mercantile** (352 South Shore Rd., tel. 360/288–2451), open daily 6 AM–10 PM, for bait, groceries, and hot food.

Before you hit the trails, stop by Port Angeles's Chamber of Commerce for two indispensable publications: The Northern Olympic Peninsula Visitor's Guide Map ($1), which shows all major roads, places of interest, information centers, recreation facilities, commercial services, and campgrounds in the area; and the Olympic National Forest and Olympic National Park Guide ($2.50), which contains detailed trail maps.

VISITOR INFORMATION The main visitor center, and the only one open year-round, is Port Angeles's **Pioneer Memorial Visitor's Center** (3005 Mt. Angeles Rd., at Race St., tel. 360/452–0330). The Department of Natural Resources publishes a *Guide to Campground and Picnic Sites*, which lists all of the free, primitive campsites within the Olympic National Park and Forest. Call ahead to reserve a permit, as some areas have quotas on the number of campers allowed at a time. You'll need a backcountry use permit to camp on all park beaches and near trails, but not for automobile camping or forest camping. Ranger stations throughout the park and forest and along the coast provide these permits as well as maps and information on camping, hiking, and current weather conditions. The **Regional National Park Headquarters** (1065 Capitol Way, tel. 360/753–5338) in Olympia covers all parks in the area. Other Olympic National Park Ranger Stations are at Elwah (tel. 360/452–9191), Heart o' the Hills (tel. 360/452–2713), Hoh (tel. 360/374–6925), Hoodsport (tel. 360/877–5254), Kalaloch (tel. 360/962–2283), Lake Crescent (tel. 360/928–3380), Quinault (tel. 360/288–2444), Soleduck (tel. 360/327–3534), and Staircase (tel. 360/877–5569).

The in-park **emergency number** is 206/452–4501. A few telephone lines also provide info for visitors: weather and campground info (tel. 360/452–0329); Olympic and Cascade avalanche hazard (tel. 360/526–6677); pass report (tel. 360/976–7623); ski report (tel. 360/479–2754); white-water hot line (tel. 360/526–8530).

WHEN TO GO Summer, when daytime temperatures run 65°F–70°F, is the height of camping season in the park. This is also when the beaches are more generally accessible, as tides are at their lowest. September and October are typically sunny, offering the best combination of good weather and sparse crowds. Winter is the wettest and coldest season, with daytime temperatures in the 40s and nighttime temperatures falling to -35°F. During winter, high-elevation hiking requires an ice axe, and most trails are inaccessible until the snow melts in April. Spring isn't bad: You can usually find a campsite without a fight, but things can be extremely wet until at least late April.

WHAT TO PACK No matter when you come, *do not* fail to bring water-repellent clothing and a pair of sturdy shoes with non-slip soles. Even in summer, warm clothes are a necessity if you plan to spend any time at higher elevations. In winter, an ice axe (and some idea what to do with it) is also needed for high-elevation excursions. Campers should have a ground mat as well as a tent—this will keep (some of) the cold from the ground from penetrating your bones as you sleep. All campers should have a stove for boiling water, a chemical or filtration water-purification kit, or iodine tablets ($3.95 at most ranger stations).

COMING AND GOING

Most visitors enter the park at Hurricane Ridge, about 17 miles inland from Port Angeles, and work their way west. You can also enter at Staircase, Elwha, Sol Duc Hot Springs, the Hoh Rain Forest, and Lake Quinault. From Memorial Day to Labor Day, Olympic National Park charges $5 per vehicle including the driver, plus $2 per additional person. Keep your receipt: It entitles you to multiple entries.

BY CAR The park is only a 100-mile drive west from Seattle. U.S. 101 circles the park, and spoke-like roads offer limited access at various points. The long stretch of U.S. 101 along the west and northwest of the park, from Kalaloch to Port Angeles, affords the best views of ocean, forest, and mountains.

BY BUS In summer, **Clallam Transit** (694 Monroe Rd., Port Angeles, tel. 360/452–4511 or 800/858–3747) provides trolley service from Railroad Avenue (west of the Port Angeles Chamber of Commerce) to the Pioneer Visitor Center in the park. Buses leave weekdays at 1 PM and 3 PM; the narrated tour is $6 and passes major points of interest. In winter, the buses go to the Hurricane Ridge ski area ($8 round-trip). Clallam Transit Bus 14 from Port Angeles to Forks also travels through the park near Crescent Lake; you can ask to be let off along the road.

WHERE TO SLEEP

Park accommodations run the gamut from lavish mountain resorts to the cold, hard ground. Lodgings inside the park are pricey, so if you're not camping, your best bet is to stay in a nearby city like budget-friendly Port Angeles. To the west of the park, try Forks and La Push; to the south, check out Quinault or Amanda Park. If you're traveling in a group, look for "cabin rental" signs outside private residences along U.S. 101 south of Forks, and on Mora Road near La Push. Almost every place offers winter rates, which are sometimes half of summer rates. The closest hostels are in Port Angeles and near the Hoh Rain Forest.

> **UNDER $50** • **Amanda Park Motel.** At $40 a night, this is the cheapest motel anywhere near Lake Quinault. Spacious rooms feature TVs and refrigerators, and are clean, quiet, and unremarkable. Three miles away are the resorts on Lake Quinault where you can rent fishing boats, and the trailheads of the Quinault rain forest hikes. *8 River Dr., behind Quinault Rain Forest Visitor Center, tel. 360/288–2237. 8 rooms.*

Hoh Humm Ranch. The suspenders-clad proprietor of this working ranch breeds antelopes, sheep, cattle, and a herd of other animals; he's glad to let you walk the grounds and help feed the llamas. Clean, comfortable rooms ($30–$40) come with a farm breakfast of cornbread, eggs, and coffee. *Near Mile 127 U.S. 101, tel. 360/374–5337. 15 mi north of Klalaloch, 20 mi south of Forks, 6 mi east of ocean. 5 rooms, none with bath. No credit cards.*

Log Cabin Resort. The cheapest way to sleep in the park is to rent one of these funky, secluded log cabins on the northwestern shore of Lake Crescent. Each has two double beds and rents for $38.40. You can cook outside over a campfire and eat at your own picnic table. The cabins are run by an otherwise pricey lodge, so a restaurant and general store (where you can rent boats or canoes) are within close proximity. Bring your own bedding. *3183 E. Beach Rd., tel. 360/ 928–3325. 18 mi west of Port Angeles on U.S. 101, then 3 mi north on E. Beach Rd. 4 cabins, none with bath. Closed Oct.–mid-May.*

Shoreline Resort. Within the Quileute Reservation, on the Pacific Coast, these wooden cabins ($42–$79) are great if you're traveling in a group. They're spacious and new, and some have kitchens and a loft with two extra beds. You'll be close to Ocean Beach, hiking, and ocean kayaking. Bring your own sheets. *Quileute Reservation, La Push, tel. 800/487–1267. 14 mi northwest of Forks off U.S. 101. 13 cabins. Wheelchair access to 1 cabin.*

➤ **UNDER $100 • Sol Duc Hot Springs Resort.** Soak your abused tootsies in the mineral pools, grab a bite in the restaurant, and sleep soundly in these vintage cabins. A grocery store and recreational equipment are available on site. The average rate for a cabin for two is $80 a night. *Soleduck River Rd., off U.S. 101, btw Forks and Port Angeles, tel. 360/327–3583. Closed Oct. 4–May 19.*

➤ **UNDER $150 • Kalaloch Lodge.** This isolated lodge on the Pacific Coast offers comfortable, basic motel rooms and cabins, as well as a dining room, a small store, and a service station. Because of its easy beach access, Kalaloch is extremely popular, especially with families. Rates are a bit high ($95–$145), but these are the only civilized digs until you hit Aberdeen, about 75 miles south. *U.S. 101, 35 mi south of Forks, tel. 360/962–2271. 18 rooms, 40 cabins. Wheelchair access.*

Rain Forest Resort Village. If you plan to hike into the Quinault Rain Forest, fish in Lake Quinault, or explore southern areas of the park, these big wooden cabins right on the lake may be worth the price. All have fireplaces, decks, refrigerators, and TVs. If you can't afford the normal summer rates ($100 for a single, $135 for two beds and a whirlpool bath), go during the off-season when they drop to $60 and $95, respectively. *516 S. Shore Rd., south of U.S. 101, tel. 360/288–2535 or 800/255–6936. 18 cabins.*

HOSTELS **Rain Forest Hostel.** Not actually in the rain forest, this independent hostel is as close as you can get and still have a roof over your head. Stay in one of two clean bedrooms, or in the huge, noisy dorm room (beds $9 a night, plus $1 linen rental). Kay and Jim, the hostel's house parents, have traveled everywhere and hiked all over the Olympics, and are glad to help you settle on a trail, a campground, or a new way of life. The kitchen is stocked, so you can buy food as you need it, and they have rain gear for loan, a motor home for families and snorers, and a huge travel-resource library. *169312 U.S. 101, 23 mi south of Forks, tel. 360/374– 2270. Btw Miles 170 and 169 on south side of hwy. Laundry. No credit cards.*

CAMPING All campgrounds inside the park are administered by the Olympic National Park Service and the National Forest Service; call the **Pioneer Visitor Center** (tel. 360/452–0330) or visit any ranger station for information. Easily accessible sites cost $8; harder-to-reach sites are free and take no reservations. Most sites have drinking water, toilets (pit or flush), tables, and fire pits. Sorry, no showers. The **Department of Natural Resources (DNR)** and a few private companies operate primitive campgrounds just outside the park. Call 360/374–6131 for DNR in Forks or 800/527–3305 for the Olympia office.

As long as you have a backcountry permit and are 100 yards from running water, 1 mile from a trailhead, and not visible from the coastal shore, you can plunk your tent down free anywhere outside of the reserved campsites.

Some National Forest campgrounds accept reservations. To make one, call the **National Recreation Reservation Center** (tel. 800/280–CAMP). You'll pay $7.50 to reserve, plus a nightly camping fee of $5–$8; you must pay in full for your entire stay when you arrive. If you don't reserve ahead, arrive early to get a site during peak season. All campgrounds below are inside the park.

Altaire. One of the most popular campgrounds in the park, Altaire's 30 sites ($8) lie on the banks of the powerful Elwha River, close to the fabulous Olympic Hot Springs. *9 mi west of Port Angeles on U.S. 101, then 4 mi south on Elwha River Rd. Closed Oct.–May.*

Heart o' the Hills. Because it's near the Hurricane Ridge entrance, Heart o' the Hills gets crowded, rowdy, and dirty in summer. Sites cost $8. *6 mi south of Port Angeles, off Hurricane Ridge Rd. 105 sites.*

Hoh. Don't come to this Olympic Park campground expecting privacy. There are a few isolated spots, but most will have you listening as your neighbors across the dirt road talk in their sleep. The campground's main selling point is it's proximity to the Hoh Rain Forest (a 2-minute walk) and major trailheads. Sites cost $8. *14 mi south of Forks on U.S. 101, then 19 mi east along Hoh River Rd. 89 sites.*

Minnie Peterson. A Department of Natural Resources campground, Minnie Peterson offers eight big sites hidden amidst green scenery. *Upper Hoh Rd., 4 mi from U.S. 101 on left side, across from Hoh River.*

Mora. This densely wooded campground gets up to 100 inches of rain per year—plan accordingly. The $8 sites are not all secluded, but the tall firs, ocean breeze, and short drive (2 miles) to Rialto Beach make this a popular place. It's also a good base for taking hikes or guided nature walks with the rangers. Come in late August or early September to see spectacular colors and Roosevelt elk. *North of Forks on U.S. 101. From U.S. 101, go west on Hwy. 110, north on Mora Rd., and follow signs. Toilets, wheelchair access.*

FOOD

You only have two options within the forest and park: Eat what you bring with you or buy from the lodges and resorts at jacked-up prices. **The Burger Shack** (tel. 360/374–9288) right outside of Hoh Rain Forest is popular for burgers ($2.15) and fries ($1.55). **J.J.'s,** on U.S. 101 just before the Quinault Lake turnoff, is open 5 AM–7 PM and will fill your thermos with coffee ($2.50) and your belly with french toast ($2.75). Otherwise, cook something over your Coleman or eat your meals in Port Angeles or Forks.

EXPLORING OLYMPIC NATIONAL PARK

U.S. 101 passes through some of Olympic National Park and a bit more of Olympic National Forest, and side roads can take you to some more pristine areas. Bicycles are allowed on only 20 trails, all of which are in the National Forest.

SHORT HIKES One of the most popular hikes in the park is the 2-mile trek to **Soleduck Falls,** which begins at the Soleduck Campground. At **Second Beach,** 14 miles west of U.S. 101 on La Push Road, an easy 1-mile trail leads to a wide beach with tide pools that is often the scene of summer parties. The **Quinault Rain Forest Nature Trail,** also known as the Big Tree Grove Nature Trail, meanders through fantastic groves of old-growth Douglas fir for 1 mile (one-way). The trailhead is at the parking area west of Willaby Creek, almost 2 miles northeast of U.S. 101 on Lake Quinault's South Shore Road.

To get away from the tourists, hike a few miles along the difficult, high-altitude **Hoh River Trail** to Glacier Meadows. The trailhead is at the Hoh Rain Forest Visitor Center (18 mi off U.S. 101, at end of Upper Hoh Road). The visitor center also has a short, paved, wheelchair-accessible trail called the **mini-loop.** Keep your eyes open for Roosevelt elk, western robins, and the largest variety of wild mushrooms (no, not that kind) in the continental United States (check with the ranger to see where and how many you can pick). The **Hurricane Hill Trail,** at the end of Hurricane Ridge Road, is 3 miles round-trip; haul your butt to the summit and you'll be rewarded with excellent views of Port Angeles and the Strait of Juan de Fuca. The first section of the trail is wheelchair-accessible.

For more inspiring views, take the 2-mile **Mt. Walker Trail** on Forest Service Road Number 2730, off the highway 5 miles south of Quilcene. The trail switch-backs through dense stands of Douglas fir and patches of rhododendron and huckleberry, before opening up at North View-point to views of Hood Canal, Mt. Rainier, Mt. Baker, and Seattle. For current trail conditions, call the **Quilcene Ranger District Office** at 206/765-3368.

LONGER HIKES Hikers and cyclists alike will enjoy the flat, 8-mile **Spruce Railroad Trail,** which connects the North Shore and Lyre River trailheads. Another option is the **Appleton Pass Trail,** which begins at Boulder Creek (at end of Elwha Rd.) and passes through lowland forest before climbing to the tops of surrounding mountains. You can hike 17 miles to the Sol Duc Hot Springs, or just over 2 miles to the less commercial Olympic Hot Springs on Boulder Creek (*see box below*).

For a longer hike combining the best of the Olympic Peninula's forest and mountain areas, take Soleduck River Road to the trailhead of the **Soleduck Trail.** This 9-mile trail passes the stunning Soleduck Falls, then follows the river through colossal Douglas fir, hemlock, and cedar, climbing steeply to meet the **High Divide Trail** at Soleduck Park. If you continue west along the High Divide Trail, you'll be rewarded with views of Mt. Olympus and the Bailey Range. The trail follows the ridge of the mountains for just over 2 miles; at Bogachiel Peak, turn north on the **Bogachiel Trail** toward Deer Lake to reenter the forest. After about 4 miles you'll reach the lake and the juncture of the **Canyon Creek Trail,** which leads you back to Soleduck Falls. The loop totals just over 17 miles and takes you over steep and mountainous terrain; take your time and think about spending two or three nights along the trail. In winter you probably won't get past **Deer Lake** without snowshoes, skis, and an ice axe. The ranger station tries to clear most trails by Memorial Day, but accessibility and conditions vary greatly from year to year; be sure to get in touch with the rangers before you set out.

BIKING Because of the lack of bike trails in the park, bikers are reduced to sharing U.S. 101 with unsympathetic trucks. Ask at a ranger station or visitors center for a list of trails open to mountain bikes. Newly dedicated in the summer of 1994, the **Mt. Muller Trail** runs along pioneer paths that date back to the late 1800s. The 13-mile loop runs along a mountain ridge, with excellent views of the Olympic Mountain Range and the Strait of Juan de Fuca, and is ideal for strong cyclists. Look for the marked trailhead on U.S. 101, just west of Lake Crescent.

The **Lower Quilcene Trail** is a beautiful 18-mile ride that runs along the forest at the edge of the Big Quilcene River. To reach the lower trailhead, drive 1 mile south of Quilcene on U.S. 101, turn right on Penny Creek Road as it leads to Forest Service Road 27, and continue 5 miles. For the upper access to the trail, follow Forest Service Road 27 another 7 miles to Forest Service Road 2750, and continue 5 miles.

Cyclists who want to see a rain forest but don't want to ride 17 miles to the Hoh Rain Forest usually head to Lake Quinault, right off U.S. 101. From U.S. 101, take Southshore Road just

Hot Rocks

You'll find two natural hot springs within the park—one is a full-fledged resort complex and the other is undeveloped and peacefully devoid of screaming kiddies. The former, Sol Duc Hot Springs (tel. 360/327-3583) is 12 miles off U.S. 101, just west of Lake Crescent, and offers cabins and a restaurant (see Where To Sleep, above) as well as hot springs that you can use for $5.50 per day. If that doesn't restore you, you can shell out $40 for an hour-long massage. Olympic Hot Springs, on the other hand, consists of seven free, undeveloped hot springs that vary in size and temperature; one even has its own waterfall. To find this spot, go south on Elwah Road from U.S. 101 and follow the signs. Once you reach the end of the road you'll have to walk the easy, 3-mile trail. When you emerge from the springs feeling like Jell-O, crash for free at the primitive Boulder Creek Campground nearby.

over a mile to the **Quinault Rain Forest Nature Trail.** Many who bike around here camp at **July Creek,** 8 miles inland from the highway on the north shore of Lake Quinault.

BIRD-WATCHING Olympic National Park offers truly outstanding bird-watching. Bald eagles soar offshore and nest in the branches of Sitka spruce, and great blue herons stalk in the coastal estuaries. In the forest, look for the large rectangular holes carved by red-headed woodpeckers in standing dead trees. Higher in the mountains you'll see gray-crowned rosy finch and blue grouse, whose booming calls attract females during the mating season. In early April, thousands of hawks congregate at the northwestern end of the peninsula on their way to breeding grounds across the Strait of Juan de Fuca. The visitor centers provide information about local birds and bird-watching guidebooks.

BOATING AND FISHING Both the **Log Cabin Resort** at 360/928–3245 (*see* Where to Sleep, *above*) and the **Fairholm General Store** (*see* General Stores, *above*) rent canoes and row-boats ($6–$7 per hr) as well as kayaks ($5.50 per hr). The best fishing spot is Lake Crescent. Boats are also allowed on Lake Quinault, but the Quinault tribe controls it and may close it to the public at any time in the event of poor weather. Most rivers in the park are dangerous and unpredictable, and closed to boating.

You don't need a fishing license in Olympic National Park, just a catch record (a self-recorded log of what you catch that is mandated by Indian fishing treaties), available from any nearby general store or sporting-goods outlet. The streams and lakes are filled with rainbow, brook, and sea-run cutthroat trout, but only Lake Crescent is home to the crescent, a particularly beautiful species of trout. Most prized of all are the huge and belligerent steelhead that spawn in coastal streams each fall. To fish for steelhead or salmon outside the park, you'll need a fishing license ($17 for three days) in addition to a free catch record. Licenses are also sold at general and sporting-goods stores.

HORSEBACK RIDING You can ride a horse in the Hoh River Valley for just $15 with **De Blary Trail Rides** (HC 80, Forks, tel. 360/457–4385), or take lessons and ride around the grounds at **Quarter Moon Ranch** (Spath Rd., Carlsborg, tel. 360/683–5863). Lessons or rides will set you back $15 per hour. Forget visions of riding solo on a thundering steed—you can only ride on some forest trails, and you'll be accompanied by a guide.

ROCK CLIMBING The park's tallest peak, Mt. Olympus, is a mere 7,965 feet high, but climbers should find enough Alpine action and varied terrain to keep them busy for a while. Ask about conditions before climbing and do your homework: Ice axes are necessary climbing equipment for much of the year. Two tour operators in Seattle—**Alpine Ascents Unlimited** (1712 N.E. Ravenna Blvd., tel. 206/522–2167) and **Mountain Madness** (4218 S.W. Alaska Suite 206, tel. 206/937–1772)—offer climbing instruction, equipment rentals, and guided excursions.

SNOWSHOEING AND SKIING The area around **Hurricane Ridge** has excellent cross-country skiing and some downhill skiing (two rope tows and one Poma lift). The best ski conditions last from mid-December through late March. One of the most popular cross-country routes is the 1.5-mile Hurricane Hill Road, just west of the parking area. A marked area near **Hurricane Ridge Lodge** (no phone), with trails and gentle hills, has been set aside for cross-country skiers, snowshoers, inner-tubers, and kids. For an old-fashioned twist on winter sports, the lodge will set you up with snowshoe rentals and lessons.

SWIMMING The Pacific is a dangerous playground this far north: Even in summer, ocean temperatures seldom exceed 50° F, and ocean currents are vicious. If you do plan to take a dip, pick up a free tide table at the nearest ranger station. The park's best swimming areas are at Lake Crescent, whose cool green water is distilled from the surrounding glacial peaks. Lake Mills (just off Elwha Road) and Lake Crescent are popular for diving.

Grays Harbor

Grays Harbor, roughly in the middle of the western Washington coastline, has the distinction of being the deepest harbor on the west coast. The harbor may offer the chance to get in on the thriving surf culture, but the surrounding cities and port towns also provide a sobering glimpse of the effects of the ailing timber economy. Stinky paper mills sit right on the water, surrounded by mountains of pulp waiting to be carted away. Side by side at the eastern extreme of the bay are the twin seaports of **Aberdeen** and **Hoquiam,** the main rest stops for tourists looking for gas, food, and lodging. Aberdeen is an unassuming place that will now go down in history as the town that spawned Kurt Cobain (of Nirvana and self-destructed rock-star fame). Excepting the random Nirvana groupie, though, most travelers end up in Aberdeen on the way to someplace else. **Westport,** at the harbor's south end, sees a greater number of visitors who come to fish for salmon and goof around in the water. In summer, people stream to **Ocean Shores** at the northern tip to surf and hang out on the beach.

When you ask people how they're doing in the cities around Grays Harbor, they look to the silent mills and calm ports, and grimace; then they crack a smile and answer "could be worse."

VISITOR INFORMATION Grays Harbor Chamber of Commerce. *506 Duffy St., Aberdeen, tel. 360/532–1924. Off Hwy. 101 on harbor. Open summer, weekdays 8–5, Sat. 8:30–5, Sun. 8:30–5; winter, Mon.–Sat. 8–5.*

GETTING AROUND The towns that line Grays Harbor lie right on U.S. 101, about 110 miles south of Forks. U.S. 101 runs through downtown Hoquiam and Aberdeen, on the northeastern shore of Grays Harbor. To access the coastal beaches from Hoquiam, take U.S. 101 to Highway 109 North and follow the signs. For Ocean Shores, take Highway 115 from Highway 109. Drive south on Highway 105 from Aberdeen to reach Westport and Grayland, on the southwestern shore of the harbor.

➢ **BY BUS** • **Grays Harbor Transportation Authority** (tel. 800/562–9730) buses serve Olympia (Bus 40 east), where you can catch a Greyhound to Lake Quinault (Bus 60), Ocean Shores (Bus 51), Westport (Bus 55), and smaller towns along the coast. Fare is 25¢ within Grays Harbor County and $1 to Olympia. The station in Aberdeen is at the corner of Wishkah and G streets; call the station in Hoquiam (3000 Bay St., tel. 360/532–2770) for transit info.

➢ **BY FERRY** • The ferry that runs between Westport and Ocean Shores is the only direct route from the north and south shores of Grays Harbor. The **Grays Harbor Passenger Ferry** (tel. 360/268–0047) charges $8 round-trip and runs daily in summer, weekends in September.

In Search of Kurt

Formerly a sleepy seaport town, Aberdeen has been thrust into the limelight for having produced Nirvana front man and grunge legend Kurt Cobain. His mother's beauty shop is still on Heron Street, and she and Kurt's teenage sister live next door. If you drive around the area where he lived—around Seventh Street, on the outskirts of town—you'll see why he didn't quite fit in. A sign at the end of the street advertises the Aberdeen Homemakers Club, and the rest of the area is a heartland stereotype of pickups and lawn flamingos.

People in Aberdeen are quick to tell you what they thought of Cobain and anyone associated with him. According to one waitress, Kurt's wife, Courtney Love is "bitchy." A guy in Hoquiam claims that Kurt was a "real freak," and "wasn't like any of the locals." (Really?) Most succinctly, the man behind the espresso counter calls Kurt a "cool guy."

WHERE TO SLEEP A slew of nondescript motels line U.S. 101, within walking distance of the Aberdeen bus station. Two of the cheapest are the **Travelure Motel** (623 W. Wishkah St., tel. 360/532–3280), which charges $33 (single) and $42 (double); and the newer and infinitely better **Olympic Inn Motel** (616 W. Heron St., tel. 360/533–4200). The latter offers huge bedrooms with cable TV, and use of a pool and laundry facilities for $43 single occupancy and $53 double occupancy. If you can afford to splurge a little, stay in Hoquiam's **Lytle House** (509 Chenault Ave., next to castle, tel. 800/677–2320), a restored Victorian B&B. Doubles, most with shared bath, go for $65–$75, and include full breakfast, evening dessert, and a stupendous view of Grays Harbor.

➤ **CAMPGROUNDS** • Miss those Gidget reruns? Stake out a campsite or a free patch of sand along with the surfer dudes and dudettes at **North Beach,** between Moclips and Point Brown (the southern tip of Ocean Shores). The area is packed in summer, but solitary souls can enjoy quiet for the rest of the year. **Ocean City State Park** (Hwy. 115, 1 mi north of Ocean Shores, tel. 360/289–3553), just south of Pacific Beach, has flat, clean sites that are anything but private. Still, some have great views, and the campground has bathrooms and a community kitchen. To reach Ocean City from Aberdeen, go west on Highway 12 to Highway 115.

FOOD As long as you're here, you might as well grab a cheap bite to eat at Aberdeen's **Liberty Tavern** (500 E. Schley, tel. 360/533–1889), where a delicious Monte Cristo sandwich goes for $3.95. The tavern's clutter would take days to examine; old tools and instruments hang from the ceiling, and portraits of locals and outlaws cover the walls. On weekends, the tavern features banjo and piano music. **Billy's Bar and Grill** (322 E. Heron St., Aberdeen, tel. 360/533–7144) is a restored corner saloon, with a long bar and a high ceiling. Try the Shrimp Broil (shrimp, mushrooms, onions, and tomatoes on a roll topped with melted cheese; $6.95). Billy's hops all night with music and jumbo (32 oz.) microbrews ($3.75). By day, **Sidney's** (512 W. Heron St., Aberdeen, tel. 360/533–6635) is a restaurant. By night it becomes the place for Generation X-types to ogle each other and flail about to live music. Come early before it gets packed.

The Grays Harbor area is one of the largest cranberry-producing regions on the west coast. The bogs bloom in June and are harvested in October, when you can visit Grays Harbor and come eye-to-eye with the results of just about every cranberry recipe known to humans.

WORTH SEEING To get a better feel of the harbor's shipping history, head to the **Grays Harbor Historical Seaport** (813 E. Heron St., tel. 360/532–8611), which features replicas of a vintage tall ship and long boats. For a little landlocked history, check out **Hoquiam's Castle** (515 Chenault Ave., tel. 360/533–2005), built in 1897 and reflecting the expensive taste of its owner, lumber baron Robert Lytle. It costs $4 to enter and view the restored Victorian interior. The informal **Grays Harbor Farmers' Market and Craft Fair** happens Wednesday and Saturday in summer along the river in Hoquiam.

OUTDOOR ACTIVITIES **Ocean Shores,** a 1960s-era resort community, and the neighboring beach town of **Copalis** are a short drive north of Aberdeen and Hoquiam on Highway 109. Both towns are popular with surfers. The best surf shop in Ocean Shores is **Octopus Garden** (773 Pt. Brown Ave., tel. 360/289–3375), where you can grab an espresso and/or rent a board ($15 for 24 hours). The water is too cold to swim in without a wet suit, but you can sunbathe on the beach in summer. If you'd rather not bare your bod to the misty air, grab a shovel and dig for razor clams.

Westport, 20 miles southwest of Aberdeen and Hoquiam on Highway 105, is the best place on Grays Harbor to charter a boat or fish. Cruise along the main Westhaven Drive to check out the numerous charter companies. **Washington Charters** (2411 Westhaven Dr., tel. 360/268–0900) will take you whale watching or fishing for salmon or bottom feeders for $22–$70 per person. The best surfing waves in the area, found off Westhaven State Park beach, can reach 10 feet. Beginners should start out far south of the jetty, where waves are more forgiving. The **Surf Shop** (tel. 360/268–0992), on Highway 105 as you enter town, rents all kinds of equipment.

Landlubbers can enjoy **Westport Light Trail Nature Walk,** which begins near the Westport Light House and runs along the edge of the Pacific Ocean, atop a dune between Ocean Avenue and

Westhaven Park Road. Cyclists, rollerbladers, and wheelchairs can all navigate the 6,000-foot-long, 8-foot-wide concrete walkway. Signs posted along the trail give information about the dune ecosystem with pen-and-ink drawings by local artist Alexandra Gallagher. The trail ends at Westhaven Jetty, where in 1993 erosion created a channel between the jetty and Half Moon Bay.

Around mid-April, more than 500,000 birds invade the muddy **Grays Harbor National Wildlife Refuge** (tel. 360/753–9467) on their way from South America to Alaska. There are no facilities and no trails, so come at high tide (when you can see the birds), bring your rubber knee boots, and brave the mud—the bird bonanza merits the effort if you're into that sort of thing. To find the refuge from Aberdeen, go west through Hoqiam toward Ocean Shores, just west of Hoquiam, turn left on Paulson Road; at the T intersection, turn right toward the airport.

Long Beach

Regression is the word in Long Beach. The town bears a striking resemblance to Coney Island in the 1950s, with everything from cotton candy and hot dogs to go-carts and bumper cars. If this is your thing, you'll have a cheap and tawdry good time at the shooting gallery and arcade, carnival rides, and seafood stands on the Pacific Highway. When you get bored, head down to the biggest beach in the west and play with the big kids—they're the ones with the sand sculptures and the $300 kites (no kidding).

You'll have to save your fantasies of scantily clad beach bunnies and bums for warmer climes: In Long Beach you get to guess if that babe in the parka is male or female.

WHERE TO SLEEP The cheapest hotels lie along the outskirts of town, and as far south as Seaview. If you've brought your camping gear, beach campgrounds abound, but sites are typically flat and exposed. Some campgrounds offer cabins with kitchens at rates that rival the cheapest budget hotels.

Driftwood RV Park & Motel. You can pitch a tent or stay in a cabin at this grassy, tree-lined lot across from the sand dunes. The cabins are just like houses, with living rooms, TVs, kitchens, bathrooms, and one bedroom each. It's not the Hilton, but you can save cash by cooking for yourself. Tent sites are $12 and cabins are $40; ask about winter discounts. *1512 N. Pacific, on Hwy. 103, tel. 360/642–2711. 1 mi from downtown. 4 cabins. Wheelchair access. No credit cards.*

Sands Motel. Sitting right on the edge of the sand dunes at the northern border of Long Beach, this motel offers small, forgettable doubles for $27 ($33 in summer). The Sands is within walking distance of everything, and the friendly owner doesn't care how many people you cram into the room. If you stay 3–6 days, the price drops to $24 a day, and a week is only $120. *Route 1, tel. 360/642–2100. North of downtown on Hwy. 103. 4 rooms.*

Sou'wester. The Sou'wester, in the the nearby town of Seaview, offers rooms and apartments in a historic lodge, and cabins adjacent to the beach. Lodge rooms are a repository of things collected over the years, including handmade quilts and original paintings and drawings. Cabins and trailers have cooking facilities, and the main lodge has a kitchen that guests can use. The eccentric proprietors also run a hostel/campground on the grounds (*see below*). *Beach Access Rd., Seaview, tel. 360/642–2545. 1 block south of intersection of U.S. 101 and Hwy. 103. 3 rooms, 6 suites, 4 cabins, 6 trailers.*

➤ **HOSTELS** • The closest HI hostel to Long Beach is in Fort Columbia State Park (*see* The Columbia River Mouth, *below*) to the east. **The Pavilion** is an unconventional hostel/campground on the grounds of the Sou'wester (*see above*) in Seaview. Bring your sleeping bag and stay in historic late 19th-century open-air stables, or pitch your tent in a small, part-cement campground. You can cook over the barbecue pit in a quiet garden; shared bathrooms and showers are in the stables. You'll be only seconds from the Seaview Pier and an untainted beach, and even closer to the hubbub surrounding guru-ish lodge owners Len and Miriam. A place in the stables costs $10; tent sites are $13.50. *Beach Access Rd., tel. 360/642–2542. 1 block south of intersection of U.S. 101 and Hwy. 103. 25 sites. Reservations advised.*

➢ **CAMPGROUNDS** • **Andersen's On the Ocean.** This private RV and tent campground is the closest to Long Beach. RV sites ($13) sadly outnumber tent sites ($10). *Hwy. 103, tel. 360/642–2231. 3½ mi north of Long Beach. 10 tent sites. Laundry, showers.*

FOOD Small, inexpensive eateries proliferate along Highway 103; most places offer seafood and diner fare. If you're cooking, head to the **Midtown Market and Deli** (Rte. 103, tel. 360/642–2326) at the stoplight in downtown Long Beach. If you just want a snack, choose from the monstrous selection of pastries baked fresh daily at **Cottage Bakery and Delicatessen** (118 S. Hwy. 103, Long Beach, tel. 360/642–4441). In Seaview, you can get a filling meal consisting of an oyster sandwich ($3.50), chili fries ($2.50), or lots of greasy-but-good seafood at the **Loose Kaboose** (Hwy. 103, tel. 360/642–2894).

Kopa Wecoma. Locals will urge you to eat here—listen to them. The name Kopa means "by the sea" in the Chinook language and the description is apt. Fresh-baked bread accompanies just about every meal, and the cod sandwich ($4.50) is an especially good deal. *901 S. Pacific Ave., tel. 360/642–4224. Open Fri.–Mon. noon–9. Wheelchair access.*

Pastimes. Elegant pillars, Oriental carpets, and gently spinning fans spruce up this café. Try the granola and yogurt ($1.75) for breakfast. Later, go for a large garden salad ($3.25) or splurge on smoked seafood fettuccine ($13.25). For dessert, an espresso float is $2.75. *5th St. at Hwy. 103, Long Beach, tel. 360/642–8303. Open summer, Mon. 8:30–5, Tues.–Sun. 8:30–5 and 5:30–9; winter, Mon.–Thurs. 8:30–5, Fri.–Sun. 8:30–5 and 5:30–9.*

WORTH SEEING If you're in Long Beach in late July, check out the **Sand-Sations** sand-sculpting festival. A granular version of Picasso's *Guernica* is rumored to have won one year, as is an exploration of the homoerotic overtones of the Judeo-Christian creation myth. Whatever the season, **Marsh's Free Museum** is home to every type of trashy souvenir imaginable. Peruse the mind-boggling collection of player pianos, old tools, guns, photographs, and doorknobs. The dubious highlight is the world's largest frying pan. The center floor is a large trinket shop.

Kite Mania

From Long Beach's boardwalk, which stretches southwest from Tenth Street to Bolstad Street, you can watch what has become the newest craze in southwestern Washington: kite flying. Fliers battle the strong offshore winds to keep control of their surging, swooping, kaleidoscopic contraptions. Some of the high-tech gliders catch so much air that their pilots are dragged along like uncooperative children. If you decide to join in, Long Beach Kites (104 Pacific Ave., tel. 360/642–2202) offers a mind-boggling collection of kites and will even rent you one for an hour or so. Just tell them you're interested in knowing more about the kites, and possibly purchasing one. They'll give you a $100 kite to test fly for about $8. You can also visit the World Kite Museum and Hall of Fame on Third Street, where you'll find a collection of kites from 14 countries, as well as information on kite making, kite history, and international kite celebrities. It's cheap (admission: $1) and actually interesting, if a little obsessive.

At the end of August, the peninsula celebrates its passion for kites with the Washington State International Kite Festival, a week-long event with theme days like Handcrafted Kite Day and Stunt Kite Day. During the festival, lodging is scarce, but attractions, such as performances by synchronized kite teams, competitions, and demonstrations of stunt kite flying, are pretty fun. For more information, contact W.S.I.K.F. (Box 387, Long Beach, WA 98631, tel. 800/451–2542).

The museum also rents clam shovels and distributes free tide tables. *400 S. Pacific Ave., tel. 360/642–2188. Open daily 9–6.*

AFTER DARK **Bent Rudder Galley.** The Bent Rudder, with its tall ceilings and long, plank floors, is distinctly boat-like (hence the name). A beer-drinking, pool-playing, dart-throwing, boot-stomping crowd comes here on weekends for the live music and dancing. Food is served at all hours; try the Rudder Burger (sautéed mushrooms, green peppers, onions, Swiss cheese, and bacon; $5.50). *1700 Pacific Ave., tel. 360/642–8330. Open daily 10 AM–2 AM. Wheelchair access.*

Heron and Beaver Pub. This welcoming little pub is a part of the posh Shelburne Inn, but feels like Olde England. Pine-green carpets, tan wood, and stained glass windows make this a relaxing place to spend the evening. You won't want to wear your black leather, but it's a nice place for a conversation over a cappuccino ($1.75), one of 15 microbrews ($2.75), or a rare single-malt Scotch whisky. *In Shelburne Inn, where Hwy. 103 meets N. 45th St., tel. 360/642–4142. Open daily 11:30–10.*

NEAR LONG BEACH

If the waters of the mighty Columbia River and the Pacific Ocean met with less violence, a huge seaport might sit at the river's mouth instead of the long stretch of undeveloped beach known as the Long Beach Peninsula. More than 2 miles wide and 28 miles long, this moody, storm-beaten peninsula boasts the largest uninterrupted stretch of sandy coastline in North America. Oddly, traditional beach activities are rare here. Locals warn that this is *not* a place to swim: Shifting sands and tremendous undertows account for several deaths each year, and strong winds make tanning and beach lounging a bone-chilling experience year-round. Instead of frolicking in the waves, most visitors walk along the short town boardwalk and take in unobstructed views of the beach and bird life from the telescopes and salt-stained benches along the way.

No vendors are permitted on the boardwalk, but the small towns on the peninsula more than compensate, with plenty of places to buy indispensable tourist paraphernalia like peninsula-shape salt and pepper shakers. Despite all the hype, visitors seem to concentrate more on the area's excellent hiking and bird-watching, especially from November to February, when migrating white trumpeter swans arrive. Look for them around the peninsula's several lakes, especially **Brisco Lake** (just north of Long Beach) and **Loomis Lake** (just south of the town of Klipsan Beach). Equal numbers of birds and bears also ramble through the inland cranberry bogs, along with the most fearful of beasts, the amateur berry-picker.

Hiking enthusiasts should make use of the miles of hiking trails at **Fort Canby, Fort Columbia,** and **Leadbetter State Park.** Trails at Fort Canby include a steep 2-mile path from the Fort Canby Road (through the campsites) to Battery 247, a World War II battlement. Another good bet is the **Coastal Forest Trail,** which begins behind the phone booth at Fort Canby General Store and winds for just under 2 miles through old-growth forest, offering stunning views of the Ilwaco boat channel. Leadbetter State Park, at the northern tip of the Peninsula, contains a 2.5-mile **loop trail** that winds through the dunes along the ocean and Willapa Bay, beginning at the parking lot. Several trails along the loop lead to isolated patches of coast. The **Long Beach Peninsula Visitor's Bureau** (tel. 360/642–2400), at the intersection of U.S. 101 and Highway 103 in Seaview, distributes brochures on hiking, lodging, dining, and attractions throughout the peninsula.

The Pacific Highway, on the western side of the peninsula, runs through Ilwaco, Seaview, Long Beach, Ocean Park, and Nahcotta. Just south of Seaview, Sandridge Road branches off and runs through Nahcotta to Oysterville. Stackpole Road, which forks off Sandridge Road in Oysterville, will get you within hiking distance (2–3 miles) of Leadbetter Point, the peninsula's northern tip. It takes just under an hour to drive from one end of the peninsula to the other.

Good news for those without wheels: **Pacific Transit System** (tel. 360/642–9418) buses cover the Long Beach peninsula area thoroughly. Bus 20 runs Monday–Saturday up and down the peninsula to Oysterville, Ocean Park, Long Beach, Ilwaco, and Chinook. You can buy a day pass from any bus driver for $1.50. Unfortunately, the bus does not go to Leadbetter Point, which is only served by **Dial-a-Ride** (tel. 360/642–9418). Dial-a-Ride also provides on-call transit service for disabled people weekdays 7 AM–10 PM, Saturday 10–6. The fare is 35¢. Cyclists can rent wheels at the **Wright Brothers Amusement** (next to Funland, Highway 103, downtown Long Beach) for $4 an hour, helmet included.

ILWACO This town lives to fish. The **Port of Ilwaco** (tel. 360/642–3143) distributes a free fishing guide that describes the possibilities: salmon, rock cod, ling cod, flounder, perch, sea bass, sturgeon, crab, tuna, and more. To get a feel for the town's less fishy offerings, drive west from the downtown stoplight to reach the beginning of the **Highway 100 Loop**. The loop passes two lighthouses, Fort Canby State Park, China Beach, the Lewis and Clark Interpretive Center, the North Jetty, and Waikiki Beach before returning to downtown Ilwaco. Every October, Ilwaco's **cranberry festival** features everything you've always secretly wanted to know about cranberries, including how to use them as an organic "marriage aid." Cranberry fun includes food booths, craft booths, contests, and tours of the bogs.

The population of Ilwaco is only 900, but its port has 800 slips. That's almost one boat for every Ilwacan man, woman, and child.

The **Ilwaco Heritage Museum** presents the history of southwestern Washington, with an emphasis on Native American history and folklore as well as the environmental impact of early pioneer settlement. The highlight of the museum is a model of the peninsula's "clamshell railroad," a narrow-gauge train that once ran along a rail bed of ground-up clam and oyster shells, transporting passengers and mail along the beach. A model of the train runs behind the museum. *115 S.E. Lake St., tel. 360/642–3446. Admission: $1.25. Open May–Aug., Mon.–Sat. 9–5, Sun. 10–2; Sept.–Apr., Mon.–Sat. 9–5 and Sun. noon–5.*

➤ **WHERE TO SLEEP** • **Heidi's Inn** (126 Spruce St., tel. 360/642–2387) costs a bit more than the surrounding motels, but the rooms here are big, comfortable, and decorated in subtle earth tones. Doubles go for $40. All rooms have refrigerators and are stocked with coffee and tea. **Chinook County Park** campground (U.S. 101, tel. 360/777–8442; closed Labor Day–Memorial Day), 6 miles east of Ilwaco, will satisfy any suburban homesickness for trailer homes and Tupperware. Sites overlook the water and cost $7.50 ($10 with water and electricity).

CAPE DISAPPOINTMENT English fur trader Captain John Meares came upon the southeastern tip of the Long Beach Peninsula in 1788. Miffed that he had failed to find the Northwest Passage, he named it Cape Disappointment. Known as "the graveyard of the Pacific," this harbor has been the scourge of sailors since the 1700s, and more than 250 ships have sunk after running aground on its treacherous sandbars. The damp, creepy **Cape Disappointment lighthouse**, first used in 1856, is one of the oldest on the West Coast and offers great views. Cape Disappointment is accessed via Soundridge Road.

FORT CANBY STATE PARK Built in 1862 to guard the mouth of the Columbia River, Fort Canby became a state park in 1957. Today, it's the best-equipped, best-looking park on the peninsula. The 1,700-acre grounds encompass deserted beaches, 16 miles of hiking trails, abandoned bunkers, and standard campsites ($11 per night) near beaches and trees. Beachcombers can pick through the debris tossed onto the shore, or watch the huge, foaming waves collapse against the Columbia River sand bar during winter storms. *Robert Gray Dr., tel. 360/642–3078 or 800/562–0990 in WA. 2½ mi southwest of Ilwaco, off U.S. 101. Admission free. Day-use area open Apr.–Oct. 15, daily 6:30 AM–dusk; Oct. 16–Mar., daily 8 AM–dusk.*

Between Fort Canby's North Jetty and the North Head Lighthouse is the 1.5-mile-long Benson Beach. The beach enjoys a view of both lighthouses and is closed to traffic, making it an excellent place for an extended stroll.

Just south of Fort Canby is the **Lewis and Clark Interpretive Center.** Displays include an exhibit on Meriwether Lewis and William Clark's 8,000-mile journey from Wood River, Illinois to the mouth of the Columbia River, undertaken between 1803 and 1807. Artwork, photographs, and original journal entries are arranged along a series of ramps that take you from the planning of the expedition to a view of the Pacific from Cape

Disappointment. *Hwy. 100, tel. 360/642–3029 or 360/642–3078. Admission free. Open summer, daily 9–5; winter, weekends 9–5. Wheelchair access.*

NORTH HEAD The **North Head Lighthouse,** one of the oldest in the area, was built in 1899 to help skippers sailing from the north who couldn't see the Cape Disappointment lighthouse. The short, wheelchair-accessible **North Head Lighthouse Trail** leads down a slight grade to the lighthouse. You can't go in, but you'll get spectacular views of the ocean and the coastline from the base. This is also one of the best places to see gray whales on their migration to and from Arctic waters. The access road is off the Highway 100 Loop, near Fort Canby State Park.

OCEAN PARK I. A. Clark, who co-founded Oysterville, felt that Oysterville's boomtown success was not conducive to a religious lifestyle. So, in 1883, he and the Reverend William Osburn founded Ocean Park, north of Long Beach, as a camp for the Methodist Episcopal Church of Portland. Once upon a time, the town piously prohibited everything from alcohol to gambling, but no more. Just one example of the hedonism that pervades today is the mid-June **Garlic Festival.** The smelly fest features garlic-laden delicacies, garlic-eating contests, garlic-peeling contests, larger than human-sized dancing garlics, and live jazz and blues, as well as a number of food stands that cheerfully ignore the festival's theme. Between festivals and the tourist season, Ocean Park is a sleepy town with inexpensive lodging and campgrounds.

➤ **WHERE TO SLEEP AND EAT** • The clientele at **Shakti Cave** (Hwy. 103, off 253rd Pl., tel. 360/665–4000) is about 80% lesbian, but the management promotes it as a place where "all women can go and feel comfortable." The secluded cabins rent for $52.82 a night and include a bedroom, living room, kitchen, and full bath. Men can stay here, but are a minority. Spend a sunny afternoon in the plant-shaded patio at **Back Porch Garden Café** (1517 Bay Ave., at Hwy. 103, tel. 360/665–5732; closed Fri.), across from Jack's Country Store. The menu changes daily but always includes soup, bread, salads, pastas, and yummy desserts like sticky sweet buns with currants and walnuts ($1.25). The chefs at **My Mom's Pie Kitchen** (Hwy. 103, at 12th St. S, tel. 360/642–2342; closed Mon.) keep irregular hours but bake beautiful pies. Try a slice of banana whipped cream, chocolate almond, sour cream raisin, or fresh raspberry for about $3. This trailer home-turned-restaurant also serves clam chowder, quiches, and sandwiches for about $6.50.

NAHCOTTA Mountains of shucked oyster shells line the piers of this tiny village, where canning factories shuck 'em, huck 'em, and ship 'em out. Just a few miles north of Ocean Beach, Nahcotta is an escape from more touristy cities to the south and provides a less sanitized vision of peninsula life. From the road it might look like there's not much here, but a closer look reveals a beautiful state park, inexpensive fresh seafood eateries, and art galleries. Once home to Chinook Indians, Nahcotta now has a growing artist population.

Let's Get Clammy

Some grown-ups feel they need an excuse to dig in the sand, so they go clamming. ("I'm not playing in the sand, I'm getting dinner.") The success rate here varies, but clamming is always a popular pastime—whether you get any or not. Don't shovel half-heartedly though—you'll be fined if you throw or leave clams you dig, regardless of size. Check with the Peninsula Visitor's Center (tel. 800/451–2542) before you start digging: Recent traces of domoic acid and red-tide toxins, naturally occurring but toxic to humans, caused 11 cases of shellfish poisoning in November 1991. Scientists monitor samples before a season can open. Locals pay $5 for a personal-use shellfish license; non-locals pay a whopping $20. For details and license information, call the Washington Department of Fisheries (tel. 206/753–6552) or the Fisheries Shellfish Lab in Nahcotta (tel. 360/665–4166). You can rent a clamming shovel just about anywhere on the coast.

Stop by **Nahcotta Naturals** (Hwy. 103 N, Nahcotta, tel. 360/665–4449) for treats like unsul-fured dried apricots, huge bags of homemade trail mix, and fresh-baked breads. In back, they serve coffee and tea, fresh soup, tofu, and veggie sandwiches at two small tables. If you don't mind eating outside, walk to the end of the Nahcotta Pier to **Bendiksens East Point**, a cannery where locals buy their seafood right out of the water. Here you can feast on shrimp cocktail (95¢) and fresh Willapa Bay oysters in the shell ($4.50 a dozen). Sit at redwood picnic tables, enjoy the views of Long Island, and lunch with the gulls.

If you've been waiting for a splurge-worthy restaurant, it's time to break out the plastic. **The Ark** (273 Sandridge Rd., tel. 360/665–4133; closed Jan.–Feb.), adjacent to old Nahcotta dock, is known for its seafood (especially oysters) and its rich desserts, such as cranberry Grand Marnier mousse and blackberry bread pudding. Entrées run upwards of $20. Less expensive, lighter food, including soup and sandwiches ($10–$15), is served a the bar.

OYSTERVILLE Oysterville bears an unsettling resemblance to the set of Little House on the Prairie. The small signs posted on the curb-side fence of each home and business tell when it was built and who lived in it. You can even tour the old town church (pick up a free historical map of Oysterville here), the schoolhouse, the late 19th-century tannery, and the houses of the mayor and other prominent citizens. The town throws a one-day Jazz and Oyster Festival in August, thus effectively coupling two of life's best aphrodisiacs. If you miss the festival, **Oys-terville Sea Farms** will sell you seven dozen oysters for $20.

LEADBETTER STATE PARK Shaped like a shepherd's crook, Leadbetter State Park is 10 miles north of Oysterville. The park's hiking trails pass through beaches, dunes, marshes, forests, bogs, and berry brambles. As you wade through a sea of blackberries, huckleberries, and strawberries, be on the lookout for one of the black bears that are common here, as well as more than 200 species of birds. The dune area at the very tip of the point is closed from April to August to protect the nesting snowy plover (it's a bird). In the winter, you can dig for razor clams. Call **Fort Canby Center** (tel. 360/642–3078) for more information.

The Columbia River

Straddling the Columbia River between Washington's Mt. Adams and Oregon's Mt. Hood, the Columbia River Gorge is the only break in the entire length of the Cascades and the only route of passage for air currents. This unique geography endows the Gorge with world-renowned windsurfing con-ditions and four distinctly beautiful seasons, offering ideal conditions for hiking, fishing, cycling, and camping. Although it might seem contradictory, many locals are passionate about hiking along the forested mountain slopes and are also supporters of and/or employed in the region's biggest moneymaker: the lumber industry. Some of the largest lumber mills in the Pacific Northwest sit along the Columbia River, especially near **Longview.** Because of the area's dependence on the lumber industry, and recent deforestation regulations spawned by the spotted owl hoopla (see Box, below), pretty much everybody here has an opinion on the preservation-versus-industry debate. Owls aren't the only things being dicussed here; the Columbia River towns of **Celito Falls** and **Dulles** were once significant summer trading cen-ters for Native American groups, and representatives of the Wyam and Wasco tribes still meet here today to barter and discuss Native American and tribal affairs.

Longview and Kelso

Although the combined population of Longview and Kelso logs in at well over 45,000, a small-town mentality prevails. The hottest nighttime activity in these parts is cruising the avenue in your flatbed. But because these overgrown suburbs are the only major towns on Interstate 5 between Portland and Tacoma, they make a good pit-stop for inexpensive gas, meals, or a night's sleep. By day, you can brave the trails of Mt. St. Helens (see Chapter 8) or the nearby national parks and Columbia River Gorge; by night, slink back here to your motel room, take a hot shower, and watch some cable TV.

Kelso was founded in the 1840s by Scotsman Peter Crawford. **Longview** came second, planned and funded in the 1920s by timber baron R. A. Long. The towns are all but indistinguishable to the untrained eye, but only Kelso can proudly call itself the "Smelt Capital of the World." Watch millions of foot-long, silvery fish shimmer their way upstream during Kelso's **Smelt Run** in January and February. The first Sunday in March, attend the **Smelt Eating Contest** held by the Kelso Eagles, a local sports team.

If Seattle and San Francisco are the Brie of west-coast cities, Longview and Kelso are the Velveeta.

VISITOR INFORMATION The **Kelso Chamber of Commerce** has very little information for nonresidents. Instead, use the services at the next-door **Volcano Center Museum and Tourist Information,** at the same phone number and address. *105 Minor Rd., off Interstate 5, tel. 360/577–8058. Open summer, daily 9–5; winter, Wed.–Sun. 9–5.*

For local park and trail information, contact the **City of Longview Parks and Recreation Department** (2920 Douglas Street, Longview, tel. 360/577–3345). The **Longview Chamber of Commerce** has a ton of information on the area and a vast selection of brochures on Longview, Kelso, and the Mt. St. Helens Volcanic Monument, as well as a *Walking Tour* guide of local historic buildings. *1563 Olympia Way, near Hotel Monticello, tel. 360/423–8400. Open weekdays 9–5.*

COMING AND GOING Interstate 5 winds its way between Longview and Kelso, parallel to the Cowlitz River. Seattle is about 125 miles north of the twin cities; Portland is 48 miles to the south. Route 4 stretches west from Longview to the Long Beach Peninsula, about 80 miles away.

➤ **BY BUS** • **Greyhound** (1136 Washington Way, Longview, tel. 360/423–7380) serves Olympia and Seattle seven times daily. One-way fare to Olympia is about $13.50; to Seattle,

A Spotty Issue

Graffiti on a Washington bathroom stall: "Due to the lumber shortage we are out of toilet paper, so wipe your ass with a spotted owl." This pretty much sums up the timber industry's attitude toward what has become known as the "great spotted owl debate" of the Pacific Northwest. The debate over the fate of this species and the forests it inhabits has been exceptionally bitter and clouded by high emotion and rhetoric on both sides. The media hasn't helped, hyping the issue as one of "owl vs. man." Environmental groups—notably the Wilderness Society, the Audubon Society, and the Sierra Club—are trying fervently to save the approximately 6,000 remaining owls, whose habitat is the old-growth forest of the Pacific Northwest. The timber industry, represented most vocally by enormous corporations like Weyerhauser, feels it depends on these very same trees. When the Department of the Interior declared the spotted owl a threatened species in 1990, it simultaneously declared about 14 million acres of land off-limits to logging, causing a predictable uproar in the timber industry. Since then the industry has made dire predictions about the number of logging jobs it will cost to save the owl, and has depicted the situation as one of elitist environmentalists versus working-class loggers. Many argue that the case is not that clear-cut (sorry), and that a fundamental restructuring of the industry (like switching to harvesting farmed trees) and of related government policy is necessary. Tell that to an unemployed logger or a dead owl.

it's about $22. Buses leave for Portland ($13.25 one-way) six times daily and to Vancouver, B.C. ($7.50 one-way) three times daily.

➤ **BY BIKE** • Some of the two-lane highways off Interstate 5 provide smooth, relatively safe rides: U.S. 101 (along the coast), Route 4 (to Long Beach), and Route 14 (along the Columbia River) are three of the most popular rides.

WHERE TO SLEEP Longview has a number of competitively priced motels, most of which are pretty similar. You can find singles in the $28–$36 price range along 15th Avenue between Route 4 and Route 432.

Electra Motel. If the mint-colored walls of this Longview hotel don't set you twitching, you can really save some money: For $32, you get two bedrooms, a bathroom, and a kitchen. *744 10th Ave., at Vanderhook, tel. 360/423–5040. 2 blocks from bus station. 8 rooms.*

Monticello Motel. Opened in 1923, this building has served as the post office, the bank, and the town saloon. Today, it's the most elegant hotel in town, with a spacious lobby filled with oil paintings and mahogany. The rooms are a little less grand, but they are spacious and well-equipped. Doubles go for about $40. *1405 17th St., Longview, tel. 360/425–9900. 20 rooms. Luggage storage, wheelchair access.*

Sterling Motor Inn. With plush mauve carpet, low vinyl chairs, and groovy lamps, rooms at this hotel recall Mike Brady's den when Greg became a hippie and redecorated (minus the door beads). At $30 a double, these large, 70s-style rooms are the cheapest in town. *1808 Hemlock St., at 18th St., Longview, tel. 360/423–6980. 34 rooms.*

➤ **CAMPING** • **Woodland Special Camp.** About a 30-minute drive south of Longview in some amazingly dense forest, these free (!) sites are huge and secluded. Bathrooms, water, picnic tables, and chairs are all easily accessible.. *From Interstate 5 north, exit in Woodinville, turn right at signal and right again at N.W. Pacific Hwy., then left on N.W. Bratton Rd. and follow signs.*

FOOD Eating in Longview and Kelso is like choosing from a freezer full of TV dinners: The labels may be different, but the food all tastes the same. Play it safe and eat at one of the pubs in town (they have unusually good food), or go to **Safeway** (Kelso Dr., at Allen St., exit 39 from Interstate 5) and take matters into your own hands.

Country Village Nutrition Shoppe & Café. This place has everything from vitamins and herbs to an espresso and smoothie bar. The café serves a daily soup and salad special ($3.90), veggie burgers ($3.75), and whole-wheat lasagna ($4.65). *711 Vanderhook Way, Longview/Kelso border, tel. 360/425–8100. Open Mon.–Sat. 9–5.*

The Masthead. This oversized, British-style pub in Longview attracts a big daytime crowd with its large Italian salads ($5), chicken sandwiches ($5), and halibut and chips ($5). At night, locals come to drink beer, kick back, and yap. On warm days, you'll have to wait for a seat on the outdoor deck. *1210 Ocean Beach Hwy., tel. 360/577–7972. Open Mon.–Thurs. 11 AM–midnight, Fri. and Sat. 11 AM–1 AM, Sun. noon–11 PM.*

Mustard Seed. A small, quiet café in a Longview used-book store. Tables are clustered between walls of books, and under an eclectic collection of art. The menu includes Oscar Wilde English Muffin Melts ($5) and Agatha Crispy Salads ($2–$4). Scrumptious homemade scones are made by the owner's mum. *In The Book Shop, 1203 14th Ave., tel. 360/425–8707. Open Mon.–Sat. 10–5:30.*

Local bars tend to be locals only, and the menfolk seem especially unfriendly to out-of-town males who upset the already-disproportional male/female ratio.

AFTER DARK If you're like the local youth, your idea of a fun evening is cruising up and down 15th Street in your car. If you're just not cool enough for that kind of action, you can head to Longview's newly restored **Columbia Theater** (1231 Vanderhook Way, at Commerce, tel. 360/423–1011). Plays, concerts, and community events are held here year-round; prices range from $4–$8.

Allen Street Bar and Grill. From the street, this place looks small and inconspicuous, but a step inside reveals high ceilings and a row of bar stools that stretches something like half a city block down a blue-tiled bar. With a surprisingly hip crowd, this is just about the only place in town to go for decent vegetarian food, a good selection of beer and wine, and live music. Reggae, R&B, and folk music plays several nights a week. *108 Allen St., Kelso, tel. 360/414-5232. Open Mon.-Wed. 11-11, Thurs.-Sat. 11 AM-2 AM. Over 21 after 9 PM. Wheelchair access.*

OUTDOOR ACTIVITIES If you're a cyclist, stop by **Longview Schwinn and Fitness Center** (1165 Commerce Ave., tel. 360/577-4481 or 800/893-BIKE). In addition to bikes, equipment, clothing, books, and a repair shop, the center has a huge ride board. They also stock free cycling maps, magazines, and newspapers. If you're planning to ride along the river, call the **Columbia River Club** (2500 E. 4th Pl. Suite 64, 360/256-1529) in Vancouver, or the **Vancouver Bicycle Club** (tel. 206/254-3018).

Columbia River Mouth

Route 4 runs west from Longview along the Columbia River, paralleling the Lewis and Clark Trail as it passes through Wahkiakum County. There's no bus service, so the only ways to see this area are through a car window, over handlebars, or from behind the sail of a windsurfer. **Cathlamet** is the only sizable town on this route before the Long Beach Peninsula. The rest of the drive offers long doses of dense forest and riverside parks. About halfway between Longview and Cathlamet is a vehicle turnoff where windsurfers park, walk across the road, and glide around undisturbed.

CATHLAMET Tiny Cathlamet's nearly abandoned Main Street is a small strip of shops (including a bank with an ATM), two restaurants, and a grocery store. **Birnie's Retreat** (83 Main St., tel. 360/795-3432) offers a different menu every day; dishes often include red snapper, prime rib, pot roast, and all-you-can-eat spaghetti. Even if you're just passing through town, you have to stop at the blue-and-white **River Rat Tap** (90 Broadway St., tel. 360/795-3581) and drink some locally brewed beer, shoot a game at their uncrowded pool table, and enjoy the best indoor river view between Long Beach and Longview. Hungry travelers can choose from a selection of "rat" burgers ($4-$5) or chili ($4.75).

B&Bs are it as far as indoor accommodations go in Cathlamet. **The Country Keeper Bed and Breakfast Inn** (61 Main Street, tel. 800/551-1691) is a meticulously restored Victorian house with polished wood floors and banisters, stained glass, and a front porch with a view of the river. Rates start at $70 (double) and include a breakfast of fresh-ground coffee, muffins, fruit, and choice of entrée. Even if you don't stay here, stop in next door at **AJ's Antiques & Espresso** for an iced cappuccino ($1.75) or one of the special concoctions like the Bavarian mint latte ($1.50).

PUGET ISLAND South of Cathlamet, Puget is a diminutive island in the middle of the Columbia River—a great place to cycle and take in the incomparable river views. Route 409 leads from Cathlamet across the **Julia Butler Hansen Bridge** to the island. This is also the place to catch the **Wahkiakum Ferry** (tel. 360/795-3301)—the only ferry on the lower Columbia River that still carries foot passengers—to Westport, Oregon.

JULIA BUTLER HANSEN REFUGE This protected area for white-tailed deer and Roosevelt elk is only a few miles west of Cathlamet. Wander around and try to spot some of the critters. Even if you don't get out, the drive though the park is a welcome diversion from Route 4 that will add only a few minutes to your travel time. *Steamboat Slough Rd, off Rte. 4, tel. 360/795-3915. Admission free. Open 24 hrs.*

SKAMOKAWA About 30 miles west of Longview, Skamokawa is a sleepy town on the site of a 2,000-year-old Native American village. Now it's trying to lure tourists with **Vista Park** (13 School Rd., tel. 360/795-8605), a waterfront recreation area with a beach, basketball and tennis courts, and unappealing campsites ($7.50-$9 a night). The chatty proprietor gives out advice and pamphlets on attractions all over the state.

East of here, try looking for a spot at **County Line Park** (2076 Route 4 E, halfway btw Cathlamet and Longview). You'll need a permit, and there is a three-day limit, but the park has bathrooms, picnic tables, and outstanding, tree-shrouded sites right on the bank of the river. Permits are available in Kelso at the **County Parks Department** (207 4th Ave. N, tel. 360/577–3030).

FORT COLUMBIA STATE PARK AND INTERPRETIVE CENTER One of 27 turn-of-the-century coastal defense units built by the U.S. Army, Fort Columbia now houses an **interpretive center** (tel. 360/777–8221; open daily 10–5 in summer), as well as a museum with displays about military family life in the early 1900s, when the fort was an active post. Attractions include underground fortifications, battlements, and the historic buildings themselves. Hike up Scarborough Hill, behind the fort, for views of the surrounding landscape and the Columbia River.

The **Fort Columbia HI Hostel** has rows of cots reminiscent of the post-op room in *M*A*S*H*, but the place itself is big and airy. You can almost always get a bed ($8.50 HI members, $11 nonmembers; linen rental 50¢), and the hostel's proximity to the park means you can arrive early and have it all to yourself. It's also near a pristine beach cove as well as blueberry and blackberry patches. Check-in is 5 PM–10 PM; curfew is 11 PM. *U.S. 101, 1 mi south of Chinook, tel. 360/777–8755. From Astoria or Ilwaco, take Pacific Transit Bus 24 to Fort Columbia (35¢). 23 beds. Laundry, kitchen, showers. Closed Dec.–Feb.*

THE CASCADES AND EASTERN WASHINGTON

8

By Kate Isaacson

Like Oregon, Washington suffers from geographic schizophrenia. Split down the middle by the Cascade Range, Washington's two halves share little in common, topographically, culturally, or otherwise. The western (and better known) part of the state is wet, mountainous, and cosmopolitan, and its liberal residents tend to look with urbane disdain at their country cousins to the east. Once you cross the Cascades, the rain stops and the people aren't so wet. As you head farther east, lush fruit farms and wineries in the foothills give way to semi-arid steppe, marked by sagebrush and desolate canyons. It comes as a real surprise to most people that large parts of Washington, like Oregon, look more like sets from a shoot-'em-up Western than a soggy land of mists and rain. Through this landscape runs the mighty Columbia River, controlled by the vast concrete span of the Grand Coulee Dam, the world's largest. Water from this dam has transformed large parts of eastern Washington from an agricultural wasteland into the fruitbowl of the nation. The dam provides the water that the Cascade Range withholds—the mountains essentially suck all the moisture out of the wet Pacific winds. Running north–south, the Cascade mountains are among the most spectacular in the world. Jagged-edged peaks, glaciers, and snowcaps provide a backdrop for pine forests, waterfalls, and rivers. If you like to hike and ski, welcome to Nirvana; but even if you've got the energy of a sloth on Valium, you should at least drive through the Cascades—it's something you won't soon forget. Highlights of the Cascades include the stunning North Cascades National Park, towering 14,408-foot Mt. Rainier, and Mt. St. Helens.

North Cascades Loop

The Rockies are higher, but they rise up from a surround- ing plateau that is already 6,000 feet above sea level. The Northern Cascades, on the other hand, don't take a run-up—many of these babies are over 8,000 feet on their own merit. And they are spectacular. No one should pass up an opportunity to spend some time here, especially since the mountains are within spitting distance of Seattle. The series of highways that connect Seattle to Lake Chelan, North Cascades National Park, Leavenworth, and a string of other little towns is known as the North Cascades Loop. From Everett (north of Seattle on I-5), follow U.S. 2 through the mountains east to Wenatchee, passing through little climbing-and-hiking-oriented hamlets, as well as "Bavarian" Leavenworth. From U.S. 2, U.S. 97 heads north through the town of Chelan. On the north side of Chelan, take Route 153 east from U.S. 97, and after passing through several small towns, meet up with Route 20, the North Cascades Highway, which winds west through the North Cascades National Park. Route 20 offers breathtaking scenery, and is one of the finest, most spectacular mountain drives in the North America. After the North Cascades, Route 20 reaches the Puget Sound in Anacortes and runs south along the water to complete the loop in Everett.

Hiking is the best way to see the Northern Cascades—and often the only way if you want to get into the rugged interior. Two of the most stunning regions, the Alpine Lake and Glacier Peak wildernesses, for example, can be appreciated only on foot. If you don't have a car, a good hiking base is Stehekin at Lake Chelan, where you can choose from a wide selection of trails and terrains. If you're not one of the hiking crowd, you can appreciate the beauty of the mountains from your car. Though it may take a while to break through the small-town Washington ice, people will warm up once they get to know you. You could easily spend a week, if not two, exploring this region.

BASICS

Most of the Cascade Range falls under the jurisdiction of one government agency or another, and who runs what can become very confusing. In the Northern Cascades, for example, there is the Wenatchee National Forest, Okanogan National Forest, Mt. Baker-Snoqualmie National Forest, North Cascades National Park, several state parks, and a host of designated wilderness areas. If you stop by the visitor information office nearest to where you are, though, they should be able to point you to the appropriate office.

VISITOR INFORMATION Wenatchee National Forest Ranger Station. *301 Yakima St., Wenatchee tel. 509/662–4335.*

North Cascades National Park Office and **Mt. Baker Ranger District**. *2105 Rte. 20, Sedro Woolley, tel. 206/856–5700.*

Okanogan National Forest Office. *1240 2nd Ave., Okanogan, tel. 509/826–3275.*

U.S. 2

The southern part of the Cascade Loop, U.S. 2 is a spectacular drive that twists and turns as it climbs into the mountains. The road's highest point is 4,061-foot Stevens Pass, which it reaches before it heads into Leavenworth (*see below*). Many Seattle residents drive up U.S. 2, park, and hike into the surrounding mountains. To the north is **Alpine Lake Wilderness**, one of the most popular hiking areas in the Cascades. The highlight of this wilderness is the **Enchantments,** a series of stunning mountain lakes. Contact the Wenatchee National Forest Ranger Station (*see above*) for more information about these two areas.

GOLD BAR Gold Bar, about 50 miles east of Seattle and 30 miles east of Everett, is one of the first small towns you hit as you drive into the Cascades on U.S. 2. It's a popular hiking base, and you can probably find out everything you need to know about the surrounding trails at the **Mountain Co.** (7th St. and U.S. 2, tel. 206/793–0221), a full-throttle outdoor store, which sells backpacking, hiking, and climbing gear, and rents snowboards ($18.95 per day), cross-country skis ($12 per day), and snowshoes ($8 per day). **Wallace Falls State Park** (tel. 206/793–0420), 2 miles northeast of Gold Bar, is one of the few undiscovered edens in the Cascades. Gorgeous campsites ($11) hidden in the woods have running water and flush toilets, as well as fire rings and tables.

INDEX The reason to stop in Index, a tight little community eight miles east of Gold Bar on U.S. 2, is to climb the sheer face of 1,000-foot-high black granite **Town Wall,** a rock precipice with a variety of knobs, ledges, and chimneys. Stop in Gold Bar at the Mountain Co. (*see above*) for climbing gear and a guide to the many trails—from beginning to advanced—that ascend the wall. The *Index Rock Climbing Guide* ($6.95) is very useful for local climbs, while *Washington Rock* ($11.95) covers all of the major climbing areas in Washington state. Non-climbers can take the easy way up via the **Index Wall Hike.** Starting behind the Bush House, the trail leads to a lookout point three-quarters of the way up the wall. It's a steep climb, but the awesome view of the Skykomish river makes it worthwhile. The free **Troublesome Creek Campground** (Mt. Baker-Snoqualmie National Forest, tel. 206/677–2414) is located in a secluded setting on the North Fork of the Skykomish River, near a nature trail and about 3 miles from some mineral springs. Take Galena Road 12 miles northeast from Index.

SKYKOMISH Twelve miles farther east from Index is Skykomish, an old town with a little library, a general store, and a hotel-café that serves excellent cinnamon buns. It's a good spot to head for breakfast or after a day of hiking. **Beckler River** is probably the best campground in the area. Set on the banks of the Beckler River, the 27-site campground has pit toilets, running water, and picnic tables. Sites are $8. A 1-mile walk will get you to a laundromat, a café, and a general store. To get to the campground, take U.S. 2 about a mile east of Skykomish and then go 2 miles north on Forest Service Road 65.

Keep driving east on U.S. 2 to **Stevens Pass** (tel. 206/973–2441). At 4,061 feet, the mountain offers perhaps the best views of the soaring Cascade Mountains. Between late fall and early spring, driving here can be treacherous, but the skiing bug brings Washington residents out in droves. Stevens Pass boasts 26 ski lifts, as well as ski-rental shops, bars, and cafés.

Leavenworth

Even Walt Disney couldn't have dreamt this place up. Smack in the middle of nowhere on the southern edge of the Cascade Mountains, this failed logging and mining community decided in the 1960s that its apple industry would not be able to pay the figurative rent. An ingenious tourism committee sifted through one ploy after another and, looking to the surrounding tree-lined mountains, decided to call itself "Leavenworth—Washington's Bavaria." If you're traveling anywhere in Washington, you're bound to be handed a pamphlet urging you toward this faux Deutschland. If you're in the area, you should ingest a grain of salt and enjoy the fruits of this distinctly American pleasure zone. After stopping for a beer and some provisions, take advantage of the surrounding land, especially the wilderness around Lake Wenatchee. With thickly forested mountains as far as the eye can see, it almost looks like . . . nahh.

Leavenworth has covered its dilapidated brick walls with Tyrolean designs and hanging flowers, and most of the town has gone full-tilt oom-pah.

Not surprisingly, this carefully orchestrated tourist town has festivals left and right—almost every weekend in summer. The big ones are **Maifest,** held the second weekend in May, which features fräuleins dancing around a maypole; and the **Autumn Leaf Festival,** held during the last week of September and first week of October. The **Leavenworth Chamber of Commerce** (703 U.S. 2, tel. 509/548–5807), open daily 8–6, provides information about the festivals. **High Mountain Recreation, Inc.** (405 U.S. 2, Leavenworth, tel. 509/548–4326 or 800/423–9380) offers guided tours of Leavenworth's sights and the surrounding countryside.

COMING AND GOING From Seattle, take I-5 north to U.S. 2 and follow it east to Leavenworth (about 120 miles). On the return trip, you can continue east a few miles on U.S. 2, then south on U.S. 97 to Cle Elum, and back to Seattle on I-90. Leavenworth itself is easily covered on foot, but you need a car to reach some of the area's best hiking trails.

WHERE TO SLEEP Looking at the hotel prices in Leavenworth, you'd think you really were in Bavaria. Choose carefully, or escape to a less expensive hotel along U.S. 2. Better yet, take a sleeping bag into the hills.

Edel Haus. If you're staying in town and the Edelweiss (*see below*) is full, you might as well stay in this beautiful old inn on the banks of the Wenatchee River. The rooms have private bath, cable TV, and a shared hot tub. Included in the $70 double rate is 50% off a lunch or dinner at the pricey gourmet restaurant downstairs (dinner entrées average $13). *320 9th St., tel. 509/548–4412. From Front St., go right on 9th St. toward the river. 3 rooms, 1 cottage. Wheelchair access.*

The Edelweiss Hotel. In the center of town, this hotel has truly barren rooms at low prices. Two hostel-style rooms are especially cheap ($18, $28 with TV and window). If you want your own sink, prices start at $24. A friendly tavern and German restaurant are downstairs. It's right in the middle of the Bavarian Village, so you can sleep soundly knowing that the pretzel-munchers around you are paying about ten times as much for lodging as you are. *843 Front St., tel. 509/548–7015. Across from Village Green. Check-in after 2 PM. Luggage storage. Reservations advised.*

Mrs. Anderson's Lodging House. The period furnishings in this historic bed-and-breakfast on the edge of the Bavarian Village give it a certain amount of charm. The price of the rooms ($44–$55 with shared bath, $63–$70 with private bath) includes a continental breakfast served in the parlor on the second floor, or outside overlooking the waters of the Wenatchee River. *917 Commercial St., tel. 800/253–8990. 10 rooms, 8 with bath. Wheelchair access (1 room).*

➤ **CAMPING** • Ask at the chamber of commerce (*see above*) about **Lake Wenatchee State Park** (tel. 509/782–1413), which has three fully equipped campgrounds. Of the seven campgrounds along **Icicle Creek Road,** the closest sites at Mile 8 are always the first to fill up. Nearby trails lead into the wilderness of Wenatchee National Forest (tel. 509/782–1413). Take U.S. 2 west ½ mile from town to Icicle Creek Road.

FOOD Of the several outdoor beer gardens in town, **Adlers** (633A Front St., tel. 509/548–7733) is the best, with live polka music (Friday–Sunday), sausages, and beer. For lunch, try the **Soup Cellar** (725 Front St., tel. 509/548–6300), a subterranean café that serves up all-you-can-eat soup and salad. The **Hansel and Gretl Delicatessen** (819 Front St., tel. 509/548–7721) is a big deli always bustling with locals and tourists. It serves hefty sandwiches ($3), quiche ($2.50), hot cider (50¢), and cheap coffee (25¢).

When in Leavenworth, do as the Bavarians do—eat and drink like a Jenny Craig escapee.

Gustav's Onion Dome's (617 U.S. 2, in Bavarian Village, tel. 509/548–4509) balcony is packed with a young crowd munching burgers ($4.75), German sausages ($3.75), and hot Rueben sandwiches ($4.75). They also serve a huge selection of ales. Come to the **Leavenworth Brewery** (636 Front St., in village, tel. 509/548–4545), just a few doors down, for a tour, a meal in the pub/restaurant, or to taste the great house microbrews (the Whistling Pig Wheat is a house favorite). Burgers, sandwiches, or German fare averages $5 at lunch. Come back on weekend nights for live jazz, blues, and rock (cover varies from zip to $3). For an authentic Bavarian dining experience, climb downstairs to **Andreas Keller** (829 Front St. tel. 509/548–6000), where you'll eat in a comfortable cave with mural-covered walls. Huge lunches start at $4.95 (polish sausage, potato salad, kraut, rye breads), and dinners start at $6.95 (bratwurst or knockwurst, salad, kraut, and rye bread). If you can feel your arteries hardening, head to the **Gingerbread House** (828 Commercial St., tel. 509/548–6592) for a variety of muffins ($1), scones, healthy soups ($1.25), and other lunch foods. Sit outside at tables or inside on tall stools and watch aspiring hippies pound out the dough for the next loaf.

OUTDOOR ACTIVITIES There are few recreational opportunities right in Leavenworth, but **Leavenworth's Parks** is a continuous complex of paved trails and developed park land along the Wenatchee River. The Leavenworth Ranger District presides over 320 miles of trails that offer excellent views of the Cascades. The trails that wind through **Icicle Valley** to the surrounding mountains are some of the most beautiful. To reach the trailheads, take Icicle Road off U.S. 2 for about 5 miles. Contact the **Forest Service** (tel. 509/782–1413) for more information. For a comprehensive grasp of outdoor recreation in the area, head to **Gator's Gravity Tours** (Cnr U.S. 2 and Rte. 20, south end of town, tel. 509/548–5102).

Ohne Gardens (3327 Ohne Rd., off U.S. 97, tel. 509/662–5785), a 9-acre public park and garden atop a once-barren mountain, overlooks the Wenatchee Valley. It costs $5 to get in, but it's definitely worth it if you have a few hours to explore: The flowers and landscaping are extraordinary.

➤ **RIVER RAFTING** • Leavenworth sits on the **Wenatchee River,** which has first-rate conditions for both white-water rafting and mellow float trips. **Alpine Whitewater** (tel. 509/662–6046 or 800/926–7238) and **Leavenworth Outfitters** (tel. 509/763–3733 or 800/347–7934) run trips ($40–$55) and provide all the necessary equipment. The season begins around April and ends in July or August.

➤ **SKIING** • Leavenworth has more than 20 miles of cross-country trails, a lighted night run, and a small downhill run. Contact the **Leavenworth Winter Sports Club** (tel. 509/548–5115) for more information. Rent your skis (or inner tubes for skidding) in town at **Leavenworth Ski and Sports center** (U.S. 2, near Icicle Rd., tel. 509/548–7864). For the best downhill skiing in the area, visit **Stevens Pass** (*see* Skykomish, in U.S. 2, *above*) or **Mission Ridge** (tel. 509/663–3200). An all-day lift ticket costs around $30 and is good until 10 PM.

North Cascades National Park

You may have to travel to Alaska to see scenery that can compare with the raw beauty of the 505,000-acre North Cascades National Park. Towering saw-tooth peaks, deep canyons, countless waterfalls, ice sheets, and more than 300 glaciers—half the total number of glaciers in the lower 48 states—make the area a true paradise for hikers and mountaineers. The park encompasses two national recreation areas, Ross Lake and Lake Chelan (*see below*); and two wilderness areas, Picket Range and Eldorado Peaks. You can reach the big lakes and the lower mountain slopes from early April to mid-October, but as you go higher, the season becomes dramatically shorter—mid-July to mid-September. Through it all runs Route 20 (North Cascades Highway), one of the most breathtaking drives in the country.

It's an eerie feeling to be hiking along and hear the boom of ice cracking, followed by the rumble as it crashes to the valley floor.

BASICS Ranger stations provide information on hikes and are a source for trail maps and backcountry permits. Backcountry permits are necessary if you plan to spend the night in a wilderness area. You'll find ranger stations, forest service offices, and information centers all over the park: at **Marblemount** (728 Ranger Station Rd., off Rte. 20, tel. 206/873–4590), **Newhalem** (502 Newhalem St., tel. 206/386–4495), and **Sedro Woolley** (2105 Hwy. 20, tel. 206/856–5700).

COMING AND GOING Route 20 runs east–west through the Cascade Mountains. To enter the Cascades from the west, take the Route 20 turn off from I–5 in Burlington, north of Seattle. To enter from U.S. 97 to the east, go west (at Okanogan) on Route 20. Route 20 between Burlington and Okanogan is extremely beautiful and should not be missed—even if you have to drive straight through (which only takes a few hours). No buses serve Route 20, so you have to hitch, hike, or rent a car.

WHERE TO SLEEP The Cascade Loop passes through a series of small towns offering a range of motels, hotels, and inns. Most motels to the east of the Cascades are north of Lake Chelan, along Highway 153 as it passes through Methow, Carlton, Twisp, and Winthrop before joining with Route 20. After you reach Highway 20, the options thin out considerably until you hit the Cascade Range in the west. The towns of Marblemount, Rockport, Darrington, and Concrete on the west end of Route 20 also hold a number of small, relatively inexpensive motels.

East of the park on the Cascade Loop, **Blue Spruce Motel's** (Rte. 20, Twisp, tel. 509/997–8852) clean but tacky rooms cost $30 a night single or double. **Trail's End Motel** (Rte. 20, Winthrop, tel. 509/996–2303) in Winthrop, the "Old West" tourist trap, is a fun place to stay on your way into the North Cascades. This central and friendly motel is the cheapest in town—doubles go for $55.

➤ **CAMPING** • Over 100 campsites dot the backcountry of the North Cascades National Park, Ross Lake, and Lake Chelan national recreation areas. Most campsites are open to the public July through August, or at other times by written request to one of the ranger stations (*see* Basics, *above*). At any time of year, you need a free wilderness permit to stay in these areas; call the ranger office at Marblemount (*see* Basics, *above*) for more information. Reservations are not really necessary, however, since only about 30% of the campsites are occupied on an average summer night.

Cascade Island. On the banks of the Cascade River, this 15-site campground run by the Department of Natural Resources is both scenic and free. A 1-mile hike will get you to a store and a café. *Tel. 800/527–3305. From Marblemount, go ⅔ mi on Old Cascade Rd., turn right on Rockport Cascade Rd., then left on South Cascade Rd. and drive 1.2 mi. Running water, toilets.*

Goodell Creek. If you're planning a rafting trip, this is a convenient place to camp—where Goodell Creek flows into the Skagit River. Sites cost $3. *Tel. 206/873–4590. 14 mi east of Marblemount and a couple mi west of Newhalem on Rte. 20. 22 sites. Pit toilets, running water.*

Newhalem Creek. Hikers love this campground next to the Skagit River because it's so close to major trailheads and features real toilets, running water, and picnic tables. Sites cost $10. *Rte. 20, tel. 206/873–4590. 15 mi east of Marblemount. 22 sites. Closed Labor Day–Memorial Day.*

FOOD Most grocery stores and restaurants lie at the far ends of Route 20. In the west, try the intimate **Mountain Song Restaurant** (5860 Rte. 20, Marblemount, tel. 206/873–2461). The best deals are the $5.25 all-you-can-eat soup, salad, and homemade bread and muffin bar, and the $3.50 breakfast buffet with fruit, yogurt, cereal, and baked goods. For something less expensive, try **Good Food** (5914 Rte. 20, tel. 206/873–2771) just a few doors down. Sit inside or at picnic tables by the river and munch on $2 deluxe burgers, $2.25 chicken sandwiches, or $3.25 soft tacos. At **Winthrop Brewing Co.** (155 Riverside Ave., tel. 509/996–3183) you can choose a salad ($7), pesto pizza ($7.25), or onion burger ($5.95). They even make their own unique microbrews. The sporadic nighttime entertainment is loud and free.

EXPLORING NORTH CASCADES NATIONAL PARK We'll say it again: The drive along Route 20 is absolutely *stunning.* The road begins at Burlington on the coast and wends its way into the Cascades and then down to Twisp and Okanogan in eastern Washington. The most interesting part is the 55-mile section between Marblemount on the western slopes of the Cascades and the Washington Pass Overlook on the eastern slopes. As you follow the twists and turns of the road, you'll be rewarded with spectacular views of glaciers, peaks, and canyons. About 17 miles east of Marblemount is the **Gorge Creek Falls Viewpoint,** where a waterfall plunges into a deep gorge near the road. Seven miles farther is **Diablo Lake Overlook,** with its view over glacial Diablo Lake. Sediment suspended in the water gives the lake a bizarre green hue. Continue another 4 miles on Route 20 and stop to take a stroll on the **Happy Creek Forest Walk.** This wheelchair-accessible nature trail offers a great look at some of the old-growth forest that once blanketed this part of the Cascades. Twenty-three miles east is the **Washington Pass Overlook,** with its dramatic views of 7,600-foot Early Winter Spires and 7,808-foot Liberty Bell Mountain.

➤ **HIKING** • North Cascades National Park has more than 345 miles of trails. Pick up trail maps and backcountry permits from ranger stations (*see* Basics, *above*). Many of the trailheads are along Route 20, between Marblemount and the Washington Pass Overlook. In addition, several trails begin off Cascade River Road, an unpaved road leading south and east from Marblemount. If you can get to Stehekin on Lake Chelan (*see below*), another unpaved road (Stehekin River Road) leads into the mountains and is a starting point for a half-dozen trails. Below is just a sample of the many fine hikes in the area.

Cascade Pass is an easy day-hike that leads to 5,392-foot Cascade Pass, which has spectacular views of glaciers and peaks to the east and west. From the pass you can head over the summit and pick up the unpaved road that runs to Stehekin (*see* Lake Chelan, *below*). A few miles below the pass, you'll find waterfalls, steep cliffs, and wildflowers. You can collapse at several campgrounds along the way, or head off along several other trails. To get to the trailhead, take the Cascade River Road from the Green Bridge in Marblemount; it's a 22-mile drive on a steep gravel road.

Easy Pass is a definite misnomer for this extremely tough hike that climbs 3,000 feet in 3 miles. It's a grunt any time of year, and ice axes are essential until Labor Day. Once at the top of Easy Pass, though, it's an easy hike (no, really) on **Fisher Creek Trail** to Fisher Basin. You can camp in the basin, which is usually carpeted with flowers, grasses, and shrubs. Fisher Creek Trail joins with **Thunder Creek Trail,** which winds its way north through silver-fir forest to Diablo Lake and Route 20. You can do the whole hike in three days, but be sure to pick up topographical maps at the ranger station. The trailhead is off Route 20 between Mileposts 152 and 153.

Lake Chelan

Covering 33,104 acres, Lake Chelan is the largest natural lake in Washington state. It is also one of eastern Washington's most expensive (and pretentious) resort areas. Fifty-five miles long and 1,500 feet deep, the glacial lake is set in an immense gorge. At the south end of the lake, **Chelan** is abuzz with Jet-skis, beaches, and ritzy resorts. Surrounding the lake on all sides are several state and national parks: Okanogan National Forest, Glacier Peak Wilderness, Lake Chelan Sawtooth Wilderness, and, farther north, **Lake Chelan National Recreation Area. Stehekin**, at the northernmost tip of the lake, is a paradise for solitude-seekers and backpackers. Stehekin can't be reached by car (though a shuttle bus does enter Stehekin from Cascade Pass), has no phone service, houses only 75 people in winter, and must have its groceries delivered by boat. The only town actually within the Lake Chelan National Recreation Area, Stehekin also serves as the starting point for strenuous hikes and mountain-bike trips into the Northern Cascades.

BASICS If you can, talk to Dell at the **Lake Chelan Chamber of Commerce**. Chelan's *Vacation Guide*, published yearly, is free at most Chelan stores and is invaluable for its inside scoops and calendar of events. *702 E. Johnson St., Chelan, tel. 509/682–3503 or 800/424–3526. Open weekdays 9–5.*

The **Ranger Station** is the place to go for information on all outdoor activities in these parts. *428 W. Woodin Ave., Chelan, tel. 509/682–2576. Open fall–spring, weekdays 7:45–4:30; summer, daily 7:45–4:30.*

In Stehekin, gather info weekdays 8–4 at the **Golden West Visitor Center** and the **Ranger Station**, both at the landing. At the visitor center, you can get a backcountry permit and make a reservation on the $5–$10 shuttle bus that heads up the valley, stopping at campgrounds on request. These information centers only have radio phones.

COMING AND GOING Chelan is a half-hour drive north from Wenatchee on U.S. 97. From Wenatchee, make sure you take the quicker and more scenic U.S. 97 Alternate Route (it's marked on U.S. 2 and U.S. 97), which runs up the west side of the Columbia River. You have to take a ferry to reach Stehekin (*see below*). **Empire Bus Lines** (tel. 509/662–2183), a subsidiary of Greyhound, offers bus service to Chelan from Seattle (5½ hrs, $34.50) and Spokane (4½ hrs, $35.50). You change in Ellensburg from Seattle, in Wenatchee from Spokane.

GETTING AROUND If you want to see anything but resorts, you'll have to pay the extortionate rates to take a ferry or plane into the National Forest, but the inaccessibility makes for thin crowds and unspoiled wilderness. Otherwise, take the $10 shuttle from Cottonwood Campground at Cascade Pass, north of Stehekin (*see below*)—accessible off Route 20 in the North Cascades. Parking next to the *Lady of the Lake* dock in Chelan costs about $4 a day or $20 per weekend; if you park at Field's Point, the closest ferry stop to Chelan, it's a more reasonable $3 a day or $15 per week.

➤ **BY BIKE** • Bikes are ideal for exploring the upper valley around Stehekin. On the south shores of Lake Chelan, **Nature Gone Wild** (109 S. Emerson, tel. 509/682–8680) rents bikes for $5 an hour. At the **Stehekin Valley Ranch** (*see Where to Sleep, below*), an 18-speed bike goes for $3.50 an hour, $18 a day.

➤ **BY FERRY** • The **Lake Chelan Boat Company** (tel. 509/682–2224) runs two boats up the lake to Stehekin every day between May 1 and October 31 (4 hrs, $21 round-trip). The scenery turns rugged, lush, and truly dramatic a short way into the trip. The ride itself is worth the fare, even if you return to Chelan the same day. No reservations are necessary. Boats leave from the dock 1 mile south of Chelan on the U.S. 97 Alternate Route.

➤ **BY BUS** • The least expensive and least publicized access to Stehekin is through the backcountry in the North Cascades. **Stehekin Valley Road Transportation System** (tel. 206/856–5703 ext.14) runs a shuttle bus to and from Cottonwood (stop by a ranger station for a map—it's accessible by car), 23 miles north of Stehekin, from May 15 to September 30. The one-way fee is $5–$10, depending on the destination in Stehekin. Two buses leave daily from the Stehekin landing ferry for the Cottonwood dock at 8 AM and 2 PM; they leave Cottonwood for Stehekin at 10:35 AM and 5 PM. You can secure a space up to two days in advance at visitor centers in Stehekin, Chelan, Marblemount, or Sedro-Woolley; at the North Cascades Visitor's Center; or by calling the Golden West Visitor Center (tel. 206/856–5703, ext. 14).

WHERE TO SLEEP The town of Chelan is packed with resorts charging sky-high prices. In Manson, a more rural community 9 miles up the lake from Chelan, you'll find more resorts. If you want to camp, go straight to Stehekin. Camping at Stehekin is free; just pick up a permit from the information office at the Stehekin dock.

Camping in Chelan instead of in Stehekin is like sleeping in your car in the Yellowstone parking lot.

➤ **CHELAN • Apple Inn Motel.** This standard motel in Chelan's city center is reliable and clean, with a hot tub, pool, TVs, phones, and air-conditioning. Rooms cost $49–$59 in summer, $30 in winter. The place fills up quickly in summer, so reserve ahead. *1002 E. Woodin Ave., tel. 509/682–4044. 41 rooms. Wheelchair access.*

Campbell's Resort. This hotel does everything right. On the expansive grounds you'll find a private beach, a pool, an espresso bar, and a restaurant, not to mention unparalleled lake views. All this can be yours for $98–$156 May–September, or $48–$78 in the off-season. Some rooms come equipped with a kitchen. *104 W. Woodin Ave., tel. 509/682–2561 or 800/553–8225. 150 rooms, all with bath. Wheelchair access.*

Mom's Montlake Motel. Just off the main street in Chelan, these fully equipped, spacious doubles go for $36–$48, depending on the season. Seventies retro furniture notwithstanding, this is one of Chelan's best budget options. *823 Wapato, tel. 509/682–5715. 10 rooms, 5 with kitchen ($10 extra).*

Parkway Motel. Small rooms ($30–$35) with wood walls come with full bath, TVs, and powerful air conditioners. This motel is right across the highway from the lake and next door to a supermarket. *402 North Manson Hwy., tel. 509/682–2822. 15 rooms. No credit cards.*

➤ **STEHEKIN • The North Cascades Lodge.** The best things about this lodge are the hot tub and the location (right at the ferry landing). Appreciate the silence that results when you have no phone, radio, or TV. Stay in standard doubles ($55), three-person cabins ($68) with a kitchen and lake view, or deluxe rooms ($65–$75) with a lake view and a king-sized bed. Deluxe cabins ($75–$82) come with kitchen and a lake or forest view and fit up to eight people. *Tel. 509/682–4494. 28 units. Bicycle and boat rental, grocery store, restaurant.*

Silver Bay Inn. If you're going to burn money, set it on fire at this plush lakefront inn. A huge, sunny room will cost you $85, with a two-night minimum; bicycles, canoes, and croquet sets are included. Two waterfront cabins with all the amenities go for $85–$120 for two people. Transportation to and from the Stehekin dock is included. *Tel. 509/682–2212. 1½ mi from landing. 2 rooms, 2 cabins. No credit cards.*

Glacier Peak Wilderness

West of Lake Chelan, the half-million-acre Glacier Peak Wilderness is one of the most rugged areas in the Cascade Range and contains more active glaciers than any other part of the United States. Peaks of 8,000 feet are commonplace, but the 10,568-foot Glacier Peak dwarfs them all. The Pacific Crest Trail runs through the wilderness and attracts thousands of hikers each year. So difficult is the terrain, however, that the trail actually runs through the valleys and not along the crest, as the name suggests. For maps and more information about Glacier Peak Wilderness, contact the Park and Forest Service information office (tel. 509/682–2576).

Stehekin Valley Ranch. This ranch offers genuine serenity at moderate prices. The 10 "tent-cabins" come with beds and kerosene lamp, hot showers, and three meals a day. The cost, including transportation from the boat landing, is $55 a night. The reservation office is at the Stehekin Landing near the Purple Point Campground. *Tel. 509/682–4677. 9 mi up Stehekin River Valley from boat landing. 12 cabins. Rafts, horses, fishing trips. Closed Sept. 23–June 13.*

➤ **CAMPING** • If you want to camp but have missed the last boat to Stehekin, try the **Don Morse Memorial City Park** (Hwy. 150, tel. 509/682–5031) in downtown Chelan. It's popular with the RV set and gets crowded in summer, but it's the cheapest place to crash in town ($20 per site). If you have a car, drive 9 miles from Chelan up South Shore Road to **Lake Chelan State Park** (tel. 509/687–3710), where wheelchair-accessible sites cost $5–$10.

In Stehekin, you can stay near the boat landing in the area known as down-valley, or you can head up-valley aboard the **Lower Valley Shuttle** ($4), which leaves four times a day from the dock to the 10-mile mark, stopping at campgrounds on request. The Visitor's Information Center (*see* Visitor Information, *above*) provides permits and information about some of the amazing, secluded campsites in the Stehekin area. **Purple Point Campgrounds,** about a half-mile north of Stehekin along the Stehekin River Road, is a great place to spend your first night before heading out into the wilderness. There are about 12 free campgrounds along the Stehekin Valley Road, and many more are accessible by trail. Site reservations and permits are issued from visitors centers and ranger stations throughout the area.

FOOD Chelan is fortified with resort-priced diners and sandwich "shoppes," most of which are downtown along Woodin Avenue (U.S. 97). Along the Manson Highway you'll find more down-to-earth options. If you need a caffeine fix, try **Flying Saucers Espresso** (116 S. Emerson St., at Woodin Ave., tel. 509/682–5129) for a mocha or a cap. In Chelan, put together some grub from the local **Safeway** (106 Manson Rd.). A good place to stop for an ice cream ($1.20), garden salad ($4), or sandwich ($4.50) is **Dogwoods** (246 W. Manson Hwy., in Chelan Plaza, tel. 509/682–8630). In Stehekin, your options are limited. The best meal awaits you at **Stehekin Valley Ranch** (*see* Where to Sleep, *above*). Non-guests with reservations can grab a bus up to the ranch for a succulent $13 country dinner. You can also get burgers at the **North Cascades Lodge** (*see* Where to Sleep, *above*).

OUTDOOR ACTIVITIES Spectacular Stehekin is the main reason to come to Lake Chelan. Stehekin is ideal for campers, hikers, anglers, and mountain climbers looking for the perfect route into the North Cascades. The elevation changes from 1,100 feet at Lake Chelan to 5,400 feet at Cascade Pass, almost 29 miles away, and the terrain is rugged and breathtaking. Near the ferry landing in Stehekin, **McGregor Mountain Outdoor Supply** stocks hiking and backpacking supplies, hunting and fishing licenses, and fishing gear.

➤ **HIKING** • The Stehekin River Road runs from the boat landing and follows the river 23 miles to Cottonwood Campground (at the trailhead to Cascade Pass). Some manageable loop trails from Stehekin are the **Purple Creek Trail,** which heads east from Stehekin before joining up with **Boulder Creek Trail** and looping back to town; and the **Devore Creek Trail** and **Company Creek Trail,** which combine to loop around 7,989-foot Tupshin Peak. For information about hikes in the area, head to the Visitor's Center at the Stehekin ferry landing. Don't forget to obtain a free backcountry permit.

Mt. Rainier National Park

"Of all the fire mountains which, like beacons, once blazed along the Pacific Coast, Mt. Rainier is the noblest." —John Muir

Actually a volcano more than a million years old (it last erupted only 150 years ago), Mt. Rainier was named Tahoma, or the Mountain of Snowiest Peak, by Native Americans. The mountain is so big it creates its own weather system, blocking the moisture that rises off the Pacific and causing some mighty nasty storms on its western side. The park consists of much more than this incredible volcanic peak, however; it also encompasses nearly

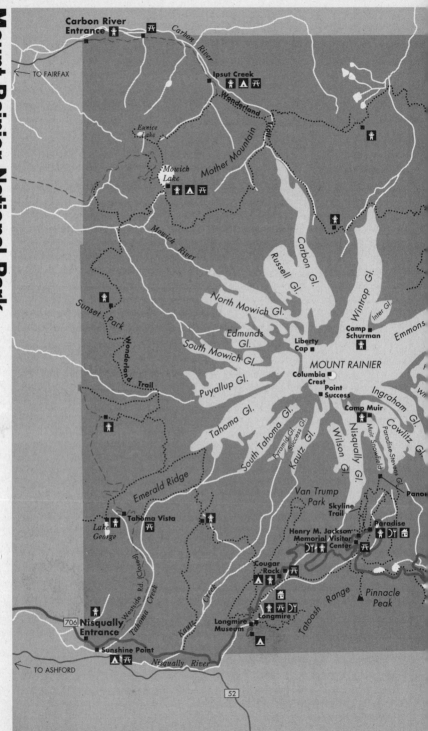

Mount Rainier National Park

Carbon River Entrance

TO FAIRFAX

Carbon River

Ipsut Creek

Wonderland

Eunice Lake

Mowich Lake

Mother Mountain

Mowich River

Sunset Park

North Mowich Gl.

Russell Gl.

Carbon Gl.

Wintrop Gl.

Inter Gl.

Emmons

Camp Schurman

Edmunds Gl.

South Mowich Gl.

Liberty Cap

Wonderland

Puyallup Gl.

MOUNT RAINIER

Columbia Crest

Point Success

Trail

Tahoma Gl.

South Tahoma Gl.

Pyramid Gl.

Success Gl.

Kautz Gl.

Wilson Gl.

Nisqually Gl.

Ingraham Gl.

Cowlitz Gl.

Camp Muir

Muir Snowfield

Paradise-Stevens Gl.

Emerald Ridge

Van Trump Park

Skyline Trail

Panor

Lake George

Tahoma Vista

Westside Rd. (Closed)

Tahoma Creek

Kautz Creek

Henry M. Jackson Memorial Visitor Center

Paradise

Cougar Rock

Longmire Museum

Longmire

Tatoosh Range

Pinnacle Peak

706 **Nisqually Entrance**

Sunshine Point

TO ASHFORD

Nisqually River

52

270

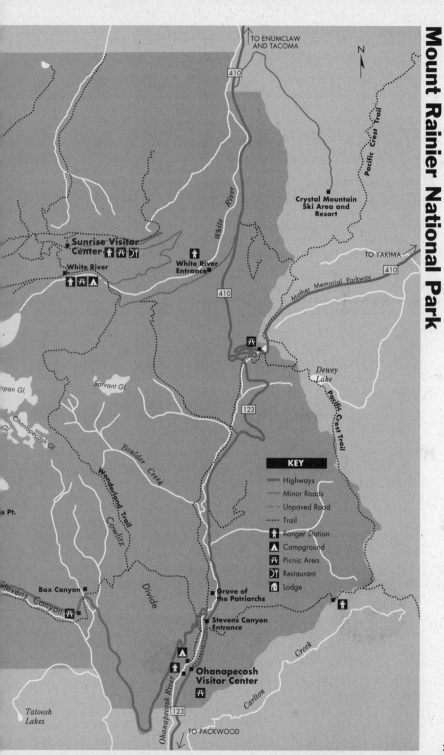

TO ENUMCLAW
AND TACOMA

N

410

Pacific Crest Trail

Crystal Mountain
Ski Area and
Resort

White River

Sunrise Visitor
Center

White River
Entrance

White River

TO YAKIMA

410

Mather Memorial Parkway

410

Dewey
Lake

Sarvant Gl.

123

pan Gl.

Ohanapecosh Gl.
Gl.

Boulder Creek

Pacific Crest Trail

KEY

Highways
Minor Roads
Unpaved Road
Trail
Ranger Station
Campground
Picnic Area
Restaurant
Lodge

Pt.

Wonderland Trail

Cowlitz

Stevens Canyon

Box Canyon

Divide

Grove of
the Patriarchs

Stevens Canyon
Entrance

Carlton Creek

Ohanapecosh
Visitor Center

Ohanapecosh River

Tatoosh
Lakes

123

TO PACKWOOD

400 square miles of surrounding wilderness: forests of towering Douglas firs, glaciers, mountain peaks, and long meadows blanketed with summer wildflowers or winter snow. Elk roam the plateaus while mountain goats pick their way over perilously steep slopes. Black-tailed deer, black bears, and an assortment of small, furry mammals, including chipmunks and marmots, also call the area home.

The park is prime terrain for hikers, backpackers, and mountain climbers. In summer, frolickers romp in the wildflowers and, in winter, skiers glide and snowshoers trudge through the thick, powdery snow.

BASICS

VISITOR INFORMATION All the information centers supply basic park information and issue free wilderness-use permits for overnight trips. The center at **Longmire** is the best resource for serious hikers. For 24-hour information on Mt. Rainier National Park roads, trails, facilities, and weather, tune your radio to AM 1610 near the Nisqually entrance.

Mt. Rainier National Park Headquarters provides weather and road information, camping and hiking tips, and ranger talks and other activities. *Hwy. 706, Tahoma Woods, Ashford, tel. 206/569–2211. 9 mi west of the park off Rte. 7. Open daily 8–4:30.*

The **Longmire Museum and Hiker Information Center** is the place to go for information on trails, maps, campgrounds, and regulations for backcountry use. The museum has historical exhibits on geology and early park exploration. This is the only center inside the park that is open daily year-round. *Tel. 206/569–2211, ext. 3317. In Longmire, 6 mi from Nisqually entrance. Visitor Center: Open Sun.–Thurs. 8–6, Fri. 8–7, Sat. 7–7. Museum: Open daily 9–5:30.*

Other information centers are the **Henry M. Jackson Memorial Visitor Center** at Paradise Alpine Plateau (east of Longmire, tel. 206/569–2211, ext. 2328); the **Ohanapecosh Visitor Center** (Rte. 123, tel. 206/569–2211, ext. 2352), 1 mile inside the park; the **Sunrise Visitor Center** (Tel. 206/569–2211, ext. 2357) at the highest point in the park accessible by car; and the **White River Hiker Information Center** (tel. 206/569–2211), 5 miles inside the park past the White River entrance off Route 410. The last office specializes in the northeast section of the park.

FEES There's a $5 fee per vehicle at all four park entrances, which are open 24 hours. Visitors entering on foot, by bicycle, or bus pay $3. After seven days you'll have to pay again. A **Golden Eagle Passport** ($25) is good for one year's admission to all federal recreation areas and national parks.

PUBLICATIONS The *Mt. Rainier Official Map and Guide*, available free at park entrances, indicates roads, campsites, and trails and gives a short introduction to the park's attractions. *The Road to Rainier* is a free newspaper that includes both park activities and local events in nearby towns; pick it up at visitor centers and local markets. Pick up a free copy of *Tahoma* in summer or *Snowdrift* in winter from any visitor center for an overview of park activities, nature walks, and special events.

WHEN TO GO Mid-July through mid-October is the best time to visit the park, mainly because most of the public roads are snow-free and accessible by car. During the winter, all access to the park is closed except the Nisqually entrance, and the main road dead-ends at Paradise. In the summer, temperatures range from 70°F to 80°F. Trails are usually cleared by July, and lower-elevation trails are clear by Memorial Day. **Paradise,** above the timberline, is the coldest section of the park, averaging 60° F in summer and dropping to way below freezing in the winter. **Longmire,** near the southwest entrance, is slightly warmer, averaging 30°F to 40°F in the winter. Snow begins to fall in late October, and winter storms are common until late spring.

GENERAL STORES You can buy a limited selection of groceries within the park at the **National Park Inn** (*see* Where to Sleep, *below*) at Longmire. Outside the park, the towns of **Ashford, Packwood,** and **Greenwater** are your last chances to shop and fuel up—you can't get gas in the park itself. Stop at **Elbe Supply** (Rte. 706, Elbe, tel. 206/569–2772), open daily 5 AM–9 PM, for groceries, hot food, and sporting goods. Just outside the Nisqually entrance, stop for fresh soup ($1.75), sandwiches, coffee, and mouthwatering pastries at the **Granley Bear Bakery** (38104 Rte. 706E, Ashford, tel. 206/569–2720). They also have a good selection of camping supplies and cross-country ski equipment.

COMING AND GOING

BY CAR To get to the park from Seattle (a 95-mile drive), take I–5 south and veer east on Highway 512, then take Highway 7 south until it hits Highway 706 in Elbe. Highway 706 takes you to the **Nisqually entrance**, near the Longmire visitor center. From the east (Yakima), travel west on U.S. 12, then take Highway 123 north to **Stevens Canyon entrance.** From Portland, drive north on I–5 and then east on U.S. 12, or north and east on Highways 7 and 706. Most people start at the Nisqually entrance (the only one open year-round) and head east through Stevens Canyon, and then north along the White River. From the northwest, Route 165 leads through the **Carbon River entrance** to Ipsut Creek Campground and Mowich Lake. This route does not connect with any others within the park, however, and is less used. The route ends at Paradise, and all other roads within the park are left unplowed from November to May. Many roads are steep and narrow; bring chains and turn your headlights on. If you need to thumb a ride, U.S. 12 offers the best odds, as it carries both Mt. St. Helens and Mt. Rainier traffic.

BY BUS Gray Line Bus Service (2411 4th Ave., Seattle, tel. 800/426–7532) runs one-day tours of Mt. Rainier National Park from May through early October; you can also catch a ride on the tour bus and stay in the park for $23 one-way. Buses leave from the Sheraton Hotel in downtown Seattle daily at 8:15 AM and drop you off at the Paradise Lodge about three hours later. Definitely reserve in advance.

WHERE TO SLEEP

If you must have the trappings of civilization, don't expect them to come cheap. **Mt. Rainier Guest Services** (55106 Kernahan Road East, tel. 206/569–2275) provides information about the two hotels in the park and takes reservations. A few miles outside the park, Ashford and Packwood have better pickings, but expect to pay at least $50 for two people in summer. Off-season, most hotels drop their rates significantly. In Packwood, try the **Hotel Packwood** (102 Main St./U.S. 12, tel. 206/494–5431), where tiny singles start at $20, and a bunk in a shared room goes for $25. The lobby has a great fireplace, and coffee and tea 'round the clock. In Ashford, the **Gateway Inn** (38820 Rte. 706E, just outside Nisqually entrance, tel. 206/569–2506)

Minty-Fresh Lodging

Wild Mint, in Ashford, is an amazing new B&B in a turn-of-the-century loggers' boarding house/bordello/saloon/barber shop. (You can still see the holes in the wooden floor made by loggers' spiked boots.) The three theme rooms (including the "celestial gypsy room," with stars on the ceiling and a canopy bed) go for $30–$65, depending on the season and whether it has a bathroom; breakfast comes in the "health conscious" or "European-style decadence" versions. Downstairs, you can buy local artwork, handmade jewelry and crafts, and essential oils. An espresso bar here vends both caffeinated and less stimulating drinks. The first Saturday of the month features local acoustic musicians, and the couches and easy chairs in the gallery act as a nucleus for conversation and a magnet for local personalities. Hwy. 706, Ashford, tel. 206/569–2674. 10 miles from the Nisqually entrance at Mt. Rainier National Park. 4 rooms, 1 with bath.

has small, clean doubles with atrocious orange carpeting for $35. You can walk to the park from here. If these are full, the park prints a pamphlet called "Accommodations," which lists 41 hotels near the park; it's available at any park entrance, visitors center, or ranger station.

HOTELS **National Park Inn.** One of the original hotels in the park, this 1917 structure was renovated in 1990. The rooms are clean and homey, and many have tree-branch bedframes and wrought-iron lamps. Tea and cookies are served daily in the comfortable lounge, strewn with sofas, tables, lamps, and a blazing fireplace. Of the two park inns, this is quieter, has nicer rooms, and is more laid-back. Singles and doubles are $60 with shared bath, $85 with private bath. *Tel. 206/569–2411. 7 mi past the Nisqually entrance, next to information center. 25 rooms, 14 with bath. Luggage storage, restaurant, post office, general store. Wheelchair access (2 rooms). No smoking.*

Paradise Inn. This inn offers spectacular mountain views and hiking trails at your doorstep. The well-preserved 1920s lobby is like something out of a movie, with cathedral ceilings, log railings, and a huge stone fireplace. The rooms themselves ($60–$85) are small, clean, and basic. Spring for a room with bath: They're bigger and have better decor. At night, the lounge is packed with loaded climbers spinning tales of their day's adventures. You'll also be close to Camp Muir and the visitors center. *Paradise, tel. 206/569–2275. 126 rooms. Luggage storage. Closed early Oct.–late May.*

HOSTELS **Whittaker's Bunkhouse.** In Ashford, 6 miles west of the park, this former logger bunkhouse offers dormitory beds for $18 in the summer ($15 off-season), plus a few double rooms with private bath for $55 ($39 off-season). *30205 Rte. 706, tel. 206/569–2439. 20 beds. Hot showers, linens.*

If you want uncrowded campsites in the summer, join the locals off Skate Creek Road, between Packwood and Ashford. The forests are lush and undisturbed, and you don't need a permit (it's not park service land). Just pull off the side of the road wherever you feel like it, and hike in.

CAMPING Mount Rainier National Park has three types of campgrounds: trailside, cross-country, and alpine. Trailside campgrounds are marked by the National Park Service and usually have toilets and are near a water source. Ask a ranger for a map marking all the campgrounds. At any of the undeveloped sites (i.e., ones that you don't have to pay for), you'll need a backcountry permit; get one at any visitors center.

Make sure you also have a map of the U.S. National Forest Zones (get one at the ranger station) so you won't be caught— and cited—for snoozing on someone's property. Only the five main campgrounds allow open fires, so you'll have to bring a portable stove. Pick up a copy of *Backcountry Trip Planner: A Hiker's Guide to the Wilderness of Mt. Rainier National Park* at any visitors center; it's an invaluable source of information for planning backcountry stays. Hikers on the Wonderland Trail will find primitive campsites every 7 or 8 miles along the trail.

Maybe the best thing about the car campgrounds is that they have drinking water and that luxury of luxuries, flush toilets. Only one, Sunshine Point, stays open year-round; the other four are closed from September to late June. Campgrounds are annoyingly crowded on weekends, and it's virtually impossible to get a spot on holidays, since they operate on a first-come, first-served basis. The only **public showers** in the park are at the Jackson Memorial Visitor Center at Paradise.

On weekends, expect to pay $5–$8 for the privilege of pitching your tent next to an RV and squatting over cold porcelain.

Cougar Rock. At an elevation of 3,180 feet, this is usually the last campground to fill up, even though it's more private than other areas like Sunshine Point. It's near several Longmire trails. Sites are $8 per night. *2.3 mi north of Longmire Visitor Center. 200 sites. Drinking water, flush toilets, firewood. Closed mid-Oct.–late May.*

Mounthaven. Just outside the Nisqually park entrance, you can pitch your tent ($10) on the grass along a gurgling stream. It's an infinitely better choice (particularly on busy weekends) than campgrounds in the park. You can also rent a little wooden cabin for $44. *38210 Rte.*

706 E., Ashford, tel. 206/569–2594. ¼ mile from Nisqually entrance. Showers, toilets, water, firewood, ice, vending machines.

Sunshine Point. Although this campground is quite scenic—it's along the banks of Tahoma Creek—sites have little privacy. The $6 sites are grabbed fast in high season. ⅓ mi from Nisqually entrance. 18 sites. Drinking water, toilets.

White River. This is the most popular campground in the park. At an elevation of 4,400 feet, it's the highest and most scenic place to spend the night. Sites cost $8. Off Rte. 410, 5 mi west of White River entrance. 117 sites. Drinking water, flush toilets. Closed Sept.–late June.

FOOD

IN THE PARK If you want somebody else to fix your food in the park, expect to pay through the nose. You have a choice of four places: In Longmire, the sit-down restaurant at the **National Park Inn** (see Where to Sleep, above) serves typical American entrées for $6–$14. At Paradise, a McDonald's-style joint at the Henry M. Jackson Visitor Center, called the **Jackson Grill** (open daily 10–7) has the cheapest food you'll find at this altitude. The soup ($2.25), salad ($2.60), and fries ($1.75) are all pretty reliable, but skip the bland veggie grain burger ($5.25). The **Paradise Inn** (see Where to Sleep, above) has the nicer and more expensive of the two park restaurants. The wood-lined dining room serves everything from hamburgers with fries ($5.50) to salmon ($16).

NEAR THE PARK For groceries, stop at the **Ashford Valley Grocery** (29716 Rte. 706, Ashford, tel. 206/569–2560), open daily 7 AM–10 PM. If you don't want to cook for yourself, you can get hot food like mini pizzas ($2.50) or kielbasa (99¢), or you can order from the deli. **Baumgartner's** (1008 E. Roosevelt E., Enumclaw, tel. 206/825–1067), at the junction of Routes 169 and 410, is the best place around for fresh baked goods, imported meats and cheeses, deli sandwiches, beer and wine, and heavenly desserts. It's open daily 10–4. The bustling **Wild Berry Restaurant** (37720 Rte. 706, tel. 206/569–2628), in a log cabin just outside Nisqually entrance, serves baked trout, pizzas, and sandwiches, as well as unusual breakfast items like crepes and burritos. The restaurant is open weekdays 11:30–7, weekends 11–8, and the owners also rent out a cabin and cottage ($60) across the street.

EXPLORING MT. RAINIER

The only way to get around the park is by car, foot, or bike. Cyclists who enjoy narrow, curving roads with steep climbs are in luck, but if you're not in terrific shape, you might be resigning yourself to considerable pain.

The park is divided into five major regions, each offering completely distinct landscapes, hikes, and activities. The **Longmire** area, in the southwest end of the park near the Nisqually entrance, was the first section of the park to be developed. In 1883, James Longmire built a health resort here where people could bathe in the mineral springs surrounded by meadows and old-growth forest. You'll find the best hiker information center here, as well as a general store, gas station, museum, and inn. The **Paradise** area, past Longmire on the main road leading from the Nisqually entrance, is the most popular area in the park; its unobstructed, year-round views of Mt. Rainier, alpine meadows, and towering forests fulfill expectations of awe-inspiring wilderness, and snowshoers and cross-country skiers flock here in winter for its unsullied powder. The **Henry M. Jackson Memorial Visitor Center** is the largest information center, and many trails begin here. On the way to Paradise from Longmire, stop at **Narada Falls** (Narada means "uncontaminated") for a cosmic view of the swirling water and an enlivening blast of icy spray. The hike down to the falls is 200 steps down a steep slope. The **Ohanapecosh** area is to the southeast, near the Steven's Canyon entrance. Here, lowland, old-growth forest covers the landscape with Douglas firs, western hemlock, and red cedar—some of these trees are 500 to 1,000 years old. The **Sunrise** area, on the northeast side of the mountain, is about two hours from Paradise. At 6,400 feet, Sunrise is the highest point in the park accessible by car; from this towering height you can survey **Emmons Glacier,** the largest glacier on Mt. Rainier. The **Carbon River** area, in the northwest, is the only section of the park inaccessible from the main road; the only way to get here is along Route 165. Once you've entered the park, the winding, unpaved roads are so difficult to drive that you'll need an entire day simply to tour this remote area. These roads are often closed due to mud slides, but in the dry summer months you can cover them without four-wheel drive. The heavy rainfall here has resulted in a lush, temperate rain forest. From November to May, only the Longmire and Paradise areas are accessible by car, but they often require chains; call the ranger service before you attempt them.

GUIDED TOURS The nonprofit **Pacific Northwest Field Seminars** (909 1st Ave., Suite 630, Seattle, tel. 206/220–4140) offers backpacking, hiking, painting, astronomy, and nature studies on and around Mt. Rainier. Seminars range from one to four days, and the average cost is $35 a day. Several seminars are accessible to the disabled. You can get more information and register at ranger stations and visitors centers.

If your dogs are tired and you just want to idle for a while, hop on the vintage Mount Rainier Scenic Railroad (Hwy. 7, Elbe, tel. 206/569–2588) and let the train take you on a 1½-hour trip to and from Mineral Lake for only $7.50.

Rainier Mountaineering Inc. is *the* place to contact for information on climbing in the park. They rent out equipment, offer climbing instruction to all you *Cliffhanger* wannabes, and lead climbs to Mt. Rainier's summit. *At the Guide House, across from Paradise Inn, Paradise, tel. 206/569–2227 (summer) or 206/627–6242 (winter). Open daily 9–5. Write to: 535 Dock St., Suite #209, Tacoma 98402.*

HIKING More than 300 miles of trails cross Mt. Rainier's backcountry. Trails are usually snow-free from about mid-July to September. For a comprehensive list of hikes, refer to *50 Hikes in Mt. Rainier National Park*, available at visitor centers.

➢ **SHORTER HIKES** • In the Longmire area, the half-mile **Trail of Shadows,** which begins just across the road from the National Park Inn, has exhibit panels on the region's meadowland ecology, its mineral springs, and James Longmire's homestead cabin. The **Rampart Ridge Trail,** a fairly steep 4.6-mile loop that branches off the Trail of Shadows, climbs to a ridge above the meadows for views of Longmire and the Nisqually Valley, as well as Mt. Rainier, Tumtum Peak, and the path of the Kautz Creek Mudflow of 1947.

At 6,800-foot **Panorama Point,** the spine of the Cascade Range spreads away to the north and south, and Nisqually Glacier grumbles its way down the slope of the mountain. The trail, probably the most crowded and attraction-packed in the park, begins and ends in the Paradise parking lot, just west of the inn. The 1¼-mile **Nisqually Vista Trail** that begins at the visitor center stays in the subalpine fir and meadow habitat but has equally dramatic views of Mt. Rainier and the Nisqually Glacier. Both trails are popular, but the Skyline Trail thins out the farther you climb. The hike to **Van Trump Park and Comet Falls** follows a 6-mile trail through a steep 2,200-foot elevation gain. A few miles into the trail you'll come to Comet Falls, a huge 320-

Between a Rock and a Cold Place

A true glacier consists of layers of snow, mixed snow and ice, and pure ice. When winter snowfall levels exceed the summer snowmelt, leftover snow accumulates, is packed in under the weight of new snow, and becomes compressed into glacier ice. Glaciers are not static: They grow with heavy snowfall and shrink from melting at the edges. Mount Rainier's glaciers move from one to two feet a day, depending on the steepness of the slope they're on. When the glacier moves, crevasses form between the ice, ready to swallow up any hikers or climbers who unwittingly pass by. More that 35 square miles of glaciers—the largest collection of glaciers in the continental United States—sit near Mount Rainier's summit. Twenty-six of the large glaciers are named, and fifty smaller glaciers remain anonymous.

foot waterfall that gushes noisily from a stone cliff. If you've made it this far, push yourself the extra mile to Van Trump Park (named after the first climber to ascend the summit). Along the way you'll see groves of wildflowers and mountain goats in late June or early July. Once you get to the top you'll be above the treeline, which clears the way for magnificent views. Check with the rangers about trail conditions—it's usually covered in snow until the summer.

The **Grove of the Patriarchs,** a 1½-mile trail along the Ohanapecosh River, wanders among the ancient, woody behemoths of the lowland forest in the park's southeastern corner. The trail begins just west of the Steven's Canyon entrance and leads over a bridge to an island covered with 1,000-year-old trees (and slimy 6-inch banana slugs). These trees have been protected from forest fires by the rushing waters to either side and are among the oldest in the Northwest. Farther upstream, the 2-mile **Silver Falls Loop** leads along the river's emerald green pools through ancient Douglas firs to the 75-foot Silver Falls and back. This beautiful trail leaves from the Ohanapecosh Visitor Center. At 6,400 feet, the **Sourdough Ridge Self-Guiding Trail,** a mile-long loop that starts at the visitors center parking area, yields magnificent views of Mt. Rainier and neighboring peaks Baker, Adams, and Glacier. The 5-mile **Sunrise–Frozen Lake–Shadow Lake Loop,** which branches off from the Sourdough Ridge Trail, has the best view of Emmons Glacier, the largest U.S. glacier outside Alaska. This route is less strenuous than the Skyline Trail at Paradise, but you may have to maneuver past steep snow patches well into July.

Carbon River is accessible only from the little-used northwest entrance to the park, so you can find solitude on all the trails along Carbon River Road, even on weekends. The 3-mile **Carbon River Rain Forest Trail,** which begins close to the Carbon River entrance, won't produce any spectacular views, but you will get close to a rainforest. The 5-mile **Carbon Glacier Loop** parallels the Carbon River through the rainforest and emerges at the snout of the Carbon Glacier, with a view of Mt. Rainier. The hike begins and ends at Ipsut Creek Campground, 5 miles beyond the Carbon River entrance.

➤ **LONGER HIKES** • The **Wonderland Trail** runs a 93-mile circle around the mountain. This 10- to 14-day hike passes through several distinct ecological zones, and even in summer hikers should be prepared for mud, rain, and snow. Elevation gains and losses average 3,500 feet for a single day's hike. You'll find primitive campsites along the way.

PARK ACTIVITIES

CLIMBING Mt. Rainier is an especially difficult lump of rock to conquer. Only experienced, equipped, and physically fit climbers should contemplate hauling themselves up its slopes. You're required to register with one of the ranger stations before attempting even the shortest climbs on the peak; they'll probably recommend tagging along with an experienced guide service, such as Rainier Mountaineering, Inc. (*see* Guided Tours, *above*). The schlep to the top is only about five miles each way on unmarked trails, but it usually takes four–eight hours because of the altitude and the snow. A year-round hazard is white-outs (when you're blinded by airborne powder snow), which can cause you to veer off onto the Paradise-Stevens Glacier (to the right of the trail), or onto the Nisqually Glacier (to the left). If you inadvertently end up on one of the glaciers, you could fall up to 250 feet in a glacier crevasse and die. Those guide services are sounding better and better, aren't they? No technical climbing equipment is necessary, since this is more akin to a steep hike in adverse conditions. Most people find an ice axe, hard hat (to protect your head from falling rock), and crampons helpful. The **Muir Snowfield trail** from Camp Muir to the top is the most common route (the climbing school follows this route). Camp Muir has shelter for about 20 climbers, if you want to unroll your sleeping bag and sleep sardine style on a long platform. (There are no reservations; it's first-come, first-served). Serious climbers can take one of the other paths obstructed by walls of ice and rock.

In 1890, Fay Fuller, an Olympian schoolteacher, became the first woman to climb to the summit of Mt. Rainier. In 1990, 8,335 climbers attempted to reach the peak; only 4,534 were successful.

BIKING Bicycles are permitted on park roads, which tend to be steep and very narrow, but the *only* place you can ride in the backcountry is on Mt. Rainier's wide, flat **West Side Road.** It

Every July over 700 cyclists participate in the Ramrod bike race that begins in Enumclaw, runs through the park, and loops back (over 100 miles). For the less ambitious, there's the Wimprod, a race that follows the same loop, but takes place over two days instead of one. Someone should look up "wimp" in the dictionary, because anyone who can finish this race definitely isn't one.

used to be open to cars, but it has been flooded several times by glacial outbursts and is considered mildly dangerous (though it hasn't washed over since 1991). You will see the road 1 mile up on the left, past the Nisqually entrance, before you hit Longmire (it isn't marked by a turnoff sign). You can ride three miles up to a dry creek, and continue through a forest for about seven more miles. Ride at your own risk: The outbursts (called Jokolype) usually occur June–October, when glacier ice is melting. If you hear the loud sound of rushing water, head for the hills (leave the bike).

SNOWSHOEING Deep snows make Mt. Rainier snowshoeing heaven. Rentals are available at the **Longmire General Store** (tel. 206/569–2411), next to the National Park Inn, for $7.25 per day. From December through April, park rangers lead two free snowshoe walks a day that start at the Jackson Memorial Visitor Center and cover 1.2 miles in about two hours. Most snowshoers head for the network of trails in the Paradise area, but the park's eastern roads, Route 123 and Route 410, are unplowed and provide an alternative route for snowshoeing.

SKIING The **cross-country** trails around Paradise are extremely popular; if you want more solitude, try the trails in and around the Ohanapecosh/Steven's Canyon area, which are just as beautiful. Visitors should never ski on the plowed main roads—the snowplow operators can't see little obstacles like you, even if you are wearing neon ski-wear. **Crystal Mountain,** near Mt. Rainier, is a downhill and cross-country ski resort with a vertical drop of 3,100 feet, a 7,000-foot summit, and 10 chair lifts. You can night ski and snowboard, too. Lessons, rentals, and repairs are available. All-day passes cost $16–$20 on weekdays, $32 on weekends. *Crystal Mountain Rd., tel. 206/663–2265. About 12 mi from Mt. Rainier, off Rte. 410. Closed mid-Apr.–mid-Nov.*

White Pass. Smaller than Crystal Mountain but less crowded, White Pass has downhill and cross-country skiing. Rentals, lessons, and snowboarding are available, as well as night skiing on Friday and Saturday. An all-day pass is $13–$18 on weekdays, $29 on weekends. *U.S. 12, 40 mi east of Mt. Rainier, tel. 509/453–8731. Closed mid-Apr.–Nov.*

Mt. St. Helens

On May 18, 1980, Mt. St. Helens rudely awoke from 123 years of sleep, gave a tremendous belch, and spewed out enough molten lava to melt itself down 1,300 feet. The explosion was triggered by a rash of over 10,000 earthquakes between March and May; the "last straw" was a 15–20 second 5.1 earthquake, which caused the bulging north flank of the mountain to slide away in the largest landslide in human history. The blast flattened 150 square miles of nearby forests, leaving tree trunks scattered over the mountainside like a pile of pick-up sticks. Hot (1500° F), stone-filled wind ripped across the land and created a 200 foot tidal wave in Spirit Lake. The 520 million tons of ash that bellowed from the belly-aching crater filled the atmosphere, creating a midday dark sky on the *east coast;* ash from Mt. St. Helens circled the entire globe in just two weeks.

Steaming volcanic mud flows called lahars, made up of a mixture of semi-melted rocks, mud, and water, streamed down the volcano's side at speeds of up to 60 miles per hour, and puddled into what is now a pumice plain on the south shore of Spirit Lake.

After years of complete desolation, little green insurgents are finally beginning to repopulate the area: Flowers, lichen, and ferns are creeping over once-fiery slabs of rock, and hopeful sprouts are poking their tips up among the toppled trees. The southern side of the mountain may still be encrusted by volcanic caves and heaping lava formations, but visitors actually benefit from the destruction: In the remains of the forests, enormous rock pinnacles once hidden by trees beckon climbers. Trails lead to views of the still-smoking crater and ash-filled lakes, and in winter, snowmobilers and cross-country skiers plow enthusiastically across the slopes.

BASICS

EMERGENCIES Dialing 911 only works from the telephone at the Pine Creek Information Station. Everywhere else, call the Skamania County Sheriff at 360/427–5047 (24 hours).

TELEPHONES The word from the phone company is that the region's area code will soon be changing to 360 (yes, that's 360). Of course, they will not say when. Being an optimistic lot, we're changing the appropriate phone codes in this book. The upshot: If you can't get through, try the old code (206).

PERMITS If you plan to climb above 4,100 feet from May 15 to October 31, you must have a permit. Call 360/247–5800 to request an application. The earliest you can reserve a permit is February 1. If you didn't plan ahead, some permits are available at **Jack's Restaurant and Store** (13411 Lewis River Rd., Hwy. 103, Cougar, tel. 360/231–4276) and **Mt. St. Helens National Volcanic Monument Headquarters** (*see* Visitor Information, *below*). Sign-ups begin at 11 AM for permits for the next day; once your name is on the list, come back at 6 PM and get in line (your name on the list only guarantees you a place in line). The permits are free and are valid from midnight to midnight on the day for which they are issued. From November 1 to May 15 you don't need a permit, but you still must register at Jack's so rangers will know where to look for you if you get lost. Winter visitors need an Oregon or Washington **Sno-Park permit** to park in plowed parking areas. The three-day $10 permits are not available at ranger stations or information centers, but many businesses in Cougar and Randle carry them—look for any store that rents or sells winter recreational equipment.

PUBLICATIONS A $2 "Mt. St. Helens National Volcanic Monument Map" is available at the main visitor center in Castle Rock, the Pine Creek and Woods Creek information stations, and the Ape Caves. This big, colorful map includes information on trails, roads, scenic views, and nearby sights, complete with estimated driving times between attractions.

GENERAL STORES Your last chances to shop and fuel up before entering the park are in **Randle,** north of the park on U.S. 12; in **Cougar,** south of the park on Route 503; and in Woodinville, Longview, Kelso, or Castle Rock along I–5. Randle and Cougar only have minimarts, so unless you want slushies and fruit pies, shop for food and camping supplies in the major towns along I–5. In Randle, **Fischer's Shopping Center** (9790 U.S. 12, tel. 360/497–5355) has groceries, sporting goods, and other goods. If you're coming from the south, stop in Woodinville at **Thriftway** (Lewis River Rd.). Just north of Thriftway on the left side of Lewis River Road is a terrific fruit and vegetable stand (open daily 10 AM–6 PM) that sells inexpensive, fresh, locally grown produce.

VISITOR INFORMATION The **Mt. St. Helens National Volcanic Monument Headquarters** offers information on mountain access, camping, and recreational activities. It also purveys all sorts of fun facts about post-eruption ecology in a slide show, a film, and other educational materials. *42218 N.E. Yale Bridge Rd., Amboy, tel. 360/247–5473 or 360/247–5472. 3 mi north of Amboy on Rte. 503. Open summer, daily 7:30–5; winter, weekdays 7:30–5.*

Coldwater Ridge Visitor's Center. Overlooking Coldwater Lake, this is the largest and most crowded visitor center in the region. Hands-on displays and exhibits focus on the biological recovery process taking place throughout the area. A video program runs continuously throughout the day. *Rte. 504, tel. 360/274–2100. Take Exit 49 off I–5, go east 13 miles on Rte. 504. Open daily 9–6.*

The **Gifford Pinchot National Forest Supervisor's Office** (6926 E. 4th Plain Blvd., tel. 360/750–5000) in Vancouver, Washington, provides forest-wide information about camping and recreational activities. Other visitor centers include the **Pine Creek Information Station** (Forest Rd., 17 mi east of Cougar, no phone), open summer only; and the **Mt. St. Helens Visitor Cen-**

ter (3029 Spirit Lake Hwy., Castle Rock, tel. 360/274–6644 or 360/274–9344). The latter is open year-round and shows a very informative slide show every half hour. From I–5 at Castle Rock, take exit 49 and go 5 miles on Route 504. The **Woods Creek Information Portal** is 6 miles south of Randle (Forest Rd., no phone).

➤ **RANGER STATIONS** • The following ranger stations distribute information about activities within the whole of Gifford Pinchot National Forest, including camping, hiking, and fire or permit restrictions: **Mt. Adams Ranger District** (2455 Hwy. 141, Trout Lake, tel. 509/395–2501); **Packwood Ranger District** (13068 U.S. 12, Packwood, tel. 360/494–5515); **Randle Ranger District** (10024 U.S.12, Randle, tel. 360/497–7565); and **Wind River Ranger District** (23R Hemlock Rd./Rte. 14, Carson, tel. 509/427–5645).

COMING AND GOING

Admission to the Mt. St. Helens National Monument is free. The two main points of entry to the monument are **Cougar,** to the south, and **Randle,** to the north. Several routes branch eastward off I–5 and eventually pass through these two towns: Route 503 is the most direct route to Cougar, and U.S. 12 takes you to Randle. Cougar is about 1½ hours northeast of Portland, and Randle is an easy 2½-hour drive south of Seattle. Another entrance to the monument is under construction along Route 504, which leads from I–5 at Castle Rock to the main visitor center. It's being extended to the western border of the monument at Coldwater Lake. If you arrive via Cougar in the south, you'll have to drive all the way around the mountain to get to the northern Clearwater Visitor Center. Decide before you go what you want to see, and allow a few hours driving time to reach the southern and northern areas of the mountain. For information on road conditions 24 hours a day, call 360/274–4038.

There is no bus service to the monument. **Greyhound** (tel. 360/624–3456) runs along I–5 and you may be able to hitch from the stops in Woodland or Castle Rock, 4 miles from the visitor center. The best way to catch a ride to the monument is to rub elbows at the visitors center on I–5, near Castle Rock.

WHERE TO SLEEP

Accommodations near Mt. St. Helens are almost entirely limited to campgrounds. Randle and Cougar both have a motel or two, but you might as well lodge along I–5, where there's more competition. The **Randle Motel** (9780 U.S. 12, ¼ mi west of Rte. 25, tel. 360/497–5346), in Randle, is the only clean spoon in U.S. 12's drawer of dirty flatware. The rooms are the cheapest in the vicinity (all have two beds; you pay $40 for using one, $50 for both), and four have kitchens at no extra charge. At **Lone Fir Resort** (16806 Lewis River Rd., Cougar, tel. 360/238–5210) you can camp ($8) or stay in a basic motel room for $38–$65 (less if you're a member of AAA). All rooms have cable TV, and most can accommodate four people ($7 per extra person).

Where to go When You're Sick of S'Mores

You can settle in for an evening of folk tunes by the fire, but if you're feeling rambunctious, do your neighboring campers (or motel dwellers) a favor and head into town. In Cougar, just about the only place to go is Jack's Wildwood Inn and Ale House (16841 Lewis River Rd., tel. 360/238–5222), where rangers, mountain men, and pink-cheeked campers mingle peacefully over a huge selection of northwest microbrews. If you're closer to the north, head to the Big Bottom Bar and Grill (U.S. 12, tel. 360/497–9982), where a gritty crew of locals gather to play pool, gamble, and drink domestics and microbrews.

CAMPING Mt. St. Helens is surrounded by campgrounds, though none lie within the monument itself. You can camp just about anywhere within the Gifford Pinchot National Forest, as long as you're at least 500 feet off the trail. The area to the north of the mountain, primarily in the "blast" area, is the Mt. St. Helens National Volcanic Monument. Most of this area here is currently the subject of geologic research, and camping is prohibited. The national forest has an extensive system of trails that encircles the mountain, and you can find secluded camping throughout the southern and western regions. If you're in the monument area, you are supposed to camp near the trail so you don't damage the rejuvenating forest ecosystem. Windy Ridge gets snow by early November, and the roads are not cleared for the public until at least Memorial Day, so keep this in mind when hiking and camping.

The campground nearest the volcano action is **Iron Creek,** 9 miles south of Randle on Route 25. Campgrounds fill up quickly on summer weekends, so you may have to settle for one farther from the mountain. For information on all other campgrounds in the forest, pick up a campground directory at any ranger station. Wilderness camping does not require a permit and is legal in any green, forested area within the monument; you can find forests primarily on the south side, but check with ranger stations for specific area restrictions.

There are several established campgrounds within the national forest. If you're hiking to the top of the crater, you might want to stay at **Campers Bivouac,** a free campground at the base of the Ptarmigan Trail, which has primitive, unmarked gravel sites with stunning views of the forested southern side of Mt. St. Helens. The campground has a toilet and a phone, and is also a good place to go if you just want to sleep next to your car. Beware: It's a very bumpy and narrow drive up, with absolutely no railing between you and the bottom of a deep canyon. The campground is 3 miles north of Highway 83, west on Forest Service Road 8100. The area is well marked with road signs. (Allow at least 10–20 minutes to creep your way up here).

Cougar Camp. These big campgrounds lie on adjacent edges of Yale Lake just north of Cougar. The sites are protected under an umbrella of trees and several have lake views. Register with the caretaker near the entrance. You'll pay $8 per vehicle. The camp opens April 22 (no reservations). *Tel. 360/238–5224. North from Route 503, just past Cougar. 45 sites. Restrooms, showers, boat launch.*

Kalama Horsecamp. This Forest Service campground isn't exactly free—they ask for donations. Ten sites sit on the banks of the Kalama River, eight with horse corrals. You'll find water, restrooms, and fire rings. The campground lies just at the border of the national monument, and offers fantastic mountain views. *Just before Cougar, tel. 360/247–5473. Traveling north on Hwy. 503, turn west on Forest Service Road 8100 and continue past Merrill Lake about 10 mi. Open year-round.*

Merrill Lake. This Department of Natural Resource campground is close to many trails, and best of all, it's free. *Just before Cougar on Rte. 503, turn left (west) onto Forest Service Rd. 8100; it's about 6 miles up the road, marked DEPT. NATURAL RESOURCES. 11 sites. Picnic areas, boat launch, toilets, potable water. Open April 16–Sept.*

FOOD

North of Mt. St. Helens, you can pick up a bite in Randle; a few restaurants along U.S. 12 serve diner-like fare. **Adams St. Helens Restaurant** (U.S. 12 and Cispus Rd., tel. 360/497–5556), on your left as you exit the monument on Highway 25, serves a variety of food, including grilled tuna with salad ($3.25). If your looking for Randle-ites, head one mile west to the small, rainbow striped **Huff 'n' Puff** (9455 U.S. 12, tel. 360/497–5721), open daily 10–10 in summer, 10–8 in winter. The menu offers some great deals; most breakfasts are $2–$3. The most popular lunch is the deluxe logger burger ($2.70), but you can also get a veggie burger ($2.70) or crisp, flaky fish 'n chips ($2.70). South of Mt. St. Helens, your only dining option is **Jack's at Mt. St. Helens** (13411 Lewis River Rd., Hwy. 503, tel. 360/236–4276). Fuel up before your big hike with breakfast concoctions (home fries sautéed with red and green peppers, onions, ham, scrambled eggs, and cheddar; $5.50); a good and basic hamburger ($3.75); or a filling vegetarian sandwich with fries ($4.95).

EXPLORING MT. ST. HELENS

If you want to explore the monument thoroughly, you'll have to spend more than a day. If you enter the monument from Randle on the north side, follow Route 25 to Route 26, a single-lane road ascending the mountain. Route 26 ends at Route 99, which dead-ends at **Windy Ridge,** the highlight of the park. Windy Ridge is as close to the crater as you can get by car, and grants a spectacular view of the volcano, leveled forests, and Meta Lake. The many viewpoints along the way to the top also serve as trailheads. The pull-off at **Cedar Creek,** on Route 99 en route to Windy Ridge, is a high vantage point where you can view the murky Spirit Lake—full of ashes and rotting trees—for a startling look at the destructive effects of the eruption.

HIKING The monument's trails not only show you the awesome effects of the 1980 eruption on the surrounding environment, but also ancient volcano formations and diverse forests that escaped the blast. The trails off Routes 99 and 26 cover the most ravaged areas and afford some of the best views of the crater. Suggested hikes are listed below, but ranger stations and information centers provide lists of other trails, an essential $2 topographical map of the monument, and trail guides.

On Mt. St. Helens you can hike across lumpy lava flows, through leveled forests, and past boulders carved into canyons by scalding liquid rock.

➢ **NORTHSIDE HIKES** • North of the mountain, **Meta Lake Trail #210,** off Route 99 on the way to Windy Ridge, is a ¼-mile, wheelchair-accessible path that leads to the banks of pond-size Meta Lake. In addition to a few trout, thousands of daphnia—black-water fleas shaped like tadpoles—survived the blast and now cover the shallow lake floor. The **Boundary Trail** runs the entire width of the national forest, but the most interesting part is a 5-mile stretch from the Norway Pass trailhead on Route 26 west to Mt. Margaret. Emerging from oases of green forest onto expanses of leveled trees, you get a sense of the drama of the blast. Closer to the crater, the **Independent Pass Trail,** 5 miles from Windy Ridge off Route 99, runs exclusively through devastated terrain, and connects with the Boundary Trail, 3 miles beyond the trailhead. The **Truman Trail** begins at the end of Route 99 on Windy Ridge, the highest elevation accessible by car, and descends for 7 miles past the Spirit Lake basin before intersecting the Boundary Trail. You'll pass very little vegetation, walking mostly through lava, ash, and pumice deposits in the bleak heart of the blast zone.

In the far northern section of the monument, the 7-mile one-way **Green River Trail** follows the Green River through an old-growth forest with huge trees that reach up to 11 feet in diameter. There are no volcanic views, since the trail winds through a valley, but the primeval forest is worth savoring in itself. The trail begins on Forest Road 2612, 3 miles west of Route 26.

➢ **OTHER HIKES** • On the southeast side of the mountain, the fairly difficult 5-mile one-way **Ape Canyon Trail #234** begins near the Lahar Viewpoint, which overlooks a plain of dried, muddy ash at the end of Route 83. The trail climbs steeply northward, between mud flows and patches of salvaged forest for 3 miles, then levels into a gray landscape called the Plains of Abraham, with evidence of both the 1980 eruption and other, more ancient ones. At the end of the trail you'll have awesome views of Mt. St. Helens, Mt. Adams, Mt. Hood, and Mt. Rainier. (The deep ravine you pass along the way is one of the places where Bigfoot has been spotted.) The **Lava Canyon Trail** begins a couple hundred yards away from the Ape Canyon Trail, but descends southeast, away from the mountain, through a canyon of ancient lava, mud flow, and 50-foot waterfalls surrounded by forest. The first half-mile is wheelchair accessible and has exhibit panels. The next 2½ miles traverse steep cliffs, and include a ladder on which you climb down into the canyon, and a horrifyingly narrow, wood-and-rope swinging bridge that stretches at least 100 feet over the canyon. It's reminiscent of something out of *Indiana Jones* (but wait, the bridge breaks in that movie, uh, never mind), and you'll have to make your way across the petrifyingly rickety old thing if you want to hike the entire trail. Who knows, the adrenaline rush could expedite your ascent back up the canyon.

The newly completed, 29-mile **Loowit Trail** circles the entire mountain, straddling the timberline. Some stretches are very strenuous, but the constantly shifting scenery reveals practically everything the monument has to offer. Most hikers take three days to complete the trail, which is accessible from several feeder trails. Consult a visitor center before taking off; camping is restricted, water sources are scarce, and it's tricky getting around the devastated north side of the mountain.

You can climb to the top of Mt. St. Helens from May 16 to October 31, but you must obtain a **climbing permit.** Hiking experience is not really necessary, but it'll take you 10 hours to hike the 4,600 feet up and back. Seventy permits a day are given out through an advance-reservation system, and the other 40 permits go out the day prior to the climb on a first-come, first-served basis. To reserve a permit, write after February 1 to Mt. St. Helens N.V.M. (42218 N.E. Yale Bridge Rd., Amboy, WA 98601, tel. 360/247–5800). You'll receive an application for the current or upcoming season to mail back. (*See* Permits, *above*, for where and how to pick them up, and where to get a permit in person.) Severe weather will mandate the use of climbing boots, ice axe, crampons, rope, and a hard hat. When the crater has a snow layer, you can walk around inside it, but camping is never allowed. Call the **Climbing Information Hotline** (tel. 360/247–5800) for details and weather conditions.

SPELUNKING The **Ape Cave Trail #239** crawls along the bulging innards of **Ape Cave,** the longest intact lava tube in the continental United States. The Ape Cave dates back to AD 39, when Mt. St. Helens released a roaring lava river. After it oozed over most of the mountain, the outside edges of the river cooled first and hardened into rock; underneath the insulating crust, the lava continued to flow for 10 miles. When the eruption ended, the lava drained out the end, leaving a long, low tube beneath the earth.

You'll be spelunking (cave-crawling) in a dark, cold, dripping-wet tunnel that extends 12,810 feet into the earth; rocks glisten in the lamp light and the howling of distant winds fills the air. The temperature inside the caves is a downright chilly 42° F, so bring at least a warm sweater. Flashlights won't cut through this inky darkness: You'll need a bright lantern, which you can rent near the parking lot for $3 until 4 PM. Ask at **Ape's Headquarters** (off Rte. 83, no phone), open summer, daily 10–6, near the parking lot, or at the monument headquarters (*see* Visitor Information in Basics, *above*) about ranger-led interpretive walks, which usually run at 11:30, 12:30, 1:30, and 2:30.

FISHING The lakes and reservoirs in the monument are bursting with fish, especially near Cougar in the south end of the Yale Reservoir, and along the Green River. Dolly Varden trout are especially plentiful here. The Lewis River, and its recreational outlets at Yale, Swift, and Merwin Reservoirs are also popular for salmon, trout, steelhead, bass, sturgeon, and smelt. A Washington State fishing license is required throughout the National Forest. Get one at **Jack's Restaurant and Store** (*see* Permits in Basics, *above*).

The north side of the mountain has nearly 30 trails open to mountain bikes. Pick up a free "Trailbike Riding Recreation Opportunity Guide" at a visitor center or ranger station.

SNOWMOBILING AND SKIING The monument has plenty of tended winter trails for snowmobiling. Cross-country ski trails from 1.8 to 6 miles are concentrated on the southern side of the monument; the most popular are the **June Lake, Swift,** and **Sasquatch** trails. On Forest Service Road 83, two large areas are cleared for cross-country skiing, snowshoeing, and

Searching for Sasquatch

Mt. St. Helens is the home of the legendary Bigfoot (or Sasquatch), who freaked out many a child in the 1970s, thanks to "In Search Of." The town of Cougar, right outside the monument off Route 503, boasts the highest number of Sasquatch sightings. Unfortunately, the hairy creature's 12- to 18-inch footprints have not been seen for about 10 years—not since Mt. St. Helens's 1980 eruption. Has the mystical beast died, or simply moved on? Rumor has it he's migrated to hipper climes, and can be seen at Nasty Girls' Exotic Dance Emporium and Auto Body in Seattle.

snowmobiling. You can rent cross country skis at **Jack's Restaurant and Store** (*see* Permits, *above*). The full ski set (skis, boots, and poles) costs $12 for one day.

Yakima Valley

Sheltered from Western Washington's heavy rainfall by the Cascade Mountains, the Yakima Valley has everything necessary to make it one of the most productive agricultural centers in the nation. The desertlike conditions, accompanied by a layer of volcanic soil and an intricate irrigation system, have produced ideal farming conditions. Of the 3,072 counties in the United States, Yakima ranks first in the number of fruit trees, and first in the production of apples, mint, and hops. The environment has also proven to be superb for vineyards; Yakima County boasts over 20 local wineries, many of which produce award-winning wines. Crops, vines, and trees don't exactly add up to a hip tourist destination, but if you're venturing off the beaten path, you could do worse than to stumble across the Victorian charm of Ellensburg and the free tastings at excellent local wineries.

Although the valley has relatively moderate weather, in winter you might want to call either **Sno-Line Report** (tel. 206/753–2150) or the **Road Report** (tel. 206/976–ROAD; 25¢ charge) before attempting to travel over the Stevens, Cayuse, Chinook, White, Snoqualmie, Sherman, Blewett, and Satus passes. The motorist information line also informs drivers of the conditions on Mt. Baker and the North Cascades Highway.

Ellensburg

There's something impressive about this Washington town that has as many espresso bars as feed stores. Ellensburg is part western outpost and part university campus, mixed together in a beautiful old town with wide boulevards and tall, leafy trees. Stroll through the historic district and you'll pass art galleries, used bookstores, an old-time hardware store, and one antiques shop after another.

With the discovery of coal and iron ore near Ellensburg in the late 19th century, this small former trading post envisioned itself becoming the Pittsburgh of the West. But on the Fourth of July, 1889, the downtown area burned to a crisp, and up with it went many of the town's aspirations. Shortly after the blaze, the mid-19th-century architecture was replaced by Victorian brick buildings, which remain to this day. Ellensburg lost out to Olympia in the bid to become the state capital, but it did become the home of the 6,000-student **Central Washington University** (9th Ave. and D St., tel. 509/925–3137), a major asset for the local economy. Today the town revolves around cattle ranching, and serves as a stop on I–90 between Seattle and Yakima.

Ellensburg is famous for its festivals, the most popular of which is the **Ellensburg Rodeo,** hyped by promoters as "the greatest show on dirt." Ranked among the top 10 rodeos in the country, the four-day Labor Day weekend event is accompanied by the **Kittitas County Fair,** with a parade and live entertainment. For ticket information, call 800/637–2444. The **Ellensburg Chamber of Commerce** (436 N. Sprague St., tel. 509/925–3137), open weekdays 8–5, provides further information about the city and the rest of the Yakima Valley.

COMING AND GOING Ellensburg is 108 miles southeast of Seattle along I–90, and 36 miles northwest of Yakima via I–82. **Greyhound** (801 Okanogan St., tel. 509/925–1177), four blocks west of the city center, offers daily bus service to Seattle (2–2½ hrs, $18), Spokane (4 hrs, $26), and Walla Walla (5½ hrs, $25). The depot has $1 lockers where you can store luggage.

WHERE TO SLEEP Most motels in town charge $35–$65 for painfully uninteresting, sometimes shabby doubles. Lodgings cluster along the two routes into town from the I–90: Cascade Way and Canyon Street.

For those with their own transport, the **I–90 Motel** (1390 Dollarway Rd., Exit 106 from I–90, tel. 509/925–9844) is about a five-minute drive from downtown and has big, clean singles for $34–$37. You'll find the cheapest rooms in town at the **Rainbow Motel** (1025 Cascade Way,

Yakima Valley

0 — 10 miles

0 — 15 km

N

TO ELLENSBURG

Union Gap

Wapato

97

Yakima

Moxee City

YAKIMA RIDGE

Donald

Toppenish R.

220

97

Toppenish

Satus Creek

YAKIMA INDIAN RESERVATION

22

Stewart Vineyards

Bonair Winery

Zillah Oakes Winery

Buena

Hyatt Vineyards

Staton Hills Winery

Zillah

Granger

Covey Run Vintners

Horizon's Edge Winery

Porteus Vineyards

Eaton Hill Winery

Sunnyside Canal

24

241

Sunnyside

Grandview

Chateau Ste. Michelle

Yakima River Winery

82

Tucker Cellars

RATTLESNAKE HILLS

Hinzerling Vineyards

Prosser

Pontin del Roza

Chinook Wines

Hogue Cellars

Yakima R.

HORSE

221

Chateau Ste. Michelle

HEAVEN

Kiona

Benton City

Oakwood Cellars

Cold R.

240

HILLS

Kiona Vineyards

Blackwood Canyon

West Richland

Richland

Columbia R.

82

395

Kennewick

182

Pasco

TO WALLA WALLA

285

tel. 509/925–3544), which has clean, smallish doubles for $35–$40. At **Harold's Motel** (601 N. Water, tel. 509/925–4141), big, inoffensive singles start at $30, and doubles start at $35. Both the Rainbow and Harold's have cable TV and coin-op laundry. If you're low on funds, you can stay in one of three funky, grass-floor tepees at the **Riverview Campground** (Canyon Road, btw Mileposts 14 and 15, tel. 509/952–6043). For only $20 per tepee, you can squeeze in up to eight people. Sure, there's barely enough room inside to stand up and walk in a small circle, but at $2.50 per person, you can't really complain.

If you're coming to Ellensburg for a festival or concert, don't assume that hotels will charge the prices we list here—some jack up their rates as much as 300%. Ain't capitalism grand?

FOOD On the way into town you'll pass diners, truck stops, and fast-food joints, but once in town, the odds of finding food that won't make a home in your arteries drastically improves. **Super 1 Foods** supermarket (200 E. Mountain View, tel. 509/962–7770) is open 24 hours and has a bakery, deli, and pharmacy. For a full selection of vegetarian and vegan products, try **Better Life** (111 W. Sixth Ave., tel. 509/925–2505).

Austin's Eats. This warehouse café with ornate, twenty-foot ceilings and partially-exposed brick walls, displays local artwork, jewelry, and homemade crafts. Folk music often fills the place, and they have live jazz on Friday nights, when they close as usual around 6, then reopen around 8 for live music. Find yourself a couch and dive into a cappuccino or one of their entrées (oases in this desert of chicken-fried steak they call Washington). Try a falafel "burger" ($3.95), hummus and tabbouleh sandwich ($3.95), Mediterranean pizza ($2.50), or a chicken pesto sandwich ($4.25). Come at night to hang out with students and a twentysomething crowd. *312 N. Main St., tel. 509/925–3012. Open daily 8 AM–6 PM.*

Mama's Cajun Cooking. Electrify your tastebuds at this little hole-in-the-wall. Mama, who really cooks all the meals, offers up formidable jambalaya ($4.75), simmered for twelve hours and served with a side of hush puppies. Also try the spicy Cajun shrimp ($5.75) or Louisiana hot links ($3.50). If you left your antacid at home, you might opt for a sandwich or burger instead (about $4). *601 Cascade Way, btw I–90 and town, tel. 509/962–3272. Open Tues., Wed., and Sun. 6 AM–2 PM, Thurs.–Sat. 6 AM–2 PM and 5–7:30.*

Valley Cafe. Ragtime piano wafts through this trendy art deco café designed in 1938. The menu includes a variety of salads (Mediterranean tortellini, $5.45), sandwiches (chicken dijon, $5.95), and steamed veggies ($5.95). The café plate ($5.45), a cup of fiery soup and an open-faced toasted french bread sandwich, is perfect for a midday meal. *105 W. 3rd St., tel. 509/925–3050. Open weekdays 11–9, weekends 9 AM–10 PM.*

See Dick and Jane Make Art

Hidden in suburbia outside downtown Ellensburg is the area's most captivating attraction, Dick and Jane's Spot (101 N. Pearl St., tel. 509/925–3224). Actually the home of artists Dick Elliott and Jane Orleman, the house is a continuously growing, whimsical sculpture, incorporating the work of 30 other artists as well. Drive by and you'll see a collage of 20,000 bottle caps, 15,000 bicycle reflectors, bicycle pinwheels, and bizarre statues, all spliced together haphazardly on the outside of the house. But Dick and Jane don't spend all their time tinkering with the house: Dick is well-known for groundbreaking "reflector art" (on public walls in New York City), Jane for poignant Munchian portraits of child abuse. Their joint masterpiece stands on private property, so don't cross the fence, but be sure to look at the recycled creation from all angles. You can deposit any donations in the box near the visitor's log.

WORTH SEEING Visit the **Clymer Gallery** (416 N. Pearl St., tel. 509/962–6416), weekdays 10–5, weekends noon–5, for a look at the work of award-winning Western artist John Clymer (1907–1989), an Ellensburg native who produced more than 80 covers for the *Saturday Evening Post*. In the same building is the Ellensburg Western Art Association's permanent collection of paintings, sculptures, and alternative media representing local and international artists. A restored art deco theater housing 40 dealers, the **Showplace Antique Mall** (103 E. 3rd St., tel. 509/962–9331) is a hangout for local shoppers browsing through vintage clothing, old photographs, and other miscellaneous items.

OUTDOOR ACTIVITIES Several good **cycling** routes surround the area. **Mountain High Sports** (105 E. 4th St., tel. 509/925–4626) rents mountain bikes for $10 per half-day, $17 for a full day, and can advise you on where to ride 'em. If you're feeling adventurous, you can explore the fairly smooth 16 miles of Upper Yakima River, or 20 miles of even more mellow Lower Yakima River Canyon on a huge, inflatable **river raft** (like the one in *Race for Your Life, Charlie Brown*). You can rent one for only $50 a day from the knowledgeable staff at **River Raft Rentals** (Rte. 4, tel. 509/964–2145).

NEAR ELLENSBURG

GINKGO PETRIFIED FOREST STATE PARK The Ginkgo Petrified Forest State Park, about 40 miles east of Ellensburg via I–90, is a fossil forest created by ancient lava flows. It's also the only place in the world where you can find petrified ginkgo, an ornamental Chinese tree. Perched on a cliff above the Columbia River, an **interpretive center** (tel. 509/856–2290) provides displays of cut and polished sections of petrified wood, as well as incredible views of the river.

ROSLYN This sleepy village, just off I–90 between Seattle and Ellensburg, functions as the backdrop for *Northern Exposure*, the quirky television series ostensibly set in Alaska. Head straight for the **Roslyn Cafe** (28 Pennsylvania Ave., at 2nd St., tel. 509/649–2763) for mouthwatering hamburgers with spinach and onions ($4) and decadent desserts. (The café is in the background of the closing credits every week.) Otherwise, quaff a few cold ones at **The Brick Tavern** (Pennsylvania Ave., tel. 509/649–2643), the oldest bar in the state. Built in 1898, the historic watering hole has a creek flowing through it. Come toast the snobby locals as they smirk at tourists—if you want to blend in, forget your camera.

One interesting thing to do here is visit the 23 **ethnic cemeteries** clustered on the mountainside near town. The graves, most of which are marked by European-style headstones, are

Get Your Farmer Tan Here

Several private farms and orchards open their figurative doors to the public and (for a fee) allow you to come and participate in seasonal harvests (usually between July and October). Make sure you wear stainable clothing; berry juice will hang around on your duds as a permanent reminder of your farmer-for-a-day experience. Call the farm ahead of time to check availability, hours, and price, and to let the farmer know you're coming. Once you arrive, remember that the person in charge most likely lives there, so follow their instructions, and respect their private property. At William and Gloria Spino's Farm (1124 Hwy. 142, Klickitat, tel. 509/369–3371) you should bring your own containers—you can pick apples, lambert cherries, and plums. At the Granger Berry Patch (Ken and Sandy Fein, 1731 Beam Rd., Granger, tel. 509/854–1413) you can spoil yourself with currants (red and black), gooseberries, raspberries, marionberries, loganberries, boysenberries, blackberries, huckleberries . . . you get the idea.

holdovers from Roslyn's early days as a bustling mining community. Roslyn lies on Route 903, about 70 miles southeast of Seattle and 30 miles northwest of Ellensburg.

Yakima

The county seat and center of valley activity, Yakima was originally established in the early 1880s at the site of what is now the town of Union Gap, a few miles south. When they discovered that city founders had bought up local property in anticipation of the railroad, Northern Pacific nimbly moved their train terminal and shipping facility 5 miles north, leaving local sharks in the dust. Today, Yakima is very much a farming town, although it also does big business as a convention center. The city ground to a halt in 1980 when Mt. St. Helens erupted; everything from computers to Cuisinarts stopped working as Yakima was inundated with 800,000 tons of ash. For the dirt on Yakima and the whole valley, contact the **Yakima Valley Visitors and Convention Bureau** (10 N. 8th St., 98901, tel. 509/575-1300), open weekdays 8:30-5, weekends 9-5.

COMING AND GOING To reach Yakima from Seattle (about 145 miles), take I-90 to Ellensburg and then head south on I-82 at Kittitas. You can also get to Yakima from Mt. Rainier (96 miles) and Mt. St. Helens in the west via U.S. 12. **Greyhound** (602 E. Yakima Ave., tel. 509/457-5131) operates three buses daily to Seattle (3½ hrs, $19) and one to Spokane (5½ hrs, $26).

One local described the surfeit of police on Yakima Valley highways as being "worse than flies on a fresh dog turd."

GETTING AROUND Yakima Transit (2301 Fruitvale Blvd., tel. 509/575-6175) local buses service the city Monday–Saturday. Renting a car is a pretty affordable option if you want to blow out of town, and it's the only logical way to explore Yakima Valley's scattered wineries. **Sunfair Auto Rental's** (1600 E. Yakima Ave., at I-82, tel. 509/248-7600) cheapest cars rent for $29 per day, $162 a week.

WHERE TO SLEEP Yakima's hotels are nothing to rave about (but neither is Yakima, for that matter). Stay away from the area around the mall, south on 1st Street: Locals refer to this run-down, drug-infested part of town as "the hole." North 1st Street is overflowing with cheap, nondescript places to spend the night.

Bali Hai Motel (710 N. 1st St., tel. 509/452-7178) is one of the least expensive motels on 1st Street. Small doubles with exposed light bulbs and cable TV go for $30. If you're looking for something more demure, break open your piggy bank and stay in the charming Victorian **Irish House Bed and Breakfast** (210 S. 28th Ave., near Yakima Ave., tel. 509/453-5474). Doubles decked out in 19th-century decor go for $60, including a full breakfast (but shared bath). The epitome of lodging mediocrity, **Econo Lodge** (510 N. 1st St., tel. 509/457-6155) provides average rooms with cable TV, free coffee, and free newspapers. Doubles are $40-$50.

➤ **CAMPING** • Since Yakima's motels pretty much suck, staying at one of the campgrounds that line U.S. 12 and Route 410 is an especially desirable alternative. Many of the sites are scattered along the rivers just west of Yakima and are close to fishing and swimming areas. Though plagued by RVs, **Yakima Sportsman State Park** (904 Keys Rd., tel. 509/575-2774) is the better of the two campgrounds in the Yakima area. About three miles from the center of town, these sites ($11) have picnic tables, fire rings, and access to showers. Take Exit 34 off I-82 and head 1 mile east. Owned and run by the Yakima tribes, scenic **Yakima Nation RV Park** (U.S. 97, tel. 509/865-2000) is south of Yakima, in Toppenish. If you don't have a tent, rent a tepee for $20 for two, $30 for up to five. Attractions include a pool, spa, and basketball and volleyball courts.

FOOD The true budget traveler would subsist entirely on Yakima's fresh fruits and vegetables. To sample cheap, delicious local crops, stop at the **Residential Fruit Stand** (1103 S. 3rd Ave., at Nob Hill Blvd.) in summer from 9 AM to dusk. Try **Folk-Lore Natural Foods** (9 N. B St., Toppenish, tel. 509/865-4772) for healthy staples and samples of old-fashioned sarsaparilla. If you have a case of the midnight munchies, slurp coffee with the locals at 24-hour **Mels Diner** (314 N. 1st St., tel. 509/248-5382); they sell standard roadside food at affordable prices. **Ali-**

cia's Fine Mexican Products (605 E. Nob Hill Blvd., tel. 509/575–0995) is a tortilla factory that sells the best prepared and frozen tamales in the Northwest. Buy them frozen ($6–$7 per dozen) or hot (89¢ each or $8.40 per dozen). It's in one of the more run-down parts of town, so keep your wits about you. Intimate **Deli de Pasta** (7 N. Front St., tel. 509/453–0571) is slightly more pricey than the diners, but worth it. For lunch, a big salad or sandwich will run you $6. At dinner try a daily special ($8) or fresh pasta. Wednesdays you get all the pasta you can eat for $9.95.

Grant's Brewery Pub. The first brew pub in North America established after Prohibition, Grant's Brewery Pub qualifies as much as a major sight as well as a place to eat and drink. They serve traditional, British-style ales produced locally by Yakima Brewing and Malting Company, located in the same building (daily tours at 2 and 3 PM). This is the home of the infamous microbrewmeister Bert Grant, a Scotsman who knows the meaning of good ale. The pub grub ($4–$6) of burgers, salads, and sandwiches complement the brew. There's live jazz and blues on weekends, when this place is as hip as it gets in town. *32 N. Front St., tel. 509/575–2922. Open Mon.–Thurs. 11:30 AM–midnight, Fri.–Sat. 11:30 AM–1 AM, Sun. 11:30–10.*

WORTH SEEING There's not much to see in town, but a few nearby sights and plentiful vineyards can keep you entertained for a day. With its collection of vintage farm machinery (like an operating windmill and apple-packing line), the **Central Washington Agricultural Museum** (450 S. Main St., tel. 509/248–0432) helps preserve Yakima's agricultural heritage. A visit to this unorthodox museum is enlightening, especially if you're a city slicker—and it's free. From Yakima, drive south through Union Gap on Main Street to the U.S. 97 overpass. Drive across, and turn right on the gravel road. The museum is open daily 9–5. In White Swan, at the end of Route 220, **Fort Simcoe State Park** (5150 Fort Simcoe Rd., tel. 509/874–2372), open daily 6:30 AM–dusk, was constructed in 1856 as an advance post of the Ninth Infantry Regiment. In 1859, the fort was abandoned and handed over to the Bureau of Indian Affairs as a center for education and the instruction of trade skills. Only five of the original military structures remain today, some of which (along with the museum) reveal the history of the fort and the Yakima tribes.

It's no coincidence that Yakima sounds like "Yucky, mon." Rolling into town, you'll gain an immediate appreciation for where you last were and a blind fondness for where you're headed.

Yakima Indian Nation Cultural Center. Set on the 1.4-million-acre Yakima Indian Reservation, the cultural center features a museum detailing the history of the 14 tribes and bands that allied in 1855 to form the Yakima Indian Nation. A recreated winter lodge features a variety of exhibits that follow the tribes back to prehistoric times. Don't miss the restaurant in the rear of the museum: They serve traditional *Luclukmu* (salmon and dumplings) for $4.25 a bowl; Indian fry bread costs 65¢ per piece. *Off U.S. 97 at Buster Rd., tel. 509/865–2800. East of Yakima near Toppenish. Admission: $4, $2 students, free Mon. in summer. Museum: Open Mon.–Sat. 9–6, Sun. 10–5. Restaurant: Open Sun.–Wed. 8–2, Thurs.–Sat. 8–8.*

OUTDOOR ACTIVITIES The **Yakima Greenway** (tel. 509/453–8280), stretching along the Yakima River between Selah and Union Gap, is 3,600 acres of developed recreational areas, including paved biking and running trails, as well as picnic areas, fishing spots, and boat landings. Three miles west of Yakima on U.S. 12, at its junction with Naches Highway and Powerhouse Road, you'll find the **Indian Painted Rocks**. Although some of the old, painted stones were destroyed by an irrigation project, the site is still a cool place to go exploring and has a hands-on display of rocks and artifacts.

➤ **MOUNTAIN BIKING AND HIKING** • West of Yakima is the colossal **Wenatchee National Forest,** which stretches all the way up to Lake Chelan along the line of the Cascades. The region around Yakima falls under the jurisdiction of the Naches Ranger District and encompasses the Goat Rocks, Norse Peak, and William O. Douglas wildernesses. Yakima provides reasonably easy access to more than 30 mountain bike trails and 100 hiking trails, most of which offer spectacular views of the forest and an occasional glimpse of local wildlife. You can rent mountain bikes for $15 a day from **Yakima Cycle Shop** (509 W. Yakima Ave., tel. 509/452–7104). For trail and camping information and forest maps, stop off at the **Naches Ranger**

Station (tel. 509/653–2205), about 18 miles northwest of Yakima on U.S. 12. From the ranger station, it takes about another 20 minutes to get into the forest.

Yakima Valley Wine Country

With more of its land hidden under vineyards than any other part of Washington, the Yakima Valley forms the heart of the state's burgeoning wine industry. Wine is now being produced at more than 75 wineries on both sides of the Cascades, making Washington the second largest producer of wines in the United States. The rich soil and warm climate, combined with its prime location—the valley is at the same latitude as Burgundy, France—means that the region's wines are sufficiently good to cause Californian and European wineries some discomfort. Although the 22 wineries of the Yakima Valley all lie close to I–82 between Yakima and the Tri-Cities (*see below*), they are not strung along a continuous driving loop. So, before you set out, obtain a free copy of *The Yakima Valley Wine Tour,* either by writing in advance to **Yakima Valley Wine Growers Association** (Box 39, Grandview, WA 98930), or by going to the Yakima Valley Visitors and Convention Bureau in Yakima (*see* Yakima, *above*). Most wineries offer daily tours and free samples from 10 to 5.

Among the vineyards closest to Yakima is the **Staton Hills Winery** (71 Gangl Rd., Wapato, tel. 509/877–2112), 10 minutes south of Yakima and just east of I–82. You can't miss the cedar, stone, and glass landmark as you head east down the highway from Yakima. The tasting room has a huge fireplace for use in winter and picnic tables outside in summer. Farther east along I–82 in Granger is **Stewart Vineyards** (1711 Cherry Hill Rd., Granger, tel. 509/854–1882), which is worth a visit in spring when the cherry trees are blooming. At any time of year, though, the views of the Yakima Valley are terrific. The oldest winery in the state is the **Chateau Ste. Michelle** (W. 5th St. and Ave. B, Grandview, tel. 509/882–3928). Dating back to the '30s, the winery has a collection of vintage redwood fermenters used nowhere else in the state. If you come in October, you can see the wine fermenting, with its cap of grape skins.

Tri-Cities

"The 4-H club [in Lancaster] ran an ever-popular Most Misshapen Potato contest. My high-school basketball team was called the Neutrons (the junior team, the Neutrinos), and had a mushroom cloud as our logo and jacket crest." From *Shampoo Planet,* by Douglas Coupland.

Douglas Coupland's Lancaster is a thinly disguised version of Richland, one-third of the semi-urban triumvirate known as the Tri-Cities. Like Los Alamos and parts of Nevada, Tri-Cities is an arid, rather desolate region best known because of its role as a center of nuclear experimentation. With a population of 33,350, Richland maintains one of the highest concentrations of Ph.Ds in the country. Although it was settled in the late 1800s, the town didn't receive much attention until the 1940s, when the government built a series of nuclear reactors here as part of the Hanford Project (a plan that established nuclear power plants across the United States). Now only one working reactor remains in the Hanford Reservation, and there is talk that it may close down. When each plant closes, it's a sigh of relief to some, but a major economic loss to many residents.

Although the Tri-Cities seem like one blobby entity, **Pasco, Richland,** and **Kennewick** are actually distinct communities. Pasco, the oldest and the poorest of the three cities, is home to a deluge of pawnshops and rotting taverns. Kennewick, the wealthiest and most populous (44,490) of the Tri-Cities, is an ever-widening suburbia complete with mini- and maximalls—it's unmistakably the focal point of local consumerism. The main reasons to come here are to enjoy the watersports, to base yourself while exploring the Yakima Valley wineries and wilderness areas, or, on a morbid note, to eyeball a rotting corpse of the nuclear age.

BASICS Richland's Chamber of Commerce (515 Lee Blvd., tel. 509/946–1651) is perhaps the best of the three cities' tourist offices. Otherwise, visit the **Chamber of Commerce** in either Kennewick (500 N. Morain St., Suite 1200, tel. 509/736–0510) or Pasco (129 N. 3rd St., tel. 509/547–9755), or try the **Tri-Cities Visitor and Convention Bureau** (6951 W. Grandridge Blvd., tel. 509/735–8486 or 800/835–0248) in Kennewick.

COMING AND GOING The Tri-Cities are in south central Washington, about 30 miles north of Oregon at the junction of U.S. 395, U.S. 12, and I–82. **Greyhound** (115 N. 2nd St., Pasco, tel. 509/547–3151) runs buses daily to Seattle (6 hrs, $35.50), Spokane (2 hrs 45 min, $21), and Walla Walla (1 hr, $8.50).

GETTING AROUND Richland and Kennewick are separated from Pasco by the Columbia River and Lake Wallula. **Ben Franklin Transit** (1000 Columbia Dr., Richland, tel. 509/735–5100) local Buses 120 and 225 run between Richland and Pasco; Bus 120 also goes between Richland and Kennewick; Bus 65 goes between Pasco and Kennewick. Routes also include West Richland and the Tri-Cities Airport.

WHERE TO SLEEP The cheapest sleep in the area is **Desert Gold Motel and Travel Trailer Park** (611 Columbia Dr., Richland, tel. 509/627–1000), which has singles ($30), doubles ($34), and tent sites ($8), as well as a pool and Jacuzzi. In Richland stay at the **Bali Hi Motel** (1201 George Washington Way, tel. 509/943–3101), where nicely decorated, comfortable doubles cost $35–$40, and you can use the pool and spa. The **Bedford Inn Bed and Breakfast** (706 Tayor, tel. 509/946–5259), also in Richland, offers two rooms in a cozy two-story house. Doubles with breakfast cost $60.

➤ **CAMPING** • Pitch your tent at **Columbia Park Campground** (6601 S.E. Columbia Dr., Richland, tel. 509/783–3711), just off U.S. 12 along the Columbia River, between Richland and Kennewick. Grassy sites cost $7–$11, and showers are included. If you want to be near the Snake River, try the **Arrowheads Campground** upriver from Sacajawea State Park. Take U.S. 12 west for four miles, then U.S. 395 north to the Hillsboro exit and turn right on Commercial.

FOOD Richland outdoes its neighbors when it comes to food. If you're a bottomless pit, shamelessly indulge in all-you-can-eat grub at **Roy's Western Smorgy** (1300 Columbia Ctr., tel. 509/725–8539), just off Route 204. You can chow on ribs, baked chicken, mashed potatoes, two large salad bars, soups, fried and steamed fish, a bunch of veggies, and more for $5 at lunch and $6.89 at dinner. **Baron's Beef and Brew** (1034 Lee Blvd., Richland, tel. 509/946–5500) serves 180 bottled beers in a sporty atmosphere. The diverse menu includes Cajun flaming chicken wings ($5) and burgers ($5), as well as an assortment of sandwiches and salads. It's also a fun place to hang out in the evening. Tucked away next to the park, **Giaccis** (94 Lee Blvd., Richland, tel. 509/946–4855) has a sunny patio packed with locals on weekends. Fresh, rich Italian dishes run $7.50–$12. For a healthy sandwich, fresh loaf of wheat bread, pastry, or espresso, **Jeamfer's** (701 George Washington Way, Richland, tel. 509/946–5514) is a laid-back bakery and café with ample seating; you can eat well for under $5, or just sip an espresso for $1.

WORTH SEEING Most of what you'll want to see in the Tri-Cities won't be in the cities at all. With the exception of a few popular festivals and the requisite historical museums, the Tri-Cities' main draw lies in the surrounding area. Recreational opportunities abound both on the area's three rivers and in the surrounding farmland and wilderness. Although it's sometimes overshadowed by Yakima, the Tri-Cities has its own successful, thriving **wine country**. Pick up a map of local wineries from the Chamber of Commerce (*see* Basics, *above*) of any of the three cities.

The **Hanford Science Center**, owned by the U.S. Department of Energy but operated by Westinghouse, uses interactive exhibits such as nuclear tic-tac-toe to teach tourists and school children about basic atomic science. You don't have to sit through a whole bunch of pro-nuclear energy bullshit—it's all nonpolitical and deals exclusively with scientific concepts. *825 Jadwin Ave., in the Richland Federal Bldg., tel. 509/376–6374. Admission free. Open weekdays 8–5, Sat. 9–5, Sun. noon–5.*

Sacajawea State Park (2501 Sacajawea State Park Rd., 2 mi east of Pasco off U.S. 12, tel. 509/545–2361 or 509/545–2315) is the former trading and fishing site of local Native American tribes, including the Yakima, Wanapum, Walla Walla, and Palouse. The park has numerous open grassy areas, perfect for picnics right on the river, though there's no camping. The Interpretative Center at the park emphasizes the history of the Lewis and Clark Expedition, which was sent out by President Jefferson in 1804 to find a land route to the Pacific Northwest.

AFTER DARK Because of the nearby college, Tri-Cities has some fun nighttime options. **The Frontier Tavern** (710 The Parkway, Richland, tel. 509/943–2133) has shuffleboard, dart boards, and $1 hot dogs in an unpretentious setting. **Silent Sams** (8300 Gage Blvd., behind Columbia Center, Richland, tel. 509/783–0434) is a bit of a slacker scene, with cheap pool and a fun crowd.

OUTDOOR ACTIVITIES If you have time, don't miss **Jupiter Dunes Wilderness Area** (tel. 509/353–2570), open year-round. It's laced with extensive hiking and off-road vehicle trails that are great for biking, and you can pitch your tent for free anywhere. Take U.S. 12 from the Tri-Cities and turn left on Pascok Highway; after 10 miles turn left at the huge yellow mail boxes and office buildings, and continue up the road for 4 miles.

NEAR THE YAKIMA VALLEY

WALLA WALLA This little agricultural town in southeast Washington is most famous for its slightly silly name. The town gets its name from the Indian word for "many waters," and the majority of Walla Walla's historic structures date back as far as the days of the Oregon Trail. **Fort Walla Walla Museum Complex and Park** (Myra Rd., at Dalles Military Rd., tel. 509/525–7703), an 1858 military reservation, features 14 vintage buildings, including the Babcock Railway Station, built in 1880 on the Northern Pacific line. It also holds the largest display of early agricultural implements in the west. During the days of the Oregon Trail, the 1836 mission of Marcus and Narcissa Whitman was a vital rest stop for pioneers on their way west. The mission has been preserved as the **Whitman Mission National Historical Site and Museum** (off U.S. 12, about 7 mi west of Walla Walla). In 1847, the work of the missionaries came to an ugly end when the mission was attacked by the local Cayeuse Indians. The massacre, which resulted in the murder of the Whitmans and the capture of most of the mission residents, was sparked by the Indians' distrust of the white man's medicine, which saved white children from a measles epidemic but not the Cayeuse, who had no resistance to the disease. Take the self-guided trail to the mass grave, the mission site, and the memorial monument. For more information about Walla Walla and the surrounding area, visit the **Chamber of Commerce** (29 E. Sumach St., at N. Colville St., tel. 509/525–0850).

➤ **COMING AND GOING** • Walla Walla lies southeast of the Tri-Cities on U.S. 12. *See* Tri-Cities Coming and Going *above*, for bus info.

Eastern Washington

As far back as the mid-19th century, politicians were advocating dividing the state along the line of the Cascades, and some fringe types today would like to see eastern Washington and eastern Oregon unite to form a 51st state called Lincoln. Bush would probably be a better name for it, because this conservative area would consist of nothing but tumbleweed and sagebrush if it weren't for irrigation water from the Grand Coulee Dam. As it is, eastern Washington is a huge farming center, encompassing fruit and vegetable farms in the west and cattle ranching and wheat fields as you go farther east. Out here, pickup trucks and horses are more than rustic affectations. Anchoring the area is Spokane, a fun, laid-back city at the far eastern end of the state.

Spokane

Spokane is like a smaller, cleaner country cousin of Seattle. Spokane takes the modernity of Seattle and mixes it with the idealistic and friendly charm of a small town. Not that Spokane is that small—it's the only real city in eastern Washington. The residents are politically, ethnically, and ideologically diverse, creating an aura of tolerance and open-mindedness. The city, bordered by several universities, caters to the tiny budgets and varied demands of a student population. Spokane has a big gay population, several good bars, dance clubs, microbreweries, all-night cafés, and cheap theater and film houses. Poet Vachel Lindsay, joining Bing Crosby and Tom Foley as famous Spokes, may have put his finger on Spokane's appeal when he wrote: "Never have I ever known better neighbors, nor do I expect to find better, ever, than those in Spokane."

BASICS Spokane Regional Convention and Visitors Bureau. *926 W. Sprague Ave., at Monroe St., tel. 509/747-3230 or 800/248-3230. Open fall–spring, weekdays 8:30–5; summer, weekdays 8:30–5, Sat. 9–3.*

COMING AND GOING It's a straight 289-mile shot from Seattle to Spokane along I–90. If you're driving the 85 miles from Grand Coulee, you need to take Route 174 south and then U.S. 2 east. From the Tri-Cities take U.S. 395 north to I-90 east. **Greyhound-Trailways** (tel. 509/624–5255) runs daily buses from Seattle (6 hrs, $26) and Portland (9 hrs, $42). The **bus depot** (1125 W. Sprague Ave.) is downtown, nine blocks west of Amtrak and one block from the Visitor's Bureau. The $1 lockers are big enough to hold a moose.

➤ **BY TRAIN** • **Amtrak** (W. 221 1st Ave., tel. 800/872–7245 or 509/624–5144) offers daily service to Seattle (7 hrs, $67) and Portland (7 hrs, $67). You can check your bags in a locker 24 hours before your train leaves for free if you have a ticket. If you're coming in late, be careful in the seedy area around the station.

GETTING AROUND Spokane has an extensive local bus system that operates from 6:40 AM to 12:15 AM. Tickets are 75¢; exact change or tokens are required. You can pick up schedules, route maps, and tokens at either the **bus depot** (W. 1229 Boone Ave., tel. 509/328–RIDE) or at W. 510 Riverside Avenue (Sherwood Mall, downtown, tel. 509/456–7277). If you have a car, a good way to explore the city is to follow the **City Loop Drive,** which takes you out of the city and into the forested residential hills of greater Spokane. Start at Stevens and Riverside streets and follow the arrowhead signs. If it's cold, you can tour Spokane's downtown via its **Skywalk System,** the second largest in the world. On this enclosed walkway, you can cover 15 blocks of shopping without hazarding the elements. Basically, it's just a glorified mall, but at least it's unusual. Rent a bike at **Quinn's** (Riverfront Park, on Howard St. Bridge, tel. 509/456–6545) for as little as $4 per hour for your basic model. Spokane has over 25 miles of trails along the Spokane River.

WHERE TO SLEEP Downtown Spokane is full of moderately priced, clean hotels, in addition to a youth hostel. A few minutes west of downtown off I–90 lies a cluster of inexpensive motels, restaurants, and supermarkets. Troll for cheap motels along 1st Avenue.

The Alpenhaus. At only $20 per single, $25 per double, the large but thin-walled rooms here are probably the cheapest you'll find in Spokane. The printed sheets and bedspreads look junky, but the rooms have full bath, cable TV, and a table and chairs. The staff don't always answer the phone. *2834 W. Sunset Blvd., tel. 509/747–0102. 15 rooms.*

Forget about sleeping in a park (especially Riverside Park). Not only are they unsafe, but they're also heavily patrolled by gung-ho cops.

Sun Tree 8 Inn. Of their two downtown branches, the newer Sun Tree at Post Street is more expensive than the smaller, older location a few blocks away on Division Street. At both locations you get clean rooms, cable TV, and a continental breakfast. Prices for Post Street start at $36 for a single, $45 for a double. At Division Street a single is $44.50 per night, and doubles are $50. *123 S. Post St., tel. 509/838–8504; 211 S. Division St., tel. 509/838-6630. Jacuzzi. Wheelchair access.*

Town Centre Motor Inn. The rooms in this standard downtown motel are stocked with TVs, refrigerators, and even a microwave for zapping those midnight snacks. Singles are $43–$50, doubles about $50–$56. *901 W. 1st Ave., btw bus and train stations, tel. 509/747–1041 or 800/247–1041. 36 rooms. Sauna, gym. Wheelchair access.*

➤ **HOSTELS** • **Spokane Youth Hostel (HI).** Built in 1910, this big, busy house has a wooden porch, a sitting room, and long-term room rentals. Because it's so big, it's not as homey as some hostels, and travelers from everywhere are always coming and going. Units have four–six beds, a kitchen, and a bathroom. Members pay $10, nonmembers $13. *930 S. Lincoln St., tel. 509/838–5968. Walk 10 blocks from downtown, straight uphill along Lincoln or Monroe Sts. Check-in 4–10 PM. 22 beds. Laundry.*

➤ **CAMPING** • **Riverside State Park**, 6 miles northwest of Spokane, is near the Little Spokane River Nature Area, hiking trails, and an equestrian center. You'll almost always be able to secure a site—there are 101 of them—at $10 per night. From Spokane, take the Monroe Street Bridge 1.5 miles north, turn left on Shannon Avenue, continue two blocks, and turn right on Northwest Boulevard; 4¾ miles later, turn left at the Riverside State Park Sign (near H Street, you can't miss it).

FOOD Downtown Spokane is chock full of culinary options that cater to the wallets of a working and student population. Old R&B tunes waft from **Great Harvest Bread Co** (816 W. Sprague Ave., btw Post and Lincoln Sts., tel. 509/624–9370), along with the scent of fresh-baked bread and bagels. At lunch you can get fresh soup, salads, and sandwiches ($4.50). Many of the breads are vegan, and the lunches are vegetarian. Dingy, dirty, and frequented by friendly homeless people, **Rasputin's** (212 Wall St., btw 2nd and 3rd Aves., no phone) is a totally disorganized slacker venture that sometimes sells $1.85 burritos, 85¢ PB&J sandwiches, and turbo coffee (50¢). If you want to find a place to crash or party, ask around here.

➤ **UNDER $5** • **Dick's.** You know how your parents are always yammering about the days when ice cream was a nickel? Well, at this pink burger stand, burgers still cost 55¢, fries are 43¢, pie á la mode is 63¢, and coffee is a mere 20¢. Eat at a picnic table out front, or take your feast to Riverfront Park a few blocks away. Be careful at night in this neighborhood. *10 E. 3rd Ave., at Division St., tel. 509/747–2481. Go south on Division until just before I–90. Open Mon.–Sat. 9 AM–1 AM, Sun. 9 AM–12:30 AM. Wheelchair access.*

➤ **UNDER $10** • **Espresso Delizioso Café.** Without a doubt, this is the coolest hangout in the city. Not only do they serve entire pots of coffee for $2.25 amid ersatz Victorian decor, but they make delicious food as well. Grab some soup with bread ($5.25), or a veggie tofu burger ($4.50) for lunch, or a more elaborate (and expensive) dish for dinner. Come hear live music (with no cover charge) on weekend nights. *706 N. Monroe St. #1, tel. 509/326–5958. Open Mon. –Thurs. 7:30 AM–11:30 PM, Fri. 7:30 AM–2 AM, Sun. 9 AM–2 AM.*

Fugazzi. Yes, those are yuppies sitting over in the corner, but this café serves great sandwiches ($5.50), salads ($3.50–$7.75), homemade granola ($2.75), and pasta and pizza. It's also strategically located downtown, making it a perfect place to linger and watch the locals scurry by. In the evening, it's intimate and dimly lit, and after dinner, it's a laid-back place to drink wine (from $2.50), beer ($2), or cappuccino ($1.50). *1 N. Post Street, tel. 509/624–1133. Open Mon. 7 AM–4 PM, Tues.–Thurs. 7 AM–9 PM, Fri. 7 AM–10 PM, Sat. 8 AM–10 PM.*

The Mustard Seed Oriental Café. This brick-walled restaurant has small tables scattered over a multilevel space, across from Riverfront Park. The menu includes hot and spicy chicken with peppers ($6.50), Szechwan shrimp ($7.50), and beef teriyaki ($6.50). Lunches average $6, including rice, salad, and soup. Dinners, which include stir-fried veggies, rice, and soup or salad, are more pricey at $7.95–$12.25. *W. 245 Spokane Falls Blvd., tel. 509/747–2689. Open weekdays 11:15–2:30 and 5–10, Sat. 11:30–2:30 and 5–10, Sun. 4–10.*

WORTH SEEING **Arbor Crest Cliff House** is the most spectacular sight in Spokane. In 1924, a guy named Royal Riblet set up this eclectic home and winery overlooking the Spokane Valley. Fortunately for us, his seventh wife left the house, which is listed in the National Register of Historic Places, for public viewing and free wine-tasting. *4705 N. Fruithill Rd., tel. 509/ 927–9463. From I–90, go north on Argonne Rd., east on Upriver Dr., and continue straight at fork on Fruithill. Open daily noon–5. No one under 21 admitted.*

Cheney Cowles Memorial Museum enthusiastically presents various local artifacts. Audiovisual exhibits explore the highs and lows of the city, and a gallery space displays the work of a new local artist every month. A small Native American collection includes a hunting diorama, baskets, and beadwork of the Plateau Indians. As part of the museum admission, you can also explore the adjacent **Campbell House** for a glimpse of Spokane's opulent past. *2316 W. 1st*

Ave., tel. 509/456–3931. On City Loop Dr. Admission: $3, $1.50 Wed. 10–5, free Wed. 5–9. Open Tues. and Thurs.–Sat. 10–5, Wed. 10–9, Sun. 1–5.

Picnic, learn about local flora, or just take in the country air at two of Spokane's many parks. On City Loop Drive, the **Finch Arboretum** (3404 W. Woodland Blvd., off Sunset Hwy., tel. 509/747–2894) is a mile-long stretch of green set along Garden Springs Creek. **Manito Park** (S. Grand Blvd., at 17th Ave., tel. 509/456–4331) is South Hill's expansive playland, with a rose garden, sailing pond, and conservatory, all impeccably kept. To get here, take Bus 2 from downtown.

Riverfront Park (507 N. Howard St., tel. 509/625–6600 or 800/336–PARK) is probably the first place any proud Spokane host takes a guest. Just north of the downtown area, Riverfront Park is the symbol of Spokane's moment of international glory—the park was built for the 1974 World's Exposition. Stroll the grounds and public market (open Wednesday–Sunday) and traverse the exhilarating Spokane Falls, around which the city was built. Although the word "park" usually conjures images of grassy hills and walkways, Riverfront Park is more of the amusement genre. Tourist facilities include a **gondola ride** over the falls, an IMAX four-story movie screen, a hand-carved, wooden **Looff Carousel**, and the carnival rides under the **U.S. Pavilion,** which becomes an ice-skating rink in winter. At night, check out the concert pavilion. Call the park for info on visiting and permanent attractions, prices, and show times. Cyclists from all over the country come to ride the **Centennial Trail**, a 41-mile multipurpose pathway that winds along the Spokane River.

Gonzaga University has put together a shrine containing Bing Crosby's Oscar and other relics in the Crosbyana Room of its Crosby Library (E. Boone St., tel. 509/328–4220). A short visit here and you'll be crooning "White Christmas" before you know it.

CHEAP THRILLS Spokane residents are always on the lookout for a new and better view of the sunset. From Riverside State Park (*see* Outdoor Activities, *below*), head west on Francis Avenue (Rte. 291), then north 4 miles on Indian Trail Road to the site of the **Indian Rock Paintings.** There are no signs, so ask for directions if you have trouble. Then hike into the hills for a spectacular view of the sunset along the Spokane River. **Cliff Park,** on a volcanic cone off 13th Avenue, affords another superb view of the setting sun.

AFTER DARK The downtown area, especially along Division Street near Riverside Avenue, abounds with small local taverns. If you only do one thing in Spokane, catch a movie at one of the city's historic movie theaters: **The Fox Theater** (1005 W. Sprague Ave., at Monroe St., tel. 509/624–0105) and the **Garland** (924 W. Garland Ave., tel. 509/327–1050) show first-run movies and charge $1.50 and $1 respectively. Call the **Arts Line** (tel. 509/747–ARTS) for information on indoor and outdoor theater, free readings, concerts, exhibitions, and shows.

Come nightfall, plant your butt on a stool at **Fort Spokane Brewery** (401 W. Spokane Falls Blvd., tel. 509/838–3809), across from Waterfront Park. This friendly downtown bar serves great microbrews (come for the subterranean brewery tour Monday–Saturday 10–6). A raucous, hard-drinking, college-age crowd gathers nightly at **The Viking** (1221 N. Stevens, tel. 509/326–2942) to guzzle, talk loudly, and generally act like Generation X. A nice, dark, predominantly gay and bi establishment, **Dempsey's Brass Rail** (909 W. 1st St., tel. 509/747–5362) has a restaurant/bar with plenty of single drinkers occupying its bottom floor, while upstairs is more lively with a dance floor, techno tunes, and Saturday Night Fever-style lighting. The vibe is friendly, and there's no cover. A more overtly gay bar, **J.S. Pumps** (415 N. Monroe St., tel. 509/352–9084) sometimes puts on drag shows and other forms of mischievous fun. Both women and men come here to drink, snack, and ogle each other.

OUTDOOR ACTIVITIES Spokane is ideally located for outdoor recreation, including fishing, cycling, camping, climbing, hiking, and horseback riding. The **Northwest Outdoor School** (tel. 509/255–5200) leads guided meadow hikes at Mount Spokane ($29), local mountain-climbing lessons ($75), introductory rock-climbing classes ($50), and a variety of backpacking instruction and guided hikes (around $125). The hills around Spokane are laced with trails, many of which wind around the shifting path of the Spokane River. **Riverside State Park** (Francis Ave./U.S. 291, tel. 509/456–3964), northwest of the city, has a paved trail that leads through a 17-million-year-old fossil forest site in Deep Creek Canyon, along with numerous other trails and picnic spots. Go to the state park office Wednesday–Friday for information on this and other trails. **49 Degrees North** (U.S. 395, tel. 509/935–6649), an hour away from Spokane, has night skiing; **Silver Mountain Ski Area** (tel. 208/756–9521), 90 minutes east in Idaho, has the world's longest gondola and is rumored to rival its southern Idaho counterpart, Sun Valley.

NEAR SPOKANE

COUER D'ALENE At the western extreme of Idaho, Coeur d'Alene (pronounced "Cortalane") is a teriffic day trip from Spokane. The pretty 33-mile drive east on I-90 passes Post Falls, Idaho, as well as a massive collection of factory outlets. If you make it to the **Greater Coeur d'Alene Convention and Visitor Bureau** (1st St. and Sherman Ave., tel. 208/664–0587) by 10 AM, you can hop on the red double-decker **Guided City Tour** (tel. 208/664–0587) bus for an hour-long historical tour ($5). Another leaves at 4 PM. When you get back from the tour, walk across the street to the longest floating boardwalk in the world. Or you can make the easy 1½-hour hike to woodsy **Tubb's Hill** (the trailhead is at the lake end of the municipal parking lot), or head down to the shops and restaurants on and around Sherman Street. If you want to stay the night, the

The least expensive place to park your car for the day in Coeur d'Alene is the municipal lot at Front Avenue and 3rd Street.

Flamingo Motel (718 Sherman Ave., tel. 800/955–2195) rents bungalows with kitchens for $35.50–$65.50 (price varies with the season).

There's one more reason to come to Coeur d'Alene: to tie the knot. Weddings are a big business here—with no blood test, no waiting, and no second thoughts—and chapels and extra-special bed-and-breakfasts cater to the starry-eyed honeymooners. Talk to the Convention and Visitor's Bureau (*see above*) for details. You just have to provide the spouse.

Coulee Dam National Recreation Area

It took 24 million tons of concrete and steel to stop the flow of the mighty Columbia River and to create the Grand Coulee Dam, the largest concrete structure in the world. Almost a mile long and twice the height of Niagara Falls, it is the world leader in the production of hydroelectric power. Behind the dam, Roosevelt Lake (actually a reservoir) was created—stretching first east and then north for 170 miles. In 1946, 150 of these miles and the land around them were designated the **Coulee Dam National Recreation Area.** Today this national park serves as a playground for all types of watersports. The area offers ample boating, fishing, sailing, waterskiing, hiking, and camping opportunities. For those seeking refuge from the masses, several free campgrounds are accessible only by boat or foot.

Built by President Roosevelt's Works Progress Administration, the dam has been smashingly successful in irrigating southeastern Washington's ailing agricultural dust bowl. At the same time, however, the Grand Coulee Dam has destroyed Native American fishing grounds that were important not only as a food source, but also as a source of the people's spiritual identity. Half of the dam was built on the Colville Tribal Reservation, and just recently the Colville tribe received restitution in excess of $75 million from the U.S. government.

Imagine Timothy Leary with a laser-powered Spirograph and you get an idea of the Grand Contacts Laser Show, the largest laser light show in the U.S. (the system cost $785,000).

BASICS Visitor's Arrival Center. *U.S. 155, just north of Grand Coulee, tel. 509/633–9265. Open May 28–July, daily 8:30 AM–11 PM; Aug., daily 8:30 AM–10:30 PM; Sept., daily 8:30 AM–9:30 PM.*

The **Grand Coulee Dam Area Chamber of Commerce** hands out the free and informative *Grand Coulee Dam Area Visitor's Guide. 306 Midway, off U.S. 155, next to Safeway, tel. 509/633–3074 or 800/268–5332. Open weekdays 8–1 and 2–5.*

COMING AND GOING To get to Grand Coulee from Spokane, take U.S. 2 to Route 174; or U.S. 2 to Route 155 from Wenatchee or Seattle. No public transit runs to Grand Coulee. To get around town in a hurry, call **C. B. Cab Co.** (tel. 509/633-3563).

WHERE TO SLEEP If you've come to see the dam, Grand Coulee City, five minutes away, is the closest place to stay. You'll shell out almost twice as much to be across the street from the dam. If your destination is the Coulee Dam National Recreation Area, stay in one of the motels that line U.S. 2, south of Roosevelt Lake (in Davenport or Wilbur) or to the east of the lake along Highway 25 (in Kettle Falls or Colville).

The friendly owner of **Center Lodge Motel** (508 Spokane Way, Grand Coulee City, tel. 509/633-0770) is more amenable to playing "let's make a deal" than most. Singles and doubles both go for $30-$35. Most of the big, air-conditioned rooms come with refrigerators and couches. Next door to the Center Lodge Motel, **The Umbrella Motel** (404 Spokane Way, tel. 509/633-1691) has smaller rooms that are equally stocked with the basic necessities. Rooms cost $25 for one person, plus $5 for each additional person. Across the street from the dam, **Ponderosa Motel** (10 Lincoln St., tel. 509/633-2100) has sunny rooms ($48-$64), a pool, and views of the dam laser show.

➤ **CAMPING** • Although the campgrounds in the southern recreation area are close to the dam and **Fort Spokane**, they are also busy and covered only with sagebrush and small shrubs. As you travel farther north up **Roosevelt Lake**, you'll find campsites that are more forested and less crowded. Exactly half of the 18 campgrounds in the National Recreation Area charge a $10 fee per-night; the other half, though not blessed with modern conveniences (e.g., flush toilets), are free. All sites are free between October 15 and May 15.

The two campgrounds in town, Canyon and Coulee Playland, are just crass mini-resorts.

FOOD The big establishments along U.S. 155 serve standard and unimaginative tourist fare, so try local spots instead. Near the dam, stop at the **Safeway** on Highway 155, or at **Good Deal Foods and Variety and Ed's Meats** (304 Mead Way, tel. 509/633-2202) for groceries and hot deli food. If you just want a cappuccino and a pastry, try **Beyond Expresso** (310 Mead Way, tel. 509/633-0847).

Serving moderately priced Chinese, Thai, and American food, **Sam Palace** (213 Main St., tel. 509/633-2921) is a good place to jolt your taste buds back to life. Come at lunch for $5 specials. **Flo's Place** (316 Spokane Way, 1 mi south of dam, tel. 509/633-3216), a funky little dive, offers friendly conversation and big portions of lumberjack food. Waffles are only $1.25, and omelets are $4.95 with hash browns and toast. **Stuck's Tavern** (122 Spokane Way, tel. 509/633-9815) is a dark bar with good food, darts, cheap beer ($1) and a laid-back, local atmosphere. Indulge in a huge Laboomba burger for $5.

NEAR GRAND COULEE

COLVILLE INDIAN RESERVATION Flanked by the Columbia River and Franklin Roosevelt Lake, the Colville Indian Reservation is one of the largest reservations in Washington. There are currently 7,700 enrolled members in the Colville Confederated Tribes (representing 11 bands). If you want to get a better understanding of frontier history, visit the free **Colville Confederated Tribes Museum and Gift Shop** (516 Birch St. tel. 509/633-0751), half a mile north of the dam via Highway 155. You'll see a sweat lodge, a tepee, historical displays, and native artifacts and artwork. Inquire here about tribal campgrounds and events, such as the **Annual Colville Confederated Tribes Pow Wow,** held on the Fourth of July weekend (and on the subsequent weekend in Nespelem, about 15 miles north of Coulee Dam). You're welcome to drive through the undeveloped, breathtaking landscape here and sleep at one of the **campgrounds**. You can't help notice the vast difference in the Native American land and the government-owned land on the other side: Except for a few highway signs, you'll feel like you've ambled onto a time-warped western frontier, while just miles away the dam puts on a million-dollar laser light show.

SUN LAKES STATE PARK About 30 miles south of the dam on Highway 17 is Sun Lakes State Park, a surreal reminder of the colossal power of nature. The highlight of the park is **Dry Falls** which, during the Pleistocene Era, was an enormous waterfall some 3½ miles wide and 400 feet high, carved out by huge ancient floods. Today, the sight of the waterfall skeleton and canyon beneath it is unforgettable. The park's Interpretive Center offers presentations on the area's geological history and a film about the great floods. *Hwy. 17, tel. 509/632–5214. Admission free. Open May–Sept., daily 10–6.*

REPUBLIC Less than an hour northeast of Grand Coulee Dam on Route 21, the town of Republic is a colorful gold mining and logging town, surrounded by the wilderness of the Okanogan and Colville National Forests. Come here from Grand Coulee and spend a night at the **Triangle J Ranch Hostel** (423 Old Kettle Falls Rd., tel. 509/775–3933), a great family ranch with a log bunkhouse with 14 beds ($10), tent sites ($6), and bed-and-breakfast rooms ($30–$40).

You could justify the trip to Republic alone with a visit to the **Stonerose Interpretive Center and Fossil Dig** (Clark St, at 6th St., tel. 509/755–2295), the source of the greatest variety of Eocene Fossils in the United States. Come early in the morning, pay $2.50, and they'll set you up with archaeological tools and a permit sticker. Head up the hill a few blocks to the site of an old lake bed and unearth 45-million-year-old fossils of plants, animals, and sea life. A curator is on site to inspect and interpret your fossil's age and origin.

VANCOUVER 9

By Marissa Levin

Vancouver welcomes the visitor like an ideal lover: with a rare and tantalizing mixture of cosmopolitanism, natural beauty, and wildness. A former logging town, port city, and railroad hub, Vancouver, the host of the 1986 World Exposition, symbolizes the rugged beauty and hearty individualism of the West, while keeping on the cutting edge of Canadian culture. No matter what time of year you visit, there is a healthy combination of urban and outdoor activities to keep you bemused. The warmer months mean lots of time in the great outdoors— swimming, lounging on the beach, waking up to crisp mountain mornings. Winters in Vancouver can be a bit of a wet blanket, but all the rain provides an easy excuse for visiting the city's excellent museums, restaurants, and cafés. Best of all, that annoying wet stuff translates into powdery snow at higher altitudes; some of the best skiing in North America lies only two hours away.

With half a million people, Vancouver is by far the largest city in the province, and is viewed by many Canadians as a hectic urban sprawl. Compared to Los Angeles or New York, however, Vancouver has a laid-back, peaceful rhythm. The one glaring exception was when Vancouver's hockey team, the Canucks, lost to the New York Rangers in game seven of the 1994 Stanley Cup Series. Who would have imagined rioting—police with tear gas, shattered glass, and more than a handful of injuries—in peaceful Vancouver? Since then, the city has slipped back into its less publicized, far more placid existence; Vancouverites still wave to each other on the street and thank their bus driver as they disembark.

Like the Inuit, who have several words for snow, Vancouverites have myriad colorful phrases for "It's raining," used in varying degrees of despair, depending on what month it is.

The only lingering sense of tension stems from a lack of unity; there's very little (besides the Canucks during a good season) that brings Vancouver together. While some minority groups— Chinese immigrants and the gay community, to name a few— have established strongly knit neighborhoods, urban Vancouver lacks a strong social fabric. And while locals sometimes interpret this as a harmful sort of separatism, it does provide Vancouver with a diversity and energy that you don't find in most Canadian cities. As a cluster of varied neighborhoods that caters to everyone from grungy anarchists to fashion-conscious yuppies, Vancouver is anything but homogenous. And one can only hope that in its search for identity, Vancouver won't lose one ounce of its character.

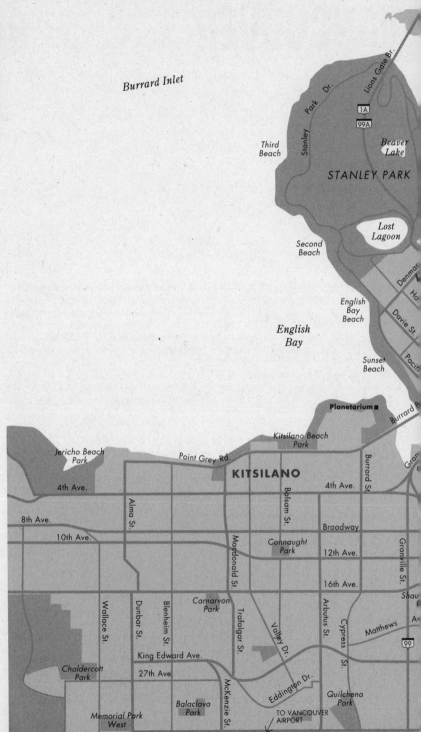

Burrard Inlet

Lions Gate Br.

Stanley Park Dr.

1A
99A

Third
Beach

Beaver
Lake

STANLEY PARK

Lost
Lagoon

Second
Beach

Denman

Ha.

English
Bay
Beach

Davie St.

English
Bay

Pacif

Sunset
Beach

Planetarium ■

Burrard R

Kitsilano Beach
Park

Jericho Beach
Park

Point Grey Rd.

Gran

Burrard St.

KITSILANO

4th Ave.

Alma St.

4th Ave.

Balsam St.

8th Ave.

Broadway

10th Ave.

Connaught
Park

12th Ave.

Macdonald St.

Granville St.

16th Ave.

Shau

Wallace St.

Dunbar St.

Blenheim St.

Carnarvon
Park

Trafalgar St.

Valley Dr.

Arbutus St.

Cypress St.

Matthews

A

99

King Edward Ave.

Chaldercott
Park

27th Ave.

McKenzie St.

Eddington Dr.

Quilchena
Park

Balaclava
Park

Memorial Park
West

TO VANCOUVER
AIRPORT

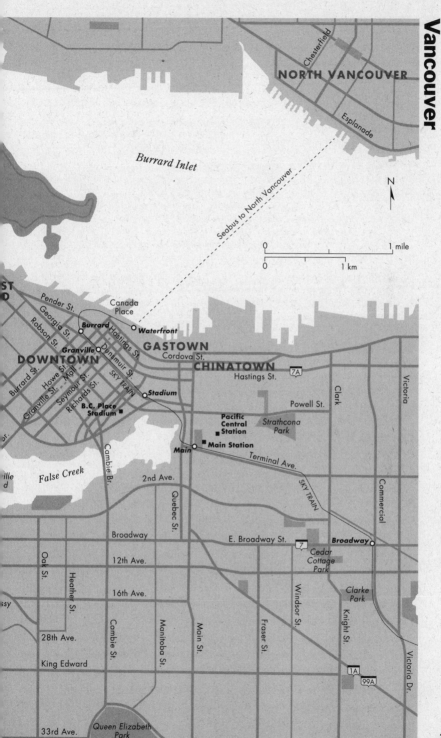

NORTH VANCOUVER

Chesterfield

Esplanade

Burrard Inlet

N

Seabus to North Vancouver

0   1 mile

0   1 km

Pender St.

Canada Place

Georgia St.

Robson St.

Burrard   Hastings St.

Waterfront

Granville   Dunsmuir St.

GASTOWN

Cordova St.

DOWNTOWN

Burrard St.

Howe St.

Granville St. — Mall

Seymour St.

Richards St.

SKY TRAIN

Stadium

B.C. Place Stadium

CHINATOWN

7A

Hastings St.

Powell St.

Clark

Victoria

Pacific Central Station

Strathcona Park

Main Station

Main

Terminal Ave.

Cambie Br.

False Creek

2nd Ave.

Quebec St.

SKY TRAIN

Broadway

E. Broadway St.

7

Broadway

Cedar Cottage Park

Commercial

12th Ave.

Oak St.

Heather St.

16th Ave.

Windsor St.

Clarke Park

Knight St.

28th Ave.

Cambie St.

Manitoba St.

Main St.

Fraser St.

King Edward

1A

99A

Victoria Dr.

33rd Ave.

Queen Elizabeth Park

Basics

AMERICAN EXPRESS AmEx has two downtown offices to deal with travel tickets, traveler's checks, and personal check-cashing. They'll hold mail for cardholders up to 30 days. *1040 W. Georgia St., tel. 604/669–2813; also on 4th floor of Bay Department Store, 674 Granville St., at Georgia St., tel. 604/687–7686. Both open weekdays 8:30–5:30, Sat. 10–4.*

LUGGAGE STORAGE Pacific Central Station (*see* Coming and Going By Train, *below*) has luggage lockers for C$1.50–C$2. The **airport** has 24-hour luggage lockers for C$1–C$4.

A good place to find general information on Vancouver's gay community is Little Sister's Bookstore (1221 Thurlow St., tel. 604/669–1753).

MAIL Vancouver's **main post office** accepts poste restante mail; the postal code is V6B 3P7. *349 W. Georgia St., tel. 604/662–5725. Open weekdays 8–5:30.*

MEDICAL AID The **Elizabeth Bagshaw Clinic** (3195 Granville St., Suite 40, tel. 604/736–7878) is an inexpensive women's clinic. Visits are by appointment only; if they don't have an opening, they'll refer you to someone else. You can also call the **Women's Health Collective** (tel. 604/736–5262) for referrals. If you're unable to pay for services, try **Pine Free Clinic** (1985 W. 4th St., tel. 604/736–2391). For prescriptions and all-purpose medical supplies, **Shopper's Drug Mart** (1125 Davie St., tel. 604/685–6445) is open 24 hours a day.

PHONES If you're at all familiar with the U.S. phone system, it should be a snap to let your fingers do the walking in Canada. Local calls usually cost 25¢—and the pay phones accept U.S. quarters, in addition to the Canadian sort. Aside from using your credit card, the most convenient way to make calls is to purchase a **BCTel phone card**, good for C$10 or C$25 worth of calls. Purchase cards at HI hostels and 7-Eleven convenience stores.

VISITOR INFORMATION The **Vancouver Travel InfoCentre** provides free maps, listings of accommodations, tons of glossy brochures, and info on the city and all of B.C. The InfoCentre also has a kiosk in the Pacific Centre Mall, at the corner of Granville and Georgia streets. *200 Burrard St., tel. 604/683–2000. Open daily 8–6.*

COMING AND GOING

BY PLANE **Vancouver International Airport** rests on an island about 14 kilometers (9 miles) south of downtown. Its small southern terminal handles flights to secondary destinations within the province. Airlines serving Vancouver International include **Air Canada** (tel. 604/688–5515), **Canadian Airlines** (tel. 604/279–6611), **American** (tel. 800/433–7300), **Continental** (tel. 800/525–0280), **Delta** (tel. 604/682–5933), **United** (tel. 800/241–6522), and **Horizon Air** (tel. 800/547–9308).

The **tourist information counter** on Level 3 provides tips on both lodging and transportation to outlying areas. **Bureaux de change** are located on either side of customs; automated machines

Run for the Border

If you're arriving by car from the United States and want your entrance into Canada to be any more memorable than crossing a state line, be sure to bring your own festive accoutrements. For most people, crossing the border is an anticlimax—U.S. citizens don't even need to show a passport as long as they can produce a driver's license (it's still a good idea to bring your passport, as some less-traveled crossing points do insist upon seeing it). Not only that, Canadian establishments accept U.S. money, although their exchange rates usually suck. You can avoid hassle and save serious bucks with a visit to any local bureau de change.

on Levels 2 and 3 take most major currencies. **ATMs** on Level 3 are connected to Interac, MasterCard, Cirrus, Circuit, Plus, and Visa. The Bank of America currency exchange, on Level 3, is open 6:30 AM–8:30 PM.

➢ **AIRPORT TRANSIT** • City buses and a shuttle service link the airport to downtown Vancouver; the drive takes 20–45 minutes, depending on the time of day. Your cheapest but least convenient option (you must transfer buses at least once) is **B.C. Transit** (tel. 604/261–5100), a municipal bus service that takes you to budget lodgings and downtown attractions for about C$1.50. To reach downtown, take B.C. Transit Bus 100 from Level 3 to Granville and 70th streets, then transfer to Bus 20 (be sure to ask the driver for a transfer when you buy your ticket). B.C. Transit buses leave from Level 3 every half hour between 5:30 AM and 12:30 AM and take 40–45 minutes. For a more convenient ride (no nasty transfers), pick up the **Vancouver Airporter** (tel. 604/244–9888) on Level 2. The service runs every 15 minutes 6:30 AM–9:30 PM, and then every 30 minutes until midnight. The shuttle stops at a number of major downtown hotels, but you can arrange to be dropped off at any downtown destination. One-way fare is C$9; it's C$15 for a round-trip ticket. A **taxi** ride downtown costs C$20–C$35.

BY CAR Vancouver is a three-hour, 226-kilometer (138-mile) drive north from Seattle along I–5, which becomes Route 99 at the U.S.–Canada border. Avoid border crossings during peak times: holiday weekends, Friday evenings, Saturday mornings, and Sunday afternoons and evenings. In other words, try to travel only when nobody else wants to. Route 1 (the Trans-Canada Highway) enters Vancouver from the east; driving time from Whistler on Route 99 is about two hours. From Hope on Route 1 it's about 1½ hours.

BY BUS Greyhound (1150 Station St., across from Main Skytrain Station, tel. 604/662–3222) is the most comprehensive bus line serving Vancouver. Destinations include Seattle (3½ hrs, C$25 one-way), Calgary (13 hrs, C$96 one-way), and some really long hauls like Toronto (67 hrs, C$279 one-way) and Whitehorse, Alaska (46 hrs, C$290 one-way). Ask at the ticket window for free maps and for the seven-day unlimited **Canada pass** (C$191). There's an ATM on the Plus, Interac, and Visa systems inside the terminal.

Quick Shuttle (tel. 604/244–3744) bus service runs between Vancouver and Seattle eight times a day. It'll pick you up at the Sandman Inn (180 W. Georgia St.) and drop you off in downtown Seattle or at the Seattle/Tacoma airport. Fares run C$26–C$33 one-way, C$47–C$60 round-trip.

Perimeter Transport (8695 Barnard St., tel. 604/266–5386) runs 1–4 buses a day between Vancouver and Whistler, from mid-November to the end of April (in other words, until the end of the ski season). From May to September shuttles leave twice daily, according to demand—be sure to reserve a seat in both directions. Prices run about C$26.75 one-way, plus tax. Buses depart from Level 2 of the Vancouver airport.

Pacific Coast Lines (tel. 604/662–8074) operates out of the Pacific Central Station (1150 Station St.), offering service between Vancouver and Victoria. Buses also leave from the Vancouver airport. The 3½-hour trip costs about C$21 one-way, and buses leave every 1–2 hours until 7 PM.

Maverick Coach Lines (tel. 604/662–8051) heads from Pacific Central Station (1150 Station St.) to Whistler (5 per day, 2½ hrs, C$13 one-way), Nanaimo on Vancouver Island (every 2 hrs, 3 hrs, C$17.50 one-way), Sechelt (3 per day, 2½ hrs, C$15 one-way), and Powell River (2 per day, 25½ hrs, C$25.50 one-way).

BY TRAIN Two major train lines operate out of Vancouver. **VIA Rail** serves most of British Columbia and mainland Canada; from Vancouver, it provides direct service to Jasper and Edmonton in Alberta, with connections to the rest of the country. **B.C. Rail,** departing from the North Shore, runs one line from Vancouver to Prince George via Whistler and Lillooet.

➢ **VIA RAIL** • The **Pacific Central Station**, which houses VIA Rail and various bus services, is next to the Main Street Skytrain station; from here you can catch several bus lines to downtown accommodations (10–20 minutes by foot). For more info on destinations and fares, stop by the InfoCentre (*see* Visitor Information, *above*) and pick up a VIA Rail guide. A valid student ID will get you a 10% discount on your ticket. *1150 Station St., tel. 604/669–3050 or 800/561–8630.*

➤ **BC RAIL** • The **B.C. Rail Station** sends trains to Prince George, with a stop in Whistler. The two-hour journey takes you past Howe Sound, a site so breathtaking that you'll wish you were stopping. Trains run daily between North Vancouver and Prince George from mid-June to mid-September and three times a week the rest of the year. Tickets cost about C$14 one-way. Daily trains also run year-round between North Vancouver and Lillooet, at the start of the Cariboo Gold Rush Trail. The station is open 6 AM–9 PM in the winter, 6:30 AM–9 PM in the summer. Tiny **lockers** are available for C$1 per day. *131 West 1st St., North Vancouver, tel. 604/631–3500 for fares and reservations or 604/631–3501 for departures and arrivals.*

BY FERRY Ferries connect the mainland with Vancouver Island, the Gulf Islands, the Queen Charlotte Islands, and other coastal destinations. **British Columbia Ferries** operates two major ferry terminals outside Vancouver: the **Tsawwassen** terminal and the **Horseshoe Bay** terminal. Call 604/277–0277 for 24-hour recorded info on B.C. Ferries, or talk to a live person (and make reservations) at 604/669–1211.

The **Tsawwassen** terminal, on Route 17 (off Route 1/Route 99), is an hour's drive from downtown. From here, ferries cruise the 38 kilometers (24 miles) to Victoria (on Vancouver Island) and through the Gulf Islands, a series of small isles between the mainland and Vancouver Island. Frequent ferries also travel to Nanaimo (on Vancouver Island) daily until 7 PM. Basic fare to Swartz Bay (on Vancouver Island) runs C$6.25 one-way. Bicycles cost an extra C$2.50; standard vehicles under 7 feet run about C$19 extra. Larger vehicles cost even more. To reach the ferry by city bus, catch Bus 601 South Delta from Bay 3 at the Burrard Station (corner of Dunsmuir and Burrard streets). Get off at the Ladner Exchange and take Bus 604 to the ferry terminal.

From the **Horseshoe Bay** terminal (tel. 604/277–0277), 30 minutes north of downtown on Route 1/Route 99, ferries sail a short distance up the coast and across to Nanaimo on Vancouver Island. Boats leave about every two hours from 6 AM to 10 PM; fares are the same as those listed above. To reach the terminal, catch the **Vancouver Blue Bus** marked HORSESHOE BAY TERMINAL from any stop on Georgia Street, in the downtown area.

HITCHHIKING If you want to go south, take the bus as far out on Granville or Oak streets as you can. Hitchhiking isn't allowed (as in it's illegal) on the east-bound Trans-Canada Highway (Route 1), so try catching a ride on one of the smaller highways. **Little Sister's Bookstore** (1221 Thurlow St., tel. 604/669–1753) has a make-shift ride-board; hostels are also a good place to hook up with drivers. If you do find a ride, remember that it can be a big, bad world out there—use your common sense.

GETTING AROUND

Although public transportation in Vancouver is easy and convenient, individual neighborhoods like Chinatown, Gastown, and downtown are best explored on foot. To see other areas such as UBC, Little Italy, or the North Shore, you'll have to rely on **B.C. Transit** buses and the **Skytrain,** a combination subway and commuter train that links the downtown core to the nearby city of New Westminster. The **Seabus,** a passenger-only ferry, connects Vancouver to North Vancouver.

Although some savvy locals may get away with riding free, visitors who don't know the system should buy a ticket: It'd be kind of humiliating to spend part of your vacation in the custody of the public transit police.

The city's major transportation hub is **Granville Street,** with a Skytrain station and stops for several bus lines. The **Waterfront Skytrain station** on West Cordova Street, down the street from the InfoCentre, also operates as a hub for buses. From the Seabus terminal on the North Shore, buses serve the entire North Shore area.

The **transit-information line** (tel. 604/261–5100) will tell you how to get to any specific address or location. If you have a car and intend to spend the day downtown, you may want to leave it in one of Vancouver's **Park 'n Ride** parking lots, which are specially designed for commuters. The closest one to downtown is on Hastings Street near the PNE (Pacific National Exhibition) site. In the morning, Bus 2 stops in front of the lot and takes you to downtown in about 20 minutes. If you park during the day, walk to nearby Arbutus Street and take Bus 14, which runs downtown about every 10 minutes. Make sure to pick up "Discover Vancouver on Transit" from the InfoCentre; it's packed with important information. You should also grab a bus schedule—they're free.

BY SUBWAY **Skytrain** (tel. 604/261–5100) is Vancouver's one-line, 22-kilometer (14-mile) rapid transit system. Trains leave about every five minutes from the Waterfront station, near Canada Place downtown, running underground through the downtown area and then above ground to New Westminster, southwest of Vancouver. You can buy tickets from machines at each station, or at convenience stores, and must carry them with you as proof of payment, since they also act as your transfer. Skytrain transfers can also be used for Seabus and B.C. Transit buses (*see below*), and vice versa. During rush hour (from the first bus to 9:30 AM and 3:30–6:30), tickets cost C$1.35 within one zone, C$2.75 for three zones. During non-peak hours the flat fare for all public transit is C$1.35. Trains run daily until 12:45 AM.

BY BUS You need exact change to ride the buses: C$1.50 for adults, 65¢ for senior citizens and children. Upon boarding the bus, you'll get a transfer that's good in that zone for up to 2 hours. Seldom will you find someone who actually knows what constitutes a zone, but if you've been on the bus for over 45 minutes, you're on your way to a two- to three-zone trip. Pick up a pamphlet that indicates destinations and their zones at the front of the bus. Books of 10 tickets are sold at convenience stores and newsstands: Look for a red-white-and-blue FARE DEALER sign. Day passes, good for unlimited travel after 9:30 AM, cost about C$3.50 for adults and are available from fare dealers and at any Seabus or Skytrain station.

BY SEABUS The **Seabus** is a 400-passenger commuter ferry that crosses Burrard Inlet between downtown and North Vancouver; it leaves from the foot of Lonsdale, a primarily residential area in North Vancouver. The ride takes 13 minutes and costs C$1.50 for adults, 65¢ for seniors and children. With a transfer, you can make connections with any B.C. Transit bus or Skytrain. Call **transit information** (tel. 604/261–5100) for details.

BY CITY FERRY The small city ferries that operate on False Creek offer a pleasant alternative to buses and trains. You can catch ferries at the following locations: the Arts Club Theater on Granville Island, the Aquatic Center at the north foot of the Burrard Bridge, the north foot of the Granville Bridge, the Maritime Museum, the False Creek Yacht Club, and B.C. Place at the old Expo site. For information call **Granville Island Ferries** (tel. 604/684–7781) or **Aquabus** (tel. 604/689–5858).

BY TAXI It's difficult to hail a cab in Vancouver. Unless you're near a hotel, you'll have better luck calling a taxi service. Try **Yellow Cab** (tel. 604/681–1111), **Black Top** (tel. 604/731–1111) or **Bonny's** (tel. 604/435–6655). Base fare is about C$2.10, plus C$1.10 for each additional kilometer. Late at night, when cab service changes from luxury to necessity, meters usually become obsolete, and drivers will barter over prices.

BY BIKE In typical West Coast fashion, the bicycle has come to replace the automobile for many environmentally conscious Vancouverites. Even drivers of big, gas-guzzling machines have a certain amount of respect for cyclists. Although the soggy Vancouver climate will hinder winter cycling, it's an ideal way to get around during the summer. Those with hard-won biker's calves will have a distinct advantage negotiating the hilly terrain. For more info *see* Outdoor Activities, *below*.

BY CAR **Rent-A-Wreck** offers rentals from C$35 per day (200 km free, then 15¢ per additional km). You must be at least 19 and have a major credit card. If you put on a great big smile, they may be willing to work out an unlimited mileage deal, depending on your destination. *180 W. Georgia St., in West End, tel. 604/688–0001; also 1085 Kingsway, tel. 604/876–7155. Open Apr.–Oct., weekdays 7–7 (Fri. until 8), Sat. and Sun. 8–5; Nov.–Mar., weekdays 7–6, Sat. 8–5, Sun. 9–3.*

Where to Sleep

In July and August, tour- ists swarm into town and hotels raise their prices about 20%—you'd better make reservations if you want a roof over your head. The rest of the year, when tourism wanes and hotels seek patronage, you'll have no problem finding a cheap place to stay on short notice.

Vancouver's cheap hotels tend to provide amenities like vibrating beds and black velvet paintings at no extra charge; they also offer a central but sleazy location, particularly in the districts of **Gastown, East Hastings St.** (a.k.a. Skid Row), and the **red-light district** (around the northern end of Granville, Seymour, and Richards streets). These prime locations provide easy access to nightlife (a prelude, some might say, to getting your money's worth out of the vibrating bed) and many of Vancouver's major sights, including Stanley Park, the Vancouver Art Gallery, and shop-lined Robson Street. Travel in pairs or groups when walking at night.

During lean tourist months, haggling for a cheaper room rate is perfectly acceptable— and looking impoverished may persuade the management to cut their prices.

The **YMCA** and **YWCA** are conveniently located and generally cleaner and more helpful, though maybe not as exciting as a downtown hotel. Student housing and youth hostels on the outskirts of town, also good budget options, offer the added bonus of easy parking (helpful if you have a car), beaches, and cycling opportunities. Check out the notice boards at the **University of British Columbia Housing Office** (2071 West Mall, tel. 604/822–2811) or the bulletin boards at the University Student Union for summer sublets of two weeks or longer. The dorms at **Simon Fraser University** in Burnaby lie in relatively quiet outlying areas that will do in a pinch.

B&Bs are a booming business in British Columbia. Several agencies have homes all over the province, including **Canada West Accommodations B&B Registry** (86607 N. Vancouver, Vancouver V7L 4L2, tel. 604/929–1424), **AAA Bed & Breakfast** (658 E. 29th Ave. Vancouver V5V 2R9, tel. 604/875–8888), and **AA Lesbian and Gay Accommodations of Canada** (tel. 604/873–2287). For a complete list, ask at the Vancouver Travel InfoCentre (*see* Tourist Information, *above*).

DOWNTOWN

Downtown, which encompasses most of the peninsula, offers the best access to the city's sights and nightlife. Rooms here cost a little more than in Gastown or on Hastings Street, but your safety is certainly worth it—mummy and daddy will sleep better. Most points of interest—including Gastown, Stanley Park, and the former site of the World Expo—are within walking distance.

Depending on the type of accommodation and the rate, a PHT (Provincial Hotel Tax) of 10% and/or the GST (Goods and Services Tax) of 7% can be added. Ask! Unless otherwise noted, you must add 17% tax to the prices listed.

➤ **UNDER C$15 • The Salvation Army.** Try this charitable organization only if you are male, desperately short on cash, and not particular about your company. Clean, institutional bunks in the dormitory cost C$9 a night. If you're genuinely hard up (i.e. absolutely broke) and they have space, they might put you up for free. Weekly rates start at C$85 per person. They start taking names at 5 PM and open the doors at 7 PM. You must leave by 7:45 AM the following morning. Don't abuse their generosity. *500 Dunsmuir St., V6B 1Y2, tel. 604/681–3406. From Stadium Skytrain station, go 4 blocks up Dunsmuir St. Guest capacity: 30. Curfew 11 PM. Wheelchair access.*

➤ **UNDER C$60 • Green Gables Bed and Breakfast.** Close to Chinatown, this quiet, comfortable B&B attracts lots of young travelers during the summer months. Carl owns the house, cooks, cleans, and desperately wants to share his knowledge of his favorite out-of-the-way spots. If there's a vacancy in one of his 7 rooms, jump at the chance. Singles cost a reasonable C$45, doubles C$59 (C$40 off-season). Don't come for the private baths—there aren't any. *628 Union St., tel. 604/253–6230. From downtown, Bus 22 to Princess and Prior Sts.; go north on Princess St., east on Union St.*

St. Regis Hotel. The clean and spacious rooms as this centrally located downtown hotel have aged a bit less gracefully than Liz Taylor—but without the multiple facelifts. Rooms cost around C$50 for one, C$60 for two. There's a C$5 charge for each additional guest. *602 Dunsmuir St., tel. 604/681–1135. From Granville St. Skytrain station, turn onto Dunsmuir St. 83 rooms. Luggage storage.*

YMCA. This aging YMCA building is smaller, older, and not as centrally located as its sister organization, a few blocks away. Still, rooms are clean, both men and women are welcome, and guests have full access to the fitness facilities. Singles cost C$33 (C$76 per week), doubles C$51. Rooms with TV sets are C$2 more, and there's a charge of C$7 for each extra person in the room. Add C$3 to the prices in summer, plus 10% PHT year-round. *955 Burrard St., tel. 604/681–0221. From Burrard St. Skytrain station, walk to cnr of Burrard and Barclay Sts. 111 rooms, none with bath. Midnight curfew. Laundry, storage lockers.*

➤ **UNDER C$70** • **Kingston Hotel.** This quaint bed-and-breakfast near the red-light district offers European-style shabbiness (much more savory than other varieties of shabby) and easy access to downtown attractions. The small bathrooms, one on each floor, are moderately clean. Compared to most hotels in the area, this is a great deal—especially for students, who get a 10% discount with an ISIC card or current school ID. Singles are C$40, doubles C$45–C$70, including a Continental breakfast. Rooms with private bath are C$12 more, and there's a C$10 fee to add an extra person. Try to make reservations at least a month in advance during July and August. *757 Richards St., tel. 604/684–9024. From Pacific Center Station, Bus 3 to Granville; walk 2 blocks to Richards St. 60 rooms, some with bath. Laundry facilities, luggage storage.*

Shaughnessy Village Bed & Breakfast Guest House. This thematically decorated conglomeration of cabins looks like it stepped out of *Something Wild.* Depending on who the other tenants happen to be during your stay (we're talking the Griswalds to the Bradys), you're either destined for a very exciting or incredibly cheesy experience. Singles are C$36–C$54, doubles C$49–C$69. *1125 W. 12th Ave., btw Granville and Oak Sts., tel. 604/736–5511. Take Bus 1 down Oak St. 240 rooms. Laundry facilities, balcony, fridge, color TV.*

YWCA. Clean, safe rooms and complete fitness facilities in the heart of downtown, within walking distance of Robson Street, Stanley Park, the art galleries, and Gastown. Women get lodging priority, but couples and families are welcome (single men can give it a try if they arrive in person—no guarantee). Rates range from C$46 for a single with hall bath to C$66 for a double (C$74 for a quintuple with hall bath); rooms with private bath are available for C$5–C$10 more. Add 10% PHT to all prices. *580 Burrard St., tel. 604/662–8188. Diagonal to Burrard St. Skytrain station. 169 rooms, some with bath. Kitchen facilities, laundry.*

ROBSON STREET

Vancouver's Robson Street was created as a way to link downtown to the West End, and make the city more "walkable." With almost as many shoe stores and sidewalk cafés as the Champs-Elysées, the street has actually attracted far more tourists than local walking commuters. When a tourist straggles into sight, most entrepreneurs hear the *ding!* of a cash register. If that *ding!* is music to your ears, then Robson Street (recently dubbed "Rodeo Drive North") should be your cup of tea. But expect to hear a particularly loud *ding!* when you're looking for a place to rest those sorry soles for the night. A tourist is a tourist is a tourist . . . .

The area south of Robson Street (around Granville and Richards streets) is sometimes known as the "red-light district." With good reason: Everything from theater to film to prostitution takes place here. While the area isn't exactly life-threatening, women may encounter some unpleasant verbal harassment—try to travel in groups. Despite the seedy atmosphere, cheap accommodations are rare. Your best bet is the **Nelson Place Hotel** (1006 Granville St., tel. 604/681–6341). Located in a grungy but fairly safe area, this 100-room hotel offers nondescript singles for C$45–C$50, and much larger, equally nondescript doubles for C$50–C$60. The most redeeming quality of this establishment is its convenient location: near bars, cinemas, and major bus lines. They've also got luggage storage, free parking, and wheelchair access. From the Pacific Central Station, take Bus 3 or 8; both stop directly in front of the hotel.

➤ **UNDER C$80** • **Barclay Hotel.** If you just gotta splurge, it don't get much better than this: a comfortable and elegant interior and a prime location, right in the center of some serious shopping action. Singles run about C$55, rooms with queen-size beds about C$70, and rooms with twin beds around C$80. For C$10, you can get an extra cot in the room. If you're coming in summer, reserve at least two months in advance. *1348 Robson St., tel. 604/688–8850. From Burrard St. Skytrain station, walk up Burrard to Robson and turn right. 85 rooms. Laundry, luggage storage.*

Tropicana Motor Inn. The only thing that could push this establishment beyond its already excessive level of tackiness (the pictures are bolted to the walls) would be Barry Manilow playing in the lounge downstairs. Sorry, no *Copa* this time around. All accommodations are one bedroom suites (with kitchenettes) that sleep two–four people for C$90. If the Tropicana is full, try the equally tacky **Riviera Motor Inn** (1431 Robson St., tel. 604/685–1301). *1361 Robson St., btw Jervis and Broughton Sts., tel. 604/687–6631. 74 rooms. Laundry, luggage storage, free parking, sauna, pool. Wheelchair access.*

GASTOWN

Gastown by day is a far different beast than Gastown by night. Between 6 PM and 9 PM (depending on the day), business owners pack up their personalized license plate holders and maple candies and head for home; they're replaced by a crowd that's anxious to live it up and knock a couple back. Safety in numbers is a good motto here—especially since lots of locals call the train tracks adjacent to Water Street home. The hotels in the area are safe and clean, but they're not particularly comfortable or cheap.

➤ **UNDER C$60** • **Chelsea Inn.** This brand new establishment is spotlessly clean and a real bargain, considering its high-rent location. None of the rooms have private baths, but the conscientious caretakers keep everything in good shape. They're out to make your stay a long and enjoyable one, and it shows. Singles are C$40, shared rooms C$25, doubles C$55. *33A W. Hastings St., at Abbot St., tel. 604/685–4243. 30 rooms, none with bath.*

Dominion Hotel. In the middle of all the action (lots of bands play in nearby bars), this brick building looks far more impressive from the outside than that it does from within. Nevertheless, it's a clean and safe—if somewhat worn—option. The bar below rocks until early in the morning so you may want to request a back room. A single or double with hall shower costs about C$45. Doubles with private shower are about C$55. Both rates include breakfast. They'll allow up to 4 people in some of the larger rooms, at C$10 per each additional person. In winter subtract C$5–C$10 from the prices. *210 Abbott St., tel. 604/681–6666. From Waterfront Skytrain station, walk east on Canada Place Way, turn right onto Abbott St. Free pick-up in summer from Greyhound/VIA Rail stations. 70 rooms, some with bath. Laundry, luggage storage.*

THE WEST END AND ENGLISH BAY

The prevalence of both the gay and elderly communities in this cohesive neighborhood creates an interesting balance between relaxation and hype. Trendy Davie and Denman streets foster a beach town atmosphere (the sound of crashing waves is real). The area has become a pricy one due to the popularity of Davie Street's out-of-control party scene, but there are still some bargains to be found.

➤ **UNDER C$65** • **Buchan Hotel.** Tucked into a quiet, tree-lined street in the West End, this neat old hotel is within easy walking distance of Robson Street, English Bay, and Stanley Park. Rooms are bright and clean, and the hotel has an Elizabethan flavor (i.e. you may want to look as presentable as possible when you arrive). Its ideal location and sedate appearance appeal to a middle-class clientele, so rates are a tad high. In summer, singles with baths cost C$60, doubles with bath are C$65; add C$5 for an additional person. Prices really take a dive here in the winter when singles go down to C$45 and doubles to C$55. *1906 Haro St., tel. 604/685–5354. 61 rooms, some with bath. From Burrard St. Skytrain station, walk to Haro St. and turn right. Laundry, luggage storage.*

➤ **UNDER C$85** • **Shato Inn.** Just around the corner from Denman Street, this small hotel offers spotless rooms and bathrooms, only five minutes from the beach. It's a bit pricy, so you won't find the usual troop of backpackers, but it is a wonderful place to catch up on some rest after a long, tiring day of lounging at the beach (poor baby). Singles run C$55–C$75, doubles C$65–C$85. Make reservations for summer visits. *1825 Comox St., tel. 604/681–8920. From downtown, Bus 3 from Robson St. to Denman and Comox Sts. 22 units, most with private bath. Wheelchair access.*

Sylvia Hotel. A stone's throw from the beach and conveniently located near English Bay, Stanley Park, and downtown, this ivy-covered hotel is the beloved site of the first cocktail bar in Vancouver. Rooms are large, clean, and extremely safe, although a little shabby furniture-wise. On the plus side, upper-level rooms have spectacular views. Singles and doubles run C$65–C$90 in the off-season; similar prices for triples make it a great deal for larger groups willing to share a room. There's a C$10 charge for each additional person. Reserve at least six months in advance for summer stays. *1154 Gilford St., tel. 604/681–9321. Bus 3 from downtown Robson St.; get off at Denman and Comox Sts. and walk 1 block west to Gilford St. 115 rooms. Laundromat across street.*

EAST HASTINGS STREET

Only a block away from touristy Gastown, East Hastings Street sees few out-of-towners. Given its affiliation with the drug and prostitution trades and the fact that it has been dubbed "skid-row," this shouldn't surprise anyone. Those who are especially brave (or poor) can find a few relatively clean, safe hotels, but no one should cruise around alone at night.

➤ **UNDER C$50** • **Heritage House Hotel.** Just south of Gastown, this hotel caters mainly to homosexual men, although everyone is welcome. On Thursday, Friday, and Saturday evenings, the hotel sponsors a drag show and sing-along karaoke parties in the bar downstairs—it can get a little noisy. Hall bathrooms are sometimes used for more than bathing (don't be surprised to find Vaseline jars in the showers), but private baths are available. Singles with bath are C$49, without C$39. Doubles are about C$50. Women traveling solo should probably head elsewhere. *455 Abbott St., tel. 604/685–7777. From Waterfront or Stadium Skytrain stations, walk up Hastings to Abbott St.; look for green awning. 110 rooms, some with bath. Laundry, luggage storage.*

Patricia Hotel. This hotel is in one of the worst parts of town, but buses stop right in front, for what it's worth. The lobby is a lot classier than the rooms. Most of the guests are monthly residents, but the fourth and fifth floors are reserved for nightly guests, mainly sailors and sports teams. Singles run C$32–C$49, doubles C$39–C$59. *403 E. Hastings St., tel. 604/255–4301. From train, bus, or Main St. Skytrain station, walk north on Main St., turn right on Hastings St. 195 rooms. Free parking.*

HOSTELS

HI Vancouver Youth Hostel. In a huge park near the UBC campus, this cheap sleep is a 20- to 30-minute bus ride from downtown Vancouver. When full, which is often, the hostel limits stays to three nights. Check in at 11 AM or you may wind up on a mattress on the floor, where you *really* don't want to be. Due to its enormous size and steady flow of traffic, the hostel is nowhere near clean. If you're hard up, you can exchange two hours of work for a free night in their dorms, which cost about C$14 a night for HI members (C$18 for non-members), including GST. Family rooms are C$2 extra per night. Cruise down to nearby Jericho Beach on one of their mountain bikes (C$18.50 per day). *1515 Discovery St., tel. 604/224–3208. From airport, Bus 100 to Granville and 70th Ave. Transfer to Bus 20 and get off at Granville and 4th Ave. Take Bus 4 to Discovery St. 285 beds, none with bath. Curfew 2 AM, lights-out 11 PM. Laundry facilities, luggage storage, kitchen access, sheet rental (C$1.50), free parking.*

Vincent's Backpackers Hostel. This backpacker's mecca, one of a chain of private hostels, is only one block from the Skytrain station, and a quick walk from downtown, Chinatown, and the VIA Rail/Greyhound station. The area sure is convenient, but it's not safe, especially for women. Rooms are old and worn, but a nice change from enormous dorm rooms. In summer, a dorm bunk is C$10, a single C$20, and a double C$25, tax included. There's a C$2 fee for non-members, or you can buy a membership for C$10. You can rent bikes for C$7 a day with a passport or C$30 deposit. The ride board downstairs is an excellent place to make travel connections on the backpacking circuit, or talk to Vincent himself—he's a veritable wellspring of budget-travel info. *927 Main St., tel. 604/682–2441. From Main St. Skytrain station, walk north and look for THE SOURCE sign. From airport, Bus 100 to Marine Dr.; transfer to Bus 3. 150 rooms, none with bath. Laundry facilities, luggage storage, kitchen access, sheet rental (C$2). No smoking, no credit cards.*

STUDENT HOUSING

Simon Fraser University. Vancouver's second-largest university, on gorgeous, isolated Burnaby Mountain, opens one hall to travelers during the summer; it's an inexpensive—but out of the way—option. The modern, well-maintained rooms are available to students, high-school groups, conferences, and families. Singles are C$18 without linen or housekeeping, C$32 with full service; doubles cost C$37. All rooms except the "bare bones" singles are subject to 15% tax (room tax plus GST). The commanding view of metropolitan Vancouver and the school's lush, peaceful setting almost compensates for the 45-minute bus ride downtown. *McTaggart Cown Hall, tel. 604/291–4503. From Metrotown Skytrain station, SFU Bus 144 to campus. 365 rooms, none with bath. Laundry facilities, luggage storage, kitchen access, free parking. Wheelchair access. Closed Sept.–Apr.*

University of British Columbia (UBC) Conference Centre. The center has a wide variety of rooms available, and prices vary accordingly. Totem Park Residence offers a bed in a single or double room with Continental breakfast for C$28 a person (with shared bathroom); the Place Vanier dorm has beds for C$20 per person. The monolithic Gage Towers, the only high rises on the UBC campus, contain hundreds of identical cubicles that house students in winter, and academics, tourists, and families in summer (when singles are almost always available). The halls are close to the beaches, and buses to downtown depart frequently from the Student Union Building next door. Singles with private bath are C$47. Full apartments, including kitchenette, living room, and private bath, are C$52–C$70. Call for reservations. *Walter Gage Residence, 5961 Student Union Blvd., tel. 604/822–1010. 1,422 rooms, some with bath. Luggage storage, laundry, kitchens (C$25). All but 50 suites closed Sept.–Apr.*

Vancouver School of Theology. Across the lawn from the UBC Conference Centre, this ponderous place looks like it should have a moat around it. The school is crammed with students during the winter but remains open to travelers year-round. Singles run about C$17 for students with ID (preferably the ISIC card), and C$30 for non-students; doubles are about C$44 for non-students and C$27 for students. Rooms and baths here are older, larger, and more worn—but cheaper—than at the conference center. *6000 Iona Dr., tel. 604/228–9031. From downtown, Bus 10 UBC to Student Union Building. In summer, 160 rooms, some with bath. Laundry facilities, luggage storage. Closed Christmas–Jan. 3.*

CAMPGROUNDS

Campgrounds in Vancouver are primarily private RV parks with only a few sites for tents. The **Travel InfoCentre** (*see* Tourist Information in Basics, *above*) supplies a parks map complete with a list of camping facilities. Most of the campsites are incredibly out of the way: With the cost of tent rental and other camping necessities, it's usually cheaper to just dorm it.

Capilano RV Park. This North Vancouver campground, under the Lion's Gate Bridge and next to a Native American reservation, charges C$16 a night. Partial hook-up runs C$21, full hook-up C$26. Add 7% GST to all prices. It's only a 15- to 20-minute walk to Stanley Park and downtown. Call for reservations. *295 Tomahawk Ave., on Vancouver side of Lion's Gate Bridge, tel. 604/987–4722. 15 camping sites, 193 RV sites. Laundry facilities, bathrooms.*

For people whose budget can only buy them a view of the stars, **Wreck Beach,** near UBC, is where people crash in summer months. Although (technically) it's not legal, their biggest problem is not the police but rather the sketchy characters that hang around the area. Inland, the bushes and back trails of **Stanley Park** may provide sufficient cover from the rain, but if safety is an issue, this isn't a great option. Try to avoid sleeping in train and bus stations or the airport: You may get rousted with unnecessary force. If you need a bath but can't pay for a room, take advantage of the free showers in the Student Union Building at UBC.

Food

If you have a little padding in your budget, definitely sample some of Vancouver's first-rate restaurants. Most are downtown in the West End, or along Broadway and Fourth Avenue in Kitsilano. The city boasts all kinds of eateries in all price ranges, but you'll find the best quality for your money at the cheap ethnic restaurants in **Chinatown, Little Italy,** and **Little India.** You can also find less common ethnic restaurants like Ukrainian, Salvadoran, Thai, and Native American scattered around the city.

Vancouver also offers zillions of picnic spots with exceptional scenery. Whether it's the field of a local high school or Stanley Park, if the sun is shining, the outdoors are without question the best surroundings for a relaxing meal. Most every corner is home to a mom-and-pop store that'll fix you up with bread and produce (though no booze). Safeway is the major supermarket of choice, and there are at least two in every district of the city. For those with slightly more expensive tastes, **Granville Island Market** and the **Lonsdale Quay Public Market** sell gourmet picnic fixings. If your accommodations have kitchen facilities, you can do some mighty fine cooking (perhaps a salmon fillet?) for a fairly reasonable price. During the summer, you can also get your hands on tons of tasty fresh fruit shipped in from the Okanagan region of Canada. When winter rolls around, don't expect to find affordable fruits or vegetables—it's cans of the Jolly Green Giant until April. Health food markets are new to these parts; they're often trendy and pricey.

Canadians are proud of their beer, and rightly so. Don't forget, this is the country that produced those classics of mid-1980s pop culture, the McKenzie Brothers.

Be sure to sample some of Canada's finest at one of the many microbreweries that have opened around the province. **Granville Island Brewery** (Cartwright St., tel. 604/688–9927) offers free tours (*see* Exploring, *below*). The alcoholic fruit ciders from the Okanagan region are excellent, especially cherry. Liquor laws in Canada are fairly strict; you can purchase alcohol only from government liquor stores or specially licensed beer and wine stores. Hours vary, but the government stores are generally not open at night or on weekends. Plan ahead. In case of late-night emergencies, you can purchase beer by the case from some pubs and bars. Most restaurants have liquor licenses, although some of the smaller family-run establishments don't.

KITSILANO

Kitsilano, or "Kits" to locals, extends from west 10th Street to the northern shore at Point Grey Road. This was once the center of the counterculture in Vancouver, but the poets and musicians have long since migrated to hipper, grungier climes; the area is now overrun by trendy shops selling bottles of organic oils to Vancouver's young professionals. Don't despair: Among the many expensive restaurants on the two main thoroughfares (West Fourth Avenue and Broadway, roughly between Alma and Vine streets) lurk a few budget joints.

➤ **UNDER C$5** • Benny's. A nice place to spend the afternoon, unless all the high schoolers from around the corner are out (or maybe that's your scene). Benny's plain bagels are 65¢ each, but you've gotta go for some of the interesting toppings. The Mex Bagel (C$4.25) comes with cheddar cheese, salsa, peppers, and avocado. *2505 W. Broadway, no phone. Open daily 8 AM–11 PM. Wheelchair access.*

Fine Wedge Pizza. This place is nothing more than a hole in the wall, but it sure serves a mean pizza for only 99¢ per slice. Expect a line at all hours. *3134 W. Broadway, no phone. Open daily 9 AM–3 AM. Wheelchair access.*

Fringe. Definitely the coolest hangout in the area. A few locals pass in and out for lunch, but at night—usually after 9 PM—it's packed with an alternative crowd that has remained loyal to the Kits area. While you're enjoying the Spinach Image (spinach salad with egg and mushrooms in a tangy balsamic vinegar and mustard dressing; C$4) or Damn It Jim (a tasty grilled cheese 'n' veggie sandwich; C$3.50), check out their vintage concert posters and the black and whites in the back room. *124 W. Broadway Ave., tel. 604/738-6977. Open Mon.–Sat. noon–2 AM, Sun. noon–midnight. Wheelchair access.*

Terron Bread. Pick up a fresh sandwich to go, or grab a loaf of one of their many kinds of breads and make your own. Mornings are very crowded. Sandwiches cost C$4, magnificent brownies C$2. *2380 W. 4th Ave., tel. 604/736-1838. Open Mon.–Thurs. 8–6, Fri. 8–6:30, Sat. 8:30–6, Sun. 8:30–5. Wheelchair access.*

➤ **UNDER C$10 • Calhoun's.** This converted warehouse is a great place to sit and veg or just chat with the locals—it's open 24 hours a day. The restaurant caters to just about everyone, serving everything from ice cream (C$1.50) to tortilla pie (C$4). Sandwiches are served on huge pieces of freshly-baked bread, and come with veggies and your choice of meat and cheese (C$4–C$5). Wash it all down with an imported or local beer. *3035 W. Broadway Ave., tel. 604/737-7062. Wheelchair access.*

Capers. The courtyard here makes for some serious people watching. The muffins (C$1.50) are baked fresh daily—as are many of the people who serve them. A tuna sandwich with a side salad goes for C$4.50; the black bean salad (C$2.95) makes a tasty meal. While the market next door is a bit pricy, it's one of the best-stocked health food stores in the city. Check the notice board in the market for rentals and other community info. *2285 W. 4th Ave., at Vine St., tel. 604/739-6676. Open weekdays 11–10, Sat. and Sun. 9 AM–10 PM; market open daily 7 AM–11 PM.*

Funky Armadillo. This place will blow your tapas off—and the drinks are good, too. For a tasty snack, try the spicy Nervous Onion Soup with melted cheese on top (C$3.50), or the bruschetta, a warm baguette with fresh tomato, virgin olive oil, and basil (C$3.50). All the pastas (C$7–C$9) are unique and filling, but don't expect any great dates with all the garlic. The bar attracts a pretty rowdy crowd after 9 PM, so come early if you want a mellow meal. *2741 W. 4th Ave., btw Stephens and MacDonalds Sts., tel. 604/739-8131. Open Mon.–Sat. 11 AM–2 AM, Sun. 10 AM–midnight. Wheelchair access.*

The Naam. If you're prone to late-night, tofu-burger attacks, you can rest easy: Vancouver's oldest alternative restaurant is now open 24 hours a day. The Naam has left its caffeine- and alcohol-free days behind, and now serves wine, beer, cappuccinos, and wicked chocolate desserts, along with its vegetarian stir-fries. Favorites include the Dragon Bowl (sautéed vegetables and tofu over rice; C$6.50) and the pan-fried potatoes with sesame seeds (C$2.25); the latter comes with a delicious miso gravy for an extra 75¢. And there's always the Naam burger (that's veggie patty to you) for C$5.50. *2724 W. 4th Ave., at Stephens St., tel. 604/738-7151. From Granville St., UBC Bus 4 or Dunbar Bus 7 to Stephens St.*

Simpatico. The best pizza in town is served at this hybrid Greek and Italian restaurant, decorated with Chianti bottles, blue-and-white checkered tablecloths, and portraits of Greek generals. The whole-wheat pizzas (C$7–C$12) are a great deal when split among two or three people. Also try the Greenpeace pizza, made with shrimp, oysters, and vegetables, or the Cannibal's Feast pizza, which comes with four meaty toppings and must be served on the other side of the room from the Greenpeace pizza to avoid unnecessary tension. *2222 W. 4th Ave., tel. 604/733-6824. Bus 4 or 7 to W. 4th Ave. and get off at Safeway stop near Vine St.*

Sophie's Cosmic Café. Sophie's collection of kitschy artifacts—including Miss Piggy and Curious George—overflows into this one-time hippie coffee shop. Filmmakers, politicians, and artists come here to munch on Sophie's middle eastern-style granola with yogurt and fresh fruit

(C$5.50). Eggs Benedict with homemade hollandaise sauce runs C$6. Although there's usually a line, Sophie's patrons are interesting enough; just kick back and enjoy the ride. *2095 W. 4th Ave., at Arbutus St., tel. 604/732–6810. UBC Bus 4 from Granville St. station, or Bus 7 Dunbar heading south. Open daily 8 AM–10 PM. Wheelchair access.*

LITTLE INDIA

Unless you are a big fan of Indian cuisine—or are interested in becoming one—Little India isn't the ultimate dining experience. The name "little" says it all. You will, however, find excellent, authentic Indian food from recipes that have most certainly been passed down through the generations. You'll know you've entered Little India (48th Street to 51st Street and Main Street) by the decorative emblems on the street lights that say PUNJABI MARKET in English and Arabic.

➤ **UNDER C$10** • **The Himalaya.** Don't be turned off by the lackluster, cafeterialike interior—the food is excellent. Order the huge buffet meal only if you're really hungry: For C$7 (lunch or dinner) you'll get salad, rice, and a number of curry dishes for both vegetarian and meat eaters—some darn spicy stuff. *6587 Main St., at 50th St., tel. 604/324–6514. From downtown, Fraser Bus 8 to 49th St. Open daily 10–9:30. Wheelchair access.*

Noor-Mahal. This place specializes in East Indian cuisine, serving up spicy and flavorful bargains. The ambiance, however, leaves something to be desired (it's hard for Formica to look anything but sterile). The C$6 *dosas* (crêpelike pancakes made with three types of flour and stuffed with curried whatnots) are yummy; vegetarians should try the hefty vegetarian version for C$9. You can choose medium, hot, or extra-hot seasonings to fire up your meal. *4354 Fraser St., at 28th Ave., tel. 604/873–9263. From downtown, Fraser Bus 8. Closed 3 weeks in Dec. Wheelchair access.*

GASTOWN

If you want value for your money, don't dine in Gastown. Head to nearby Chinatown or even downtown to avoid the tourist mark-up. If you do happen to collapse from low blood sugar at the feet of the "Gassman" statue itself, be selective.

➤ **UNDER C$5** • **Cottage Deli Soup and Sandwich.** A standard deli with a pleasant patio and views of the train yards and the mountains, this little restaurant serves a variety of sandwiches for around C$5. *205 Water St., tel. 604/688–0844. Open daily 10:30–3.*

➤ **UNDER C$10** • **Tomato Fresh Food Cafe.** Even non-tomato people will dig this vibrant 1947 diner (they do everything down to smoking the turkey on the premises). There are a number of non-tomato items on the menu (the house roasted turkey sandwich with cranberry sauce goes for about C$5) but the grilled-tomato, cheese, onion, pesto sandwich (C$7.25) is delicious. The fruit and vegetable juice bar serves healthy drinks for C$2.50–C$3.75. This place is also a great bet for your morning (and afternoon and evening) latte (C$2.75)—served in a brightly colored bowl fired by a neighborhood potter. *3305 Cambie St., at W. 17th St., tel. 604/874–6020. Open Tues.–Sat. 9 AM–10 PM, Sun. 9–3. Take-out open Mon.–Sat. 7:30–6:30.*

➤ **Under C$15** • **Only Seafood Café.** While the rest of the neighborhood has gone to s—, this neighborhood fixture—it's been in business for over 75 years—has remained what it has always been: a hole in the wall that serves up huge portions of fish 'n' chips and fried-fish steaks for C$7–C$11. *20 E. Hastings St., at Carroll St., tel. 604/681–6546. Open summer, daily 11–9; winter, weekdays 11–7:30, weekends until 9 PM.*

THE WEST END

This corner of downtown attracts a young, fashion-conscious crowd, and is a favorite gathering place of the gay community. Although Davie Street was once considered one of the sleazier parts of town, off-beat stores and restaurants have gradually crept into the area, making it an upscale, popular hangout. Plenty of inexpensive restaurants line Denman Street.

The far end of Davie and Denman streets, near their intersection at English Bay, is a great place to catch the ongoing fashion parade from a sidewalk café, or to get a bite after a bike ride in nearby Stanley Park.

➤ **UNDER C$5** • **Did's Pizza.** Come here for yummy pizza slices (C$3) served by young punksters with nose rings and lots of attitude. The quasi-cyberpunk decor and graffiti-covered walls attract hungry clubbers who pour out onto the sidewalk after the nightclubs close. *630 Davie St., tel. 604/689–8866. Wheelchair access. Open Mon.–Sat. noon–3 AM, Sun. noon–midnight.*

Elbow Room Coffee Shop. Attached to an old house, this tiny, bustling coffee shop serves good, hearty breakfasts all day long. You can get eggs any style, killer blueberry or apple-cinnamon pancakes (C$4.75), or regular lunch food (including cheeseburgers; C$5.25). You'll find that the gum-chewing, bouffant-bedecked waitresses adhere fairly rigorously to the sign on the wall: FOOD AND SERVICE IS OUR NAME, ABUSE IS OUR GAME. *720 Jervis St., a few blocks off Robson St., tel. 604/270–0647. Open weekdays 7:30–3:30, weekends 8:30–3:30. Wheelchair access.*

English Bay Bagelry. New Yorkers may not express such enthusiasm, but the bagels here knock the lox off the competition, hands down. The bagel breakfast (C$4) is a great deal; it comes with a two-egg cheese omelet, a bagel with cream cheese, and fruit salad. Sandwiches run about C$4, and a solo bagel with cream cheese costs C$2.10. Go crazy and try their inventive flavored cream cheeses on the supreme cheese-onion bagel. *1184 Denman St., #102, at cnr of Denman and Davie Sts., tel. 604/683–2846. Open daily 7 AM–11 PM ('til 2 AM in summer). Wheelchair access.*

Jump Start. If you can ignore all the health and fitness hype at this little shoebox of an establishment, it's a good place to pick up fat-free potato chips and healthy lasagna (C$4) for a picnic at English Bay. *965 Denman St., tel. 604/688–6833. Open Mon.–Sat. 9–7, Sun. 10–7. Wheelchair access.*

Pastameli. Unless you're lucky enough to get one of the few tables outside, this is definitely a "to go" operation. They make great hoagies (C$4.50) and deli sandwiches (served with pasta salad; C$4). If you're looking for a bigger meal try one of their pastas (around C$7.50). The oven-fresh pizza is made to order. *1120 Denman St., tel. 604/688-8182. Open daily 9 AM–midnight. Wheelchair access.*

Souvlaki Place. This little Greek joint near English Bay caters to people on the go—mostly hungry bike riders. Souvlaki is only C$4.25, and falafel and spanakopita each run about C$4. Keep in mind that you're paying for the food, not the service. *1181 Denman St., tel. 604/689-3064. Open daily 11–10:30. Wheelchair access.*

Whale. If you're fed up with hangover cures that involve greasy home fries, head to Whale: Their tasty fruit-and-vegetable drinks are a good cure for throbbing, don't-touch-me-or-I'll-yack headaches. Try the Whale Doctor, a filling concoction of apple, lemon, banana, and yogurt for C$3.50. Black bean, cucumber, and sprout sandwiches go for C$4.25. Everything is vegetarian. *1110 Denman St., tel. 604/669-7278. Open daily 8 AM–9:30 PM. Wheelchair access.*

➤ **UNDER C$10** • **Bud's.** Covered in Formica from top to bottom, this is not the ultimate resting stop. Ignore the grease-stained menus and concentrate on the large and tasty portions of fish 'n' chips. Two-piece cod or halibut dinners run C$8.25–C$9.50, and they have a good variety of beers and B.C. cider (C$3.50)—definitely worth sampling. *1007 Denman St., at Nelson St., tel. 604/683-0661. Open daily 11:30–9 (until 8 PM in winter). Wheelchair access.*

Clearwater Cafe. This trendy restaurant—complete with bleached-wood furniture and sponged walls—saves itself with a very atypical menu. The homemade royal sunflower paté (made with a vegetable base of sun-dried tomatoes, sunflower seeds, carrots, and sweet potatoes; C$6) is served with cucumber and red onion on grain toast. The Won Hoppers (C$9) are veggie wontons in tomato misu soup served with rice. *1030 Denman St., tel. 604/688-6264. Open Mon.–Sat. 10 AM–11 PM, Sun. 10:30–10. Wheelchair access.*

Doll and Penny's Café. The mannequins in drag above the entrance are beacons for this casual restaurant, which caters mainly to Vancouver's gay community. They offer huge Sunday brunches, great burgers for C$8, and pesto linguine for C$8.25. After the bars close at 2 AM, the café fills with patrons in search of a late-night snack. *1167 Davie St., tel. 604/685–3417. Open Mon.–Thurs. 8 AM–3 AM, Fri. and Sat. 8 AM–4 AM, Sun. 8 AM–1 AM. Wheelchair access.*

Hamburger Mary's. Whether it's 2 AM or 5 PM, this is a popular meeting spot for both gays and straights. Chatty servers dish up tasty appetizers like Coney Island fries (C$3.50) and spicy chicken wings (C$3.50) in a space that tries hard to look like a 1950s diner. Gourmet burgers go for about C$6; the apple pie is killer and well worth C$3. Move the party here after the bars have closed: Mary's serves booze into the wee hours. *1202 Davie St., at Bute St, tel. 604/687–1293. Open Mon.–Wed. 6 AM–3 AM, Thurs.–Sun. 6 AM–4 AM. Wheelchair access.*

Nonyu Baba. This simple, family-run restaurant serves excellent cuisine from Singapore on utilitarian Formica tables. Try the black-bean chicken (C$8) or Peranakim (curry) chicken (C$8)—both are damn spicy. The tofu with prawns is delicious. The Assam seafood soup is a house specialty. Wash it all down with jasmine tea. *1118 Davie St., near downtown, tel. 604/687–3398. Open weekdays 11:30–2:30 and 5–10:30, weekends 5 PM–10:30 PM.*

The Planet. Follow their invitation and "explore the ever evolving planet" via the superb, well-conceived menu. The chicken satay (grilled chicken on skewers; C$5.45) is delicious but dainty, while the jumbo-sized jambalaya (Cajun seafood stew with a tomato base; C$8.45) is simply filling. The bar sees some serious action on the weekends, and the bartenders usually put on a show when things seem like they might die down. On Sundays you can even groove to live music. *910 Granville St., tel. 604/257–6200. Open daily 11:30 AM–midnight (Fri. and Sat. until 1 AM). Wheelchair access.*

Stepho's. Near Nonyu Baba (*see above*), this popular restaurant offers huge portions of cheap Greek food, including lamb, beef, pork, chicken, or prawn souvlaki served with pilaf, potatoes, and Greek salad (C$8.50). A veggie pita sandwich runs C$4.25. The excellent tzatziki (yogurt and cucumber dip) costs C$3.75. The restaurant walls are laden with Metaxa bottles and posters of Greek antiquities. Plan on waiting in line for a table. *1124 Davie St., tel. 604/ 683–2555. Open daily 11:30–11:30. Wheelchair access.*

COMMERCIAL DRIVE

Now that there are more convertible Saabs in Kitsilano than throaty vintage Pontiacs, the people who prefer second hand clothes to $100 jeans have migrated to Commercial Drive, or "the Drive." This may look like a run-down forgotten part of town, but it's just a ploy to avoid another yuppie invasion. Besides the great number of Italian restaurants in **Little Italy** (on the Drive, between Venables and Broadway Sts.), there are plenty of good cafés where the lesbian community gathers; "Lesbian Avenger Recruitment Now" T-shirts are all the rage. To reach Commercial Drive, take Bus 20 (labeled VICTORIA) from downtown Granville Street. To return downtown, take the bus labeled GRANVILLE. The Broadway Skytrain station, on the corner of Broadway and Commercial, is about a 10-minute walk from most spots.

➤ **UNDER C$5 • Uprising Bread Bakery.** This small, co-op bakery just off Commercial Street makes amazing breads; the yeast-less, sourdough-pumpernickel is C$2.35 a loaf. They display an array of scones, muffins, and cookies in their tiny corner store, and also sell a few light lunch items. Awesome sandwiches (it's the yummy bread) cost around C$4, and quiche is about C$3. They'll give you 20% off day-old bread, but you have to ask. *1697 Venables St., off Commercial Dr., tel. 604/254–5635. From Hastings St. downtown, Victoria Bus 20. Open weekdays 8–6, Sat. 9–6. Wheelchair access.*

➤ **UNDER C$10 • Circling Dawn Organic Foods.** It's the only place in the city where you'll never have to wonder, "Is this organic?" A newly-renovated café in back boasts a deluxe juice and vegetable bar: Look no further for your wheatgrass fix (C$3). Fresh soup with bread runs C$3.50, and pancakes are C$5. If you're on the run, pick up fresh organic produce straight from the farm. It's a good place to meet fellow free spirits—a notice/ride board hangs in the corner in case you need your chakras balanced or a ride to the Dead show. *1045 Commercial Dr., at Napier St., tel. 604/255–2326. Open daily 10–9. Wheelchair access.*

La Quena Coffee House. Staffed by volunteers who work in exchange for a place to hold events and express progressive ideas, this non-profit restaurant serves primarily vegetarian Mexican and Latino food. A black-bean burrito costs C$6, à la carte burritos are C$4. Stir-fry on rice (C$5) is best washed down with *chai* (spiced Indian tea). The open, relaxed atmosphere makes it a good place to meet people, even if the interior is a bit shabby. The restaurant sponsors folk music and ongoing political events almost every night. *1111 Commercial Dr., 3 blocks south of Venables St., tel. 604/251–6626. Open daily 11–11; kitchen closes at 7 PM. Wheelchair access.*

Waa Zu Bee. The name definitely reflects the funky attitude at this eclectic hangout. Glittering mermaids on the walls look out on a crowd that's as diverse as the menu. If you're in the mood for spicy, try the ragin' Cajun catfish on a baguette (C$8). The brie-topped chicken (C$8) is slightly tamer, but just as good. *1622 Commercial Dr., tel. 604/253–5299. Open Mon.–Sat. 11:30 AM–1 AM, Sun. 11:30 AM–midnight. Wheelchair access.*

➤ **UNDER C$15** • **Spumante's Cafe.** Like most of the other Italian joints in Little Italy, this is strictly a family operation. It doesn't take too much imagination to picture Mama in the back yelling at Papa for making the linguini too wide. Not only is this food good, but the portions are so big they'd make the Pope cry. The price is a bit rich—the 38 different combo plates run C$9 for lunch and C$15 for dinner—but it's worth it. Try the smoked salmon bow-tie pasta in cognac and cream sauce with prawns (C$14.95 at dinner). All combo plates come with a pasta and entrée. Pasta, salads, and soups can be ordered à la carte. *1736 Commercial Dr., tel. 604/253–8899. Open Tues.–Fri. 11:30–2:30 and 5–10, Sat. 5–10. Wheelchair access.*

ROBSON STREET

Most of the restaurants in this tourist-only part of the city deserve nothing more than a shrug (and maybe a chuckle). Still, keep your eyes open: In between the T-shirt stands and shoe stores there are some worthwhile bargains to be found.

➤ **UNDER C$5** • **Bagel Street Cafe.** The bagels here are good, but they're lots better with stuff on 'em. The veggie (C$3.50) and tuna (C$4) melts are filling, while the brie and blueberry bagel (C$3.50) is perfect for your sweet tooth. *1090 Robson St., tel. 604/688–6063. Open Mon.–Sat 8 AM–11 PM, Sun. 9 AM–11 PM. Wheelchair access.*

Bread Garden. Check out the scene and enjoy java and baked goods at this 24-hour, cafeteria-style café. Peanut butter-chocolate chip cookies are C$1, and great big Rice Krispies treats are C$1.50. *812 Bute St., at Robson St., tel. 604/688–3213. Wheelchair access.*

Ezogiku. If you can ignore the sterility of this restaurant (it sorta feels like a giant bathroom), the big bowls of Ramen are absolutely incredible. Over 30 different kinds of Ramen dishes are prepared, and most cost about C$5. *1329 Robson St., no phone. Open daily 11–11. Wheelchair access.*

Pizzarico's. Come meet Ross the pizza god (he's the owner) and listen to him engage absolutely everyone in conversation while you enjoy a fat slice of basic cheese (C$3) or a daily special like Cajun chicken (C$4). *766 Robson St., across from Eaton's, tel. 604/669–2900. Open weekdays 7:30 AM–10 PM, Sat. 11–10. Wheelchair access.*

➤ **UNDER C$10** • **Allium.** The minute you walk in, the yellow sponged walls and floral prints make you feel like you've entered the secret garden. Most everything on the menu includes an ingredient from the allium family (garlic and its relatives). Try the homemade soup and quiche combo for C$5, or a sandwich on homemade grain bread for C$4. The great big raspberry scones (C$2.50) are delicious. *1885 Commercial Dr., tel. 604/253–4224. Open Mon.–Sat. 10–5. Wheelchair access.*

Cactus Club Cafe. This restaurant in the heart of Tourist Land attracts a lot of attention with its loud disco tunes, full bar, and gorgeous staff. You'll have so much fun that the food is sure to taste a bit better than it really is—they hope. There's a burger—beef, chicken or veggie (C$6.50–C$7)—for everyone, but make sure to save room for some Elvis Ice Cream Pie—a heavenly mocha-Kahlua-Oreo concoction for C$5 a slice. *1136 Robson St., tel. 604/687–3278. Open Mon.–Sat. 11:30 AM–1 AM, Sun. 11:30 AM–midnight. Wheelchair access.*

Mongolia Grill. Choose the ingredients (seafood, vegetables, and everything in between) and then let them turn up the heat (you specify hot, medium, or mild). They'll weigh what you've chosen, cook it to your specification, and toss it over steamed rice for a healthy, filling meal. Vegetarians get 20% off. *818 Thurlow St., 2 doors from Robson St., tel. 604/683–8834. Open daily 11–11. Wheelchair access.*

GRANVILLE ISLAND

Granville Island houses a ton of fine restaurants that you could blow all your money on. A better choice is to eat reasonably at the cafeteria at the **Emily Carr School of Art and Design** (1399 Johnson St., tel. 604/844–3800), where you can get a full meal for under C$5. To appreciate the alternative flavor of the island's gastronomic elements, hit the **public market** and put together a picnic, or buy a hot dish at one of the many stands. The options are virtually unlimited, ranging from natural peanut butters to fresh tortellini. Even if you don't buy anything, you might enjoy just wandering around and checking out the interesting food; it's truly a feast for the senses.

➢ **UNDER C$10** • **Isadora's Cooperative Restaurant.** This cooperatively-owned, non-profit restaurant serves up healthy lunches and dinners with some quirky combinations of ingredients. Try a salmon-fillet burger (C$6.50) or a West Coast salad (C$7), and tackle a slice of rhubarb pie (C$3) for dessert. *1540 Old Bridge St., next to theater, tel. 604/681–3748. Open weekdays 7–11 and 11:30–9, weekends 9–9. Wheelchair access.*

Dessert and Coffeehouses

What do a group of women debating the future of the information highway have in common with two men discussing the diaper of choice? All of this chit-chat, arguing, and exchanging of ideas is most likely going on within one of the zillions (and that's putting it lightly) of cafés around Vancouver. As is true with most North American cities, the rapid influx of java joints has sent both the conference room and bar scene into hibernation.

Cafe Calabria. Step off Commercial Drive and into this Old Country coffee bar, complete with a groaning copper espresso machine and a plaster replica of Michelangelo's *David* wrapped in a flag from the homeland. Italian tourist posters, movie star photos, and handful of regulars round out the picture and provide the perfect atmosphere for an aromatic espresso or frothy cappuccino (C$1.25–C$2.25). *1745 Commercial Dr., tel. 604/253–7017. Open daily 8 AM–midnight. Wheelchair access.*

Coffee Klatch. If the buzz of tourists on Robson Street is beginning to make your head spin, walk that extra block toward Stanley Park to this mellow spot. Sip a latte (C$2.10) and pull yourself together. *1319 Robson St., tel. 604/689–2899. Open daily 6:30 AM–midnight.*

Crumbles. Although coffeehouses are a dime a dozen in these here parts, the comfy atmosphere at Crumbles—both inside and out on the sidewalk patio—makes for several quality hang-out hours. If fat-free muffins (C$1) give you the creeps, they also serve a number of pasta salads (C$3.25) and sandwiches (around C$4). *1001 Denman St., tel. 604/683–8640. Open weekdays 7 AM–midnight, weekends 7:30 AM–midnight. Wheelchair access.*

Delaney's. Most popular with the area's gay crowd, this new addition to caféville serves up one of the best lattes (C$2.05) around. For a splurge, try the pecan caramel cake (C$3). *1105 Denman St., at English Bay, tel. 604/662–3344. Open daily 6 AM–midnight.*

The Edge. Come here to find out what's up in the gay community. Along with a number of other spots along this strip of Davie Street, this café is big with late-night partyers on their way back from events like Phallic Phridays at Celebrities (*see* After Dark, *below*). *1148 Davie St., tel. 604/689–4742. Open weekdays 6 AM–4 AM, weekends 24 hours.*

Lost Cafe. Located in the midst of corporate Vancouver, this tiny café—it's about the size of a freight elevator—appears lost in all the downtown shuffle. The same can be said for most of the patrons (you'll know you're here by the line of mountain bikes and skateboards parked out front). Try any of the sandwiches (about C$4), served on sourdough bread so fresh that it sticks to the roof of your mouth. *3-732 Davie St., tel. 604/662–8767. Open daily 11 AM–midnight.*

Not Just Desserts. Welcome to sin city. This dessert and coffee place may serve meals, but why eat real food when there are seven kinds of killer cheesecake (C$4 per slice) to sample. A piece of their gargantuan double-chocolate fudge cake (C$4.25) can satisfy four people, or two if you want to stay awake for the next week. They also serve alcoholic coffees and espresso drinks. *1635 E. Broadway, 1 block from Broadway Skytrain station, tel. 604/877–1313. Open Mon.–Thurs. 10 AM–midnight, Fri. and Sat. 10 AM–1:30 AM. Wheelchair access.*

Exploring Vancouver

If you're only in Vancouver for a few days, you'd be wise to restrict your explorations to the downtown core, even though you'll miss some of the more eclectic neighborhoods and most of the outdoor activities. Even without a whole lotta time, a thorough downtown visit will give you Stanley Park, the Vancouver Art Gallery, Chinatown, Gastown, The West End, and Robson Street—all of which are within reasonable walking distance. You don't have to go too far out of your way—just a short ferry ride across False Creek or a bus ride up Granville Street—to add artsy and avant-garde Granville Island to your agenda.

One of the major sights outside the downtown core, the University of British Columbia (UBC) sits on a huge preserve called The University Endowment Lands. Here you'll find the excellent Museum of Anthropology, several gardens and beaches, and lots of student culture (cafés, restaurants, bookstores) on nearby streets. North Vancouver, across the Burrard Inlet, has a few points of interest that are often missed by the average tourist—don't let the hassle of the commute get in your way. Finally, areas like Commercial Drive and Kitsilano are not so much tourist attractions as diverse neighborhoods that provide a respite from the beaten path (plus some excellent shopping opportunities). When weather permits, explore the core of the city on foot or by bike; for a tour of outlying areas you'll need to take public transit—unless you're in training for the American Gladiators.

Because weeks can go by without one ray of sunshine during the winter, locals become slaves to Apollo during the summer.

Worth Seeing

B.C. PLACE Looking back, it seems appropriate that the theme of Vancouver's Expo '86 was transportation. A majority of the 20 million visitors came, saw, and then went just as quickly as they arrived. Today the main site of the Expo has been turned into an urban residential area named the **Plaza of Nations.** The outdoor amphitheater occasionally hosts special events, but other than these random occurrences, there's only one worthwhile reason to visit—the brightly lit white orb suspended on the horizon. That giant golf ball is actually the **Omnimax Theater,** now part of **Science World** (1455 Quebec St., tel. 604/687–7832), a science museum that's pretty darn cool. If you happen to be a science star, the exhibits may be a bit elementary (they're geared towards children); but most of them are informative, interesting, and entertaining. And no matter who you are or what your interests, the 27-meter, spherical screen will blow your mind.

Adjacent to the Plaza of Nations you'll find **B.C. Place Stadium** (777 S. Pacific Blvd., tel. 604/661–7373). Home to Vancouver's professional football team, the B.C. Lions, this air-supported, domed stadium is affectionately referred to as "the marshmallow in bondage." Most big name bands that come through town play here. For schedules and tickets, contact Ticketmaster at 604/280–4444. If you're a real sports buff, head over to the **B.C. Sports Hall of**

Downtown Vancouver

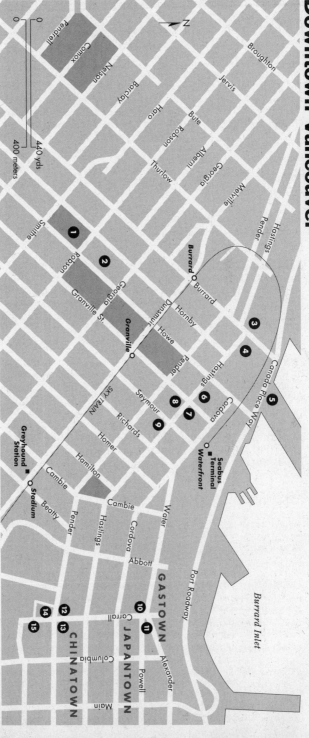

While you're at the stadium, take a look at the memorial to Terry Fox. He lost his leg to cancer and still managed to run 5,342 kilometers (3,339 miles) across Canada (he died before completing the trip) to raise money for medical research. You'll find the monument on the west side of the stadium at Robson and Beatty streets.

Fame (Gate A inside the stadium, tel. 604/687–5520) for some firsthand info on the province's finest athletes.

CANADA PLACE Originally built as the off-site pavilion for Expo '86, this massive structure rests just ½ kilometer (⅓ mile) from B.C. Place. Both are easily accessed via Skytrain (Canada Place is next door to the Waterfront Station). The extreme design mimics Sydney's Opera House with its peaked fabric-roof representing sails (if you didn't get the ship theme, just smile and nod). On a sunny day, walking around on the "deck" is a pleasant way to take in spectacular views of the harbor and the North Shore—if you can see pasts the hordes of tourists doing the same.

The same building houses the **CINEMAX Theater** (tel. 604/ 682–4629 or 604/682–6422 for box office), which shows special IMAX movies created for its five-story screen. Its flat, square screen doesn't give the viewer the same sensation of motion as the Omnimax at Science World (*see above*), but if you've never seen a five-story movie (they're sometimes shown in 3-D), it might be worth the admission price just to check it out. The theater is located at the north end of Canada Place.

CHINATOWN You'll know you're in Chinatown when you encounter old Chinese men yelling out the prices of their fresh fruits and vegetables, and butchers brutally hacking at raw meat in the shop windows. The elegant Chinese dragons over the lampposts beginning at East Hastings Street and Main Street are another good indication that you've arrived. Vancouver's Chinatown took off after an influx of Chinese immigrants came to Canada as railway workers in the early 20th century. Today it's the third largest Chinatown in North America (behind San Francisco and New York). An afternoon stroll in this area offers an eye-opening look at a racially diverse Vancouver that you might otherwise miss.

Breeze through the numerous herbal shops and discount porcelain stores that center around Pender and Keifer streets, or spend some worthwhile time at the **Dr. Sun Yat-Sen Classical Garden** (578 Carroll St., at Pender St., tel. 604/689–7133)—the

Take a moment at the Dr. Sun Yat-Sen Classical Garden to consider whether or not you're actually a butterfly dreaming you're a person—or just enjoy the most peaceful spot in all of Chinatown.

first authentic classical garden built outside China. If the spiritual history behind the structures and vegetation interests you, there are several guided tours given daily through the garden. Tai chi classes are offered weekly (call for schedules). Otherwise, just sit and enjoy the (hopefully) sunny day. Admission runs C$4.50 (C$3 students). While you're in the neighborhood, check out the **Sam Kee Building** (8 W. Pender St.), recognized by Ripley's Believe it or Not! as the narrowest structure in the world. When the city confiscated Chang Toy's land in 1913 in order to widen a city street, Mr. Toy demonstrated his anger by actually building on the remaining six feet. The building measures six feet by 100 feet on the outside—only 4 feet, 10 inches on the inside. Try fitting your queen-size bed into that baby!

GASTOWN During the mid-1800s, "Gassy" Jack Deighton (named for his fast talking—honestly) opened the first saloon pub in Vancouver. For many years it was one of the slimiest sections in the city until the town transformed Jack's old stomping grounds into a commercial and tourist area in 1971. Gastown's action centers on **Water Street,** at the end of which you'll find a statue of old Gassy himself. The brick buildings and old-fashioned lampposts give the street a rustic quality, but there's not much to see and do; the area is only a few blocks long and easily managed on foot as part of a day's meanderings. Scattered amongst the usual tourist traps are a few galleries and some surprisingly funky and esoteric shops (*see* Shopping, *below*). Check them out during the day: After dark the area fills with leering neighborhood drunks.

GRANVILLE ISLAND Originally a tidal mud flat, this once-small area was built up to its present size when the city dredged nearby False Creek and dumped the debris on the island. An

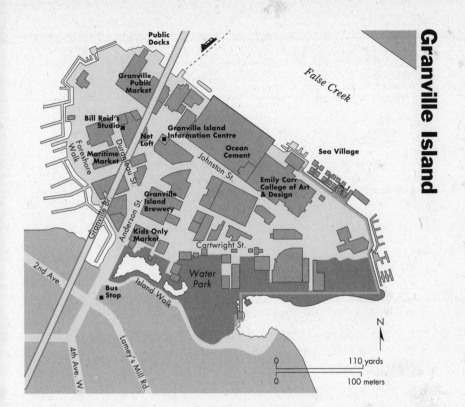

Public
Docks

Granville
Public
Market

False Creek

Bill Reid's
Studio

Granville Island
Information Centre

Net
Loft

Foreshore
Walk

Maritime
Market

Duranleau St.

Johnston St.

Ocean
Cement

Sea Village

Granville Br.

Anderson St.

Granville
Island
Brewery

Emily Carr
College of Art
& Design

Kids Only
Market

Cartwright St.

2nd Ave.

Island Walk

Water
Park

Bus
Stop

N

4th Ave. W.

Lamey's Mill Rd.

0   110 yards
0   100 meters

unsightly jumble of tin warehouses, cranes, and logging-industry leftovers occupied the area until 1971, when the federal government bought the island with plans to build a public market and artisans' studios, and to instigate various marine activities. With the opening of the public market in 1979, the industrial wasteland was imaginatively and artistically transformed into a cultural center and popular restaurant and shopping area. City workers painted the rusty tin with vibrant hues of yellow, blue, and red, and the docks now house passenger ferries instead of logging boats. Although the touristy and artificial parts of Granville may far surpass the average person's tolerance for plastic and neon, tourists and locals are still drawn to the island by the market, the theater, and several quality restaurants.

To get a general feel for the island, head down Cartwright Street past a number of different galleries and shops. The owners are warm and friendly even though it's obvious that few people have come to actually buy. Cartwright Street meets Johnston Street at the **Emily Carr College of Art and Design** (1399 Johnston St., tel. 604/687–2345), which looks more like a playground than a college. If school isn't in session, peak through the windows and into their enormous studio spaces. Keep going up Johnson Street and you'll find your way to the **Granville Island Public Market**. Although it's pricey, the food looks so good that you can enjoy the aesthetics without actually eating (yeah, right). They have everything from fresh produce to kick ass Cajun chicken, and the crowds are always fun to watch. Across the street from the public market you'll find the **Granville Island Information Center** (1592 Johnston St., tel. 604/666–5784). Stop here for college tours and all your information needs.

Walk in the door of the nearby **Granville Island Brewery** (tel. 604/688–9927) as a prelude to a stroll (or stagger) along the coast. The brewery, started in 1894, produces an unpasteurized natural beer available only in British Columbia. Half-hour brewery tours run twice a day during the summer at one and three. Tours and post-tour beer sampling—score!—are both free.

Those interested in Native American art will undoubtedly want to stop by the studio of Haida artist **Bill Reid** (behind Blackberry Books in the Net Loft shopping complex). The most respected and renowned carver in the province, Reid is responsible for several impressive works around the city (*see* Vancouver Public Aquarium and the UBC Museum of Anthropology, *below*). Although you can't visit the studio, you can view his work through its large windows. There are also a number of interesting (though often overpriced) shops in this complex.

From Granville Island, consider taking a stroll or bike ride along the **False Creek seawall,** which is easily accessible from the island. The path starts behind the water park and follows the creek east. You can also ride or walk west from the island to **Vanier Park** and **Kits Beach.**

Parking is free for up to three hours on the island, but it's scarce on weekends. Avoid the indoor garages, which can charge a hefty fee. Other transport options include ferries from the downtown Aquatic center (at the south end of Thurlow Street) or from Vanier Park (call Granville Island Ferries, tel. 604/684–7781)—both cost under C$2. False Creek Bus 50 from Gastown or downtown will deposit you about a five-minute walk from the island. If you want to go right to the island itself, take a UBC, Granville, Arbutus, or Oak bus from downtown to Granville and Broadway; ask for a transfer and then switch to Granville Island Bus 51.

THE LOOKOUT! AT HARBOUR CENTER Swallow your pride and engage in one of the cheesiest experiences that Vancouver has to offer. Pay the steep admission price and you'll get a 167-meter (553-foot) ride to the top of Harbour Center on the glass-enclosed elevator, plus a spectacular 360° view of Vancouver. Admission, good all day, includes a 12-minute slide show letting you in on what it's really like to live in such a gorgeous—and soggy—place. The slide show isn't worth pulling yourself away from the view for; nor is dining at the Revolving Restaurant. *555 W. Hastings St., tel. 604/689–0421. Admission: C$5.75, C$3.75 students. Hours vary, depending on weather; call for schedules.*

ROBSON SQUARE No matter where you wander in Vancouver, you'll wind up at Robson Square sooner or later. That was the intent Vancouver architect Arthur Erickson (designer of the Museum of Anthropology), who designed the square as a gathering place for the city. The complex contains the Vancouver Art Gallery and Erickson's concrete-and-glass structure, which replaced the old court buildings in 1981. Although Erickson's structure comes across as extremely modern, he put a lot of effort into preserving the fundamental elements of the former building. In the square, you'll also find government offices, the law court, a food fair, and an outdoor ice-skating rink (on Robson St. between Hornby and Howe Sts.). The hangout factor is pretty high here; there's usually a preponderance of vendors on the sidewalk peddling their wares—most often silvery jewelry and T-shirts.

STANLEY PARK Give your tired tootsies a break and collapse at will on this 1,000-acre wooded park, complete with beaches, Douglas fir and cedar forests, and spectacular views. Best of all it's all only a few blocks from the downtown core. Officially established in 1889 and named after Lord Stanley (then Governor-General of Canada), Stanley Park is the city's giant playground, where children and adults alike come to let loose and enjoy Vancouver's beauty.

Loads of walking and biking trails criss-cross the virtually pristine forests that comprise a large section of the park. In other areas, you can find rolling lawns, gardens, and recreational facilities. The 9-kilometer (5½-mile) **seawall promenade** is ideal for walking, biking, or roller-skating; it starts at the foot of Georgia Street and runs along the circumference of the park. On the way you'll pass a replica of the figurehead of the SS *Empress of Japan,* a trading vessel that sailed between Vancouver and Asia. It's about as interesting as it sounds, even if it is a good navigational tool. Nearby you'll find **Lumberman's Arch,** a huge archway dedicated to Vancouver's lumberjacks, and the Vancouver Public Aquarium (*see below*). The crowded **Children's Zoo** and miniature railway are open daily 10–5, admission free.

If you keep walking along the seawall, it continues under the Lions Gate (or First Narrows) Bridge to **Prospect Point,** which offers an excellent view of the North Shore Mountains. The promenade passes Second Beach, First Beach (*see* Beaches, *below*), and finally culminates at English Bay Beach and the West End neighborhood. It would take you a long time to explore the park completely on foot but it's a great way to spend a day if you have some extra time and want to work off a few of those excess meals. If the walking idea doesn't thrill you, biking is an enjoyable and feasible alternative. Be careful, though—in-line skaters tend to think the path belongs to them.

Lost Lagoon, at the entrance to the park, provides a home for several species of the Canadian goose and the extremely rare Trumpeter swan. As you travel east, you'll pass **Deadman's Island,** a former burial ground for local Salish Native Americans, now used as a naval training base (hmmm . . .). Take the obligatory picture at the nearby cluster of totem poles. The **Brockton Oval,** a cinder running track, has hot showers for those in need—you know who you are. The park and facilities are open to everyone during the day, but many people call the park "home" at night. Be cautious.

Vehicle traffic in Stanley Park goes one-way. Beach Drive to the west becomes Park Drive heading north and continues all the way along the seawall path. That means if you're driving and you miss your turn-off, you have to go the entire way around the park to get back. Although parking is plentiful it's really not necessary unless you're arriving with lots of equipment for a major picnic or baseball game. The **information booth** in the parking lot (near the park entrance on Georgia Street) gives out free maps, as do the bike-rental places. During the summer, you can take a city bus around the perimeter of the park, so keep your transfer.

➤ **VANCOUVER PUBLIC AQUARIUM** • One of Vancouver's most popular tourist attractions draws crowds of visitors to its daily orca and beluga whale shows. Schedules are posted outside the aquarium. One of the coolest aspects of this place, the humid **Amazon Rain Forest Gallery,** lets you walk through a rain forest environment, complete with piranhas, giant cockroaches, alligators, tropical birds, and jungle vegetation. There's also a display of the underwater life of coastal British Columbia—a tad depressing if you think about the conditions under which these animals live. That—and the steep admission price—may inspire you to get your views of beluga whales and harbor seals in their natural habitat, on your way to Vancouver Island. The bronze statue of a killer whale in front of the aquarium was donated by the B.C. artist, Bill Reid, whose most famous statue is in the Museum of Anthropology at UBC. *In Stanley Park, tel. 604/682–1118. Admission: C$8. Open summer, daily 10–8; winter, daily 10–5:30. Wheelchair access.*

UNIVERSITY OF BRITISH COLUMBIA The province's largest university, UBC sits on a huge piece of land at the most western point of the city. The campus is easily accessible to beaches, gardens, and a wonderful museum; it's definitely worth the 20-minute bus ride from downtown. Even if museums aren't usually your thing, make an exception for the **UBC Museum of Anthropology** (*see* Museums and Galleries, *below*), with its huge collection of Native American artifacts, and the **UBC Botanical Garden** (*see* Parks and Gardens, *below*), which contains a Japanese garden and an Alpine garden, among others. After viewing the museum, head just south of the building to Beach Trail 4, which leads out of Point Grey. There's usually a lot of activity on the point around sunset, including drumming circles and dancing. Although these are informal gatherings among friends, most people are eager to receive newcomers. The view is spectacular.

Several bus lines run from the city center to the university, so distance shouldn't deter you from visiting. All buses stop in front of the Student Union Building, which contains a cafeteria, a student lounge, bulletin boards (probably the best place in the city to find rides and sublets), and **The Pit,** the extremely popular student pub (*see* After Dark, *below*). Take either Bus 4 or Bus 10 from downtown Granville Street, or Bus 31 from the Broadway Skytrain station. The campus is quite large and spread out, though, so it's much easier to explore by car or bike.

YALETOWN Although this area, centered on Cambie Street between Richards and Bently streets, may be suffering from the Kitsilano syndrome (yuppies! yuppies! yuppies!), the art scene keeps the neighborhood as down to earth as possible. If contemporary art turns you on, this is the area to find it: Galleries display everything from Chihouly glass to Motherwell oils. A number of local artists' studios are also in the area. To get here, take the Skytrain to Stadium Station and walk down Cambie Street. Otherwise, take Fraser Bus 8 down Main Street and get off on Cambie Street.

Museums and Galleries

Museums and galleries dot the entire greater Vancouver area. Specialty museums, such as the **B.C. Sugar Museum** (123 Rogers St., tel. 604/253–1131) or the **Capilano Fish Hatchery** (Capilano Regional Park, off Capilano Rd., tel. 604/666–1790), may interest those eccentric few; if that's you, pick up the *Where* guide from the InfoCentre for complete listings. There are also a number of private galleries in the area that show contemporary, avant-garde works. Many of these are located on the 1000 block of Cambie Street, and in the heart of downtown between Howe and Broughton streets, north of Robson Street. The **Buschlen Mowatt Gallery** (1445 W. Georgia St., btw. Nicola and Broughton Sts., tel. 604/682–1234) has a great collection of contemporary artists including Sam Francis and Helen Frankenthaler. Galleries make a good—and free—way to get your dose of visual art; museum admission fees can get steep, even with a student discount. Try going on free or discount days. Call the **Arts Hotline** (tel. 604/684–ARTS) for info.

CANADIAN CRAFT MUSEUM For art with a practical twist, check out the wonderful furniture, dishes, and a number of other homespun crafts on display here. The building itself is worth a look, even if you couldn't care less about what's inside. *639 Hornby St., behind Cathedral Pl., tel. 604/687–8266. Admission: C$2.50, C$1.50 students. Open Mon.–Sat. 9:30–5:30, Sun. noon–5.*

ROEDDE HOUSE MUSEUM Notable B.C. architect Francis Rattenbury—designer of the Vancouver Art Gallery and the Parliament Buildings in Victoria—really hit home with this Victorian house, designed for Mr. Roedde, the first bookbinder in Vancouver. Luckily, the Roedde House Preservation Society has protected this house and the Barclay Heritage Square upon which it sits. It's convenient to Robson Street, so stop by and take a look. *1415 Barclay St., at Broughton St., tel. 604/684–7040. From Robson St., walk a few blocks to Barclay St., or take Robson Bus 3. Open Mon., Wed., Fri. 10–5. Wheelchair access.*

SCIENCE WORLD When you first saw the movie *Big* didn't you want to date—or at least befriend—Tom Hanks? Well, the giant keyboard at this mostly hands-on museum is probably the closest you're ever gonna get. Although Science World may sound like a purgatory of incomprehensible little symbols and bad-smelling fluids, it's not. Housed in the gigantic geodesic dome built for Expo '86, the museum is devoted to giving visitors a variety of tangible science experiences. While most exhibits and performances are aimed primarily at children, big kids—and that means you—will also enjoy losing their shadow, blowing giant bubbles, and picking up rocks that glow in the dark. The upstairs **Omnimax Theater** (*see* B.C. Place in Worth Seeing, *above*), the museum, and the building itself are unforgettable. Parking is pretty steep, but you should be able to find free spaces along nearby streets. *1455 Québec St., at Terminal Ave., tel. 604/268–6363. Skytrain to Science World/Main St. Admission to Science World and Omnimax: C$8–C$17, depending on number of Omnimax movies you see. Open daily 10–5 (until 7 in summer).*

UBC MUSEUM OF ANTHROPOLOGY Even if you're just walking past, the intensely imaginative Museum of Anthropology building will immediately pique your interest. Vancouver architect Arthur Erickson, who also designed Robson Square and the Law Courts, created a wonderful balance between the concrete-and-glass structure and the surrounding nature. Inside, you'll find incredible exhibits on architectural design and Northwest Coast First Nation art. The **Great Hall** contains totem poles, dug-out canoes, and various ceremonial bowls and dishes embellished with imaginative representations of Pacific Northwest wildlife. The placement of the totem poles illustrates the contrasting northern and southern carving styles, while the giant glass window behind the display allows you to experience the exhibit as though you stumbled upon these masterpieces in their natural setting. The displays have all been carefully designed, so pay close attention not only to what you're seeing but also to how the experience of each gallery differs. (Some are very open and exposed while others may make you feel like you're all alone, creeping around a store after closing time.) Oftentimes,

Come on Tuesdays when the UBC Museum of Anthropology is open late (until 9 PM) and admission is free, and enjoy a beautiful sunset and some good rhythms.

there are people hanging out in front of the museum at Point Grey Cliffs, drumming and dancing. *6393 N.W. Marine Dr., on UBC Campus, tel. 604/822–3825. Admission: C$4, C$2 students; free Tues. Open daily 11–5 (Tues. until 9); closed Mon. in winter.*

VANCOUVER ART GALLERY In a neoclassical building at one end of Robson Square, the Vancouver Art Gallery is something of a city gathering place: People loll around on the steps and lawns before, after, or instead of viewing the exhibitions. The gallery features rotating displays of painting, sculpture, photography, video, and graphic arts, plus a permanent collection of works that span four centuries. You won't want to miss the wing that contains many of the best works by Emily Carr, one of Canada's most famous artists. *750 Hornby St., tel. 604/682–5621. Admission: C$5, C$2.50 students. Open Mon.–Sat. 10–5 (Thurs. until 9), Sun. and holidays noon–5.*

VANCOUVER MARITIME MUSEUM You can learn a lot—perhaps a bit more than you'd want—about the history of Vancouver's port and the marine activity of British Columbia in this maritime museum. Just outside the museum, the *St. Roch,* the R.C.M.P. vessel that made the first trip through the Arctic Northwest Passage (in both directions), is open to the public. Nearby **Heritage Harbor** contains several restored sailing vessels that you can explore—inside and out. *1905 Ogden Ave., in Vanier Park, tel. 604/257–8300. Admission: C$5, C$2.50 students. From downtown, take Bus 22 or a Granville Island ferry. Open Oct.–Apr., Tues.–Sun. 10–5.*

VANCOUVER MUSEUM If you have some time—and a hefty chunk of money—you may want to check this place out. With an emphasis on Vancouver's history, and the art and culture of the region's native peoples, the museum's collection consists largely of reconstructed displays of everyday life, from a Victorian parlor to a trading post. If you've been to the Royal British Columbia Museum in Victoria, you might find it a little disappointing in comparison. Still, the temporary exhibitions that pass through here are usually worthwhile. *1100 Chestnut St., in Vanier Park, tel. 604/736–4431 or 604/736–7736 for exhibition info. From downtown, take Bus 22. Admission: C$7.50, C$3.75 students. Open spring–fall, daily 10–9; winter, Mon.–Sat. 10–5.*

Parks and Gardens

Even in the biggest metropolitan area in British Columbia, Mother Nature still carries a bit of clout. It would be near impossible to ignore the massive mountain views and lush vegetation, so Vancouver has made a point of incorporating as many natural escapes into the urban fabric as possible. You'll recognize this effort in the city's numerous parks and gardens—you'd have to be color blind to miss all the green. Those frolicking in Vancouver's recreational areas shouldn't be surprised to end up in the middle of a rather messy sloshball game or ultimate Frisbee tournament; Vancouverites tend to leave their big-city attitudes at home.

PACIFIC SPIRIT PARK This 100-acre park, generally called the **University Endowment Lands** by locals, is a relatively wild haven only 15 minutes from downtown Vancouver. Over 50 kilometers (31 miles) of trails offer excellent opportunities for hiking, biking, and horseback riding through stands of trembling Aspen and old-growth fir and cedar forests. Amenities are few, but you will find toilets (whew!) and park maps. To reach the park, take Bus 4 or 10 from downtown to the UBC bus loop, then walk across campus to Southwest Marine Drive, past Point Grey and the botanical gardens.

QUEEN ELIZABETH PARK The ingenious plan to transform two former stone quarries into spectacular ornamental gardens has created spectacular views and a great place to hang. Along with some really fascinating (and beautiful) gardens, there are lots of grassy, sloping lawns and the **Civic Arboretum,** a living museum of trees and shrubs indigenous to the coastal region. The park is a fair distance from downtown, but garden lovers will find the trip well worth it. Although the park itself is free, the domed **Bloedel Conservatory,** in the middle of the park, is not. Those who shell out the entrance fee will be rewarded by an interesting and well-presented display of exotic plant and animal life in a desert environment. Come on a rainy day and feel like you're outside and dry at the same time: The conservatory offers a 360 degree view of the surrounding area. *33rd Ave., at Cambie St., tel. 604/872–5513. From Granville* and Robson Sts., Cambie Bus 15. Conservatory admission: C$3, C$1.50 students. Open spring–fall, weekdays 9–8, weekends 10–9; winter, weekdays 9–5, weekends 10–5.

STANLEY PARK This huge park offers beaches, forests, trails, views, and outdoor activities in a refreshing expanse of green—right near downtown (see Worth Seeing, above).

UBC BOTANICAL GARDEN Regardless of how you feel about gardens, the UBC Botanical Garden deserves at least a browse. More likely than not, they'll suck you in for at least an hour or two. Although the Nitobe Memorial Japanese Garden (see below) is the main attraction here, the **E. H. Longbrunner Alpine Garden** is also worth a visit. The Alpine Garden, located at the base of Thunderbird Stadium, covers 2.5 acres and displays mountain flora from most parts of the world. For info and maps, go to the Botanical Garden office (6501 N.W. Marine Dr., tel. 604/822–9666), near the Nitobe Memorial Garden. 6250 Stadium Rd., btw 16th Ave. and S.W. Marine Dr., tel. 604/822–9666. From downtown, Bus 10 or 41. Admission: C$4, C$3 students. Combined admission with Nitobe: C$5.25, C$4 students. Open daily 10–6.

➤ **NITOBE MEMORIAL GARDEN** • Across the road from the UBC Museum of Anthropology sits this serene Japanese garden dedicated to Japanese educator, scholar, publicist, and diplomat Dr. Inazo Nitobe. Although considered the most authentic Japanese garden outside Japan, the Nitobe Garden nonetheless exhibits telltale signs of its Pacific Northwest roots (no pun intended): The Japanese landscaper used many indigenous trees and shrubs, which he trained and pruned according to Japanese tradition. In one corner of the garden sits an authentic **Tea Garden** and **Tea House** used for the Tea Ceremony—a must-see if you're interested in Japanese tradi-

The circular walk around the Nitobe Garden is said by some to represent man's journey through life; to others, it's just a circular walk around a garden.

tion. If not, this is still a great place to calm your travel nerves. 1903 West Mall, UBC, tel. 604/228–4208. Admission: C$2.25. Open daily 10–dusk; closed weekends in winter. Wheelchair access.

VAN DUSEN BOTANICAL GARDEN This golf course-cum-garden houses one of the most comprehensive collections of ornamental plants in Canada. Come in springtime to see the flowers at their peak. Hard-core plant/landscaping types will love this 55-acre park, but others may decide that the C$4.50 entrance fee is a bit too steep. If the fee is holding you back, free tours are given Sunday at 2, or by reservation. Admission is half price October–March. Most of the garden is wheelchair accessible. 5251 Oak St., at 37th Ave., tel. 604/266–7194. From downtown, Oak St. Bus 17 to 37th Ave.

VANIER PARK This grassy park has an excellent view of downtown and the West End, and is prime kite-flying terrain: treeless and vast. A few minuscule beaches line the west end. Even if the rain destroys your plans for a relaxing day in the park—which it probably will—the **H. R. MacMillan Planetarium** (1100 Chestnut St., tel. 604/736–3656) is reason enough to visit. Check out a laser show on the 20-meter dome for a guaranteed escape from reality. Call for show times; prices depend on the performance. Next to the main building, the **Gordon Southam Observatory** has a Zeiss refractor telescope that lets you see the stars, moon, planets, and galaxies. Obvious fact: It works especially well when it's not raining. Both the Planetarium and Observatory are wheelchair accessible. If you still have time, be sure to check out the Maritime Museum and the Vancouver Museum (see Museums and Galleries, above), also located in the park.

Beaches

For a big city, Vancouver offers an amazing number and variety of beaches. An almost continuous string of beaches runs from Stanley Park to UBC, some of which are only a few steps from the city core, while others are fairly secluded. Hardy Canadians and foolhardy tourists alike withstand the icy water just for a skinny-dipping/hypothermia story to tell 'round the campfire. Unfortunately, nowadays they're also telling a lot of stories about nearly being swept away in an oil slick. The pollution can get especially bad at **Wreck Beach** and **English Bay**; call the Parks Department of the City of Vancouver to get the scoop on the latest conditions (tel.

604/257–8400). Logging debris does wash up on the sand rather frequently, which can mean loads of entertainment for the kids and infinite frustration for beach-loving environmentalists.

Vancouver's main bathing beaches (Wreck Beach excluded) have lifeguards from Victoria Day to Labor Day, daily 11:30–9. Note that liquor is prohibited in parks and on beaches (except, it seems, at Wreck Beach—those who choose to hang out here tend to ignore most rules anyway). All beaches are free and usually have nearby bathhouses that are surprisingly clean.

While the beaches listed below are the most well-known and best-equipped in Vancouver, there's an especially nice spot at **Ambleside Park** in West Vancouver, across the Lions Gate Bridge. The gay scene is particularly hopping here. Take any "West Vancouver" bus (except during rush hour, when restrictions apply); call West Vancouver Transit (tel. 604/985–7777) for more info.

KITSILANO BEACH Often referred to simply as Kits Beach, this is the place to go for the stereotypical West Coast beach scene: scantily clad and well-toned people on a never-ending quest to check out all the other scantily clad and well-toned types. It's by far the busiest beach and its proximity to several restaurants and pubs makes it a real party spot. As you head toward Vanier Park, it quiets down some. Facilities include tennis courts, a playground, and a huge, heated saltwater pool that is usually filled with children getting an early start on their Kits beach social skills.

POINT GREY BEACHES If you start at the end of Point Grey Road and travel west towards the University of British Columbia, you will hit, in succession, **Jericho Beach, Locarno Beach,** and **Spanish Banks.** All have both sandy and grassy areas which become progressively less crowded as you head farther west. Spanish Banks is generally considered the most mellow of the Vancouver Beaches. Jericho Beach, adjacent to a huge park and a youth hostel, is a favorite gathering place for volleyball players and ultimate Frisbee fanatics—sometimes they organize tournaments. Point Grey Road offers some good bike-riding terrain. Bus-goers can take the UBC Bus 4 from downtown. Get off at any stop after Burrard Street and walk down any street to the right (west), and you'll be sure to hit the shore. The farther down 4th Street you go, the more remote the beach.

WRECK BEACH If you continue walking along the beach just past Point Grey (site of the Museum of Anthropology), you'll hit Wreck Beach, Vancouver's unofficial nude beach: Nude bathing is technically illegal but the police have decided to ignore these less-than-threatening lawbreakers. To reach the beach, most people climb down the cliff from Marine Drive at UBC. The beach isn't marked, so look for a bike rack and people at the top of the stairs.

Come to Wreck Beach if you're especially open-minded, or especially nude.

A lot of people make Wreck Beach their home. Some peddle an obscenely large array of wares, including soft drinks, pizza, English trifle, falafel, and various smokable substances. Others have set up stands for massage or hair braiding. The atmosphere is generally peaceful and non-threatening, assuming you don't feel threatened by nude peddlers. Although most people are mature and cool about all the nakedness, women often complain of "spectators" and the rather slimy men who call this place home. Be careful not to watch the sun go down and then find yourself alone with any of them—few play with a full deck. *From UBC bus loop, follow University Blvd. west 4 blocks to S.W. Marine Dr., turn right, and look for Beach Trail 6.*

WEST END BEACHES You'll find the West End Beaches next to downtown, on the other side of False Creek. **Second Beach** and **Third Beach,** along Beach Drive in Stanley Park, are large family beaches. Second Beach has a guarded saltwater pool and both have concession stands and washrooms. In addition, they are both readily accessible to English Bay and the restaurants and cafés along Denman and Davie streets. Many people come down after work to stroll or watch the amazing sunsets.

Farther along Beach Drive, at the foot of Lewis Street, is **Sunset Beach,** a fairly long and narrow stretch of sand. Much quieter than English Bay and the Stanley Park beaches, it offers ample parking and an excellent view of Vanier Park. A lifeguard is on duty, but don't expect any facilities. It's only a five-minute walk to the bustling West End cafés and restaurants, though, so you probably won't starve to death.

Festivals

Vancouver's mountains and beaches provide a spectacular setting for a variety of festivals and seasonal events. Make sure to pick up an updated listing of concerts, exhibits, and other festivities at the InfoCentre (see Visitor Information in Basics, above). The **Arts Hotline** (tel. 604/684–ARTS) is a good source of info, or pick up the arts magazine *Playboard* at the InfoCentre. The number of events is inversely related to the rainfall, meaning summer weekends are filled with activities. In the winter you'll have to come up with alternative forms of entertainment, preferably involving a bottle of wine, a bearskin rug, a roaring fire, and . . .

➤ **JANUARY** • After ringing in the New Year in Robson Square (a slightly more sedate version of Times Square), locals bring their hangovers to the annual **Polar Bear Swim.** The event takes place on the beach at English Bay, and involves a bunch of people getting their jollies off jumping into freezing-cold water. The intrepid participants add humor to the event with wacky costumes and props. Most people only watch (and point, and laugh).

➤ **FEBRUARY** • In early to mid-February, the Chinese community celebrates **Chinese New Year** with music, dancing, and fireworks. Look for information on specific events along Keifer and West Pender streets. The festivities take place—surprise—in Chinatown (see Worth Seeing, above).

➤ **JUNE** • Vancouver sizzles during the last 10 or so days in June, when hundreds of jazz performers and jazz lovers come to town for the annual **DuMaurier International Jazz Festival** (tel. 604/682–0706). Big names from all over the world come to play jazz and blues in venues ranging from theaters to nightclubs. Tickets aren't cheap, but the shows are hot. Purchase tickets through Ticketmaster (tel. 604/280–4444), or check the *Georgia Straight* for schedules. A booklet of comprehensive information can be found at almost any corner store about a month before the festival begins. To kick off this huge event, free performances are given on Water Street in Gastown the first weekend of the festival.

➤ **JULY** • July 1 is **Canadian Independence Day.** The best place to get into the spirit of things is along the waterfront on Granville Island, at English Bay, or at Kit's Beach. They all have a number of food venues and fireworks shows at night (tel. 604/666–8554). During the third weekend in July, folk musicians and fans alike converge on Jericho Park for the **Vancouver Folk Music Festival,** performed on six stages for three days. The festival, devoted to expanding people's conceptions about the folk-music genre, attracts over 12,000 people each day. Ticket prices vary from year to year, but weekend passes are usually the most affordable option. For more information, contact the Vancouver Folk Music Festival (3271 Main St., tel. 604/879–2931).

The **Sea Festival** in late July is one of Vancouver's most happening summer events; unfortunately organizers have toned it down slightly over the years due to some overly boisterous crowds. Traditionally, everyone gathers around English Bay for nautical displays, a parade, and an excellent fireworks show. For the most part, that hasn't changed; the only difference these days are the large number of armed guards who also attend the festivities. The Sea Festival also includes the conclusion to the annual **Nanaimo to Vancouver Bathtub Race,** when brave souls cross the Strait of Georgia in creative porcelain contraptions. For information, call 604/684–3378.

➤ **AUGUST** • Aviation fans flock to the town of Abbotsford, 72 kilometers (45 miles) east of Vancouver, to witness the **Abbotsford International Air Show,** usually held in early August. You'll catch both military and civilian aeronautical demonstrations, including acrobatic teams and soloists. There's a C\$40 entry fee per carload (maximum of six people); walk-in spectators pay C\$10 (all prices include GST). For information about the event, contact the Abbotsford International Air Show Society (tel. 604/852–8511 or 604/533–3713).

➤ **OCTOBER** • With Vancouver and Seattle establishing themselves as the new hot spots for the film industry, it's no surprise that the **Vancouver International Film Festival** is turning heads in Hollywood. The festival generally debuts some of the most promising films for the upcoming year at venues around town. For schedules and prices call 604/685–0260.

Shopping

With specialty stores scattered all through the city, Vancouver is both a shopper's paradise and nightmare: You can find anything you've ever wanted here, but you may have to go literally from one end of the city to the other before you find it. There are a number of large shopping malls in the downtown area. **Pacific Center Mall,** at Granville Street and Robson Street, is the city biggie. The main shopping areas in the downtown districts are the **Granville Street Mall, Robson St.,** and **Gastown.** Before you go nuts with the plastic, remember that Vancouver's downtown exists for the tourist. Don't expect to find a single bargain, though you may find something you can't live without.

DOWNTOWN The **Granville Street Mall** is an outdoor pedestrian shopping area that stretches between Smithe and Hastings streets. Cars are not allowed on the mall, but buses are (it's a major public-transport hub). Outdoor street vendors sell their wares off makeshift tables, while the offbeat and reasonably-priced shops attract a trendy crowd. This is the place to find inexpensive jewelry and trashable sunglasses, along with many flyers about what's happening in the city.

GASTOWN Here you'll find innumerable opportunities to pick up that totem pole key chain you've always wanted. Sprinkled among the kitsch vendors are a few interesting shops. **The Inuit Gallery** (345 Water St., tel. 604/688–7323) has gorgeous Inuit sculptures and Northwest Coast masks and jewelry, but unless you intend on spending a few thousand, look but don't touch. For a more affordable souvenir, consider a pair of moccasins or a Cowichan sweater from nearby **Hill's Indian Crafts** (165 Water St., tel. 604/685–4249).

Several excellent new and antiquarian bookstores are scattered in this area. **MacLeod's Books** (455 W. Pender, tel. 604/681–7656) has a large collection of Western Canadiana and numerous books on Inuit and native Northwest Coast cultures. **The Women's Book Store** (315 Cambie St., tel. 604/684–0523) offers works by feminist and lesbian writers, and also has a good notice board and info on the gay scene.

Deck yourself out for Vancouver's night life on West Cordova Street, between Cambie and Hamilton streets. There are a number of terrific new and used clothing stores, antiques shops, and a bohemian coffeehouse, all of which offer some of the most affordable finds in town. **Bassix** (217 W. Hastings St., at Cambie St., tel. 604/609–7734) sells a large assortment of magazines generally not available at local newsstands.

West of Gastown, in the **West End,** you'll find coffeehouses, restaurants, and some of the best shopping in Vancouver. **Little Sister's Book and Art Emporium** (1221 Thurlow St., at Davie St., tel. 604/669–1753) carries an extensive collection of books written by or about homosexuality, as well as sex tools, cards and videos. The front entrance to the store is loaded down with information ranging from apartment rentals to theater announcements.

If you have more time than money, try the gigantic, 300-stall flea market at 703 Terminal Avenue, just a five-minute walk from the Science World Skytrain station. The market takes place every Saturday, Sunday, and holiday from 8 to 4.

KITSILANO This mucho trendy area around West 4th Avenue and Broadway offers the kind of variety that you would expect from a university community. Holistic bookstores, chic clothing boutiques, Greek specialty markets, surfshops, and Native American jewelry stores stretch down several blocks. If you are looking to rent a wetsuit for the chilly surf, or need a good tune-up for your snowboard, you'll find a large concentration of sports-equipment stores on West 4th Street between Burrard Street and Cypress Street. The best mountaineering store in town, **Coast Mountain Sports** (2201 W. 4th St., tel. 604/731–6181) is pricey (as are all mountaineering shops), but the salespeople are incredibly knowledgeable about the merchandise and the area.

ROBSON STREET Vancouver's principle fashion drag is lined with cafés, book shops, and dress shops. People-watching here is as entertaining as shopping, and definitely cheaper. You'll find the most affordable shops between Granville Street and Howe Street, where stores like **2ND SKIN** (720 Robson St., tel. 604/683–7607) and **Underground** (710 Robson St., tel. 604/684–6398) offer vintage Charlie's Angels T-shirts and body piercing, much to the chagrin of those heading toward the pricier, upscale Robson Street establishments.

After Dark

In Vancouver, like most other places, that old scientific principle holds true: Money leaves your wallet at a velocity directly proportional to the alcohol content of your blood. If you keep hold of the reins, however, you'll find that it's possible to go out and have fun, and not wake up with an empty wallet—that is, if you're over 19, the legal drinking age in B.C. For the lowdown on entertainment, pick up *The Georgia Straight,* a free weekly publication available in any corner store, coffeehouse, and most retail stores. *The Westender* has similar information at a 25¢ price. Alternative establishments like **Underground** (*see* Shopping, *above*) often carry *Grind,* a free monthly that lists raves and obscure clubs. *Angles* serves the gay and lesbian community and offers complete listing of gay and lesbian bars and clubs, as does *Xtra,* the Vancouver gay and lesbian bi-weekly paper. Once again, you'll have to resort to **Ticketmaster** (tel. 604/280–4444) for your major concert and theater ticket needs.

Bars and clubs start getting lively around 10 or 11 and close at 2. A few late-night restaurants become after-hours bars, but you usually have to order something to eat if you want a place to sit.

Most nighttime hot spots are located around Granville, Richards, and Seymour streets, south of Robson Street. This is also the city's red-light district, so don't be surprised to find the Vancouver Symphony Orchestra playing a couple of blocks away from a XXX theater; in fact, the two elements together might make for a really interesting evening's entertainment. Gastown also has several pubs, and most first-run movies play in theaters along the Granville Mall.

For a change of pace from the typical bar/dance-club scene, head to Commercial Drive, the center of the lesbian community and home to a number of small Italian, Portuguese, and Latin American restaurants featuring live music and dancing. Most of the evening spots are on Commercial Drive near Venables Street and First Avenue.

PUBS **The Blarney Stone.** This Irish pub in Gastown ranges from lively to raucous. Most of the people here during the day should list this place as their billing address; at night the bar is crowded with tourists and blue-collar workers. Live bands play Tuesday through Saturday and get the Guinness-swilling crowd dancing. *216 Carrall St., tel. 604/687–4322. Cover: C$5–C$6 on weekends. Open Mon.–Sat. 11 AM–2 AM, Sun. noon–midnight.*

Jeremiah's. If home isn't so convenient, the next best thing may be a relaxed evening at this place. You can get a full dinner, a couple of beers, a little pool, and something sporting on TV—why not just move in? The staff is very mellow and could care less if you sat here all day without ever ordering (if you're in a hurry, don't expect quick service). *3681 W. 4th Ave., at Alma St., tel. 604/734–1205. Open daily 11 AM–midnight. Wheelchair access.*

Kingshead Creative Food and Brewery. If you are a big fan of acoustic-guitar covers of Paul Simon and Van Morrison, then hold up here: The nightly one-man show pretty much sets the mood. If you're here for lunch or dinner, order a large basket of lipps (chicken strips) for C$8—they're awesome. *1618 Yew St., in Kitsilano, tel. 604/733–3933. Open weekdays 7:30 AM–1 AM, Sat. 8 AM–1 AM, Sun. 8 AM–midnight.*

The Pit. This student pub on the UBC campus is often frequented by non-students, despite complaints of overcrowding by UBCers. The Pit sometimes has live music, but people mostly come for cheap beer and the opportunity to mingle with hordes of students from everywhere imaginable. *In Student Union Building at UBC, tel. 604/822–2901. Open weekdays 9–midnight, weekends 9–4.*

Rose and Thorne. Anybody over 25 will definitely be in the minority in this trendy downtown pub. The clever decor will make you feel like you're in an English parlor, with its comfy sofas and wood touches. Only the slightly scraggly, yet very hip clientele suggests otherwise. This is a popular place to meet friends for a pint and a game of darts before hitting the clubs; it can get darn crowded on weekends. *757 Richards St., tel. 604/683–2921. Open Mon.–Sat. 11 AM–1 AM, Sun. 4–midnight.*

Shoot Straight and Don't Scratch

There are a number of good places to play pool in Vancouver, all with strikingly different character. Things tend to get pricy as the hours stack up, but it probably won't cost you any more than your average night on the town.

- *Automotive Billiards Club is a true pool-shark paradise with 17 tables. If you lose, drown your sorrows with an amazing espresso milkshake (C$4.25). Shoot until 2 AM every night of the week. 1095 Homer St., at Helmcken St., tel. 604/682–0040.*

- *Bar None provides a truly upscale pool experience. Wait for one of the four tables with drink or pizza in hand—Sid's downstairs has a full bar plus pizza for C$3.50 a slice. You won't find any avid pool players here—most people come to see and be seen. Bar None stays open 'til 2:30 AM every night except Sundays, when it's open until midnight. 1222 Hamilton St., at Davie St., tel. 604/689–7000.*

- *Lamplighter's Pub may not be the classiest place in town, but there's generally a good-sized crowd waiting for one of the three tables. They offer cheap, basic pub fare like cheeseburgers (C$3.75) and spaghetti (C$4.25). Most people here are staying in the upstairs Dominion hotel, so complete inebriation doesn't stand in the way of finding home. Things get a little sketchy after dark. There is live music nightly, and a cover on weekends. 210 Abbott St., off Water St., tel. 604/681–6666.*

- *Soho Cafe, a stylish and chic pool hall, has 11 tables at C$8–C$12 per hour, depending on when you play. The tables are usually open during the day, although the place crowds with business people eating lunch. At night you'll have to wait, so take the opportunity to munch on the clubhouse sandwich (C$5.40). This joint doesn't shut its doors until 3 AM, except Sunday when it's more like 12:30 AM. 1144 Homer St., at Davie St., tel. 604/688–1180.*

- *Woodstock attracts the down-to-earth college crowd. The weather outside directly reflects your odds of getting one of the six tables inside: If it's rainy just sit down and make yourself comfy. Whatever the wait, chow on some damn tasty burgers (C$4.50) or chips and salsa (C$2.25). Pool prices run C$8–C$12 per hour, depending on the time and day. 2836 W. 4th St., tel. 604/739–7286.*

Unicorn. Located in tourist central (the Plaza of Nations), Unicorn cashes in on sight-seeing induced fatigue. The touristy location makes the beers a bit pricy, but it's pleasant and convenient if you need to take a load off. Learn to do an Irish jig on Thursday, Friday, or Saturday nights when the band goes full force. *770 Pacific Blvd., tel. 604/683–4436. On Plaza of Nations at north end of Cambie St. Bridge. Open Sun.–Wed. 11:30–10, Thurs. 11:30 AM–midnight, Fri. and Sat. 11:30 AM–1 AM. Wheelchair access.*

CLUBS Expect a hefty cover charge across the board on weekends; prices vary during the week. The majority of clubs don't have dress codes, but you can expect a line outside most places on Friday and Saturday nights. Arrive slightly early, go on weeknights, or just give up and rent a movie. The drinking age in B.C. is 19 and clubs do card for entry.

Celebrities. This multi-level, revamped warehouse in the West End is the hot spot for the gay community. On weekends there are usually theme nights (like the oh-so-catchy Phallic Phridays), advertised all around town and in the paper *Xtra*. Even though they close at 2 AM, this is one of the wildest places to be at night. *1022 Davie St., tel. 604/689–3180. Open 8 PM–2 AM.*

Glass Slipper. Offering all kinds of jazz in a smoky, dimly-lit setting, this is the place to take either a really good date or a really bad one. If it's good the music will make it even better; if it's bad the poor lighting will help. Shows start around 9 PM. *2714 Prince Edward St., tel. 604/877–0066. At 12th and Kingsway Aves. Cover C$6, unless special performance. Open daily 9 PM–2 AM. Wheelchair access.*

Graceland. Finding the alley entrance to this trendy club can be slightly tricky, but just keep looking. Graceland plays a variety of dance music accompanied by funky slide shows and pulsating lights. Some nights focus on one type of music, like funk, indie, or reggae. Dress to impress and don't forget your attitude: They check for it at the door. *1250 Richards St., tel. 604/688–2648. Open daily 9 PM–2 AM.*

Luv-A-Fair. If it's good music and a diverse crowd you seek, look no further. Once you get past all the alternative rock chicks in their newest Seattle-influenced fashions, there are lots of people who just want a good place to dance; they don't really care about or even notice who's there and who's not. Music includes everything from the Sex Pistols to Captain and Tenille. *1275 Seymour St., tel. 604/683–2134. Cover: C$5; free on Tues. Open daily 9 PM–2 AM.*

Odyssey. Another major dance emporium similar to Celebrities (*see above*), this cheesy place is hugely popular with gay West Enders. Expect lots of techno. *1251 Howe St., tel. 604/689–5256. Open daily 8 PM–2 AM.*

Town Pump. This Vancouver institution has hosted big-name and up-and-coming live bands for years. Most fall roughly in the rock-n-roll genre, within which they range from hard rock to garage bands to mellower, folk-oriented music. It's a restaurant during the day, so there's plenty of tables where you can take refuge after one too many rockers has stepped on your feet. Poor ventilation makes it a non-smoker's nightmare. *66 Water St., at Abbott St., tel. 604/683–6695. Cover depends on show. Open daily 5 PM–2 AM.*

Warehouse Cabaret. Playing primarily dance music, this club injects Vancouver with a little soul. Even if you don't have an iota of rhythm, don't hold back from coming here; they've got some of the best music in town. Thursdays are reserved for classic funk. *871 Beatty St., near B.C. Place Stadium, tel. 604/684–1313. Cover: C$5.*

Yale Hotel. Located in a sleazy part of town, this friendly hotel hosts R&B bands in its lounge. It's been here for years and is a bit of an institution for the city's true musicians (and those who think they're true musicians). Jam sessions are held Saturday 3 PM–7:30 PM and Sunday 3 PM–midnight, so if you're looking to make it big or find some people to jam with, here's your chance. The locals who hang out here are a mixed bunch: Expect some harassment if you're a woman on your own. *1300 Granville St., at Drake St., tel. 604/681–YALE. Cover depends on performance. Live music Tues.–Fri. 9 PM–1:30 AM, Sat. 3 PM–7:30 PM, Sun. 3 PM–midnight.*

Yuk Yuk's. This is your standard stand-up comedy club, with acts ranging from hilarious to the give-me-a-break quality. What do you expect with a name like Yuk Yuk's? Wednesday nights are reserved for new talent, so if you want to try your hand at humor, here's your chance for public humiliation. The club is located on the Plaza of Nations. *705 Pacific Blvd., tel. 604/687–LAFF. Cover: C$3–C$9. Open Wed.–Sat. 7 PM–1 AM.*

FILM In addition to first-run cinemas, Vancouver has several artsy and alternative movie houses. **The Ridge** (3131 Arbutus St., at W. 16th Ave., tel. 604/738–6311) plays esoteric films, and **Pacific Cinematheque** (1131 Howe St., tel. 604/688–FILM) shows foreign films. **The Paradise Theater** in Granville Mall (919 Granville St., tel. 604/681–1732) is the best deal in town: They show triple features of recently released mainstream movies for half the price of a single film in a normal movie theater.

Outdoor Activities

When the sun shines over Vancouver, cyclists and joggers burst out in full force, and windsurfers pound the beach in increasingly growing numbers. The city's parks, including Pacific Spirit and Lynn Canyon, and the nearby mountains, offer excellent hiking terrain and numerous opportunities to saunter through the woods. And when the snow starts falling, there aren't many who don't head for the mountains, skis in tow. Three ski resorts lie within an hour's drive of the city, and **Whistler** (*see* Near Vancouver, *below*)—with some of the best skiing in North America—is just two hours away.

HIKING AND BIKING

Because Vancouver is a very environmentally conscious city, bike riding has become a preferred mode of transportation. Bike lanes are very common as are trails in all the bigger parks: You'll see mad cyclists speeding through Stanley Park and terrorizing pedestrians at every turn. For some really excellent scenery, try the bike lane at the **Stanley Park Sea Wall**. A bike trail also runs along the water starting at **Granville Island** and then heads west through **Vanier Park**. For a longer ride, take West 4th Avenue or Point Grey Road out to **UBC**. Here, you'll find a number of challenging mountain-bike trails in forested areas. Another popular route runs along the north or south shores of False Creek.

Several bike shops on downtown Denman Street near Stanley Park rent bicycles. **Bayshore Bicycles** (745 Denman St., tel. 604/688–2453) rents almost-new mountain bikes for about C$6 an hour, C$15 per half day, and C$20 for a full day. They're open daily 10 AM–6:30 PM. **Seymour Cycle** (710 Denman St., tel. 604/688–1077), across the street, only carries various types of Peugeot's. Bikes are about C$4 an hour, C$15 per half day, and C$20 for 24 hours. The shop is open daily 10 AM–6 PM, but they'll stay as late as 8 PM on sunny days.

If you're planning to stay in the area for a while and want to roll on wheels of your own (without spending big bucks), Bayshore Bicycles sells its old bikes in September.

On the hiking end of things, **Pacific Spirit Park** has an expansive trail system of over 48 kilometers (30 miles). **Capilano Regional Park,** on the North Shore, is a good place for a

---

Trail Tidbits

For the lowdown on hiking in Vancouver, try the Federation of Mountain Clubs of B.C. (1367 W. Broadway, tel. 604/737–3053). Next, pick up some equipment at Western Canada Wilderness Committee Store (20 Water St., tel. 604/683–8220), a non-profit store geared towards increasing environmental consciousness, or the Mountain Equipment Co-Op (428 W. 8th, near Cambie St., tel. 604/872–7858), which has lots of equipment, an incredible book section, and a useful notice board.

scenic, if not too strenuous, walk. For more of a challenge, try hiking up to the Lions, two snowy peaks at the **Cypress Bowl Recreation Area** (tel. 604/926–5612) in the North Shore Mountains. At the top you'll find refreshing ponds of melted snow, the perfect place to hold your own Polar Bear Swim (*see* Festivals, *above*). You'll get another good hike going from Cypress Falls Park to Cypress Bowl. It's 15 kilometers (9½ miles) and very strenuous, but just think of how accomplished you'll feel at the top. To reach Cypress Bowl, take exit 8 off the Trans-Canada Highway in West Vancouver.

WATER SPORTS

The Thompson, Chilliwack, and Fraser rivers are the principal rafting rivers in southwestern British Columbia. The Fraser River has whirlpools and big waves, but Thompson and the Chilliwack offer some serious white water. Rafting trips range from three-hour rides to multi-day excursions, and most are rather expensive. Day trips hover around C$70, while three-day trips are about C$200. Some well-qualified guide companies include: **Kumsheen** in Lytton (tel. 604/455–2296 or 800/482–2269), **Hyak** (tel. 604/734–8622), and **Canadian River Expeditions** (tel. 604/738–4449).

You can rent windsurfing equipment from several places on the west side of town, including **Windsure** (Jericho Beach, tel. 604/224–0615). If you're an inexperienced surfer, they have instruction packages ranging from C$31 to C$125, depending on the time you need. Rentals cost C$15 per hour, including wetsuit, Windsurfer, and life jacket; a five-hour rental goes for C$60. On Mondays they offer two hours for the price of one, and the same offer applies to women on Tuesdays.

SKIING

In the North Shore Mountains near Vancouver, there are three ski areas that are perfect for novice skiers or for those wanting a quick fix between trips to big-daddy **Whistler** (*see* Near Vancouver, *below*). The largest area, **Cypress Park** (tel. 604/926–5612; snow report 604/926–6007), has the best runs and is less than an hour away from downtown via Highway 1 in North Vancouver. Equally close to the city (up Hwy. 1 and Capilano Rd. past Capilano Canyon Regional Park), **Grouse Mountain** (tel. 604/986–0661; snow report 604/980–6262) has extensive night skiing and a typical après-ski scene. **Mt. Seymour** (tel. 604/986–2261; snow report 604/879–3999) has the highest elevation in the area, making the snow somewhat better. To get here from downtown, head up Highway 1 to Route 13 (Mt. Seymour Road). For the best cross-country skiing, go to **Hollyburn Ridge** (tel. 604/922–0825) in Cypress Park.

Near Vancouver

If you have the time and/or inclination, the outskirts of Vancouver offer a vast array of things to do, including a few museums for those who enjoy meeting people in period costumes. If that does nothing more than cheese you out, check out the excellent skiing or the excellent parks, which offer hiking, climbing, spelunking, and a number of other outdoorsy pastimes.

WHISTLER

The New Whistler—a ski resort with prices to kill your budget in one fell swoop—rests on the former dump site of the small, funky town that used to be Whistler before the developers rolled through. This glitzy pseudo-village is packed with bars, restaurants, and hotels, all with remarkably similar personalities (nouveau-bland) and prices (steep). However, you have to balance the irritating aspects of Whistler with its undeniable beauty and access to some of the best skiing, hiking, and biking in Canada.

COMING AND GOING B.C. Rail (131 W. 1st St.; tel. 604/631–3500 for reservations or 604/631–3501 for schedules) runs from Vancouver to Whistler several times daily for C$14 one-way. **Perimeter Transport** (8695 Barnard St., tel. 604/266–5386) buses scoot between Whistler and Vancouver six times a day (C$26 round-trip); reserve in advance.

WHERE TO SLEEP The HI Whistler Hostel is the only cheap place to stay in town. Set in a beautiful wooden building with windows overlooking the lake, this super-comfy hostel has a big kitchen, a friendly atmosphere, and no lockout (sweet). It's also an easy walk to town. Beds cost C$18 for nonmembers, C$13.50 for members, and C$20 in winter. Reserve ahead. If you arrive by train, the conductor can drop you at the hostel; if you arrive by bus, get off at the Husky Station and follow the train tracks east. To get here by car, take Route 99 and turn off on Alta Lake Road. *5678 Alta Lake Rd., tel. 604/932–5492.*

OUTDOOR ACTIVITIES This is it: the reason that people spend exorbitant sums of money to stay and eat in places that are all expensive clones of each other. It's the skiing, it's the hiking, it's the biking, it's the sheer beauty of the place. So now you know.

➤ **SUMMER SPORTS** • Mountain bike rentals are available by the hour from **Jim McKonkey's Sport Shop** (tel. 604/932–2311), **Pumphouse Fitness Center** (tel. 604/932–1984), and **Blackcomb Ski and Sport** (tel. 604/932–3142). The shops have bike trail maps that indicate levels of difficulty. Most bike rentals will cost you about C$20 a day.

In the Whistler area, numerous hiking trails traverse **Garibaldi Park,** heading to Nairn Falls, Brandywine Falls, and Cheakamus Lake. Trail maps are available at the information booth at the conference center. If you're interested in horseback riding, **Whistler Trail Riding** (tel. 604/932–6623) conducts one- and three-hour rides in the valley. Don't expect to be handed a beautiful Arabian and then set off into the sunset. They do not rent horses, they simply offer guided trips on horseback.

There are beaches without lifeguards at Lost Lake Park, Alpha Lake Park, Wayside Park, and Rainbow Park. Lost Lake, the smallest and warmest, has a diving raft. You'll find grassy areas, picnic tables, and washrooms at each beach. All five of the lakes around Whistler are stocked with trout, though the area around Dream River Park is one of the most popular fishing spots. A little farther away, try Cheakamus Lake, Daisy Lake, and Callaghan Lake.

➤ **WINTER SPORTS** • British Columbia offers some of the best skiing in North America. The vertical drops at **Blackcomb** (the longest in North America at 5,280 feet) and **Whistler** (5,020 feet) put them in pretty high standing. Both mountains have high-speed chair lifts and get over 450 inches of snow annually. Blackcomb has over 80 trails and Whistler has over 90, while Blackcomb stays open during the summer months for glacier skiing. You'll find the cheapest place to rent equipment—and the most knowledgeable staff—at **Wild Willies Ski Club** (7011 Nesters Rd., on Hwy. 99, tel. 604/938–8036).

Warning: An addiction to skiing may wipe out your budget. People have been known to go to great extremes, like scrapping the rest of their travel plans and beginning a career at the Swig & Schuss Bar and Grill, just for one more lift ticket.

Near Whistler Village, the most popular cross-country spots are the 15 kilometers (9½ miles) of **Lost Lake Trails** (tel. 604/932–6436) or the Whistler golf course, perfect for beginners. Any of the logging roads in Garibaldi Park, especially those around Garibaldi Lake (which have warming shelters) and the trail to Callaghan Lake, are also good for cross-country skiing.

SQUAMISH

The dull hum of machinery and the orange lights of the pulp mill remind you that Squamish is, in fact, an industrial town. With the exception of a new café downtown (one can almost hear the old timers complaining about "them damn artsy-fartsy city folks"), Squamish oozes hardworking small townness. However, it also attracts a fairly large contingency of outdoors people, specifically rock climbers who come to scale its world-famous granite walls. Besides Cleveland

Avenue, which functions as the main drag and tends to close down early, there is literally nothing to do in this sleepy town.

People come to Squamish to climb, camp, and climb again. Don't come here for a good learning experience; the ascents are popular with some of the most renowned climbers in the world. The message from them is clear: Climb or get out of the way.

If you're gonna stay the night, camping at **Psych Ledge**—which bears a striking resemblance to a mossy enchanted forest—is your best bet, hands down. If a little bit of wet doesn't bother you, the spots are free and frequented by a friendly, free-spirited group of visitors who are most likely in town to do some—what else?—rock climbing. You'll find this place off Route 99 past Shannon Falls, just below the Klahanie Restaurant and Campground.

COMING AND GOING B.C. Rail's Vancouver–Prince George train stops in Squamish for about C$8 one-way; service is daily in the summer, three times a week in the winter.

ELSEWHERE NEAR VANCOUVER

Do you feel like you've seen it all, but still have a day to spare? Are you sick of rubbing elbows with people who seem to see everything through the lens of a camera? Have obviously retouched glossy pamphlets begun to irritate you? If so, here are a few non-tourismo activities to soothe your soul.

AIBC WALKING TOUR Even though the phrase "walking tour" probably conjures up a nightmarish image of camcorders and fanny packs, far more Vancouver residents than tourists take the Architectural Institute of British Columbia up on its offer. Not only are the tours free (always a bonus), but they offer a unique perspective into the history of the downtown area, especially if you have a particular interest in architecture and urban design. Tours last approximately two hours. *103–131 Water St., in Gastown, tel. 604/683–8588. Tours Tues.–Sat. at 2 PM.*

CAPILANO REGIONAL PARK The park (tel. 604/985–7474) charges a C$6.25 entrance fee (C$4.50 students), but it's well worth it for a day of breathtaking seclusion. The highlight of any visit is the century-old **suspension bridge** that spans 150 meters. Before you step onto the bridge, watch out for testosterone-wacked visitors who get their kicks by making things as unstable as possible for everyone else. (It may be necessary to remind them that if you fall, they fall.) Bring a picnic: The restaurant here should pay you to eat. To get here, take a westbound Bus 246 from downtown Georgia Street. Get off at Richwood Drive and Capilano Road, one block from the park entrance. In summer the park is open daily 8 AM–9 PM. Call for changing hours during the winter.

CYPRESS FALLS PARK Despite the less-than-formidable size of this park, it's easily accessible and offers some of the best hiking and skiing in the Vancouver area. Even the easiest trails lead to beautiful waterfalls. The harder trails—still rather short (one hour max)—end at hidden cliffs; a plunge into an icy lake can make even the hottest day manageable. Cypress Bowl ski area connects with the falls, though the hike is a long and often crowded one. For more information about skiing and hiking at Cypress Bowl, call 604/926–6007. To get to the park from downtown, catch Horseshoe Bay Bus 250 at Georgia and Granville streets. Get off at **Park Royal** and transfer to the Cypress Park Bus 253. Get off at Woodgreen Place and walk to the large baseball field; across the field is the trail leading to the lower waterfall—by far the more worthwhile of the two falls.

LIGHTHOUSE PARK Follow the main trail (Beacon Lane) to the focal point of the park: Point Atkinson Lighthouse, where the views are as close to orgasmic as they get. The lighthouse itself has been closed to visitors, but the outside and surrounding areas make great spots for picnics, hiking, climbing, and general romping. To get here, take Bus 253 from Park Royal (*see* Cypress Falls Park *above*) and get off at the intersection of Keith Road and Marine Drive. Turn right onto Marine Drive (if you're facing the water) and follow the signs to Lighthouse Park—about ½ mile. *Tel. 604/922–1211. Open 24 hours.*

LYNN CANYON PARK Locals come here to sun themselves on the rocks and swim in the icy water below. Some daredevils partake in cliff jumping, but exercise extreme caution—every year at least one careless person dies. The natural waterslides created by the rocks will thrill the cold-blooded—and freeze their asses off. The suspension bridge at this park is less crowded and longer than the one at Capilano (*see above*), and what's more, it's free. Although the bridge itself is spectacular (and not for those prone to vertigo), don't stop here: Numerous dirt paths lead through the forest. The **Lynn Canyon Geology Center,** at the park entrance, has information on the park and an extremely helpful and informative staff (ask them for waterslide specifics). The center also has a small display area and lots of information on current environmental issues throughout the province. *3663 Park Rd, in Lynn Canyon Park, tel. 604/987–5922. Take Bus "C" to Longdale Quay; transfer to Bus 229 toward West Lynn and get off at Peters Rd. Open daily 10–5; closed weekends Dec.–Jan.*

WEST COAST "D" BREW Escaping the city doesn't necessarily mean running for the hills. Come here to find out a little more about yourself, and your traveling companions, as you're led through the one-hour processes of brewing your own beer. The possibilities are infinite: You can make anything from light lagers to dark ales, *and* booze as you learn—regular beers are sold for 50% off store prices. You can also make your own wine, for approximately C$3 per bottle. The one stipulation is that the fermenting process takes two weeks, so it's only a good idea for those on an extended stay or those returning to the area. Designing your own labels is part of the creative process. *29 East 2nd Ave., tel. 604/875–0600. Open Thurs. and Fri. 10–8, Sat. and Sun. 10–5.*

VANCOUVER ISLAND 10

By Marissa Levin and Helen Lenda

North America's largest Pacific island stretches 460 kilometers (285 miles) from one end to the other, protecting the coast of British Columbia from the brute force of the open ocean. Separated from the mainland a few million years ago, the island seems to bask in the bliss of separation. Absence may make the heart grow fonder, but Vancouver Island is perfectly content on its own. In the south you'll find Victoria, B.C.'s most British city. The east coast alternates between commercialized towns where salmon fishing reigns supreme, and tranquil provincial parks filled with trees and trails. To the west, in Pacific Rim National Park, the secluded stretch of white sand at Long Beach gives way to the treacherous West Coast Trail, where land and cliffs staunchly resist the pounding water.

Hanging out in Victoria is inevitable and well worth your while, but you should motivate yourself to see the natural surroundings up-island as well. Most visitors nest on the east side, which is easily accessible along Route 1 and Route 19 all the way up to the northernmost settlement at Port Hardy. The west coast is far more difficult to reach; only one major road (Route 4) goes all the way across the island, and no roads run along the coast, except for a couple of short stretches between Victoria and Port Renfrew and between Ucluelet and Tofino. But fewer tourists means a more natural environment—instead of other cars, your company will likely be deer, bears, sea lions, and orca whales. Information centers in most west-coast towns make even the most far-removed places, like Tofino, at the northern tip of Pacific Rim National Park, feasible for visitors. Geriatric hippies will return your hello with a big smile and happily assist with inquiries (they'll also probably try to bum a smoke, thanks to a steep price hike on cigarettes in British Columbia). Safety is not an issue in any area, even for women traveling alone. Your main problem may be money: Much of the island (especially Victoria) thrives on tourism, and prices can be exhorbitant.

If you talk politics with locals, you'll inevitably get an earful about the controversy between logging companies and environmental-interest groups in British Columbia. The logging conflict is heated in many areas around the island, but mainly on the west coast, near Clayoquot Sound. In 1993, the temperate rain forest here was sentenced to be logged by the British Columbia Parliament. Locals are less than pleased, and they may urge you to visit the area near Tofino and join in their protest against logging. Other than this, few issues rock the island; the locals like to keep things relaxed.

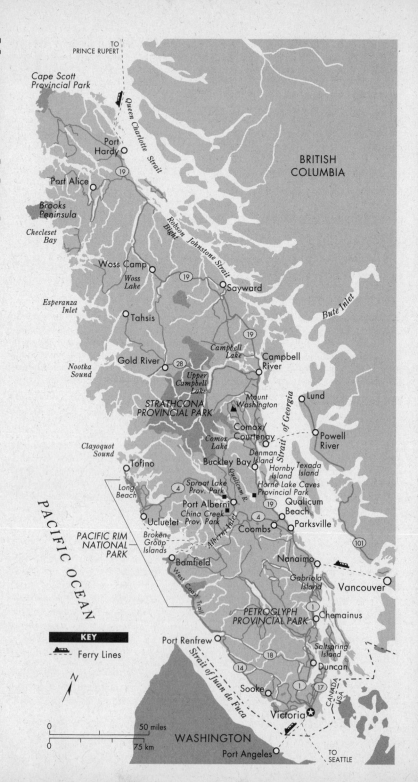

Vancouver Island

TO PRINCE RUPERT

Cape Scott Provincial Park

BRITISH COLUMBIA

Port Hardy

Queen Charlotte Strait

Port Alice

Brooks Peninsula

Checleset Bay

19

Robson Bight

Johnstone Strait

Woss Camp

Woss Lake

19

Sayward

Esperanza Inlet

Tahsis

Bute Inlet

Strait of Georgia

19

Campbell Lake

Gold River

28

Upper Campbell Lake

Campbell River

Lund

Nootka Sound

STRATHCONA PROVINCIAL PARK

Mount Washington

Comox Lake

Comox/ Courtenay

Powell River

Clayoquot Sound

Tofino

Denman Island

Buckley Bay

Hornby Island

Texada Island

Long Beach

4

Sprout Lake Prov. Park

Qualicum R.

Horne Lake Caves Provincial Park

Qualicum Beach

PACIFIC RIM NATIONAL PARK

Ucluelet

Port Alberni

China Creek Prov. Park

19

4

Coombs

Parksville

101

Broken Group Islands

Alberni Inlet

Bamfield

Nanaimo

West Coast Trail

Gabriola Island

Vancouver

PETROGLYPH PROVINCIAL PARK

1

Chemainus

PACIFIC OCEAN

KEY

Ferry Lines

Port Renfrew

18

Saltspring Island

14

Duncan

Strait of Juan de Fuca

Sooke

1

17

CANADA USA

Victoria

0   50 miles
0   75 km

WASHINGTON

Port Angeles

TO SEATTLE

Victoria

You'll hear it repeated again and again because it's true: Victoria is a city for the newlywed and the nearly dead. The abundance of senior citizens, swank shops, and tourist souvenirs are evident the moment you enter the Inner Harbour. But don't write Victoria off as another *Golden Girls* episode just yet. The newlyweds may not be as noticeable, but the longer you stay, the more you'll see that moony romanticism is not a choice here, it's a contagious fever. Suddenly, you too will be spending the evening feeding swans in Beacon Hill Park or reading poetry that you would have found cheesy a week ago in a poorly lit boho coffeehouse. Because it subsists on tourism, Victoria is forced to retain an innocent, almost Disneyland quality. Besides the typical tourist attractions, the city has some genuinely beautiful gardens, historic buildings, and a sunny climate—a rarity in soggy British Columbia.

Victoria tries, sometimes too hard, to preserve its British identity, and you're likely to find traditional English products and stores long since out of style in England itself. But leave behind the Inner Harbour, with its touristy tackiness, and you'll get a strikingly different perspective on the small city. Along Johnson Street to the north and Blanshard Street to the east, life becomes real again. In these less central spots, elderly women hang the laundry on lines, and kids race each other on Big Wheels. Unfortunately, the tourist climate has permeated most of the city financially: Victoria can be damned expensive. But some of the finer things—a walk around the Inner Harbour or a nap at the beach—are still free. While you're here, make sure to talk with locals (and not just the man at the currency exchange); for the most part they're incredibly friendly people who will extend themselves to ensure you have a good time.

BASICS

AMERICAN EXPRESS This handy office cashes checks, holds client mail, and replaces lost checks. *1203 Douglas St., at Fort St., tel. 604/385–8731. Open weekdays 8:30–5:30, Sat. 10–4.*

BUREAUX DE CHANGE The easiest way to change money is just to withdraw it from an ATM; the money comes out magically Canadian. However, you actually pay a hidden commission since banks charge about US$3–US$5 per withdrawal. The best place to exchange traveler's checks is **Custom House Currency Exchange.** *815 Wharf St., tel. 604/389–6001; and 1140 Government St., same tel. Open daily 7 AM–8 PM.*

EMERGENCIES While Canadian citizens enjoy the benefits of socialized medicine, foreigners do not; a visit to the doctor costs the same as in the United States. If you need a late-night pharmacy, **Save-On Food and Drugs** (3510 Blanshard St., at Saanich Rd., tel. 604/475–3301) is open until midnight.

LAUNDRY If you're not staying at the amenity-rich hostels, you can wash your duds at **Maytag Laundry** (1309 Cook St., btw Yates and Johnson Sts., tel. 604/386–1799), open daily 7 AM–10 PM; or **Prestige Laundry** (255 Menzies St., 2 blocks before Thrifty's, tel. 604/386–2220), open weekdays 7:30 AM–10 PM and weekends 9–8.

PHONES AND MAIL BC Tel phones work just like those in the states, except most of their phones accept credit cards and phone cards as well as coins. Phone cards are convenient little things that you buy at the hostel or Zombies (*see* Food, *below*); you dial a code imprinted on your card and don't have to pay cash. The cards are more convenient than coins, but cost more than using a Visa. The **post office** (815 Yates St., tel. 604/953–1351) is open weekdays 8:30–5.

VISITOR INFORMATION The **Tourism Victoria** office, in the Inner Harbour, has a competent staff who will help with tickets, tours, and room reservations. You could spend most of your vacation here wading through the B&B brochures. *812 Wharf St., right on Inner Harbour, tel. 604/382–2127. Open summer, daily 9–9; off-season, daily 9–5.*

COMING AND GOING

BY CAR Several major highways pass through Victoria. Route 1 (the Trans-Canada Highway) heads north up the east coast of the island. Route 1 becomes Route 19 after Nanaimo, and

Upper
Harbour

1

**Train
Station**

Herald St.

Fisgard St.

2

3

**City
Hall**

Cormorant St.

Pandora Ave.

Johnson St. Bridge

Store St.

4

8

Johnson St.

5

Broad St.

KEY

i Tourist Information

6

**Post
Office**

Yates St.

7

Trounce Alley

9

i

View St.

Wharf St.

**Eatons
Centre**

Langley St.

Government St.

**Harbour
Square Mall**

Fort St.

10

11

Inner Harbour

Broughton St.

Blanshard St.

Douglas St.

Gordon St.

13

Courtney St.

Humboldt St.

**Windsor
Court**

14

Burdett Ave.

**Blackball
Ferries**

12

Collinson St.

15

**Bus
Depot**

Belleville St.

Humboldt St.

Blanshard St.

N

Quebec Ave.

18

19

Menzies St.

16

20

Kingston St.

17

Elliot St.

Academy Close

0   200 yards

21 **22**

23

Southgate St.

0   200 meters

Superior St.

24

Sights ●

Bastion Square, **6**

Beacon Hill
Park, **24**

Carr House, **17**

Chinatown, **2**

Craigdarroch
Castle, **11**

Fernwood Village, **8**

Helmcken
House, **20**

Maritime Museum
of British
Columbia, **7**

Ogden Point, **23**

Parliament
Buildings, **16**

Royal B.C.
Museum, **18**

Royal London Wax
Museum, **15**

Thunderbird
Park, **19**

Lodging ○

Backpacker's
Hostel, **10**

Battery Street Guest
House, **22**

Cherry Bank
Hotel, **14**

Craigmyle Guest
House, **9**

Empress Hotel, **12**

James Bay Inn, **21**

Renouf House, **3**

Salvation Army, **4**

Selkirk Guest House
(HI), **1**

Victoria Hostel
(HI), **5**

YWCA, **13**

runs all the way to Port Hardy, the northernmost city on the island. Route 14 heads west from Victoria and then north to Port Renfrew; and Route 17 shoots northeast to the town of Sidney. If you're headed to Tofino and Ucluelet, you'll have to take Route 19 north and veer west at Route 4, which crosses the island to Pacific Rim National Park.

BY BUS **Pacific Coach Lines** (tel. 604/662–7575) sends buses from downtown Victoria to downtown Vancouver (3 hrs, C$40). **Island Coach Lines** (tel. 604/385–4411) services all of Vancouver Island; the Victoria–Nanaimo run costs C$28. Both lines operate from the **Victoria Bus Depot** (700 Douglas St., at Belleville St., tel. 604/385–4411), open daily 9–5. Stuff your bag into their lockers for C$1.50 per 24 hours. The depot doesn't stock maps or bus schedules, but you can get them free at Tourism Victoria (*see* Visitor Information, *above*).

BY TRAIN **Esquimalt and Nanaimo Railway** (450 Pandora Ave., tel. 604/383–4324, or 800/561–8630 in Canada) leaves daily for Nanaimo and Courtenay on the east coast.

BY FERRY Linking downtown Victoria and Seattle, the plush ships of the **Victoria Line**—equipped with a cappuccino bar, lounge, and gift shop—are the biggest thing to hit Canada since Ann Murray. The government sank major money into this project to boost tourism, and you, the tourist, reap the benefits. It's far cheaper and nicer than the competition. The ferry leaves Victoria daily at 7:30 AM for the 4½-hour trip to Seattle; it returns from Seattle at 1 PM daily. You'll pay C$49 one-way for a car and driver; a passenger ticket is C$25, and bicycles are C$5. *Victoria: Ogden Point, 185 Dallas Rd., tel. 604/480–5555. Seattle: Pier 48, South Jackson St., tel. 206/625–1880.*

B.C. Ferries run to Victoria and the Gulf Islands from the Tsawwassen and Horseshoe Bay terminals in Vancouver (95 min, C$6.25, C$2.50 bicycle, C$25.75 vehicle, one-way) eight times daily in the off-season and every hour in summer. Expect long lines and delays for vehicles in summer. *1112 Fort St., tel. 604/656–0757 or 604/386–3431. Open daily 7 AM–10 PM.*

The **Victoria Clipper** for passengers only flits between Pier 69 in Seattle and Victoria's Inner Harbour (3 hrs, C$90 round-trip). Ferries leave both Seattle and Victoria four times daily in summer, once daily in winter. Reserve ahead if you take this one, but why not take the Victoria Line (*see above*) instead for way cheaper? *Victoria: Inner Harbour, 254 Belleville St., tel. 604/382–8100. Seattle: Pier 69, 2701 Alaskan Way, tel. 206/448–5000 or 800/888–2535.*

Black Ball Transport, Inc. travels between Port Angeles, Washington, and Victoria (1½ hrs, US$6.25, US$25 car) four times daily in mid-summer. You can't make reservations. *Victoria: 403 Belleville St., tel. 604/386–2202. Port Angeles: Tel. 206/457–4491.*

Victoria Express Passenger Ferries also sends boats between Port Angeles and Victoria's Inner Harbour (1 hr, US$20 round-trip). Ferries run daily May 23–October 31. *Tel. 604/361–9144, 206/452–8088, or 800/633–1589.*

Washington State Ferries runs two boats a day in summer (one in winter) from Sidney, about 30 kilometers (17 miles) north of Victoria, through the San Juan Islands to Anacortes, Washington (3–3½ hrs). Foot passengers pay US$6.50; car and driver pay US$33. Drivers should show up an hour ahead. Call for reservations in summer. *Tel. 206/464–6400 or 800/84–FERRY in WA; 604/381–1551 or 604/656–1531 in Victoria. From Victoria, take Bus 70 (toward Pat Bay) from cnr of Douglas and View Sts.*

BY PLANE **Air British Columbia** (tel. 800/663–3721) flies between Seattle and Victoria (C$150 one-way) and between Vancouver and Victoria (C$90 one-way). **Canadian Airlines** (tel. 604/382–6111) has similar one-way fares. **Kenmore Air** (tel. 800/543–9595) flies from Seattle to Victoria for about C$85 in the summer months. Victoria's **airport** (201–1640 Electra Blvd., tel. 604/363–6600) is 27 kilometers (17 miles) north of town on Route 17. The **Airport Bus** (tel. 604/475–2010) runs between the terminal and major downtown hotels every half hour (50 min, C$13). Make reservations for pick-up from town.

GETTING AROUND

Downtown Victoria centers around the **Inner Harbour,** the hub for both ferries and tourist attractions. The bus depot, train station, and youth hostel all lie near this crowded patch, and most other budget accommodations are within a 15-minute walk. The downtown section spreads out in a simple grid. Douglas, Blanshard, and Government streets, all running north–south, are the primary commercial streets. Wharf Street lies along the water and intersects with Bastion Square and the "old town." The University of Victoria is northeast of downtown past the Oak Bay neighborhood. City buses run throughout the city, linking downtown with outlying areas, but your feet will probably be your main means of transportation.

BY BUS The efficient **B.C. Transit** buses (tel. 604/382–6161) cost C$1.35 for one zone and C$2 for two (which you'll rarely need). A Super Day Pass (C$3) is good for one day's unlimited travel. Bus drivers don't make change. Pick up day passes at 7-Elevens, the Tourism Victoria information center, and many shopping centers. Get a free schedule from the tourist office or from bus drivers for 25¢. The corner of Douglas and Yates streets downtown is a major hub for city buses, which run from around 6 AM to 12:30 AM.

BY BIKE OR SCOOTER Do like the Victorians do and scoot around town on two wheels. **Budget** (727 Courtney St., at Douglas St., tel. 604/388–7874) rents bikes for C$5 an hour or C$15 a day, and scooters for C$8 an hour or C$30 a day. **Harbour Rentals** (843 Douglas St., btw Humboldt and Courtney Sts., tel. 604/384–2133) has scooters for C$25 a day, and bicycles for C$15–C$20 a day. They also rent motorcycles for C$50 a day. Deposits are always required. **Sports Rent** (611 Discovery St., at Douglas St., tel. 604/385–7368) rents Rollerblades for C$15 per day; mountain bikes are C$20–C$45 per day.

WHERE TO SLEEP

You'll have no trouble finding a cheap sleep in Victoria—but in July and August you should definitely reserve in advance. The few budget digs close to town are highly publicized and fill up fast. Don't be afraid to stay outside downtown; great places are scattered throughout interesting neighborhoods like Fernwood (see Worth Seeing, below). If the places listed below are full, your cheapest and closest choices are the flimsy budget motels on Gorge Road near Douglas Street. Decent rooms run about C$50–C$60. You won't find any English charm here, but the scene at the nearby Denny's-style restaurants could be considered cheap late-night entertainment.

In case you're curious, a double room at the **Empress Hotel** (721 Government St., tel. 604/384–8111), the ostentatious landmark overlooking the Inner Harbour, will set you back C$195–C$335. You're better off loitering in the lobby, gathering disdainful stares because of your sagging pockets filled with not-quite-complimentary ashtrays.

➢ **UNDER C$50** • **Salvation Army.** A block from the youth hostel downtown, the Army has brand-new, squeaky-clean dorms and private rooms—for men only. Dorm beds are C$15 including breakfast; private single rooms cost C$19 with no meal. Ask about weekly and monthly rates. *525 Johnson St., at Wharf St., tel. 604/384–3396. 100 beds. Dorm lockout 9–3:30. Wheelchair access.*

YWCA. Close to downtown and the Inner Harbour, the YWCA rents private rooms with shared baths, but only to women and only in summer. The linoleum floors and freshman-dorm decor won't thrill you, but singles cost C$31 and doubles C$46. Guests have access to the gym and the pool. *880 Courtney St., tel. 604/386–7511. From bus depot, take Douglas St. to Courtney St. and turn right. 13 rooms, none with bath. Laundry, luggage storage. Wheelchair access. Closed Oct.–May.*

➢ **UNDER C$75** • **Cherry Bank Hotel.** This old-fashioned hotel is short on amenities (no phones or TVs) but rich in character. The burgundy wallpaper and fluffy furniture make it feel like an ersatz bordello. Attic rooms have skylights, and rooms with kitchens cost the same as those without 'em. Ask to stay in the charming older section. Singles run C$35–C$55, doubles C$55–C$75, including full English breakfast. *825 Burdett Ave., at Quadra St., tel. 604/385–5380. 5 blocks from Inner Harbour. 26 rooms, 19 with bath. Free parking, 1-day luggage storage. Reservations advised.*

James Bay Inn. The rooms can get hot and noisy in summer, and, though clean and comfortable, show their age. Singles cost C$55–C$65, doubles C$70, and twins C$48–C$72. Off-season, rates go down about C$8. *270 Government St., at Toronto St., tel. 604/384–7151. 3 blocks behind Parliament Buildings. 48 rooms, 38 with bath. Luggage storage.*

BED-AND-BREAKFASTS Because new B&Bs pop up every year, it's worth calling a B&B registry to get the latest scoop. They include **B&Bs in Heritage Homes** (809 Fort St., tel. 604/384–4014), **Victoria B&B** (1054 Summit Ave., tel. 604/385–2332), and **Garden City B&B Registry** (tel. 604/479–9999). B&Bs get cheaper the farther you go from the center of town.

Battery Street Guest House. Owner Pamela Verduyn has reason to be proud about her six-room Victorian home, stuck away on a sleepy residential street near Beacon Hill Park (a block from the beach), and rightly so. The price for spacious, immaculate rooms includes a deluxe breakfast spread. You'll face hot competition for the two doubles with bath (C$85), though the other doubles (C$65) and the single (C$45) are equally nice. *670 Battery St., tel. 604/385–4632. From downtown, follow Government St. past Parliament Buildings south for 15 min. Luggage storage. Reservations advised.*

Craigmyle Guest House. In an old residential neighborhood next to Craigdarroch Castle (*see* Worth Seeing, *below*), this quality B&B features a huge living-room fireplace and a filling, yummy English breakfast. Singles go for C$65; doubles are C$80–C$95; and rooms for four or five people are C$130–C$155. *1037 Craigdarroch Rd., tel. 604/595–5411, fax 604/370–5276. From downtown, walk 1½ km (1 mi) up Yates St., or take Bus 11 or 14 from Douglas St. 17 rooms. Reservations necessary.*

Renouf House. In the heart of the Fernwood district, this place does double duty as a newly renovated "Bunk and Breakfast" downstairs (C$17.75 a bed) and a full-blown B&B upstairs (singles C$35, doubles C$45–C$50). Every morning you'll feast on an all-natural, homemade breakfast buffet in an entirely smoke-free environment. If they're full, another three-room house (one room with bath) takes the overflow. *2010 Stanley Ave., tel. 604/595–4774. Take Bus 10 (toward Haultin) from Douglas and Fort Sts.; get off at George and Dragon Pub, walk down Gladstone Ave. 1 block, left on Stanley Ave. 8 dorm beds, 5 rooms, none with bath.*

HOSTELS **Backpacker's Hostel.** A worn old house in the quiet Fernwood neighborhood, about 15 minutes from the Inner Harbour, this private hostel vacillates between ultra-laid-back and wild and crazy. David Burgess, who runs the place, is a walking tourist info center. One bunk room is reserved for women only, while the rest are coed. Bunks cost C$10, twin rooms C$25, breakfast included. Reserve well ahead for the "honeymoon suite"—a double bed with a private bath (C$30). *1418 Fernwood Rd., tel. 604/386–4471. Take Bus 10 from Douglas St. downtown, or from bus depot, and go north on Douglas St., right on Fort St., straight to Fernwood Rd. Laundry, luggage storage, kitchen and frequent BBQs, bike rental, TV, free coffee.*

Selkirk Guest House (HI). If you don't mind the 40-minute walk or 10-minute bus ride from downtown, head for this Victorian house overlooking the water. The hostel welcomes responsible backpackers and families with kids; pets are allowed but smoking is not. Double rooms cost C$35–C$45; dorm space runs C$14 for HI members, C$16 for nonmembers. Check in before 9 PM if possible. *934 Selkirk Ave., tel. 604/389–1213, fax 604/389–1313. Bus 14 (toward Craigflower) from downtown, get off at cnr of Craigflower and Tillicum, walk 1 block north to Selkirk, turn right, go 150 meters; house is back from street on left. 16 beds, 2 private rooms (1 with bath). Check-in 4 PM–11 PM. Kitchen, canoes, row boats. Call ahead.*

Victoria Hostel (HI). The best deal for your money is probably this spiffy, newly renovated youth hostel. You couldn't ask for a better location (near the water five minutes from the bus station), and the talkative staff will point you toward cool places in town. Bunks cost C$13 for HI members, C$18 for nonmembers; family and group rooms are C$2 extra. Rates lower slightly in winter. Reserve ahead in summer. *516 Yates St., tel. 604/385–4511, fax 604/385–4511. From bus depot, right on Belleville St., right on Government St., left on Yates St. after many blocks. 104 beds. Laundry, luggage storage, linen rental C$1.50. Wheelchair access.*

STUDENT HOUSING **University of Victoria Bed and Breakfast.** From May to August, the university opens its student housing to the public, and lots of foreign-exchange students take advantage. Choose between an institutional but clean single (C$32) or a double with twin beds (C$47). Prices include linens and breakfast. Reservations in July and August. *Housing and*

Conference Services, University of Victoria, tel. 604/721–8396. Northeast of downtown past Oak Bay; 20-minute ride from Inner Harbour on Bus 4, 11, or 14. Laundry, pay phones. Wheelchair access.

CAMPING If you camp around Victoria, don't expect the idyllic conditions that prevail on the rest of the island. At times, Winnebagoes outnumber trees, and prices may make you want to head indoors. Like all accommodations in B.C., campgrounds fill quickly in summer, so make reservations, especially if you plan to arrive late in the day.

Thetis Lake Campground. Families flock to this campground, which features not only hiking trails around the lake but also great salmon fishing nearby. Sites cost C$15 for two people. *1938 Rte. 1, tel. 604/478–3845. 10 km (6 mi) from downtown; follow Dallas Rd. by car or take City Bus 50 and get off at Colwood overpass. Island Coach Lines bus toward Nanaimo lets you off at Thetis Lake Park. 100 sites. Showers, laundry, electricity 50¢, water 50¢.*

Victoria West KOA. If you want to feel like you're really camping and don't mind some distance from town, this is the place. Superb, tree-filled, grassy sites cost C$19–C$24 for two. *Rte. 1, tel. 604/478–3332. Halfway btw Nanaimo and Victoria. Take Island Coach Lines toward Nanaimo; get off at Malahat Chalet, cross hwy. and walk south; look for driveway with sign. 100 sites. Showers, laundry, swimming pool.*

FOOD

Eating well on a budget in Victoria should not be a problem. Plenty of restaurants cluster downtown, but some hidden goodies lie outside the city center as well. You can easily stuff yourself for under C$10—even for less than C$5. Chinatown and a few other exceptions aside, Victoria has little in the way of ethnic restaurants. On the other hand, you'll have no trouble finding fish 'n chips or pie. Vegetarians have an array of choices, and most restaurants exhibit at least a modicum of health consciousness. Because Victoria is on an island, the prices of import groceries are high. Therefore it's usually easiest and cheapest to eat out rather than searching for your favorites at corner stores. The one real supermarket is a 20-minute walk from downtown.

The only bagel store in town, as well as the local skater hangout, **Benny's Bagels** (132–560 Johnson St., Market Sq., tel. 604/384–3441) serves an extremely popular cheese melt for C$4.25. **Barb's Place** (310 St. Lawrence St., tel. 604/384–6515), a floating shack anchored at Fisherman's Wharf, serves fresh seafood chowder (C$2), or fish and chips (C$4.50) cooked in vegetable oil and wrapped in newspaper. At **Growlies** (615 Yates St., tel. 604/383–2654), just up from HI hostel, you can sample a Canadian perogy platter (a knish-like thing—dough stuffed with cheese, potatoes, and onions) for C$5.45, breakfast eggs for C$4, or hefty salads and sandwiches for C$5.50. Redubbed the "Rising Prices Bakery" by disgruntled locals, **Rising Star Bakery** (1320 Broad St., btw Johnson and Yates Sts., tel. 604/386–2534) still bakes excellent, inventive breads, which are quickly snatched up for about C$2 each. Beware of the hot food: It's not worth the money.

➤ **UNDER C$5 • Demitasse Coffee Bar.** Walk into this quiet, artsy café to take in the aroma of freshly ground beans and the sight of colorfully painted ceilings, fake columns, and wooden tables. You won't get the most food for your bucks, but you will find pale intellectual types busily avoiding Victoria's beer-drinking, hockey-watching mainstream. Try the hummus, tomato, and sprout sandwich (C$4.75); deep-chocolate cake (C$3.50); or homemade granola with fruit and yogurt (C$3.45). *1320 Blanshard St., at Johnson St., tel. 604/386–4442. Wheelchair access. Open weekdays 7 AM–10 PM, weekends 8 AM–10 PM.*

Eugene's on Broad Street. This cafeteria-style restaurant may look nothing like Greece, but it definitely tastes authentic. All the recipes are Eugene's own, and he takes special pride in the *rizogato*, his Greek rice pudding (C$2.25). Spanakopita goes for C$3.50, and souvlaki is C$4.75. *1280 Broad St., btw Yates and View Sts., tel. 604/381–5456. Open Mon. 8–6, Tues.–Thurs. 8–8, Fri. 8–9, Sat. 10–5.*

Q Café. The huge patio outside and the 24-hour schedule make this place extra-appealing. A typical menu of salads and sandwiches (C$4.95), chicken pie (C$4.25), coffee, and desserts satisfies a very atypical crowd—the most ethnically, sexually, and otherwise diverse in the city. *1701 Government St., tel. 604/384–8831. Cnr of Government and Fisgard Sts., across from Harmonious Gate entrance to Chinatown. Wheelchair access. Open 24 hrs.*

Zombies. Originally open only at night, the best pizza place in town has finally given a nod to those of us who also experience daylight. If you don't mind watching plastered people stuffing their faces, late nights are the best time to experience some alternative pizza culture. Make sure to check out the excellent murals on the bathroom wall. The veggie pesto slice (C$1.25) is your best bet for food. *1219 Wharf St., tel. 604/389–2226. BYOB. Wheelchair access. Open Tues.–Sun. 11 AM–4 AM, Mon. 11 AM–3 AM.*

➤ **UNDER C$10** • **Japan Foods.** Because this place just looks like a hole in the wall, it remains undiscovered even by most locals. Expect a typical Japanese menu at low prices: California rolls cost C$3.95 for eight pieces, tuna sushi is C$1.50, tempura goes for C$7, and they have a wide selection of beers (C$3.50). *734 Yates St., btw Blanshard and Douglas Sts., tel. 604/386–3116. Wheelchair access. Open weekdays 11–8, Sat. noon–8.*

John's Place. This popular joint is stocked with a jukebox, snug booths, and old movie posters—and the food isn't half bad either. For breakfast try the fluffy Belgian waffles (C$6.50). The spinach and cheese tortellini (C$8.50) is undeniably the house favorite at lunch and dinner. John is known for his decadent baked goods, like mile-high apple pie (C$3.75). Expect a wait for Sunday brunch. *723 Pandora Ave., at Douglas St., tel. 604/389–0711. Wheelchair access. Open Mon.–Sat. 7 AM–10 PM (until 11 PM in summer), Sun. 8 AM–10 PM.*

Caffeine in the Bloodstream

In the last year and a half, Victoria has started to look and feel more like Seattle than Mother England, thanks in great part to the coffeehouse explosion. Now, even devout tea-timers crowd the profusion of java joints that have sprung up all over town. Below are three of the best.

- *Java. One of the only alternative hangouts in Victoria, Java proves that hardcore coffee culture has finally, thankfully, crossed the Strait of Juan de Fuca. Among the sketching artists, chess players, and local bands, you can get some damn good coffee (double latte C$3.25) and great desserts (C$2–C$4). Check out the entertainment schedule for upcoming shows. 537 Johnson St., at Wharf St., tel. 604/381–BEANS. Wheelchair access. Open Sun.–Thurs. 10 AM–midnight, Fri.–Sat. 10 AM–1 AM.*

- *Mocambo Café. If you need an escape, sidle upstairs to this very comfortable, mellow café and enjoy a book or write a long letter. You can get a light meal of homemade soup (C$2.25) and salad (C$3.50) or just enjoy a fantastic cappuccino (C$1.75). 1028 Blanshard St., at Fort St., tel. 604/384–4468. Wheelchair access. Open Mon.–Sat. 7–7.*

- *Zackery Bean. In addition to drinking a latte (C$2.50) and munching on homemade cookies (C$1.25), you can hone your pool skills or peruse the cluttered bookshelf—they promise a free coffee for every donated book. This place is always crowded with folks just passing the time. 719 Yates St., at Douglas St., tel. 604/480–1163. Open Mon.–Thurs. 7 AM–midnight, Fri.–Sat. 7 AM–2 AM, Sun. 8 AM–midnight.*

Nirvana Green Cuisine. Since markets selling produce are scarce in this town, you may need this cafeteria-style vegetarian restaurant to assuage your fears of developing scurvy. The salad-bar options (C$5.95 per pound) range from raw vegetables to pasta salads and change on a daily basis. Sandwiches (C$4.50) and healthy desserts (C$1.50–C$3) are offered as well. *560 Johnson St., Market Sq., tel. 604/385–1809. Open daily 11–8.*

The Re-Bar. The chatty clientele, multicolored walls, and frescoed floor combine to convince you that although you may be ingesting a wheatgrass sports drink (C$2.75), you're having fun, dammit. The low-fat food and the juice bar attract all kinds, from athletes to granolas. Try the Szechuan noodle salad (C$7.25) or enchiladas (C$8.25). *50 Bastion Sq., btw Wharf and Government Sts., tel. 604/361–9223. Open weekdays 7:30 AM–10 PM, Sat. 8:30 AM–10 PM, Sun. brunch 11–3.*

Szechuan Exotic Chinese Cuisine. Ten minutes from downtown, the Exotic cooks the best Szechuan food in the city. Make sure you're hungry, because they serve huge portions; it's best to go with a group so you can sample more dishes. The Szechuan noodles (C$7) are outstanding. *855 Caledonia Ave., at Quadra St., tel. 604/384–0224. Wheelchair access. Open Mon.–Sat. 11:30–2 and 4:30–10.*

➤ **UNDER C$15 • Pagliacci's.** If you're in the mood to splurge, try Victoria's best Italian restaurant. There's almost always a line and service can be slow, but the food and the ambience are stupendous. You'll find live music in the evenings, tarot reading by Sadie on Tuesday afternoons, and Sunday brunch (a real treat). Pasta dishes like the Manhattan Transfer (pesto and sun-dried tomatoes) go for around C$10, and full dinners run about C$15. The desserts are to die for. You're guaranteed to leave stuffed and smiling. *1011 Broad St., btw Fort and Broughton Sts., tel. 604/386–1662. Open Mon.–Sat. 11:30 AM–1 AM, Sun. 11 AM–midnight.*

MARKETS The one real supermarket within walking distance, **Thrifty's** (Menzies St.) is a 20-minute walk down Wharf Street from downtown (right at Belleville, left at Menzies). You'll find a few small convenience stores scattered about the city: **Ideal Food Market** (640 Yates St., tel. 604/383–5415) is just up the street from the Victoria Hostel. **Red Mango** (1725 Quadra St., tel. 604/385–2827), in the Fernwood neighborhood, carries some unusual imported specialties like rice-paper candy and goat cheese. The best health-food market is **Viteway Foods** (1019 Blanshard St., tel. 604/384–5677).

WORTH SEEING

Victoria has some genuinely interesting and worthwhile sights, plus several more created solely to draw in tourist dollars. Most attractions center around the Inner Harbour, where summer tourists outnumber locals. Other attractions lie within a block or two of this area. For the sights you can't reach on foot, make use of the public transit system.

A number of excellent museums and galleries proffer the Victorian era after which the city was named. An active historical society has restored a few heritage homes and parks that allow you to step back in time to the days of parasols, bustles, and the Empire, all within a somewhat incongruous West Coast context. The three most interesting heritage homes include the Helmcken House and Carr House (*see below*), and **Point Ellice House** (Pleasant St., near Bay St. Bridge). For more information on Victoria's heritage homes, call **Heritage Properties Branch** (tel. 604/387–4697).

BEACON HILL PARK You can't help feeling content with the world at Beacon Hill Park, where kids chase after roaming peacocks and ducks while their parents picnic on grass crowded with wildflowers and willow trees. For a view of the shore, head east to the Dallas Road border of the park, where a number of staircases lead down to the beach. Gaggles of locals hang out here eternally with beers and buds. *Monday Magazine* (which inexplicably comes out on Thursdays) lists upcoming summer concerts in the outdoor band shell. You can play baseball at the field, see the swans in Goodacre Lake, or bring a picnic, but you *must* make your way to this park. From the Inner Harbour, walk south down Douglas Street past the bus depot. It's generally safe at night, but use common sense, especially if you're alone.

BUTCHART GARDENS You've seen billboards for it since you left Northern California; now here it is, painfully expensive entrance fee and all. You'll soon forget your empty wallet when you see the absolutely exquisite gardens and kaleidoscope of flowers. In 1904 the Butcharts, Portland Cement Company barons, initiated the beautification of an old quarry. The 50-acre site now contains several specialty gardens: Bridges and walkways lead to a sunken garden, a Japanese garden, an English rose garden, and an Italian garden. Pack a picnic and take advantage. In July and August, fireworks light up the sky every Saturday evening. *800 Benvenuto Ave., tel. 604/652–4422. Take Bus 75 (toward Central Saanich) from downtown. By car, take Scenic Marine Dr., Douglas Rd., and Beach Dr. to Rte. 17 North, a 21 km (13 mi) drive. Admission: C$4.50–C$9.50. Open June 15–Aug., daily 9 AM–10:30 PM; off-season evening hrs vary.*

CARR HOUSE Emily Carr, one of Canada's most celebrated artists, was born here in 1871. Carr studied in San Francisco, London, and Paris, and spent much of her time focusing on local native crafts. She is best known for her colorful, almost primitive depictions of the Northwest, though later in life she wrote several books. The autobiographical *Book of Small* tells of her early childhood; her descriptions in the book were used as the basis for the restoration of her home. The guided tours are embellished with anecdotes and theater vignettes of her life. *207 Government St., near Belleville St., tel. 604/387–4697. In James Bay area, a short walk from Inner Harbour. Admission: C$3.75. Open June 16–Sept. 26, Thurs.–Mon. 11–5.*

CRAIGDARROCH CASTLE Just outside downtown is the opulent home of British Columbia's first millionaire, Robert Dunsmuir, who oversaw coal mining for the Hudson's Bay Company. Virtually none of the Dunsmuir's furniture remains inside this pointy, haunted-looking house (built between 1887 and 1890), but you can still see the stunning carved-oak walls and staircase and the rich wood paneling throughout the 39 rooms. Climb 87 steps to the fifth floor for an excellent view of downtown Victoria. *1050 Joan Crescent, tel. 604/592–5323. Walk down Fort St. (a.k.a. Antique Row), or take Bus 10 or 11 down Yates St. Admission: C$5, C$4 students. Open June 16–Aug., daily 9–7:30; Sept.–June 15, daily 10–5.*

DOWNTOWN VICTORIA The bustling downtown area sits between the Inner Harbour, Cook Street, and Pembroke Street. Most commerce is concentrated on Douglas and Blanshard streets; Government Street is set aside for tourists and has plenty of English boutiques and restaurants. You'll probably just want to wander around this area, but as you go, keep your eye out for some points of interest. **Bastion Square,** between View and Yates streets near the harbor, exists to look good, with its gas lamps, cobblestone streets, and fussy shop fronts. It also provides the perfect place to look out at the harbor.

The British side of Victoria has rubbed off on Chinatown as well: The area is simply too touristy and expensive to have the feel of a bustling, semi-seedy, genuine Chinatown—like what you'll find in San Francisco or Vancouver.

Chinatown's shops and restaurants center around Fisgard Street. This area is distinguished by the Harmonious Gate, a red, imperial-looking Chinese gate at the Government Street entrance. Fan Tan Alley, just off Fisgard Street, claims not only to be the narrowest street in North America but also to have a scandalous past as the gambling and opium center of Chinatown.

Bordering Pandora Avenue and Government Street is **Centennial Square,** the oldest part of Victoria. The buildings in this area date from the 1880s and 1890s. Check out the three-story **Victoria City Hall,** originally built in 1878. The design incorporated high, arched windows; the clock tower was added in 1891. For a great view, walk up Douglas Street to the front of the building. **Fisherman's Wharf,** east of the Inner Harbour, is not only a beautiful hangout but the best place to pick up some fresh fish right off the boat—as long as you're an especially early riser with access to a kitchen. From the tourist information center head toward the Parliament Buildings and down Belleville Street past Laurel Point Inn.

FERNWOOD Welcome to working-class Victoria. It's refreshing to see a part of this city where people actually live; tricycles are turned over on front lawns and remnants of toilet paper pranks litter the trees. A walk around the neighborhood will remind you that there is life after tourism. Make sure to stop by the Red Mango (*see* Markets, *above*) and **Fernwood Village,** the main shopping area and community center, lined with good food and low-key stores. Also check out the inspirational, community-run **Inner City Farm** on Mason Street for fresh produce.

HELMCKEN HOUSE If late nineteenth-century life, Dr. John Helmcken, or painfully outdated medical tools are of particular interest to you, then fit this into your agenda. The former residence of pioneer Dr. Helmcken has been accurately restored and contains a rare and interesting collection of antique medical paraphernalia, as well as a frightening display of old medical tools—stuff only David Cronenberg could appreciate. The staff wears period costumes and are happy to relate little anecdotes. *Cnr of Douglas and Belleville Sts., east side of B.C. Museum, tel. 604/387–4697. Admission: C$3.25, C$2.25 students. Open May 5–Oct., daily 11–5; Dec. 18–31 for special Christmas program. Closed Dec. 25–26.*

MARINE DRIVE This drive takes about an hour, including stops, and makes a fine day's bike ride as well. Starting from Fisherman's Wharf or Beacon Hill Park, follow Dallas Road and then Beach Drive along the water, past blissful ocean views and several of Victoria's ritziest homes. Take the road past Oak Bay to the **University of Victoria** (tel. 604/721–UVIC), which has a good museum and student-sponsored cultural events, or continue along Arbutus Road to **Mt. Douglas Park,** where you'll find little beaches. You can reach Butchart Gardens by taking Route 17 north.

The beautiful old tombstones and angelic statues at **Ross Bay Cemetery** (Dallas Rd., btw Memorial and Fairfield Sts., tel. 604/598–8870), on the waterfront along Marine Drive, will convince you that the dead really are headed to a better place. This cemetery holds the tombs of some of Victoria's most famous citizens: Sir James Douglas, first governor of B.C.; coal baron Robert Dunsmuir; artist Emily Carr; and Billy Barker, of gold-rush fame. Try to find the grave of politician John Dean, who had his tombstone erected many years before his death. Even if the idea of tromping on someone's ancestors freaks you out, consider stopping here—this place is right on the water and truly beautiful. Catch a guided tour, complete with historical anecdotes, three times a week for C$5. To reach the cemetery by public transit, take Bus 2 from Douglas and Fort streets downtown and get off on Gonzales Avenue.

PARLIAMENT BUILDINGS You'll eventually find the lawn in front of the Parliament, a great place to have a picnic, throw a Frisbee, or nap after a morning of running around. On the top of the stone edifice, check out the gold-plated statue of Captain George Vancouver, the first person to circumnavigate Vancouver Island. On the lawn are a statue of Queen Victoria in her younger days and a giant sequoia, a gift from the state of California. At night, the building is festively lit by more than 3,000 tiny bulbs.

Don't just look at the outside; take one of the free and entertaining half-hour tours given all day. The hosts tell funny anecdotes and will point out features like the ceremonial entrance opened only for the Queen of England. You'll also learn about the structure of government in British Columbia, based on the nearly 600-year-old British system. Tours are conducted in six languages during summer and three in winter. Ask the guide about debates, which are open to the public daily from 2 to 6—they're free and much more stimulating than *The People's Court. 501 Belleville Ave., btw Government and Menzies Sts., tel. 604/387–3046. Open weekdays 8:30–5, weekends and holidays 9–5.*

Take Bus 2 from Douglas and Fort streets to Crescent Street and Quimper Road to reach Victoria's peaceful Chinese cemetery (tel. 604/384–0045), where small stone markers sit among wildflowers next to the rocky shore. It'll bring out the Taoist in you.

ROYAL B.C. MUSEUM This excellent museum should be one of your first stops and could be among the highlights of your entire trip. A comprehensive collection of British Columbian artifacts takes you from the region's first indigenous people to the Anglos who came later. The walk-through exhibits include a full-scale reconstruction of a Victorian cobblestone street lined with storefronts, a Kwakiutl Indian House surrounded by totem poles, and a life-size mammoth. Piped-in sound effects and olfactory sensations accompany the displays. Plan at least five hours to see it, maybe more. Particularly interesting is the chronicling of native history before and after the invasion of the Europeans; the native masks are compelling as well. Your ticket is good for two days, so it might be worth asking around your hotel for a used ticket. The pre-recorded tours are not really necessary. *675 Belleville St., btw Government and Douglas Sts., tel. 604/387–3701. Admission: C$5, C$3 students, C$2 disabled. Open June–Aug. daily 9:30–7; off-season, daily 10–5:30.*

The totem poles next to the museum in **Thunderbird Park** (cnr Belleville and Douglas Sts.) almost always have a tourist posing for a picture in front of them. The Indian Arts and Crafts Society and the Royal B.C. Museum produce small art demonstrations for free: It's pretty neat to watch someone carve a totem pole before your very eyes. Schedules vary, so ask when the next demonstration will be.

MUSEUMS AND GALLERIES

The **Royal B.C. Museum** (*see above*) is probably the finest museum you'll visit in a long time. Don't miss it.

ART GALLERY OF GREATER VICTORIA You'll find a hodgepodge of interesting pieces here. The collection of Asian art includes the only Shinto shrine outside Japan, on permanent display in the Japanese garden. The museum itself is a Victorian mansion in the swanky Rockland district (near Craigdarroch Castle). Unfortunately for this gallery, local Emily Carr left the bulk of her work to the Vancouver Art Gallery. *1040 Moss St., tel. 604/384–4101. Take Bus 11 or 14 from Fort and Douglas Sts. Admission: C$4, C$2 students; free Thurs. after 5 PM. Open Mon.–Sat. 10–5, Thurs. 10–9, Sun. 1–5.*

MARITIME MUSEUM OF BRITISH COLUMBIA Dugout canoes, model ships, Royal Navy charts, photographs, uniforms, and ships' bells chronicle Victoria's seafaring history. The entrance fee is pretty steep, and they offer no student discounts, so if you've already seen the Maritime Museum in Vancouver you may want to skip it. *28 Bastion Sq., tel. 604/385–4222. Admission: C$5. Open June and Sept., daily 9–6; July and Aug., daily 9–8:30, Oct.–May, daily 9:30–4:30.*

ROYAL LONDON WAX MUSEUM Across from the Parliament in the old Steamship Terminal, the Royal London Wax Museum houses more than 200 life-size wax figures, from Elvis to the Wizard of Oz. Not surprisingly, the Canadian mountie, the Beefeater, Charles and Di, and Queen Victoria go over the best in this land of Anglophiles run amok. Check out the reproductions of the British crown jewels. Madame Toussaud is to blame for the outrageously lame addiction to wax figures—see if you can't stick a wick in Princess Di's do. *470 Belleville St., on the Inner Harbour, tel. 604/388–4461. Admission: C$7, C$6 students. Open daily 9–9.*

CHEAP THRILLS

For a fabulous hike, walk up **Fort Rodd Hill.** Its restored barracks and artillery stations were built in 1895 as a defense station for the harbor. You may even spot a deer among the turn-of-the-century defense batteries—they're usually out and about at dusk. While you're here be sure to check out the **Fisgard Lighthouse,** perched on the cliff with the spectacular ocean behind it. Built in 1859, it's the oldest lighthouse on the west coast of Canada. *Fort Rodd Hill: At entrance to Esquimalt Harbour, tel. 604/363–4662. Take Bus 50, get off at Western Exchange. Open daily 10–5:30. Lighthouse closes at 5.*

If it's foggy, walk down to Ogden Point on Dallas Road. With visibility at a maximum of 5 feet in every direction, you really feel like you're on the ethereal path to the afterlife.

Mt. Douglas Park has several hiking trails that lead to ocean views, a beach, picnic areas, and a playground. Hike up to Summit Lookout cliff for a view of Cattle Point across the water. None of the hikes is very long or strenuous, but you may want to bring water if the most exercise you've had lately is taking your pack on and off. *Tel. 604/387–4363. Catch Bus 28 at Douglas and Yates Sts. downtown; get off at Majestic and Ash Sts. and walk 20 minutes down Ash St.*

For an incredibly picturesque view of Victoria, head to **Mt. Tolmie Park.** On a clear day you can see across Haro Strait to the Washington Cascades, and if you're really good you'll be able to pick out Mt. Baker. Catch Bus 4 from Douglas and Yates streets downtown.

FESTIVALS

Every year Victoria hosts a variety of fun and fabulous festivals; ask at the tourist office for a schedule. Those listed below are just a taste of what the city has to offer (basically, they'll use anything as an excuse to put on a party).

MAY If you usually smirk at mimes and subway guitarists whose repertoires consist of the slow and fast versions of *Layla*, the **International Busker's Street Festival** (tel. 604/383–2663) will change your opinion of street performers considerably. Come watch and listen to talented people who are eager to teach, chat, and strut their stuff in Market Square. On May 20, the town shifts into high gear for the **Victoria Day Parade** (tel. 604/382–3111) in honor of Queen Vic's birthday. The action centers around Douglas Street downtown. Food stands and vendors crowd the streets; schools and most workers get the day off. **The Swiftsure Lightship Classic** international boat race (tel. 604/592–2441) takes place in the Inner Harbour and the surrounding marina. Pack a picnic and set up camp on the Parliament lawn. Watch out for cops; on days like this they're out in full force and will nab you for anything.

JUNE During the last week in June, more than 250 musicians from around the world come to Victoria for the annual **Jazz Fest International** (tel. 604/388–4423). The same big names from the Vancouver jazz festival also play at this one; prices are equivalent to a regular jazz concert. **The Victoria International Boat Race** (tel. 604/382–5744), on June 22–23, draws some of the world's fastest crew teams, including those from Oxford and Harvard. Walk across the Johnson Street Bridge and hang out along the bike path for a great view.

JULY **Canada Day** (tel. 604/382–2127) is a national holiday commemorating Canada's achievement of dominion status on July 1, 1867. Most people sit and watch fireworks on the Parliament Building lawn or in Beacon Hill Park. During the last week in July, **Folk Fest** (tel. 604/388–5322) celebrates Canada and all things Canadian. For eight days the Brits step aside and native traditions are highlighted through music, dance, food, and crafts.

AUGUST In early August, the **First People's Festival** (tel. 604/387–3701) celebrates the culture of Canada's native people. Events include dance demonstrations, storytelling, potlatch (a native feast), and canoe rides on the Inner Harbour. The world-famous **Classic Boat Festival** (tel. 604/385–7766), a display of antique wooden boats in the Inner Harbour, happens August 30–September 1. **SunFest** (tel. 604/388–4423) is a world-beat music festival at which you can pretend you're in Jamaica, basking in the sun.

SHOPPING

DOWNTOWN The ubiquitous, gorgeous flower arrangements downtown weren't placed there just for decoration—their purpose is to aesthetically stimulate the tourist shopper and keep those dollars flowin'. Shops on Government Street between Yates and Wharf streets hawk everything from English woolens and bone china to exotic teas, Irish lace, and Scottish tartans. Take a walk down Trounce Alley, off Government Street between View and Fort streets, for some great

Thrift Town

Victorians don't seem to know a good thing when they've got it, as evidenced by the abundance of thrift stores that haven't been picked over—gold mines of clothes, furniture, and . . . stuff. You can find everything from vintage Mickey Mouse clocks to 18th-century furniture, but move quickly: The best items change hands more frequently than Charlie's Angels after Farrah left. Four of the best spots are St. Vincent de Paul (840 View St., tel. 604/382–3213), the Salvation Army Thrift Store (525 Johnson St., directly behind HI hostel, tel. 604/384–3755), the Goodwill Thrift Store (560 Yates St., tel. 604/385–5811), and Value Village (1810 Store St., tel. 604/380–9422). Go crazy.

boutique shopping. If you're a mall rodent, **Eaton's** on Government Street is your best bet. The fourth-floor food court has an international array of affordable eats.

The **Western Canada Wilderness Committee** gives out lots of literature on environmental issues and sells environment-oriented products, the profits from which go to preserving the B.C. wilderness. This politically active committee also sells excellent books on hiking and exploring the wilderness areas of B.C., and organizes occasional excursions and trail-building projects around the island. Other branches are in Nanaimo and Vancouver. *19 Bastion Sq., Suite 102, tel. 604/388–WCWC, fax 604/388–9223.*

Even if the two tapes you're schlepping around are your favorites, everything gets stale at some point. Lyle's Place (726 Yates St., tel. 604/382–8422) is the cheapest spot for used and new tunes, and the counter is covered with the latest word on concerts and local jams.

JOHNSON STREET Head north on Government Street to Johnson Street for funky new- and used-clothing shops. **Second Hand Roses** (101–561 Johnson St., tel. 604/386–3440) has a wide array of used Doc Martens and wacky jewelry. Victoria's closest thing to a head shop, **Off the Cuff** (587 Johnson St., tel. 604/386–2221), sells a plethora of offbeat collectibles. A sign in front of the cashier reading THOU SHALT NOT FUCK AROUND WITH OUR STOCK helps set the mood. Across the street, the **Great Outdoors Store** (570 Johnson St., tel. 604/386–8778) sells and rents every piece of outdoor equipment you can think of, including snowboards, camping gear, and skis. This is a great place to find out about and sign up for trips around the island. Another good place for outdoor equipment is **Ocean River Sports** (1437 Store St., tel. 604/381–4233). With a bulletin board filled with trip and job information, a very knowledgeable staff, and a great book selection, this the place to stop when you're missing a few essentials.

OAK BAY The neighborhood of Oak Bay is considered by many the most British in Victoria, and thus in Canada. Come here to find tea cozies, biscuits, royal-family trees, and wool sweaters. Most storefronts sport original detailing from the '30s. The **Oak Bay Theater** has been altered to house new shops and galleries, but it remains architecturally impressive. The area is about 10 minutes from the Inner Harbour, near the University of Victoria. To get here, take the free Oak Bay Explorer bus (a vintage double-decker) from downtown in front of the Empress Hotel, or take Bus 4 from Douglas Street.

AFTER DARK

Because it's flooded with restless students, Victoria has no lack of nightlife. You can always count on a few standard bars and clubs as reliable diversions, but pick up one of the free weeklies in cafés and restaurants around town to find out what's new. *Monday Magazine* is the most

Where to Go to Escape from Your Vacation

- *Every Woman's Books. This nonprofit, volunteer-operated organization offers books by and about women. Come here to find out what's happening in the lesbian community throughout the island. 635 Johnson St., tel. 604/388–9411.*

- *Munro's Books. A huge bookstore with many works by local authors, this is a good place to pick up a novel by Emily Carr or a historical work on Victoria. They occasionally host signings for local authors. 1108 Government St., tel. 604/382–2464.*

- *Snowden's. This is the best used bookstore around, although patience is required to wade through endless rows of books and old men reading pornos. 619 Johnson St., tel. 604/383–8131.*

comprehensive. *The Look Weekend Planner* in the *Times-Colonist Daily* also lists events. Canada's most British city has a high concentration of friendly but pricey pubs. Check the windows of pubs and restaurants for upcoming events; political groups often organize fund-raising parties for worthy causes.

PUBS AND BARS **Bartholomews.** Welcome to the Cheers of Canada. The clientele never changes: See if you can match the regular with his butt print on the stool. It's easy to imagine Norm himself ordering up some greasy fish and chips (C$5) and perhaps even an exceptionally good salad (C$6). During warmer months, take advantage of the patio. Live music plays every night except Monday. *777 Douglas St., beneath Executive House Hotel, tel. 604/388–5111. Wheelchair access. Open Mon.–Sat. 7 PM–2 AM, Sun. 7 PM–midnight.*

BJ's Lounge. BJ's is the only gay bar in the city, so expect it to be packed. The place booms with live music Fridays and Saturdays; it's also got a pool table, darts, and music videos playing constantly. *642 Johnson St., beneath Carleton Plaza Best Western, tel. 604/388–0505. No cover. Wheelchair access. Open Mon.–Sat. noon–1 AM, Sun. noon–midnight.*

The George and Dragon. This fun pub features live music Monday, Tuesday, Thursday, and Friday, and laser karaoke on Wednesday. The Thursday night blues jams are particularly cool. *1302 Gladstone St., at Fernwood St., tel. 604/388–4458. No cover. Open daily 10 AM–11 PM.*

Hunters. Most nights a DJ plays the newest canned tunes to a university crowd, but he takes a break on Sundays for live jazz shows that attract older locals. This place just opened, so it's in mint condition, with a huge, beautiful brass and wood bar. Expect to wait in line on weekends. *759 Yates St., tel. 604/384–7494. No cover. Wheelchair access. Open Mon.–Sat. 11:30 AM–1:30 AM, Sun. 11:30 AM–midnight.*

Spinnakers. The first brew pub in Victoria serves homemade pints to down with your kidney pie, while taking in the waterfront view. Live bands often accompany the drinking here, but the joint's recently gotten very touristy. *308 Catherine St., tel. 604/386–BREW. Wheelchair access. Open daily 7 AM–10 PM.*

MUSIC AND DANCE CLUBS **The Forge.** DJs spin Top-40 dance music for everyone from alienated slackers to alienated yuppies. *919 Douglas St., in the Strathcona Hotel, tel. 604/383–7137. No cover. Open Tues.–Sat. 8 PM–2 AM.*

Harpo's Cabaret. A longstanding Victorian favorite, Harpo's has some of the best music in town and often features big names as well as local bands. Styles range from rock-and-roll to soul to alternative. Cover charges vary according to who's playing. *15 Bastion Sq., tel. 604/385–5333. Open daily 7 PM–2 AM.*

Hermann's Dixieland Inn. This joint features jazz every night of the week, and it's worth checking out. Hermann's is a fully licensed restaurant, so in order to booze you have to eat. *753 View St., tel. 604/388–9166. Cover: $3–$5. Open Tues.–Fri. 11:30 AM–1 AM, Sat. 4 PM–midnight, Sun. 4 PM–9 PM.*

Julie's. Squeeze your butt into some spandex and head to this Top-40 dance party. It's fun to watch the scene even if you're not into it. Refrain from wearing torn jeans or you'll be curtly rejected at the door. *603 Pandora Ave., beneath Victoria Plaza Hotel, tel. 604/386–3631. Cover: $2. Wheelchair access. Open daily 8 PM–2 AM. Closed Mon.–Tues., Sept.–May.*

Rumors Cabaret. Boogie over to this dance club, popular with the gay and lesbian crowd. The best DJ in town spins disco and house all night long. If you can't dance to house . . . get over it! Or down cocktails and play pool with the hip regulars. *1325 Government St., tel. 604/385–0566. No cover. Open Mon.–Sat. 9 PM–2 AM, Sun. 9 PM–midnight.*

Near Victoria

THE GULF ISLANDS

Anchored between the mainland and Vancouver Island, the Gulf Islands vary in accessibility, amenities, and population density. Some have no running water and virtually no inhabitants.

They are all enchantingly beautiful, however, and the uninhabited ones are particularly fun to explore. All sorts of people take advantage of their remoteness, some to grow their own food, others to work on their art. Saltspring Island is the largest and most commercial, while **Penders, Mayne,** and **Saturna** are some of the more remote. In Galiano you'll find a happy medium.

B.C. Ferries (1112 Fort St., Victoria: tel. 604/656–0757 or 604/386–3431; Vancouver: 604/669–1211; Saltspring: 604/537–9921; Outer Gulf Island: 604/629–3215), open daily 7 AM–10 PM, runs daily ferries to the islands from Victoria's Swartz Bay (a 30-minute drive north on Highway 17 from Victoria), to Fulford Harbour on Saltspring Island (10 daily, C$15.50 vehicle only, C$4.25 passenger, round-trip); to Galiano (4 daily, C$16.50 vehicle, C$4.25 passenger); and from Tsawwassen near Vancouver to the Gulf Islands two–four times daily (C$30.75 vehicle only, C$7.75 passenger, one-way, return $14.75, $3.75 passenger).

SALTSPRING ISLAND The most populated and touristed of the Gulf Islands, Saltspring is easily accessible from Duncan or Victoria and from Vancouver on the mainland. You'll find all the essentials in **Ganges,** the island's main village, where art galleries, trendy boutiques, and espresso bars share the pavement with a grocery store and a post office. A number of the local galleries are worth checking out, and every year **Artcraft,** a summer-long arts-and-crafts fair, exhibits the art of more than 200 Gulf Island artists. Don't leave without seeing **Ruckle Park** (tel. 604/653–4209), a nifty restored farm. You can camp here for C$9.50 per night (no reservations accepted).

Although Saltspring is the largest of the Gulf Islands, it still makes an excellent getaway from sightseeing; you can finish the book you've been carrying around for the past two weeks or catch up on journal entries.

A number of easily accessible walking and biking paths crisscross the island, and kayaking is always an option. Ask at the **Travel Infocentre** (121 Lower Ganges Rd., tel. 604/537–5252) about other activities. During summer, another information center (2810 Fulford Ganges Rd., tel. 604/653–4254) opens up at Fulford Harbour in the Fulford Inn parking lot.

➤ **GETTING AROUND** • **Saltspring Transit** (tel. 604/537–4737 or 604/537–1846) will take you to the Fulford ferry dock (headed to Victoria) or the Long Harbour dock for C$5. If you don't catch the bus at one of the main terminals, flag it down at any safe location along the route. **Saltspring Taxi** (tel. 604/537–9712) has 24-hour service around the island, including the ferry terminals, and all cars have bicycle racks. You can rent bikes for C$15 a day at **Island Spoke Folk** (tel. 604/537–4664) in Ganges. For a C$5 fee, they'll deliver mountain bikes right to the ferry terminal. From the terminal, Ganges is a hilly 18 kilometers (11 miles). You can rent a scooter for C$50 a day at **Rainbow Rentals** (364 Lower Ganges Rd., tel. 604/537–2877).

➤ **WHERE TO SLEEP** • Most B&Bs start at around C$45 a night for two people, but some places get away with charging city rates for rural family homes. If you come in the off-season or shop around, you should be able to find something in your price range, even if you have to bargain with the owner. Stop by the tourist office for a complete price list.

Although a bit out of town (10 minutes by car) it's well worth the extra time and effort to get to **Emily's Cottage** (1390 Sunset Dr., off Vesuvius Rd., tel. 604/537–5474). The fully equipped romantic two-room cottage with breakfast costs C$50. The **Arbutus Court Motel** (770 Vesuvius Bay Rd., tel. 604/537–5415) is near the beach and the best pub in town. You get a choice between a sea or an orchard view; the surroundings are breathtaking. All rooms have private baths (doubles C$48–C$65), and eight come with a kitchen (C$55–C$75). **Cushion Lake HI Hostel** (640 Cushion Lake Rd., tel. 604/537–4149) is open year-round. It's about 2½ kilometers from Ganges, within walking distance of the beach and the lake. Trek out here on your own or give Mike, who runs the place, a call; he might come pick you up from the ferry. A bed costs C$13 for members, C$16 for nonmembers.

➤ **FOOD** • The **Saltspring Nature Works** (158 Fulford-Ganges Rd., tel. 604/537–2325) is a natural-foods market with beautiful fresh produce and great sourdough baguettes. They also serve a few deli items like focaccia pizza. The **Vesuvius Neighbourhood Pub** (Vesuvius Ferry Landing, tel. 604/537–2312), on the north end of the island, will entertain you with darts, an indoor fireplace, and an outdoor barbecue Monday–Saturday 11:30 AM–12:30 PM and Sunday

11 AM–midnight. They have live entertainment on weekends. The basic burger costs C$5.95; soup and salad combos are C$6.50. **Dagwood's Diner** (350 Upper Ganges Rd., tel. 604/537–9323) attracts big breakfast and lunch crowds year-round, and offers dinner as well in summer. The breakfast special is C$3.75, but to go all out, order the deluxe version (C$5.25). Hamburgers (C$4–C$6.50) range from basic to gourmet.

GALIANO ISLAND Part of Galiano's intrigue lies in the visible metamorphosis this once-remote island is now experiencing. Though most of Galiano remains wooded and uninhabited, a number of B&Bs have popped up in the last couple of years, and it's obvious that this offbeat spot has been spotted and plotted on the map. Galiano may not be as exotic as you expected, but it's a great place to get a tan or to camp (especially if you make it up to Dionisio Point Provincial Park). If you want to act out your Robinson Crusoe fantasies, you'll have to look elsewhere.

➤ **BASICS** • The closest thing to a visitor center is the **Galiano Island Visitor Association** booth (Sturdies Bay Rd., tel. 604/539–2233) 200 yards up from the ferry terminal. There is no public transportation for the island, but a private **bus** connects the Hummingbird Pub (tel. 604/539–5472) to Montague Harbour Provincial Marine Park Campground (tel. 604/387–4363). Expect to hitch or walk to most destinations north of Montague Harbour.

➤ **WHERE TO SLEEP** • One of the few reasonably priced B&Bs, **La Bevengerie** (Montague Harbour Rd., tel. 604/539–5392) has artfully decorated singles (C$50) and doubles (C$50–C$80), all with private bath. The tasty breakfast, hot tub, and ferry pick-up are added bonuses. **Montague Harbour Provincial Marine Park** (tel. 604/387–4363) packs in the crowds and the fun: Beaches, a forest, and boats are yours to frolic with. Four people camp for C$12. Unspoiled **Dionisio Point Provincial Park** (tel. 604/387–4363) is on the least accessible (northern) part of the island. You'll have to hitchike to get here but it's worth it. Up to four people can camp for C$6 from March until the end of October. If you scuba dive, take advantage of some intense marine life. To get here, follow Parlier Pass Road by car, on bike if you're a badass, or by thumb.

➤ **FOOD** • If someone asks you, "How about some hummer," they mean a burger at the **Hummingbird Pub** (Sturdies Bay Rd., tel. 604/539–5472). Grab that hummer (C$6) or a pot pie (C$7) between 11 AM and 10 PM. The "pub-bus" runs between Montague Harbour and the restaurant from 5 PM to 11 PM daily July–August. Bands play on weekends, but on any night it's the most happening place in town. At **Café Chaos** (Sturdies Bay Rd., tel. 604/539–2001), breakfast (served all day) is the best thing on the menu. Lunch items like hummus and pita or a chicken burger cost C$4–C$6. The café is usually open weekdays 8 AM until 9 or 10 PM, weekends 9–9.

➤ **OUTDOOR ACTIVITIES** • This island is heaven for outdoor types. Sailing, kayaking, and hiking in the forest are the main events, but you can use your imagination. Most kayaking trips are run by **Gulf Island Kayaking** (tel. 604/539–2442). Guided tours with instruction cost C$65 for a full day or C$48 for four hours (including equipment). Rentals are C$33 per day for a single kayak and C$55 for a double. The office is on the left-hand side of the main road as you get off the ferry.

ELSEWHERE NEAR VICTORIA

DUNCAN AND CHEMAINUS An hour's drive north from Victoria lies Duncan, dubbed the City of Totems for the large number of carved poles that adorn the town. The **Travel Infocentre** (381 Trans-Canada Hwy., tel. 604/746–4421) is well marked on the main highway. You'll find a couple tourist attractions/traps in the area. The **British Columbia Forest Museum Park** (RR 4 Trans-Canada Hwy., tel. 604/746–1251) features hands-on displays and a steam train ride around the 100-acre park. Admission for adults is C$7; students pay C$6. On the south end of town at the **Native Heritage Center** (200 Cowichan Way, tel. 604/746–8119), artisans carve wood and weave local Cowichan sweaters.

Further north, between Duncan and Nanaimo, the tiny town of Chemainus has carved itself a place on the map with its downtown revitalization project, which started in 1980. When the town's mainstay, the local mill, threatened to close, the townspeople preserved their history on walls turned into giant canvasses. Now the downtown area is a virtual outdoor art gallery, boasting 29 murals of mostly native subject matter (with lots on totem poles and animal themes), which explain the history of people interacting with the forest. If you're driving by, stop and check out this curiously successful project. The **Travel Infocentre** (9758 Chemainus Rd., tel. 604/246–3944) is open daily 9–5 between May 22 and September 5. The **Chemainus Hostel** (9694 Chemainus Rd., tel. 604/246–2809), on the main drag, is clean and pretty enough, but most people move on quickly to Victoria or up to Port Alberni. To get to Duncan or Chemainus by car, take Route 1 from Victoria.

SOOKE This town is best known for **All Sooke Day,** held on the third Saturday of July, when loggers come from all over to participate in shows and competitions. A 7 AM pancake breakfast kicks it all off. If you aren't particularly interested in the games, listen to the live music or peruse the arts-and-crafts stalls. The day comes to a close with a big barbecue of salmon and meat. Admission is C$6 for adults and C$4 for students (food costs extra). The **Sooke Travel Infocentre** (2070 Phillips Rd., cnr of Sooke Rd., tel. 604/642–6351) can recommend great hikes in the area. To reach Sooke from Victoria, take Bus 16 or drive approximately 35 kilometers (22 miles) west of Victoria on Route 14.

If you want to get your ass kicked, wave a Greenpeace flag during the log-rolling competition in Sooke.

East Sooke Park, an extensive wilderness park close to Victoria, is great for those who don't have time to explore the whole island but want to experience some fine hiking trails and gorgeous beaches. The **Coast Trail** is the longest and most strenuous of the hikes—a six-hour trek that follows the coast all the way from Iron Mine Bay to Becher Bay on either side of Sooke. Shorter hikes like the **Anderson Cove Trail** cover easy terrain in about two hours. Before starting any hikes, you should stop by the **park office** (tel. 604/474–PARK) just beyond the parking lot. The entire southwest coast of the island from Sooke to Port Renfrew has several secluded beaches. Look for trails leading down to the water.

Eastern Vancouver Island

A trip up the east coast on Route 1 (which magically transforms into Route 19 in Nanaimo) will give you a chance to witness a startling metamorphosis in the character of the island; in case you hadn't heard before, it ain't all like Victoria. Vancouver Island spreads out in a stunning array of mountains, waterways, and so many trees you start to wonder if they really are endless, like the logging companies say. Unfortunately, you're won't be the only person to discover the island's charms. The traffic on Route 19 near Nanaimo can bring Friday-night rush hour to mind, and roadside signs direct you to a grim assortment of strip malls and cheesy resorts. But head off the main highway and you'll soon leave the world of the Winnebago behind. The landscape becomes more rural, and tent-toting travelers will welcome the sight of several provincial parks, some good fishing, and whale-watching. Those who want more culture than the local logger's bar may want to visit Hornby and Denman islands—both refuges for bohemian types with an artsy-craftsy bent.

VISITOR INFORMATION Hikers should definitely pick up a map from **Maps B.C.** for detailed topographical information; write or call. *Maps B.C., Ministry of Environment, Parliament Bldgs., Victoria VAV 1X5, tel. 604/387–1441.*

The **Ministry of Environment, Land, and Parks** provides information on the provincial parks in the northern half of Vancouver Island, including road conditions, advice on equipment, trails, and fire restrictions. *District Manager, Parks and Outdoor Recreation Division, Rathtrevor Beach Provincial Park, Box 1479, Parksville VOR 2SO, tel. 604/248–3931 or 604/755–2483.*

GETTING AROUND A car is the best way to get up the coast, but **North Island Transport** (tel. 604/949–6300) and **Island Coach Lines** (tel. 604/753–4731) offer service all the way to Port Hardy, at the island's northern tip. Train service goes only as far as Courtenay (*see* Coming and Going, in Nanaimo, *below*).

Nanaimo

Most island travelers pass through Nanaimo at one point or another, either on their way to the Vancouver ferry or on the highway north. But the town deserves more than a quick zip-through. Like most points on the eastern coast, the landscape encompasses protected bays, sequestered islands, and sharp, precipitous mountains. Nanaimo has historically been a quiet port community, and its recent explosion of uncouth strip malls and tract houses has left long-time residents bitter, not only about the visual eyesores but about soaring taxes as well. All the same, residents are extremely welcoming and will undoubtedly point you in the direction of a Nanaimo bar, the town's delectable dessert (*see box, below*).

Nanaimo's second source of fame, after the Nanaimo bar, is the annual **Nanaimo to Vancouver International Bathtub Race.** The first fateful race, held in 1967, saw nutty contenders pile into creative bathtub contraptions and motor 55 kilometers (34 miles) across the Strait of Georgia to Vancouver's Kitsilano Beach. The rowdy event has since been expanded to include a week of family-oriented festivities called the **Marine Festival,** held in mid-July.

BASICS **Around the World Travel Services** does all things AmEx does. Call ahead if you need to change big money. *163 Commercial St., at Bastion St., tel. 604/753–2282. Open weekdays 9–5:30, Sat. 9–5.*

Travel Infocentre. They'll give you a sketchy map of the area free, but they sell a better one for C$2.95. *266 Bryden St., at Rte. 19, tel. 604/754–8474. Open May–Sept., daily 8–7; Oct.– April, weekdays 9–5.*

Western Canada Wilderness Committee. This is the place to get information on current logging issues. They also sell detailed maps. *70 Church St. #2, downtown off Rte. 19, tel. 604/754–9740. Open daily 10–5.*

COMING AND GOING From Victoria, take Route 1 north 111 kilometers (65 miles) to Nanaimo. **Island Coach Lines** (cnr of Comox and Terminal Aves., tel. 604/753–4731) runs several daily buses to Nanaimo from Victoria (2½ hrs, C$15.40 one-way), and Vancouver via Horseshoe Bay (2¾ hrs, C$17.55 one-way). Lockers for backpacks cost C$1 for 24 hours. The **Esquimalt and Nanaimo (E&N) Railway** (321 Selby St., downtown, tel. 800/561–8630) runs between Victoria and Courtenay, passing through town around 11 AM on the northward journey and 3 PM on the southward trip.

➤ **BY FERRY** • **B.C. Ferries** (tel. 604/753–6626) runs several times daily between Departure Bay, 2 miles from Nanaimo, and both Horseshoe Bay, north of Vancouver (1½ hrs), and Tsawwassen, south of Vancouver (2 hrs). You'll pay about C$6 (C$21.50 per car). They don't take reservations; arrive at least one hour before departure (earlier in summer). Take Hammond Bay Bus 2 from downtown to Departure Bay.

GETTING AROUND If you come by ferry, you'll arrive in Departure Bay. Follow Stewart Avenue south to downtown and the north–south Route 19 (a.k.a. Terminal Avenue, Nicol

Death by Chocolate in Five Layers

Chocolate lovers, beware! Nanaimo's famous culinary specialty does not involve seafood, as one might expect from a port town, but decadent layers of butter, chocolate, graham crackers, almonds, and coconut. This sumptuous dessert, known as the "Nanaimo Bar," is available at several bakeries in town. The Scotch Bakery (87 Commercial St., tel. 604/753–3521) opened in 1892 and has been a local favorite ever since. Several miles out of town, the Columbia Bakery (2151 Bowen Rd., tel. 604/758–7219) serves Nanaimo bars as well as croissants, muffins, and a variety of breads.

Street, the Island Highway, and the Trans-Canada Highway). You can easily walk around the downtown area, but since Nanaimo is spread along the waterfront you'll want to take a **city bus** (tel. 604/390–4531) to outlying areas. The Travel Infocentre (*see* Basics, *above*) gives out free schedules. The fare is C$1.25, C$3 for a day pass; exact change is necessary. The Gordon Street Exchange, near the Harbour Park Mall, is the bus hub.

WHERE TO SLEEP Nanaimo has no less than two small hostels, as well as several bed-and-breakfasts and a few budget motels strung along the highway. Your best bet, both aesthetically and economically, is to camp. Always make reservations in summer, when even the dives get crowded.

Big 7 Economy Motel. These well-maintained singles (C$36) and doubles (C$40) are decorated in the full spectrum of rusts, beiges, and browns. Request a waterbed and dream you're back in the '70s. Rooms cost less off-season. *736 Nicol St. (Rte. 19), tel. 604/754–2328. 5 min south of city center. 59 rooms.*

Carey House Bed and Breakfast. The unfussy atmosphere and huge English breakfast will make you feel like you've been adopted by a British aunt who happens to like international houseguests. The single (C$30) and double (C$45) rooms share a bath, while the basement suite (C$50) has its own. *750 Arbutus Ave., tel. 604/753–3601. Take Bus 3 two stops to Townsite Rd., right on Arbutus, walk 1½ blocks. 3 rooms.*

Tally-Ho Island Inn. This hotel shares the same building with the bus depot, so you have no excuse if you miss your bus. Clean, comfortable double rooms (even if you're single) run C$68–C$88 in the summer, C$62–C$72 off-season. *1 Terminal Ave., at Comox Rd., tel. 604/753–2241 or 800/663–7322. 101 rooms.*

➤ **HOSTELS** • **Nicol Street Mini Hostel.** This amiable hostel charges C$13 per bed for HI members and C$15 for nonmembers. The "sugar shack," a tiny room with one double bed, runs C$15 per person. You can camp on a lawn with harbor views for C$7.50. *65 Nicol St., tel. 604/753–1188, or 604/754–9697 for reservations. 5 km (3 mi) south of Departure Bay. 24 beds, 6 tent sites. Registration 4–11 PM. Laundry, kitchen.*

Thompson's Hostel. This place is a little farther from town than the Nicol Street hostel, but it has easy access to nearby swimming, canoeing, and kayaking (with free equipment). Beds cost C$12, tent sites C$5. They'll pick you up at the bus terminal from 6 to 9 PM, and drop you off in the morning. Thompson's accepts international travelers only—in a rare switch, Canadians can pretend to be American (though it won't work unless you have ID). *1660 Cedar Rd., off Rte. 1, tel. 604/722–2251. Take Bus 11 from downtown. 12 beds. Laundry, kitchen. Reservations necessary.*

➤ **STUDENT HOUSING** • **Morden Hall** and **Dunsmuir House** on the Malaspina College campus overlook the city. Sleep in a single for about C$20 and relive your dorm days. Clean rooms come with refrigerators and share a bath with an adjoining room. *750 4th St., tel. 604/754–6338. 2 km (1 mi) from downtown. Take Hayward or Fairview bus to Wakesiah and 4th Sts., walk uphill. Check-in 8 AM–4 PM weekdays. Laundry. Wheelchair access. Reservations advised. Closed Sept. 1–April 31.*

➤ **CAMPING** • **Jingle Pot Campsite and RV Park** (4012 Jingle Pot Rd., tel. 604/758–1614) makes a good back-up if the more scenic sites are full. Tent sites cost C$12 for two people. Take the bus to Rutherford Mall, walk uphill (10 min) to Jingle Pot Road.

Brannen Lake Campsite. The roomy sites on this wooded, 160-acre working farm are adjacent to a lake and hiking trails that lead off into the woods. Tent sites cost C$13 for two people (C$1 per extra person). *4228 Biggs Rd., tel. 604/756–0404. 6 km (4 mi) north of ferry terminal. Take bus to Rutherford Mall, walk uphill. 60–80 sites.*

Newcastle Island Provincial Park. The best camping around is a short passenger-ferry ride away. The park has amazing beaches and forests and *no cars*. Sites cost C$9.50 each. They don't have showers here, so be ready to stink. *2930 Trans-Canada Hwy., tel. 604/387–4363. Ferries (tel. 604/753–5141) leave hourly 10–7:30 for Newcastle Island. 18 sites.*

FOOD Nanaimo has several reasonably priced eating troughs. The **Dinghy Dock Pub** (Protection Island dock, tel. 604/753–2373) gently rocks as you eat burgers, pizzas (after 5 PM), or eccentric specialties like the excellent Cajun-style blackened halibut burger (C$8.50). Take the Protection Island ferry (tel. 604/753–8244) from Front Street. **Smiley's Pizza Pie House** (21 Nicol St., tel. 604/753–4831 or 604/753–9322) offers the best pizza in town (slices C$2, C$3 with soda) and good pasta, too. It's near the Nicol Street hostel, but for the truly lazy, delivery is free.

Filthy McNasty's Café. The smiling young staff at this low-key joint downtown serve ravioli (C$9), sandwiches (C$6–C$7), and homemade rolls fresh from the oven. The B52 latte (C$6.95), with kahlua, Bailey's, and Grand Marnier, is a heavy-duty treat. Hostel cardholders get 15% off everything. *14 Commercial St., tel. 604/753–7011. Open daily 8 AM–10 PM; kitchen closes at 9.*

Gina's Mexican Café. For hefty Mexican food, climb up to this fuchsia and purple downtown restaurant. A soft beef taco costs C$7.50, a vegetarian burrito C$7. If you can squeeze in dessert, try a fruit burrito (C$3). *47 Skinner St., behind the courthouse, tel. 604/753–5411. Open weekdays 11–9, Sat. noon–10, Sun. 2–8.*

WORTH SEEING The **Nanaimo Art Gallery** (900 5th St., tel. 604/755–8790), on the Malaspina College campus, exhibits the work of local, national, and international artists. Every summer, the gallery puts together the Festival of Banners, which showcases locally made banners throughout Nanaimo's streets. Above the waterfront, the **Nanaimo District Museum** (100 Cameron St., tel. 604/753–1821) features complete reconstructions of scenes from past island life. The museum is renovating displays at the **Bastion,** a structure built by the Hudson's Bay Company in 1853 on Nanaimo's waterfront.

AFTER DARK Do like Nanaimo natives and hang out in a pub or coffeehouse after dark. For a smoky version of the former, try the **Red Brick Saloon** on Church Street. **Queen's** (34 Victoria Crescent, btw Albert St. and Island Hwy., tel. 604/754–6751) is a booming pub with a full menu, live music every night—mainly R&B with some reggae and indie thrown in—and free pool on Sundays. For your java fix, try the **Nanaimo Coffee Roasting Company** (18 Commercial St., tel. 604/754–5471), **Javawocky** (90 Front St. #8, on the waterfront, tel. 604/753–1688), or **Thistledown Books and Coffee Shop** (15 Commercial St., tel. 604/755–1840), where you can drink your espresso amid a collection of used books.

OUTDOOR ACTIVITIES Nanaimo has parks galore and an array of water sports. **Kona Bud's Beach Rentals** (2855 Departure Bay Rd., tel. 604/758–2911) rents Windsurfers and canoes for C$10 an hour. **North Island Water Sports** (2755 Departure Bay Rd., tel. 604/758–2488) rents kayaks for C$40 (single) or C$75 (double) per day; both are at the beach at Departure Bay. **Sun Down Diving** (610 Comox Rd., tel. 604/753–1880) and **Sea Fun Divers** (300 Terminal Ave., tel. 604/754–4813) rent scuba-diving equipment for C$50 a day. **Chain Reaction** (4 Victoria Crescent, tel. 604/754–3309) has mountain bikes for C$12 a day.

Piper's Lagoon Park, north of town off Hammond Bay Road, is great for taking in the sunset or wading out to tiny islands nearby. **Morrell Sanctuary** (1050 Nanaimo Lakes Rd., tel. 604/753–5811), a second-growth forest above town, has 11 kilometers of nature trails, some wheelchair

Gourmet School Cafeteria

During the school year (September–June) the students in the Professional Cook Training Program at Malaspina College (900 5th St., tel. 604/755–8770 for reservations) cook up everything from cafeteria food to gourmet dinners, and they only charge enough to cover their costs. Three-course meals, served Thursdays, cost only about C$10 for lunch and C$18 for dinner—expect fine cuisine and fussy gourmet service. Try to arrive at the end of the semester, when the budding chefs have mastered their art.

accessible. **Petroglyph Park** (Rte. 19, several km south of town) is written up in all the tourist literature, and while it's worth a roadside stop, graffiti and vandalism have severely damaged these impressive ancient Native American rock carvings.

Head out to **Newcastle Island** for an afternoon of biking, walking, swimming, and picnicking (*also see* Camping, *above*). The **Perimeter Trail** (2½ hrs) takes you by Giovando Lookout, a great place to watch for eagles. For a shorter walk, follow the **Shoreline Trail** to Mallard Lake and the Lake Trail back to town (1 hr). To reach the island, take a 15-minute passenger-ferry ride (C$4 round-trip, C$1.50 for bicycles). The **ferry** (tel. 604/753–5141) leaves hourly 10 AM–7:30 PM every day between May and October, and on "sunny weekends" off-season, from the wharf behind the Civic Arena, just north of downtown Nanaimo on the highway. Nearby **Gabriola Island** is bigger and more populated, but it's still great for cycling and scuba diving. Ferries for Gabriola leave Nanaimo daily, every hour from 6:30 AM to 10:45 PM (C$3 round-trip, C$8.25 for vehicles).

Parksville

Parksville is Vancouver Island's answer to Waikiki, though nobody may have asked. In summer, tourists flock to the town's long, wide beach, especially during the **International Sandcastle Competition** (late July) and the **National Beach Volleyball Championships.** Although a multitude of lodges, waterfront motels, and private campgrounds fill the area, you'll be hard-pressed to find a room in July and August, when it seems all of Canada is hitting the beach. If you like seaside towns but hate the crowds, **Qualicum Beach** is a mellower version of Parksville, just north on Route 19.

VISITOR INFORMATION **Parksville Travel Infocentre.** *1275 E. Island Hwy., tel. 604/248–3613, fax 604/248–5210. 3 km (2 mi) south of town. Open May–Sept., daily 9–9; Oct.–Apr., weekdays 9–5.*

COMING AND GOING Island Coach Lines stops in Parksville on its Nanaimo–Campbell River run; the bus stop is on Harrison Street, one block west of the highway. Route 19 (Island Highway) runs right through Parksville, becoming the town's commercial strip for several miles.

WHERE TO SLEEP Chock full of amenities and greenery, **Rathtrevor Beach Provincial Park Campground** (Island Highway, along Rte. 19, 3 km from town, tel. 604/755–2483) is one of the most sought-after in all of British Columbia. They have no reservations, so you may have to join the queue at the crack of dawn in summer (the campground is closed November–March). Sites cost C$15.50. If you prefer four walls and a ceiling to au naturel, the slightly worn **Park View Motel** (196 E. Island Highway, a.k.a. Rte. 19, tel. 604/248–3331) is very near the bus stop. Rooms run C$58 in summer, C$45 in winter. Be prepared for the highway traffic to interrupt your dreams. With a central location and tent sites (C$13.50 for two) on the beach, **Park Sands Beach Resort** (105 E. Island Highway, a.k.a. Rte. 19, tel. 604/248–3171) is pretty sweet. The adjacent RVs and cottages don't really mar the experience. From the bus stop, walk to the highway and cross it. The resort closes November–March.

FOOD Parksville has more than its fair share of fast-food and family-style diners. For a healthier alternative, try the small **Thank Goodness Café** (166 W. Island Hwy., on Rte. 19, tel. 604/248–4566), which serves fresh quiche and salad (C$6.50), soup (C$2.50), lattes (C$1.95), as well as muffins and breads baked on site. The **Sand Bar Pub** (Island Hwy., on Rte. 19 downtown, tel. 604/248–4744) offers standard pub grub, including heaping nachos (C$6.75), steaks (C$12.55–C$16.25), and a Thursday night all-you-can-eat pasta bar.

NEAR PARKSVILLE

RATHTREVOR BEACH PROVINCIAL PARK Drive a few kilometers south from Parksville and you'll reach the long, sandy beaches and warm waters (average summer temperature 70°F) of Rathtrevor Park. You're free to explore the forest, marsh, and field habitats; rangers offer natural-history tours on summer days. The 174-site campground (*see* Where to Sleep, in Parksville, *above*) is well known for its amenities and fills up extremely fast in summer. Even if you don't camp, Rathtrevor is an ideal place to spend an afternoon swimming or walking. For details, contact the **Ministry of Parks, Strathcona District** (Box 1479, Parksville VOR 250, tel. 604/248–3931 or 604/755–2483).

CATHEDRAL GROVE Considered a sacred place by Native Americans, this mammoth thicket features centuries-old Douglas fir and western red cedar rising like pillars from a floor of spindly ferns. The ancient branches screen out the sun to form a cathedral-like ceiling high above your head. This is one of the few remaining areas of its kind on the east coast; the logging industry has long since changed the landscape of the rest of Vancouver Island. Though the park is extremely crowded in summer, you can still find a secluded glade and stop to read or nap under the shade of a giant cedar. From Parksville, drive west 32 kilometers (20 miles) on Route 4 to get here.

HORNE LAKE PROVINCIAL PARK Tucked deep in the woods, this park features a great series of caves, varying from huge, empty chambers to small crawlways. Three of the limestone caves are open all the time to intrepid explorers, but **Riverbend Cave,** with a total of 383 meters (1,259 feet) of mapped passages, is accessible by guided tour only. **Island Pacific Adventures** (101 Horne Lake Caves Rd., tel. 604/757–8687) gives tours from June to September and rents caving helmets (C$5). The turnoff for Horne Lake is on Route 19, about 15 kilometers north of Qualicum Beach. From here, another 15 kilometers (mostly gravel) brings you to the park entrance. If you don't want to drive back when you're done, you can spend the night at the relatively primitive **Horne Lake Campground** for C$6 per site.

Whether you plan to brave the Horne Lake caves solo or with a guide, bring good walking shoes, a warm sweater, and a flashlight.

Hornby and Denman Islands

In the '60s and '70s, the undisturbed and peaceful aura of Hornby and Denman islands attracted rural hippie types whose agricultural interests extended beyond growing pot in the backyard. The two islands support not only organic farming, but also a thriving artistic community; craftspeople and artists often open their small galleries or studios to the public. Ask at the tourist office for the brochure that lists galleries and open studios, or just look for signs on the road. The main attraction of the islands, however, remains their stunning natural beauty and variety. Even in relatively busy summer months, the islands move at a slow, if not standstill, pace.

On Hornby, **Tribune Bay Provincial Park** and **Whaling Station Bay** have fine, sandy beaches. **Little Tribune Bay** is a nude beach for those who prefer to let the sunshine in. At low tide, you can see the cool petroglyphs at **Tralee Point** (the beach at the end of Ostby Road), or make your way to **Helliwell Provincial Park,** where fauna-packed hiking trails lead along the Helliwell Bluffs; look out for sea lions, eagles, herons, seals, and beavers. From the Hornby ferry dock, a wooded trail leads east to **Ford's Cove,** where you'll find a small store, wharf, and art gallery. The walk takes about half an hour one-way; ask at the Hornby Island Resort for directions to the trailhead.

Waste Not, Want Not

Hornby's residents have developed an amazingly complete recycling project that has eliminated the need for a dump or garbage collection on the island. Except for a few nonrecyclable items, all waste is sorted and brought to the Recycling Center off Central Road. Stop by the Free Store, where people bring any reusable items like clothes, books, and dishes. If you're in the market for a new sofa or a pair of socks, check out the store between 9 AM and 1 PM Thursday through Saturday. One woman's garbage is another's living-room furniture.

Denman Island is larger and slightly less hippified than Hornby. Expect to see orchards, small farms, and the occasional deer as you travel around. Many visitors zip through to Hornby, ignoring Denman altogether, but this island has a lot to offer on its own. Though its beaches can't rival Hornby's, the island's forested parks are worth checking out. **Boyle Point Park,** on the southern end of East Road near the Denman–Hornby ferry dock, has a 1-kilometer trail that leads to land's end, overlooking the Strait of Georgia and the Chrome Island Lighthouse. From **Fillongley Park** on the island's north side, a number of trails and old logging roads lead through the entire northwestern quarter of the island. The map on Denman's brochure (available at the tourist office; *see below*) outlines several of the trails, but the actual paths are unmarked, so be prepared to do some map deciphering out in the bush.

VISITOR INFORMATION The **Denman General Store** doubles as a **Travel Infocentre** (1069 Northwest Rd., tel. 604/335–2293). Here you can pick up the free, comprehensive visitor's guide *The Undiscovered Gulf Islands.* The store also changes money. There are no banks on the islands, although the **Hornby Co-Op** (*see* Food, *below*) will change money.

COMING AND GOING B.C. Ferries (tel. 604/339–3310) sail between Buckley Bay (on Route 19) and Denman every hour (15 min, C$2.75 round-trip, C$7 per vehicle). Buses and trains traveling up the coast stop near the ferry terminal. To get to Hornby, cross the island (11 km, or 7 mi) by car, foot, or thumb to reach a second dock, where a 10-minute ferry ride takes you to Hornby's Shingle Spit dock (say that five times fast) every hour. Round-trip from Buckley Bay to Hornby is C$5.50, C$14 per vehicle (bikes ride free).

GETTING AROUND On Hornby, most of the activity centers around Tribune Bay, on the side of the island opposite the ferry dock. Again, ask for a ride or stick out your thumb if you don't want to walk the 10 kilometers (6 miles); or call the **Hornby Blue Bus** (tel. 604/335–0715), a funky 1960s International Harvester. The cost of this ride is whatever you can talk the driver into. **Cycledeli Bicycle Shop** on Denman (3646 Denman Rd., tel. 604/335–1797) rents mountain bikes for C$10 per hour or C$25 per day; the owner can point you toward the best biking trails. **The Hornby Island Off Road Bike Shop** (tel. 604/335–0444), next to the Co-Op market, rents mountain bikes as well.

WHERE TO SLEEP Accommodations on the islands start at about C$50 for a double (less off-season) and are always booked through July and August. The quality and quantity of B&Bs on both islands are high, but be sure to call ahead. Campers will find more options on Hornby, in the form of large, private campgrounds.

➤ **HORNBY** • **Bradsdadsland Resort.** This privately owned campground near the ferry docks has oceanfront campsites and is run by Brad (on his dad's land, apparently). With prior notice, two campers without a vehicle pay C$17. *Shingle Spit Rd., tel. 604/335–0757, off-season 604/681–6673. Open mid-May–mid-Sept. Lockout 11 PM–8 AM. Hot showers, flush toilets, laundry. Reservations accepted.*

Hornby Island Resort and Thatch Pub. This multifunction complex (*see also* Food, *below*) has double rooms (C$60) and five-person cabins (about C$600 a week), both of which must be reserved months in advance, as well as a campground that usually has space if you come early. Campsites are C$16. *Shingle Spit Rd., adjacent to ferry dock, tel. 604/335–0136. Coin-op showers, laundry.*

Tribune Bay Campground. Right behind the Co-Op, this place is set amid lawn and trees right in the heart of everything. Bring your own firewood and drinking water. Sites are C$18 for two people. *On Saltspring Rd., a continuation of Central Rd., tel. 604/335–2359. Hot showers 4 hrs a day. Closed Sept. 3–May 23.*

➤ **DENMAN** • **Denman Island Guest House.** This turn-of-the-century farmhouse offers easygoing hospitality, rustic rooms, and abundant country breakfasts. Singles are C$40, doubles C$50, and additional people C$10. *3808 Denman Rd., up from the ferry dock, tel. 604/335–2688. 5 rooms, none with bath.*

Sea Canary Bed and Breakfast. The centrally located Sea Canary has views of Baynes Sound and Vancouver Island from its garden and breakfast room. Four modern double rooms with shared baths go for C$50–C$60; the suite with private bath is C$75–C$85. *3305 Kirk Rd., tel. 604/335–2949. From ferry dock, left into downtown Denman, left on Kirk Rd.*

Fillongley Provincial Park. This lovely green park on the beach features a horrible little campsite with ten crammed-together stalls separated by cement blocks. Each site (C$9.50 for two people) has a fire pit, but there are no showers. *Tel. 604/ 755–2483. Follow Denman Rd. 4 km (2 mi), turn left onto Swan Rd., follow signs. Closed Nov.–mid-Apr.*

The beach fronting Fillongley Park is a clam lover's heaven, with more clams than anyone knows what to do with. Visitors can claim up to 75 clams a day for personal consumption, so come hungry.

FOOD The food here is good and not too expensive, but your choices are extremely limited. If you're camping, bring groceries. The small grocery store in Buckley Bay will sell you the basics, but you'll find better prices in Courtenay, Nanaimo, or Parksville.

➤ **HORNBY** • The grocery store, restaurant, and cafés are concentrated at the end of Central Road near Tribune Bay. If the **Co-Op** (Rural Rte. 1, at Central Rd., tel. 604/335–1121)—a combination grocery store, post office, gas station, and hardware store—doesn't have what you're looking for, you probably won't find it on the island. The Co-Op and adjacent **Ringside Market,** a grassy area with small shops and food stands, are the focal points of the community. Next to the Co-Op, popular **Vorizo Café** (5305 Central Rd., tel. 604/335–2464) specializes in Mexican dishes like quesadillas (C$5) and burritos (C$4.50); they also have an espresso bar. Next door at **Jan's Café** (tel. 604/335–1487) you can get breakfast until 11 AM, burgers (C$5), sandwiches (C$4–C$5), and luscious desserts (C$3). **The Pub** (4305 Shingle Spit Rd., tel. 604/335–0136), in the Hornby Island Resort, jams with live music about three times a week. The building, made of local rock and wood, is adorned with works by local craftspeople. The bar offers four beers on tap (C$2.50–C$4.50 a pint) as well as mixed drinks (C$4–C$6).

A few farms sell organic produce—visit **Even'side Farm Market** (1985 Central Rd., tel. 604/ 335–2231) for seriously fresh veggies. The **Cardboard House Bakery** (Central Rd., tel. 604/ 335–0733) is known around town for its creative breads (try the carrot-herb loaf for C$2.50), cinnamon buns (C$1.25), quiches (C$1.75), and espresso bar. Adjoining the bakery, **Pizza Galore** will fill you with salmon pizza and seven varieties of vegetarian pie. A slice costs C$3.75; full pizzas range from C$10–C$18.

➤ **DENMAN** • Restaurants and such are concentrated "downtown," next to the docks for ferries to Buckley Bay. The **Denman Island Store and Café** (1069 Northwest Rd., tel. 604/ 335–2293) offers tofu burgers for C$4.75 and meat burgers for C$5. Down the street, the **Kaleidoscope Market** (1055 Northwest Rd., tel. 604/335–0451) serves cappuccino in an outdoor picnic area. Both the store and the market have a small selection of groceries. For a more swish dining experience, the **Denman Island Restaurant** (3808 Denman Rd., in Denman Island Guest House, tel. 604/334–2688) has a changing menu based on fresh seafood and local produce Wednesday–Sunday 4:30–9:30 PM. A complete dinner runs about C$15, but the food, atmosphere, and garden views are worth the money.

CHEAP THRILLS To find out if any concerts, plays, or other events are happening while you're here, check the bulletin board at the Hornby Island Co-Op (*see* Food, *above*). During the first ten days in August, the **Hornby Festival** is an eclectic combination of musical, theatrical, and dance events. For more information call the Hornby Festival Society (tel. 604/335–2734).

Comox and Courtenay

What these adjacent towns lack in tourist attractions, they make up for in recreational opportunities and mellow attitude. Use them as a base for exploring extraordinary Strathcona Provincial Park nearby (*see below*) and the hiking and skiing trails of Mt. Washington and the Forbidden Plateau. The towns themselves are primarily commercial centers for logging and fishing. The area is one of the fastest-growing in Canada, as the recent rash of commercial strips and residential development should make abundantly clear. But you need only head a few kilometers west toward the mountains to return to farms, pasture, and dense, dark forests. The **Travel Infocentre** (2040 Cliffe Ave., a.k.a. Route 19, tel. 604/334-3234) hands out a crappy map for free and good one for money each day from 8:30 to 4:30.

COMING AND GOING **Island Coach Lines** (tel. 604/334-2475) stops in Courtenay several times daily on its north- and southbound runs. The trip from Nanaimo (C$15.40) takes two hours; from Port Hardy (C$43) it's 5½ hours. All buses drop you at the **bus depot** (27th St., tel. 604/287-7433), where you can also catch city buses. **B.C. Ferries** runs between Comox and Powell River on the mainland (1 hr 15 min, C$6 one-way, C$21.50 vehicle). Courtenay is the terminus of the **E&N Railway** (tel. 800/663-8249); trains leave once a day for Victoria from the station off Cumberland Road.

For the maximum scenery in a single weekend, catch the ferry from Vancouver to Victoria, drive north to Comox along the east coast of the island, take the ferry to Powell River, and return to Vancouver via the Sunshine Coast.

WHERE TO SLEEP Ask at the tourist office for the brochure listing bed-and-breakfasts; reserve ahead to avoid getting stuck in motel bland-land. The cheapest indoor accommodation around is **North Comox Hostel** (4787 Lake Trail Rd., tel. 604/338-1914), close to a series of hiking trails and swimming in Comox Lake. Beds in double rooms are C$12.50 for HI members, C$15 for nonmembers. Bonnie the owner plans to rent out a smattering of tent sites for summer at around C$10. Call ahead to be picked up from the bus or train station. To reach the hostel from downtown Courtenay, go up 5th Street and right on Lake Trail for 4 kilometers. **Greystone Manor** (4014 Haas Rd., tel. 604/338-1422), 6 kilometers south of Courtenay in Royston, is a 76-year-old house that looks right out on Comox Harbour. The place is decked out with antiques, a wood-burning stove, and pretty print wallpaper. The huge, yummy breakfast will keep you going for half the day. Singles cost C$49 and doubles C$63 at this no-smoking B&B. Look for the sign on Route 19 or, if you take the bus, ask the driver to let you off at Hilton Road.

FOOD Budget dining in the area consists of little more than fast-food joints. For picnic supplies, check out the enormous and piquantly named **Overwaitea Foods,** in the Driftwood Mall on Route 19. Consume said supplies at nearby Lewis Park, just off Route 19 in the center of Courtenay. The exceptional **Leewand Brew Pub** (649 Anderton Rd., Comox, tel. 604/339-5400) serves seafood, pasta, and Mexican dishes in the C$7-C$11 range and sandwiches for C$4.50; wash it all down with some home-brewed beer. **Zorba's Restaurant** (1832 Comox Ave., Comox, tel. 604/339-3222) has large portions of souvlaki (C$14), lamb (C$14), and Greek salad, as well as a number of pizzas (C$11-C$17). The hodgepodge decor may not win any awards, but the food is tasty and the service incredibly friendly.

OUTDOOR ACTIVITIES For hiking and camping equipment, look in at **Mountain Meadow Sports** (368 5th St., Courtenay, tel. 604/338-8999). They carry the book *Hiking III*, which has extensive listings and maps of hikes all over central Vancouver Island. *See* Strathcona Park, *below,* for info on skiing.

Campbell River

This unremarkable town, apparently named in a burst of unoriginality, sits right at the mouth of the Campbell River. Much more commercial than the other towns along the coast, Campbell River looks like one big free-enterprise zone, overrun with shopping centers and industry. But people don't come here for the architecture; they come to catch fish. Dubbed the "Salmon Fishing Capital of the World," Campbell River swarms with fishing enthusiasts, from Hollywood stars to wealthy Vancouverites, who vie to snare the enormous tyee and chinook salmon. Skilled anglers have landed some of the biggest salmon ever caught on a line just off this coast. Every year on the first weekend in July, Campbell River has a festival called—what else?—**Salmonfest,** with a fishing derby, a parade, and fireworks. If you don't fish, Campbell River (like Comox and Courtenay) makes a viable base for exploring Strathcona Provincial Park.

VISITOR INFORMATION *Campbell River Travel Infocentre. 1235 Shoppers Row, tel. 604/287-4636. Open July–early Sept., daily 8–8; mid-Sept.–June, daily 9–5.*

COMING AND GOING Route 19 runs north–south through Campbell River, and Route 28 heads west from town. Campbell River is 107 kilometers (65 miles) from Nanaimo and 220 kilometers (144 miles) from Victoria. **Island Coach Lines** (1290 Cedar Ave., across from courthouse, tel. 604/287–7151) runs buses to Nanaimo (2 hrs 45 min, C$19.80) and Victoria (5 hrs, C$35). Once a day, a bus heads north to Port Hardy (4 hrs, C$39). Scoot around town on the buses of **B.C. Transit** (tel. 604/287–RIDE) for C$1.

WHERE TO SLEEP Room rates soar during high season (June–October), when you'll be lucky to find a lean-to for under C$45 a night. Most of the motels and campgrounds are along the Island Highway (Route 19); the campgrounds usually double as RV parks, so if you want to get in touch with nature, go to Strathcona (*see below*).

At the **Above Tide Motel** (361 Island Hwy., on Rte. 19, tel. 604/286–6231), you can gaze out on Discovery Passage (the nearest body of water) from every room. The place gets a fair share of traffic noise, but rooms are clean and cheap: Singles go for C$39–C$49, doubles for C$44–C$54, and triples for C$54–C$64. **Pier House Bed and Breakfast** (670 Island Hwy., on Rte. 19 across from Discovery Pier, tel. 604/287–2943), once the town's courthouse, is stuffed with Victorian relics. It's convenient but also gets a little noisy. Singles run C$50–C$60, doubles C$60–C$70, rooms with twin beds C$75–C$85, including an elegant breakfast. Overlooking the Strait of Georgia, the clean but characterless **Vista Del Mar Hotel** (920 South Island Hwy., on Rte. 19, tel. 604/923–4271 or 800/661–4311) caters to a fishing clientele with charters and a boat launch. Singles run C$38–C$42, doubles C$48–C$52, and twins C$52–C$57.

➤ **CAMPING** • The **Campbell River Fishing Village & RV Park** (260 S. Island Hwy., on Rte. 19 2 km south of town, tel. 604/287–3630) caters primarily to RVs, but you can rent tent sites for C$15. The highway noise and treeless setting suck, but in a pinch it's a clean place to pitch your tent. Sites cost C$14–C$18 at the **Parkside Campground** (6301 Gold River Hwy., 5 km west of town, tel. 604/287–3113), but it's closed September–March. Woodsy **Elk Falls Provincial Park Campground** (Off Hwy. 28, tel. 604/755–2483), 6 kilometers (4 miles) west of Campbell River, charges C$9.50 per site. You won't find any showers, but you can always take a chilly dip in the river.

FOOD Quality restaurants are not Campbell River's strong point, but a few decent choices exist. **Super-Valu** market in the Tyee Plaza sells groceries daily 9–9. The **Royal Coachman Inn** (84 Dogwood St., tel. 604/286–0231) is a pub-like restaurant complete with dart boards, fireplace, and an array of draft beers. Pasta runs C$7–C$9; seafood dishes go for C$11 and up. Best of all, it's open until midnight. **Piccadilly Fish 'n Chips** (798 Island Hwy., a.k.a. Rte. 19, tel. 604/286–6447) operates out of an English double-decker bus on the main drag. They'll set you up with halibut and chips (C$5–C$7) or a scallop burger (C$7) to enjoy on the "upper deck" or take to go. **Pumpernickel's** (940 Island Hwy., a.k.a. Rte. 19, tel. 604/287–7414) serves espresso drinks (C$1.25–C$3), sandwiches (C$6–C$8), salads (C$5–C$8), and luscious desserts (C$3–C$5). Local artwork adorns the walls, and the evening hours (until 8 PM on weekdays, 10 PM on weekends) attract a young crowd.

WORTH SEEING You can catch and kill salmon on the water, or you can visit the **Quinsam River Salmon Hatchery** (4217 Argonaut Rd., tel. 604/287–9564), open daily 8–4, and watch them being born. Take a free self-guided tour and admire millions of shiny baby fish idly flapping their gills. To reach the hatchery, take Route 28 toward Gold River and follow the signs. **Quadra Island,** 15 minutes by ferry from Campbell River, is a popular half-day or day trip. The island has a number of hiking trails as well as the **Kwaginlth Museum and Cultural Centre,** which displays costumes, masks, and artifacts of local tribes. Ferries leaves hourly from the Campbell River waterfront (C$2.50 round-trip, C$7 per vehicle). "Lumberjack Mike," a wooden replica of a logger astride a huge western red cedar, towers above the downtown shopping district. If the statue's heroic pose entices you to learn more about logging, take a "Timbertour" with **Timberwest** (tel. 604/286–3872), a logging company that "manages" forests across the island. The free tours take you to a potentially loggable second-growth forest, an actual logging site, or a sawmill; they run three times a week May–September. Check at the booth in the travel infocentre (*see* Visitor Information, *above*).

OUTDOOR ACTIVITIES This area is good for scuba diving, sea kayaking, and canoeing. If you can scrape up about C$55 per day to rent scuba equipment at **Beaver Aquatic** (760 Island Hwy., a.k.a. Rte. 19, tel. 604/287–7652) or **Sea Fun** (tel. 604/287–3622), you'll be rewarded with crystal-clear views of eels and octopi. (Divers must be certified.) **C.V. Sea Kayaks and Canoes Ltd.** (760 Island Highway, a.k.a. Rte. 19, tel. 604/287–2650) rents and sells kayaks and canoes, and gives lessons and tours as well. Kayaks go for C$35 (single) or C$55 (double) per day; canoes are C$20.

➤ **FISHING** • You don't have to own a yacht to have fun dangling a line over **Discovery Pier** on Campbell Harbour, near the Government Wharf (C$1 per visit). If you're obsessed, splurge on a fishing charter; the cheapest you'll get will run C$50. Depending on the season, the waters swarm with salmon of almost every type: blueback, coho, chinook (or king), northern coho, and tyee. You might even land a steelhead trout. The infocentre (*see* Visitor Information, *above*) has a vast supply of brochures on fishing charters and equipment rentals.

Strathcona Provincial Park

Animals that exist nowhere else but on Vancouver Island roam free in the 570,000 acres of rugged mountain wilderness encompassed by Strathcona Provincial Park. You can spy Roosevelt elk, coastal black-tailed deer, Vancouver Island wolves, and cheeky Vancouver Island marmots (the wolves' prey) in the park's undeveloped areas. Strathcona piles up superlatives: The 2,200-meter (7,220-foot) **Golden Hinde**, in the center of the park, is the highest point on the island. The spectacular **Della Falls**, in the southern section, is the highest waterfall in Canada—tons of water crashes down 443 meters (1,452 feet), jumping over three cascades and spewing spray in all directions. The park's multitude of lakes and campsites attracts summer canoeists, anglers, and wilderness campers. In summer, hikers climb Strathcona's peaks; in winter, alpine and nordic skiers glide across the **Forbidden Plateau** and **Mt. Washington,** which lie just outside the boundaries of the park. Lodging, restaurants, equipment rental, and visitor centers cluster around Buttle Lake and Forbidden Plateau.

VISITOR INFORMATION B.C. Parks (1812 Miracle Beach Dr., Black Creek, tel. 604/337–5121), open weekdays 8–4:30, covers all the parks in northern Vancouver Island. You can also stop by the **ranger station** (no tel.) just after the entrance to Buttle Lake; they keep flyers and maps in the kiosk at the portal. If you plan to go backpacking, ask **Maps B.C.** (Ministry of Environment, Land, and Parks, Stathcona Zone, 1812 Miracle Beach Drive, Black Creek, B.C. V9J 1K1, tel. 604/336–5121) for National Topographic Series, Scale 1:50,000, F/11 Forbidden Plateau, and F/12 Buttle Lake.

WHEN TO GO During summer, you'll have mild hiking weather in the daytime, although snow sometimes lingers even at the lower elevations into July. Be prepared for cool evenings and the possibility of rain at any time. Snow generally falls from November through March and

So, You Wanna Land a Fish?

Trout (rainbow, cutthroat, steelhead): The best time of year for trout is in the winter (January–April), though you can catch them year-round. These sharp-toothed poissons may be smaller than their salmon sisters, but they taste delicious barbecued, baked, or grilled.

Salmon: Salmon fishing is done in tidal waters throughout Discovery Passage; each local fisherman seems to have a favorite spot. Blueback (young coho) season is April–June; coho season runs June–September; you'll catch springs April–September; and northern coho season is in September and October. The big ones that everyone lusts after, the tyee or chinook, have their season July–September.

gets steep and deep on the high plateaus and on the peaks. Ski season kicks in around the same time.

COMING AND GOING From Campbell River, follow Route 28 west 48 kilometers (30 miles) to the park entrance. The main highway continues west to Gold River, while a secondary road leads into the park, past Buttle Lake. If you're hitching, try standing near the beginning of Route 28, after the turnoff from Route 19 north of Campbell River. The Forbidden Plateau, a little finger of land pointing to the western coast, is inaccessible by car from Buttle Lake. You can get there on a loose gravel road from Comox and Courtenay on the coast. For skiing, **Woods Mountain Ski Park** and **Mt. Washington Ski Area** lie approximately 19 kilometers (12 miles) from Courtenay; look for the turnoff on Route 19.

WHERE TO SLEEP If you appreciate nature but need a bathroom and running water, Comox and Courtenay are the towns closest to the Forbidden Plateau (*see* Comox and Courtenay, *above*). To access Buttle Lake, you could stay in Campbell River, but if you want to explore the main body of the park, you're better off crashing at one of the two official campgrounds or splurging at the Strathcona Park Lodge just north of the lake.

Strathcona Park Lodge. On the shore of Upper Campbell Lake, this lodge is like a fantastic summer camp. Cabins, dorms, and a dining hall are spread across the woody hillside. The lodge offers outdoor education classes, canoeing and kayaking trips, ropes courses, and guided hikes. Cabins (two–eight people) go for C$80–C$115, double rooms for C$50–C$95, and campsites for C$15. *Rte. 28, tel. 604/286–8206. From Campbell River, drive 45 km (28 mi) west on Rte. 28. Breakfast, lunch, and dinner available. Closed Dec.–Feb.*

➤ **CAMPING** • The two official park campgrounds, which have a total of 161 campsites, are perched at the edge of lovely Buttle Lake. Hikers traveling in the backcountry can camp anywhere they choose, so long as they are more than 1.6 kilometers (1 mile) from the road and a reasonable distance from water sources. Both official campgrounds have fire pits.

Buttle Lake. This campground makes a great base for day hikes along the lake, where hopeful anglers vie for trout. A long beach stretches along one side of the campground, but most sites (C$12) are woodsy and private. *From the park turnoff on Rte. 28, follow paved road. 85 sites. Curfew 11 PM. Water, toilets, firewood. Closed Oct.–Apr.*

Ralph River. At this campground on the delta of the Ralph River, sharp-eyed campers can spot bear, deer, and elk. Nearby trails lead to meadows and bubbly creeks. Sites go for C$9.50. *Follow secondary highway (Buttle Lake Rd.) from Rte. 28. 75 sites. Water, toilets, firewood.*

FOOD Unless you're skilled at hunting marmot, haul your groceries from Campbell River. The only restaurant in the park is at **Strathcona Park Lodge** (Rte. 28, tel. 604/286–8206), where you can get buffet-style meals in the Whale Room. Simple but plentiful breakfasts cost C$7.50, lunch is C$8.50, and dinner runs C$13.50.

OUTDOOR ACTIVITIES Locals call Strathcona "a small version of the Rockies," thanks to the great hiking, fishing, and skiing around here.

➤ **HIKING** • Around Buttle Lake, you'll find a plethora of trails ranging from 3 kilometers to 11 kilometers. Two short paths, **Lupin Falls** (½ km) and **Karst Creek** (2 km), cover moderate terrain and are easily reached from the road that runs past Buttle Lake. At the southern end of the lake, beyond the Ralph River campground, a 6-kilometer trail leads to **Bedwell Lake**. After a steep climb, the trail opens up into subalpine terrain, and at the lake you'll find tent sites and pit toilets.

With a little luck, you can catch your dinner in Buttle Lake. You'll need a freshwater license, which you can buy at the Strathcona Park Lodge (six-days C$21, annual C$33).

To hike around the Forbidden Plateau, head to the Mt. Washington Nordic Lodge (about 30 km from Rte. 19; look for the turnoff in Courtenay). From here you can take the easy **Paradise Meadows Loop** (2.2 km) or continue farther up to a number of lakes. From Great Central Lake, accessed from Port Alberni, a 16-kilometer trail leads to the magnificent **Della Falls**. The route can be muddy and unpredictable; check with park rangers (*see* Visitor Information, *above*) before heading out.

➤ **SKIING** • **Forbidden Plateau (Wood Mountain Ski Area)** and **Mt. Washington** are both popular destinations for skiers. Mt. Washington, the more developed of the two areas, has cross-country and downhill facilities; Forbidden Plateau has a few lifts and a rope tow. Tickets run about C$30 on weekends, less on weekdays. You can reach both areas from Courtenay; the turnoff is clearly marked on Route 19. **Island Coach Lines** (tel. 604/334–2475) operates a ski bus during winter.

Port Hardy

Most visitors pass through this quiet fishing town at the end of Route 19 en route to somewhere else. Not only is Port Hardy the entryway to the Cape Scott Provincial Park on the northernmost tip of the island, but B.C. Ferries runs from here to Prince Rupert, with connections west to the Queen Charlotte Islands and north to the Alaskan Panhandle (*see* Chapter 11). Weary travelers can hole up in town for a night before taking a ferry or heading into the park. The **Port Hardy Travel Infocentre** (7250 Main St., tel. 604/949–7622) will load you up with more maps and brochures than you'll ever need.

COMING AND GOING Port Hardy lies at the northern terminus of Route 19; it's 230 km (140 mi) from Campbell River, 375 km (229 mi) from Nanaimo, and 485 km (297 mi) from Victoria. **Island Coach Lines** (7210 Market St., tel. 604/949–7532) sends daily buses to Campbell River (C$40), Nanaimo (C$58.65), and Victoria (C$70), with a separate daily bus to Vancouver via Nanaimo. In summer, an extra bus meets the night ferry from Prince Rupert.

➤ **BY FERRY** • **B.C. Ferries** (tel. 604/669–1211) makes the 15-hour, C$95 (C$51 in winter) trip between Port Hardy and Prince Rupert once every two days in summer and once a week in winter. The summer boat leaves 7:30 AM and arrives at 10:30 PM (either direction); in winter, the ferry leaves at 4:30 PM and arrives at 9 AM. A double cabin runs about C$30, but most people just spread their sleeping bags on the lounge floor. **North Island Transport** (tel. 604/949–6300) runs a shuttle bus (C$4.50) from the major hotels in Port Hardy to the terminal, which is 3–4 miles south of Port Hardy at Bear Cove; otherwise, call a **taxi** (tel. 604/949–8000).

WHERE TO SLEEP Make reservations in July and August, when tourists descend on Port Hardy. Check with the Infocentre (*see above*) for a current listing of B&Bs. A bit out of town, the **Pioneer Inn** (4965 Byng Rd., tel. 604/949–7271 or 800/663–8744) gives you the most for your money, including TVs, faded '70s furniture, and a secluded woodsy setting. Singles are C$50–C$56, doubles C$64–C$68. What the **Seagate Hotel** (8600 Granville St., tel. 604/949–6348) lacks in character, it makes up for in central location. Spacious, clean singles are C$50–C$69, doubles C$55–C$74, and triples C$60–C$79; for about C$5 extra, you can get a view. From Route 19, turn right on Hardy Bay Road and right on Granville Street.

A Whale Rub

Look for the area called Robson Bight, a few miles south of Port Hardy near the town of Port McNeil. Orca whales like to beach themselves on the shore here and rub against the round, smooth pebbles on the beach; no one is quite sure why. This favorite tummy-massage spot is now an ecological preserve, and observers must take special care not to disturb the whales as they scratch.

Recently, Robson Bight has become an item of contention between the logging industry, (which, ever the villain, wants to log the area upriver) and environmentalists, who fear that debris from logging will pile up in the water and on the beaches and deter the whales from stopping to scratch their bellies.

Adjacent to the Quatse River Salmon Hatchery, the **Quatse River Campground** (5050 Hardy Bay Rd., tel. 604/949–2395), open October–April, has grassy tent sites for C$12. Take Coal Harbour Road east from Route 19. The **Sunny Sanctuary Campground** (just south of Rte. 19 and Hardy Bay Rd. junction, tel. 604/949–8111) abounds with RVs in spring, but has a small grassy area where you can pitch your tent for C$8–C$10 (one–two people).

FOOD Rest assured that Port Hardy will never be featured in *Gourmet* magazine as a culinary destination. But if you need to fill your stomach before hopping on a ferry or heading out to Cape Scott, there are a few decent options. The **Family Baker** (7030 Market St., tel. 604/949–8122) is a combination bakery/deli that serves sandwiches (C$3–$5), salads (C$3), and soup (C$1.50), as well as row upon row of baked treats. Just across the street, the **Hardy Rock Cafe** (Market St., tel. 604/949–7625) blasts classic rock at jarring decibel levels and serves everything from a cajun prawn burrito (C$7) to gyros (C$6.25) and pizza (C$8–$12.50).

Cape Scott Provincial Park

The native Kwakiutl once roamed this lush, lonely rain forest, before a small colony of Danes tried to settle it and were brutally defeated by the elements. At the northernmost point of Vancouver Island, 60 kilometers (36 miles) east of Port Hardy, Cape Scott Provincial Park has defied civilization's attempts to conquer it. Now only animals—sea lions, otters, elk, deer, bear, cougars—dominate the 90,000 acres of scenic wilderness. No highways infiltrate the park; it's the domain of experienced and well-equipped hikers willing to tackle the demanding peaks, trek into the wilderness, and sleep in dense foliage. You should expect plenty of rain to soak you at all times of the year, but when it's clear you'll be rewarded with spectacular views.

A network of trails carved through the wilderness by enterprising Danish colonists still remains. Trails lead from the parking lot at the entrance (along San Josef Road). A 2½-kilometer (1½-mile) wheelchair-accessible trail runs to **San Josef Bay,** where the San Josef River spills into the ocean. Hikers will pass the old **Henry Ohlsen home,** which functioned as the Danes' store and post office in the early 1900s. From San Josef Bay, a trail leads across Mt. St. Patrick (422 meters) to **Sea Otter Cove** (about 10 km); parts of the trail can only be accessed at low tide. A 23.6-kilometer (14-mile) trail, also beginning in the parking lot, leads to **Cape Scott;** it passes by **Nels Bight,** a wide bay with one of the finest beaches in the park. All trails are often overgrown and/or muddy.

VISITOR INFORMATION There are no visitor information centers even remotely near the park; stop by the **B.C. Parks** zone office in Black Creek just north of Courtenay, or write for information to Ministry of Parks (District Manager, Box 1479, Parksville VOR 2SO, tel. 604/248–3931). The Port Hardy Infocentre (*see above*) can also give you a brochure on the park. Pick up Sheets I/9 and I/16 of the National Topographic Series Maps, Scale 1:50,000, Index No. 102, at a map shop anywhere in British Columbia.

No matter when you go to Cape Scott, it'll probably be the rainy season. Trails and campsites are perennially soggy, and high winds barrel through from time to time as well.

COMING AND GOING A combination of public highways and logging roads lead 60 kilometers (36 miles) west from Port Hardy to the park. From Route 19, turn left onto Holberg Road just after the Hardy Bay Road turnoff into Port Hardy, and go 48 kilometers (30 miles) to Holberg—the rest is logging road. Exert extreme caution at all times when driving the narrow gravel logging roads, with trucks whizzing by. While there's no public transit to the park, **All Kinds Trips and Charters** (tel. 604/949–7952) runs buses and boats from Port Hardy mid-June–September. For C$30, they'll bus you to the trailhead; for C$70, they'll pick you up by boat from Nissen Bight at the far end of the park and return you to Port Hardy.

WHERE TO EAT AND SLEEP **Western Forest Products** (tel. 604/956–4446) has a 14-site campground on the San Josef River just outside the park boundary. Inside the park, there are no official campgrounds, so wilderness camping is permitted almost everywhere you won't sink. The more popular areas (near San Josef Bay along the park's southern coast and at Nels Bight on the northern boundary) provide fresh water, as does the east end of Nissen Bight and Guise Bay. Bring your own food and boil all water.

PACIFIC RIM NATIONAL PARK

Pacific Rim National Park

Big, bodacious Pacific Rim National Park is Canada's first official marine park, although a third of it isn't under water. On a map, the park looks like a distorted hat, with land-bound brims and a watery crown. This luxuriant stretch of diverse terrain is actually three very different parks in one, but no part is easily accessible from any other. To the north lies the packed white sand of **Long Beach,** which stretches between the whale-watching towns of Tofino and Ucluelet on the bay. Barkley Sound, chock-full of the tiny bits of land called the **Broken Group Islands,** lies between Long Beach and the **West Coast Trail.** The rugged trail winds through miles of rain forest and watery bogs from the town of Bamfield south to Port Renfrew. The easiest way to access Pacific Rim is through Port Alberni, east of the park along Route 4. Each of the three sections—Long Beach, the Broken Group Islands, and the West Coast Trail—provides completely different recreational opportunities. You can beachcomb, kayak, or hike, although not all in the same day or place.

FEES The park charges a parking fee of C$5 a day. Reservations to hike the West Coast Trail cost C$25 per person.

WHEN TO GO If you want to conquer the West Coast Trail, come in summer, when you're less likely to freeze to death or be pummeled by incessant rain. The tourist season in Long Beach begins with the whale migration from mid-March through April; high season then kicks in and goes through October. The meteorologically inclined descend on the area during the winter to watch the spectacular winter storms; you're not advised to attempt this from your dome tent, however.

FESTIVALS Festivities in Port Alberni focus on that utterly edible fish, the salmon. Every year on Labor Day weekend, the **Salmon Festival** draws eager anglers from all over North America hoping to win the Fishing Derby and claim the C$20,000 first prize. From early to mid-August, the town hosts the **NHL Salmon Derby,** when hockey personalities, mostly from the Vancouver Canucks, raise money for charity by hooking fish (instead of each other). The **Pacific Rim Whale Festival,** held in both Tofino and Ucluelet from late March through early April, celebrates the migration of the gray whale. About 19,000 Pacific grays pass through Vancouver Island's west coast during this season. In addition to watching the mammoth creatures (which tend to look more like exposed boulders than animals), you can take part in educational programs, art shows, and other special events. Call for more info (tel. 604/725–3113 in Tofino, 604/726–4641 in Ucluelet).

This is black bear country, and the land belongs to them before anyone else. Remember that bears can run, swim, and climb faster than humans—and they're hungrier than you, too. For more info, pick up the bear pamphlet at any information center.

Port Alberni

In the center of Vancouver Island, on Route 4, Port Alberni is the last major town on the way to the park if you're coming from the east coast. There's no reason to stop here unless you need a change from the great outdoors—like a restaurant, a movie, or a standard motel. Port Alberni was quite the bustling town when the railroad ran. Now the main attraction is the paper plant, which looks even more demonic than most in contrast to its peaceful mountain setting. The **Port Alberni Travel Infocentre** (Rte. 4, tel. 604/724–6535, fax 604/724–6560) is open daily 8–8 in summer, daily 9–5 in winter.

The Robertson Creek Hatchery allows you to see how salmon survive. Although you can take a tour year-round, the best months to visit are September and October, when the mature fish

371

return to spawn. You can watch the entire process, beginning with the adult fish spawning and ending with the maturation of the eggs. The self-guided tours are free. *Tel. 604/724–6521. On the Stamp River at the end of Grand Central Lake, 18 km (11 mi) from Port Alberni off Great Central Lake Rd. Open daily 8 AM–4 PM.*

COMING AND GOING Driving from Victoria, take Route 1 north to Route 4 west; if you're coming from the northern part of the island, take Route 19 to Route 4. **Island Coach Lines** (4541 Margaret St., Port Alberni, tel. 604/724–1266) stops in towns all along the island's east coast. Daily buses run to Victoria (3½ hrs, C$26.40 one-way) and to Tofino (2 hrs, C$15). **Orient Stage Lines Ltd.** (tel. 604/723–6924) also serves Port Alberni and Tofino.

The boat *M.V. Lady Rose* is not just a way to reach Pacific Rim National Park; it's an experience. This Scottish masterpiece, built in 1937, departs three times a week from the Argyle Street Dock at the Alberni Harbour Quay and steams down the Alberni Inlet to Bamfield. The round-trip takes about nine hours. The ship sails on Tuesday, Thursday, and Saturday, and also on Friday in summer. During summer, there are additional sailings through the Broken Group Islands to the town of Ucluelet that leave on Monday, Wednesday, and Friday; the round-trip is about 11 hours. Fares run C$15–C$18 one-way and C$30–C$35 round-trip, depending on your destination. For reservations and information, stop by the office in the Alberni Harbour Quay. Daily and weekly kayak rentals are also available at the same number and address. *Alberni Marine Transportation, Inc., Port Alberni, tel. 604/723–8313 or 800/663–7192 (Apr.–Sept.), fax 604/723–8314.*

WHERE TO SLEEP Port Alberni has the standard blah motels for around C$40–C$50 per night per double. A few private campgrounds are on Route 4 and on Redford Street near the junction of Routes 4 and 4A, but the provincial park campgrounds (*see* Near Port Alberni, *below*) are cheaper and better.

Friendship Lodge. At this no-frills operation, you'll get a bed on the linoleum floor and like it. A single is C$25 (C$35 with breakfast, C$50 with full board). Semiprivate rooms cost about C$5 less. Some rooms have sinks, but for more complete ablutions you must use one of the immaculate hall bathrooms. *3978 8th Ave., tel. 604/723–6511. 14 rooms, none with bath. Luggage storage.*

Roger's Creek Bed and Breakfast. One more night of motel decor might send you over the edge? The solution is Rogers Creek. Comfortable doubles go for C$45; twins are C$55. *4405 Elizabeth St., tel. 604/723–4371. Across from Rogers Creek Park. 3 rooms, none with bath.*

➤ **CAMPING** • **Dry Creek Public Campground.** Situated next to a creek and trees near the Alberni Harbour Quay, this campsite offers sites for C$6–C$13 per vehicle. Happily, the campground reflects the beauty of the surrounding area rather than the industrial feel of the city. *4225 Wallace St., off 3rd Ave., tel. 604/723–6011. Showers, flush toilets. Closed Oct.–mid-May.*

FOOD Budget dining in Port Alberni is generally mediocre. Wherever you stay, you're bound to be near a **Safeway** (3756 10th Ave., tel. 604/723–6212; or 359B Johnston Rd., tel. 604/723–5000). The **Alberni Harbour Quay,** a touristy shopping complex on the waterfront, has a few decent places, but you might want to walk a few blocks to the far more authentic **Blue Door Café** (5415 Argyle St., tel. 604/723–8811), open daily 5 AM–3:30 PM. Patrons who look remarkably like Archie Bunker feast on massive meat 'n potatoes fare, including burgers (C$7) and sandwiches (C$6). The **Swale Rock Café** (5328 Argyle St., tel. 604/723–0777) is the closest you'll come to hip in this sleepy town; stop by Sunday–Thursday 7 AM–9 PM, Friday–Saturday 7 AM–10 PM. The homemade bread is heavenly, as is the seafood club (C$7). For dinner try the seafood fettuccini (C$10)—don't fret, bread comes with it.

OUTDOOR ACTIVITIES Fishing is fun in these parts (because everyone catches at least one), but it's also big business. Before embarking on an adventure, head to the travel infocentre for the *Sport Fishing Guide,* which will clue you into the do's and don'ts. A one-day fishing license costs C$3.75 at sporting-goods stores (there's one in Harbour Quay), hotels, or service stations. Expect a chartered fishing trip to cost at least C$80. **Alberni Pacific Charters** (5440 Argyle St., tel. 604/724–3112) is the biggest and cheapest charter company. Kayaking is also a pricey venture—C$50 for three hours of instruction with all equipment included. The best place to sign up for lessons or rent equipment is **Alpha-Wave Adventures** (5425 Argyle St., tel. 604/723–0026).

NEAR PORT ALBERNI

SPROAT LAKE West of Port Alberni on Route 4, **Sproat Lake Provincial Park** (tel. 604/248–3931) is known for its prehistoric petroglyphs. Carved by an unknown people, these ancient stone carvings depict the spirits that inhabited the forests, mountains, skies, and waters of the native Canadian world. The park is split into two segments, one north of Route 4 and one south along the lake. The petroglyphs are in the park's lower segment, an easy hike from the lake's sometimes-sunny shores.

Take your pick between two provincial park campgrounds: The forested **Upper Campground** has 44 sites, and the **Lower Campground** by the shores of Sproat Lake has 15. Both offer picnic facilities, easy trails around the lake, showers, and swimming. Expect a huge crowd during July and August. The sites cost C$10 and are open all year on a first-come, first-serve basis (like all provincial campgrounds). While you're at the lake, have a look at the **Martin Mars Water Bombers** (tel. 604/723–6225), the largest fire-fighting boat planes in the world.

Long Beach

Bordered by Tofino to the north and Ucluelet to the south, this section of the park is by far the most accessible and hence the most visited. Long Beach consists of 7 miles of beautiful white sand, guarded by the sea below and dense forest and cliffs above. To those who have been spoiled by a coastal hometown, Long Beach may seem like just another beautiful beach, but visitors are willing to fight serious crowds (during late July and August) to get here. It's best to come during tidal changes, at sunrise or sunset, when Long Beach is truly spectacular. If it's sunny, pack a picnic and climb up onto the rock islands (they're islands if the tide is high and exposed rock if it's low).

You can't camp on Long Beach, but if you stay close to the parking lot, where washed-up logs separate sand from cement, you can probably catch some inconspicuous z's.

At the southern end of Long Beach, off Route 4, lies the town of **Ucluelet,** the whale-watching capital of North America. Ucluelet (pronounced you-CLUE-let) has totally devoted itself to the sea. People come from all over to fish, watch whales, scuba dive, and surf—an influx that causes the small town to swell

A Gray Whale Feeding Frenzy

What do Baja and Pacific Rim National Park have in common? Nothing much, besides the migration of the gray whale. In January, herds of pregnant females travel from the Arctic to the warm waters of Baja, Mexico, to give birth. Soon after the calf is born, the whole family begins a migration back up to colder water. As they pass the coast of Vancouver Island, hunger hits and they begin the filter-feeding process. They don't have teeth; instead they filter in an enormous amount of organisms from the water through their baleen, a horny screen of sorts in their mouths. This filter feeding occurs close to shore, where the whales can dig into the sand but still come up for water every three to five minutes. The bingeing lasts a couple months, during which an enormous entourage of tourists climb into small boats for the whale-watching season. You can spot gray whales by the spurts of water they shoot 3–4 meters (10–12 feet) into the air every three to five minutes. If you're lucky, you might see an orca (killer whale).

to several times its ordinary size from spring through fall. Although Ucluelet is currently going through substantial changes to better cater to tourists (adding new restaurants and lodgings, etc.), it's much more industrial than neighboring Tofino.

At the end of Route 4 on the northern tip of Long Beach, **Tofino** is another excellent whale-watching spot along the west coast. It abounds with beachfront resorts, motels, and several unique B&Bs. Tofino is smaller and more popular than Ucluelet with those who prefer a mellow, laid-back atmosphere. Groups of Volkswagen-driving, guitar-playing types don't seem to scare off the families, more of whom visit each year to partake in activities geared toward all budgets and levels of athletic ability (*see* Outdoor Activities, *below*).

The area supports a myriad of art galleries. The most dazzling is the **Eagle Aerie Gallery** (350 Campbell Rd., Tofino, tel. 604/725–3235), which displays the silkscreen compositions of artist Roy Vickers, known for his bold use of color and purity of line. Vickers, the son of a Tsimshian fisherman, designed the gallery based on a traditional west coast longhouse, an artistic accomplishment in itself.

VISITOR INFORMATION The **Ucluelet Travel Infocentre** (620 Peninsula Rd., tel. 604/726–4641) runs a seasonal travel info office at the Tofino/Ucluelet Junction from July to August. In Tofino, the helpful staff at the **Travel Infocentre** (380 Campbell St., downstairs from Chamber of Commerce, tel. 604/725–3414) hands out brochures on whale-watching and excursions to Meares Island, as well as local menus, weekdays 11–5.

Long Beach Visitor Information. Get info here on trail conditions and camping as well as cougar or bear alerts. For stuff in advance write to the Superintendent, Pacific Rim National Park, Box 280, Ucluelet V0R 3A0. *Pacific Rim Hwy. (Rte. 4), tel. 604/726–4212. 2 km north of Tofino/Ucluelet junction. Open mid-Mar.–Sept., daily 10–6.*

Wickaninnish Centre. This place offers a historical and ecological overview of the area, complete with displays, murals, films, and talks on the ecology of the Pacific Northwest. *Tel. 604/726–4701. South end of beach; follow signs. Wheelchair access. Open mid-Mar.–Sept., daily noon–5.*

COMING AND GOING From Port Alberni, Route 4 runs west to Tofino, Ucluelet, and the Long Beach section of the park. In summer, you often have to fight heavy traffic along the highway. **Island Coach Lines** (4541 Margaret St., Port Alberni, tel. 604/724–1266) operates a few buses daily between Port Alberni and Tofino and Ucluelet for about C$15. The **M.V. Lady Rose** (tel. 604/723–8313, fax 604/723–8314) sails from Port Alberni to Ucluelet (*see* Coming and Going, in Port Alberni, *above*).

WHERE TO SLEEP There are no formal accommodations or restaurants in the park. The closest places for such things are Tofino and Ucluelet. You can't camp on the beach, but several campgrounds occupy the bluffs above the beach.

➤ **UCLUELET** • While the town has its fair share of bed-and-breakfasts, their prices would sink most budget travelers—rooms start at C$40 and go up. The cheapest are **Bayview B&B** (238 Mavis St., tel. 604/726–7175), 3 miles north of Ucluelet, and **Bumble Bee B&B** (1235 Peninsula Rd., tel. 604/726–2550); both have clean double rooms for C$50. You can crash on a cot in the Bumble Bee's living room for 10 bucks. The prices at the **Ucluelet Hotel** (250 Main St., tel. 604/726–4324) help alleviate the barren atmosphere. Singles and doubles are a mere C$25–C$35, depending on the room. Dimly lit cabins on the boat/hotel at the **Canadian Princess Fishing Resort** (Boat Basin, tel. 604/726–7771 or 800/603–7090) are decked out like Disneyland's Pirates of the Caribbean. Clean, small doubles cost C$49, C$59 in summer; the Captain's Cabin (C$69, C$79 in summer) has its own bath. Look left as you enter Ucluelet on Peninsula Road and you can't miss the place.

➤ **TOFINO** • Budget travelers, it's time to pitch your tent. There's no hostel here, and rooms under C$30 are scarce. If you decide to spring for a room, B&Bs are your best bet. The tourist office in Tofino (*see* Visitor Information, *above*) has a complete list with prices. Several privately owned beachfront campground resorts line the highway just outside town. The **Dolphin Motel** (1190 Pacific Rim Hwy., tel. 604/725–3377) is a standard roadside crash pad with singles for C$38–C$66, doubles for C$42–C$66, and twins for C$52–C$66. Prices drop in the off-season. **Midori's Place** (370 Gibson St., tel. 604/725–2203) offers rooms with bath and breakfast for C$50 per single, C$55 per double. You'll pay a few bucks extra at the waterfront **Paddler's Inn** (320 Main St., tel. 604/725–4222), but the scrumptious breakfast and airy rooms are worth the C$50–C$75 per double. They close mid-October–March.

➤ **CAMPING** • **Bella Pacifica Resort and Campground.** This campground right on Macken-zie Beach would be fabulous if not for the high prices and the gaggle of RVs blocking your view of the water. A space for two costs C$18.50–C$26.50, all hookups included. Reserve at least seven days in advance. *Tel. 604/725–3400. About 3½ km (2 mi) out of Tofino. Free hot show-ers, laundry, ice machines. Closed Oct.–Mar.*

Green Point. This drive-in campground has fire pits and flush toilets, and it's open year-round. Sites cost C$14 and fill up fast. During summer, they use a waiting-list system; stop by to get a number and instructions on when to come back, usually in one to three days. *Rte. 4, tel. 604/726–4245. Halfway btw Ucluelet and Tofino. 94 sites. No credit cards.*

Pacific Rim Resort Campground. This spiffy, spotless campground has bathrooms, picnic tables, and an arcade. The sites cost C$20 for two and an additional C$4 for each person. Hookup and water are C$3 each. *1481 Pacific Rim Hwy. (Rte. 4), tel. 604/725–3202. 10 min south of Tofino. 284 sites. No credit cards.*

Schooner Cove. Sites are right above the beach, but it's a 10-minute walk to get there. Tides completely submerge this place in winter. Sites are C$6 per tent, first come, first served. *Rte. 4, tel. 604/725–2479. 15 km north of Tofino/Ucluelet junction. Pit toilets, water. Closed Sept. 30–May 1.*

FOOD Considering that the population of the area is over 2,000, restaurant options are not all that extensive. Stock up on groceries before you come.

➤ **UCLUELET** • At least the food's better than the movie at **Porky's 2** (1950 Peninsula Rd., tel. 604/726–7577). Their cheap, greasy eats will cure your hangover. Grab fish and chips (C$6) or a Porky's burger (C$3) daily 11 AM–9 PM. The original Porky's (308 Neill St., tel. 604/725–3921) is in Tofino. The **Wickannish Restaurant** (tel. 604/726–7706), 16 kilometers (10 miles) north of Ucluelet, occupies a spiffy wooden lodge on the beach. Seafood is the primary dish; the clam chowder is especially tasty. Entrées range from C$11 to C$20. The restaurant closes mid-October–mid-March.

➤ **TOFINO** • Tofino offers great food, shining views, and an utterly friendly atmosphere. The only bummer is price. If you're in no position to throw down the Visa card, several markets carry quality groceries at a reasonable cost. The **Tofino Co-Op** (140 1st St., tel. 604/725–3226) sells organic foods, baked goods, camping supplies, and standard groceries. **Organic Matters** (637 Campbell St.), open Monday–Saturday 10–5, is a fully equipped organic market.

The inexpensive **Alley Way Café** (tel. 604/725–3105), behind the bank at Campbell and 1st streets, serves a Canadianized, ultrahealthy form of Mexican cuisine each day 10–10 between May and September. The vegetarian burrito (C$5.50) is stuffed with tofu, sautéed corn, onions, and other veggies. You can also get a clam burger (C$5.50) or tabouli salad (C$3.75). Inside a striking glass-and-wood building, the **Common Loaf Bake Shop** (180 Campbell St., tel. 604/725–3915) will feed you luscious cinnamon rolls and Tofino bars (the local version of the Nanaimo bar). It's open summer, daily 8–9, winter 8–6, and the outstanding baked goods make the wait worthwhile. They sell day-old bread at reduced prices (C$1.25), and in the evenings you can get pizzas with fresh ingredients and whole-wheat crusts (about C$7). **The Loft** (346 Campbell St., tel. 604/725–4241), open daily 7 AM–10 PM, serves wholesome food in grand proportions. Try the eggs Benedict (C$7.95).

OUTDOOR ACTIVITIES Feel free to explore a number of well-mapped and -maintained hik-ing trails. The seasonal Information Centre stocks maps of the eight Long Beach trails, which range from 1 to 5 kilometers. (If you come in the off-season, the Tofino Travel Infocentre offers the same map.) The **Wickaninnish Trail,** which connects Long Beach and Florencia Bay to the south, is a great hike for the eager and adventurous. This was once part of the land route from

Tofino to Ucluelet. For an easier hike, try the **Spruce Fringe Trail,** a 1.5-kilometer loop that explores the Sitka spruce area fronting the ocean, or the short but excellent **Rain Forest Trail.**

The gray whales appear en masse between mid-March and April. Remember that going out to have a peek means entering their world; many charters will obnoxiously follow any whale they spot, cruising almost on top of them so passengers can get better views. The best way to see the peaceful creatures is from a respectful distance. To find out about all the companies, go to the information center in Tofino. **Chinook Charters** (450 Campbell St., tel. 604/725–3431) and **Zodiac Whale Watching** (568 Campbell St., tel. 604/725–3330 or 800/666-9833) in Tofino are the two cheapest outfits; a two-hour whale watching trip costs about C$35.

In the mad rush to catch sight of the elusive, mammoth whales, few stop to think about what effect the armada of charter boats has on the animals themselves.

The **Tofino Sea Kayaking Company** (320 Main St., tel. 604/725–4222) rents kayak equipment and offers lessons for C$35 an hour. Single kayaks go for C$38 a day, doubles for C$65. The company also runs day trips to Meares Island (4 hrs, C$48), the Duffin Passage Islands (2½ hrs, C$36), and others. They also sell charts of Clayoquot Sound and Tofino Harbour.

Surfers brave the icy Pacific here, too, in one of the only places to ride the waves in Canada. **Live to Surf** (1182 Tofino Hwy., Tofino, tel. 604/725–4464) rents boards for six hours (C$25).

Hot Springs Cove consist of a series of pools in natural rock formations. Because of their isolation, they're much less crowded than most hot springs, and the ocean view makes them spectacular. Several companies run half-day trips here for about C$55. Check with the Tofino Infocentre to get the names and rates of other companies. At the springs, clothing is optional, and most visitors opt to go au naturel.

NEAR LONG BEACH

MEARES ISLAND This little island's virgin rain forest became a hot spot for the Tofino environmental movement in 1980, when the Friends of Clayoquot Sound formed to rescue the island from logging operations. When the logging company decided to start cutting, Tofino residents staged a protest that encouraged visitors from all over the continent to visit the island and witness the incredible beauty that was about to be destroyed. Eventually, Meares Island was officially declared a tribal park by the Clayoquot and Ahousaht Native Indian Bands, permanently forbidding logging. Boats to the island operate out of Tofino, and you can hike the tribal park trails. An easy walking loop starting from the dock takes about 2½ hours and passes through lush vegetation; gung-ho hikers can embark on longer trails off the main path. For C$20, **Nuu-Chah-Nulth Booking and Information** (tel. 604/725–2888 or 800/665–9425) will drop up to four people off on the rocks and pick them up at the same spot at a designated time. Don't get lost, because there's nothing here but nature. Check the Tofino Travel Infocentre (*see* Visitor Information, *above*) for the different companies offering boat trips, or stop by the marinas. **Tofino Sea Kayaking Company** (tel. 604/725–4222) has introductory kayak trips to the island and a guided tour of the Big Tree Trail for C$35 per person.

Broken Group Islands

The Broken Group Islands, a cluster of more than 100 islands and islets in the Barkley Sound, are a kayaker's wet dream. The turbulent waters surrounding these 100-plus islands teem with sea lions, seals, and whales. The Broken Group's inaccessibility makes a trip here a true adventure. The water supply is very limited in the off-season: You may opt to carry your own, and you should certainly treat or boil any water used on the island. You're not allowed to light fires on the islands, so bring a stove if you want to cook. There are no trash cans; be prepared to take out everything you bring in. No one should attempt to visit here alone, and you should definitely arrange a boat ride back to Tofino. Make sure to carry a marine chart to navigate through the reefs. The C$8 Canadian Hydrographic Service Chart has navigation information on one side and a complete description of the history, hazards, campsite facilities, and fishing regulations of the islands on the reverse side. You can buy it at most marinas and fuel docks, or order it by mail from Canadian Hydrographic Society, Chart Sales Distribution Office, Institute of Ocean Sciences, 9860 W. Saanich Rd., Box 600, Sidney, B.C. V8L 4B2.

Most people who come here are not only outdoor badasses but strong kayakers as well. Experienced paddlers can rent kayaks from the **Tofino Sea Kayaking Company** (*see* Outdoor Activities, in Long Beach, *above*). If you come from Victoria, you might stop at **Ocean River Sports** (*see* Shopping, in Victoria, *above*) to find out what kind of kayaking, sailing, or hiking trips they have scheduled.

COMING AND GOING The only way to access these islands is by boat. Private charters are available but very costly. To find out more about charter companies, contact the **Ucluelet Travel Infocentre** (620 Peninsula Rd., tel. 604/726–4641). The most spectacular way to get from Port Alberni to the Broken Group Islands, Bamfield, and Ucluelet is aboard the old Scottish-built freighter *Lady Rose* (*see* Coming and Going, in Port Alberni, *above*), which passes through gorgeous scenery and will drop you off and pick you up at a prearranged time and place.

WHERE TO SLEEP There are eight campgrounds on the Broken Group Islands. All are open May–September and have access to pit toilets and fire pits (though you must bring your own water). The park doesn't take reservations for campsites, but the Tofino Travel Infocentre (*see* Visitor Information, in Long Beach, *above*) offers detailed maps of where the sites are and how to access them. They also carry the Hydrographic Service Chart.

West Coast Trail

Some of the most spectacular and challenging coastal wilderness ever trudged across by creatures in boots and backpacks stretches 75 kilometers (46 miles) between the tiny towns of **Bamfield** and **Port Renfrew.** This section of the coast is known as the "Graveyard of the Pacific," because of the number of ships that have smashed against the rocks and sunk off its treacherous shores. After the SS *Valencia* ran aground in 1906, killing passengers and crew, the Canadian government constructed the West Coast Trail to help shipwrecked sailors reach safe ground. Upgraded by the Canadian Parks Service in the late 1970s, the trail follows the coast, offering smashing views of the sea, dense forest, sandstone cliffs, and an untouched landscape abounding with wildlife. Black bears and snakes slink about, while sea otters and gray whales sun and spout along the shore. The coast is blistered with caves and craggy rock formations, and the waterfalls and swimming holes along the route allow you to sit and soak your aching feet.

Unfortunately for the nature-loving tenderfoot, only experienced, competent hikers should attempt the West Coast Trail. The first 10 kilometers (6 miles) north from Port Renfrew are possibly the most difficult part, but no part of the trail is a smooth stroll through the park. How the Canadians expected half-drowned sailors to traverse this landscape is anyone's guess. You'll encounter a variety of terrain, including muddy tropical rain forest, sticky bogs, steep slopes, deep gullies, and high cliffs crossed by a series of wooden ladders. Rain drenches the landscape most of the year, resulting in slippery boardwalks, mud slicks, and treacherous footing on decomposing logs. Rivers cutting across the trail can only be crossed in manually powered cable cars. Finishing the trail has become major fodder for bragging among travelers. When you're done, you too can stop others on the street to tell them what a stud you are.

You can approach the trail from either end. Hike, hitch, or drive 5 kilometers (3 miles) from Bamfield to the **Northern trailhead.** If you come from Victoria, you'll start at the **Southern trailhead** in Port Renfrew (*see* Coming and Going, *below*). Although you could tackle the trail in about a week, most veterans advise taking at least 10 days to appreciate the beauty along the way. A new rule instituted last year to protect the environment limits use of the trail to 52 hikers per day, plus a few spaces set aside for stand-by hikers. You must make an advance reservation, which cost C$25 per hiker, by calling Pacific Rim National Park (tel. 604/728–1282) at least seven days in advance. You can also reserve by calling **Discover B.C.** (tel. 800/663–6000 in Canada and U.S., 604/387–1642 outside) between 6 AM and 6 PM. Spaces fill up quickly, so call as early as you can.

Backpackers should bring food, a means for cooking it, a water purifier, and the full barrage of all-weather camping gear. You'll also need enough cash (at least C$15) to pay for two ferry crossings. The **Gordon River Ferry** (tel. 604/647–5430, call for times), at the southern trail-head near Port Renfrew, is privately run, while the **Nitinat Narrows Ferry**, about 32 kilometers (20 miles) along the trail, is run by the park. Nitinat Narrows ferries run daily 9–5 from May 12 to September 30. To contact the ferry, dial 0–711 for a Campbell River Radio Telephone Operator and ask for Nitinat Raven. The call number is N692932.

VISITOR INFORMATION The best places to find information are the **Park Registration Centres** at either end of the West Coast Trail. They distribute essentials like contour maps (C$5) and tide tables. You must register here to hike the trail. The center at the northern end of the trail (tel. 604/728–3234) is at Pachena Bay, 5 kilometers (3 miles) south of Bamfield. At the southern end, the office is next to the Port Renfrew Recreation Centre (tel. 604/647–5434). The recommended map for hiking the trail is West Coast Trail, Port Renfrew-Bamfield (scale 1:50,000, contour interval 100 feet). If you want to look it over ahead of time, order it from the Superintendent, Pacific Rim National Park, Box 280, Ucluelet, B.C. V0R 3A0 (tel. 604/726–7721, or 604/726–4214 mid-Mar.–Sept.). Contact the **Western Canada Wilderness Committee** in Victoria (201 Bastion Sq., tel. 604/388–9292) for literature on the environmental issues in the West Coast Trail area.

COMING AND GOING Most visitors drive 1½ hours from Port Alberni into Bamfield, at the northern end of the trail, along a gravel logging road. From Victoria, it's a 92-kilometer (56-mile), two-hour ride along Route 14 to Port Renfrew in the south.

➤ **BY BUS** • The **Pacheenaht Band Bus Service** (4521 10th Ave., Port Alberni, tel. 604/647–5521) operates on call during summer between Port Renfrew and Bamfield. One-way fare is about C$25 (C$20 for students). **Western Bus Lines Ltd.** (4521 10th Ave., Port Alberni, tel. 604/723–3341) runs every Monday, Wednesday, and Friday between Port Alberni and Bamfield (2 hrs, C$17). The bus leaves from the Western Bus Lines/Island Coach Lines Depot in Port Alberni (4541 Margaret St., Port Alberni, tel. 604/724–1266) and from the Tides and Trails Café (cnr of Frigatte and Bamfield Rds.) in Bamfield. Reservations are recommended.

No public buses run between Victoria and Port Renfrew, but a few shuttle services cover that route. **Knight Limousine Service, Ltd.,** also called **Port Renfrew Connector** (3297 Douglas St., 2nd floor, Victoria, tel. 604/475–3010), leaves twice daily from Victoria at 7:30 AM and 2 PM and stops at the trail-registration center on its way to Port Renfrew. One-way fare is C$25. Reservations are required, and it's possible to arrange a pickup from the Victoria youth hostel. The **West Coast Trail Express** (tel. 604/985–4301) leaves Victoria at 8 AM and arrives in Bamfield at 11:40 AM. The return trip leaves Bamfield at 1 PM and arrives in Victoria at 4:45 PM. For a pre-hike thrill, fly to the trail via **Hanna's Air Saltspring** (tel. 604/537–9359). Prices vary for these trips from Vancouver to Port Renfrew and Bamfield; it's pricier than a bus, but you'll get an amazing perspective on what lies ahead.

WHERE TO SLEEP Designated campsites are scattered along the West Coast Trail, mostly on or near the beaches, but you shouldn't encounter too many objections no matter where you decide to sleep. Should you need to spend the night in Port Renfrew or Bamfield, there are one or two decent options. **Gallaugher's West Coast Fish Camp** (Beach Rd., Port Renfrew, tel. 604/647–5535 or 604/746–5469) has four minimalist cottages with showers and fully equipped kitchens on the San Juan River (C$40–C$50 for two people). **Orca II Bed and Breakfast** (44 Tsongoray Rd., Port Renfrew, tel. 604/647–5528), one block from the beach at San Juan Bay, may not be the nicest place you've ever stayed, but it's far more comfortable than the front seat of your rent-a-wreck. Singles (C$35–C$40) and doubles (C$50) have shared bath and come with breakfast. In Bamfield, the CYHA-affili-ated **Sea Beam Hostel** (c/o General Delivery, Bamfield V0R

With 270 people living in the town of Bamfield, you're more likely to find a neighborhood barbecue than a restaurant. Stock up on groceries before you come—the same goes for Port Renfrew.

1B0, tel. 604/728–3286) provides a common room with a fireplace ideal for trading stories about the horrors and exhilarations of the West Coast Trail. It's C$15 per night for a dorm bed; camping costs C$12. Call for directions.

BRITISH COLUMBIA 11
AND THE ALASKAN
PANHANDLE

By Helen Lenda and Marisa Gierlich

For most Alaska-bound travelers, British Columbia blurs into a long, scenic thor-oughfare, a series of eats and sleeps and long highways. Haste is understandable: British Columbia's forests are incredible, but they're being logged; its rivers are powerful, but they're being dammed; its people are friendly but rarely more than just "nice"; and wild climate, scenery, and characters await at the end of the road, in Alaska. The best part of traveling in B.C. is the ease of doing so. Roads are well-marked and well-maintained, and provincial travel-information centers tell you what you need to know about lodging, restaurants, tourist attractions, and road conditions. Furthermore, the provincial parks that appear every 50 miles or so on all main highways provide leafy respites from the road and, more often than not, contain primitive, self-registration campgrounds.

Before driving north toward Fairbanks on the Alcan (also called the Alaska) Highway, give your car a thorough going-over, make sure your tires (including the spare) are in good shape, and prepare for a bumpy, muddy, incredible ride. Before veering west into Alaska, the Alcan takes you into the Yukon, the Canadian region that became a household word during the gold rush, when a day's panning could be more lucrative than a lifetime in a traditional job. **Whitehorse** is the region's capital and transportation hub, but **Dawson City**, where relics of the lawless frontier abound, retains more of a gold-rush-era feel.

Alaska's Panhandle, also called Southeast Alaska, straggles down the coast between the Gulf of Alaska and Canada like a crumpled tail. This is the Alaska most often seen by tourists. Every summer, cruise ships carry thousands of vacationers through the waters off the Panhandle. The whole of Southeast Alaska consists of a series of islands, bays, channels, and inlets, all dominated by awesome ice fields and glaciers.

The border between Alaska and the Yukon is only open 9–9; the crossings between Washington and British Columbia are open 24 hours. You should bring a passport to enter Canada from the United States, even if it doesn't quite feel like another country.

Because the region is so watery, cars just aren't that useful: Many Panhandle communities aren't even connected by road. Instead, residents and travelers alike use the **Alaska Marine Highway**, a system of ferries serving the region's isolated communities. Fortunately, the ferries don't have to brave the fury of the Gulf of Alaska, sticking instead to the inland bays and channels that make up the famed Inside Passage.

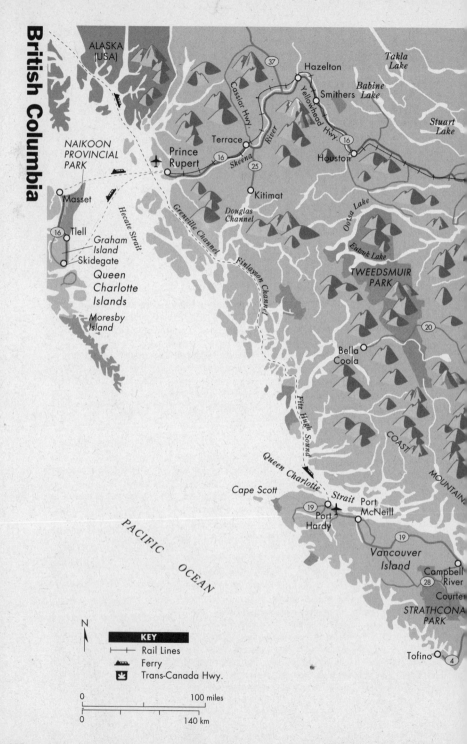

British Columbia

ALASKA (USA)

Takla Lake

(37)

Hazelton

Babine Lake

Yellowhead Hwy.

Smithers

Cassiar Hwy.

Stuart Lake

NAIKOON PROVINCIAL PARK

Terrace

(16)

Houston

(16)

Prince Rupert

Skeena

(25)

River

Masset

Kitimat

Douglas Channel

(16)

Tlell

Hecate Strait

Ootsa Lake

Graham Island

Skidegate

Grenville Channel

Eutsuk Lake

Queen Charlotte Islands

Finlayson Channel

TWEEDSMUIR PARK

Moresby Island

(20)

Bella Coola

Fitz Hugh Sound

COAST

Queen Charlotte Strait

MOUNTAINS

Cape Scott

Port McNeill

(19)

Port Hardy

Vancouver Island

(19)

PACIFIC OCEAN

Campbell River

(28)

Courte

STRATHCONA PARK

Tofino

(4)

N

KEY
Rail Lines
Ferry
Trans-Canada Hwy.

0   100 miles

0   140 km

ALBERTA

Grande Cache

JASPER NATIONAL PARK

Vanderhoof

John Hart Hwy.

Yellowhead

Prince George

Cariboo Hwy.

Barkerville

BOWRON LAKE PARK

Quesnel

Quesnel Lake

MOUNT ROBSON PARK

COLUMBIA MOUNTAINS

Kinbasket Lake

WELLS GRAY PARK

FRASER

Williams Lake

PLATEAU

Cariboo Hwy

Fraser

Clearwater

MONASHEE MOUNTAINS

Adams Lake

100 Mile House

Shuswap Lake

Cache Creek

Lillooet

Kamloops

Okanagan Lake

Vernon

Oyama

Merritt

Kelowna

Westbank

Peachland

Whistler

Pemberton

Lytton

Summerland

Penticton

Powell River

GARIBALDI PARK

CATHEDRAL PROV. PARK

Squamish

Howe Sound

Harrison Hot Springs

MANNING PARK

CANADA

USA

Nanaimo

Vancouver

Port Alberni

Duncan

NORTH CASCADES NATIONAL PARK

Victoria

Port Angeles

TO SEATTLE

The Alaska Highway

Between Kamloops and Dawson Creek, the Cariboo and John Hart highways keep you moving past logging towns and former fur-trading and gold-mining posts. These now-peaceful burbs were once controlled by the British-owned Hudson's Bay Company, a fur-trading monopoly that sidelined in imperialism and murder in the name of profit. The Cassiar Highway branches off the Cariboo at Prince George and continues north. The Alcan Highway, the major route connecting Canada and Alaska, officially begins farther on, at Dawson Creek.

If you're driving north for the pure adventure of it, the Alcan (as in Alaska–Canada) Highway is the only way to go. The two-lane route extends 1,519 miles between Dawson Creek, British Columbia, and Delta Junction, Alaska (just east of Fairbanks). This stretch passes through steep mountain ranges and land roamed by sheep, moose, and caribou. The winding road, unpaved in parts and always under construction, is slow going at times and murder for anyone prone to car sickness. But the Alcan isn't so much about getting somewhere, it's about enjoying the long, scenic, rural—and did we say long?—ride.

For an idealized view of life in these parts circa 1900, rent Robert Altman's "McCabe and Mrs. Miller," a film starring Warren Beatty and Julie Christie as endearing capitalists braving the Northwest frontier.

Until the Alcan officially begins at Dawson Creek, most of the "towns" along the highway are just truck stops—gas stations, motels, auto-repair shops, and fast-food joints lined up along both sides of the road. These tend to be anticlimactic after a long day's drive, but they make efficient, relatively cheap pit stops. If you're planning on spending the night indoors, keep in mind that rates at in-town motels are about 30% less than those at the isolated lodges off the highway. However, camping is the accommodation of choice: Provincial park campgrounds are everywhere, and the primitive sites usually cost about C$9–C$12 a night. Private campgrounds, usually part of motel/gas-station complexes, run C$10–C$15 a site and often provide hot showers and laundry facilities. The entire drive from Seattle to Fairbanks should take between six and 10 days. Highlights along the way include Muncho Lake, Stone Sheep Provincial Park, Liard Hot Springs, and the vast Kluane National Park.

BASICS Travel "Infocentres" (clearly marked by red-and-blue signs) carry information on attractions, accommodations, and weather and road conditions. For some important pre-trip dirt, write the tourist offices in Whitehorse or Dawson Creek (*see below*) for an Alaska Highway info packet.

MONEY The U.S. dollar is very strong in Canada and is widely accepted, though you'll generally get crappy rates unless you change money at a bank. Banks are open weekdays 9–5:30. Gas stations and hotels are the second-best options for money exchange. You'll find ATMs throughout Canada that accept Visa and American Express as well as Plus and Cirrus affiliated bank cards.

WHEN TO GO The best month to drive the Alcan is May, before the kids and mosquitoes get out of hand. That said, the weather in May is unpredictable—plan for wind, rain, and bouts of sunshine. The weather in summer is usually just fine, and, consequently, July and August see the most traffic on the Alcan. The highway is a nightmare in winter: The road is battered by snow and sleet, and most hotels and restaurants go into hibernation.

PUBLICATIONS The *Milepost* (C$18.95), put out by Vernon Publications, is the Alaska Highway bible and is available at gas stations, hotels, and cafés along the way. The *Adventure Guide to the Alaska Highway* (Hunter Publishing Inc., C$15.95) is another informative and well-written publication.

COMING AND GOING Several bus companies serve the Alaska Highway and surrounding areas. **Greyhound** (tel. 604/662–3222 or 800/661–8747 in Canada) goes north to Whitehorse and west to Prince Rupert. A seat on the daily bus from Dawson Creek to Whitehorse costs C$161 one-way. **Alaska Direct** (tel. 403/668–4833) has extensive connections in Alaska but it ain't cheap: Whitehorse–Fairbanks one-way costs $120. **Norline Coaches** (tel. 403/668–

3355) serves mostly Yukon destinations. Whitehorse to Dawson City costs C$68 one-way on Norline. **Alaskon Express** (tel. 800/554–2206) runs from Whitehorse to Fairbanks for a whopping $155 one-way.

AlaskaPass, Inc. (tel. 907/766–3145 or 800/248–7598) offers a comprehensive travel pass that allows unlimited walk-on passage on Alaska Marine Highway ferries (which serve the Panhandle's Inside Passage), as well as free rides on the Alaska Railroad, Alaskon Express, and four bus, ferry, and train companies in British Columbia and the Yukon. From May through October, an eight-day pass costs $499, a 15-day pass $629, a 30-day pass $879, and a 45-day pass $929. The only restriction on the pass is a $50 surcharge imposed on ferry travel originating in Bellingham, Washington. In winter, prices drop about 30%. Calculate your costs before you buy; the pass is worth the money only if you plan on doing *a lot* of traveling.

Kamloops

Kamloops is still getting used to its size and has yet to outgrow its awkward adolescence. A full third of its commercial enterprises were established as recently as 1993, when the town hosted the Canadian Summer Games and the World Fly Fishing Championships. Handily located at the confluence of the Thompson and North Thompson rivers, 220 miles northeast of Vancouver, Kamloops had its start as a logging and mining town. It now makes a very convenient, if not particularly picturesque, place to eat, sleep, and stock up on tourist info.

Indiscreet strip malls and fast-food chains greet visitors on the outskirts of town. Kamloops's historic core, centered around Victoria Street and Third Avenue, is a little easier on the eye and offers all the necessities: Movie theaters, pubs, and laundromats abound, and there are even a few hip-hop/skate-rat clothing shops thrown in for good measure. During summer, **Riverside Park** is a popular sunset strolling spot, and the **Wanda Sue Paddlewheeler** (1140 River St., at 10th Ave., tel. 604/374–7447) runs scenic two-hour tours up the Thompson River (C$10 per person). The **Kamloops Museum and Art Gallery** (207 Seymore St., tel. 604/828–3576), open from May to September, features an interesting selection of photographs and modern and pop art.

BASICS Travel Infocentre. *1290 W. Trans-Canada Hwy., tel. 604/374–3377. Southern edge of town, off Aberdeen Mall exit. Open weekdays 8–8, weekends 8–6.*

COMING AND GOING Kamloops is 356 kilometers (220 miles) of expressway from Vancouver. For 24-hour information on which of the several highways connecting the cities is

How the Alcan Came to Be

For a road, the Alaska Highway has a fascinating history. After the Japanese attack on Pearl Harbor in 1941, the security of Alaska became a top-priority concern. Canadian objections to plans for an overland route connecting the Lower 48 to Alaska melted away, and, in a back-breaking effort, 11,000 soldiers and 7,000 civilians built the road in eight short months. Covering 1,519 miles and crossing 130 bridges, the highway was a major feat of engineering. After all the sweat and toil, it was never important in the war, though it has had profound effects on both the United States and Canada. The virtually unexplored regions of northern British Columbia, the Yukon, and Alaska were suddenly linked with "civilization." Further, the 3,000 African-American soldiers who worked on the highway won recognition that was crucial in achieving a fully integrated army. Historic mileposts that mark natural and man-made points of interest were set up along the highway in 1992 in celebration of the highway's 50th anniversary.

preferable, call the **Road Report** (tel. 604/371–4997). For info on public transportation to the city, call **Greyhound** (tel. 604/374–1212); for info on buses within Kamloops, call **Kamloops Transit** (tel. 604/376–1216).

WHERE TO SLEEP Plenty of chain motels on the highway greet road-weary travelers with open arms, but driving a few extra miles into the city center will save you C$10–C$15 on a room. Stop in at the Travel Infocentre (*see above*) for brochures on campgrounds and B&Bs.

Fountain Motel. The clean but boring rooms at this motel come with TVs and phones. A night here will set you back C$40 for a single, C$50 for a double, C$60 for a triple, or C$68 for one of the two triples with kitchenettes. *506 Columbia St., tel. 604/374–4451, fax 604/374–2469. 4 blocks from city center. 22 rooms.*

Plaza Motor Hotel. While it ain't *the* Plaza, this hotel sits on the town's main intersection, above a bar frequented by burly roughneck types. Tattered double rooms cost C$55 a night. *405 Victoria St., at 3rd Ave., tel. 604/372–7121. 85 rooms.*

➤ **HOSTELS** • **Old Courthouse Hostel (HI).** Housed in the town's 1909 provincial courthouse, this hostel has beautifully kept dorms (C$13.50 members, C$18.50 non-members) as well as private rooms (C$31.50 members, C$50 non-members) that sleep up to three people. Check-in is 7–1 and 4–11:30 daily. *7 W. Seymore St., at 1st Ave., tel. 604/828–7991, fax 604/828–2442. 68 beds, 3 private rooms. Laundry, luggage storage, kitchen.*

FOOD In a town where fast-food reigns supreme, health nuts can get their fix at **The Zone Organic Market** (444 Victoria St., tel. 604/828–7899); their soups (C$2.75) and salads (C$2.75–C$4) come with hefty hunks of homemade bread. The chef's daily specials, usually Mexican dishes, are dependably filling and run about C$5.25. The popular **Kelly O'Bryan's** bar (235 Lansdowne St., btw 1st Ave. and 3rd Ave., tel. 604/828–1559) is open daily 11 AM–midnight and serves giant portions of chicken wings, stuffed mushrooms, and fried zucchini (each C$2.75). If it's your birthday, come in for a free prime-rib dinner (normally C$11.95).

The Cariboo Highway

The Cariboo Highway is a 440-kilometer (275-mile) stretch of Highway 97 between Kamloops and Prince George. The GOLD RUSH TRAIL signs that line this well-paved two-lane road leave little doubt as to its origin. The six-hour drive between these two cities follows the same route as the old Cariboo Wagon Trail that prospectors traveled from the bustling port of Vancouver to Barkerville, the region's richest mining town. Attractions like **100 Mile House** and **70 Mile House** are named for their distance from Goldpan City (now just a bend in the Fraser River), the first place that a prospector hit pay dirt in the early 1860s. History aside, the Cariboo has a distinct rhythm to it. Services are available about every 64 kilometers (40 miles); between stops you'll find ample opportunities for camping and plenty of small motels in woodsy settings.

Although the hub towns along the Cariboo Highway teem with useful services, most have about as much charm as a pair of wet wool socks. Because of the many pulp mills that thrive in this region, the towns also tend to smell a bit like wet wool socks.

CACHE CREEK This T-shape town at the junction of the Trans-Canada (Hwy. 1) and Cariboo (Hwy. 97) highways is little more than an oversized pit stop. But the town's cheap motels and restaurants, as well as its proximity to Seattle (just a seven-hour drive away), make it a good overnight stop. In summer, the staff at the **Travel Infocentre** (1340 Hwy. 97, in Chevron station, tel. 604/457–5306) can tell you what's going on around town. When that center closes (September to June), ask at the **general store**. This venerable institution is across from the **Desert Motel** (1069 Hwy. 1, just south of junction, tel. 604/457–6226), where you'll find clean single (C$45), double (C$55), and triple (C$65) rooms with phones and TVs, as well as a heated pool. The less-than-hospitable **Sage Hills Motel** (1390 Hwy. 97, just north of junction, tel. 604/457–6451) has cheaper rooms (C$30 single, C$40 double, C$45 triple) that all come with TVs, phones, and a substantial layer of grime.

WILLIAMS LAKE Williams Lake is the biggest town between Cache Creek and Quesnel. Travelers arriving at the end of the 203-kilometer (126-mile) drive north from Cache Creek are slammed in the senses as woodsy shores and serene lakeside towns give way to gas stations, strip malls, and pulp mills. Those who approach from the north, on the other hand, are relieved by the oasis of pristine beauty provided by the lake. The **Williams Lake Stampede,** held annually on a weekend in mid-July, is the biggest fair in the region. It draws fans of rodeo, pie-eating contests, and barn dancing from all over Canada.

The best thing to do in Williams Lake is mooch off relatives with lake-front property. Otherwise, head 45 minutes south out of town on Highway 97 to the **campground** in the provincial park on the shores of Lac La Hache; it's open May–October, and sites go for C$9.50. Stock up on brochures and maps at the **Travel Infocentre** (1148 S. Broadway, off Hwy. 97, tel. 604/392–5025) at the south end of town. On City Hall Street there are two supermarkets, **Safeway** (open daily 9–6) and **Overwaitea** (open Mon.–Sat. 9–6); chain restaurants and gas stations are scattered around town. If you have an extra 15 minutes or just want to stretch your legs, the **Scout Island Nature Center** (south side of town, off Hwy. 97, tel. 604/398–8532) is worth a look. A trail leads you around this little island, where occasional signs provide info about local plants and animals.

QUESNEL This big-time logging town 120 kilometers (72 miles) north of Williams Lake is the biggest city on the Cariboo Highway. Quesnel tries to entice the just-passing-through tourists to stay awhile by promoting its three big attractions: **Barkerville Historic Park** (*see box, below*); **Billy Barker Days,** a river fair and rodeo held every year on the third weekend in July; and the **Riverfront Trail Walk,** a pretty 3-mile loop that leads along two rivers and through the city center. (You can park your car and start the walk at Ceal Tingley Park.) All are worthwhile if you're in town, but they're nothing to stop for in and of themselves. The well-stocked **Travel Infocentre** (703 Carson Ave., off Hwy. 97, tel. 604/992–8716 or 800/667–0143 in B.C.) is open daily 9–4 and shares space with the **Quesnel and District Museum** (705 Carson Ave., tel. 604/992–9580), with a notable collection of regional memorabilia; admission is C$1.50. The eight square blocks that constitute Quesnel's city center hold a fair number of cheap restaurants, a **Safeway** market (Reid St., tel. 604/992–6477), and a few gas stations.

Quesnel has plenty of affordable accommodations. The friendly family at **Good Night Inn** (176 Davie St., tel. 604/992–2187) rents clean rooms with TVs and garage-sale decor for

Barkerville Historic Park

Founded by Billy Barker, who struck gold on William's Creek in 1862, Barkerville was once the largest city north of San Francisco and west of Chicago. It was also North America's most important Chinese community north of San Francisco and a mecca for fortune seekers hoping to repeat Barker's lucky strike. Today the town is a full-scale living-history museum. For those not turned off by "historic recreations," it's worth the hour's drive east of Quesnel. The town's wooden buildings and plank sidewalks are original, and some establishments—including a Chinese restaurant, an excellent bakery, and a dry-goods store—are open for business from mid-June to early September. During summer, the town goes into high gear with horse-pull contests, wagon races, and theater performances, and everything is run by fully costumed people who act as if they've time-warped back to 1870. In season, the park operates daily 8–8, and admission is C$5.50 (C$3.25 students). For the rest of the year, you can wander the deserted buildings freely at any time of day. Hwy. 26, tel. 604/994–3332.

C$40–C$55, depending on the season, how many people you want to stuff in one room, and the manager's mood. The inn even boasts an indoor pool. Eight kilometers (5 miles) north of Quesnel, the **Lazy Daze Campground** (off Hwy. 97 at 10 Mile Lake Rd., tel. 604/992–3282) has virtually unlimited tent space for C$12 a site (including hot showers and laundry facilities). Four C$28 rooms sleep three each. They're often booked, so call ahead.

Prince George

Prince George has been booming since the 1800s, when the Hudson's Bay Company established a fur-trading post here. Prince George's commercial importance increased yet again when the railway was built right through it just after the turn of the 20th century. The town that resulted is surprisingly pleasant, with no less than 120 parks within the city limits. The **Fraser Fort George Regional Museum** (323 20th Ave., tel. 604/562–1612) features a thorough exhibit on Prince George's history from its founding in 1802 by trapper Simon Fraser.

The Cassiar Highway, to the west of the Alcan, may be a quicker way to Alaska (depending on road conditions), but it's certainly not the easiest way up. A road that's unpaved for 150 miles and serves as an emergency landing strip for airplanes hardly inspires one to relax and switch on the cruise control.

Besides being a major crossroads for people heading up the Cassiar and Alaska highways, Prince George is the headquarters for a number of reforestation organizations that hire throngs of college-age Canadians to plant trees during summer—for info, contact **Roots Reforestation** (tel. 604/562–4884). As a result, despite the squat, square blocks of motels and convenience stores, downtown Prince George has a bit of bohemian flair. On weekend nights you can even hear live blues and rock at the **Urban Coffeehouse** (1188 6th Ave., tel. 604/562–6762). The **Other Art Café** (1148 7th Ave., tel. 604/561–1553) serves great coffee and vegetarian food. It also presents live jazz, blues, funk, and reggae nightly in summer (weekends only in winter). During the day, groups of four or more can call the **Pacific Western Brewing Company** (641 N. Nechako Blvd., tel. 604/562–2424), 2 miles north of Prince George, to arrange a free tour and tasting.

BASICS The **Travel Infocentre** (1198 Victoria St., tel. 604/562–3700) has the most comprehensive regional info, but if you just want a city map and the scoop on local happenings, stop by **Mosquito Books** (1209 5th Ave., tel. 604/563–6495).

COMING AND GOING From Kamloops, Prince George is nearly a full-day drive: 611 kilometers (381 miles), switching from Highway 1 to Highway 97 at Cache Creek. From Prince George, it's another 725 kilometers (450 miles) to Prince Rupert, the jumping-off point for the lush Queen Charlotte Islands (*see below*). The **B.C. Rail Station** (1108 Industrial Way, tel. 604/564–9080) sends trains primarily to the south; one-way fare to Vancouver is C$100. Trains depart the **VIA Rail Station** (tel. 604/564–5233) for destinations all over Canada. Call **Greyhound** (tel. 604/564–5454) for the scoop on long-distance buses.

WHERE TO SLEEP Most affordable lodgings are clustered along the highways on the outskirts of town. Downtown, the streets get rowdy at night, so solo travelers should stay alert. The clean and relatively quiet **Connaught Motor Inn** (1550 Victoria St., btw 15th St. and 16th St., tel. 604/562–4441 or 800/663–6620 in B.C.) has singles for C$35, doubles for C$49, and triples for C$55. From May to September, the **KOA Campground** (Hwy. 16, west of town, tel. 604/964–7272) offers a heated pool, laundry, and a convenience store. It's mostly for RVs, but it does have a decent grassy area set aside for tents (C$15 for two people), and two log cabins (C$55) that sleep up to four.

FOOD There are quite a few ethnic restaurants downtown—Indian, Hungarian, German, Japanese—but most overcharge and serve piddling portions. The reigning favorite is the **Oriental Inn** (955 Victoria St., btw 9th Ave. and 10th Ave., tel. 604/563–6432), where C$6.50 gets you a greasy combo plate of egg rolls, chow mein, and a chicken, beef, or pork dish. Vegetarian fare is available upon request. **Café Maia** (4th St., at Brunswick Ave., tel. 604/564–7859) is a funky bistro that serves fresh salads (C$3.25–C$5.50), veggie and chicken burgers (C$6.50), and souvlaki (C$7.95 with chicken, C$10.95 with prawns). The café is open weekdays 8 AM–10 PM, Saturday 9 AM–11 PM, and Sunday 10–6.

NEAR PRINCE GEORGE

THE YELLOWHEAD HIGHWAY This 720-kilometer (450-mile) stretch of paved, two-lane highway extends from Prince George to the port town of Prince Rupert, following the valleys of the Nechako, Bulkley, and Skeena rivers along the route of the Canadian National Railway. There's not much in the way of services between towns, so keep an eye on your gas tank. **Terrace**, 584 kilometers (365 miles) from Prince George, where the Yellowhead and Cassiar highways meet, is the biggest town, with a good selection of motels and restaurants.

The John Hart Highway

The 414-kilometer (259-mile) stretch of Highway 97 between Prince George and Dawson Creek passes through some amazingly diverse country that affords plenty of opportunities for camping and fishing. Along the 188-kilometer (118-mile) expanse between Prince George and the Mackenzie Junction, you'll find four lakes with public campgrounds: **Bear, Summit, Carp,** and **McLeod.** Bear and McLeod lakes both have provincial park campgrounds with pit toilets, fire rings, and picnic tables; sites are C$7–C$12. Summit and Carp lakes have extremely basic, free forestry campgrounds. As you pass McLeod Lake, the highway starts to climb. Past the scenic **Bijoux Falls** rest area, you'll reach the highway's summit at **Pine Pass** (elevation: 884 meters), where a turquoise lake sits against an imposing ridge that is part of the Rocky Mountains. North of here, the evergreens give way to poplar, aspen, and birch, as the highway descends into the Peace River valley. Small gas stations and cafés pop up every hour or so, and the restaurant at **Whiskers Bay,** 130 kilometers (81 miles) north of Prince George, is open 24 hours a day.

CHETWYND Other stops along the highway are more scenic but tend to shut down without warning. Chetwynd, on the other hand, is about the only point between Prince George and Dawson Creek where you are sure to find a room and a meal at any time of year. The local **Travel Infocentre** (5200 North Access Rd., next to a caboose on the east edge of town, tel. 604/788-3345) is open weekdays 9–4:30. The relatively modern **Pinecone Motor Inn** (5440 52nd Ave., tel. 604/788-3311) has clean singles for C$45, doubles for C$50, and triples for C$55 as well as a restaurant that serves filling omelets (C$4.50), sandwiches (C$3.50–C$6.95), and dinner entrées (C$7.95–C$12.95) daily 6 AM–11 PM. The **Windrem Motel** (5201 S. Access Rd., tel. 604/788-2460) is a combination motel and campground. Tent sites go for C$15, including electricity and water, and cabins go for C$38 (C$46 with kitchenette).

Dawson Creek

The Alaska Highway is Dawson Creek's raison d'être. Most out-of-towners set foot in Dawson Creek for only as long as it takes to leave it and head north to Alaska. You'll find a **Safeway** (tel. 604/782-2854) and a **K-Mart** (tel. 604/782-3391), as well as plenty of gas stations and auto-parts stores on Eighth Street, just south of Highway 97. The **Museum and Travel Infocentre** (8th St., at Hwy. 97, tel. 604/782-9595), open daily 8–8, is an old railway station filled with memorabilia from the highway-building 1940s. Next door, in what used to be a grain elevator, the **Dawson Creek Art Gallery** (101-816 Alaska Ave., tel. 604/782-2601) displays local artists' work on walls surrounding a winding staircase.

The "Mile Zero" post at the corner of Eighth and 102nd streets (a block south of the Infocentre) is Dawson Creek's biggest attraction: Snap a photo of the official beginning of the Alcan, and get the hell out of this square, flat town.

WHERE TO SLEEP AND EAT Since being downtown is of no real importance, you're better off staying at one of the budget motels along Highway 97 (called Alaska Avenue in the southwest part of town, Eighth Street in the southeast, and 120th Avenue elsewhere). The **Trail Motel** (1748 Alaska Ave., tel. 604/782-8595) caters to executive types but has decent rates:

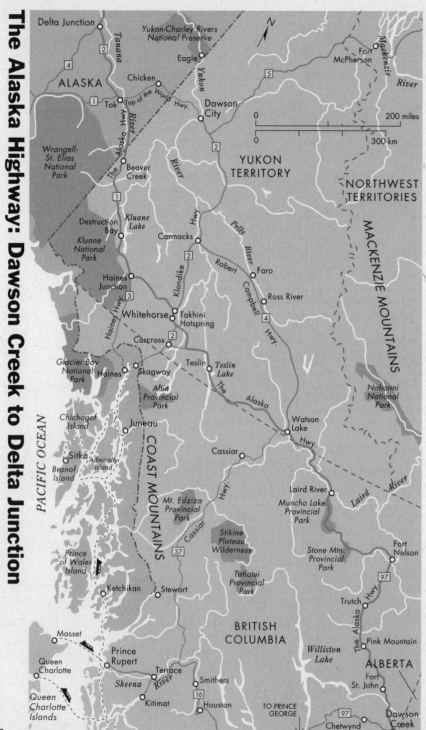

The Alaska Highway: Dawson Creek to Delta Junction

Delta Junction

Yukon-Charley Rivers National Preserve

Tanana

2

4

ALASKA

Chicken

Tok

Top of the World Hwy.

The Alaska Hwy

Eagle

Yukon

5

Fort McPherson

Mackenzie River

1

Dawson City

Wrangell-St. Elias National Park

Beaver Creek

River

2

YUKON TERRITORY

NORTHWEST TERRITORIES

0   200 miles

0   300 km

1

Destruction Bay

Kluane Lake

Kluane National Park

Carmacks

Klondike

Hwy.

Pelly River

Robert

Campbell

Faro

Ross River

MACKENZIE MOUNTAINS

Haines Junction

3

2

Whitehorse

Takhini Hotspring

4

Hwy.

Nahanni National Park

Carcross

2

Teslin

Teslin Lake

The

Alaska

Glacier Bay National Park

Haines

Skagway

Atlin Provincial Park

Watson Lake

Hwy

Chichagof Island

Juneau

Cassiar

PACIFIC OCEAN

Sitka

Branof Island

Admiralty Island

Laird River

Laird River

Muncho Lake Provincial Park

Mt. Edziza Provincial Park

Cassiar Hwy.

COAST MOUNTAINS

Prince of Wales Island

Stikine Plateau Wilderness

Stone Mtn. Provincial Park

Fort Nelson

37

Ketchikan

Stewart

Tatlatui Provincial Park

The Alaska Hwy

97

Trutch

Masset

BRITISH COLUMBIA

Williston Lake

Pink Mountain

ALBERTA

Queen Charlotte

Prince Rupert

Terrace

Skeena River

Smithers

16

Houston

TO PRINCE GEORGE

Fort St. John

Queen Charlotte Islands

Kitimat

97

Chetwynd

Dawson Creek

Singles are C$50, doubles C$55, triples C$60. The **Airport Inn** (800 120th Ave., tel. 604/782–9404) is run by a congenial family that keeps the newly renovated rooms in great shape. Singles are C$35, doubles C$45, triples C$49. The **Dawson Creek Diner and Deli** (8th St., at 102nd St., tel. 604/782–1182) has made-to-order pizzas (C$6–C$10 small, C$11–C$14 large), salads and sandwiches (C$3.50–C$4.95), and daily specials (less than C$10) to eat in or take on the road. **The Orion** (910 102nd Ave., tel. 604/782–8297) serves Chinese dishes without MSG, and anything can be made vegetarian. Try the chicken chow mein (C$6.50) or the honey-and-garlic spare ribs (C$7.50), or ask for some vegetable chop suey with ginger (C$5.95).

Dawson Creek to Watson Lake

The southernmost part of the highway between Dawson Creek and Fort Nelson is relatively quick, easy driving. North of Fort Nelson, however, the scenery changes dramatically from bleak, low hills to rocky, jagged peaks. Services show up less frequently, and prices for gas, food, and lodging increase substantially. You can cover the major stretches in a day if you don't stop at any of the sights, but to do so would be a shame, since some of the Alcan's major attractions—Stone Mountain Provincial Park, Muncho Lake, and Liard Hot Springs—are here. If the weather's behaving, consider spending a night at Muncho Lake to break up the long, twisty expanse between Fort Nelson and Watson Lake. Otherwise, you can fill up on homemade food and baked goods at **Shepherd's Inn** (Mile 72, tel. 604/827–3676). The bannock bread (a large griddle biscuit) with jam is C$1.95 and worth it. The Inn also has one of the nicest gift shops along the highway, making it a favorite stop among Alcan veterans.

FORT NELSON Fort Nelson is the standard first-night stop along the highway, 300 miles north of Dawson Creek. Once you start north from here, there's not much in the way of services for another 320 kilometers (200 miles). The town is a mile of gas stations, motels, and auto shops. Friendly locals stage a free "Welcome Visitors" program consisting of tidbits of local folklore at 6:45 nightly at the **Phoenix Theater** (halfway through town, on west side of hwy., tel. 604/774–7469). The **Fort Nelson Museum** (north end of town, on west side of hwy., tel. 604/774–3536) houses memorabilia from Fort Nelson's fur-trading days. The museum is open daily 9–7:30, May to September only; admission is C$1.50. The **Travel Infocentre** (5319 50th Ave., tel. 604/774–6400 or 604/774–2541 in winter) is open May to September, daily 8–8. The staff (mostly UBC students home for the summer) is helpful and provides great Alaska Highway brochures for free.

> **WHERE TO SLEEP AND EAT** • A bunch of motels line the highway, all with about the same rates and the same funky carpets and bedspreads. The exception is **Home on the**

Fort Nelson is an environmentalist's nightmare: Logging is the main industry, followed by natural-gas scrubbing (purifying gas for home use) and chopstick production. In fact, the world's largest chopstick factory bangs out five million pairs a day at a Mitsubishi-owned plant just outside town.

Let's Go Curling, Eh?

In case someone puts this question to you, be prepared. Canadian curling has nothing to do with Arnold's biceps or Farrah's hair. It was originally a Scottish game—like boules, but played on ice. Teams of four hurl squat, 40-pound curling stones at tees (the "goals") with circles drawn around them. Players sweep the ice with brooms vigorously in order to influence (somehow) the direction of the hurled stone. Every player gets a crampit (a spiked metal plate) with which to dig into the ice so they don't slip during all the action. If this sounds like riotous fun, you may have already hurled a few too many.

Hill B&B (5612 51st St., tel. 604/774–3000), where owners Fern and Jack provide comfy rooms (singles C$40, doubles C$50), breakfast, and use of a Jacuzzi. If you have time, they'll arrange a private curling lesson (*see box, above*). The **Blue Bell Motel** (4103 50th Ave., tel. 604/774–6961) has tidy singles (C$35), doubles (C$45), and triples (C$50), and is attached to a 24-hour restaurant and gas station.

Unless you grab supplies from the **IGA supermarket** (4823 50th Ave. S, tel. 604/774–2791) and have a picnic along the river south of town, don't expect eating in Fort Nelson to be exciting or particularly healthy. Try the new pub at the **Trapper's Inn** (halfway through town, on west side of hwy., tel. 604/774–6935). The young chef makes a good *donair*—the Canadian rendition of a Greek lamb kebab—in a pita with homemade tzatsiki (yogurt-and-cucumber sauce) for C$6.50. You can also get a variety of hot open-faced sandwiches for C$3.95–C$6.

STONE MOUNTAIN PROVINCIAL PARK Stretching from Mile 373 of the Alcan to Mile 380, Stone Mountain Provincial Park is the place to spy the stone sheep (the long-legged, short-haired beasts, slightly larger than bighorns) that are indigenous to the mountains of northern British Columbia and the Yukon. At Mile 373, **Summit Lake** (elevation: 1,318 meters) marks the highest point on the highway. The lake makes a good picnic spot, and there is a spectacular 6-kilometer (3.75-mile) hike to the Flower Lakes from a well-marked trailhead on the south side of the highway. From May to October, you can set up your tent at the **Stone Mountain Provincial Park Campground** (just off the highway) for C$9.50 a night. Sites are exposed to the wind, so bring a warm sleeping bag.

MUNCHO LAKE Be careful as you approach Muncho Lake (Mile 456)—people tend to slam on their brakes as they round the bend and catch sight of the stunning turquoise water. The aqua glow comes from a combination of oxidized copper leached from the mountains of the Sentinel Range (on the north shore) and limestone deposits from the northern extreme of the Rocky Mountain Range (on the south shore). **Captain Gunness** (tel. 604/776–3411) runs nightly boat tours of the lake at 6 PM from Strawberry Flats Campground, and at 7:30 PM from Highland Glen and the provincial park campground; shell out the C$8 fee if you're interested in the history, geology, and folklore of the area.

In addition to sleeping at **Highland Glen Lodge** (Mile 462, tel. 604/776–3481), you can take in the view, pick up some homemade bread (C$4 per loaf), and watch the lake's only float plane take flight. Double rooms are C$55, triples C$62. Also available are tent spots (C$10) and log cabins (C$25 per person). The provincial park **campground,** just north of Highland Glen, has 30 lakeside spaces for C$9.50 a night.

LIARD RIVER HOT SPRINGS The natural hot springs in **Liard River Provincial Park** (Mile 497, tel. 604/776–7343) are the hands-down-favorite stopping point among butt-weary trav-

The Yukon

For the most part, casual travelers don't experience the oft-conjured Yukon of nostalgia—of aurora borealis, vast wastelands of frozen tundra, and toothless old miners. For many, the Yukon is synonymous with money in the form of precious metals. Even today, miners continue to bring gold out of them thar' hills. But if you talk to modern Yukoners, like the waitress who came for her sister's wedding six years ago and never left, or the gas-station owner who is now free from the "terminal bureaucracy" of the States, you'll see that greed is not all that draws people here. Even if you just buzz through on the Alaska Highway, hitting only the big cities (Dawson City and Whitehorse), the grandeur of the Kluane range and the size of the potholes provide sufficient testimony to the extreme nature of this singular place. For maps and brochures on the region, write to Tourism Yukon (Box 2703, Whitehorse, Y1A 2C6, tel. 403/667–5340).

elers. A wooden boardwalk leads from the parking lot to two pools, the shallow Alpha (108°F) and the deeper Beta (98°F), surrounded by a mini-tropical ecosystem that supports plants and fish not normally found this far north. Each pool has a changing room and bathroom. The hot springs are free; the grassy spots at the nearby campground cost C$12 a night. They're both open year-round, but the campground fills up quickly in summer and on holiday weekends. At **Trapper Ray's Café** (Mile 497, tel. 604/776–7349), you can feast on good homemade soups (C$2.50) and sandwiches (C$5.50); breakfast is served all day.

> *"There are strange things done, in the midnight sun / By the men who moil for gold. /And the Arctic trails could tell such tales / That will make your blood run cold."—Robert Service, "The Cremation of Sam McGee"*

Watson Lake

Just north of the Yukon border at Mile 635, Watson Lake is the gateway to the Yukon. The one requisite stop in this town is **Signpost Forest,** where a homesick soldier working on the highway put a sign marking the distance to his hometown. More than fifty years later, there are approximately 21,000 such signs—made of everything from freeway on-ramp markers to spray-painted Frisbees—tacked onto tall wooden planks here. A few shops charge C$15 to make one for those who can't think up some clever method of their own. The **Visitor Information Center** (tel. 403/536–7469), open daily 9–9, is on the edge of the Signpost Forest. It has a high-quality exhibit on Yukon history and a concise, informative slide show. They'll try to sell you tickets to the **Canteen Show** (June–August at 8 PM; C$15) in the tent next door, but the USO-style vaudeville is an acquired taste. Instead, walk the 3-kilometer (2-mile) interpretive trail around **Wye Lake**, one block north of the Alaska Highway.

WHERE TO SLEEP Once again, what you see is what you get—budget hotels are scattered on both sides of the highway, not varying much in quality or price. Mid-way through town, **The Big Horn Hotel** (tel. 403/536–2020) is brand new and still undiscovered by tour buses. Clean rooms decorated in blue and oak go for C$85 in high season, C$50 in low season. The **Cedar Lodge Motel** (222 Adelia Trail, just south of town, tel. 403/536–7406) has small, slightly worn, but clean cabins for C$55–C$65 per twosome, plus C$10 for each additional person. The **Downtown RV Park** (105 8th St. N., off hwy. at south end of town, tel. 403/536–2646) is mostly a gravel parking lot, but they have a few tent sites (C$10) and are open year-round.

FOOD Since none of the restaurants in Watson Lake has great food, choose a place based on its people-watching potential. A steady stream of locals crowd the café in the **Belvedere Motel** (609 Frank Trail, just off hwy., tel. 403/536–7712) for hot sandwiches (C$4–C$6.50) and salads (C$5.50). You can also grab a beer in their lounge, open Monday–Saturday until 2 AM, Sunday until 10 PM. **Tag's Deli** (in Chevron station, across from Signpost Forest, tel. 403/536–7422) is open daily 6 AM–midnight for greasy chicken, fries, and donuts, as well as fresh subs. Tag's doubles as a laundromat and gossip central.

Watson Lake to Whitehorse

This stretch of the Alcan is just a prelude to the phenomenal natural goodies lurking north in Kluane National Park. Watson Lake, the biggest town this side of Whitehorse, is a fine place to stock up on gas and groceries and do laundry. If you can hold out a while to sleep, stop at the **Rancheria Hotel** (Mile 710, tel. 403/851–6456), an hour and a half past Watson Lake, where cozy doubles go for C$58, and lakeside campsites cost C$14 (call 403/851–9800 for camping info). An adjacent 24-hour café serves incredible muffins, tarts, and cinnamon buns (C$1.50). Fill up, because between Teslin (the next town after Watson Lake) and Whitehorse there's a long stretch of nothing but you and the road.

TESLIN Teslin was around for a long time before it got labeled Mile 804 of the Alaska Highway. Tlingit people have inhabited the area where the Nisutlin River flows into Teslin Lake for centuries, and the town was officially established as a Tlingit trading post in 1903. Today it has the largest Indian population in the Yukon Territory and handmade Indian crafts are sold all over the place. The **George Johnston Museum** (on hwy., tel. 403/390–2550), open daily 9–7, is named after a Tlingit man known for his trapping and photography. For C\$3, you can peruse the thorough display of gold-rush memorabilia, Indian artifacts, and photos of Tlingit people. There isn't much to hold you overnight, but the marina at the north end of the Teslin River bridge is a great place to spread a picnic. If you do want to crash here, the **Yukon Motel** (Mile 804, tel. 403/390–2575) has clean, newly renovated rooms (C\$50–C\$68) that overlook the lake.

Whitehorse

Set alongside the Yukon River, Whitehorse is home to two-thirds of the Yukon's population, and its 20,000 residents have created a big-city atmosphere in the middle of the wilderness. Casual conversations with locals lend the impression that half of Whitehorse's population came north for two weeks and ended up staying. It may be that they were simply overcome with joy at seeing the first real city—complete with an **Arts Center** (Yukon Pl., on hill above Takhini neighborhood, tel. 403/667–8575), a movie theater, and several worthwhile museums—since Dawson Creek, just over 1,440 kilometers (900 miles) south.

The Alaska Highway was built through Whitehorse 50 years ago. However, tens of thousands of gold seekers had already passed through the town during the 1898 Klondike rush. Today the main draws are the outdoor sports—hiking, mountain biking, river trips—that bring a fresh crowd of eager twentysomethings to Whitehorse each summer. If you camp at Robert Service Campground (*see* Where to Sleep, *below*)—one of the Yukon's few tents-only campgrounds—and have a good pair of hiking shoes, Whitehorse can be a few days of great fun.

BASICS The **Visitor Reception Center** on the Alaska Highway has information about the region and shows an interesting slide show on the history of Whitehorse. The **Visitor Information Center** (302 Steele St., tel. 403/667–2915) is open May–September, daily 8–8 (Oct.–Apr. until 5). They have still more brochures and will point you toward hotels, restaurants, and the like.

COMING AND GOING Whitehorse is at Mile 918 of the Alaska Highway. It constitutes, roughly, the halfway mark between Dawson Creek and Fairbanks, Alaska. Many people abandon the Alcan here and head north up to Dawson City on the Klondike Loop (*see below*).

Hitching is fairly common on the roads around Whitehorse, though catching a long-distance ride can be a pain. The best spots are along the Alaska Highway, on the outskirts of downtown. Caution, as always, is the watchword (i.e. don't take any rides from hirsute, monosyllabic men named Bulldog).

➤ **BY BUS** • The **bus terminal** (2191 2nd Ave., near Olgilvie) is on the northeastern side of downtown near the Yukon River, two blocks from the Qwanlin Mall. From here **Norline** (tel. 403/668–3355) has service to Dawson City (C\$70), Carmacks (C\$27), and other points in western Canada. **Greyhound Lines of Canada** (tel. 403/668–3225) goes to Vancouver (around C\$250), Edmonton (C\$200), and other points in the United States and Canada. **Alaskon Express** (tel. 403/668–3225) has service to Anchorage, Fairbanks, Skagway, and Haines.

➤ **BY PLANE** • The **Whitehorse Airport** (tel. 403/667–8440) is off the highway on the west side of town. **Air North** (tel. 403/668–2228) has service to Fairbanks (C\$197 one-way) and Juneau (C\$386 one-way), as well as to Dawson City. **Canadian Airlines** (tel. 403/294–2000) runs to most major Canadian destinations and has discounts for people under 25. **Alkan Air** (tel. 403/668–6616) flies to Dawson City. **Delta Express** (tel. 403/668–6804) also has flights to Anchorage and Edmonton. On weekdays, **Whitehorse Transit** (tel. 403/668–8381) buses marked HILLCREST run between the airport and downtown several times during rush hour and a few times during the rest of the day; the fare is C\$1.25. Only four run on Saturday and none runs on Sunday. Your only other options are to hitch or take a cab.

GETTING AROUND Downtown Whitehorse is laid out on a rectangular grid, bordered by the Yukon River to the east and the Alaska Highway to the west. Main Street runs perpendicular to the river and is, naturally, the center of activity. The town sprawls into several small suburbs that branch off along the highway. **Whitehorse Transit** (tel. 403/668–8381) operates local buses Monday–Thursday from 6:15 AM to 7 PM, Friday until 10 PM, with limited service Saturday and none on Sunday and holidays. You can pay C$1 one-way or C$3 for an all-day unlimited ticket, which you buy from the driver.

WHERE TO SLEEP If you want to avoid the bustle of town, try **Barb's Bed and Breakfast** (64 Boswell Crescent, tel. 403/667–4104), a modern, private home in Whitehorse's Riverdale suburb. Doubles go for C$60–C$65. The **98 Motel** (110 Wood St., tel. 403/667–2641) lets rooms with shared bathrooms, worn brown carpet, and wood-paneled walls for C$45, plus a C$10 key deposit. The bar next door is fairly noisy until it closes at 11 PM. On the far end of town near the bus terminal, the **Roadhouse Inn** (2163 2nd Ave., tel. 403/667–2594) looks dilapidated, but the C$45–C$70 rooms are generally sanitary and comfortable. The upstairs rooms have TVs and bathrooms. The recently renovated **Capital Hotel** (103 Main St., tel. 403/667–2565) attempts to capture an 1898 gold-rush feeling. Singles are around C$55, doubles C$65, and triples C$75. The architecturally lacking **High Country Inn** (4051 4th Ave., near Lowe St., tel. 403/667–4471) was once an HI hostel, but has remade itself to appeal to the tour-bus crew. It now has 20 hostel beds (C$18 HI members, C$20 non-members) and a few private rooms (C$50 single, C$75 double), as well as a restaurant. About 3 kilometers (2 miles) south of downtown, the **Robert Service Campground** (S. Access Rd., tel. 403/668–3721) has about 30 tent sites (C$10.50) laid out along the woods by the Yukon River. The campground is equipped with bathrooms, pay showers, and free firewood, but there's no potable water.

FOOD Main Street has several decent restaurants, but some of the better spots are tucked away in other parts of downtown. The **Blue Lizard Café** (4159 4th Ave., tel. 403/667–2936) makes great 10″ pizzas for C$10 and lasagna for C$8. The healthy (if small) meals at **No Pop Sandwich Shop** (312 Steele St., tel. 403/668–3227) draw hippies and yuppies, artists and local bureaucrats. The No Pop also has a full bar and does a lot of coffee and dessert business. Veggie burgers go for around C$4.50. The busy **Talisman Café** (2112 2nd Ave., tel. 403/667–2736) serves an assortment of homemade dishes such as Cajun seafood (C$10), homemade pasta with pesto (C$8.50), and a Middle Eastern plate (C$7.95). If you're just passing through on the highway, stop at **Claire's** (tel. 403/668–5631) in the Whitehorse Airport for some of the cheapest eats in town: A beef or veggie burger is about C$5, the daily pasta special C$6.50.

WORTH SEEING The **Yukon Historical and Museums Association** (3126 3rd Ave., tel. 403/667–4704) gives daily tours of historic downtown buildings. The association also sells maps outlining self-guided walking tours for C$1.

MacBride Museum. Memorabilia from Whitehorse's history is presented in this downtown log cabin. Fans of gold-rush lore, railway mementos, and pioneer stuff will find this very exciting. *1st Ave., at Wood St., tel. 403/667–2709. Admission: C$3, C$2 students. Open May and Sept., daily noon–4; June and Aug., daily 10–6; July, daily 9–6; Oct.–Apr., Sun noon–4.*

S.S. Klondike National Historic Site. This historic site contains a 210-foot stern-wheeler built in 1937. On board the boat are a number of cabins containing photos and uniforms dating to the era when boats were the major means of transportation into the Yukon. The highlight, however, is just romping around the old boat. *2nd Ave., at S. Access Rd., on bank of Yukon River, tel. 403/667–4511. Admission free. Open mid-May–early Sept., daily 9–7:30.*

Yukon Transportation Museum. This fantastic hands-on museum next to the airport displays everything from snowshoes and dog sleds to airplanes and railway cars in the context of Yukon history. The highlight is the 1920s-era *Queen of the Yukon,* the first commercial plane to serve the territory. *Whitehorse Airport, tel. 403/668–4792. From downtown, take Alaska Hwy. to airport or take HILLCREST bus. Admission: C$3. Open June, Wed.–Sun. 10–6; July–Sept., daily 10–6.*

AFTER DARK You can usually find some activity at the hotel bars downtown. Try the **98** (100 Wood St., tel. 403/667–2641) for a saloon atmosphere and a crowd that looks like it's been here since the gold rush. The **Taku Hotel** (4109 4th Ave., tel. 403/668–4545) is popular among Yukon yuppies (yes, there is such a thing). You can hear live music, usually blues or folk-rock, at the bar in the **Capital Hotel** (103 Main St., tel. 403/667–6525); there's no cover charge. **Foxy's** (2141 2nd Ave., tel. 403/668–3092) is a fun hangout frequented by an outdoorsy crowd. The theater arts come to Whitehorse in the form of summer spectacles with names like *The Fabulous Gold Pan Digger Sisters*. Tickets for these extravaganzas—aimed at the fiftysomething RV set and often involving can-can girls in pantaloons—go for C$15.

OUTDOOR ACTIVITIES

➤ **HIKING** • The **Yukon Conservation Society** (302 Hawkins St., at 3rd Ave., tel. 403/668–5678) gives free, guided nature walks May–September. They also publish a pamphlet on local hikes and mountain-bike trails, available for C$5. **Miles Canyon** offers a network of trails along the cliffs above the Yukon rapids. To find the trailheads, take Second Avenue south to South Access Road, which leads to Miles Canyon Road, where you'll see signs for the canyon.

The extensive **Grey Mountain Road Trail** follows a ridge that affords great views of the town and valley. For the trailhead, cross the bridge by the S.S. *Klondike* National Historic Site and follow Lewes Road, making a left on Alsek Road and another left at the first set of traffic lights. You'll need six–eight hours to walk the entire trail.

➤ **CANOEING** • The **Kanoe People** (tel. 403/668–4899) may not know how to spell, but they do know their paddles. Guided day and evening trips down the Yukon River start at around C$50; a two-week, 460-mile trip costs around C$350 per canoe. If you don't mind the 30-minute drive, **Frits Admiral and Diane Jones** (Hotsprings Rd., off North Klondike Hwy., tel. 403/633–4562) run a less touristy operation and will tailor a package to your budget and skill level. Pre-set packages include a C$50 full-day trip with picnic lunch. You can also just rent a canoe for C$20 a day or a mountain bike for C$15 a day.

Whitehorse to Tok

It's an awfully long haul from Whitehorse to Tok, Alaska. This portion of the Alaska Highway is the final leg of the Yukon drive and runs along the eastern edge of Kluane National Park and passes the sort of scenery that inspires expensive coffee-table books. It's also the part of the highway that makes some people swear never to do it again: The unstable permafrost beneath the road's surface creates frost heaves and potholes the size of small swimming pools. Though some people do it in a day, give yourself a break and plan to stay somewhere along the road. Waking up to the vast peaks of the Kluane is worth the extra night.

HAINES JUNCTION The aptly named Haines Junction is just a handful of motels and cafés clustered around the intersection of the Alaska Highways and Haines Road. Most visitors who pass through here are on their way to Kluane National Park, just west of town. The junction itself can be confusing: If you're heading down the Alaska Highway toward Fairbanks, turn right at the junction; if you want to go to Haines or Skagway, keep going straight. The **Kluane National Park Visitor Center** (Alaska Hwy., 1 block east of junction, tel. 403/634–2345) is open daily 9–9. Stop in to collect park info and see their slide show. The bar at the **Kluane Park Inn** (Alaska Hwy., tel. 403/634–2261), open daily 7 AM–2 AM, is the favorite place for a post-hike beer and pool game. For lodging, take the Alaska Highway a short ways north of the junction to the **Stardust Motor Lodge** (tel. 403/634–2591), where C$55 gets you a comfortable double with a private bathroom; the friendly Swiss owner can point you to nearby hiking trails. **Madley's General Store** (Alaska Hwy., tel. 403/634–2200) is open daily 9–9 and sells everything from fresh produce to camping gear and fishing flies.

KLUANE NATIONAL PARK A visit to Kluane is one of those experiences that may cause you to find yourself, sometime in the future, approaching a stranger with a "Kluane" T-shirt or bumper sticker and breathlessly asking "Have you been there, too?" Most people heading to Alaska just whiz by on the highway, content to ogle the rugged Kluane Range through the haze of road grime on their car windows. But if you're at all into hiking, make an effort to spend at least an afternoon on one of the park's trails.

Tucked into the southwestern corner of the Yukon, Kluane became a national park in 1972. Its interior is dominated by vast ice fields and massive mountains, including **Mount Logan**, Canada's highest peak. The region drops off into the Pacific Ocean in the west and rises to meet the Kluane Range in the east. Because of the harsh climate and technically demanding terrain, the park's interior is unexplored by all but serious mountaineers. On the glacial fringe, however, there are some great trails for those who want just a day hike or a few nights on the trail. The **Kluane National Park Visitor Center** in Haines Junction (*see above*) stocks trail and topographical maps and is an essential stop for anyone planning to explore the park.

Kluane Lake is the largest lake in the Yukon. Covering 154 square miles, it looks like the ocean from some angles and can be as temperamental. The winding highway around the lake can be equally treacherous, as most people drive it with one eye on the road and the other on the scenery.

The Alaska Highway runs into the park's edge at Haines Junction and continues north; south of Haines Junction, the park is bordered by Haines Road. Hiking trails are spread pretty evenly throughout the park. Those in the north traverse a more barren landscape than those in the south. No lodging is set up inside the park, so wild camping is the name of the game; get the lowdown from the visitor center in Haines Junction. The nearby towns of Haines Junction, Beaver Creek, and Burwash Landing all have government-run campgrounds as well as motels, gas stations, and cafés.

SILVER CITY GHOST TOWN Silver City is about 5 kilometers (3 miles) down a dirt road off the Alaska Highway at Mile 1,020. This collection of dilapidated cabins was once a busy trading post on the wagon road from Whitehorse to the Klondike, complete with a roadhouse and Mountie barracks. Today it makes for an eerie Kodak moment, especially if you have black-and-white film.

TOK The town of Tok is the first sizable Alaskan town you'll hit driving north on the Alaska Highway. It's bound to be a disappointment: If Tok's "Handcrafted Alaskan Souvenir" shops, trading posts, and RV parks were condensed into two city blocks, it might be a cute little community. Instead, Tok is a sprawling mess at the junction of the Alaska and Glenn highways. Many of the town's structures are less than two decades old, built to replace older ones destroyed by a fire that raged through here in 1980. The city was originally founded as a base for workers on the Alaska Highway. The name (which rhymes with "poke") is a shortened version of the original name, Tokyo Camp, which in turn was a bastardization of the Athabascan word *tokai*, meaning "creek." Because of anti-Japanese sentiment during the war, it was shortened to Tok.

➢ **BASICS** • Tok lies on the Alcan, 716 kilometers (447 miles) from Haines Junction and 328 kilometers (205 miles) from Fairbanks, Alaska. It's also connected by road to Dawson City, 299 kilometers (187 miles) away on the Top of the World Highway (*see below*). **The Tok Visitor Center** (Tok Cutoff, off Alaska Hwy., tel. 907/883–5775), open daily 7 AM–9 PM, gives out free cups of coffee (or some approximation thereof) and offers an interesting natural history display, a wildlife slide show, and a message board, as well as the usual brochures.

➢ **WHERE TO SLEEP** • Tok's hotel rates skyrocket for the summer season (after June 1), but if you call ahead to reserve, some places will cut you a deal. As usual, motels are found along the two highways. From May 15 to September 15, you can spend a cheap night ($7.50) at the casual **Tent Hostel** (Mile 1322.5, tel. 907/883–3745), 13 kilometers (8 miles) west of town. Everyone sleeps in a big tent with two partitions, some heat, and a kitchen area. You must have a sleeping bag and tolerance for the rustic sharing of space. From the Alcan, go south on Pringle Drive and follow HOSTEL signs. You can sleep in a quiet, no-frills room at **Tok Saveway** (Tok Cutoff, 2 blocks south of Tok Junction, tel. 907/883–5389) at the same $60–$65 rate (double occupancy) year-round. Attached to Saveway is a 24-hour gas station/convenience store. The **Stage Stop B&B** (Glenn Hwy., just south of Tok Junction, tel. 907/883–5338) is run by a friendly Californian named Mary who has an excellent little sleeping cabin ($45 for up to three people); the bathroom is a short walk away in the main house. Three other rooms go for $50–$65 a night.

➢ **FOOD** • If Tok has a heart, it must be **Fast Eddy's Restaurant** (Alaska Hwy., just south of Tok Junction, tel. 907/883–4411). Locals and travelers congregate here over tasty pizzas

($10–$15), gigantic burgers served with crinkle fries ($5.50), and a fresh all-you-can-eat salad bar ($5), daily from 6 AM to midnight. If you've got $10.95 burning a hole in your trousers, check out the dinner special (salad, veggies, potatoes or rice, bread, and choice of salmon, halibut, or ribs) at the **Gateway Salmon Bake** (next to Fast Eddy's, tel. 907/883–5555). You can also try an authentic buffalo burger here for $6.50.

The Klondike Loop

"Klondike Loop" is the local name for the 523 kilometers (327 miles) of **Yukon Highway 2**, the 104 kilometers (65 miles) of **Top of the World Highway**, and the 174 kilometers (109 miles) of **Taylor Highway** that connect the towns of Whitehorse, Dawson City, Eagle, Chicken, and Tok. Most people traveling by car take the Alaska Highway between Whitehorse and Tok in one direction and the Klondike Loop in the other; it's a good way to break up the monotony and get a glimpse of how back-country people live (and drive) in these parts. The Klondike Loop between Whitehorse and Dawson City (Yukon Highway 2) is not too different from the Alaska Highway: two lanes, well-paved, and crowded June–August. North of Dawson City, however, the adventure begins. The Top of the World and Taylor highways are both unpaved, curvy, narrow, by turns muddy and dusty, and fun as hell to drive if your car can take it. From the road, glimpses of the Dawson Range and Sitz Mountains to the south and east, and of the Ogilive Mountains to the northwest, will leave you slack-jawed. Gas stations and hotels are scarce, so fill up in Tok or Dawson City and plan on camping, doing the whole thing in one day, or staying the night in Eagle.

Dawson City

Just 200 miles from the Arctic Circle, Dawson City was a boomtown of the 1898 gold rush. The population dwindled along with the gold, but little else has changed since then. Dozens of buildings are maintained as historic sites, and the decrepit structures that have gone neglected are as much a part of Dawson's charm as the registered landmarks.

Pull into Dawson City in the good ol' summertime and bask in the midnight sun. When you're within spittin' distance of the North Pole, darkness doesn't fall all summer, and there are only a few hours of dusk each night.

Dawson City's fabulous youth hostel and multiple camping opportunities make it a great place to bunk down for a few days, whether it's to absorb a little history or to party with the college students who come here for summer jobs in the tourist industry.

BASICS **Dawson City Visitor Center**. Housed in a replica of the original Dawson City Dry Goods Store, this office has useful listings of lodgings and restaurants, informative videos, and excellent, free walking tours of the town (10:30 AM daily in summer). Front St., at King St., tel. 403/993–5566. Open mid-May–mid-Sept., daily 9–9.

The Dirt on Mushing

Animal-rights activists beware—Tok is known as the sled dog capital of Alaska (not an inconsiderable distinction, considering that mushing is the official state sport). One out of every three residents is involved in the sport in one way or another, and many visitors come just to pick up a pup. The racing season begins in November and culminates with the mid-March "Race of Champions." If you're interested in the sport (or in raising a fuss about its implications) head to the Tok Dog Mushers Association (Alaska Hwy., just north of Tok Junction, tel. 907/883–6874) for info, films, and fanfare.

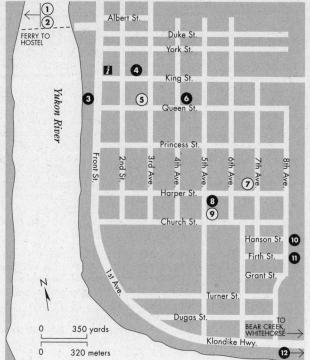

COMING AND GOING The best route to Dawson City is the Klondike Highway from White-horse. The Top of the World Highway connects Dawson City to Eagle, Chicken, and Fairbanks (via Tok); it starts at the ferry landing on the Yukon River's west bank.

➤ **BY BUS** • **Norline Coaches** (tel. 403/668–3355) runs a bus between Dawson City and Whitehorse three times a week (6 hrs, C$68). Buses leave from in front of the **Chevron Gas Shack** (5th Ave., at Princess St., tel. 403/633–3864).

➤ **BY PLANE** • The **Dawson City Airport** is 19 kilometers (12 miles) out of town on the Klondike Highway, just past the Hunker Road turnoff. **Air North** (tel. 403/993–5110) has flights to Whitehorse (C$170) and Fairbanks (C$195) with connections to other cities. There is no public transportation to or from the airport, but the **El Dorado** (tel. 403/993–5451) and **Downtown** (tel. 403/993–5346) hotels have limo services and can usually accommodate a few extra bodies for C$10 each. Most B&Bs will send a car for their guests.

GETTING AROUND Downtown Dawson City's dirt roads and boardwalks stretch along the banks of the Yukon River along a grid planned 100 years ago. You can see Dawson City on foot, but many sites are a ways out of town and accessible primarily by car, bike, or guided tour. A free ferry (really a drive-on, wobbly raft) leaves from Front Street 24 hours a day; it travels across the Yukon River to West Dawson, the hostel, and the Top of the World Highway.

WHERE TO SLEEP Hotels in Dawson City are expensive. Your best options are to camp or stay at the hostel. The **5th Avenue Bed and Breakfast** (705 5th Ave., at Church St., tel. 403/993–5941) has spacious singles for C$50–C$72 and doubles for C$72–C$82, depending the size of the room and whether it contains a private bath. Breakfast includes fresh-baked muffins and scones. From May to October, the **Midnight Sun Hotel** (3rd Ave., at Queen St., tel. 403/993–5495) charges C$85 for a double plus C$10 for each extra person. Ask for a room in the annex if you want silence. The modern **White Ram Manor B&B** (7th Ave., at Harper St., tel. 403/993–5772) has an outdoor hot tub, a large deck, and a communal kitchen. Doubles are C$60 in low season and C$75 in high season.

➤ **HOSTELS** • **Yukon River Hostel**. On a grassy hill across the Yukon River from town, this hostel is in a woodsy cabin complex. A dorm bed is C$12 for HI members, C$15 for non-members. Tent sites go for C$6 per person. The communal cabin, which is equipped with a wood-burning stove, books, and games, is a great place to meet fellow travelers. There's no lockout or curfew. They have no phone, so for reservations write to Dieter Reinmuth, Box 32, Dawson City, Yukon Y0B 1G0. *From town, take free 24-hr ferry across Yukon River, then take first left. 16 beds. Luggage storage, kitchen. Closed Oct.–May.*

➤ **CAMPING** • Take the free ferry across the Yukon River from Front Street to reach the government-run **Yukon River Campground** (C$8 a site), where you'll find bathrooms and free firewood, but no potable water. The **Guggie Ville** campground and RV park (Bonanza Creek Rd., tel. 403/993–5008), about 1.5 kilometers (1 mile) south of town, is a tourist-ridden RV hell hole with a dozen grassy tent spaces (C$10 a night) and excellent shower, kitchen, and laundry facilities. Intrepid and/or extremely broke travelers have been known to hop the free ferry over to West Dawson to a tent city set up by squatters just across from the Yukon River Campground. Young backpackers and summer-job seekers congregate here, blithely disregarding the signs that read NO CAMPING DUE TO ENVIRONMENTAL HEALTH CONSIDERATIONS.

FOOD If you can spare C$32, take the *Yukon Lou* ferry to a small island on the Yukon for the all-you-can-eat **Pleasure Island Barbecue** (tel. 403/993–5482). The boat ride and feast take about 2½ hours; reserve a seat at Birch Cabin on Front Street. Otherwise try **Klondike Kate's** (3rd Ave., at King St., tel. 403/993–6527), open daily 7 AM–11 PM. Locals crowd the place for breakfast (C$4), pita sandwiches (C$4–C$6), homemade soups (C$3.50), and pasta (C$6–C$10). The patio is especially popular for lunch. **Marina's** (5th Ave., at Princess St., tel. 403/993–6800) is open daily 11 AM–midnight for the best pizza in the Yukon (C$8–C$15) and tasty subs (around C$6.50).

WORTH SEEING **Bonanza Creek** was simply known as Rabbit Creek before gold was discovered here in 1896, starting the Klondike gold rush. **Dredge Number 4** (docent tours daily between 9:30 AM and noon) and the original **Discovery Claim** that made this place famous are at Miles 8 and 13 of Bonanza Creek Road, which branches off the Klondike Highway 5 kilometers (3 miles) from town. Those who don't have their own vehicle are stuck hitching or shelling out C$30 for a ride with **Gold City Tours** (Front St., at Queen St., tel. 403/993–5175).

The **Dawson City Museum**, housed in the 1901 Territorial Administration Building, chronicles the town's gold-rush heyday with turn-of-the-century clothes and gadgets. The information on the techniques of gold mining is a must for *cheechakos* (tenderfoots) ready to stake a claim. A theater also shows movies on local history daily at 11 AM, 2 PM, and 4:30 PM. *5th Ave., tel. 403/993–5291. Admission: C$3.50, C$2.50 students. Open June–Aug., daily 10–6; May and Sept., Tues., Thurs., and Sat. 1–4; Oct.–Apr., by appointment only.*

Stern-wheelers were vital to Yukon trade because they could navigate rivers that afforded as little as 18 inches of water under their wheels. The stern-wheeler "Keno," dry-docked along the banks of the Yukon River on Dawson City's Front Street, is one of the few stern-wheelers that remains intact.

The **Jack London Interpretive Centre** is a one-room log cabin featuring a collection of photographs and memorabilia from the writer's residence in the Klondike. There is a 45-minute reading of London's work daily at 1 PM. *8th Ave., at Firth St., tel. 403/993–6317. Admission free. Open June–mid-Sept., daily 10–noon and 1–6.*

The **Palace Grande Theatre** was once known as the biggest, bawdiest show hall in the North, staging opera, wild-west shows, and whatever else came to town. The Canadian government restored the theater in the 1960s, and it's now home to the **Gaslight Follies** theater group. Cheesy vaudeville shows and melodramas are performed on alternate nights May–August; tickets cost C$11–C$13. During the day, you can catch a free guided tour (2:30 PM daily) that includes a showing of *City of Gold*, a film depicting Dawson's pre-restoration days. *King St., btw 2nd Ave. and 3rd Ave., tel. 403/993–6217.*

The **Robert W. Service Cabin** is a memorial to the English-born Yukon poet whose most famous piece is "The Shooting of Dan McGrew." Service lived here while he composed much of the poetry that has come to immortalize life in the Yukon. You don't get to go inside, but an actor reads poetry and fills you in on Service's life and times; it doesn't cost anything to attend the readings. *8th Ave., at end of Hanson St., tel. 403/993–5462. Readings May–Aug., daily at 10 AM and 3 PM.*

AFTER DARK Excluding the Keno Lounge (*see* box, *below*), **Diamond Tooth Gertie's** is *the* entertainment spot for Dawson City tourists (at least for those over age 19, the legal gambling age). You hand over C$4.75 to get in and C$5 for drinks; whatever else you have in your pockets goes to the one-armed bandits, blackjack dealers, and roulette wheel that prey upon the happy, drunken clientele. The can-can shows, which ostensibly haven't changed since the real Diamond Tooth Gertie owned the joint 100 years ago, are free. The floor shows are held every day of the week, at 8:30 PM, 10:15 PM, 11:30 PM, and 1 AM. *4th Ave., at Queen St., tel. 403/993–5575. Open mid-May–early Sept., Mon.–Sat. 8 PM–2 AM.*

If you prefer not to risk the remainder of your travel funds, you can try the **Midnight Sun** (3rd Ave., at Queen St., tel. 403/993–5495), a hotel bar popular with young seasonal workers for its dance floor and karaoke. **Gold City Tours** (Front St., at Queen St., tel. 403/993–5175) runs a nightly shuttle (C$9) up to the **Midnight Dome,** a viewpoint that provides a fabulous view of the town and its surrounding mountains and rivers. It can also be reached via a 2-kilometer (1.25-mile) trail that leads uphill from the east end of King Street, or by car (the turnoff from the Klondike Highway is clearly marked).

NEAR DAWSON CITY

CHICKEN Beautiful Chicken, Alaska (population 25) was once a settlement for the miners who worked the tributaries of Forty Mile River. Gold is still mined here in the summer, though mostly by people who commute from Tok or Fairbanks. Chicken consists of one cool café, one saloon, and one mercantile store. It serves primarily as a lunch stop for dusty travelers and a gas stop for those who failed to fill up in Tok or Dawson City. The businesses are owned by a young couple who have lived here for six years and are full of stories about their experiences in the woods. They also make great burgers ($6) and fresh berry pie ($3.50), and will let you pitch a tent for free.

For a long time, Chicken was called Ptarmigan, after a bird common to the area. When the town was incorporated, residents had to write down its name but couldn't agree on the spelling. In pragmatic northern style, they changed the name to the more familiar Chicken.

EAGLE Only one, grueling dirt road leads to Eagle. The views for the last 32 kilometers (20 miles) are breathtaking, however, and this serene community on the banks of a wide bend in the Yukon River is a fine place to while away some time. Originally Athabascan land (what remains of the native village is south of town on First Street), Eagle was taken over by white miners in the late 1800s and pretty much died in 1910 when someone struck it big in Fairbanks. The U.S. Army established a fort here in 1914, but it was dismantled a short four years later, leaving behind a host of

A New Twist on Toe Sucking

Drink long and hard before you stop at the Keno Lounge in the Westmark Dawson Inn (5th Ave., at Harper St., tel. 403/993–5542). The house specialty is the "Sour Toe Cocktail." For a mere C$5 extra, you can have the drink of your choice served with—no kidding—a dry and shriveled, severed human toe instead of an olive. This will entitle you to membership in the exclusive "Sour Toe Club," established by Captain Stevenson (the guy who owns the toes).

sturdy buildings that now serve as museums. In summer, the Historical Society gives a walking tour ($3) of the town at 10 AM daily.

Eagle is a favorite stopping point for Yukon river trips. The **Eagle Trading Co.** (1 Front St., tel. 907/547–2220) pretty much owns the town. You can stay in one of their woodsy doubles ($60) overlooking the river, or shell out $15 per site to pitch a tent in their campground (closed in winter). The latter has no water, only outhouses, but it's in a grassy area on a hill above the town. Their restaurant serves shrimp baskets ($6.75), hamburgers ($4), and chef salads ($5.75); the store has some fresh produce and a good selection of health foods.

DELTA JUNCTION When the Alaska Highway was built, the Richardson Highway already ran between Delta Junction (Mile 1,422) and Fairbanks. This means that Delta Junction, 144 kilometers (90 miles) from Tok, is technically the terminus of the Alaska Highway. So, get out of your car, stretch your legs, and congratulate yourself. The **Delta Visitor Center** (tel. 907/895–5069), at the junction of the two highways, provides all necessary maps, brochures, and souvenirs. The **Delta Junction Hostel** (Main St. N, tel. 907/895–5074), 5 kilometers (3 miles) off the highway, has 10 beds at $7 a night.

Prince Rupert and Queen Charlotte Islands

The port city of Prince Rupert, on Kaien Island off the coast of British Columbia, is the jumping-off point for the ferries and cruise ships that ply the waters of the Inside Passage, which separates British Columbia and the Alaskan Panhandle. The city also serves as a hub for ferries heading south to Vancouver Island and west to the remote Queen Charlotte Islands, as well as for trains and buses heading east to Prince George and other destinations within British Columbia. The city is not much of a tourist draw in and of itself—the main activity here seems to be figuring out how to stay out of the fog and rain that typically blanket the area.

While you could easily breeze through Prince Rupert in a day or less, the Queen Charlotte Islands, 50 miles to the west, are another story entirely. The Queen Charlottes consist of two big islands, **Graham** and **Moresby**, and over 100 smaller ones that pockmark a long, skinny strip between the Hecate Strait and the Pacific Ocean. Rain forests, rocky beaches, and long inlets define the landscape, and the travelers who come here are generally outdoorsy types who want to kayak, backpack, fish, or just loll around in a gorgeous, secluded environment. Whether you spend a week or a month exploring these islands, you can be sure that you will leave without seeing all there is to see.

Prince Rupert

Prince Rupert is the heart of British Columbia's transportation system. Blessed with one of the world's deepest harbors, the town got its start as the western terminus of the Grand Trunk Pacific Railway in the early 1900s. Today, ferries, planes, buses, and trains meet up in Prince Rupert, meaning that for most people who find themselves here, the town is merely a stopover. Given the area's persistent drizzle and limited number of attractions, however, they're not missing all that much.

If you have some time to spend, a good place to educate and entertain yourself is in the **Museum of Northern British Columbia** (100 1st Ave. E, in Infocentre, tel. 604/624–3207). The small museum has an impressive collection of artifacts documenting the history of the region, from the native people who inhabited the coast as far back as 5,000 years ago to the development of the town in the early parts of this century. If this doesn't satisfy you, head down Second Street (towards the water) to the **Kwinitsa Railway Museum** (in VIA Rail Station, on waterfront, tel. 604/627–1915 in summer or 604/624–3207 in winter). This small building, originally a stop along the Grand Trunk Pacific Railway, was moved to Prince Rupert to house exhibits chronicling the history of the area's railroads.

BASICS Prince Rupert's main **Travel Infocentre** (100 1st Ave. E., tel. 604/624–5637 or 800/667–1994) is open May–September daily 9–9, October–April weekdays 10–5. A branch office is housed in the Park Avenue campground, a short walk from the ferry docks (*see* Where to Sleep, *below*). Don't be misled by the large MAIL sign on the government building on Second Avenue—this is *not* the place to buy stamps or mail letters. Rather, head to **Shopper's Drug Mart** (300 3rd Ave., tel. 604/624–2151), where you can do both; it's open weekdays 9–9, Saturday 9–6, Sunday 11–5. The local AmEx agent is **Express International Travel Limited** (333 3rd Ave. W, tel. 604/627–1266), open weekdays 8:30 AM–5:30 PM, Saturday 9–5.

COMING AND GOING Kaien Island is 721 kilometers (447 miles) west of Prince George on the Yellowhead Highway (Hwy. 16) and 1,543 kilometers (959 miles) north of Vancouver. The ferry dock is approximately 2 kilometers (just over a mile) from downtown. Walk east along Highway 16, which becomes Park Avenue, or call **Skeena Taxi** (tel. 604/624–2185) for a C$5–C$6 ride into town.

➤ **BY BUS** • Buses leave the **Greyhound Depot** (822 3rd Ave. W, tel. 604/624–5090) for Prince George (11 hrs, C$80), continuing on to Vancouver (23 hrs, C$162). The depot is open weekdays 8:30–8:30 and weekends 9–11:15 and 6–8:30 PM; sizable **luggage lockers** cost C$1 per 24 hours.

➤ **BY FERRY** • Terminals for both **B.C. Ferries** (tel. 604/624–9627) and the **Alaska Marine Highway** (tel. 604/627–1744 or 800/665–4614 in Canada) are at the extreme southwestern end of town, about 2 kilometers (just over a mile) from the city center along Highway 16. B.C. Ferries makes the trip south to Port Hardy on even-numbered dates during June, July, and September, and on odd-numbered dates during August, leaving Prince Rupert at 7:30 AM and reaching Port Hardy at 10:30 PM; the one-way fare is C$95 per passenger, C$190 per vehicle. During the winter, B.C. Ferries operates to Port Hardy once weekly, leaving Prince Rupert at noon on Friday and arriving at 8 AM the following day. In summer, B.C. Ferries also sends daily ferries east to the Queen Charlotte Islands (6–8 hrs, C$20.75 per passenger, C$79 per vehicle); in winter, service is cut back to three ferries weekly. Alaska Marine Highway ferries sail from Prince Rupert to points north, including Ketchikan (6 hrs, C$38 per passenger, C$75 per vehicle), Juneau (24 hrs, C$104 per passenger, C$240 per vehicle), and Skagway (32 hrs, C$124 per passenger, C$286 per vehicle).

➤ **BY PLANE** • Both **AIRBC** (112 6th St., tel. 604/624–4677) and **Canadian Air** (Rupert Square Mall, 500 2nd Ave. W, tel. 604/624–9633 or 604/624–9181 for reservations) have several flights daily to Vancouver (C$280 one-way). The airport is on nearby Digby Island, but you must check in at the airlines' respective downtown offices and then take a shuttle (C$10) to the island.

➤ **BY TRAIN** • VIA Rail (end of 2nd St., on waterfront, tel. 604/627–7589 or 800/561–8630 for reservations) runs to Prince George three times a week (12½ hrs, C$78). From Prince George, it is a 60-hour ride to Vancouver (C$246). Prices drop by 30% to 50% if you book a week in advance.

WHERE TO SLEEP The loads of travelers that arrive on the daily ferries, trains, and buses in summer cause Prince Rupert's accommodations to fill up fast. If you'll be among these hordes, call ahead for motel or B&B reservations. Although it's a bit shabby, the **Oceanview Motel** (950 1st Ave. W, tel. 604/624–6259) is one of the better deals in town: Singles are C$30–C$40, doubles are C$34–C$44, and triples are only C$47. To get here from the ferry terminal, follow Park Avenue to town, then veer left onto First Avenue. Tucked between the waterfront shops east of town in Cow Bay, **Eagle Bluff B&B** (201 Cow Bay Rd., tel. 604/627–4955) offers great views of the water, breakfast, and doubles for C$55 with shared bath or C$60 with private bath. Winter rates drop C$5. From the town center, take Third Avenue East to the waterfront and turn left. **Pioneer Rooms** (167 3rd Ave. E, tel. 604/624–2334), just east of downtown, has tiny rooms, shared bathrooms, and simple cooking facilities. At C$20 for a single and C$30 for a double, the 18 rooms fill up fast. To find it from the ferry terminal, follow Park Avenue to town and veer right on Third Avenue East.

> **CAMPING** • Convenient, grassy **Park Avenue Campground** (1750 Park Ave., tel. 604/624–5861 or 800/667–1994) sits just between the ferry terminals and town. RVs dominate, but there is a small, sloped tent area with sites for C$9. A **Tourist Infocentre** next to the camping office opens during the summer. **Prudhomme Lake Provincial Park** (tel. 604/847–7320), open April–November, is 20 kilometers (12.5 miles) east of town on Highway 16 and extremely difficult to reach without a car. Once you get here, however, you'll find forested sites (C$9.50) with access to trails and pit toilets.

FOOD Prince Rupert has all kinds of restaurants, from seafood to Greek to Chinese. Try **Smile's Seafood Café** (113 Cow Bay Rd., on waterfront, tel. 604/624–3072) for oyster or shrimp sandwiches (C$7–C$8), or clam chowder (C$2.75). For a quick fix, **Northwest Subs N' Stuff** (526 3rd Ave., tel. 604/624–SUBS) offers both meat and vegetarian submarine sandwiches (C$4.50–C$6.50), small salads (C$1), and homemade soups (C$1.25). The **Cow Bay Café** (205 Cow Bay Rd., on waterfront, tel. 604/627–1212) serves small portions of tasty dishes such as spinach pesto quiche (C$5.95), grilled-chicken salad (C$6.95), and spinach pie (C$6.95). **Rodno's Pizza** (716 2nd Ave. W., tel. 604/624–9797), which looks decidedly drab from the outside, has checkered tablecloths, zippy Greek music, and decent Greek food; specialties include moussaka (C$10), souvlaki (C$4.50), and Greek salad (C$4–C$8). They also serve a dozen varieties of pizza (C$9–C$15). **Fairview Restaurant, Imperial Gardens,** and **Stardust** all advertise (and deliver, with similar results and prices) "Chinese and Canadian Cuisine"; all three are on Third Avenue.

The flamboyantly named Lambada's Cappuccino Dessert Bar (505 3rd Ave. W, tel. 604/624–6464) is Prince Rupert's definitive breakfast spot. Come by early to join at least half the town for a well-made espresso drink and some fresh pastries.

Queen Charlotte Islands

The remote Queen Charlotte Islands, dotted with rain forests and lined by rocky beaches, move at their own, relaxed pace. Tourism is increasing, especially in the form of groups on outdoor adventure trips, but logging and fishing are still the economic mainstays of the islands' 6,000 or so inhabitants. The harsh bald spots left by clear cutting assault the eyes of visitors and are even visible from the deck of the ferry from Prince Rupert. Steps have been taken to preserve much of this pristine wilderness, however: After protesting logging on Lyell Island in the mid-1980s, local Haida Indians succeeded in forcing the creation of a national park reserve to protect the southern half of Moresby Island. Haida culture is highly visible throughout the region in other ways. **Ninstints,** a Haida village on Anthony Island, just south of the reserve, contains a number of the remarkable totem poles for which this group is famous and has recently been declared a World Heritage Site by UNESCO.

Most visitors first set foot on the Queen Charlotte Islands at Skidegate Landing on Graham Island. **Queen Charlotte City,** the island's biggest town and home to most of the guide companies that operate in the region, stretches along the shoreline about 4 kilometers (2.5 miles) to the west of the landing. Heading 45 kilometers (28 miles) north along Highway 16 on Graham Island, you pass the village of **Tl'ell** and an entry point to the expansive **Naikoon Provincial Park.** Another 25 kilometers (12.5 miles) brings you to **Port Clements,** a quiet village known for its strange yellow tree, advertised as the "Golden Spruce." (To find this arboreal mutant, drive about 15 minutes through town; the spot is well-marked.) From Port Clements, the highway continues about another 40 kilometers (25 miles) to the island's north coast and the twin towns of **Masset** and **Old Masset.** Masset contains the **Detkatla Wildlife Sanctuary,** a critical resting point for migrating waterfowl such as mallards, sandbill cranes, and Canadian geese. A bird-watching walk, run by the Habitat Conservation Fund, leads from Old Masset Cemetery Road, just east of town off Tow Hill Road. Old Masset is a Haida community.

The northern end of Moresby Island is a short ferry ride south from Graham Island's Skidegate Landing. **Sandspit,** Moresby's largest community, is just east of the island's Alliford Bay ferry landing. Float planes leave Sandspit's airport to shuttle visitors down to South Moresby Island, or back to the mainland (*see* Coming and Going, *below*). From Sandspit, logging roads lead south to camping areas at **Grey Bay** and **Moresby Camp,** south of which the roads end, giving way to a national park reserve.

BASICS To find out more about the park reserve, visit or call Sandspit's **Canadian Parks Reserve** office (tel. 604/637–5344). On Graham Island, **Joy's Island Jewelers Ltd.** (604/559–4742), about halfway between the ferry terminal and Queen Charlotte City, houses the island's main Travel Infocentre. During the summer, an additional Infocentre operates in Masset: Look for the small booth on your right as you drive into town, or call 604/626–3982.

COMING AND GOING You can only reach the Queen Charlotte Islands by air or sea. Most people arrive on **B.C. Ferries** (tel. 604/669–1211) from Prince Rupert (*see* Coming and Going in Prince Rupert, *above*). **Harbour Air** (tel. 604/637–5350) has daily flights from the Sandspit Airport on Moresby Island to Prince Rupert (C$160 one-way). **Canadian Regional Airlines** (tel. 800/663–3502) offers daily flights to Vancouver; the cost is about C$400 round-trip, but travelers under 25 may be eligible for a special C$99 one-way fare.

GETTING AROUND The lack of public transportation on the islands makes it hard to get around without a car. Rental cars are available in Queen Charlotte City from **Twin Services** (209 3rd Ave., tel. 604/559–4461) and **Rustic Car Rentals** (605 Hwy. 33, tel. 604/559–4641). Rentals are about C$50 per day, but you can often get a discount if you book through a motel or B&B. Locals are good about picking up hitchhikers; the stretch between the ferry terminal and Queen Charlotte City is the best place to get a ride. Reliable cab companies on Graham Island include **Pete's Taxi** (tel. 604/559–8622) and **Twin Services** (tel. 604/559–4461); a ride from the ferry landing to Queen Charlotte City should run C$6–C$8.

WHERE TO SLEEP Most of the year, you'll have no trouble getting a reasonably priced (C$25–C$35) room in one of the islands' hotels, motels, or B&Bs. The exception is summer— during this time, have a reservation or expect to end up paying dearly for a room. Campers get a break, as there are good campgrounds near every town.

➤ **QUEEN CHARLOTTE CITY • Gracie's Place.** On Queen Charlotte City's main drag, Gracie's has four comfortable rooms, each with its own entrance. The inn is just a few steps from the handful of shops that comprises the city center. Singles are C$50, doubles C$60 (C$20 more with kitchenette). *3113 3rd Ave., tel. 604/559–4262. From ferry, follow hwy. into Queen Charlotte City; Gracie's is on north side of street, midway through town.*

When camping on the Queen Charlotte Islands, whether you're in the middle of nowhere or at a crowded campground, be sure to hang your food in a tree to keep it away from the islands' elusive but still significant bear population.

Jo's Bed & Breakfast. This small B&B offers proximity to the ferry, fabulous breakfasts, and reasonable rates (C$25 single, C$35 double). Don't expect a luxury suite, however—this place is a real home, complete with overworked mother (Jo) and young son. *4813 Skidegate Rd., tel. 604/559–8865. From ferry, walk uphill on Skidegate St.; look for white house with matching fence. 4 rooms, none with bath. No credit cards.*

Premier Hotel. Built in 1910, the central Premier Hotel is one of Queen Charlotte City's oldest structures. Each of the 11 rooms is different: There's a small single with shared bath (C$25), a spacious one-bedroom suite with kitchenette and balcony (C$60 for one person, C$65 for two), and a few options in between (C$40–C$55). *3101 3rd Ave., across from waterfront, tel. 604/559–8415.*

Spruce Point Lodging. On the beach in Queen Charlotte City's western end, this small inn has spotless singles (C$50) and doubles (C$60), all with balconies overlooking Hecate Strait. Breakfast is delivered to each room in the morning. There is also a basement "hostel," consisting of a shared bath and kitchen connected to three bedrooms, each with two beds (C$17.50 per person). *609 6th Ave., tel. 604/559–8234. Follow main road through town, turn left on 6th Ave. and follow signs. 7 rooms.*

➤ **TL'ELL** • **Misty Meadows Provincial Park.** This popular summer campground is in the forest between Highway 16 and the coast, close to a cool beach. Private sites cost C$9.50. Bring your own food; there are no stores nearby. *Write: c/o Bag 5000, 3726 Alfred St., Smithers V0J 2N0, tel. 604/847–7320. From ferry landing, take Hwy. 16 about 45 km (28 mi) north. 30 sites. Pit toilets.*

Tl'ell River House. The newly refurbished rooms here all feature private baths and TVs; some have river views. Because there aren't many non-camping choices in this area, rates are inflated: Singles are C$65, doubles C$70. *Beitush Rd., tel. 604/557–4211. Take Hwy. 16 north from ferry about 40 km (25 mi) and turn right just before Tl'ell River bridge. 10 rooms. Restaurant.*

➤ **MASSET AND NAIKOON PARK** • **Agate Beach Provincial Park.** This beachfront campground rents exposed, often windy sites for C$9. Campers huddle in a small shelter with a wood stove on rainy days; when it's sunny, they hit the immense beach. *Contact: c/o Bag 5000, 3726 Alfred St., Smithers, tel. 604/847–3720. 25 km (12.5 mi) east of Masset. Pit toilets.*

Alaska View Lodge B&B. Directly above the beach on the rain forest's edge, this romantic, isolated B&B is in prime whale-watching country. There are two rooms in the main house (C$50 single, C$70 double) and two rooms in the guest house (C$60 single, C$80 double). *Tow Hill Rd., tel. 604/626–3333. From Masset, drive 12.5 km (8 mi) toward Tow Hill (part gravel).*

Masset Haida Lions RV Park. Just east of Masset, this campground has grassy sites (C$8) and friendly managers. The Detkatla Wildlife Sanctuary, across the road, is a prime bird-watching area. Firewood and coin-operated showers are available. *1044 Tow Hill Rd., tel. 604/626–3382. Take Hwy. 16 east from Masset about 1 km (under a mile). 26 sites.*

Naikoon Park Motel. This motel's somewhat gloomy green exterior may not seem appealing, but its small rooms are clean and warm. Singles and doubles are C$35, C$50 with kitchenette; triples are C$40, C$55 with kitchenette. There's nothing but wilderness around here, so be sure to bring supplies. *Tow Hill Rd. Lot 14, tel. 604/626–5187. 9 rooms.*

➤ **MORESBY ISLAND** • **Grey Bay Campground.** This free campground consists of a few pit toilets and 11 grassy tent sites spread out along a beach south of Sandspit on Grey Bay. It takes about 45 minutes to drive here from Sandspit, and the (mostly logging) roads can be rough. Campers should check with Timberwest (tel. 604/637–5436), the logging company that owns the campground, for current access info.

Moresby Island Guest House. With eight rooms, two shared baths, and a well-stocked communal kitchen, this Sandspit guest house feels a bit like the set of *Eight Is Enough.* Singles run C$25–C$35, doubles are C$50. *Beach Rd., facing ocean, tel. 604/637–5305. About 13 km (8 mi) from ferry landing. Laundry.*

Seaport B&B. Kayakers frequent this small place, across the road from the water's edge in Sandspit. It is the oldest B&B in the Queen Charlottes and one of the most reasonable, with C$25 singles and C$35 doubles. Breakfast often includes muffins and breads from Jo's B&B on Graham Island (*see above*). *Beach Rd., tel. 604/637–5698. 8 beds, none with bath.*

FOOD You'll find the most options (about four of them) in Queen Charlotte City; the farther you go from this port town, the fewer choices you have. Prices are generally 10%–20% higher than in mainland British Columbian towns. Those camping away from the major towns should stock up before heading out, because virtually no supplies are available in remote parts of the islands. Cooking for yourself is a less expensive and tastier alternative. There's a grocery store in Queen Charlotte City's **City Centre** building (3rd Ave., tel. 604/559–4444), and you can get fresh bread and muffins at the nearby **Saunders Bakery and Crafts** (312 2nd Ave., tel. 604/559–4625).

➤ **QUEEN CHARLOTTE CITY** • The Sea Raven Seafood Restaurant (3rd Ave., tel. 604/559–4773) is a popular place for dinner; visitors come for the seafood and locals come to watch hockey games on the bar's TV. Try the salmon dinner (C$15) or halibut and chips

(C$9). **Summerland Pizza and Steak House** (2600 3rd Ave., tel. 604/559–4588) serves decent pizza and Greek specialties. Twenty nine variations on pizza run C$9–C$18, depending on size; moussaka, lamb chops, and ribs go for C$14–C$16. To put a slightly smaller dent in your wallet, eat at **John's Café** (City Centre building, 3rd Ave., tel. 604/559–4240), where you can enjoy either Chinese (C$8–C$15) or Canadian (C$7–C$10) dishes in a no-frills diner atmosphere.

➤ **TL'ELL** • The **Tl'ell River House Restaurant** (Beitush Rd., tel. 604/557–4211) makes a good stop for egg breakfasts (C$5–C$10), lunch sandwiches (C$8–C$10), and dinner entrées (C$12–C$15). Desserts run about C$4, and the cheesecake is rumored to be out of this world. For an espresso fix, head to **Body Currents Gallery** (tel. 604/557–4211).

➤ **MORESBY ISLAND** • If you're traveling around Moresby Island, Sandspit is the place to fill and/or stock up. **The Sandspit Inn** (Airport Rd., tel. 604/637–5334) has a restaurant that serves burgers (C$7), sandwiches (C$7–C$10), and soups (C$2–C$3). **Dick's Wok Inn** (Copper Bay Rd., tel. 604/637–2275) is the island's answer to Chinese cuisine. For a quick snack, look for **The Bun Wagon** (often parked on Copper Bay Rd. across from school, tel. 604/637–5446) for fish 'n' chips, sandwiches, or milkshakes. You can pick up groceries at **Supervalu Store** (Beach Rd., tel. 604/637–2249).

OUTDOOR ACTIVITIES

➤ **HIKING** • For guided hikes, check with **Queen Charlotte Adventures** (Hwy. 16, right after Infocentre, tel. 604/559–8990) in Queen Charlotte City. **Naikoon Provincial Park,** in the northeastern corner of Graham Island, has trails for day hikes and overnight backpacking. From the Naikoon Picnic area in Tl'ell, a 5-kilometer (3-mile) trail leads along the river to what remains of the ship *Pesuta*, which ended its days here in 1928. Look for otters along the way, and expect to walk at least two hours each way. One of the most popular hiking areas is around **Tow Hill,** about 25 kilometers (15.5 miles) east of Masset. One trail winds its way up Tow Hill to two viewing platforms, one facing east to **Rose Spit** (the northeastern tip of Graham Island) and the other west to **Agate Beach**; the climb should take about 25 minutes. A second, shorter trail takes you to the **Blow Hole** rock formation on the beach; the Blow Hole may or may not be visible, depending on the tide. The 10-kilometer (6-mile) **Cape Fife Trail** takes you from Tow Hill across to Fife Point on the island's eastern coast; tent sites at Fife Point make this a good overnight trip. For the truly rugged, an 89-kilometer (55-mile) trail leads down the east coast from Rose Spit to the Tl'ell River bridge. The trail is rough in parts and usually takes 4–5 days. Before heading out, backpackers must register with the **Naikoon Park Headquarters** (Box 19, Naikoon Provincial Parks, Tl'ell, B.C. V0T 1Y0, tel. 604/557–4390) on Highway 16 in the north end of Tl'ell. You can also call, write, or visit the Headquarters for maps and other information on area trails.

On northern Moresby Island, a trail leads from the far end of Grey Bay along rocky beach and through dense forest to **Cumshewa Head**, a spiritual spot to Haida people. The hike takes about 15 hours both ways. Before driving out to Grey Bay, check with **Timberwest** in Sandspit (Beach Rd., tel. 604/637–5436) to see which roads are currently active logging routes. Southern Moresby Island is pristine country for backpackers, primarily because it's so difficult to get here. Check at a Travel Infocentre (*see* Basics, *above*) or **Greenwood Travel Services** (tel. 604/559–8455) for current transportation information.

➤ **FISHING** • The bountiful supply of fish in the islands' many streams and ocean inlets lures vacationing notables such as Jimmy Carter to the Queen Charlottes. Spring is the time for salmon and halibut, while in winter, particularly around Christmas, the steelhead trout practically jump into your arms. A number of companies offer day and overnight fishing trips from Queen Charlotte City; check at a Tourist Infocentre (*see* Basics, *above*) or with Greenwood Travel Services (*see above*) for more details and prices.

➤ **KAYAKING** • Queen Charlotte City's shoreline is a popular place to jump in the water for a half- or whole-day kayaking adventure. **Moresby Mountain Sports** (Spruce Point Lodge, 609 6th St., tel. 604/559–8234) offers kayak rentals and guided trips around northern Moresby. Queen Charlotte Adventures (*see above*) also leads kayak trips to South Moresby.

The Alaskan Panhandle

The tiny fishing communities that dot the islands and peninsulas of Southeast Alaska are linked to one another by the Alaska Marine Highway, a ferry system that threads its way through the channels of the Inside Passage. Mammoth glaciers and snowcapped peaks share the region with over a dozen towns, ranging from sleepy villages like **Wrangell** to Alaska's bustling capital city, **Juneau**. In your travels here, you will inevitably see (and smell) some of the innumerable cruise ships that haul passengers up and down the coast. Pollution from the ships now obscures some of the famed views, and if you happen to be in one of the small towns when a ship disgorges its passengers, watch out: It's like getting swept up in a half-off sale of Lawrence Welk memorabilia. If you're prepared to camp, though, it's easy to get away from the touristy towns and lose yourself in the glorious scenery. You're bound to get wet—it rains like hell much of the time—but it's still worth it. Unfortunately, the cost of seeing some of the Panhandle's finest sights, such as Glacier Bay, is often prohibitive. If you're traveling alone, try to team up with others to help reduce the cost of boat charters and equipment.

If you do any traveling in the Panhandle, you'll spend plenty of time on ferries and see plenty of water—much of it falling on you from overhead.

BASICS If anyone can help you navigate your way through the Panhandle, the **Alaska Division of Tourism** (tel. 907/465–2010) can. And if they haven't got an answer, they'll refer you to local visitor centers or chambers of commerce.

COMING AND GOING

➤ **BY BUS** • Many of the communities in Southeast Alaska are only accessible by ferry, which obviously limits bus service. Several bus companies do serve the region, but the immense distances between towns can drastically inflate the price of a ticket. **Alaskon Express** (tel. 800/544–2206) carries passengers between Haines, Skagway, Anchorage, Fairbanks, and the Yukon town of Whitehorse, as well as a number of smaller destinations in between.

The flat terrain in many parts of the Panhandle is ideal for long bike trips, which allow you to explore the countryside at your own speed.

➤ **BY FERRY** • The **Alaska Marine Highway** (tel. 800/642–0066) is the primary source of transportation in Southeast Alaska. Summer traffic on the ferry system is heavy, and reservations for vehicles must be made far in advance. During the fall, the system cuts back its service and runs less frequently through the spring. The price for a walk-on ferry ticket is fairly cheap—usually $20–$30 for a three- to five-hour ferry ride between towns. Costs add up once you start factoring in a bike or a kayak (an extra $10–$15) or a car ($25 for a 6-hour journey, $174 for a 36-hour trip). If you'll be traveling extensively by ferry, consider purchasing an **AlaskaPass** (*see* Coming and Going, in The Alaska Highway, *above*).

➤ **BY PLANE** • Small aircraft remain an essential part of transportation in Alaska, particularly in the Bush and outlying island communities. Prices vary, but expect to pay anywhere

Into the Woods

Intrepid travelers should look into the option of staying at one of the rustic Forest Service cabins that are scattered along the Panhandle. The cabins rent for $25 a night and must be reserved in advance. Most can only be reached via privately chartered boats or float planes. Cabins are located in Glacier Bay National Park near Juneau, in remote areas near Skagway, in Misty Fjords National Monument, and on Prince of Whales Island near Ketchikan. Call the Forest Service in Juneau (tel. 907/586–8751) for reservations.

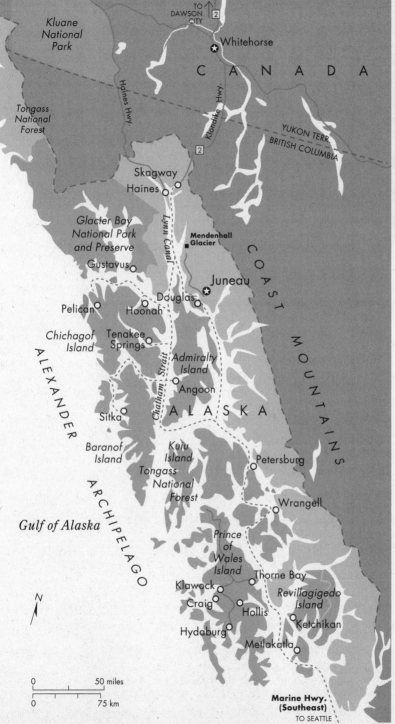

Kluane National Park

Tongass National Forest

C A N A D A

TO DAWSON CITY

2

Whitehorse

Haines Hwy.

Klondike Hwy.

2

YUKON TERR.
BRITISH COLUMBIA

Skagway

Haines

Glacier Bay National Park and Preserve

Lynn Canal

Mendenhall Glacier

Gustavus

Juneau

Douglas

Pelican

Hoonah

Chichagof Island

Tenakee Springs

Chatham Strait

Admiralty Island

Angoon

C O A S T   M O U N T A I N S

Sitka

A L A S K A

Baranof Island

Kuiu Island

Tongass National Forest

Petersburg

Wrangell

Gulf of Alaska

A L E X A N D E R

A R C H I P E L A G O

Prince of Wales Island

Thorne Bay

Revillagigedo Island

Klawock

Craig

Hollis

Ketchikan

Hydaburg

Metlakatla

N

0   50 miles
0   75 km

Marine Hwy. (Southeast)
TO SEATTLE

from $100 per hour of flight. Two of the many local airlines include the Haines-based **LAB Flying Service** (tel. 907/789–9160), which provides service between nine towns along the Panhandle, and **Wings of Alaska** (tel. 907/789–0790), which flies out of Juneau to 10 Panhandle destinations.

➤ **HITCHHIKING** • Hitching is still fairly popular and acceptable in Alaska. Short rides are plentiful on the more heavily traveled roads, but if you need to make a longer, cross-country jaunt, the going can be slow.

Ketchikan

Alaska's "Gateway to the North," bustling Ketchikan sprawls beneath vast forests at the southern end of the Panhandle, 900 miles south of Anchorage and 90 miles north of Prince Rupert. The site was originally a Tlingit fishing community; later, it became the first port of call for steamships heading north. Today, Ketchikan's port is invaded by cruise ships daily. Thus, the city affords northbound backpackers not only their first chance to glimpse eagles scanning the Alaskan waters for salmon, but their first encounter with masses of septuagenarians scanning Alaskan shops for souvenirs. Fortunately, the city also contains an impressive collection of Tlingit, Haida, and Tsimshian totem art. The ancient Tongass rain forest, quite unvisited by the leisure-suit crowd, is also nearby. Ketchikan's biggest attraction, however, is actually 20 miles to the east: **Misty Fjords National Monument** (*see* Near Ketchikan, *below*) is a 2.3-million acre enclave of glacial cliffs, massive waterfalls, and rushing streams and rivers.

BASICS The **Ketchikan Visitor Information Bureau** (131-V Front St., tel. 907/225–6166) gives out free self-guided walking-tour maps. A number of tour operators work out of the information bureau; city tours run about $10 per hour. The **Forest Service,** in a new wooden building on Mill Street, is scheduled to open in the near future. Until then, the large, pink **Tongass Visitor Center** (Mill St., at Stedman St., tel. 907/225–3101) is the place to go for info on local hikes and Forest Service cabins. Check out the center's natural history displays and video on Misty Fjords National Monument. The Center is open daily in summer, weekdays in winter. The **Alaska Employment Service** (2030 Sea Level Dr., Suite 220, tel. 907/225–3181), midway between the ferry terminal and old town, is the place to find out about job openings in can-

What Does It All Mean?

Sure, they're beautiful, but what do they mean? If you're tired of staring in ignorant admiration at the totem poles of the Northwest Coast, recognizing a few figures will help you read the totem stories.

• *Dzonokwa, represented by a huge face with pursed lips and often adorned with black paint, is a female bogeyman who lurks in the woods.*

• *Hokw-hokw, a bird-monster known for splitting the skulls of humans to munch on their brains, is noted for his very long, straight beak.*

• *Sisiutl is a scaly sea serpent who may bring either good or evil, and can transform himself into a bazillion other forms.*

• *Thunderbird, a creature capable of swooping down on whales and carrying them off for dinner, typically has curled horns and the beak of an eagle or hawk.*

• *Watchmen, charged with guarding the village and watching the sea, are small, crouched men with tall hats; they are usually found atop Haida poles.*

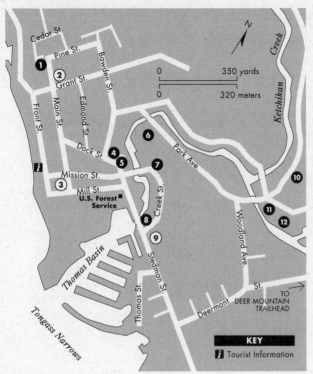

Sights ●
Chief Johnson
Totem Pole, **5**
City Park, **10**
Creek Street
Funicular, **7**
Deer Mountain
Hatchery, **11**
Dolly's House, **8**
Kyan Totem Pole, **1**
Salmon Falls, **6**
Tongass Historical
Museum, **4**
Totem Heritage
Center, **12**

Lodging ○
Ketchikan Youth
Hostel, **2**
New York Hotel, **9**
Union Rooms, **3**

KEY
i Tourist Information

neries and national parks. You can mail letters and buy stamps at Ketchikan's main **post office** (Tongass Ave., tel. 907/225–9601), just north of the ferry terminal.

COMING AND GOING The **Alaska Marine Highway** terminal (3501 Tongass Ave., tel. 907/225–6181) is at the northern end of Ketchikan, 1 mile from the new part of town and 2 miles from the old town. A bus runs between terminal and town every 20 minutes on weekdays; the fare is $1. A taxi to the center of town costs about $8.

The Ketchikan Airport is on nearby Gravinia Island. **Alaska Airlines** (tel. 907/225–2141 or 800/426–0333) charges $174 round-trip for its Ketchikan–Juneau flight. The **Ketchikan Gateway Borough Ferry** whisks passengers to and from the airport ($2.50). It docks just south of the Alaska Marine Highway terminal.

GETTING AROUND The center of Ketchikan lies between the car and pedestrian tunnel and the Thomas Basin boat harbor. Walking will get you everywhere except to Ward Lake, 5 miles north of town; Totem Bight State Park, 10 miles north; and Saxman Native Village, 2.5 miles south of town. The city operates a limited number of buses (tel. 907/228–6625) around town and to the ferry terminal Monday–Saturday; most routes cost $1 and have service every 20 minutes until 6:45 PM.

WHERE TO SLEEP Rates at newer hotels hover around $70 for a single, occasionally dipping to $60 in the winter. The **New York Hotel** (207 Stedman St., tel. 907/225–0246) gives you plenty of character for your dollar, with lots of dark wood paneling and antiques. Singles or doubles with continental breakfast go for $80 in summer and $50 in winter. **Union Rooms** (319 Mill St., tel. 907/225–3580) gives you a shabby cubbyhole of a single for $40 or an equally run-down double for $50. Ketchikan has a number of B&Bs. Singles typically start at $50, doubles at $60–$70.

It's easier to get a tan in rainy Ketchikan than it is to come by a cheap, comfortable room.

➤ **HOSTELS** • For dorm-style digs, your best bet is the **Ketchikan Youth Hostel**, in the basement of the United Methodist Church and open from Memorial Day to Labor Day. HI members pay $7 for a foam mattress on the floor; non-members pay $10. *400 Main St., tel. 907/225–3319.*

➤ **CAMPING** • **Signal Creek Campground**, on Ward Lake, is popular among hikers who laugh in the face of soggy sleeping bags. It offers 25 sites, which rent for $5 a night, but is open in summer only. Fish and firewood are readily available and there is a wheelchair-accessible pit toilet. To get here, hitch a ride or drive Tongass Highway out to the pulp mill; turn off at the WARD LAKE sign and follow the dirt road. The most convenient campground is the **Ketchikan RV Park** (Tongass Ave., 1 mi from downtown, tel. 907/225–6166). Nineteen sites rent for $5 each. Campers can take a shower ($1.50, towel included) or do laundry (75¢) at the **Seaman's Center** (423 Mission St., tel. 907/225–6003). Backpackers in search of wilderness adventure should contact the **Forest Service** (*see* Basics, *above*) for info on camping and remote cabins in the Ketchikan backcountry.

FOOD You'll find a core of restaurants downtown along the waterfront and in the Creek Street area. Others are on Tongass Avenue near the Plaza Mall. For a quick, inexpensive meal, graze the salad bar at **Tatsuda's Supermarket** (Stedman St., tel. 907/225–4125), a few blocks past Creek Street. You can also pick up supplies at **Supervalu Supermarket** (3816 Tongass Ave., tel. 907/225–1279), a block north of the ferry terminal. **Annabelle's** (326 Front St., tel. 907/225–6009) serves a mean cup of chowder for $5 and sandwiches for $7–$10. At **Chico's** (435 Dock St., tel. 907/225–2833) you can pick up a plate of enchiladas for $8 or a gyro lunch special for about $6. The old-fashioned **New York Café** (207 Stedman St., tel. 907/225–0246) will satisfy any and all cravings for Norman Rockwell prints, omelets ($9), sandwiches ($7–$10), and burgers ($8–$10). The **5-Star Café** (5 Creek St., tel. 907/247–7827) serves excellent black-bean burritos ($7) and 10 different espresso drinks (about $2 a shot).

WORTH SEEING The best way to explore Ketchikan's major attractions is to pick up a free walking-tour map of the town from the visitor center (*see* Basics, *above*). Historic/touristy Ketchikan centers around **Creek Street**, a boardwalk on pilings that once housed the Panhandle's most notorious brothels. For $2.50, you can tour **Dolly's House** (24 Creek St., tel. 907/225–6329), a former brothel that reputedly looks exactly as it did when Dolly was in charge. A block away, $2 gets you in to the **Tongass Historical Museum** (629 Dock St., tel. 907/225–5900), which focuses on a different side of the region's history, with impressive exhibits on the region's Indian cultures and Ketchikan's rise as the "Salmon Capitol of the World." If you're here during a salmon run, you can catch a glimpse of these famed fish as they struggle upstream through the **Salmon Falls Fish Ladder,** just under the bridge on Park Avenue (uphill from the museum). If nothing is jumping at the ladder, continue up Park Avenue to the **Deer Mountain Salmon Hatchery,** where approximately 300,000 salmon and trout get their start every year. The fish are released to freshwater lakes and streams after one–two years.

Two of the most famous totem poles in the region are just outside the Tongass Historical Museum, on Dock Street. **Raven Stealing the Sun**, near Ketchikan Creek, tells the story of Raven, who stole the heavens from a giant and brought them to the world. Farther down the street is the **Chief Johnson Totem Pole**, a replica of the original carved in 1901 in honor of Raven's wife, Fog Woman, who brought salmon to the world. The **Totem Heritage Center** (601 Deermount St., accessible from Park Ave., tel. 907/225–5900) is dedicated to teaching about and preserving native Southeast Alaskan culture. For $2, you can see the center's collection of 33 magnificent totems salvaged from abandoned villages. A ways north of town, you can join the cruise-ship hordes at **Totem Bight State Historical Park** (Tongass Ave., tel. 907/247–8574), which contains a longhouse and 15 Haida and Tlingit totem poles. If you aren't completely totemed-out by this time, trek a few miles south of Ketchikan to **Saxman Native Village.** Tlingit people resettled here in the 1880s at the urgings of missionaries; today, the village features a totem park, clan house, and carving center where you can watch carvers at work.

OUTDOOR ACTIVITIES The moderate, 3-mile hike to the summit of **Deer Mountain** ends with an exhilarating, panoramic view of Ketchikan. The more adventurous may want to continue along the ridge to **Blue Lake,** and the truly in-shape may want to continue the full 10 miles to **John Mountain.** The forest service at the **Ketchikan Ranger District** (tel. 907/225–3101) has topo maps and info about trail conditions. They can also point you to some of the many other trails in the area.

Southeast Exposure (507 Stedman St., tel. 907/225–8829) rents two-person kayaks ($45 per day) for trips to the Naha River Trail, Wolf Creek Trail, and George Carroll inlets. You can even kayak to some Forest Service cabins. They give lessons to novices, and lead expeditions ranging from six hours in local inlets ($70) to eight days in Misty Fjords National Monument—don't get any funny ideas, because this one costs $1,110 per person.

NEAR KETCHIKAN

MISTY FJORDS NATIONAL MONUMENT Created by receding glaciers and reshaped by volcanic activity, Misty Fjords is an immense amalgam of diverse geologic formations and ecosystems about 20 miles east of Ketchikan. Running north–south through the area is **Behm Canal,** a 50-mile-long inlet pierced by **New Eddystone Rock,** a 237-foot volcanic plug. Wildlife flourishes in the temperate rain forests, peat bogs, and mountainous country. **Alaska Cruises** (tel. 907/225–6044) makes a 10-hour trip from Ketchikan through the monument for $125 round-trip, including breakfast, lunch, and afternoon snack.

PRINCE OF WALES ISLAND Long ignored by tourists, forest-blanketed Prince of Wales Island is gradually being discovered by folks who come here for the solitude and the good fishing. Ferries land in **Hollis,** but **Craig,** 31 miles to the west, has a bar scene (which can get out of hand on occasion) and a few small inns. The Hollis–Craig Road is the only paved thoroughfare on the island, leaving hundreds of gravel roads for mountain bikers (and logging trucks). Check with the **Forest Service** in Craig (tel. 907/828–3304) for suggestions on safe roads, fishing holes, and hiking trails.

During the summer, an **Alaska Marine Highway** ferry (tel. 907/225–6181) runs six days a week between Ketchikan and Hollis on the east side of the island ($40 round-trip). Several float planes fly from Ketchikan to Hollis ($70 one-way); try **Temsco Airlines** (1249 Tongass Ave., tel. 907/225–9810). Once on the Island, you can rent a car from **Allstar Rent-a-Car** (tel. 907/755–2424), but be prepared for gravel.

Wrangell

Package tourism has yet to trample Wrangell, and you'll most likely encounter small-town friendliness and hospitality here: The diminutive downtown is really one sleepy, nondescript block. Wrangell draws travelers because it provides easy access to the interior and is a jumping-off point for journeys up the Stikine River to the LeConte Glacier and the Anan Bear Observatory. One of the best times to swing through town is during the first weekend in February, for **Tent City.** This footloose party is held annually to celebrate the gold-rush era; one of the best events is the "Shady Lady Fancy Dress Ball." But if you want to witness a real blowout, don't miss the famous **Fourth of July** festivities, for which residents begin preparing in early June.

SYMPTOMS OF WRANGELLITIS:
Saying hello to strangers on the street • Inexplicable cravings for sourdough doughnuts • Talking excessively with your neighbor at the coffee counter • Conversing with Tlingit totems in your dreams.

BASICS When in Wrangell, use only the last four digits of phone numbers for local calls. For long-distance calls, dial 01 first. For collect or credit-card calls, dial 00.

The folks at the **Forest Service** can answer questions about hiking trails and recreation cabins. They also maintain an information board beside the ferry terminal. *525 Bennett St., tel. 907/874–2323.*

Visitor Information Center. *Outer Dr., at Bruger St., tel. 907/874–3901. Open mid-May–mid-Sept., daily 9–5 and when cruise ships arrive; office (but not phones) closed in winter.*

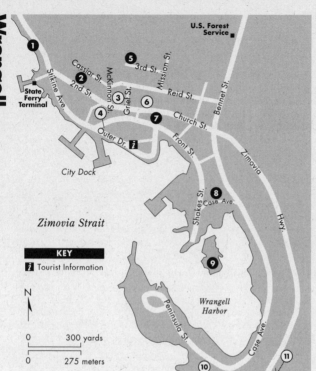

Wrangell

Sights ●

Chief Shakes
Gravesite, **8**

KikSetti Totem
Park, **7**

Mt. Dewey
Trailhead, **5**

Petroglyph Beach, **1**

Shakes Island, **9**

Wrangell
Museum, **2**

Lodging ○

City Park
Campgrounds, **11**

First Presbyterian
Church Hostel, **6**

Rooney's Roost, **3**

Sourdough
Lodge, **10**

Stikine Inn, **4**

U.S. Forest
Service ■

City Dock

Zimovia Strait

KEY

i Tourist Information

N

| 0 | 300 yards |
| 0 | 275 meters |

*Wrangell
Harbor*

COMING AND GOING **Alaska Marine Highway** (Stikine Ave., tel. 907/874–2021) ferries sail to Ketchikan six days a week (6 hrs, $24 one-way) and to Juneau every day (12–18 hrs, $56 one-way). **Alaska Airlines** (tel. 907/874–3308) flies daily to Ketchikan (around $100), Juneau ($120), and Anchorage ($285).

GETTING AROUND Island geography has kept urban sprawl at bay (literally). Almost everything is accessible by foot except the Stikine River, Anan Bear Observatory, and LeConte Glacier. A few of the hiking trails start on the outer reaches of the island, but taxi services can get you there more quickly than walking. Try **Porky's Cab Co.** (tel. 907/874–3603).

WHERE TO SLEEP Wrangell doesn't get many tourists and consequently lacks cheap hotels. The cheapest roof over your head is at the **First Presbyterian Church Hostel** (Church St., tel. 907/874–3534), open June–September, where you can unroll your sleeping bag for $10 a night. **Rooney's Roost** (206 McKinnon St., at 2nd St., tel. 907/874–2026) is a B&B with a bit of character that is close to downtown; rooms cost $50–$55. Rooms at the clean, modern **Sourdough Lodge** (1104 Peninsula St., tel. 907/874–3455), which has a sitting room and a big porch, run between $50 and $65. The bland, modern **Stikine Inn** (107 Front St., in center, tel. 907/874–3388) has rooms for $50–$80; make reservations in summer. You can camp for 24 hours free at the small picnic area in the **City Park** (off Zimovia Hwy., about 1 mi south of town); it has fire pits, shelters, and bathrooms.

FOOD You'll find most restaurants downtown on Front Street. Those interested in a do-it-yourself meal should head for **Benjamin's Supermarket** (223 Brueger St., tel. 907/874–2341), near the information center and city hall. For a real diner atmosphere, try the **Diamond C Café** (215 Front St., tel. 907/874–3677), where french toast costs around $4 and a shrimp burger is around $6. A soup-and-salad lunch (served from noon until the soup runs out) is only $3.50 at the **Dock Side Restaurant** (109 Front St., tel. 907/874–3737); dinner entrées, such as the much-acclaimed deep-fried prawns, run $12–$18. If you're craving a pizza, get one for

$7–$12 at **Maggie's and Sons** (Front St., tel. 907/874–2353); finish it off with a sizable ice-cream cone for $1.25.

WORTH SEEING Chief Shakes V was a prominent Tlingit during the mid-1800s, when Russian, British, and American traders were vying for control of the area. His remains are buried at the **Chief Shakes Gravesite** (Case Ave.), marked by two totems depicting killer whales. To see a replica of his tribal house, walk to **Shakes Island** (accessed from Shakes St., just past the Marine Bar). The house and totems on this small island were constructed and carved in the late 1930s as a Civilian Conservation Corps (CCC) project and dedicated during a potlatch attended by over 1,000 people in 1940. The interior of the house can be viewed by appointment only; call 907/874–3747. The small but jam-packed **Wrangell Museum** (2nd St., tel. 907/874–3770) houses the decorative post that graced Chief Shakes's original tribal house, as well as a Tlingit ceremonial dance blanket, a samurai warrior helmet, and exhibits on the local fishing and timber industries. Admission is $2.

For a glimpse farther back into history, check out **Petroglyph Beach,** a series of stone carvings of spirals, eagles, and ravens found a few minutes' walk north of the ferry terminal. The carvings date back about 8,000 years; archaeologists are unsure who is responsible for them. The best time to see the petroglyphs is at low tide.

AFTER DARK Live music flows with the beer at the **Stikine Bar** in the Stikine Inn (107 Front St., tel. 907/874–3511). The historically minded can toss one back at the **Marine Bar** (274 Shakes St., tel. 907/874–3005), built on the original site of the Russian fort Redoubt St. Dionysius.

OUTDOOR ACTIVITIES Along the Stikine River, which begins on the mainland 5 miles north of Wrangell, is the **Chief Shakes Hot Springs,** 22 miles from town, and the 55-mile-long **Grand Canyon,** whose cliffs tower as high as 1,000 feet. **T. H. Charters** (tel. 907/874–3613) will take you on an eight-hour cruise up the river in a 50-foot boat for $125. If you prefer a bird's-eye view, contact **Sunrise Aviation** (Wrangell Airport, tel. 907/874–2319) about their 45-minute sightseeing tours ($75) over the Stikine River and the LeConte Glacier. The **Anan Bear Observatory,** a Forest Service facility some 30 miles (as the crow flies) east of Wrangell, is another popular destination: In July and August, black and brown bears, bald eagles, and harbor seals come here to feed on the spawning salmon. T. H. Charters will take you here for $125; the trip takes 5–8 hours. The Forest Service cabin at Anan Bay is one of the district's most popular, and can be reserved at Wrangell's Forest Service office (*see* Basics, *above*) for $25 a night.

Drop a line at Highbrush Lake and Thom's Creek (30 and 40 miles from town, respectively) for steelhead and cutthroat trout as well as salmon. Be on the lookout for deer, bear, and moose that come here after the same prey.

The closest hiking to town is a steep, 30-minute trek up **Mt. Dewey**. Your effort will earn you a striking view of Wrangell and Zimovia Strait; look for the trailhead near the end of Third Street. A few miles south of town, a mile-long trail leads to a view of **Rainbow Falls** and **Chicago Pass**; the trailhead is across from the Shoemaker Bay Harbor parking lot. Off this trail is the **Institute Creek Trail,** a rugged 3-mile path that leads through spruce and hemlock forest and muskeg to the Shoemaker Overlook, which offers a view of the narrows.

Petersburg

Alaska's "Little Norway" was named for its turn-of-the-century Norwegian founder, Peter Buschmann. Today, Petersburg remains very much under the influence of the old country. They celebrate Norwegian independence day with a **Little Norway Festival** every May 17, signs in stores greet you with a hearty "Velkommen," and the town even has an incongruous (for Alaska) Scandinavian aura of prosperity and order. Thankfully, Petersburg is not too touristy. Without fighting for space, you can amuse yourself hiking or cross-country skiing all over Mitkof Island, where the town is situated, or visiting LeConte Glacier to the south on the mainland.

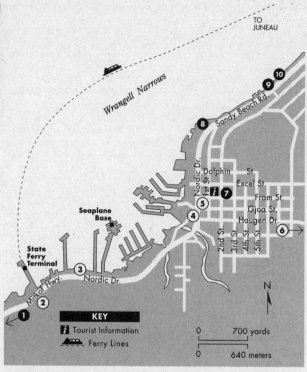

TO JUNEAU

Wrangell Narrows

Sandy Beach Rd.

Nordic Dr.

Dolphin St.

1st St.

Excel St.

Fram St.

Gjoa St.

Haugen Dr.

2nd St.

3rd St.

4th St.

5th St.

Seaplane Base

State Ferry Terminal

Mitkof Hwy.

Nordic Dr.

N

Sights ●
Blind Slough, **1**
Clausen Museum, **7**
Eagle's Roost Park, **8**
Frederick Point Boardwalk, **10**
Sandy Beach Recreation Area, **9**

Lodging ○
Jewells by the Sea, **3**
Narrows Inn, **2**
Scandia House, **5**
Sing Lee B&B, **4**
Tent City, **6**

KEY
𝑖 Tourist Information
Ferry Lines

0   700 yards
0   640 meters

BASICS When making telephone calls within the Petersburg area, dial only the last four digits. The **Petersburg Employment Service** (102 Haugen Dr., tel. 907/772–3791) lists job openings at local canneries; the best time to look for work is the last week in June, just before the season opens. The **Forest Service** office (Nordic Dr., tel. 907/772–3871) is above a **post office,** and the **Visitor Information Bureau** (1st St., at Fram St., tel. 907/772–3646) is usually staffed by an additional Forest Service representative. Stop in for a free town map and the *Viking Visitor Guide.* The office is open in summer, weekdays 8–4:30, Saturday 10–2, Sunday noon–4; in winter, weekdays 10–3.

COMING AND GOING The **Alaska Marine Highway** terminal (Mile 1 Zimovia Hwy., tel. 907/874–3711 or 907/874–2021) is just a mile from downtown. In the summer, Petersburg is served daily by one northbound and one southbound ferry. **Alaska Airlines** (tel. 907/772–4255) runs one daily flight through Petersburg to Seattle and another to Anchorage. The airport is 1 mile east of downtown on Haugen Drive. Sneakers or walking shoes (and perhaps rain gear) are prerequisites for getting around Petersburg. There's no bus system, so taxis are useful for scooting to and from the airport and ferry terminals; try **City Cab** (tel. 907/772–3303).

WHERE TO SLEEP It's easy to a find clean, comfortable room here, but you'll have to pay a fair sum. Charming, historic **Scandia House** (110 Nordic Dr., tel. 907/772–4281) rents doubles with private bath for $75 ($60 with shared bath); breakfast is included. The **Narrows Inn** (Mile 1 Mitkof Hwy., tel. 907/772–4288; closed Oct.–April), across from the ferry terminal, has singles for $60 and doubles for $70. For a homier stay, try one of the local B&Bs: **Jewells By the Sea** (806 S. Nordic Dr., tel. 907/772–3620) is close to the ferry terminal and charges $55 for a single and $65 for a double; **Sing Lee Bed and Breakfast** (Sing Lee Alley, tel. 907/772–4700), right downtown, charges $60 for a single, $70 for a double.

➤ **CAMPING** • Seasonal cannery workers and down-on-their-luck locals are regulars at **Tent City** (Haugen Dr., 1 mi east of town, tel. 907/772–3033), a tent community that looks like it might have been designed as a set for *Grapes of Wrath*. Tents are perched on wooden platforms and cost $4 a night. You get the use of the restrooms, firewood, and coin-op showers. A few blocks from downtown, **LeConte RV Park** (Haugen Dr., at Fourth St., tel. 907/772–4680) is dominated by RVs, though a few tents have been sighted here. Sites are $5 per night or $30 per week.

Kato's Kave, off Sing Lee Alley, is a large, dark, cover-free club where local folk dance to live music on a big floor every night but Sunday.

FOOD The best place to buy groceries is **The Trading Union** (Nordic Dr., tel. 907/772–3881), on the northern end of the main drag. Try **Harbor Lights Pizza** (28 Sing Lee Alley, tel. 907/772–3424) for lasagna ($6) or pizza ($10), or stop in at the **Homestead Café** (217 Main St., tel. 907/772–3900), for a hefty ham-and-egg breakfast or Viking burger (both $7). Vegetarians will appreciate the $6 tofu-salad sandwiches at **Helse** (Sing Lee Alley, near Nordic Dr., tel. 907/772–3444), a popular lunch place.

WORTH SEEING Mitkof Island's few attractions are spread out, and, since there is no public transportation, getting around is a pain. All you need is your feet to reach the downtown **Clausen Memorial Museum** (203 Fram St., tel. 907/772–3598). Displays provide information on the Tlingit and the early white immigrants to the area, as well as on the fishing trade that keeps the town thriving. Also within easy walking distance is **Eagle's Roost Park** (Nordic Dr., just north of Petersburg Fisheries), which, according to locals, is the best place to spy bald eagles. Just off the Mitkof Highway, 18 miles south of town, is the **Blind Slough Recreation Area,** a popular summertime swimming and picnic site. In late fall and winter, the region becomes bird heaven for hundreds of trumpeter swans who come to enjoy the Norwegian hospitality (i.e. not getting shot at). The area's best attraction is also the most difficult to access: **LeConte Glacier,** 25 miles to the southeast, is the southernmost active tidewater glacier in North America. Several local businesses run cruises and flights to the glacier; prices range $75 to $200 for half- to full-day excursions. Check with the Visitor Information Bureau (*see* Basics, *above*) or **Viking Travel** (106 N. Nordic Dr., tel. 907/772–3818) for more information.

Beginning just past the Sandy Beach Recreation Area on Sandy Beach Road, the mile-long Frederic Point Boardwalk, which leads through muskeg and thick forest to the beach, is a popular route for evening walks. Keep an eye out for bears.

OUTDOOR ACTIVITIES **Raven's Roost Trail** is a difficult, 4-mile trail that begins on the south side of the airport and leads through muskeg and forest to a Forest Service cabin; contact the Forest Service (*see* Basics, *above*) for reservations. In winter, most of the trails and old logging roads around Petersburg are taken over by cross-country skiers. Especially popular are the **Three Lake Loop** and the **Twin Creek Ski Trail,** both south of town. **Tongass Kayak Adventures** (tel. 907/772–4600) runs no-experience needed, five-hour paddle trips around the harbor and up Petersburg Creek. The trips cost $45 per person and can be booked through Viking Travel.

Sitka

Once known as "the Paris of the Pacific," Sitka, on the western coast of Baranof Island, continues to embody the cultural diversity that has marked its history. The focal point of downtown is St. Michael's Church, a strange wooden structure topped by an onion dome that dates back to the days when Sitka was a bustling Russian township. Before the Russians took over, Sitka was the home of the Kiksadi clan of the Tlingit tribe. At the turn of the 19th century, a Russian fort was built a little too near Sitka for the Tlingits' liking, and battles erupted; sadly, the Tlingits were badly beaten and forced to retreat. The Russians soon established control over the area, and by the 19th century the town was booming from the fur trading, ice making, and shipbuilding industries. In 1867, the area changed hands again, coming under the American flag after a ceremony on Sitka's Castle Hill. And it was here that, in 1959, the first 49-star flag was raised, welcoming the new state of Alaska to the Union.

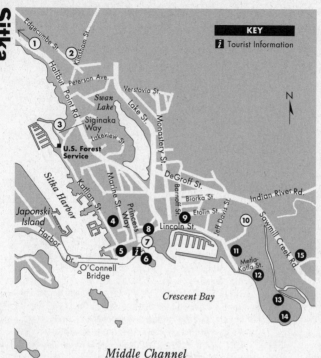

Sitka

KEY

i Tourist Information

N

Sights ●

Alaska Raptor
Rehabilitation
Center, **15**

Castle Hill, **5**

Centennial
Building, **6**

Russian Bishop's
House, **9**

Russian
Blockhouse, **4**

Russian
Memorial, **14**

St. Michael's
Cathedral, **8**

Sheldon Jackson
Museum, **11**

Sitka National
Historical Park, **12**

Tlingit Fort, **13**

Lodging ○

Sheldon Jackson
College Dorms, **10**

Sitka Hotel, **7**

Sitka Youth
Hostel, **2**

Starrigavan
Campground, **1**

Wild Strawberry
Inn, **3**

Edgecumbe St.
Kimsham St.
Halibut Point Rd.
Peterson Ave.
Swan Lake
Verstovia St.
Lake St.
Siginaka Way
Lakeview St.
Monastery St.
U.S. Forest Service
DeGroff St.
Sitka Harbor
Katlian St.
Marine St.
Barnoff St.
Biorka St.
Indian River Rd.
Japonski Island
Princess Way
Etolin St.
Lincoln St.
Jeff Davis St.
Sawmill Creek Rd.
Harbor Dr.
O'Connell Bridge
Metla-Katla St.

Crescent Bay

Middle Channel

BASICS The **Sitka Convention and Visitor Bureau** (330 Harbor Dr., tel. 907/747–5940), in the Centennial Building near Crescent Boat Harbor, is open weekdays 8–5. They give out free town maps, brochures, and accommodation and tour-company listings. The **Forest Service** (No. 109 Totem Square Bldg., 201 Katlian St., tel. 907/747–6671) has free literature on hiking, camping, and natural history and accepts cabin reservations.

COMING AND GOING Sitka has no municipal bus system, but a carefully planned day on foot shouldn't wipe you out completely—most attractions are downtown and within walking distance of one another. **Southeast Diving and Sports** (203 Lincoln St., tel. 907/747–8279) rents mountain bikes for $4 per hour, $12 for a half-day, or $20 overnight.

➢ **BY FERRY** • **Alaska Marine Highway** (tel. 907/747–8737) ferries pass through Sitka about five days a week in summer. The one-way fare for the nine-hour Juneau–Sitka route is $26; the 22-hour Ketchikan–Sitka trip is $54 one-way. The small ferry *LeConte* also makes the Juneau–Sitka voyage, calling in at the remote villages of Angoon, Tenakee Springs, and Hoonah along the way. The ferry terminal is about 6 miles from downtown Sitka. Two tour companies meet each ferry and whisk travelers downtown: **Baranof Tours** (tel. 907/747–1016) charges $2, while **Prewitt Tours** (tel. 907/747–8443) charges $2.50.

➢ **BY PLANE** • **Alaska Airlines** (tel. 907/966–2266) flies daily between Anchorage and Sitka (about $360 round-trip; reserve well ahead). The airport is less than 2 miles from downtown Sitka on Japonski Island. **Prewitt Tours** (tel. 907/747–8443) shuttles passengers between the airport and town for $2.50.

WHERE TO SLEEP For a small city, Sitka offers a surprisingly wide range of accommodations. Pick up the current listings from the visitor bureau (*see* Basics, *above*). The 50-year-old **Sitka Hotel** (118 Lincoln St., tel. 907/747–3288), which charges $55 for a double room with bath, is the cheapest hotel in town.

Wild Strawberry Inn. The ceiling in the main TV room of this popular, rustic waterfront B&B is covered with fishing poles, and the rest of the decor is equally seaworthy. Singles are $62, doubles $75. *724 Siginaka Way, on waterfront, tel. 907/747–8883 or 800/770–2628. 8 rooms, 1 with bath. Reservations advised.*

➤ **HOSTELS** • The **Sitka Youth Hostel (HI)** operates June–September in the basement of the United Methodist Church. Members pay $7 ($10 nonmembers) for a bed in a gender-segregated dorm and use of a well-equipped kitchen and comfortable TV/sitting room. Lockout is 8:30 AM–6 PM daily, and the curfew is 11 PM. Bring a sleeping bag. *303 Kimsham St., at Edgecumbe Dr., tel. 907/747–8356 (summer only) or 907/747–8425. 20 beds. No credit cards.*

➤ **STUDENT HOUSING** • **Sheldon Jackson College** rents its downtown dorm rooms to the public when school is out (mid-May–mid-August). They charge $30 per single and $50 per double in a new dorm, $25 per single and $40 per double in an older building. Linen is included, and you can get meals in the cafeteria. *801 Lincoln St., tel. 907/747–2518 in summer or 907/747–5201 in winter.*

➤ **CAMPING** • The Forest Service's **Starrigavan Campground** is less than a mile north of the ferry terminal, at the end of Halibut Point Road. The sites ($5) are close to water, toilets, picnic tables, fire pits, and firewood. The Forest Service runs another campground 13 miles from the ferry terminal, **Sawmill Creek Campground,** where you can camp for free on one of nine primitive sites for up to 14 days. Unless you're up for a very long walk, Sawmill is accessible by bike or car only: Follow Halibut Point Road to Sawmill Creek Road and bear left at the pulp mill.

FOOD Stock up on bread and cheese at **Lakeside Grocery** (Halibut Point Rd., near Katlian St.); to add fresh or smoked salmon to your picnic, stop by **Alaskan Harvest** (320 Seward St., tel. 907/747–6867) near the center of town. True to its name, the **Bayview Restaurant** (407 Lincoln St., tel. 907/747–5440) has seats overlooking the water where you can sample Russian specialties such as piroshkis (small pastries filled with eggs, beef, and spices; $7.50) and Russian-style halibut ($8). **Coffee Express** (104 Lake St., tel. 907/747–3343) has create-your-own sandwich specials (around $6) and homemade soup ($3). Head to **Ginny's Kitchen** (236 Lincoln St., tel. 907/747–8028) for cheap fast food, such as hot dogs ($1.25), sandwiches ($5.25), and sundaes ($2.25). You can get bagels with lox ($3.25) or fried bread ($2) at the **Fisherman's Cookhouse,** a small stand in front of the cinema on Lincoln Street. The **Sheldon Jackson College** cafeteria (Sweetland Hall, Lincoln St., tel. 907/747–2506) serves up not-bad dorm food. A breakfast feast is $4.50, lunch is $5.50, and dinner is $8.

WORTH SEEING If you're interested in Sitka's Native American and Russian heritage, you'll have plenty to explore, including forts, churches, museums, and battle sites. You will, however, likely be joined in your quest for local lore by a phalanx of cruise-ship passengers on shore leave. Bummer. If you have little time in Sitka, consider a one-hour tour: Both **Baranof Tours** (tel. 907/747–1016) and **Prewitt Tours** (tel. 907/747–8443) lead guided walks around town for about $10 ahead.

Alaska Raptor Rehabilitation Center. This highly respected research facility and hospital for injured birds of prey includes a clinic, classroom, auditorium, and special patient housing (called mews). An hour-long tour costs $10 per person. *1101 Sawmill Creek Rd., tel. 907/747–8662. Go left from Lincoln St. onto Lake St., right on Sawmill Creek Rd., left at first dirt road after Indian River. Open Mon.–Sat. 9–5, Sun. 9–4.*

Castle Hill. On October 18, 1867, Russia surrendered control over the territory of Alaska to the United States on this spot. Castle Hill is also where, on July 4, 1959, the first 49-star American flag was raised, marking Alaska's admission to the Union. The hill offers a good view of the surrounding downtown area, the harbor, and Mount Edgecumbe, a dormant volcano. From Castle Hill, a short walk up Marine Street brings you to the **Russian Blockhouse,** a replica of the structure that marked the divide between Russian and Tlingit Sitka in the 1820s. *Follow trail beginning at Harbor Dr. or take stairs at cnr of Katlian St. and Lincoln St.*

Centennial Building. In addition to a visitor-information center, the Centennial Building is home to the **Isabel Miller Museum,** which features a permanent collection of Tlingit, Russian, and Victorian artifacts, as well as a large-scale model of Sitka in 1867. The building also features an auditorium where the Sitka folk-dance troupe **New Archangel Dancers** (tel. 907/747–8443) performs traditional Russian dances in the summer. *330 Harbor Dr. tel. 907/747-3225. Next to Crescent Boat Harbor. Admission free. Museum open mid-May–mid-Sept., daily 8–5; mid-Sept.–mid-May, weekdays 10–4.*

Russian Bishop's House. Built in 1842, the house's first and most famous inhabitant was Bishop Innocent, canonized as the "Apostle to America" for his early missionary work with native Alaskans. The National Park Service bought the house, undertook a $5 million restoration project, and now gives tours of the premises. *Lincoln St., tel. 907/747–6281. Admission free. Open summer, daily 8:30–4:30; open winter only for 2:30 PM tour Tues., Thurs., and Sat.*

St. Michael's Cathedral. This gray wooden church, topped with an onion-shaped copper cupola, is home to a hefty collection of Russian Orthodox silver- and gold-plated icons. Originally built in 1848 under Bishop Innocent, the church was destroyed by fire in 1966 and rebuilt 10 years later. *Lincoln St., tel. 907/747–8120. Admission: $1 donation requested. Open summer, Mon.–Sat. 11–3, Sun. noon–3.*

Sheldon Jackson Museum. On the Sheldon Jackson College campus south of downtown, this museum has an impressive collection of Native Alaskan artifacts, gathered primarily by Presbyterian missionary Sheldon Jackson over 100 years ago. Writer James Michener did much of the research for his historical novel *Alaska* here. *104 College Dr., tel. 907/747–8981. Follow Lincoln St. out of town to campus. Admission: $2; free students and under 18. Open mid-May–mid-Sept., daily 8–5; mid-Sept.–mid-May, Tues.–Sat. 10–4.*

Sitka National Historical Park. The oldest national park in Alaska commemorates the Battle of Sitka, in which the Russians defeated the Tlingit in 1804. The park contains an astounding array of totem poles and decorative house posts set along a mile-long trail. A grassy meadow adjacent to the trail is all that remains of Tlingit Fort, in which several hundred Tlingits barricaded themselves for a final stand against the Russians. The **Visitor Center** (open daily 7:30–6) houses an audiovisual display about the battle as well as the **Indian Cultural Center** (tel. 907/747–6281), where (in summer only) you can talk with Native Alaskan wood carvers, jewelers, and clothing designers. *Lincoln St., past Sheldon Jackson College. Park open daily 5 AM–10 PM.*

FESTIVALS The **Sitka Summer Music Festival** is held every June and draws international chamber musicians to Sitka. Concerts can be crowded, so break your bad habits and make a reservation. A single concert costs around $12; a festival pass runs about $60. *Festival offices: Centennial Bldg., 330 Harbor Dr., tel. 907/747–6774.*

OUTDOOR ACTIVITIES The Forest Service (*see* Basics, *above*) provides trail and camping info and gives out a helpful guide, *Sitka Trails.* One of the most popular trails close to town is the relatively easy, 6-mile **Indian River Trail,** which leads through muskeg and old-growth forest to a roaring waterfall. The trailhead is next to the Public Safety Academy on Sawmill Creek Road. On a clear day, the **Gavan Hill Trail** (trailhead just past 510 Baranof Street) offers views of Sitka and the surrounding area at the end of a steep 3-mile climb. Similarly, the **Mount Vestovia Trail** leads almost 3 miles up difficult, often muddy switchbacks to meadows with great views. The trailhead is 2 miles out of town on Sawmill Creek Road, near the Kiksadi Club. Hikers going solo can leave their names with the **Fire Department** (209 Lake St., tel. 907/747–3233) as a safety measure. (They'll come collect what's left of you if you fail to return.)

➤ **KAYAKING** • For the adventurous, Sitka is a perfect place to sea-kayak, and even novices can try a one- to three-day trip. You can arrange for kayak rentals and Forest Service cabins ($25) at the base of Mount Edgecumbe or near the White Sulfur Hot Springs on Chichagof Island to the north. **Baidarka Boats** (201 Lincoln St., tel. 907/747–8996) rents double kayaks for around $40 a day and provides an hour of instruction for up to four people for $25; guided tours are $120 a day per person.

Haines

Hollywood descended on Haines in 1989 to film its version of Jack London's classic *White Fang* (starring super-slacker Ethan Hawke), but, with no movie theater in town, most residents had to wait two years for the film to come out on video. Natural entertainment is the thing in Haines, which is known as "Valley of the Eagles," in honor of the more than 3,500 bald eagles that come in fall and winter to feast on salmon in area streams.

Sitting on a heavily forested peninsula between the base of the spectacular Coastal Mountain Range and Portage Cove, Haines and the surrounding area are dotted with salmon-rich rivers and valleys filled with wildlife. Tlingit, Chilkat, and Chilkoot people were the first to settle the area, which later became a base camp for both local gold prospectors and travelers on the Jack Dalton Trail, which ran up to the Yukon. Still a crossroads of sorts, Haines is the meeting point of two of Alaska's most important transport arteries, the Alcan Highway and the Alaska Marine Highway ferry system. As a result, Haines, unlike Skagway, feels like a real town rather than a living memorial to the past.

Haines is also a regional art center. Several impressive galleries, workshops, and an Indian dance center are all dedicated to maintaining indigenous arts and traditions—even a short time exploring them will provide a good sense of local culture and history. The town swells with visitors in August when it plays host to the annual **Southeast Alaska State Fair,** which brings folk music, dancers, logging contests, food, and art displays to town for an entire week of down-home festivities.

BASICS The staff at the log-cabin **Visitor Information Center** answers questions competently and gives out the useful *Haines Sentinel.* The center may allow backpackers to stow gear here for the day. *2nd Ave., at Willard St., 2 blocks from Main St., tel. 907/766–2234. Open May–Sept., daily 8–8; Oct.–April, weekdays 8–5 and when cruise ships arrive.*

Rangers are in and out of the **Alaska State Parks** office (Main St., tel. 907/766–2292), but between 8 AM and 9 AM you can usually catch them for questions on hiking and camping in the Haines area.

COMING AND GOING The 155-mile Haines Highway originates in Haines and meets the Alcan Highway for connections to the interior. You'll pass through Canada on this route, so have the proper identification ready. Whitehorse, Canada, is 225 miles northeast. You can rent a car from motels in town for about $45 per day; try **Affordable Cars** in the Captain's Choice Motel (2nd St., at Dalton St., tel. 800/478–2345).

➤ **BY FERRY** • The **Alaska Marine Highway** ferry terminal (tel. 907/766–2111) is less than 5 miles north of town on Lutak Road. One ferry runs daily to Skagway (1 hr, $14 one-way); another goes to Juneau (4½ hrs, $20 one-way). **Haines Shuttle** (tel. 907/766–3138) charges $5 for a ride between town and the ferry terminal. **Haines Skagway Water Taxi** (tel. 907/766–3395) will transport you to Skagway in their small boat (2 daily, 1½ hrs, $18). Look for the boat at the harbor just south of the junction of Beach Road and Main Street.

➤ **BY BUS** • **Alaskon Express** (tel. 800/544–2206) runs from Haines to Anchorage ($194 one-way), Whitehorse ($79 one-way), Fairbanks ($169 one-way), and other points in Alaska and Canada. Buses leave three days a week in summer (two days a week in winter) from the Hotel Halsingland at Fort Seward and from the Wings of Alaska office on Second Avenue.

➤ **BY PLANE** • The **Haines Airport** is about 5 miles out of town on the Haines Highway. **Haines Airways** (tel. 907/766–2646), **LAB Flying Service** (tel. 907/766–2222), and **Wings of Alaska** (tel. 907/766–2030) all fly from Haines. Typical one-way fares are $60 to Juneau and $30 to Skagway.

➤ **HITCHHIKING** • For travelers heading north, Haines is the best place to catch a ride into the interior. Check ferry schedules to see when tourist-bearing cars will be coming off the boats and wait for them at the junction of Haines Highway and Main Street, about a mile from

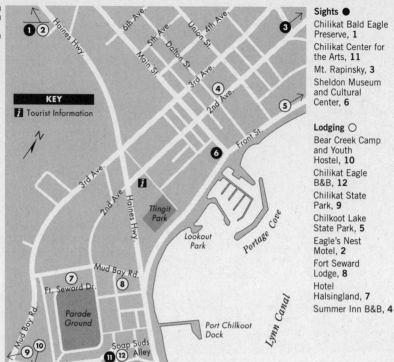

Sights ●

Chilikat Bald Eagle Preserve, **1**

Chilkat Center for the Arts, **11**

Mt. Rapinsky, **3**

Sheldon Museum and Cultural Center, **6**

Lodging ○

Bear Creek Camp and Youth Hostel, **10**

Chilikat Eagle B&B, **12**

Chilikat State Park, **9**

Chilkoot Lake State Park, **5**

Eagle's Nest Motel, **2**

Fort Seward Lodge, **8**

Hotel Halsingland, **7**

Summer Inn B&B, **4**

KEY

i Tourist Information

downtown. The corner of Front Street and Lutak Road is the best spot to catch a short ride out to the ferry terminal.

GETTING AROUND Haines is surrounded by the Chilkat River and the Lynn Canal and is divided in two by the Haines Highway. The Fort William H. Seward Historic District occupies the area south of the highway and holds a number of hotels and Native Alaskan arts centers. Restaurants, gift shops, the boat harbor, a few hotels, and the museum are all north of the highway. The State Fairgrounds are about a mile's walk down the Haines Highway.

WHERE TO SLEEP Because it's an important point of connection between southeast Alaska and the Interior, Haines gets very busy during summer. Fortunately, the town has motels, B&Bs, campgrounds, and a hostel that, together, offer enough beds to accommodate just about everybody, except during ultra-busy periods such as the Fourth of July and the mid-August Southeast Alaskan State Fair. Even then, you can always squeeze in a tent at the Eagle Camper Park (*see* Camping, *below*). Residents on the outskirts of town will often let visitors pitch a tent in a field or yard—be sure to get permission.

A motel is a motel is a motel in Haines—variations are slight, and most are around Fort Seward on the south side of town. The clean, well-lighted **Eagle's Nest Motel** (Mile 1 Haines Hwy., tel. 907/766–2891) has singles for $60, doubles for $70, and triples for $80. The Victorian **Hotel Halsingland** (13 Ft. Seward Dr., tel. 907/766–2000; closed Nov.–Mar.) has well-worn, shared-bath singles ($30) and doubles ($40); rooms with private baths run $75–$80. **Fort Seward Lodge** (Mud Bay Rd., at Haines Hwy., tel. 907/766–2009 or 800/478–7772) is a former bowling alley that now has comfortable, shared-bath single ($55) and double ($65) rooms.

Chilkat Eagle Bed & Breakfast. Unless you're allergic to cats, this historic B&B is a great bet for stimulating conversation, a good night's sleep, and a tasty breakfast. The owners will fortify you with home-grown fare and local stories. Spacious singles with shared bath are $55, doubles are $65. *67 Soap Suds Alley, at west side of Fort Seward, tel. 907/766–2763. 2 rooms, none with bath. No credit cards.*

Summer Inn Bed & Breakfast. This 1912 B&B is simply decorated, though the bathroom does have an antique claw-foot tub. There are no TVs or phones in the rooms to interfere with your rest, and you get a full breakfast of pancakes or quiche in the morning. Ask for a room with a view of Lynn Canal. Prices range from $55 for a single to $85 for a triple in summer; prices fall $10 in winter. *247 2nd Ave., btw Dalton St. and Union St., tel. 907/766–2970. 5 rooms, none with bath.*

➤ **HOSTELS • Bear Creek Camp and Youth Hostel (HI).** This rustic hostel was recently upgraded by ambitious new management. Dorm beds are $12 for HI members, $15 for nonmembers. Cabins with two bunk beds and one double bed cost $37, and tent sites are $5 plus $2.50 per additional person. Free transport to and from the ferry terminal is provided. *Small Tract Rd., tel. 907/766–2259. Follow Mud Bay Rd. south and take gravel Small Tract Road 1 mi. 20 dorm beds, 5 cabins, 8 tent sites. Laundry, kitchen, showers.*

➤ **CAMPING •** Of the area's four public campgrounds, the waterfront **Portage Cove** (Beach Rd., off Haines Hwy., tel. 907/766–2292) is closest to town. No-vehicle tent sites are $6 and come with bear caches, fire pits, and wheelchair-accessible pit toilets. Eight miles southwest of town on Mud Bay Road, the quiet **Chilkat State Park** (tel. 907/766–2292) encompasses both forest and waterfront sites. You can stay in one of 32 secluded sites for $6; the park contains pit toilets and a water pump. Next to scenic, salmon- and trout-rich Chilkoot Lake, **Chilkoot Lake State Park** (Lutak Rd., 11 mi north of town, tel. 907/766–2292) offers $8 tent sites with fire pits, toilets, and a water pump.

FOOD **Food Center Market** (3rd Ave., at Dalton St., tel. 907/766–2181), open Monday–Saturday 8:30–8 and Sunday 11–7, is the place to pick up groceries. Those with stomachs as big as their eyes may want to invest in the **Port Chilkoot Potlatch** (tel. 907/766–2000), a $20 all-you-can-eat salmon bake, held nightly 5–8 in a replica of a Tlingit tribal house on the parade grounds of Fort Seward. **Porcupine Pete's** (Main St., at 2nd Ave., tel. 907/766–9199) has big windows for watching the action on the street and serves decent pizza ($10–$20), sandwiches ($6–$8), and ice cream.

Chilkat Restaurant and Bakery. This is probably the best deal in Haines: Every Friday night you can get all-you-can-eat Mexican food for $12. The eat-until-you-can't soup-and-salad bar, also $12, happens every night. Fresh-baked bread, muffins, and all kinds of pastries are also available. *5th Ave., at Dalton St., tel. 907/766–2920. Open summer, Mon.–Sat. 7 AM–9 PM and Sun. 9–9; winter, Mon.–Sat. 7:30 AM–3 PM.*

Mountain Market. Stop in here for a latte ($2.50), a brownie ($1.60), and a delicious array of healthy goodies such as the "tofuna" sandwich (made with tofu and tahini; $5) or the broccoli-and-cheddar rice bake ($4.50). The Market is a hip hangout as well as the local source for organic groceries. *Haines Hwy., at 3rd Ave., tel. 907/766–3340. Open weekdays 7:30–7, weekends 9–6.*

WORTH SEEING. Haines's most celebrated sight is the 48,000-acre **Chilkat Bald Eagle Preserve,** the fall and winter home for thousands of bald eagles. The park entrance is 18 miles from town. Within Haines itself you'll find plenty of local art.

Sheldon Museum and Cultural Center houses a collection of artifacts, photographs, jewelry, woven blankets, baskets, and more. Exhibits relate the histories of early pioneers, the native Chilkat and Chilkoot cultures, and the sea and land transportation routes that have been critical to the town's development. Two 25-minute videos on the bald eagles and Haines are shown daily at 1:30 PM. *25 Main St., tel. 907/766–2366. Admission: $2.50. Open mid-May–mid-Sept., daily 1–5; mid-Sept.–mid-May, Sun., Mon., and Wed. 1–4.*

Southeast Alaska State Fairgrounds, a 40-acre site 1 mile south of town, hosts the week-long state fair every August. The fair involves everything from Russian folk dancers and log-rolling contests to music performances and endless food booths. Newly installed on the fairgrounds is

Dalton City, a mini gold-rush town created as a set for *White Fang,* where you'll find dogsled demonstrations, Tlingit carvers, and more souvenir shops than you thought possible. Dalton City is open May through September; admission is $6.

CHEAP THRILLS Go gallery hopping through town to see sculptors, weavers, and basket-makers practicing their crafts. The **Alaskan Indian Arts** building (Ft. Seward, tel. 907/766–2160), **Chilkat Valley Arts** (307 Willard St., tel. 907/766–2990), the **Whale Rider Gallery** (2nd St., at Willard St., tel. 907/766–2540), and the **Northern Arts Gallery** (301 Willard St., tel. 907/766–2318) are particularly good.

AFTER DARK The **Chilkat Center for the Arts** (Theatre Dr., tel. 907/766–2020), housed in a former cannery on the south side of the Fort Seward parade grounds, presents a variety of productions. The traditional **Chilkat Dancers** perform almost every summer night at 8 PM; tickets are $8. The center also hosts **ACTFEST,** the Alaska Community Theatre Festival, for one week every other April, as well as the occasional film screening.

Join the locals for a game of pool and a pitcher of Juneau's own Alaskan Amber beer at the happening **Fogcutter Bar** (Main St., tel. 907/766–9109), or relax at the more mellow **Harbor Bar** on the waterfront (bottom of Main St., tel. 907/766–2444). **Lookout Park,** right next to the boat harbor along Front Street, has a small covered sitting area where folks often come on summer nights to smooch and watch the action on the waterfront.

OUTDOOR ACTIVITIES Hikers should pick up the free pamphlet *Haines is for Hikers* from the visitor center. Day hikers can try a view-filled 4-mile loop that leads past the summit of **Mt. Riley** via Mud Bay Road. The 7-mile **Saddle Trail** is a more strenuous hike that leads from the top of Young Road to the 3,920-foot peak of Mt. Ripinsky. You can also start at the opposite end, from the trailhead just east of Mile 7 of the Haines Highway; the views are spectacular either way. Another all-day hike leads almost 7 miles from Chilkat State Park (*see* Camping, *above*) to **Seduction Point,** taking you along the shoreline and through the forest, providing stunning views across the Chilkat Inlet to the Davidson Glacier.

➤ **BIKING** • Sockeye Cycle (Portage St., Ft. Seward, tel. 907/766–2869) leads three-hour mountain-bike tours ($60) and rents bikes ($6 per hour, $30 per day). A hilly but scenic ride from Haines leads 7 miles along the half-paved, half-gravel Mud Bay Road to Chilkat State Park.

➤ **RIVER RAFTING** • Water signs, and anyone else with $70 to spare, can take the four-hour float trip through the Chilkat Bald Eagle Preserve, led by **Chilkat Guides** (Beach Rd, at Portage Rd., tel. 907/766–2491). Knowledgeable and enthusiastic guides point out wildlife and features of the natural landscape. A picnic lunch is included.

Skagway

Poor William Moore. When the riverboat captain sailed into this inlet in 1887 to claim it for himself, he had every hope of cashing in on the gold rush; he even built a dock and set up trail tolls throughout his new town. The gold-hungry miners who arrived in Mooresville 10 years later, however, ignored Mr. Moore entirely and renamed the place Skagway, turning it into a wild, gold-crazy town. Back in 1898, one oft-quoted law officer condemned Skagway as "little better than a hell on earth." The notorious Jefferson Randolph "Soapy" Smith owned a saloon in Skagway, and it was from here that he oversaw the activities of what is said to have been the largest band of gangsters in North America. The saloons, brothels, hotels, and restaurants that sprung up during the 1898 rush are now museums, false-fronted stores, and refurbished hotels.

Ask a local to tell you the story of how good guy Frank Reid and his 101-man vigilante team washed local gangster Soapy down the proverbial drain.

Ten miles from Skagway, the settlement of Dyea (population: 25) is the starting point for the treacherous **Chilkoot Trail,** a 33-mile route along which thousands of prospectors—with thousands of pounds of gear and equipment—poured like ants toward the gold country. Today, the

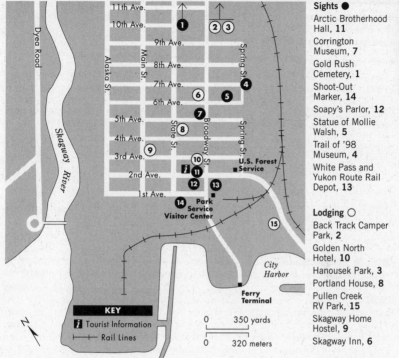

Sights ●

Arctic Brotherhood Hall, **11**

Corrington Museum, **7**

Gold Rush Cemetery, **1**

Shoot-Out Marker, **14**

Soapy's Parlor, **12**

Statue of Mollie Walsh, **5**

Trail of '98 Museum, **4**

White Pass and Yukon Route Rail Depot, **13**

Lodging ○

Back Track Camper Park, **2**

Golden North Hotel, **10**

Hanousek Park, **3**

Portland House, **8**

Pullen Creek RV Park, **15**

Skagway Home Hostel, **9**

Skagway Inn, **6**

KEY

i Tourist Information

┼┼ Rail Lines

trail is a walking museum, and the hike from one end to the other is, for many travelers, a highlight of their Alaskan adventures.

BASICS The **Skagway Convention and Visitors Bureau,** in the unusual, driftwood-laden Arctic Brotherhood Hall, hands out brochures on local attractions and lodgings. Pick up a copy of the free newspaper, *Skagway Alaskan,* for information on the area's history and current happenings. *Broadway St., btw 2nd and 3rd Aves., tel. 907/983–2854. Open mid-May–Sept., daily 8:30–5.*

The **Forest Service** operates a small information office across from the train depot; stop by to reserve one of the two recreation cabins in the area (*see* Outdoor Activities, *below*) or to learn about Southeast Alaska's Tongass National Forest. *2nd Ave., at Spring St., tel. 907/983–3088. Open May–Sept. Sun., Mon., and Thurs. 10–1 and 2–5; Tues., Wed., Fri., and Sat. 8–11:30 and 12:30–5.*

COMING AND GOING The **Klondike Highway** (*see* The Klondike Loop, *above*) leads from Skagway to Canada. Whitehorse is 110 miles away; Dawson City is 435 miles away.

➤ **BY BUS** • One **Alaskon Express** (tel. 907/983–2241 or 800/544–2206) bus leaves at 7:30 AM daily for Whitehorse (3 hrs, $52) in the Yukon Territory; three a week go to Anchorage (2 days, $199) and Fairbanks (2 days, $194). Buses leave from the downtown Westmark Hotel (3rd Ave., at Spring St.). **Alaska Direct Buslines** (tel. 800/770–6652) provides cheaper service from Skagway to Whitehorse ($35) and Anchorage ($180).

➤ **BY FERRY** • There is one boat daily from the **Alaska Marine Highway** terminal (bottom of Broadway, tel. 907/983–2941) to all points on the Marine Highway, including Haines (1 hr, $14) and Juneau (7 hrs, $26). **Haines Water Taxi** (5th Ave., at Broadway St., tel. 907/766–3395) runs two boats daily to Haines (1½ hrs, $18).

➤ **BY TRAIN** • In summer, financially stable visitors can take the five-hour journey from Skagway to Whitehorse ($90 one-way) on the historic, narrow-gauge **White Pass and Yukon Route Railroad** (tel. 907/983–2217). The train takes you as far as the town of Fraser, on the Canadian border; a bus then delivers you to Whitehorse.

➤ **BY PLANE** • The airstrip that runs between the Skagway River and Alaska Street is served by **Skagway Air Service** (tel. 907/983–2284), **Wings of Alaska** (tel. 907/983–2442), and **LAB Flying Service** (tel. 907/983–2471). You'll pay about $30 to Haines, $70 to Juneau.

GETTING AROUND Most of downtown Skagway is in the Skagway Historic District, a three-by-seven-block area. The most outlying downtown attraction, the Gold Rush Cemetery, is less than 2 miles from the center, so you can manage on foot. The Chilkoot Trail, near Dyea, is less accessible. **Frontier** (tel. 907/983–2512), **Klondike** (tel. 907/983–2075), and **Pioneer** (tel. 907/983–2623) are tour companies that charge about $10 to take you to the trailhead, but hotels often provide free transportation for their guests. **Sockeye Cycle** (5th Ave., at Broadway St., tel. 907/983–2851) rents bikes for $6 per hour or $30 per day.

WHERE TO SLEEP The **Golden North Hotel** (30 Broadway St., tel. 907/983–2294) is stuck in the 1890s—it's even haunted by the ghost of a woman who died of consumption here while waiting for her fiancé to return from a gold-prospecting mission. Well-worn rooms are decorated with maps and other artifacts from the gold-rush. Singles go for $43–$65, doubles for $49–$81. **Portland House** (5th Ave., at State St., tel. 907/983–2493) has some of the cheapest singles ($30) and doubles ($45) in town—if you don't mind the heat and aroma of the restaurant downstairs wafting into your room. Once a house of ill repute, **Skagway Inn** (Broadway St., at 7th Ave., tel. 907/983–2289) is now a B&B. It still peddles the atmosphere—if not the wares—of the olden days in heavily decorated rooms that rent for $55–$70.

➤ **HOSTELS** • **Skagway Home Hostel.** This private hostel in a historic house, just two blocks from the main drag, treats guests almost like family. Hostel and home are one and the same, and guests and managers share the bathroom, living room, and kitchen. Guests are even required to do one chore per day. If you give a few hours' notice, you can join the family for dinner ($5), or contribute your own creation and eat for free. One manager is a backcountry ranger for the Chilkoot Trail; she's a great source of info on hikes around Skagway. Beds cost $12. The two couple's rooms have double beds and rent for $34 each. *3rd Ave., near Main St., tel. 907/983–2131. 40 beds. Curfew 11 PM. Laundry ($3). No credit cards.*

➤ **CAMPING** • The city-run **Pullen Creek RV Park** (tel. 907/983–2768) is geared towards RVs but has some tent spaces ($8), as well as clean restrooms and showers. It's right off the docks downtown, next to Pullen Creek Park. **Hanousek Park** (14th Ave., at Broadway St., tel. 907/983–2768) has RV sites as well as wooded tent sites ($8), showers, and fire pits; it's walking distance from most attractions. If the above two are full, the **Back Track Camper Park** (12th Ave., at Broadway St., tel. 907/983–3333) allows tent camping ($8) in a patch of green surrounded by gravel. Before hitting the Chilkoot Trail, most hikers crash at the free Forest Service **Dyea-Chilkoot Trailhead** (tel. 907/983–2921), about 9 miles from Skagway. Some people also camp for free at **Yakutania Point and Smuggler's Cove**, a beautiful and popular picnic area that becomes a party scene at night. The fact that it's not legal does not deter some from following the small footbridge at the west end of First Avenue in search of a quiet spot off one of the several trails that start here.

FOOD The **Corner Café** (4th Ave., at State St., tel. 907/983–2155) is a plain, popular diner that serves croissant sandwiches ($7) for lunch as well as veal-cutlet or pork-chop dinners ($11). Cafeteria-style **Broadway Bistro** (Broadway St., btw 3rd Ave. and 4th Ave., no phone) covers all the bases with espresso ($1.75) and "Alaska-size" muffins ($3) for breakfast, reindeer-sausage sandwiches ($8) for lunch, and pasta ($9–$11) or smoked-salmon calzone ($9) for dinner. Tiny **Sweet Tooth Café** (Broadway St., at 3rd Ave., tel. 907/983–2405) is an ice-cream parlor that also serves humble fare such as buttermilk pancakes ($4) and cheeseburgers ($5) daily 6–6.

If you're not a vegetarian already, Skagway's ubiquitous reindeer sausage might just push you over the edge.

Northern Lights Pizzeria. This busy restaurant dishes up good-sized portions of pasta ($9–$11), so-called Mexican entrées ($13–$16), a variety of pizzas, and Greek and seafood dishes. The Alaskan Dungeness crab goes fast, even at $17 a shell. *Broadway St., at 4th Ave., tel. 907/983–2225. Open May–Sept., daily 11–11.*

Prospector's Sourdough Restaurant. Come here in the morning for sourdough hot cakes ($5), shrimp or crab omelets ($9), or a reindeer-sausage breakfast ($7.50). Poor Rudolph. For dinner, try the whopping seafood sampler ($20); it includes crab, salmon, halibut, prawns, and scallops, a serious seafaring fish fest. Prospector's gets busiest at lunch; otherwise you'll have plenty of elbow room. *Broadway St., at 4th Ave., tel. 907/983–2865. Open mid-May–mid-Sept., daily 6–9.*

WORTH SEEING Downtown Skagway—Broadway Street in particular—has a seemingly endless number of historical sites and buildings in various stages of renovation. Pick up a walking-tour map from the visitor center (*see Basics, above*) and explore the past in present-day Skagway, or take a guided walk with the staff of the **Klondike Gold Rush National Historical Park visitor center.** Back when the railroad ran right down Broadway Street, this center was the train station. Today this restored building holds a variety of programs about Skagway's history and an exhibit room with old photos showing the characters and equipment of the gold-rush era. The film, *Days of Adventure, Dreams of Gold,* is composed of hand-colored, original photographs and is worth checking out. Walking tours led by rangers leave several times daily. *2nd Ave., at Broadway St., tel. 907/983–2921. Open late May–Sept., daily 8–6; June–Aug., daily 8–8.*

Corrington Museum. When you're saturated with the T-shirt and reindeer-sausage shops on Broadway Street, a few minutes here can be quite restorative. This strange little museum in the back of Corrington's Store offers a peek into the history of the 49th state through exhibits and more than 30 pieces of scrimshaw, carved to depict everything from the Bering Land Bridge theory to the opening of the Alaska Pipeline. *5th Ave., at Broadway St., tel. 907/983–2580. Admission free. Open May–Sept., daily 9–9.*

Gold Rush Cemetery. Skagway's most notorious outlaw and most beloved local hero now reside together forever in this cemetery, about 30 minutes' walk from downtown. Jefferson Randolph "Soapy" Smith and good guy Frank H. Reid both bit the big one in a gunfight on July 8, 1898. (A small marker at the corner of First Avenue and State Street commemorates the spot where they did each other in.) Right behind the cemetery (follow the short dirt path) are the beautiful, 300-foot **Reid Falls,** named after our hero. *Follow State St. until it turns into 23rd Ave.; take first dirt road on right to cemetery.*

Trail of '98 City Museum. This museum contains an eclectic collection of gold-rush memorabilia, as well as exhibits on native crafts and history. Outside the museum stands Locomotive 195, which carried materials north for the construction of the Alaska Highway on the White Pass and Yukon Route Railroad from 1943 to 1946. *Spring St., end of 7th Ave., tel. 907/983–2420. Admission: $2, $1 students. Open June–Aug., daily 8–6; May–Sept., daily 9–5.*

AFTER DARK Red Onion Saloon. This 100-year-old former bordello is the best place in Skagway for beer, pizza, and live rock music. When the saloon was moved from Sixth Avenue

The Angel of White Pass

A tiny statue in front of the playground on Sixth Avenue honors the indomitable Mollie Walsh, who traveled alone to Skagway in 1897 and opened a restaurant for prospectors along the White Pass Trail. After being wooed by numerous lonely gold-seekers, she married and moved to Seattle, where, in a rather grisly ending to a colorful life, she was murdered. An old lover of hers in Skagway commissioned the statue to honor Walsh for having "fed and lodged the wildest, gold-crazed men generations shall surely know."

to its current location, it was accidentally installed backwards; what is now the front was originally the back. *2nd Ave., at Broadway St., tel. 907/983–2222.*

Eagle's Hall. The long-running Broadway show (Skagway's Broadway, that is), *The Days of '98,* is, for a musical comedy about the gold-rush days, pretty good. A professional cast takes to the Eagle's Hall stage to depict the life and times of Soapy Smith. The best night to catch the show, however, is July 8, the anniversary of the fatal shoot-out between Soapy Smith and Frank Reid, when the performance is followed by a celebratory "wake" beside the graves of Smith and Reid. Cast members lead the way and share, with the audience, a case of champagne sent north by one of Soapy's descendants. *6th Ave., at Broadway St., tel. 907/983–2545. Tickets: $14. Shows nightly at 8:30.*

OUTDOOR ACTIVITIES In addition to the not-to-be-missed Chilkoot Trail (*see* Near Skagway, *below*), several trails, ranging from easy to experts-only, start right downtown. Most accessible are the **Dewey Lakes Trails.** The easier of the two is the short jaunt to Lower Dewey Lake; more strenuous is the 3-mile hike to Upper Dewey Lake, where you'll find a rustic cabin with messages from past hikers. The snowy bowl of Upper Dewey is a spectacular sight in itself, but locals will tell you that the really magnificent views are from **Devil's Punchbowl,** 1 more mile up an alpine trail. Back down at sea level, take the short trail leading from the footbridge at the southern end of the airport runway to **Yakutania Point and Smuggler's Cove**, a great picnic spots on sunny days. The Klondike Gold Rush National Historical Park visitor center (*see* Worth Seeing, *above*) hands out the slick *Skagway Trail Map,* which has directions to these and other trails in the area.

NEAR SKAGWAY

CHILKOOT TRAIL Hikers come to Skagway just to hike the 33-mile Chilkoot Trail that leads from nearby Dyea to Bennett, Canada, and once served as the main thoroughfare for prospectors heading into the Yukon. One of the most photographed images of the gold rush is the unbroken line of heavily-laden prospectors trudging up the rocky slope from Sheep Camp to Chilkoot Pass; this is still the most challenging stretch of trail. Set aside three or four days for the trek, and check with the Forest Service in Skagway (*see* Basics, *above*) for complete trail and weather information, a *Hiker's Guide,* and Canadian customs forms before setting out. You must also obtain a free trail permit from the Dyea Ranger Station, about half a mile from the trailhead.

In the 1870s, the thousands of gold seekers who walked the Chilkoot Trail were required by law to transport a year's supply of provisions with them into Canada.

To get to the trailhead, 10 miles from Skagway, contact one of the three tour companies in town (*see* Getting Around, *above*). At the end of the trail, wobble over to the Bennett train station and either ride back to Skagway ($60) or go by train and bus to Whitehorse (about $50). The train runs from Lake Bennett every day except Saturday; check with the White Pass and Yukon Route Railroad (*see* Coming and Going, *above*) in Skagway before the hike for precise times and prices.

Juneau

Spread out along the mainland coast below Mt. Juneau and Mt. Roberts, Alaska's third-largest city is accessible only by boat or plane: Like most of Southeast Alaska, Juneau's main link to the outside world is the Alaska Marine Highway ferry system. This hasn't dampened Juneau's progress, however, as this gold-mining boomtown has grown into a small but cosmopolitan city. In recent years, several attempts to relocate the capital nearer to Anchorage and Fairbanks have been futile: Federal, state, and local government offices remain here, sandwiched between the Gastineau Channel and the Coast Mountains.

There are more miles of mining tunnels under and around Juneau than there are paved roads.

Visitors will find plenty to keep them occupied in and around town. You can spend mornings grubbing for salmon in the Gastineau Channel, pan for gold in the afternoon, and relax in a bar or dance the night away in downtown club. Surrounding Juneau are some breathtaking parks and nature preserves, including the **Mendenhall Glacier**, just 13 miles away in the

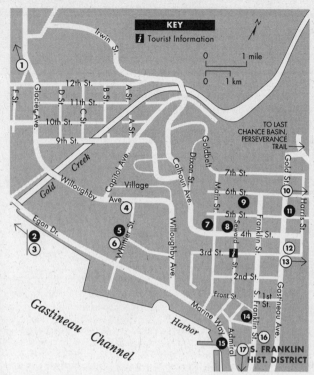

KEY

i Tourist Information

Sights ●

Alaska State Capitol, **8**

Alaska State Museum, **5**

Alaska Steam Laundry, **14**

Chapel By The Lake, **2**

Four-Story Totem, **9**

Juneau-Douglas City Museum, **7**

Marine Park, **15**

St. Nicholas Russian Orthodox Church, **11**

Lodging ○

Alaskan Hotel, **16**

Bergmann Hotel, **13**

Breakwater Inn, **1**

Cashen Quarters, **12**

Driftwood Lodge, **3**

Inn at the Waterfront, **17**

Juneau International Hostel, **10**

Prospector Hotel, **6**

University of Alaska Dorms, **4**

Juneau Ice Fields. The area's most popular attraction is the 3-million-acre **Glacier Bay National Park and Preserve,** with 16 expansive tidewater glaciers. The smaller but equally spectacular **Tracy Arm Glacier** and **Sawyer Glacier,** south of Juneau, also provide a good chance to get up close and personal with these massive ice monsters.

BASICS

LAUNDRY The Harbor **Washboard** (1114 Glacier Hwy., near Douglas Bridge, tel. 907/586–1133) is open Monday–Saturday 9–9 and Sunday 9–6. **The Dungeon Launderette** (4th St., at Franklin St., no phone) is open 8–8 daily.

LUGGAGE STORAGE Lockers are available at the airport and ferry terminal (*see* Coming and Going, *below*), and downtown at **The Alaskan Hotel** (167 S. Franklin St., tel. 907/586–1000) and the **Juneau-Douglas City Museum** (114 W. 4th St., tel. 907/586–3572).

VISITOR INFORMATION Information booths can be found at the waterfront Marine Park, the airport, and the ferry terminal. You can also get your questions answered at the **Davis Log Cabin,** a replica of a 19th-century Juneau log cabin where volunteer staffers provide brochures and advice. *134 3rd St., at Seward St., tel. 907/586–2201. Open summer, weekdays 8:30–5 and weekends 9–5; winter, weekdays 8:30–5.*

Centennial Hall is the area headquarters of the **Forest Service.** You can pick up free hiking handouts here, or buy a comprehensive booklet, *Juneau Hiking Trails* ($3), and a number of natural-history and wildlife books. *101 Egan Dr., tel. 907/586–8751. Open mid-May–mid-Sept., daily 8–5; mid-Sept.–mid-May, weekdays 8–5.*

Juneau

COMING AND GOING

BY FERRY The **Alaska Marine Highway** terminal (tel. 907/465–3941) is 15 miles northwest of town on the Glacier Highway. You can make connections from here to all points on the Marine Highway, including Bellingham, Washington (3 days, $226 one-way) and Skagway (7 hrs, $26 one-way). **Mendenhall Glacier Transport** (tel. 907/789–5460) takes ferry passengers downtown or to the airport for $5. **Eagle Express** (tel. 907/789–5720) does the same for $6. If you're broke, walk 2 miles along Glacier Highway toward Auke Lake to catch a **Capital Transit** city bus (tel. 907/789–6901) to downtown; these run every hour and cost $1.25.

BY PLANE The **Juneau International Airport** is 9 miles from downtown on the Egan Expressway. Both **Alaska Airlines** (tel. 907/789–0600) and **Delta** (tel. 800/221–1212) have daily flights between Juneau and Seattle (about $125 one-way). Alaska Airlines also flies to Anchorage, Ketchikan, and other Alaskan cities. **Capital Transit** (tel. 907/789–6901), the city bus line, runs between downtown and the airport every hour for $1.25. **Eagle Express** (tel. 907/789–5720) offers courtesy transportation from the terminal for guests at certain hotels; others pay $6 for the 15-minute ride downtown. **Mendenhall Glacier Transport** (tel. 907/789–5460) buses travel between the airport and the ferry terminal; the cost is $5 one-way. A taxi between the airport and downtown is about $15.

GETTING AROUND

The heart of downtown is, typically enough, Main Street, which stretches from the waterfront up toward the mountains. The bulk of Juneau's attractions, restaurants, and shops all fan out from Main Street. Since urban sprawl is restricted by the waterfront on one side and the mountains on the other, Juneau winds its narrow way down the Gastineau Channel into the so-called Valley, a mini suburb where most of the locals live. Excursions north into the Valley and beyond can be tackled by public bus or, since the roads are fairly flat, by bicycle.

BY BUS **Capital Transit** (tel. 907/789–6901) provides bus service from downtown to Douglas Island and Lemon Creek, but the main route loops between downtown and Mendenhall Valley. Buses typically run every hour and cost $1.25; schedules are available on buses.

BY BIKE You can bike to the Mendenhall Glacier and other outlying sights, such as the Chapel by the Lake and the Salmon Hatchery (*see* Worth Seeing, *below*). **Mountain Gears** (210 N. Franklin St., tel. 907/586–4327) rents mountain bikes for $6.50 per hour or $25 per day; in winter, they also rent snowboards for $25 per day.

WHERE TO SLEEP

Juneau has its fair share of beds, but in summer, the choice ones fill up quickly. Your cheapest options are the youth hostel, right downtown, or the university dorms and campgrounds south of town. Rates for hotels and B&Bs start at about $60 for a double.

➢ **UNDER $60** • **Alaskan Hotel.** Built in 1913, this downtown hotel maintains the rich Victorian style of its heyday and is listed in the National Register of Historic Places. Rooms come equipped with oak headboards and antique light fixtures. A single with a shared bath is around $45, a double $55; singles and doubles with private baths are $60–$70. *167 S. Franklin St., tel. 907/586–1000. 40 rooms, 18 with bath. Luggage storage, laundry, airport/ferry shuttle bus.*

The Bergmann Hotel. A boarding house for miners when it opened in 1913, the Bergmann is a rustic, weathered place just three blocks from downtown. Rooms are small, but they have some cool furnishings left over from the mining era. Singles go for $45, doubles for $55. *434 3rd St., tel. 907/586–1690. Take Mendenhall Glacier Transport bus ($5) from ferry. 42 rooms. Luggage storage, laundry.*

➢ **UNDER $70** • **Cashen Quarters B&B.** The rooms in this downtown house are clean and quiet, with a well-worn, familiar air. A suite with a kitchenette goes for $55, doubles are $65, and a two-bedroom suite is $85. An abundant breakfast is included. *315 Gold St., at 3rd St., tel. 907/586–9863. 5 rooms. Open mid-May–Sept. Reservations advised.*

The Driftwood Lodge. Around the corner from the Alaska State Museum and just a five-minute walk from city center, this motel has large, worn rooms, and one wheelchair-accessible two-bedroom apartment with kitchenette ($95). Singles cost around $60 ($65 with kitchenette), doubles are just a few dollars more. *435 Willoughby Ave., tel. 907/586–2280. 62 rooms. Laundry, ferry shuttle.*

Inn at the Waterfront. Three blocks from downtown, this former brothel is directly across from the cruise ship terminal at the base of Mt. Roberts. Narrow halls lead to small but comfortable rooms. Singles cost $42 with shared bath and $59 with private bath; doubles are $51 and $68. Continental breakfast and use of a steam bath are included in the rates. *455 S. Franklin St., tel. 907/586–2050. 21 rooms, 17 with bath. Luggage storage.*

➤ **UNDER $130** • **The Breakwater Inn.** These spotless rooms have balconies overlooking the Gastineau Channel and the Aurora Boat Harbor. Although the main highway separates the hotel from the harbor, the view is still worth the extra few bucks. Both singles and doubles go for $95. *1711 Glacier Ave., at 17th St., tel. 907/586–6303. 1 mi from downtown. 49 rooms. Luggage storage, ferry/airport shuttle.*

The Prospector Hotel. The Prospector recently received a face-lift at the hands of new management, so the already clean, large rooms have gotten even better. Many rooms have waterfront views, but the cheapest singles are stashed in the basement. The rates are $90–$130. *325 Whittier St., at Willoughby Ave., tel. 907/586–3737. 5-min walk from downtown. 57 rooms. Luggage storage.*

HOSTELS **Juneau International Hostel (HI).** Perched on a hill above the downtown waterfront, the hostel has cramped single-sex rooms full of bunk beds and a living room with a fireplace. Beds cost $10, plus one chore. The maximum stay is three days. The 11 PM curfew and 9–5 lockout are strictly enforced. *614 Harris St., at 6th St., tel. 907/586–9559. Kitchen.*

STUDENT HOUSING From late May through early August, the **University of Alaska** rents beds in four-bedroom suites for $35 a night. Space is limited—call ahead for availability. *Housing Lodge, 4300 University Drive, tel. 907/465–6443. 12 mi NW of town, near Mendenhall Glacier; take UNIVERSITY bus.*

CAMPING **Auke Village Campground.** Just under 2 miles west of the ferry terminal and close to the beach, this 12-site campground was originally a Tlingit camp. Sites cost $5. *Glacier Hwy., tel. 907/586–8800. From downtown, take AUKE BAY bus and walk 4 mi west. Firewood, flush and pit toilets.*

Mendenhall Lake Campground. The facilities at this campground on Mendenhall Lake, 14 miles from downtown, include wood, water, and pit toilets. The campground accommodates both RVs and tents; sites are $5 per night. *Montana Creek Rd., tel. 907/586–8800. From downtown, take city bus to junction of Mendenhall Loop and Montana Creek Rd. and walk 1 mi to campground entrance. 61 sites.*

ROUGHING IT Ferry travelers who arrive late or leave early in the morning often roll out their sleeping bags in the sheltered picnic area at the Auke Bay terminal and meet no objections from Marine Highway officials. Other campers bed down along **Perseverance Trail,** off Basin Road just up the hill from downtown, although bears like this spot, too.

FOOD

The dining scene in Juneau covers all bases; you can grab a taco, salad, burger, bagel, or espresso for less than $5 from a downtown food cart, or splurge on fresh seafood or authentic Italian food in a real restaurant. Grab a quick bite at the deli and salad bar in **Foodland Supermarket** (615 Willoughby Ave., tel. 907/586–3101), open daily 7 AM–9 PM. If you have access to cooking facilities, you can pick up fresh crab and salmon at the **Aurora Boat Basin** (Egan Dr., near Highland Dr.).

➤ **UNDER $5** • **Boarding House Bakery.** There's isn't much space in this one-room bakery (maximum sit-down capacity hovers around 10), but you will find plenty of fresh baked goods.

Soups, salads and sandwiches cost $4–$5. *245 Marine Way, tel. 907/586–BAKE. Across from Marine Park. Open daily 7–6.*

➤ **UNDER $10** • **Channel Bowl.** "Food doesn't need to look pretty to taste good," grumbles the cook at this local breakfast retreat. He's right: This local bowling alley serves large, scrumptious breakfasts. Try the egg-and-potato dish called Thor's Mt. Jumbo ($6). *608 Willoughby Ave., downtown, tel. 907/586–1165. Open Mon.–Sat. 11–11, Sun. noon–11.*

The Fiddlehead Restaurant and Bakery. Juneau's most famous health-food restaurant even has its own cookbook. Toss back a few herbal teas while friendly staff bring you a bean burger ($7) for lunch or granola pancakes ($7) for breakfast. Upstairs, pay a $2 cover charge to hear live music six nights a week (jazz on Friday and Saturday). *429 Willoughby Ave., next to Driftwood Lodge, tel. 907/586–3150. Open daily 6:30 AM–10 PM.*

Oriental Express. In defiance of the Italian mural adorning its entry staircase, this informal basement restaurant serves mostly Asian cuisine. Try the scallop or shrimp stir-fry ($8.50–$9.50) or one of five kinds of chow mein ($7–$8). *210 Seward St., near Franklin St., tel. 907/586–6990. Open weekdays 10–10, weekends 11–10.*

3rd Street Pizzeria. Midway between the hostel and downtown, this small place attracts locals and travelers, but it's a bit too far uphill for cruise-ship visitors. Watch the world out of big windows while you munch on an unusually elongated 15″ pizza; vegetarian pies are $18, pepperoni pies $14. *3rd St., at Franklin St., tel. 907/463–5020. Open weekdays 11:30–3:30 and 5–9, Sat. 1–9:30, Sun. 2–9:30.*

The place to kick back and soak up the local scene is Heritage Coffee Co. and Café on South Franklin Street, Juneau's caffeine king since 1974.

➤ **UNDER $15** • **Armadillo Tex-Mex Café.** Armadillo is a small, popular café serving hot stuff like barbecued chicken or chicken enchiladas for around $10. The atmosphere is casual: Patrons place their orders at the counter and take a seat. On those few, precious sunny days, tables are placed outside. *431 S. Franklin St., across from cruise ship terminal, tel. 907/586–1880. Open Mon.–Sat. 11–9, Sun. 4–9.*

Fernando's. If you can swallow Alaskan Tex-Mex, why not Alaskan Mexican? Fernando's is a low-key establishment serving Mexican classics. La Favorita ($13) is a combination plate that comes with a beef taco, an enchilada, and a chile relleno. Fernando's Special Burrito claims to be "the big daddy of burritos." *116 N. Franklin St., tel. 907/463–3992. Open Mon.–Thurs. 11–9, Fri. and Sat. 10–10.*

Fisherman's Wharf. Fresh seafood, a dockside view of the waterfront, and outdoor seating make Fisherman's Wharf popular with tourists and locals alike. Salmon and chips is around $8, clams are $6, and Dungeness crab is $14. *2 Marine Way, tel. 907/586–2727. Open mid-May–mid-Sept., 11–7; mid-Sept.–mid-May, weekdays 11–3.*

Sorrento. This place on a prime wharf location has large picture windows that look out onto the busy Gastineau Channel. Italian and seafood specialties (with lots of rich sauce) include linguini and clams ($14), shrimp scampi ($9), and tortellini ($14). *2 Marine Way, on Merchant's Wharf, tel. 907/463–4626. Open daily 12–2 and 5:30–10.*

➤ **UNDER $20** • **Thane Ore House Halibut Salmon Bake.** For $17.50, you can inhale all the salmon, halibut, barbecue beef ribs, salad, baked beans, and corn bread you want. If you show up at 6:30 PM, you can watch Thane Ore House's gold-rush show, the *Gold Nugget Revue*, for an additional $7.50. Hmmm. *Thane Rd., 4 mi from town, tel. 907/586–1462. Open May–Sept., daily noon–9 PM. Free transportation from downtown hotels.*

WORTH SEEING

Juneau's two museums and most of its other worthwhile attractions are in the downtown area, but several sights, including the spectacular Mendenhall Glacier and the Alaska Brewing and Bottling Co., are a drive or bike ride away. Massive columns mark the entryway to the **Alaska State Capitol** on Fourth street, home to the governor's office and State Senate and open for free tours on summer weekdays.

THE ALASKA STATE MUSEUM If you need a museum fix, you could do worse than this— it's one of Alaska's best. The informative and comprehensive collection has exhibits on Native Alaskans, including artwork and a 40-foot walrus-hide whaling boat. *395 Whittier St., tel. 907/465–2901. Follow Marine Way to Egan Dr., turn right on Whittier St., Admission: $2. Open mid-May–mid-Sept., weekdays 9–6 and weekends 10–6; mid-Sept.–mid-May, Tues.–Sat. 10–6.*

THE ALASKAN BREWING AND BOTTLING CO. Barley and hops connoisseurs have a chance to witness the beer-brewing process in action, sample the ambrosial end-product, and perhaps even grab a six pack for later. Free tours are given every half-hour. *5429-A Shaune Dr., tel. 907/780–5866. From downtown, take city bus to the corner of Glacier Hwy. and Anka St. in Lemon Creek (before airport); follow Anka St. 2 blocks and take a right on Shaune Dr. Open mid-May–mid-Sept., Tues.–Sat. 11–4:30; mid-Sept.–mid-May, Thurs.–Sat. 11–4:30.*

CHAPEL BY THE LAKE This small, unadorned Presbyterian chapel was constructed between 1954 and 1958 out of 48-foot spruce logs. Through the window behind the pulpit, you can catch a great view of the Mendenhall Glacier and surrounding terrain. *Adjacent to University of Alaska campus above Auke Lake, 12 mi northwest of downtown, tel. 907/789–7592. Take city bus to university. Always open.*

THE GASTINEAU SALMON HATCHERY If you've always wondered about those fish that risk "life and fin" to reproduce, here's your chance to get the lowdown. Tours of the hatchery include an opportunity to spy on salmon swimming up a fish ladder through an underwater viewing window. If you prefer to eat the scaly beasts rather than admire them, you can cast a line from the dock next to the building. *2697 Channel Dr., tel. 907/463–4810. From downtown, take city bus to Mendenhall; get off at Bartlett Memorial Hospital, cross expressway and walk back toward downtown about 3 min. Admission: $2.75. Open mid-May–mid-Sept., weekdays 10–6 and weekends noon–5; mid-Sept.–mid-May, by appointment only.*

THE JUNEAU-DOUGLAS CITY MUSEUM This small museum devotes most of its five-room exhibit space to the life and times of Juneau's gold mines and miners. *144 W. 4th St., at Main St., tel. 907/586–3572. $1 donation requested. Open mid-May–mid-Sept., weekdays 9–5, weekends 11–5; mid-Sept.–mid-May, Thurs.–Sat. noon–4:30 and by appointment.*

ST. NICHOLAS RUSSIAN ORTHODOX CHURCH This white, odd-shaped wooden building with bright blue trim is the oldest original Russian church in the state. It was constructed in 1893 by and for the predominantly Tlingit members of the Russian Orthodox faith. *326 5th St., at Gold St., tel. 907/586–1023. $1 donation requested. Open May–Sept., daily 8–6; winter hrs may vary.*

At the corner of Sixth and Seward streets, at the top of a block-long set of stairs, is one of Juneau's finest and tallest works of art: the Four-Story Totem Pole, a 45-foot red cedar carved in 1940.

SOUTH FRANKLIN HISTORIC DISTRICT Compacted into a few city blocks at the heart of downtown is an amalgam of touristy shops, cafés, sculptures, historic buildings, bars, and scores of people trying to take it all in. At the corner of South Franklin Street and Marine Way is a large, iron **Raven and Eagle** sculpture depicting the yin-yang into which each individual in the Tlingit tribe is born (to achieve perfect balance, an eagle is supposed to marry a raven). Two blocks up, on the left-hand side of the street, is the old **Alaska Steam Laundry** (174 S. Franklin St.), built in 1901 and now reincarnated as the Emporium Mall. The mall houses a café, a bookstore, and several gift shops, and the walls are covered with an impressive display of super-enlarged photographs of old Juneau.

CHEAP THRILLS

Marine Park, at the end of Seward Street downtown, is where travelers, street musicians, and state employees on lunch break all cross paths. During the summer, you can pass a Friday evening under the midnight sun at one of the **Concerts in the Park** series. At the southern end of Marine Park is the **Juneau Public Library**. Located on the seventh floor of a parking garage, the library's deck is the perfect place to sit back and look out over Gastineau Channel.

In April, Juneau plays host to the ever-popular **Alaska Folk Festival** (tel. 907/364–2801), a week of no-holds-barred music and dancing. In early summer, the Juneau **Jazz 'n Classics** (tel. 907/586–3485) attempts to serve up these two musical styles on the same plate, with concerts, workshops, and even a few free performances.

AFTER DARK

While Juneau's nightlife may never pose a threat to London's, the city does offer a little bit of almost anything you need to get you through the night, from dancing, theater, jazz, and rock-and-roll to wee-hour hikes on long summer days, when night, as such, barely exists. The **Perseverance Theatre** (914 3rd St., tel. 907/364–2421) has persevered through 13 seasons. A variety of highbrow productions, often by Alaskan writers, are staged from September through May. During the summer, the troupe caters to tourists with *The Lady Lou Revue,* yet another musical comedy depicting the Klondike gold rush of 1898.

The Red Dog Saloon (278 S. Franklin St., tel. 907/463–3777) is, to quote a local, "Juneau's number-one tourist trap." The swinging doors and sawdust-covered floors pull in the tourists like flies—icky. When cruise ships are not in port, the saloon actually features some good local bands. **The Alaskan Bar** (167 S. Franklin St., tel. 907/586–1000), with its low-hanging lights, wooden bar, balcony, and Victorian decor, is a comfy, not-too-crowded place to sip a drink and catch some blues, folk, or country-rock. **The Fireweed Room,** upstairs at the Fiddlehead Restaurant (429 Willoughby Ave., tel. 907/586–3150), features weekend jazz trios and nightly piano music, along with an occasional special act; cover is usually $2 on weekends. **The Penthouse** (175 S. Franklin St., tel. 907/463–4141), way up on the fifth floor of the Senate Office Building, is a dance club.

OUTDOOR ACTIVITIES

HIKING Juneau is surrounded by more than 25 trails, many of which are easily accessible and can lead you away from the city lights in minutes. The Alaska Natural History Association publishes a comprehensive guide to the area, *Juneau Trails,* available for $3 at most bookstores and at the Forest Service information center in Centennial Hall (*see* Basics, *above*). Ask the Forest Service for free individual trail maps as well. Follow Gold Street up to Basin Road to find the popular 3-mile **Perseverance Trail.** The wide, easy trail leads through the valley of Gold Creek, with spectacular views of waterfalls along the way and occasional glimpses of relics from the Perseverance Mine, which operated here at the turn of the century. **Mt. Roberts Trail** is also easily accessed from town; its trailhead is atop a flight of stairs at Sixth and Nelson streets, a few blocks from the youth hostel. Switchbacks lead through just under 3 miles of forest to "The Cross," a replica of an earlier cross erected by a Catholic priest in 1908. From here, another half-mile of steep alpine trail brings you to Gastineau Peak; continue 1 more mile to Mt. Roberts. Both peaks offer great views of Juneau, Douglas, and the Gastineau Channel. Less challenging, but equally scenic, is the 3-mile **Dan Moller Trail** on Douglas Island. To reach the trailhead, walk over the Juneau-Douglas bridge, turn right onto Cordova Street, then left onto Pioneer Avenue; it's on the right past 3185 Pioneer Avenue. Wooden boardwalk and often muddy patches of trail lead gently uphill through muskeg and forest to the Dan Moller cabin, which may be reserved for overnight use through the Forest Service (*see* Basics, *above*).

CHARTER TRIPS This may be the time to splurge. **Alaska Rainforest Tours** (369 S. Franklin St., Suite 200, tel. 907/463–3466) takes small groups (six people maximum) on three-day camping trips to the spectacular Tracy Arm Fjord and glaciers, several hours south of Juneau. The personalized trip, aboard a 32-foot boat, may be an alternative to the expensive prospect of visiting Glacier Bay: You get similar scenery, but fewer tourists. The $300 price tag is still steep, but you'll get your money's worth. Ask about "last-minute excursions"—people filling empty spots on this trip and others organized by Alaska Rainforest Tours are often offered 20%–40% discounts the day before departure. **Glacier Bay Tours and Cruises** (76 Egan Dr., Suite 130, tel. 907/463–5510 or 800/451–5952) leads day cruises to Tracy Arm Fjord; half-day boat trips run about $130. Contact either company for chartered fishing trips, river rafting, or "flightseeing" tours.

HELICOPTER RIDES Yes, it's painfully expensive, but if you're ready to throw down some cash, a tour by helicopter will be an experience you'll never forget. Several companies in Juneau will fly you over the heads of moose, mountain goats, and other wildlife on your way to a glacier landing, where you'll spend 15–30 minutes walking on the ice and learning about glacial geology. Both **ERA Helicopters** (tel. 907/586–2030) and **Temesco Helicopters** (1650 Maplesden Way, tel. 907/789–9501) charge about $150 per person.

KAYAKING **Alaska Discovery Expeditions** (5449-4 Shaune Dr., tel. 907/586–1911) rents kayaks and conducts guided tours for as long as 10 days. Rentals run $40 (single) and $50 (double) per day; a popular kayak route is along the northern coastline of Douglas Island.

PANNING FOR GOLD What trip into gold-rush country would be complete without a shot at striking it rich? The easiest place to pan is at the **Gold Creek Salmon Bake** (Last Chance Basin, end of Basin Rd., tel. 907/586–1424). If you fork over $20 for the all-you-can-eat feast, the hosts will provide you with a pan and instructions. **The Alaska Division of Mines** (tel. 907/364–2111) can direct you to other spots, such as **Ready Bullion Creek** on Douglas Island.

SKIING The **Eagle Crest Ski Area** (Douglas Island, tel. 907/586–5284), just 12 miles from downtown, is the local ski resort, with 30 downhill and three cross-country trails. Equipment rentals cost about $20, and full-day adult lift tickets are $24; Nordic passes cost $7 (full-day).

Near Juneau

MENDENHALL GLACIER

This murky blue glacier is one of Juneau's most popular attractions, and one of the most accessible glaciers in Southeast Alaska (just 12 miles from downtown Juneau). Larger than the state of Rhode Island, Mendenhall Glacier is one of 38 glaciers that extends from the 1,500-square-mile Juneau Ice Field. The immense natural wonder, which recedes 25 to 30 feet each year, supports several trails, ranging from easy, half-mile photo ops to long, hard hikes. The **East Glacier Trail** is a 4-mile loop that leads from the visitor center (*see below*) to Nugget Creek, where you can watch the water spill into the lake below. The **West Glacier Trail** (also 4 miles) begins near the Mendenhall Lake Campground (*see* Camping, *above*) and follows the edge of the lake, offering different angles on the glacier along the way. **Mendenhall Glacier Transport** (tel. 907/789–5460) offers several tours of the city and glacier ($12.50 for 2½ hrs). The do-it-yourself version is to catch the city bus through the Mendenhall Valley to the Mendenhall Loop Road and get off at Glacier Spur Road; from here it's a flat, 2-mile walk to the visitor center.

BASICS The **Forest Service Visitor Center** is equipped with a video room, small exhibits, and a telescope for ice-field viewing. Interpreters from the center lead guided walks on the shorter trails during the summer months. *Tel. 907/789–0096. Open May–Sept., daily 8:30–5:30; Oct.–April, weekends 9–4.*

GLACIER BAY NATIONAL PARK

Probably one of Southeast Alaska's most spectacular (and expensive to reach) attractions, this vast preserve stretches from the western side of the Chilkat Range to the Pacific Ocean and Cape Fairweather. In between lie more than 3 million acres of wilderness and 16 aqua-blue and white tidewater glaciers, which—in a mighty roar and crash—drop, or calve, small icebergs into the inlets of Glacier Bay. For more than a century, scientists and naturalists (most notably John Muir, who visited in 1878) have explored and written about Glacier Bay with wonder. Wildlife abounds here—you might see bears, mountain goats, seals, otters, and moose. While here you get to experience the evolution of an ecosystem: as the glaciers recede they uncover an ancient algae crust that can be traced forward along the evolutionary ladder to the moss, alder scrub, spruce trees, and, finally, spruce forests that populate the mountains and cliffs of the park.

On your way to Glacier Bay, you'll most likely fly into the small rural community of **Gustavus**, where friendliness prevails. Originally a Tlingit site, Gustavus was first homesteaded by three honeymooning couples around 1915, and grew slowly in the ensuing decades. Today, the close-knit community remains slow-paced and agriculturally based, supplying Glacier Bay tourists with lodging, food, and other services. Ten miles away, within the park, is **Bartlett Cove,** where you'll find Glacier Bay Lodge, the campground, and the dock.

BASICS For information about the preserve, call the **Glacier Bay National Park and Preserve** (Gustavus, tel. 907/697–2230) or the **Gustavus Visitors Association** (tel. 907/697–2358).

COMING AND GOING The preserve is about 70 miles from Juneau but is only accessible by expensive float planes or chartered tours. From Gustavus, you can bike or hitchhike to the **Bartlett Cove Campground** (*see* Where to Sleep, *below*), right outside the park, or call **TLC Taxi** (tel. 907/697–2239) for a $9 ride. You can also take the **Glacier Bay Lodge Bus** (Bartlett Cove, tel. 907/697–2225), which meets every Alaska Airlines flight, for $8. The three B&Bs and the Gustavus Inn provide bikes for their guests to roam around the few dirt roads in the area. You'll still need a boat to get up near the glaciers.

➤ **BY PLANE** • The easiest way to enter to the park is to catch one of the daily flights offered by **Alaska Airlines** (tel. 907/789–0600), **Wings of Alaska** (tel. 907/789–0790), and **Glacier Bay Airways** (tel. 907/789–9009). The 20-minute flight from Juneau will cost you $90 round-trip; discount tickets are sometimes available during the summer.

➤ **BY BOAT** • Any way you look at it, a trip "up bay" (as locals say) to view the glaciers is going to burn a hole in your wallet. The Juneau-based **Glacier Bay Tours and Cruises** (76 Egan Dr., Suite 110, tel. 907/463–5510) will bring you close to the spectacular calving glaciers and wildlife for a hefty $153. Additional bonuses include a well-informed naturalist, lunch, and endless coffee on board.

WHERE TO SLEEP Lodging options in Gustavus and Bartlett Cove run the gamut from free camping in a temperate rain forest to pricy dorms and reasonable B&Bs. Within the park itself, **Glacier Bay Lodge** (Bartlett Cove, tel. 800/451–5952) rents beds in six-person dorms for $28 each, with one wheelchair-accessible toilet and shower for each dorm room. **Good River** (tel. 907/697–2241), in Gustavus at the end of Good River Road, rents homey rooms for $50 (single) and $70 (double); you can also pay $50 for a rustic log cabin for two, complete with a doorless "outhouse with a view." **Bartlett Cove,** a quarter mile from the Glacier Bay Lodge, is a free campground with mossy sites set among Sitka spruce trees. The park service is very serious about bear-proofing here: They give a camper orientation daily at 11:30 AM and 7 PM at the backcountry office (tel. 907/697–2627).

OUTDOOR ACTIVITIES Although many visitors whiz through the area in a mere day, and experience only the boat trip up Glacier Bay, those with some time to spend can try hiking, fishing, and kayaking around Gustavus.

➤ **HIKING** • The **Bartlett River Trail** is a 3-mile loop that leads past an estuary popular with migrating waterbirds; the well-marked trailhead is about half a mile from the Lodge, on the road leading to Gustavus. Midway between the lodge and Gustavus is the beginning of the 2-mile **Bartlett Lake Trail,** an unmarked path that takes you to a hidden lake. To find the trail from Gustavus, walk or bike along the road to Bartlett Cove until it turns 90° west; follow the pavement about 1 mile to an overgrown path and continue another mile to the old shed at the trailhead. Another popular walk is the 10-minute trek through dense forest to the wreckage of a National Guard plane that crashed in the 1970s. The trail begins from the road leading to Bartlett Cove, about 2 miles before the paved road to the Bartlett Lake Trail; it's marked by a vertical piece of metal (resembling a bumper) on the east side of the road. The unmarked 14-mile **Point Gustavus Trail** connects Bartlett Cove and the mouth of the Goode River, several miles west of Gustavus; ask at the ranger station in Bartlett Cove for directions or, from Gustavus, head west to Goode River and follow it to the beach.

➤ **SEA KAYAKING** • If you have a few days and yen for adventure, leave the tour boats behind and explore Glacier Bay in a sea kayak. Those who do it say there's no comparison to the serenity of the waters and the excitement of a night spent listening to the thunder of a continually calving glacier. **Glacier Bay Sea Kayaks** (Gustavus, tel. 907/697–2257) can set you up in a two-person kayak for $35–$50, depending on the length of the trip, and give you tips about navigating the waters and camping in the wilderness of Glacier Bay. Juneau-based **Alaska Discovery** (234 Gold St., tel. 907/697–2411) leads guided, one-day trips ($95) from Bartlett Cove.

ADMIRALTY ISLAND

Across Stephen's Passage from Douglas Island is **Admiralty Island,** known to the Tlingits as *Xootsnoowu,* or "Fortress of the Bears." This million-acre wilderness preserve offers supreme opportunities for hiking, kayaking, and canoeing. The island has been designated a National Monument to preserve the native forests and wildlife, in particular the giant Alaskan brown bears that easily outnumber humans here. The **Admiralty Lake Recreation Area** is a 110,000-acre expanse that is off-limits to cars. Winding through Admiralty Island is the 25-mile **Cross-Admiralty Canoe Route,** a favorite with expert paddlers; contact the Forest Service in Juneau (*see above*) for more information. You can see bears at a safe distance at the **Pack Creek Brown Bear Sanctuary,** on the island's east coast. The best time to spot them is during the July and August salmon runs. Visitors to Pack Creek must get a permit from the Forest Service in Juneau before camping. On the west side of Admiralty is **Angoon,** a tiny Tlingit fishing village where people still live in 16 communal tribal houses.

COMING AND GOING **Alaska Marine Highway** ferries run from Juneau to Admiralty Island twice weekly in summer; a round-trip ticket is $48. **Wings of Alaska** (tel. 907/789–0790) flies between Juneau and Angoon ($70 one-way) several times daily.

CHICHAGOF ISLAND

Chichagof Island, west of Admiralty Island, is dotted with tiny communities like **Tenakee Springs,** with its smelly, sulfurous hot springs, and **Pelican,** a fishing community best known for its bar scene. Both towns are good escapes for travelers who want nothing more than to disappear into the Alaskan outback.

TENAKEE SPRINGS Tenakee Springs (population: 150), near the island's east coast, was once known as the "hellhole of Alaska," serving as a hideaway for notorious outlaws such as Soapy Smith and his gang. Today, the town's popularity stems from the sulfur hot springs that bubble out of the ground and into a community bathhouse at 108°F. The bathhouse, at the ferry dock, is open 24 hours, with separate times for men and women. If you're traveling between Sitka and Juneau by ferry, and the ferry stops in Tenakee Springs during the hours designated for your gender, you'll have just enough time to jump in for a 10- or 15-minute soak (no bathing suit required). If 15 minutes just isn't enough, you can stay over in Tenakee—but be prepared to spend several days, as the Sitka and Juneau ferries stop in this tiny village just two or three times a week. The ferry from Juneau costs $44 one-way. **Wings of Alaska** (tel. 907/789–0790) also serves Tenakee Springs with daily flights from Juneau ($60 one-way).

Tenakee Springs is the place to come if you want nothing more than a hot soak and a snooze.

If you do decide to stay, check out the rustic cabins at **Snyder Mercantile** (tel. 907/736–2205), at the head of the dock; they have cold running water, outhouses and minimal cooking facilities. A single or a double costs only $30, but bring your own sleeping bag, towel, and flashlight (outhouses are no fun in the dark).

PELICAN Pelican, an active fishing community of about 250, sits on the opposite side of Chichagof on Lisianski Inlet. The entire town is laid out along one narrow boardwalk built on pilings above the water; the only automobile is the town garbage truck. There's not much to do here, but the town does have quite a reputation for partying, especially on the Fourth of July. **Norm Carson** (tel. 907/735–2460) is a one-man tour company: He'll take you sport fishing, whale watching, hiking, and even rent you a spartan beach cabin for $50 a night. A day on his 21-foot boat runs $125 per person. The most historic spot for a night's sleep in Pelican is **Rosie's Plaza** (on boardwalk, tel. 907/735–2265), run by Rose, who throws a no-holds-barred Fourth of July celebration for the fishing community every year and lets rooms for $65.

ANCHORAGE AND THE GULF COAST

12

By Alison Huml

Anchorage's appeal for shoestring travelers is limited. Sure, it has almost every-thing you could want from a city, including a performing arts center and an acclaimed reper-tory theater, but for someone who has just staggered out of the wilderness smelling like a chunk of gorgonzola, Anchorage's main attractions are more mundane: a hot shower, a soft bed, real food, and protection from the small aircraft they call mosquitoes.

But you can get those things in any number of Alaskan towns. What makes Anchorage inter-esting to budget travelers is its location and convenience. The city is the hub for Alaska's road and rail networks, making it easy to reach some of the state's most spectacular scenery. In just a few hours you can be in Prince William Sound to the east, the Kenai Peninsula to the south, or Denali National Park (see Chapter 13) to the north. We're not talking day trips here—that would be impossible, and stupid to boot—but it is feasible to nip back to the city for a bit of R&R between wilderness campaigns.

Whenever travel writers wax lyrical about snowy peaks and frolicking wildlife, the overwhelming urge is to smack 'em in the head, but flowery prose is unavoidable when you talk about the Gulf Coast—the place is extraordinarily beautiful. Despite the lube job Exxon did on it, Prince William Sound remains a highlight of any trip to Alaska. The crash of calving glaciers echoes through steep fjords, while the 10,000-foot peaks of the Chugach Mountains form an impressive backdrop. The Kenai Peninsula is more crowded than the Prince William Sound because it's so easy to reach from Anchorage, but it offers a similar landscape of ice, water, and rock, spotted with cool little fishing villages like Homer and Seward. If you really want to get away from it all, continue south from the Kenai Peninsula to Kodiak Island, the fog-shrouded home of the giant Kodiak bear. Swimming throughout the rich waters of the Gulf of Alaska are killer whales, porpoises, otters, and seals, as well as the halibut and salmon for which the huge Alaskan fishing fleets vie. On land, particularly if you hike and camp, you're likely to see caribou, bears, eagles, and even wolverines.

Anchorage

Few people travel to Alaska to see a big city. You didn't have your mind on fancy restaurants and boutiques when you loaded your backpack with a tent, toilet paper, and enough insect repellent to wipe out entire species. But Anchorage is a major point of entry for travelers to Alaska, as well as the nerve center of Alaska's transport networks, so you're bound to wind up here sometime.

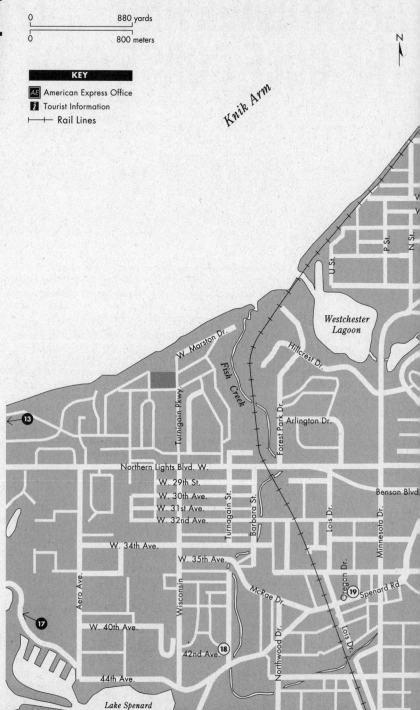

Anchorage

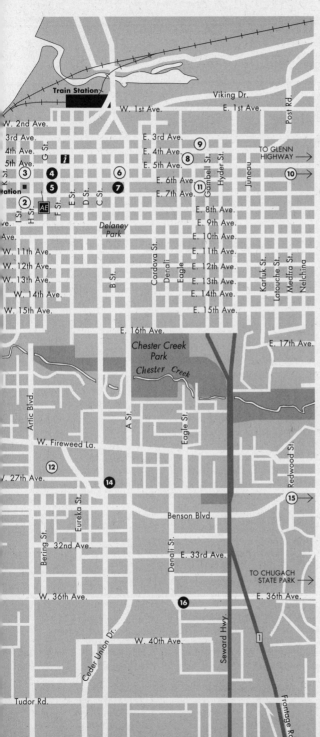

Sights ●

Alaska Aviation Heritage Museum, **17**

Alaska Experience, **5**

Anchorage Museum of History and Art, **7**

Earthquake Park, **13**

Heritage Library and Museum, **14**

Knowles Coastal Trailhead, **1**

Loussac Public Library, **16**

Performing Arts Center, **4**

Lodging ○

Alaska Budget Motel, **9**

Alaskan Samovar Inn, **11**

Alaska Pacific University, **15**

Anchor Arms Motel, **8**

Anchorage International Hostel (HI), **2**

Chelsea Inn, **19**

Inlet Inn, **3**

International Backpackers Inn/ Hostel, **10**

Midtown Lodge, **12**

Sixth and B B&B, **6**

Spenard Hostel (HI), **18**

The city's setting, on the shores of Cook Inlet and fronted by the Chugach Mountains, is lovely, but Anchorage itself is quite ugly. It sprawls across the countryside, and even its flashiest modern towers appear drab next to Alaska's immensity. Many Alaskans look upon Anchorage's urban pancake with the same scorn Californians reserve for Los Angeles. In fact, some refer to the city as Los Anchorage. Although it's impossible to get away from the wilderness completely in Alaska—even in Anchorage, moose roam the park trails—the city does have a different feel from other Alaskan towns. For starters, it's huge by Alaskan standards: 250,000 people, fully half the state's population, live here. And unlike other Alaskans, who work in fishing and oil, most of the city's residents are employed in banking, government, or transport. They're also young: The average age here is 28, giving the city a noticeable energy and drive.

Anchorage itself is young, too. Although Captain Cook navigated Cook Inlet in 1778, the city only got its start with the construction of the Alaska Railroad, which was completed in 1917. Boom and bust periods followed major events: an influx of military bases during World War II; a massive build-up of Arctic missile-warning stations during the Cold War; and most recently, the discovery of oil at Prudhoe Bay and the construction of the Trans-Alaska Pipeline. Oil and fishing drive Alaska's economy, and with the decline of both industries, unemployment is on the rise.

BASICS

AMERICAN EXPRESS The downtown **American Express** office (700 G St., cnr of 7th Ave., tel. 907/274–5588) offers full financial and travel services weekdays 7:30–5:30. The office is hidden inside the huge Arco building (on the left-hand side as you enter). For evening and weekend service, Bus 3 will take you to the AmEx in Boniface Mall (5530 E. Northern Lights Blvd., Suite 5, tel. 907/333–8585), open weekdays 9–6:30 and Saturday 10–5:30.

LUGGAGE STORAGE You can stash your bags across from baggage claim in the domestic terminal of **Anchorage International Airport** (tel. 907/248–0373) for $3–$5, daily 5:30 AM–1:30 AM. The kindly **Anchorage International Youth Hostel** (700 H St., between 7th and 8th Aves., tel. 907/276–3635) lets you store luggage for $1 a day if you're not a guest and for free if you are.

VISITOR INFORMATION You'll find racks of pamphlets in the airport, but all the advice you'll ever need is available at the **Log Cabin Information Center.** The knowledgeable staff is not allowed to give recommendations, but they'll load you down with pamphlets in response to your questions. Be sure to pick up a free *Anchorage Visitors Guide* with a map and downtown walking tour, and invest a quarter in a map of paved city trails for biking and running. *546 W. 4th Ave., at F St., tel. 907/274–3531, or 907/276–3200 for recorded events hotline. Open daily June–Aug. 7:30–7, May and Sept. 8:30–6; Oct.–Apr. 9–4.*

Rangers at the **Alaska Public Lands Information Center** will fill you in about camping and hiking on public lands in Alaska. The center also has natural history exhibits, free films at 12:15 and 3:30 in summer, topographic maps, and a trip-planning computer. *605 W. 4th Ave., tel. 907/271–2737. Catercorner from Log Cabin. Open daily 9–6.*

COMING AND GOING

BY CAR You can enter Anchorage on one of two roads: the **Glenn Highway** (a.k.a. Highway 1) to the northeast or the **Seward Highway** to the south. The Glenn leads 35 miles north to Wasilla, where it connects with the Parks Highway to Denali (237 miles) and Fairbanks (359 miles). If you stay on the Glenn, you come to Glennallen (187 miles), where you can pick up the Richardson Highway and the Tok Cut-Off. The Seward Highway leads south to Seward (127 miles) via Girdwood and Portage, and connects with the Sterling Highway to Homer. *The Milepost* ($18.95), an extensive mile-by-mile guide to Alaska highways, is available at bookstores and gas stations across Alaska. Points of interest along the roads, campgrounds, and road conditions are painstakingly detailed.

BY BUS Anchorage has no long-distance bus station. Big buses drop passengers off at hotels or at the hostel. Lots of bus routes are actually package tours arranged through hotels—independent travelers can tag along if there's space. Reserve in advance for all buses; most lines only run from mid-April to mid-September. **Alaskon Express** (tel. 907/277–5581 or 800/544–2206) is the most comprehensive bus line, with service south to Seward ($35), north to Fairbanks ($109), east to Glenallen ($55), Tok ($99), and Valdez ($59), and southeast all the way to Skagway ($199). It picks up at the major downtown hotels, or you can flag down a bus at any point en route. Alaskon's **Gray Line** (547 W. 4th Ave., tel. 907/277–5581) has package tours to Valdez that, space permitting, will accept single travelers ($67). The youth hostel also runs some van shuttles and mini-tours; check with the front desk.

The **Homer and Seward Bus Lines** (720 Gambell St., at 7th Ave., tel. 907/278–0800) will shuttle you south to Homer ($38) and Seward ($30), with additional stops in Soldotna and Kenai. Bus service only runs in summer, however. If you're heading to Denali, **Moon Bay Express** (tel. 907/274–6454) and the **Alaska Backpacker Shuttle** (tel. 907/344–8775) offer the cheapest fares; both charge $35 one-way, $60 round-trip, and pick up from the youth hostel daily at 8 AM. **Alaska Welcomes You!** (tel. 907/349–6301) offers transportation and package tours for the physically challenged. A 2½ hour tour of Anchorage costs $29; a deluxe eight-to 14-day tour of the Kenai Peninsula and Denali goes for upwards of $2,000.

BY TRAIN In summer (May 18–Sept. 19), the **Alaska Railroad** (411 W. 1st Ave., at F St., tel. 907/265–2494 or 800/544–0552) has daily train service from Anchorage to Seward (4 hrs, $50 one-way, $80 round-trip), Denali (8 hrs, $69, $88 June 19–Sept. 4), and Fairbanks (4 hrs, $99, $125 June 19–Sept. 4). Service in winter is more limited. To reach downtown from the station head south on F Street up the hill for a brisk five-minute walk.

BY PLANE Anchorage International Airport is served by about 20 major airlines and several smaller intrastate carriers. Domestic carriers include **Alaska Airlines** (tel. 800/426–0333), **Continental** (tel. 800/525–0280), **Delta** (tel. 800/221–1212), **Northwest** (tel. 800/225–2525), **United** (tel. 800/241–6522), and **MarkAir** (tel. 800/478–0800). Intrastate flights are expensive, but they're often your only option, since roads are few and far between. A round-trip flight to Fairbanks usually costs $160, to Nome $380, $150 to Valdez, and $280 to Sitka. Periodic price wars force fares down. Intrastate carriers serving the Kenai Peninsula, Kodiak, and the bush include **Era Aviation** (tel. 907/426–0333), **MarkAir** (tel. 907/243–4700), and **Reeve Aleutian Airways** (tel. 907/243–4700). Charter and flightseeing (sightseeing in a plane) excursions also fly out of Lake Hood, adjacent to Anchorage International Airport, and out of Merrill Field, 2 miles east of downtown on 5th Avenue.

➤ **AIRPORT TRANSIT** • Anchorage International Airport is 6 miles southwest of downtown, about 20 minutes by bus or car. **People Mover** (tel. 907/343–6543) runs Bus 6 between the airport and downtown five times a day on weekdays for $1. The **Alaska Backpacker Shuttle** (tel. 907/344–8775) will whisk you downtown, or out to the campgrounds for about $10. Groups of three or four can hire a taxi and split the $15 charge between them; taxis loiter outside the baggage claim area on the lower level.

GETTING AROUND

The major attractions, the youth hostel, the train station, and most of the bus stops are **downtown**. This area is laid out in a 15-block grid: Numbered avenues run east–west; alphabetically ordered streets run north–south. West of A Street, which bisects the city, the streets have letter names (B Street, C Street, and so forth); east of A Street, they have proper names (Cordova, Denali, Eagle, etc.). You can wait a long time for a bus, but luckily it's easy to get around this area on foot. If you get lost, it helps to remember several distinct landmarks: Cook Inlet is to the west, Ship Creek (look for the masts) lies to the north, and the Chugach Mountains are to the east. Although Anchorage is a relatively safe city, try not to get lost in the rougher side of downtown (east of Gambell Street, among 1st and 5th avenues).

During Prohibition, when Anchorage went dry, everyone headed out to the Spenard neighborhood to get trashed and meet a nice lady for an hour or so.

South of downtown is the rest of Greater Anchorage, or the "Anchorage Bowl," accessible by erratic public transportation. **Midtown,** the city's commercial district, has a smattering of budget lodgings amid shopping malls, car dealerships, and neighborhood bars. **Spenard,** which extends from Midtown to the airport, is a funky, up-and-coming district with a big twenty-something bar scene. Buses run from downtown to outlying areas during the day; the only way back at night is to walk—a bad idea—or take a cab.

BY BUS **People Mover** buses leave from the downtown transit center (6th Ave. and H St., tel. 907/343–6543 or 907/343–4775) and traverse the entire Anchorage Bowl. Transferring is difficult, since bus routes seldom intersect. Buses run infrequently, especially at night and on Sundays, and may arrive early or late. You pay 90¢ for a token (buy them at the transit center), $1 for a ticket, and 10¢ for a transfer. Purchase route maps and timetables for $1 from the bus driver, the transit center, or most newsstands.

BY TAXI Folks don't stand around in the cold long enough to hail taxis in Anchorage—they telephone for one instead. The main companies are **Alaska Cab** (tel. 907/563–5353), **Checker Cab** (tel. 907/276–1234), and **Yellow Cab** (tel. 907/272–2422 or 907/694–5555). **Anchorage Taxicab** (tel. 907/278–8000) has wheelchair lifts. Fares start at $2, with an extra $1.50 for each mile. Taxis may be your only option if you stay out after 10 PM, when most buses stop running, or if you travel to one of the rougher parts of town, like Spenard or east downtown.

BY BICYCLE If you have strong legs and can afford the rental prices, biking is a great way to explore Anchorage in the summer. The city has more than 125 miles of bike trails, including the 11-mile **Knowles Coastal Trail,** which runs along Cook Inlet. At **Downtown Bicycle Rental** (145 6th Ave., at B St., tel. 907/279–5293), bikes (including tandems) go for $10–$14 a day. **Anchorage Coastal Bicycle Rentals** at Adventures and Delights (414 K St., at 4th Ave., tel. 907/279–1999), a block from the coastal trail, rents bikes with locks and helmets daily 9–6; your standard 10-speed goes for $25 a day, mountain bikes for $30. It may be worth it to buy a used bike for $35–$40 if you're here for a while; look through the newspaper's classified ads to find one.

WHERE TO SLEEP

In the summer, budget lodging in Anchorage is an oxymoron. Even the cheapest hotels run $60–$70, and they're often seedy and lacking in character. Splitting the cost of a room with friends won't save you much, since many hotels have a surcharge for extra guests. The best way to avoid the jacked-up rates is to visit Anchorage before June or after August, when the crowds thin and hotel prices drop about $30 per room. In summer, make reservations at least one or two months ahead, especially for weekends.

The two HI hostels, one right downtown and the other in Spenard, are by far the cheapest and best places to crash. **Alaska Pacific University** (4101 University Dr., tel. 907/564–8238) rents out spotless dorm rooms for about $25; call for availability. You can find plenty of cheap but nasty lodgings at the undesirable east end of downtown. Midtown and Spenard are sprinkled with budget motels, but they're inaccessible except by bus or taxi.

Bed-and-breakfasts are often a good alternative to the bland hotels. Although B&Bs cost $45–$75 per night, the price includes breakfast and sometimes transport. Beware of some fleabag B&Bs in Spenard; though some charge as low as $20 for a room, it's not worth the risk of having your possessions ripped off, or worse. For more information about B&Bs, contact **Alaska Private Lodgings** (Box 200047, Anchorage 99520, tel. 907/248–2292), or browse through the listings in the *Anchorage Visitors Guide* (*see* Visitor Information, *above*).

➤ **UNDER $60 • Alaska Budget Motel.** Though on the seedy side, the rooms are perfect for groups, with plenty of floor space for sleeping bags or roll-away beds. Doubles go for $59; tack on an extra $10 for each additional person you stuff in (up to six). A few blocks from downtown, the hotel is safely insulated from the rough 4th Avenue nightlife. *545 E. 4th Ave., tel. 907/277–0088. Btw Eagle and Gambell Sts.; walk or take Bus 45 from downtown. 24 rooms. Luggage storage.*

Inlet Inn. Location and cleanliness are the only exciting features of this small, bland hotel. Two blocks north of the youth hostel, the Inlet is the only other budget lodging in the center of town, with easy access to buses, restaurants, and bars. Doubles with shared bath cost $44, $60 or more with private bath. Some basement rooms are slightly cheaper. *539 H St., tel. 907/277–5541. Btw 5th and 6th Aves., 1 block north of transit center. 84 rooms, some with bath. Luggage storage, free shuttle from airport. Wheelchair access.*

Midtown Lodge. A few miles from the airport and downtown, this cabin-style lodge is set well away from busy Arctic Boulevard. The spartan cubicles share baths. Their appeal is economic, not aesthetic: Singles cost a mere $44, doubles $49. Prices drop even lower in winter. Grab free coffee and rolls in the morning, and free snacks in the afternoon. *604 W. 26th Ave., tel. 907/258–7778. Btw Firewood Ln. and Northern Lights Blvd.; take Bus 9 from downtown. 55 rooms, none with bath. Laundry, kitchen.*

➢ **UNDER $90 • Alaskan Samovar Inn.** On a busy street on the east side, several blocks from downtown, the only good thing about this brown hotel is its location next-door to the Homer and Seward Bus Lines (*see* Coming and Going, *above*). Bleak doubles go for $86–$97 ($30 less in winter). They advertise "Jacuzzi in every room," but when you see the piddly bathtub with water jets, you may want your money back. Skip the hotel restaurant. *720 Gambell St., at 7th Ave., tel. 907/277–1511. 65 rooms. Luggage storage, free shuttle from airport.*

Anchor Arms Motel. The rooms may not be pretty, but they're damn big. Each comes with a kitchen, which is fortunate since you won't be able to eat out after you spend $89 for a double. The east-side neighborhood is on the sleazy side—the bar around the corner posts: NO PIMPS OR PROSTITUTES ALLOWED. *433 Eagle St., btw 4th and 5th Aves., tel. 907/272–9619. Walk or take Bus 45 from downtown. 42 rooms. Laundry, luggage storage. Wheelchair access.*

Chelsea Inn. This sparkling new three-story hotel is in the southwest end of Spenard—several miles from downtown but close to cool hangouts. Small, clean doubles with shared bath and lounge are $90; doubles with private bath are $105 (add $10 for each extra person). Noise from nearby train tracks and traffic may bother light sleepers. *3836 Spenard Rd., at Oregon Dr., tel. 907/276–5002. Take Bus 6 from airport, Bus 7 from downtown. 32 rooms, some with bath. Luggage storage, no-smoking rooms. Wheelchair access.*

Sixth and B B&B. One of the best B&Bs is right downtown, and it's home to the "Far From Fenway Fan Club." Devoted Red Sox fan Peter Roberts rents out two doubles ($38–$68 in high season) and a spacious upstairs loft ($58–$98 for two, $15 for extra people). You get a spotless, antique-crammed room, and license to graze in the kitchen or tool around on a bicycle for free. *6th Ave. and B St., tel. 907/279–5293. 3 rooms, 1 with bath.*

HOSTELS **Anchorage International Hostel (HI).** Just 1½ blocks from the city bus terminal and a 10-minute walk from downtown, this is the cheapest and most popular place to stay. Many travelers on their way to or from Denali, Fairbanks, and the canneries crash here, making this a good place to get a ride or the scary truth about gutting fish. The midnight curfew throws a soggy blanket on your nightlife, but a security guard who works until 2 AM might let you in. Beds cost $12 members, $15 nonmembers. Guests must do a 15-minute chore before they leave. The Backpacker's shuttle runs here from the airport for $5. *700 H St., btw 7th and 8th Aves., tel. 907/276–3635. 80 beds, none with bath. Midnight curfew, lockout 10–5. Laundry, luggage storage, ride board, pay phones, kitchen, TV lounge. $2 shower fee for non-guests.*

Even if you haven't reserved at the hostel, you should still be able to get a bed if you line up by 4:30 PM. Travelers on long-distance buses and trains don't blow into town until after 5.

International Backpackers Inn/Hostel. If Ed and Chris don't have a bunk ($12–$15 per night) available in one of five houses within a square block, they'll find space for you in a massive tent ($10 per night). You can also pitch your own tent for $10. This place has no curfew, but it's far from downtown. You'll have to put up with slimy bathrooms, crusty kitchens, and permanent guests. Try to stay in the yellow house (#325)—it's just as cramped but cleaner and brighter than the others. The Alaska Backpacker Shuttle (*see* Coming and Going, *above*) runs here from the airport for $7.50. *3601 Peterkin St., at Mumford St., tel. 907/274–3870. From downtown, take Bus 45 to Bragaw and Peterkin Sts.; walk west 3 blocks down Peterkin. 45 beds. Laundry, kitchen, luggage storage.*

Spenard Hostel (HI). This mellow hostel used to take overflow from the main hostel downtown, but it's now a separate entity. If you want to escape amped backpackers and downtown bustle and get some quiet instead, this is the place. They don't enforce a lockout or curfew, and you can use laundry machines for free. Beds go for $10 for HI members, $12 for nonmembers. *2845 W. 42nd St., off Wisconsin Ave., tel. 907/248–5036. 36 beds. Kitchen, luggage storage.*

CAMPING Public campgrounds all lie inconveniently outside the city. **Eagle River,** 13 miles north on the Glenn Highway, is one of the best, with beautiful sites ($10) in a valley and new bathrooms. Just north of town, **Centennial Camper Park** (8300 Glenn Hwy., tel. 907/333–9711) is the city's main public campground. It's surrounded by 85 acres of woods, complete with ski trails and a ball park—but even all those trees won't block the highway noise. Rest rooms, pay phones, and a grocery store are all nearby. Sites cost $10 a day for Alaska residents, $13 otherwise, and a spot is always available. To reach Centennial, take the Muldoon Road turnoff, make the first left on Boundary Road, go left into the park, and follow the blue signs; or take Bus 3 or 75 from downtown. The Alaska Backpacker Shuttle (*see* Coming and Going, *above*) will take you from the airport to either campground for $10.

Lion's Park (5800 Boniface Pkwy., ½ mi south of Glenn Hwy. on right, tel. 907/333–9711) is a smaller, lesser known public campground (60 sites), with wooded sites ($10), prison-like bathrooms, and its share of noise. **Golden Nugget Camper Park** (4100 DeBarr Rd., across from Costco, tel. 907/333–5311) has a few grassy tent spots among the gravel ($10); the showers and laundry are a hell of a lot cleaner than at public grounds.

FOOD

Anchorage has plenty of places to eat; the problem is finding somewhere affordable. The main drag, 4th Avenue, is lined with restaurants that pack 'em in and charge top dollar for Denny's-style cuisine. If you're going to shell out for a meal, head outside downtown for some excellent ethnic cuisine. The Mediterranean food at **Aladdin's** (4240 Old Seward Hwy., tel. 907/561–2373) will knock you on your butt, but dinner runs $15–$20. A crêpe dinner will set you back $10 at the nearby **French Connection** (4300 Old Seward Hwy., tel. 907/563–2528). Do-it-yourself meals are the cheapest way to go. Both **Safeway** (1400 W. Northern Lights Blvd., btw Spenard Rd. and Minnesota Sts.) and **Carr's** (1650 W. Northern Lights Blvd., across from Safeway; other location at Gambell and 13th Sts.) are open 24 hours.

Two blocks west of Loussac Library, the Bagel Factory (36th Ave. and A St.) serves 14 different kinds of bagels and nine kinds of cream cheese. That means altogether . . . a lot of combinations.

➤ **UNDER $5** • **Federal Building Cafeteria.** Come eat with the suits at this civic cafeteria. Full breakfasts are $3.50, sandwiches $3 or less, and hot entrées $4. The decor is better than your high school cafeteria, but the food's about the same. After 1:30 you get $1 off most food. *111 8th Ave., at A St., tel. 907/277–6736. Go right after main entrance. Open weekdays 7–3:30.*

Java Joint. Hands down, this two-story hot-pink coffeehouse is the hippest thing going. The people couldn't be friendlier, nor the coffee more addictive (tall latte $2). Delicious, fluffy scrambled eggs with jalapeños, cheese, and a side of toast are only $2.50. Sandwiches run $4, and mouth-watering 12-inch pizzas with toppings like prawns, artichoke hearts, or mesquite chicken go for $8.50–$10.50 at night. Check out the message board and calendar of evening events (*see also* After Dark, *below*). *2911 Spenard Rd., btw Fireweed St. and Northern Lights Blvd., tel. 907/562–5555. Take Bus 7 from downtown. Open Sun.–Thurs. 6 AM–midnight, Fri. and Sat. 8 AM–2 AM.*

Side Street Café. This new downtown café next to Darwin's Theory bar draws an international crowd looking for hot food and temporary shelter during hostel lockout hours. The food is decent and cheap: A bowl of fresh chicken and white-bean chili with a bagel goes for only $3.50; espresso is $1.50. *428 G St., btw 4th and 5th Aves., tel. 907/258–9055. Open weekdays 7 AM–8 PM, Sat. 7–5, Sun. 8–4.*

Taco Grande. Since 1977, this food trailer has been serving great, dirt-cheap Mexican food in a lot a block down from the homeless shelter. The beans are fresh and the prices couldn't be lower (bean burritos $1.60). Ask for it hot and spicy and it'll make you cry. *Cnr E. 3rd Ave. and N. Post Rd. 5-min walk from downtown, or take Bus 45. Trailer is on right as you face mountains (west). Open weekdays 11–6.*

White Spot Café. At this tiny diner, squeezed between shops and bars downtown, the food is greasy, filling, and remarkably cheap. Leonora, the feisty old woman who's been running the place for 33 years, serves you quickly, even if it's not exactly what you ordered. Pancakes go for $2.75 and a burger with fries costs $3.25. Veggies' only lunch option is a plate of fries. *109 W. 4th Ave., at A St., tel. 907/279–3954. Open daily 6:30 AM–7 PM.*

➤ **UNDER $10** • **Cyrano's Books and Café.** Come to this little coffeehouse/bookstore to write letters, browse for books, or see an evening art film or Andean musical performance at the downstairs movie house. The food, including dynamite carrot cake ($2.50) and spicy chicken gumbo (Friday–Saturday only; $4.50), is excellent. Even vegetarians have a wide choice. Check the entrance hall for musical and literary events. *413 D St., off 4th Ave., tel. 907/274–2599. Open Oct.–May, daily 10–10; June–Sept., daily 8–10.*

The Natural Pantry. This cafeteria-style restaurant serves vegetarian and healthy foods; locals chat about tai chi and carrot juice amid decor that hasn't changed in two decades. Meals are fresh and natural, but portions are small. You can fill up at the all-you-can-eat (the magic words) salad bar for $4.50–$5.50. Also try the light quiche ($4–$4.50) and blackberry cider ($1–$1.50). *Plaza Mall, 300 W. 36th Ave., at A St., tel. 907/563–2727. In Midtown, 2 blocks west of Loussac Library; take Bus 11, 60, or 93 from downtown. BYOB. Open weekdays 10–7:30, Sat. 10–6.*

➤ **UNDER $15** • **Gwennie's Old Alaskan Restaurant.** Gwennie's is the kind of place where the waitresses call you "honey" and portions are so enormous they hang off your plate. In the southern end of Spenard, this rustic, pioneer-style place looks touristy but isn't. The breakfast special of eggs, two pancakes, and bacon goes for $4.50; a crab omelet with reindeer sausage is $9; for dinner, try the Fisherman's Platter ($15.95) with king crab, oysters, scallops, shrimp, and fish. *4333 Spenard Rd., tel. 907/243–2090. Take Bus 7 from downtown. Open daily 6–10.*

Maharaja's. The best Indian restaurant in town serves a variety of meat and vegetarian dishes (entrées $10 and up), including breads and traditional chicken dishes cooked in the tandoori oven. You're surrounded by Indian music and tapestries while you eat. Try the chicken *tikka* (tandoori chicken marinated in yogurt, tomatoes, and onions; $11). *328 G St., btw 3rd and 4th Aves., tel. 907/272–2233. BYOB. Open weekdays 11:30–2, Sun.–Thurs. 5:30–9:30, Fri. and Sat. 5:30–10. Reservations advised.*

Thai Cuisine. Terrific food and swift service at this Thai restaurant draw the yupaks (young urban professional Alaskans) who want to "do lunch." Tasty vegetarian and meat dishes cost $6–$10. Two favorites are *pad Thai* (fried noodles with prawns and peanut sauce; $6.95) and stir-fry shrimp curry ($8.95). Round out the meal with a sweet Thai iced tea ($1.50). *444 H St., btw 4th and 5th Aves., tel. 907/277–8424. Open weekdays 11–10, Sat. 11–10, Sun. 4–10. Reservations advised.*

➤ **UNDER $25** • **Villa Nova.** From the outside, this restaurant in a strip mall called "Plaza Z" looks like a pizza joint, but it's one of the finest restaurants in town. Dishes like vegetarian rigatoni and fresh halibut with mango salsa run $15.95–$17.95. Owner and chef Sophia says if she ever took the pricey *cacciucco* (seafood stew; $25.95) off the menu, "people would scream." *5121 Arctic Blvd., at International Airport Rd, tel. 907/561–1660. Take Bus 9 from downtown. Open Mon.–Sat. 11–2 and 5–10.*

WORTH SEEING

Most of Anchorage's sights are downtown, within spitting distance of each other and of many hotels and restaurants. The few that are farther out—including some museums and parks—require time, determination, and a bus to reach.

ALASKA AVIATION HERITAGE MUSEUM This surprisingly fascinating museum on the south shore of Lake Hood holds photos and films of the early Alaskan bush pilots, vintage flying uniforms, and 20 historic aircrafts. From the museum, you can watch today's bush pilots in action as they take off from the Lake Hood Seaplane Base, the largest seaplane airport in the world. *4721 Aircraft Dr., tel. 907/248–5325, or 800/770–5325 in AK. Take Bus 6 (infrequent) from downtown or Bus 93 from Midtown. Admission: $5. Open Mon.–Sat. 9–7, Sun. 9–6.*

ALASKA EXPERIENCE Watch 40 minutes of Alaskan landscapes on a three-story, 180° wraparound screen that's guaranteed to make you dizzy. It's billed as one of Anchorage's great attractions, but the mildly engaging *Alaska Experience* has nothing that you can't see for yourself (for free) by driving a short ways out of Anchorage. The newly added Earthquake attraction will add another $5 to your $6 ticket ($10 if you buy them together); it's informative, but it wouldn't frighten a Californian. *705 W. 6th Ave., at G St., tel. 907/276–3730. Across from transit center. Open summer, daily 9–9; winter, daily noon–6; film shown on the hour.*

ANCHORAGE MUSEUM OF HISTORY AND ART The largest museum in Alaska houses a collection of art that ranges from prehistoric to contemporary. You can breeze through the permanent collection of Alaskan artists on the first floor—the only works of interest are portaits and paintings by Fred Machetanz, George Ahgupuk, and James K. Moses. Upstairs, an exhibit traces Alaskan history and features life-size reconstructions of native homes. *121 W. 7th Ave., btw A and C Sts., tel. 907/343–4326. Admission: $4, under 18 free. Open May 15–Sept. 15, daily 9–6; off-season, Tues.–Sat. 10–6, Sun. 1–5.*

The Anchorage Bowl runneth over with parks, ranging from the 4,000-acre Far North Bicentennial Park in South Anchorage to dinky corner lots.

CITY PARKS **Delaney Park** (the "park strip") downtown runs from A Street to P Street between 9th and 10th avenues. Originally built as a firebreak, the park now sports flower gardens, picnic areas, ball fields, and tennis courts. It's a great place to jog or watch summer softball games. A series of plaques at **Earthquake Park,** on West Northern Lights Boulevard in South Anchorage, are dedicated to the devastating 1964 earthquake, which sent much of this neighborhood sliding into Cook Inlet. The **Knowles Coastal Trail** runs through part of the park, with views of downtown and the inlet.

HERITAGE LIBRARY AND MUSEUM This tiny museum in the National Bank of Alaska houses an outstanding collection of Native American artifacts as well as an archive of newspapers and books. Ask the librarian to show you around the collection of Aleut baskets and contemporary ivory carvings. *National Bank of Alaska, 301 Northern Lights Blvd., at C St., tel. 907/265–2834. Take Bus 3 from downtown. Admission free. Open weekdays 1–5.*

LOUSSAC PUBLIC LIBRARY Anchorage's big, elegant library, in a Midtown park, has several lounges and study areas where you can escape city life. Rest your bones in the Ann Stevens Room, furnished like someone's private study. The Alaska Collection, housed in its own three-story wing, includes artwork, historical archives, and a copy of every book ever writ-

Oil Makes the Art Go Round

If you've noticed that Alaskan museums are not exactly competitive with the Met, don't blame it simply on a lack of artistic interest or taste. Because freight is so expensive, the cost of shipping (let alone insuring) exhibits from the lower 48 is prohibitive. Alaska also lacks the population to support museums the way other states can. Oil companies put up most of the money for art exhibits, which explains why many end with a "Tribute to the Alaskan Pipeline," models of oil riggers, or "Oil makes the world go round" diagrams.

ten about Alaska. *3600 Denali St., at 36th Ave., tel. 907/261–2845. Take Bus 2 from downtown or 93 from Midtown; Buses 97, 90, 75, and 60 stop nearby. Admission free. Open Mon.–Thurs. 9–9, Fri. 9–6, Sat. 10–6, Sun. noon–8.*

CHEAP THRILLS

Most people come to Alaska for the wilderness and find the urban atmosphere of Anchorage a bit depressing. But you can escape the city by wandering through a park, heading out on the **Knowles Coastal Trail** (*see* Getting Around By Bicycle, *above*), or finding a high vantage point to look at the Chugach Mountains. You can gaze out on Cook Inlet from the **Captain Cook monument** at 3rd Avenue and L Street. If you want to see the salmon run in **Ship Creek,** head for the viewing platform on Whitney Road, north of downtown across the Ship Creek Bridge. Another peaceful place is **Westchester Lagoon,** where children feed the ducks. To get here, take C Street south to Hillcrest and turn right. On a summer night, nothing beats watching national collegiate teams play baseball at **Mulcahy Park** (16th Ave., at A St.).

FESTIVALS In summer, Anchorage puts on a kite-flying event, a Renaissance festival, and celebrations of colonial and native heritage. For info on fishing derbies on the Kenai Peninsula and the awesome annual bluegrass festival in Talkeetna, ask at the visitor center. Have a ball at February's **Fur Rendezvous** (tel. 907/277–8615), a 10-day celebration of Alaska's long fur-trapping and trading history, with fur auctions, sled-dog races, Eskimo blanket tosses, crafts fairs, square dancing, and whatever else the locals can think of. This is a serious party break from the long winter. In March, the infamous **Iditarod Sled Dog Race** (tel. 907/376–5155) begins in Wasilla, near Anchorage, and continues 1,049 miles north to Nome. The trail was once an important trade route from Seward to the interior; today, it's an endurance challenge and a chance to see some of the best dog-mushing in the world.

SHOPPING

Wandering around downtown Anchorage, you'll find an abundance of souvenir shops selling native crafts like ivory or bone carvings; but for the real thing, go to the **Taheta Arts and Cultural Group Co-op** (605 A St., tel. 907/272–5829), a cooperative of Eskimo/Indian and Aleut artisans selling their arts and crafts.

You can rent mountaineering and camping equipment at **Alaska Mountaineering and Hiking (AMH)** (2633 Spenard Rd., tel. 907/272–1811) and **REI** (1200 W. Northern Lights Blvd., tel. 907/272–4565). The studly staff at AMH will field your mountaineering questions and hook you up with equipment, guides, and even rides. For the cheapest outdoor rentals around, head to the Moseley Sports Center at **Alaska Pacific University** (4101 University Dr., tel. 907/564–8314). Tents rent for $10 a day, $30 a week; stoves are $2 a day; and cross-country ski packages are $7 a day, $28 a week. From downtown, take Providence Drive toward the mountains to University Drive and turn left into campus; the sports center is the grey building, second on your right.

AFTER DARK

Anchorage has a decent arts scene, including a repertory theater and occasional opera. For the scoop on upcoming cultural events, contact the **Performing Arts Center** (tel. 907/343–1948). The *Anchorage Daily News* lists events and nightlife in its Friday edition. For most, Anchorage's nightlife—if not life in general—revolves around beer. Luckily, the city is so large and diverse that you'll find every kind of bar. Check out the evening events held downstairs at the downtown café **Cyrano's** (*see* Food, *above*), which range from writing groups to film screenings to music. Otherwise, head for the bars downtown or in the colorful Spenard neighborhood, the hip site for new coffeehouses and performance spaces. Whatever you do, don't miss the espresso bar **Java Joint** (*see* Food, *above*), which draws the friendliest crowd of all ages. There's something happening almost every night (check the schedule taped to the counter), but Wednesday night is the most popular: Starting at 8, an Irish folk music jam comes together and people jig and square dance on a packed floor.

Downtown Anchorage is quiet at night, but it has a couple of booming bars. **Darwin's Theory** (426 G St., tel. 907/277–5322) is packed with men who are low on the evolutionary ladder. Guys (buddies) will probably be treated to at least one round, but women will feel like a side of beef. **Legal Pizza** (1034 W. 4th Ave., tel. 907/274–0686), a popular downtown restaurant, has live folk and bluegrass music nightly in summer; for the price of a cup of tea you can listen for hours. To see an arty film, join the too-hip intellectuals at **Capri Cinema** (3425 E. Tudor Rd., tel. 907/275–3799). Take Bus 75 from downtown and prepare to shell out $6 for a ticket.

Blue Moon. It's primarily a gay bar, but the huge downstairs dance floor and slammin' music attract people of all genders, races, and sexual orientations. The upstairs bar features karaoke almost every night. Tuesday is country-music night, Wednesday is cross-dressing, and on weekends you have to line up to get in and boogie. *530 E. 5th Ave., btw Fairbanks and Eagle Sts., tel. 907/277–0441. Cover: $2–$3. Open Mon.–Thurs. 1 PM–2:30 AM, Fri. 1 PM–3 AM, Sat. 3–3; Sun 3–2:30.*

Chilcoot Charlie's. Spenard Road is lined with sleazy bars and strip joints with names like "Great Alaskan Bush Company," but Charlie's is the most infamous of them all. This Anchorage institution is packed on weekends with people wearing everything from flannel shirts to tight-fitting zebra-print skirts. The interior, a cross between a log cabin and a labyrinth, includes several bars and two stages for live bands. *2435 Spenard Rd., tel. 907/272–1010. Cover: $3. Open Sun–Thurs 11:30 AM–2:30 AM, Fri.–Sat. 11:30 AM–3 AM.*

Fly By Night Club. It bills itself as a sleazy bar, but it's actually a charming, unpretentious— dare we say, even yuppie—place. Mr. Whitekeys, the owner and piano player, and his band play classic '60s rock and blues. The Fly By Night's infamous Whale-Fat Follies, a raunchy, satirical musical about Alaskan life, plays in mid-summer; tickets are $10 and reservations are essential. *3300 Spenard Rd., tel. 907/279–7726. Open Tues.–Sat. 4 PM–late.*

Kaladi Brothers' Coffeehouse. At the best espresso bars around the state, they serve Kaladi Brothers' coffee. Their main coffeehouse attracts mainly an older crowd. Dim lighting and excellent live jazz or folk on weekends make this romantic place the site of much yuppie scamming. *68th Ave., at Frontage St., tel. 907/344–5483. Take Bus 101 or head north on New Seward Hwy. Open Mon.–Thurs. 6 AM–10 PM, Fri. 6 AM–11 PM, Sat. 7 AM–11 PM, Sun. 8 AM–10 PM.*

Mea Culpa. This former auto-body shop, now a Spenard coffeehouse, is painted aqua blue with a yellow Windsurfer stuck on the roof. The inside is plastered with student art. Thursday–Saturday nights local bands from grunge to folk take the stage. *229 W. Fireweed Ln., at C St., tel. 907/272–3492. Take Bus 60 or 90 from downtown; Bus 97, 2, or 75 gets within 2 blocks. Cover: $1–$3. Open Mon.–Wed. 7 PM–9 PM, Thurs.–Fri. 7–midnight, Sat. 9–midnight, Sun. noon–6.*

OUTDOOR ACTIVITIES

Many Alaskans consider Anchorage an insult to nature, but most visitors will be shocked by how wild the elements remain. Moose frequently wander into the suburbs and even downtown,

The Avenue of Ill Repute

If you thought all of Anchorage was laid out in perfect city blocks, then you definitely missed Spenard, the city's coolest neighborhood. Curving its way past some of Anchorage's seediest establishments, Spenard Road was the winding path taken by drunk patrons of Joe Spenard's speakeasy during Prohibition days. Today, it's lined with bars, pawn shops, and hole-in-the-wall restaurants. This may be the place where you find a secondhand steal, or the place where you lose your wallet. To reach Spenard Road, follow I Street south from downtown; it curves to the west and splits into Spenard Road and Minnesota Drive.

and it's not uncommon to find bears taking a constitutional in one of the city's greenbelts. You can also see beluga whales in Cook Inlet and beavers in Campbell Creek, just one block off Dimond Boulevard.

➤ **HIKING** • Hiking trails crisscross the entire Anchorage area, but some of the best hikes are in 495,000-acre **Chugach State Park,** which rims the Anchorage Bowl to the south and east. Valleys, lakes, and towering peaks make this a perfect place to hike, fish, and camp. People Mover Bus 92 can take you to the trailheads for many of the area's best hikes. Several trails start at the Glen Alps park entrance (take Bus 92 to cnr of Hillside Dr. and Upper Huffman Rd.; go east on Upper Huffman Rd. and up Toilsome Rd.). The most popular trail is **Flat Top Mountain,** a 3½-mile trek up a 4,500-foot peak. From the top on a clear day, you have a magnificent view of Denali. Other good hikes beginning at Glen Alps include **Powerline Trail** (11 mi round-trip), **Ramp and Wedge peaks** (11 mi round-trip), and **Williwaw Lakes,** a scenic trail (13 mi round-trip) leading to several beautiful alpine lakes. For information about other treks in the area, pick up hiking maps from the **Alaska Public Lands Information Center** (605 W. 4th Ave., tel. 907/271–2737), or invest in the comprehensive *55 Ways to the Wilderness in Southcentral Alaska,* available at outdoor shops and bookstores.

Alaska Women of the Wilderness (P.O. Box 773556, Eagle River, AK 99577, tel. 907/688–2226) operates testosterone-free, low-cost trips and educational courses.

➤ **ROCK CLIMBING** • Climbers call the rocks in nearby Chugach State Park "Chugach crud" because they're so crumbly. Beginners can tackle **Boy Scout Rock,** off the Seward Highway before Girdwood; pick up the guide *Chugach Rock Climbing* at AMH (*see* Shopping *above*) first. The best nearby climbing is on the granite faces of **Archangel Park** in the Mat-Su Valley (*see* Near Anchorage, *below*). You can clamber indoors on the awesome new walls (ability levels 5.2–5.14) at the **Anchorage Gymnastics Association** (525 W. Potter Dr. #4, btw C and Arctic Sts., tel. 907/563–3041). Four hours cost $6; you can rent a harness and shoes for $2.50 apiece.

The University of Alaska at Anchorage and Alaska Pacific University have collaborated in an **Alaska Wilderness Studies Program** (tel. 907/786–1468). Courses range from short programs on rock climbing for teachers to full expeditions and wilderness education courses. A nine-day trek through Lake Clark National Park, plus four days of instruction, costs $670.

So you wanna ride a llama? Pat Barnes (tel. 907/376–8472) has the sweetest deals around. A weekend pack trip, including transportation, food, gear, and said llama, is only $130.

➤ **FISHING** • You need a license to fish in Anchorage's 19 creeks, four rivers, and many lakes. Contact the **State Department of Fish and Game** (tel. 907/344–0541) for more information. Licenses for one day for non-Alaskans are $10. Grayling and trout are around all year, but salmon fishing is a summer thing. If you want the lowdown on hot fishing spots, call 907/349–4687 for a recorded message.

➤ **KAYAKING** • You can kayak on many of the city's lakes and lagoons, including Goose Lake, Jewel Lake, and Westchester Lagoon, but most people head down to Whittier (*see* Prince William Sound, *below*) to let their kayaks into the Prince William Sound. **Adventures and Delights** (36th Ave. and C St., tel. 907/276–8282) rents double kayaks to experienced paddlers only ($55 one day, $45 additional days). **REI** (2710 Spenard Rd., tel. 907/272–4565) rents single kayaks ($40 a day, $35 additional days). The water is damn cold, so you should know how to upright yourself immediately. Also, don't get too close to glaciers—they may calve and crush you. Finally, be aware of dramatic tide changes—as much as 30 feet in some places.

Near Anchorage

Anchorage may not be the "real Alaska," but it makes one hell of a good base from which to explore it. Within striking distance lie Denali National Park (*see* Chapter 13, Fairbanks and the Bush) to the north, the Kenai Peninsula to the south, Prince William Sound to the east, and the Lake Clark National Park to the west. And if you don't have your own transport, Anchorage is one of the best places in Alaska to snag a ride; just hang around the youth hostels or listen to the Bush Line (AM radio 890, KBBI). In other words, you'll never feel too anchored down.

MATANUSKA-SUSITNA VALLEY

The Mat-Su Valley, as it is known, actually consists of two valleys created by the Matanuska and Susitna rivers. Lying north of Anchorage and cut in half by the Glenn and George Parks highways, the valley is the site of Alaska's only farming community. Farming in Alaska was actually President Roosevelt's idea, part of his New Deal plan to help the depressed Midwest. In 1935, 203 families relocated here, but the majority couldn't hack it and hightailed it back to Kansas.

In the Mat-Su Valley, "Attack of the Killer Tomatoes" seems a distinct possibility. Long summer days mean vegetables grow to Chernobyl-inspired proportions—80-pound cabbages are mere appetizers.

The **Glenn Highway** (Highway 1) runs north from Anchorage to Palmer. From Palmer, the Glenn forks east to Glenallen, and the **George Parks Highway** runs to Fairbanks, 380 miles away. It passes Denali National Park, roughly midway between Anchorage and Fairbanks. During the stretch between Palmer and Denali you'll pass outstanding views of the Alaska range. Beyond the park is the heart of Alaska; the road is flanked by birch, spruce, and aspen forests. The highway is paved and well-traveled, and hitching is usually easy.

PALMER The center of the Mat-Su Valley farming community, 40 miles north of Anchorage, Palmer looks like something from a Swiss calendar, with its old barns and log houses silhouetted against craggy Pioneer Peak. On the nearby farms (on the Bodenburg Loop off old Palmer Highway) you can pick your own raspberries and other fruits and vegetables. The biggest shindig of the year is the annual **Alaska State Fair,** held during the last week of August, when the valley's mongo veggies go on display. A bed at the **Sheep Mountain Lodge** (Mile 113, Glenn Hwy./Hwy. 1, tel. 907/745–5121), a hostel with superb mountain views, costs only $12 a night. Call ahead for a reservation (and have your Visa or MasterCard handy).

About 8 miles north of Palmer along the Glenn Highway is the turnoff for **Hatcher Pass Road,** which links with the George Parks Highway. Open only in summer, the road leads to the 277-acre **Independence Mine State Historic Park,** which has a visitor center and several restored gold-mining buildings. The views from the road of glaciers, lakes, and valleys are outstanding. Locals head up here to hike or pick berries. Also off the Glenn Highway is **Musk-Ox Farm** (tel. 907/745–4151), home to over 100 musk ox, which look like a mix between a sheep and an ox. Their fur, known as qiviut, is used to make very expensive coats, hats, and scarves. It's collected in early summer—usually mid-April to June—by combing the animals. If you're feeling adventurous, volunteer to comb a musk ox for the farm. The owners claim the animals are tame, and they're secured, so you've got nothing to worry about—climb into the stall and go to it. Admission is $5 and tours are given daily from May to September. About an hour's drive north of Palmer is the **Matanuska Glacier,** a massive sheet of ice some 27 miles long and 4 miles wide. You can walk to the glacier if you pay a small fee to cross private land. A $7.50 camping fee includes admission.

Get a Stiff One at the Bird House

About 20 miles from Anchorage along the Seward Highway, look for the large, tacky blue bird that adorns the entrance to the Bird House bar. Built around the turn of the century, this small cabin has been slowly sinking into the soft mud of Turnagain Arm to the point where the floors and the bar now tilt at crazy angles. The walls and ceiling are at least a foot thick with business cards, bogus checks for millions of dollars, and underwear stapled there by passing tourists. The only thing more wacky than the inside are the proprietors themselves. The grandmotherly bartender who just served your beer may offhandedly lift her apron to reveal an oversize (but rather hairy and lifelike) erect penis. Minors can come in and look, but they can't touch and they won't be served alcohol.

WASILLA If you head north from Anchorage on the George Parks Highway, you come to Wasilla, home of the **Iditarod Trail Sled Dog Race Headquarters** (Mile 2.2, Knik Rd., tel. 907/376–5155). Open year-round, the headquarters displays dog sleds, clothing, and videos of the grueling race, held each March. If you're absolutely riveted by this sled-racing stuff, there's also the **Knik Museum and Sled Dog Mushers Hall of Fame** (Mile 14 on Knik Rd., tel. 907/376–2005).

LAKE CLARK NATIONAL PARK

Lake Clark National Park and Preserve rises from tidal flats to the precipitous Chigmit Mountains, 120 miles west of Anchorage across Cook Inlet. The Aleutian and Alaska ranges meet here, and the isolated interior of the park is choked with mountains, lakes, and rivers. One of those mountains, Mt. Redoubt, suffered disastrous incontinence in 1990 when it could no longer hold its ash. Accessible only by air, Lake Clark is virtually untouched and well set up for experienced and intrepid hikers. Backpacking, river-running, and fishing are the main draws. The park superintendent (222 W. 7th Ave. #61, Anchorage, tel. 907/271–3751) can provide you with specific information about the area, including topographic maps. Unless you camp, be prepared to shell out vast amounts to stay in hunting and fishing lodges. Similarly, you'll pay through the nose to charter a plane in Anchorage, Kenai, or Homer—flights generally cost $200–$250 per hour.

Another way to reach the park is on a scheduled flight to Port Allsworth, inside park boundaries, on **Lake Clark Air** (tel. 907/278–2054) for $280 round-trip. **MarkAir** (tel. 800/627–5247) has a scheduled flight to Lake Illiamna, along the borders of the park. From here, you can take the mail plane to the small border towns of Nondalton or Port Allsworth, on the southwest shore of the lake. This is only a little cheaper, but you get the added benefit of spending some time at Lake Illiamna. Bring absolutely everything you need, because you won't find any convenience stores in this wilderness.

Kenai Peninsula

The Kenai Peninsula is popular for three reasons: It's unbelievably beautiful, it's near Anchorage, and you can get to it by road—nothing to be sniffed at in Alaska. Not surprisingly, Anchorage residents consider the peninsula their backyard, heading down here in droves on weekends and vacations to camp, fish, and hike. You can get away from it all if you try, but if you're looking for some kind of hermit-like solitude, you're in the wrong place.

The Kenai Peninsula, flanked on one side by Cook Inlet and on the other by Blying Sound and Prince William Sound, stretches 250 miles south from Anchorage into the Gulf of Alaska. This region supports itself through tourism and fishing—the peninsula has set records for halibut and salmon catches, and each of its towns has a fishing fleet and canneries. Fishing draws a lot of visitors, but you won't be disappointed if you just come for the scenery. Like the Panhandle and Prince William Sound, the Kenai Peninsula has its fair share of fjords, glaciers, and impressive mountains. And whether you're trekking through the mountains or bouncing around on a boat in Ketchemak Bay, you'll see unbelievable wildlife. The towns of Kenai and Soldotna are basically convenient places to load up on supplies (Kenai is home to the world's largest K-mart), but Homer and Seward are truly charming. Homer, in particular, is a fantastic fishing village with a thriving art and cultural scene.

Bicyclists should avoid riding down the Seward and Sterling highways on weekends at all costs. Obnoxious RVs and trucks will practically rub up against you.

Two roads serve the Kenai Peninsula. The **Seward Highway** stretches 127 miles south from Anchorage to Seward, on the eastern coast of the peninsula. It's an exhilarating 2½-hour drive along Turnagain Arm near Anchorage and through the mountains farther south, but be prepared for weekend traffic in summer; locals and tourists swarm in to fish the Kenai River. At Mile 90 of the Seward Highway you'll hit the turnoff (Tern Lake Junction) for the **Sterling Highway,**

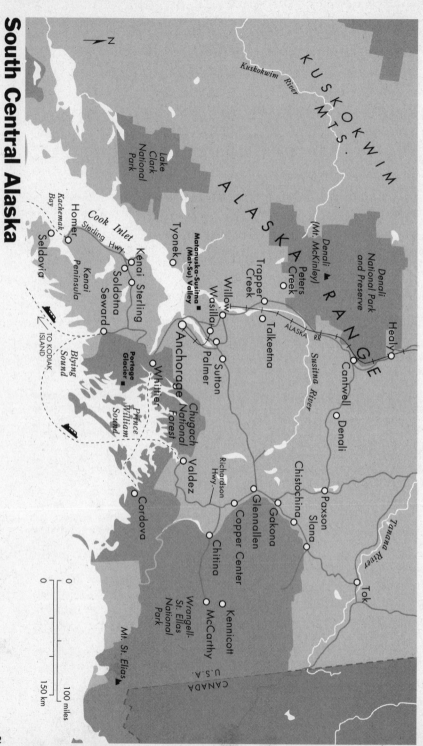

South Central Alaska

K U S K O K W I M   M T S.

Kuskokwim River

Denali
National Park
and Preserve

(Mt. McKinley)
▲ Denali

Healy

A L A S K A   R A N G E

ALASKA RR

Cantwell

Denali

Lake
Clark
National
Park

Peters
Creek

Trapper
Creek

Talkeetna

Susitna River

Chistochina

Slana

Paxson

Tanana River

Tok

Cook Inlet

Sterling Hwy.

Kachemak
Bay

Homer

Seldovia

Kenai
Peninsula

Soldotna

Kenai

Sterling

Seward

Tyonek

Matanuska-Susitna
(Mat-Su) Valley

Willow

Wasilla

Anchorage

Palmer

Sutton

Blying
Sound

TO KODIAK
ISLAND

Portage
Glacier

Whittier

Chugach
National
Forest

Prince
William
Sound

Valdez

Cordova

Richardson Hwy.

Glennallen

Gakona

Copper
Center

Chitina

Kennicott

McCarthy

Wrangell-
St. Elias
National
Park

Mt. St. Elias ▲

CANADA
U.S.A.

0

100 miles

0

150 km

452

which heads west across the peninsula before running down the west coast to Soldotna, Kenai, and finally Homer, 220 miles south of Anchorage. Remember to leave your lights on for the length of the highways—it's the law.

Seward

Seward, the only major town on the east side of the Kenai Peninsula, is doubly appealing—it's both drop-dead bee-yew-tiful and accessible by a three-hour drive from Anchorage. Named after William H. Seward, the secretary of state who arranged the purchase of Alaska from Russia in 1867, the town was once a buzzing seaport and important commercial center. In 1902 Seward was chosen as the starting point for the state railroad and, a few years later, for the Iditarod Trail, a dog-sled trail used to transport freight to Nome. The town boomed for a long time, but the apocalyptic 1964 earthquake—and tidal waves that followed—ravaged the boat harbor and 90% of the town's economy. While shipping and fishing remain important, tourism is now the town's lifeline—major cruise lines stop here between buffets. For most of the year, Seward is a quiet, unobtrusive place with a couple of grocery stores and a few town drunks. But in summer, the town swarms with with tourists, cannery workers, and sport and commercial fishermen.

As its deep port attracts more and more cruise ships, Seward is losing its sense of small-town community, but it's gaining lots of money. Prices have soared, though if you camp and eat carefully you can still leave with a few bucks in your pocket.

To the north, the town is ringed by stunning glaciers and mountains. **Mt. Marathon** is the most prominent peak and the site of an annual Fourth of July footrace to its 3,022-foot summit and back. You can get very close to **Exit Glacier,** a finger of the massive Harding Icefield, on the road from Seward, and several trails lead right up to the glacier. To the south lie Resurrection Bay and the Chiswell Islands, where you'll see marine life ranging from sea lions and otters to porpoises and whales. To the south and west are the magnificent Kenai Fjords, almost inaccessible and virtually untouched until the 1989 *Exxon Valdez* oil spill. The fjords are an outstanding collection of ice-blue glaciers that spill into steep bays. Getting into this glacial wonderland requires a chartered plane or ferry tour, but the hiking and backcountry camping opportunities make it worth the extra time and money.

BASICS The **Visitor Information Cache** (cnr 3rd Ave. and Jefferson St., tel. 907/224–3094), in an Alaska Railroad railcar, offers brochures, maps, and coffee for a quarter. It's open daily 11–4 from June to August. In winter, contact the **Seward Chamber of Commerce** (tel. 907/224–8051) for lists of hotels, restaurants, sights, and events, as well as the pamphlet "65 Free Things to Do in Seward."

Definitely swing by the **Kenai Fjords National Park Visitor Center** (1212 4th Ave., on boat harbor, tel. 907/224–3175), open daily 8–7 in summer, weekdays 8–noon and 1–5 in winter. The outgoing staff brim with facts; watch a free slide show, or join them for an interpretive walk in summer. Weekdays 8–5, the **U.S. Forest Service** (4th Ave. and Jefferson St., tel. 907/224–3374) provides info on the Seward district of the Chugach National Forest, including trails, camping, and cabins. No hotel in town has laundry facilities, so you'll have to get acquainted with **Seward Laundry** (804 4th Ave., tel. 907/224–5727).

COMING AND GOING For driving info, *see* the Kenai Peninsula introduction, *above.* Many people hitchhike on the Seward Highway, the only road that goes in or out of town. Take the trolley ($1) to the edge of town and point your thumb north. Not much civilization awaits between Seward and Anchorage, so bring food and be prepared to camp along the way.

➤ **BY BUS** • **Homer and Seward Bus Lines** (6th and Railway Aves., tel. 907/278–0800) runs daily between Seward and the Samovar Inn in Anchorage (*see* Where to Sleep, in Anchorage, *above*); fare is $35 one-way. **Alaskon Express** (tel. 907/277–5581 or 800/544–2206) also goes from Anchorage to Seward for $35, and the downtown Anchorage youth hostel (tel. 907/276–3635) usually runs a weekly shuttle to Seward for $25 one-way.

➤ **BY TRAIN** • The **Alaska Railroad** (tel. 907/265–2494 or 800/544–0552) connects Seward and Anchorage once daily in summer and on weekends only during the last three weeks of September (4½ hrs, $50 one-way, $80 round-trip). The hokey narration as you pass amazing sights marks this as the domain of package tourists. The train stops at a depot in the Small Boat Harbor, north of downtown. From here, walk or take the trolley ($1) into town.

➤ **BY FERRY** • The **Alaska Marine Highway** (5th and Railway Aves., tel. 907/224–5485) runs ferries weekly to Homer (17½ hrs, $96), Kodiak (4½ hrs, $54), Valdez (14 hrs, $58), and Cordova ($96). Service stops four times during summer when the ferry goes on extended week-long cruises of the Aleutians.

GETTING AROUND The main part of town is only about a mile long and a few blocks wide, and it's easily manageable on foot. Fourth Avenue is the main drag, leading from the Small Boat Harbor—filled with restaurants, shops, and the eponymous small boats—to the ferry terminal at the south end of town. Downtown is a two-block stretch of 4th Avenue between Railway Avenue and Adams Street. If you're pooped, call **PJ's Taxi** (tel. 907/224–5555) or **Independent Cab** (tel. 907/224–5000). Outlying areas, including Exit Glacier, some campgrounds, and several B&Bs, are hard to reach unless you have a car or are willing to hitchhike. You can rent a bike around the Small Boat Harbor at **Murphy's Motel** (911 4th Ave., at D St., tel. 907/224–8090) or **Charter Option** (tel. 907/224–2026). A new charter may be able to give you a lift out to Exit Glacier; ask at the Visitor Information Cache (*see* Basics, *above*) if it's up and running.

WHERE TO SLEEP Most hotels are smack in the main part of town. As more cruise ships pull into Seward and fill up the rooms, hotels are tacking on additional charges and asking a fortune. Camping is one of your best options; both public and private grounds have grassy spots on or near the water. Bed-and-breakfasts start at around $60 and are often far from the center. **By the Sea Bed and Breakfast** (611 Adams St., tel. 907/224–3401) is one of the few downtown B&Bs. Reserve early for one of its spacious doubles with views (around $75). The **New Seward Hotel** (cnr 5th Ave. and Washington St., tel. 907/224–8001 or 907/224–2378), the cheaper half of the high-priced Best Western next door, gives you a large but chintzy double with bath for $92 ($82 with shared bath). Ask about doubles in the basement for $58. The best place in town is by far the Van Gilder (*see below*).

➤ **UNDER $50** • **Niko's** and **Tony's**. Niko's, a pizza parlor, rents 10 no-frills rooms upstairs; Tony's, the bar next door, has nine equally spare ones. Each charges about $50 for a room in the off-season, $60 in summer (less if you negotiate on a slow night or stay a week). Ask the bartenders for more information. *Niko's: 133 4th Ave., at Washington St., tel. 907/224–5255. Tony's: 135 4th Ave., tel. 907/224–3045. No credit cards accepted.*

Van Gilder Hotel. Not only is this hotel furnished with antiques, it's also a full-fledged National Historic Site (built in 1916). "Pension rooms" with shared bath are $50 per single or double. Rooms with private baths go for $85; you pay even more for views of the inlet. *308 Adams St., btw 3rd and 4th Aves., tel. 907/224–3079. 26 rooms, some with bath.*

➤ **UNDER $80** • **Taroka Inn.** This family-run inn should be your next stop if the Van Gilder is booked, or if you want your own kitchen (and a massive room). It's a good value at $75 per double, plus $10 for each extra person. If you're traveling with a herd, this is your place. *235 3rd Ave., at Adams St., tel. 907/224-8975. 9 rooms. Check-in 4–6 PM. Kitchen.*

➤ **HOSTELS** • **Snow River-Seward Hostel (HI).** A groovy German couple has fixed up this hostel, 16 miles from Seward and surrounded by woods. The Anchorage youth hostel often arranges van trips here, and Homer and Seward Bus Lines (*see* Coming and Going, *above*) can drop you off, but once you're here, you ain't going nowhere without wheels. It's time to either hang with nature or trek the nearby Lost Lake Trail. Members pay $12, nonmembers $15. The hostel has no phone, so contact the HI folks in Anchorage (tel. 907/276–3635) to reserve a bed. *Box 425, Seward, AK 99664. At Mile 16 off Seward Hwy. (Hwy. 9). Kitchen. No credit cards.*

➤ **CAMPING** • In summer, you can plunk down in any marked camping area on the **water-front** along Ballaine Avenue. Much of the park here is paved for RVs, but you'll find grass for tents just south of Jefferson Street, near the rest rooms. This is a safe, friendly place to camp and share your food or fire with other travelers, but it gets jammed in July and August. Leave the $6 fee in the drop-off box. A five-minute shower is $1 at the harbormaster's public rest rooms (1300 4th Ave.). Seward has strict rules about camping in non-designated areas, so roughing it is largely a matter of avoiding the authorities. As always, you can join the **Tent City** at the canneries, far from the town center, but your best bet is just to crash on the waterfront and hope to avoid the officials who come by and check tents to see if you've paid.

Three miles south of downtown, **Miller's Landing** (tel. 907/224–5739) juts out into the bay, offering 40 campsites among the trees. You can easily hitch a ride down here, and the private sites ($10) are convenient for setting off in your boat or kayak. Other options are to camp at **Forest Acres Park** at Hemlock and Dimond streets or at **Spring Creek** (tel. 907/224–3331) across the bay.

FOOD Seward has a handful of excellent—and expensive—steak and seafood restaurants, but the cheaper places are bland and boring. Most restaurants line 4th Avenue. Head downtown for pizza and burger joints and to the Small Boat Harbor for seafood. You can get groceries at **Bob's Market** (207 4th Ave., tel. 907/224–3644) downtown or at the 24-hour **Eagle Quality Center** (Mile 2, Seward Hwy., tel. 907/224–3698). The cheapest hot lunch around is on the third floor of the **Seward Senior Citizens Center** (336 3rd Ave., tel. 907/224–5604). A full meal of large proportions, including drink and dessert, costs $5, and is served at noon.

➤ **UNDER $5 • Resurrect Art Gallery and Coffee House.** This unassuming brown church has been transformed into the best place to spend an hour (or more) in Seward. As you sip your latte ($2), savor homemade baklava ($2), or chow on a burger with broccoli and cheese ($3), you can look up at the excellent work of local artists. Also check this place out for music and eclectic events, especially on Friday nights. *3rd Ave., btw Madison and Jefferson Sts., tel. 907/224–7161. Wheelchair access. Open weekdays 8–6 (Fri. until 10), weekends 9–6.*

➤ **UNDER $10 • Mainstreet Café.** This clean downtown café with faux-brick walls, ship paintings, and a friendly cook packs in locals and tourists for the best breakfast in town, served until 11 (1 PM on weekends). Chow on a huge bowl of oatmeal with raisins ($3) or a veggie omelet ($6.50). For lunch grab an excellent bowl of oyster stew ($4) or a turkey sandwich ($4.25). *205 4th Ave., tel. 907/224–3068. Wheelchair access. Open daily 6–3 PM.*

➤ **UNDER $15 • Apollo Restaurant.** The Apollo does Italian, Greek, Mexican, and pizza—all with a certain "je ne sais quoi." You can't go wrong with anything on the menu, especially the massive calzones (meat $12.95, veggie $13.95) or the shrimp Apollo (shrimp with mushrooms, garlic, onions, and wine; $16.95). Lunch entrées go for $5.95–$9.95 and medium pizzas are $11.95–$19.95. *229 4th Ave., tel. 907/224–3092. Wheelchair access. Open daily 11–11.*

Peking. You have to swing by this place at least once to get a taste of some of the best Chinese food around. Every inch of the walls is covered in red, gold, and ornate decorations, and every table is filled. Order the excellent tofu with vegetables ($9.50). Lunch specials, served 11:30–3, are a great deal at $5.45–$6.45. *338 4th Ave., tel. 907/224–5444. Downtown at Jefferson St. Open 11:30–11.*

➤ **UNDER $25 • Ray's Waterfront Bar and Grill.** This classy restaurant is all brass and wood, with big windows overlooking the harbor and mountains beyond. Ray's serves huge steaks and local seafood, with salad and bread, for about $20. If that's out of your range, get a taste of Ray's by ordering a bowl of choice clam chowder ($4.75); or head to the bar for the same view and good burgers and fries ($5.95). *Small Boat Harbor, tel. 907/224–3012. Open summer, daily 11–11; shorter hrs off-season.*

WORTH SEEING The whole point of coming to Seward is to get outside among those magnificent mountains and glaciers. If you're pooped or nursing a melon-size blister, Seward has a few minor diversions, most of which involve obsessive re-creations of the '64 earthquake.

Resurrection Bay Historical Society Museum (3rd Ave. and Jefferson St., tel. 907/224–3902), housed in the town's senior center, has a gripping collection of photos of the '64 quake and aftermath; an exhibit on the Iditarod Trail; and a small collection of Eskimo art objects. Admission is $1, and it's open in summer, daily 11–5. **Seward Community Library** (5th Ave. and Adams St., tel. 907/224–3646), open weekdays noon–8, Saturday noon–6, features exhibits of local photography, an heirloom quilt, and a 1927 Alaskan flag. You can rest on the old sofas and easy chairs and browse through current magazines and newspapers. In summer, the library shows a daily program on the 1964 earthquake, including a film and a slide show for a $1.50 donation. Affiliated with the University of Alaska's marine research program, the **Seward Marine Center** (3rd Ave., btw Washington St. and Railway Ave., tel. 907/224–5261) has only recently opened its exhibits to the public. Check out the obscenely big whale skulls and four small aquariums filled with sea life. Call for a schedule of daily films and lectures. It's open summer, weekdays 11–5, Saturday 8–noon and 1–5.

Check out the zany and creative houses at Miller's Landing, 3 miles south of town, which sport weird chimneys, funky doors, and wild paint jobs—one house looks like a pot-bellied stove, and all of them are precariously perched on stilts.

AFTER DARK At night, locals, fishermen, and tourists all speed to the bars, most of which are downtown on 4th Avenue between Adams Street and Railway Avenue. Offering live music (usually country) on weekends, the **Yukon** (cnr 4th Ave. and Washington St., tel. 907/224–3063) and **Thorn's Showcase Lounge** (208 4th Ave., tel. 907/224–3700) pull in the crowds. **Tony's** (135 4th Ave., tel. 907/224–3045) is the most popular bar downtown, while **Ray's** (*see* Food, *above*) is the place for a classy drink on the water. The **Liberty Theatre** (304 Adams St., tel. 907/224–5418) shows second-run movies nightly.

OUTDOOR ACTIVITIES You have a choice of several good day hikes in and around Seward, and anglers from around the world set their fishy sights on the town's Silver Salmon Derby in August.

➢ **HIKING** • **Two Lakes Trail,** an easy 1-mile (round-trip) walk through the woods and along the lakes at the base of Mt. Marathon, begins at the park behind the Alaska Vocational Center (cnr of 2nd Ave. and B St.). The trailhead for the more difficult hike up to the summit of **Mt. Marathon** is at the west end of Jefferson Street. Another long trek leads to **Caines Head State Recreation Area,** a 6,000-acre park on the shore of Resurrection Bay, some 6 miles south of Seward. The preserve has hiking trails, fishing areas, and the remains of an old World War II fort. You can reach the trail at Lowell Point, at the end of Lowell Drive. Water taxis to Caines Head are also available from Miller's Landing (*see* Campgrounds, *above*) for $25 round-trip. The popular **Resurrection River Trail** begins at Mile 7.5 of Exit Glacier Road. The first 8 miles are relatively level, until you reach a recreation cabin; then the trail climbs 1,000 feet and continues another 8 miles to the **Russian Lakes Trail.** For more info, contact the Forest Service or the Visitor Information Cache (*see* Basics, *above*).

Every Fourth of July, Seward hosts a race up to the summit of Mt. Marathon; it takes the studly runners less than an hour to finish, but if you're sane it should take about three.

➢ **FISHING** • Weekenders from Anchorage flock to Seward to fish. Unfortunately, charters into Resurrection Bay cost hundreds of dollars; check the offices along the harbor or write to the chamber of commerce (*see* Basics, *above*) for a list of companies. Impoverished slobs like us can always fish off the harbor docks or from the beach in the waterfront area, but be sure you have a valid license. Inquire at the harbormaster for licenses and places to rent equipment; **Charter Option** (Small Boat Harbor, tel. 907/224–2026) is sure to have what you need.

➢ **KAYAKING** • **Alaska Treks 'n' Voyages** (tel. 907/224–3960 or 907/276–8282) rents kayaks from $30 a day to experienced paddlers and offers guided trips along the coast from Lowell Point for $85–$95 a day. If you know what you're doing, this is a thrilling way to see Resurrection Bay up close.

KENAI FJORDS NATIONAL PARK The steep coastal canyons of the Kenai Fjords were formed by glaciers carving their way through the surrounding mountains to the sea. For many people, the fjords are *the* reason to visit Seward, and they might be the most breathtaking thing you'll ever see. If you take a boat tour, you'll probably see more marine life than anywhere else in the state—the trips are well worth the money. Several boat charters, including **Kenai Fjords Tours** (tel. 907/224–8068) and **Mariah Charters** (tel. 907/224–8623 or 907/243–1238), give full-day tours of the fjords for $85 and half-day tours of Resurrection Bay for $54. Some smaller boats offer 2½-hour tours for $19.95 if you just want a quick look around (check around the Small Boat Harbor for specials, which come and go). Kenai Fjords National Park also encompasses the 300-square mile Harding Icefield and the glaciers it has spawned. The icefield and most of the glaciers (except Exit Glacier; *see below*) are inaccessible to all but the most experienced adventurers. If you have the moolah, you can always charter a plane and see it from above.

The **Kenai Fjords National Park Visitor Center** (Small Boat Harbor, Seward, tel. 907/224–3175), open daily 8–7 in summer and weekdays 8–7 in winter, stocks information about the various areas of the park, including Exit Glacier and Resurrection Bay. This is also the place to reserve cabins ($25) at Aialik Bay and Placer Creek, off Resurrection River Trail. The center presents films and evening talks daily during summer and hosts an Exit Glacier nature walk. Check out *A Guide to Alaska's Kenai Fjords* ($9), by David William Miller.

EXIT GLACIER Exit Glacier is part of Kenai Fjords National Park, but it stands out because it's so accessible. From Mile 3.7 of the Seward Highway, a 9-mile road leads to the Exit Glacier ranger station. From here, you can take a short nature trail right to the base of the glacier, or follow a longer (1 mi) nature trail to gain some elevation and still view the glacier close-up. The early portions of these trails are wheelchair accessible. A difficult 10-mile (round-trip) trek next to the glacier leads to the edge of the **Harding Icefield**—it'll take all day and all your energy, but it's completely worth it. A primitive campground lies near the glacier. For those without wheels, a tour company plans to cover Exit Glacier for about $15; inquire at the visitor center (*see below*) for an update. You can also walk or hitchhike the 9 miles to the glacier.

Le Barn Appetit (tel. 907/224–8706), a bed-and-breakfast off the Seward Highway at Exit Glacier Road, gives tours of the glacier for about $15; double rooms are $60 and the healthy food is scrumptious. For more information, swing by the **Exit Glacier Visitor Center** (tel. 907/224–3462), where the rangers can give you the skinny in summer, Monday–Thursday 8–5 and Friday–Sunday 8–7.

Soldotna

Most travelers only stop in Soldotna if they want to fish or if they need a base for exploring the Kenai National Wildlife Refuge (*see box* Kenai National Wildlife Refuge, *below*). Homesteaded after World War II, Soldotna was for many years a mere pit stop along the highway near Kenai. In recent years, though, the population has grown to 3,700, and the town has become something of a giant discount shopping mall for the Kenai Peninsula. The **Kenai River,** which runs right through town, attracts thousands of sport fishers who vie for king salmon every year. Nearby **Kasilof River** is also popular for salmon, and **Deep Creek** jumps with halibut. Get your fishing license from the **Alaska Department of Fish and Game** (34828 K-Beach Road, Suite E, tel. 907/262–9368). Boat tours and fishing charters are available in town, or you can rent fishing gear and your own canoe for $35 a day from **The Sports Den** (44176 Sterling Hwy., tel. 907/262–7491) or from locals on the side of the road looking to make an extra buck.

VISITOR INFORMATION The bulky **Kenai Peninsula Visitor Center** (Mile 95.5, Sterling Hwy., at K-Beach Rd., tel. 907/262–1337), open daily 9–7 in summer and weekdays 9–5 in winter, carries information on Soldotna, Kenai, and nearby areas. Pick up a *Soldotna Visitor Services Directory* for lists of B&Bs, charters, and restaurants.

COMING AND GOING Soldotna is on the Sterling Highway, which heads west from its junction with the Seward Highway before running down the western side of the peninsula. Soldotna is also the turnoff for people heading to Kenai, 11 miles away. **Homer and Seward Bus Lines** (tel. 907/278–0800) stops in Soldotna on the way from Anchorage to Homer (4 hrs, $30 one-way).

Unless you fish seriously, what the hell are you doing in Soldotna? Save your money and stay in a town that's not a strip mall.

WHERE TO SLEEP AND EAT Campgrounds and bed-and-breakfasts beat out overpriced, nondescript hotels like the $60-a-night **Duck Inn** (Mile 3, Kalifornsky Beach Rd., tel. 907/262–5041). See the visitor center (*see* Visitor Information, *above*) for a list of B&Bs. Prices rise about 25% for three weeks in July, during the salmon run. The two city campgrounds (tel. 907/262–7359) are both on the river and fill up quickly during the summer fishing season. Both have water and pit toilets and cost $7 a night. One of them, **Centennial Campground** (Centennial Park Rd., off K-Beach Rd. at Sterling Hwy.), has 160 sites, including some beautiful ones on the river. **Sal's Klondike Diner** (44619 Sterling Hwy., near the bridge, tel. 907/262–2220) is open 24 hours, and you should stop here even if you bypass the rest of Soldotna. They serve tasty, nongreasy diner food to friendly fishermen; half the clientele seem like they eat here every day.

Kenai

On a bluff overlooking Cook Inlet, Kenai is the peninsula's largest town—a sprawling urban metropolis by Alaskan standards. Kenai is an industrial center for oil, which employs most of the town's residents; and commercial fishing, which provides seasonal work in the canneries. Sport fishing is popular along the Kenai River, which empties into the inlet just south of downtown. You can cover everything worth seeing downtown in a couple of hours. Attention K-mart shoppers: the world's largest **K-mart** (10480 Spur Hwy., tel. 907/283–7616) is right here in Kenai. Fill up on supplies before you head out to Seward, Homer, or your fishin' hole. If you want to hang around, head for the nearby wilderness areas, including the Kenai National

Combat Fishing: Fighting the Reds

Much of the Kenai Peninsula is besieged in summer with tourists and locals with fishing fever. On Friday nights you can usually find a line of trucks rushing out of Anchorage for a little "combat fishing." Anglers are literally shoulder to shoulder during red-salmon openings, especially on the popular Russian River, at Mile 53 of the Sterling Highway. Combat fishing sounds violent, but it isn't—you'll just think an army has invaded when you see a juggernaut of anglers wearing camouflage jackets, hip-waders, and T-shirts that read SPAWN 'TIL YOU DIE. *The salmon runs are usually so thick that everyone gets at least one delicious red to barbecue.*

If you're planning a fishing trip on the Kenai or anywhere else in Alaska, check with the Alaska Fish and Game Department for scheduled river openings. Fish and Game closely monitors this region, and you'll be allowed to fish only in certain rivers during designated times and with a valid license. Fines are steep, so make sure you know what's open and what's not. If you see a river where no one else is fishing, chances are it's closed. You can buy a fishing license all over the Kenai Peninsula at bait stores and even at gas stations with minimarts. Non-residents of the state can get special three-day ($15) and 14-day ($30) licenses.

Wildlife Refuge (*see box,* National Wildlife Refuge, *below*) and the Captain Cook State Recreation Area (*see box below*).

Stop to check out the mouth of the **Kenai River** from the bluffs just south of downtown. On a clear day, you can see Cook Inlet, Mt. Redoubt, and Mt. Iliamna (the last two are volcanoes over 10,000 feet high). During incoming tides, look for beluga whales, which swim up the river to feed. Two good viewing sights in Old Town are at Main and Mission streets and farther west on Alaska Way. You can also walk along the beach, accessible from either Alaska Way (down a trail to Meeks Crossing) or Spruce Street.

Kenai was founded by Russian fur traders in the 18th century, and **Old Kenai** still has some historic buildings, as well as a calm, quiet feel that distinguishes it from the main highway. Get a walking-tour map of the old town from the visitor center (*see below*). The **Russian Orthodox Church** (Mission Ave.) has a pretty exterior, and you can see the inside on summer afternoons for a $1 donation. The **Kenai Fine Arts Center** (cnr Cook and Main Sts., tel. 907/283–7040), open Monday–Saturday 10–4, is also worth a visit. The small but well-kept gallery exhibits the work of some talented local artists.

VISITOR INFORMATION The **Chamber of Commerce Visitor Center** stocks brochures, lists hotels and charters, and offers a good walking tour of Old Kenai. Look for a neat display of native artifacts and historic paraphernalia in an adjoining room. *402 Overland Ave., at Main St. off Kenai Spur Hwy., tel. 907/283–7989. Open spring, fall, weekdays 9–5; summer, weekdays 9–5, weekends 10–4.*

COMING AND GOING Kenai is connected to the rest of the peninsula through Soldotna, 11 miles away. From the Sterling Highway in Soldotna, take the Kenai Spur Highway straight into town, or take K-Beach Road to Bridge Access Road, which meets the Kenai Spur just east of downtown. Together, the two routes are known as the Kenai Loop. **Homer and Seward Bus Lines** (tel. 907/278–0800) stops in Kenai ($30 from Anchorage, $17 from Homer).

WHERE TO SLEEP AND EAT Most travelers to Kenai camp for free near one of the canneries or rough it illegally, since the municipal campground no longer permits overnight camping. Hotels are annoyingly expensive: The **Uptown Motel** (47 Spur View Dr., tel. 907/283–3660), **Katmai Hotel** (10800 Kenai Spur Hwy., tel. 907/283–6101), and **Kenai Kings Inn** (10352 Spur Hwy., tel. 907/283–6060) all charge $90 and up for a double. Your only alternatives are the B&Bs listed at the visitor center (usually $50–$60 per double). Otherwise, get out of Dodge.

Food prospects are equally bleak. One of the best deals is the 24-hour **Katmai Pines Lodge** (Katmai Hotel, tel. 907/283–6101), just east of downtown, where huge omelets and sandwiches go for $6–$7. **Paradiso's** (Main St. and Kenai Spur, tel. 907/283–2222) has good but pricey Italian and Mexican food.

Captain Cook State Recreation Area

The 4,000-acre Captain Cook State Recreation Area lies some 25 miles north of Kenai, well off the tourist track. This peaceful coastal stretch of Cook Inlet encompasses a beautiful beach, rivers and lakes, tree-filled picnic areas, and free camping. Agate hunters beachcomb on the shore while anglers fish and canoe in Stormy Lake and Swanson River. To get here, take the Kenai Spur Highway until it turns into North Kenai Road. On the way you'll be treated to the sight of offshore oil platforms and petrochemical plants. For information, contact Alaska State Parks, Kenai District (Box 1247, Soldotna 99669, tel. 907/262–5581).

Homer

Artists only need two things to survive—beautiful scenery and cheap rent—and Homer's got them both. In the green hills at the southwest end of the Kenai Peninsula, the town overlooks alpine peaks, glaciers, and steep-sided fjords; check your pulse for signs of life if you're not inspired. Cutting into the peninsula is **Kachemak Bay,** where you can spend a dreamy day fishing, boating, or bird-watching. But unlike many Alaskan towns, Homer is not just a base for exploring nearby marine and wilderness areas—the town itself is worth seeing. A small fishing village complete with coffee shops, art galleries, fine food, and a great local paper, Homer has a reputation as an artists' community and has attracted a creative, alternative-minded population. If it weren't for the view and the fishing, you'd think you had momentarily stepped out of Alaska.

Sadly, the secret is out, and Homer becomes something of a zoo in summer. The Homer Spit, a 4½-mile sandbar jutting into Kachemak Bay, is the hub of all the activity. Hundreds of campers pitch their tents in the sand here; it looks as if an army had hit the beaches. It's not just out-of-state tourists who wash up in Homer; the town is also a popular weekend retreat for Anchorage residents. In summer, year-round Homerites avoid the touristy spit and stay holed up in their quiet homes in the hills.

When you're not soaking up the atmosphere, get out on a boat in Kachemak Bay to fish or check out marine life. **Gull Rock,** a small rock island in the bay that's covered with birds on every inch, is a great photo op. You could also spend a day exploring the communities of **Seldovia** and **Halibut Cove** and the trails that wind through **Kachemak Bay State Park.** Homer hosts a few worthwhile festivals, including the **Spring Arts Festival** in April/May, with performances and exhibits by local artists, and the **Concert on the Lawn** in August, a day-long outdoor fête featuring local musicians.

BASICS The **Visitor Information Center** (tel. 907/235–5300), open daily 9–9, is on the spit before the first boardwalk. The center has camping information and a useful guide to visitor services. You can also get info at the **Chamber of Commerce** (tel. 907/235–7740) on Ocean Drive, or at the **Pratt Museum** (3779 Bartlett St., tel. 907/235–8635).

The **Alaska Maritime National Wildlife Refuge Visitor Center** has information on the coastal areas of Kachemak Bay. The very helpful staff offers a useful price list of the different boat tours. *202 W. Pioneer Ave., tel. 907/235–6546. Open daily 8:30–5.*

COMING AND GOING Homer lies at the end of the Sterling Highway, 220 miles south of Anchorage. The beautiful drive is often crowded with traffic, especially on weekends. Hitching is common, fairly safe, and easy, especially between Soldotna and Homer, a route well-traveled by locals. You'll find plenty of places to camp along the way if you can't get a ride. Also give the "bush line" at radio station KBBI a try; people frequently offer rides on the air in exchange for paying half the gas.

Radio station KBBI broadcasts a "bush line" where you can exchange messages with friends or ask for a ride on a private plane or boat. To leave a message, call 907/235–7721. You may not have any luck, but one woman got a plane ride all the way to Katmai National Park.

➤ **BY BUS** • **Homer and Seward Bus Lines** (455 Sterling Hwy., tel. 907/235–8280) shuttles you from Homer to Anchorage for $38, to Seward for $35; the bus will stop in Soldotna or Kenai upon request. Rides down to the spit cost $2 extra.

➤ **BY FERRY** • The ferry *Tustumena* sails weekly from Homer to Seldovia (3 hrs, $18), Kodiak (10 hrs, $48), and Seward (1½ days, $96), though this is a roundabout way to reach Seward. It also runs to the Aleutian Islands four times during summer. The local office is near the end of Homer Spit on the right. *Tel. 907/235–8449. Open weekdays 10–noon.*

➤ **BY PLANE** • If you're in a tizzy to get to Homer quickly, **ERA** (tel. 907/235–5205), **MarkAir** (tel. 907/235–5533), and **Southcentral Air** (tel. 907/235–6171) all fly from Anchorage for about $60 one-way. Smaller airlines with scheduled and charter flights to Seldovia,

Kechemak Bay, or Katmai National Park include **Gulf Air** (tel. 907/235–8591) and **Kachemak Air** (tel. 907/235–8924). The airport is off Lake Street, just north of Beluga Lake.

GETTING AROUND Getting around Homer is a little difficult on foot, because the two main areas—downtown and the spit—are about 5 miles apart. Three streets form the triangle of downtown: Pioneer Avenue, the Homer Bypass, and Lake Street. Pioneer has the biggest share of shops, art galleries, and restaurants. To help you scoot around, **Quiet Sports** (144 W. Pioneer Ave., tel. 907/235–8620) rents mountain bikes, including lock and helmet, for $12 per half day, $20 per full day. Homer Spit Road leads 5 miles out to the end of the Spit, where you'll find all the fishing, boating, and tourist action. If you lack wheels, hitchhiking is the only practical way to get between downtown and the spit (a taxi ride costs $10). Heading out from downtown, stand on Ocean Drive at the base of the spit, or on Homer Bypass or Lake Street before they intersect. Leaving the spit, stand anywhere on the roadside. Most traffic heads onto the spit in the morning and off in the evening.

WHERE TO SLEEP Most people camp in Homer, but the town has a wide range of lodging, from no-frills bunks to B&Bs. Most hotels are within walking distance of downtown. Get a complete B&B listing from the chamber of commerce, or book through a referral agency for no charge: Try **Homer Referral Agency** (tel. 907/235–8996, fax 907/235–2625), **All Points North Travel** (tel. 907/235–2575 or 800/770–2575 in AK), or **Central Charters** (tel. 907/235–7847, or 800/478–7847 in AK).

➢ **UNDER $60** • **Ocean Shores Motel.** Scattered over three grassy acres of oceanfront, this motel has standard rooms ($60, $50 with shared bath) that you can stuff as many people as you want into. Rooms with kitchenettes are $80, and rustic cabins (which have the best ocean view) go for $55. *3500 Crittenden Dr., tel. 907/235–7775. Just off Homer Bypass at Pioneer Ave. Wheelchair access.*

SunSpin Guesthouse. For breakfast and a cheap bunk ($22) downtown, you can't beat Randi Somers's clean and welcoming B&B. Doubles go for $50, and you can get a private bath and sauna (sweet), or an apartment for only $75. *358 E. Lee Dr., tel. 907/235–6677, or 800/391–6677 in AK. From Pioneer Ave., take Svedlund Dr. north, first right onto Lee Dr. 6 bunk beds, 3 rooms, 1 apartment. Free transport from airport. Wheelchair access. No credit cards.*

Driftwood Inn. Even with its new gray paint job, this hotel looks like it just washed ashore. Inside, though, you'll find a fireplace in the lobby and comfy upstairs rooms with shared bath ($68, $78 for bay view). The downstairs doubles ($74, $82 with view) have private baths. You can do cartwheels in the two huge rooms that sleep four or more ($100–$110). *135 W. Bunnel Ave., tel. 907/235–8019, or 800/478–8019 in AK. At Bishop's Beach, just off Main St. south of Homer Bypass. 21 rooms, 12 with bath. Kitchen, laundry. Wheelchair access downstairs.*

Heritage Hotel. Right downtown lies this quiet, unpretentious historic log hotel. Older rooms with dark wood paneling, sinks, and shared bath go for $65 in the thick of the tourist season (mid-June–mid-Aug.), and for as low as $40 in winter. Bigger, newer rooms with private bath cost $15 more. *147 E. Pioneer Ave., at Main St., tel. 907/235–7787, or 800/478–7789 in AK. 43 rooms, some with bath. Wheelchair access.*

➢ **UNDER $100** • **Land's End.** This beautiful resort sits at the very end of the Homer Spit, jutting out into Kachemak Bay. In summer, rooms with double beds cost $75, with twin beds $100; ocean views are extra. Even if you can't afford the rooms, stop in at the restaurant or bar to check out the fantastic view. *4786 Homer Spit Rd., tel. 907/235–0400. 63 rooms. Luggage storage. Wheelchair access.*

➢ **HOSTELS** • **Seaside Farm.** Small private cabins rent for $35–$50 and hostel-style bunks are $12, but most people crash on the lawn ($6 per tent). Travelers who show up with only seeds in their pockets are put to work in exchange for shelter. A large outdoor shed known as the "pavilion" is the big hangout: It's stocked with a functional TV, a VCR, a stove, and a

If you missed Woodstock, head to Seaside Farm. A visit to this working farm overlooking the ocean, where you can mingle with scores of transients like yourself, is an essential Homerian experience.

barbecue. You may want to avoid the sewage-water showers. *Mile 4.5, East End Rd., tel. 907/235–7850 or 907/235–2670. 5 mi from town (Pioneer Ave. turns into East End Rd.). Kitchen, shower $4. Open summer only (some cabins available year-round). No credit cards.*

➤ **CAMPING** • All over the peninsula you'll hear stories about the 5-mile, tent-spackled Homer Spit—summer home to tourists, cannery workers, and other temporary residents. Sites are exposed to the cold, wind, and rain (flee to the Salty Dawg Saloon for shelter; *see* After Dark, *below*), and theft is a problem. The tents lie close to the road, which is busy at all hours—a good thing, since you'll have to hitch the 3–5 miles into town. You can camp in any designated beach area for $3 a night or $30 for 14 days (pay next to the visitor center). You'll find water and rest rooms just off the road, and you can shower ($3.75) and do laundry (wash $2, dryer $1) at the well-worn **Homer Spit Campground** (3735 Homer Spit Rd., tel. 907/235–3160). For more information, stop at the visitor center or the harbormaster.

You can find more sheltered, woodsy sites ($3) with good views of the city below at the **Homer City Campground** (off Bartlett St.), but you'll miss out on the friendly camaraderie of the spit. The campground is about a mile north of downtown; from Pioneer Avenue, go north on Bartlett Street and left on Fairview, and you'll see it on the right. Don't forget to check out the $6 tent sites at the Seaside Farm (*see* Hostels, *above*), where there's always room for one more.

FOOD Homer has plenty of excellent, reasonably priced restaurants, including a few with peninsula-wide reputations—Fresh Sourdough Express, Café Cups, and Smoky Bay. For groceries and a salad bar, go to the **Eagle Quality Center** (436 Sterling Hwy., tel. 907/235–2408), open 24 hours. Fast food is served up daily 11–8 on the spit at **Glacier Drive-In** (3789 Homer Spit Rd., tel. 907/235–7145), but when it's this cheap (burgers $3) it's gotta be greasy. The best breakfast deal is at the **Kachemak Bowl** (672 East End Rd., tel. 907/235–8666), a bowling alley that serves a whomping stack of stellar sourdough pancakes ($4.50); if you can clean your plate, you should be on TV.

If your head aches for a caffeine fix and heavyweight conversation, head to Latitude 59° (Lakeside Mall, on Lake St. off Pioneer Rd., tel. 907/235–5935). You can have your coffee whipped up two dozen ways (75¢–$4).

➤ **UNDER $5** • **Smoky Bay Co-operative.** This natural-foods store carries organic produce, healthy desserts, and Ben and Jerry's ice cream (well, it's natural). At the counter you can pick up cheap, filling vegetarian entrées, soup, and good coffee (breakfast and lunch only). Most of all, it's a great place to hang out and meet people. Check the bulletin board outside for events, rides, and messages. *248 W. Pioneer Ave., at Bartlett St., tel. 907/235–7252. Open weekdays 8–8, Sat. 8:30–7, Sun. 10–6.*

Two Sisters Espresso-Bakery. While the tourists mob Sourdough Express, steal away to this small, woman-run café. Relax over a potent latte ($2) and a freshly baked cookie ($1) as you watch the cooks hand-knead dough for their orgasmic pizza ($3). Save room for chocolate cheesecake ($2.75) or tasty soup and sandwiches. *106 W. Bunnell Ave., tel. 907/235–2280. Opposite Driftwood Inn (see Where to Sleep, above). Open daily 8–6.*

➤ **UNDER $15** • **Café Cups.** This homey downtown restaurant has an artsy, laid-back atmosphere and delicious food. It's a little pricey (dinner entrées run $10–$18) and the service is slow, but you can still get a good deal: The early bird breakfast (7–9 AM) of two eggs, home fries, and toast is $3; and scrumptious sandwiches like the Mediterranean (olive tapenade, garlic, eggplant, tomatoes, and provolone) and the spinach-nut-veggie burger go for $6.50 at lunch. Sit inside for art and conversation, outside for cribbage and chess. *162 Pioneer Ave., across from library, tel. 907/235–8330. Wheelchair access. Open daily 7 AM–10 PM.*

Fresh Sourdough Express Bakery and Restaurant. This restaurant started out as a bakery van and soon became famous for its sourdough bread; now it's mobbed all summer. The organic food's delicious, if a bit expensive: Try the all-you-can-eat breakfast ($8), sourdough sandwiches ($6–$7), or the excellent desserts. You can take home a loaf of their famous non-fat bread for $3. *1316 Ocean Dr., at base of spit, tel. 907/235–7571. Wheelchair access. Open summer, daily 7 AM–10 PM; winter, daily 8 AM–4 PM.*

Neon Coyote. For something hot 'n' spicy, head to the rear entrance of this nondescript restaurant and order one of the best Mexican meals you'll find this far north. They serve choice huevos rancheros ($5.75) and chicken and cheese enchiladas ($8). Salads ($3.50–$7); sandwiches, including the excellent grilled chicken pita ($7.50); burgers ($5–$7); and fish 'n' chips round out the menu. *435 E. Pioneer Ave., tel. 907/235-6226. Open weekdays 10–8:30, Sat. 10–6.*

WORTH SEEING Because so many artists live in Homer, this Alaskan town feels positively hip and free-spirited. Take a stroll through the small, free galleries downtown to check out what the muse hath wrought. All carry the free guide *Downtown Homer Art Galleries.* Two of the best are **Bunnell Street Gallery** (106 W. Bunnell Ave., across from Driftwood Inn, tel. 907/235-2662) and **Ptarmigan Arts** (471 Pioneer Ave., tel. 907/235-5345).

Don't leave without checking out the **Pratt Museum,** whose beautiful displays include marine aquariums, natural history exhibits, and local artwork. The highlight is the downstairs exhibit "Darkened Waters—Profile of an Oil Spill," an honest, moving depiction of the 1989 *Exxon Valdez* spill. While you're here, pick up tourist information about Homer. *3779 Bartlett St., at Pioneer Ave., tel. 907/235-8635. Admission: $3, $2 students. Open May–Sept., daily 10–6; Oct.–Dec. and Feb.–Apr., Tues.–Sun. noon–5.*

The **Homer Spit,** a 4½-mile arm of sand and gravel, is one of the world's longest natural spits and the hub of the town's tourist trade and fishing industry. In Small Boat Harbor at the end of the spit, you'll find Homer's 700-boat fishing fleet, fish canneries, and a few touristy souvenir shops and restaurants. Worn wooden boardwalks connect clusters of buildings. Check around to see if any trophy-size halibut, weighing several hundred pounds, are on display—they're quite a sight. With a license you can fish off the end of the spit or in the "fishing hole," a small lagoon stocked with pink, silver, and king salmon. Buy a license and rent gear at the **Homer Rental Center** (on the spit, tel. 907/235-2617); poles go for $10 a day. Otherwise, join the hordes for some clamming or beachcombing, or rent a horse from **Trails End Horseback** (tel. 907/235-6393) and head up into the hills; a four-hour ride is $65.

CHEAP THRILLS Homer is so beautiful that it's fun just to hop in a car and take a drive along some the scenic roads. **East End Road,** which starts out as Pioneer Avenue, heads east from downtown and winds along the coast for miles, ending at some remote villages. **Skyline Drive** follows the ridges above town, offering fantastic views of the spit and Kachemak Bay; you can get there from East Hill Road (off East End Rd.) or West Hill Road (off Sterling Hwy.).

AFTER DARK If you want to spend your nights with hard-drinking fishermen, head for the **Salty Dawg Saloon,** about 4 miles up the spit. Housed in a historic wood-shingled building with a mini-lighthouse on top, the dimly lit, low-ceilinged bar features live music several nights a week. **Pier One Theatre** (Pier One warehouse, tel. 907/235-7333), next to the fishing hole midway down the Spit, has excellent summer performances. The show starts at 7:15 Thursdays and Sundays, 8:15 Fridays and Saturdays; call ahead for tickets ($8–$9) or buy them at several places around town, including Latitude 59° (*see* Food, *above*).

OUTDOOR ACTIVITIES One fine way to spend a day is puttering around in Kachemak Bay, with its stunning views of glaciers, mountains, and marine wildlife. Don't let the huge number of boat-tour operators bewilder you; the U.S. Fish and Wildlife Service and the **Alaska Maritime National Wildlife Refuge** (*see* Basics, *above*) have a list to help you compare prices and destinations. **Dano Gregg** will be your water taxi, your mountain-biking guide, your drinking buddy, you name it—and he'll beat any other charter's price. The easiest way to track Dano down is by leaving a message for him on the bush line (tel. 907/235-7721), or try his cellular phone (tel. 907/399-3009).

If you want to spend some time outdoors, Dano's the man. Dano Gregg migrates back to Homer for the months of May to October every year to live out of his three vans on the spit and take visitors around the Bay in his skiffs.

The **Center for Alaskan Coastal Studies** (book through Rainbow Tours, tel. 907/235-7272) is a nonprofit educational organization that offers an all-day trip to Peterson Bay for $49, where a naturalist will help you explore tide pools and forest areas. Bring lunch, rubber boots, warm duds, and rain gear. Rainbow Tours also offers a $10, 90-minute cruise to Gull Island (a seabird rookery) and a tour of Seldovia for $36 round-trip. A number of other companies offer short trips around Gull Island or to the villages across the bay; contact **Central Charters** (tel. 907/235–7847) to book a spot on a tour boat.

True North Kayak Adventures (contact Central Charters, *see above*) will give you a personal one-day kayak tour of Kachemak Bay—even if you don't know the foggiest about what to do. Bring your rain gear and $140 for equipment, instruction, lunch, and a water taxi. **Kayak'atak** (tel. 907/234–7425) and several rental outfits in Halibut Cove (again, contact Central Charters) will entrust their kayaks to experienced paddlers for $45 (single) or $70 (double). Reserve a kayak in advance. **Discovery Adventures** (tel. 907/235–6942) gives three-hour guided canoe trips around Homer for $54 and day trips on the peninsula for $73. You can rent canoes here for about $18 a day.

NEAR HOMER

HALIBUT COVE A little village on Ismailof Island, Halibut Cove is home in summer to about 150 people, mostly fishermen and artists. Although touristy, the town is still charming. All the houses are built on stilts over the water, with boardwalks running between them. A couple of hours is plenty to see the island. Look for quiet beaches and trails in the interior and far side. The **Phenomenal Trees Walk** is a short, pretty trail (phenomenal might be pushing it) through the woods to a bluff overlooking the bay. The town's three **art galleries** include one displaying Diana Tillion's paintings, done with octopus ink. The food is superb but pricey at the **Saltry** (tel. 907/296–2223)—dinner (served 4–9) will cost you about $25. Lunch (served noon–4) may be more realistic: Homemade soup, organic salad, fresh baked bread, and creamy cheesecake go for around $10. Make reservations. The boat *Danny J.* makes a noon trip to Halibut Cove ($35) with a stop at Gull Island, and an evening trip ($17.50) to eat at the Saltry. Book through Central Charters (tel. 907/235–7847 or 800/478–7847 in AK).

KACHEMAK BAY STATE PARK Whether you mountain bike, hike into the mountains and glaciers, ski, or stick to the shore to explore tide pools, Kachemak Bay State Park is well worth the trip. In the bay itself, you're likely to spot whales, sea otters, seals, and the occasional bald eagle circling overhead. Most of the poorly maintained trails that run through the park cover steep, rugged terrain. The **Grewingk Glacier Trail** is the exception—an easy 7-mile (round-trip) trek that starts near the Rusty Lagoon Campground and offers fabulous views of Grewingk Glacier. In 1994, the Forest Service also cleaned up the trail to **Poot Peak**. Climbing the 2,600-foot peak is still dangerous in wet weather, though, since the shifting scree (rock debris)

Kenai National Wildlife Refuge

Dall sheep, caribou, moose, and waterfowl roam these two million acres of wetlands and forests, which cover the western Kenai peninsula (north to Turnagain Arm and south to Kachemak Bay). You can often see the wild things as you drive by on the Sterling Highway from Homer, Kenai, or Soldotna, but the best way to meet them is by venturing into the refuge itself. You'll find campsites and about 200 miles of hiking trails, some through wet and swampy lowlands. There are two long canoe trails, the 80-mile Swanson River Route and the 60-mile Swan Lake Route, each of which takes about a week to complete. If you have the money, you can charter a plane or boat into the remote areas. For information, contact the Kenai Wildlife Refuge Visitor Center (tel. 907/262–7021) in Soldotna. The center is up in the hills on Ski Hill Road, off K-Beach Road near the junction with the Sterling Highway.

is slippery. The 7-mile round-trip (6–7 hr) hike begins at Halibut Cove Lagoon. You can choose from several primitive campsites in the park—be aware that the weather is extremely variable. For more info, contact the **Homer Ranger Station** (tel. 907/235–7024) or **Alaska State Parks, Kenai Area** (tel. 907/262–5581). You reach the park by boat or plane; snag a water taxi (2 daily, $50 round-trip) through **Central Charters** (tel. 907/235–7847), or give Dano a buzz (*see* Outdoor Activities, in Homer, *above*).

The beautiful view you've been gawking at across the bay from Homer is of Kachemak Bay State Park, a 250,000-acre wilderness of glaciers, mountains, and jagged coast.

SELDOVIA One of the oldest settlements on Cook Inlet, Seldovia once thrived as a fur-trading post, fox-farming area, and center for a booming herring and salmon industry. Today, the quiet town makes an excellent day trip from Homer. Much of Seldovia was destroyed by the '64 earthquake, but a small remaining section of the old boardwalk, as well as the town's back roads, preserves the look of an earlier Seldovia. The **Otterbahn Trail** is a short, easy walk from the back of town to scenic Outside Beach, where you can camp. To stay the night, try **Annie McKenzie's Boardwalk Hotel** (tel. 907/234–7816) or **Crow Hill B&B** (tel. 907/234–7410). The best food is at the **Kachemak Kafé** (907/234–7494).

To get to Seldovia, take the state ferry (tel. 907/235–8449), which runs across the bay from Homer most Wednesdays and some Tuesdays ($32 round-trip). Several private companies, including **Kachemak Bay Adventures** (tel. 907/235–8206), **Rainbow Tours** (tel. 907/235–7272), and **Central Charters** (tel. 907/235–7847) run boats more frequently for $35–$40. All the tours give you about two hours ashore.

Kodiak Island

When the spring rains have greened the mountains and stark valleys, Kodiak looks like a tropical island that has lost its way in the northern Gulf of Alaska, 250 miles southwest of Anchorage and almost 100 miles off the Kenai Peninsula. Kodiak, Afognak, and several smaller islands form a 5,000-square-mile archipelago of rough coastal and mountain terrain. About half of the island's 15,500 residents live in the town of **Kodiak**; the rest are scattered along the nearby roads or in coastal villages. Most of the island is still untamed wilderness, refuge to the huge Kodiak brown bear and an abundance of plant and wildlife; in the bays around the island, sea otters, porpoises, and sea lions mate and proliferate. The few roads are centered around the town of Kodiak, so access to remote areas is only possible by boat or float plane. The weather year-round is cool and mild, though it's foggy or soggy much of the time.

Odd as it may seem, the Moonies (the Unification Church) are a huge presence in Kodiak. They own lodges, charter boats, and canneries, including the mega-cannery International Seafood. Some locals laud them as model citizens, but others say they try to induce the town's sleep-deprived workers to join the cult/religion.

Kodiak's abundant natural resources have long supported a thriving human population. The first settlers arrived over 7,000 years ago, and by the Koniag period (AD 1200–1800), a highly developed society had formed, with 10,000–15,000 natives living in dozens of coastal villages. When Russian fur traders arrived in the late 18th century, they nearly wiped out the native population through war, slavery, and disease. In 1792, the Russian colony moved from Three Saints Bay to the protected waters of St. Paul Harbor, where the town of Kodiak now sits. Kodiak still bears evidence of Russian influence, from archaeological ruins to the Russian Orthodox Church downtown.

In the succeeding decades, Kodiak had a rocky, colorful history, undergoing its share of booms and declines. In 1912, the mainland volcano Mt. Katmai erupted, covering Kodiak in ash and blacking out the island for over 60 hours. During World War II, Kodiak became the command center for America's Aleutian Campaign and was fortified against attack with gun emplacements and concrete bunkers, some of which remain today. Crab fishing boomed after the war,

Cannery Row: Working the Slime Line

Working in a salmon cannery is a popular endeavor for students looking to make money over the summer break, and chronic travelers seeking seasonal work. You must be a U.S. citizen or have a green card to work the canneries; no special skills are needed for this labor-intensive industry, but you should be aware of some things before you commit yourself to cannery row.

- **The work is a bitch.** You should be in great health before you start and expect to have ruined it by the end of salmon season. Many canneries have only one work shift, so when salmon deliveries are made you have to work incredibly long hours—a 20-hour shift with only four hours off is not unusual. (You get breaks about every two hours and a half-hour break every four.) In canneries with two shifts, you work 12 hours on and then 12 hours off as long as the fish keep coming. The cannery usually provides free coffee in the break room, but a lot of workers pop amphetamines to keep themselves going. And you sign a contract when you start, so quitting in the middle of the job could be a legal hassle.

- **The pay can suck.** Base pay for cannery workers is usually just a few dollars over minimum wage. But you can still make a lot of money—as much as $3,000—if the salmon run is good and you work a lot of overtime. You'll be so exhausted after work, you won't have the strength to go out and blow your paycheck. If the salmon run is small, there may be no work and hence no money.

- **Rent is a rip-off.** If you insist on having a roof over your head, you may lose all your hard-earned money to a greedy landlord. You're better off camping, although the nearest campground could be far—a real bummer after a 20-hour shift. Some towns have ordinances that ban camping near the cannery, but you can often skirt the law if you're careful. Look for good tree cover or some other feature that will hide your tent from the eyes of the law.

- **You'll hate their guts.** If you've never worked in a cannery, chances are you'll get the lowliest job—working the slime line. This is just as horrible as it sounds; it involves gutting the fish, although some aspects of the grisly process are now automated. You will be issued waterproof pants, jacket, boots, and gloves that are supposed to keep you dry and reasonably clean as you spend hundreds of repetitive hours deveining, beheading, or degilling fish. The rain gear, as it's called, does a pretty good job, although there's nothing to protect you from getting fish guts all over your face. And don't think you won't smell like a fish—wear only clothing you can throw out when the season is over.

- **Beware of dragger-processors.** The prison ships of the fishing fleet, dragger-processors are large behemoths that net and process fish. If you think working in a land-based cannery is bad, try doing the same job at sea when you can't leave even if you want to. Dragger-processors are often at sea for a month or more, and you're trapped like a sockeye in a gill net.

interrupted only by the disastrous earthquake of 1964, which destroyed 40% of the town's business district and cost millions in damage. Once again, Kodiak was rebuilt, and it now has a huge fishing fleet of more than 2,000 boats.

People who grow up on Kodiak Island are called "rock children." They're not crusty urchins as the name implies, just people in closer touch with the earth than most of us.

To the visitor, the town of Kodiak may seem inconsequential, a mere foothold on the vast, wild island. But things are changing. The native lands, which comprise much of the undeveloped territory outside Kodiak National Wildlife Refuge, are steadily being logged. And business is growing as Kodiak vies to replace Anchorage as the tourist and trade center of south central Alaska. The bustle of the dock and harbor now spills into the business district nearby, and the hills hold a growing residential area. Today, Kodiak is still wild, remote, and beautiful, but in 10 or 20 years all that may have changed.

BASICS

AMERICAN EXPRESS This office does the whole financial and travel-service shtick. *202 Center Ave., tel. 907/486–6084. Open weekdays 8:30–5:30, Sat. 10–3.*

EMPLOYMENT OFFICE To hook up with work in the canneries, or other work around Kodiak, head here. *309 Center Ave. tel. 907/486–3105. Btw Rezanof Dr. W. and Mill Bay Rd. Open weekdays 9–5.*

LAUNDRY AND SHOWERS **Ernie's Laundromat and Showers** is downtown across from the boat harbor. Showers cost $3.25; you pay $1.50 to wash your clothes and 25¢ for a spin in the dryer. *218 Shelikof St., tel. 907/486–4119. Open summer, Mon.–Sat. 8 AM–10 PM, Sun. 8–8; winter, daily 8–8.*

VISITOR INFORMATION The **Visitor Information Center** is at the end of Center Street, along with the ferry terminal and the chamber of commerce. Here you can find out about sights, camping, and hotels, as well as boat and air charters. Pick up the free and comprehensive *Kodiak Visitor's Guide. 100 Marine Way, tel. 907/486–4782, fax 907/486–6545. Open weekdays 9–5, weekends 10–3.*

The **Alaska State Park Office, Kodiak District,** in Ft. Abercrombie State Historic Park, arranges use of the group recreation area at Abercrombie and the wilderness cabins on Shuyak Island. The staff also conducts historical walking tours and naturalist programs several times a week. Check out the videos and photos of the World War II Aleutian Campaign. *Tel. 907/486–6339. Open weekdays 8–noon and 1–5.*

The **Kodiak National Wildlife Refuge Visitor Center** has information on hiking, wildlife, cabins, private lodges, and air and boat charters in the refuge. Chat with the helpful staff before heading out in the wilderness; they give out loads of advice—including info on where the bears are. The center itself has some beautiful displays, including a giant relief map of the island group and films about Kodiak. *1390 Buskin River Rd., tel. 907/487–2600. 4 mi west of downtown and ¾ mi from airport. Open weekdays 8–4:30, weekends noon–4:30.*

COMING AND GOING

BY FERRY The ferry *Tustumena* makes the 10-hour run weekly from Kodiak to Homer ($48), Seward ($54), Valdez ($98), Cordova ($98), and nearby Port Lions ($20). Service halts four times during summer when the ferry makes a week-long trip to the Aleutians, leaving from Kodiak and heading to Dutch Harbor; the round-trip journey costs $400. Check the ferry schedule to avoid getting stuck in Kodiak for a week. *100 Marine Way, at Center St., tel. 907/486–3800. Open weekdays 8–5.*

BY PLANE Flying to Kodiak costs more than traveling by ferry but is (obviously) faster. **MarkAir** (tel. 800/478–0800) and **ERA** (tel. 800/426–0333) fly several times a day between Anchorage and Kodiak. The regular fare is $282 round-trip, but if you buy a ticket 14 days in advance and stay over on Saturday night, it's only $174. You pay about the same for this restricted fare as you would to go by bus from Anchorage to Homer and then by ferry to Kodiak, so if you don't care about seeing the Kenai Peninsula, flying is the way to go. MarkAir also has an unlisted fare of $80 on flights from Homer to Kodiak that go via Anchorage, but you have to ask to get it. The Kodiak airport is 5 miles southwest of downtown, off Rezanof Drive. The **Airporter Shuttle** (tel. 907/486–7583) runs between the airport and downtown for $5.

Air is the main way to reach the Kodiak National Wildlife Refuge, neighboring islands, and native villages. The best deals going are the $99 mail flights offered by MarkAir (*see above*)—significantly cheaper than chartering a flight at $400 an hour. For your money, you'll fly for two–three hours, visiting several small communities for a brief stint as their mail is dropped off; after the work is done your pilot may do a little flightseeing and bear-watching with you. Air charters include **Uyak Air Service** (tel. 907/486–3407), **Island Air Service** (tel. 907/486–6196), and **Pen Air** (tel. 907/487–4014). Bad weather often delays flights.

GETTING AROUND

Kodiak the town sits on the northeast corner of Kodiak the island. To the north are the small islands of Afognak and Shuyak; to the southwest stretches the rest of Kodiak Island, including the Kodiak National Wildlife Refuge and several small coastal villages. Only 100 miles of road (largely unpaved) cover Kodiak. The main road, **Rezanof Drive,** heads northeast from downtown Kodiak to Ft. Abercrombie 4 miles away. **Pasagshak Bay Road** begins at Mile 30 of the **Chiniak Highway** (the main thoroughfare from town to the west coast, most of which is unpaved), and leads 16 miles to a campground and the Fossil Cliffs. The only other road is a 12-mile scenic drive to Anton Larsen Bay, beginning at Mile 4.7 of Rezanof Drive West. Out of town, the land along these roads is mostly undeveloped and uninhabited. Downtown Kodiak is easily walkable. Center Street runs from Rezanof Drive south to the ferry dock; just to the west, **Marine Way** begins at Rezanof and curves around the harbor to intersect with Center. The area in between is jammed with shops and restaurants, many hidden in the alleys of the "mall."

If you want to explore Kodiak Island and have a stomach of steel, ask around at the docks to see if you can bum a ride on a tender boat, which makes two- to three-day excursions to pick up fish from boats around the island.

BY CAR If you can't afford to fly (*see* Coming and Going, *above*), renting a car is the next-best way to see Kodiak's wilderness. **Rent-a-Heap** (tel. 907/486–5200), not surprisingly, has the cheapest cars around ($27 a day plus 27¢ a mile). **Budget** (tel. 907/486–5815) charges $30 a day plus 28¢ a mile. For long-distance driving, get a $45 rental with unlimited mileage from **National** (tel. 907/456–4751).

BY BIKE Kodiak is an awesome place to explore on a mountain bike. You can rent one for $20 a day at **Elkay's Bicycle Shop** (Rezanof Dr., near Center St., tel. 907/486–4219), open Monday–Saturday 10–6.

WHERE TO SLEEP

Most hotels and B&Bs are downtown, within walking distance of the ferry dock. Options are limited, so it's wise to make a reservation. The visitor center has a list of about 10 B&Bs in Kodiak, most offering doubles for $55 or more. **Kodiak Bed and Breakfast** (308 Cope St., tel. 907/486–5367), run by Mary Monroe in her modern, single-story house, is highly recommended and within walking distance of downtown. Singles are $60, doubles $72. If it's full, the more frou-frou **Country Bed and Breakfast** (1415 Zentner Ave., 1 mi from town, tel. 907/486–5162) has similar rates. The friendly owners, Ken and Sally Van Dyke, will give you a free lift from the ferry or airport. At all costs, avoid the grungy **Kodiak Star Motel** (119 Yukon St.).

Unfortunately, campgrounds lie 2–4 miles from downtown and are definitely no fun to reach without a car. Most transients and cannery workers camp at Gibson Cove (*see below*), the closest grounds to downtown and the canneries. Also check the message board outside **Kraft's Gro-**

cery Store (111 Rezanof Dr., tel. 907/486–5761); sometimes people advertise their cheap rooms or $10 bunk beds here.

Shelikof Lodge. The rooms are clean but stuffy and smell of smoke. Ask to see a few first, because size varies a lot. Singles are $60, doubles $65, and triples $70. You can buy a tasty meal or a stiff drink downstairs at the Fox Inn bar and restaurant. *211 Thorsheim St., tel. 907/486–4141. Off Lower Mill Bay Rd. behind McDonald's. 38 rooms.*

Buskin River Inn. This comfortable place is an excellent alternative to the Westmark Hotel downtown, with friendly service, large rooms, and views of the woods and river. Costly doubles go for $110 and singles are $100. The airport locale is inconvenient unless you're waiting for connecting flights. The hotel restaurant, Eagle's Nest, is getting increasingly popular. *1395 Airport Way, tel. 907/487–2700 or 800/544–2202. 5 mi southwest of downtown, off Rezanof Dr. 51 rooms. Laundry, luggage storage. Wheelchair access.*

WILDERNESS CABINS Kodiak **National Wildlife Refuge** (1390 Buskin River Rd., Kodiak 99615, tel. 907/487–2600) rents out nine rustic four-bunk cabins right on the refuge for only $25 per night, with a maximum stay of seven days. The cabins are assigned by lottery; write for an application and return it by January 2 for April–June dates, and by April 1 for July–September dates. **Alaska State Parks, Kodiak District** (SR Box 3800, Kodiak 99615, tel. 907/486–6339) rents out four cabins on Shuyak Island, a beautiful kayaking spot 54 miles north of Kodiak. Each cabin has eight bunks and costs $25 per person per night. Write for an application; reservations are accepted up to six months before the rental date. **Afognak Adventures** (tel. 907/486–6014) keeps three rustic cabins on Afognak Island, 30 miles north of Kodiak. The cabins sleep up to six and cost $50 a night; you might be able to stay free in early summer before they're ready for rental. For a complete list of private cabin rentals and wilderness lodges, contact the visitor center or the chamber of commerce (*see* Visitor Information, *above*).

CAMPING Kodiak is loaded with good campgrounds, but all except one lie several miles from downtown. For information on state campgrounds, contact **Alaska State Parks** (tel. 907/486–6339); for the city campground, contact **City of Kodiak, Parks and Recreation** (tel. 907/486–8103). All campgrounds have water and pit toilets. If you're broke, head about 5 miles out of town in any direction to open, undeveloped land, but remember that much of the land near the road is private or owned by Native Americans.

Buskin River State Recreation Site. This place ranks a distant second to Ft. Abercrombie (*see below*). The 18 campsites ($6, 14-day limit) are more like exposed gravel lots, but nearby Buskin River and the beach are pretty picnic sites and popular places to fish. *4½ mi southwest of town off Rezanof Dr., just past Refuge Visitor Center.*

Ft. Abercrombie State Historic Park. Next to the remnants of a World War II naval gun emplacement, these beautiful tents-only sites ($6) are hidden in the woods away from the road. No reservations are taken, but there should be space. Foot trails follow the coast to Miller Point, where you can spy whales and sea otters. Trails also circle trout-filled Gertrude Lake. *The Cry of the Wild Ram,* Alaska's longest-running play, is performed in an amphitheater in this park every August. *Tel. 907/486–6339. 4 mi northeast of town, off Rezanof Dr.*

Gibson Cove Transient Worker Campground. Kodiak's only long-term camping area is inhabited mostly by cannery workers. There's little privacy, lots of camaraderie, and cheap rent ($3 a night per person). Near the gravel sites (some with wooden platforms), trails lead to a pretty beach or up into the hills, so you can temporarily escape the smell of fish. Amenities are decent; you get proper rest rooms with hot showers. *Off Rezanof Dr., 2 mi southwest of downtown. As road rises to a crest, turn on unmarked gravel road.*

Pasagshak River State Recreation Site. Forty miles from town on Pasagshak Road, seven free, primitive sites (14-day limit) line a gorgeous, rugged coastline. Potable water is available. This area is used mostly as a fishing and picnicking spot.

FOOD

Wander down Center Street or through the mall for a look at your choices—plenty of fast food and cheap, mediocre restaurants. Big grocery stores include **Kraft's** downtown and **Safeway** on

Mill Bay Road. You can sip a high-priced latte ($2.50) and munch on quiche ($5.75) at the stuffy **Harborside Coffee and Goods** (Shelikof Ave., tel. 907/486–5862) across from St. Paul Harbor. The best restaurant in town is the pricey **2nd Floor Restaurant** (116 W. Rezanof Dr., above Peking Restaurant, tel. 907/486–8555), where a superb plate of fresh sushi goes for $16–$24. You won't find many locals here—they've had enough of raw fish.

Beryl's. A family crowd feeds on staples like hamburgers ($5), sandwiches ($4.45–$5.45), and ice cream. The vegetarian garden burger ($6.25) is divine. Sip an espresso for $1.50, or be bold and go for the ice cream sundae ($2.50). *202 Center St., tel. 907/486–3323. In alley next to First National Bank. Wheelchair access. Open weekdays 6:30–6 and weekends 8:30–6.*

If you swing by the old Russian Orthodox Church (Mission Rd., tel. 907/486–3854), ask if the sisters are holding any public dinners. Every so often they rustle up an excellent, all-you-can-eat Russian meal in the church basement for less than $10.

Henry's. This classy bar (by Alaskan standards) has a multi-page menu offering everything from chicken chow mein ($7.50) to excellent hamburgers ($5.75). Fishermen regularly fill up here before heading out to sea. *512 Marine Way, in the central mall, tel. 907/486–3313. Wheelchair access. Open 11 AM–midnight.*

Road's End. The food here is much better than anything in town, but you have to drive 40 miles to get it. Try a thick steak, or the breakfast special of two eggs, sausage, toast, and hash browns ($3.75), while looking out over hills and beach. It's well worth the trip—you can even spend the night in a room upstairs for $60. *Mile 42, Chiniak Hwy., tel. 907/486–2885. 40 mi southwest of downtown; Rezanof Dr. turns into Chiniak Hwy. Wheelchair access. Open 7 AM–10 PM.*

WORTH SEEING

The **Alutiq Archaeological Repository Center** (215 Mission Rd.) is a new museum and archaeological research center funded by the *Exxon Valdez* oil spill settlement. Doors will open on June 1, 1995; inquire at the visitor center for current info.

ALUTIQ CULTURE CENTER This small but expanding museum was established to preserve the culture of Kodiak's Native Americans. The carefully prepared displays of books, photographs, and artifacts—including an excellent exhibit on kayaks—offer a native perspective that is decidedly lacking in the other museums. Local archaeologists may be on hand to answer questions about their work. *Rezanof Center, 214 W. Rezanof Dr., tel. 907/486–1992. Admission free. Open weekdays 9–5.*

BARANOV MUSEUM This museum lies inside the historic Erskine House. Built in 1808, the structure was used as a warehouse for otter pelts by both the Russian-American and Alaska Commercial companies, and later it became a family home. Today, the museum holds a small, extremely well displayed collection of archives and historical artifacts, including Alutiq bone pieces and grass baskets, and Russian samovars, icons, coins, and trading beads. Notice, though, how the museum never mentions the Russians' slaughter of the natives. *101 Marine Way, at Center Ave., tel. 907/486–5920. Admission: $2. Open summer, weekdays 10–4, weekends noon–4; winter, Mon.–Wed., Fri. 11–3, Sat. noon–3. Closed Feb.*

HOLY RESURRECTION ORTHODOX CHURCH Founded in 1794, the church dates from the original Russian colony on Kodiak. It's had several face-lifts and renovations over the years, but the original exterior cupolas and the interior iconographic decoration remain. To see the interior, attend a regular church service or pop by and see if the door is open. *Mission Rd., tel. 907/486–3854. Services Thurs. 7:30 PM, Sat. 6:30 PM, Sun. 9:30 AM.*

KODIAK NATIONAL WILDLIFE REFUGE Encompassing 1,865,000 acres, the refuge takes up two-thirds of Kodiak Island, plus small parts of Uganik and Afognak islands. No roads lead into the area—you get here only by float plane or boat (*see* Coming and Going, *above*), so most visitors never see it. The refuge overflows with wildlife; most impressive, it's home to the Kodiak bear, the largest living carnivore on earth. In fact, the refuge began in 1941 as an effort to protect the bear (as well as other species). Some 2,500 of them live on the island; they grow to 1,200 pounds and are an awe-inspiring sight. The refuge is open to hiking, camping, and fishing. You can also rent one of nine recreational cabins (*see* Where to Sleep, *above*). Local air services run chartered flights and scheduled bear-watching flights over the refuge. Check with the Wildlife Refuge Visitor Center (*see* Visitor Information, *above*) before you head out. The rangers can give you up-to-date info on the best areas to hike and spot bears, and clue you in on special preparations.

VENIAMINOV MUSEUM Few tourists know about this museum, hidden in St. Herman's Theological Seminary. It houses an extensive and intriguing collection of Russian Orthodox artifacts—Alutiq-style church objects and vestments, books, and an excellent set of icons—all of which document a blending of Russian and native cultures. *414 Mission Rd., tel. 907/486–3524. 3 blocks west of Center Ave. Admission free. Open in summer by appointment; call at least 24 hrs in advance.*

CHEAP THRILLS

One of the best (and cheapest) ways to see Kodiak Island is to rent a car and get out of town. **Chiniak Highway** is a beautiful 42-mile drive along the coast, with plenty of hiking, picnic, and fishing spots along the way, and an old World War II airstrip and military bunkers at the end. At Mile 30 is the turnoff for **Pasagshak Bay Road,** a 17-mile scenic drive that passes a campground and picnic area before reaching the **Fossil Cliffs** (accessible only at low tide) at the end of the road. You can dig for fossilized ivory and tools that were used hundreds of years ago, or find them lying on the sands of **Fossil Beach.** Plan on a day to cover both roads.

Geologocally speaking, Kodiak is eroding. Meanwhile, frenzied archaeologists from all over are quickly trying to bag whatever fossils they can find before they go under water.

You can always join Kodiak locals in one of their kooky annual events: the **King Crab Festival** in May includes a carnival and the world's only "Survival Suit Race," and the **Pillar Mountain Golf Tournament,** in late March, features a par-70 golf course with just one hole, which runs up the side of the entire mountain. For more info, contact the chamber of commerce (*see* Visitor Information, *above*).

AFTER DARK

They say Alaskan towns are all bars and churches—Kodiak is a little weak on churches, but you'll find bars aplenty in or near the mall. The **Mecca** (302 Marine Way, tel. 907/486–3364), known as a major meat market, has music and dancing most nights and gets pretty wild. For a friendly, mellower atmosphere and local gossip head to either **The Village** (tel. 907/486–3412) or **Henry's** (tel. 907/486–3313), both in the mall. You can always catch a (sort of) first-run movie at the **Orpheum Theater** (102 Center Ave., tel. 907/486–5449) for $5.

The Cry of the Wild Ram is a historical drama about Alexander Baranov (1747–1819), a major figure in Russian-controlled Alaska who helped found the Russian colony and build up the fur trade on Kodiak in the 1790s. The play, which Kodiak locals have performed annually since 1966, is staged outdoors at the Frank Brink Amphitheater at Ft. Abercrombie, overlooking Monashka Bay. See it on weekend nights at 8 in early to mid-August. *Kodiak Arts Council, tel. 907/486–5291. Tickets: $15 reserved, $12 regular, $10 students.*

OUTDOOR ACTIVITIES

HIKING Trails in Kodiak are poorly marked, rarely maintained, and difficult to follow, but they cover some gorgeous territory. Get a list of trails and advice from the Visitor Information Center or the Kodiak National Wildlife Refuge Visitor Center (*see above*), or visit **Backcountry Sports** (2102 Mill Bay Rd., tel. 907/486–3771) Monday–Saturday 10–7 for hiking info, topos, and camping equipment and rentals. One recommended trail is **Pillar Mountain,** starting at the top of Pillar Mountain Road and descending steeply down the mountain's southwest side for 4 miles. The difficult but well-marked **Barometer Mountain Trail** leads 5 miles up to the summit of Barometer Mountain, where you get phenomenal views of the island; the trailhead is on a small road that leads off Chiniak Highway just behind the airport runway. **Near Island Trail** is an easy meander through the woods and beaches, beginning at the NORTHEND PARK sign at the end of the bridge; take Trident Way from downtown Kodiak to Near Island. If you take the first right from Trident Way onto Bay Road and continue left onto Dog Road, you'll overlook **St. Herman Boat Harbor,** where sea lions hang out and sun themselves.

KAYAKING Kodiak's coast offers some of the best kayaking in the world. You can take an afternoon trip around Near Island, to Anton Larsen Bay, or through the sheltered waterways of Shuyak Islands, 50 miles north of Kodiak. **Backcountry Sports** (*see above*) has everything you need; single kayaks cost $30 a day, standard doubles are $40 ($50 for a Kepler). Talk to Arthur Schultz while you're there; he'll tell you where to go and even take you there himself for a fee. **Wavetamer** (tel. 907/486–2604) also offers kayak rental, instruction, and guided trips. Call in advance to reserve a space.

Prince William Sound

If you visit Anchorage without making the effort to see Prince William Sound, you should be shot. It is one of the highlights of any trip to Alaska. What's more, it's only a few hours away and accessible by train and road. Ringed by the Kenai Peninsula to the west and the Chugach Mountains to the north, Prince William Sound is more than 15,000 square miles of bays and deep fjords overlooking snow-topped mountains, massive glaciers, and wilderness. Amid this magnificence swim whales, porpoises, seals, and sea lions. It sounds corny, but nature plays on a grand scale up here. Sadly, when Exxon screws up, it also does so on a grand scale. Prince William Sound and its wildlife are still recovering from the effects of 11 million gallons of crude oil dumped into the water when the *Exxon Valdez* ran aground near Valdez in March 1989 (*see box, below*).

When most people think of halibut, they imagine a flounder-like flatfish that fights like a wet paper bag. But Alaskan halibut are often more than 300 pounds, and most closely resemble a garage door with an attitude.

Whittier, Valdez, and Cordova are the only major towns on the sound, and only Valdez can be reached by road (you reach Whittier by train from Portage). Valdez makes most of its money from the Trans-Alaska Pipeline, which terminates here, but each town also has a sizable fishing fleet and a host of pleasure craft. Fishing is a religion up here. During summer, the towns hold one fishing derby after another, for salmon, halibut, or the hell of it. The place that retains the most fishing-town charm is Cordova (Valdez has plenty of derbies, but is referred to by Cordovans as "Val-disease").

The prime time to visit is midsummer, when the foggy and rainy weather clear to give you a good view. September and June are less touristed and the weather is still fair. The easiest way to see Prince William Sound is to take the train to Whittier from Anchorage, or to drive to Valdez along the Glenn and Richardson highways. If you really want to get a feel for the sound, take the ferry to or from one of the ports on the Kenai Peninsula (*see Kenai Peninsula, above*). The boat stops at Whittier, Valdez, and Cordova and swings by the Columbia Glacier as well. But don't stick just to the water's edge. If you can, take a trip from Cordova down the Copper River Highway through the Copper River Delta. The delta is a nesting ground for millions of migratory birds, but you're also likely to see moose, beavers, bears, and even wolverines, especially if you hike some of the trails. Most spectacular of all the sound's treasures is the **Columbia Glacier,** a blue-white ice sheet several miles across. The state ferry and numerous small boat operators can take you close to this behemoth, which periodically calves, sending thousands of tons of ice crashing into the waters of the sound.

Whittier

Whittier may be the major gateway to Prince William Sound, but you would never know it—this is not a happening town. It's a bizarre place: Over half of the 900 residents live in an abandoned World War II military high-rise, Begich Towers; the other half live in a crumbling stack of 1950s condos; and the rest of Whittier's buildings are battered or deserted warehouses, canneries, or military structures. Overall, Whittier doesn't have much to hold your attention except for its perch on Prince William Sound. From Anchorage, Whittier is the closest jumping-off point for the sound; it also has less boat

Don't plan on withdrawing any moolah in Whittier—they don't even have an ATM, let alone a bank.

traffic than most ports, so it's a good place to kayak. If you're headed to Valdez or Cordova on the ferry from Whittier, you're in for a scenic cruise that passes the awesome Columbia Glacier. Avoid spending the night in Whittier unless you're prepared to camp—lodging options are grim.

VISITOR INFORMATION The **Visitor Information Center** (no phone) is in a railroad car next to the tracks, across from the harbormaster. The center, open daily 11–6 in summer, sells railroad tickets and gives out a few brochures and a town map.

COMING AND GOING To get to Whittier, you first need to get to Portage, and the train ain't gonna take you there. **Homer and Seward Bus Lines** (tel. 907/278–0800) will drop you off in Portage en route from Anchorage to Homer or Seward for $22. The **Backpacker Shuttle** (tel. 907/344–8775) also runs to Portage from Anchorage for $17.50. The Portage train depot is at Mile 86.5 on the Seward Highway, 1 mile north of the turnoff to Portage Glacier. From Portage, the **Alaska Railroad** (tel. 907/265–2494, or 907/265–2607 for recording) runs several times a day to Whittier ($13 one-way, $16 round-trip). The 45-minute ride winds through the mountains and several long tunnels built by the military in World War II.

The state ferry *Bartlett* sails from Whittier several times a week for Valdez and Cordova (7 hrs, $58), passing the magnificent Columbia Glacier. The ferry dock is on the harbor side of the railroad tracks, next to the "triangle" of shops. For information, call the **Alaska Marine Highway office** (tel. 907/272–4482) in Anchorage.

GETTING AROUND Whittier is so small you can easily cover it on foot—there's nowhere to drive even if you do have a car. The railroad tracks divide the town in two: The small boat harbor, ferry dock, and triangle of shops and restaurants are on the north side; the hotels and Begich Towers are on the south side. The only legal place to cross the tracks is on Whittier Street, inconveniently located on the far west side of town; if you cross anywhere else, you have to negotiate several rows of tracks and railroad cars, and you'll be fined heavily if you're caught.

WHERE TO SLEEP If by some ugly twist of fate you're stuck in Whittier for the night, let's hope you brought your tent. The **Whittier Campground,** on the south end of town behind Begich Towers, is by far the nicest place to spend the night. Sites look like gravel parking spaces and cost $5 a night (drop payment into the collection box at the entrance), but a nearby waterfall forms the pretty backdrop. Water and pit toilets are available. If you're without a tent, give the **Whittier B&B** (tel. 907/472–2396) a buzz. They'll set you up in a double inside Begich Towers for $50 a night. Otherwise your only options are the dilapidated **Sportsman Inn** (Eastern Ave., far eastern end of town, tel. 907/472–2352), with doubles for $60–$65, or the **Anchor Inn** (Whittier St., center of town, tel. 907/472–2354), where double rooms go for $55–$60; the cockroaches will hang up your coat at both joints.

FOOD For breakfast, lunch, or dinner go to the **Sportsman Inn** (tel. 907/472–2316); the restaurant far outshines the shabby hotel. The excellent cook serves up a seafood omelet ($8.25), pancakes ($4.45), deep-fried halibut ($13.25), and "Willy's Special," pizza with mushrooms and various meats—a medium ($13.95) is enough for two to share. You'll also find several restaurants in the triangle. The best of the bunch is **Cafe Orca** (tel. 907/472–2496), where you can wash down your Sante Fe bagel (bagel with spicy sun-dried tomato spread; $2.75) or fresh sandwich (around $6) with a steaming hot latte ($2). Huge windows overlook the sound.

OUTDOOR ACTIVITIES With its breathtaking views of Prince William Sound and several glaciers, the area around Whittier is perfect for hiking your brains out. Two popular treks are the 8-mile round-trip **Portage Glacier Trail** and the easier 8-mile round-trip to **Second Salmon Run.** The trailhead for the Portage Glacier hike is near the tank farm, about 1½ miles west of town along a gravel road. Lots of uphill walking is involved, but the views of the glacier and Passage Canal are well worth it. The trail to the salmon runs starts behind the Sportsman Inn; follow the dirt road up the slope, keep right when you reach the first fork, and then go left at the second. The first salmon run is less than a mile away. In summer, king and silver salmon head upstream to spawn. The second salmon run is 3 miles farther on, but the views of **Billings Glacier** should keep you going.

You can rent kayaks from **Prince William Sound Kayak Center** (tel. 907/472–2452, or 907/562–2866 in Anchorage); singles are $40 a day, doubles $60 a day. If you're anxious about going off on your own, join one of their trips. Two-day outings (the minimum) cost $90–$115.

Valdez

If you have a car, a trip to Valdez (pronounced val-DEEZ) may be the best way to see Prince William Sound. The Richardson Highway connects the town with Anchorage and the interior, whereas neither Whittier nor Cordova is even accessible by road. At the extreme north end of Prince William Sound, Valdez sits at the head of the Valdez Arm, a 12-mile natural fjord. The bay to the south and the sawtooth mountains to the north will blow you away—if the sky ever clears long enough for you to see them. Most spectacular of all is the Columbia Glacier, one of Alaska's most famous and photographed attractions. The state ferry as well as several small boat operators lead tours to the glacier from Valdez (see Worth Seeing, below); don't miss out.

If you're looking for a town with solitude and character, hop the ferry to Cordova as soon as possible.

Because the city's harbor is ice-free all year, Valdez was the entry point for people and goods heading to the interior during the gold rush of 1897–98. The first route to the goldfields took prospectors over the treacherous Valdez Glacier; many died trying to get across. The natives showed the prospectors a better route, which is now the Richardson Highway. Riches continue to come from the interior, but today it's black gold that pours into Valdez, the southern terminus of the Trans-Alaska Pipeline. In general, if you don't fish for a living here, you work for the oil companies.

The *Exxon Valdez* oil spill (see box, below) was not the first environmental catastrophe to strike the area. Valdez was completely leveled in the 1964 Good Friday earthquake, whose epicenter was only 45 miles west of the city. Eyewitness accounts report that the ground liquefied, forming huge waves that destroyed almost every structure in the town. Not surprisingly, residents were wary of rebuilding on such unstable land, so they voted to move the town 4 miles west to its current location. Although some of the old town's buildings were transported to the new site, most of Valdez is less than 25 years old and looks like it was put up overnight.

BASICS The **Visitor Information Center** (Fairbanks Dr., btw Egan and Pioneer Drs., tel. 907/835–4636 or 907/835–2984), open daily 8–8 from May to mid-September, is staffed by clueless teenagers who look up from their *Sassy* only long enough to point you to the brochure racks. Make free local calls here and check the supremely handy info board for B&B listings. Another info board and phone hooks you up with charters and activities in town. The **harbormaster** (N. Harbor Dr., tel. 907/835–4981) sells $3 shower tokens and lets travelers make local calls for free. The rest rooms are open 24 hours a day. **Valdez High School** (cnr of Hazelet Ave. and Robe River Dr.) has an indoor pool and free showers open to the public a few hours each day.

COMING AND GOING The scenic Richardson Highway begins at Egan Drive in Valdez and stretches to Glennallen, 115 miles north. From the junction at Glennallen you can take the Glenn Highway 187 miles to Anchorage or continue on the Richardson Highway to Delta Junction or Tok.

➢ **BY BUS** • **Gray Line** (tel. 907/835–2357 in Valdez or 907/277–5581 in Anchorage) cruises daily to Valdez from Anchorage via Glennallen (10 hrs, $59). Make advance reservations as an individual traveler, not as part of a tour. You can hop off at Glenallen for $39 and get a bus connection to just about anywhere. In Valdez, the bus depot is at the **Westmark Hotel** on the harbor. Other companies come and go each season—check with the visitor center.

➢ **BY FERRY** • The ferry dock for the **Alaska Marine Highway** (tel. 907/835–4436) is a five-minute walk south of town, just off Hazelet Avenue. The ferry *Bartlett* connects Valdez with Cordova (5 hrs, $30) and Whittier (7 hrs, $58) several times a week.

➢ **BY PLANE** • Both **Alaska Airlines** (tel. 800/426–0333) and **Mark Air** (tel. 907/835–5147 or 800/627-5247) have regular flights between Anchorage and Valdez for about $99 one-way. The airport is 6 miles from the town center on Airport Road, off the Richardson Highway. No buses connect the airport to downtown, so call **Valdez Yellow Cab** (tel. 907/835–2500); the trip is a flat $7, plus $1 for each additional person.

GETTING AROUND The center of Valdez is small and easily walkable, all the better since there's no public transport. The two main streets are Egan Drive and Fairbanks Drive, where

The Exxon Valdez Oil Spill

Few people had heard of Valdez before March 1989, when the oil tanker Exxon Valdez ran aground on Bligh Reef near the town, dumping 11 million gallons of crude oil—the largest spill in U.S. history—into pristine Prince William Sound. No one had ever prepared for a disaster of this magnitude. Engulfed in the oil, birds, fish, and sea mammals died by the thousands. Aside from the environmental damage, the spill wiped out the fishing season for the huge Prince William Sound fleets. But oil, it seems, is still a money-maker whether you're pumping it into a car or scrubbing it off rocks. Thousands of people headed for Valdez, where they earned big bucks in the clean-up effort, hosing down beaches, polishing rocks, and rescuing wildlife. Valdez's population quadrupled to 12,000. Even the fishing boats got in on the action, taking Exxon to the cleaners for about $3,000 per day per boat to help pick up the oil. And while Prince William Sound was awash with oil, Valdez was awash with cash. At night, the clean-up crews hit the town bars and restaurants in droves. Prices went through the roof (and in Alaska the roof is pretty high).

So what was the Exxon Valdez doing in the narrow channel leading to the town? The most northerly ice-free port in Alaska, Valdez was chosen in 1974 as the terminus of the Trans-Alaska Pipeline, which brings crude oil 800 miles south from the oilfields of Prudhoe Bay. When the Valdez went aground, it had just taken on a full load at the marine terminal. Conceivably, so had Captain Joseph Hazelwood, since he was charged with being drunk (not to mention away from the helm) at the time of the accident. The prosecution, however, wasn't able to prove anything at the captain's trial. In August 1994, the court ruled that Exxon pay $286.8 million in damages to local fishers, a figure much lower the $895 million that had been asked for. This decision was essentially a coup for Exxon. A few weeks later, however, the court awarded punitive damages of 5 billion dollars, and though the Sound may never be exactly as it was, and that figure won't ruin Exxon, the money will go a long way toward restoring the communities here.

you'll find the museum, the library, and most hotels and restaurants. North Harbor Drive at the harbor is another small hub of activity, with several restaurants, the harbormaster, and some RV parks. Lots of people rent cars in Valdez to drive up to Wrangell St. Elias State Park; try **Valdez U-Drive** (tel. 907/835–4402) or **Avis** (tel. 907/835–4774), both at the airport terminal. If you're just tooling around town, Valdez U-Drive gives you a free ride to their office and charges just $35 a day; you'll pay $52 to drive long distances. Avis charges $39 with unlimited mileage but has incredibly rude service.

WHERE TO SLEEP The oil spill put Valdez on the map and on the itineraries of RVers, cruise lines, and package tours. Prices for lodging have skyrocketed. Your best bet is to bring your tent or reserve at a B&B, of which Valdez has dozens; the visitor center (*see above*) has a free directory, or you can call **One Call Does It All Reservation Service** (tel. 907/835–4988 or 800/242–4988). The cheapest beds in town are at **Airport Valdez Mancamp** (100 Glacier Dr., across from airport, tel. 907/835–5990). Five white, institutional block buildings were erected to house workers cleaning up the oil spill. You can join the construction crews here for $36 a night.

Otherwise, Valdez's hotels are basically the same—comfortable, conveniently located, and expensive. All have an adjoining restaurant and bar, and, except for the Valdez Motel, all are wheelchair-accessible. With doubles for $95, the **Totem Inn** (Richardson Hwy., just west of Meals Ave., tel. 907/835–4443) and the **Valdez Motel** (Egan Dr., tel. 907/835–4444) are the cheapest choices. The two largest hotels, the **Valdez Village Inn** (cnr of Egan Dr. and Meals Ave., tel. 907/835–4445 or 800/478–4445) and the **Westmark Valdez** (Fidalgo Dr., near boat harbor, tel. 907/835–4391), both cost $130 for a double. If you can, get one of the cabins ($80) at the Valdez Village Inn; they include a kitchenette and can sleep up to six people. If you come in early or late summer, or if the season is slow, you might be able to talk your way down to winter prices—about $50 a night.

➤ **CAMPING** • Aside from **Bear Paw Camp Park** (Small Boat Harbor, off Meals Ave., tel. 907/835–2530), camping in Valdez isn't much fun. Bear Paw charges $15 for two people in a tent and has pristine, secluded spots on a hill overlooking the harbor. The ultra-clean showers and laundry room are a good place to hang out and escape the mosquitos.

Valdez's other campgrounds are noisy and far from town, and most of the unofficial camping areas are marshy outposts for an empire of mosquitoes. Most campgrounds don't have phones; for general info or reservations (groups of ten or more), call **Valdez Parks and Recreations Department** (tel. 907/835–2531). **Valdez Glacier Campground** (Airport Rd., 7 mi from downtown) has over 60 sites for $7, but that's about all there is to recommend it. Behind the airport and a short walk from the glacier, the campground is cold, noisy, and frequented by bears. Water and pit toilets are available.

South Harbor Campground, or "Hotel Hill," is a tent city of cannery workers off South Harbor Drive. Set on an exposed hill overlooking the small boat harbor, it's a good place to meet restless youths and exchange information, though there's little privacy, plenty of late-night noise, and a real possibility of theft. Camping here used to be free, but the campground now charges $5 a night or $75 a month for a spot on a wooden platform, with pit toilets and water. Fees are collected infrequently.

➤ **ROUGHING IT** • If you come by car, you'll pass some gorgeous areas along the highway where you could camp in the woods. Otherwise, try the north end of town just off Mineral Creek Drive, on the far side of the river. You can also camp in the woods or bushes off Egan Drive or anywhere west of downtown, but the mosquitoes and damp weather will make you miserable after a few hours.

FOOD The dearth of good eating in Valdez makes scrumptious Cafe Valdez (*see below*) even more appealing, but so far it's only open for lunch. Save your money and stomach lining by checking out the salad bar, hot soups, deli counter, and bakery at **Eagle Quality Center** (313 Meals Ave., 1 block from Richardson Hwy., tel. 907/835–2100). It's open 24 hours and has a microwave where you can heat up frozen meals. Though locals recommend it, avoid the greasy slop dished up at **Oscar's** (103 N. Harbor Dr.).

➤ **UNDER $10** • **Alaska Halibut House.** So you're eating fast food; at least it's fresh, affordable local seafood. The specialty here is a basket of deep-fried halibut with french fries ($7). If you hate fish, they also serve breakfast and burgers, and there's a salad bar. *Cnr of Meals Ave. and Fairbanks Dr., tel. 907/835–2788. BYOB. Wheelchair access. Open daily 6 AM–11 PM.*

Cafe Valdez. In a nondescript strip mall, Cafe Valdez rustles up at least three great homemade stews or soups a day, some baked treats, and fresh sandwiches (about $6). Seafood jambalaya with extra spice and a side salad goes for $6.75. The café is officially open only for lunch, but the cook says that as long as you see a light and hear some music, you can stop in for coffee and maybe a muffin in the morning. *310 Egan Rd., near Tatitlek Ave., tel. 907/835–5455. Wheelchair access. Open daily 11:30–3:30.*

Sugarloaf Restaurant. The Village Inn may charge extortionate rates for its rooms, but the casual restaurant next door serves up good, basic food at decent prices. A stack of pancakes goes for $4, and a blackened cajun burger with fries is $6.50. *Cnr of Richardson Hwy. and Meals Ave., tel. 907/835–4445. Wheelchair access. Open daily 6 AM–11 AM and 5 PM–10 PM.*

Valdez Christian Book and Coffee Shoppe. The shoppe serves up homemade soup in a bread bowl with unlimited extra helpings (yee-haw) for $4.50; also grab one of Bob's monster cookies ($1.25). The atmosphere is uncomfortable—you eat in a silent bookstore surrounded by extremely polite Christians—so you might want to order to go. *126 Pioneer St., off Meals Ave., tel. 907/835–5881. Open weekdays 9–6, Sat. 10–5.*

➤ **UNDER $15** • **No Name Pizza.** This seedy-looking joint has a lot more character—and much better pizza—than Pizza Palace at the harbor. Full pies cost $12 and up. For a huge meal all to yourself, try the $9 pizza bomb, a 12-inch pizza folded in half. *Egan Dr., btw Chenega St. and Meals Ave., tel. 907/835–4419. In the Valdez Center Mall.*

WORTH SEEING The **Valdez Museum** is a fascinating place to wile away an afternoon. The entrance is dominated by a 1907 Ahrens steam fire engine and a lighthouse lens made of 68 glass prisms from Hinchinbrook Island. But the real treasures are the history displays, especially the reconstruction of a gold-rush miner's cabin and saloon. The museum has surprisingly little on the oil spill. *Cnr of Tatitlek Ave. and Egan Dr., tel. 907/835–2764. Admission: $2. Open mid-May–mid-Sept., daily 9–7; off-season, Tues.–Sat. 9–7.*

The **Trans-Alaska Pipeline,** which turned Valdez into a thriving town, has become a tourist attraction in its own right. The 800-mile pipeline transports oil from the North Slope fields in Prudhoe Bay to the marine terminal at Valdez, where the oil is loaded onto tankers to be shipped south. Completed in 1977, the pipeline was built to withstand earthquakes, the Arctic climate, and Alaska's rugged terrain, including rivers and mountain ranges. This feat of engineering cost $8 billion, the most ever spent on a private construction project. Alyeska Pipeline Service Company gives free two-hour tours of the pipeline terminal, where you can watch tankers being loaded and learn all the interesting statistics (from the oil companies' perspective, of course). Tours leave from the airport several times daily in summer; reserve a spot by calling 907/835–2686. For additional information, contact the Public Affairs Department of **Alyeska Pipeline Service Company** (1835 S. Bragaw St., Anchorage 99512).

The **Columbia Glacier** is the second-largest coastal glacier in North America, flowing 40 miles from the Chugach Mountains to Prince William Sound. The face of the glacier is 4 miles wide and 100–300 feet high, and the surrounding water is covered with icebergs. It's amazing to watch the glacier calve—a huge sheet of ice breaks off and explodes into the water below. The Alaska Marine Highway ferry (*see* Coming and Going, *above*) passes the glacier on its trips from Whittier to Valdez and Cordova (except for the Monday excursion). If you want to get even closer, take one of the small boats that wind their way through the icebergs almost to the face of the glacier. Trips costs about $80 per person; try **Columbia Glacier Cruises** (tel. 907/835–2357 or 800/544–2206) or **Stan Stephens Charters** (tel. 907/835–4731 or 800/992–1297), or get a list of tour operators from the visitor center.

AFTER DARK The **Black Gold Recreation Hall** (tel. 907/835–2531), on Waterfall Drive north of the park strip, has Ping-Pong and pool tables, TV, and magazines, and is a popular hangout for restless young people Monday–Saturday 8 AM–10 PM. After the recreation hall closes, try one of the hotel bars or the **Glacier Bar** (113 Fairbanks Rd., tel. 907/835–4794), which gets especially crowded on weekends, when classic-rock cover bands play. If you like a rough crowd, head to the **Acres Bar** (Richardson Hwy. and Airport Rd., tel. 907/835–5055).

OUTDOOR ACTIVITIES You can wind your way through Valdez on many a fine hiking trail. This waterfront town also hosts a few festive summer fishing derbies (*see below*). Valdez Bay is a calm place for beginners to learn how to kayak, and the white waters of Keystone Canyon challenge both kayakers and river-rafters.

➤ **HIKING** • **Mineral Creek Trail** is a moderate day hike through a green canyon, with a rushing creek below and waterfalls all around. The first 5½ miles are along a gravel road (accessible by car), but the last mile is a rough, snowy foot trail that leads to the Old Stamp Mill, which once processed gold ore. If you don't have a vehicle, the entire 13-mile loop will take about six hours. To reach the trailhead, go north on Hazelet Avenue, turn left on Hanagita Street, and right on Mineral Creek Drive, and then take the first right onto Mineral Creek Canyon, an unmarked gravel road. The road crosses the river and continues into the hills.

Farther from town is the trail to **Solomon Lake,** which begins across from the Solomon Gulch Fish Hatchery on Dayville Road, 10 miles from town. The 1½-mile trail ends at the lake and reservoir, rewarding hikers with views of Valdez and the bay. The hike includes two very steep inclines: one on a long flight of wooden stairs, the other over a muddy slope with only a rope to help you keep your balance. After these, the trail is flat and smooth all the way to the lake.

Goat Trail is a hike through historic Keystone Canyon. The path was once part of the Valdez Trail to Eagle, an important route to the interior from 1909 until 1945, when the Richardson Highway was completed. The trail begins just past Horsetail Falls in Keystone Canyon (Mile 13½ on Richardson Hwy.) and continues for 5 easy miles to the original bridge over Bear Creek, which is now unsafe to cross. Expect great views of Mother Nature.

➤ **FISHING** • You can fish almost anywhere in Valdez, except for the 200-yard security zone around the oil terminal and the area near the Solomon Gulch Fish Hatchery. Contact the visitor center (*see* Basics, *above*) about the Halibut Derby in late May, the Silver Salmon Derby in August, and the Pink Salmon Derby on July 4th. **Dockside Marine Fish Gear** (225 N. Harbor Dr., tel. 907/835–2683) has information, licenses, and equipment.

➤ **KAYAKING AND RIVER-RAFTING** • ANADYR Adventures (203 N. Harbor Dr., tel. 907/835–2814), by the small boat harbor, rents kayaks and leads three-hour guided trips in Valdez Bay for $52. A spectacular day trip to Shoup Glacier will set you back $140. **Keystone Raft and Kayak Adventures** (Mile 16.5, Richardson Hwy., tel. 907/835–3008) leads five daily raft trips (around $40) down Keystone Canyon and charters kayak trips and longer raft trips of up to 10 days.

Cordova

"You can't get there from here" really does apply to Cordova. No roads or train tracks lead to this isolated burg at the eastern end of Prince William Sound. You come by air or by water, or you don't come at all. There's something to be said for solitude: Cordova, unlike Whittier and Valdez, has a small-town appeal that doesn't rely solely on its scenic setting. If you only hit one town on the sound, this should be it. A real sense of community pervades Cordova, though the situation changes in summer, when outsiders flock in for jobs on boats and in the canneries, doubling the population. Copper originally put the town on the map: Cordova was chosen in 1906 as the port for a railroad bringing copper from the Kennecott Mines. The copper gave out in 1938, and now most of the 2,400 permanent residents make their money from fishing. Bars, hotels, and restaurants cater to the fishermen, and the whole town suffers when fishing is bad.

Whatever Cordova's attractions, they are insignificant compared with the majesty of the surrounding land. Sitting in the shadow of Mt. Eccles on Orca Inlet, Cordova has literally hundreds of square miles of pristine wilderness in its backyard. The Copper River Delta, a web of glaciers, rivers, streams, and marshes that fan out from the Copper River, is a sanctuary for birds, bears, and moose. Through this wilderness runs the 50-mile Copper River Highway (see below), which ends at the collapsed Million Dollar Bridge. Just driving along this highway makes a visit to Cordova worthwhile.

Longtime resident Sheelagh Mullins moved to Cordova when a "magical man" convinced her to accompany him to a "town where no road leads." If the proposed highway connecting Chitnia and Cordova is ever completed, the Mullinses may have to move again.

BASICS The **Cordova Chamber of Commerce** (1st St., btw Adams and Browning Aves., tel. 907/424–7260) is a tiny office supposedly open Monday, Tuesday, and Friday 1:30–5 (its hours are actually random). Most people go to the **Cordova Historical Museum** (see Worth Seeing, below) for information. It distributes free brochures and a useful walking-tour map, as well as information on lodging and sights. The only information office open every weekday 8–5 is the **U.S. Forest Service, Cordova Ranger District** (2nd St., btw Browning and Adams Aves., tel. 907/424–7661), on the third floor of the Old Post Office. Here you can pick up info on Prince William Sound and the Copper River Delta, plus a comprehensive 15-page handout on trails in the area.

Get the crud off your clothes at **Whirlwind Laundromat** (cnr of 1st St. and Adams Ave., tel. 907/424–5110), where a wash is $3 and a spin in the dryer is 25¢. You can grab a shower ($3) daily 8–5 at the **harbormaster** (end of Nicholoff Way., on New Harbor, tel. 907/424–6400). Otherwise, try **Bob Korn Swimming Pool** (cnr of Railroad and Nicholoff Sts., tel. 907/424–7200); call or check the door for posted hours.

COMING AND GOING The most popular way to reach Cordova is on the **Alaska Marine Highway.** The ferry leaves Valdez (5 hrs, $30) and Whittier (7 hrs, $58) several times a week for Cordova, and it passes the Columbia Glacier. Three times a month, you can sail from these ports to Seward, Homer, Kodiak, and the Aleutian Islands. The ferry dock (tel. 907/424–7333) is about 1½ miles west of town off Orca Inlet Road. It's a long, uphill trek into town, so you may want to call **Wild Hare Cabs** (tel. 907/424–3939) for a ride ($4 flat fee) or store your backpack at the ferry office on your left, two blocks from the dock (it's open during departures and arrivals).

The other way to reach Cordova is by plane—worth the expense if you're desperate to save a few hours or want to go straight from Anchorage to Cordova. **Mark Air** (tel. 907/424–5982 or 800/627–5247) flies round-trip from Anchorage for a day of sightseeing ($163). A $180 package includes your flight, rental car, and hotel for one night. **Alaska Airlines** (tel. 800/426–0333) has three daily flights from Anchorage ($112 round-trip) or Fairbanks ($228 round-trip). Charter companies like **Ketchum Air Service** (tel. 907/424–7703) or **Cordova Air Service** (tel. 907/424–3289) can get you to nearby islands and villages for about $400 an hour. You may be able to split the cost; call ahead to ask if anyone else is going when you want to go. The **Reluctant Fisherman Inn** (tel. 907/424–3272) runs a shuttle from the airport to town for $9, even if you don't stay there.

GETTING AROUND Although residential Cordova sprawls wide, the town's small business center is easily explored on foot. Most restaurants, hotels, and bars lie within a few blocks of 1st Street, between Council and Adams avenues. Nicholoff Way, off Railroad Avenue, is where you'll find a massive grocery store, the harbormaster, and the New Harbor. The ferry dock is 1½ miles west of town.

To reach the Million Dollar Bridge and Childs Glacier, rent a car or grab a shuttle. **Footloose Tours** (see Worth Seeing, below) will treat you to a guided trip for $35. You can rent a car from **Imperial** (tel. 907/424–5982), at the airport's MarkAir terminal, for about $65 per day. The **Reluctant Fisherman Inn** (407 Railroad Ave., tel. 907/424–3272) rents out a handful of cars ($45) and vans ($50); you get the first 50 miles free, and then it's 25¢ per mile. If you need a cab, call **Wild Hare** (tel. 907/424–3939). They're available 24 hours and will give you a lift to the ferry for $4.

WHERE TO SLEEP Unless you've reserved ahead for a cheap room at the Alaskan Hotel (see below), your best option is to check into one of Cordova's B&Bs. At all costs, avoid the

Reluctant Fisherman Inn; you'll pay out the nose (over $100 a night) for average rooms and snotty service.

➤ **UNDER $45** • **Alaskan Hotel.** The rooms above this old-time bar are clean and cheap: Doubles cost $35 with a shared bath (slap on $20 if you want your own bath). Rooms are directly over the bar, so you'll hear music and noise all night, every night. *1st St., btw Adams and Browning Aves., tel. 907/424–3288.*

Cordova Hotel. The bar may look seedy, but the rooms upstairs are clean, simple, and relatively isolated from the noise downstairs. Doubles without a bath cost $40. *1st St., btw Adams and Browning Aves., tel. 907/424–3388. Above Cordova Bar. 20 rooms, 12 with bath.*

➤ **UNDER $75** • **Cordova Rose Lodge.** Despite the name, don't expect a frilly rose theme—it's strictly maritime on this superbly renovated, landlocked 1924 barge. Your hosts, the Gleins, can give you a lift to their floating pad on the Odiak Slough, and will rustle up a full breakfast. Doubles with private bath are $65, with shared bath $55. *1315 Whitshed Rd., tel. 907/424–ROSE. 5 rooms, 4 with bath. No credit cards.*

Harborview B&B. Run by the same spunky woman who operates Footloose Tours (*see* Worth Seeing, *below*), Harborview has rooms that really let you stretch and make yourself at home, and it's close to downtown. All rooms have private bath, phone, and kitchen access. Doubles run $55 a night. *Observation Ave., off 1st St., tel. 907/424–5356. 5 rooms. Wheelchair access.*

Oystercatcher B&B. John and Mary Davis let two rooms in their cozy downtown home overlooking the sound. Rooms go for $50, including full breakfast. *Cnr of 3rd St. and Council Ave., tel. 907/424–5154. 2 rooms, neither with bath. Kitchen, laundry. No credit cards.*

➤ **CAMPING** • Camping outside official areas is commonplace, though you obviously don't have the luxury of running water or toilets, and you'll be at least a mile from town. It's a long steep walk to **Ski Hill,** but you'll find privacy and incredible views. You can also camp at **Eyak Lake,** either at Nirvana Park about a mile from town or deeper into the woods off Lake Avenue. Many people also camp at **Hippy Cove,** the bluff near the ferry dock, although there was a shooting here some time ago. Wherever you camp, take precautions against foraging bears. The **U.S. Forest Service** (tel. 907/424–7661) maintains remote cabins (usually $25 a night) around Prince William Sound and the Copper River Delta; contact the office for reservations.

From May to September, you can pay to camp officially at the **Odiak Camper Park.** At this sorry-looking gravel lot on Whitshed Road about two miles from town, RVs, trailers, and tents sit cheek to jowl. You won't have much privacy or shelter from the wind, but you do get a great view of the inlet and tidal flats, and sites are only $3. Register 24 hours a day with the police (Railroad Ave., near Nicholoff Way, tel. 907/424–6100).

FOOD Take break from the crap you've been eating and indulge at the Cookhouse Cafe (*see below*); this new place will serve you a meal you'll never forget. You can still get cheap and greasy food downtown by following hungry fisherman to **Club Cafe,** in an alley behind the Club Bar on 1st Street. Starting at 6 AM, you can get a cheap breakfast of two eggs, two sausages, and hash browns for $2.75. Pick up the cheapest groceries at the mammoth **Alaska Commercial Company** on Nicholoff Way (tel. 907/424–7141).

➤ **UNDER $5** • **Baja Taco.** The owner of this converted school bus/taco stand is always busy serving excellent, cheap Mexican food to fishermen at the harbor. Try the veggie Mex plate, huevos rancheros, or a burrito (each about $5). *Nicoloff Way, at the harbor next to Napa Auto Parts, tel. 907/424–5599. Open weekdays 7:30–4, Sat. 9–4, Sun. 10–4.*

➤ **UNDER $10** • **Ambrosia Pizza.** This slightly stuffy restaurant serves huge slices of pizza and Italian dishes. The $6 lunch specials include spaghetti, ravioli, and a mini-pizza big enough for two. Medium pizzas loaded with fresh toppings run about $16.75, but the mother of all pizzas, with every known topping, is $19.75. You can grab a slice for just $2. *1st St., at Browning Ave., tel. 907/424–7175. Wheelchair access. Open weekdays 11–10, weekends 4–10.*

Homeport Restaurant. Fill up on cheap home cookin' in the basement of the Baptist Church. Thursday night is an all-you-can-eat food feast ($7). A few fishermen mix in with the families here, and travelers are welcomed and encouraged to eat seconds. *Cnr of 1st St. and Adams Ave., tel. 907/424–3465. Wheelchair access. Open Mon.–Sat. 5 PM–10 PM.*

Killer Whale Café. This is one of the few cafés in Cordova where you'll want to spend time. They whip up great pastries and espresso, as well as spinach salad ($7.50) and sandwiches ($7–$8). You can browse through a small, eclectic bookstore downstairs. *1st St., btw Council and Browning Aves., tel. 907/424–7733. BYOB. Open weekdays 8–4, Sat. 8–3.*

➢ **UNDER $15** • **Cookhouse Cafe.** Hallelujah! An Alaskan restaurant that uses spices other than salt and pepper. If amazing dinners like fresh grilled salmon on polenta ($12.95) and appetizers like clam pizza ($6) or superb Ceasar salad ($6.95) are too much of a burden on your wallet, come for lunch. Salmon with soup is only $5.50 and sandwiches are under $5. On Sunday mornings, sit yourself down at a large white picnic table, check out beautiful local art-work, and dig into apricot-stuffed French toast ($5.50) and other brunch specialties. The menu changes frequently, so you can (and will) make several trips. *1 Cannery Row, at 1st St., tel. 907/424–5926. Midway btw ferry dock and town. BYOB. Wheelchair access. Open Mon.–Thurs. 6 AM–3 PM, Fri.–Sat. 6 AM–9:30, Sun. 9–2.*

WORTH SEEING Because Cordova is so isolated, you don't have to go far from town before you're all alone in the wilderness. The 48-mile Copper River Highway (*see below*) provides the main access to the glaciers, hiking trails, and wildlife of the Copper River Delta. For a laid-back afternoon, wander through the boat harbor, one of the five largest in Alaska, where you can watch fishermen repairing nets. Listen carefully and you'll hear that many of them are speaking Russian. If you start talk-ing to some of them (almost all speak English, too), they'll probably offer you a free filet, if not a free ride out with them the next morning.

If you want to see what happens to the fish after it's caught, or if you're investigating job opportunities, take a free tour of North Pacific Cannery (tel. 907/424–7175). Call before you show up, wear sturdy shoes, and bring a little cash if you want to buy some seafood.

➢ **CORDOVA HISTORICAL MUSEUM** • This small, engaging museum overflows with an unlikely mixture of Cor-dovan artifacts: the lens from the Cape St. Elias lighthouse, a rare three-man kayak from the early 1900s, and an assort-ment of curios thrown in for good measure. The museum is also *the* place to get visitor information. Next door, the Cor-dova Library (tel. 907/424–6665) shows films on Cordovan history on Saturday evenings in summer. *1st St., btw Adams and Browning Aves. Admission free. Open summer, Tues.–Sat. 1–5 and Thurs. and Sat. 7–9; off-season, Tues.–Sat. 1–5.*

➢ **LAKE EYAK** • Surrounded by woods and mountains, Lake Eyak stretches for miles behind the town. You can see the lake from Power Creek Road to the west or from the Copper River Highway to the east. In summer, Eyak is popular among local residents, who come here to windsurf, jet ski, or just paddle. Check out the salmon swimming in the creeks nearby.

Copper River Delta

The highway to Million Dollar Bridge runs through the Copper River Delta, a vast area of marshes and tidal flats that provide nesting grounds for literally millions of birds. Trum-peter swans, Canada geese, blue herons, and eagles are all here. You might also spy moose and bears from the highway, but you can appreciate better of the delta by hiking and camping away from the road. Pick up a map showing all the trails and campsites from the U.S. Forest Service (see Basics, above). If you know how to fish, you won't go hungry in summer—coho, sockeye salmon, and Dolly Varden trout abound in the rivers and streams that flow through the delta.

➤ **COPPER RIVER HIGHWAY** • Don't leave Cordova without taking a drive down the Copper River Highway. Sure it's tough to get hold of wheels, but make the effort. If you can find some other travelers to split the cost, you can rent a car (*see* Getting Around, *above*). Otherwise, take a five-hour tour with **Footloose Tours** (tel. 907/424–5356); for $35, a van whisks you from the ferry, throwing in a bag lunch and a little history, too. The highway runs 50 miles east of Cordova along the bed of an old railway. The story of the railroad, built in the early 1900s to transport copper from the rich Kennecott Mines, is remarkable in itself: In just four years, workers laid 200 miles of track over the wet, unstable land of the Copper River Delta and completed an engineering feat once thought impossible—a bridge spanning two glaciers.

That bridge, known as the Million Dollar Bridge, lies at the end of the Copper River Highway. One of the spans was destroyed during the 1964 earthquake, but the remaining half is one of Cordova's most spectacular sights. You can still walk (or drive carefully) onto it, venturing out over the huge Copper River. Looking to the right, you see the face of **Miles Glacier,** a few miles away. To the left is massive **Childs Glacier,** whose face rises a sheer 300 feet. A road leads to a viewing platform and picnic/camping area, where you can get a closer look.

The glacier rumbles and cracks, and periodically calves huge chunks into the river, sometimes splashing water all the way onto the opposite bank. These splashes can strand salmon on the beach for bears or people to pick up—"glacier fishing," as it is known, does not require a license.

AFTER DARK As in most Alaskan towns, when Cordovans go out, they make a beeline for the bars (not that there's anywhere else to go). Some downtown bars, like the **Cordova Hotel** (1st St., tel. 907/424–3388) and **Club Bar** (1st St., tel. 907/424–3405), are kind of seedy. To hang out with local characters and get an earful of fishing tales, pull up a stool at the **Anchor Bar** (1st St., tel. 907/424–3262), or try the long, antique counter at the **Alaskan Hotel and Bar** (1st St., tel. 907/424–3288). Live music has been known to emanate from the Alaskan and the **Powder House** (Mile 2, Copper River Hwy., tel. 907/424–3529), a lakeside joint that's a step up from the other bars, with good music and even better sushi on Fridays.

OUTDOOR ACTIVITIES The U.S. Forest Service (*see* Basics, *above*) distributes an excellent 15-page overview of trails in the area. Most trails begin off the highway, miles out of town, but a few are within walking distance. **Crater Lake Trail** is a stunning 2½-mile climb up the back of Mt. Eyak, with good views of the delta and Lake Eyak, but the 1,500-foot ascent is tough going. The lake itself is set in an alpine bowl, half-covered with snow and ice. The trail begins 2 miles north of town off Power Creek Road, opposite Skaters' Cabin. **Power Creek Trail** starts 7 miles north of town at the end of Power Creek Road and climbs 3 miles past Ohman Falls through the mountain basin. A poorly marked 5½-mile ridge connects the two trails, creating a 12-mile hike from trailhead to trailhead. Other trails ascend **Ski Hill** and **Mt. Eyak** from 5th Street near Browning, or from Whitshed Road near the reservoir.

Mt. Eyak Ski Area (tel. 907/424–7766) has a chair lift and downhill and cross-country ski trails. The skiing is decent, but the season varies as wildly as the schizoid weather. **Muskeg Meander,** at Mile 18 on the Copper River Highway, also has cross-country trails.

FAIRBANKS AND THE BUSH

13

By Alison Huml

Most visitors to Alaska never get farther north than the Panhandle or Anchorage, so they can't truly come to grips with the immensity of a state one-fifth the size of the continental United States. Only as you head north to Fairbanks and beyond—into the bush, as Alaskans call it—does the scale and emptiness of the land become apparent. Much of this area consists of mountain ranges and hundreds of miles of tundra bearing no signs of human life whatsoever. This means no roads at all, not even dirt ones—a foreign concept for anyone weaned on take-out windows and six-lane super highways. The lone road that does run north into the Arctic Circle is the only lifeline to the oil fields on the coast of the Beaufort Sea. The only way to reach the other parts of this region—dogsleds aside—is to walk or fly. Although commercial airlines now run regular flights and package tours to a few remote destinations, the bush remains largely the domain of Alaska's legendary bush pilots, who ferry people and supplies to outlying settlements and Eskimo towns across the state. Most pilots operate out of Fairbanks, the last outpost of "civilization" in this wilderness. Don't expect to find the Metropolitan Opera here, however—despite its urban veneer, Fairbanks is the kind of city where a housewife's tasks may include hacking up a moose and putting it in the freezer for winter.

Those who, like most Alaskans, meet the land on its own terms will find the bush more magnificent than their wildest imaginings. The bush is the glacier-covered peaks of the Alaska range, the hundreds of thousands of lakes that dot the flat expanse of the North Slope, the cloud-wrapped mass of Mt. McKinley in Denali National Park, and the ice floes glowing in the midnight sun on the Arctic Ocean. More than anything else, though, it's the realization that, in the grand scheme of things, you're pretty insignificant (nothing personal).

Fairbanks

Sprawled along the banks of the Chena River, Fairbanks is the second-largest city in Alaska. It sits at the geographic heart of the state in a sea of thick spruce, willow, and birch forests. On a clear day, you can see several of the glacier-covered peaks of the Alaska Range, nearly 75 miles to the south; to the north, the White Mountains dominate the horizon. More than anything else, it's the city's setting, smack in the middle of millions of acres of wilderness, and the promise of access to remote corners of Alaska that draws visitors. Fairbanks's location at the point where the Alcan Highway, which connects Alaska to the Lower 48, comes closest to meeting the Dalton Highway, the only overland access to the oil fields at Prudhoe Bay, makes it a hub of sorts. Even if you're just passing

The magical aurora borealis (the northern lights) is best viewed from Fairbanks between mid-August and April.

Fairbanks

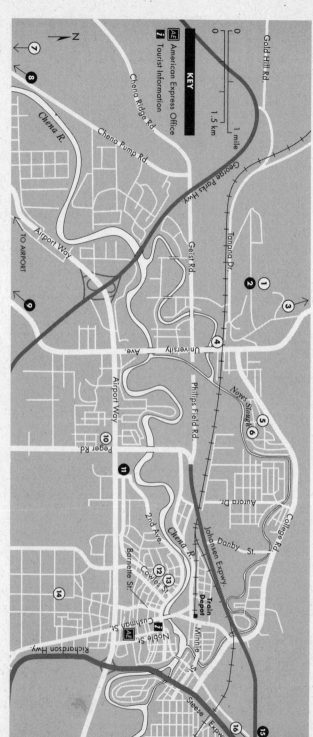

484

through, make time for a quick visit to the city's excellent museum or a performance at the university—you won't find much along those lines further north.

The town of Fairbanks has spread out from the original downtown area that developed around founder E. T. Barnette's "cache" (an Alaskan term for a storage room). Barnette had originally hoped to open a trading post much farther east. When the stern-wheeler he had chartered in 1901 could make it no farther up the shallow Chena River, Barnette unloaded his supplies to await a boat with a shallower draft, but ended up making Fairbanks his home. When gold was discovered 16 miles away in 1902, hundreds joined him.

The best time to visit Fairbanks is in March, when airfares and lodging rates plummet. March is also a good time to explore the surrounding hills and bush, because the muskeg (swampy ground that's impassable in summer) is still frozen solid, making it possible to reach many remote areas via snowmobile or dogsled.

BASICS

AMERICAN EXPRESS **Vista Travel Incorporated** is the local AmEx representative. This downtown office provides travel and financial services and will hold cardholders' mail. *1211 Cushman St., tel. 907/456–7888 or 800/528–4800 for lost cards or traveler's checks. Open weekdays 8:30–6, Sat. 10–4.*

VISITOR INFORMATION The **Alaska Public Lands Information Center (APLIC)** provides valuable information on Alaska's state and national parks and makes campground reservations. The exhibits on Alaska's wildlife and regional areas are useful if you're planning a trip to the more remote areas of the bush. *250 Cushman St., at 3rd St., tel. 907/456–0527. Open June–Aug., daily 9–6; Sept.–May, Tues.–Sat. 10–6.*

The extremely helpful staff of the **Fairbanks Visitors and Convention Bureau** provides information about lodging, camping, recreation, and shopping. If you're looking for a B&B, browse through their binders, complete with photos. Also pick up the free *Visitor's Guide*, which has a pull-out city map. *550 1st Ave., tel. 907/456–5774 or 907/456–4632. Where Cushman St. Bridge crosses Chena River. Open May–Sept., daily 8–8; Oct.–Apr., daily 8–5.*

COMING AND GOING

If you're making a beeline to Fairbanks from Anchorage, you can get a one-way flight for $78. Another option is to get a group together and rent a car. Even with drop-off charges, renting can be a relatively cheap way to go, especially if **Payless Car Rental** (tel. 800/729–5377) in Anchorage is still offering its special deal: If you arrive in Fairbanks and return the car within 24 hours, you pay a flat $50.

BY BUS Many of the bus companies listed below operate only from mid-May to mid-September, and it's always advisable to reserve ahead. There is no central bus terminal, so call for pick-up and drop-off points. **Denali Express** (405 L St. and 612 4th Ave., tel. 907/274–8539 or 800/327–7651) and **Fireweed Express** (tel. 907/452–0521) will haul you down to Denali for $25 one way, $45 round trip; it costs $5 more to take your bike. Denali Express continues down to Anchorage for a grand total of $105 one way. **Alaskan Express** (Westmark Inn, 1521 S. Cushman St., tel. 907/456–7741) buses meet the southeastern Alaska ferry in Haines and Skagway and then drive to Fairbanks through Canada. The fare of $169 from Haines and $194 from Skagway does not include lodging during the one-night stopover in Beaver Creek. Fairbanks to Anchorage (via Tok, *not* Denali) costs $109.

BY TRAIN Across the Chena River from the tourist office, the **train depot** (280 N. Cushman St., tel. 907/456–4155) is the northern terminus of the Alaska Railroad. In summer, the northbound train arrives daily from Anchorage at 8:30 PM, and the southbound train departs daily at 8:30 AM. One-way fare from Anchorage with a stopover in Denali is $135 (12 hrs). The Fairbanks–Denali fare is $47 (4 hrs). City buses stop running after 7 PM, so unless you're staying at a hostel or B&B that provides transportation from the station, your only option after this hour is a cab.

BY PLANE The **Fairbanks International Airport** is about 4 miles southwest of town. It is not served by city buses, so your best option is to take a taxi to town for about $10 (unless your B&B or hostel will send a car for you). Several car-rental companies have counters at the terminal, but you should make reservations up to a week in advance for economy cars, especially on weekends. Almost all flights to Fairbanks originate in Anchorage. Carriers include **Alaska Airlines** (tel. 800/426–0333), **American** (tel. 800/433–7300), **Delta Airlines** (tel. 800/221–1212), **MarkAir** (tel. 800/627–5247), and **United Airlines** (tel. 800/241–6522). Both Alaska Airlines and MarkAir have flights to northern destinations such as Barrow and Nome, but bush planes often charge less.

Fairbanks is the gateway to most of the bush communities farther north. Several tiny airlines have government mail contracts to these villages, serving as their only link to "the outside." Space permitting, you can book a seat on these flights, but consider carefully where you'll end up—many Eskimo villages take a dim view of tourists. If you just want to go along for the ride, you won't have any problem, but a seat on a round-trip mail run costs about $200. **Frontier Flying Service** (tel. 907/474–0014) has regular service to more hospitable far-north bush communities such as Anaktuvuk, Bettles, and Nome. Be sure to arrive at least one hour before takeoff, so as not to lose your space to extra cargo.

HITCHHIKING It's fairly easy to get a lift to Fairbanks from Anchorage or Denali National Park on the well-traveled George Parks Highway. Forget trying to hitch from the Alaska (Alcan) Highway: Most drivers are heading to Anchorage and will leave you stranded in Tok, a sort of hitcher's purgatory where the road to Anchorage branches off.

GETTING AROUND

Fairbanks's downtown area is centered around Cushman Street, which runs north–south about 4 miles east of the University of Alaska. The airport is roughly the same distance northeast of downtown. Most fast-food chains, grocery stores, and shopping malls are along College Road or Airport Way; both streets parallel the Chena River. The University of Alaska at Fairbanks sits at University Avenue and College Road, on the highest hill in the city. At this end of College Road you'll find a few restaurants, a health-food store, and two sporting-goods stores that cater to students, locals, and backpackers.

BY BUS Fairbanks is a sprawling city and can be a little difficult to get around. **Metropolitan Area Commuter Service (MACS)** buses serve all the campgrounds, major shopping areas, and the university for $1.50 ($3 for a day pass), but they stop running at 7 PM. **Transit Park** (Cushman St., at 5th Ave., tel. 907/456–6623) is the local bus depot; pick up a schedule here or at the visitor center (*see* Visitor Information, *above*). The **G.O. Shuttle Service** (tel. 907/474–3847 or 800/478–3847) hits Fairbanks's hot spots. For $10, you can hop on and off the shuttle route throughout one full day.

BY CAR OR BIKE The best way to see Fairbanks is by bike or car. Car rental is pricier here than in Anchorage, and no one offers unlimited mileage, so be sure to ask how much each additional mile will set you back. **Rent-A-Wreck** (2105 Cushman St., on south side of Airport Way, tel. 907/452–1606) has cars for $35–$40 a day. You can rent bicycles at **Lucky Sourdough Tourist Trap** (402 Barnette St., tel. 907/456–2522) and **Beaver Sports** (2400 College St., tel. 907/479–2494) for $18 per 24 hours, plus a $250 deposit.

WHERE TO SLEEP

Fairbanks has seen a tourist boom in recent years, which means that there are budget hostels and B&Bs on every block. In short, unlike in other parts of Alaska, in Fairbanks there's no reason to pay big bucks for a cubicle in a charmless dive.

BED-AND-BREAKFASTS Most B&Bs offer singles during the summer for $40–$50 and doubles for $50–$85. The proprietors are great sources of information and will usually send a car for you to the airport or train station. Unfortunately, the better places fill up fast, so reserve well in advance, especially in summer. All of Fairbanks's B&Bs are listed in the *Visitor's Guide*, available at the visitor center (*see* Visitor Information, *above*); the following are some of the best values.

Ah Rose Marie. This 65-year-old downtown farmhouse, complete with a friendly cat and dog, has been revamped and now boasts a spiral staircase and lots of windows. In warm months, breakfast (fresh fruit and eggs) is served in the enclosed front porch. Singles start at $50, doubles at $65. *302 Cowles St., btw 3rd and 4th Aves., tel. 907/456–2040. 8 rooms, 2 with bath. No credit cards.*

Bell House. This old house enjoys a convenient downtown location and is filled with Victorian-style antiques, three cats, and a collection of 200 bells (hence the name). Rooms all have double beds and go for $55–$65. Breakfast consists of fruit and muffins in summer, heartier fare in winter. *909 6th Ave., at Cowles St., tel. 907/452–3278. 3 rooms, none with bath.*

Birch Grove Inn B&B. This warm cedar house sits among three acres of birch trees, a little ways north of town. The rooms, decorated with Alaskan artifacts, run from $45 in low season to $80 in high season. The owners here will bend over backwards to make sure you have a great stay. A different homemade breakfast (such as sourdough blueberry pancakes) is served daily. *691 Depauw Dr., tel. 907/479–5781. 3 rooms, none with bath. Closed Oct.–Jan.*

Birch Haven Inn. Northeast of downtown, this modern wooden house has four rooms with private bath for $60–$90. One of the owners is a pilot who is familiar with the area and can direct you to nearby hiking trails. *233 Fairhill Rd., ¾ mile from Steese Hwy., tel. 907/457–2451.*

HOSTELS **Fairbanks International Youth Hostel** changes location like a criminal on the lam. At press time, no one knew where they would be next. Check with the AYH for the latest information, or contact the manager at 907/456–4159; he's desperately searching for a permanent site. At least six private hostels have sprouted to fill the gap. If you like your hostels fun and grungy, try **Billie's Backpacker Hostel** (2895 Mack Rd., at Westwood Way., tel. 907/479–2034), about 1 mile from University Avenue, or **Fairbanks College Bunkhouse** (1541 Westwood Way, tel. 907/479–2627); these pack in travelers for $13.50 and $15, respectively. The company, especially at Billie's, is cosmopolitan, but the beds and showers are scary.

Alaska Heritage Inn and Hostel. This B&B/hostel is loosely affiliated with Hostelling International. B&B rooms go for $30 (single) and $40 (double), while each of the seven dorm bunks go for $16.20 the first night ($2 less if you're an HI member) and $13 the next. Tent sites ($5 per person) are also available. *1018 22nd Ave., at Gillam St., tel. 907/451–6587, fax 907/488–7899. From downtown, walk 15 min south down S. Cushman St. Closed to short-term visitors Oct.–May. No credit cards.*

North Woods Lodge and Hostel. If you have your own wheels and/or don't mind being out in the scenic boonies a few miles from town, the North Woods is a find. Tent sites are $7, spots in the sleeping loft go for $15, and cabins cost $25 for one or $40 for two. A luxurious loft for four is $50. Your excellent host, Tom Rinder, will show you the nearby trails and the enormous hot tub. *George Parks Hwy., tel. 907/479–5300 or 800/478–5305, fax 907/479–6888. Take first left off Chena Ridge onto Chena Pump Rd.; after 2 mi turn right onto Roland Rd., then right again onto E. Chena Hills Rd.; you'll see lodge on right.*

CAMPING All the hostels listed above offer tent spaces for $5–$7. If these are full, try one of the following campgrounds; all are close to MACS bus routes.

Chena River State Recreation Site. This wooded campground lies right on the banks of the river, about 1½ miles from the university and smack in the midst of swarms of mosquitoes. Sites go for $12 a night. There are no showers or stores nearby. *University Ave., at Chena River. Fire pits, picnic tables, toilets, water.*

John Alfonsi Sr. Memorial Campground. In a wooded area in the northwest corner of the university, this is the cheapest campground in town. Be cautious, however: Thefts have been reported here. Sites go for $15 per week or $4 per day. You can shower, do laundry, and get something to eat at Wood Center, a student activities building about a 15-minute walk away. *University of Alaska, tel. 907/474–7355. 13 sites. Toilets, water.*

Norlite Campground. This clean, safe, private campground is 2 miles out of town. Sara, the friendly owner, keeps a benevolent eye on everything. Campsites are about $8, $15 with car. *1660 Peger Rd., at Airport Way, tel. 907/474–0206. 59 sites. Groceries, laundry, picnic area, showers, snack bar, visitor information.*

FOOD

Food is expensive here, even by Alaskan standards. If you're on a tight budget, make use of the kitchen facilities available at all of the B&Bs and hostels listed, or fire up your camp stove. The area around the intersection of University Avenue and Airport Way has spawned a number of cheap mega-supermarkets such as the 24-hour **Safeway** and mammoth **Fred Meyer.** Be sure to indulge your sweet tooth at **Hot Licks** (3549 College Rd., at University Ave., tel. 907/479–7813 and 29 College Rd., tel. 907/451–0566), where the ice cream is made on the premises. For $16.95 you can join the crowds of tourists in an orgy of delicious grilled fish at **Salmon Bake,** in the Alaskaland theme park on Airport Way (*see* Worth Seeing, *below*).

For $12.95, you can participate in another all-you-can-eat gorge-fest of Mongolian barbecue at **Golden Shangai** (1900 Airport Way, tel. 907/451–1100), open daily 11:30–10, until 11 on Friday and Saturday. They also serve standard Chinese dishes (about $9). The **University of Alaska Cafeteria** (in Wood Center, on campus) serves institutional fare whose main redeeming quality is its price: Hot entrées cost $2–$3.

UNDER $5 **Bun on the Run.** This dinky white trailer with a striped awning may look funny, but the two women who own the place do all their baking right here. Cinnamon rolls, muffins, and sandwiches ($4) are all fresh and delicious. A cup of freshly ground coffee with a cinnamon roll costs about $2.25. *College Rd., in parking lot of Beaver Sports, about ¼ mi from University Ave. Open summer, Mon.–Sat. 8–6.*

Souvlaki. Near the train depot, Souvlaki serves traditional Mediterranean dishes as well as American food. Vegetarian selections include a pita with spicy falafel ($3.75) and Greek salad ($3.95). *112 N. Turner St., tel. 907/452–5393. Across bridge from visitor center. Open summer, weekdays 10–8, Sat. 10–6; winter, Mon.–Sat. 10–6.*

Whole Earth Grocery and Deli. Health food has finally come to Fairbanks (via air freight, of course). Whole Earth serves up healthy sandwiches on homemade bread and has a variety of deli salads as well as a do-it-yourself salad bar. Sandwiches run $3.25–$4.25. *1157 Deborah St., near University Ave., tel. 907/479–2052. Open weekdays 10–7, Sat. 10–6, Sun. noon–5.*

UNDER $10 **Gambardella's Pasta Bella.** This busy, downtown Italian joint guarantees good food and garlic breath. Lunch and take-out specials include gourmet pizzas ($9.95–$14.50), spicy Italian-sausage lasagne ($7.50, $9.50 with salad), and subs on homemade bread ($2.95–$5.50). You'll pay $9–$15 for the sit-down dinners after 5 PM, $3.25 more for the not-to-be-missed cheesecake. *706 2nd Ave., 4 blocks west of visitor center, tel. 907/456–3417. Wheelchair access.*

Plate & Palette Gallery Café. This huge café serves gourmet lunches and dinners. As you nibble on your lunchtime spinach salad with brie ($7.25), sandwich ($4–$6.50), or lentil-walnut burger ($6.95), other patrons mill around and gaze at the local artwork on the walls. Desserts are exotic, with such choices as blueberry-amaretto mousse ($3.75). Dinner gets pricey— entrées with foreign names go for $14.95–$17.95. *310 1st Ave., btw Dunkel and Noble Sts., tel. 907/451–9294. 3 blocks from visitor center. Open Mon.–Thurs. 10–7, Fri. 10 AM–midnight, Sat. 11–6. Wheelchair access.*

Sam's Sourdough Café. This place near the university has food that's less greasy than the well-worn diner atmosphere might lead you to expect. Excellent breakfasts, such as fresh veggie omelets ($6.75) and their special sourdough pancakes ($4), are served all day. A basket of fries and fried chicken or a complete dinner special goes for $7.95. *3702 Cameron St., at University Ave., tel. 907/479–0523. 1 block south of College Rd. Open weekdays 6 AM–10 PM, weekends 7 AM–10 PM. Weelchair access.*

WORTH SEEING

Pat Walsh of **VanGo Tours Inc.** (tel. 907/455–6499, fax 907/455–4126) offers an insider's tour of Alaska. Her specialty tour, "Faces of Alaska—Lifestyle Sampler," starts at $50 for a half day and takes you into the homes of local farmers, artists, and dog mushers, as well as around the city. She also arranges tours to remote bush villages and homesteads. **Alaska Sightseeing Tours** (553 1st Ave., tel. 907/452–8518) and **Gray Line** (Westmark Fairbanks, 10th and Noble Sts., tel. 907/452–2843 or Westmark Inn, 1521 Cushman St., tel. 907/452–5816) both offer highly impersonal tours of Fairbanks's hot spots for $22 and $23, respectively. You're better off buying a $10 day pass on G.O. Shuttle Service (*see* Getting Around, *above*).

Don't let anyone sucker you into going to Cripple Creek Resort, a reconstructed gold-mining village in Ester. It's nothing more than a tourist trap that shoves turn-of-the-century gold-rush shtick down the throats of unsuspecting visitors.

ALASKALAND If you have a perverse interest in tacky theme parks, you might be entertained by the Disneyland-goes-Old West quality of this one. Entrance to the grounds, with various exhibits on gold mining and Athabascan Indian villages, is free, but they try to lure you into all sorts of pricey and disappointing amusements. *Airport Way, at Peger Rd., tel. 907/459–1087. Open summer, daily 11–9.*

CREAMER'S FIELD Creamer's Field is a large, flat, open area that attracts more than 100 varieties of migratory birds, and the old dairy homestead here has been converted into the offices of the State Migratory Waterfowl Refuge. A 2-mile path winds through the refuge and affords excellent bird-watching opportunities. *1300 College Rd., tel. 907/451–7059. Next to Alaska Dept. of Fish and Game. Admission free.*

GOLD DREDGE NUMBER 8 The only gold dredge open to the public, Gold Dredge Number 8 was in use from 1928 to 1959. Today, you can take a tour and try to earn back the $10 admission fee by panning for gold. *1755 Old Steese Hwy., tel. 907/457–6058. Open summer, daily 9–6.*

STERN-WHEELER DISCOVERY You can take a cruise on the Chena and Tanana rivers aboard this antique stern-wheeler, but you'll have to pay through the nose ($25) and mingle with a gaggle of tourists. The four-hour trip includes a stop at a re-creation of an Athabascan Indian village and a dogsledding presentation. Cruises run May–September, daily at 8:45 AM and 2 PM. *Alaska Riverways, Dale Rd. Landing near airport, tel. 907/479–6673.*

UNIVERSITY OF ALASKA AT FAIRBANKS Built on top of the largest hill in Fairbanks, this university is renowned for its Geophysical Institute and Agricultural and Forestry Experiment Station Farm. It also contains some educational attractions for the general public, the most rewarding of which is the **UAF Museum.** The exhibits on history and the natural sciences are divided into Alaska's five main cultural and ecological regions—Southeast, Interior, Aleutians, Southwest, and Arctic—and give an overview of this huge and diverse land. Exhibits include the remains of a mammoth, a mastodon, and Blue Babe, a 38,000-year-old steppe bison. Look for the saber-toothed tiger's claw marks on Babe.

If it's hot and sunny, try taking a dip in the Gravel Pits, flooded quarries near the end of the airport runway. To find them, go south along University Avenue until you hit a maze of unmarked dirt roads, then follow a car filled with beach chairs or coolers. If no one fitting this description passes by, ask a local to point you in the right direction.

The UAF Museum also offers two worthwhile performances. From June through August, **Northern Inva Performances** (tel. 907/474–7505) presents demonstrations of Eskimo storytelling, songs, and athletics. Shows take place Tuesday–Sunday at 3 PM and 7 PM. The **Aurora Dome** (tel. 907/474–6944) breaks out into full color for a show on the aurora borealis. A ticket for *either* performance costs $10, and it's $15 for both; purchase tickets in the museum. *Museum tel. 907/474–7505. Admission: $4. Open summer, daily 9–8; shorter hrs off-season.*

If you've come to Alaska to see big critters, visit the university's **Large Animal Research Station,** home to musk-oxen, caribou, reindeer, and moose. Tours are given from June to August on Tuesdays and Saturdays at 1:30 PM and 3 PM, Thursday at 1:30 only. In September, you can catch a tour on Saturday at 1:30 PM. If you don't want to pay to get in, however, you can still see the animals roam around by walking behind the station at Mile 1 Yankovich Road, off Ballaine Road. *Tel. 907/474-7207 for tour info. Admission: $5, $2 students.*

AFTER DARK

Many residents head out of town to party. The coolest new hangout is the **Crazy Loon Saloon** (2999 George Parks Hwy., tel. 907/455-4487), five miles south of town. The Crazy Loon has good music and a college-age crowd. The rowdiest party is at the **Howling Dog Saloon** (2160 Old Steese Hwy., tel. 907/457-8780) in the town of Fox, about 11 miles north of Fairbanks, where you can dance to rock and R&B. The sand volleyball court outside is also the sight of a lot of action; it's easy to rotate into a game. Right across the street is the **Fox Roadhouse** (tel. 907/457-8780), a country and western two-stepper's heaven that also serves pricey steaks and seafood.

Back on the outskirts of Fairbanks, **Ivory Jack's** (2581 Goldstream Rd., tel. 907/455-6666) and the **Pump House Saloon** (Mile 1.3 Chena Pump Rd., tel. 907/479-8452) are upbeat nightspots. **The Boatel** (tel. 907/479-6537), about 2 miles from downtown on Airport Way, is the antithesis of upbeat; their self-bestowed moniker is the "sleazy waterfront bar." Don't be intimidated if the bartender shouts at you for your drink order—just shout it right back.

If you can't stay in Alaska year-round to see the changing of the seasons and the aurora borealis, LeRoy Zimmerman's "Crown of Light" show at the **Ester Firehouse Theater** (tel. 907/479-2500) in the town of Ester (7 miles south of Fairbanks on the George Parks Hwy.) is the next best thing. The performance starts at 8 PM daily and costs $5. If you'd rather have a quiet drink in Ester, try the **Golden Eagle Saloon** (tel. 907/479-0809), where you can just sit and make small talk with the bartender or the locals.

OUTDOOR ACTIVITIES

The best hiking near Fairbanks is out in Chena River State Recreation Area (*see below*). Dick Bouts of the **Bureau of Land Management** (tel. 907/474-2366) can provide info on some really strenuous, off-the-beaten-track trails. Easier 3- to 12-mile hikes can be found along the **Skarland Trails** on the west ridge of the University of Alaska campus; trail maps are available at the **UAF Museum** (*see* Worth Seeing, *above*). The **Birch Hill Ski Area,** off the Steese Highway, has 1- to 3-mile trails for easy walking and berry picking.

CANOEING The Chena River, which runs right through the center of town, flows gently enough that canoers can paddle both up- and downstream. The most popular canoeing outing is the **Tanana River trip,** which starts at the end of Chena Pump Road and goes for 60 miles to the town of Nenana, where you can catch a train back to Fairbanks. If you're a masochist, you can do this trip in a day; mere mortals may want to take two. **Beaver Sports** (2400 College St., tel. 907/479-2494) rents canoes for $24 a day.

In the winter you can take guided dogsled trips: You even get to drive your own team, a feat that will undoubtedly impress the folks back home.

DOG MUSHING So you really want an adventure? If you've ever been curious about what Alaska is really like in the winter, this is one way to find out. The best time to plan a dogsled trip is March. **VanGo Tours** (tel. 907/455-6499) offers a dogmushing workshop and wilderness day trip for $40-$75 per person. **Tivi Kennels** (tel. 907/832-5569) offers a more leisurely sled ride starting at $25 per person. Most companies provide you with arctic outer wear.

Near Fairbanks

CHENA RIVER STATE RECREATION AREA

This area, about 25 miles east of Fairbanks, encompasses the Chena River basin, a valley framed by Alpine hills. The Chena Hot Springs Road, which runs through a 25-mile stretch of the recreation area—Mile 26 to Mile 51—is paved, so car-rental companies will let you bring their vehicles here. You can choose from a range of primitive and developed campgrounds and a number of hiking trails that wind through the area's tundra and hills. **Angel Rocks** is a tough 3½-mile (round-trip) hike that runs along the river before veering past some rocky outcroppings that afford excellent views of the Alaska Range. The trail starts just before Mile 49 of Chena Hot Springs Road (turn right before the bridge). The **Granite Tors Trail** is a strenuous 12-mile circuit that crosses the tundra, passing two groups of tors (granite pinnacles); the trailhead is at the Mile 39 campground. If you're up for a real trek, try the **Chena Dome Trail,** a 30-mile trek that begins at Mile 50.5 and heads into the mountains ringing the valley. Allow three–four days and pack in all the supplies you'll need (including water and firewood).

Mile 37 of Chena Hot Springs Road is notorious for flooding after a heavy rain; it's unwise to try it in wet weather unless you have a four-by-four that can haul ass.

WHERE TO SLEEP You don't need reservations for the **Mile 27** or **Mile 39 campgrounds,** whose wheelchair accessible facilities include fire pits, picnic tables, bathrooms, and water. Sites cost $6 per night at both campgrounds. **Twin Bears Camp** (Mile 30 Chena Hot Springs Rd. tel. 907/451–2753) sits on the shore of a small lake and has a big recreation hall heated by a wood stove, a dining hall with cooking facilities, a laundry, and 12 unheated cabins that sleep about 50 people all told. The generators work only when the temperature tops 20°, so there's no electricity in winter. If you want to stay in any of the four primitive cabins in the recreation area, **North Fork** (Mile 48 Chena Hot Springs Rd.) is the easiest to reach. The others are about 6 miles off the road but may as well be in the next state: Bogs and river crossings make the trip hellish except in winter, when everything is frozen solid. For reservations, information, and maps, contact the **Alaska Division of Parks** (3700 Airport Way, Fairbanks, tel. 907/451–2695).

If you crave a hot bath or a cold drink after a grueling day of hiking, canoeing, or skiing, try the **Chena Hot Springs Resort** (Mile 57 Chena Hot Springs Rd., tel. 907/452–7867). The resort's swimming pool, hot pool, and whirlpools are open to the public for $8. The resort also has a full bar and a large dining room open for breakfast, lunch, and dinner; the food is surprisingly fresh and delicious. A dish like pasta primavera goes for $9, while hamburgers are $6. You can camp here, but the setting is not as picturesque as in the recreation area. Hotel rooms are expensive ($70–$100), but two cabins (sans running water) go for only $25 a night.

Denali National Park

Roughly translated from an Athabascan language, Denali means "the High One." If you're lucky enough to catch a glimpse of this 20,320-foot mountain through its self-spun cloak of clouds—especially when it shines white, then gold, during the summer midnight sunset—you'll know why. Although the U.S. Geological Survey lists the mountain's name as Mt. McKinley, the name Denali is more frequently used by Alaskans, who acknowledge that this mountain had a name long before the white explorers first saw it.

Denali National Park and Preserve is much more than a single great mountain, however—it's 6.9 million acres of pristine Alaskan territory. Whether you're backpacking, camping, climbing, or fishing, you're bound to exhaust yourself long before you exhaust the possibilities of the terrain. In addition to Denali, several other peaks topping 13,000 feet are found here. And, in the lowlands, the tundra and taiga forests are fed by swiftly flowing glacial rivers, and the only trails are those made by wild caribou, moose, wolves, and bears.

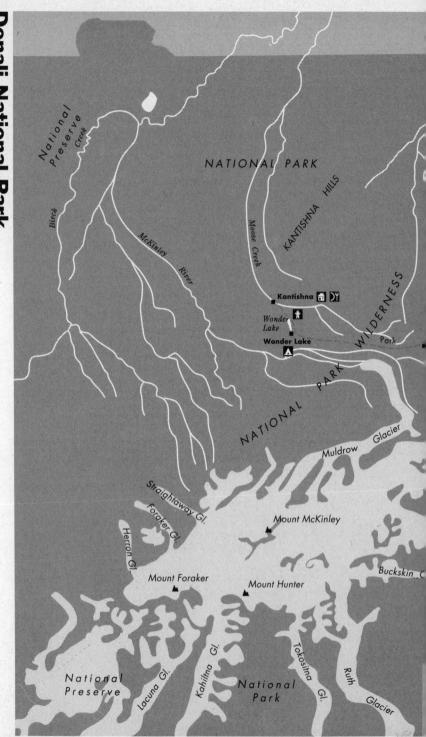

National Preserve

Birch Creek

National Park

McKinley River

Moose Creek

KANTISHNA HILLS

Kantishna

Wonder Lake

Wonder Lake

WILDERNESS

Park

NATIONAL PARK

Muldrow Glacier

Straightaway Gl.

Foraker Gl.

Herron Gl.

Mount McKinley

Mount Foraker

Mount Hunter

Buckskin

National Preserve

Lacuna Gl.

Kahiltna Gl.

National Park

Tokositna Gl.

Ruth Glacier

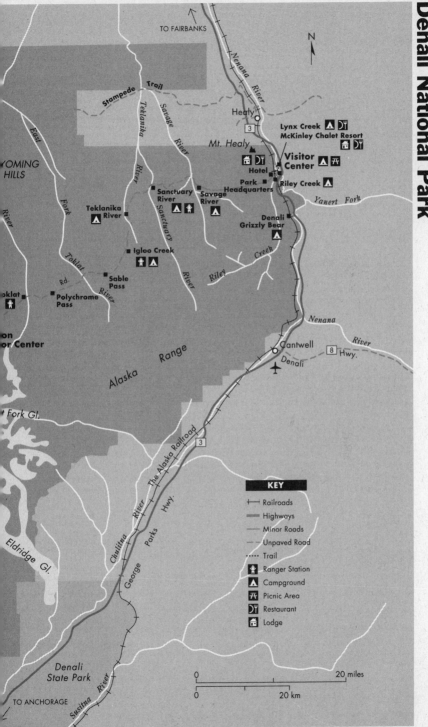

TO FAIRBANKS

N

Healy

Lynx Creek 🔺 🍴
McKinley Chalet Resort 🏠 🍴

Mt. Healy

Hotel 🏠 🍴

Visitor Center 🔺 ⛱

Park Headquarters

Riley Creek 🔺

Yanert Fork

WYOMING HILLS

East Fork River

Sanctuary River 🔺 🚹

Savage River 🔺

Teklanika River 🔺

Denali Grizzly Bear 🔺

Igloo Creek 🚹 🔺

Sable Pass

oklat

Polychrome Pass

on or Center

Alaska Range

Riley Creek

Nenana River

Cantwell
Denali

8 Hwy.

Fork Gl.

Eldridge Gl.

The Alaska Railroad

Chulitna River

George Parks Hwy.

3

KEY

├┼┤ Railroads
▬▬ Highways
── Minor Roads
─ ─ ─ Unpaved Road
········ Trail
🚹 Ranger Station
🔺 Campground
⛱ Picnic Area
🍴 Restaurant
🏠 Lodge

Denali State Park

TO ANCHORAGE

Susitna River

0 _____ 20 miles
0 _____ 20 km

Denali National Park

493

The park is sectioned into 43 backcountry units whose use is closely monitored by the rangers, so crowds are not a problem. The only time you'll feel crowded is at the visitor center at the park entrance or when riding a bus. Once you're actually in the park, you never have to see another human. You can lose yourself in the land—permanently, if you're not careful. You do

The bus system, which serves the single 85-mile road into the park, keeps Denali both accessible and unspoiled: Most private vehicles are not allowed beyond the Savage River Ranger Station at Mile 12.

need to observe unit closure boundaries—in order to make it hard for anyone to plead ignorance, the park service hands everyone a map showing clearly whether particular units are open or closed. You'll not only be fined if you're caught in a closed area, but you'll also be endangering yourself and the habitat of your fellow animals.

Be aware that very few trails traverse the park. If you plan any long hikes, estimate being able to cover half the distance you might normally cover on a maintained trail. Also, be prepared to get wet. Numerous streams and rivers crisscross the park, and a hike of any duration will mean passing through them, since there are no bridges (and if a stream doesn't soak you, a rain cloud almost certainly will).

BASICS

VISITOR INFORMATION Begin planning your trip to Denali before you reach Alaska. The park gets more than half a million visitors each year, most of whom come during the summer. This means that during the warm months it can be almost impossible to get spots in campgrounds or on shuttle buses. Make reservations for both the shuttle bus and campgrounds by calling 800/622–7275 in Alaska and the continental United States (except Anchorage) or 907/272–7275 from everywhere else. You can pay the park fees by credit card over the phone. The park's entrance fee is $5 per family, $3 per person. Call **Park Headquarters** (tel. 907/683–2294) for more information about fees.

The **Alaska Public Lands Information Center (APLIC)** in Fairbanks (*see* Visitor Information, in Fairbanks, *above*) will give you a map of the park and a copy of the park's informative paper, *Denali Alpenglow,* but you can no longer reserve bus seats and campgrounds from here.

Visitor Center (VC). If you've disregarded all the sage advice above and blown into Denali with no reservations, hightail it over here. This is the only place to make in-person campground reservations, and you can only make them a maximum of two days in advance. You can pick up a **backcountry permit** at the backcountry desk; you'll be assigned a zone, weighted down with bear-proof containers, and treated to a movie on bear encounters (to backcountry preparation what *Red Asphalt* is to driver's ed.). *On park rd, ½ mi off George Parks Hwy., tel. 907/683–1266. Open late May–mid-Sept., daily 7–6.*

Taiga and Tundra

Forest designated taiga (a Russian word meaning "land of little sticks") consists of small spruce, aspens, birch, and balsam poplar. Taiga forest grows in low valleys and river basins, where it's wet and relatively warm. From afar, this type of forest looks open and accessible, but it's actually a hiking nightmare, as a result of the dense bushes that grow among the trees. Tundra begins where the taiga forest stops, at around 2,700 feet. This kind of terrain is characterized by small shrubs and miniature wildflowers, as well as low-bush cranberries, lingonberries, and crowberries. Tundra can be moist, with swampy fields of tussocks (low vegetation), or dry and brittle. You can join the rangers at Denali's Eielson Visitor Center (Mile 66) weekly for an easy nature walk through the tundra.

PUBLICATIONS *Denali Alpenglow* is a free paper published once a year by the park. Available at APLIC offices, the VC, and several visitor-information centers in Alaska, it will answer most of your questions about the park. Also sold at the VC bookstore and APLIC is the essential *Backcountry Companion* ($8.95), by park naturalist Jon Nierenberg, who provides a practical assessment of the various backcountry units in Denali.

The mosquito isn't Alaska's unofficial state bird for nothing. In summer, turbo mosquito repellent, mosquito coils, and yes, even those dumb-looking head nets are worth bringing. After a few days, you'll be wishing you'd brought a flamethrower as well.

WHEN TO GO When you visit Denali depends largely on your fortitude. If you like to mush dogs or cross-country ski, late February, March, and early April are best—the icy, pristine beauty is amazing. Big advantages during these late winter months are the lack of crowds, mosquitoes, and bears. You'll rarely have days above freezing, though, and you should be well-versed in the vagaries of weather in extreme northern latitudes.

Spring breakup, which occurs anytime from mid-April to mid-May, is miserable throughout Alaska. This is when the snow and ice start melting, and everything turns to muck. June, July, and August—the warmest months—are the most popular in the park. During these months, the tundra flowers bloom, the days are long, and lower elevations are green and lush.

WHAT TO PACK If you have the guts to come to the park in winter, you should already be experienced enough with extreme cold weather to know what to pack. If, like most people, you come in the summer, you won't encounter extreme temperatures, but you should be prepared for temperatures from 30° to 90°. You can count on rain during your visit; you'll want gear such as a waterproof jacket and pants that slip on easily over clothing. Above all, make sure your tent is water-resistant and bug-proof. Footwear should be sturdy—hiking boots that provide good ankle support will be helpful if you go into the rugged backcountry—and you should be sure always to have a dry pair of socks in reserve. Lightweight, Neoprene socks provide the best insulation.

Bring along some foot-size, leak-proof plastic bags. If your shoes get wet while hiking, you can don your dry socks once you make camp, slip the plastic bags over your feet, and put your wet boots back on.

SUPPLIES **The Mercantile,** at Mile 1.4 of the park road, sells a limited selection of groceries, beer and wine, camping fuel, and film. It's also the only place to buy gas (at outrageous prices) in the park, and has the only public showers ($2). A **post office,** open daily 7 AM–10 PM, is right next door. Outside the park, **Lynx Creek** (Mile 238.6 George Parks Hwy., tel. 907/683–1240) sells some groceries, prepared foods, camping supplies, and gas.

Doing Denali

Each summer, hundreds of climbers attempt to scale North America's highest mountain, whose vertical relief is greater than that of Mt. Everest. Of the hundreds that try it, only half reach the peak; many are stopped by powerful storms that drive temperatures down to unlivable levels. Two routes to the top have been dubbed the Orient Express and the Autobahn in honor of the high numbers of Asians and Germans, respectively, who perished on them. The youngest successful climber was a 12-year-old Boy Scout; an elderly blind woman has also made it to the summit. The first successful summer ascent occurred in 1913. During the first successful winter ascent, in 1967, the temperature was -168°, adjusted for wind chill.

COMING AND GOING

The marked entrance to the park is off the George Parks Highway, which connects Anchorage and Fairbanks. The drive from Anchorage takes about five hours; from Fairbanks, about two. All buses between the two cities will let you off at the park. It's also pretty easy to hitchhike here. (The youth hostel in Anchorage is a good place to find a ride or a hitching buddy.) **The Alaska Railroad** (tel. 907/265–2494 in Anchorage) provides direct, daily service to the park from Anchorage (8 hrs, $85) and Fairbanks (4½ hrs, $45). The park depot is just a short walk

If you're leaving Denali for Anchorage, be forewarned that you can't catch a shuttle bus from inside the park in time to catch the daily 12:30 PM train that leaves from just outside the park—plan to spend your last night at Morino campground instead.

from Morino campground. Buses are cheaper and faster (though less scenic) than the train. **Denali Express** (tel. 800/327–7651) runs between the park and Anchorage ($35) and Fairbanks ($25). **Moon Bay Express** (tel. 907/274–6454) and the **Backpacker Shuttle** (tel. 907/344–8775) both leave from the downtown Anchorage youth hostel for Denali ($35). **Fireweed Express** (tel. 907/452–0521) will shuttle you from Fairbanks to Denali for $25.

The gravel Denali Highway is seldom used because it is, literally, hell on wheels. Dust and flying rocks from passing vehicles are a major problem, especially since people drive so fast. If you get a rock through your oil pan or have some other kind of mechanical mishap, you'd better have a high limit on your credit card—tow trucks and auto repairs don't come cheap here. This is an excellent road for mountain bikes, though, as long as you carry extra tires, tubes, and a small repair kit. You should also have some sort of water-purification system.

GETTING AROUND

A single 85-mile road runs into the park from the entrance near the George Parks Highway. The only private vehicles allowed beyond the Savage River Ranger Station, 12 miles from the park entrance, are those bearing folks camping at Teklanika River (*see* Camping, *below*).

The Denali Highway

If you want to get a great look at the Alaska Range, drive the Denali Highway, a rough gravel road that connects the George Parks Highway with the Richardson Highway, 130 miles to the east. The Denali Highway, open summer only, starts at Cantwell, about 27 miles south of the Denali National Park entrance. The views of the Alaska Range, including Mt. McKinley (Denali), are outstanding. You're also likely to see bears, porcupines, beavers, caribou, moose, ptarmigans (the state bird, known locally as "stupid chickens"), and trumpeter swans. Grayling and lake trout abound in the many lakes and clear streams that lie just off the highway. If you go hiking off the highway, be sure to take topographical maps, because there are no trails. You can camp anywhere along the road or stay at one of the three campgrounds along the route. Food and gas are available every 20 miles or so. The three best places to make pit stops and inquiries about the location and condition of local trails are: the Tangle River Inn (Mile 22), the McClaren Lodge (Mile 41), and the Gracious House (Mile 82). Rich, at the Tangle River Inn, also rents canoes and sells topographical maps for two nearby canoe/kayak routes: the Delta River Canoe Route and the Upper Tangle Lakes Canoe Route.

BY BUS The park's **shuttle buses** leave the visitor center every 30 minutes between early morning and late afternoon. You must book a time and obtain a coupon from the VC (*see* Visitor Information, *above*) to board these shuttles. Once upon a time, these buses were free; now a seat on the shuttle costs $12 to Toklat, $30 to Eielson Visitor Center (Mile 66), and $30 to Wonder Lake at the end of the road. At press time, the park was planning a three-day discounted shuttle-bus pass—ask about it at the VC or over the phone when you make your reservations.

Once you're a few miles past the center, you can get on and off these buses at will to hike and explore, but if a bus is full, it will not stop to pick you up. The next bus with a space, and/or the last bus of the day, will always make room. **Camper buses** run less frequently throughout the day—about five go round-trip daily during the busiest part of summer. These buses, which have a luggage area for backpacks and bicycles, are reserved for campers with packs and back-country or campground permits. Prices are the same as for the shuttle bus. The free **Riley Creek Loop Bus** leaves the VC every half hour and makes a 1-mile loop, with stops at the Denali Park Hotel, Morino campground, and the train depot. If you're hitchhiking, you can use the **courtesy buses** run by the big lodges to get to and from the George Parks Highway.

BY BIKE No special permit is required to bike in Denali, but biking is allowed *on the park road only*. Mountain bikes are preferable, as the road is unpaved past the Savage Creek Ranger Station. The road is relatively level, but it gets dusty on dry days, and you can lose almost all visibility when a bus passes. **Denali Mt. Bike** (inside park, tel. 907/322–0716) rents bikes for a scandalous $25 a day.

WHERE TO SLEEP

Camping is the way to go in Denali, not only because it heightens the experience of being in the wilderness, but because local hotels and cabins charge an arm, a leg, and your firstborn. Most campgrounds are only open in summer. Your best bet for an indoor sleep is the **Denali Hostel**, which offers spanking-clean bunk-style rooms, showers, kitchen facilities, and break-fast for $22 a night. All ages are welcome, and there's even a room for couples. The owners will transport you to and from the park for free. *Tel. 907/683–1295. Coming from park toward Healy on park road, turn left on Otto Lake Rd. and continue 1½ mi.*

HOTELS AND CABINS Break out your credit card: Hotels and cabins are expensive and cater mostly to tour groups. Hotel rates average $100, while cabins hover around $80. Cabins are much quieter than hotels, which tend to have thin walls, but they often lack private bath-rooms. Three clean places are clustered around the park entrance: **Denali Crow's Nest Log Cab-ins** (tel. 907/683–2723), **Denali Cabins** (tel. 907/683–2643), and **Denali Grizzly Bear Cabins and Campground** (tel. 907/683–2696). The **Denali Park Hotel** (tel. 907/683–2215) is the only lodge inside the park and is close to the railroad station and shuttle buses, but rooms cost over $100. Reservations are necessary at all places.

CAMPING Campgrounds in Denali are generally well maintained. All except Morino require reservations. Potable water is available at all campgrounds, but you won't find any laundry facilities or showers. Three campgrounds—Riley Creek, Savage River, and Teklanika River—are open to both RVs and tents. Campgrounds with tent camping and bus access are Sanctuary, Igloo, and Wonder Lake. There are no campfires allowed at Sanctuary, Wonder Lake, or Morino, but the others all have fire grates.

Sleeping in the backcountry is as wild as camping gets. Be sure you know the rules of minimal-impact camping—this will insure that you don't leave any marks on the environment and it doesn't leave any on you. You're on your own once you enter the backcountry, and you should be prepared to handle emergencies. Help could be several hours or even days away if you are injured. Pick up your backcountry permit at the VC (*see* Visitor Information, *above*).

➤ **INSIDE THE PARK • Igloo Creek.** Situated on beautiful Igloo Creek, about 34 miles from the park entrance, this tents-only campground has sites for $12 a night. Nearby Igloo Mountain is a moderate climb that requires no technical gear. Ask a ranger about the best route up the mountain.

Morino. This wooded campground is reserved for backpackers without vehicles. Just 1½ miles from the park entrance, Morino is near the train depot and the Mercantile, the park's only general store, and is a great place to meet other backpackers. Sites are $3.

Riley Creek. Half a mile from the park entrance, this campground is one of only three at which you can park a vehicle. It's also one of the easiest places to snag a space. A night of picnic tables, plenty of trees, and obnoxious squirrels can all be yours for $12.

Sanctuary River. On the banks of a large glacial river 22 miles from the park entrance, this campground is near Primrose Ridge, a popular hiking area. Sites are $6.

Savage River. One of only two park campgrounds with a view of Denali, Savage River allows vehicles. The campground is 12 miles from the park entrance. Sites are $12.

Wonder Lake must have gotten its name either because the view of Denali is so wonderful from here, or because it's a wonder you can see Denali through the clouds of mosquitoes.

Teklanika River. Of the three campgrounds open to vehicles, this one lies deepest in the park. There aren't many trees and the ground is rather flat, so if someone's making noise, you'll hear it at every campsite. The best sites are along the riverbank. Sites cost $12.

Wonder Lake. Eighty-five miles from the park entrance, this campground has the best view of Denali. Several tent sites ($12) face the mountain from the side of a hill. Head nets and mosquito repellent are strongly advised.

➤ **OUTSIDE THE PARK** • **Denali Grizzly Bear Cabins and Campground.** Near the park entrance, Grizzly Bear has showers, laundry, and a small general store. Well-kept tent sites are $15. *Mile 231.1 George Parks Hwy., tel. 907/683–2696.*

Lynx Creek. These campsites are a little bare, but you get showers, a store, great food, and a pub. Sites are $15 a night. *Mile 238.7 George Parks Hwy., tel. 907/683–1240.*

FOOD

Bring food from Anchorage or Fairbanks if you can. Goods in the small grocery stores near the park cost 1½ times as much as they do in the cities. The bigger lodges and cabin complexes all have restaurants, but your only choice for a reasonably priced meal nearby is **Lynx Creek Pizza** (Mile 238.6 George Parks Hwy., tel. 907/683–2547), just north of the park entrance, where you can get a slice of pizza and a drink for less than $5. Lynx Creek also has a bar that becomes something of a meat market at night.

If you make the 10-minute drive south of the park entrance to **Perch** (Carlo Creek, off George Parks Hwy. at Mile 24, tel. 907/683–2523), you'll be rewarded with an absolutely amazing breakfast. Rangers and local guides flock here for the homemade breakfasts (served daily 6 AM–1 PM). You *must* try the french toast ($4) made from their own fresh-beaked bread. Lunch isn't served, but you can buy a box lunch for $5.50. Dinner (served 5 PM–10 PM) gets gourmet and pricey; you'll pay $15–$25 for an elegant meal.

EXPLORING DENALI

If you're disabled or disinclined to venture into the wilderness, you can still get a good sense of the land by riding the park bus along the 85-mile road to Wonder Lake. From the road, you're likely to see caribou, moose, and grizzly bears. But if you can, get out and walk—you can hike for miles without ever losing sight of the road. Out in the backcountry, how you explore Denali is very much up to you—the park covers 6.9 million acres, and many of these acres have no trails to lead you around.

ORIENTATION PROGRAMS Try to catch the free half-hour **dogsled demonstrations** (usually at 4 PM) at the Park Headquarters and Dog Kennels, at Mile 3.4 of the park road. The park uses dogsled patrols during the winter, and the powerful animals are truly something to behold.

Showtimes are posted at the main visitor center (*see* Visitor Information, *above*) and in park buses. The visitor center also presents two valuable, free 10-minute slide shows: One is a general overview of the park; the other focuses on the backcountry.

HIKING Two free ranger-led "Discovery Hikes" are offered daily in different areas of the park. Most are strenuous, and they generally last four to six hours. Often involving climbs, these hikes are a good way to explore this pathless wilderness. The ranger will also be able to answer your questions about most of the flora, fauna, and geography of the park. Information on the hikes is posted at the visitor centers and on campground bulletin boards. No registration is needed—just show up at the appointed place and time.

Trailheads for the few maintained trails in the park lie between the Park Headquarters and the main visitor center. The book, *The Nature of Denali* ($4), available at the visitor center, describes the trails; the best of the bunch is the moderate 4-mile hike up to the **Mt. Healy overlook** and back. The trailhead is behind the Denali Park Hotel (follow the trail signs); most hikers quit when they reach the overlook, but the trail continues on to Mt. Healy. If you make it out to the Eielson Visitor Center, head up the trail that begins north of the center and leads to **Thoroughfare Ridge**. It will take you less than an hour to reach the top, and, if the weather is clear, you'll get a great view of Denali. Take a shuttle bus into the park in order to survey the terrain before you set out into the backcountry. If you plan to hike out of sight of the park road, bring along a topographical map of the area. Remember there are no bridges over the many streams, so prepare to get your feet wet. On warm days, small creeks can turn into numbingly cold, churning rivers from the snowmelt.

Ridges often have slopes made of loose crumbling rock called schist or scree. Crossing a scree slope can also be difficult because you sink to your knees in the stuff and your boots get filled with it.

Ridges and streambeds generally provide the easiest hiking. Low-lying flat areas are usually marshy and tussocky (full of low vegetation), making for pretty miserable hiking. If you need to cross this terrain, just relax and take your time slogging through it.

Primrose Ridge and the **Polychrome** and **Eielson** rest areas are popular spots to begin moderate hikes; all are easily reached via shuttle. Well-maintained, beautiful, and quite steep, the **Horseshoe Lake Trail** (1½ miles round-trip) begins where the railroad track crosses the park road, between the main visitor center and the Morino campground. Don't overlook this trail just because it's near the more populated and accessible areas of the park. You can often see beavers, moose, and birds on this trail. Find a quiet place to sit by Horeshoe Lake and watch its beaver lodge—it's not hard to catch a glimpse these animals at work.

BIRD-WATCHING More than 150 species of birds—including golden eagles, red-throated loons, and arctic terns—migrate to Denali every summer. The area around Wonder Lake has many small ponds and lakes where you can observe waterfowl, including a loons' nest on the northern side of the lake. Ask a ranger for the best birding areas at any given time of the year.

FISHING No permit is needed to fish within the Denali National Park. Although most rivers are too heavily silted for fish, you can find a few clear streams where you can catch trout. Wonder Lake is good for fly-fishing.

RAFTING Several rafting companies will take you for a white-water ride down the icy, class-four Nenana River. Operators provide waterproof gear, and some tours include a riverside lunch with a campfire. The river is run in two sections: The part south of the park entrance is comparatively easy, while the northern section is extremely wild. Only very experienced rafters should attempt this section of the river—several people have died on it. Operators include **Denali Raft Adventures** (tel. 907/683–2234) and **McKinley Raft Tours** (tel. 907/683–2392). Two-hour trips cost $35–$40.

The Arctic Circle and the Bush

Travelers come here for one of two rea- sons: just to say they've been above the Arctic Circle (tour companies can take care of that whim for $50–$100), and because northern Alaska is one of the last pristine wildernesses on earth—so far, humans have had little significant impact up here. Whether you want to climb the jagged peaks of the **Brooks Range** or hike across the vast Arctic tundra, what you will find here is untrammeled nature. Apart from a few scattered Eskimo settlements, the Alaska Pipeline, and the oil fields of Prudhoe Bay, this enormous expanse belongs to birds, bears, and caribou. Fairbanks is the starting point for almost all travel north of the Arctic Circle. The only road that runs into it—the Dalton Highway (*see below*)—starts in Fairbanks, and many of the region's bush pilots operate out of that city, as well. Except for the area immediately off the Dalton Highway, the Arctic Circle is accessible only by air. If you're planning on camping and hiking, don't come unprepared. There are no maintained trails for you to follow, and no one is around to help if you screw up.

You'll find the tamer side of the bush in Nome, a product of the 1898 gold rush; and the soft side of the Arctic Circle in "larger" towns such as Barrow, the northernmost settlement in the Americas. Most hotels in Barrow start at $90 per night, and food is also expensive, so grab your tent and stuff your pockets with granola bars before heading up. In addition to the smaller bush airlines, both Alaska Airlines and MarkAir have established routes and one-day or overnight package deals for less than $400. Unfortunately, these tours tend to shuttle you through with only a superficial glance from a tour bus window. If you're going to blow your dough on one trip up to the Arctic, slap your money down for a ticket to the culturally rich town of Anaktuvuk.

Anaktuvuk Pass

The Inupiat name Anaktuvuk translates roughly as "the place where the caribou shit," which, considering the modesty of caribou, should give you an indication of the wildness of this area. The village of Anaktuvuk lies on the Anaktuvuk River in the **Gates of the Arctic National Wildlife Preserve's** Brooks Range. Flying into the village will take your breath away (or bring your lunch up), as the pilot skirts mountain peaks and dips into the wide valley of Anaktuvuk Pass. An odd collection of trailers with plywood additions, this remote indigenous village must have all building materials, heavy equipment, and vehicles flown in. Few who live in Alaskan bush villages care for tourists, but those in Anaktuvuk Pass are remarkably tolerant of outsiders. The displays at both the **Simon Panaek Museum** (341 Mekiana Rd., tel. 907/661–3413) and the connected **Hans van der Laan Brooks Range Library**, open weekdays 8:30–5, will introduce you to the local Eskimo culture and the wilderness of the Brooks Range. The one camp in town is **Nunamiat Camp** (1038 Illinois St., tel. 907/661–3026 or 907/661–3220); a bed in a room that sleeps three–four goes for about $165 a night, including three meals. The camp's small restaurant (tel. 907/661–3123) serves standard fare such as hamburgers ($5). You'll get laughed at if you ask about a room with a private bath or flush toilets, but there are showers. If you're camping on your own, make sure you pitch your tent far enough from town that your stuff won't be an easy target for curious kids.

If you're a serious and experienced backpacker—you know how to read a topographical map, use a compass, and dress suitably for the terrain—and you like your camping wild, rugged, and cold, this is the place to be. ATV (all-terrain vehicle) trails extend only a few miles from the village—after that, you're on your own. Expect many stream crossings and plenty of hiking through boggy muskeg. The weather here can change quickly, and you can run into freezing temperatures even in summer. At higher elevations, the mountain passes have snow year-round. Before you set out, check in with the Park Service cabin next to the airstrip to let them know where you're going and when you'll be back. The Gates of the Arctic National Park and Preserve is a minimum-impact preserve. Make sure you know the park regulations before you start your trip, and be smart about the wildlife in the area, especially the bears. To prevent

ARCTIC OCEAN

Chukchi Sea

Barrow   Pt. Barrow
Wainwright   Alaktak
        Atkasuk   Prudhoe
                        Bay
                    Deadhorse

Point Hope   LOOKOUT   RIDGE
        BAIRD   MTS   Colville River
Noatak   CONTINENTAL DIVIDE   BROOKS   RANGE
National   Noatak   Anaktuvuk Pass
Noatak   Preserve   River
Cape Krusenstern   Kobuk Valley   Gates of the Arctic
National   Katzebue   National   National Park
Monument   Park   and Wildlife
Shishmaref   Preserve   Dalton Hwy
        ARCTIC   CIRCLE
Wales   Bering   Selawik   Bettles
Land Bridge   National Wildlife
Teller   National Preserve   Reserve   Kanuti Flats
        Koyukuk   National
SEWARD PENINSULA   National   Wildlife
    Council   Wildlife   Refuge   Livengood
Nome   Refuge
    Moses   Koyukuk   Baker   Fairbanks
    Point   Nulato   Yukon River
Norton Sound   Unalakleet   Nowitna National
            Wildlife Refuge
Bering   St. Michael   Innoko   Denali   Denali
Sea   National   National   Hwy
    Scammon Bay   Wildlife   Park   Cantwell
            Refuge   Denali
Hooper Bay   Holy Cross   (Mt. McKinley)   Willow
    Yukon Delta   Aniak   Palmer
    National
    Wildlife   Anchorage
    Refuge   Bethel   Tyonek
            Lake   Kenai   Whittier
Kuskokwim   Togiak   Clark   Seward
Bay   National Wildlife   National
    Refuge   Park   Homer
Platinum   Togiak
    Aleknagik   N
    Dillingham
    Naknek   Katmai
    King Salmon   National
    Egegik   Park
Bristol Bay   Ugashik   Port Lions
        Kodiak   Kodiak
ALASKA PENINSULA   Port Heiden   National
        Wildlife   Kodiak
    Chignik   Refuge   Island   Gulf of Alaska
Port
Moller

KEY
Rail Lines

0   100 miles
0   150 km

The Alaskan Bush

501

ingesting some nasty parasites, purify all your drinking water, especially at lower elevations. **Frontier Flying Service** (tel. 907/474–0014) offers two scheduled flights daily into Anaktuvuk from Fairbanks (about $250 round-trip) and also provides tours and tips on backpacking in the area.

Barrow

Just 4 miles south of Point Barrow, the northernmost point in the United States, Barrow is a remarkable town. Many people come here just to see the "midnight sun," which doesn't set for 82 days from late May to early August. The flat area around Barrow was formed as the polar ice cap retreated from the north slope of the Brooks Range after the last Ice Age. Formally called the North Slope, this region is home to the Inupiat Eskimos who have hunted whales, walrus, seals, and polar bears here for centuries. Today, Barrow is the seat of the North Slope Borough and the government and cultural center for the people of this region. If

Standing on the black sands of Barrow's beaches at 2 AM and gazing across the white ice floes of the Arctic Ocean is a singular experience.

you're looking to purchase native crafts, the **North Slope Borough** offices has the best prices and selection. It's in the turquoise building at the far eastern end of Agvik Street and is open weekdays 8:30–5.

Traditionally, whaling has provided the basic means of subsistence for the Inupiat, and they celebrate their whaling heritage every summer with *nalakatuqs*, or whaling festivals. Although whaling is still practiced, its economic importance has been overshadowed by the revenues generated by the North Slope natural gas leases. As a result, this town of 3,000 perched on the edge of the Arctic Ocean has almost total employment and very high wages. It has its share of problems, too, however. Though Barrow is officially "damp" (meaning alcohol can only be imported for personal use, and not bought or sold), the town still faces a serious drug and alcohol crisis, and the beauty of its surroundings stands in stark contrast to the dirty condition of its streets and beaches.

COMING AND GOING   Barrow is not geared toward the budget traveler. The cheapest way to see the town is on a one-day package tour with **MarkAir** (tel. 800/258–2746) or **Alaska Airlines** (800/468–2248) for $383. Once in Barrow, you won't have any problem getting around: Oil money has created the most reliable bus system in Alaska, but nobody seems to use it. Empty

Camping on Barrows's beach is frowned upon, but if you're determined to try, wander out of town a ways. As a backpacker, you'll stick out like a frostbitten thumb, but you should be okay if you keep two rules in mind: Don't leave any valuables lying around, and don't expect your unguarded tent to remain where you left it.

buses roll up and down the town every 20 minutes and cost only $1; the main bus station is opposite the MarkAir terminal on Ahkovak Street. Street signs are nearly as rare as surfboards up here—they all get knocked down by cars and trucks in the winter. Just ask locals for directions.

WHERE TO SLEEP AND EAT   The **UIC-N.A.R.L. Hotel** (tel. 907/852–7800) offers the cheapest doubles around ($90). It's 4 miles out of town, but there's express bus service from downtown that runs three times daily. The **Airport Inn** (1815 Momegana St., tel. 907/852–2525) and the **Top of the World Hotel** (1200 Atvik St., tel. 907/852–3900) are top-of-the-line places. A double at the Airport costs $130 ($120 in cash); a similar room at the Top of the World is $150.

Food prices in Barrow are equally outrageous. If you haven't brought supplies with you, head to **A.C. Stuaqpak** (Agvik St., at Kiogak St.), which is open daily 9 AM–midnight and sells groceries and deli and bakery fare. The two best restaurants in town are **Arctic Pizza** (125 Apayuak St., near Pisokak St., tel. 907/852–4222), where small pizzas go for $15; large pizzas with the works are $48 (!!). The **Teriyaki House** (Ahkovak St., opposite Alaska Airlines, tel. 907/852–2276) serves Japanese and Chinese specialties; sushi is $3.90–$5.90 for two pieces. Both restaurants are open daily from 11:30 to 11.

Dalton Highway

The Dalton Highway extends due north from Fairbanks into the Arctic Circle and all the way to the Arctic Ocean. The 415-mile route crosses the Yukon River and the Brooks Range before ending at the Prudhoe Bay oil fields. Built in the 1970s during the construction of the Trans-Alaska pipeline, this gravel road is the major supply route for the oil fields and the only road running above the Arctic Circle. At press time, the Dalton Highway was officially open to the public only as far as Disaster Creek at Mile 209. However, public pressure may lead to the opening of the road all the way to Deadhorse, 10 miles south of Prudhoe Bay. The oil companies object to public use of this highway because of the heavy truck traffic—and consequent poor visibility due to dust kicked up by commercial trucks—on this narrow road.

The highway offers access to the rugged **Brooks Range**, which crosses northern Alaska from east to west, and the **Gates of the Arctic National Park,** which lies to the west of the highway. No trails or visitor centers exist in the park, so to visit it you must be completely self-sufficient. Tundra, rough-hewn valleys, and 6,000-foot sawtooth ridges offer a unique trekking experience for the intrepid. Many people drive or hitch to **Dietrich,** just south of the Disaster Creek checkpoint, and walk into the park. Topographical maps are a necessity, and you must keep a sharp lookout for bears.

You can get groceries and gas at the Yukon River (Mile 56) and at Coldfoot (Mile 175). Otherwise, there are *no services* for travelers along the 415 miles of this nasty, dusty, gravel road until you reach Deadhorse (if the road is even open to Deadhorse, that is). If you do reach Deadhorse, you can pay exorbitant prices for gasoline (about twice the price as in Fairbanks) and buy a bag of potato chips, but that's about it. If your vehicle breaks down, you can get a tow from either Yukon Bridge or Coldfoot for $5 per mile. You should only drive pickup trucks or four-by-fours on the Dalton Highway—RVs are not recommended.

GUIDED TOURS The **Northern Alaska Tour Company** (Fairbanks, tel. 907/474–8600) shuttles visitors 115 miles up the Dalton Highway to the Arctic Circle from Fairbanks in their small vans and minibuses. The all-day tours cost about $95 and include lunch and snacks. A better, more expensive trip ($145) involves driving up and flying back, and for $30 extra includes a boat ride on the Yukon River to Stevens Village, an Athabascan fishing camp. The flight back is worth the extra money for the outstanding views of the Yukon Flats and the Ray and White mountain ranges.

Nome

If you thought the wild frontier towns were a faded part of America's past, you haven't been to Nome. This weather-beaten town is a living reminder of a gold-rush boomtown. But unlike Dawson City, with its Klondike glitz, Nome represents the grittier side of the gold rush—when hungry, crazy-eyed men would kill you for looking at 'em the wrong way. Gold mining is still the major industry in Nome, although it's hard to say whether the prospectors or the saloons are raking in the dough faster. Nome is one of the few places in Alaska's remote northern areas to remain "wet," meaning you can legally buy and sell alcohol. Folks fly in from all over the

Bad News Bears

Bears along "Haul Road" (as the Dalton Highway is known) are pretty savvy when it comes to getting a free meal. Many hang around Dietrich or other small settlements near the road and raid garbage dumps, so you should be extra careful with your food. Many people carry firearms for protection against bears—it's legal to kill a bear in defense of life or property (including your tent), as long as you report it. Just make sure you shoot straight—a wounded bear will shred you.

northwest to party here. At times, Nome's nightlife resembles a saloon scene from a B-grade western, and bar brawls are common.

Nome lies in the midst of a treeless tundra on the southern coast of the Seward Peninsula, a thinly populated region jutting out of western Alaska into the Bering Strait, toward Siberia. The western tip of the peninsula is believed to be the remainder of a land bridge that once joined the Americas with Siberia. Gold washes down the rivers onto the beaches, and a handful of prospectors still work small claims a nugget's throw from the town's main street. The law established in the original 1898 gold rush states says that anyone can establish a gold claim on the beach—all you have to do to stake your claim is to work it. The minute you leave, however, you forfeit all rights to that claim.

A couple of years ago in one of Nome's saloons, a bartender leaped over the bar and slit the throat of a patron he hated, but accidently got the wrong man. The victim lived, and the bartender is still working in Nome. Do yourself a favor and don't bring up the subject, especially in a bar.

Nome's gold-mining history is definitely its main attraction—the town is littered with rusting gold dredges. The dredges aren't safe, and it's illegal to walk within half a mile of them. Three gold dredges still operate around the clock. The **Carrie McLain Museum** (Front St., at Lanes Way, tel. 907/443–2566), in the basement of the library, has information on Nome's wild gold rush past and is open daily in summer from 10 to 7. Upstairs, the **Kegoayah Kozga Library** (tel. 907/443–5133) holds a rare book collection with first editions of books on Alaska. At 7:30 nightly, the **visitor center** (see Visitor Information, *below*) hosts an informative, often lively talk by a Nome local. You can sit elbow-to-elbow with locals with a story to tell at the **XYZ Center** (Front St., at north end of City Hall), where local crafts are also sold. From September to May, the XYZ provides an excellent lunch (usually including reindeer, blueberries, and other foods native to the area) for Nome elders at noon; visitors are welcome. You'll pay less than $5 for your meal and get a chance to meet fascinating people.

On warm summer days, head out to **Anvil Mountain** (elevation 1,100 feet) for stellar views of the coast and the wildflowers. Another diversion in this town is to try and hit one of its wacky races, held throughout the year. The most famous is the infamous Iditarod Sled Race in March (see box, *below*). Others include the **Homemade Raft Race** (June), the **Bering Sea Ice Golf Classic** (March), or the **Bathtub Race** (Labor Day). More conventional is the **Anvil Mountain Run,** held every July 4th, that starts on Front Street and heads up the mountain and back. The record time so far is one hour and 11 minutes.

BASICS

AMERICAN EXPRESS American Express Travel Service (Front St., near visitor center, tel. 907/443–2211) takes care of money and mail for cardmembers.

VISITOR INFORMATION The **Nome Convention and Visitor's Bureau (NCVB)** has town maps and information about practically everything on the Seward Peninsula, from gold panning to excursions to Siberia (only about an hour away by plane). The NCVB can tell you which Eskimo towns are hospitable to visitors and even provide you with a contact before you leave. *Front St., at Hunter St., across from City Hall, tel. 907/443–5535 or 800/478–1901. Open weekdays 8:30–6:30.*

COMING AND GOING

All roads may lead to Rome, but none go to Nome, at least not from southern Alaska. **Alaska Airlines** (tel. 800/426–0333) and **MarkAir** (tel. 800/258–2746) both have a couple of flights daily. Most flights to Nome originate in Anchorage and cost approximately $400 round-trip, although advance purchase tickets may cost less. Once you're in Nome, small gravel roads lead to coastal villages within a 300-mile radius.

GETTING AROUND

You won't need a car to maneuver around Nome, but you can rent one to get out to the remote villages accessible on surrounding gravel roads. **Budget** (tel. 907/443–5598), **Bonanza** (tel. 907/443–2221), and **Stampede** (tel. 907/443–5252) all rent compact pickups and four-wheel-drive vehicles for $55–$75 a day. People here will often pick up hitchhikers, although cars going your way may be few and far between. Be prepared to camp and bring along plenty of food and water.

WHERE TO SLEEP

Hotels in Nome range from overpriced and clean to overpriced and dirty. Even the **Nugget Inn** (Front St., next to visitor center, tel. 907/443–2323, fax 907/443–5966), Nome's premier tourist hotel, which charges $95 for a double with an ocean view, has walls so thin you can hear your neighbor sneeze. Luckily, Nome has bed-and-breakfast accommodations that are not only cheaper but also slightly more soundproof. **Betty's Igloo** (1st Ave., at K St., tel. 907/443–2419), about five blocks from Front Street, has double rooms that come with breakfast for $70. **June's B&B** (231 E. 4th, tel. 907/443–5984) is a small house with extremely friendly owners; a double room and breakfast is $65. A group of at least three can get an apartment for $85–$160 a night: **Nanuaq Manor** (tel. 907/443–5296), **Polar Arms Apartments** (tel. 907/443–2661), and **Stampede Apartments** (tel. 907/443–3838) all have short-term rentals for small groups. Wherever you go, make sure you look at any room before you pay for it, and avoid the **Polaris Hotel** at all costs.

CAMPING Nome has no designated campgrounds, but camping is permitted on the beach and anywhere alongside the gravel roads that cross the peninsula. Most people pitch camp east of the town's seawall, which protects Front Street

The lack of darkness in summer months and the dearth of trees can add to a camper's distress when nature calls—the midnight sun casts a bare bottom in a particularly unflattering light.

M*U*S*H

Nome is probably best known as the finish line of the Iditarod, the hair-raising, world-famous 1,200-mile dogsled race that takes place every March. The official starting point is in Wasilla, just outside Anchorage. The mushers cover slightly different routes each year and must pass through 20 checkpoints along the way. The checkpoints also serve as food drops for the teams, and vets are on hand to examine the dogs—the vet can pull sick or exhausted dogs out of the race. A musher need only finish with five dogs from his or her original team, which usually consists of 15–20 dogs. These dogs are surprisingly small, around 35 pounds, and must have tough feet, bristly hair that doesn't easily freeze, and plenty of endurance. Many people mistakenly think of sled dogs as purebred huskies or malamutes. A true sled dog is really a mutt that's been carefully bred for the right qualities.

One of the most bizarre Iditarod entrants is a man who races an entire team of poodles every year. The team never places very well, and often they don't even finish. It's pathetic to watch film clips of this musher pulling his dogs up after they've dropped exhausted onto the snow and frozen into it—the sound of ripping poodle fur is extremely unpleasant.

from the onslaught of the Bering Sea in winter. Finding bathrooms can be a real problem, though—the portable toilet at the city park could gag a maggot. Fortunately, bars and restaurants usually don't mind if you use their bathrooms. You can shower for $3 at **Blizzard Laundromat** (West St., at Seppala Dr., tel. 907/443–5353) or for $4 at the **Recreation Center** (E. 6th Ave., northern edge of town, tel. 907/443–5431).

FOOD

Nome has two grocery stores: **Hanson's Trading Company** (Bering St., at 4th Ave., tel. 907/443–5454) and **Alaska Commercial Company** (Front St., tel. 907/443–2243). An average restaurant meal costs $10–$15. **Pizza Napoli** (Front St., tel. 907/443–5300), **Nachos** (Front St., tel. 907/443–5503), and **Twin Dragon** (Bering St., tel. 907/443–5552) are all decent. **The Polar Club Café** (Front St., tel. 907/443–5191), open 24 hours, is the best value in Nome. This place doesn't look inviting from the outside (or from the inside, for that matter), but you can get a hot pancake breakfast here for less than $5. The all-you-can-eat lunch and dinner buffets are a good deal for $10–$15. **Fat Freddies** (Front St., tel. 907/443–5899) provides broad views of the Bering Sea and serves tasty food, including excellent burgers with fries ($6) and a salad bar.

The Board of Trade bar, also known as the BOT, is an utter dive, but it's a great place to buy ivory carvings—it won't take long before you're approached. You can do the best bargaining around closing time.

AFTER DARK

Nome is infamous for its rowdy nightlife. You should be careful at night, particularly if traveling alone: Some real hard cases roam around Nome after dark. It's easy to meet friendly locals, but you should probably leave well before closing time and keep your wits about you in order to ensure your safety. All of Nome's bars are clustered around the visitor center and the Nugget Inn on Front Street and are within easy stumbling distance of each other. **The Anchor Tavern** is Nome's idea of an upscale bar, but "upscale" is a relative term. **The Breaker's Bar** is another good spot, with a similar atmosphere to the Anchor Tavern. **The Polaris Bar** and the **Board of Trade** (known affectionately by the locals as the "BOT") are both dives, but they usually feature decent rock bands. There is some debate over which of the two is sleazier, but you're more likely to see a fight at the BOT.

Walrus Ivory

Nome is the place to buy walrus ivory, because most of the carvers live in the small villages north of town. Walrus ivory falls into one of two categories: fresh or fossil. Only Eskimos can legally harvest and carve fresh walrus ivory. If you have moral objections to ivory, don't buy it. However, you should understand that Eskimos have been hunting these animals for 28,000 years, and this activity is a central part of their culture and economy. If you're buying ivory, make sure it's signed by the artist. Most carvers have distinctive designs or animal shapes for their carvings, but a signature almost guarantees its authenticity. Watch out for gift shops selling elephant ivory. Elephant ivory is strikingly white and has usually been carved into a precise design by a machine. Walrus ivory is off-white or slightly yellowish and, if it's been hand carved, has no sharp ridges or angles. Many ivory objects have also been carved from the fossilized remains of woolly mammoths; this kind of ivory has a unique brownish color.

Near Nome

TELLER A small Eskimo village (population 200) at the end of the 71-mile Nome–Teller Road, Teller huddles on a small sand spit on the west coast of the Seward Peninsula. The town gained some notoriety when a local, Libby Riddles, became the first woman to win the Iditarod Race. The inhabitants are now used to seeing the odd stranger drive in and take a look around, but it's still a fairly rare event. You should be on your best behavior and realize that this is a small, close-knit community where you'll be regarded with a lot of curiosity. The drive to Teller through the tundra alone is worth the trip, but bring along your own munchies—the general store here is expensive.

It's startling to realize that this weather-beaten little village exists in the same country that brought you Disneyland.

COUNCIL A little more than 70 miles northeast of Nome, Council is a favorite spot for locals because it has—wonder of wonders—trees! (Nome residents' eyes will light up when they tell you about Council's arboreal attractions.) The drive itself is outstanding, especially when you go around desolate Cape Nome. Only 13 miles east of town, the cape offers spectacular views of the coast. As you head farther down the road, be on the lookout for wildlife.

Index

Notes

A T-SHIRT FOR YOUR THOUGHTS . . .

After your trip, drop us a line and let us know how things went. People whose comments help us most improve future editions will receive our eternal thanks as well as a Berkeley Guides T-shirt. Just print your name and address clearly and send the completed survey to: The Berkeley Guides, 515 Eshleman Hall, U.C. Berkeley, Berkeley, CA 94720.

Your Name _____

Address _____

_____ Zip _____

Where did you buy this book? City _____ State _____

How long before your trip did you buy this book? _____

Which Berkeley Guide(s) did you buy? _____

Which other guides, if any, did you purchase for this trip? _____

Which other guides, if any, have you used before? (Please circle)
Fodor's   Let's Go   Real Guide   Frommer's   Birnbaum   Lonely Planet
Other _____

Why did you choose Berkeley? (Please circle as many as apply)
Budget information   More maps   Emphasis on outdoors/off-the-beaten-track
Design   Attitude   Other _____
_____

If you're employed: Occupation _____

If you're a student: Name of school _____ City & state _____

Age _____ Male _____ Female _____

How many weeks was your trip? (Please circle) 1 2 3 4 5 6 7 8 More than 8 weeks

After you arrived on your trip, how did you get around? (Please circle one or more)
Rental car   Personal car   Plane   Bus   Train   Hiking   Biking   Hitching
Other _____

When did you travel? _____

Where did you travel? _____
_____

The features/sections I used most were (please circle as many as apply):
Basics   Where to Sleep   Food   Coming and Going   Worth Seeing   Other

The information was (circle one):
Usually accurate   Sometimes accurate   Seldom accurate

I would _____ would not _____ buy another Berkeley Guide.

These books are brand new, and we'd really appreciate some feedback on how to improve them. Please also tell us about your latest find, a new scam, a budget deal, whatever—we want to hear about it.

For your comments:

_____

_____